Since first publication in 1993, *Nations and Politics in the Soviet Successor-States* edited by Ian Bremmer and Ray Taras has established itself internationally as the first genuinely comprehensive, systematic and rigorous analysis of the nation- and state-building processes of the fifteen new states which grew out of the 1991 collapse of the Soviet Union. *New States, New Politics: Building the Post-Soviet Nations* succeeds and replaces the editors' earlier book with a new collection of specially commissioned studies from the world's foremost specialists. This fully revised second edition has some new authors; improved and more up-to-date maps; as extended section on Russia and its nations; and the valuable new reference feature of extended chronologies which document the landmark events in post-Soviet nation-building. The whole text has been updated and expanded and is re-set throughout. Far from eradicating tensions among the former Soviet peoples, the disintegration of empire has seen national minorities rediscovering long-suppressed new identities. National identities loom larger, and national conflict even more firece than ever before. The contributors to *New States, New Politics* once again bring together historical and ethnic background with penetrating political analysis to offer a fresh, up-to-date and unique record of the different roads to self-assertion and independence being pursued by these young nations. This new edition will confirm *New States, New Politics* as essential reading for students and specialists alike, and for anyone concerned with the new politics of the former Soviet Union.

# New States, New Politics:
# Building the Post-Soviet Nations

# New States, New Politics:
# Building the Post-Soviet Nations

*Edited by*

IAN BREMMER
*Hoover Institution, Stanford University*

*and*

RAY TARAS
*Tulane University*

CAMBRIDGE
UNIVERSITY PRESS

Published by the Press Syndicate of the University of Cambridge
The Pitt Building, Trumpington Street, Cambridge CB2 1RP
40 West 20th Street, New York, NY 10011–4211, USA
10 Stanford Road, Oakleigh, Melbourne 3166, Australia

© Cambridge University Press

First published 1997

*New states, new politics: building the post-Soviet nations* succeeds and
replaces *Nations and politics in the Soviet successor states*, published by
Cambridge University Press in 1993 (0 521 43281 2 hb, 0 521 43860 8 pb)

Printed in Great Britain at the University Press, Cambridge

*A catalogue record for this book is available from the British Library*

*Library of Congress cataloguing in publication data*

New states, new politics: building the post-Soviet nations / edited
    by Ian Bremmer, Ray Taras.
        p.   cm.
        Includes bibliographical references and index.
        ISBN 0 521 57101 4. – ISBN 0 521 57799 3 (pbk.)
        1. Former Soviet republics – Politics and government.
    2. Nationalism–Former Soviet republics. I. Bremmer, Ian A. (Ian
    Arthur), 1969– . II. Taras, Ray, 1946– .
JN6511.N48   1996
320.9171'247'09049–dc20   96–12565   CIP

ISBN 0 521 57101 4 hardback

ISBN 0 521 57799 3 paperback

# Contents

# Maps

# Tables

# Notes on contributors

**Muriel Atkin** is Associate Professor of History at George Washington University. She received a Ph.D. in history from Yale University. She is the author of the monographs *The Subtlest Battle: Islam in Soviet Tajikistan* and *Russia and Iran, 1780–1828* as well as numerous articles on Tajikistan and Russian Soviet relations with Iran.

**Ian Bremmer** is National Fellow at the Hoover Institution, Stanford University and President of the Association for the Study of Nationalities. He has published extensively on problems of Soviet transition and disintegration including, *Soviet Nationalities Problems* (1990) with Norman Naimark, *Nations and Politics in the Soviet Successor States* (1993) with Ray Taras, and the forthcoming *Understanding Nationalism: Ethnic Minorities and Nation-Building in the Post-Communist States*.

**Robert Conquest** is Senior Research Fellow at the Hoover Institution, Stanford University. He has authored and edited numerous books on Soviet and international affairs, including *The Nation Killers, The Harvest of Sorrow, The Great Terror, Stalin: Breaker of Nations*, and *The Last Empire: Nationality and the Soviet Future*. Much of his work has recently been published in Moscow, St. Petersburg, and Kiev.

**William Crowther** is Associate Professor of Political Science at the University of North Carolina, Greensboro. He has conducted research and has written extensively on democratization and political transitions in Moldova and Romania and interethnic relations. He is presently writing a volume on cultural determinance of the democratization process in Southeastern Europe.

**Nora Dudwick** is a Research Associate at the Institute for European, Russian, and Eurasian Studies, George Wahsington University. She received her Ph.D. in Anthropology from the University of Pennsylvania in 1994, where she wrote on politics and national identity in Armenia. Since September 1987, she has visited and conducted research in Armenia on seven occasions, and is presently completing a project on the cultural construction of violence in Armenia. She is the author of a number of articles on the subject.

**John Dunlop** is Senior Fellow at the Hoover Institution, Stanford University. He is a specialist on contemporary Russian politics, Russian nationalism, and empire. He is author of many studies which treat the position of ethnic Russians in the former Soviet Union, including *The Faces of Contemporary Russian Nationalism, The New Russian Nationalism,* and, most recently, *The Rise of Russia and the Fall of the Soviet Union.*

**Gail Fondahl** is Assistant Professor in the Faculty of Natural Resources and Environmental Studies Geography Programme, University of Northern British Columbia, and a Research Fellow at the Institute of Arctic Studies, Dartmouth College, New Hampshire. She is currently researching indigenous rights to land and resources and evolving land tenure systems among the Siberian peoples and is completing a volume entitled *Reindeer Herders and Railroad Building; The Cultural Ecology of Trans-Baykalia.*

**Allen Frank** received his Ph.D. in Central Eurasian Studies in 1994 at Indiana University, Bloomington. He is a specialist on Islam and native religion in the Middle Volga region, with a special interest in the region's Islamic manuscripts. His current research involves Muslim saints and shrines of the Middle Volga region.

**Gregory Gleason** is Associate Professor of Political Science and Public Administration at the University of New Mexico. He is the author of a number of articles on Russian and Central Asian public policy as well as the forthcoming *Central Asian States: Discovering Independence,* to be published by Westview Press in 1996. He has conducted field research in Central Asia under the auspices of a number of institutions including the USSR Academy of Sciences and the Uzbekistan Academy of Sciences. During 1994, he worked for a year in the Central Asian republics implementing a program on democratic development sponsored by the US Agency for International Development.

**Shireen Hunter** is Senior Visiting Fellow at the Centre for European Policy Studies (CEPS) in Brussels and a Senior Associate at the Center for Strategic and International Studies (CSIS) in Washington DC. Her articles have appeared in many major journals, including *Foreign Affairs, Foreign Policy, SAIS Review, Current History,* the *Washington Quarterly* and the *Middle East Journal.* Dr. Hunter's latest book is *The Transcaucasus in Transition: Nation-Building and Conflict.*

**Eugene Huskey** is Associate Professor of Political Science and Director of Russian Studies at Stetson University in Florida. In addition to Kyrgyz politics, he has interests in Russian law and government. Among his publications are *Russian Lawyers and the Soviet State*, and *Executive Power and Soviet Politics* (editor). He is currently writing a book on the Russian presidency.

**Bohdan Krawchenko** is Professor of Political Science at the University of Alberta. He has written extensively on Ukrainian politics and national identity, including *Ukraine After Shelest* and *Social Change and National Consciousness in Twentieth Century Ukraine*.

**Stephen Jones** is Associate Professor of Eurasian Studies at Mount Holyoke College. He has written extensively on Georgian affairs in specialist journals and books. His own book, *The Georgian Democratic Republic: 1918–21*, will be published in 1996.

**Alexander Motyl** is Associate Director of the Harriman Institute at Columbia University and Vice President of the Association for the Study of Nationalities. He is the author of *Dilemmas of Independence: Ukraine after Totalitarianism, Sovietology, Rationality, Nationality: Coming to Grips with Nationalism in the USSR*, and the editor of *Thinking Theoretically about Soviet Nationalities* and *The Post-Soviet Nations*. He is currently completing a manuscript, entitled *Fighting Words: Confrontations with Revolutions and Revolutionaries*.

**Nils Muiznieks** received his Ph.D. from the University of California, Berkeley, and presently is Director of the Latvian Center for Human Rights and Ethnic Studies in Riga. His research focuses on national movements and state development in the Baltics, and he has published widely both in the West and in the Baltic press.

**David Nissman** received his doctorate from Columbia University in Turkic Studies. Author of *The Soviet Union and Iranian Azerbaijan* and numerous articles on ethnic identity and relations in the Middle East and Central Asia, he has conducted extensive research in Turkmenistan. He presently serves as a Fellow in the Seminar on Turkic Studies at Columbia.

**Martha Brill Olcott** is Professor of Political Science at Colgate University. She has been studying Soviet nationality problems since 1973; since then, she has traveled to the USSR more than fifteen times, and has spent nearly three years in residence in eleven of the fifteen successor states. Her most recent publications include *The Kazakhs* (2nd ed., Hoover Institute, 1995) and *The New States of Central Asia* (USIP, 1995).

**Jane Ormrod** is a doctoral candidate in the Department of History at the University of Chicago. She has presented work on Russian peasant popular culture and has conducted research and field work in Russia and the North Caucasus. She is currently investigating cultural self-representation and the development of ethnic and national identity among the peoples of the North Caucasus.

**Toivo Raun** is Professor in the Department of Central Eurasian Studies at Indiana University and Executive Vice President of the American Association of Baltic Studies. He is a specialist of Estonian nation-building and political development and has published numerous books and articles on the topic, including *Estonia and the Estonians* (Hoover, 2nd ed, 1993).

**Alfred Senn** is Professor in the Department of History at the University of Wisconsin, Madison. An expert in Lithuanian politics as well as Soviet sport, he has conducted extensive field research on the national movement in Lithuania. Professor Senn has published widely in the West and much of his work has been translated into Lithuanian. He has also authored several books, including a treatise on the road to independence in Lithuania, *Lithuania Awakening* (California, 1990).

**Ray Taras** was educated in Canada, England, and Poland, and has served on the faculty of universities in Canada, England, and the United States. He has published a number of books on comparative politics including *The Road to Disillusion: From Critical Marxism to Postcommunism in Eastern Europe* (1992) and *Polish Communists and the Polish Road to Socialism: A History of Self-Destruction* (1993). Taras's previous books with Cambridge University Press are *Ideology in a Socialist State* (1984) and *Nations and Politics in the Soviet Successor States* (1993), with Ian Bremmer.

**Michael Urban** is Associate Professor of Politics in the University of California, Santa Cruz. His recent books include *More Power to the Soviets: The Democratic Revolution in the USSR, An Algebra of Soviet Power: Elite Circulation in the Belorussian Republic 1966–86,* and the edited volume, *Ideology and System Change in the USSR and East Europe.* Currently, his research focuses on the development of a party system in Russia, and the evolution of Russian political identity and political language.

**Ronald Wixman** is Professor in the Department of Geography at the University of Oregon. Since the age of seventeen, he has made over twenty-five trips to Eastern Europe, the USSR, and the Middle East, where he has studied ethnic, cultural, religious, and ethno-territorial problems. To date he has published two books and a number of articles on these issues; his handbook of Soviet nationalities (*The Peoples of the USSR: An Ethnographic Handbook*) has become the standard reference on the various nationalities and ethnic groups of the USSR.

**Jan Zaprudnik** is a graduate of Louvain University and received his doctorate at New York University. He has taught in the Department of History at Queens College and has served as correspondent and Editor at Radio Liberty. Dr. Zaprudnik has contributed articles on Belarus to numerous volumes, including *Handbook of Major Soviet Nationalities, The Journal of Byelorussian Studies*, and *ZAPISY of the Byelorussian Institute of Arts and Sciences.*

# Preface

The sudden and dramatic disintegration of the former Soviet Union at the beginning of the 1990s is now history. The causes and processes of collapse have undergone microscopic analysis, while the birth of new states has encouraged a growing compilation of new country studies. To be sure, comparative research has not been altogether ignored as a meaningful framework of inquiry, but there is surprisingly little of it. It is as if post-Sovietologists remain unconvinced that the fifteen new states are really states, that they will endure, or that they represent the political embodiment of important new nations.

A natural hesitancy exists to regard the politics of any new states, especially smaller or "unhistoric" (not having a lengthy history as an independent state) ones, as of equal significance to that of their established, much written about brethren. The importance of studying Russian politics is self-evident, not least because its leaders have claimed the dubious distinction of being the legal successor to the USSR. There were no quarrels with the Russian Federation inheriting the Soviet Union's place as a permanent member of the United Nations Security Council. It is Russia again that is unofficially treated as the eighth member of the Group of Seven economic powers; Russia's president is now a regular guest at the annual G-7 summits. By contrast, there is a reluctance on the part of many scholars to spend much time examining political developments in the other fourteen states, considered more as splinters rather than successors of the USSR. Studying the non-Russian Eurasian states is still viewed by many in the post-Soviet field as specialized scholastic research rather than exemplary scholarly enterprise.

Using a common framework to conduct analysis of all the Soviet successors is significant for a number of reasons. Firstly, as is the case in any comparative research, it facilitates the discovery of parallel political processes and patterns that would go unnoticed in an intensive single case study. The new states have inherited a set of common problems – for example, authoritarian politics – but at the same time they differ considerably in terms of their respective political methods and goals, such as the desirability and scope of regional cooperation. The ultimate legacy of Soviet rule, as well as the significance of the many differences that exist among the post-Soviet regions, may best be considered only from a broad comparative perspective.

Secondly, the post-Soviet states compete for power, status, allies, and investment. Clearly, they cannot all avail themselves of the same means in order to "best" their interstate rivals. Only by skillfully experimenting with institutions and processes in order to discover their comparative advantage will some states progress, while others will be left behind. Here it is not the *comparability* of the starting points but the *divergence* in path development that merits careful examination.

Thirdly, by investigating the politics of all the Soviet successors we learn more about the key actor in the region, Russia. As elsewhere in international relations, equality among sovereign states is a fiction; invariably, regional hegemons emerge, secondary powers become identifiable, and peripheral states are created. This hierarchization of states is of great analytical importance. The practical consequences of Russia consolidating its position as regional hegemon, and subsequently reestablishing itself as a great power, are all too obvious. From the perspective of Russia's weaker neighbors, we can catch a glimpse of what may lie ahead.

Having thought out the framework for *Nations and Politics* and run with it for the better part of two years, we were as relieved as excited when the final manuscript found its way to the out box. It had been an ambitious undertaking: we hoped to marshal into a comprehensive theoretical framework over twenty specialists analyzing every corner of the former Soviet Union, grappling with urgent issues that had not yet made it into the popular consciousness. When at last the book was complete, we quickly became psychologically accustomed to the notion that our work was indeed over. It was thus with mixed feelings that we decided to try our hands at the post-Soviet context.

At first glance, there was good reason to leave well enough alone. The story of the Soviet denouement and of the rise of nations has become familiar to students and specialists alike. The Soviet Union fell apart, *Nations and Politics* documented the national movements that accompanied and, indeed, brought about the collapse, and the successor states were free to go about their business.

But this constitutes only a part of a larger story about how states evolve into recognized actors within the international system. *New States, New Politics* sets as its principal objective understanding the state-building process underway in the Soviet successors. Recognizing national development and, where applicable, early trappings of statehood from the Soviet period and earlier, it sets out to explain the important political events that have marked the successor states in their first five years of existence. The contributors to this volume evaluate both, and, consider their degrees of independence. The chapters track the search for new political roles undertaken by these nations and their success in defining them. At some level, of course, international relations have taken the place of the provincial relations previously dominant in Eurasia. But here, too, we encounter a further paradox: political relations in Russia's "near abroad" are not really international relations of the kind found in most parts of the world. They are shaped by centuries of both Russian domination and quests for expanded autonomy on the part of the oppressed peoples. When the argument is made that all of these developments nevertheless represent an improvement upon the instability and oppression of the Soviet period, *New States, New Politics* asks whether this instability and oppression has not, in fact, increased fifteen-fold.

The collapse of the Soviet Union thus may have radically altered the state-centered analysis, but it by no means eliminated it. Accordingly, as this book's focus remains firmly on nations, we shun a mechanistic state-centered approach and consider the extent to which national political aspirations have themselves been incorporated into state structures, as well as the fate of those nations which have suffered under those new state structures. Because the contributors to this volume are seasoned specialists on their particular countries, we are able to present a rich empirical canvas of post-Soviet development. Moreover, because they have, in various ways, pioneered new theoretical approaches to the general study of nationalism, *New States, New Politics* also highlights the inroads made into nationalities studies.

Let us outline the structure of this volume. Part I is an introduction describing how Soviet studies were transformed into nationality studies at the beginning of the 1990s, and assessing the importance of this paradigmatic shift. It also inquires whether the many new theories about the former Soviet nations are well founded, considering the political realities of the region. The introduction then offers a typology of relationships between nations that is applicable both in the Soviet and post-Soviet contexts.

If there is a new political center, it is clearly dependent on Russia's resolve to return to that role. Part II of the volume, "Russia and its nations," carefully examines the state of the new union. Its first chapter chronicles the political shifts in the Russian Federation under president Yeltsin and examines Russian attitudes to their minorities, the Russian diaspora and the independent states. The following three chapters offer extensive treatment of the regions within Russia where the nationalist explosion has most troubled Moscow authorities – the Middle Volga, the North Caucasus and Siberia.

Part III provides specialized analyses of the non-Russian successor states, including case studies of politics in the new states of Eastern Europe – Ukraine, Belarus and Moldova. In part IV, we turn to the Baltics – Lithuania, Latvia and Estonia. The Caucasus – Azerbaijan, Armenia and Georgia – are the subjects of part V, and part VI presents case studies of Central Asia's emergent states – Kazakhstan, Uzbekistan, Tajikistan, Turkmenistan and Kyrgystan.

The conclusion reassesses the boom in nationalities studies in the 1990s, and advances a framework for mapping ethnic mobilization in the midst of the collapse of empire, as well as for testing its sustainability during the next stage of political development. This chapter then applies the framework of relations posited in the introduction to the post-Soviet context. Finally, it considers relations between nations from the perspective of international relations theory, which in recent years has also been influenced by the unprecedented political developments in the Eurasian regions.

In addition to the theoretical insights and original empirical research that we hope this volume provides, *New States, New Politics* also presents extensive data compiled in appendices to help readers more easily use the volume as a reference work. To this end, we have included political chronologies which appear at the end of each chapter, and identify key caesurae and facts from the Soviet nationalities explosion to the state building of the post-Soviet 1990s.

We hope that readers caught up in the daunting but absorbing pursuit of comparing politics in nations – especially nations as extraordinary as those emerging in Russia and in its shadow – will enjoy a rewarding journey through *New States, New Politics*.

Academic appointments can be funny. Each of us has taken turns at National Fellowships at the Hoover Institution – one per volume. There must be some luck in that, but beyond good fortune it is hard to overstate the support, intellectual and financial, offered by the Hoover Institution, and especially Visiting Research and National Fellows coordinators Tom Henriksen, Richard Staar, Deborah Ventura and Wendy Minkin. We also wish to express our sincere appreciation to Bob Andrews, Paul Chzranowski and Gerry Dzakowic at Lawrence Livermore National Laboratory, for their far-sightedness and continued enthusiasm.

Much of the trepidation of putting together this revisited work was reduced by the knowledge that we were continuing to work with Cambridge University Press. John Haslam, editor and our principal go-between, assured the high professional quality of the volume. Our ultimate thanks go to Michael Holdsworth, whose understanding of the publishing business and willingness to work with two (at times) taxing personalities made *Nations and Politics* the success it was and *New States, New Politics* the sort of volume we can be proud of. His sensibilities are professional, he prods gently when needed, and he's great fun to drink with. Cheers, Michael . . .

In redesigning this book to cope with the many and varied needs of the scholars, researchers, and students who will be using it, we relied upon the suggestions of many reviewers, colleagues, and our own students. We would like to especially thank Jeff Chinn at the University of Missouri, Columbia; Bruce Parrott at Johns Hopkins University; and Stephen White at Glasgow University for taking the time to consider *Nations and Politics'* many strengths and weaknesses, filling out burdensome and extensive questionnaires (composed, of course, by Michael Holdsworth) and helping us make difficult decisions about how to make *New States, New Politics* an even better piece of work.

We would also like to acknowledge the constructive suggestions which have been made by a number of scholars concerned with nationalities questions. The following have read parts of the manuscript and offered valuable insights: Rogers Brubaker at the University of California, Los Angeles; Graham Allison and Roman Szporluk at Harvard University; Michael Rywkin at City College of New York; Larry Diamond and Alex Inkeles at the Hoover Institution, Stanford University; and Mark Beissinger at the University of Wisconsin, Madison.

Michael Nichols assisted the editing process by typing and re-typing at moment's notice. Administratively, Karen Kimball at Lawrence Livermore National Laboratory took much of the trauma out of organizing a workload that all too often seemed monumental.

But we cannot leave our acknowledgements without expressing our unending goodwill to our editorial assistant Cory Welt, at Stanford University, who devoted a not insubstantial portion of his best years to tracking down the problems upon problems that arose daily with the manuscript. Aside from singlehandedly compiling the appendices which appear at the end of each chapter (a more daunting research assignment would be hard to find), he followed up on nearly every inconsistency, problematic citation, and missing piece of analysis we were able to find in the book. If our readers find *New States, New Politics* that much more coherent, thorough, and readable than its predecessor, they should save their last thank you, as we have, for Cory.

*Stanford University*
*1996*

# Part I
# Introduction

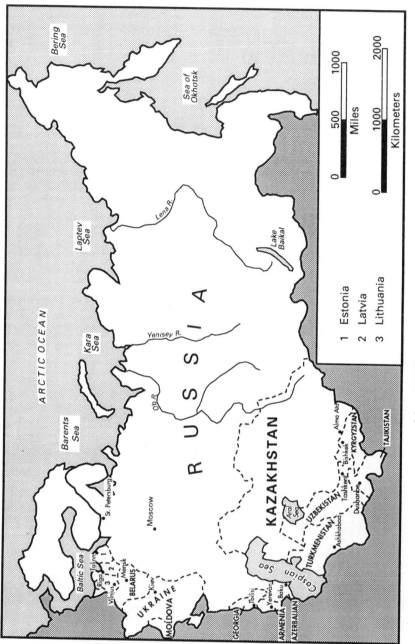

Map 1.1 The Soviet successor states

# 1　Post-Soviet nationalities theory: past, present, and future

IAN BREMMER

Having suffered through the distress of economic crises, the siege and devastation of war, and the terror of Stalin, the Soviet Union survived tremendous adversity. Yet, after seventy years of Soviet rule preceded by centuries of Tsarist rule, it was national conflict that proved the most fundamental threat to Soviet stability. Demands for national autonomy, sovereignty, and ultimately independence surfaced with a vengeance, bringing about the disintegration of the Soviet state system. That this came as a surprise to Soviet citizens and Sovietologists alike is a serious understatement.

In retrospect, it seems a foregone conclusion that national explosion would prove the undoing of the Soviet system. After all, the Soviet Union was perhaps the most extensive single case of the conflict and coexistence of national groups in history. While precise estimates vary, there were more than 100 nations in the Soviet Union, *most* of which laid claim to Soviet territory as their homeland.[1] All of these nations, with varying degrees of voluntarism, had been incorporated into the multinational framework of a single state.

The politico-demographic situation in the former Soviet Union makes the importance of nationalism particularly difficult to gauge. Members of national groups typically lived together, with Armenians, Chuvash, Kyrgyz, Turkmen, Yakuts, and others living in generally ethnically homogeneous regions. Even more significantly, administrative divisions and ethnic divisions within the Soviet Union were largely delineated along the same territorial lines. For this reason, regional movements in the Soviet Union tended to be national in *form*, regardless of content. Environmental groups in Uzbekistan, anti-nuclear groups in Kazakhstan, Belarus and Ukraine, and workers' movements in autonomous republics within the RSFSR were all assailed by Gorbachev (and, indeed, Western scholars) as nationalist. In each of these cases, however, the extent to which these organizations deserve a nationalist title is open to question.[2]

The peculiar logic of the post-Soviet context raises its own problems. Freed to varying extents from Moscow-based rule, the fifteen Soviet union republics effectively became successor nation-states. But while the post-Soviet states engaged in nationalizing processes, they did not necessarily become states of and for their respective titular national groups.[3] According

3

to their constitutions, at least, most have claimed to represent all the peoples on their territories, not just the titular group for which their republican predecessors had been formed. Again, the impact of nationalism varies greatly.

This chapter attempts to clarify the issues at stake regarding the conduct of post-Soviet nationalities relations. The first section introduces the analysis by considering the origins of Soviet nationalities policies, tracing Marxism and Leninism in relation to the national question. The chapter then turns to consider developments connected with the Soviet nationalities explosion and the collapse of Soviet rule. In the third section, a comprehensive framework is presented for analysis of the underlying cleavages leading to national conflict in the Soviet and post-Soviet contexts. The chapter concludes with an assessment of the changing factors underpinning national relations in the Soviet successor states. It is hoped that such an analysis will shed light upon not only post-Soviet cases but also the articulation of nationalism more broadly, particularly in today's increasingly interdependent world system where greater understanding of the national phenomenon is essential for the avoidance of large-scale conflict.

## Traditional approaches toward the Soviet nationalities question: Marxism and Leninism

Traditional explanations of nationalism started from analyses of the state. Nationalism has been a principal ideological current since the time of Napoleon, and the political imperative of successive Empires – Ottoman, Hapsburg, British, and Russian, to cite a few – has been to disarm national aspirations, whether through force, provision of economic development, or skillful use of intrigue within indigenous elites.

It is useful to recall, however, that nationalism has often been thought responsible for the suppression of individual rights and initiative. In his study, *The Myth of the Nation and the Vision of Revolution*, J.-L. Talmon wrote of late nineteenth-century Europe in these terms:

> Far from constituting the basic element and goal of society, from being his own autonomous lawgiver and free and equal partner to the social contract, as he was seen in the eighteenth century, man was made to appear more and more a function of collective forces, past traditions, the social setting, the organizational framework, the spirit of the nation, the Zeitgeist, their milieu, group mentality, finally the race . . . Not man, therefore, but the nation, was the measure of all things, and the dominion of the dead was depicted as infinitely more potent than the deliberate decisions of the living.[4]

In some respects, therefore, the ideology of nationalism is reminiscent of the ideology of communism.[5] In states governed by nationalist or communist principles, the individual is important only as the embodiment of collective spiritual values. Man is no more the starting point of communism than he is the starting point of nationalism. But let us again invoke Talmon and consider a description that might aptly convey the relationship between nation and individual in the USSR. Talmon concluded about Europe on the eve of World War I: "Every nation was a world of its own, a unique blend. Since it fashioned countless men and determined their fate and well-being, the nation's interests, the imperatives of its particular situation, the conditions favoring its survival, cohesion, strength and influence contained its truth, morality and justice."[6]

Despite their apparent similarities, however, World War I revealed the inherent contradiction between socialist and nationalist ideologies. The leaders of the Second International believed that war could not break out between proletariats in different states because class loyalty was considered to transcend national loyalty. For them, socialism was viewed "as the purified product of the endeavors of European liberalism and democracy, and the crowning achievement of an ancient common European heritage."[7] The swift mobilization of war machines in Russia and Germany thus came as a bitter disappointment to most socialist leaders.[8]

Probably the most realistic of all Marxist currents concerning the national question was put forward by two Austrian socialist thinkers of the 1920s, Karl Renner and Otto Bauer. Contrary to Luxembourg and even Lenin, who generally recognized the progressive nature of national struggles, the Austro-Marxists were committed to the notion of an "evolutionary nationalism" that incorporated the history and traditions of a nation in the forging of a socialist order. Furthermore, as Talmon observed, they saw it as "the aim and destiny of socialism to enable the lower orders, for so long kept out of the national community, to join the national culture, to become co-heirs of the national heritage." As the Austro-Marxists contended, "Far from being anti-national, from working for the disintegration of the national community and for the effacement of its distinctness, socialism was aspiring to raise the nation to much loftier heights."[9]

Renner and Bauer ultimately underestimated the explosive nature of nationalism, which could so quickly derail the socialist project. As Talmon noted, they had failed "to grasp the demoniacal, obsessive character of nationalist passion. They genuinely believed in the possibility of drawing and maintaining a line between the legitimate urge for collective self-expression and the passion for ascendancy, power, prestige and domination. A socialist nation could not by definition become imperialistic."[10] But the Soviet Union had clearly become an imperialist state, as illustrated by its signing of the secret protocol to the Ribbentrop–Molotov pact in August 1939, its aggression against Finland during the Winter War of 1939–40, Stalin's "sphere-of-influence" agreement with Churchill concluded in Moscow in October 1944, and finally his understanding of the 1944 Yalta treaty which left Soviet-liberated territories in Eastern Europe to Generalissimo Stalin's discretion. For other nations of the USSR – the peoples of former Turkestan, of Georgia, Armenia, and Azerbaijan – Soviet imperialism had been witnessed earlier – from 1921, when the Menshevik governments of the Transcaucasus were overrun, to 1927, when the last of the Basmachi revolts in Uzbekistan was crushed.

There was something peculiar about the formation of the Soviet state that went beyond the issue of Marxist experimentation. Following Alexander Gerschenkron, who studied the linkage between nation-building and industrialization,[11] Roman Szporluk underscored the fact that the Russian industrial revolution had preceded the processes of modern nation-building, and consequently, "Marxism had taken hold before nationalism."[12] The country's liberal nationalists were swept aside by the Bolsheviks and failed to have much of an influence in either elite circles or among the population. From the outset, Russia was slow in building a liberal civil society and a modern nation. But Szporluk also showed how "relations between nations, and not just classes, played a vital role in determining the outcome of the Bolshevik Revolution." These included more illiberal Russian nationalists opposed to Communists who were convinced that the Bolsheviks "would best be able to preserve the territorial unity of Russia against the separatism of its non-Russian nationalities."[13] In a similar vein, Isaac Deutscher identified the nationalist dilemma of the Bolsheviks in 1917: "The Leninists still believed that socialism demanded equality between nations; but they also felt that the reunion of most, if not all, of the Tsar's dominions under the Soviet flag served the interests of socialism."[14] These early calculations by certain Russian nationalist and Communist circles were to govern the formative years of the Soviet imperial state.[15]

So far we have discussed Marxist rather than Marxian approaches to the nationalities question. In Szporluk's study of Marx's early writings on German nationalism, he found a contemptuous attitude toward German backwardness as represented by its bourgeoisie, which lagged far behind its English and French counterparts in undertaking a world-historical mission. Yet by focusing on social relations, Marx was unprepared to attribute a historical role in social development to the nation. Szporluk concludes: "There can be no doubt that he considered nationality to be a minor factor, a 'dependent variable,' in the process of social development."[16] Nationalism was a historically determined phenomenon that emerged as a result of the rise of capitalism and was primarily a device of the imperialists, who could use it as a means to further their own parochial class interests by unifying the entire society.[17] But nations would eventually fade away in favor of a new community based upon class solidarity. The capitalist nation-state system would thus force itself into ruin.

Given this thesis, it is not surprising that many second-generation Marxists felt incapable of offering a doctrinal guide for the managing of national revolutions. There was nothing in Marx's model of successive social formations that pointed to nationalism as a historic force capable of accelerating or retarding progress to the next stage of development. Accordingly, the only solution to the national problem required the elimination of national differences.[18]

Before the Bolshevik Revolution, Lenin discounted the significance of nationalism and supported a policy of regional autonomy, whereby state political-administrative divisions would not be based upon ethnic lines.[19] After the revolution, however, many of the nations which had successfully gained their freedom from Tsarist Russia – such as the independent Soviet republics of Azerbaijan, Armenia, Belorussia and Ukraine – were firmly opposed to domination from an imperial center. It thus became increasingly apparent to Lenin that the formation of a stable union would require substantial concessions to national rights.[20]

Lenin was caught uncomfortably between two poles, needing a modicum of national assimilation for state survival but unwilling to alleviate the national crisis through substantive action for fear of destabilizing the union. Consequently, even though assimilation of national groups was the desired goal, Lenin deemed it necessary to erect a facade of equality and sovereignty. He compromised by allowing the creation of a federal Soviet Union based upon the dictum "national in form, socialist in content."[21]

The structure of the Soviet system was divided into four levels of regional, ethnically-based administrative-political units. Institutions were set up identically within each level, with replications of not only party and state apparatuses but also cultural, scientific, and educational facilities. The primary nationalities policy enacted to support the new structure was *korenizatsia* (nativization), through which national cultures were promoted and members of nationalities were given preference for state-controlled benefits such as education, housing, and employment. Economic policy underpinned Soviet support for nationalities, based upon the premise of giving to each according to his needs and taking from each according to his ability. Economic leveling was thereby mandated, with government subsidies following policies of redistribution. It was, in essence, a massive state program of nation-based affirmative action.

Lenin's nationalities policy was transitional, since while many nations were allowed to remain distinct, it was anticipated that they too would eventually be assimilated. Paradoxically, where nations did not exist, they were created, with the intention of accelerating their inevitable demise.[22] Yet Soviet power never gave legitimate expression to the national aspirations of the peoples who were subordinated to it. While the Soviet leadership neither launched a *Kulturkampf* against nationalities nor tried to forcibly Russify them following the October revolution, "socialist in content" meant that the ambiguous Soviet culture was presumed to dominate all other cultures save the Russian.[23] And suspicion of the central leadership about all but the most ritualistic manifestations of nationalism in the periphery exacerbated the sense of colonization felt by local peoples. As one observer put it, "The effort to cast all aspects of life in an ethnic mold brought ethnic considerations into areas that would otherwise have remained unaffected by them and gave sinister political implications to relatively harmless manifestations of ethnic assertiveness."[24]

Even within the limited parameters of Soviet federation, all national groups were not treated equally. Only fifty-three of the over one hundred Soviet nations were eventually identified with a particular territory and so afforded rights by virtue of their national status – the so-called "titular" nationalities.[25] Fully half or more of the Soviet Union's national groups had *no* political recognition as nations. Of the fifty-three titular nationalities, fifteen were designated by the highest status of Soviet Socialist Republics (SSRs) or "union republics," which together encompassed the entire union. Directly accountable to and within the territories of the union republics, in order of descending status, were twenty Autonomous Soviet Socialist Republics (ASSRs), eight Autonomous Regions (*oblasti*), and ten Autonomous Areas (*okruga*).[26] The rights and responsibilities of each of these formations were enumerated in the Soviet Constitution, including areas of dependence, guaranteed institutions, and rights of autonomy. Significantly, obligations under Soviet rule were the same for all national groups while only the fifteen union republics were granted the right to secede.[27]

Closer analysis of the secession issue uncovers a central dilemma of Soviet nationalities policies – the need to justify the contract between union republics and the Soviet state. Under this contract, each republic was responsible for carrying out the policies of the Soviet center and participating fully in socialist development. Should the republics be inclined to leave the Union, their option to do so was guaranteed by the Soviet state. The reasoning was based upon a circular logic. Given a right to secession, the republics would pledge to acknowledge a union under Soviet leadership; in return for such a pledge, nationalities would choose not to enact their right to secession. National instabilities would be constrained by a freely entered arrangement, thus providing the justification for empire that lay at the foundation of the Soviet Union.

*De jure* nationalities policy was far divorced from Soviet reality, however. Neither Lenin nor any of his successors ever harbored any intention of allowing the republics to exercise their right to secede. Instead, Soviet central authorities provided a package of economic benefits to the republics, to be used largely at the discretion of local elites, in exchange for republican compliance with Soviet rule. This deal effectively "bought off" the loyalties of target leadership cadres, such as economic managers, trade union officials, administrative and party heads, and intellectuals. Those not fortunate enough to be so targeted were effectively excluded from the nationalities contract.

Reliance upon national passivity to maintain the stability of the union was therefore not left to a legal framework. Instead, the Soviet center hoped to undermine the fomenting of "nationalism in content" through the coopting of key actors in the periphery.[28] Throughout the Soviet period, Russian migration to the non-Russian republics was extensive, indoctrination through schools and youth groups was maintained at a high level, religious organizations were repressed, and local economies were made dependent upon the Soviet center. Massive bureaucratic institutions were created, emanating from Moscow with symmetrical lines of authority reaching down to the local level. Particularly in the non-Slavic areas, the Soviet center attempted to convince the varied nations that they had no culture prior to the Soviet period. This movement constituted the Stalinist "merging of nations" [*sliyanie*] and the Brezhnevite "creation of a new historical society – the Soviet people [*sovietsky narod*]."

Soviet leaders improvised on the national question, rather than extrapolating from Marx (as they did in other areas such as economics and culture). Perhaps the Soviet state would not have been better served by an identifiably Marxian approach to the subject; especially concerning this potent force, the theories of Marxist writers systematically wavered often in a way transparent to even unideological and illiterate groups – thereby calling into question the viability of Marxism as a guide to action generally. The inability to incorporate a *de jure* dynamic for national development in Soviet doctrine essentially stems from this inadequacy.

## The Soviet nationalities explosion

Contrary to Lenin's reasoning, the road to socialism turned out to be insufficient incentive to maintain the integrity of the Union. Beginning in earnest in 1988, national explosions rocked the entire country and, by the end of 1991, the Soviet Union had disintegrated with all fifteen union republics having achieved independence and more than twenty ASSRs, autonomous regions, and autonomous areas having declared sovereignty and formed national movements with widespread popular support.

With the possible significant exception of coopted local elites (the so-called "state-dependent sector"), Soviet citizens never came to feel that a Soviet nation existed. Even among Russians, the Soviet state was effectively thought to be the natural extension of the Russian nation. And while the potential ramifications of a tougher nationalist policy are unclear (i.e. dissolution of sub-union administrative-political units or reorganization along non-ethnic lines), there should be no doubt that the same Soviet policy that coopted national elites also allowed for the persistence of strong popular national feelings. Consequently, the Soviet Union could emasculate the Orthodox Church, but it could not stop people from believing its tenets; it could teach marches praising the victories of Marxism-Leninism in the schools, but it could not cease the singing of ethnic songs at home; it could publicly Sovietize its people, but it could not strip them of their national identities. On the whole, Soviet policies of integration met with failure.

This analysis does not imply that nations had a tradition of challenging Soviet policy. Indeed, while many socialist principles were widely criticized under Khrushchev, little significant dissidence arose over the nationalities question for most of Soviet rule.[29] Instead, outward adherence to Soviet policies was given, while much of the substance of day-to-day life remained the same. The Soviet policy of "national in form, socialist in content" was turned on its head, giving way in practice to socialist in form, national in content. Soviet rule was circumvented, but not challenged, through subterfuge and corruption.

It was only after Gorbachev came to power that national groups directly confronted Soviet authority. Several factors worked in conjunction to bring about this dramatic change. Those Sovietologists undertaking class analysis have been quick to point out the nefarious effects of perestroika upon the interests of the industrial proletariat.[30] Yet a parallel process set off by perestroika, though less perceptible, was also damaging to the interests of national elites in the Soviet Union. This process involved *khozraschet* (self-accounting) and the related tightening of public monitoring of accounts; attacks on corruption; large-scale reductions in state-sector employment; and cutbacks in center-periphery capital transfers. The net effect was to economically alienate republican elites who could previously count on comfortable (and, in many cases, lavish) living standards.

Thus dissatisfied with the increasingly disadvantageous content of the nationalities contract, national elites were further spurred by glasnost, which allowed widespread criticism of the Soviet regime with lessened fear of retribution. Those who had previously chosen to "exit" were given a "voice" and motivated to air their grievances openly.[31] Together, the Soviet "carrot" of economic incentive diminished, and its authoritarian "stick" became less ominous as the state apparatus appeared fragmented and weak. Soviet suppression of national preferences became ineffectual at a time when Soviet socialism had become inextricably linked with imperialism in the minds of discontented national groups. If the Communist order had succeeded in bringing about forced *sblizhenie* (coming together) of the peoples of the Soviet Union, glasnost and perestroika could not help but produce their spontaneous *otdalenie* (distancing).

The most serious national uprisings against Soviet rule rose in the union republics. There are four factors which help to explain this. Firstly, only in the union republics did legitimate contractual grievances form the central plank of national demands. This dissent was strongest in the Baltics where, because of the Molotov-Ribbentrop Pact, no legitimate basis for their incorporation into the union existed. In other union republics, while the validity of the initial contract was acknowledged, the titular national movements demanded that the Soviet center recognize their right of secession. This was even true of Russia, which in 1990 joined its republican brethren in declaring itself sovereign.

Secondly, the state-dependent sector, which stood to lose the most from a sudden shift in Soviet policy, was most extensive in the union republics. To the extent that elite mobilization had been responsible for national uprising, movements among the republican national movements were successful.

Thirdly, national rights of the union republics had been most staunchly supported by Soviet policy. This support especially applied to linguistic and cultural autonomy. These nations would thus expect easier consolidation in the transition period.

Finally, union republics were the most ethnically homogeneous administrative divisions in the Soviet Union. According to 1989 Soviet census data, titular nationalities of union republics were majorities in all but Kazakhstan, where they represented a plurality of the population.[32] This situation was typically not the case in the autonomous republics, such as in Bashkhortostan, Buryatia, Karelia, Komi, Mari, Mordvinia, Udmurtia, and Sakha, where titular nationalities did not even comprise a plurality of the population.[33]

But while national expression throughout the union republics clearly opposed Soviet rule, the related demands were emphatically *not* total independence, as most national movements sought to dissolve the existing union in order to create a new one based upon more satisfactory, looser arrangements.[34] With the exception of the Baltics, only Georgia consistently rejected all calls for a new union treaty and pushed for complete secession. And while elite dissimilation may appear particularly strong in explaining anti-Soviet nationalist demonstrations, such an explanation is less compelling for other expressions of national sentiment which were either markedly less anti-Soviet, lacked reference to the Soviet state altogether, or embraced continued Soviet rule. This is first and foremost the case of the non-titular nationalities.

Following many of the union republican declarations, a large number of non-union republic-based national groups voiced demands for sovereignty (included among them the Abkhaz Checheno-Ingush, Chuvash, Karelian, Komi, Mari, Tatar, and Udmurt ASSRs and autonomous regions and areas including Adygei, Chukotka, Gorno-Altai, Karacharo-Cherkessia, Komi-Permyak, Koryak and South Ossetia).[35] Yet almost without exception, these movements challenged republican (most typically Russian), as opposed to Soviet, rule. These conflicts came from the peculiar existence of nations within nations, a phenomenon which may be referred to as *"matrioshka* nationalism." Reactionary movements resulted, with further consolidation of republican power making the republican government an immediate and dangerous threat. The same demonstrations asserting the rights of national movements in the union republics often hurt national movements in the autonomies as a direct consequence.

Tracing the nationalities explosions in the Soviet Union thus demonstrates a multiplicity of national interactions; the direct challenging of Soviet rule does not accurately describe national movements across the board. Some movements demanded independence, others opted for more limited increases in national autonomy; some attacked party representatives, Soviet army installations, and state institutions, while others targeted neighboring ethnic groups. It is not that the relationships of these movements with the Soviet state were fundamentally different from one another, but rather that other relationships with neighboring national groups were often themselves considered to pose a more immediate problem. National movements under the shadow of Soviet collapse were thus not simply reactive in opposing Soviet rule, but were interactive with the complex national structures around them. For a fuller understanding of these developments, we must consider a framework for national analysis.

## A framework for national analysis

Traditional Sovietology was Moscow-based, top-down, and monolithic. That there were strong ideological and practical factors underlying this approach is beyond question; most notable among them are the Cold War context of Western scholarship and the relative inaccessibility of Soviet sources. But whatever the motivations, the Soviet Union came to be viewed as a unified bloc, and most internal Soviet cleavages were either dismissed or ignored. To the extent that the Soviet periphery was recognized as worthy of analysis, nationalities were perceived as reacting to and dependent upon center-initiated policies. The few scholars working on the Soviet periphery through this period were effectively marginalized.

It was only after the national explosions under Gorbachev that the study of Soviet nationalities became significant. Sovietologists immediately focused upon the factors contributing to destabilization.[36] Why had the Soviet Union suddenly fallen apart? What, if anything, could be done to keep the process from progressing further? And, as research agendas changed in the post-Soviet context, how did the Soviet Union remain together in the first place?

These questions implicitly identified the inadequacy of state-centric nationalities analysis. Indeed, much has been written recently about the importance of a "perspective from below" – a regional approach discarding many of the methodological assumptions latent in traditional Sovietology, putting the overworked paradigm of state-civil society relations on the backburner and making corporatism no longer satisfactory.[37] But if the perspective from below recognized that post-Soviet methodology must consider nations first and foremost, the question of how to formulate such an approach remained. Post-Sovietology illuminated the failings of Sovietological analysis without offering a comprehensive theoretical framework to replace it. As a consequence, post-Soviet nationalities studies have continued to be characterized by the methods of area-studies rather than the canons of social science.[38] In the same vein as Stephen Cohen's revisionist replacement of the totalitarian school of Sovietology, a thorough alternative to the state-centric framework is desperately needed in the study of post-Soviet nationalities.[39]

In formulating such an alternative, we proceed from an analysis of the varied national relationships within the former Soviet Union, breaking national conflict into its constituent actor-types: center, titular nationality, and non-titular nationality. The use of the term *center*, as opposed to state, here recognizes the Weberian notion of that institution which holds a monopoly over the right to use coercive force.[40] In most cases, center and state are interchangeable. Traditionally, this was true of the Soviet Union. But the use of the term "center" also allows for a more accurate portrayal of the so-called "neocolonial" relationships between imperial powers and underdeveloped states, where authority lies outside the state in question. The ties between ruler and ruled may be discrete and indirect. The ruled may have gained a nominal sense of "statehood," but the national sentiment levied against perceived outside exploitation is no less substantive. Following Soviet collapse, as we shall see, the locus of analysis shifted somewhat, but the term has lost none of its utility.

The *titular nationality* is the nation which, for any number of economic, demographic, cultural, or political reasons, has been vested with administrative power in a given region. In Russia it is the Russians, in Moldova the Moldovans, in Sakha the Yakuts, and so on. The titular nationality has a special relationship with the state, being in a position of privilege *vis-à-vis* those nations not so empowered – the *non-titular nationalities*.

Although defined clearly under Soviet law, an analytical categorization of "titular" must show it to be a relative modifier. In other words, while "titular" relates to the special status of a nation in relation to the center, this status varies widely in a state with hierarchical titular rank. Nations may be considered titular in relation to other nations in certain contexts (i.e. titular Russians and non-titular Georgians in Russia; titular Uzbeks and non-titular Tajiks in Uzbekistan) while not in relation to others (non-titular Russians and titular Georgians in Georgia; titular Tajiks and non-titular Uzbeks in Tajikistan), depending upon their relative hierarchical status.

Table 1.1. *Patterns of inter-ethnic relations*

| | A | B | C | D |
|---|---|---|---|---|
| | Center | First-order titular nationality | Second-order titular nationality | Non-titular nationality |
| A  Center | | Integration | Integration | Assimilation |
| B  First-order titular nationality | Liberation | Competition | Domination | Domination |
| C  Second-order titular nationality | Collusion | Liberation | Competition | Domination |
| D  Non-titular nationality | Collusion | Liberation | Liberation | Competition |

Under Soviet rule, titular distinctions were particularly nuanced. Equality could be the foundation of a relationship between titular nationalities (on the union republican level – Estonians and Latvians, Armenians and Azeris), but it often was not (straddling different levels – Russians and Bashkirs, Uzbeks and Karakalpaks). Accordingly, it is useful to speak of *first-order* (union republic – Belarusans, Kyrgyz, Ukrainians) and *second-order* (ASSR – Abkhaz, Chechens, Yakuts) titular nationalities. Once again, in the post-Soviet context, the emergence of new states alters the framework for titular groups, but the same basic characterization applies.

Given these four actor-types, there are fifteen different possible interactions: center (*A*) – first-order titular nationality (*B*); *A* – second-order titular nationality (*C*); *A* – non-titular nationality (*D*); *B* – *A*; *B* – *B*; *B* – *C*; *B* – *D*; *C* – *A*; *C* – *B*; *C* – *C*; *C* – *D*; *D* – *A*; *D* – *B*; *D* – *C*; and *D* – *D*.[41] Nationalism, defined as the political ideology aspiring towards the congruency of nation and center, plays a role in each.[42] Although the magnitude of this role will likely be determined or at least constrained by the relative strength of the center, its *form* may be expected to change depending upon the interaction. Nationalism is thus not only Janus-faced, pointing upwards towards the state and downwards towards constituent peoples, but it also looks across to other nations.[43] These interactions may be shown graphically as dyads on a 4 × 4 matrix (see table 1.1).

This table represents the hypothesized objectives of each actor-type, given a certain interaction. Each of these interactions may be briefly outlined. The center's interaction with all titular nationalities is one of *integration*, whereby the center attempts to establish a singular set of overarching norms and values (and thus a singular "nation") to maintain social cohesion. Nationalism among the titular nationalities undermines the ability of the center to apply direct and unitary rule. Titular nationalities are therefore allowed many of the trappings of nationhood – language, cultural rite and ritual, education, and so forth – but are made to subscribe to fundamental economic and political norms of the larger state system. Center-driven motivations to maintain a position of strength in relation to the periphery thus lead to integrative policies. The Soviet center's relationships with Azeris, Bashkirs, Evenks, Georgians, and Uzbeks all fall under this category.

The center's relationship with non-titular nationalities follows the somewhat different pattern of *assimilation*. While the center's desire for relative strength remains, it feels for any number of reasons – historical, ideological, cultural, or demographic – that gradual integration is unnecessary. Instead, the center seeks to make the non-titular nationalities an undifferentiated part of the state culture. Linguistic rights are not protected; cultural practices, if not forgotten altogether, are weakened; and so on. Denied rights of their own as nations, non-titular nationalities find it very difficult to maintain their national heritage. This process was exemplified by relations between the Soviet state and the Jews, republican minorities such as Tabasaranis and Laks in Dagestan, Finns in Karelia, and the "peoples of the north" in Siberia. Ultimately, the expected outcomes in center policies towards titular and non-titular nationalities are both consistent with the traditional "perspective from above" – analyzing the Soviet state's justifications and actions towards its constituent nations in maintaining the integrity of the union – the essential difference between them is one of time-frame.

The interaction of first-order titular nationalities with the center was the traditional referent frame of the Soviet periphery – the "perspective from below" – and manifests nationalism as *liberation*. This relationship takes into account titular nationalities' hopes to thwart external rule and claim independence for themselves. Nations no longer wishing to yield to the diktat of central authority and desiring both a monopoly of control over the state apparatus and the ability to impose their norms and values upon their own populations first require liberation from the broader state-system.

Nationalism as liberation may manifest itself through demands for increased regional control of economic mechanisms, as it did among the Soviet republics of Central Asia, or through drives for independence, as it did in the Baltics and Georgia. It may also affect the leading titular or "hegemonic" nation of an empire. The Russians were not only the titular nationality of the RSFSR; to some extent, they were also the titular nationality for the entire Soviet Union. Historically, to quote Paul Goble, "Russians were offered the choice of being free or being powerful"; they chose the latter.[44] Yet many reconsidered their decisions in the throes of imperial crisis, pressing instead for liberation from the burdens of empire which for centuries led to the desecration of Russian national values and supporting the creation of a Russian nation-state.

Titular nationalities' intentions to improve their position *vis-à-vis* other titular nationalities of the same order are expressed in terms of *competition*. Desire to attain self-determination leads the titular nation to view as threatening other nations which it perceives as either encroaching on its own position or potentially able to make such an encroachment. Similar to the behavior of states in the international arena, the existence of mutually desired scarce resources creates a zero-sum relationship between titular nations, resulting in competition.[45]

Nationalism as competition can occur at all levels of national relations: between Uzbeks and Tajiks, Armenians and neighboring Turks, and, of course, Russians and Western nations. The focus of competition may be easily distributable (natural resources such as precious metals, oil, food), or it may be more absolute (land, political power), leading to a variance in the expected difficulties of conflict resolution. Rival claims over territory comprise the most long-standing and pernicious objects of competition (the conflict between Armenia and Azerbaijan over Nagorno-Karabagh provides one of the most obvious examples); easily observable indicators such as economic indices and military force levels also often lead to intense conflict. No matter what the immediate cause of dispute, however, the underlying motivation for competition remains constant.

The relationship between titular nationalities and lower order titular and non-titular nationalities is one of *domination*. By virtue of their privileged status, titular nationalities reap educational, employment, and social benefits. Lower-order titular and non-titular nationalities represent a threat to this near-monopoly – domination is the logical response. This relationship was expressed commonly in Russian relations with Bashkirs, Buryats, Chechens, Evenks, Jews, Tatars, Tuvans, and many other nations within the RSFSR. Here the relativistic use of "titular" comes into play, with second-order "titular" nationalities dominated as non-titular nationalities in relation to the hegemonic Russian nation. Similarly, Georgian relations with Abkhaz and Ossetians in Georgia, Azeri relations with Armenians in Azerbaijan, and, more recently, Latvian, Lithuanian, and Estonian relations with Russians in the Baltics all display this essential characteristic of domination.[46]

Yet, just as first-order titular nationalities express nationalism to keep lower order and non-titular nationalities from acquiring the fruits of power – be they economic, political, cultural, or otherwise – lower order and non-titular nationalities express nationalism to attain those privileges from which they are excluded. Paralleling the actions of first-order titular nationalities toward the center, this is also nationalism as *liberation*, whereby lower order and non-titular nationalities attempt to achieve self-determination. If developments in Chechnya against Russian rule provide one particularly explosive example, nationalism as liberation among lower-order titulars such as the Abkhaz, Buryats, Komi, North Ossetians, Tatars and Turans fit this model equally well.

Lower-order titular and non-titular nationalities interacting with the center are in perhaps the most interesting position, expressing nationalism as *collusion*. Ultimately non-titular as a consequence of center-initiated policy, they none the less find themselves most threatened by the titular nations directly above them. These ruling nations pose the greatest danger to lower-order titular and non-titular nationalities, and only the center possesses the power to restrain them. Accordingly, collusion surfaces as the national analog to the age-old Islamic tenet "the enemy of my enemy is my brother." Lower-order titular and non-titular nationalities collude with the center to guarantee some small degree of autonomy, favoring such mechanisms as a strong unitary state apparatus to keep the titular nationalities above them in line.[47] Particularly in the case of Bashkir, Buryat, Chukchi, Chuvash, Karachai, and Tatar relations with the Soviet center, nationalism as collusion was apparent.

Finally, there are interactions between non-titular nationalities which also express nationalism as *competition*. While mimicking titular-titular relationships through competition over such scarce resources as property rights, housing, and basic sustenance, non-titular nationalities typically lack the organizational skills and resources to engage in direct competition with one another. Yet, in the relatively small number of cases where this is not the case, such competition may be fierce. Dagestan provides perhaps the best example, with a host of non-titulars engaged in competition with one another (Kumyks and Avars, Lezgins and Avars, Lezgins and Kumyks, and so on). Relations between Meshketian Turks and Kyrgyz in Uzbekistan, and Russians and Crimean Tatars in Ukraine have also reflected non-titular competition.

This framework describes the basic nature of relationships among actors found in the Soviet and post-Soviet arenas. To move from the sketches provided here to a more concrete analysis, however, requires three major provisos. Firstly, room to maneuver exists within each interaction and the objectives of a given actor may be pursued in many different ways, from the most gradual policies to the most radical. Liberation may be a demand for greater cultural and economic autonomy, or it may be a secessionist movement. Competition could emerge as the imposition of tariffs over trade, or it could express itself as armed conflict. Many factors assist in determining the means involved, including the specific nature of actor grievances, the existence and consequent severity of a relationship of dependency, the internal and or external support for the pursuit of given means, and the perceived potential of success and the consequences of failure.

Secondly and relatedly, these relationships discuss dispositions towards action and not abilities. Vast power imbalances may make a preferred strategy impossible to employ. Hence the relative quiescence of Baltic national movements for nearly half a century of Soviet rule, despite a strong disposition towards liberation. Weighing the real and grave dangers of voicing opposition and the likely prospects of success provides a straightforward explanation of "ethnic stability" under Soviet empire.

Thirdly, as is evident from the matrix, actors are constantly involved in multiple relationships, which often make the logical expression of nationalism seem hypocritical in practice. For example, first-order titular nationalities may employ the rhetoric of liberation when dealing with the center, while at the same time rejecting such claims (and exerting domination) when they are made by lower-order titular or non-titular nationalities within their borders. Viewed in this context, Russian President Yeltsin's criticism of Gorbachev's infringement of Baltic sovereignty through economic blockade and troop movement in 1990–91 is consistent with his policies of repression against the wayward Chechen republic.

Different impulses may also be found among the same nations, leading to contradictory expressions of national sentiment. These impulses are not mutually exclusive, but represent competing simultaneously-operating motivations which may lead not only to the strengthening or weakening of "traditional" state-building but also of the articulation of those demands. For example, cooperation may occur among titular nationalities instead of competition, as a tactic which persists in the face of another relationship perceived to be of greater immediate importance (i.e. liberation from the Soviet center).[48] Hence the close coordination of the Baltic national movements in the Gorbachev era, only to be replaced by cooling and eventual competitive relations (particularly in the economic sphere) with the collapse of Soviet power.

Few scholars have recognized the potential effects of these varied relationships on the expression of national sentiment. Szporluk's division of Russian nationalists into "empire savers" and "nation builders" – two starkly different sentiments each grounded in the primacy of different national interactions – is a start in this direction.[49] "Empire savers" focus on the titular nationality/non-titular nationality interaction, expressing nationalism as domination.[50] "Nation builders," alternatively focus on the Russian relationship with the Soviet center, and so seek liberation from empire.[51] Continuing with Szporluk's categorization, not all non-Russian nationalists are empire destroyers. While such a tendency may have existed throughout the Soviet periphery, it was often diluted or even overwhelmed by other impulses, equally nationalist, which played themselves out against other nations. Only a case-by-case consideration of national agendas, dynamic national forces, and pertinent social cleavages enables clear determination of which impulses predominate.

## Nationalities in the post-Soviet context

Far from having created stability, the collapse of the Soviet Union resulted in a dramatic increase in the amount and the intensity of ethnic conflict. Between wars in Armenia and Azerbaijan, Georgia, Tajikistan, Moldova, and Chechnya, not to mention serious ethnic discontent from Kiev to Kyzyl, almost no corner of the former Soviet Union has been free of ethnic tension. Indeed, the volatility of the post-Soviet context is unparalleled even in the final days of Soviet power. Given the disintegration of what had been for seventy years a structure of multinational empire, how can we understand the continuing cycles of discontent in the Soviet successor states?

There are two key developments affecting post-Soviet nationalities relations which have underpinned the increase in ethnic tension – the replacement of a single Soviet center with fifteen new centers and, subsequently, the emergence of a Russia-dominated post-Soviet order. The first development was both immediate and dramatic, as – upon the demise of the Soviet Union – first-order titular nationalities became centers unto themselves. Existing as they did in different environments with varied arrays of titular and non-titular nationalities under their rule, each of these centers had their own interests to protect against the others. In essence, the post-Soviet context replicated over and over again the Soviet nationalities matrix presented in the previous section.

But while the structure of national interactions remained largely unchanged, the power balances underlying it had altered significantly. Given the post-Soviet governments' lack of popular legitimacy and their tenuous authority over local constituencies, the dangers posed by autonomy-seeking titular and non-titular nationalities became greater than ever. If liberation from the Soviet monolith seemed increasingly plausible once cracks began to show in the empire's foundations, Soviet-era second-order titular prospects for independence were magnified by the ascendancy of successor states which lacked foundations entirely.

The consequences for post-Soviet nationalities relations have been enormous. Centers with little if any preparation for self-rule have attempted to quickly assimilate potential national dissenters in the hopes of shoring up their own political authority. Ironically, the long-term prospects of assimilation are likely greater in the post-Soviet context than they had been for the Soviet state, for the national ideas of the Soviet successors are more compelling than the vague supranationalism that the communist empire had to offer. But in the more immediate future, as the viability of the successor states themselves is an open question, the prospects of peaceful nation-building remain tenuous.

Part of the reason for this expectation of instability is that the devolution of power that accompanied Soviet collapse had by no means reached a logical conclusion with the independence declarations of 1991. New first-order titular nationalities, previously firmly nested under the Soviet matrioshka, saw no reason that they too could not become centers. Sensing opportunity, the new titulars were quick to revolt. Thus the sudden challenges posed by the Chechens and Tatars in Russia, the Poles in Lithuania and the Gagauz in Moldova. And in regions where open ethnic conflict had already been brewing, Soviet collapse only made matters worse. The bloody war over Karabagh intensified with the end of Soviet power, as the Armenians stepped up their demands for independence from a weak and newly-independent Azerbaijan. So too Abkhazians and Ossetians sought to rid themselves of Georgian rule, while Georgia was still deeply in the throes of state-building.

Collusionary trends were also in evidence. In Ukraine, Soviet collapse effectively gave Russians in Crimea – dominant in the peninsula – first-order titular status. Crimean Russians moved quickly to liberate themselves from Ukraine (and reintegrate with Russia), demanding greater rights from Kiev and organizing referenda on independence. But for the disenfranchised Crimean Tatars, who effectively had become non-titulars in their own homeland, the incentives were different. Instead of renewing demands for autonomous control of the Crimean peninsula, the Tatars came out in favor of strengthening a unitary Ukrainian state. When the Ukrainian government, concerned about alienating the Russian population and exacerbating an already tense ethnic situation, proved less than forthcoming to Crimean Tatar interests, the Tatars turned not to secession but to support of the Ukrainian national movement, Rukh. Nationalism as collusion was clear among the Tatars, and it occurred similarly among Russian non-titular majorities throughout the autonomies of the Russian Federation.

A final result of changes in the post-Soviet power balance was the development of competitive relations among the new centers or, put another way, the initiation of international relations in what had become an anarchic post-Soviet realm. Competition for scarce resources among union republics that had been veiled by the umbrella of Soviet power and had only started to emerge as a troublesome source of conflict under Gorbachev came out in full force after Soviet collapse. This expressed itself most often intra-regionally, as it did over water and other resources in Central Asia, and energy and land in the Caucasus. A similiar competition emerged among the Russian autonomies, although with less force than it had among the Soviet successors, given relative power capabilities.

If the emergence of centers in the former-Soviet periphery was the immediate consequence of Soviet collapse, the post-Soviet context soon after bore witness to a second important development: the reemergence of a dominant center seeking regional hegemony. Never having forgotten its imperial roots, the Russian government quickly began to see its own state interests as contiguous with those of the former-Soviet landmass. This was evidenced concretely by Russian efforts to coordinate military defense zones throughout the former Soviet Union, control key economic infra-structure (in particular, energy import and export), and push through poli-cies of dual citizenship. Hence the establishment of the Commonwealth of Independent States, originally expected by Western analysts to be a figleaf for the peaceful severance of ties between the former Soviet republics but, from the Russian perspective, created to serve as the mechanism for repub-lics' reintegration into an imperial structure.[52]

As a result of this second development, a new form of collusion emerged – between Russia and the titular and non-titular nationalities out-side Russia – with the intention of undermining the fledgling sovereignties of the successor states. Post-Soviet titular nationalities increasingly looked to Russia as an answer to their political problems, putting aside their own claims for independence in favor of a Russian dominated post-Soviet system. Hence Abkhazians and Ossetians, seeking to undermine Georgia's renegade policies and get Georgia back into the CIS, requesting and receiv-ing Russian military assistance. Similarly the leaders of the Lezgin and Talysh movements in Azerbaijan, who looked to Russia for support in their efforts to gain greater leverage *vis-à-vis* the Elcibey and, later, Aliev govern-ments. The aptly-labelled "neo-Soviet" forces in Tajikistan, colluding with Russian "peacekeeping" forces, provide yet a third textbook example.

But these collusionary relationships notwithstanding, there remain essen-tial differences between Soviet and post-Soviet empire-building. Most sig-nificantly, the underlying logic of post-Soviet center-periphery relations is neo-Russian imperialism, an ethno-nationalist motivating force. Accord-ingly, the post-Soviet Russian center harks back to the Tsarist Empire in seeking to assimilate on the basis of a Russian national, not a supra-national, idea. This makes it possible, if onerous, for fellow Slav Ukrainians and Belarusans to consider themselves part and parcel of a new empire, but it makes the prospects for the Central Asians, Caucasians, and even Balts more ominous.

This has made especially destabilizing the issue of Russian minorities outside Russia. Scattered throughout the former Soviet Union, the Russian minorities according to the 1989 census comprised 25.3 million of the populations of the non-Russian Soviet republics. But not only do the Rus-sian minorities themselves pose a threat to post-Soviet governments; they have also brought the threat (and in several cases the reality) of intervention on their behalf from the Russian homeland.[53] The ethnic motivations behind Russian expansionism make Russian minorities' prospects of col-lusion transcend the purely strategic. The dangers are particularly great in regions where Russians are concentrated on specific territories, such as in northeast Estonia, northern Kazakhstan, and Transneister Moldova.

How then will national relations develop in the post-Soviet context? Our theoretical framework led us to expect extremely complex and fragmented nationalities movements in a Soviet Union under transition, with conflicting objectives sought not only by different national groups but also different tendencies appearing within the same national group. To the extent that preexisting power structures have remained intact since the disintegration of the Soviet system, we expect such dynamics to persist in the successor states. The preliminary overview presented in the final section of this chapter substantiates these hypotheses, further arguing that the resurgence of the Russian center, coupled with the existence of fifteen weak, post-Soviet centers-in-becoming, creates a climate propitious for heightened instability and ethnic conflict. Beyond this, it is impossible to draw further conclusions without rigorous, case-by-case consideration. It is to this approach that we now turn.

## Notes

1 There has been considerable debate on nation counting in the former Soviet Union, particularly concerning the difference between the ill-defined Soviet conceptions of "nation" and "ethnic group." See S.I. Bruk, "Ethnicheskie protsessy i voprosy optimizatsii natsional'no administrastivnogo deleniia v SSSR," *Natsional'nye problemy v sovremennykh usloviiakh* (Moscow: Institute of Marxism-Leninism, CPCC, 1988), pp. 128–143; and M.A. Abdullaev, "Osobennosti razvitiia dukhovnoi kul'tury malykh narodov SSSR v usloviiakh sovershenstvovaniia sotsializma," *Filosofiia razvivaiushchegosia sotializma* (Moscow: 1988), pp. 139–144.

2 There is, of course, another side to this problem. Cleavages which appear national in form by virtue of continued association with co-nationals may well become nationalist in content. Similarly, even though groups may be mobilized for diverse non-national purposes, to the extent that they are perceived as national movements, this perception may become self-fulfilling.

3 On the nationalizing state and its use in the post-Soviet context, see Rogers Brubaker, "Ethnic Nationalizing States in the 'Old' Europe, and the New," in Ian Bremmer, ed., *Understanding Nationalism: Ethnic Minorities and Nation-Building in the Post-Communist States* (forthcoming) and related works by Brubaker on this topic.

4 J.L. Talmon, *The Myth of the Nation and the Vision of Revolution* (London: Secker and Warburg, 1981), pp. 544–545.

5 Peter Zwick convincingly demonstrates the commonalties between the two in his *National Communism* (Boulder, CO: Westview, 1983).

6 Talmon, *Myth*, p. 545.

7 *Ibid.*, p. 162.

8 In a similar way, few could have expected (Andrei Amalrik is a distinguished exception) that "taking the lid off totalitarian communism would lead to national conflicts as bitter and pervasive as have recently occurred in the Soviet Empire" (Andrei Amalrik, *Will the Soviet Survive Until 1984?* [New York: Harper and Row, 1970] ). The internationalism of Rosa Luxemburg seems an anachronism in the denouement of the USSR.

9 Talmon, *Myth*, p. 162.

10 *Ibid.*, p. 163.

11 Alexander Gershenkron, *Economic Backwardness in Historical Perspective* (Cambridge MA: Harvard University Press, 1979).

12 Roman Szporluk, *Communism and Nationalism* (New York: Oxford University Press, 1988), p. 223.

13 *Ibid.*, p. 229.
14 Isaac Deutscher, *Stalin: A Political Biography*, 2nd edn (New York: Oxford University Press, 1967), p. 243.
15 They also became the target of nationalist *revindications* when Gorbachev's *demokratizatsia* policies provided nationalist leaders with the legitimacy to articulate and aggregate their views.
16 Szporluk, *Communism*, p. 51.
17 Walker Connor, *The National Question of Marxist-Leninist Theory and Strategy* (Princeton: Princeton University Books, 1984), pp. 5–20.
18 Hélène Carrère d'Encausse, *Decline of an Empire: The Soviet Socialist Republics in Revolt* (New York: Newsweek Books, 1979), p. 46.
19 Ronald Suny, "The Revenge of the Past: Socialism and Ethnic Conflict in Transcaucasia," *New Left Review*, November-December 1990, no. 184, pp. 5–6.
20 It is significant that there was support among some Marxists for this position. Most notable was Tatar revolutionary Sultan Galiev, who advanced the notion of "proletarian nations," where entire nations on the periphery were thought to be subordinate to the imperialist center. Class and national cleavages on the periphery could be thought to coincide and, following this reasoning, could be cultivated simultaneously. See Alexander A. Bennigsen and S. Enders Wimbush, *Muslim National Communism in the Soviet Union: A Revolutionary Strategy for the Colonial World* (Chicago: University of Chicago Press, 1979), pp. 41–45.
21 Connor, *National Question*, pp. 45–61.
22 This process led to the creation of modern national identities in Central Asia and the strengthening of national identities in the Caucasus.
23 Lenin's shift from a policy of regional autonomy to one of assimilation foreshadowed more ominous developments after his death. The accession to power of Stalin led to a deterioration of national rights in the Soviet Union. The national egalitarianism which had prevailed under Lenin became national regimentation and hierarchy. Russia was acknowledged to be the greatest nation while many others (most notably Chechens, Germans, Kalmyks, and Crimean Tatars) were deported by the hundreds of thousands to Central Asia and Siberia, punished *qua* nations for crimes against the Soviet Union. Russification took place to a far greater extent under Stalin, and "somewhat national in form, Russian in content" became the rule.
    It is ironic, however, that mass national identities were strengthened by Stalin's internal passport system, under which nationality was officially reported. The strength of Soviet policies of preference can be clearly seen in the decisions of ethnically-mixed marriage descendants, who invariably chose to affiliate themselves with their local titular nationality. Given the choice, it was deemed preferable to be Russian only in Russia.
24 Paul B. Henze, "The Specter and Implications of Internal Nationalist Dissent: Historical and Functional Comparisons," *Soviet Nationalities in Strategic Perspective* (London: Croom Helm, 1985), p. 15.
25 "Nation" and "nationality" are used indiscriminately throughout this chapter. The distinction in Soviet usage is an artificial one, based upon the Stalin-propagated notion of hierarchical relations among nations.
26 In reality it was even messier, with some administrative units having two titular nationalities.
27 Three factors underlay the Soviet administrative distinctions. Firstly, each union republic bordered upon a foreign state. Were this to be otherwise, secession would leave a hole in the center of the union, an impractical arrangement for the republic and an intolerable one for the Soviet Union. Secondly, larger, concentrated nations typically merited a higher administrative bracket. The vast majority of nations in the former Soviet Union are numerically small – usually numbering in the tens of thousands but

occasionally as few as several hundred. Other nations, most notably the Tatars, had populations spread across the Soviet Union. Not deemed to constitute a credible threat to the stability of the union, they were not granted the right to secede. (Distinctions between ASSRs and Autonomous Regions and Areas were largely based upon the size of the national group as well.) Thirdly, nations which did not have their homeland within the Soviet Union but were instead part of a diaspora fell into a lower administrative bracket. When this was the case, demands for statehood were either already actualized elsewhere or otherwise would be focused in the homeland.

With few exceptions, these factors applied evenly throughout the Soviet Union. The Buryats, Karelians, and Tuvans – each bordering on foreign states and as large or almost as large as, for example, the Estonians and Moldovans – were the only nations which had been denied union republic status despite their apparent suitability. The Karelian case is interesting in that it was initially afforded union republic status upon its admission into the USSR in 1940 but was downgraded to ASSR in 1956, because of concerns about its size and the possibility of an outbreak of Finnish nationalism in the area. Thus, while there may have been elements of arbitrariness in categorization (and, indeed, strong elements of fictitiousness – in particular, the attempted legitimizing of Soviet treatment of the Jews through the creation of a national Jewish territory, Birobidzhan, in Siberia), for the most part administrative status was delineated according to a consistent plan.

28  The recognition of the power of nationalism did not only lead to sanction. The power of Russian nationalism was used instrumentally by Stalin (as was organized religion) during World War II. When mass mobilization became an immediate necessity, Stalin called the citizens to fight for Great Russian nationalism and the *Rodina* (Motherland), not socialism.

29  The few exceptions include isolated assertions of linguistic autonomy and anti-Stalinist sentiment during the Brezhnev years.

30  See, for example, Anders Aslund, *Gorbachev's Struggle for Economic Reform* (Ithaca: Cornell University Press, 1989); Marshall I. Goldman, *Gorbachev's Challenge: Economic Reform in the Age of High Technology* (New York: W.W. Norton, 1987); and Ed A. Hewett, *Reforming the Soviet Economy* (Brookings: Washington DC, 1988).

31  See Albert O. Hirschman, *Exit, Voice, and Loyalty* (Cambridge: Harvard University Press, 1970).

32  Barbara A. Anderson and Brian D. Silver, "Aspects of Soviet Ethnic Demography," unpublished paper. University of California, Berkeley, February 1991.

33  Russians are typically the majority group in these cases, often vastly outnumbering the titular nationality. In 1989 the population in Buryatia was 70 percent Russian and 24 percent Buryat; in Karelia, 74 percent Russian, 10 percent Karelian; and in Mordvinia, 67 percent Russian, 33 percent Mordvin (see Appendix A).

34  Central Asia is the most gradualistic of the cases, as fundamental national issues there were neither ones of sovereignty or independence. Greater autonomy over economic matters had not so much been demanded as requested. Calls for linguistic, religious, and cultural autonomy were only somewhat stronger. The primary demand had been for help, particularly on the environmental front (with regards to the Aral issue), but also economically. Central Asian states, lacking both infrastructure and promising non-Soviet regional alternatives, found themselves reliant upon the continued support of the center. These problems necessitated the immediate attention of all Central Asians; national sovereignty did not assist in their solution.

35  This list does not exclude the numerous "counter-movements" of ethnic Russians in the peripheral autonomous republics, Azeris in Armenia, Armenians in Azerbaijan, and so on.

36  Examples of this focus include Robert Conquest, ed., *The Last Empire: Nationality and the Soviet Future* (Stanford: Hoover Institution Press, 1986); Nadia Diuk and Adrian

Karatnycky, *The Hidden Nations: The People Challenge the Soviet Union* (New York: William Morrow and Co., 1990); and Bohdan Nahaylo and Victor Swoboda, *Soviet Disunion* (New York: The Free Press, 1990).

37 This scholarship includes Lubomyr Hajda and Mark Beissinger, eds., *The Nationalities Factor in Soviet Politics and Society* (Boulder, CO; Westview, 1990); Gregory Gleason, *Federalism and Nationalism: The Struggle for Republican Rights in the USSR* (Boulder, CO: Westview, 1990); and Graham Smith, *The Nationalities Question in the Soviet Union* (London: Longman, 1991).

38 See, for one notable example among many, the well-documented but none the less insular *Studies of Nationalities in the USSR Series* (published by Hoover Institution Press), a collection of ethnographic "thick descriptions."

39 Stephen Cohen, *Rethinking the Soviet Experience* (New York: Oxford University Press, 1986). Such a framework would also have usefulness in the study of national relations outside and, of course, within the Soviet successor states themselves. The resurgence of nationalism in the post-colonial period was not a phenomenon specific to the Soviet Union, and much as examples for understanding national group relations are usefully drawn from outside the Soviet Union, so too applications of its methodology should not be confined to its former borders.

40 Max Weber, "Politics as a Vocation," in H. H. Gerth and C. Wright Mills, eds., *From Max Weber: Essays in Sociology* (London: Routledge and Kegan Paul, 1948), pp. 77–78.

41 In an ethnocratic state, when center and titular nationality are more or less synonymous, there are only three relationships: center / titular nationality (*A*) – non-titular nationality (*B*); *B* – *A*; and *B* – *B*.

42 This is a variation on the widely accepted definition of nationalism presented by Ernest Gellner. See Gellner, *Nations and Nationalism: New Perspectives on the Past* (Ithaca: Cornell University Press, 1983), pp. 1–7.

43 Anthony D. Smith, *Theories of Nationalism* (London: Macmillan, 1971).

44 Paul Goble, "Imperial Endgame: Nationality Problems and the Soviet Union," unpublished paper, November 1990. p. 3.

45 And once again signs of weakness in the power of the center, like anarchy in the international realm, would serve as the catalyst for the competition.

46 Interestingly, second-order titular nationalities could thereby express nationalism *vis-à-vis* non-titulars, as the Kabardinians in Kabardino-Balkaria have against the non-titular Noga.

47 It should therefore come as no surprise that Russian nationalists often denied nationalist movements in these areas as fomented by the KGB (assumedly under Gorbachev's control).

48 This can work in reverse as well. A titular nationality may cooperate with the center because a competitive relationship with a neighboring titular nationality is considered more important. Note that the case is slightly different for the lower-order titular and non-titular nationalities, whose collusionary relationship with the center is *not* temporary because its resolution of the more "pressing" matters (conflict with the dominant titular nationality) necessitates its becoming a first-order titular nationality itself. The relationship then becomes one of liberation from the center, but no longer between center and lower-order titular or non-titular nationality.

49 Szporluk, "Dilemmas of Russian Nationalism," *Problems of Communism*, July/August, 1989, pp. 15–35.

50 Significantly, from this perspective union republican nationalities are considered to be lower-order titular.

51 Both categories may be aptly titled "empire savers," with the only substantive distinctions being *size* of empire (since the RSFSR may hardly be considered a nation), but Szporluk's distinction none the less applies.

52 Also not to be ignored is the widespread currency among Russian policymakers of the term "Near Abroad", referring to the non-Russian states of the former Soviet Union. This has shown clearly the extent to which Russia believes that there remaines a special entity which can be accurately conceived through traditional interpretations of international relations.

53 The potential danger of such collusion has been revealed by Russian Foreign Minister Kozyrev, who has repeatedly stressed that the Russian government reserves the right to intervene militarily to protect the rights of Russians living in the Near Abroad.

# Part II
# Russia and its nations

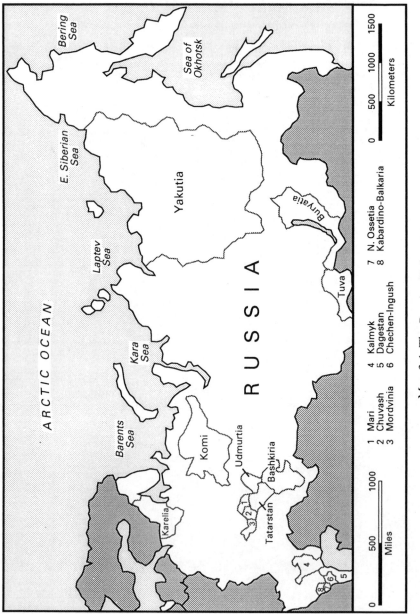

Map 2.1 The Russian Federation

1 Mari
2 Chuvash
3 Mordvinia

4 Kalmyk
5 Dagestan
6 Chechen-Ingush

7 N. Ossetia
8 Kabardino-Balkaria

# 2  Russia: in search of an identity?

JOHN B. DUNLOP

Since 1987, when Mikhail Gorbachev's programs of glasnost and demo-cratization began to set off chain reactions of convulsive political change, ethnic Russians have been a people in quest of an identity. During the seventy years of communist rule, most Russians had come to accept the regime's attempt to identify their interests as a people with those of the USSR as a whole. This identification had been reinforced structurally: unlike the other fourteen union republics, the Russian Soviet Federated Socialist Republic (or RSFSR for short) had deliberately not been given many of the institutions enjoyed by the other republics; there was, for example, no Russian KGB, no Russian MVD, no Russian Academy of Sciences, and no television channels or radio stations geared specifically at the interests of ethnic Russians. Strikingly, there was not even a Russian Communist Party, while all the other republics possessed their own party organizations.

The obvious aim behind this denial of structural parity to the Russian Republic was to bind Russians, the lynchpin ethnos of the Soviet Union, as closely as possible to the USSR as a whole. There is evidence that the regime was to a considerable degree successful in achieving this goal. Nationalities specialist Yuri Arutyunyan has noted that, "the concepts of 'Union' and 'Russia' in the minds of Russians are one and the same."[1]

This conjoining of the concepts "Russian" and "Soviet" was further emphasized by the fact that some twenty-five million Russians lived in the minority republics. This migration of Russians to the periphery had served to dilute the political and economic clout of the titular peoples of the other republics. In the Russian Republic, on the other hand, Russians lived compactly, comprising 81.5 percent of the population, thereby making Russia the third most ethnically homogeneous republic in the union after Armenia and Azerbaijan. As two Estonian scholars have noted, this vast movement of Russians to the periphery was a demographic policy specifically directed from the center, whose purpose was the formation of a nationally-mixed population in every region of the Soviet Union.[2] In Estonia, they report, the number of Russians grew from less than 25,000 in 1945 to 475,000 in 1989. The aim behind the regime's encouragement of such migration was to create a supra-ethnic "Soviet people" who would speak Russian but be ethnically and culturally mongrelized.

## An empire which is not an empire

Western commentators have frequently applied the term "Russian empire" both to pre-revolutionary Tsarist rule and to the post-revolutionary Soviet state. This imprecise use of terminology serves to skew and to distort the position of Russians under both the Tsars and the Soviets. The nationalities specialist, the late Hugh Seton-Watson, was wont to underline his conviction that the Tsarist empire should not be regarded as an ethnic Russian empire. "The government of the Russian Empire," he stressed, "was based on the principle of autocracy. All Russian subjects owed allegiance to the Tsar, who was responsible only to God. Provided that they loyally obeyed him, they enjoyed his protection regardless of whether they were Russian by speech or religion."[3] It was only toward the end of the nineteenth century, Seton-Watson notes, during the reigns of Alexander III and Nicholas II, that the Tsarist government began to adopt a conscious policy of Russification. "The previous policies," he writes, "had been made in the name of a monarch responsible to God. Russification was a policy made in the name of the Russian nation. It assumed that Russians were superior to the other subjects of the tsar . . ."[4]

If the Tsarist empire cannot, except for its closing years, be termed a Russian empire, much less can the Soviet empire be so considered. As Carl Linden pointed out in 1983, "the [Soviet] party-state in its strict conception acts not in the name of those it rules but as a proxy of the future 'communized' humanity freed of political rule and no longer separated into nation-states. By its ideology the Soviet party-state is the revolutionary replacement of the Russian nation-state, not its continuation."[5] However, in practice, as Linden notes, considerations of *Realpolitik* often required the Soviet regime to tap the energies of Russian patriotism as a "secret additive" to its power. This was especially true during Brezhnev's long reign, which witnessed a marked decline in the mobilizing power of the official ideology. During the Brezhnev years, an ideologically illicit "Russian imperial nationalism" was used to prop up a decaying Marxism-Leninism.

If the Soviet Union could not legitimately be termed a "Russian empire," neither could Russians be called an "imperial people." As Alain Besançon commented in 1983, the position of Russians in the USSR differed in important ways from, say, the position of the English or the French in the British and French empires. "To have an empire," Besançon explained, "one must have a privileged people, an essentially military means of conquest, and limited goals. The Russian people has no privileges. It has 'advantages' certainly, as the surest ally of communism, and party leaders are often drawn from its ranks, even in the national republics." However, Besançon went on, "These advantages [of the Russians] are not rights. Moreover, they are compensated for by heavier obligations, exemption from which is considered by the Russians to be a privilege of the non-Russian nationalities. A Russian who enjoys privileges as a Communist owes his privileges to his communism, not to his Russianness."[6]

With the exception of the Central Asian peoples, Russians in the Soviet Union did not live noticeably better than did the titular peoples of the minority republics. Debilitating poverty, wretched roads, and environmental degradation were the norm in the Russian Republic as they were throughout the USSR. Russian patriotic thought was carefully monitored and, where deemed necessary, suppressed by a watchful censorship. Some Russian nationalist spokesmen, such as Vladimir Osipov, editor of the well-known *samizdat* journal *Veche*, found themselves undergoing long prison sentences for preaching "the Russian idea."

However, while they lived badly and were not an "imperial people" in the Western sense of that term, ethnic Russians were encouraged by the regime to take pride in the fact that they belonged to a "great power." As Milovan Djilas observed in 1988: "It's true that the ordinary Russian bears the main burden of empire, without sharing its blessings. But the fact is: almost every Russian, lowly or elevated, embraces with enthusiasm the idea of Russian aggrandizement and takes for granted that he has to make sacrifices for it."[7] In a perverse sense, therefore, if Djilas is correct, imperial pride took the place of economic well-being for many ethnic Russians.

## Russians witness a fragmentation of empire

The years 1990 and 1991 witnessed an almost textbook case of the collapse of an empire. The multinational Tsarist Empire – only 45 percent of whose populace were ethnic Russians – had, as is well known, been on the verge of breakup in 1914. Through a combination of coercion, cunning, flexibility, and considerable luck, the Bolsheviks had been able to render this dying empire, albeit with somewhat altered borders, viable for another seventy years, and indeed to expand its direct influence into Eastern Europe and Afghanistan, with its indirect influence spreading throughout the world. In hindsight, we can see that this vast empire began to suffer from degeneracy and "imperial indigestion" during the Brezhnev period. The "bleeding wound" of Afghanistan served gradually to sap the fading imperial will of the Russian people at the same time as the emergence of the Solidarity movement in Poland represented a mortal threat to continued Soviet hegemony in Eastern Europe.

At home, in the USSR, a complementary process was at work. As the Soviet specialist in inter-republican migration, Viktor Perevedentsev, has noted, a sudden break (*perelom*) in migration patterns became observable in the mid-1970s.[8] Up until then, there had been a marked net outflow of Russians to the other republics; around 1975, this pattern reversed, and a net inflow into the RSFSR became noticeable. To cite Perevedentsev's figures, during the years 1966–1970 the Russian Republic experienced a net outmigration of 598,000 persons; during the period 1971–1975 the figure was 195,000. In the years 1976–1980, by contrast, Russia experienced a net immigration of 725,000; during the period 1979–1988 the net inflow was 1,767,000. Central Asia, on the other hand, which until the mid-1970s had been a recipient of large inmigration, began to witness a population outflow. Thus during the years 1976–1980 Central Asia (excluding Kazakhstan) experienced a net outmigration of 245,000; for the years 1979–1988, the figure was 850,000. The comparable figures for Kazakhstan were 414,000 and 784,000. From being a "donor" republic, the RSFSR had become the largest "recipient" republic in the Soviet Union.

The gradual loss of Russian "imperial will" during the draining war with Afghanistan was therefore accompanied by a dramatic end to ethnic Russian penetration into the periphery. Yuri Arutyunyan of the Institute of Ethnography in Moscow noted in 1991 that this dramatic outmigration from the periphery was due, in significant part, to the fact that the "socio-professional" status of Russians in the minority republics was steadily declining. "In Tbilisi," he reported.

> the Russians find themselves in a lower socio-occupational status than the indigenous Georgian population. For a long time, they did not seriously compete with the Georgians, who perform more qualified and prestigious work. In Tallinn, the coefficients of occupational prestige for Russians and for the indigenous ethnic groups are nearly the same, because of high competitive abilities of the Russians and Estonians. In Kishinev, radical changes have been observed: in the 1970s, the Moldavians had lower occupational prestige on average than the Russians, but this difference had evened out by the 1980s . . . In Tashkent, in the 1970s the Uzbeks lagged far behind the Russians in prestigious occupations; towards the 1980's the difference evened out . . .[9]

Losing their competitive advantage *vis-à-vis* the titular peoples of the periphery was a factor powerful in inducing Russians to contemplate returning to their home republic.

The tumultuous events of 1987–1991 came as a profound shock for ethnic Russians living in the periphery, whose numbers were already being depleted by significant outmigration. Suddenly, many of them found themselves deemed "foreigners" in what they had considered their own land. The following letter from Dushanbe, where some 190,000 Russians lived, captures the sense of panic and indignation which came over many Russians living in the periphery during the late 1980s:

> Dear comrades, mothers and fathers, brothers and sisters!

> The Russian-langue populace of the capital of Tajikistan, the city of Dushanbe, appeals to you!

> Agitated by the outrages of fanatical crowds, by the bloodletting, by the blind hatred, and by the pillaging, we appeal to you for help! The lives of children, women, and old men are under threat! The compromising tactics of the [Soviet] government and its fear to take decisive action to halt the disorders assist the raging of anarchy and of religious [i.e. Muslim] fanaticism.[10]

Or there is this letter describing the fate of ethnic Russians living in the republic of Azerbaijan:

> And now Russians have become refugees in their own country [note the implied assumption that Azerbaijan is Russian]. When has this ever happened?! Perhaps only during the time of the Great Fatherland War ... Our gratitude to the military! They evacuated the civilian population from Baku, both Russians and mixed families.[11]

The unexpected headlong collapse of the Soviet Empire, and, with it, of the historic Tsarist Empire during the period 1987–1991 came as an agonizing surprise to Russians living in the periphery as well as to those in the RSFSR. The fast-moving breakup of the empire placed before Russians a stark choice which historian Roman Szporluk has aptly described as one between "empire saving" and "[Russian] nation-building."[12] It was a choice which most Russians, including Mikhail Gorbachev and Boris Yeltsin, had never expected to have to make.

## Gorbachev and the Russian Republic

Perhaps no Russian was more taken by surprise by the lightning collapse of the "inner" Soviet empire than the Soviet president and Communist Party general secretary. From the time of his accession in 1985, Gorbachev had repeatedly shown himself to be blind and insensitive to ethnic issues. An ardent "Soviet patriot," Gorbachev fought hard to preserve the "Russian"/"Soviet Union" identification in the minds of Russians which had served as vital cement for the unitary Soviet state during the pre-perestroika period.

Once glasnost and democratization had begun to loosen the Soviet federation Gorbachev found himself in an unexpected squeeze between two groups which thoroughly detested one another but for whom, for different reasons, the political and economic autarchy of the Russian Republic was a high-priority desideratum. The first group was a conservative alliance of neo-Stalinists, National Bolsheviks, and Russian nationalists who, in a sense, wanted to resurrect policies which had obtained during the reigns of Tsars Alexander III and Nicholas II. The decaying official ideology of Marxism-Leninism was to be boosted by potent doses of Russian imperial nationalism. As for the Russian Republic, members of the conservative coalition insisted that it be granted the same institutions – and especially a Russian Communist Party – as were enjoyed by the minority republics.

Another group, who were sworn opponents of the conservatives, also emerged to champion the cause of Russian autarchy. This was a coalition of so-called "democrats," whose standard bearer was, of course, Boris Yeltsin, and who advocated turning the RSFSR into an economically and politically sovereign republic, with the USSR becoming a confederation of fully self-governing republics. (The conservative coalition, by contrast, believed that Russia should suppress the separatist leanings of the periphery, by force if necessary.) Throughout his period of rule, Gorbachev attempted to counter the agendas of these two powerful coalitions. Contrary to the wishes of the conservatives, he struggled to maintain the traditional structural asymmetries, whereby the RSFSR was denied institutions – such as its own Academy of Sciences – enjoyed by the other republics. Like Brezhnev before him, Gorbachev wanted to preserve the "Russian/USSR" linkup in the minds of ethnic Russians. Contrary to the goal of the increasingly powerful democrats, he struggled to maintain the USSR as a unitary state, permitting only a modest and largely cosmetic devolution of power to the republics.

Despite vigorous and determined efforts on the part of Gorbachev and his followers, they were unable to plug the dike against the rising waters of Russian autarchic sentiment. In 1990, over Gorbachev's objections, the conservative alliance brought into existence a Russian (*Rossiiskaya*) Communist Party, under the leadership of outspoken neo-Stalinist tribune, Ivan Polozkov. In the same year, Russia also gained its own trade union organization, Komsomol, and Academy of Sciences.

Once Boris Yeltsin had succeeded in achieving election as chairman of the RSFSR Supreme Soviet – in late May 1990 – and in declaring the republic's sovereignty, Gorbachev was forced grudgingly to acquiesce to the Russian Republic's gaining the trappings of a "normal" Soviet republic – its own KGB, MVD, and State Committee for Defense and Security; its own television channel and radio station, as well as newspapers officially published by the Russian Republic; and, finally, the activization of a previously dormant and largely symbolic RSFSR Foreign Ministry. These developments succeeded in bringing Russia into a state of rough ethnic "parity" with the other union republics.

Once Yeltsin had gained election as RSFSR chairman in May of 1990 and Russia had declared her sovereignty in June, the Gorbachev "center" began actively to encourage the Russian autonomous formations to declare their full sovereignty from the RSFSR. This strategy was presumably pursued to weaken the power of Yeltsin and of the democrats around him. In the words of then Yeltsin supporter, RSFSR people's deputy Oleg Rumyantsev, executive secretary of the RSFSR Constitutional Commission: "[Gorbachev] would have earned a place in Russian history as a great reformer had he not made his principal error, the error of tearing Russia apart. Russia does not forgive such transgressions, for Gorbachev bears a great political blame for the anti-Russian direction of his politics."[13] Rumyantsev noted that "even prior to the first [RSFSR] Congress, a law conflicting with the RSFSR was drafted [by the center] to proclaim all autonomous areas located on the territory of the Russian Republic as subjects of USSR rule."

In this case, too, Gorbachev failed in a determined effort to fragment the unity of Russia. Among the autonomous formations of the RSFSR, only Tatarstan refused officially to participate in the elections for the RSFSR president, in June, 1991, and only it refused to sign the union treaty as a part of the RSFSR. The Soviet president's concerted attempts to fragment the Russian Republic were no more successful than his frenetic efforts to preserve the unity of the USSR.

## Boris Yeltsin and Russia in 1991

The leader of the Russian democratic forces in 1991 was Boris Yeltsin, a former high-ranking party official, who channeled his uncommon energy and political savvy into a position rivaling, then surpassing, that of Gorbachev in terms of authority and power. Yeltsin's election as RSFSR president in June 1991 gave him the popular legitimacy that Gorbachev lacked. In a high-stakes contest, Yeltsin used his strong popularity with ethnic Russians, as well as with the other peoples of the USSR, to force repeated concessions from the center.

The assumption of power in the Soviet Union's largest republic by a maverick who had officially broken with the communist party and its legitimizing ideology served to move the breakup of the "inner" Soviet empire along at a blistering pace. The Russian Republic's declaration of sovereignty in June 1990 was the first important nail which Yeltsin drove into the coffin of the USSR, and his conclusion of a Commonwealth of Independent States with other republics in December 1991 buried the USSR for good.

One significant result of Yeltsin's election as head of the Russian Republic was that it induced Russians to begin to see the RSFSR as a discrete political and economic entity, something apart from and opposed to the USSR. In 1989, at the first USSR Congress of People's Deputies, conservative Russian nationalist writer Valentin Rasputin had attracted attention when he had exclaimed, "perhaps it is Russia which should leave the [Soviet] Union . . ."[14] These words had been uttered carpingly, and their intention had been to underline the absurdity of such a development. One year later, Russia had declared its sovereignty, and a separate political existence for Russia no longer seemed such an absurdity.

In directly challenging Gorbachev and the center, Yeltsin for the first time embossed the dichotomy "Russia/USSR" upon the minds of contemporary Russians. In a series of pitched battles with the center, Yeltsin, as had been noted, gradually acquired for Russia institutions already enjoyed by the other republics – a Ministry of Internal Affairs, television channel, and so forth. In May of 1991, after a crippling miners' strike, the center grudgingly agreed to transfer control of the mines in the Kuzbass, Rostov, and Komi regions to the jurisdiction of the Russian Republic. Each of these political victories served to advance the cause of Russian autarchy.

In addition to acquiring for Russia the trappings of a normal Soviet republic, Yeltsin also began to sign a number of treaties and economic agreements with the other union republics. In December 1990, for example, a full year before the Commonwealth of Independent States, he signed an important treaty with the Ukrainian Republic in which both parties agreed to:

- recognize each other as sovereign states . . .
- protect the rights of their citizens residing on the territory of the other party;
- recognize and respect the territorial integrity of the Russian Federation and Ukraine within the existing boundaries in the USSR.[15]

It will be noted that this signed agreement between the RSFSR and Ukraine explicitly recognized the existing boundaries separating the two republics. Given the fact that the USSR was in the process of fragmenting into sovereign republics, the question of boundaries took on added importance. Unlike Yeltsin and his allies, a number of ethnic Russians, as we shall see, believed that the extant borders separating the RSFSR and Ukraine, as well as those dividing Russia and other republics, were unfair and historically unjustifiable. They believed that the RSFSR represented a truncated entity which could in no way be considered the legitimate heir of prerevolutionary Tsarist Russia.

Yeltsin's approach to the minority peoples of the RSFSR, who comprised approximately 18.5 percent of the republic's population, was, in 1991, to be as accommodating and flexible as possible: "the autonomous [formations of the RSFSR]," he maintained in March of that year, "can take as much sovereignty as they can administer. We can agree to all of that. But they will have independently to answer, of course, for the well-being of their people. We make one condition: they will have to take part in a federation treaty with Russia. I underline: we will not let anyone pull Russia down."[16] On the symbolic level, Yeltsin scored points with RSFSR minorities, and especially Muslims, by appointing a dynamic Chechen, Ruslan Khasbulatov, as his deputy chairman.

What was Yeltsin's view in 1991 of the position of the twenty-five million Russians living outside the Russian Republic? "It is the duty of

Russia and of its Supreme Soviet and leadership," he observed in March of that year,

> somehow to help them. But understand me: It is impossible to defend people with tanks. After that, their lives would be more complicated. It is necessary to put our relations with those republics on a juridical foundation, one of international rights, which we are presently doing. In that case, any fact of discrimination against the Russian populace [on the part of another republic] can be juridically resolved, and we can apply sanctions against this or that republic or state. For example, we have concluded treaties with Latvia and Estonia, and they are now amending their laws in a number of instances . . .[17]

Given this changing situation, Yeltsin believed that Russians living in the periphery must choose what is most convenient for them: "If they want to return to Russia," he pledged, "then we will create proper conditions for them there." To which he added: "Incidentally, in our treaties with the [other] republics we provide compensation [to Russians] for loss of property incurred in the process of leaving that republic . . ."[18]

To summarize, Yeltsin's role in recasting and redefining the role of ethnic Russians within the "inner" Soviet empire was pivotal. By officially recognizing the sovereignty and the present boundaries of the other republics, he contributed *de facto* to rendering Russians living in those areas "foreigners." From then on, Russians in the periphery had to decide whether to become, say, Latvian or Uzbek citizens, or to emigrate back to Russia. By opting decisively for Russian "nation-building" and by firmly rejecting "empire saving," Yeltsin helped deal a heavy blow to the world's last major empire and also liberated Russians so that they could get on with the task of solving their monumental economic and social problems.

## The view in 1991 from a revived Russian foreign ministry

Under Brezhnev, the post of RSFSR foreign minister had been a symbolic one, since the Russian Republic's interests had been wholly subordinated to those of the USSR as a whole. In the fall of 1990, a thirty-nine-year-old specialist in international affairs, Andrei Kozyrev, was appointed to the post of RSFSR foreign minister, and he immediately began to elaborate upon Yeltsin's view of a new role for Russians in a revamped confederation. In his numerous writings and public statements, Kozyrev took note of the fact that the tendency in Western Europe in recent decades had been toward integration, not disintegration. The task at hand, he believed, was to bring about a similar process of integration on the territory of the former unitary Soviet state, on the basis of full sovereignty for each constituent republic.

"Usually the opponents of this process," Kozyrev observed, "point to the fact that the [present] republican borders inaccurately represent the ethnic make-up of the population." His rejoinder to this argument: "Let this be the case. But does this mean that the republics must now carry on endless territorial disputes with one another? Germany and France conducted wars for centuries over Alsace and Lorraine until they finally understood the principle of a civilized resolution of an ancient conflict. They simply made the border conditional."[19]

Kozyrev expressed a firm conviction that a sovereign Russia had a good chance of reconstituting the Soviet Union, or at least a major part of it: "as Russia learns to stand on its own," he wrote in a piece which appeared in *The New York Times*, "a democratic Russia will become a national center of gravity for the other sovereign republics . . ."[20] The new treaties and agreements which the RSFSR concluded with such republics as Ukraine, Belarus, Moldova, and Kazakhstan were, he maintained, intended to provide "an alternative to disintegration." *De facto*, the new agreements laid "the basis for a new union."[21]

One wondered at the time whether Kozyrev's views on reintegration might not represent wishful thinking. Could the union in fact be reconstituted on the basis of granting full political and economic sovereignty to its members? Aleksandr Tsipko, then deputy director of the Institute of International and Economic and Political Research of the USSR Academy of Science, was one who held that it could not. "If the Federation Council will rule the country," he predicted, "then, of course, the country will once again be ruled by the head of the largest republic, that is, by Russia."[22] Russians like Kozyrev, Tsipko believed, were suffering from "the inertia of imperial thinking." Not all the republics which sought full independence from the USSR would in the future opt for reintegration with Russia, and for the specific reason that Tsipko cited. Indeed, one wondered whether in the long run the paths of the USSR's three Slavic and its eight Trans-Caucasian and Central Asian republics lay in the same direction.

## The "hardliners" and Russia

Together with the Gorbachev "center" and the Yeltsin "democrats," the so-called hardliners represented a third major political force impacting the future of the Russian Republic. With strong representation in such elite institutions as the KGB, the party bureaucracy, the military command, and the Soviet military-industrial complex, this group was in a position to attempt to impose its will on the Russian Republic and on the union as a whole. In January 1991, the hardliners played the key role in attempting a *putsch* in the Baltic and they were, of course, supporters of the August, 1991 coup. There was, however, as has been mentioned, a basic contradiction in their position. On the one hand, they were vehement champions of the unity of the Soviet state; on the other hand, paradoxically, they were ardent defenders of Russian autarchy, a stance which de facto served to weaken the very cohesion of the USSR which they sought to preserve.

An example of the "empire saving" obsession of the hardliners was the open letter which a number of them wrote to Boris Yeltsin, in his capacity as chairman of the RSFSR Supreme Soviet, in January 1991.[23] The authors of this truculent letter included such well-known conservative Russian nationalist writers as Valentin Rasputin (who had served, at Gorbachev's request, as a member of the Presidential Council), Vasilii Belov, and Vladimir Krupin (chief editor of the journal *Moskva*), and proto-fascist publicists Aleksandr Prokhanov, Eduard Volodin, and Karem Rash. The letter's signatories assailed Yeltsin for supporting the desire of the Baltic republics to secede from the USSR. Underlining the "historical rootedness of Russia in the Baltic lands," the authors maintained that Yeltsin's primary task as head of the Russian Republic was to safeguard ethnic Russians and Eastern Slavs living in the periphery.

Even worse than Yeltsin's perceived sins against the unity of the Soviet Union was, the authors believed, his conniving in the breakup of Russia itself. "Only a politician indifferent to the fate of the Fatherland," they wrote scornfully, "could hand out willy-nilly free economic zones and sovereignties on the territory of Russia, dismembering the Russian state." And they concluded sternly: "Taken as a whole, your [i.e. Yeltsin's] actions can be simply defined as the disintegration of the USSR and the destruction of Russia, neither of which was created by you, and it is not up to you to decide their fate." For Russian nationalists like Valentin Rasputin and proto-fascists like Aleksandr Prokhanov, Russia and the USSR were the same thing. In such a reading, Latvia and Armenia, say, were as much a part of "Russia" as were the Russian cities of Moscow and Khabarovsk.

In the eyes of the hardliners, thus, "Russia" was an indivisible entity that had to be preserved, by force if necessary. Minority separatist leaders like Landsbergis of Lithuania or Gamsakhurdia of Georgia were seen as violent enemies of Russia who had to be removed from office. Some hardliners also advocated that the fourteen minority republics be abolished and replaced by American-style states which would belong to a "Pan-Russian Republic." In economics, some of them opposed all market reform; others countenanced a "Pinochet model" or "South Korean model" of authoritarian modernization. In summary, it was clear that the hardliners sought to replace the Soviet empire, which was rooted in Marxism-Leninism, with a resurrected Russian Empire, such as the one that began to emerge in the Tsarist period during the reigns of Alexander III and Nicholas II. The bankruptcy of such a strategy was forcefully pointed out by Alain Besançon in 1983: "Once the ideological magic [of Marxism-Leninism] has been destroyed," he wrote,

> there would be only one source of magic left – the imperial or colonial
> legitimacy of the Russian people in a world that today is entirely

decolonized. This anachronistic legitimacy would immediately stimulate the resistance of the non-Russian nations, who would call forth their own legitimacies, necessitating military occupation. The Russian people is not sufficiently populous for that task.[24]

## Solzhenitsyn's program of Russian "nation-building" in late 1990

In late 1990, three months after the Russian Republic had declared its sovereignty, two major Soviet newspapers, *Komsomol'skaya pravda* and *Literaturnaya gazeta*, published Nobel prize winner Aleksandr Solzhenitsyn's programmatic brochure *Rebuilding Russia* in a print-run of over twenty-five million.[25] Given its huge readership, the brochure inevitably served as a catalyst for ethnic Russians to begin thinking about the future of the Soviet empire.

On the subject of the future of the USSR as a unitary state, Solzhenitsyn sided decisively with Yeltsin and the democratic "nation-builders" against Gorbachev and the hardliners. The Soviet Union, he contended, had no future as a single state. Centrifugal developments and separatist tendencies had, he believed, proceeded to a point where the union could be held together only at the cost of enormous bloodshed. An additional factor, he noted, was that Russians had been so debilitated by seventy years of communist rule that they simply lacked the strength to maintain an empire. "We have to choose firmly," Solzhenitsyn declared, "between an empire that first of all destroys us [i.e. ethnic Russians] ourselves, and the spiritual and bodily salvation of our people." He noted that Russia became stronger once it had cut Poland and Finland loose and that postwar Japan surged in vigor after abandoning its expansionist dreams.

Unlike Yeltsin and the democrats, Solzhenitsyn believed that Russia herself should take the initiative in disbanding an empire that was in fact killing her. He consequently urged that eleven of the Soviet republics be cut loose from Russia whether they wanted this or not. He held that Russia should concentrate on resuscitative "nation building" uncluttered by debilitating alliances or confederations with former Soviet colonies.

While Yeltsin and the democrats were prepared to recognize the present boundaries separating Russia and the other republics, Solzhenitsyn, for his part, wanted to redraw some of those boundaries if that should prove to be the will of the populace, as expressed through plebiscites. Thus in the case of the Central Asian republic of Kazakhstan, he believed that the republic's northern tier, which was heavily settled by Russians, should be ceded to Russia, while its southern part, largely populated by Kazakhs, should be free to choose to remain with Russia or go its separate way. (Angered over Solzhenitsyn's views, crowds of ethnic Kazakhs reportedly staged burnings of those Soviet newspapers which carried the text of his brochure.)

With regard to the Eastern Slav republics of Ukraine and Belarus, Solzhenitsyn expressed a hope that their populations would choose to remain in union with their Russian brethren. He proposed the formation of what he called a Pan-Russian Union (*Rossiiskii soyuz*) to accomplish this purpose. (Yeltsin's advisor on nationalities' questions, RSFSR congresswoman Galina Starovoitova, noted that the term "Slavic Union [*Slavyanskii soyuz*]" would be preferable for what Solzhenitsyn had in mind, "otherwise there is discrimination in the very title.") Aware that separatist sentiment had been growing in Ukraine, especially in the republic's western regions, Solzhenitsyn stated categorically that the people of Ukraine should not be held in union with Russia by force. Rather, he contended, the populace should be free to express its will through the vehicle of referendums, on an oblast by oblast basis. Implicit in Solzhenitsyn's comments was a belief that Ukraine was likely to split, with its western regions voting for independence and its eastern regions electing to remain together with Russia. In Belarus, in his view, separatist tendencies were not strong.

As for the non-Russian peoples of the RSFSR, Solzhenitsyn argued that those autonomous regions, such as Tatarstan, whose historical borders were fully enveloped by the Russian Republic, would have to share the future fate of the Russian people, though their ethnic, economic, and religious needs should receive maximum attention. The Russian Council of Nationalities, one of the few worthy Soviet institutions in Solzhenitsyn's opinion, should, he believed, serve as a forum for the enunciation of such needs. Those minority peoples of the RSFSR who enjoyed external borders could, in his view, secede from Russia if that should prove to be the will of their populace expressed through a plebiscite.

Solzhenitsyn took pains to warn that the dismemberment of the Soviet Union should not occur chaotically, "like the Portuguese fleeing from Angola," but rather in an orderly fashion carefully prepared by specialists. Particular attention, he emphasized, should be paid to ensuring the rights of all minority peoples, including ethnic Russians living in the Soviet periphery.

To conclude, Solzhenitsyn's anti-imperial model for the reconstitution of Russia had, of course, nothing in common with the vision of a unitary state promulgated by Gorbachev and the hardliners. It also, however, differed in significant ways from Yeltsin's concept of a "democratic" confederation of sovereign republics. Solzhenitsyn believed that such a body would likely serve to bog Russia down in imperial residue and would therefore slow down or prevent the recovery of her health. The answer, Solzhenitsyn contended, was for Russia fairly and democratically to adjust her borders with the neighboring republics and then get on with the business of "nation-building" unencumbered by deleterious alliances.

## Russian public opinion in 1989–91 on the question of retaining an empire

Before the advent of glasnost, Western analysts had little hard data at hand with which to assess the opinions of ethnic Russians living in the Soviet Union. To fathom the workings of the Russian mind, analysts were reduced to such arcane pursuits as scrutinizing the favorite novels of Russians; examining the comment book of an exhibit given by a popular Russian nationalist artist; and dissecting the films to which Russians flocked in great numbers.[26] Due to a lack of trustworthy information, Western observers at times succumbed to a temptation to exaggerate the significance of such lurid developments as the emergence on the political scene of a violently anti-Semitic organization, called Pamyat, in May of 1987.

The polls showed persuasively that ethnic Russians during 1989–91 were growing accustomed to the fragmentation of the empire and that they, by a significant margin, refused to countenance the use of force to hold it together. A marked "deimperialization" of the Russian psyche appeared to be occurring.

To demonstrate the speed of this shift, one need merely cite the results of a poll which was conducted in the Russian Republic by VTSIOM in the fall of 1989, and then contrast its results with two subsequent polls taken in the RSFSR in May and September of 1990. In the 1989 poll, the results of which were published in the weekly magazine *Ogonek*, 63.4 percent of the RSFSR citizens contacted gave a high priority to preserving "the unity and cohesion of the USSR."[27] By contrast, only 10.6 percent of Armenians, 10.2 percent of Balts, and 30.9 percent of Ukrainians accorded it a high priority. This poll therefore showed that "empire saving" sentiment remained strong among Russians in the fall of 1989.

Six months later, in May of 1990, shortly before Yeltsin was elected chairman of the RSFSR Supreme Soviet, VTSIOM conducted a new poll of 1,517 persons in twenty areas of the RSFSR.[28] This poll yielded markedly different results from the one in 1989. On the question of what the future relations of the RSFSR to the "center" should be, for example, the respondents held:

18% – that relations should remain the same as at present;

35% – that the economic and political rights of Russia should be expanded but that the final say in all questions should remain with the "center";

43% – that Russia should receive political and economic independence (up to and including leaving the USSR);

4% – other.

A major shift in Russian public opinion had occurred. For more than 43 percent of RSFSR respondents, the bonds conjoining "Russia" and "the USSR" had been severed.

Another intriguing result of this poll was that growing numbers of ethnic Russians were prepared to countenance the granting of added political clout to the autonomous formations of the RSFSR:

> 20% – stated that the power of the autonomous regions in the RSFSR should remain the same as at present;

> 57% – stated that the economic and political rights of the autonomous regions should be broadened, but that the final say in all questions should remain with the RSFSR as a whole;

> 20% – stated that the autonomous regions should receive economic and political independence (up to and including leaving the RSFSR);

> 3% – other.

The responses to this question seemed to demostrate that there was considerable popular support within the RSFSR for the position embraced by Yeltsin, namely, that the autonomous formations be offered broad self-rule in exchange for their remaining members of the Russian Republic.

A poll taken by VTSIOM four months later, in September 1990, showed an even more pronounced shift in public attitudes.[29] This poll contacted 1,458 persons residing in twenty-five population points within the Russian Republic. Here is what the respondents felt concerning the proper relationship of the RSFSR and the "center":

> *Should the organs of the Soviet Union have the right to revoke or halt the decisions of the Russian Federation?*
>
> 23%   – They should have the right
> 52.5% – They should not have that right
> 24.5% – Difficult to answer

> *Should the organs of the Russian Federation have the right to revoke or halt the decisions of the organs of the Soviet Union?*
>
> 48.1% – They should have that right
> 21.9% – They should not have that right
> 30.2% – Difficult to answer

On questions which concerned the position of the autonomous formations within the RSFSR, the respondents were of the following opinion:

*What variant of the organization of the Russian Federation seems preferable to you?*

28.6% – One historically-formed state with special rights for the national-territorial formations
47.8% – A federation in which the national-territorial formations, regions, and oblasts enjoy full rights
23.7% – Difficult to answer

*The autonomous formations should have the right to leave the Russian Federation if a majority of their populace should favor it*

55.9% – Yes
27.8% – No
16.3% – Difficult to answer

*On their own territory, the laws of the autonomous formations should take the precedence over the laws of the Russian Federation*

26.5% – Yes
46.6% – No
26.8% – Difficult to answer

This September 1990 poll, thus, offered strong support for Yeltsin's policies of pursuing sovereignty for the Russian Republic and of offering a broad degree of self-rule to the autonomous formations within the RSFSR. The respondents, as can be seen, were even prepared to let the autonomous formations secede from Russia, if their populace expressed such a preference through referendums.

## Russians in 1991 on the use of force to retain the "inner" empire

The protracted, bloody war in Afghanistan appears to have gradually drained ethnic Russians of a willingness to support the use of Russian lives to preserve the so-called "outer" Soviet empire. By the beginning of the 1990s, this sentiment had spread to the issue of the forcible preservation of the "inner" Soviet empire. When, for example, the central authorities attempted to call up reservists in southern Russia for use in Azerbaijan in January 1990, there occurred a revolt on the part of the reservists' mothers and families, and an organization called "mothers against mobilization" came into existence.[30] In August of the same year, the newspaper *Izvestiya* reported that conscripts' mothers had rallied in the Russian provincial city of Perm' to protest the failure of the commandant of the local military district to meet with them. The mothers had been demanding that their sons serve only in the RSFSR and not be sent to the Caucasus or to Central Asia.[31]

In January of 1991, when the "center" orchestrated a *putsch* against the lawfully elected Baltic parliaments and their presidents, similar anti-imperial sentiments emerged among ethnic Russians.[32] On January 16, just three days after "Bloody Sunday" in Vilnius, the polling organization VTSIOM contacted 962 persons living in thirteen cities of the RSFSR. Their reaction to the attempted coup was:

*Do you approve or do you condemn the actions of the troops?*

29% – Approve
55% – Condemn
16% – Difficult to answer

In Moscow and Leningrad as it was then still known, cities which represented the political "wave of the future" for much of the rest of the RSFSR, the reaction was even more decisive. Less than 15 percent of Leningraders came out in support of the troops' actions, while in Moscow the figure was 15.4 percent.[33]

Another important indicator was the feelings of young Russians, of the so-called "upcoming generation." In early 1991, the magazine *Reader's Digest* asked the Institute of Sociology of the USSR Academy of Sciences to conduct an RSFSR-wide poll of the attitudes of young Russians aged 18 to 25.[34] On the critical question of whether or not the minority Soviet republics should be permitted to secede from the union, the young Russians who were contacted felt as follows:

70% –Yes
19% – No
11% – Undecided

The findings of such polls indicated a marked willingness on the part of ethnic Russians to let those republics who wanted to leave the USSR to do so. It might be asked, however, how such results tallied with those of the March 1991 referendum, in which approximately 71 percent of RSFSR voters reportedly voted to preserve the union. (Approximately the same percentage, roughly 70 percent, voted to institute the post of president of the RSFSR, i.e. supported Boris Yeltsin and his agenda.)

A first point which should be made is that the language in which the referendum was couched was deliberately vague. Voters were asked: "Do you consider necessary the preservation of the Union of Soviet Socialist Republics as a renewed federation of equal sovereign republics, in which the rights and freedom of the individual of any nationality will be fully guaranteed?"[35] This language was notably ambiguous and did not overtly contradict the "Yeltsin model" of a renewed confederation of fully sovereign republics. There may have also been tampering with the vote in parts of the Russian provinces.

In the more politically advanced areas of the Russian Republic, the referendum did quite poorly. In Boris Yeltsin's home base of Sverdlovsk city (now renamed Ekaterinburg), for example, only 34.4 percent voted for Gorbachev's "renewed federation," while in both Moscow and Leningrad the figure was only slightly above 50 percent. This was hardly a ringing endorsement of the Soviet president and of his policies.

## The views of Russians living in the periphery in 1989–91

Like the views of ethnic Russians living in the core Russian Republic, the attitudes of Russians in the non-Russian periphery were changing with considerable rapidity, and in a direction favorable to the interests of the titular peoples of the minority republics. In the republic of Estonia, for instance, where 475,000 Russians made up the bulk of the non-Estonian populace, polls taken in 1989 and 1990 showed considerable changes in attitude.

By early 1991, when the regime attempted a coup in the Baltic, ethnic Russian sentiment had shifted even more decisively in the direction of sympathy for the independence of the Baltic republics. This shift was politically significant, inasmuch as Russians comprised 34 percent of the population of Latvia and 30.3 percent of the population of Estonia. (By contrast, they made up only 9.4 percent of the population of Lithuania.) In a critical February 1991 plebiscite of the populace of Latvia, 73.6 percent of those voting supported Latvian independence. Since only 54 percent of Latvia's population was ethnic Latvian, this meant that hundreds of thousands of Russians had to have supported the Latvians in their bid for secession. A similar result obtained in the Estonian referendum, with 77.8 percent of those voting supporting independence for the republic.[36]

During approximately the same time frame, in January 1991, *Moscow News* published the result of a poll of 1,005 ethnic Russians living in nine minority republics and in one autonomous formation of the RSFSR, which had been taken in November and December of 1990.[37] Published under the heading "Do the Russians Want to Flee?" the poll offered a useful snapshot of ethnic Russian sentiment in the Soviet periphery (see table 2.1).

In Central Asia (excepting Kazakhstan) and in Georgia approximately a third or more of ethnic Russians wanted to be repatriated to Russia. In Estonia, Western Ukraine, and Kazakhstan, the percentage of Russians desiring to return to the RSFSR stood at 20 percent or higher. These figures suggested that the de-Russification of the periphery would continue at a rapid pace in coming years; indeed, in certain republics, the process might snowball and result in "Russian flight" from areas of Central Asia and the Caucasus. The devolution of power to the republics corresponded objectively to a retreat of Russians from the periphery.

Table 2.1. *Do the Russians want to flee?*

*Are you on the whole satisfied or dissatisfied that you live in precisely this republic?*

| Republic | % satisfied | % dissatisfied | % difficult to answer |
|---|---|---|---|
| Estonia | 51 | 19 | 30 |
| Latvia | 75 | 7 | 18 |
| Western Ukraine | 36 | 21 | 44 |
| Georgia | 62 | 22 | 16 |
| Azerbaijan | 86 | 6 | 10 |
| Kazakhstan | 73 | 11 | 16 |
| Kyrgyzstan | 56 | 4 | 40 |
| Tajikistan | 61 | 25 | 14 |
| Uzbekistan | 64 | 11 | 25 |

*Do you have the desire to leave for Russia or would you like permanently to reside in this republic?*

| Republic | % leave for Russia | % remain | % difficult to answer |
|---|---|---|---|
| Estonia | 23 | 50 | 27 |
| Latvia | 16 | 65 | 19 |
| Western Ukraine | 26 | 44 | 31 |
| Georgia | 37 | 36 | 26 |
| Azerbaijan | 5 | 68 | 27 |
| Kazakhstan | 20 | 63 | 17 |
| Kyrgyzstan | 31 | 2 | 26 |
| Tajikistan | 37 | 38 | 25 |
| Uzbekistan | 38 | 36 | 26 |

# The August 1991 coup and the Soviet Union's collapse

If the entire Gorbachev period witnessed a rapid succession of dramatic events, then high drama continued in the Russian Republic in the second half of 1991. In June, the republic's bid for full sovereignty received a significant boost when Boris Yeltsin bested five opponents and was elected president of the RSFSR, with 57.3 percent of the vote.

After months of bitter rivalry, Yeltsin and Gorbachev had succeeded in April of 1991 in coming to rough agreement concerning the political and economic shape of a future Union of Sovereign States. The scheduled signing of the union treaty, which was set for August 20, precipitated the failed coup of August 18–21. That political earthquake, in turn, set off powerful aftershocks which would be felt for years. Like the Bolshevik *putsch* of 1917, the failed August coup appeared to constitute a critical twentieth-

Table 2.2. *National composition of the RSFSR, 1989*

| Nationalities | Population | in % |
|---|---|---|
| Total population | 147,022,000 | 100.0 |
| Russians | 119,823,000 | 81.5 |
| Tatars | 5,587,000 | 3.8 |
| Ukrainians | 4,411,000 | 3.0 |
| Chuvash | 1,764,000 | 1.2 |
| Dagestani | 1,764,000 | 1.2 |
| Other | 13,673,000 | 9.3 |

*Source: Natisional'nyi sostav naseleniya SSSR* (Moscow: Finansy i statistika, 1991).

century turning point. In its immediate aftermath, the Communist Party was outlawed, the KGB was weakened, and the Soviet "center" was marginalized to a point of irrelevancy. The Ukrainian vote for full independence on December 1 nailed down the lid on the coffin of what had until recently been the USSR.

The death throes of the Soviet center required that the Russian Republic step in and gradually assume many of its functions. This development, however, served to strain relations with the minority republics, which clearly suspected that the new confederation of sovereign states being championed by Yeltsin and his team was in fact a mask for increased ethnic Russian political and economic control. The prospects for a viable confederation appeared therefore to be dim at best.

Similarly, Yeltsin's expressed hope that the minority peoples of the RSFSR would prove to be satisfied with real autonomy ran into serious obstacles in the post-coup period. The Chechens declared their full independence from Russia, and Yeltsin had to back down from an unwise declaration of emergency rule in Checheno-Ingushetia. Tatarstan, too, began to take steps toward achieving complete independence.

A week after Ukraine declared its independence, Yeltsin and the leaders of Ukraine and Belarus (Leonid Kravchuk and Stanislau Shushkevich) signed the "Belovezhskii accords" forming a Commonwealth of Independent States (*Sodruzhestvo nezavisimykh gosudarstv*). On December 12, the Russian parliament ratified the Belovezhskii agreement by a vote of 188 to 6. The next week, the Russian government seized control of the Kremlin, the Soviet Foreign and Interior Ministries, and the USSR KGB. And on December 25, 1991, after the parliament voted overwhelmingly to change the name of the republic from RSFSR to the Russian (*Rossiiskaya*) Federation (or simply Russia), workers lowered the red hammer-and-sickle flag

from atop the Kremlin, and the red, white, and blue Russian tricolor was
raised in its place.

The headlong breakup of the historic Russian and Soviet empires understandably served to shock and bewilder many present-day Russians. Some,
however, saw in it an opportunity for the Russian nation's redemption. In
an interview with the newspaper *Pravda*, the influential Russian nationalist
spokesman, Igor' Shafarevich, called for Russia to turn away from dreams
of reclaiming an empire and to engage instead in salvific nation-building.
"How shall we live," he asked, "now that the USSR has broken up and
Russia remains alone with herself?" He answered his own question thus:

> The relations of the nations of the USSR had, it seems, become
> intertwined into a tangle that human reason lacked the strength to
> undo. Now that tangle has been sliced apart by fate. Looking about
> after the initial shock, we see that Russia can be a viable country within
> its new boundaries, can stand much more firmly on its feet than did the
> previous USSR. First of all, this is still an enormous country, retaining
> part of [the USSR's] exceedingly rich natural resources. It is a country
> with a large and cultured populace; it is larger than Japan; larger than
> France and united Germany taken together; larger than Brazil and
> Argentina.

And Shafarevich continued:

> But what is most striking is that this country is, to a rare degree,
> ethnically homogeneous. Of the fifteen republics of the former USSR,
> Russia occupies the third place (after Armenia and Azerbaijan) in the
> percentage of titular people to total population: 81 percent are [ethnic]
> Russians, and 86 percent consider Russian to be their native language
> ... Russia is now ethnically more homogeneous than Czechoslovakia,
> Belgium, Spain, or Great Britain. Of course, in addition to Russians,
> there live in Russia more than 100 peoples, and Russians, given their
> numerical dominance, bear a special responsibility so that the cultural
> and spiritual life of those peoples should develop freely.[38]

Shafarevich's summons for Russians to bravely accept the loss of empire
and to get on with the business of "nation-building" was not met resolutely
by all, however. (And Shafarevich himself soon abandoned his position and
became an outspoken empire-saver). Writing in the no. 45, 1991 issue of
the reformist weekly *Moskovskie novosti*, Sergei Razgonov, for example,
reflected despairingly:

> Let us total up the losses. We have given away the Baltic, ceded
> Crimea, and we are going to sell the Kurile Islands ... Lord, will we
> really once again be reduced to the size of Vladimir-Suzdal' Rus' or of
> the Serpukhovsk princedom? No, no, I am not weeping for the empire,
> although, of course, it is painful that it will soon not be easy to take a

> stroll along Tallinn's Vyshgorod, to sit with friends in the cafes of
> Riflis, or to warm oneself on the beaches of Koktebl' ...

And Razgonov continued his lament:

> We [Russians] are no longer one-sixth of the earth's surface ... But we
> continue to carry within ourselves one-sixth of the globe – from Riga to
> Shikotan. It is a scale we have become accustomed to. Ah, how difficult
> it is to part with it. ... From that former Homeland, we will be
> required to emigrate, all of us, to the last man.[39]

This disoriented sense of loss experienced by Russians as they cast about
for a post-imperial national identity could, of course, serve as a breeding
ground for extremist currents and ideologies. In the Russian presidential
election in June 1991, a charismatic proto-fascist demagogue, Vladimir
Zhirinovsky, came in a surprising third with 7.8 percent of the vote. Zhirinovsky's message was and remains a crudely simple one: ethnic Russians
should take back the empire and put the minority peoples in their place.

## Independent Russia: the initial array of forces

Yeltsin's first government team was made up of inward-looking *democrats*
who focused their energies on internal Russian political and economic
reform. These "Young Turks" (as the press was quick to dub them)
included first deputy prime minister Gennadii Burbulis; deputy prime ministers Egor Gaidar, Aleksander Shokhin, and Sergei Shakhrai; Foreign Minister Andrei Kozyrev; Minister of Justice Nikolai Fedorov; and Minister for
the Press and Mass Media Mikhail Poltoranin. Having asserted the primacy
of Russian national interests in the battle against the Soviet center in 1991,
this team continued to pursue a "Russia first" policy upon independence.
The policies they adopted, in economic reform in particular, exhibited an
intent to resolve Russia's own crises regardless of the impact reform measures (such as price liberalization) would have on the other newly-
independent states. Despite their alleged commitment to the new CIS, the
Russian leadership proved as eager as the heads of other states to pursue
their own national interests without worrying unduly about those of their
neighbors.

The pro-Western stance articulated by the democrats (which came to be
known as "Atlanticism") was not the only position available to Russian
politicians inclined towards democratic reform. While the "Atlanticists"
regarded with relative equanimity Russia's loss of superpower status, many
former "democrats" found the experience so painful that they began, in
later 1991 and early 1992, to move decisively to the political right. Loss
of territory and population, as well as the immediate havoc which Soviet
collapse wreaked on the economy, contributed to a wrenching sense of
national humiliation and abasement in many. As Vsevolod Rybakov noted

in his essay "Will Russia Become a Great Power?", "the possession of an enormous nuclear arsenal is sufficient in our time for people to fear us, but not to respect us . . . That is not much for 'greatness'."[40]

Out of such a concern arose a grouping of *democratic statists*, one of the leading spokesmen of which was Sergei Stankevich, Yeltsin's state councillor for political affairs. Rather than a self-abnegating "Atlanticism," Stankevich preferred the line of "Eurasianism," (taken from an interwar emigre movement of the same name) which recognized that "our state emerged and grew strong as a unique historical and cultural amalgam of Slav and Turkic, Orthodox and Muslim components . . ."[41] Russia or, more precisely, "Eurasia" was thus a very different country from the Western democracies and her geopolitical needs were markedly different ones.

The democratic statists also took a much harder line towards the "near abroad" than did the Atlanticists. According to Stankevich, Russia had "a thousand-year history and legitimate interests" in such republics as the Baltic states, Moldova, and Georgia.[42] While the "democratic statists" argued among themselves as to the scope of Russia's natural sphere of influence – some discarded the Baltics while others would include the entire Caucasus and Central Asia – they agreed that, in relations with former Soviet republics, Russia should not be afraid to use her muscle as a "great state" to achieve her desired aims.

The struggle among the wide array of democrats and democratic statists that took place in 1992 occurred against the background of a growing coalescence of the extreme right (or pure *statists*). As the dynamic proto-fascist politician Vladimir Zhirinovsky observed during an October 1991 interview: "In a rich nation my program would not go over very well. But in a poor, embittered country like Russia, this is my golden hour."[43] The gnawing sense of loss of empire combined with rising anger over the republic's dire economic position served to prepare the ground for a potential triumph of an extremist ideology. As for the discredited communists, many in the hard right welcomed the demise of Marxist-Leninist ideology, which had complicated their program considerably, while at the same time they invited former communists into the ranks of the "opposition of patriotic forces."

To varying degrees, the statists supported a return to one-party rule and a command economy, the restoration of the USSR's borders, and even armed opposition to the current regime. Repeatedly emphasizing that they saw little difference between the "democrats" and the "democratic statists," the front's leaders viewed their opponents as being traitors and witting or unwitting dupes of the CIA and other Western intelligence agencies.

As Russia entered the new year of 1993, the country appeared to be riven and divided as seldom before, mired in a new "Time of Troubles." Upper echelon struggles over independent Russia's new political and economic course was only one indicator of this. The economic situation had steadily worsened. Organized crime had begun to exert a strong influence on virtually all forms of private business. Relations with a number of the former union republics seemed maximally strained. Finally, surging nationalist sentiment among Russia's minorities and breakaway leanings among Russians living in regions like the Far East placed the future integrity of the Russian Federation in doubt.[44] It was in this context that a situation of *dvoevlastie* (dyarchy, or dual power) emerged, in which the growing conflict between proponents and opponents of economic reform and democratization, and of the decentralization of Russia and, alternatively, the recreation of the USSR, heightened to a hitherto unknown degree.

## 1993: Dvoevlastie and parliamentary elections

Throughout 1992, Yeltsin had found himself increasingly at loggerheads with the Russian parliament. Given the monumentality of the economic and social problems facing Russia – and also the fact that many members of the old Communist party were carrying out obstructionist tactics in the parliament and in soviets at all levels – Yeltsin had sought to amass as much power as possible. Future clashes between a president seeking expanded powers and a parliament staking out its turf appeared inevitable.

A series of three gatherings of the Congress of People's Deputies, beginning with the Seventh Congress held from December 1–14, 1992, set the stage for the political battle which was to paralyze the government for the better part of 1993. Over the course of the three Congresses, Yeltsin narrowly survived multiple attempts to strip him of his powers. While he personally survived, the President was forced to surrender a number of his leading allies, including Yegor Gaidar who was replaced as prime minister by the centrist Viktor Chernomyrdin.

Yeltsin moved to end the ten-month crisis of *dvoevlastie* on September 21, 1993, when he issued a decree which dissolved both the Congress of People's Deputies and the Supreme Soviet and called new parliamentary elections for December 12.[45] Parliament did not react kindly to the decree. It declared Vice President Rutskoi the new acting president of Russia and approved a motion proposed by deputy Sergei Baburin to provide severe penalties – including the death penalty – for those committing actions aimed at forcefully changing Russia's political system. Several hardline former military and security officials were appointed to key positions in the parallel opposition "government." Rutskoi and parliamentary deputies refused to vacate the White House (the parliamentary building). De facto supporting the parliament was the Constitutional Court, which announced that Yeltsin's decree was not in accord with the Constitution.

In the two weeks that followed the decree, the potential for a violent resolution to the conflict increased. The White House's electricity, gas, and telephone lines were turned off. After Stanislav Terekhov, leader of the pro-Rutskoi Union of Officers, led an attempt to seize the CIS military communications center (a policeman and a woman died in the exchange of fire), police and OMON troops fully blockaded the White House.

On October 3, several thousand demonstrators left their mass rallies in support of parliament and hardliner forces and headed to the White House, where they quickly overwhelmed a heavy police cordon reluctant to open fire. After more than twelve hours of attempting to maintain neutrality, the defense ministry grudgingly agreed to a phased storming of the White House. Once the military had come on board, it proved relatively easy for the presidential side to achieve victory. The White House was successfully assaulted on October 4, and the leaders of the rebellion were taken into custody. In all, official figures placed the number of casualties at 145 dead and 733 wounded.[46] It had been the largest loss of life in Moscow since the time of the Bolshevik coup seventy-six Octobers earlier.

Though his victory had been of the narrowest possible kind, Yeltsin found himself suddenly catapulted into a uniquely advantageous position. *Dvoevlastie* had ended abruptly, and a new Constitution embodying a "presidential republic" was scheduled to be voted on in a referendum accompanying the December 12 elections. While Moscow lived under emergency rule for two weeks, throughout Russia existing soviets at all levels – most of which had openly sided with the Supreme Soviet – were disbanded. The July draft of the Constitution was sharpened and toughened in the November draft, essentially to reduce the autonomous republics to the same status as the nonethnic-based oblasts, krais, and federal cities.

While conditions seemed ripe for a reemergence of reformist forces which had begun to lose ground over the year, the December elections graphically showed that ten months of *dvoevlastie* had taken a heavy toll. In voting to the 225 seats of the 450-seat Duma that were reserved for party lists, the four democratic parties together managed to accumulate only 34 percent of the vote. The Communist Party received 12 percent, the Agrarians 8 percent, the Women of Russia gained an unexpected 8 percent, and the right-of-center Democratic Party of Russia gained 5.5 percent. Arkadii Volsky's Civic Union, which had exerted a significant political influence in 1992, was decisively rejected by voters with less than 2 percent of the vote. But the most spectacular, and best publicized, upset in the elections was the 23 percent of the vote handed to extremist Vladimir Zhirinovskii's Liberal Democratic Party.[47]

The elections constituted an undeniable setback for prodemocracy and promarket forces in Russia. Among the causes for this reversal were the sense many voters had that Gaidar's reforms had failed and in failing had damaged the economic prospects of the country; general concern that Russia was rudderless and drifting; and disillusionment with establishment politicians in the wake of ten painful months of *dvoevlastie* rule. Other reasons included the upsurge in Russian self-awareness that was occurring as ethnic Russians came increasingly to reject their old Soviet identity and sought a return to national roots; a concomitant anger over the increase in separatist sentiment in non-Russian regions of the Russian Federation; a growing sense that Russia had ceased to be a great power; and, finally, a rising concern among Russians about the plight of their coethnics in the "near abroad."[48]

## 1994 and beyond: Defining Russia's future

Given the conservative makeup of the lower chamber of the new parliament and the continuing activity of communist and neo-fascist groups, many Russian political commentators expressed concern that 1994 could be as volatile as the previous year. The dramatic resignations of the reformers First Deputy Prime Minister Yegor Gaidar and Finance Minister Boris Fedorov in January contributed to the speculations of impending instability. The first eight months of 1994, however, saw Russia settle into a state of relative political calm.

At the same time, however, in 1994 there continued a trend which had begun the year before of increasing alienation from Western states and active intervention in the affairs of the "near abroad." Reversing his previous position and now seemingly embracing the "Eurasianist" line of the democratic statists, Foreign Minister Kozyrev clearly enunciated the Russian government's new foreign policy, which included adamant rejection of NATO expansion into Central and Eastern Europe, wary cooperation with NATO and the UN in the ongoing conflict in the Balkans, and renewed attention to the "plight" of Russians and Russian-speakers in the "near abroad." This latter plank rapidly evolved to a point to which both government officials and Duma deputies could approvingly speak of efforts to recreate a unified space within former USSR borders, and Kozyrev could openly state on several occasions that Russia presumed the right to intervene militarily to defend the rights of Russians in neighboring countries. Active Russian support, in the form of troops, weapons, and training, of breakaway regions in other countries of the CIS (Moldova's Transdniestria, Georgia's Abkhazia, Azerbaijan's Nagorno-Karabakh) and apparent "palace coup" atempts (in Azerbaijan), as well as a continued role as protector of Tajikistan's neo-Communist regime, enforced the perception that Moscow had slid into a familiar role as imperial center.[49]

## Mass opinion on restoring the "inner" empire, 1992–1994

To the casual observer it might appear that, following the breakup of the USSR, the masses of ethnic Russians abandoned the relative lack of belligerence which had characterized their attitude toward the minority peoples of the USSR during the transition years 1989–1991 and once again came to embrace aggressive "empire-saving" views. This, however, has manifestly not been the case. What is true is that a weighty majority of ethnic Russians perceived, and continue to view, the collapse of the Soviet Union as having been a tragedy, for which they blame the Gorbachev and Yeltsin leaderships. "From the beginning of 1992 to this day [i.e. July 1994]," Sociologist Igor Klyamkin has observed, "more than two-thirds of those polled – Russian citizens belonging to all social groups and adhering to all political parties and to all leaders in the electorate – express regret over [the breakup of the Soviet Union]."[50]

This gnawing sense of regret over the loss of empire should not, it needs to be stressed, be seen as equivalent to a conviction that the Soviet Union must be reestablished. "That idea," Klyamkin has underlined, "is also unpopular. Depending on how the question is formulated, it attracts from one-fifth to one-third of respondents."[51] Unlike certain Russian elites – for example the military officer corps – the Russian masses do not believe that the clock can be turned back or the USSR can be reconstructed.

As has been noted, Russians had over the course of the Soviet period largely lost a sense of themselves as a distinct ethnic group. As Lev Gudkov of the polling organization VTSIOM observed in early 1994: "For Russians, the chief role in their self-definition was until recently played by the view of themselves as citizens of the USSR, as Soviet people. Neither language, nor culture, nor the past, nor traditions had a significance comparable to the perception of themselves as citizens of the Soviet state. From 63 percent to 81 percent of ethnic Russians called their homeland not Russia but precisely the USSR (among Russians living in the non-Russian union republics, that percentage, on the whole, was higher, and it grew larger as one moved from 'West' to 'East' – i.e., from the Baltics to Central Asia.)"[52]

When the USSR fell apart in December 1991 and fifteen sovereign republics emerged from the rubble, Russians were unexpectedly forced to begin to see themselves as "citizens of the Russian Republic" rather than as citizens of a supraethnic USSR. As Andrei Ryabov of the Gorbachev Foundation in Moscow explained the results of a survey conducted in ten regions of Russia during the spring of 1994: "If in the spring of 1993, 42.4 percent of respondents considered themselves to be citizens of Russia, by this year [1994] the figure has grown to 54.1 percent, while those who consider themselves citizens of the USSR have dropped from 13.7 percent last spring to 10.4 percent this spring."[53]

Increasingly seeing themselves as citizens of the Russian Republic, Russians came to view the majority of the former union republics – Ukraine and Belarus obviously constituted exceptions – as something distinct and "other." While, as Ryabov has noted, 64.2 percent of Russian respondents wanted Russia to "play a more active role in the post-Soviet space," and only 14.5 percent were opposed, almost half of the respondents (47.3 percent) opposed Russia's offering any economic assistance to other former union republics (while 29.4 percent approved of such aid). These sentiments could, and undoubtedly should, be construed as, in a sense, neo-imperial in nature, but, as Ryabov underlines, "only 15.5 percent of respondents are prepared to use military force against neighbors in the case of conflicts with them or in the event of their infringement of the rights of their Russian-language populace." The loss of Russian lives was thus deemed to be too exorbitant a price to pay for increased political leverage in the "near abroad."

The breakup of the USSR in December 1991 was accompanied by the blitz-formation of the Commonwealth of Independent States, an entity which, for some ethnic Russians, held out the hope that a new union could gradually be constructed on its foundation. Igor Klyamkin has recalled: "In February 1992, when we asked [Russian citizens] about priorities of state-building, 18 percent of those polled were 'for' the reestablishment of the union, 50 percent preferred the strengthening of inter-state ties within the framework of the CIS, while 20 percent strove toward the strengthening of Russian (*rossiiskaya*) statehood."[54]

But, Klyamkin went on: "By April of 1994, the situation had altered: the percentage of those hungering for a reestablishment of the USSR had de facto not changed, the strengthening of the CIS was now favored by 30 percent of our compatriots, while the strengthening of Russian statehood now garnered 41 percent of respondents. We monitored public opinion over the entire course of this period [1992–early 1994], and the tendency for admirers of the CIS to diminish and for adherents of Russian state independence to increase grew unswervingly."

To summarize the complex and rapidly changing mood of Russian citizens unveiled by VTSIOM, "Obshchestvennoe mnenie" and other Russian polling organizations: ethnic Russians during 1992–94 consistently regretted a loss of empire but, in the majority, began to regard that loss as irreversible. Logically, they came to focus their attention upon the narrow political and economic interests of their own republic, increasingly losing confidence in the CIS as an integrating mechanism. While the Russians wanted Russia to play a more active role in the near abroad – which they regarded as a vital Russian sphere of interest – they generally rejected a use of force in achieving that aim.

## Mass opinion on Russia's relations with the other former republics

Public opinion polls taken during 1992–94 revealed that Russians held markedly differing views about the wisdom of reintegrating with the various former union republics. A poll taken by "Obshchestvennoe mnenie" in fourteen Russian cities during September of 1992 revealed the following percentages of respondents favoring a "new union" with these regions and republics:

| | |
|---|---|
| Ukraine | 24.0% |
| Belarus | 23.0% |
| Kazakhstan | 12.0% |
| Central Asia | 3.5% |
| Transcaucasia | 2.3% |
| The Baltics | 5.0%[55] |

Not surprisingly, Russians felt closest to their Eastern Slav brethren, the Ukrainians and Belarusans. A March 1994 Russia-wide poll revealed that 21 percent of respondents believed that it would be worthwhile to form a union with Belarus even if it involved economic hardship for Russia; 42 percent said that there was no need for such an unprofitable union; and 29 percent were undecided. The corresponding percentages for Ukraine were: 31, 44, and 25.[56]

This was scarcely a ringing endorsement of immediate union with Ukraine and Belarus. When the same respondents were asked by the poll whether or not it would be advisable for Russia to reduce gas supplies to Ukraine over non-payment of debts, 72 percent agreed that such a step would be appropriate; 17 percent disagreed; and 11 percent were indifferent.

Igor Klyamkin noted in 1994 that, while Russians theoretically favored integration with the Republic of Belarus, only 9 percent of those polled wanted such a union if it were accompanied by economic losses for Russia; 56 percent flatly rejected such a loss-making reintegration.[57]

## Russians and the "hot spots" of the near abroad

Polls taken during 1992 and 1993 demonstrated that citizens of Russia were unenthusiastic or ambivalent concerning the use of Russian troops to regulate conflicts in so-called hot spots of the near abroad. A June 1992 survey taken in the capital by the Moscow Sociological Agency found 57 percent of respondents opposed to using military force to regulate conflicts in the near abroad; 24 percent called for diplomatic measures on Russia's part; and 33 percent were prepared to use economic measures to quell the conflicts.[58]

Approximately a year later, a Russia-wide poll asked respondents what should be done with the "Russian-language population" in Tajikistan, where a bloody civil war was occurring. The results of the poll showed a lack of agreement over what should be done:

32% – defend them by political means;
16% – pull them out immediately;

16% – send in the troops;
13% – do nothing;
23% – unable to answer[59]

A Russia-wide survey taken in September 1993 by sociologists working for the "VP" polling service found similar confusion among those polled.[60] Respondents were asked: "In many republics located on the territory of the former Union there currently exist hotbeds of armed conflict – should Russian [rossiiskie] troops be in those places or not?" The response to this question was as follows:

17% – yes, to quell a conflict;
27% – yes, but only to defend the ethnic Russian [russkoe] population;
49% – no, they should not be there;
 7% – difficult to answer

Russian citizens were to a significant degree concerned over the fate of their coethnics living in the near abroad, and many favored the use of economic and diplomatic pressure to defend that populace against perceived oppressive policies by the titular peoples of the former minority union republics. The respondents were, however, completely divided on the issue of whether or not to send in troops to suppress political conflicts or to defend the interests of ethnic Russians.

## The migration dimension: an "in-gathering" of Slavs?

Migration to Russia from the near abroad has served during the period 1992–1994 as a kind of "objective correlative" to ethnic Russian empire-saving sentiment expressed in public opinion polls. The outmigration during this period generally continued the tendency seen from the mid-1970s onwards: namely, an outflow of population to Russia from both Central Asia (excluding Kazakhstan, which, due to its ethnic mix, was a special case) and Transcaucasia.[61]

Writing in 1993 migration specialist, Viktor Perevedentsev, foresaw: "The majority of the Russian (or, if you will, Russian-language or 'European') population will inevitably leave [Central Asia] even if ideal ethnic relations should prevail in that region."[62] In a similar vein, an official with the Russian Federal Migration Service predicted in mid-1993: "Most likely a majority of the three million Slavs who live [in Central Asia] will emigrate to Russia."[63]

Why are Russians leaving the four Central Asian republics and the three republics of the Transcaucasus in such large numbers? Obviously, fear of interethnic violence and of civil war represent key factors. Such fears override what might otherwise be interpreted as hospitable environments. The newly independent republic of Tajikistan, for example, could accurately be termed a Russian client state; the Russian military has recently played a major role in enabling Tajikistan's former communists to emerge supreme in a bloody civil war. Tajikistan has designated Russian as a language of international communication and has not set a deadline for record-keeping in the republic to be transferred to Tajik, a language which, as the 1989 USSR census showed, only 3.5 percent of the republic's Russians were able to speak.[64]

But despite such overtures to its Russian populace, Tajikistan has witnessed a mass flight of Russians from its territory. According to the Russian Federal Migration Service, by early 1994, approximately 300,000 of the 380,000 Russians and Russian speakers living in Tajikistan had already departed the republic.[65]

In Kyrgyzstan there has been no civil war and the republic boasts a progressive, pro-Russian president, Askar Akaev. Russian television programming and Russian newspapers are readily available, and a Slavonic Academy has been opened to provide higher education to Russian-speakers. Despite this seemingly auspicious setting, a net total of 100,000 persons, a majority of them Russians, departed the republic in 1993. The outmigration during the previous year of 1992 was similar in scope. If this pattern of Russian flight were to continue, a journalist for the newspaper *Izvestiya* has concluded, then soon "[T]he republic will be turned into a Turkish monolith."[66]

In contrast to Tajikistan and Kyrgyzstan, Uzbekistan appears to be indifferent as to whether or not the Russians remain. *De facto*, Uzbekistan is taking steps that inevitably must drive the Russians out. Between 1989 and 1992, a reported 23 percent of the Russian-speaking population of Uzbekistan left the republic.[67]

Recently, the Uzbek leadership has begun actively assisting the process of Russian outmigration. Election districts have been gerrymandered (village areas being merged with urban ones) so that fewer and fewer Russian-speakers are elected to the legislature. Russians and Slavs are being removed from all positions of authority; no Russian-speaker, for example, currently heads an oblast in the republic. Because of such developments, it is not surprising that many Russians have actively sought to leave Uzbekistan. If not as marked, similar conditions have held in the other Central Asia and Transcaucasus republics.

If migration specialists like Yurii Arutyunyan and Viktor Perevedentsev are correct, then it appears that the remaining years of this century are likely to witness a mass "in-gathering" of Russians and Slavs into Russia, Ukraine, and Belarus from Central Asia and Transcaucasia. While the Russian government could, theoretically, attempt to reconstruct a Russian empire in the periphery without a significant presence of Russians and Russian-speakers there, the task obviously would be a formidable one.

It is therefore understandable why some Russian nationalist spokesmen, such as Solzhenitsyn, advocate focusing exclusively upon reintegration with Ukraine, Belarus, and Kazakhstan – where almost nineteen million Russians lived at the time of the 1989 USSR census – and allowing the other former union republics to go their own way. Public opinion polls taken among Russian citizens during 1992–1994 tend, as we have seen, to provide support for Solzhenitsyn's views, which, however, are not shared by influential "empire-saving" Russian elites.

## Russia and its minorities

On the eve of the breakup of the USSR in 1991, Russians did not manifest a high rate of hostility toward their republic's ethnic minorities. Thus when a Russia-wide 1991 poll of 5,000 persons asked the question: "Is there a nationality toward whose representatives you feel hostility?" only 20–35 per cent of those polled answered in the affirmative. Minorities most often singled out for dislike were the so-called peoples of the Caucasus: Armenians, Azerbaijanis, Georgians, Chechens, and Gypsies.[68]

The animus against these particular groups was, Russian sociologists explained, due largely to the fact that they were peoples with a strong sense of ethnic solidarity who were more successful than Russians in commerce, and they were suspected of comprising criminal mafias. Inter-ethnic violence occurring in the Caucasus was another factor behind Russian dislike of these peoples. Finally, these groups were darker in complexion than many Russians and thus came to be racially denigrated as "blacks" [*chernie*].

Once the USSR broke apart in December 1991, dislike of Russia's minorities and of many of the titular peoples of the former union republics began to escalate. Animosity toward titular peoples such as the Estonians, Moldovans, and Uzbeks, who had pushed hard for sovereignty, began to grow, while detestation of the "peoples of the Caucasus" also shot upward. Traditional animosities – such as dislike of Jews and Tatars, "who played an important role in the mechanism of the self-identification of Russians"[69] – also received a new boost, although anti-Semitism and anti-Tatar sentiment remained moderate in scope. The withering away of Russians' view of themselves as a supra-ethnic "Soviet people" served to increase enmity toward the republic's minorities: increasingly it became "us" (ethnic Russians) against "them" (non-Russians).

The polls track this rising incidence of prejudice graphically. At the end of 1992, VTSIOM polled 1,009 residents of Moscow, asking them: "Have you formed a positive or negative attitude toward, for example . . .?"[70] The percentages were as follows:

| | not formed | positive | negative |
|---|---|---|---|
| Ukrainians | 30 | 67 | 3 |
| Jews | 36 | 56 | 8 |
| Tatars | 36 | 53 | 11 |
| Moldovans | 46 | 47 | 7 |
| Latvians | 46 | 47 | 7 |
| Armenians | 29 | 37 | 34 |
| Georgians | 31 | 36 | 33 |
| Gypsies | 36 | 31 | 33 |
| Chechens | 33 | 27 | 40 |
| Azerbaijanis | 28 | 26 | 46 |

Ten months later, in October 1993, VTSIOM conducted a Russia-wide poll which asked respondents a similar question: "How do you most often relate to . . .?"[71] The percentages were as follows:

| | negatively | positively |
|---|---|---|
| Chechens | 48 | 35 |
| Gypsies | 48 | 39 |
| Azerbaijanis | 43 | 43 |
| Armenians | 45 | 41 |
| Uzbeks | 20 | 61 |
| Estonians | 16 | 64 |
| Jews | 17 | 68 |
| Tatars | 13 | 71 |
| Ukrainians | 7 | 81 |
| Russians | 2 | 91 |

It should be noted that much of the animosity identified by these polls was not based on personal contact. Thus, for example, at the time of the late 1992 VTSIOM survey, only 31 percent of the respondents had ever encountered a Chechen. Only 6 percent of respondents had had frequent contact with Chechens.[72] One worrisome result revealed by the polls was that Russian young people were entertaining more hostile feelings toward Gypsies and Chechens than were older respondents.[73]

Lev Gudkov and Oksana Bocharova of VTSIOM have noted another significant result revealed by the polls: "It is characteristic that the growing uneasiness and great-power dissatisfaction [of Russians] with regard to Ukraine as a [sovereign] political formation is not reflected in attitudes toward Ukrainians as an ethnic group – here one observes maximal benevolence and closeness."[74] The sense of oneness felt by Russians toward Ukrainians apparently overcame any resentment provoked by Ukrainian state-building efforts.

The polls also revealed a growing sense among Russians that the republic's minorities had already obtained too great an influence. In 1990 and 1993, VTSIOM conducted Russia-wide polls that asked respondents: "Do you agree that today non-Russians exert an excessive influence in Russia?"[75] The percentages were as follows:

| Year | Agree | Disagree | Difficult to answer |
|------|-------|----------|---------------------|
| 1990 | 40    | 56       | 4                   |
| 1993 | 54    | 44       | 2                   |

Interestingly, while hostility toward non-Russians living in their midst was growing, the masses of ethnic Russians continued to entertain moderate views concerning the degree of self-rule to be granted the autonomous republics within Russia. In late 1992, when VTSIOM asked Moscow residents, "Do you believe that the peoples inhabiting the territory of Russia have a right to form sovereign states independent of Russia?" the percentages were as follows:

| | |
|---|---|
| yes | 47 |
| no | 38 |
| difficult to answer | 15[76] |

Of all the minority formations in Russia, the secession-prone Republic of Chechnya under its tempestuous president, General Dzhokhar Dudaev, has represented the greatest headache for the Russian government in the post-Soviet period. Among conservative Russian elites, there early emerged a conviction that force needed to be employed to return Chechnya to the fold. The Russian masses, by contrast, have consistently taken a more nuanced view of the problem. When, for example, a summer 1994 Russia-wide poll conducted by "Obshchestvennoe mnenie" asked respondents what should be done about Chechnya, it obtained these results:

40% – Russia should take no decisions with regard to Chechnya until the internal conflicts in the republic are resolved

23% – Moscow should recognize Chechnya as an independent state

16% – The Russian government should conduct negotiations with the leaders of Chechnya concerning special conditions for the republic's remaining in the Russian Federation

5% – Moscow must at any price – including the use of force – preserve Chechnya within the Russian Republic.[77]

## The view of conservative elites

While the Russian masses have in the period following the collapse of the Soviet Union generally been ambivalent and hesitant concerning a reconstituting of the Soviet empire, conservative elites, such as the Russian military officer corps have exhibited few such reservations. Shortly after the demise of the USSR, the All-Army Officers's Assembly – an organization consisting largely of ethnic Russians – met in Moscow. About 2,000 officers attending the convention were polled by the Moscow branch of VTSIOM and by the Association of Military Sociologists.

As reported in February 1992, 71 percent of the officers polled supported the reestablishment of one state within the borders of the USSR.[78] A weighty 63.1 percent of the officers polled also believed that in future years a single army of the CIS would be preserved.[79] In apparent contradiction with this sentiment, 57 percent of respondents feared that "in the near future there could be armed conflicts between Russia and the other republics of the CIS."

Asked which former Soviet politicians they approved of, the officers gave President Nursultan Nazarbaev of Kazakhstan an impressive 65.3 percent rating, with Vice President Rutskoi coming in second (36.1 percent) and outspoken "empire-saver" Colonel Viktor Alksnis, an ethnic Latvian, third (28.7 percent). President Yeltsin was fourth with a 20 percent rating. The high ratings for two non-Russians – Nazarbaev and Alksnis – showed that in early 1992 many Russian officers remained convinced "Soviet patriots" and were relatively indifferent to narrow Russian national concerns. President Nazarbaev and Colonel Alksnis received support from the officers because it was felt that they, like General Rutskoi, might be able successfully to reassemble the "space" of the former Soviet Union.

Despite the clear neo-Soviet, supraethnic "empire-saving" views held by the officers, when they were asked: "[I]n which of the former union republics would you prefer to serve?" they replied as follows:

| | |
|---|---|
| Russia | 58.3% |
| Ukraine | 15.2% |
| Belarus | 8.1% |
| Baltics | 2.1% |
| Kazakhstan | 1.1% |
| Moldova | 0.3% |
| Central Asia | 0.1% |

Obviously the officers were aware that there were regions of the former Soviet Union which were increasingly inhospitable to a Russian presence. If permitted to choose, the officers therefore opted to stay out of Central Asia, Kazakhstan, the Baltics and Moldova. (Transcaucasia was apparently not on the list of regions mentioned in the poll, but one presumes that few, if any, officers would have wanted to serve in that politically unstable area.)

Two polls taken among Russian officers over the course of the summer of 1994 showed that "empire-saving" sentiment was notably on the rise in their ranks. In a poll of instructors and students at Russian military academies in Moscow, 76 percent of the respondents supported General Aleksandr Lebed, head of the Russian Fourteenth Army in Trans-Dniestria in Moldova, for the post of Russian defense minister; Deputy Defense Minister Boris Gromov came in second with 19 percent backing.[80] The sitting defense minister, Pavel Grachev, received no support at all. Both Generals Lebed and Gromov were presumably seen by those polled as tough "empire-savers" who would vigorously advance Russia's interests throughout the territory of the near abroad.

When asked what politicians might be expected to be successful in the upcoming 1996 presidential elections, 49 percent of respondents picked a political centrist, Prime Minister Viktor Chernomyrdin, but, ominously, 40 percent selected neo-fascist demagogue Vladimir Zhirinovsky, who had repeatedly pledged to reassemble the "space" of the former Soviet Union and then to divide it into approximately 100 supraethnic American-style states. Under Zhirinovsky's scheme, which was tantamount to a program of ethnocide, all of the former minority union republics – and of the autonomous formations within the Russian Federation – were to be abolished.

In the same poll of instructors and students at Moscow military academies, an overwhelming 94.5 percent of respondents advocated that the Russian government adopt "policies oriented toward [Russian] national interests and, in the first instance, toward the countries of the CIS; priority is given here to Belarus and Ukraine."[81] Another summer 1994 poll taken among Russian officers from all service branches on behalf of the German Social Democratic Party's Friedrich Ebert Foundation found that 62 percent of the respondents believed "Russia requires 'authoritarian rule' to solve its problems," while 80 percent aspired to "Russia's restoration as a great power respected in the entire world."[82]

An investigative report published on the pages of the mass-circulation weekly *Argumenty i fakty* in late 1993 concluded that "a majority of the [Russian] officers do not accept the foreign policy of Russia."[83] Russian generals and other military officers were said strongly to oppose the withdrawal of troops from Eastern Europe, the Caucasus, and the Baltics. The Belevezhskii Accords, which had led to the formation of the CIS in December 1991, were vilified as "a betrayal of the interests of the state."

The views of one officer were seen by *Argumenty i Fakty* as typical: "The military [the officer declared] live by the idea of the state. We are convinced that the division of the USSR into separate states . . . is a short-lived event . . . The politicians will be swept aside if the Union is not soon reestablished under another name. The Armed Forces will find the means to 'convince' them of this."

It will be noted that a significant evolution had taken place in the minds of Russian officers since early 1992, following the breakup of the USSR. From being strong "Soviet patriots," dedicated to restoring the Soviet Union and to resurrecting the concept of a supraethnic "Soviet people," the officers had gradually evolved into Russian nationalists and imperialists who sought to establish Russian political, economic and military hegemony over the entire "space" of the near abroad. A similar evolution has taken place among other conservative Russian elites, such as the leaders of the military-industrial complex. Indeed, many self-styled Russian "centrists" have also evolved in such a direction.

## The invasion of Chechnya and its aftermath

The Russian invasion of Chechnya on December 11, 1994, an event preceded by the so-called "phony war" of August–December, represented, as we can see now, a key turning point in modern Russian politics. Russia's blitzkrieg offensive was intended to be a crushing blow which would impress not only Russia's restive minorities but also the newly independent states of the CIS, as well as the Western powers.

An article appearing in the reformist weekly *Moscow News* sought to summarize what it saw as the principal motivation behind the Russian leadership's decision to take action: "[T]he ex-USSR republics," the newspaper wrote

> ... have begun to treat Moscow without proper respect: Estonia
> declares even more loudly its claims for the Pechorskii district;
> Lithuania is closing the military transit to Kaliningrad; and Azerbaijan
> and Kazakhstan are contending for their rights to Caspian oil. At the
> latest [December 1994 OSCE] summit in Budapest none of the close or
> distant neighbors backed Yeltsin's stand on the inadmissibility of
> expanding NATO. Thus, the first interest in the Chechen adventure is a
> demonstration of, and the desire to show the world, that Russia still
> has enough strength.[84]

Rather than achieving a blitzkrieg victory, the combined military, MVD and marine forces which poured into Chechnya soon found themselves bogged down in a bloody war with a determined and able opponent. Seven months after the invasion, the Russian forces had yet to achieve their goal of forcing unconditional surrender upon the Chechens, though they had managed to inflict heavy human and material losses upon them and their republic. In mid-February of 1995, Russian human rights commissioner Sergei Kovalev – the leading domestic critic of the war – estimated that 24,500 civilians had perished in Groznyi, the capital of Chechnya, a figure which, he said, included approximately 7,300 women and 3,700 children.[85]

In indiscrimately attacking civilian targets in Groznyi and throughout the republic, the Russian forces, as Sergei Yushenkov, chairman of the defense committee of the Duma has remarked, directly violated "many international conventions and even the Charter of the International Tribunal [Nurnberg]."[86] Among Russia's egregious violations of international law were the carpet bombing of civilian targets; the widespread use of cluster bombs against peaceful inhabitants; and the employment of the Grad and Uragan rapid-volley-fire artillery systems against civilians, a practice specifically prohibited by the Geneva Conventions. There was also the brutal mistreatment of Chechen prisoners, many of them innocent civilians, at notorious "filtration" centers established in Mozdok, Stavropol', Groznyi and Pyatigorsk; this mistreatment took the form of severe beatings, burnings with cigarettes, and occasional murders.[87]

The invading Russian forces themselves suffered heavy casualties. In mid-to-late March 1995, the military correspondent for *Moscow News*, Aleksandr Zhilin, estimated that the combined Russian army and MVD forces had already lost "about five thousand men."[88]

While prior to the invasion the Chechens had not been closely united around their tempestuous president, General Dzhokhar Dudaev, once the Russians poured in, the Chechens then closed ranks, as was their centuries-old tradition, against a foreign invader. President Yeltsin's sweeping claims that the Russian forces were opposed by Chechen "bandits" represented an attempt to scapegoat the Chechens as a kind of collective Medellin cartel. The invasion and Yeltsin's crude attempts collectively to denigrate the Chechens inevitably transformed the conflict into a "people's war" for perhaps a majority of Chechens, who then flocked to Dudaev's banner. Some Russian commentators began to make reference to Professor Samuel Huntington's intriguing 1993 article appearing in *Foreign Affairs*, entitled "The Clash of Civilizations?"[89] Would Russia, these commentators wondered, soon find herself in a "civilizational" war with the Muslim peoples of Russia, the "near abroad," and even of the "far abroad"? Russian nationalist writer Aleksandr Solzhenitsyn was one who thought it was possible; he sternly warned his fellow countrymen: "The opening of military actions against Chechnya is a serious political mistake. Whatever the result . . . it will bring political harm, chiefly in our relationship with the Caucasus and with the Muslim world in general."[90]

Aware of a possible "civilizational" dimension to the war against Chechnya, the Russian leadership employed a combination of carrots and sticks in an effort to prevent Muslims at home, within the CIS, and elsewhere from becoming actively involved in backing Chechnya's secessionist effort. Chechnya's close neighbor, the autonomous republic of Ingushetiya, was on several occasions bombed and shelled, as was the adjacent republic of Daghestan. The head of the Foreign Intelligence Service (SVR), Academician Evgenii Primakov, a specialist on the Arab world, paid a visit to

Jordan, the site of a large Chechen diaspora, to promote a hands-off approach. Similar pressure was exerted upon Turkey, which is also home to a major Chechen diaspora. Russia moved ahead with a plan, strongly opposed by the United States, to sell a nuclear reactor to Iran. An attempt by three non-Muslim autonomous republics – Chuvashia, Tuva, and Sakha (Yakutia) – to prevent military draftees in their lands from being sent to war in Chechnya was countered by the Russian government.

What did ethnic Russians themselves feel about the war? For the most part, it emerged, they disapproved of it. Thus, for example, a Russia-wide poll taken in late January and early February of 1995 found 72 percent of respondents opposed to the invasion, with only 16 percent approving it.[91] Given the general mood of passivity and anomie prevalent among the Russian masses, however, such disapproval did not translate into large demonstrations against the leadership's actions. The passivity of the masses enabled Yeltsin and the "power ministers" to continue to prosecute the war, in quest of a humiliating unconditional surrender by the Chechens.

Russian academic specialists in ethnic affairs have virtually uniformly condemned the invasion as both unnecessary and foolhardy. Yeltsin's ethnic affairs adviser, Emil Pain, for example, a member of the Russian presidential council, vigorously opposed the war from the beginning and consistently advocated a negotiated settlement.[92] The former chairman of the State Committee for Nationality Affairs, Valerii Tishkov, termed the invasion "a grandiose, unjustified war," asserting that "the variant of a state associated with Russia" would have been acceptable to the Chechen leadership, including General Dudaev. "I am deeply convinced," Tishkov stated, "that up until 23 November 1994 there did not exist any fatal inevitability of a Chechen war; rather there existed possibilities for resolving the crisis. It would have been worthwhile for Yeltsin to pick up the phone ... and invite Dudaev to fly to the Kremlin ..."[93] Two academics who have broken with this general pattern and have supported the war effort have been Andranik Migranyan, a member of the presidential council, and Aleksandr Tsipko.[94]

In his above-noted comments concerning the war, Valerii Tishkov implicitly placed much of the onus for the invasion on Minister for Nationalities and Regional Affairs Nikolai Egorov, an agricultural specialist by training. "It is not enough to be born in the Caucasus to be an expert on the Caucasus," Tishkov observed caustically. The well-known Russian political scientist, Fedor Burlatskii, has for his part speculated that Egorov, an ethnic Russian Cossack, may well "have been ruled by the emotions of being a Cossack" when he pressed for an invasion of Chechnya.[95] (Another key figure in the so-called "party of war," Oleg Lobov, the powerful secretary of the Russian Security Council, was also a Cossack, one said to be proud of his ancestry).

Egorov's ethnic background is significant because, as traditional guardians of Russia's borderlands, the Russian Cossacks, and especially those living in the country's southern regions, have often experienced a sense of competition and rivalry with the Muslim mountain peoples of that area. For Yeltsin therefore to place a Cossack from southern Russia – and especially one completely untrained in ethnic studies – in charge of nationalities affairs in Russia was to invite trouble, and, not surprisingly, trouble soon reared its head.

The December 1994 invasion of Chechnya can be seen as part of a Russian nationalist spasm which shook the top Russian leadership during late 1994 and early 1995. This spasm followed directly on the heels of Yeltsin's political "shift to the right" in mid 1994, and, like Gorbachev's earlier such "shift to the right," in late 1990 and early 1991, it led directly and swiftly to ethnic bloodshed. The two key figures behind the emergence of what came to be called "the party of war" were General Aleksandr Korzhakov, head of Yeltsin's Security Service, and First Deputy Prime Minister Oleg Soskovets.[96]

In addition to generating a war in Chechnya, the nationalist spasm also facilitated an attempt by elements in the top leadership to establish an independent Russian course in economics which would, to a considerable extent, have detached Russia from the global economy. "The backpedaling on economics," one Western journalist has written, "appears to be of a piece with the move toward war."[97] The central figures in this economic backpedaling process were the aforementioned Oleg Soskovets and Vladimir Polevanov, head of the State Property Committee.[98]

The invasion of Chechnya, journalist Nikolai Petrov has underlined, led to "the growth of ethnic intolerance in society and to a torpedoing of the very idea of multi-national statehood."[99] In order to succeed as a viable modern state, however, Russia was obviously required to elaborate and to defend the concept of *rossiyanin*, i.e., of a citizen of the Russian Federation without regard to ethnicity. A failure to do so would increase the likelihood of "civilizational" war with other minority peoples of Russia. Worse still, the unleashing of Russian imperial nationalism could serve to exacerbate relations with the newly independent states of the CIS, and such strains could, in turn, result in threatending consequences for the region and for the world at large.

Unfortunately, the period of the Chechnya war has witnessed a growth of imperial nationalism among some ethnic Russians. Thus when, in early 1995, a Russia-wide poll asked respondents: "Do you agree that it is necessary to strive to create a state in which [ethnic] Russians are officially recognized as the chief nation?" the answer was:

43% – I agree
38% – I disagree

9% – I am indifferent

10% – Difficult to answer[100]

In similar fashion, a survey of Russian college-level students in early 1995 found that 50 percent of the sample opposed marriage with representatives of other nations, while 40 percent maintained categorically that, "Russia is for the [ethnic] Russians." Of the sample, 30 percent confided that they had voted for neo-imperialist Vladimir Zhirinovsky in the December 1993 elections.[101] Such aggressive sentiments among Russia's students did not bode well for the country's minorities or for the neighboring states of the CIS.

## Conclusion

The tumultous processes which resulted from Gorbachev's accession in 1985 and his destabilizing programs of glasnost and democratization for the first time in seventy years required that ethnic Russians begin consciously to define their relations to the "inner" Russian empire. Faced with a choice between "empire-saving" and "nation-building," the masses of ethnic Russians at first began to tilt in the direction of nation-building. The rapid de-ideologization of the Russian popular psyche following the breakup of the USSR led Russians increasingly to view themselves as a discrete ethnic group rather than as "Soviet people."

While the rapid de-ideologization of Russians was a development to be welcomed, there were nonetheless numerous pitfalls accompanying it. Animosity began to grow among Russians toward a number of the titular peoples of the near abroad for allegedly mistreating the millions of Russians on their territories. Hostility also grew toward the "peoples of the Caucasus" and other minorities within the Russian Republic itself. Adroit and unprincipled demagogues such as Vladimir Zhirinovsky and neo-Nazi "fuhrer" Aleksandr Barkashov rose up to exploit these animosities.

The invasion of Chechnya in December 1994 represented a giant step backwards in the sphere of ethnic relations. As Fedor Burlatsky has observed: "[E]vents in Chechnya turned the Russian political spectrum upside down. Nationalist Vladimir Zhirinovsky became the most active adherent of Yeltsin's policies – not only on Chechnya but also on budgetary issues, the war against crime, and implementing a hardline course of defending Russian national interests *vis-à-vis* the CIS and the West." Looking to the future, Burlatsky foresaw the possibility of "less democracy and a less-free market" in Russia, as well as "a harder line in the international arena."[102] While the polls showed that many Russians continued to be politically moderate, as a people they were becoming less tolerant in their attitude toward non-Russians, and it was not clear that Russians would ultimately be able to elude political snares set by skillful demagogues and extremists such as Vladimir Zhirinovsky, General Aleksandr Rutskoi, and Gennadii Zyuganov, head of the Communist Party of the Russian Federation, all of whom announced that they were running for the Russian presidency.

During the course of a 1988 interview, the late Milovan Djilas prophesied the Soviet Union's imminent demise and remarked concerning the impending emergence of a Russia shorn of empire:

> We are talking about the natural expiry of an unnatural and tyrannical regime which is bound to come, as surely as the British and French empires had to face their demise when the time was ripe. The Russian people would benefit the most. They would gain a free and more prosperous life and yet remain, undoubtedly, a great nation . . . I believe that a reduced but self-confident, opened-up Russian state would induce much less brooding in the Russian people and make them a happier race . . .[103]

As we have seen, public opinion polls at first showed that a majority of ethnic Russians were prepared, albeit perhaps grudgingly, to agree with Djilas' view. But by 1996, this "nation-building" orientation among Russians had begun noticeably to wane, and it became increasingly possible that unscrupulous "empire-savers" might yet have their day.

## Notes

1 From Yuri V. Arutyunyan, "The Russians Outside Russia," in Marco Buttino, ed. *In a Collapsing Empire* (Milano: Feltrinelli, 1993), p. 142.
2 From Klara Hallik and Marika Kirch, "On Interethnic Relations in Estonia," in *ibid.*, pp. 149–151.
3 Hugh Seton-Watson, *The New Imperialism* (Chester Springs, PA: Dufour Editions, 1961), p. 23.
4 *Ibid.*, pp. 30–31.
5 Carl A. Linden, *The Soviet Party-State: The Politics of Ideocratic Despotism* (New York: Praeger, 1983), p. 95.
6 Alain Besançon, "Nationalism and Bolshevism in the USSR," in Robert Conquest, ed., *The Last Empire* (Stanford, CA: Hoover Institution Press, 1986), pp. 10–11.
7 "Djilas on Gorbachov," *Encounter*, October, 1988, p. 7.
8 From Viktor I. Perevedentsev, "Population Migrations between the Republics in the USSR," in Buttino, ed., pp. 21–29.
9 Yu. V. Arutyunyan, "The Russians Outside Russia," p. 141.
10 In *Literaturnaya Rossiya*, September 28, 1990.
11 In *Sobesednik*, no. 6, 1990.
12 See Roman Szporiuk, "Dilemmas of Russian Nationalism," *Problems of Communism*, July-August, 1989, pp. 16–23.
13 Oleg Rumyantsev, "Russian Reform: The Democratic Position," unpublished essay, *circa* March, 1991.
14 In *Literaturnaya gazeta*, June 14, 1989.
15 From *Moscow News*, no. 48, 1990, p. 9.
16 In *Komsomol'skaya pravda*, March 14, 1991, p. 2.
17 *Ibid.*

18 *Ibid.*
19 In *Novoe vremya*, no. 9, 1991, p. 91.
20 From *The New York Times*, November 25, 1990, p. Ell.
21 In *Stolitsa*, no. 6, 1991, pp. 6–7.
22 See "Spor o Rossii," *Novoe vremya*, no. 13, 1991, p. 7.
23 In *Sovetskaya Rossiya*, January 19, 1991.
24 Besançon, "Nationalism," p. 11.
25 The text of the brochure appeared in the September 18, 1990 issues of
   *Komsomol'skaya pravda* and *Literaturnaya gazeta*. English edition: *Rebuilding Russia*
   (New York, NY: Farrar, Straus and Giroux, 1991). For an analysis and for a
   discussion of Russian reactions, see my essay "Solzhenitsyn Calls for the
   Dismemberment of the Soviet Union," *Report on the USSR*, December 14, 1990, pp.
   3–4.
26 See Klaus Mehnert, *The Russians and Their Favorite Books* (Stanford, CA: Hoover
   Institution Press, 1983); Vladislav Krasnov, "Russian National Feeling: An Informal
   Poll," in Conquest, ed., *The Last Empire*, pp. 109–130; and "Two Films for the
   Soviet Masses," in the collection of my essays, *The New Russian Nationalism* (New
   York: Praeger, 1985), pp. 60–74.
27 See *Ogonek*, no. 43, 1989, p. 4.
28 See *Argumenty i fakty*, no. 21, 1990, pp. 2–3.
29 See *Moskovskie novosti*, no. 40, October 7, 1990, p. 9.
30 On the January 1990 events, see "V Krasnodare posle mobilizatsii," *Komsomol'skaya
   pravda*, January 28, 1990, p. 1.
31 In *Izvestiya*, August 14, 1990.
32 On the attempted *putsch*, see John B. Dunlop, "Crackdown," *The National Interest*,
   Spring, 1991, pp. 24–32, and "The Leadership of the Centrist Bloc," *Report on the
   USSR*, February 8, 1991, pp. 4–6. See also "Litva-yanvar' 1991: Otchet gruppy
   nezavisimykh voennykh ekspertov soyuza 'Shchit'," *Russkaya mysl'* (Paris), February
   22, 1991, special appendix, pp. i-iv. Excerpts from the "Shchit" report appeared in
   *Moskovskie novosti*, no. 9, March 3, 1991, p. 10.
33 For the results of the poll, see *Komsomol'skaya pravda*. January 18, 1991, p. 1.
   *Moskovskie novosti*, no. 4, 1991, pp. 8–9, and "Russian Radio," January 22, 1991.
34 *Moskovskie novosti*, no. 4, 1991, pp. 8–9, and "Russian Radio," January 22, 1991.
35 In *Reader's Digest*, March, 1991, pp. 49–54.
36 Ann Sheehy, "Updated Fact Sheet on Questions in March 17 and Later
   Referendums," Radio Liberty Report via *sovset'*, *March 14, 1991*.
37 See *The New York Times*, March 5, 1991, p. A3.
38 "Rossiya naedine s soboi," *Pravda*, 2 November 1991.
39 *Moskovskie novosti*, no. 45, 1991.
40 "Stanet li Rossiya velikoi derzhavoi?" *Nezavisimaya gazeta*, 20 June 1992.
41 "Derzhava v poiskakh sebya," *Nezavisimaya gazeta*, 28 March 1992.
42 *Rossiiskaya gazeta*, 23 June 1992.
43 *Boston Globe*, 21 October 1991.
44 Paul Goble, cited in "Things Fall Apart," *The Economist*, 30 January 1993.
45 Before concluding its summer session, the Khasbulatov-led Supreme Soviet had drafted
   amendments to the Constitution and to the Criminal Code that were to be brought
   before the Tenth Congress, scheduled to be held in November. These amendments
   were designed to reduce Yeltsin's power radically, transforming him into a ceremonial
   head of state. The amendments to the Criminal Code, in particular, would have
   imposed criminal penalties for refusal to comply with parliamentary decisions. Yeltsin
   apparently felt that he had to make a preemptive strike. See Robert Sharlet, "Russian
   Constitutional Crisis: Law and Politics under Yeltsin," *Post-Soviet Affairs* 9, no. 4
   (1993), p. 326.

46 "Chislo postradavshikh vo vremya sobytii 3–4 oktyabrya v Moskve ustanovleno," *Izvestia*, 25 December 1993.

47 See Kronid Lybarskii and Aleksandr Sobyanin, "Fal'sifikatsiya-3," *Novoe Vremya*, no. 15, 1995, pp. 6–12. It should be noted, however, that there may have been extensive vote-rigging by local election commissions leading to the misrepresentation of perhaps as many as 9–11 million votes.

48 On Zhirinovskii and the results of the December 1993 elections, see John Dunlop, "Zhirinovsky's World," *Journal of Democracy*, 5, no. 2, April 1994, pp. 27–32.

49 A new threat to Yeltsin rule also appeared to hover on the horizon in 1994 – a third putsch, which this time would be spearheaded by elements in the military. Throughout the year, Yeltsin's control on the armed forces appeared tenuous: military chief of staff Mikhail Kolesnikov and Defense Minister Pavel Grachev attempted to wrest control of the border guards and of other armed units on Russian soil through the parliament and the Russian Security Council (although these efforts failed). On this, see *Komsomol'skaya pravda*, 24 July 1994; *Izvestia*, 17 June 1994; and *Novaya ezhednevnaya gazeta*, 15 July 1994. More ominous was the growing popularity of General Aleksandr Lebed', the outspoken and conservative head of the Fourteenth Army in Transdniestria, whose blatant insubordination in regularly denouncing both Yeltsin and Defense Minister Grachev was met only with mild reprimands and attempts at conciliation. In June of 1995, Lebed resigned his commission and became a candidate for election to the Russian presidency. One public opinion poll showed him leading the pack. With Lebed's popularity, the prospect of a Pinochet-type regime coming to power in Russia (by legal or illegal means) became a distinct possibility.

50 Igor' Klyamkin, "Integratsiya nachinetsya 'snizu'," *Delo*, July, 1994, pp. 1–2. For the results of polling conducted concerning these issues by "Obshchestvennoe mnenie," see *Argumenty i fakty*, no. 35, 1994, p. 2.

51 *Ibid.*

52 Lev Gudkov, "Natsional'noe soznanie: versiya Zapada i Rossii" *Rodina*, no. 2, 1994, pp. 14–18. For valuable polling data on ethnic Russians living both in the RSFSR and in certain minority union republics before the breakup of the USSR, see: *Russkie, etno-sotsiologicheskie ocherki* (Moscow: "Nauka," 1992).

53 "Integratsiya – eto vam ne reanimatsiya," *Obshchaya gazeta*, no. 19, May 13–19, 1994, p. 7.

54 In Klyamkin, "Integratsiya nachinaetsya 'snizu'."

55 Ostankino Television, September 27, 1992 in Radio Free Europe-Radio Liberty, *Russia & CIS Today*, September 28, 1992, p. 990/27.

56 Interfax dispatch cited in Radio Free Europe – Radio Liberty, *Daily Report*, April 13, 1994, p. 3.

57 Klymakin, "Integratsiya nachinaetsya 'snizu'."

58 Moscow Radio, June 27, 1992 in *Russia & CIS Today*, June 29, 1992, p. 006/06.

59 *Izvestiya*, August 14, 1993, p. 5.

60 *Segodnya*, September 14, 1993, p. 2.

61 On recent migration trends into Russia from the near abroad, see my essays, "Will a Large-Scale Migration of Russians to the Russian Republic Take Place Over the Current Decade?" *International Migration Review*, Fall 1993, pp. 605–629, and "Will the Russians Return from the Near Abroad?" *Post-Soviet Geography*, April 1994, pp. 204–215.

62 V.I. Perevedentsev, "Migratsiya naseleniya v SNG: opyt prognoza," *POLIS*, no. 2, 1993.

63 *Nezavisimaya gazeta*, June 2, 1993, p. 3.

64 Much of the information on Russian outmigration from Central Asia is taken from my *Post-Soviet Geography* article cited in footnote 52.

65 *Nezavisimaya gazeta*, January 20, 1994, p. 5.

66 *Izvestiya*, December 4, 1993, p. 5. The Russian ambassador to Kyrgyzstan, Mikhail Romanov, has cited a host of reasons for the Russian exodus: "the danger of being close to an area of conflict; the worsening of interethnic problems; the law on language . . . [and] difficulties in finding appropriate schools for children, since more and more institutions of learning are switching to instruction in Kyrgyz." When in May of 1993, Kyrgyzstan introduced its own currency, this served to unsettle many Russians, who felt keenly the loss of a "legitimate" ruble and the concomitant end to a valued link to Moscow. The wage and benefits differential obtaining between Russia and Kyrgyzstan was another factor prompting Russian outmigration. Wages, pensions, and scholarship stipends were said to be three, five, and even ten times lower in Kyrgyzstan than in Russia. *Kuranty*, February 17, 1993, p. 5. *Novoe vremya*, no. 2, 1994, pp. 10–11. Ostankino Television, October 31, 1993 in *Russia & CIS Today*, October 31, 1993, pp. 0779/33.

67 *Nezavisimiya gazeta*, January 20, 1994, p. 4.

68 "Sotsial'naya napryazhennost': diagnoz i prognoz," *Sotsiologicheskie issledovaniya*, no. 3, 1992, p. 18.

69 See "Ierarkhiya etnicheskikh stereotipov naseleniya," in Intertsentr VTSIOM, *Ekonomicheskie i sotsial'nye peremeny: monitoring obshchestvennogo mneniya*, no. 1 (January 1994), pp. 17–19. On anti-Semitism before the breakup of the USSR, see Lev Gudkov and Alex Levinson, *Attitudes toward Jews in the Soviet Union: Public Opinion in Ten Republics* (New York: The American Jewish Committee, 1992).

70 In *Moskovskii komsomolets*, January 12, 1993, p. 2.

71 In "Ierarkhiya etnicheskikh stereotipov naseleniya."

72 See "Chechenskii mif," *Novyi vzglyad*. no. 44, 1992, p. 3.

73 In "Ierarkhiya etnicheskikh stereotipov naseleniya."

74 *Ibid.*

75 "Novyi russkii natsionalizm: ambitsii, fobii, kompleksy" in Intertsentr VTSIOM, *Ekonomicheskie i sotsial'nye peremeny*, no. 1, 1994, pp. 15–17.

76 *Moskovskii komsomolets*, January 12, 1993, p. 2.

77 NTV, September 18, 1994 in *Russia & CIS Today*, September 19, 1994, p. 0671/27.

78 *Nezavisimaya gazeta*, February 5, 1992.

79 "Armiya i vlast'" *Gospodin narod*, no. 2, 1992.

80 "Za kogo armiya?" *Novoe russkoe slovo* (New York), August 4, 1994.

81 *Ibid.*

82 *Daily Report*, September 9, 1994, p. 1. The article appeared in the no. 36, 1994 issue of *Der Spiegel*.

83 "Armiya mezhdu vchera i zavtra," *Argument i fakty*, no. 44, 1993, pp. 8–9.

84 "Who Stands to Gain from the Invasion?" *Moscow News*, December 23–29, 1994, p. 2.

85 In *The Moscow Times*, February 26, 1995, pp. 18–19. (It should be noted here that, by the time Groznyi came to be bombed and shelled, it had become a largely ethnic Russian enclave, due to the fact that many of the city's Chechen residents had by then fled to the homes of relatives in the mountains. To punish the Chechens, Russian troops were thus killing mass numbers of their fellow Russians.)

86 In *Crossroads* (Jamestown Foundation), February 1995, pp. 5–6, 13–15.

87 See *Literaturnava gazeta*, March 1, 1995, p. 10 and *Monitor* (Jamestown Foundation), June 1, 1995.

88 *Moscow News*, March 17–23, 1995, p. 2.

89 In *Foreign Affairs*, Summer 1993, pp. 22–49.

90 In *Argumenty i fakty*, nos. 1–2, 1995, pp. 1 and 3.

91 Reported in *Transactions*, April 14, 1995, pp. 6–8. For other polls relating to Chechnya, see Intertsentr VTsIOM, *Fkonomicheskie i sotsial'nye peremeny*, no. 1,

1995, pp. 7–8; *Opinion Analysis: USIA*, M-39–95, March 3, 1995; and *Rossiiskaya gazeta*, June 21, 1995.

92 Presentation at Center for International Security and Arms Control (CISAC), Stanford University, March 9, 1995.

93 In *Novoe vremya*, no. 15, 1995, pp. 22–23. On Lobov, see *Izvestiya*, May 13, 1994, p. 5. On Egorov, see *Moscow News*, December 16–22, 1994, p. 4.

94 For Migranyan's views, see *Nezavisimya gazeta*, January 17, 1995, p. 1. For Tsipko's, see *Rossiiskava federatsiya*, no. 1, 1995, pp. 2–3.

95 In *Nezavisimaya gazeta*, January 31, 1995, p. 2.

96 On Korzhakov, see *The New York Times*, January 5, 1995, p. A6; *The Boston Globe*, January 29, 1995; and *The Moscow Times*, December 4, 1994, p. 14. On Soskovets, see *Izvestiya*, January 19, 1995, p. 5.

97 In *Boston Globe*, January 17, 1995, p. 31.

98 On Polevanov and his activities, see *Kommersant*, no, 3, 1995, pp. 10–11; *Financial Times*, December 22, 1994, p. 4; and *The Economist*, January 7, 1995, pp. 60–61 and January 21, 1995, pp. 62–63.

99 In *Novoe vremya*, no. 5, 1995, pp. 6–9.

100 In *Ogonek*, no. 19, 1995, p. 17.

101 In *Argumenty i fakty*, no. 13, 1995, p. 12

102 "Yeltsin: A Turning Point," *Transitions*, March 15, 1995, pp. 8–9.

103 "Djilas on Gorbachov," *Encounter*, November 1988, p. 30.

# Russia: chronology of events

*March 1985*

11    The Communist Party Central Committee confirms the choice of Mikhail Gorbachev as General Secretary.

*April 1985*

Boris Yeltsin is appointed head of the Central Committee Construction Department.

*July 1985*

1    Eduard Shevardnadze is appointed a full Politburo member and Yeltsin is named to the Secretariat.
Eduard Shevardnadze is appointed foreign minister.

*December 1985*

Yeltsin replaces Viktor Grishin as first party secretary of Moscow.

*February 1986*

18    Yeltsin is made a candidate member of the Politburo.
26–8    Twenty-seventh Party Congress is held in Moscow. Gorbachev stresses the importance of restructuring, acceleration, and intensification of the economy. Prominent dissidents Anatolii Scharansky and Yurii Orlov are released from prison.

*December 1986*

Andrei Sakharov is freed from internal exile in Gorky.

*January 1987*

Gorbachev advocates "democratization" (secret ballot, multiple-candidate elections) at a Central Committee party plenum.

*March 1987*

At a session of the Secretariat of the RSFSR Writers' Union, conservatives begin an attack on reform.

*May 1987*

Mathias Rust lands his plane in Red Square, resulting in the replacement of Defense Minister Sokolov with Colonel General Dmitrii Yazov.

The nationalist group Pamyat' holds a demonstration in Moscow. Yeltsin agrees to meet with members.

*June 1987*

Aleksandr Yakovlev is made a full member of the Politburo. Local elections are held with multiple candidates. 57 percent of candidates elected in the RSFSR are non-Communists.

*August 1987*
7-Sept. 29    While Gorbachev is on vacation writing *Perestroika*, Ligachev and KGB head Chebrikov step up their attacks on his policies.

*October 1987*
21    At a Central Committee plenum, Boris Yeltsin is viciously attacked, leading to his removal from the Politburo.

*November 1987*

Yeltsin is removed from his post as first party secretary of Moscow, to be replaced by Lev Zikov.

*January 1988*

At a Central Committee plenum, Gorbachev assails Brezhnevite "stagnation," following which several monuments to Brezhnev are pulled down.

*March 1988*
15    The conservative Nina Andreeva letter is published in *Sovetskaya Rossiy*.

*June 1988*

At the 19th Party Congress, proposals include elections to a new legislature, a more powerful presidency, free elections by secret ballot, and transfer of most administrative powers to the soviets. Yeltsin is denied a request for rehabilitation.

*August 1988*

The secret protocols of the Molotov-Ribbentrop pact are published in *Sovetskaya Rossia*.

*September 1988*
30    At a plenum of the Central Committee, Ligachev is demoted, Vadim Medvedev is elevated to full Politburo membership and made head of the ideological commission; Chebrikov is made head of the legal commission; Vladimir Kryuchkov is appointed head of the KGB; Boris Pugo is

appointed head of Party Control committee; Yakovlev is appointed head of the international commission; Anatolii Lukyanov is appointed Soviet vice-president; Vitallii Vorotnikov is given the token post of RSFSR president; and Aleksandr Vlasov is appointed RSFSR prime minister and made candidate member of the Politburo. Gromyko retires.

*October 1988*
1     Gorbachev is selected chairman of the USSR Supreme Soviet (equivalent to president).

*March 1989*
26     Elections to the new USSR Congress of People's Deputies are held. In his Moscow district, Yeltsin wins nearly 90 percent of the vote against a party-backed opponent. Several prominent party leaders are defeated, even in uncontested races.

*April 1989*
At a meeting of the Central Committee, it is announced that 74 of the 301 full members of the Central Committee have "resigned," and 24 new members are introduced.

*May 1989*
The first session of the Congress of People's Deputies opens and continues through June. The proceedings are televised and widely seen throughout the country. Gorbachev is elected president of the Soviet Union by a nearly unanimous vote.
In elections to the Supreme Soviet, Yeltsin, Gavril Popov, Sergei Stankevich, Yurii Afanasev, and Tatiana Zaslavskaya – all prominent reformers – are defeated. Aleksei Kazannik resigns his place in the Supreme Soviet in favor of Yeltsin.

*July 1989*
Strikes occur in Kuznetsk and Vorkuta.
29–30     388 reform-minded deputies form the Inter-Regional Group of People's Deputies, with Yeltsin, Afanasiev, Sakharov, Popov, and Viktor Pal'm (an Estonian), as co-chairmen.

*October 1989*
Gorbachev issues a 15-month ban on strikes, but the Supreme Soviet adopts more moderate legislation permitting strikes except when they would endanger lives, health, or the economy. 16,000 miners in Vorkuta strike two weeks later.

*December 1989*

At the second session of the Congress of People's Deputies, the parliamentarians vote 1,139 to 839 against discussing the possible revision or repeal of Article Six of the constitution which guarantees the Communist Party a leading role in government.
Andrei Sakharov dies.

*February 1990*

4    In the largest unofficial demonstration in Moscow in sixty years, some 200,000 people call upon the Communist Party to surrender its monopoly on power.

7    The Central Committee agrees to give up the Party's monopoly on power.

25    50–100,000 demonstrators march against the Communist Party in anticipation of the forthcoming RSFSR Supreme Soviet elections.

*March 1990*

The USSR Congress of People's Deputies approves the creation of a "strong presidency" to replace the traditional collective head of state – the 42-member presidium.

14    Gorbachev is elected president by a vote of 1,542 to 368 (with 76 abstentions). Reformers do well in elections to the RSFSR Congress of People's Deputies – Democratic Russia bloc wins 55 of 65 seats in Moscow and 25 of 34 seats in Leningrad.

*May 1990*

1    At May Day celebrations in Red Square, thousands jeer Gorbachev and the Soviet leadership. After 20 minutes of heckling, Gorbachev departs.

29    Yeltsin is narrowly elected chairman of the RSFSR Supreme Soviet in third-round voting.

*June 1990*

The RSFSR Congress of People's Deputies votes overwhelmingly for sovereignty.
The new RSFSR Communist Party holds its founding congress, and Ivan Polozkov is chosen first party secretary.

*July 1990*

15    400,000 rally in Moscow calling for Party leaders to be taken to trial.
At the 28th Party Congress, Boris Yeltsin announces his resignation from the Communist Party, Gorbachev is reelected general secretary, Yakovlev is not elected into the Central Committee, and a new Politburo made of the first

party secretaries of the 15 republics, plus Gorbachev and 9 others, is established.

*September 1990*

The RSFSR Supreme Soviet adopts Shatalin and Yavlinskii's "500-day plan" for economic reform.
70,000 gather in a demonstration calling for the resignation of Ryzhkov's government.
Yeltsin is involved in a mysterious car accident.

*October 1990*

Gorbachev wins the Nobel Peace Prize.
The Supreme Soviet adopts a law on public associations providing legal guarantees to newly-created political parties.

30 Thousands gather outside KGB headquarters to commemorate the victims of totalitarianism in a ceremony organized by Memorial.

*November 1990*

7 Following official Revolution Day ceremonies, Yeltsin

and Popov participate in anti-government ralllies.

17 At a session of the Supreme Soviet, Lt. Colonel Viktor Alksnis gives Gorbachev thirty days to shift away from the reformers or else face the threat of removal.

*December 1990*

1–2 The hardline parliamentary faction Soyuz is created.
Foreign Minister Shevardnadze resigns, warning of an approaching dictatorship.

22 An anti-government letter signed by 53 hardliners is published in *Sovetskaya Rossiya*.

*January 1991*

14 Valentin Pavlov is confirmed as new Soviet Prime Minister.
15 Alexander Bessmertnykh is appointed foreign minister and Boris Pugo becomes interior minister.
16 Gorbachev proposes the temporary suspension of the 1990 Law on Press but backs down when liberal deputies protest.
20 100–300,000 march to the Kremlin to protest the crackdown in Lithuania.

*February 1991*

19 Yeltsin calls upon Gorbachev to resign.
22–24 Two large pro-Yeltsin rallies and one anti-Yeltsin rally are held in Moscow.

*March 1991*

10    Several hundred thousand demonstrators gather in Moscow in support of Yeltsin.

17    The referendum on preserving the Union is held, and 71 percent of voters in the RSFSR (75 percent turnout) support the union. Simultaneously, 70 percent of voters in Russia elect to hold Russian presidential elections.

25    Following a 21 March decree of the Supreme Soviet banning an upcoming demonstration in Moscow, the USSR Cabinet of Ministers declares that all demonstrations are forbidden in Moscow until April 15.

28    More than 100,000 Yeltsin supporters defy the ban on demonstrations.

*April 1991*

5    The RSFSR Supreme Soviet votes 607–228 (with 100 abstentions) to give Yeltsin broad emergency powers.

*May 1991*

12    Gorbachev and Yeltsin meet with the heads of the RSFSR autonomous republics and agree in principle to making the autonomies subjects of the Union Treaty.

21    Two leaders of Democratic Union are arrested by the KGB for calling for the overthrow of the USSR.

31    The Statute of the Russian Orthodox Church is registered by the RSFSR Ministry of Justice.

*June 1991*

12    Boris Yeltsin is elected RSFSR president with 57 percent of the vote. Runner-up Ryzhkov receives 17 percent and Vladimir Zhirinovsky gets 8 percent.
The RSFSR Supreme Soviet approves a draft law "On the Languages of the Peoples of the RSFSR."

17    Gorbachev and leaders of seven republics sign a new draft Union Treaty.
At a session of the USSR Supreme Soviet, the heads of the KGB, military, and Ministry of Internal Affairs voice their support for Pavlov's demand for extraordinary powers for the Cabinet of Ministers.

21    The USSR Supreme Soviet votes 262–24 against discussing transferring power to Pavlov. Gorbachev jokes with reporters that "the coup is over."

*July 1991*

1    The Movement of Democratic Reforms, headed by Yakovlev and Shevardnadze, announces its formation.

3    Shevardnadze resigns from the Communist Party.

20 Yeltsin issues a decree "departifying" all state organizations and bodies on Russian soil.

23 In a letter published in *Sovetskaya Rossiya*, three future leaders of the August coup appeal for the overthrow of the Russian government.

24 Gorbachev announces that he and leaders of 10 republics have agreed on disputed power-sharing provisions in the proposed Union Treaty.

*August 1991*

4 Gorbachev begins a vacation in Crimea.

16 Yakovlev resigns from the CPSU and warns of an approaching coup.
The Union Treaty is published in the press, and it is announced that the signing will occur on 20 August.

19–22 Soviet hardliners stage a coup, detaining Gorbachev in the Crimea and announcing the temporary rule of the State Committee for the State of Emergency (GKChP). The coup fails to gain popular and military support and does not succeed. Gorbachev returns to Moscow.

24 Gorbachev resigns as General Secretary of the CPSU and disbands the Central Committee as well as the USSR Cabinet of Ministers.

29 USSR Supreme Soviet votes 283–29 (with 52 abstentions) to ban the activites of the Communist Party.

*September 1991*

2 A State Council is formed which is made up of Gorbachev and the heads of all republics planning to stay in a new confederation.

6 Leningrad adopts the name St. Petersburg.
The State Council recognizes the independence of the Baltic states.

*October 1991*

4 All the leaders of the former republics, except for the Baltic states, sign a treaty on an economic community.

18 Gorbachev and 8 republic leaders agree to an economic union based on a plan by Yavlinsky.

20 Yeltsin transfers control of the USSR Ministry of Internal Affairs to the RSFSR.

23 The State Council disbands the USSR KGB.

31 The Russian Congress of People's Deputies confirms the tricolor flag as the Russian state flag.

*November 1991*

6 Yeltsin issues a decree abolishing the CPSU and the

Communist Party of Russia on Russian soil and nationalizes their property.

14  In Novo-Ogarevo, the leaders of seven former union republics (Russia, Belarus, and the Central Asian republics) agree to create a Union of Sovereign States. But on the 25th, the seven leaders decline to sign the treaty when Gorbachev summons them to do so.

*December 1991*

7–8  Yeltsin, Kravchuk, and Shushkevich establish the Commonwealth of Independent States and choose Minsk as its capital.

9  Gorbachev holds a meeting with Yeltsin and Nazarbaev. He later announces his opposition to the CIS and calls for the convening of the USSR Congress of People's Deputies and the holding of a referendum on the CIS and the Union Treaty.

10  Gorbachev meets with military officials and asks them to support him as Soviet commander-in-chief. Yeltsin addresses the same group of military officials the next day, reminding them of a recent 90 percent pay raise and asking them for support.

12  The Russian parliament ratifies the Minsk agreement on the creation of the CIS with a vote of 188–6. It also votesto annul the 1922 treaty which established the USSR.

16  The Russian parliament declares itself the legal successor to the USSR Supreme Soviet and votes to take over its assets. Three days later, Russian officials seize control of the Kremlin, the foreign and interior ministries, and the KGB.

22  Several thousand gather in Moscow to protest the dissolution of the USSR.

25  The Soviet flag is lowered from atop the Kremlin and is replaced by the Russian tricolor.
Gorbachev resigns marking the formal dissolution of the Soviet Union.

26  Russian parliament votes to change the name of the republic from the RSFSR to the Russian Federation (or Russia).
Russia assumes the Soviet seat on the United Nations Security Council.

*January 1992*

12  In the wake of the 1–2 January price deregulation, parliamentary chairman Ruslan Khasbulatov beseeches Yeltsin to replace the government or else the parliament will be forced to do so by constitutional means.

*February 1992*

9 Tens of thousands gather on Manezh Square in a demonstration organized by the procommunist "Working Russia" movement to demand the reestablishment of the Soviet Union and the dismissal of Yeltsin's government. A smaller, pro-Yeltsin demonstration is held in front of the parliament building.

8–9 A Congress of Civic and Patriotic Forces is held in Moscow with the participation of Vice-President Alexander Rutskoi. Two days later, Yeltsin signs a decree limiting the responsibilities of Vice-President Rutskoi.

23 Militia clash with procommunist demonstrators.

*March 1992*

2 Khasbulatov shuts down a parliamentary commission, chaired by Lev Ponomarev and Father Gleb Yakunin, which had been investigating the activity of the August coup plotters.

3 Valerii Tishkov is appointed chairman of the State Committee for Nationalities Policy.

10 Leaders of twenty-five nationalist and communist groups announce the creation of a joint Council of Opposition Movements.

14 The Democratic Party of Russia led by Nikolai Travkin and the People's Party of Free Russia headed by Vice-President Alexander Rutskoi hold a Conference of Social Forces and agree to work together.

15 Mass demonstrations held in Moscow, St. Petersburg, and elsewhere in support of resurrecting the USSR.

17 10,000 gather in Manezh Square for an antigovernment demonstration.

30–31 The Federation Treaty is signed by all 89 subjects of the Russian Federation with the exception of Tatarstan and Chechnya. Bashkortostan signs only after concluding a special agreement allowing the republic broader rights in various spheres of government.

*April 1992*

3 First Deputy Prime Minister and Yeltsin confidante, Gennadii Burbulis, resigns.

6 At the Sixth Russian Congress of People's Deputies, a proposal for a vote of no-confidence in the government is narrowly defeated by a vote of 447–412 (with 70 abstentions).

10 Congress approves the Federation Treaty 848–10 (with 40 abstentions).
Congress votes 492–313 (with 64 abstentions) for Yeltsin's

economic program, 32 votes short of the necessary majority.

12    The government submits its resignation in the face of a rejection of its economic program as well as a proposal to retract Yeltsin's right to appoint ministers without parliamentary approval.

14    The proposal on curbing Yeltsin's powers fails, and Yeltsin is permitted to stay on as prime minister and rule by decree through 1992. The Congress also adopts the economic program. The cabinet withdraws its resignation the next day.

19    20–70,000 gather in Moscow in support of disbanding the Congress of People's Deputies.

20    Congress ratifies the CIS agreement 548–158.

*May 1992*

1    20,000 communist supporters gather at October Square on May Day to protest the government's policies.

7    Pavel Grachev becomes Minister of Defense.

21    The coalition Civic Union is formed with the participation of the Free Russia People's Party (led by Rutskoi), Travkin's Democratic Party, Arkadii Volsky's Renewal Party, and the parliamentary faction Smena-New Policy.

*June 1992*

1    A committee of procommunist opposition parties led by Sergei Baburin is established in Omsk and calls for Yeltsin and his supporters to be put on trial for destroying the Soviet Union.

3    Moscow mayor Gavril Popov resigns after being attacked for his radical reform policies. His deputy Yurii Luzhkov succeeds him.

12    The ultranationalist Russian National Assembly holds a congress in Moscow.

15    Yegor Gaidar is appointed acting prime minister.

22–23    Several thousand gather at a demonstration at the Ostankino television center organized by the procommunist group Labor Moscow to demand airtime for programs sympathetic to their views. When militia attempt to break up the rally, fighting ensues and more than 75 people are injured.

*July 1992*

4    More than forty pro-reform political groups, including Democratic Russia and the Russian Democratic Reform Movement, meet to discuss organizing a political bloc. On 9 December, they agree to establish the Democratic Choice bloc.

7  Constitutional Court proceedings open to determine the constitutionality of Yeltsin's 1991 decrees banning the Communist Party and expropriating its property.

29  Yeltsin proposes amendments to the draft constitution granting broader presidential powers.

*September 1992*

28  The leaders of most of Russia's republics issue a statement declaring their support for the Supreme Soviet and Khasbulatov.

*October 1992*

1  Distribution of vouchers for the mass privatization program begins.

8  Yeltsin issues a decree taking away the premises of the Gorbachev Foundation. A police blockade is formed to prevent foundation employees from entering the office.

9  Parliament approves a law revoking Yeltsin's right to appoint the cabinet directly.

12  25 members of the nationalist organization Pamyat raid the offices of the newspaper *Moskovskii Komsomolets* and demand information on authors of articles about the group.

19  Valerii Tishkov, chairman of the State Committee for Nationality Affairs, resigns citing opposition in the legislature to his policies.

22  Several thousand participate in an anti-Yeltsin demonstration in Moscow.

24  The National Salvation Front holds a congress in Moscow. Sergei Baburin, Gennadii Zyuganov, and Ilya Konstatinov are among those elected co-chairmen of the movement. Protest gatherings organized by the Federation of Independent Trade Unions are held throughout Russia. In Moscow an estimated 10,000 demonstrators participate.

25  Labor Moscow holds its founding congress in Moscow.

28  Yeltsin bans the National Salvation Front on the grounds that it calls for the violent overthrow of the government. Yeltsin also issues a decree banning the parliamentary guard, under Khasbulatov's direct supervision.

*November 1992*

The Union of Russian Governors issues a statement calling for an extension of Yeltsin's special powers, due to expire at the end of the month, and rejecting any changes in the government's composition.

24  Yegor Yakovlev is removed as chairman of Ostankino Television for violating a presidential order to restrain from broadcasting information on the North Ossetian-Ingush conflict.

25   Facing heavy criticism, staunch Yeltsin supporter Mikhail
     Poltoranin resigns his posts as Minister of Press and
     Information and deputy prime minister.

30   Constitutional Court concludes its proceedings on the
     Communist Party. It upholds the ban on the Party's top
     bodies but repeals it for local party organizations.

## December 1992

1–14  The Seventh Congress of People's Deputies is held in
      Moscow. Yeltsin calls for a political ceasefire and accuses
      Khasbalutov and a majority of the congress of seeking to
      block reform and establish a dictatorship of the legislature.
      The Congress adopts an anti-Yeltsin "Appeal to the Russian
      People."

1    Yeltsin issues a decree on "Questions of the Defense of the
     Rights and Interests of Russian Citizens outside the Bounds
     of the Russian Federation."

5    Two proposals for amending the constitution to dilute
     Yeltsin's powers of government appointment fail to pass by
     4 votes and 1 vote.
     The Congress rejects Yeltsin's nomination of Gaidar as
     prime minister by a vote of 486–467 (with 22 abstentions).
     In response to a call by Yeltsin for a referendum to break
     the political impasse between the president and parliament,
     thousands gather at demonstrations both for and against
     such a referendum.

7    Deputies approve a constitutional amendment allowing for
     the private ownership of land. The President and the
     Democratic Russia movement support a referendum on the
     question, for which Democratic Russia had collected 1.8
     million signatures.

11   Yeltsin agrees to the opposition's demand to dismiss
     Burbulis as his chief advisor, a position to which he was
     appointed in November.

14   In a second-round of voting, Viktor Chernomyrdin is
     selected as prime minister with a vote of 721–128.
     In an address to the council of CSCE foreign ministers,
     Foreign Minister Andrei Kozyrev delivers a hardline speech
     on foreign policy, acknowledging an hour later that he was
     only warning what it would be like if the political
     opposition were to gain power.

## Janurary 1993

3    Yeltsin and George Bush sign the START II treaty in
     Moscow.

13   Yeltsin issues a decree ordering the government to take all
     necessary measures to restrain organizations which violate

the constitutional order and promote ethnic or religious strife.

30   Despite its illegal status, the National Salvation Front holds its first session outside of Moscow.

*February 1993*

13–14   Communists hold a congress attended by 650 delegates with the aim of recreating the Communist Party of Russia.

16   Yeltsin declares that presidential envoys are to become part of Russia's local administrations.

20–21   Stanislav Terekhov, leader of the hardline Officers Union, organizes a meeting of serving and retired officers from the armed forces and the ministries of security and internal affairs.

23   On the first "Defenders of the Fatherland Day," 20–40,000 hardline supporters gather and calls to overthrow the government by violent means are heard.

*March 1993*

12   Parliament votes against amendments to the draft constitution giving increased power to the president. They also vote to cancel the upcoming referendum.
Yeltsin and his supporters walk out of a Congress session.

20   In a television address, Yeltsin announces the imposition of "a special regime." Vice-President Rutskoi denounces the decree as unconstitutional, and the Constitutional Court agrees.

24   Yeltsin issues a decree on the "activities of executive bodies," but it contains no mention of special rule.

28   No-confidence votes are held against both Yeltsin and Khasbulatov. 617 deputies vote for Yeltsin's removal, with 268 against (689 votes were needed for the motion to be binding). Only 339 deputies vote to remove Khasbulatov, with 558 against (517 votes were needed for this motion). Pro-Yeltsin demonstration attracting an estimated 100,000 people takes place near the Kremlin. A rival, hardline demonstration attracts approximately 30,000.

29   Congress approves the wording of the four questions to be asked in the April 25 referendum. The electorate is to be asked if they trust the president, approve of his socioeconomic policies, and support early presidential and parliamentary elections.

*April 1993*

22   The Procurator General announces that top officials will be held for questioning regarding allegations of corruption made by Rutskoi.

23    Yeltsin removes Rutskoi from his post as Minister of Agriculture.

25    The referendum is held. 59 percent express confidence in Yeltsin; 53 percent, in his economic reforms. 32 percent support early presidential elections while 43 percent favor early parliamentary elections.

*May 1993*

1    When police attempt to prevent hardline demonstrators from marching on Red Square, violence ensues. One policeman later dies of injuries sustained in the fight. Both the government and parliament are accused of instigating the riot.

9    Anti-Yeltsin Victory Day demonstrations proceed peaceably.

*June 1993*

2    The Democratic Party of Russia refuses to participate in a coalition agreement with its former Civic Union allies, the People's Party of Free Russia and the All-Russia Union Renewal.

5    The Constitutional Assembly convened by Yeltsin to discuss the draft constitution begins proceedings. Disagreements break out between the government and parliament, as well as between Moscow and the regions.

*July 1993*

12    433 of 585 delegates at the Constitutional Assembly vote to approve a draft constitution which gives the president wide-ranging powers including the right to dissolve parliament.

24    The government announces the withdrawal of all pre-1993 Russian banknotes from circulation. The origins of this decree were uncertain as, two days later, Yeltsin issued a decree relaxing the terms for trading in old rubles.

*August 1993*

13    Yeltsin proposes the creation of a Federal Council to be made up of two representatives of each of the 89 subjects of the federation. The Council of the heads of the Republics agrees to the idea a few days later.

*September 1993*

1    Yeltsin suspends both Rutskoi and his ally First Deputy Prime Minister Vladimir Shumeiko pending the results of a probe into allegations of corruption.

18    Gaidar returns to government through his appointment as First Deputy Prime Minister.

19    Moscow Procurator Gennadii Ponomarev declares that the charges of corruption against Rutskoi are unfounded.

19–20    Deputies spend the night in the White House (parliament building) because of rumors that Yeltsin was intending to disband parliament, by force if necessary.

21    Yeltsin issues Decree No. 1400 dissolving the Congress of People's Deputies and the Supreme Soviet and setting new elections to parliament for 12 December.
The Supreme Soviet votes to impeach Yeltsin and elects Rutskoi acting president.
The army pledges neutrality in the conflict.
A rally in support of parliament is held, initiating a series of pro-parliamentary demonstrations over the next several days.

22    The Constitutional Court declares Yeltsin's decree unconstitutional.

23    An emergency session of the Congress of People's Deputies is convened.
A policeman and woman civilian are killed in a failed attack on CIS military headquarters led by Stanislav Terekhov, leader of the Officers' Union. Government troops move to blockade the White House, which has its electricity, water, and telephone service cut off.

26    A crowd of 10,000 gathers in front of the Moscow City council in support of Yeltsin.

29    Yeltsin gives deputies an ultimatum to leave the White House by October 4.

30    Representatives of 62 Russian regions threaten Yeltsin with "political and economic reprisals" if he does not lift the blockade of the White House.

30–1    Church-mediated compromise fails.

*October 1993*

3    Supporters of hardline groups leave their demonstrations and storm the police cordon around the White House. Armed mobs seize the nearby mayor's office, police headquarters, and other installations. A battle for the Ostankino television station begins and lasts through the night.

4    Yeltsin issues a state of emergency.
Army troops enter Moscow and begin a siege of the White House which ends successfully late in the day. More than 100 die and hundreds are wounded. Khasbulatov, Rutskoi, General Albert Makashov, and others surrender.

5    Opposition groups and newspapers are suspended, as well as the Moscow city and district soviets.

6    Yeltsin calls upon all local soviets to voluntarily disband. Constitutional Court Chairman Valerii Zorkin resigns.

7    Yeltsin temporarily suspends the Constitutional Court. He also issues a decree which permits him to appoint the heads of regional administrations.

9    Yeltsin issues a decree dissolving all soviets lower than regional or republican-level.

10   Yeltsin issues a decree providing for direct elections to the Federation Council (rather than have representatives be appointed).

16–17  The pro-government electoral bloc "Russia's Choice" holds its founding congress in Moscow, as does Sergei Shakrai's Party of Russian Unity and Accord.

22   A provision making the republics sovereign states is dropped from the draft constitution.

*November 1993*

7    A few hundred Communist supporters disobey a ban on Revolution Day demonstrations in Moscow. Several hundred more observe the holiday in a protest outside of the city.

10   Of 21 parties which had presented petitions with the required 100,000 signatures, 13 are permitted to enter the electoral race.

*December 1993*

12   Elections to the 450-seat State Duma and the 178-seat Federation Council are held, as well as the referendum on the constitution. 55 percent of eligible voters are reported to have participated in the referendum, of which 58 percent support the constitution. In elections to the Duma, Vladimir Zhirinovsky's Liberal-Democratic Party wins the largest popular vote (23 percent). Including the single-mandate seats, Russia's Choice becomes the largest faction with 96 seats (21 percent); the Liberal-Democratic Party gets 70 (16 percent); the Communist Party, 65 (14 percent); and the Agrarian Party, 47 (10 percent). The rest of the seats are divided primarily between four other parties and blocs (PRES, Yabloko, Women of Russia, Democratic Party of Russia) and independent candidates.

*Janurary 1994*

12   Yeltsin ally Vladimir Shumeiko is eleccted chairman of the Federation Council.

14   Ivan Rybkin, member of the Agrarian Party, is elected chairman of the State Duma.

16   Yegor Gaidar resigns his post as First Deputy Prime Minister and Minister of Economics. Finance Minister Boris Fyodorov resigns four days later.

24   Valerii Zorkin is reinstated to the Constitutional Court

after being forced to resign as chairman in the aftermath of the October events.

*February 1994*

2 In the first reported election results of regional parliaments, 40 of 45 seats in the Penza oblast legislature go to former Communists. Local elections continue in many rounds throughout the year with similar results.

*April 1994*

2–3 At a party congress of the Liberal-Democratic Party, delegates elect Zhirinovsky party leader until 2004.

25 Duma deputy and prominent banker Andrei Aizderdzis is shot dead outside of his apartment.

28 The "Civic Accord" document, which calls upon all signatories to refrain from violence in pursuing political goals and other destabilizing activity, is signed by Yeltsin, Chernomyrdin, parliamentary chairmen, regional leaders, and representatives of parties, trade unions, and other organizations (100 leading businessmen and bankers sign the following week).
The pro-reform Liberal Democratic Union of "12 December," led by Boris Fedorov and Irina Khakamada, is officially registered as a new parliamentary faction.

*May 1994*

1 Communist and trade union-organized May Day demonstration transpires peacefully.

16 Nikolai Egorov replaces Sergei Shakrai as Minister for Nationalities Affairs and Regional Policy.

*June 1994*

12 The parliamentary faction Russia's Choice is officially subsumed into a new party, Russia's Democratic Choice. At the congress where the decision is made, Yegor Gaidar, who is selected as party chairman, calls for the establishment of a single market on the territory of the former USSR.

*August 1994*

31 Democratic Russia and Konstantin Borovoi's Party of Economic Freedom sign an agreement on political cooperation.

*September 1994*

9 At a meeting of the Union of Russian Governors, regional heads passed a resolution deeming it "inadvisable" to hold elections for local chief administrators before 1996.

17   A nationalist congress, Russian Frontier, is held in
     Kaliningrad.
21   A committee to create a United Movement of Social
     Democrats is organized in Moscow, with the participation
     of Aleksandr Yakovlev, Gavriil Popov, Anatolii Sobchak,
     and Stanislav Shatalin. Popov's Russian Movement for
     Democratic Reforms and Democratic Russia sign an
     agreement on political alliance.
24–25 The founding congress of the United Democratic Center
     attracts 320 participants from 30 parties and movements
     and 55 regions and republics, largely without the
     participation of prominent Moscow democrats.
27   Fyodorov and Irina Khakamada announce the creation of a
     Coordinating Council of Liberal Organizations, which
     includes their own Liberal Democratic Foundation and
     Liberal Women's Foundation as well as other
     organizations.

*October 1994*

5    Yeltsin signs a decree affirming that regional chief
     administrators are to be appointed by the president for a
     transitional period of unspecified length.
6    An interfactional group of deputies, Economic Union, is
     created. The Union supports the economic reintegration of
     CIS states and seeks to work with likeminded deputies in
     other post-Soviet states.
20   The organizing committee of the Congress of Russian
     Communities, led by Dmitrii Rogozin, holds its founding
     meeting attended by 80 delegates from 55 cities and
     regions.
11–14 The ruble falls by more than 900 to the dollar (30 percent)
     in one day, prompting the forced resignations of acting
     Minister of Finance Sergei Dubinin and head of the
     Central Bank Viktor Geraschenko. Tatyana Paramonova
     is appointed acting chairwoman of the Central
     Bank.
17   Dmitrii Kholodov, the military correspondent for
     *Moskovskii Komsomolets*, is killed by a bomb planted in an
     attache case.
18   Russia's Choice, Yabloko, and the Dec. 12 Liberal
     Democratic Alliance hold their first joint meeting since the
     Duma was elected.
27   Chernomyrdin's cabinet survives a no-confidence vote of
     194–54 (with 55 abstentions). 226 votes were needed for
     the motion to pass.
     Hundreds of thousands participate in anti-government
     demonstrations across the country sponsored by the
     Federation of Independent Trade Unions of Russia.

28    In a speech to the State Duma, Aleksandr Solzhenitsyn criticizes reformers and brings applause from communists and Zhirinovsky supporters.

30    Sergei Mavrodi, the head of the MMM investment fund whose collapsed pyramid scheme earlier in the year landed Mavrodi in jail and cost thousands of investors their investments, wins a seat in the Duma in an election to replace a murdered deputy.

## November 1994

1    Communist deputy Valentin Martemyanov is fatally assaulted and dies on 5 November.
Yevgenii Yasin is appointed Minister of Economics, replacing Aleksandr Shokhin.

7    Several thousand participate in a Revolution Day rally at which speakers call for civil disobedience and a general strike in order to overthrow the government.

## December 1994

6    Yuri Belyayev, who had been elected chairman of the nationalist National Republican Party of Russia the day before, survives an assassination attempt.

7    Yuri Kalmykov resigns his post as Minister of Justice.
Fyodorov's parliamentary faction, the December 12 Liberal Democratic Alliance, is dissolved by the Duma because it lacks the requisite number of supporters.

11    Yeltsin announces the deployment of troops to Chechnya. (For more on the war in Chechnya, see the North Caucasus chronology.)

13    In a vote of 289–4 (with 1 abstention), the State Duma asks Yeltsin to use all political means possible to end the crisis in Chechnya.

## Janurary 1995

10    *Nezavisimaya Gazeta* publishes a Federal Counterintelligence Service report which accuses several foreign academic institutions and foundations of collaborating with the United States government to undermine Russia's political and economic development.

26    In an interview, Vladimir Shumeiko defends the expanded role in government of the head of Yeltsin's security service Aleksandr Korzhakov.

28    The political association Regions of Russia, led by the president of the Union of Petroleum Industrialists Vladimir Medvedev, is established. The group supports the suppression of Chechnya's secessionist movement.

*February 1995*

1    LDPR Deputy Sergei Skorochkin is killed, making him the third Duma parliamentarian to be murdered.

6    The Russian Social Democratic People's Party (the former People's Party of Free Russia) expels their chairman Aleksandr Rutskoi and his followers for their establishment of the nationalist Derzhava movement, which is considered incompatible with the RSDPP's own principles.

8    An estimated 500,000 coal miners take part in a one-day warning strike to protest the government's wage debt.

12–13    The Democratic Alternative party, led by Grigory Yavlinsky, holds its founding congress.

14    Vladimir Tumanov is elected chairman of the Constitutional Court.

18–19    The Russian Party of Social Democracy (led by Aleksandr Yakovlev), the Foward, Russia! party (led by Boris Fyodorov), and the Great Power Revival People's Patriotic Movement (led by former Zhirinovsky ally Viktor Kobelev) hold their founding congresses. The All-Army Officers' Assembly, organized by Stanislav Terekhov, changes its name to the All-Russia Officers' Assembly and elects Vladislav Achalov its chairman.

*March 1995*

1    Well-known television personality and director of Russian Public Television Vladislav Listyev is assassinated.

13    Oleg Zverev, president of the Union of Entrepreneurs, is murdered.

16    The Federal Border Service and the Russian Orthodox Church issue a statement of cooperation.
The right-of-center Party of People's Conscience, led by Aleksei Kazannik, holds its founding congress is Omsk.

25    Yeltsin issues a decree to combat extreme nationalist and fascist groups.

*April 1995*

2    The founding congress of Aleksandr Rutskoi's Derzhava movement is held in Moscow and attended by 886 delegates from 62 regions, including Viktor Alksnin, Viktor Aksyuchits, Mikhail Astafyev, and Nikolai Pavlov.

7    The State Duma passes a law which declares that the highest official of a region or republic is to be chosen by popular election.

12    Thousands participate nationwide in protest demonstrations organized by the Federation of Independent Trade Unions.

19    In honor of the 50th anniversary of the World War II

victory, the Duma passes a law granting amnesty to about 300,000 prisoners.

25  Yeltsin announces his intent to support two centrist electoral blocs led by Chernomyrdin ("Russia is Our Home") and Rybkin in the December parliamentary elections.

# 3    The North Caucasus: confederation in conflict

JANE ORMROD

## History, nation and identity

Embracing nineteen native national groups[1] and a significant ethnic Russian diaspora,[2] the North Caucasus region is one of the most ethnically and linguistically diverse regions in the world. Three main ethno-linguistic groups – Altaic, Indo-European and Ibero-Caucasian – are represented in the region. The diversity of linguistic subgroups renders many of the national languages mutually incomprehensible. The geography of the North Caucasus facilitated the preservation of this diversity: the mountainous terrain isolated the population groups, creating conditions conducive to the persistence of a multiplicity of languages and dialects.[3]

At least until the mid-twentieth century, the diversity of the North Caucasian groups was also expressed in tribal or clan identity. For example, decisions to fight against the Russians in the Caucasian Wars of the nineteenth century were made not by Caucasian national groups but by tribal federations.[4] While the tribal federations had begun to dissolve by the early twentieth century, the clan structure remained strong, and social identity based on a local, clan consciousness was prominent in the early decades of Soviet power.[5]

Despite the fragmentation of the North Caucasian population into various linguistic, ethnic, tribal and clan groups, the inhabitants are unified by broad, cultural similarities. Contact between North Caucasian groups extends back for centuries, and various cultural and economic practices were broadly adopted throughout the North Caucasus.[6] Hence, the North Caucasian ethnic groups exhibit similar wedding rituals, family customs, architecture, styles of dress, forms of epic narrative in folklore, notions of justice, and even the retention of similar pagan practices in both Christian and Muslim rituals.[7]

The broad, North Caucasian *gorskii* (mountaineer) identity was realized in a variety of alliances. The North Caucasian force, lead by the Imam Shamil, opposed Russia in the nineteenth-century Caucasian Wars and embraced most of the North Caucasian ethnic groups. The Christian Ossetians, perhaps wary of Shamil's aim to establish a North Caucasian emirate governed by strict adherence to *shariat* (Koranic law), did not join his forces.[8] Regardless, the Ossetians, like the Muslim groups, were caught up

96

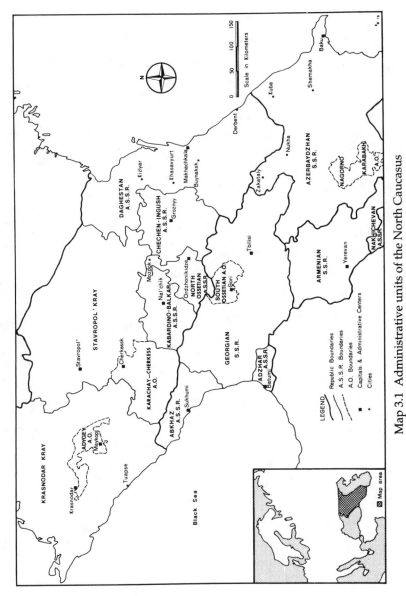

Map 3.1 Administrative units of the North Caucasus

Used with permission of Ronald Wixman (*Language aspects of ethnic patterns and processes in the North Caucasus*, Chicago, 1980).

by the repressions which followed the Russian victory. Ossetians joined the wave of North Caucasian immigration to Turkey in the last half of the nineteenth century.[9] And the Civil War struggle – in which diverse North Caucasian peoples united under the sheik Uzun Khadzhi to defeat Denikin's forces – drew in even the Ossetians.[10] Such conflicts, particularly the lengthy Caucasian War and its brutal aftermath, fueled anti-Russian sentiment in the North Caucasus and fostered a broad sense of identity based on resistance to Russian encroachments.

The *gorskii* identity was sufficently strong that the North Caucasian peoples formed a relatively independent political alliance, extending across the Caucasus, that remained intact from 1918 to 1921. The Mountain Republic (*Gorskaia Respublika*) was created in early 1918. In 1921, after the Bolsheviks had consolidated power, the Republic was made into an Autonomous Republic, and the territories of Dagestan were unified into a separate, Dagestan Autonomous Republic. In 1922, the Mountain Autonomous Republic was reduced further, with the creation of separate Adygei, Chechen, Karachai-Cherkessian and Kabardino-Balkarian Autonomous Regions (*Oblasti*). The Mountain Republic was fully dissolved in 1924, when its remaining territories were divided into the North Ossetian and Ingush Autonomous Regions. The Chechen historian A. Avtorkhanov argues that the destruction of the Mountain Republic and the creation of new national republican formations was undertaken against the will of North Caucasian leaders at the initiative of the centre, with the intention of splitting up the historically rebellious North Caucasian groups and shattering their viable political union.[11] Breaking up the Mountain Republic reduced the threat of a North Caucasian alliance against Soviet power. Less convincingly, some Soviet ethnographers have argued that the diverse North Caucasian nations could not be settled peaceably into a single republic, and therefore had to be separated into several autonomous republics and regions.[12]

In any case, the new national formations had no analogue in the North Caucasian past. Until this time, alliances had been formed on a local, tribal, or clan basis or, at other times, were a product of a general North Caucasian *gorskii* loyalty. The new groupings united various dialect and clan groups which had distinct identities. The Balkars, for example, were actually comprised of several Turkic linguistic groups: the Balkan, Chegem, Khulamtsan, Bezeng, and the actual Balkars.[13] In Dagestan, where there is no titular national group (the name "Dagestan", like "Yugoslavia", refers to a geo-political entity, and not an actual ethnic or national group), the officially recognized national groups sometimes contained more than one ethnic group. Thus the Andi-Dido and Archi peoples of Dagestan were grouped together with the Avar national group: they shared the Avar written language and official cultural institutions and were listed in the 1959 census as Avar.[14]

Soviet efforts to foster these new "national" identities were considerable. The creation of written languages for many of the groups was a first step in this direction, and was underway in the 1920s.[15] Knowledge of Arabic was widespread among Muslim clergy, but most of the North Caucasian population was illiterate.[16] By the end of the 1920s, newspapers were being published in many of the national languages. However, throughout the 1920s and early 1930s, the written languages and national language schools met with little enthusiasm from the local population. The local regimes had difficulty finding people who were willing to work (or to train for work) as teachers or newspaper correspondents. Publishing activity was minimal.[17] Furthermore, enrollment of children in schools was low.[18]

Indifference on the part of the North Caucasian groups – both peasants and intelligentsia – to participate in the development of their "national" cultures suggests that these cultures were not, at least in the 1920s and early 1930s, an important part of their identity. N.G. Volkova and L.I. Lavrov have characterized North Caucasian national consciousness in this period as a local, clan consciousness, together with a "parallel consciousness" of a "huge ethnic society" of North Caucasian *gortsy*. Initially, the North Caucasian peoples exhibited little consciousness of themselves as members of their officially recognized, national groups.[19]

Only after twenty years of Soviet power did official national identity begin to emerge. Currently, it forms the basis of ethnic and political discourse in the North Caucasus. This transformation in ethnic consciousness has been fostered by a number of developments which served, on the one hand, to distinguish the particular national groups from the sea of culturally and historically similar groups of *gortsy* and, on the other hand, to supplant clan loyalties with a vision of a larger national community.

Although not embraced with immediate enthusiasm by their national groups, literary languages were an important prerequisite for the development of a modern national community. Fellow nationals, most of whom – unlike members of a village or clan community – will never meet, are, through the printed word and the dissemination of the idea of the nation, joined in an abstract community.[20] By the mid-1930s, North Caucasian national groups were showing signs of cultural development. A national intelligentsia had become active. Using the national languages, scholars and writers recorded native folklore and wrote works of fiction and scholarship.[21] Significantly, the Chechen rebellion of the late 1930s was led by members of the intellegentsia: the writer Khasan Israilov and the jurist Mair-Bek Sharipov.[22] However, the events of the late 1930s, particularly the Cyrillization of the national languages and the purges of the national intelligentsia, hindered the development of the North Caucasian national cultures.[23] The curtailment of national language education under Khrushchev in the late 1950s posed another obstacle to cultural development.

A crucial event in the development of national identity in the North

Caucasus was the deportation, in 1944, of the entire populations of the Karachai, Balkar, Ingush, and Chechen national groups. The official explanation of this policy was that these groups had conspired with the occupying German forces during the Second World War. However, a more likely motive was the Soviet government's desire to weaken the force of rebellion and eliminate possible Turkish sympathy in the region.[24] The deported groups were resettled in areas of Central Asia, Kazakhstan, and Siberia, and their former territories were assimilated into the lands of the surrounding republics and regions of the North Caucasus.[25] Ultimately, the mass deportations at the gunpoints of the NKVD further enforced notions of national identity: on the basis of official national identity, some peoples were deported and others were not. If, in the earlier decades of the twentieth century, it was possible to speak of the North Caucasian nationalities as groups without distinct national histories, this was no longer true after 1944.

In 1956, the Khrushchev government granted the deported peoples the right to return to their homelands.[26] The names of their former regions were restored and the exiled peoples returned, in massive numbers, almost immediately. However, the actual process of resettlement did not always proceed smoothly. In many cases, returning people arrived in their former territories only to find that, during the years of their exile, their former villages had been resettled by others. Former territorial divisions and boundaries were not always restored.[27] As a consequence, clashes between peoples ensued. In the case of Ingush-Ossetian boundary disputes, a full resolution and cessation of violent confict has yet to be achieved. Owing to the circumstances of resettlement, North Caucasians were drawn into conflict and mutual hostility on the basis of national identities which had begun, in the early 1920s, as ethno-linguistic designations with little resonance in popular consciousness.

In the late 1980s, under Gorbachev, the development of national identity was greatly facilitated by the policy of glasnost and the easing of Russian assimilationist pressure. The future of national languages and national language education became an important issue throughout the North Caucasus. Educational reform occurred quickly. In the late 1980s, a group of Karachai linguists compiled a new Karachai-Russian dictionary, wrote textbooks for schools, and began working to implement a national language education programme in Karachai schools.[28] In Chechnya, the grade one class of 1990 was the first class of students in a new curriculum. Work on a Chechen thesaurus, with the intent of rendering borrowed Russian words into Chechen forms, was underway.[29] Scholars and pedagogues began work on an Ossetian dictionary and Ossetian history texts, and developed a new educational curriculum.[30] National cultural development was a chief concern of the national political movements in the North Caucasus. During the last years of Soviet power in particular, demands for national sovereignty or enhanced republican status were largely expressions of cultural anxiety and demands for cultural sovereignty.

The freedom granted to the Soviet press under Gorbachev greatly facilitated – and was, arguably, a necessary condition for – the development of modern, national identities among the peoples of the North Caucasus. For the first time, the North Caucasian ethnic groups were able to disseminate, through the organs of mass media and public speech, ideas of common national history, culture, and political interests. Scholars were able to research and publish on topics that had, in the Soviet period, been suppressed for their nationalist or anti-Soviet implications. In the last years of Soviet power, North Caucasian cultural and political elites developed and presented images of nationhood which found resonance in popular consciousness.

Since the collapse of Soviet power in 1991, the discourse of national and ethnic identity among the peoples of the former Soviet Union has been based almost entirely on concepts of the national state, whether fully sovereign or as a part of a republican structure. In the North Caucasus, national identity – rather than tribal or broadly North Caucasian – is the framework for discussion among North Caucasians and with other groups, and is disseminated through the print media and television. While, during the Gorbachev years, demands for national autonomy were focused on concerns of cultural self-determination, the North Caucasian demands of the post-Soviet period have broadened to include demands for heightened economic and legislative autonomy. At the extreme the Chechen republic has sought full independence from the Russian Federation.

Historically, the relations of the North Caucasian peoples with Russia have been hostile, and the historical memory and self-representation of the North Caucasian peoples is closely tied to struggles against the Russians.[31] Following the collapse of the Soviet Union, these relations – at least as manifest in political relations – have begun to change. Cooperation with Moscow has, for some North Caucasian national politicians, emerged as a vehicle for the possible enhancement of the national status of their own republics with respect to other North Caucasian national groups. However unwelcome Russia's past intrusions into the North Caucasus have been, Russia is, in principle, a powerful ally and mediator of conflict within the North Caucasus. Furthermore, the economic difficulties faced throughout the former Soviet Union pose severe challenges to the emerging national states, and to endanger economic ties Russia is likely to deepen, rather than ease, these difficulties. Hence, all the North Caucasian nations, with the exception of Chechnya, have chosen to negotiate with Russia to remain within the Russian federal structure, but with greater autonomy in their internal affairs. While the ongoing war between Russia and Chechnya will heighten North Caucasian suspicion of and hostility toward Russia, the economic motivations to participate in a Russian federal structure remain intact.

Apart from relations with Russia, the territorial situation of the North Caucasian national groups is complicated by internal problems of shared territory. In the cases of Kabardino-Balkaria and Karachaevo-Cherkessia, two titular nationalities share state structures. This was, until the split of Checheno-Ingushetia in 1992, also the case for the Chechens and the Ingush. Aside from these latter two, only the Ossetians and Adygei are the sole titular nationalities in their republics. In Dagestan, ten non-titular national groups – the Avars, Aguls, Dargins, Kumyks, Laks, Lezgins, Nogai, Rutul', Tabasaran and Tsakhurs – are officially recognized as the Peoples of Dagestan.[32] The drawing and redrawing of boundaries and the deportations and resettlements of the Soviet period complicate territorial questions yet further.

Given the incompatability of blurry boundaries and shared territories with the concept of the national state as a geographical and political entity, the North Caucasus is remarkably peaceful. Cultural and political self-consciousness in the North Caucasus involves multiple and shifting identities. Notions of national identity are meshed in a context of long-standing, broadly North Caucasian loyalties. The latter have been realized in a political assembly, the Federation of North Caucasian peoples. A shared identity of North Caucasian peoples does not – particularly in the case of hostilities between the Ingush and Ossetians – successfully mediate all the competing claims of the national groups. However, the strength of this identity helps to explain the willingness of most North Caucasian peoples to tolerate ill-defined boundaries and shared political power.

The following sections will focus more closely on events in each of the North Caucasian republics. In addition, three large cultural groups – the Nogai, the Cossacks, and the Russians – will be considered separately. The populations of these groups do not live compactly within a single republican territory but are spread throughout various areas of the North Caucasus. This chapter will also address the growing problem of refugees who have fled from troubled regions to seek refuge in other North Caucasian republics.

## The North Caucasian republics

### Adygeia

From the time of its creation in 1922 until 1991, the Adygei territory had Autonomous Region, rather than Autonomous Republican, status within the Krasnodar District (*Krasnodarskii krai*). According to data from the 1989 census, the region had the highest percentage of ethnic Russians – 68 percent – of all the North Caucasian Territories, although this figure also includes Cossacks. The titular national group, the Adygei, constituted only 22.1 percent of the population.[33] While since the collapse of Soviet power, ethnic Russians have tended to leave the North Caucasus for the territories of Russia, there have been no reports of significant out-migration of Russians from Adygei. Relations between the Russians and Adygei appear to be peaceful and stable. The creation of the Adygei Republic in 1991 evoked no hostility from local Russians, nor has there been any evidence of tensions in the following years. The constitutional project ongoing in Adygeia has proceeded smoothly, with delegates from the Russian Federation working together with Adygei representatives[34] Political relations between Adygei and Russia also appear friendly at a more local level, as an economic cooperation agreement between Adygeia and the Krasnodar District was signed in 1994.[35]

The Kuban Cossacks have, for over two hundred years, lived in close proximity to the Adygei. Indeed, with respect to their national dress and cultural practices, the Kuban Cossacks resemble more closely the Adygei than other Cossack bands. Since the early Soviet period, the two groups have maintained peaceful relations.[36] The Kuban Cossacks have appeared to be supportive of the enhancement of republican sovereignty in Adygeia. At the founding meeting of the All-Kuban Cossack Union in October 1990, Cossack delegates addressed an announcement to the Adygei, expressing their desire for friendly and supportive relations.[37] More recently, the Cossacks of the republic of Adygei have expressed some anxiety about their representation within the republic. At a session of the Legislative Assembly of the republic in October 1994, Cossack delegates emphasized that "the interests of all peoples and nationalities of Adygeia" must be expressed in the republic's legislation.[38] However, such statements seem to be an expression of concern to preserve stable political relations between the two groups, rather than a Cossack perception of unjust treatment in Adygeia.

With the enhancement of Adygei republican status in 1991, Adygei interest in fostering their national culture and national community has been expressed in political institutions within the republic. In particular, the republic created in 1991 a special commission to enhance ties between the Republic and expatriate Adygei living in Turkey, with the purpose of stimulating a "national-cultural rebirth" within the republic.[39]

General North Caucasian identity appears vital in Adygeia. Since 1991, a Committee on Land Reform in Adygeia has been working on a proposal for an exchange of land with the Krasnodar District. More specifically, the Committee proposed to exchange 50–60,000 hectares of its pasture and arable land close to the city of Krasnodar in return for 25,000 hectares of coastal land. The expressed motivation for this exchange on the part of the Adygei was to bring them closer to the other peoples of the North Caucasus, in this case the Abkhaz and Shapsug peoples. In June 1994, the Committee spoke with some confidence about the likelihood of this exchange. However, the Russian Ministry for National and Regional Policy denied the existence of a firm agreement, commenting only that Adygeia might arrange to rent this land from the Krasnodar District.[40]

The flourishing of national and North Caucasian identity in Adygeia has not, thus far, hindered the cooperative relations of the Adygei with either the Russian republic or ethnic Cossacks. This situation appears stable: given the persistence of peaceful negotiation and cooperation between these groups following the collapse of Soviet power, there is little reason to expect tensions to escalate in the near future.

### Chechnya

While a number of North Caucasian republics have threatened to separate from the Russian Federation, Chechnya, characterized by its aggressive nationalism, is distinguished as the only republic to have actually proclaimed its full independence. Since November 1991, when Dzhokhar Dudaev's government declared Chechnya to be a sovereign state, popular support for Chechen sovereignty has been very strong.[41] Even in the course of the brutal war with Russia, Chechens have continued to support – as well as fight and die for – the idea of an autonomous Chechnya.

A number of factors account for why Chechnya alone has pursued complete sovereignty with such force. First, a sense of national identity, animosity toward Moscow, and anxiety about national survival was intensified by the 1944 deportation of the Chechens. Combined with the history of Russian repression during the Caucasian Wars, recollection of the deportations offers both a powerful national narrative of attempted genocide at the hands of Russia, and also a common Chechen experience and unifying force in social consciousness. Chechens express pride in their aggressive resistance to Russian encroachment and in their retention of their language and culture in the face of pressure to assimilate.[42]

Second, unlike the other deported nationalities (Karachai, Balkar, and Ingush), the Chechens were the demographically dominant group in their Autonomous Republican formation. In 1989, Chechens represented 57.8 percent of the population of Checheno-Ingushetia, while the Ingush accounted for only 12.9.[43] As a majority in their autonomous republic, the Chechens had opportunities even in the Soviet period to strengthen their national culture and institutions, to acquire political experience, and to develop political confidence. As early as the 1960s and 1970s, the Chechen intelligentsia was active in its encouragement of the national culture. Its more vocal and nationalist elements called for heightened respect for Chechen ethnic and religious practices, and enhancement of Chechen language education.[44] Islam has remained a strong force among Chechens. The Islamic University in Groznyi was founded in 1991 and, in 1994, 4,000 Chechens made the pilgrimage to Mecca.[45]

A third factor accounting for Chechnya's move towards full independence is its lack of quarrels or conflicts with other North Caucasian groups. Even the split, in 1992, of Checheno-Ingushetia did not erupt into violent conflict. The Ingush decision to remain within the Russian federal structure provoked no animosity from the Chechens, nor did it weaken the Chechen independence movement. From its inception, Dudaev's government, called the All-National Chechen Congress, addressed primarily the national aspirations and concerns of the Chechens, leaving the Ingush to their own political affairs. Because of its peaceful relations with the surrounding groups, Chechen national animosity has been directed toward Russia, rather than toward other North Caucasian groups.

General Dzhokhar Dudaev and his Chechen All-National Congress seized power after the August 1991 coup attempt in Moscow. He was able rapidly to mobilize support for his nationalist platform and was elected president on 9 November 1991.[46] Boris Yeltsin immediately contested the election, issued a warrant for Dudaev's arrest and sent troops to Groznyi. However, Dudaev's National Guard blocked the Russian troops at the airport, and the Russian parliament, reversing Yeltsin's decision, recalled the troops. The Chechens refused to return the weaponry that the Russian and former Soviet armies had left in the Republic. Yeltsin's aborted attack fueled Dudaev's anti-Russian, nationalist rhetoric and provided a rallying point for Chechen nationalists.[47]

While Dudaev's separatist policies were widely supported, among Chechens, support for Dudaev himself was less enthusiastic. There was concern over Dudaev's tendency toward authoritarian rule, a concern voiced even by clan leaders and elders.[48] These suspicions received some confirmation when, following a clash between Dudaev and Chechen parliamentarians in June 1993, Dudaev suspended parliament and set up a Temporary Council.[49] In the course of 1993 and early 1994, opposition groups began to strengthen and civil strife reached the level of armed conflict. However, the leaders of the most powerful opposition movements – Ruslan Labazanov, Umar Avturkhanov, and former speaker of the Russian Parliament Ruslan Khasbulatov – were unable to form a united opposition. Thus, in August 1994, Dudaev was able to repel opposition attacks in Groznyi.[50] The opposition movements retained sufficient strength to continue their activities into the fall of 1994. By mid-October, however, the opposition movements lost much local support with the revelation that the Russian government had given them substantial financial and military assistance. On 17 October 1994, Dudaev appeared on national television and called on Chechens to "defend the homeland from the representatives of Russian aggression.[51]

Civil unrest – which Russia itself had sponsored – provided an excuse for Russia to launch an air attack on Chechnya on 26 November 1994, allegedly to "stabilize" the Chechen political situation.[52] Ironically, the Russian attack on Chechnya did accomplish the stated Russian objective of quelling civil unrest. As an indignant Ruslan Khasbulatov observed,

Russian "pirate raids" on the Chechen Republic served to strengthen Dudaev's hold on power. In the face of Russian aggression, the oppositionist, anti-Dudaev loyalties collapsed and Chechen fighters rushed to defend Groznyi.[53]

Prior to the invasion, Russia had a number of other concerns about the Chechen republic, and these in combination led to and helped to justify the decision to invade. By late September 1994, Russian Federal vice-premier Serge Shakhrai issued a statement outlining Russian discontent with the situation in Chechnya, and justifying Russian interference in the affairs of the republic.[54] First and foremost, Russia did not recognize the legitimacy of Dudaev's election to the presidency, the split of Checheno-Ingushetia, or Chechen independence. Not wanting to give any implicit recognition of Dudaev's government, Russian leaders refused to negotiate with Dudaev. In Russia's official view, Chechnya remained a subject of the Russian Federation and of Russian internal affairs. Consequently, Russian interference was not subject to international law.

Dudaev's designation of Chechnya as a "free economic zone" provided another excuse for Russian interference. The "free economic zone" of Chechnya was, in Shakhrai's words, a "criminal zone", and amounted to the protection of criminal elements and the creation of a mafia-like web of crime. Thus, Chechnya was accused of assisting in the transportation of contraband, currency, weapons, and narcotics to such centres as Moscow, London and the Far East.[55] While there was invariably some truth in the accusations, anti-Chechen sentiment and discrimination in Russia has been fuelled by such highly-exaggerated depictions, both in popular and official discourse, of the Chechens as thugs and mafiosi, even describing Chechnya as a "Sicilian" type of society.[56]

Russian propaganda has portrayed Chechens as Islamic fundamentalists and terrorists.[57] Shakhrai argued that Chechen nationalism and religious revival have created dangerous circumstances for Russians living in Chechnya, as over 200,000 have left the republic since Dudaev's government was formed, a proportion that can only be matched in the North Caucasus by, possibly, Ingustetia and North Ossetia. The Russian outmigration from Moscow is, in this view, justified in moving against the Chechen government to ensure the safety of ethnic Russians.[58]

Chechen mismanagement of their own affairs, in the Russian view, led to chaos in the transportation system. According to Shakhrai, disruption on railway lines in Chechnya was jeopardizing Russia's links with Dagestan and compromising normal relations between the two nations. Similarly, Russia accused Chechnya of failing to regulate air traffic, with unapproved and unscheduled flights out of Groznyi creating dangers in Russian airspace.[59]

Chechnya's oil industry and a Russian desire to retain control in this sphere received much attention in the Western press. In Russian accounts, the oil issue was less prominent. Contrary to the image of Chechnya as an "oil-rich" region, the republic produces little of its own oil. None the less, Chechnya's refining industry produces a significant amount of Russia's aviation oil, and a pipeline linking Russia with southern oil producers runs through Chechen territory.[60] While concerns about the oil industry and supply may have contributed to Russian opposition to Chechen separatism, these concerns were not sufficient to prevent Russia from destroying much of the industry's infrastructure in the course of the invasion.

A confluence of Russian concerns and propaganda, therefore, precipitated the invasion of Chechnya. Not to be excluded is the possibility that elements in the Russian leadership had wearied of Chechnya's refusal to cede its independence and felt that a short, successful war would serve the dual purpose of quelling Chechen separatism and enhancing the popularity of Yeltsin's government within Russia.

The war, however, has been neither short nor successful. The November 26 air strikes and Russia's conditions for negotiation with the Chechens – namely, Dudaev's resignation and Chechen disarmament – made peaceful settlement all but impossible. Russia officially launched its invasion of Chechnya on December 11, 1994. Faced with determined Chechen fighters, the Russian forces were unable to capture Groznyi until January 26, 1995, when the Chechen parliament building finally fell to Russian forces. By this time, much of the city had been destroyed. The invasion progressed slowly, with the Chechen forces gradually losing mainland territory and retreating into the mountains. The casualties, on both sides, numbered in the thousands.[61] Tens of thousands of Chechen refugees have been forced to flee the republic.[62] Although the Russians have the military power to capture the lowlands of Chechnya, the Chechens probably will continue to fight indefinitely from bases in the mountains, as they have done in their long history of conflict with Russia.

The reaction of the other North Caucasian republics to the Russian invasion of Chechnya was restrained, and none of these governments officially offered military aid to Chechnya. However, many of them did offer other forms of aid to Chechnya. In particular, Ingushetia and Dagestan have accepted masses of Chechen refugees.[63] President Aushev of Ingushetia attempted to mediate the crisis and arrange negotiations between Russian and Chechen leaders: these efforts were blocked by Yeltsin's refusal to meet with Dudaev.[64] The North Caucasian popular response to the attack on Chechnya was less restrained, as volunteers from the other North Caucasian republics, particularly Ingush and Dagestani, joined the Chechen struggle. Abkhaz fighters, whose struggle against Georgia had been assisted by Chechen volunteers, also offered support to Chechnya.[65] Nevertheless, the governments of the other North Caucasian republics appeared anxious neither to jeopardize their relations with Russia nor to risk the destruction that Chechnya has suffered. The possibility that Chechnya's armed resistance to Russia could spread and lead to a massive, North Caucasian war has not proved substantial. However, the struggle may foster anti-Russian sentiment, as well as anxiety about republican autonomy, throughout the North Caucasus.

The Chechens face the devastation of the infrastructure of their territory and the prospect of a long exile as refugees in other North Caucasian territories. It is unlikely that these setbacks will diminish the force of Chechen national identity. Destruction and exile are part of Chechen history. Earlier experience of and recovery from disaster, in the Caucasian Wars and the 1944 deportations, contributed to the strengthening of Chechen national resolve and unity. The war with Russia will likely retard the development of elite culture and cultural institutions in Chechnya, but the experience will also fuel Chechen national defensiveness and contribute to the national narrative of Russian repression.

## Ingushetia

Although the Ingush shared republican status with the Chechens for nearly sixty years, they have not only a distinct language, but also distinct relationships with the surrounding North Caucasian national groups. Territorial conflicts between Ingush tribes and Terek Cossacks have been ongoing since the 1860s.[66] The Ingush have also been involved in territorial disputes with the North Ossetians. Aside from the Ingush's desire to remain within the Russian Federation,[67] their particular relations with the North Ossetians, their distinct language, and their compactly-settled territory have contributed to their willingness to split the former Republic of Checheno-Ingushetia. In 1988–1989, before Chechnya had undertaken to separate from the Russian federal structure, 60,000 Ingush citizens signed a petition calling for the formation of an autonomous Ingush republic.[68] On 8 January, 1992, the Chechen parliament announced the restoration of the 1934 border between Chechnya and Ingushetia.[69] Although both the Chechen and Ingush Councils of Elders objected government officials in Chechenya and Ingushetia negotiated the creation of two republics.[70] Despite some initial conflict over the territorial divisions,[71] the separation was resolved peacefully and no lasting tensions between the two republics are apparent.

The focus of the Ingush conflict with the North Ossetians is the territory, in the Prigorodnyi region of North Ossetia, which was granted to the North Ossetian ASSR following the 1944 deportation of the Ingush and was not restored to the Ingush upon their return to the North Caucasus in 1957. As early as the 1970s, the Ingush petitioned the Soviet government asking for the return of this territory, and complained of Ossetian discrimination against Ingush living in the region. Armed clashes between Ossetians and Ingush has occurred periodically since the Ingush returned from exile.[72]

The escalation of this conflict in the early 1990s was spurred by the decision of the Supreme Soviet of the North Ossetian ASSR, in September

1990, to suspend the right of Ingush to live in North Ossetia.[73] Throughout 1991, the Ingush resisted this demand. In March 1991, following an address by Boris Yeltsin which seemed to condone Ingush claims to the territory, armed Ingush attempted to seize Ossetian homes in the Prigorodnyi region.[74] In the Ingush city of Nazran thousands of Ingush demonstrated to demand restoration of the Prigorodnyi territories and expressed a willingness to use armed force if necessary.[75] In response, the Ossetian authorities in the Prigorodnyi region imposed a curfew, formed a National Guard, and began armed retaliation for Ingush aggression.[76] The violence continued to escalate throughout 1992. By mid-1993, masses of Ingush – as many as 71,000 – had been forced to flee from North Ossetia to Ingushetia.

The republic of Ingushetia, experiencing difficulties accommodating this flood of refugees looked to Russia to help negotiate a settlement with North Ossetia. Such a settlement, it was hoped, would restore to the Ingush some of the disputed territories. Some support for this aspiration lay in the Russian Federal decree "On the Rehabilitation of Repressed Peoples,"[77] which sought to restore to deported peoples their previous national-territorial status. North Ossetia, however, was not willing to cede territory to Ingushetia, particularly since they were attempting to accommodate their own refugees from the South Ossetian war with Georgia.

As a result of the political impasse, the three sides – Ingushetia, North Ossetia and Russia – entered into negotiation. As the negotiations faltered, Russia attempted to take the lead. Martial law was declared in the Prigorodnyi region in July 1993.[78] A Temporary Administration was established and a Russian peacekeeping force was dispatched to the territory to oversee the return of the refugees. However, these measures were not sufficient to restore peace to the region and allow the refugees' safe return. Armed battalions on both the Ossetian and Ingush sides hindered the efforts of Russian peacekeepers to maintain order, and neither side was willing to make any concessions. The North Ossetians argued that Ingush and Ossetians in Prigorodnyi would be unable to live peacefully side by side, while Ingushetia would not renounce its claims on the Prigorodnyi territory.[79]

Similarly, both sides found fault with the Russian government's handling of the affair. North Ossetian leader Aklsarbek Galazov argued that provision for territorial rehabilitation in the Law "On the Rehabilitation of the Repressed Peoples" failed to consider demographic changes in the territories in question and had incited the Ingush to attempt to seize parts of the Prigorodnyi region. Ingush President Ruslan Aushev, for his part, criticized the Russian Federation's unwillingness to enforce its own law in restoring Ingush territory, and the inability of Russian peacekeepers to ensure the peaceful return of Ingush refugees to Prigorodnyi region. Aushev threatened to call a referendum on whether Ingushetia should follow the lead of the "fraternal" Chechen people and leave the Russian federation, thus becoming a subject of international law.[80]

In December 1993, Russian President Boris Yeltsin met with Galazov and Aushev in the neutral territory of Kabardino-Balkaria. The three signed a statement proposing that: Ingushetia renounce its territorial claims; North Ossetia admit the possibility of Ossetians and Ingush living together in the Prigorodnyi region; the refugees be permitted to return to their places of residence; and local armed units be disbanded.[81] This was further enforced on 26 June 1994, with the signing of the Beslan Agreement "On the Regulation of Restoring Refugees and Forced Migrants" to their places of previous residence in the Prigorodnyi region.[82] The negotiations, however, were tense and the Beslan Agreement was satisfactory to neither the North Ossetian nor the Ingush.

As of early 1995, the majority of refugees still had not returned to the Prigorodnyi region, and reports of violence continued. Ingush refugees alleged that Ossetian villagers prevented their return and were continuing to burn Ingush homes.[83] Ruslan Aushev accused the Ossetians of resettling the returning Ingush in isolated "reservations" rather than at their original places of residence. Thus resettled, the Ingush were unable to obtain employment or pensions. Galazov countered with the argument that, since many Ingush homes had been destroyed, a full and immediate repatriation was impossible. Aushev looked to Russia to force North Ossetia to abide by the terms of the Beslan Agreement and permit the return of the Ingush to their original territories;[84] but the Prigorodnyi situation remains in a state of irresolution.

Although Aushev threatened to consider full sovereignty for the republic, Ingushetia appears unlikely to secede from the Russian Federation. Despite some dissatisfaction with Russian efforts to mediate the Prigorodnyi conflict, Ingushetia continues to look to Russia for support. Russia has, within limits, supported Ingush repatriation, while other neighbors have shown no inclination to involve itself in the affair.[85] In turn, Ingushetia has accommodated large groups of Chechen refugees, but not officially offered military support to Chechnya in its war with Russia. Despite the cultural and historical similarities and friendly relations between the Chechen and the Ingush, Ingushetia is unlikely to jeopardize its alliance with Russia.

## Kabardino-Balkaria

The creation, in 1922, of a republic which combined Kabardinians and Balkars as the two titular nationalities is puzzling. Their languages are not mutually understandable. The Kabardinians have closer linguistic and historical ties to the neighboring Cherkess, while the Balkars are closer to the Karachai.[86]

The Balkars are a demographic minority in the republic. In 1989, they comprised only 9.4 percent of the population, while the Kabardinians and Russians represented 48.2 percent and 32 percent respectively.[87] The Balkars were among the groups deported in 1944, and the Balkar territories were turned over to the Kabardinian ASSR and resettled. While they were permitted in 1956 to return to the newly reconstituted Kabardino-Balkar ASSR, they were not, in all cases, permitted to rebuild their homes in their former territories.[88] They are now settled compactly in approximately one-fifth of the republican territory.[89]

Balkar consciousness of continuing injustice and discrimination is poignant and long-standing and has set the tone for political relations in Kabardino-Balkaria. While conflicts between Kabardinians and Balkars have never reached the level of violence of the Ingush-Ossetian conflict, there were, in the late 1950s, reports of clashes between Balkars and Kabardinians in some of the collective farms in which Balkars had been resettled.[90] Balkar dissatisfaction with the 1956 repatriation was not confined to territorial grievances, and Balkar discussions of past unfairness and harsh treatment have continued into the 1990s. The destruction of Balkar cemetaries and monuments during the time of their exile remains a sore point for Balkars, and the Balkar press has charged Kabardinians, as well as Ossetians, with responsibility.[91] The press has reported that, following their repatriation, Balkars were subject to discrimination within the republic and in the former USSR generally. Reportedly, Balkar students had more difficulty gaining admission to universities and receiving permission to defend dissertations than other national groups.[92] In 1994, the National Council of the Balkar People reiterated their complaints of discrimination, arguing that unfair treatment of the Balkars was persisting in the Republic. Delegates complained that Kabardinians represented 90 percent of military special forces personnel, and that the republican political structure was dominated by Kabardinians.[93]

In November 1990, the Balkar territorial and political claims met with cooperation from the Kabardino-Balkar government, and a commission was formed to study the "restoration of the historically Balkar regions." However, a year later, the First Congress of the National Council of the Balkar People announced plans to form a separate Balkar republic, arguing that "the national state structure of the Kabardino-Balkar republic did not permit [the Balkar people] to realize in full measure their rights as full subjects of the republic."[94] Ultimately, the Balkars modified their demands, and in July 1994, asked for enhanced sovereignty in their territory, explicity renouncing demands for separation from Kabardino-Balkaria. They continued to complain of discrimination and alleged that funds allocated for compensation for deported people were misappropriated by the Kabardino-Balkarian government.[95] Significantly, the Balkar Council has argued that its demands would be supported by Russia, as these demands accorded with the Russian law "On the Rehabilitation of the Repressed Peoples." The republican leadership, in turn, accused the Balkar council of trying to destabilize socio-political relations within the republic. Reactions from the Congress of the Kabardinian People were more openly hostile, with one delegate remarking that "the Balkars are the sort of people who need repressing."[96]

The Balkar claims for recognition of their territorial and political rights have hindered the formation of a stable constitutional structure in the Kabardino-Balkarian republic. As late as October 1993, Kabardino-Balkaria had not yet dismantled its Soviet era political and administrative structures, as disagreements between the Kabardinians and Balkars held up the process of parliamentary reform.[97] By late 1993, an agreement had been reached to form a government on the basis of national representation according to the demographic proportion of each national group within the Republic. Furthermore, a resolution could be passed only if approved by a two-thirds majority of the deputies of *each* ethnic group. While this agreement allowed parliamentary and constitutional reform to begin, it is possible that the difficulties of attaining the level of agreement necessary for passing resolutions and crafting legislation will hinder parliamentary and legislative reform yet further.

Relations between Russia and Kabardino-Balkaria do not appear to be tense. However, Russia has not recently played a prominent political role in Kabardino-Balkaria, largely because the disagreements internal to the republic have stalled constitutional negotiations with Russia. At the same time, the conflicts between the Kabardinians and Balkars have been restrained, not provoking Russian interference. The Balkars dropped their demands for full sovereignty, opting instead to negotiate with the Kabardinians for greater power in their own territories. There is no indication that these conflicts are likely to reach the level of armed confrontation.

## Karachaevo-Cherkessia

Like Kabardino-Balkaria, Karachaevo-Cherkessia unites two titular national groups which are distinct both linguistically and culturally, sharing only those aspects of cultural identity common to most North Caucasian groups. In 1989, the two titular nationalities of Karachevo-Cherkessia, the Karachai and Cherkess, accounted for 31.2 percent and 9.7 percent of the population respectively. Russians comprised an ethnic plurality, with 42.4 percent of the republic's population.[98] In addition, two national minority groups – the Abazin and Nogai – numbered approximately 30,000 and 20,000.[99]

In the late 1980s, the native ethnic groups devoted varying efforts to the development of national culture. By 1989, numerous national-language schools were opened: 817 Karachai schools; 91 Cherkessian schools; 115 Abazin schools; and 39 Nogai schools. As non-titular national groups in the Soviet Union, the Abazin and Nogai had suffered from neglect of their cultures. Therefore, popular interest in these cultures has been slower to develop,[100] and most Abazin and Nogai activity has been centered primarily in the republican capital of Cherkessk.

Interethnic relations within the republic have been relatively peaceful, and a new constitution is being written. In 1994, representation of the national groups in the parliamentary executive were in close correspondence with their demographic proportions. The representatives comprise: eleven Russians; eight Karachai; four Cherkess; three Abazin; and three Nogai.[101]

Karachai grievances have created some instability in the political affairs of the republic. The Karachai were among the groups deported from the North Caucasus in 1944 and, like the Balkar, now share a state with groups who were not subject to deportation. Furthermore, the Karachai have perceived themselves as victims of discriminatory treatment even following their repatriation. The Karachai report that they suffered hindrances with respect to educational and career advancement. Until the fall of Soviet power, members of the Karachai did not hold socially or politically sensitive positions within the Karachaevo-Cherkessian Republic, even within their own, largely Karachai territories.[102] However, where the Balkars hold the Kabardinians responsible for discriminatory treatment, the Karachai claim to have suffered directly at the hands of ethnic Russians.[103] Karachai resentments, therefore, do not bring their national identity into conflict with North Caucasian identity.

Nevertheless, the Karachai, in the late 1980s and early 1990s, expressed some aspirations to independent republican status. In November 1991, a general meeting of the Karachai announced to the Russian Supreme Soviet their desire to secure their autonomy and "complete rehabilitation" from the consequences of their deportation. According to a Radio Moscow report, the Karachai group announced that, if their demands were not met, an Extraordinary Council of People's Deputies of Karachai would simply create republican structures on its own authority, as Dudaev's government had done in Chechnya.[104] Like similar Balkar claims to autonomy in the late Soviet and early post-Soviet years, the Karachai demands have been modified. The Karachai appear satisfied with their level of representation at the republican level in Karachaevo-Cherkessia, and with their political presence more locally, in their own region.[105]

However, as the Karachai threat to republican stability has appeared to wane, ethnic Russian discontent has been on the rise. Unlike some of the other North Caucasian regions, Karachaevo-Cherkessia has not experienced significant out-migration of ethnic Russian elements.[106] *Rus'*, an organization promoting Russian cultural protection, has gained considerable popularity among Russians in Karachaevo-Cherkessia, and has some sympathy among local Cossacks as well. *Rus'* has, for example, opposed the construction of various mosques in the republic, arguing that Russian Orthodoxy must be protected from the encroachment of "alien faiths". Support for such opinion indicates that the development of North Caucasian ethnic cultures in the republic may be perceived by some local Russian elements as a cultural threat. The organization has proposed that the regions inhabited largely by ethnic Russians – mainly industrial and resort regions in the Cherkess area of Karachaevo-Cherkessia – either be administered by ethnic Russian bodies or be permitted to separate and join the Krasnodar District.[107] The popularity of this organization indicates considerable unease among ethnic Russians living in relatively stable areas of the North Caucasus. It is difficult to discern the extent to which an organization such as *Rus'* poses a threat to the republic of Karachaevo-Cherkessia. Given that the Speaker of the People's Assembly of Karachaevo-Cherkessia appears at least somewhat sympathetic to *Rus'*, the force of ethnic Russian discontent and its capacity to upset the current political stability in the republic must be considered seriously.

## North Ossetia

The ethnocultural situation of the Ossetian people in the North Caucasus is complicated by religious factors. Unlike the majority of the North Caucasian peoples, who are Muslim, the majority of Ossetians are Orthodox Christian. While this religious difference may have deterred the Ossetians from joining Shamil's struggle against the Russians in the nineteenth century, they nevertheless allied with other North Caucasian groups during the Civil War and were included in the North Caucasian Mountain Republic of 1918 to 1922. The cultural similarities and shared history of the Ossetians and the other North Caucasian peoples has made a common identity among these groups possible despite religious differences.[108]

The Ossetian national community includes three dialect groups. The Tual have lived mainly in South Ossetia, within the Georgian republican structure. The Digor and Iron dialect groups occupy North Ossetia, where the Iron constitute the vast majority. The Digor account for only about one-eighth of North Ossetians,[109] and their designation as an officially recognized national group was eliminated in the late 1930s. Among the Digor, some thirty to forty percent are Muslim. Although only 15 to 20 percent of Iron are Muslim, they are a numerically larger group than the Digor Muslims.[110] Christian and Muslim Ossetians have in common many traditional cultural practices: the wedding ceremonies, certain family customs and wake rituals are identical, and are "national, rather than religious" in character.[111] While Christian and Muslim Ossetians retain distinct religious identities, and Iron and Digor retain a consciousness of linguistic distinction, there is – according to Ossetian informants from all of these categories – little friction between the groups, and intermarriage is socially acceptable.[112]

The Christian Ossetians, then, are not strangers to Islam: indeed, various Muslim names have been adopted by the Christian Ossetians.[113] The religious differences of the Christian Ossetians and the Muslim peoples of the North Caucasus have not played a divisive role in political relations and have not entered the discourse between these groups, nor has the Ossetian government expressed concern about the rise of Islamic consciousness in the North Caucasus. Similarly, Ossetians do not speak of a common bond of Orthodox Christianity as a reason for alliance between themselves and either Cossacks or Russians.

Ossetian national identity is strong, even in the North Caucasian context, and has been sharpened by the South Ossetian war with Georgia and the conflicts between the Ossetians and Ingush in the Prigorodnyi region. Members of the intelligentsia in the North Ossetian capital, Vladikavkaz (formerly Ordzhonikidze), have expressed anxiety that national culture, especially in the larger cities, has been eroded by Russification. Particularly troubling was the observation that refugees from South Ossetia exhibited higher competence in the Ossetian language and closer adherence to traditional Ossetian customs. As in other regions of the North Caucasus, cultural revitalization is underway: new history texts and programs for national language education were completed by 1992.[114]

Relations with Russia have been variable. Ossetia's constitutional project has been underway and, as of mid-1994, the Republic was beginning to reach a "federal agreement" with Russia. However, the agreement was hindered by an Ossetian desire for greater autonomy in the spheres of economic decision-making and control of the republic's resources. The agreement between Russia and Ossetia has also been stalled by Ossetian dissatisfaction with the Russian handling of the conflicts in the Prigorodnyi region.[115] North Ossetian objection to the Russian policy and activity in the Prigorodnyi region began as early as 1991, with the advent of the Russian republican law "On the Rehabilitation of Repressed Peoples".[116] In a 1991 survey, 97 percent of North Ossetians polled felt that the borders of North Ossetia should not be altered.[117]

The Prigorodnyi conflicts, which are described above in the discussion of the Ingush Republic, have sharpened anti-Ingush feeling among the Ossetians. As a consequence, Russia's role as mediator and peacemaker has been difficult, as no solution was satisfactory to both the Ingush and Ossetians. North Ossetians have objected to the Russian failure to support Ossetian demands that citizens from Ingushetia refrain from crossing the border, "propagandizing" to keep Ingush in the Prigorodnyi region and assisting them in armed struggle. There is also some local, armed resistance on the part of North Ossetians to the resettlement of the Ingush.[118]

In October 1994, North Ossetian president Aksarbek Galazov responded aggressively to Russian criticism of the Ossetian implementation of the process of Ingush repatriation and the ongoing conflict in the region: "If we are found guilty of breaking laws, if the opinion is reached that the republic of North Ossetia doesn't control the situation, then this could lead to direct Presidential (i.e. Russian Federation) rule. Our people will not accept this and I, as a representative elected by the people, will be forced to lead a national liberation movement.[119] North Ossetia clearly objects to Russian encroachment in its internal affairs and, like the Ingush Republic, is willing to threaten separation from the Russian Federation. However, the republic is equally hesitant to follow the Chechen example and act upon its separatist rhetoric. Like all the North Caucasian republics, North Ossetia formally protested the Russian invasion of Chechnya. However, the Russian government appears confident of North Ossetia's unwillingness to be drawn into direct conflict with Russia. Indeed, Russia has used a number of North Ossetian locations as bases for both military operations and negotiations in the war with Chechnya.

The South Ossetian war with Georgia was important in strengthening Ossetian national identity and heightening a need for national state building. The war ensued in 1989, when the Georgian government annulled South Ossetia's autonomous regional status, and began to subside in July 1992, with the arrival of Russian peacekeepers and the creation of a Tripartite Commission between Russia, Georgia and South Ossetia.[120] During the war, North Ossetia rallied to the defence of the South Ossetians, sending food, and medical and military aid. North Ossetian volunteers joined the South Ossetian guard. North Ossetia has also housed masses of South Ossetian refugees: in September 1991, the number of refugees registered in Vladikavkaz exceeded 80,000.[121] In mid-1994, 40,000 refugees still remained in North Ossetia.[122] As a consequence of the war, concepts of Ossetian nationhood and the North Ossetian role in the conflict between Georgia and South Ossetia have been the focus of much attention.

The Ossetian intelligentsia views North and South Ossetia as a single nation, which was divided after the Bolshevik Revolution in a "Bolshevik experiment" intended to fragment and weaken the Ossetian nation and assimilate its people into the Georgian and Russian nations. Ossetians bolster their claims to South and North Ossetia by identifying themselves as descendents of the Alans, who, they claim, had occupied both territories for centuries.[123]

Maintaining this view of a single Ossetian national territory, North Ossetians have sought an official role in the regulation of conflict in South Ossetia. They obtained this as a party in the four-sided Control Commission, along with Georgia, South Ossetia, and Russia.[124] South Ossetia remains eager to exit from Georgia and join the Russian Federation and the republic of North Ossetia, although it no longer tries to achieve this through armed conflict with Georgia. South Ossetian leader Liudvig Chibirov has argued that, since South Ossetia has received the majority of its economic and technical assistance from Russia (Russia even pays South Ossetian peacekeepers), locating the South Ossetian Republic within the Russian Federal structure makes administrative sense.[125]

The complex North Ossetian political situation makes its relations with Russia similarly complex. In the context of the Prigorodnyi regional conflict, relations with Russia are tense; in the situation with South Ossetia, however, Russia appears in a friendly, potentially helpful capacity. North Ossetia is likely to undertake full separation from and conflict with Russia only if Russia directly and severely encroaches on North Ossetia's present degree of autonomy. However, a strong North Ossetian identity and aspirations to strengthening, and perhaps expanding, its national boundaries have led the Republic to demand considerable autonomy within the federal Russian structure.

### Dagestan

Uniting ten official, non-titular national groups within its borders, the republic of Dagestan is remarkable for its stability and peaceful climate. The majority of national groups appear content to remain within the republic. In April 1991, thirty-nine out of fifty-four regional soviets (*raisovety*) in Dagestan supported a resolution for sovereignty and the creation of a Dagestan republic. For the most part, the fifteen regional soviets opposing the creation of a sovereign Dagestan represented national groups which had expressed some aspiration to split from Dagestan. Since then, however, these demands for autonomy have been withdrawn, as most have expressed satisfaction with a parliamentary system. Furthermore, following the disbanding of the Soviets in late 1993, the reorganization of the electoral districts resulted in no single national group dominating within any district.[126]

In Dagestan, the expression of ethnicity through the discourse of the national state has not been as forceful as elsewhere in the former Soviet Union. With few exceptions, the peoples of Dagestan are drawn together in identity based on years of common history and Islam. The popularity of the Shamil Popular Front Party indicates the vitality of the historical experience of the Caucasian Wars in national consciousness.[127] Dagestan is, in some respects, the centre of Islam in the North Caucasus: Makhachkala, the capital of Dagestan, is the seat of the Muslim Spiritual Board of the North Caucasus and Dagestan. Religious consciousness among the Muslim peoples of Dagestan is strong, and multiethnic, Islamic political movements, such as the Islamic Democratic Party, have attracted broad support.[128]

Dagestanis – both political elites and citizens in general – appear to be guided by a perception that the multiethnic character of the republic must be expressed in its institutions, and that no one national group should be able to dominate. Accordingly, the reorganization of electoral districts was meant to inhibit political solidarity along the lines of ethnicity. Similarly, Dagestani politicians resisted the creation of the office of president within their republic following Yeltsin's victory over the Russian parliament in October 1993. The Dagestan parliament argued that the special, multinational character of Dagestan is unsuitable for presidential rule, and better reflected in a parliamentary system.[129] These sentiments had been expressed

Table 3.1. *Concentration of ethnic groups in the North Caucasus and Dagestan, 1989*

| Territory | National group | % of territorial population |
|---|---|---|
| Dagestan | Avar | 27.5 |
| | Agul | 0.8 |
| | Dargin | 15.6 |
| | Kumyk | 12.9 |
| | Lak | 5.1 |
| | Lezgin | 11.3 |
| | Nogai | 1.6 |
| | Rutul' | 0.8 |
| | Tabasaran | 4.3 |
| | Tsakhur | 0.3 |
| | Russian | 9.2 |
| Adygeia | Adygei | 22.1 |
| | Russian | 68.0 |
| Checheno–Ingushetia | Chechen | 57.8 |
| | Ingush | 12.9 |
| | Russian | 23.1 |
| Kabardino–Balkaria | Kabardin | 48.2 |
| | Balkar | 9.4 |
| | Russian | 32.0 |
| Karachaevo–Cherkessia | Karachai | 31.2 |
| | Cherkess | 9.7 |
| | Russian | 42.4 |
| North Ossetia | Ossetian | 53.0 |
| | Russian | 29.9 |

*Source:* 1989 census data, *Argumenty i fakty*, no. 13, March 1991, p. 1.

a year earlier in a referendum, where the majority of citizens of Dagestan opposed the introduction of a presidency, favouring a parliamentary system instead.[130]

The strength of multiethnic Dagestani identity is not absolute, and competing loyalties among some elements of the population have arisen. As elsewhere in the North Caucasus, the consequences of the 1944 deportations have created strife. In Northern Dagestan, the Akkintsy, who are ethnic Chechens, were deported and have expressed dissatisfaction with their repatriation. In attempts to recover their former territories, the Akkintsy have entered into conflict, even into violent clashes, with the neighbouring Avars and Laks. Their demands, however, do not extend to sovereignty or unification with Chechnya, and the conflicts with the Avars and Laks appear to have eased. The Akkintsy seem content to remain within Dagestan, provided that the government address questions of territorial restoration or compensation.[131]

Since the collapse of Soviet power, only three separatist movements of significance have been reported in Dagestan. None of these groups holds the Dagestan republic or its government responsible for the conditions which motivated the desire to separate. In 1990, the Kumyk movement *Tenglik* ("Equality") announced its intention to create a national Kumyk state, and Kumyk deputies in the Dagestan Congress called for greater sovereignty in the territories with a large Kumyk population.[132] The proponents of Kumyk independence have argued that the years of Soviet power and Russification have stunted the development of Kumyk national culture, and that cultural sovereignty is the only way to rectify this situation.[133] Toward the mid-1990s, however, Kumyk aspirations to separate statehood appeared to be weakening, and are not hindering political processes in the Republic of Dagestan.

Also in the early 1990s, the Lezgins expressed a desire for separation in order to unite the Lezgin territory, which is split roughly equally between Dagestan and Azerbaijan.[134] In December 1991, the All-National Congress of Lezgins called for the creation of a "national-state formation, Lezgistan", which would unite the Lezgin populations and territories.[135] Similarly, a third national group within Dagestan, the Nogai, have called for a separate state in order to strengthen ties with the large, Nogai populations in other regions of the North Caucasus.[136] In both cases, these demands have not been met, but neither group has stirred significant dissent within the republic.

Dagestan faced a crisis in the summer of 1994. A serious epidemic of cholera, possibly originating in Mecca and contracted by Dagestani pilgrims, spread through the republic. The epidemic was exacerbated by a decrepit water purification system. Dagestan lacked the resources – both technical and financial – necessary to control the spread of the disease. The government was forced to turn to Moscow for assistance.[137] This circumstance illustrates the practical necessity for many North Caucasian states of maintaining good relations with Russia. Because of the weakness of Dagestan's economic and technical development and Moscow's ability to offer assistance, Dagestan has benefitted from its inclusion in the Russian federal structure.

Nevertheless, the motivations for continuing alliance with Russia have not been strong enough to overcome Dagestani support for Chechnya in the war with Russia. The Dagestan government immediately protested the Russian attack, and has accepted large groups of Chechen refugees. Although the government has officially denied extending military aid to Chechnya, Dagestani fighters have, apparently on their own volition, joined the Chechen forces. In mid-December, shortly after Russia's invasion of

Table 3.2. *The populations of North Caucasian ethnic groups, 1989*

| Ethnic group | Population |
|---|---|
| Abazin | 601,000 |
| Agul | 19,000 |
| Adygei | 125,000 |
| Avar | 34,000 |
| Balkar | 85,000 |
| Chechen | 957,000 |
| Dargin | 365,000 |
| Ingush | 237,000 |
| Kabardin | 391,000 |
| Karachai | 156,000 |
| Kumyk | 282,000 |
| Lak | 118,000 |
| Lezgin | 466,000 |
| Mountain Jews | 19,000 |
| Nogai | 75,000 |
| Ossetian | 598,000 |
| Rutul' | 20,000 |
| Tabasaran | 98,000 |
| Tsakhur | 20,000 |

*Source: Naselenie SSSR: po dannym vsesoiuznoi perepisi naseleniia 1989* (Moscow, 1990), pp. 37–40.

Chechnya began, villagers in Northern Dagestan captured a detachment of soldiers, along with their weapons and six tanks. The soldiers were sent on to Groznyi as prisoners of war.[138] This display of support on the part of Dagestan citizens suggests that a common, North Caucasian identity, or, at least, mutual animosity toward the Russians, is strong. However, the reluctance of the Dagestan government to involve itself actively in the conflict is significant. As in the case of Ingushetia, Dagestan's restraint suggests that, barring the expansion of Russian aggression outside Chechnya, the war in Chechnya is unlikely to erupt into a full-scale, North Caucasian conflagration. While Dagestanis have exhibited solidarity with the Chechens, the refusal to become deeply involved in the struggle indicates that North Caucasian identity is mediated by national self-interest and the serious consequences of severely alienating Russia.

Dagestani identity is the most multifaceted in the North Caucasus. Aside from the identity of particular national groups, the concept of "Dagestan" has strong resonance. A deep religious consciousness and sense of North Caucasian historical identity add further dimension to Dagestani identity.

What is remarkable is that these various alliances seem to coexist with little conflict.

### Groups without territories: Nogai, Cossacks, ethnic Russians, and Refugees

Among the non-titular national groups of the North Caucasus, three large dispersed and diaspora groups – the Nogai, Cossacks and ethnic Russians – constitute an important subgroup. They are distinguished by: their demographic distribution, as populations dispersed throughout the North Caucasus; their lack of coherent geographic boundaries; and their difficulties in creating political communities and an effective political voice in the absence of either titular national status or claims to a compactly settled, North Caucasian homeland.

The Nogai, the remnants of a once great nomadic steppe people, occupy a territory that was once the huge Nogai steppe, and now are spread throughout various North Caucasian republics. The largest Nogai groups are settled in Karachaevo-Cherkessia and Dagestan, with some in the Chechen and Ingush territories.[139] With the exception of groups living in Dagestan, the Nogai have had little opportunity for sustained cultural development. In the years of Soviet power, they lacked the cultural institutions – such as theatres, schools and clubs – that would facilitate this. Furthermore, in the Soviet period, positions of social or political leadership were generally assigned either to ethnic Russians or to representatives of of the titular national groups of these regious.[140] As a non-titular national group in territories with titular nationalities, the Nogai have been dominated and their cultural development stunted. Only recently have the Nogai of Karachaevo-Cherkessia been able to create national language schools and obtain representatives in the republican executive organs of government.[141]

In Dagestan, where all the national groups are non-titular and the ethnic Russian population is small, the Nogai have had greater cultural and political independence. Furthermore, in Dagestan, the Nogai live more compactly than elsewhere and have experienced less interaction with other ethnic groups. Only in the Nogai region of Dagestan, where Nogai represent up to 75 percent of the student population in schools, has Nogai-language instruction been available at all educational levels.[142] Significantly, the most active political activity and the only Nogai movement for national sovereignty has come from the Nogai of Dagestan.[143] The lack of a single Nogai territory has made claims for national sovereignty difficult, and the Nogai of Dagestan have received little active support from Nogai groups elsewhere. By the mid-1990s, Nogai interest in sovereignty appeared to have weakened.

Similarly to that of the Nogai, the demographic situation of the Cossack groups in the North Caucasus obstructs the creation of a national-state formation. The Cossacks suffered severe repression during the years of Soviet power. In 1919–1920, entire Cossack settlements were eliminated and their populations deported to Siberia, in fulfillment of an official policy of "de-cossackization" (*razkazachivanie*). During collectivization, alleged Cossack kulaks were resettled in Central Asia and Kazakhstan.[144] The Cossack population that remained is dispersed throughout all of the North Caucasian republics. Furthermore, the Cossacks were never officially recognized by the Soviet government as a national group, and have generally listed themselves as either Russian or Ukrainian on Soviet censuses.

Cossacks began arriving in the North Caucasus regions as early as the last half of the sixteenth century.[145] In 1860, the Black Sea Cossack band divided itself into the Kuban and Terek bands. In 1916, when Cossacks were last enumerated, the populations of these bands were 1,367,000 and 255,000 respectively.[146] Prior to the Revolution, the Cossacks offered military support to Russia, and they fought against Shamil in the Caucasian Wars. Traditionally, Cossacks view themselves as closely linked, both culturally and ethnically, with Russia, although they maintain a self-perception of a separate social, Cossack identity. This historical alliance with Russia has complicated Cossack relations with other North Caucasian groups. However, the Cossacks share a history of repression at the hands of Soviet power.

The Kuban Cossacks, who inhabit the territories of Stavropol' and Krasnodar, do not live in the mountainous heart of the Caucasus. Their contact with non-Russian North Caucasian national groups is mainly confined to groups in the Adygei and Karachaevo-Cherkessian territories. Despite a history of pre-revolutionary conflict between the Cossacks and these groups, recent relations have been peaceful. In Adygeia, Cossacks have expressed solidarity with enhanced sovereignty in the republic since the collapse of Soviet power. Cossacks participate in Adygei politics, and their concerns, thus far, have been limited to ensuring fair political representation.[147] In Karachaevo-Cherkessia, relations between the Kuban Cossack groups and other North Caucasian national groups are less relaxed. Cossacks there have shown strong support for the interests of ethnic Russians, assuming an active role in Russian cultural revival and demanding heightened autonomy in the Russian-dominated territories of the republic. Kuban Cossacks have also expressed resentment toward the Russian federal government for its failure to offer decisive support for Cossack territorial claims.[148]

The Terek Cossacks, with populations in North Ossetia, Dagestan, Chechnya, and Ingushetia have experienced greater friction with the North Caucasian national groups and have a complicated cultural identity. On one hand, almost five centuries of close contact between the Terek Cossacks and neighboring ethnic groups have led to the development of common cultural traits. Traditional Terek Cossack male dress more closely resembles that of Caucasian groups than of ethnic Russians or Ukrainians.[149] On the other hand, since the collapse of Soviet power, Terek Cossacks have entered into armed confrontation with some North Caucasian groups, particularly the Ingush. Concerned about ethnic Russian outmigration from Chechnya and Ingushetia, Cossacks have threatened to separate their territories from those republics. Like the Kuban Cossacks however, Terek Cossacks have also complained of a lack of support from Moscow.[150]

In 1992–1993, the Terek Cossacks demonstrated a North Caucasian loyalty in the Georgian-Abkhaz conflict: Cossack volunteers joined Chechen fighters in defence of the Abkhaz. However, in the Russian invasion of Chechnya, the Cossacks have shown support for Russia. In early December 1994, as tensions between Chechnya and Russia mounted, Yeltsin announced to the Terek Cossacks that his government would consider issues of Cossack cultural revival and the unification of Cossack communities.[151] This gesture of support from the Russian government may have encouraged the Terek and Kuban Cossacks to send four battalions to the Russian side, in support of "the process of restoration of constitutional order in Chechnya.[152]

Like the Nogai, Cossacks face the challenge of defining a national territory, as the Cossack population is not compactly clustered in one discrete territory. The Cossacks have been inclined to demand autonomy or separation from the republics in which they reside in the form of relatively small, dispersed territorial settlements. They are one of the most aggressive and culturally militarized groups in the North Caucasus. Cossacks have, at times, allied with and, at other times, against other North Caucasian nationalities. Their willingness to involve themselves in armed struggle has alienated both Russia and various North Caucasian groups. However, the Cossacks appear to have maintained close relations with the local, ethnic Russian diaspora. Furthermore, they can count on the support of a considerable network of equally aggressive Cossack bands, which extends from Ukraine to Kazakhstan and into Siberia.

Since the Soviet period, ethnic Russians have accounted for a large segment of the North Caucasian population. In 1989, in all republican territories but Dagestan, Russians comprised more than 25 percent of the total population. In Karachaevo-Cherkessia and Adygeia, they outnumber any of the titular national groups.[153] Perhaps because of their demographic presence in these two republics, Russians in these regions have elected to remain and to organize themselves politically. However, in other republics, particularly Ossetia, Ingushetia, and Chechnya, large groups of Russians have left to reside in Russia proper.[154]

Aside from fears of political instability and rising North Caucasian nationalism, Russians may have been motivated to depart to take advantage of economic opportunities outside of their home republic. Even some ethnic North Caucasians, particularly Chechens and Ossetians, have relocated to such centres as Moscow to pursue these opportunities.[155] Especially in the case of Chechnya, however, ethnic Russian fears of instability and anti-Russian sentiment have induced many to depart. In 1991, following Dudaev's rise to power, over 19,000 left the Republic.[156] By 1994, this figure was reported to be over 200,000.[157]

Although Terek and Kuban Cossacks have sought to protect the ethnic Russian population in the North Caucasus, large segments of this population have elected to leave rather than to organize themselves politically. Unlike the Nogai and the Cossacks, many ethnic Russians display little consciousness of a North Caucasian homeland and continue to identify themselves with Russia. Aside from Cossack influence, ethnic Russians are unlikely to pose a widespread challenge to North Caucasian stability. However, perceived mistreatment of ethnic Russians could provoke the Russian government to interfere more directly in North Caucasian affairs.

Finally, since the break-up of the Soviet Union, the presence of refugees from various North Caucasian groups has grown in the North Caucasus. In September 1991, as a consequence of the struggle between South Ossetia and Georgia, over 80,000 refugees were registered in North Ossetia.[158] In mid-1994, although circumstances in South Ossetia were relatively stable, approximately 40,000 of these remained in North Ossetia. Ingushetia has, according to its government's statistics, accommodated 71,000 refugees from the Prigorodnyi region of North Ossetia. Although resettlement is beginning, circumstances in the Prigoridnyi region have remained unstable and the outflux of the refugees has been very slow.[159] Masses of refugees from Chechnya – whose numbers may ultimately be in the hundreds of thousands – have fled mainly to Ingushetia and Dagestan, and some to North Ossetia.[160]

Although refugees have not, as of 1996, caused any political unrest in the territories of the North Caucasus, their poverty represents a drain on the economic resources of the republics which house them, and their large numbers strain the availability of housing and employment.[161] In North Ossetia, large groups of South Ossetian refugees were settled in Pioneer Camp facilities and resorts: some North Ossetians feared that the compact settlement of large groups of impoverished South Ossetians could lead to a rise in crime and social tension.[162] In the case of the many Chechen refugees in Dagestan and Ingushetia, the possibility of sustained political and even military activism on the part of the Chechen refugees could jeopardize security and relations with Russia in these republics.

## The North Caucasus in the Russian Federation: hostility in alliance

In October 1991, émigré Chechen historian A. Avtorkhanov, a figure of considerable respect throughout the North Caucasus, issued the following pronouncement on Chechen television in both Chechen and Russian languages: "The Ingush are our brothers; the Ossetians are our brothers; the Terek Cossacks and peoples of Dagestan are our brothers. We must unite in a federation, or else we will never be able to administer our affairs free from the Russians."[163] The call for the creation of a strong North Caucasian Federation was echoed in 1992 by the Ingush and Chechen Councils of Elders. Opposing the creation of separate Ingush and Chechen states, the elders hoped to encourage greater political and institutional unity in the North Caucasus generally, rather than the creation of more national-state formations.[164] Given the cultural similarities of the North Caucasian peoples and the considerable solidarity and common identity among them, the notion of a North Caucasian Federation is not entirely unfeasible. Indeed, the republic of Dagestan exemplifies such a federation: it unites several North Caucasian nationalities on an equal, non-titular basis and has proven to satisfy the majority of its peoples.

In August 1989, representatives of sixteen North Caucasian groups attended the founding congress of the Assembly of Mountain Peoples of the Caucasus, later renamed the Confederation of North Caucasian Peoples. At the time of its inception, the Confederation hoped to form a North Caucasian Federal Republic, which would be fully sovereign and exist outside the Russian Federation.[165] However, the Confederation has fallen short of these initial goals, as only Chechnya has exhibited a desire for full independence from Russia. Furthermore, the governments of the various North Caucasian republics have been in the process of creating stronger national-state structures and negotiating with Russia for enhanced sovereignty within their republics. If Dagestan is to be considered as an example of the North Caucasian federal idea, it is important to recognize that the discourse of national state territories based on ethnic group has not been part of the Dagestan experience. Elsewhere in the North Caucasus, national, rather than broadly North Caucasian, concerns have remained in the forefront.

Through the early 1990s, the Confederation of North Caucasian Peoples has come to resemble a supra-national organization, but on a North Caucasian scale. The Confederation acts largely as an advocacy body, encouraging negotiation and peacemaking within the North Caucasus and articulating North Caucasian interests outside of the region. The Confederation supported both the South Ossetians and the Abkhaz in their struggles with Georgia. It has addressed statements to Georgian President Eduard Shevardnadze and to Boris Yeltsin criticizing Georgian military action and accusing Russia of building relations with Georgia to the detriment of the North Caucasus.[166] In the case of Chechnya, representatives of the Congress met with Russian representatives, criticizing the Russian leadership for disseminating discriminatory, anti-Chechen propaganda and seeking to resolve the crisis with Chechnya through force rather than negotiation.[167] The Confederation also has something of a military presence, as it has dispatched to both Abkhazia and Chechnya batallions of volunteer fighters from various regions of the North Caucasus.[168]

The Confederation of North Caucasian Peoples tried, without success, to mediate the conflicts between North Ossetians and Ingush in the Prigorodnyi region. Tension between North Ossetian and Ingush delegates has been evident at meetings of the Confederation.[169] Russian mediation in the conflict has also not been entirely successful, but the Russian presence as mediator carried more weight with both the Ingush and the Ossetians, and Russia performed a much more visible role in the negotiations between the two sides.

A number of factors account for the fact that Russia, rather than the Confederation of North Caucasian Peoples, has maintained a strong federal presence in the North Caucasus. Russia is an internationally recognized state and a world power, while the Confederation's political status is unclear. Russia also possesses greater, potentially coercive, political and military power. Thus, Russia is a more effective ally and is in a stronger position to perform a mediating role. Furthermore, Russia is in a position to offer economic and professional assistance, as it did during the cholera epidemic in Dagestan. Finally, the tragic consequences of Chechnya's defiance of Russia have illustrated the risks incurred by not heeding Russian interests. For all but the Chechens, national interest is understood to be best served by negotiating for some degree of self-determination within the Russian federal structure.

The Confederation of North Caucasian Peoples has a political presence in the North Caucasus and genuinely reflects an identity shared by its peoples. However, the vocal proponents of a North Caucasian Federation have been representatives of the older generations, such as Avtorkhanov and the Councils of Elders. The formative political experiences of the younger generation have included participation in the development of modern, national discourse, beginning in the Gorbachev era. Cultural survival is represented as national survival; hence, ethnic empowerment is achieved through the building of the national state. The North Caucasian national republics that have grown from this experience have a strong resonance in popular consciousness. North Caucasians, with few exceptions, have continued to identify with and actively support each other, though this solidarity is balanced and even outweighed by more recent notions of national self-interest.

Historic enmity between Russia and the North Caucasian peoples, Russian aggression in Chechnya, and anti-Caucasian propaganda in Russia has alienated the peoples of the North Caucasus. Nevertheless, the political and economic advantages of Russian federalism are compelling. Accordingly the Russian invasion of Chechnya did not provide the impetus for a general, North Caucasian departure from the Russian federal structure. However, if Russian interference in the affairs of the North Caucasus spreads to the other republics, then the North Caucasian commitment to Russian Federalism is likely to diminish. Having survived the brutal Caucasian Wars of the nineteenth century, the genocidal deportations of 1944, pressures to assimilate into the cultures of the larger nations of Georgia and Russia, and, since the collapse of Soviet power, wars with these two larger powers, the peoples of the North Caucasus have perceived themselves as targets for attack and aggressive defenders of their cultural and territorial integrity. The ongoing Russian attempts to compel Chechen integration by military force serve only to reopen past wounds and revive national narratives of Russian aggression.

## Notes

I would like to thank the Association of Universities and Colleges of Canada for the financial assistance that made my fieldwork in 1992–1993 possible. I also acknowledge the useful contributions of James R. Harris in the preparation of this chapter.

1 *Naselenie SSSR: po dannym vsesoiuznoi perepisi naseleniia 1989* (Moscow, 1990), pp. 37–40. These native groups are: Abazin; Avar; Agul; Adygei; Balkar; Dargin; Mountain Jews (*Evrei gorskie*); Ingush; Kabardin; Karachai; Kumyk: Lak; Lezgin; Nogai; Ossetian; Rutul'; Tabasaran; Tsakhuri; and Chechen.

2 *Argumenty i Fakty*, no. 13, March 1991, p. 1. Data from the 1989 census shows the percentage of ethnic Russians to range from 9.2 percent in Dagestan to 68 percent in the Republic of Adygei. However, significant out-migration of ethnic Russians has been ongoing in the region since the 1989 census data was gathered.

3 Ronald Wixman, *Language Aspects of Ethnic Patterns and Processes in the North Caucasus* (Chicago: University of Chicago, Dept. of Geography, Research Paper No. 191, 1980), pp. 86–98.

4 *Ibid.*, pp. 89–90

5 N.G. Volkova, L.I. Lavrov, "Sovremennye etnicheskie protsessy", E.P. Prokhorov, ed., *Kul'tura i byt narodov Severnogo Kavkaza* (Moscow: Nauka, 1968), p. 330; Wixman, *Language Aspects*, p. 113.

6 V.S. Uarziati, *Kul'tura Ossetin: sviazy s narodami kavkaza* (Ordzhonikidze: Ir, 1990), pp. 6–7.

7 Ethnographical and historical study of the broad, North Caucasian culture has been considerable. See especially Uarziaty, *Kul'tura Ossetin*; Volkova and Lavrov, "Sovremennye etnicheskie protsessy, p. 330; A. Avksent'ev, *Islam na Severnom Kavkaze*, p. 168; Ia.S. Smirnova and A.I. Pershits, "Izbeganie", *Sovetskaia etnografiia*, no. 6, 1978, pp. 61–70; Ia. Smirnova, *Semia i semeinyi byt narodov Severnogo Kavkaza* (Moscow: Nauka, 1983); Wixman, *Language Aspects*, pp. 102–103; A. Bennigsen and S.E. Wimbush, *Muslims of the Soviet Empire* (Bloomington, IN: Indiana University Press, 1986), p. 149.

8 P. Henze, "Fire and Sword in the North Caucasus", *Central Asian Survey*, vol. 2, no. 1, July 1993, pp. 17, 32–33.

9 Dzeps Kimmer, "Severnyi Kavkaz: god 2000", *Sovetskii Dagestan*, no. 1, 1991, pp. 41–44.

10 A. Uralov (A. Avtorkhanov), *Narodoubiistvo v SSSR* (Munich, 1952), p. 10.

11 Uralov (Avtorkhanov), *Narodoubiistvo*, pp. 10, 21–22; see also Kh.M. Berbekov, *K voprosu ob obrazovanii natsional'noi gosudarstvennosti Kabardino-Balkaria*

(Nal'chik), 1960, pp. 15, 20; Wixman, *Language Processes*, p. 137; Robert Conquest, *The Nation Killers: the Soviet Deportations of Nationalities* (London: Macmillan, 1960), p. 23.

12 Volkova and Lavrov, "Sovremennye etnicheskie protsessy", p. 330; "Scholars Identify Pressing Ethnic Issues", *Izvestiia*, March 22 1988, p. 3, in *Current Digest of the Soviet Press (CDSP)*, April 13, 1988, pp. 1–4 (interview with ethnographer L.M. Drobizheva and demographer Iurii Poliakov).

13 V. Kozlov, *The Peoples of the Soviet Union*, trans. P.M. Tiffen (Bloomington, IN: Indiana University Press, 1988), p. 156.

14 Wixman, *Language Aspects*, pp. 172–174.

15 In the 1920s, the languages were written in Latin characters; in 1938, the Latin script was changed to Cyrillic.

16 A.G. Trofimova, "Razvitie literatury i isskustva", *Kul'tura i byt narodov Severnogo Kavkaza*, p. 303.

17 *Ibid.*, p. 310.

18 V.I. Fil'kin, *Partiinaia organizatsiia Checheno-Ingushetiia v gody bor'by za uprochenie i razvitie sotsialisticheskogo obshchestva* (Groznyi: Checheno-Ingushskoe Nauchnoe Izdatel'stvo, 1963), p. 98.

19 Volkova and Lavrov, "Sovrmennye etnicheskie protsessy", p. 330.

20 Benedict Anderson, *Imagined Communities* (London: Verso, 1983), p. 15.

21 Trofimova, "Razvitie literatury i isskustva", pp. 311–312.

22 V. Kharlamov, "Kogo razdeliaet Terek," *Pravda*, November 4, 1991, p. 2.

23 A. Avtorkhanov, "Forty Years of Sovietization of Checheno-Ingushetiia", *Caucasian Review*, no. 10, 1960, p. 8.

24 Wixman, *Language Patterns*, p. 148.

25 A. Nekrich, *The Punished Peoples* (New York: Norton, 1978). Discussion of the deportations in the Soviet literature began to appear only in the late 1980s. See especially N.F. Bugai, "K voprosu o deportatsii narodov SSSR v 30-40kh godakh," *Istoriia SSSR*, no. 6, 1989, pp. 135–144; N.F. Bugai, "Pravda o deportatsii chechenskogo i ingushkogo narodov," *Voprosy istorii*, no. 1, 1990, pp. 32–44; V.N. Zemskov, "Massovoe osvobozhdenie spetsposelentsev i ssyl'nykh (1954–1960 gg.)," *Sotsiologicheskie issledovaniia*, no. 1, 1991, pp. 5–26.

26 V.N. Zemskov, "Massovoe osvobozhdeniie spetsposselentsev," p. 26.

27 Nekrich, *The Punished Peoples*, p. 149.

28 Interview, Cherkessk, October 9, 1991.

29 Interviews, Groznyi, October 21–23 1991.

30 Interviews, Vladikavkaz, October 16, 1991, 15 June 1992.

31 L.I. Klimovich, "Bor'ba ortodoksov i modernistov v Islame," *Voprosy nauchnoi ateizma*, no. 2, 1966, p. 85.

32 *Argumenty i fakty*, no. 13, March 1991, p. 1 (from 1989 census). The Rutul', Aguls and Tsakhurs have no written language of their own: the Agul use the Lezgin written language, while the Aguls and Tsakhurs use Azeri. See Bennigsen and Wimbush, *Muslims of the Soviet Empire*, p. 169.

33 *Argumenty i fakty*, no. 13, March 1991, p. 1.

34 *Nezavisimaia gazeta*, October 22, 1994, p. 3.

35 *Ibid.*

36 S. Shipunova, "Kazaki Kubani," *Sovetskaia Rossiia*, April 13, 1991, p. 3.

37 *Ibid.*, p. 3.

38 *Nezavisimaia gazeta*, October 22, 1994, p. 3.

39 *Nezavisimaia gazeta*, August 13, 1991.

40 *Nezavisimaia gazeta*, June 10, 1994, p. 3.

41 L.S. Perepelkin, "Chechenskaia respublika: sevremennaia sotsial'no-politicheskaia situatsiia," *Etnograficheskoe obozrenie*, no. 1, 1994, pp. 3–15.

42  Fieldwork observations, 1991.

43  *Argumenty i fakty*, no. 13, March 1991, p. 1. Like the Ingush, the Karachai and Balkar represent minority groups in their republican state formations.

44  Kh.Kh. Bokov, *Internatsionalizma na dele* (Moscow: Nauka, 1984), pp. 152–169.

45  *Nezavisimaia gazeta*, July 27, 1994, p. 3.

46. *Pravda*, November 11, 1991, p. 1.

47  *Nezavisimaia gazeta*, November 20, 1991, p. 3.

48  *Cegodnia*, December 24, 1993, p. 2.

49  *ITAR-Tass, FBIS*, Report on the Former Soviet Union, Russian National Affairs, June 5, 1993

50  *Nezavisimaia gazeta*, August 31, 1994, pp. 1, 3.

51  *Nezavisimaia gazeta*, October 18, 1994, p. 3.

52  *Nezavisimaia gazeta*, December 3, 1994, pp. 1, 3.

53  *Nezavisimaia gazeta*, December 8, 1994, p. 3; *Nezavisimaia gazeta*, December 16, 1994, p. 1.

54. *Nezavisimaia gazeta*, September 27, 1994, pp. 1, 3. At this time, Shakhrai did not argue for a Russian military attack on Chechnya.

55  *Ibid.*, p. 1.

56  L.S. Perepelkin, "Chechenskaia respublika," p. 10.

57  *Reuters News Service*, January 24, 1994.

58  *Nezavisimaia gazeta*, September 27, 1994, p. 3.

59  *Ibid.*, pp. 1, 3.

60  L.S. Perepelkin, "Chechenskaia respublika," p. 6.

61  *Reuters News Service*, January 17, 1995.

62  *Ibid.*, January 24, 1995.

63  *Ibid.*

64  *Nezavisimaia gazeta*, December 8, 1994, p. 1. Dudaev did meet with Russian Minister of Defense, Pavel Grachev, in the Ingush capital of Nazran. Clearly no settlement was reached as the Russian invasion began three days later.

65  *Nezavisimaia gazeta*, December 16, 1994, p. 1; *Reuters News Service*, January 17, 1995.

66  Iu. Karpov, "K probleme ingushskoi avtonomii," *Sovetskaia etnografiia*, no. 5, 1991, p. 29.

67  In December 1991, a referendum showed popular support for Ingush separation from Chechnya and retention of federal ties with Russia.

68  *Izvestiia*, May 30, 1989.

69  *FBIS, Report on the Former Soviet Union*, Russia, January 9, 1992, p. 55.

70  *Ibid.*, January 8, 1992, pp. 62–63; January 13, 1992, p. 38.

71  *Ibid.*, 14 January 1992, p. 53.

72  Nekrich, *The Punished Peoples*, pp. 158–159.

73  *Nezavisimaia gazeta*, April 25, 1991, p. 3.

74  *Nezavisimaia gazeta*, March 28, 1991.

75  *Izvestiia*, November 21, 1991, p. 1.

76  *Pravda*, November 29, 1991, p. 1.

77  *Ibid.*

78  *Nezavisimaia gazeta*, October 10, 1994, p. 3.

79  *Izvestiia*, October 13, 1993, p. 7; *Rossiiskie vesti*, December 7, 1993, p. 2.

80  *Rossiiskie vesti*, December 7, 1993, p. 2.

81  *Ibid.*

82  *Nezavisimaia gazeta*, June 28, 1994, p. 3.

83  *Nezavisimaia gazeta*, October 10 1994, p. 3; *Nezavisimaia gazeta*, November 12, 1994, p. 3.

84  *Nezavisimaia gazeta*, October 10, 1994, p. 3.

85 In 1991, Dzhokhar Dudaev assured the North Ossetian government of his neutrality. *Argumenty i fakty*, no.46, November 1991, p. 1. There have been no reports since of any official Chechen involvement.

86 Wixman, *Language Aspects*, pp. 137–139.

87 *Argumenty i fakty*, no. 13, March 1991.

88 *Nezavisimaia gazeta*, March 14, 1991, p. 3.

89 *Nezavisimaia gazeta*, July 19, 1994, p. 3.

90 Fadeev, ed., *Ocherki istorii Balkarskogo naroda*, p. 98.

91 V. Dzidzoev, unpublished paper on Balkarian nationalism and attitudes toward other North Caucasian peoples as represented in the Balkarian press, delivered at the *Pervaia mezhdunarodnaia konferentsiia po osetinovedeniiu*, Vladikavkaz, October 1991.

92 *Ibid.*

93 *Nezavisimaia gazeta*, July 19, 1994, p. 3.

94 *Nezavisimaia gazeta*, March 14, 1991, p. 3.

95 *Nezavisimaia gazeta*, July 19, 1994, p. 3.

96 *Ibid.*

97 *Nezavisimaia gazeta*, October 20, 1993, p. 3.

98 *Argumenty i fatky*, no. 13, March 1991, p. 1.

99 S.A. Arutiunov, Ia.S. Smirnova, G.A. Sergeeva, "Etnokulturnaia situatsiia v Karachaevo-Cherkesskoi Aftonomnoi Oblasti," *Sovetskaia etnografiia*, no. 2, 1990, p. 28.

100 *Ibid.*, p. 23.

101 *Nezavisimaia gazeta*, July 21, 1994, p. 3.

102 Interviews: Cherkessk, Karachaevsk, 1991; also Arutiunov, Smirnova and Sergeeva, "Etnokulturnaia situatsiia," p. 27.

103 *Ibid.*

104 Radio Moscow, November 27, 1991, *Radio Liberty: Report on the USSR*, no. 49, December 6, 1991, p. 34.

105 *Nezavisimaia gazeta*, July 21, 1994, p. 3.

106 *Ibid.*, p. 3.

107 *Ibid.*

108 See Uarziati, *Kul'tura Osetin: sviazy s narodami kavkaza*, Introduction.

109 Interview with Ruslan Bzarov, *Pervaia mezhdunarodnaia konferentsiia po osetinovedeniiu*, Vladikavkaz, October 1991.

110 I am indebted to the Ossetian historian Ruslan Bzarov for his information. The figures are approximate, as no official statistics have been compiled for these categories.

111 Kh.V. Dzutsev, Ia.S. Smirnova, *Semeinye obriady osetin* (Vladikavkaz: Ir, 1990), pp. 35, 56–72.

112 Interviews, *Pervaia mezhdunarondnaia konferentsiia po osetinovedeniiu*.

113 E.Kh. Apazheva, presentation on Kabardinian-Ossetian connections, *Pervaia mezhdunarodnaia konferentsiia po osetinovedeniiu*.

114 Fieldwork observations, particularly interviews with school principals, directors, and curriculum officials in Vladikavkaz, June-August 1992.

115 *Nezavisimaia gazeta*, June 17, 1994, p. 3.

116 "Zakon RSFSR o reabilitatsii repressirovannykh narodov," published in *Sovetskaia rossiia*, May 7, 1991, p.3.

117 *Nezavisimaia gazeta*, May 12, 1991, p. 3.

118 *Nezavisimaia gazeta*, June 28, 1994, p. 3; *Nezavisimaia gazeta*, October 10, 1994, p. 3.

119 *Nezavisimaia gazeta*, October 10, 1994, p. 3.

120 *FBIS Report on the former Soviet Union, Caucasus*, November 15, 1993.

121 *Sovetskaia rossiia*, September 17 1991, p. 1.

122 *Nezavisimaia gazeta*, August 31 1994, p. 3.

123 Declaration composed by delegates to the Plenary Session of the Pervaia *mezhdunarodnaia knoferentsiia po osetinovedeniiu*.

124 *Nezavisimaia gazeta*, September 29, 1994, p. 3.

125 *Ibid.*,

126 *Nezavisimaia gazeta*, August 24 1994.

127 *Nezavisimaia gazeta*, November 18 1993, p. 3.

128 A. Glebova, "Musul'mane sobiraiutsia v khadzh," *Novoe vremia*, no. 30, June 1991, pp. 12–14; *Nezavisimaia gazeta*, February 26, 1991, p. 2; *Nezavisimaia gazeta*, August 24, 1994, p. 3.

129 *Nezavisimaia gazeta*, August 24, 1994, p. 3.

130 *FBIS Report from the former Soviet Union, Russian National Affairs*, v. 205, 26 October 1993, p. 52.

131 *Sovetskaia Rossiia*, April 9 1991, p.2; *Nezavisimaia gazeta*, April 15, 1991, p. 3.

132 *Nezavisimaia gazeta*, January 24, 1991, p. 3.

133 D. Khalidov, "K soglasiiu cherez reformy", *Sovetskii Dagestan*, no. 2, 1991, p. 20.

134 *Izvestiia*, July 23, 1990, p. 2.

135 *Pravda*, December 9, 1991, p. 1.

136 *Nezavisimaia gazeta*, January 24, 1991, p. 3; *Nezavisimaia gazeta*, May 18, 1991, p. 3.

137 *Nezavisimaia gazeta*, August 24, 1994, p. 1 and August 26, 1994, p. 3.

138 *Nezavisimaia gazeta*, December 20, 1994, p. 1.

139 K.P. Kalinovskaia, G.E. Markov, "Nogaitsy – problemy natsional'nykh otnoshenii i kul'tury," *Sovetskaia etnografiia*, no. 2, 1990, p. 15. Little data is available on Nogai in Chechnya and Ingushetia.

140 *Ibid.*, p. 17.

141 S.A. Arutiunov, Ia.A. Smirnova, G.A. Sergeeva, "Etnokul'turnaia situatsiia," p. 23; K.P. Kalinovskaia, G.E. Markov, "Nogaitsy."

142 *Ibid.*, p. 18.

143 *Nezavisimaia gazeta*, January 24, 1991, p. 3; May 18, 1991, p. 3.

144 *Sovetskaia Rossiia*, April 13, 1991, p. 3.

145 S.A. Kozlov, "Poplnenie vol'nykh kazach'ikh soobshchestv na Severnom Kavkaze v XVI-XVII vv.," *Sovetskaia etnografiia*, no. 5, 1991, pp. 47–55.

146 "Kazachestvo," *Bol'shaia sovetskaia entsiklopediia* (Moscow, 1973), pp. 175–177.

147 *Sovetskaia Rossiia*, April 13, 1991, p. 3; *Nezavisimaia gazeta*, October 22, 1994, p. 3.

148 *Nezavisimaia gazeta*, July 21, 1994, p. 3; *Izvestiia*, December 4, 1991, p. 1.

149 S.A. Kozlov, "Popolnenie vol'nykh kazach'ikh," p. 54.

150 *Nezavisimaia gazeta*, September 15, 1991, p. 3; *Nezavisimaia gazeta*, April 18, 1991, p. 3.

151 *Nezavisimaia gazeta*, December 3, 1994, p. 1.

152 *Nezavisimaia gazeta*, December 23, 1994, p. 3. From an announcement by Vladimir Naumov, chairman of the Union of Russian Cossacks.

153 *Argumenty i fakty*, March 13, 1991, p. 1.

154 *Nezavisimaia gazeta*, July 21, 1994, p. 3.

155 I have not found any reliable figures on the numbers of North Caucasians in Moscow. Many are not officially registered. Their presence, however, is widely reported in the Russian press and this is confirmed by my own fieldwork in Moscow.

156 *Izvestiia*, November 27, 1991, p. 1.

157 *Nezavisimaia gazeta*, September 27, 1994, p. 1.

158 *Sovetskaia Rossiia*, September 17, 1991, p. 1.

159 *Nezavisimaia gazeta*, October 10, 1994, p. 3.

160 *Reuters News Service*, January 24, 1994. In mid-January, United Nations officials produced the following estimates of refugee influx to other North Caucasian

republics: 100,000 to Ingushetia; 42,000 to Dagestan; 10,000 to North Ossetia. However, 260,000 additional refugees were not accounted for in this figures, and many of these may also have fled to these republics.
161 *Nezavisimaia gazeta*, October 10, 1994, p. 3.
162 Fieldwork observations, Vladikavkaz, 1991–1992.
163 Groznyi, Chechen Republican Television Station, October 22, 1991.
164 *FBIS, Report on the Former Soviet Union, Russia*, January 8, 1992, pp. 62–63; January 13, 1992, p. 38.
165 *Nezavisimaia gazeta*, January 31, 1991, p. 3.
166 *FBIS, Report on the Former Soviet Union, Caucasus*, November 10, 1993, pp. 96–97.
167 *FBIS, Report on the Former Soviet Union, Russian National Affairs*, December 15, 1993, pp. 69–70.
168 *Ibid.*; *Nezavisimaia gazeta*, December 16, 1994, p. 1. As of December 12, 1994, the Confederation of North Caucasian Peoples had sent between 800 and 1,000 fighters to Chechnya.
169 *FBIS, Report on the Former Soviet Union, Russian National Affairs*, December 9, 1993, p. 50.

# North Caucasus: Chronology of events

*August 1989*

Representatives of sixteen North Caucasian groups attend the founding congress of the Assembly of Mountain Peoples of the Caucasus.

*1990*

In Dagestan, the Kumyk movement *Tenglik* (Equality) calls for the creation of a Kumyk republic.

*September 1990*

The Supreme Soviet of the North Ossetian ASSR suspends the right of Ingush to live in North Ossetia.

*October 1990*

The All-Kuban Cossack Union holds its founding congress.

*November 1990*

In Kabardino-Balkaria, a commission is formed to examine the possibility of restoring Balkar autonomy in their historical lands.

*January 1991*

Adygeia is upgraded from an autonomous region to an ASSR.
The Islamic University of Groznyi is founded in Checheno-Ingushetia.

*February 1991*

North Ossetia requests presidential rule.

*March 1991*

Armed Ingush attempt to seize Ossetian homes in the Prigorodnyi district of North Ossetia. The Ossetian authorities in the Prigorodnyi district impose a curfew, form National Guard, and begin armed retaliation. Several are killed, and the conflict leads to the flight of more than 70,000 Ingush from North Ossetia.
In the Ingush city of Nazran, thousands demonstrate to demand a restoration of the Prigorodnyi district to Ingushetia and express a willingness to use armed force if necessary.

17    In the all-union referendum on preserving the union,

support for the union in the North Caucasus is as follows: Dagestan – 83 percent (81 percent turnout); Kabardino-Balkaria – 78 percent (76 percent); Kalmykia – 88 percent (83 percent); North Ossetia – 90 percent (86 percent); Checheno-Ingushetia – 76 percent (59 percent).

*April 1991*

In Dagestan, 39 out of 54 regional soviets support a resolution for sovereignty.

*May 1991*

Checheno-Ingushetia declares a "Justice Day" for the rehabilitation of repressed peoples.
Yeltsin issues a decree "On the Rehabilitation of the Repressed Peoples," which promises to restore to deported national groups their national-territorial status.
Dagestan issues a declaration of sovereignty.

*June 1991*

The Congress of the Chechen People reaffirms an earlier decision to rename Checheno-Ingushetia the Chechen Republic of Nakhnichichi.

*August 1991*

General Dzokhar Dudaev and the Chechen All-National Congress seize power in Checheno-Ingushetia.

*October 1991*

Adygeia signs an economic agreement with the surrounding Krasnodar district.
A Northern Ingush Republic is proclaimed.

*November 1991*

9   Dudaev is elected president of Checheno-Ingushetia.
Parliamentary elections take place in Checheno-Ingushetia, and the parliament resolves to nationalize all enterprises and ministries in the republic.
Dudaev declares Chechnya to be a sovereign state.
Yeltsin imposes a state-of-emergency and orders troops to Checheno-Ingushetia but rescinds his decree after encountering stiff opposition in the Russian parliament.
At the First Congress of the National Council of the Balkar People, delegates announce plans to form a separate Balkar republic.
Karachai leaders asks the Russian Supreme Soviet to assist in securing their autonomy and complete rehabilitation.
The Confederation of Mountain Peoples of the Caucasus is established.

*December 1991*

2    A referendum is held in Ingushetia on separating the region from Checheno-Ingushetia. A majority of the population approves of the change.

In Dagestan, the All-National Congress of Lezgins calls for the creation of a national state-formation called Lezgistan.

*January 1992*

8    The Chechen parliament declares that the border with Ingushetia should be restored.

*March 1992*

1    Opposition forces in Chechnya temporarily occupy radio and TV centers before being seized by the Chechen national guard.

12    The Chechen parliament issues a declaration of independence.

20    A law is adopted which creates an Ingush republic.

21–22    The parliament of the Confederation of Mountain People resolves to set up a defense committee and joint armed forces.

28    A referendum is held in Karachevo-Cherkessia on keeping the republic united, in contradiction with Yeltsin's 5 February draft law to divide it into separate Karachai and Cherkess autonomous oblasts.

*May 1992*

4    Armed Kumyks and Laks confront each other in Dagestan over a decree establishing a new Lak settlement on ostensibly Kumyk territory. Police prevent the confrontation from intensifying.

*June 1992*

4    The Russian Supreme Soviet formalizes the establishment of the Ingush republic.

*September 1992*

27    In Kabardino-Balkaria thousands gather at a demonstration protesting the arrest of Musa Shanibov, the chairman of the Confederation of Mountain Peoples, and a confrontation with police ensues. Shanibov is released following the imposition of a brief state-of-emergency.

*October 1992*

2–4    At a congress, the Confederation of Mountain Peoples changes its name to the Confederation of the Peoples of the Caucasus. Leaders suggest revoking the Federation Treaty and demand withdrawal of Russian troops from the region

and recognition of the independence of Chechnya,
Abkhazia, and South Ossetia.

4    A new protest is held in Nalchik to demand the resignation
of the president of Kabardino-Balkaria. The demonstration,
which was organized by the Congress of the Kabardinian
People, ends when the government agrees to remove Interior
Ministry units from government buildings, give the
Congress television airtime, and halt the trials of those who
had volunteered in the fighting in Abkhazia.

17    The Congress of Kabardinian People holds a conference
blaming the republican government for the tensions in the
republic and announces that they will continue to provide
assistance to Abkhaz troops until Georgia withdraws.

31–1    Armed conflicts occur between Ossetians and Ingushetians.

*November 1992*

        Ingush guerillas enter Vladikavkaz.

2    Yeltsin declares a month-long state of emergency in North
Ossetia and Ingushetia.

10–12    Russian troops enter Ingushetia.
Sergei Shakhrai is appointed head of administration in
North Ossetia.
Dudaev declares a state of emergency in Chechnya and
appeals to Chechens to defend the republic's independence.

17    An agreement is reached to disengage Russian and Chechen
troops in North Ossetia and Ingushetia.

*January 1993*

10    The formation of the first territorial district for MVD
Internal Troops, to be located in the North Caucasus, is
announced.

*February 1993*

28    Ruslan Aushev is elected president of Ingushetia with 99.99
percent of the uncontested vote (turnout was 92.7 percent).

*March 1993*

6    North Ossetian Supreme Soviet recognizes South Ossetia as
an independent state.

25    More than 10,000 Lezgins demonstrate near the
Azeri-Dagestani border to demand the unification of the
Lezgin people.

29    Martial law is declared in the Prigorodnyi district of North
Ossetia, and a Temporary Administration is established
with a Russian peacekeeping force to oversee the return of
Ingush refugees.

*April 1993*

11    30-year-old multi-millionaire Kirsan Ilyumzhinov is elected president of Kalmykia, winning over 65 percent of the vote (over 80 percent turnout).

17    Dudaev issues decrees dissolving Chechnya's parliament and government and imposing direct presidential rule.

18    Parliament annuls all of Dudaev's decress except that disbanding the government.

19    Chechnya's Constitutional Court issues a ruling which agrees with parliament.

22    The Second Congress of Ossetian People ends in Vladikavkaz. North Ossetian parliamentary speaker Akhsarbek Galazov casts doubt on any possibility for reunion with South Ossetia.

30    At Ilyumzhinov's request, Kalmykia's Supreme Soviet dissolves itself in order to establish a "professional parliament" made up of only 25 of the 130 deputies.

*June 1993*

4    Military units loyal to Dudaev storm two buildings to prevent the holding of a referendum on the presidency and early elections called for by the Chechen parliament (and disband an opposition meeting.) 14 are killed in the firefight.
Dudaev suspends the parliament and establishes a Temporary Council.

19–20    At a congress of the Balkar people, delegates declare that they seek the restoration of pre-1944 territorial boundaries and the return of Balkars deported in that year.

*August 1993*

1    Viktor Polyanichko, the head of the interim administration in North Ossetia and Ingushetia, is assassinated.

*September 1993*

22    Dudaev declares his support for Yeltsin in the latter's conflict with the Russian parliament.

*December 1993*

12    Chechnya does not participate in Russian parliamentary elections.
North Ossetian and Ingush leaders Galazov and Aushev sign a statement with Yeltsin proposing that Ingushetia renounce its territorial claims on the Prigorodnyi region, North Ossetia permit the return of refugees, and local armed units be disbanded.

25    Yeltsin signs a decree on the rehabilitation of the Kalmyk

people and support for their cultural revival and
development.

In Makhachkala, the capital of Dagestan, a rally is held to
mourn the murder of Arsen Bairamov, a Duma candidate,
and request Yeltsin to disband the Dagestan parliament and
declare Duma elections there invalid.

Musa Shanibov, the president of the Confederation of
Peoples of the Caucasus, acknowledges that the
establishment of armed forces for the Confederation is
illegal and insists that the organization has no troops of its
own.

Yeltsin announces that the government will consider issues
of Cossack cultural revival and the unification of their
communities.

*January 1994*

16    Galazov is elected president of North Ossetia with over 66
percent of the votes cast.

*March 1994*

11    Ilyumzhinov announces that Kalmykia's constitution will be
abolished.

*April 1994*

5    Kalmykia adopts the "Steppe Code" in lieu of a
constitution, providing the republic with a 27-seat
parliament (the People's Khural). The Code makes no
mention of republican sovereignty.

*May 1994*

2–5    Clashes between Lezgins and Azerbaijanis take place in
Dagestan following a quarrel which led to the deaths of
two Lezgins.

28    The third Congress of the Shapsug people opens in Sochi.
Numbering 10,000, the Shapsug have called for the
restoration of the Shapsug autonomous district of
the Krasnodar krai which was abolished by
Stalin.

*June 1994*

12–13    In Chechnya, at least eight people are killed in clashes
between government and opposition troops.
Balkar leaders call for the establishment of a separate
Balkar republic.

26    North Ossetia and Ingushetia sign the "Beslan Agreement,"
which provides for the return of Ingush refugees to the
Prigorodnyi region of North Ossetia.

27    The Spiritual Board of Muslims and Council of Imams of

Kabardino-Balkaria warns that dividing the republic will only result in inter-ethnic violence.

*July 1994*

1    Valerii Kokov, the president of Kabardino-Balkaria, signs a power-sharing treaty with Russia similar to that which Tatarstan signed in February.
Balkar leaders renounce demands for separation and ask for enhanced sovereignty in their territory.

23    In Chechnya, opposition leaders call on Yeltsin to recognize the Provisional Council as the only legal government body in the republic.

*August 1994*

2    Umar Avturkhanov, head of the Chechen Provisional Council, claims the opposition controls most of Chechen territory.

8    The Provisional Council announces the formation of an alternate Chechen government in the Nadterechnyi region.

10    In Grozny, the first Congress of the Chechen People since the nineteenth century is held, and about 2,000 delegates attend. Delegates advise Dudaev to declare martial law and full mobilization. They also vote to launch a holy war if Russian troops invade Chechnya.

12    In Chechnya, a state of emergency is declared and full mobilization of the male population begins.

16    Ruslan Khasbulatov is appointed head of the State Council in Chechnya.

*November 1994*

26    Russian forces attempt to launch an undercover attack on Chechnya. Several officers and soldiers are captured.

*December 1994*

11    The Russian invasion of Chechnya is officially launched.

31    Russian troops enter Groznyi.

*Janurary 1995*

11    After a brief truce, fighting resumes in Chechnya.

26    Russian troops capture Groznyi.

*February 1995*

10    Chechens abandon Groznyi as their central base of operations. Fighting continues in towns and villages throughout Chechnya.

25    The People's Party of Kalmykia, led by Duma deputy Khulakhachiyev and opposing Kalmyk President

Ilyumzhinov, holds its founding congress in the city of
Elista.

*March 1995*
    23   North Ossetia becomes the fourth republic to sign a
power-sharing treaty with Moscow.
    26   Parliamentary elections are held in North Ossetia.

# 4 The Middle Volga: exploring the limits of sovereignty

ALLEN FRANK AND RONALD WIXMAN

Currently the Middle Volga region is one of the two most ethnically hetero-geneous regions of the Russian Federation. Unlike the Northern Caucasus region, however, in which the primary issues of ethnic relations center on Russian rule over ethnically non-Russian peoples and territories, in the Middle Volga there are two major players in the issues surrounding ethnic relations and policies. Here the Turkic speaking, culturally Moslem Tartars enjoy a prominent role in determining the situations of their neighbors relative to the Russian regime, former Soviet policies and current ethnic relations. Historically, the Christian Russians vied for influence over the local populations with the Moslem Tatars. A conflictual history of ethnic asssimilation centering on the struggle for supremacy between these two dominant peoples left the various Finnic and Hunnic peoples of the Middle Volga trapped between the "Tartar wolf" and the "Russian bear."

The Middle Volga is distinctive in a number of important ways in Russian and Soviet history. It was the first significant non-Russian area incorporated into the Muscovite State. Similarly, it was here that the Orthodox Church (as a cultural-ideological center) and the Russian Empire (as an imperial state) learned to deal with non-Russian, non-Orthodox subject peoples and how to establish policies aimed at ruling and assimilating them. In addition, in the Middle Volga they had to compete with culturally and economically dominant Tatars who held sway not only over local non-Russians, but over the Russians themselves for 300 years.

The Middle Volga also holds special significance as the site where the Moslem-Turkic Tatars were defeated by the Mucovite state. This signalled the beginning of the Russian *reconquista*.[1] Indeed, St. Basil's Cathedral – an image which is synonymous with the city of Moscow – was constructed in commemoration of the defeat of Islamic forces by Christian Muscovites. In recognition of this victory, as well as of the liberation of all formerly Christian lands which, in the minds of the Russians at the time, were held by Islamic peoples (notably Constantinople and Jerusalem), a new Christian symbol appeared atop Russia's churches – the cross over the crescent.[2]

It was also in the Middle Volga that the Russians, under the precedent set by St. Steven of Perm,[3] enacted a policy of creating literary liturgical languages and tolerating, to some extent, the minorities for whom they were created. Later, St. Steven's policies were adopted less out of a sense of Christian benevolence than as a stop-gap measure to impede the Islamization of the local (and later the Soviet) government supported ethnic groups by providing them with ethnic institutions of their own. This support included the preservation of their spoken languages, the establishment of literary native languages; the recognition of non-Russian, ethnic liturgical languages by the Eastern Orthodox Church; and, at times, even the creation of ethnic territories.[4]

By the late fifteenth century, it had already become apparent to the Russians that ethnic, linguistic, and cultural Tatarization went along with the spread of Islam. As the animist Finnic speaking peoples (the ancestors of the Mordvinians, Mari and Udmurts) and even a significant portion of Slavs adopted the Moslem religion under the influence of the Tatars, they also assumed a Tatar identity. The Tatars, like the Turks of the Caucasus, Turkey, and Central Asia, maintained an open ethnic system under which one could become a legitimate member of the dominant ethnic group by accepting and adopting their cultural norms and language.[5] The same was true of the Russians, in that the acceptance of the primacy of Russian Orthodox religion and the Russian language led to the ethnic assimilation of non-Russians.[6] Thus, the ethnic leitmotif of the sixteenth century through to the twentieth was characterized by a competition between the Tsarist and Soviet regimes and the Russian and non-Tatar peoples of the Middle Volga.[7]

This ethnic game of dominance, and the use of interethnic relations, is still being played out today in the post-Soviet era. One major change, however, is that now, with modernization and common awareness of their situation, some of the local peoples of the region, most notably the Bashkirs and Chuvash, have managed to use this Tatar/Russian rivalry to their own advantage.

## Historical setting of the Middle Volga

Archaeologists have uncovered traces of the Paleolithic culture in the Middle Volga, making the region an ancient center of human civilization. The ancestors of the region's Finno-Ugric nationalities, while their origins remain unclear, inhabited the region before the arrival of Turkic nomads, in the sixth century, and of Slavic colonists. The extension of Russian power in the Middle Volga proper (the groups discussed above were located on the periphery) is a relatively recent occurrence by Old World standards, dating to the conquests of the khanates of Kazan and Astrakhan in 1552 and 1556. Until then, the Middle Volga was politically dominated by Turkic, Inner Asian states, based either locally, in the Middle Volga region, or more remotely, on the steppe. The political history of the region actually begins with the migration into the area of the Turkic Bulghars, a nomadic group, in the seventh or eighth century. The Bulghars dominated a series of lucrative trade routes and traded with the local Finno-Ugrians, presumably extracting a degree of tribute from them as well. In the late ninth and early tenth centuries, many, if not most, of the Bulghars converted to Islam. These Bulghars became, in communal terms, the ancestors of the region's Tatar Muslim population, while those who retained their native religion became the ancestors presumably of the modern-day Chuvash.

The incorporation of large, Muslim, and "animist" communities into the Russian state resulted in an alternating adoption and abandonment of policies aimed at both converting these somewhat alien, menacing communities, and integrating them into the Muscovite, and later, Imperial Russian systems.

Christianization and the repression of Islam and "animist" traditions began soon after the conquest of Kazan. Numerous Tatar communities were converted to Christianity at this time.[8] These communities retained their identities and remained very separate from the Muslim Tatars. In the 1740s, large-scale conversions of the Finno-Ugric and Chuvash communities took place, and were accompanied by the destruction of hundreds of mosques and sacred groves.[9] However, in Bashkiria, where non-Russians formed the vast majority of the population, the provincial authorities were able to keep the missionaries out and large numbers of Mari, Udmurt, Chuvash, and Tatar peasants migrated there to avoid Christianization.

The integration of elements of the Muslim population into the system of state service commenced in the reign of Ivan the Terrible. Beginning in the 1740s, the provincial authorities in Bashkiria launched efforts to integrate the Islamic clergy into the Russian administrative system, appointing "loyal" mullahs for the administration of Islamic law in Muslim communities, and providing these mullahs with salaries. In 1788, Catherine the Great authorized the formation of the Orenburg Muslim Spiritual Assembly, responsible for the administration of the empire's Muslim communities in the Volga-Ural region and Siberia. As a result of their integration into the Russian administrative system, the Islamic clergy took the lead in promoting a unified Islamic identity for the communities under their jurisdiction. The basis of this emerging identity were the Bulghars, who had remained in Tatar historical memory as the ancestors which had first converted to Islam.[10]

This era of cooperation began to wane in the first half of the nineteenth century, when the ruling elites of Russia started to conceive of the empire as being a specifically Orthodox and ethnically Russian one. As a result, and along with increasing conflicts with Ottoman Turkey, both Russian bureaucrats and the Russian Orthodox clergy found cause to suspect their Muslim subjects, the vast majority of which inhabited the Middle Volga, as a potential Turkish "fifth column," and thus potentially disloyal. In this sort of atmosphere, the Russian authorities began to express concern over the Tatarization and Islamization of the region's Finno-Ugric and Turkic communities. This concern animated Russian religious policy in the Middle Volga until the beginning of the twentieth century. The traditional Russian policy of equating communal status with religious affiliation bonded easily with the older Inner Asian religious conception of communal and ancestral religious affiliation that was common to the region's Finno-Ugric and Turkic communities, be they Muslim, Christian, or "animist." This combination resulted in very stable communal religious identities that have remained intact to the present day.[11]

The second half of the nineteenth century brought great changes to the economic and cultural life of the Middle Volga region. By this time, as a result of ongoing Russian colonization that had begun before the Russian conquest of Kazan, the majority of the region's population was ethnically Russian. In addition, the region had started to undergo gradual industrialization which, along with the resulting expansion of commercial activity, not only benefited Russian capitalists, but was instrumental in stimulating the creation of a wealthy Tatar (and to a lesser extent Chuvash) bourgeoisie. Under the influence of European ideas, as well as current pan-Turkic ideology, the Tatar bourgeoisie was especially active in promoting the idea of a Tatar national identity, as opposed to the older "Bulghar" identity current among Middle Volga Muslims since the late eighteenth century. It was this new Tatar elite that was to articulate and lead the Tatar "national" movements during the revolutions of 1905 and 1917.[12]

## The people of the Middle Volga

### Finno-Ugrians

The most populous Finnic group are the Mordvins who, together with the Maris, form the so-called Volga Finnic language family. The Mordvins actually form two separate ethnic groups, the Moksha and the Erzia, whose members have hsitorically conceived of themselves as two separate peoples, but who were seen as one people by their Russian and Muslim neighbors.[13] Linguistically, Erzia and Moksha are closely related but mutually unintelligible, and they constitute two separate literary languages.

Retaining their native "animist" religion until the 1740s, the Mordvins, along with other Finno-Ugric and Turkic groups in the region, were then subjected to a policy of mass forced conversions to Eastern Orthodoxy. Despite the disruption that these conversions caused, they were essentially successful, especially among the Mordvins, who, along with the Komi, were the only peoples in the Middle Volga region completely Christianized. Nevertheless, the Mordvins retained many of their former religious conceptions which Russian missionaries classified as "pagan."

The Mordvins are generally thought to have been the most Russified of the Volga-Ural nationalities, and ethnographic accounts since the end of the eighteenth century have typically depicted them as being on the brink of cultural extinction. Nevertheless, their ability to maintain their identity through the centuries, at least in the rural milieu, is in no small part due to their adherence to ancestral and communal religious conceptions common throughout Inner Asia. The Mordvins inhabit their own "national" republic, but large and numerous Mordvin communities are found in Penza, Simbirsk, and Saratov districts, as well as in Tatarstan.

The Maris (formerly known as Cheremis) are the least populous of the region's Finno-Ugric groups but have, ironically, been the most successful in maintaining the use of their language and native religious practices.[14] Linguistically, the Maris can be divided into three groups: the Hill (kuryk) Maris, who inhabit the right bank of the Volga; the Lowland (olyk) Maris, who inhabit the left bank of the Volga, and the Eastern Maris, who primarily inhabit Bashkortostan, but are also found in Tatarstan, and in the Perm and Ekaterinburg oblasts. The Hill Maris speak a distinct form of the Mari language and use their own special literary language, while the Lowland and Eastern Mari speak mutually intelligible dialects and use the Lowland Mari literary language.

The basis of Mari communal identity is religious affiliation. The Hill Mari and a large part of the Lowland Mari were converted to Eastern Orthodoxy in the eighteenth century. However, resistance to Christianization was widespread among the Maris, and communities were sharply defined along religious lines. The "unbaptized" Maris refer to their religion as *chi marii vera* (the real Mari faith) and to Christian Mari religion as *rushla vera* (the Russian faith).[15] The Eastern Maris remain almost entirely "unbaptized," and as a result of living in the Turkic Muslim Bashkortotstan, they bear many cultural traits of material culture and language. The Maris live primarily in Mari El, Bashkortostan, and the Nizhnii Novgorod and Viatka oblasts.

The Udmurt (formerly known as Votiak) and Komi languages belong to the Permic branch of the Finno-Ugric language family.[16] The Udmurt language is divided into a number of mutually intelligible dialects, but, as with the Maris, religious affiliation determined traditional lines of communal distinction. The majority of Udmurts were converted to Christianity in the 1740s; nevertheless, large communities of Udmurts, particularly in Bashkortostan, retained their own religious traditions, which the Bashkir Udmurts refer to simply as *Inmarly Oskon* (God's faith).[17]

The northern Udmurts, living roughly north of the city of Izhevsk, have tended to retain the most archaic material culture but are the most Christianized and Russified. The southern Udmurts, among whom are nearly all of the "unbaptized" Udmurts, share many cultural features with their Muslim Tatar and Bashkir neighbors.[18] The Udmurts mainly inhabit their "national" republic, Udmurtia, but large communities are also located in Tatarstan, Bashkortostan, and the Viatka and Perm oblasts.

The Komi are the smallest of the Finno-Ugric nationalities in the Middle Volga. The Komi are divided into two groups: the Komi proper, or Zyrians (the pre-revolutionary designation), who inhabit the Komi Republic, and the Komi-Permiaks, who inhabit an autonomous okrug within the Perm oblast.[19] The ancestors of the Komi were the so-called Permians, and linguistic and archeological evidence indicate that in the seventh- or eighth-century occupation of the lower Kama River by Turkic nomads, they migrated north, into the taiga and tundra regions west of the Ural Mountains. As a result, the cultural and historical development of the Komi occurred outside of the cultural and historical milieu specific to the Middle Volga. Nevertheless, the Komi were by no mean isolated from the rest of the world. The Komi lands, Permia, were known to the Vikings as Bjarmia, and the ancestors of the Komi were apparently involved in trade with the Scandinavian merchants. In the twelfth century, the area came under Novgorodian influence, and in the fourteenth century, St. Stephen of Perm converted the Komi to Christianity, and even developed a Komi alphabet. While engaging in agriculture, fishing, hunting and reindeer herding, the Komi were accomplished merchants and financiers and accumulated considerable wealth trading their goods with their Samoyed and Vogul neighbors to the east.

## Turkic groups

After the Tatars, the Chuvash are the most numerous nationality in the Middle Volga. It is not clear when the ancestors of the Chuvash came to the area but in all likelihood it was in the sixth century or later. Chuvash forms its own branch of the Turkic language family.[20] Also, Chuvash comprise the only Turkic group in the Middle Volga region which is not predominantly Muslim, and it is thought that the ancestors of the Chuvash were Volga Bulgarians who did not convert to Islam in the early tenth century.

In terms of their material culture, the Chuvash share many features with their Finno-Ugric neighbors, especially the Maris. In fact, their Turkic affiliation was only widely recognized in the late nineteenth century; many ethnographers had, until then, assumed that the Chuvash were Finno-Ugrians. Like most of the Finno-Ugrians, the Chuvash were largely converted to Christianity in the 1740s, but numerous communities, particularly in Bashkortostan, retained the "Chuvash faith." However, by the late nineteenth century Christianity began to play an important role in the creation of a Chuvash national identity. The Chuvash today inhabit, for the most part, their "national" republic, Chuvashia, but large Chuvash communities are also located in southern Tatarstan, Bashkortostan, and the Simbirst oblast.

The most numerous, and dominant, ethnic group in the Middle Volga, after the Russians, are the Tatars.[21] Descendants of the Volga Bulgarians, who converted to Islam in the early tenth century, the Tatars speak a Turkic language more closely related to modern Kazakh and Crimean Tatar, suggesting the gradual migration of steppe nomads into the Tatar lands up until the Russian conquest. The Tatars are overwhelmingly Muslim, although a number of Tatar-speaking communities are Eastern Orthodox Christians whose ancestors were converted during the reign of Ivan IV, the so-called *kriashens*. Tatar is also used as a *lingua franca* by Mari, Chuvash, Udmurt, and Bashkir communities in Bashkortostan and Tatarstan, and is used as a first language by several Mari and Mordvin communities in those republics.

Tatars divide themselves into several subgroups. The largest are the so-called Kaan Tatars, who are the most numerous group, and who speak the so-called Central Dialect. The second group are the Mishers, with their own dialect, who live primarily west of the Volga River and in Bashkortostan. Tatars live primarily in Tatarstan, northern Bashkortostan, and the Cheliabinsk oblast.[22]

The last major Turkic group are the Bashkirs, a formerly nomadic group that have to a large degree preserved a clan and tribal social structure. The ethnic history of the Bashkirs is extremely complex. Many ethnographers and linguists believe that the early ancestors of the Bashkirs were the ancestors of those Hungarians who did not migrate westward in the prehistoric era.[23] In any case, the Bashkirs became Muslims during the age of the Golden Horde. Despite commonly heard claims to the effect that the Bashkirs, as nomads, were "lightly," "superficially," or "nominally" Muslims, Bashkir legends of origin, tribal and clan histories, and legends of Islamization unambiguously indicate the importance of Islamic identity and its role in maintaining communal cohesion. The Bashkirs share cultural features with the Tatars, including Islam, and mutually intelligible languages (indeed, some "Bashkir" dialects are almost indistinguishable from Tatar). Nevertheless, they have retained a separate identity. This is in part, the result of having retained clan and tribal affiliation, largely lost among the Tatars, but was especially reinforced by the Rusian practice of conferring upon the Bashkirs special status, similar to that conferred upon Cossack communities, allowing them favorable tax status and landowning rights in exchange for military service.[24]

## Ethnic and national aspirations at the time of the Revolution

One of the results of the Middle Volga's ethnic history is that no single dominant ethnic movement emerged. Given the cultural linguistic and territorial overlap they experienced, as well as their location deep within the Russian heartland, the peoples of this region had little opportunity to pursue independence. Indeed, few, if any of the peoples other than the Tatars, had developed either the sense of national consciousness or the leaders necessary to provide and sustain the impetus for a nationalist fervor until recently.

No ethnic independence movements arose among the Komi, Komi-Permyaks, Udmurts, or Mordvinians. Essentially, they accepted the dictates of the Russian, and later Soviet, government and benefited from the latter's fear of Tatarism. This was even more true of the Chuvash and Bashkirs, whose cultures and physical locations were far closer to that of the Tatar empire, and initial conversion of the Tatars to Islam created a strong affinity between the Chuvash and the Tatars. That the Tatars were culturally dominant in the region, and the Chuvash were Christian, could not overshadow the Chuvash concerns regarding the real dominance in the region of and by ethnic Russians. The Russians not only controlled the area politically, but worse, Russian settlers and urban dwellers continued to migrate into the Middle Volga region, further threatening the Chuvash and other populations with loss of land and autonomy.

The situation of the Bashkirs was even worse than that of the Chuvash. No one questioned the legitimate existence of a distinct Chuvash people and language. However, to most Tatars, and to the vast majority of Russians and others, the Bashkirs were either: a cultural subdivision of Tatars in the same way that Cossacks were a "subdivision" culturally of Russians or Ukrainians, and not a distinct people based on their cultural differences and historical past; a semi-nomadic social group of Tatars; a group of as yet "backward," uneducated, and uncivilized Tatars; or a group of people closely related to the Tatars who should simply be helped in their Tatarization by everyone else. Thus the very existence of a distinct Bashkir people as different from Tatars was in doubt not only as a result of Tatar nationalism, which claimed that they were Tatars, but also due to the Russian perception of them as such. Indeed, one could argue that had the Soviet regime chosen to finish the Tatarization of the Bashkirs by classifying them as Tatars and by establishing for them the Tatar literary language, then that process may have been completed by now.[25]

At the time of the October Revolution, many Tatar intellectuals and conservative religious leaders were thoroughly in support of either pan-Islamic or pan-Turkic movements (the former more religious in nature, the latter more secular, nationalist and modernist). In virtually all cases, the Tatar leadership demanded strong ties with other Turkic and Islamic regions of the USSR, and from this grew a movement to create a great Tatar state in the Middle Volga region that would comprise the lands of the Tatars, Bashkirs, Chuvash, Mari and Udmurt peoples (something akin to the lands of the Kazan Khanate that existed until their defeat by Ivan IV and their incorporation into the Muscovite State). Their goal was to achieve autonomous republic status within the framework of the Soviet system, and this republic would, by default, be dominated by Tatars. The name of this state was to have been *Idel Ural* (Idel is the Tatar name for the Volga, and Ural was for the Ural mountains and river). Among Tatar nationalists the dream of this Volga-Ural state, in which Tatars would achieve a position more similar to that which they had in the past, has never died.

The Chuvash, without making any specific linguistic or cultural demands, let it be known that they favored the establishment of a Middle Volgan state in line with Tatar proposals. In 1918, leaders of the Chuvash and Mari peoples formally requested that the Soviet government create this Middle Volgan state, as the ethnic Russians were of greater danger to the Chuvash and Mari ethnic interests than the Tatars. It seems fairly clear that the support for Idel-Ural by the Chuvash and Mari was less pro-Tatar than an attempt to exploit the fears of the new Soviet State to their best advantages. By posing as somewhat pro-Tatar they could expect to gain sympathy and support from the far more politically and numerically powerful Tatars, and also use this as leverage to gain cultural, religious and linguistic autonomy from the Russian government.[26]

Although Bashkirs expressed strong dislike for the culturally dominant Tatars, they, like the Chuvash and Mari, were more concerned with the threats posed by Russian agricultural settlements in Bashkir territory and the consequent loss of pasture land which ensued in the nineteenth century. The real threat of Russsian dominance and governmental preference for Russian settlers to obtain land in non-Russian areas superceded any hypothetical threat from Tatars. The Bashkirs found themselves in a very difficult ethnic situation at the time of the revolution, caught between the culturally and economically dominant Tatars and the land-hungry Russians.

Among the Bashkirs, a handful of nationalists arose. Led by Zeki Valedi Togan (Zeki Validov) this small group pressed for the creation of a separate Bashkiria (Bashkortostan). They opposed the notion that Bashkirs were, in effect, Tatars and that their lands should be incorporated into a Tatar-dominated state. On the other hand, they supported the idea that Bashkirs should continue to use standard Tatar as their literary language, as they had done in the past. To most Bashkirs, the Tatar threat was economic and political, but virtually all Bashkirs accepted the high status of a Tatar language and thought of Tatars as close kinsmen. The leadership of the Bashkirs thus found a way of using anti-Tatarism to court Russian protection, and Tatar national aspirations as leverage against the Russians. This dualistic playing off of Tatar and Russian interests continues to the present day.

## Soviet policy

As a result of World War I and the Russian Revolution, Finland, Estonia, Latvia, Lithuania, Poland (which then included Western Ukraine and the western part of Belarus), Ukraine, Georgia, Azerbaijan, Armenia, the Central Asian Khanates, and other areas of the Russian Empire declared their independence. Bessarabia (Moldova) was incorporated into the newly expanded Romanian state, and the Northern Caucasus established quasi-independence in a shaky alliance between numerous ethnically diverse peoples of the region and local Cossacks. To comprehend what happened in the Middle Volga during the early Soviet Period it is essential to recognize that little of Russia's multi-ethnic state remained. In fact, one ethnically diverse area existed to pose any challenge to Moscow's central authority in 1919 – the Middle Volga. It had been the region in which the Muscovite State first learned about ethnic diversity and applied ethnic, language and religious policies, and it was subsequently the first region of the USSR in which a distinct nationality policy was applied. Here the Soviets established their famous policy of *razmezhevanie* (division) which was later applied throughout the Moslem regions of the USSR (Central Asia, Transcaucasia, and the Northern Caucasus). This policy was designed to split the Moslem peoples of the USSR into groups that were large enough to maintain distinct ethnic identities yet small enough to be controlled absolutely by the Soviet center. As Bennigsen and Lemercier-Quelquejay state, "the policy involved breaking up the large mass of Muslim and Turkic-speaking populace into fragments and then putting the pieces together into the required number of units, each of them having an exact territorial demarcation.[27]

The Middle Volga was the first region of the USSR in which a centrally planned nationalities policy was administered. It is not by accident, then, that the first ethnically based territory established in the Russian Soviet Federated Socialist Republic (RSFSR) was the Bashkir ASSR, proclaimed on March 23, 1919, a full year before the creation of the Tatar ASSR. The maintenance of separate Bashkir and Tatar territorial and administrative divisions was clearly aimed at undermining a pan-Turkic movement and preventing the creation of the Idel Ural State which, at the time, was supported by a majority of the peoples indigenous to the Middle Volga.

Not only was each officially recognized people to have, in Bennigsen and Lemercier-Quelquejay's words, "an exact territorial demarcation," but the actual boundaries themselves became a tool of Soviet policy. Through the manipulation of boundaries the Soviets could incite existing territorial conflicts and thereby further divide peoples and preserve Muscovite (Soviet) control, or they could create them. While the cases of the Caucasus (both Northern and Trans-Caucasian) and Central Asian regions are well known, less is said of the Middle Volga, where this policy originated.

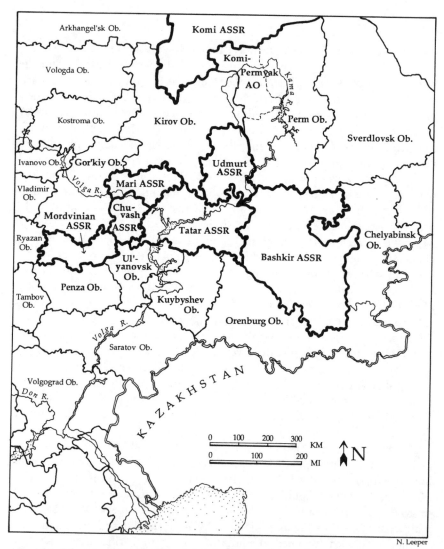

N. Leeper

Map 4.1 Administrative divisions of the Middle Volga

With the creation of the Bashkir ASSR arose a bitter antagonism between Tatars and Bashkirs. The Ufa district, an area populated primarily by Tatars, and the town of Ufa itself (an important Tatar city), were included within the territorial limits of the newly founded Bashkir autonomy. This created for the first time a serious rift between Tatars and Bashkirs over territory. Not only did the establishment of a distinct Bashkir autonomy prevent the formation of Idel Ural, but it also exacerbated Tatar-Bashkir ethnic relations. By so doing the Soviets also promoted a distinct Bashkir ethnic identity by providing the Bashkirs with a territorial state named after them. In addition to this, a distinct Bashkir literary language was created in 1923, despite the fact that, at the time of the Revolution about one third of the Bashkirs already considered Tatar, not Bashkir, their native language.

The primary reason for the creation of many of the Middle Volga autonomies was not merely to recognize the rights of local ethnic groups to territorial and cultural integrity (although this explains support afforded the Tatars themselves). As has been mentioned, the fact that the Bashkirs received the first ASSR clearly indicates the calculated political nature of the decision to single out that specific group for support: i.e. at a time when such a policy had the best chance to thwart the creation of Idel Ural, the Tatar dominated state. In fact, the policies to grant limited autonomy and cultural identity to the Chuvash, Bashkirs, and Mari, in particular, appear to be designed for one ultimate purpose – to diminish Tatar influence.

The majority of the peoples of the Middle Volga actually benefited as a result of Soviet anti-Tatarism and anti-pan-Turkism and from the concept that if the government tried to push Russification (among the Mari, Udmurts, Chuvash, etc.) there would be an anti-Russian and perhaps Tatar backlash among them. Thus, Soviet policy, in this respect, closely mirrors that of Tsarist Russia. In spite of their self-serving motives, the Soviet's actions resulted in a positive externality for the ethnic groups – namely, official support for the native languages and cultures of the Chuvash, Komi, Komi-Permyaks, Mordvinians, Mari, Udmurts, and Bashkirs.

Whereas prior to the Revolution one could hardly speak of nationalism as a process among any of the Middle Volga peoples (with the sole exception of some of the Tatar elite), the establishment of national autonomies bearing the names of the various indigenous peoples, the promotion of native literary languages, the development of native elite, and a well-educated populace, served to create "modern nations." There is no question today that there are distinct Bashkir, Mari, Chuvash, and Udmurt peoples, and that there is a far stronger sense of self identity among them today than existed prior to the Revolution of 1917. Only among the Tatars is there a strong antagonism toward the Soviet regime on account of the Tatar sentiment that they were not able to fulfill their destiny in becoming a great nation, and that all surrounding peoples were supported "over them."

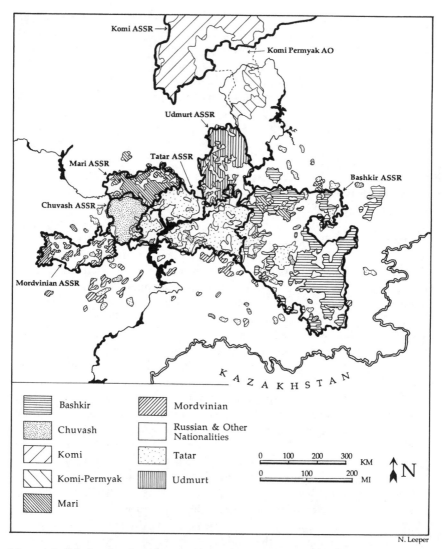

Map 4.2 Ethnic distribution of the Middle Volga nationalities. From *Mira* (Moscow, 1968).

The Soviets hindered the progress of Tatarization through the careful manipulation of official history. Official histories of the Tatars and their ethnic relations point out that the peoples of the Middle Volga were ruthlessly subjugated and brutalized by the Tatar Mongol hordes; exploited shamelessly by Tatar merchants; and forced to practice Islam against their will by Tatar mullahs. They were "liberated" from this heartless oppression only by the grace and benevolence of the Russian people, Tsarist officials, and the new Soviet government.[28]

Historiography, in general, has been an important component of ethnic relations in the USSR. The Tatars, specifically, resent the depiction of both their ancestors and themselves in officially sanctioned history books. While the Russians point to a lack of civilization and culture among the Tatars in their own history books, Tatars emphasize that among the words borrowed by the Russians from a people ostensibly uncivilized and illiterate are *karandash* and *bumaga* – words for black stone (graphite pencil), and paper.

They object to the negative descriptions of not only their activities in the Middle Volga, Kazakhstan, and Central Asia, but also their conquest of Kiev and Russia itself. The Tatars freely admit to their Mongol ancestors' having conquered other peoples, but they prefer to characterize their rule as a period of benevolent empire and not ruthless oppression. They view themselves as builders of civilization, improving the lives of the less-advanced peoples much as the Europeans, Japanese, and Chinese tried to do with their empires. There is some evidence to support this point of view, as during the 300 years of Tatar rule over what is now central Russia and Ukraine, Slavs were permitted to maintain their languages, religious practices (in fact, about 200 Russian Orthodox monasteries were constructed during this time), and local leaders – a sharp contrast to the rule of the Europeans and the Russians in their own empires.

At a meeting at the Institute of Ethnography in Moscow in the summer of 1985, a number of papers were presented by American and Soviet ethnographers on ethnicity and nationalism. Among the examples presented were the defeat of Native Americans, of the Serbs at Kosovo Polje by the Turks, of the Fall of Kiev to the Tatar Mongols, and of the Tatars by Ivan the Terrible were presented. Although the Soviet scholars present at the meeting were quick to recognize the importance of how history treating the conquests of the Native Americans, Serbs, and Russians produced the rise of nationalism among these same groups, they failed to recognize the same for the rise of Tatar nationalism in their country. They simply did not see a correlation between the depiction of Ivan IV as conqueror of Tataria in the history books (described as the liberation from the Tatar yoke) and the rise of Tatarism.

The official Russian histories depict Ivan IV as a virtual demon. On every issue he is portrayed negatively, except on the unification of Russia and the defeat of the Tatars, for which he is lavishly praised. Although Russians may celebrate Ivan's role in defeating the Tatars of old, Tatars in the Soviet Union were not afforded the opportunity to share in what they consider to be the glorious past of their ancestors: e.g. the defeat of the Kievans, and the establishment of a Tatar empire. Official Soviet histories denigrated the tsars, the Orthodox Church, capitalism, the old Russian aristocracy, and feudalism, they almost always extolled the incorporation of non-Russian lands into the Russian state because it brought Russian language and culture to the "culturally less fortunate" inhabitants. According to official Soviet texts (the only texts sanctioned for publication in the USSR during its existence), the defeat of the Kazan, Astrakhan and the Crimean Tatars was progressive because it brought Russian culture to them. The process of incorporation is always referred to as either liberation from oppression or a benevolent offer of an improved quality of life, neither of which could be refused. At worst, incorporation could be seen as the lesser of two evils, as "enlightened" Russian culture (such as it was) had to be preferable to Tatar "enslavement."

Most of the people of the Middle Volga feel threatened by the increasingly large number of Russians in their midst, a problem that was compounded by the Soviet policy of language assimilation in the schools. Once Soviet power was firmly established, the use of non-Russian language education in the schools within the Russian Federation was curtailed, with only a few exceptions. Until Khrushchev came to power, native languages were widely used along with Russian (a required medium for instruction). With the so-called Khrushchev reform, where people could choose which language schools to send their children to, most Komi, Komi-Permyaks, Udmurts, Mari, and Mordvinians elected to send their children to Russian schools as they perceived their own languages as useless to the future betterment of their children.

Among the Chuvash, the situation was somewhat better as their population is far more compact. The majority of Chuvash lived in the Chuvash ASSR, where they also formed a distinct majority (something that was true for none of the above mentioned peoples). Bashkirs and Tatars were two of the four peoples of the RSFSR (Yakuts and Buryats being the other two) for whom native language education was available through the tenth grade. Clearly this support for the Bashkirs is related to the Soviet desire to prevent their Tatarization through support for their ethnicity, language, and territory.

With Khrushchev much of the former support for ethnic cultures and languages began to diminish as part of a policy promoting ethnicity in the context of "national in form, socialist in content." With this policy came a push for greater assimilation and uniformity. Throughout the Khrushchev era Russian cultural norms and language were pushed and fewer native institutions were promoted. By the time Brezhnev was in power virtually no regular native-language education was available to any of the peoples of the RSFSR other than the Tatars, Bashkirs, Yakuts, and Buryats. Through interviews with members of these groups it became obvious that their autonomies, by the 1960s were in name alone. Official publications like *Pechat' SSSR* or *Vestnik Statistiki*, which indicate the number of books, newspapers, magazines, etc. printed in different languages, give the impression that there is a host of literature available in the languages of this (and other) regions of the USSR. However, when asked about publications and titles in their native languages all informants indicated that few native language newspapers or magazines are, in fact, in those languages. The titles appear in the native language, but the text, for the most part, is in Russian with only a few articles in native tongues. Furthermore, books with titles and title pages in native languages most frequently have their text solely in Russian. Thus in the statistical compilations of data these publications are listed as being in native langauges, but in fact are almost exclusively in Russian. Thus, by the 1960s the Komi, Komi-Permyaks, Udmurts, Mordvinians, and Mari saw the virtual end of support by the state for their cultures.

As the people of the Middle Volga are relatively small in number, live in scattered settlements among other nationalities (especially Russians), and often live outside the autonomies where native language instruction and ethnic institutions are present, they are witnessing the extinction of their respective languages and cultures. Even Bashkirs have expressed deep concern. Through the period of perestroika, Bashkirs in Bukhara, Tashkent, Moscow, and St. Petersburg (Leningrad) openly discussed their concerns about what they characterized as the tenuous situation regarding continued Russian or Soviet support of Bashkir ethnic institutions (native language use in printing, the media, and education, as well as preference in leadership positions in regional government). In the Bashkir ASSR (now Bashkortostan), according to the 1989 census, Bashkirs comprised only about one fifth of the total population, and were outnumbered by both ethnic Tatars and Russians. Bashkirs cite the examples of the other Middle Volga peoples who, from the late 1950s through the early 1970s, lost almost all of their ethnic privileges. Many Bashkirs firmly believed that the same would happen to them when the Soviets no longer felt threatened by the Tatars. As such, the Bashkirs had good reason to maintain close ties (or at least the appearance of such) with the Tatars. This gave them two advantages: (1) it ensured that the Bashkirs would continue to receive high levels of support from the Soviet government and preferential treatment in Bashkortostan, and (2) in the event that Soviet support was withdrawn, an alliance with the Tatars offered the Bashkirs a countervailing force.

The Tatars, too, were keenly aware of their precarious situation. One of the primary problems for the Tatars is that only a very small percentage of the entire Tatar population resides in Tatarstan (according to the 1989 census 1,765,000 Tatars – only 26.5 percent of all Tatars in the USSR). Even if one adds to this the approximately 1,121,000 Tatars who lived at that time in Bashkortostan (the Bashkir ASSR), where they comprised 28.4 percent of that republic's total population, as well as the Tatars of the Chuvash (36,000), Mari (44,000), Mordvinian (47,000), and Udmurt (110,000) ASSRs, one is still only talking about 47.0 percent of all Tatars in the USSR. Adding to this the Tatar population of the entire Middle Volga and its surrounding environs, the total comes to about 4,326,000 Tatars, or still only 65 percent of the Soviet Tatar population.[29] It is not difficult to understand, then, why the Tatars maintain a broader conception of what constitutes their "traditional" territory, and why they have and will continue to strive toward the creation of the Idel Ural state.[30]

This also puts the Tatar leadership in Tatarstan in a dual position. On the one hand, they are the ethnically Tatar (as opposed to the Russian and members of other ethnic communities) leaders of Tatarstan. In this, like other officials they are *Tatarstani* and represent the interests of all citizens of that republic. On the other hand, and in particular with the changes in the Russian Federation since the collapse of the Soviet Union, they are the representatives of the entire Tatar population of all of Russia.

Economic development of the Middle Volga region has been one of the most rapid during the Soviet period. The expansion of transport in the northern part of European Russia and the development of the rich forest and coal resources of these areas resulted in a massive migration of Russians to the Komi region. During World War II many people were sent to develop the resources of the area, and by 1959 the Komi people comprised 30.4 percent of the total population of their homeland while Russians had risen to 48.4 percent (almost half the total population). By 1989 with further development of the Pechora coal fields and related industries and a continued influx of Russians, the Komi came to represent only 23.3 percent (less than one fourth) and the Russians 57.7 percent of the total population of the area.

Similarly, the discovery of oil and natural gas in Tatarstan and Bashkortostan led to great development there as well, and with economic development came a large influx of Russians and other non-natives. World War II, with its shifting of industries eastward from central Russia, led to a rapid development of industries in these two important territories. In addition to petro-chemical industries, machine building and other heavy industrial complexes were expanded, and Tatarstan was targeted for greater development. Here KAMAZ, one of the largest industrial complexes in the entire Soviet Union was located at Naberezhnye Chelny (Brezhnev). Located between a number of important Soviet industrial centers, Tatarstan and Bashkortostan, with their own rich fossil fuel-based industries, could not help but become major centers of Soviet development.

This development, however, was not necessarily a blessing. Russians,

Ukrainians, and other Soviet citizens immigrated by the hundreds of thousands. By 1959 the number of Russians in Tatarstan had grown to 1,252,000 and by 1989 to 1,575,000. In Bashkortostan their relative numbers grew to 1,417,000 in 1959 (compared to only 738,000 Bashkirs), and in 1989 to 1,548,000. Immigration is not the only problem that the Tatars and Bashkirs had to face. Along with it came massive urban development, which totally changed the character of these areas. Needless to say with such rapid urban and industrial development came serious environmental concerns.

In addition to these problems, we must also consider who it was that benefited from this development. All people interviewed of the local populations of Tatarstan and Bashkortostan (this includes all citizens, not just the titular peoples) complained that the revenues generated by the exploitation of the natural resources did not benefit those territories. Repeatedly one heard that less than 1 percent of the revenues generated by the development of Bashkortostan's oil reserves remained in, or were returned to, Bashkortostan. Universally the feeling among the peoples of this region was that Moscow and the Soviets benefited, but that Bashkortostan and Tatarstan lived in poverty.

This played a major role in the post-1991 events as local Russian workers strongly supported their republics' autonomy movements. This was not over ethnic rights, but rather over the desire to improve their lives in their own regions. In this, Russians, Ukrainians, Jews, Udmurts, and Tatars could join together in common cause as citizens of Tatarstan. Here they were all Tatarstanis, Bashkortostanis, and so on. For Tatars and Bashkirs, this was highly advantageous as they could find natural allies in their otherwise dangerous Russian neighbors. Over issues of sovereignty, political autonomy, and economic autonomy Tatars and Russians in Tatarstan, and Bashkirs, Tatars and Russians in Bashkortostan could stand together.

## Demographic trends

In order fully to appreciate the current situation in the Middle Volga, the sense of security (or insecurity) of its various peoples as to their ethnic survivability and other ethno-political issues, it is important to examine their populations and rates of population growth as well as current levels of native language retention.

Population statistics and rates of growth often explain the security peoples feel as nations. In cases of relatively large and rapidly growing populations (e.g. the Uzbeks, whose population increased by 177.4 percent between 1959–1989), there tends to be a relatively high degree of security with respect to their ethnic survivability. In Uzbekistan, the large Uzbek population does not feel threatened by the numerically small numbers of ethnic Russians, regardless of the amount of control they have. Ethnically,

Table 4.1. *Population growth of the peoples of the Middle Volga, 1959–1989 (in 1000s)*

| Nationality | 1959 | 1970 | 1979 | 1989 |
|---|---|---|---|---|
| Tatars | 4,765[a] | 5,931[a] | 6,185 | 6,646 |
| Chuvash | 1,470 | 1.694 | 1,751 | 1,839 |
| Bashkirs | 989 | 1,240 | 1,371 | 1,449 |
| Mordvinians | 1,285 | 1,263 | 1,192 | 1,154 |
| Udmurts | 625 | 704 | 714 | 776 |
| Mari | 504 | 599 | 622 | 670 |
| Komi | 287 | 322 | 327 | 345 |
| Komi-Permyaks | 144 | 153 | 151 | 152 |

[a] In the 1959 and 1970 censuses, no distinction was made between Volga and Crimean Tatars. The Tatar population in this table for 1959 and 1970 includes the Crimean Tatars as well.

the survivability of Uzbeks was not in question. Conversely, where a group has a relatively small population and a low rate of natural increase (e.g. the Estonians increased only 0.7 percent between 1959 and 1989) they feel threatened. Ethnic security is at risk in Estonia, where the Estonians feel directly threatened by the presence of large numbers of ethnic Russians whose immigration threatens their already precarious existence as a distinct group with control over their own national territory.

Table 4.2 reflects the population change among the peoples of the Middle Volga region from 1959 to 1989. (The figures for Russians, Latvians, Estonians, and Uzbeks are used for comparisons). Tables 4.1 and 4.2 illustrate one major demographic obstacle for many of the peoples of this region. Only the Tatars, Chuvash, Bashkirs, and Mordvinians had populations equal to or greater than one million persons in 1989. The Udmurts and Mari had between three-quarters and two-thirds of a million persons, and the Komi and Komi-Permyaks only totalled about half a million persons. Table 4.2 indicates the rates at which these populations have grown between the 1959 and the 1989 census periods. The Bashkirs and Tatars experienced relatively high rates of growth (46.5 percent and 39.5 percent respectively); the Mari (32.9 percent), Chuvash (25.1 percent), and Komi (20.2 percent) experienced moderate growth; and the Komi-Permyaks (5.6 percent) and Mordvinians (−10.2 percent) saw markedly low rates of expansion.

Table 4.2 also indicates that between 1979–1989, all of the peoples of the Middle Volga experienced a rapid decline in rates of population growth. To some extent, the lower figures reflect not only a shrinking birth rate but also a recently-intensified degree of Russian assimilation (especially

Table 4.2. *Percent rates of population change among selected Soviet nationalities, 1959–1989*

| Nationality | 1959–1989 | 1979–1989 |
|---|---|---|
| Tatars | 39.5 | 7.4 |
| Chuvash | 25.1 | 5.0 |
| Bashkirs | 46.5 | 5.7 |
| Mordvinians | −10.2 | −3.2 |
| Udmurts | 19.5 | 4.6 |
| Mari | 32.9 | 7.7 |
| Komi | 20.2 | 5.5 |
| Komi-Permyaks | 5.6 | 0.7 |
| Russians | 27.1 | 5.6 |
| Estonians | 3.8 | 0.7 |
| Latvians | 4.2 | 1.4 |
| Uzbeks | 177.4 | 34.0 |

among the Komi-Permyaks and the Mordvinians). Similarly, the lower rate of growth among the Bashkirs may represent a significant level of Tatar assimilation (especially in the western part of Bashkortostan, where Tatars form a distinct majority, and where historically there was a high rate of Tatarization). For all of the peoples examined, the annual rate of natural population growth for the period 1979–1989 is below 1 percent, and only the Mari and Tatars experienced rates which are analytically significant.

It is also important to examine patterns of population distribution. With few exceptions, a member of an ethnic group was not entitled to native language education, media, or other materials which promote the preservation of native language culture, when residing outside that person's own ethnic republic. The only exception in the Middle Volga are the Tatars, who had ethnic institutions throughout the Soviet period in both the Tatar and Bashkir republics. Table 4.3 indicates the percentage of each ethnic group residing within the borders of its respective ethnic autonomy in 1959 and 1989. The figures provided for the 1959 and 1989 census indicate a universal decline in all cases of peoples residing within the borders of their respective republics. The most significant changes are those of the Komi-Permyaks (87.5 percent to only 62.5 percent), the Bashkirs (74.6 percent to 59.6 percent), and the Udmurts (76.2 percent to 66.5 percent). Only among the Tatars, the Mordvinians, and the Komi was this change not significant. Furthermore, only the Komi (84.6 percent) have a significant majority residing within its own republic, and only the Komi-Permyaks, Bashkirs, and Udmurts have 60 percent or more of their people residing within their homelands. Among the Chuvash and Mari, the percentage was

Table 4.3. *Population (in 1000s) and percent of total population of each nationality residing within its own autonomy, 1959 and 1989*

| Nationality | Population (in 1000s) | | Percent | |
|---|---|---|---|---|
| | 1959 | 1989 | 1959 | 1989 |
| Tatars | 1,345 | 1,765 | 27.1 | 26.5 |
| Chuvash | 770 | 907 | 52.4 | 49.2 |
| Bashkirs | 738 | 864 | 74.6 | 59.6 |
| Mordvinians | 358 | 313 | 27.9 | 27.1 |
| Udmurts | 476 | 497 | 76.2 | 66.5 |
| Mari | 279 | 324 | 55.4 | 48.3 |
| Komi | 245 | 292 | 85.4 | 84.6 |
| Komi-Permyaks | 126 | 95 | 87.5 | 62.5 |

slightly less than 50 percent, and among the Mordvinians a mere 27.1 percent. The situation of the Tatars is slightly more complicated since they have enjoyed ethnic rights in both Bashkortostan and Tatarstan.

Given such a dispersed population, and coupling this with the fact that outside their own autonomies the members of these Middle Volga ethnic groups were not entitled to ethnic institutions of their own, their situations are precarious. To this we must add that by the early 1960s the use of Komi, Komi-Permyak, Mari, Mordvinian, Udmurt, and Chuvash was eliminated as a medium of instruction in the schools even within their own republics. In all, there is a tremendous pressure on these peoples to shift to the use of Russian as the primary language of daily life. The native languages were offered only as electives in the school system.

Only among the Tatars and Bashkirs has native language education been available through the tenth grade (the same level as was available to Belarusans and Ukrainians in their republics). The situation of the Mordvinians and the Mari is particularly bad as a high proportion of their populations reside outside of their native territories (about three quarters of the Mordvinians and half of the Mari); and in both cases their native language is divided into two non-mutually intelligible dialects, which means that there are very few people able to preserve either of them. To make matters worse, in most cases, even within these so-called ethnic homelands the titular group is not in the majority. The Mordvinians, for example, comprise only 32.5 percent of their autonomy. Similar statistics are present in the Komi autonomy, where hundreds of thousands of Russians have flocked to the rich forests and Pechora coal fields. All of these peoples thus live in isolated territories in which power is vested in the surrounding Russian majority (and often in Moscow itself) and not with the titular nationality groups.

Table 4.4 indicates the distribution of peoples in the Middle Volga and adjacent territories (oblasts) in 1959 and 1989. The names of the oblasts and territories are used here the way they appeared in the 1959 and 1989 published census volumes for the reader's convenience and reference (the new names appear in parentheses). One can see both the extent of population dispersion among the various ethnicities and the degree to which they form tiny enclaves surrounded by great numbers of Russians. This pattern suggests that the promotion and retention of native language and culture is problematic. Also, although the table states that the Russians actually form a minority in the Komi-Permyak Autonomous Oblast (AO), the situation is somewhat misleading. The Komi-Permyak AO is relatively small in both size and population, and is a division of Perm Oblast, which as a whole contains 2.6 million Russians and only 123,371 Komi-Permyaks. In fact, in 1989, Perm Oblast contained more Tatars (150,460) than Komi-Permyaks.

In both 1959, and 1989 the titular groups of the Middle Volga, with the exceptions of only the Tatars, Chuvash, and Komi-Permyaks, were out-numbered within their own territories by ethnic Russians. The only significant change that took place between these two years was that in the Bashkir ASSR (Bashkortostan), the combined population of the Tatars and Bashkirs rose to slightly over 50 percent of the population. Even there, however, the Russians out-numbered either the Bashkirs or the Tatars as separate groups. Only in the Chuvash ASSR (Chuvashia) and the Komi-Permyak AO are the titular group in a significant majority position (68.8 percent for the Chuvash and 59.7 percent for the Komi-Permyaks). In 1989 the titular groups in all other cases comprised less than 50 percent of the total populations within their own autonomies. In some, like the Bashkirs in Bashkortostan (21.9 percent), the Mordvinians in Mordvinia (32.5 percent), the Udmurts in Udmurtia (30.9 percent), and the Komi in their republic (23.3 percent), the titular groups comprised less than one third of the total population of their own autonomies. It must also be considered that the more ethnically mixed a region is, the greater the use of Russian as a common language will be. When Russians, Ukrainians, Lithuanians, Chuvash, Jews, and Bashkirs live together they all use Russian as a means of common communication. Thus, the influence of Russians and their language is much higher than their mere statistical presence in a given territory would suggest.

Table 4.4 also indicates the great Russian presence that exists throughout the Middle Volga and adjacent areas. In all of the oblasts (i.e., non-autonomous national territories), the Russians comprised a minimum of 72 percent of the local populations. More important is their total population in these oblasts – 21,297,000. Adding the total population of ethnic Russians within the autonomies of the region themselves (5,946,000) to those in the surrounding oblasts, their population of 27,243,000 in 1989 gives them total dominance over the "island" populations of these relatively

Table 4.4. *Population (in 1000s) and percent of total population of select nationalities in Middle Volga administrative units, 1959 and 1989*

| Nationality | Population (in 1000s) | | Percent | |
| --- | --- | --- | --- | --- |
| | 1959 | 1989 | 1959 | 1989 |
| **Tatar ASSR (Tatarstan)** | **2,850** | **3,642** | | |
| Tatars | 1,345 | 1,765 | 47.2 | 48.5 |
| Russians | 1,252 | 1,575 | 43.9 | 43.2 |
| Chuvash | 144 | 134 | 5.0 | 3.7 |
| Mordvinians | 33 | 29 | 1.2 | 0.8 |
| Udmurts | 23 | 25 | 0.8 | 0.7 |
| **Chuvash ASSR (Chuvashia)** | **1,098** | **1,334** | | |
| Chuvash | 770 | 907 | 70.2 | 68.0 |
| Russians | 264 | 357 | 24.0 | 26.8 |
| Tatars | 31 | 36 | 2.9 | 2.7 |
| Mordvinians | 24 | 19 | 2.2 | 1.4 |
| **Bashkir ASSR (Bashkortostan)** | **3,340** | **3,943** | | |
| Bashkirs | 738 | 864 | 22.1 | 21.9 |
| Russians | 1,417 | 1,548 | 42.4 | 39.3 |
| Tatars | 769 | 1,121 | 23.0 | 28.4 |
| Chuvash | 110 | 119 | 3.3 | 3.0 |
| Mari | 94 | 106 | 2.8 | 2.7 |
| Mordvinians | 44 | n/a | 1.3 | n/a |
| Udmurts | 25 | n/a | 0.8 | n/a |
| **Mordvinian ASSR (Mordovia)** | **1,000** | **964** | | |
| Mordvinians | 358 | 313 | 35.8 | 32.5 |
| Russians | 591 | 386 | 59.1 | 40.0 |
| Tatars | 39 | 47 | 3.9 | 4.9 |
| **Udmurt ASSR (Udmurtia)** | **1,337** | **1,606** | | |
| Udmurts | 476 | 497 | 35.6 | 30.9 |
| Russians | 759 | 945 | 56.8 | 58.8 |
| Tatars | 72 | 110 | 5.4 | 6.8 |
| Mari | 6 | 10 | 0.4 | 0.6 |
| **Mari ASSR (Mari El)** | **648** | **749** | | |
| Mari | 279 | 324 | 43.1 | 43.3 |
| Russians | 310 | 356 | 47.8 | 47.5 |
| Tatars | 39 | 44 | 6.0 | 5.9 |
| Chuvash | 9 | n/a | 1.4 | n/a |
| Udmurts | 2 | n/a | 0.4 | n/a |
| **Komi ASSR (The Komi Republic)** | **806** | **1,251** | | |
| Komi | 245 | 292 | 30.4 | 23.3 |
| Russians | 390 | 722 | 48.4 | 57.7 |
| Tatars | 8 | 26 | 1.1 | 2.1 |
| Chuvash | 3 | 11 | 0.4 | 0.9 |

Table 4.4. *(cont.)*

| | Population (in 1000s) | | Percent | |
|---|---|---|---|---|
| Nationality | 1959 | 1989 | 1959 | 1989 |
| **Perm Oblast** | **2,993** | **3,091** | | |
| Russians | 2,420 | 2,595 | 80.9 | 83.9 |
| Tatars | 166 | 150 | 5.5 | 4.9 |
| Komi-Permyaks | 136 | 123 | 4.5 | 4.0 |
| Bashkirs | 40 | 52 | 1.3 | 1.7 |
| Udmurts | 22 | 33 | 0.7 | 1.1 |
| Chuvash | 15 | n/a | 0.5 | n/a |
| Of which: | | | | |
| **Komi-Permyak AO** | **217** | **159** | | |
| Komi-Permyaks | 126 | 95 | 58.1 | 59.7 |
| Russians | 71 | 57 | 32.7 | 35.8 |
| Tatars | 6 | n/a | 2.8 | n/a |
| **Gorkiy Oblast** | **3,591** | **3,720** | | |
| Russians | 3,382 | 3,522 | 94.2 | 94.7 |
| Tatars | 67 | 59 | 1.9 | 1.6 |
| Mordvinians | 64 | 37 | 1.8 | 1.0 |
| **Kirov Oblast** | **1,916** | **1,694** | | |
| Russians | 1,761 | 1,532 | 91.9 | 90.4 |
| Mari | 53 | 44 | 2.8 | 2.6 |
| Tatars | 41 | 46 | 2.1 | 2.7 |
| Udmurts | 22 | 23 | 1.1 | 1.4 |
| **Ulyanov Oblast** | **1,117** | **1,396** | | |
| Russians | 869 | 1,017 | 77.8 | 72.9 |
| Tatars | 97 | 159 | 8.7 | 11.4 |
| Mordvinians | 73 | 61 | 6.5 | 4.4 |
| Chuvash | 60 | 117 | 5.4 | 8.4 |
| **Penza Oblast** | **1,510** | **1,505** | | |
| Russians | 1,312 | 1,296 | 86.9 | 86.1 |
| Mordvinians | 109 | 86 | 7.2 | 5.7 |
| Tatars | 62 | 81 | 4.1 | 5.4 |
| Chuvash | 6 | n/a | 0.4 | n/a |
| **Kuibyshev Oblast** | **2,258** | **3,263** | | |
| Russians | 1,848 | 2,720 | 81.8 | 83.4 |
| Mordvinians | 115 | 116 | 5.1 | 3.6 |
| Chuvash | 102 | 117 | 4.5 | 3.6 |
| Tatars | 74 | 114 | 3.3 | 3.5 |
| **Orenburg Oblast** | **1,829** | **2,171** | | |
| Russians | 1,297 | 1,568 | 70.9 | 72.2 |
| Tatars | 121 | 159 | 6.6 | 7.3 |
| Mordvinians | 95 | 69 | 5.2 | 3.2 |

Table 4.4. *(cont.)*

| Nationality | Population (in 1000s) | | Percent | |
|---|---|---|---|---|
| | 1959 | 1989 | 1959 | 1989 |
| Bashkirs | 30 | 53 | 1.6 | 2.4 |
| Chuvash | 21 | 21 | 1.1 | 1.0 |
| **Chelyabinsk Oblast** | **2,977** | **3,618** | | |
| Russians | 2,372 | 2,930 | 79.7 | 81.0 |
| Tatars | 190 | 225 | 6.4 | 6.2 |
| Bashkirs | 88 | 161 | 3.0 | 4.4 |
| Mordvinians | 31 | n/a | 1.0 | n/a |
| Chuvash | 11 | n/a | 0.4 | n/a |
| **Sverdlovsk Oblast** | **4,044** | **4,707** | | |
| Russians | 3,560 | 4,177 | 88.0 | 88.7 |
| Tatars | 158 | 184 | 3.9 | 3.9 |
| Mari | 20 | 31 | 0.5 | 0.7 |
| Mordvinians | 18 | n/a | 0.4 | n/a |
| Bashkirs | 15 | 42 | 0.4 | 0.9 |
| Chuvash | 15 | n/a | 0.4 | n/a |

small Middle Volga peoples. Even the Tatar population, the only people of the Middle Volga with a sizeable population, in this region totalled only 4,326,000 and pales in comparison with that of the Russians. In addition, the Middle Volga and adjacent regions are completely surrounded on all sides by more ethnically Russian territories. Even the nearby parts of north-western Kazakhstan have a huge Russian majority.

Russian domination of the Middle Volga does not merely consist of numerical superiority. Most decisions concerning major economic issues, policies regarding education and media, and virtually all other important matters for the seventy years of Soviet rule were made in Moscow and not locally. In addition, under Soviet rule, Russians controlled virtually all industry and commerce. Even when a "local" was in charge who was of "native origin," the real decision-making power was in Moscow or in a ministry far away and under Russian control.

Russian was the official language, and Russian culture was promoted both officially and through practical realities of daily life. Little, if any, educational or media materials were available in native languages. Even the Tatars and Bashkirs, who did have access to native language education, often sent their children to Russian schools because the quality of native language schools was markedly inferior, and because attending Russian schools would allow their children greater opportunity to succeed in the Russian-dominated society. There was a strong bias on many levels against

Table 4.5. *Total populations (1000s) of select nationalities in the Middle Volga and surrounding areas, 1989*

|  | 1989 | |
|---|---|---|
|  | In autonomies | In entire region |
| Russians | 5,946 | 27,243 |
| Tatars | 3,149 | 4,326 |
| Chuvash | 1,171 | 1,426 |
| Bashkirs | 864 | 1,172 |
| Mordvinians | 361 | 730 |
| Udmurts | 522 | 578 |
| Mari | 430 | 505 |
| Komi | 292 | 292 |
| Komi-Permyaks | 95 | 123 |

Based on population statistics available in the 1989 census.

those who were raised in "native schools." Although it was officially claimed that these children were not prepared for various jobs (either because they did not speak Russian well enough, or their technical skills were too low), this was also a less than subtle way of encouraging parents to acculturate their children to Great Russian language and culture. This parallels in some ways the distinct bias against children whose parents taught their children religion or who went to churches or other religious institutions. It is important to note that even in the native language schools some subjects, such as science, mathematics, and ideology were available only in Russian, and the so-called native language schools would best be referred to as bilingual schools.[31]

The rates of linguistic Russification – the process by which individuals shift to speaking Russian as their primary language – and ethnic Russification – the process by which non-Russians acculturate to the point that they take on Russian ethnic identity – are relatively high among those Eastern Orthodox peoples in close cultural contact with the Russians and for whom Russian language and culture represented "high" culture in society. This is true for the Mordvinians, Udmurts, Komi and Komi-Permyaks, as all of these Finnic peoples share common cultural traits with the Russians. A weaker Russian influence was in evidence among the Mari, as they are not Eastern Orthodox and lack the same cultural ties to Russian culture as do the other Finnic peoples mentioned above. However, by 1989 the rate of Russification even among the Mari had become significant.

The Chuvash are one of the most interesting peoples in this regard, as they form a transition between Eastern Orthodox Russians and Finnic peoples on the one hand and Turkic Moslem Tatars on the other.

Table 4.6. *Native language retention among the Middle Volga*
*nationalities (i.e. percentage considering the language of their own*
*people to be their native tongue), 1959 and 1989*

| Nationality | 1959 | 1970 | 1979 | 1989 |
|---|---|---|---|---|
| Tatars | 92.1 | 89.2 | 85.9 | 83.2 |
| Chuvash | 90.8 | 86.9 | 81.7 | 76.4 |
| Bashkirs | 61.9 | 66.2 | 67.0 | 72.3 |
| Mordvinians | 78.1 | 77.8 | 72.6 | 67.1 |
| Udmurts | 89.1 | 82.6 | 76.4 | 69.6 |
| Mari | 95.1 | 91.2 | 86.7 | 80.8 |
| Komi | 89.3 | 82.7 | 76.2 | 70.4 |
| Komi-Permyaks | 87.6 | 85.8 | 77.1 | 70.1 |

Historically, the Chuvash formed the base on which the modern Tatar
nation was formed (Volga Bolgars), and from them the Tatars adopted
Islam. The western Bolgars, as was previously discussed, rejected Islam and
adopted Eastern Orthodoxy under the auspices of the Russians and the
Russian Orthodox church, who supported them in order to prevent their
Tatarization. The Chuvash, then, derive a strong identity from their Bolgar
past which makes them dissimilar from the Russian people, and although
they feel no strong ties to the Tatars, there is a historical bond between
these peoples. In spite of this, by using native language retention as a measure, they now display a significantly lower level of linguistic assimilation
than do most of the other Middle Volga peoples. They continue to form
a distinct majority in their own republic (68 percent in 1989), and Chuvashia has the lowest relative Russian population of any ethnic territory in
the region (only 26.8 percent).

A clear trend in native language retention is discernable among virtually
all of the peoples of the region. Between 1959 and 1989 there was a significant decline among members of each group listing the language of their
own nationality as their first language. There was also a corresponding
increase in the percentage of peoples declaring Russian to be their native
tongue. In all cases except that of the Bashkirs, the levels of native language
retention fell significantly between 1959 and 1989. The level of decline
ranged from 11 percent among the Mordvinians to 18.9 percent among
the Komi.[32]

The statistics on the Bashkirs are indicative of the success of Soviet
nationality policy in preventing their Tatarization. As was discussed above,
the Russians actively pursued policies designed to prevent the spread of
Tatar influence. As a result, they not only created the Bashkir ASSR, they
also created a Bashkir literary language in 1923 and promoted educational
use of this language to a greater extent than all but three other languages

of the RSFSR (Tatar, Yakut and Buryat). A strong policy of affirmative action toward Bashkirs during the Soviet period was also important in the push for a developed, distinctly Bashkir, people and identity. Bashkirs, more than most other peoples of the RSFSR, benefited from a policy of elevating individuals based on their ethnic background (identity) to leadership positions on a local level. This also helped preserve Bashkir as an important language in Bashkortostan. The Bashkirs thus have been very proprietary where their language is concerned, and the percent of Bashkirs listing their native tongue as primary rose from 61.9 percent in 1959 to 72.3 percent in 1989.

It is interesting to note, however, that the rate of linguistic assimilation among Bashkirs is higher within their republic than without. This would seem to indicate that although Bashkir language and culture are strong and important influences, they are still heavily affected by the presence of large numbers of Tatars in Bashkortostan; in fact, almost exactly as many Tatars as Bashkirs lived in Bashkortostan in 1989. That there are few Bashkirs living in the Tatarstan is further evidence of the potency of the Tatar assimilation influence over the closely related Bashkirs.

In general, however, language retention rates within the various Middle Volga republics tend to be higher than those outside these regions. In 1989, the Tatar ASSR could boast one of the highest rates of native language retention (96.6 percent of all Tatars in Tatarstan declared Tatar their native language). Among the other peoples in 1989 it ranged from 88.5 percent among the Mordvinians in Mordvinia to 74.4 percent among the Komi in their republic. Nonetheless, the proportion of the populations among the Middle Volga nationalities maintaining their own native languages has eroded greatly since 1979 (see tables 4.6 and 4.7). Among the Mordvinians and Komi, in the ten year period from 1979 to 1989, the proportion of members living in their republics and speaking their own languages as native tongues declined, respectively, from 93.8 percent to 74.4 percent and from 97.3 percent to 88.5 percent.

Indicators of native language retention for the Middle Volga nationalities in the USSR on the whole in 1989 also show significant levels of native language loss in all cases except among the Bashkirs and Russians. These figures, coupled with the high rate of peoples living outside the borders of their own republics (see table 4.3) indicate a fairly high rate of denationalization among all of the non-Turkic culturally Moslem peoples of the region.

Given the demographic factors of relatively low birth rates and widely dispersed populations coupled with the presence of large numbers of non-natives (Russians and others) living among them, it is not surprising to find that the native languages of the Finnic speaking peoples of the Middle Volga are in decline. In practical terms, knowledge of Russian and its use in daily affairs is far more a reality for these peoples than it ever was for Estonians, Uzbeks, or Georgians in their respective republics. Realistically

Table 4.7. *Percentage of native language retention among the Middle Volga nationalities within their respective autonomy (1979, 1989) and within the USSR (1989)*

| Nationality | In own autonomy | | In USSR |
|---|---|---|---|
| | 1979 | 1989 | 1989 |
| Tatars | 98.9 | 96.6 | 83.2 |
| Chuvash | 97.6 | 85.0 | 76.4 |
| Bashkirs | 57.7[a] | 74.7[b] | 72.3 |
| Mordvinians | 97.3 | 88.5 | 67.1 |
| Udmurts | 93.2 | 75.7 | 69.6 |
| Mari | 97.8 | 88.4 | 80.8 |
| Komi | 93.8 | 74.4 | 70.4 |
| Komi-Permyaks | 92.2 | 82.9 | 70.1 |

[a] Within their own autonomy, 1.0 percent considered Russian and 41.4 percent considered Tatar to be their native language.
[b] Within their own autonomy, 4.6 percent considered Russian and 20.7 percent considered another language of the USSR (most Tatar) to be their native language.

speaking, it is only the Tatars and Bashkirs who at the time of the 1991 coup were in any position to have strong national cultures and native language institutions. Russian dominated "Democratic" opposition united around Boris Yeltsin.[33] On the one hand, TOTs supported political democratization, private property, and the privatization of public property; on the other hand, it also promoted a specifically Tatar agenda calling for the creation of a unified Tatar school system, as well as the creation of an independent Tatar Academy of Sciences. More importantly, it embraced the principle of the sovereignty of the Tatar people, demanding a referendum to be put before all the peoples of Tatarstan. It also called for the creation of a national congress for all Tatars in the USSR as a means of asserting Tatar national sovereignty. TOTs also passed resolutions calling for the defence of the rights of the Tatar population of Bashkortostan, and the strengthening of Islam among Tatars.[34]

The Declaration of Sovereignty of Tatarstan taken by the parliament of Tatarstan in August of 1990 had little immediate effect on the region's political situation, but was a strong encouragement for the creation of new Tatar political organizations. By the end of 1990, a number of new Tatar political parties had formed, and had more agendas directed towards more specific constituencies. These included the Union of Tatar Youths, named *Azatlyk* which was essentially the youth wing of TOTs and the Tatar Party of National Rebirth (*Ittifak*), which had a strong Islamic focus, and which called directly for an independent Tatar state, and the primacy of the Tatar language in Tatarstan. Other groups with more cultural agendas also came into being at this time. Among these were the *Iman*, the Tatar youth wing of the Association for Islamic Culture in Eastern Europe, which called for the return and reconstruction of destroyed mosques and support for Islamic cultural institutions. Another such group was the Bulghar National Congress, which developed out of the Club for the Supporters of Bulghar Culture, and transformed their agenda for the promotion of Bulghar identity into a political one.[35]

As the authority of the Communist Party gradually declined in Tatarstan in late 1990 and throughout 1991, the Tatar national movement came to perceive their chief foes as the Russian democrats. Led by Boris Yeltsin, the Russian democrats supported independence movements in the various Union Republics, especially in the Baltic republics, as a way of weakening the authority of the Communist-dominated Soviet Union. However, they strongly opposed similar movements within the administrative base of their power, the Russian Federation, especially that of the Tatars, which was particularly energetic.

With the final collapse of the Soviet Union in December 1991, the Tatar national movement was faced with a daunting political situation. The Tatar Republic had become a part of an independent Russian Federation, in which the status of the former Soviet Autonomous Republics was far from clear. Whereas in the former Soviet Union, Russians had made up slightly more than half of the overall population, in the Russian Federation they numbered over 80 percent of the population. Furthermore, the balancing force of the regional Communist Party, in which Tatars were well represented, was now gone, and the Tatars were left to face the Russian democrats alone. The Russian democrats, naturally, expressed concerns for the rights of Russians in Tatarstan, who constituted nearly half of the population.

In early 1992, the Russian Federal government proposed the signature of a Federation Treaty between the federal government and the various "national" republics. Tatarstan, Ingushetia, and Chechnya refused to sign, and instead, in March of 1992 the long-debated referendum was held on the "sovereignty" of Tatarstan.[36] The period before the referendum was politically tense, but nowhere in Tatarstan, or elsewhere in the Volga region, did political conflicts turn violent. This restraint is possibly attributable to the historical lack of overt ethnic conflict in the Middle Volga region, as well as to the powerful and unsettling impression left by the ethnic violence in Moldova, the Caucasus, and Central Asia. In any case, the referendum passed by a small majority, supported by the vast majority of Tatars, most of the small, but electorally important Chuvash and Mari communities, and by a small percentage of Russian voters as well, who saw the referendum as a means of diminishing Moscow's central authority and asserting more local control over resources.

The Tatar nationalists and the Russian democrats disagreed on the significance of the resolution, the former saying it was an endorsement of Tatarstan's independence, and the latter saying it was too vaguely worded to mean anything. In reality, the results convinced the Parliament of Tatarstan to pursue a policy that would not take the politically perilous step of unilaterally announcing independence, but would nevertheless retain the claim to real autonomy as a means of extracting concessions from the Federal government, thereby maintaining local elites' control over the republic's resources. As a result of Yeltsin's political problems, including the parliamentary electoral victory of the Communists and Vladimir Zhirinovsky in December 1993, this policy was able to bear fruit; in February 1994, Tatarstan signed a bilateral treaty with the Russian Federation which established a formal fiscal relationship between the Federation and Tatarstan. This ability to extract a bilateral treaty set an important precedent for Russia's other "national" republics.

## Bashkortostan

Bashkortostan is the most ethnically diverse republic in the Middle Volga region, and its political activity has been strongly influenced by the region's ethnic and historical particularities. In 1989 the republic's titular nationality, the Bashkirs, comprised only 22 percent of the republic's population, with Russians making up 39 percent and Tatars 28 percent.[37] As a result, each of the three groups has formed its own cultural and political organization and has remained suspicious of the others. In addition to these three major nationalities, the republic's Mari, Chuvash, German, Jewish, Ukrainian, Greek, and Azerbaijani communities have also formed their own cultural and political organizations.[38]

Bashkortostan's Party apparatus was traditionally less receptive to perestroika and glasnost than Tatarstan's, and this peculiarity inhibited the development of independent political activity. The first independent cultural organization to emerge in Bashkortostan was the "Shtern" Jewish Cultural Club in July of 1988. Of more significance in terms of local national politics was the formation of the Ufa branch of the Tatar Cultural Club, formed in November of 1988, which in January 1989 became the Tatar Public Center (TOTs) of the Bashkir republic.[39] The Bashkir Republic's branch of TOTs was especially vocal on issues concerning the republic's Tatar minority, which actually formed the majority of the republic's Muslim population. These protests on the part of the Tatars in part addressed the republic's Soviet political arrangement, dating from the formation of the Bashkir Republic in the 1920s, in which Bashkir elite, as representatives of the republic's titular nationality, retained political and economic privileges.

In response to the well organized and articulate Tatar political activity, the Bashkirs formed a cultural organization in March of 1989, called *Ak Tirma* (White Yurt), and an independent political organization in December of 1989, called the Bashkir National Center (BNTs) *Ural*.[40]

Despite the differences between the Tatar and Bashkir political organizations, both supported and participated in the drafting of Bashkortostan's Declaration of Sovereignty, which was issued by the republic's Supreme Soviet in October of 1990.[41] The declaration was similar to the other declarations of sovereignty made across the Russian Federation in its desire to establish more local control over resources and finances while stopping short of formally declaring independence from the Soviet Union.

The movement toward local sovereignty was especially opposed by leaders of the Russian plurality. As a response to the debates on sovereignty underway in 1990, elements of the Russian population began forming their own political organizations to counter the move toward sovereignty, which they saw as leading toward the break-up of the Soviet Union and Russia and resulting in local independent states politically dominated by non-Russians. Moreover, the Russians were also distressed at the criticism (engendered by the policy of glasnost) of Russia and its historical role in the region. The first Russian organization to emerge was the Ufa Historical and Patriotic Assembly, which was formed in February of 1990. Primarily a cultural organization, in March of 1992 it transformed itself into a more overtly politically-oriented group called the *Rus'* Social Organization.[42]

Ethnic Russian political activity was not limited to *Rus'*, but also included the formation of the Organization of Volga Cossacks in April 1991.[43] Contrary to the popular equation of Cossacks with Slavic groups, there also emerged in Bashkortostan a Muslim Cossack organization as well, called the *Watan* Bashkir Cossack Cultural and Historical Society.[44]

The Declaration of Sovereignty's main consequence in Bashkortostan was the intensification of ethnic politics in the republic. The main Bashkir organizations remained primarily concerned with establishing Bashkir as the republic's official language, and retaining Bashkir cultural autonomy in the republic as well as the Bashkirs' favorable political position. The Tatars, on the other hand, were especially concerned with promoting the cultural and political rights of their own constituency, which they felt had been suppressed during the Soviet era. The Tatars were also encouraged by the energy and success of Tatar organizations in Tatarstan, and by the success of Tatarstan's sovereignty referendum in March of 1992. Political relations between Tatars and Bashkirs could be cooperative at certain levels. For example, in April of 1992 a "round-table" was convened between the leaders of Tatarstan's main pro-independence party, Ittifak, and leaders of the Bashkir National Center, as well as the more independence-oriented Bashkir National Party.[45]

In March of 1992 Bashkortostan, unlike Tatarstan, signed the Federation Treaty with Russia, only, however, after the Bashkir representatives were able to extract provisions from Moscow ensuring more local control over economic matters. In September of 1993, Bashkortostan's parliament refused to recognize Yeltsin's decree dissolving the Russian Parliament, and in December of that year, the Bashkir parliament declared the republic's control over all of its natural resources. Following the example of Tatarstan, Bashkortostan signed a bilateral treaty with Russia in February 1994, superceding the Federation Treaty of 1992. As a result, Bashkortostan was able to extend even more control over its economy and resources.[46]

## Chuvashia

Independent political activity among the Chuvash in the 1990s has been colored by the demographic and historical peculiarities of this, the third largest nationality in the Russian Federation. As we have seen, by the early twentieth century Chuvash national identity was largely expresssed in terms of identification with Eastern Orthodoxy, and in a wider sense this association with Russia has had an effect on post-Soviet political expression as well. Specifically, the Chuvash have avoided the adversarial stance toward the Russian Federation that has been more characteristic of the Tatar national movement.

Moreover, because the Chuvash form a large majority within their titular republic, they have been able to avoid the political marginalization experienced by the Mordvin, and to a lesser degree, Mari national movements. Roughly half of the overall Chuvash population resides outside of the borders of Chuvashia proper, and the large Chuvash communities in Tatarstan and Bashkortostan are also politically active, both in the context of local republican politics, and within the larger common Chuvash organizations.

Before the collapse of the Soviet Union in December of 1991, the political leadership of the Chuvash Republic took steps similar to those undertaken in the other national republics of the Middle Volga. In October 1990, the Supreme Soviet of the Chuvash republic announced a "declaration of state sovereignty," and adopted a new constitution early in 1991.[47]

One of the early Chuvash national organizations was the Chuvash Social and Cultural Center headquartered in Cheboksary, the Chuvash capital. The Center was already active before the collapse of the Soviet Union and published a newspaper entitled *Vuchakh*. A unified independent Chuvash national movement emerged after the collapse of the Soviet Union, in response to the new political situation. The Chuvash National Congress was formed in Cheboksary in October of 1992. This organization was formed to articulate and defend the national and cultural interests of the Chuvash people, both within Chuvashia and beyond its border. The primary focus of the group, judging from the proceedings of its constituent meeting, was cultural, and included demands for increased Chuvash-language education, the preservation of national traditions, and the promotion of Chuvash language and publishing.[48]

At the same time, the group also made a number of political demands and articulated their understanding of Chuvashia's status *vis-à-vis* the Russian Federation. With respect to Chuvashia's relations with Russia, the Chuvash National Congress did not call for outright independence from Russia, but devoted considerable attention to the meaning of the 1990 declaration of sovereignty. The Chuvash National Congress declared the origin of Chuvash statehood to have been the formation of Volga Bulgaria in the ninth century, and declared the current Chuvash Republic to be a continuation of Chuvash statehood. More substantively, the Chuvash National Congress called for strengthening the republic's sovereignty by drafting a new constitution that would include a citizenship law and increase local (Chuvash) control over taxation, cultural, and educational policies. The Congress also called for the division of state property in Chuvashia between the Chuvash Republic and the Russian Federation. Essentially, the Chuvash National Congress supported the same sort of relationship with the Russian Federation that the leadership of both Tatarstan and Bashkortostan were working toward: one that came short of formal independence, in which "sovereignty" signified local control by local political and cultural elites over the region's economic and cultural life. The Chuvash National Congress also called for the formation of a special commission for nationality issues to coordinate policy within the government and between the republic's various nationalities.[49]

## Udmurtia

The political situation in Udmurtia developed quite differently from that in Tatarstan and Bashkortostan. The republic's Party apparatus was relatively conservative, and the Udmurt intelligentsia was small, disorganized, and unsure of its position or power. The earliest assertions of Udmurt cultural rights were couched in terms upholding Leninist nationality policy, and until late 1989, Udmurt nationality questions were generally discussed in the Party within the parameters of official glasnost. One of the first independent organizations to form was the "Udmurt Cultural Club," which was founded in the capital of Udmurtia, Izhevsk, in January of 1988 by N. V. Simonov, an engineer. In 1988 and 1989, similar Udmurt organizations appeared elsewhere in Udmurtia, and outside of it as well. At its inception, the Udmurt Cultural Club was primarily concerned with fostering Udmurt culture and self-awareness at the grass-roots level and declined an overt political role.[50] As a result of both rising tensions throughout the Soviet Union and local pressures, in October 1989 the Supreme Soviet of Udmurtia issued a series of directives addressing ethnic concerns in Udmurtia. These directives announced the intention to widen the use of the Udmurt language in public life and increase Udmurt cultural awareness.

However, the directives fell short of addressing the more controversial issue of Udmurt langauge education, which was to become a primary plank of the Udmurt national movement.[51]

In December 1989, a more politically motivated group, the Society for Udmurt Culture, formed. This group sought to unify the various Udmurt cultural clubs and make more coherent and focused policy demands. The Society was primarily concerned with reestablishing Udmurt-langauge education, which had been eliminated in Udmurtia in the 1980's, and with redressing the demographic imbalance between Udmurts and Russians in the republic.[52]

Motivated by local pressures, and by the example of other Union and Autonomous Republics, the Supreme Soviet issued a "Declaration of Sovereignty" in September of 1990, affirming Udmurtia to be a sovereign entity. As in Tatarstan, the main result of this declaration was to encourage Udmurt cultural organizations in the drive for educational and political reform.

In November 1991, the various Udmurt cultural and political organizations convened in Izhevsk for the First All-Union Congress of Udmurts. This congress was attended by delegates from across the Soviet Union, including the Chairman of the Supreme Soviet of Udmurtia, V. K. Tubylov, as well as by representatives of Tatar and Mari organizations located in Udmurtia. The congress led to the formation of a political umbrella organization called "the All-Udmurt Association *Udmurt Kenesh*." The resolutions of the congress included demands for redressing the republic's demographic imbalance and restoring Udmurt-langauge education. Another resolution announced the congress' desire not to secede from Russia.[53]

Soon after the collapse of the Soviet Union in December, 1991, a small Udmurt independence movement developed in Udmurtia. The Society of Udmurt Culture has been the most active in seeking independence, and is supported in this undertaking by the large and well organized Tatar organizations in Udmurtia and Tatarstan. This organization has also actively promoted the resurrection of Udmurt, animist religious traditions by organizing sacrifice festivals.

Nevertheless, the overriding fact in the movement for Udmurt political autonomy is that Udmurts constitute barely 30 percent of the republic's population and many of the most transitional and culturally aware Udmurt communities lie outside of the republic – in Tatarstan, Bashkortostan, and in Perm and Ekaterinburg oblasts, where, ironically, native language education has been retained. This demographic imbalance, where Russians constitute well over half of the population, has resulted in Russian political control over the republic's parliament. Thus, it was understandable that the Udmurt Parliament ratified the Federation Treaty with the Russian Federation in March of 1992. At the same time, the small, but energetic,

Udmurt cultural associations and independence movement will undoubtedly continue to wield a degree of political influence.

## Mordovia

The case of Mordovia offers a sharp contrast to the energetic political activity evident in Tatarstan and Bashkortostan. This contrast indicates the variegated intensity of ethnic politics from one republic to the next in the Middle Volga. Although the Mordvins constitute the largest Finno-Ugric nationality in Russia, and one of the largest nationalities in the Middle Volga region, they nevertheless are perhaps the least consolidated nationality in the area, divided as they are into two ethnic groups that are in many respects distinct. Historically, Mordvins have been the most Russified of the Middle Volga nationalities. In their titular republic they constitute about a third of the population, while the bulk of the Mordvin population at large is scattered in rural communities to the south and east of the republic. In addition, the Mordvin intelligentsia is still relatively small and politically weak.

These demographic and cultural problems are compounded by the political peculiarities of the Mordvin republic. Here, the authorities' opposition to an independent Mordvin national movement is not so much attributable to the large proportion of Russians, since Russians form majorities or pluralities in nearly all of the region's republics. Rather, Mordovia retained one of the most politically conservative Party organizations in Russia. This conservatism can be partially attributed to the presence of a disproportionately large share of prison camps in Mordovia during the Soviet era, in which large numbers of political prisoners were incarcerated from the 1930s.

Despite such obstacles, in April of 1990 representatives of the Mordvin intelligentsia were able to form an independent national movement devoted to defending the interest of the Mordvin nation. This organization took the name the Mordvin *Mastorava* Society for National Rebirth and held its constituent congress in Saransk, the Mordvin capital. The texts of the resolutions taken at the congress were published in Mordvin literary journals and offer insights into the cultural and political concerns of the Mordvin intelligentsia at that time, as well as the sorts of obstacles that this organization faced from local political elites.[54]

The organizers of the congress expressed concerns regarding the social and demographic problems faced by the Mordvins and also protested policies and activities they felt threatened the future of the Mordvin nation as a whole. First and foremost, the participants decried the steady outmigration of Mordvins from their titular republic, the overall decline of the Mordvin population during the Soviet era, and the resultant "national nihilism." They attributed this decline to Soviet policies in general and were critical of local republican authorities for refusing to accept responsibility for this situation, for continuing to pursue "anti-national" policies, and for having "hindered in every possible way the movement's establishment and registration." The leaders of the movement singled out for special criticism the "anti-Erzia and anti-Moksha propaganda" conducted in the Party newspaper *Sovetskaia Mordoviia.*

More concretely, the movement's leaders called for bilingualism within the republic, for Mordvin-language education, for the inclusion of Mordvin history and culture within educational curricula, and for the creation of a department of Finno-Ugric studies within the Mordvin State University. The movement rejected the use of the ethnonym "Mordvin," preferring instead the term "Erzia and Moksha," and called for changing the name of the Mordvin republic to the "Erzia and Moksha republic." It also called for closer cultural ties with Hungary and Finland, and for the return to local control of closed territories within the republic that had been under the authority of the GULag.

Since its formation, however, the Mastorava movement has been unable to substantially influence political debate in Mordovia, which has retained much of its conservative political character.

## Mari El

The political situation in the Mari El republic is in many respects similar to that in Udmurtia. In their titular republic the Maris form only 43 percent of the population, and this proportion is the result of a long decline that occurred over the course of Soviet rule. This decline has been accompanied by a steady Russification of the Maris, and it has been these two factors that are the chief concerns of the Mari independent political organizations (in addition to the lack of political representation for Maris in their own republic, where in 1992, Maris only constituted 20 percent of the deputies in the Mari republic's Supreme Soviet). Despite the Declaration of Sovereignty of the Mari republic taken in October of 1990, all of the republic's official political discourse and higher education has been carried out exclusively in Russian. The language issue has been the primary concern of the main Mari political movement, *Mari Usham*, which has concerned itself with increasing Mari language education.[55]

The cultural situation of the Maris in the Mari republic, whose name the Mari Parliament officially changed to Mari El in early 1992, is further weakened by the fact that the large, and culturally and ethnically conscious Eastern Maris, live outside of the republic, primarily in Bashkortostan.

An interesting aspect of the Mari national movement has been its attempts to revitalize Mari native religious beliefs, despite the fact that the majority of Maris are Eastern Orthodox Christians. This revival is expressed in part by creation of the Sacred *Chimari-osh-mari* Mari Union, a pagan religious organization, which has organized large Mari communal prayers and sacrifices during both the tsarist and Soviet eras.[56] In addition, numerous collections of Mari traditional prayers and incantations are published in the Mari capital, Ioshkar-Ola.[57]

## The Komi Republic

The political and cultural situation of the Komis within their republic is the weakest of all the region's Finno-Ugric peoples. The massive influx of settlers into the region during the course of the Soviet era has reduced the Komi to only 23 percent of their republic's population. The Komi-Permyaks, while constituting a majority within their autonomous region within Perm district, suffer severely from poverty and Russification, which has blunted their own cultural awareness.

Despite the political marginalization of the Komis in their own homelands, they have formed a number of political movements. Komis have been especially active in larger movements comprising the Finno-Ugric peoples in Russia in general. This includes the International Congress of Finno-Ugric Peoples held in the Komi capital Syktyvkar in May of 1992, and sponsored by the Supreme Soviet of the Komi Republic, and the rival, and more independent First All-Russian Meeting of Finno-Ugric Peoples held in Izhevsk in May of 1992.[58]

## Conclusion

The Middle Volga has historically been a borderland between the Inner Asian and European worlds, as well as an economic link along the great Eurasian trade routes and between the worlds of the agriculturalist and the steppe nomad. These peculiarities have contributed greatly to the region's complex ethnic diversity and political history, as well as the millenium-long coexistence in the region of Eastern Orthodox, Islamic, and pagan communities. Until the 1917 Revolution, it was religion which served as the primary means for communal identity in the region. Yet these divisions did not completely inhibit the emergence of a common set of religious ideas and conceptions common to the region's Finno-Ugric and Turkic inhabitants, regardless of religious affiliation.

One of the region's fundamental paradoxes is the impact of the Russian state on the region's Inner Asian inhabitants. On the one hand, Russia has dominated the area politically since the sixteenth century, and demographically since the eighteenth, and the assimilation of the region's Finno-Ugric and Turkic communities has been a recurring policy goal of Russian, and later Soviet administrators. On the other hand, the survival of these communities has been in no small part facilitated by policies enacted by the same Russian and Soviet administrators. These administrators have consciously attempted, and quite often succeeded, in maintaining the region's indigenous Inner Asian religious and communal identities. Of course, the survival and development of these communal and national identities is first and foremost evidence of the flexibility and adaptability of the region's Inner Asian communities.

Today, the Middle Volga is Russia's largest multi-ethnic region, and is home to Russia's largest minority nationalities, including the Tatars, Chuvash, Mordvins, and Bashkirs. As such, there can be little doubt that Russia will continue its historical development as a multi-ethnic state, in which the cultural and political concerns of Russia's minority nationalities will have to be taken into account at the highest levels of the Russian government. Of primary concern to these nationalities is the re-establishment of native language education eliminated during the Brezhnev era. The eventual independence from Russia of the region, or its constituent republics, seems unlikely at present, although by no means unthinkable. The success of Bashkortostan's and Tatarstan's political elites in concluding bilateral treaties with the Russian Federation suggest that these elites have more to gain from remaining within Russia than without it. More decisively, the region's majority Russian population has played, and will continue to play, a central role in the region's political life.

## Notes

1 This *reconquista* is as important in Russian history as that of Spain under Ferdinand and Isabella in Spanish history. The seizure of Kazan symbolized more than the defeat of the Tatars and the liberation of the Russian lands; it marked the beginning of an expansion into Islamic lands that culminated with the seizure of the Crimea, Transcaucasia, the North Caucasus, and the Khanates of Central Asia. This push against Islam also manifested itself in Russian support for liberation movements by various Christian peoples within the Ottoman Empire (Serbs, Bulgars, Greeks, Armenians, Romanians, and others) and a series of wars against Ottoman Turkey in the 19th century.

2 This is a feature which any visitor to the major Russian churches in the Soviet Union could not fail to miss. Indeed, even inside the Kremlin it is the dominant cross figure.

3 S. Steven of Perm both single-handedly converted the Komi peoples to Eastern Orthodoxy and established a Komi liturgy (and thereby a Komi literary language) in the fourteenth century.

4 The success of this policy in preventing the Tatarization of the peoples of the Middle Volga led to its being repeated later in the Baltics, where the Germans, Swedes, and Poles threatedned Russia as a result of their influences on the Finns, Latvians, Lithuanians, and Estonians. Just as early tsars had supported the use of Volga Finnic and other languages to stop the Tatarization of those peoples, with the incorporation of the Baltic region the languages and cultures of the native peoples were supported and promoted so as to weaken Swedish, German and Polish influences. This policy was also applied in the Caucasus region in order both to weaken Persian influence upon the Georgians, Armenians and Azeris, and to prevent the unification of the North Caucasian Moslem peoples into a single, anti-Russian (later Soviet) group. See Ronald Wixman, *Language Aspects of Ethnic Patterns and Processes in the North Caucasus*

(Chicago: University of Chicago Department of Geography Research Series, no. 191, 1980).

5 This system is distinctly different from the French and English systems, which promoted the adoption of their respective languages, religions, and cultures, but which precluded the actual ethnic assimilation of non-Europeans into their nations. Thus, no North African, Asian, or Arab could be considered an Englishman or Frenchman.

6 This was the mechanism by which a great number of Finnic and Baltic peoples were added to the native Russian and Belarusan peoples between the tenth and nineteenth centuries.

7 One of the most interesting manifestations of this conflict was the establishment of Nizhny Novgorod (Gorky) as a trading city to rival the great Tatar trading city of Kazan. It was hoped that the new city would weaken Tatar influence in the Middle Volga, and it proved to be a valuable source of competitive information about the Tatars for the Russian/Soviet governments.

8 For discussions of Kriashen ethnic history, see: Iu. G. Mukhametshin, *Tatary-kriasheny*, (Moscow: Nauka, 1977); F. S. Baiazitova *Govory tatar-kriasheb v sravitel'nom osveshchenii* (Moscow: Nauka, 1986).

9 Cf. A. N. Grigor'ev, "Khristianizatsii nerusskikh narodnostei kak odin iz metodov natsional'no-kolonial'noi politiki tsarizma v Tatarii," *Materialy po istorii Tatarii* I (Kazan: Tatgosizdat, 1948), pp. 226–283; Chantal Lemercier-Quelquejay, Les missions orthodoxes en pays musulmans de moyenne-et basse-volga," *Cahiers du monde russe et sovietique*, 8 (1967), 369–403.

10 Allen J. Frank, "Islamic Regional Identity in Imperial Russia: Tatar and Bashkir Historiography in the Eighteenth and Nineteenth Centuries," Ph.D. dissertation, Indiana University, Bloomington, 1994, pp. 18–48.

11 Thus, for example, while Russian missionaries were likely to see Tatar-speaking Mari communities in Bashkiria, who wore Tatar clothes and spoke Tatar, as becoming part of the tatar Muslim community, the basis for their communal affiliation was most likely Mari animist ancestor spirits and shrines, even this sort of affiliation was not immediately apparent. The exception to this was the Tatar "new converts" (*novokreshchenye*) who had been forcibly baptized in the eighteenth century, but retained Islamic identities and continued to practice Islamic rituals in secret. Members of this group eventually all changed their status back to Muslim by the first decade of the twentieth century.

12 There is a voluminous literature on this aspect of Tatar history see, for example, A. Rorlich, *The Volga Tatars* (Stanford: Hoover Institution Press, 1986); Serge A. Zenkovsky *Pan Turkism and Islam in Russia.* (Cambridge, MA: Harvard University Press, 1967).

13 See N.F. Mokshin, *Etnicheskaia istorii mordvy* (Saransk: Mordovskoe knizhnoe izdatel'stvo, 1977); Tovio Vuorela, *The Finno-Ugric Peoples* (Indiana University Uralic and Altaic Series, Vol. 39, 1964), 221–236.

14 For ethnographic surveys of the Maris, see K. I. Kozlova, *Ocherki etnicheskoi istorii mariiskogo naroda* (Moscow: Izdatel'stvo Moskovskogo Universiteta, 1978); Vuorela, *The Finno-Ugric Peoples*, pp. 237–264.

15 Allen Frank, "Mari-language sources on Mari Practices in the Soviet Period," *Eurasian Studies Yearbook*, 66 (1994), 77–86.

16 For ethnographic and historical surveys of the Udmurts, see V. E. Vladykin and L. S. Khristoliubova, *Ethnografiia udmurtov* (Izhevsk: Udmurtiia, 1991); V. V. Piimenov (ed.), *Udmurty: istoriko-etnograficheskie ocherki* (Izhevsk: UdIIaL IrO RAN, 1993); Vuorela, *The Finno-Ugric Peoples* pp. 265–282; for a study on the Udmurts of Bashkkortostan, see L. S. Khristoliuhova and T. G. Minniiakhmetova, *Udmurty Bashkortostana: istoriia, kul'tura, sovremmenost'* (Ufa: Ministerstvo kul'tury Respubliki Bashkortostan, 1994).

17 Information collected by the author in the village of Baishady, Bashkortostan, in May of 1992 from Tatiana Minniiakhmetova.

18 There also exists a small sub-group of Udmurts called Besermens. These communities, while speaking a dialect of Udmurt, conceive of themselves as a separate people and inhabit the Cheptsa River valley of northern Udmurtia. The Besermens living in close proximity to Russians and Orthodox Udmurts are Christians; those living in close proximity to Muslim Tatars are Muslims. The effect of these religious divisions on Besermen identity remains unclear. The origin of the Besermens is also debatable, but they share many cultural traits with the Chuvash and are thought to be descended from the Bulghar ancestors of the Chuvash. See T. I. Tepliashina *Iazyk besermian* (Moscow: Nauka, 1970) and D. M. Iskhakov, *Istoricheskaia demografiia tatarskogo naroda XVIIi-nachalo XX vv.)* (Kazan: Akademiia Nauk Tatarstana, 1993), 86–89.

19 For the ethnic history of the Komi, see L. P. Lashuk, *Formirovanie narodnosti komi* (Moscow: Izdatel'stvo Moskovskogo Universiteta, 1972); for an ethnographic survey, see Vuorela, *The Finno-Ugric Peoples* pp. 283–304.

20 For the ethnic history of the Chuvash, see V. F. Kakhovskii, *Proiskhozhdenie chuvashshkogo naroda* (Cheboksary: Chuvashshkoe knizhnoe izdatel'stvo, 1965); N. A. Ashmarin, *Bolgary i chuvash* (Kazan: Tipografiia universiteta, 1902).

21 For general ethnographic information on the Tatars, see *Tatary Srednego Povolzh'ia i Priural'ia* (Moscow: Nauka, 1967).

22 For a discussion of the ethnographic divisions of the Tatars, see D. M. Iskhakov *Etnicheskie gruppy tatar Volgo-Ural'skogo regiona,* (Kazan: Akademiia Nauk Respublika Tatarstana, 1993).

23 For the most complete survey of Bashkir ethnic history, see R. G. Kuzeev, *Proiskhozhdenie bashkirskogo naroda,* (Moscow: Nauka, 1974).

24 Frank, *Islamic Regional Identity*. There also exists a small group of Eastern Orthodox "Bashkirs" called the Nagaibaks, who are the descendants of Christian Turkic Cossacks and who inhabit Cheliabinsk district. See Iskhokov, *Etnograficheskie gruppy*, pp. 140–144.

25 The Bashkirs found themselves in a similar position to that of the Ukrainians and Belarusans in terms of attitudes toward them. Just as the Tatars saw the Bashkirs as close kinsmen who should give up their "dialect" and shift to pure Tatar, give up their ethnic "peculiarities" and adopt those of the culturally "more advanced" Tatars, so saw the Russians their Ukrainian and Belarusan brethren. Many Russians continue to see Ukrainians and Belarusans as backward Russians who spoke dialects of Russian. Russian chauvinists do not see Belarusans and Ukrainians as inferior people, but rather as having inferior cultural traits. In the same way, Tatars do not see Bashkirs as ethnic inferiors but rather as culturally backward Tatars. Important in both cases is that it is the culture and language of the "lesser brother" that is considered inferior, and not the people themselves. Therefore, with help they can be brought into the modern world through education and they can then become pure Russians or Tatars as the case may be.

26 See Zenkovsky, *Pan Turkism* pp. 165–208; Pipes, *The Formation of the Soviet Union,* pp. 155–172; and E. H. Carr. "Some Notes on Soviet Bashkiria," *Soviet Studies,* 8, no. 3 (1957), 217–225.

27 Alexander Bennigsen, Chantal Lemercier-Quelquejay, "Les missions orthodoxes," p. 126.

28 See *Ocherki po istoni Bashkirskoi ASSR* (Ufa: Akademiya nauk SSSR, Bashkirskii filial institut istorii, yazyka i literatury, 1959).

29 This area would include all of the ASSR's (now called autonomous republics – ARs) in the region, as well as the Gorky (Nizhegorod), Kirov (Vyatka), Kuibyshev (Samara), Orenburg, penza, Perm, Saratov, Sverdlovsk (Yekaterinburg), Ulyanov (Simbirsk), and Chelyabinsk Oblasts, in which about 1,071,000 Tatars resided in 1989 (see table 4.4).

30 The Tatars have not been static in their desire for change. In 1990, they demanded greater ethnic rights and even full republic (Soviet Socialist Republic, equal in status to the other fifteen constituent republics) status for Tatarstan. They also insisted that Tatar become the official language of the republic and that all inhabitants be forced to learn Tatar. For a more thorough examination of the ethnic demands of the Volga Tatars during the Soviet Period, see Ayse Azade-Rorlich, *The Volga Tatars: A Profile in National Resilience* (Stanford: Hoover Instition Press, 1986).

31 The presence of Russians correlates isomorphically with the percentages of non-Russians who employ Russian as their primary language. It is important to recognize, however, that the influence of the Russians over others is not equal with respect to all peoples. For example, Russian influence on kindred Belarusans and Ukrainians is far greater than it is on the Turkic-speaking Moslem Uzbeks and Kazakhs. See Ronald Wixman, "Territorial Russification and Linguistic Russianization in Some Soviet Republics," *Soviet Geography: Review and Translation*, 22, no. 10 (1981), 667–675. Accordingly, one should expect to see that Russians have a much stronger influence on those peoples of the Middle Volga whose cultures are closer to their own (i.e. Eastern Orthodox peoples and not Moslems.) This hypothesis is substantiated by the information in tables 4.6 and 4.7, which indicate the levels of native language retention for the peoples of the Middle Volga in 1959, 1970, 1979, and 1989.

32 The 11 percent change among the Mordvinians masks the relatively rapid rate of their ethnic assimilation by the Russians. One can reasonably conclude that the decline in Mordvinian population took place primarily among those Mordvinians who had listed Russian as their primary tongue in earlier census periods and through marriage. The same is true for the Komi-Permyaks.

33 Damir Iskhakov, "Neformal'nye ob'edineniia v sovremennom tatarskom obshchestve," *Panorama* (Kazan), 1991 (2), 28–35.

34 The activity of TOTs was not limited to Tatarstan, but was carried out by branches throughout the Middle Volga where ever there were substantial Tatar communities, as well as elsewhere in the Soviet Union, including in Moscow, Leningrad, Kiev, Tashkent, Kazakhstan and Siberia. See "Platforma TOTsa," *Panorama* (Kazan), 1991 (2), 15–27.

35 Iskhakov, "Neformal'nye ob'edineniia," pp. 29–30, 32–34.

36 Vladimir Todres, "Bashkortostan Seeks Sovereignty – Step by Step." *Transition* I/7, 58–59.

37 Todres, "Bashkortostan," p. 56.

38 M. N. Guboglo (ed.), *Etnopoliticheskaia mozaika Bashkortostana* (Moscow: TsIMO, 1993), VII, pp. 137–171.

39 G. T. Khusainova, "Natsional'nye dvizheniia v Bashkirii v 80-kh – nachale 90-kh godov," *Stranitsy istorii Bashkirskoi Respubliki: novye fakty, vzgliady, otsenki* (Ufa: IIIaL BNTs UrO AN SSSR, 1991), pp. 141–143; *Etnopoliticheskaia mozaika*, III, pp. 50–62.

40 Khusainova, "Natsional'nye dvizheniia," pp. 143–146; *Etnopoliticheskaia mozaika Bashkortostana* (Moscow: TsIMO, 1992), II, pp. 102–117.

41 *Etnopoliticheskaia mozaika Bashkortostana* (Moscow: TsIMO, 1992), I, pp. 132–140.

42 *Etnopoliticheskaia mozaika*, III, pp. 116, 118–128.

43 *Etnopoliticheskaia mozaika*, III, pp. 118–122.

44 *Etnopoliticheskaia mozaika*, II, pp. 212–215.

45 "Istoricheskaia vstrecha," *Zamandash* (Ufa), April 29, 1992.

46 Todres, "Bashkortostan," pp. 57–58.

47 *Chuvash"en*, October 7, 1992, p. 5.

48 *Chuvash"en*, October 7, 1992, pp. 2–3.

49 *Chuvash"en* October 7, 1992, pp. 10–15.

50 "Obshchestvo udmurtskoi kul'tury," *Ponimat' drug druga: o problemakh mezhnatsional'nykh otnoshenii v Udmurtskoi ASSR* (Izhevsk: Udmurtiia, 1990), p. 78.

51 "Sovershenstvovat' national'nuiu politiku: doklad biuro na plenume obkoma KPS," *Ponimat' drug druga: o problemakh mezhnatsional'nykh otnoshenii v Udmurtskoi ASSR.* (Izhevsk: Udmurtiia, 1990), pp. 89–110.

52 "Obshchestve udmurtskoi kul'tury," pp. 74–80.

53 *Materialy pervogo vsesoiuznogo s"ezda udmurtov 22–23 noiabria 1991 goda* (Izhevsk: Udmurt Kenesh, 1992).

54 Allen Frank (trans.), "Resolution of the First All-Union Congress of the Mordvin Mastorava Society for National Rebirth," *Ural-Altaische Jahrbuecher*, 64 (1992), 153–155.

55 Ksenofont Sanukov, "Mariitsy: proshloe, nastoiashee, budushchee," *Izvestiia TOTs*, 5a (May 1992), 3.

56 Boris Bronshtein, "Iazycheskie ritualy sovershaoiutsia otkryto," *Izvestiia*, July 20, 1993.

57 N. S. Popov (ed.), *Marii kumaltysh mut* (Ioshkar-Ola: Marii kniga izdatel'stvo); V. N. Petrov (ed.), *Marii iu* (Ioshkar-Ola: Marii kniga savyktysh, 1993).

58 "Obraschchenie k parlamentam finno-ugorskikh respublik i obshchestvennosti finno-ugorskikh narodov," *Izvestiia TOTs* 7 (9–21 of June, 1992), 3; *Dokumenty, priniatye pervym vserossisiskim s'ezdom finno-ugorskikh narodov* Izhevsk: 1992.

# Middle Volga: Chronology of events

*January 1988*

The Udmurt Cultural Club is founded in Izhevsk.

*November 1988*

A Tatar Cultural Club is formed in Ufa, Bashkortostan.

*February 1989*
17–19    The Tatar Social Center, formed in the summer of 1988, holds its founding congress and announces its support for Tatarstan's sovereignty.

*March 1989*

The Bashkir cultural organization *Ak Tirma* (White Yurt) is founded in response to an upsurge in Tatar cultural activity in the republic.

*October 1989*

The Udmurt Supreme Soviet issues a series of directives aimed at increasing the use of the Udmurt language and advancing Udmurt culture.

*December 1989*

The Bashkir National Center (BNTs) "Ural" is founded. The Society for Udmurt Culture is formed and sets as its primary goal the reintroduction of Udmurt-language education.

*April 1990*

The constituent congress of the *Mastorava* society, formed to promote the interests of the Mordvin people, is held in the Mordvinian capital of Saransk.

*August 1990*
30    The Komi and Tatar ASSRs issue declarations of sovereignty, upgrading their status to union republic.

*September 1990*

A state of emergency is declared in Mordovia banning all rallies, meetings, and city and rayon soviet sessions in response to a mounting public movement against the republican leadership.

20    The Udmurt ASSR declares its sovereignty, upgrading its status to union republic.

*October 1990*

*Azatlyk*, the Union of Tatar Youths, and *Ittifak*, the Tatar Party of National Rebirth, are formed in Tatarstan.

10    The Bashkir ASSR issues a declaration of sovereignty, upgrading its status to union republic.

11    The Komi-Permyak autonomous oblast declares sovereignty.

24    The Chuvash ASSR issues a declaration of sovereignty, upgrading its status to union republic. The Mari ASSR declares sovereignty in October as well.

*December 1990*

13    The Mordovian ASSR drops the word autonomous from its name but does not declare sovereignty.

*March 1991*

12    Ethnic Germans in the USSR hold a conference to request the recreation of a Volga German ASSR.

17    In the all-union referendum on preserving the union, support for the union in Middle Volga republics is as follows: Bashkortostan – 86 percent (82 percent turnout); Chuvashia – 82 percent (83 percent); Komi – 76 percent (68 percent); Mari-El – 80 percent (80 percent); Mordvinia – 80 percent (84 percent); Tatarstan – 88 percent (77 percent); Udmurtia – 76 percent (74 percent). Tatarstan boycotts a second question on establishing the post of RSFSR president.

*April 1991*

20    The Tatar Supreme Soviet modifies the republican constitution to incorporate its sovereign status.

*May 1991*

Protestors demonstrate against holding RSFSR presidential elections in Tatarstan.

Mintimer Shamiev, chairman of the Tatar Supreme Soviet, announces that Tatarstan will not sign the Union Treaty unless it is accorded equal status with the union republics.

*June 1991*

12    Tatarstan does not hold Russian presidential elections. Instead, Tatar presidential elections are held, and Shamiev is elected president in an uncontested vote.

*August 1991*

Tatar President Shamiev expresses his support for the coup

leaders in Moscow and orders the dispersal of a crowd which gathers in central Kazan' in support of Yeltsin. The opposition gathers 30,000 signatures calling for Shamiev's resignation.

*October 1991*

15–22 In Tatarstan, nationalist organizations call for the republic's full independence. Rallies to commemorate the anniversary of the sixteenth-century Russian conquest of Kazan' coincide with a Supreme Soviet meeting. Nationalist leaders threaten the Supreme Soviet with civil disobedience if it fails to pass a resolution on independence. The Supreme Soviet of Tatarstan adopts a resolution and calls for a republican referendum to be held on the question.

*November 1991*

26 The First All-Union Congress of Udmurts is held in Izhevsk. Delegates assert their support for sovereignty but not independence. The congress leads to the formation of the All-Udmurt Association *Udmurt Kenesh*.

*December 1991*

15 In second-round elections in Mari-El, Vladislav Zotin, parliamentary chairman, is elected president with 59 percent of the vote, defeating Anatolii Popov (15 percent).

22 In second-round elections in Mordovia, Vasilii Guslyannikov, head of the republic's Democratic Russia chapter, is elected president, defeating parliamentary chairman Nikolai Biryukov.

23 The Congress of the Baskhir People announces its intention to work for the creation of an independent Bashkir state. The decision is condemned by the Tatar Public Center of Bashkiria.

*February 1992*

1–2 At an All-Tatar Congress (*Kurultai*), a Tatar National Assembly (*Milli Malis*) is elected as a shadow parliamentary body. Delegates issue their own declaration of independence for Tatarstan.

*March 1992*

In Bashkortostan, the Ufa Historical and Patriotic Assembly, a Russian cultural organization, renames itself the Rus' Social Organization and adopts a more political stance.

21 In a referendum in Tatarstan, 61 percent of voters (82 percent turnout) affirm Tatarstan's sovereign status.

28    Tatarstan sends a proposal to Bashkortostan regarding the formation of a Volga-Urals confederation.

28–29    The first session of the Milli Majlis is held, and delegates proclaim the Majlis to be the supreme representative body of the Tatar people and give it the right to repeal laws adopted by Tatarstan's government. Tatar officials refuse to recognize the Majlis.

*April 1992*

20    Leaders of the Tatar pro-independence party Ittifak and of the Bashkir National Center and the Bashkir National Party hold talks aimed at cooperation between the two peoples.

*May 1992*

16    The First All-Russian Meeting of Finno-Ugric Peoples is held in Izhevsk. The International Congress of Finno-Ugric Peoples is held in the Komi capital of Syktyvkar in May as well.

23–24    The First Congress of Peoples of Tatarstan is held. The congress supports Tatarstan's declaration of sovereignty. Supporters of the Federal Treaty are not permitted to air their views and walk out.

*June 1992*

19–21    The World Congress of Tatars attracts more than one thousand participants.

*August 1992*

13    The presidents of Tatarstan, Bashkortostan, and Sakha issue a joint statement warning the Russian government that they will seek to further their republics' sovereignty if Moscow ignores their legal rights.

21    Bashkir clergy establish their own board of the Muslims of Bashkortostan.

*October 1992*

8–9    The Chuvash National Congress holds its founding conference in Cheboksary which is attended by 1,000 delegates. The Congress declares its support for increased sovereignty, but not independence.

*November 1992*

6    Tatarstan's parliament ratifies the republic's constitution, which declares that Tatarstan is a sovereign state associated with the Russian Federation on the basis of a treaty.

*December 1992*

2    The leadership of the Tatar Milli Majlis calls for the

creation of a Confederation of Peoples of the Volga and
Ural Regions.

*April 1993*

2–3    The Mordvinian Parliament votes to abolish the post of
republican president and vice-president, blaming the
popularly elected president Vasilii Guslyannikov for the
republic's economic woes.

25    In a referendum in Bashkortostan, a majority of voters elect
to change the republic's status to that of a sovereign state
within the Russian Federation.

*June 1993*

24    Tatarstan recalls its representative to the Constitutional
Assembly, saying that the assembly was ignoring Tatarstan's
special status.

*December 1993*

12    Tatarstan's leadership encourages the republican population
to boycott the Russian parliamentary elections. Only 14
percent of eligible voters come out to vote. In a referendum,
the Komi republic's voters fail to approve the introduction
of a presidential post.

17    In Bashkortostan, Murtaza Rakhimov, parliamentary
chairman, is elected president with 60 percent of the votes
(Rafis Kadyrov receives 29 percent).
Parliamentary elections are held in Mari-El.

24    The Bashkortostan Parliament adopts a constitution
containing clauses that conflict with the Russian
constitution.

26    In Chuvashia, Nikolai Fyodorov (former Russian Finance
Minister) is elected president in second-round balloting,
defeating Communist-supporter Lev Kurakov.

*February 1994*

15    After two years of negotiations, Tatarstan signs a
power-sharing treaty with the Russian government which
recognizes that Tatarstan is a state united with Russia on
the basis of the constitutions of the two states and the new
bilateral treaty. In substance, the treaty does not appear to
give Tatarstan any benefits it had not already procured.

17    The Komi republic adopts a new Constitution which affirms
its sovereign status.

*May 1994*

8    In the Komi republic, Yuri Spiridonov, the ethnic Russian
parliamentary chairman, is elected head of state, defeating
Vyacheslav Khudaev, the Komi chairman of the Council of

Ministers. 36 percent of the electorate participate.
Parliamentary elections are held simultaneously.
20    The Komi-Permyak autonomous oblast holds parliamentary
elections.

### July 1994
18    The prime minister of Bashkortostan, Anatolii Kopsov,
resigns when he is accused of misuing state funds for
personal gain. He is replaced by first deputy prime minister
Rim Bakeev.

### August 1994
3    Bashkortostan President Murtaza Rakhimov signs a
power-sharing treaty with Yeltsin (the third such treaty in
Russia).
27    Parliamentary elections are held in Chuvashia (with
second-round voting the following week).

### November 1994
27    In Mordovia, parliamentary elections are held
unsuccessfully, as only a few of the nominees receive the
percentage of votes needed to attain a seat.

### January 1995
7    In a meeting in Cheboksary, several republican leaders
propose that a Congress of Peoples of Russia be convened
to resolve nationality problems in Chuvashia. They also
propose that the governmental Council of Heads of
Republics be revived.
12    Chuvash President Nikolai Fyodorov issues a decree
exempting the population of Chuvashia from having to
participate in the combat in Chechnya.
17    Farid Mukhametshin, the former chairman of Tatarstan's
parliament, is appointed Prime Minister to replace
Muhammad Sabirov.

### March 1995
5    Tatarstan and Bashkortostan hold parliamentary elections.
In Tatarstan, widespread violations are reported. Most of
the seats go to local officials and industrial directors.
26    Udmurtia holds parliamentary elections, and most of the
seats go to communists. A simultaneous referendum on
introducing a republican president is rejected by 64 percent
of voters.

### April 1995
19    Udmurt prime minister Aleksandr Volkov is elected head of
state by parliament.

28    Tatar opposition forces convene a "shadow parliament" at
      the founding conference of the People's Council of
      Tatarstan.

# 5   Siberia: assimilation and its discontents

GAIL FONDAHL

Siberia, the land beyond the Urals and north of Kazakhstan, comprises 75 percent of Russia. Rich in fossil fuels, minerals, timber, hydropower potential, and furs, it is sparsely populated. But while it is people-poor, with only 22 percent of Russia's population, it is peoples-rich. Over thirty peoples, numbering from a few hundred to several hundreds of thousands, claim part of Siberia as their homeland (see map 5.1, table 5.1), and essentially all of the Commonwealth's other nationalities can be found here. Over half a millennia of Russian colonization has left its mark on the demographic makeup of this vast area: the peoples of Siberia currently constitute a mere 4 percent of the total Siberian population.

It is this combination of great wealth of resources and small numbers of indigenous peoples which fuels national tensions in Siberia. Most indigenous nations enjoy nominal autonomy, in the form of autonomous districts and provinces, but limited control over the development of their homelands. Resources flow west from their lands to the center, with little benefit or remuneration. They see the environmental degradation that accompanies the exploitation of these resources undercutting the basis of their traditional economic activities – reindeer, sheep and cattle pastoralism; hunting and trapping; fishing and sea-mammal harvesting. They question the benefits of services provided by the state, such as universal education, which develops aspirations for a "more civilized" way of life while providing few opportunities for upward mobility in either "traditional" or newer professions. With heightened expectations, and greater contacts with the outside world, indigenous Siberians are weighing the gains from membership in a powerful empire against the losses in terms of cultural vitality. Here, as elsewhere in the former USSR, the myth of fraternal relations has unraveled, to be replaced by accusations of internal colonialism. As Siberian peoples attempt to regain control over their lands and its resources, they increasingly propound a separation of indigenous and non-indigenous geographies.

Most chapters of this book focus on nationalities which form the majority of the population in their own titular areas. In Siberia *prishlie* – "newcomers" (mainly Russians, but including Ukrainians, Tatars, Jews, and individuals from essentially every other nation of the former USSR) –

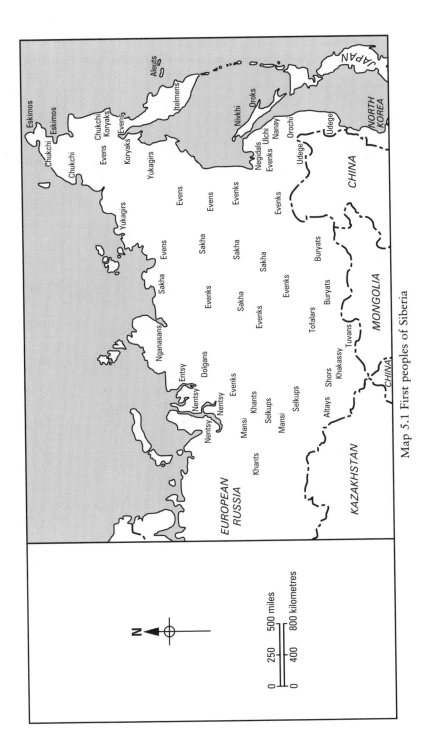

Map 5.1 First peoples of Siberia

Table 5.1. *Population of Siberian people, 1926–1989*

|  | 1926 | 1959 | 1970 | 1979 | 1989 |
|---|---|---|---|---|---|
| Buryat (000s) | 237 | 252 | 313 | 350 | 417 |
| Sakha (000s) | 241 | 236 | 25 | 327 | 380 |
| Altay (000s) | 39 | 45 | 55 | 59 | 69 |
| Khakassy (000s) | 53 | 56 | 65 | 69 | 78 |
| Tuvans (000s) | 60 | 100 | 139 | 165 | 205 |
| Shors (000s) | 17 | 15 | 17 | 16 | 17 |
| *Peoples of the North (1989 Census List)* | | | | | |
| Total | 121,512 | 131,111 | 153,578 | 158,324 | 184,448 |
| Nentsy* | 13,217 | 23,007 | 28,705 | 29,894 | 34,665 |
| Evenks | 38,805 | 24,151 | 25,471 | 27,294 | 30,163 |
| Khanty | 17,334 | 19,410 | 21,138 | 20,934 | 22,521 |
| Evens | 2,044 | 9,121 | 12,029 | 12,523 | 17,199 |
| Chukchi | 12,221 | 11,727 | 13,597 | 14,000 | 15,184 |
| Nanay | 5,860 | 8,026 | 10,005 | 10,516 | 12,023 |
| Koryaks | 7,439 | 6,287 | 7,487 | 7,879 | 9,242 |
| Mansi | 6,095 | 6,449 | 7,710 | 7,563 | 8,474 |
| Dolgans | 656 | 3,392 | 4,877 | 5,053 | 6,945 |
| Nivkhi | 4,076 | 3,717 | 4,420 | 4,397 | 4,673 |
| Selkups | 1,630 | 3,768 | 4,282 | 3,565 | 3,612 |
| Ulchi | 723 | 2,055 | 2,448 | 2,552 | 3,233 |
| Itelmens | 859 | 1,109 | 1,301 | 1,370 | 2,481 |
| Udegey | 1,357 | 1,444 | 1,469 | 1,551 | 2,011 |
| Saami* | 1,720 | 1,792 | 1,884 | 1,888 | 1,890 |
| Eskimos | 1,293 | 1,118 | 1,308 | 1,510 | 1,719 |
| Chuvans | 705 | n/a | n/a | n/a | 1,511 |
| Nganasans | 867 | 784 | 953 | 867 | 1,278 |
| Yukagirs | 443 | 442 | 615 | 835 | 1,142 |
| Kets | 1,428 | 1,019 | 1,182 | 1,122 | 1,113 |
| Orochi | 647 | 782 | 1,089 | 1,198 | 915 |
| Tofalars | 413 | 586 | 620 | 763 | 731 |
| Aleuts | 353 | 421 | 451 | 546 | 702 |
| Negidals | 683 | n/a | 537 | 504 | 622 |
| Entsy | 482 | n/a | n/a | n/a | 209 |
| Oroks | 162 | n/a | n/a | n/a | 190 |
| *Other peoples of the North†* | | | | | |
| Alyutor | | | | | c. 2,000 |
| Kerek | | | | | 100 |
| Taz | | | | | 300 |
| Chulimtsy | | | | | 300 |
| Todzha | | | | | ? |

dominate numerically (table 5.2). Indeed, Russians have outnumbered Siberian peoples for about three centuries.[1] The percentage of indigenous representation varies by area, but in almost all political-administrative divisions above the *rayon* level indigenous persons constitute less than one-quarter of the population (table 5.3). Only in the Tuvan Republic and the Aga Buryat Autonomous Okrug do the indigenous populations (Tuvans, Buryats) exceed that of the non-indigenous population. Where rapid industrial development and concomitant large-scale immigration of laborers has occurred, such as that experienced in the West Siberian oil fields, the indigenous representation has dropped most precipitously: the Khants and Mansi at the last census (1989) made up only 1.4 percent of their titular territory's population, a mere one-tenth of their relative representation in 1959.

Simple characterization of relations between the Siberian peoples and newcomers poses an impossible task. At various times and in various regions they have evidenced hostility, friendship, awe, disdain, trust, distrust, exploitation and charitable aid. Instances can be pointed to where individuals of each group viewed members of the other as saviors or destroyers.

Further exacerbating the problem is the fact that throughout the history of Russia and the USSR we have very few sources which give us the uninterpreted, unedited, uncensored indigenous view of such relations. Accounts of "historical" relations between the indigenous and immigrant population of Siberia are reconstructed largely, if not exclusively, from the writings of non-indigenous observers. Indeed, only in the last several decades, with the creation of literary languages by the Soviets, have most of the Siberian

---

\* The Saami live to the west of the Urals, mainly on the Kola Peninsula; many Nentsy live in the Nenets Autonomous Okrug, also to the west of the Urals. Thus both are "Peoples of the North," but the Saami (and part of the Nentsy) are not Siberians.

† These peoples were not included in previous censuses but are now being considered for inclusion. The Shors and Teleuts (see text) may also join the official list of "numerically small peoples of the North," as may a number from the European North.

*Sources:* A. Pika and B. B. Prokhorov (eds.), *Neotraditsionalizm na Rossiyskom Severe* (Moscow, 1994), p. 195; I. S. Gurvich (ed.), *Etnicheskoe razvitie narodnostei Severa v sovetskiy period* (Moscow: Nauk, 1987), p. 67; Chauncy Harris, "A Geographic Analysis of Non-Russian Minorities in Russia and its Ethnic Homelands," *Post-Soviet Geography*, 34, no. 9 (1993), table 4; "List of Indigenous Peoples of the North," (unofficial) from the Russian Federation Ministry of Nationalities and Regional Affairs, provided to the author by Gail Osherenko.

Table 5.2. *Population of Siberia, total and indigenous*

| Year | Total population (000s) | Indigenous population (000s) | % indigenous | % increase in non-indigenous population from previous census |
|---|---|---|---|---|
| c. 1700 | | | 50 | |
| 1790 | 934.3 | 303.4 | 32 | |
| 1897 | 5,730.0 | 861.9 | 14 | |
| 1911 | 9,366 | 1,064.0 | 11 | 68 |
| 1926 | 12,309.0 | 788.0 | 6 | 42 |
| 1939 | 16,674.0 | 816.9 | 5 | 38 |
| 1959 | 22,559.0 | 957.5 | 4 | 36 |
| 1970 | 25,353.4 | 1,205.9 | 5 | 12 |
| 1979 | 28,615.0 | 1,378.6 | 5 | 13 |
| 1989 | 32,099.0 | 1,617.9 | 5 | 16 |

*Source:* James Forsyth, *A History of the Peoples of Siberia. Russia's North Asian Colony, 1581–1990* (Cambridge: Cambridge University Press, 1992), pp. 100, 190, 405; last column calculated from Forsyth, *A History of the Peoples of Siberia*, p. 405.

Table 5.3. *Percent of population belonging to titular nation in titular administrative unit (AO = Autonomous Okrug)*

| Current name | 1926 | 1959 | 1970 | 1979 | 1989 |
|---|---|---|---|---|---|
| Altay republic | 43 | 24 | 28 | 29 | 31 |
| Buryat republic | 34 | 20 | 22 | 23 | 24 |
| Aga Buryat AO | 88 | 48 | 50 | 52 | 55 |
| Ust–Orda AO | 60 | 34 | 33 | 34 | 36 |
| Tuva republic | 75 | 57 | 59 | 61 | 64 |
| Khakass republic | 49 | 12 | 12 | 12 | 11 |
| Sakha republic | 82 | 47 | 43 | 37 | 33 |
| Taymyr (Dolgan–Nenets) AO*† | | | 17 | 15 | 13 |
| Yamalo–Nenets AO | | 22 | 22 | 11 | 4 |
| Khanty–Mansi AO | | 14 | 7 | 3 | 1 |
| Chukchi AO | | 21 | 11 | 8 | 7 |
| Koryak AO | | 19 | 19 | 16 | 17 |
| Evenki AO | | 34 | 25 | 20 | 14 |

* Autonomous Okrugs were created in 1930.
† Dolgans did not appear in 1959 census.

*Sources:* See table 5.1; Chauncy Harris, "A Geographic Analysis of Non-Russian Minorities in Russia and its Ethnic Homelands," *Post-Soviet Geography*, 34, no. 9 (1993), table 4.

peoples been able to write, and thus record their observations and feelings, their histories. And only much more recently have they been allowed to express openly in the press any opinions which are critical of relations between the Russians and themselves. There is also a dearth of information on relations *among* the various peoples of Siberia within the Soviet-period literature, with that available mainly limited to statistics on intermarriage.

For the purposes of this chapter, Siberia lends itself to classification in five groups: the "Peoples of the North," Southern Siberia, Buryatia, Sakha, and Tuva. The chapter considers the Peoples of the North in greatest detail, then draws parallels and contrasts with developments in interethnic relations which characterize the other peoples of Siberia.

## The Peoples of the North

Over two-dozen numerically small nations (under 50,000 persons each) inhabit the tayga and tundra zones of Siberia (See table 5.1).[2] Linguistically represented are the Ugrian (Khant, Mansi) and Samoedian (Nenets, Enets, Nganasan, Sel'kup) branches of the Uralic family of languages; the Turkic (Dolgan, Tofalar) and Tungus/Manchu (Evenk, Even, Nanay, Negidal, Orochi, Oroki, Udegey, Ulchi) branches of the Altaian family of languages, the Kett language group (Kets), the Eskimo-Aleut language group (Eskimo, Aleut), and the Paleoasiatic grouping of little internal coherence (Chukchi, Chuvan, Koryak, Itelmen, Yukagir, Nivkhi). Economically, these peoples have depended on reindeer pastoralism, hunting and trapping, sea mammal hunting, or fishing, or most commonly a combination of these activities. Land use thus was based on harvesting locally available, renewable resources. Because of the environmental conditions, the Peoples of the North required large territories to support small populations.

As early as 1918 the Soviet state categorized these linguistically, racially, and economically differentiated peoples as a group to be handled with one set of policies.[3] Peoples from the Arctic littoral to the Amur Basin, those living on the eastern flanks of the Urals and those of the western rim of the Pacific were all designated "small peoples of the North" (*malie narody Severa*).[4] Uniformity in the state's policy towards these peoples has evoked similarities in development of their national consciousness. Northern peoples themselves now employ this grouping in order to demand increased rights and recognition of their distinct cultures.

### *Historical Background: Interethnic Relations in the Pre-Soviet Period*

In 1581, with Yermak's crossing of the Urals to attack Kuchum's Siberian Khanate, the Russian state officially began its conquest of Siberia. However for almost 500 years prior to this historical watershed, Nentsy, Khants and, Mansi had conducted trade across the northern Urals, exchanging fur, walrus ivory, and other products of the northwestern Siberian forests and Arctic littoral for western goods from Novgorod and then Muscovy. In fact, while a desire for more furs stimulated the Russian expansion into Siberia, one impetus for opening a *southerly* route was the increasing hostility of the Nentsy to Russian incursions across the northern Urals at the turn of the fifteenth century.[5]

The more southerly route brought Russians first into Khant and Mansi lands. These peoples, who already paid tribute to the khan of Sibir, responded to initial attempts at levying further taxes on them with fierce resistance.[6] Using superior military technology (firearms), but also promises of release from payments to the khan, Russian forces soon prevailed. Throughout the taiga and tundra zones of Siberia this would be the model for conquest: a show of strength was often enough to achieve compliance of the indigenous population to the imposition of *yasak* – the fur tribute required by the Tsar, especially when accompanied by offers of aid against other perceived oppressors. Russians had firearms; natives did not. Indigenous groups soon saw Russians as possible – and powerful – allies in their battles against each other and joined these well-armed forces to crush long-standing opponents. Russians quickly learned to exploit the intertribal animosities to their own advantage. Historian George Lantzeff, in a review of the seventeenth-century literature, found Khants and Russians fighting Nentsy, Khants and Russians allied against Mansi, Yukagirs battling Chukchi with the help of Russians, and Evenks joining Russians in subjugating Buryats. Within nations, the Russians exploited inter-clan hostilities as well, to conquer recalcitrant groups.[7]

Russians moved rapidly across Siberia. By 1650 most of the northern peoples paid yasak to the Tsar's coffers. *Ostrogs* raised alongside indigenous settlements, at the confluences of rivers and at portage termini, acted as collection points for the fur tribute as well as foci for trade and retreats during times of rebellion. For the peoples of the North, compliance with the demands of yasak and other burdens imposed by the Tsarist state was neither unanimous nor continuous. When dealt with unfairly, an all too frequent occurrence, indigenous peoples rebelled. An attempt to raise the yasak in 1606 caused Nentsy in the region of Mangazeya, and Khants along the Ket River to revolt. In 1609–1610 Khants tried to evict Russians who had occupied their homelands.[8] Further to the east the Evenks and Evens revolted in 1662. The Chukchi most effectively resisted Russian domination, and continued to function as a semi-independent nation well into the nineteenth century.

Indigenous responses to the conquest and imposition of tribute were not limited to armed revolts. When provincial officials increased yasak rates or demanded other services, the hunters often petitioned Moscow to rule against local corruption. A second line of recourse was simple refusal to pay yasak. To avoid the inevitable confrontation in which this resulted, some native groups migrated deeper into the taiga, temporarily escaping their economic tormentors. More drastic measures involved assassinations of Russians, and in at least one case a mass suicide in protest.[9]

Moscow's, then St. Petersburg's, greatest interest in Siberia, and more specifically, in its native peoples, was in ensuring an uninterrupted flow of furs from the hinterland to the center.[10] To achieve this, tsarist governments repeatedly issued decrees denouncing exploitative practices. In the initial stages of conquest, yasak paid to the Tsar was to be no higher than that levied by former powers (khans); later, the yasak collectors were strictly prohibited from addending levies for their own profits. Unregulated trade was forbidden in order to protect the indigenous population. However, stories abound of highly usurious practices, the most common being unfair trading deals, especially those involving Russians attempting to get traders drunk before negotiating. Deceit was not a Russian monopoly, however. Fur trappers, for instance, rubbed sable pelts with coal in order to garner the higher prices paid for the more valuable, darker species.[11]

The preceding depiction of Siberian-Russian contact in the Siberian North draws a picture of conflict and animosity. As the immigrant population of Siberia grew, the indigenous peoples and Russians increasingly lived in close proximity and dealt with each other in realms other than trade. While laws expressly prohibited many contacts, including unregulated trade, land leasing by Russians from natives, and the cohabitation of indigenous persons and common Russians in the same village,[12] these laws were difficult to enforce. Native and Russian villages were often separate but adjacent. Intermarriage became increasingly common, and Russians employed indigenous persons to fish, herd deer, cut hay, gather firewood and berries, and carry out innumerable other tasks. Natives adopted some items of Russian dress, domestic implements and tools, and other elements of material culture, and an increasing number learned to speak Russian. At the same time, Russians adopted much indigenous technology for surviving in the severe Siberian environment: clothing, transport and hunting equipment, foodstuffs and preparation techniques, etc. Some Russians learned to speak the local languages; most often the terminology of work incorporated many words from the indigenous languages.

Unlike many other parts of the world, the State enacted no large-scale policy of genocide; in fact, as mentioned, tsars repeatedly issued protective measures, in order to ensure that indigenous peoples would be able to continue to provide the state with furs. However, local officials rarely implemented these decrees, and the indigenous northerners met oppressors both in government agents and private traders. Officials overlooked crimes against indigenous persons by immigrants, and themselves frequently ignored state decrees on humane treatment. They mistreated hostages (whom they were officially allowed to keep to ensure continued yasak payments by fellow clansmen), even starving them at times, and condoned the use of alcohol in trading. Military campaigns against indigenous settlements involved rape, murder, kidnapping, and pillaging. The conquest and colonization of northern Siberia severely impacted the native population. Introduced diseases to which there was no immunity caused phenomenal death rates. Moreover, the demand for fur tribute in areas where there had been none before meant a restructuring of the indigenous economy away from purely subsistence concerns, and a decrease in food production. When and where this contributed to declining nutritional status, the depredations of disease were even more greatly felt.[13] Finally, cultural anomie in the face of foreign incursion and subjugation undoubtedly further undermined peoples' resistance to the new diseases. Populations of a number of the peoples (Khants, Mansi, Evenks, Nanay) by the Revolution had declined by as much as 30 to 40 percent.[14]

## The Soviet period: interethnic relations

Before the Revolution, we might surmise that many indigenous peoples had little reason to distinguish between state official and private trader or colonist in terms of the treatment they could expect to receive. Any initial impressions of the tsarist government as ally or protector would have faded quickly. This view of government changed, if briefly, after the Revolution. During the early years of Soviet power, the peoples of the North did invest some hopes in the new government as a better ruler and even as a protector of their interests. Many indigenous nations still see the 1920s (prior to collectivization) as a period of great cultural development, which the new Soviet state supported. To these early decades date the creation of literary languages, the establishment of educational institutions (at first nomadic), universal suffrage, and many other institutions which many indigenous persons view positively. In 1924 the Russian government created a special "Committee of the North" to protect the interests and oversee the development of the peoples of the North. This dedicated group of scholars helped institute the State's policy of *korenizatsiya* ("indigenization") in Siberia, encouraging indigenous political participation in the new governmental structures (the *soviets*).[15] It played a role in defining the identity of many of these peoples as nations, both in the eyes of the state and among the peoples themselves.[16] A culminating step was the establishment of national *okrugy* for a number of the Peoples of the North in 1930 (map 5.2).

If paternalistic, early Russian Federation policy attempted to provide some degree of protection to the northern peoples. The Committee for the North espoused what is now referred to as "internationalization" (*internatsionalizatsiya*), a process which in theory combined the best specific, national (*natsionalno-osobennoe*) traits of these "primitive" cultures with the universal (*internatsionalno-obshchee*) traits of the more advanced (*Russian*) culture.[17] Internationalization would hypothetically

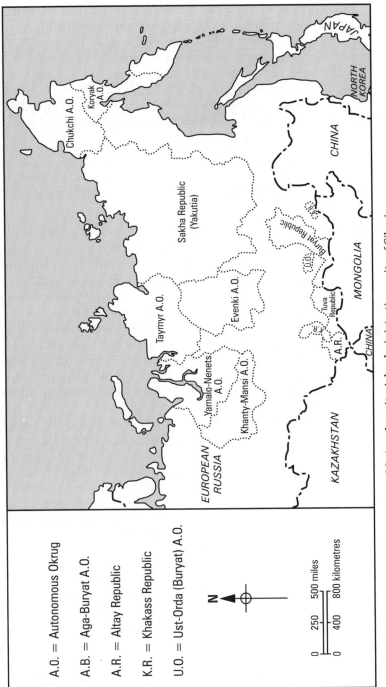

National territorial–administrative units of Siberia

A.O. = Autonomous Okrug

A.B. = Aga-Buryat A.O.

A.R. = Altay Republic

K.R. = Khakass Republic

U.O. = Ust-Orda (Buryat) A.O.

avoid both extremes of complete assimilation or complete isolation. To achieve it, national traits had to be nurtured, not obliterated.

Natives initially looked to the Committee and to the new Bolshevik government to resolve some of their conflicts with the growing Russian population. Paramount in the list of protestations in the early twentieth century were the issues of Russian encroachment on indigenous homelands and of hunting competition and habitat destruction. For instance, delegates to a 1926 meeting in the Turukhansk region complained that

> Russians, invading the taiga, ravage the graves of our ancestors, rob indigenous caches, steal foxes from Tungus [Evenk] traps. Hunting dogs of the Russians chase the easily frightened Tungus reindeer through the taiga.... And there have been cases where Russians have killed domestic reindeer.'[18]

At this meeting and others elsewhere, native representatives appealed to the state to exclude Russians (and also Buryats) from hunting, and to protect the forest from burning by the *prishlie*.[19] Soviet officials responded by assigning clans specific hunting areas (allegedly the most valuable), and prohibiting access to these by Russians. However, enforcement of the prohibition was nigh impossible. Russians continued to encroach upon indigenous hunting areas, complaining that it was unfair that the indigenous peoples had special areas set aside, but could also hunt on "free lands" (i.e. the ones open to the Russians) and that they began hunting prior to the official commencement of hunting season.[20] When indigenous persons pleaded with Soviet officials totally to halt colonization by Russians, governmental officials flatly condemned this attitude.[21] The only answer left appeared to be self-imposed isolation, a retreat beyond the borders of Russian settlement. In some instances native groups assumed a "scorched earth" policy, burning winter hunting grounds to stop the advance of Russian hunters and stabilize the boundaries of their shrinking territory.[22]

The creation of nine national *okrugy* for eight of the Peoples of the North must have seemed a promising step in terms of gaining a degree of autonomy. However, the majority of Peoples of the North received no such titular administrative unit.[23] Those who did gained little. As immigrants continued to pour into Siberia, the population of the national *okrugy* became increasingly non-indigenous. Native peoples usually received figurehead posts in the okrug government and party apparatus, but exercised minimal power over decisions on the development of resources and allocation of lands to the various state ministries and their enterprises.

By the mid-1930s any hopes of indigenous northerners must have faded, with state pursuance of policies of collectivization and sedentarization in the North. It also became clear that the state not only did not intend to limit Russian colonization, but indeed encouraged it. Local control over local affairs increasingly eroded. Two autonomous *okrugy* were abolished.[24] Moreover, cooptation replaced integration as the state's policy toward a number of the Peoples of the North. Central authorities deemed several nations too small to deserve their own literary language and halted the development of these, closing, or simply failing to support indigenous language presses. Some peoples (e.g. the Chuvans, Entsy, and Oroks) actually lost official recognition as distinct nationalities, as witnessed by their disappearance from the censuses (table 5.1). On the other hand, the Peoples of the North continued to receive a number of benefits from the state, such as affirmative action policies for admittance to universities and free travel to medical care facilities. These benefits have served to encourage native individuals (including children of mixed marriages) to identify themselves as such, at least officially, and may have played a role in keeping alive the identity of the peoples not recognized by the state.[25]

Indigenous northerners identify the 1960s and 1970s as especially damaging periods for their cultural vitality.[26] During these decades the pace of industrial development of Siberia greatly increased, and with it the degradation of their homelands. The conversion from collective to state farms throughout the North meant the consolidation of small single-nation villages into larger multinational ones; in the 1960s the number of farms decreased by 60 percent.[27] With increasing rarity did indigenous persons hold leadership positions on the larger farms. Removed from their birthplace, torn from the resource base upon which they depended, large numbers were alienated from employment in traditional activities, and from participation in subsidiary activities such as wild-food gathering. State officials increasingly effectively enforced the compulsory education policy, which meant that more and more native children ended up in boarding schools, often far removed from their parents. Northerners condemned this system for nurturing a culture of dependency on the dominant nation.[28]

Interference proceeded hand in hand with neglect: while forcing sedentarization and compulsory education, the State failed to provide the needed infrastructure in terms of housing, medical care facilities, and transport. Living conditions in Siberia's rural areas, where most (74 percent) of the indigenous population lives, are among the worst in Russia.[29] Native peoples have routinely suffered unemployment and underemployment, with trivial compensation for low-skilled work.[30] Interethnic conflict is exacerbated where job discrimination favors *prishlie*, especially in "traditional" activities: for instance, in the northern Chita Oblast, qualified Evenks greatly resented the loss of well-paid positions as state hunters to Russians.[31] The disorientation that accompanies current conditions in the North increasingly finds its expression in high rates of alcohol usage, violence, homicide and suicide. Life expectancy for Siberian people runs 16–18 years lower than the average for the RSFSR, largely due to alcohol-related accidents and violent deaths.[32]

Besides the malaise caused directly by state policies, northern peoples now also openly condemn that caused by the *prishlie* themselves. In areas where non-indigenous immigration has been greatest and resource exploitation activities most dramatic, tensions are severe, fueled by violent and other criminal activities of the *prishlie* against indigenous persons. Evenks living near the Baikal-Amur (BAM) railroad protest the widespread poaching of both deer and the game and fur animals on which they depend by *Bamovtsy*, workers on the railroad. Evenk women further south complain of increased rates of sexual assault by gold workers. Infrastructure may be limited, but the existing roads allow *kommersanty* to ply liquor among, and prey on, the indigenous population.[33] To date most published accounts concentrate on non-indigenous attacks on native persons, and fail to indicate widespread retaliation, as has occurred between the Sakha and Russians and the Tuvans and Russians (see below). Yet numerous anecdotes of violent attacks by indigenous persons on *prishlie* suggest two-way traffic.

## The post-Soviet period: tentative reforms, few gains

Glasnost allowed the open discussion of problems, and facilitated the formation of an "Association of the Numerically Small Peoples of the North" to lobby for improved rights and improved implementation of existing rights of the northern peoples. Here, referring to table 1.1 (see p. 14), we see not contention among "non-titular" groups, but rather cooperation for a common goal. With only advisory powers, the Association, formed in 1989, nevertheless successfully attained high visibility in policy circles. It put forward a platform of juridical guarantees of traditional land use and control of all resources, surface and subsurface, for the indigenous population of the North.[34] It also lobbied for USSR, then Russian, ratification of Convention 169 of the International Labor Organization, which upholds indigenous peoples' rights to control their "economic, social and cultural development," and requires the state government to "guarantee effective protection of their rights of ownership and possession" of their land and resources.[35] Republican, provincial, regional, and village associations of numerically small peoples complete a hierarchy of organization attempting to promote indigenous rights.

The Peoples of the North groups continue to stress the primacy of control over land and resources to their cultural survival. Russian Federation legislation has responded in part to some native demands, granting increased rights in terms of access to and control over renewable resources.[36] However, existing legislation is internally contradictory, and open to great variability in interpretation and thus implementation. Moreover, legislation at both the federal and regional level awaits the passage of a federal "Law on the Legal Status of Indigenous Numerically Small Peoples", as called for in other Russian legislation.[37] This proposed law has experienced an erosion of powers granted to Peoples of the North in its successive drafts.

While new legislation offers specific, if limited, protection of rights, the general process of democratization ironically has reduced the Northern peoples' political power base, due to the large numbers of immigrants and the current integration of indigenous and non-indigenous spheres of activity. With free elections, indigenous peoples can no longer hope to achieve a majority of votes even in most village administrations, let alone at the *rayon* level. Both the absolute and relative number of elected representatives of the northern peoples decreased in the 1989 and 1990 elections, most markedly at the lower (*rayon* and settlement) levels of government.[38] In less than 43 percent of all settlements registered as "national" do indigenous peoples comprise more than 50 percent of the population. Moreover, many of these settlements were until recently considered "futureless" (*neperspektivnye*) by the government, and were slated for closing.[39] While the government has reversed its position on this issue, and has even called for the consideration of re-establishing liquidated villages, there are no monies to do so.[40]

Indeed, as elsewhere in the former USSR, problems of cultural survival have been exacerbated by the financial collapse of the region. Attempts in the early 1990s to create more culturally-sensitive educational curricula and to provide better housing, social, and medical services to indigenous peoples have faltered due to lack of funds. The situation in the North is exacerbated in that this region was heavily subsidized by the government, and much of those subsidies have been withdrawn.

The new Russian government has not yet formulated a coherent policy toward indigenous people nor toward the North's regional development.[41] Leading scholars on the Siberian people[42] suggest a policy based on the concept of "neotraditionalism." Neotraditionalism propounds a move away from the policies of modernization/assimilation, pursued from the 1930s onward, toward one of genuine indigenous self-government at the lowest level (i.e. of indigenous villages), state protection of traditional activities (reindeer herding, hunting, etc.), and emphasis on meeting internal needs of indigenous communities over state procurements or market demands. It criticizes the recent emphasis on devolution of power to autonomous *okrugy* as not benefiting the indigenous nations themselves, due to the demographic realities discussed above.[43] It holds that the "severe economic conditions in the North" demand a "genuine revival" of 'traditional' northern economic activities simply to survive the current economic crisis, that the "rebirth of traditionalism" in herding, hunting, etc., is a "grim reality with no alternative" given the financial collapse of the government. This analysis, if bleak, concurs with bioregionalist approaches proposed by indigenous peoples themselves, which argue that self-government, including control over local resources, is the only path to ensuring both environmentally and culturally sustainable development of Russia's northern expanses.

### Relations to the International Circumpolar Community

The Association of the Peoples of the North has forged ties with several international indigenous groups (World Council of Indigenous Peoples, Inuit Circumpolar Council, Sami Council) which work for Fourth World rights. The Peoples of the North are familiarizing themselves with the benefits and drawbacks of land claims settlements and other political agreements negotiated by foreign indigenous people of the Arctic and Subarctic with their respective states. Increasingly, connections are forged at lower levels, via cultural exchange programs and attendance at economic and other conferences.[44] Perhaps most attention has been paid to the Siberian Eskimos, whose population straddles the international border.[45] Cut off from communications with their relatives across the international border only in 1948, the Russian Eskimosy have now re-established ties with the American Yupik population on St. Lawrence, with a great potential for politicized common agendas. With much publicity, relatives were allowed once again to visit each other in 1988. Since its formation in 1977 the Inuit Circumpolar Conference (ICC)[46] invited the Russian Eskimos to participate at its tri-yearly meetings: they were finally able to do so in 1989.

The Eskimos, and neighboring Chukchi, also have begun to participate in the plans to establish an international park straddling land on both sides of the Bering Sea (Chukotka and Alaska). However, park planning has failed to incorporate in any systematic or comprehensive way the input of the people who live within or near the proposed park territory. International projects, such as this one, however well-intentioned, may hinder future self-determination efforts of the indigenous Siberians people.

## Southern Siberia: Altays, Khakassy, Shors

As in Northern Siberia, the indigenous peoples of southwest Siberia identify the most significant threat to their continued cultural viability as stemming from incursions of an industrialization program over which they have had no control, and the concomitant loss of land and degradation of the environment which has threatened "traditional" activities. Southwestern Siberia, an area of high mountains alternating with undulating plains, is home to nomadic pastoralists of Turkic linguistic stock, who traditionally herded sheep, cattle, and horses. Over the last century and a half, immigrants streamed into the area, both as agricultural colonists and in association with the development of mining centers and metalworks. Most recently, *prishlie* came to mine ores which use in their processing the coal of the nearby Kuznetsk Basin (Kuzbas). As with the northern people, the numerical inferiority, ever increasing, of the South Siberian Turkic peoples holds little promise for real political autonomy based on the present titular administrative units.

The identities of these peoples as Shors, Altays, and Khakassy were forged, fairly successfully, during the Soviet period. Here, as elsewhere in the USSR, the creation of one literary language for each of these peoples contributed to the internal unification of a number of related groups as self-conscious nations. Prior to the October Revolution, none of these three (groups of) peoples identified itself with a single, encompassing name. The Altays and Khakassy were divided into a number of tribes and territorial groups, and the Shors identified themselves primarily by clan. This did not however, preclude pan-nationalist aspirations before the Revolution. The national histories of these peoples are similar enough to consider together; in fact nationalist aspirations have coalesced in both the earlier part of this century and more recently.

The Altays actually consist of two groups with distinct languages, a northern group comprising the Tubulars, Chelkans, and Kumandas, and a southern group comprising the Telengits, Telesy, Teleuts, and Altays.[47] These various groups fell under Western Mongol (Oirot) rule from the fifteenth century to the eighteenth. The defeat of Dzhungaria by China signified a change in rulership. Then, in the mid nineteenth century, the Russian Empire wrested this area from China, and the Altays became subjects of the Tsar. Venerating their Mongol connections, nationalists of the early twentieth century would borrow "Oirot," the term initially also used by the State to identify the peoples now known collectively as the Altays.

With the establishment of Russian power, Russian peasant immigrants, attracted by the rich pasture lands, soon began to flow into the area. Land reform in 1899 stipulated a redistribution of land based on needs for subsistence family farming (18 *desyatins*, or approximately 20 *hectares* per family).[48] This of course greatly eroded the land base of the semi-nomadic indigenous herders, who needed extensive tracts of pasture, and who did not recognize private ownership in any event.

The Khakass nation included the Kacha, Sagay, Bel'tir, Kyzyl and Koybal "tribes".[49] Their union with the Russian empire dated to the early 1600s, when the various tribes pledged allegiance to the Tsar in return for protection from multiple tribute payments (to Mongols and Kyrgyz as well as Russians).

Nationalist movements developed among the Altay and Khakass intelligentsia in the late nineteenth century and the early twentieth. Among the Altays, the movement was tied to a messianic religious movement, Burkhanism, which acknowledged the visitation of Oirot Khan to an Altay shepherd.[50] This Khan preached a doctrine that was both anti-Christian and anti-Russian. The movement among the Khakassy apparently did not have the same religious character, though the choice of the name, Khakassy, for the fledgling nation evoked a history of great depth, referring to the Khyagasy of Chinese chronicles.[51] In the early twentieth century, with the tsarist regime weakened by the 1905 revolution, Khakass nationalists attempted to free themselves from tsarist control by a transfer of land and administration to clan organizations.[52] However, tsarist officials refused to recognize the indigenous reforms.

During the tumultuous months following the October Revolution, Altay and Khakass nationalists joined to consider the creation of an independent Turkic peoples' republic, which would have included these two groups as well as perhaps the Tuvans or the Kazakhs.[53] While the new Bolshevik government forbade the formation of such an independent unit, the People's Commissariat for Nationalities initially accepted the concept of an Oirot-Khakass autonomous territory within Russia. However, in the early 1920s the state established two separate administrative units, the Oirot Autonomous Oblast and the Khakass *Uezd*. The latter was given national okrug status in 1925, then elevated to an autonomous oblast in 1930.

The Soviet state also established a Shor National Okrug, Gornaya Shoriya, in 1929. In all three areas the indigenous populations may have been a majority at the time of creation of the national administrative units.[54] Rapid influx of Russian and other immigrants during the early years of the Soviet industrialization drive quickly changed this situation. By the end of World War II, the Khakassy constituted less than 20 percent of the population of their designated homeland; prior to the war (1938), Shors had decreased to 13 percent of Gornaya Shoriya's inhabitants.[55] This national okrug was disbanded in 1939, and the land became part of the Kemerovo Oblast. Here we have a situation analogous to that of the Even-Okhotsk National Okrug: Gornaya Shoriya's existence may have been seen as an impediment to the development of the rich coal deposits of the Kuzbas as well as the associated iron deposits of the okrug itself, and the titular population considered small enough to disenfranchise without consequence to the State.[56]

The consequences to the Shors, though, were significant. In simple demographic terms the growth of the Shor population was almost three percentage points below that of the RSFSR average between 1959 and 1970 (7.98 percent, vs. 10.7 percent),[57] and between 1970 and 1979 the Shor population actually declined by almost 3 percent. Besides the abolishment of their autonomous territory, the Shors faced the closing of predominantly Shor farms and of Shor villages.[58] Forced emigration from rural areas increased the number of Shors working in the mines of the region. Social malaise of the indigenous population was expressed as it was further north: suicide rates and fatal accidents grew, especially in the wake of increased alcohol and drug abuse.[59]

The Altay suffered a less dramatic but nonetheless telling fate. Too obviously an echo of lingering aspirations, the designation "Oirot" was changed to "Altay," and "Gorno Altay" substituted for "Oirot" in the autonomous oblast's name in 1948. Altay nationalists had apparently continued to nurture the idea of a sovereign Oirotia, and remained in contact with "Oirots" in Sinkiang.[60] By renaming this nation, the State sought to sever psychological as well as tangible connections to related peoples beyond the boundaries of the USSR.

The end of the 1980s witnessed both divisive and unifying movements among these South Siberian peoples. On the one hand, the Soviet policy of consolidating various tribes or territorial groups into cohesive nations did not fully succeed: the Teleuts, for instance continued to request recognition as a nation distinct from the Altays.[61] On the other hand, the various South Siberian peoples cooperated in creating a Siberian Cultural Center (SCC, based in St. Petersburg) as a union of national activists from Khakassy, Altay, and Shors.[62] The SCC lobbied for increased national autonomy of the South Siberian peoples, an improvement in the situation of native languages, and protection from degradation caused by industrialization. Within the SCC, founded in 1989 by Khakass intellectuals, "an increasing consensus about the necessity of restoring the historical unity of these three nationalities, separated from each other by centuries of Russian colonial administration" prevailed.[63]

SCC membership spanned the political spectrum from radical separatists to more conservative "sovereignists". Some dreamt of an independent South Siberia Turkic republic, reminiscent of the vision of Oirotia earlier in this century. Pragmatists pointed to basic demographic problems inherent in establishing such a republic – the indigenous peoples are now minorities throughout their homelands. A less radical component of this movement proposed establishing indigenous administration over an archipelago of rural areas which do still have a indigenous majority.

Khakhassia declared its status as a republic of the Russian Federation, separate from the Krasnoyarsk Kray, in 1990, a move which the Russian parliament confirmed in 1991. Khakassy comprised only 11 percent of the population. Since they are geographically concentrated, the regional association of indigenous peoples, *Tun*, called for the establishment of an autonomous region within the republic. It also lobbied for a bicameral republican government, with at least half the seats in one of the two chambers, the Council of Nationalities, dedicated to Khakassy, and a prerequisite of Khakass nationality applied to the positions of prime minister, parliamentary chair, and minister of culture. Such platforms incurred the wrath of Russian and Cossack factions, who accused the association of separatist tendencies. While some of Tun's radical members do espouse separation, the group as a whole has not, rather working to ensure avenues for Khakass participation in the republic.[64]

Khakassia's relations remain tense with the Krasnoyarsk Kray, from which it separated. In 1994, the Khakass government banned the export of most goods produced in the republic to the neighboring kray; allegedly in retaliation, the Krasnoyarsk Kray constructed a customs post between the two political-administrative entities.[65] Again, the extent to which we can consider Khakassia's decision a result of ethnic politics is cloudy, given the demographics of the republic.

The Gorno-Altay autonomous oblast also declared sovereignty, first as an ASSR, then as a republic (1992). Breaking away from the Altay Kray, it removed itself from one "matrioshka" of administrative nesting. In its sovereignty decree, the republic claimed exclusive rights to its natural resources,[66] a position upheld by the Federal Treaty of 1992 for republics. But again, only 30 per cent of the population of the Altay Republic is Altay and discussion of secession from the Russian Federation has been minimal.[67]

## Buryatia

The Buryats, living to the west and east of southern Lake Baikal, and north of the border with Mongolia, are one of two Mongol peoples of the Russian Federation (the Kalmyks being the other). Traditionally pastoral nomads, raising sheep, horses, and some cattle, they adopted agriculture in increasing numbers during the nineteenth century. Russians most heavily influenced the Buryats living to the west of Lake Baikal, many of whom converted to Eastern Orthodoxy. The Buryats differ little ethnically from the Mongols across the international border: anthropologist Caroline Humphrey describes them as "those northern Mongol tribes which decided they wished to remain in the Tsarist Russian Empire" in the 18th century.[68] This choice stemmed from lower taxes and greater freedom of movement under the tsar than under the Khalka Mongol leadership.

While Russians began to penetrate Buryat homelands as early as the seventeenth century, contact between the two peoples remained minimal. Russians settled in villages, Buryats continued to nomadize. This difference in lifestyles, which limited interaction between the two peoples, would become the basis for tensions between them, for the Buryat economy depended on extensive use of land for grazing livestock.

Interethnic conflicts began by the late eighteenth century, as increasing numbers of (mainly Russian) immigrants moved into the Buryat homelands, and gradually dispossessed the Buryat of their ancestral territory. Disputes reached a critical level in the early twentieth century, when the Tsarist government proposed a land reform, similar to that proposed for the Altay region, which granted equal territory to each household, regardless of ethnic identity or economic activity. The area to be allocated, as in the case of the Altay, was calculated to meet the needs of peasant farmers (15 *desyatins*, or roughly 17 hectares, per male) not transhumant pastoralists (who migrate twice-yearly), and would be owned individually, not collectively.[69] Under this reform Buryat communities would lose up to half of their lands, threatening their nomadic way of life. Tsarist reforms also eliminated an administrative system which guaranteed Buryat governance of predominantly Buryat areas.[70]

In response to these reforms, to continued Russian immigration, and especially to the land tenure issues, a vital Buryat nationalist movement developed around the turn of the century.[71] Members of the Buryat intelligentsia in vain petitioned St. Petersburg to regain local self-government. They condemned the tsarist government for its land policies and unwillingness to limit Russian colonization. Within the intelligentsia grew increasingly schismatic factions. One supported a separate Mongolian state, essentially a re-creation of the Mongol Empire.[72] Another worked for greater political and cultural autonomy within the Russian state. The latter held greatest power at the time of the Revolution, with most Buryat leaders subscribing to socialism, but not Bolshevism.[73]

As a first step towards territorial autonomy, the new regime (Bolsheviks) in 1918 granted the Buryats *aimaks* – their own administrative areas, equivalent to *rayons*, scattered among the Russian villages. Two years later, with the formation of the Far Eastern Republic, the Buryat nation was temporarily split politically. In 1921 the constitution of the Far Eastern Republic created an "Autonomous Buryat-Mongol Oblast"; the following year the Soviet government established a Buryat–Mongol Autonomous Republic. These two were merged to form one single Buryat–Mongol ASSR in 1923. From the very beginning, Russians outnumbered Buryats in the ASSR (table 5.3).[74]

It was not the demographics, however, but rather retribution for supposed nationalist and even pan-Mongolist "deviations" that in 1937 caused the reduction of Buryat titular territory. Most of the members of the Buryat intelligentsia, who had played a critical role in shaping the early policy of the Buryat–Mongol ASSR, were denounced as Japanese spies and purged. The ASSR was carved up into three titular units (see map 5.2), with 12 percent of its former territory given to the Chita and Irkutsk Oblasts.[75] This lost land constituted some of the richer agricultural and pastoral areas of the republic. During 1937 the state also instituted a number of new privileges for settlers in the Eastern reaches of the country, which increased the flow of Russians into Buryatia.[76] By 1959 Buryats only accounted for 20 percent of the ASSR's population, though since then the indigenous population has grown faster than the Russian population. The two groups tend to remain separate, living in different villages or different sections of Buryatia's villages and towns.

Glasnost evoked a resurgence in nationalist activity in Buryatia. More radical nationalists lobbied for the return of the original name, from which "Mongol" was dropped in 1958.[77] They also demanded re-consolidation of the Buryat homeland to its pre-1937 borders. The Buryat Republic government called for a "legal and political evaluation" of the 1937 decree (1991), but in 1993 officially recognized the constitutional status of the Aga and Ust-Orda Buryat Autonomous Okrugs, simply stating the "necessity" of increasing cultural and economic ties.[78] Buryats apparently supported the 1990 declaration of sovereignty put forward by the republic's Supreme Soviet, which upgraded the republic to SSR status, and claimed control over all natural resources,[79] and the subsequent move to "sovereign" status as a republic within the Russian Federation. Legal code now guarantees equal status of the Buryat and Russian languages.[80] A new legislative body, the People's Khural, evokes the title of pre-Soviet, Mongol-influenced institutions, in form if not content. Nationalist debate took an interesting turn in the spring and summer of 1994, during campaigning for the first presidential election in Buryatia, mainly between Leonid Potapov, a Russian who espoused "gradualism" in economic policy and Alexander Ivanov, a Buryat and a "reformer." While political leanings of the Republic's population determined the outcome, Potapov's case was helped by the fact that he, the Russian, spoke Buryat, and Ivanov did not, a fact the press gave much play. Potapov resoundingly defeated Ivanov with 72 percent of the votes in the second round of voting. The post-election mood was bittersweet, as many Buryats felt that it should be a Buryat who served as the first president of the Republic, but, apart from economic leanings, considered Ivanov's ties to Buryat culture disputable.

The Buryats are experiencing a significant renaissance in culture, even if its potential is sapped by the critical financial situation of the whole Russian Federation. Buddhism enjoys a vibrant revival. Daily radio and TV broadcasting include Buryat-language programming. Environmental causes are promoted in the name of preserving the Buryat homeland. The government recently publicly condemned the "limiting of the public function of the Buryat language," the "practical liquidation of folk trades and handicrafts, the ecological traditions of the peoples of Buryatia, and the persecution and victimization of the traditional religions of the peoples" under Stalin's and others' rule.[81] Separatist tendencies are minimal, but among the intelligentsia, the possibility of recreating a larger, pre-1937 Buryatia still lends spice to late-night conversations, if as a remote dream.[82]

### Interethnic relations: Buryats and the "Peoples of the North" (Evenki)

Buryatia's northern *rayony* embrace homelands of the Evenk nation, and the republic has addressed this fact by establishing a number of national (Evenk) rural administrations (former *selsovety*) and one Evenk national *rayon* (Baunt).[83] Another *rayon* (Kurumkan) in the republic is currently considering pursuing status as a national region. Supposed to improve federal funding opportunities, Evenki in the Baunt Evenk National Region feel that, to date, the status has not in any way helped their situation. At the same time, ethnic hostility between the Evenk and Buryat appears minimal; rather, as elsewhere, both groups focus on the problems introduced by an immigrant population which has no intention of long-term residence in the republic. Legislation mentioned above which condemned repression of Buryat culture also condemned, specifically, similar repression of Evenk culture, language, and religion within the republic.[84]

## Buryat links with Mongolia and beyond

The relationship between Buryats and Khalka Mongols has often been one of uneasy alliance, relying on cultural ties to overcome political hostilities. At the turn of the century, pan-Mongolists on both sides of the border sought the creation of separate Mongol state. Meanwhile, both the tsarist and the Soviet government attempted to make use of the Buryats' close linguistic and cultural affinity to Mongolians to draw Outer Mongolia into an ever closer dependency relationship. As the Mongolian People's Republic had little of its own educated elite, the Soviets sent Buryats to staff major positions.[85] Members of the Buryat intelligentsia straddled the divide, sometimes to advance their own nationalist political agendas, trying to "extract favorable treatment for Buryats at home in return for political work carried on in Outer Mongolia".[86] While some Buryats probably felt their role as brokers and intermediaries between the Russian and Mongolian cultures to be a positive one, promoting progress while buffering against cultural anomie, Mongols allegedly resented the dominance of a westernized, modernized leadership, and considered the Buryats traitors to true Mongolian culture.[87]

Today Buryats again travel in greater numbers to Mongolia, but as cultural emissaries of the Buryat, not Soviet, Republic. The "more backward" Mongolia serves as a repository for oral traditions, songs, folkways, and material culture that Buryats feel they have lost under the Soviet regime. Mongolia also serves as reserve for spheres of Buryat ecological knowledge and adaptation destroyed during Soviet years: for instance scientists have recently initiated a program to reintroduce sheep breeds formerly raised on the steppe of this region and well adapted to the harsh climate, but displaced by Soviet planners due to lower productivity indices.[88] The breeds still predominate in Mongolian husbandry.

Of greater visibility are the international ties being forged with Buddhists from other parts of the world. The Dalai Lama, and several slightly less renowned figures of world Buddhism, have visited the Buryat Republic, speaking to "sell-out" crowds. Literature on Buddhism is ubiquitous, in both cities and remote villages. Cultural, religious, and ecological revival are imminently intertwined for the Buryats, the western division between these spheres makes little sense to "reborn" Buddhists.

# Sakha[89]

The Republic of Sakha (formerly the Yakut ASSR) is one of Russia's most richly endowed regions in terms of natural resources. From this republic come essentially all of Russia's diamonds and much of its gold, as well as coal, timber and other resources. In 1989 the titular nation, the Sakha (Yakuts), comprised about 33 percent of the population; various Peoples of the North another 2 percent.[90] Turkic in origin, the Sakha migrated from the southwest to their current home with horses and cattle, and retained transhumant pastoralism, substituting reindeer in the northernmost regions of Yakutia, where the other animals failed to thrive. They both fought and intermarried with the local population (Chukchi, Evenks, Evens and Yukagirs).

Russian penetration of this area began in the early 1600s. The Sakha initially welcomed the newcomers, but due to repressive governmental actions soon began to clash with them. A major revolt against Russian occupation occurred in 1642, and the town of Yakutsk was burned in 1681.[91] Eventually, though, the Sakha began to work for the government as tribute collectors and in other official positions. Increased contact between the two peoples led to assimilation, but this did not always mean Russification: Russian colonists were often "Yakutisized," adopting the native language and economic activities.[92]

By the early twentieth century, a Sakha intelligentsia preached a strongly nationalist doctrine. The Yakut Union, founded in 1906, demanded the return of all lands which had been expropriated by the state, by monasteries, and by other Russian groups.[93] Subsequent Tsarist repression of the Union's leaders only further fueled interest in revolutionary ideas. During the prolonged Civil War in Yakutia, Sakha participated on both sides, hoping that the new order which each side promised would bring greater self-determination.

In 1921, in the midst of the Civil War, Sakha founded a cultural organization, "Sakha Omuk" to promote their interests. Members of this organization spanned the political spectrum, the most "radical" preaching pan-Turkism. The organization survived until the late 1920s, when the state initiated an anti-nationalist campaign. Many members of the Sakha intelligentsia were purged over the course of the next decade. This, and the collectivization drive, met with much resistance in Yakutia.

The Yakut ASSR was established in 1922. In 1924, with the discovery of gold in its southerly region (the Aldan), Russians began to immigrate in large numbers. From the 1930s on, convict labor increased the numbers of immigrants substantially. While in 1926 the Sakha still comprised the vast majority (82 percent) of their titular republic's population, by 1959 their share had dropped to less than half (table 5.3).[94] Once again, it is this demographic situation, and the feeling that Russian industry has ruined the

Sakha environment for Russian profit, which has fueled the resurgence of overt nationalism in the last decade. Sakha feel that they have benefited little from the mineral wealth of their republic. Indices of living conditions fall well below the Russian average. Major mining areas have been deemed ecological disaster zones, unfit for the pursuance of traditional activities. Conversely, Russians resent the affirmative action programs which benefit the Sakha (and other indigenous nations) in both higher education and job placement.

Records of severe interethnic clashes in Yakutia date to 1979. A Ukrainian human rights activist, who was exiled to Yakutia, recounted incidents of ethnic hostility between Sakha and Russians, such as beatings and attacks, as well as rancorous graffiti.[95] Racial incidents, including mass brawling and large demonstrations, continued to occur throughout the 1980s in the capital city of Yakutsk. The demonstrations mainly involved young Sakha protesting police inaction over the interethnic clashes.[96] In the last few years, the contours of conflict have shifted, to lie increasingly between the *prishlie* and the Sakha *cum* old-timer Russians. The latter two groups generally find much common ground in their positions on environmental destruction and resource exportation (from the republic) which little benefits locals.[97]

The year 1990 saw the revitalization of "Sakha Omuk" as an organization for preserving and reviving Sakha culture. In the autumn of the same year, the Yakut Supreme Soviet upgraded the status of the ASSR, and renamed it the Yakut-Sakha SSR. Even though non-Sakha constituted a majority of the population, Sakha dominated the political positions of the ASSR; thus this pronouncement certainly was interpreted as much a nationalist move as a regionalist one. However, the Sakha government has made it clear that its major concern is economic, not political, autonomy.

The Sakha Republic's constitution, adopted in 1992, declared that the republic possesses exclusive ownership of land, minerals, and other resources of Sakha (Article 5), and the Supreme Soviet transferred all enterprises to republican ownership.[98] In the same year the Russian and Sakha governments signed an economic accord that granted Sakha 32 percent of the resource rents from diamonds and 11.5 percent of the resource rents for gold.[99] However, Sakha's exclusive claims over land and natural resources contradict the Russian constitution and the Federal Treaty of 1992. One of Sakha's most pressing political concerns is the refusal of the Russian Government to accept its constitution.

While economic conditions have not improved in the republic under President Nikolaev's rule, rates of decline at least compare favorably with neighboring regions of Siberia, which in combination with a relatively stable government, has led to lower out-migration from the republic.[100] The Sakha republic government participates in the Northern Forum, a non-profit international organization of regional governments, which was founded in 1991 to enhance opportunities for northern leaders to exchange ideas on economic, environmental, cultural, and social issues. Sakha has been able to attract a number of foreign investors, including firms from the US, Austria, Japan, South Korea, South Africa and Canada, both for resource and infrastructure development. The government has paid special attention to developing local expertise for addressing the "transition to market relations", investing heavily in post-secondary education. (A Faculty of Economics was recently opened at Yakutsk State University, and *in toto* the Sakha government spent 18 billion rubles on the university in 1993.) Some see this as nationalist policy, as 70 percent of those enrolled at the university are indigenous persons.

## Interethnic relations: Sakha and the "Peoples of the North"

"For minorities in the Yakut republic, assimilation is complicated and perhaps less advanced because the surrounding dominant population is not Russian but Yakut".[101] The little information available on "titular–nontitular" relations in the Sakha republic suggests that Sakha indeed have "dominated" the numerically smaller Peoples of the North (see table 1.1). When in 1930, a number of the "Peoples of the North" received national *okrugy*, fifteen national *rayony* were set up within the Yakut ASSR for the Evenks, Evens, Yukagirs, and Chukchi.[102] Five national *rayony* for the Evenks alone covered one-third of the Yakut ASSR's territory. However, in 1933 Sakha held the highest administrative position in ten of the fifteen *rayony*.[103] The Peoples of the North have been increasingly Sakhasized: the number of Evenks who speak Evenk, for instance, continues to decrease, but it is Sakha which is often adopted, not Russian.[104]

To protect their cultures and reassert self-determination, numerically smaller Peoples of the North have demanded greater political and cultural rights from the republican government. The republic's new constitution has met this challenge at least partially, in principle: it guarantees these northern people inalienable rights to "management and use of land", and to "defense against any form of forceful assimilation or ethnocide, or encroachment on ethnic distinctiveness."[105] It also allows the creation of self-governing, national administrative-territorial formations (regions, villages, councils, etc.) for the Peoples of the North.[106] Well before the constitution had been drafted, the government created a new titular unit for the Even people, the Even–Bytantaisk *rayon*.[107] Top leadership positions in this *rayon* have gone to Evens.

While such moves indicate progress for the Peoples of the North living within the Sakha republic, other developments suggest a deterioration of status. No further national regions have been formed.[108] The clan-family communes, which have been created, and which serve both as economic units and self-governing entities at the level of the former rural councils, experience severe problems of "self-financing." As northern subsidies falter here as elsewhere in Russia, transport becomes unaffordable, and "traditional" economic activities insupportable. Indicators of social malaise, already high rates of alcoholism, and (often-associated) suicide and homicide among the Peoples of the North climbed further in the early 1990s.

At the republican level, structural changes in governmental organization, paralleling those at the Russian Federation level, may have made the collective voice of the peoples of the North less audible. Formerly, the Sakha government included a ministry of the Peoples of the North, but the ministry was demoted to a mere department within a newly-formed ministry for all national groups in the republic. Numerically small peoples (Evenks, Evens, Yukagirs) viewed this re-organization as a step in the wrong direction, an erosion of their ability to effectively put forward their specific demands. Still, some detect a "new solidarity" developing between Sakha and Peoples of the North, based on "both a sense of shared roots but also shared responsibility for the fate of minorities who have in the past suffered from Yakutization as well as Russification."[109]

## Tuva

Tuva presents a special case in the study of national relations in Siberia and indeed in Russia. Firstly, nominally independent from 1921 until 1944, Tuvans remember a recent past of greater sovereignty. Secondly, of all the autonomous units (above *rayon* level) in Siberia, only in Tuva does the titular nationality predominate. Indeed, Tuvans form a substantial majority (64 percent) of the republic's population. Thirdly, recent interethnic conflicts, specifically those between Tuvans and Russians, had a particularly violent character, stimulating a massive exodus of Russians from the republic.

These unique characteristics do not negate the fact that the same tensions which fuel interethnic discord in other areas of Siberia are also at work in Tuva. The Tuvans are primarily pastoralists, herding sheep, cattle, and horses in isolated highland pastures of their alpine republic. Linguistically Turkified Mongols, with some Turkic, Samoyed, and Ket ancestry, many subscribe to the Buddhist faith. But Tuvans have watched their traditional way of life erode under policies of collectivization of the pastoral economy, attempted annihilation of the Buddhist faith, and denial of Mongolian elements of their culture. The area, like the rest of Siberia, has experienced large-scale immigration. Receipts from the extraction of mineral resources, a major source of the area's wealth, have not profited the indigenous population, which experiences high unemployment and one of the lowest standards of living in Russia.

While most of Siberia has been under Russian rule since the seventeenth century, Russia never conquered Tuva. Wedged between Russia, China, and Mongolia, and separated from them by lofty mountains of the Sayan,

Altay and Tannu-Ola ranges, Tuva enjoyed periods of relative independence from external subjugation. In its worst years, its population fell victim to taxation by both the Russian and Chinese empires.

Russian settlement of Tuva accelerated in the early nineteenth century, as peasants, traders and miners were drawn to the area. Manchu China considered Tuva a natural extension of Mongolia, over which it exerted control, and tried to restrain Russian penetration into the area. The Treaty of Peking (1860) allowed Russians to trade in Uryankhai, as Tuva was then known, as well as throughout Mongolia, but forbade permanent Russian settlements. However, China was unable to enforce such restrictions, and the loss of land to Russian settlers increased tensions between the indigenous and immigrant population. Moreover, Russian merchants employed exploitative practices similar to those used elsewhere in Siberia. Tuvans implored the local governmental officials to limit this exploitation, and then began to protest more vehemently, at times resorting to violence. In turn, Russians called for Tsarist military protection against "native attacks and revolts."[110] Eventually (1885), the Tsar decreed that a Russian frontier *okrug* with a Russian administration be established to deal with issues of Russian trade in Tuva.

Gold mines attracted Russians as early as the 1830s, and by the 1870s drew large numbers of immigrants. Permanent settlements could now be established if limited to 200 Russians. Tuvans provided the mines with foodstuffs, and were occasionally hired on as miners.

While increasingly tied economically to Russia, Tuvans still looked south to their cultural roots. Many aspired to a united Tuva and Mongolia. With the onset of the Chinese Revolution, Tuva provided forces to fight for Western Mongolia's independence. The question of its own fate arose. Tuvan leaders turned to Moscow to ask that Tuva be included in Russia, and in 1914 the Tsarist government proclaimed a protectorate over Tuva. This appears to have encouraged Russian settlement, for the Russian population grew from 2,100 to 8,200 between 1910 and 1916.[111]

During the years immediately prior to and after the October Revolution, the political status of Tuva was unclear.[112] Shortly after the February Revolution, Russians in Tuva held a congress to support the Provisional government. Meanwhile, at least some members of the Tuvan elite looked elsewhere for leadership, entering into relations with both Mongolia and China. Others sought independence: "the Uryankhai people declare that from now on they are free from the Russian government, that they will govern themselves in full independence and consider themselves a free people, dependent on no one".[113] Shortly after the Revolution Soviet power was declared, and the new Soviet government proposed that Tuva join the Russian Federated Republic as a national territory. Relations with Russians deteriorated during the course of the Civil War, however, when both Red and White forces confiscated Tuvan livestock for food and transport.

Tuvans retaliated by destroying Russian settlements.[114] Meanwhile both Chinese and Mongols used the breakdown of order to increase their presence in Tuva, and to put forward claims to the region.[115]

In 1921 the Uryankhai *Kray* Soviet allowed the Tuvan people to democratically decide their future: they voted for the establishment of an independent government. Thus a nominally independent Tannu-Tuva (the Tuva People's republic) was established, under Soviet supervision, and viewed by both the USSR and China as a buffer state. Russians living in Tuva were given the status of privileged foreigners, rather than granted full citizenship. The first political leader of the Tuva People's Republic, Prime Minister Donduk, was a confirmed pan-Mongolist and Buddhist. His government declared Lamaism the state religion, required religious training for young Tuvans, and supported reunification with Mongolia.[116] Buryat and Kalmyk religious leaders supported this revivalist movement, and played an active role in its propagation.[117] Fearful of a pan-Mongolism allying the Tuvans with the Khalka Mongols, Buryats and Kalmyks, the Soviet government decided to act. It encouraged the substitution of Tuvan geographic names for Mongol ones, and emphasized the Turkic ancestry of the Tuvans, by introducing a literary language based not on a Mongol, but on a "neo-Turkic latinized alphabet"[118] In 1929, a Soviet-orchestrated purge replaced Donduk with Solchak Toka, a Moscow-trained, dependable communist.[119] The USSR also successfully encouraged the granting of full citizenship to the Russian inhabitants.

In 1944 the Little Khural, a body of thirty persons parallel to the USSR's Central Committee, petitioned the latter body for Tuva's admission into the the USSR. Tuva was accordingly incorporated as an autonomous *oblast* in the RSFSR, and was elevated to ASSR status in 1961. Kolarz, analyzing the reasons for the Soviet take-over, suggested that the economic resources the region offered and the strategic position it held *vis-à-vis* some of the Soviet Union's other resources ("a fortress guarding the approaches to the Kuzbass") were not the only reasons prompting absorption.[120] He noted that the Tuvan communists, following the Soviet policy of stressing the Turkic elements of Tuvan culture, emphasized their ethnic links to the Altay and Khakassy when lobbying for a merger with the USSR.[121] Kolarz surmised that the Altay and Khakassy might similarly stress these links in arguing an opposite movement:

> From the point of view of Oirot nationalists in particular, there was no reason why these peoples should belong to the Russian Empire instead of uniting with the Tuvinians in an independent state. As long as there was an independent Tuva, there was always the possibility that Oirots and Khakassians might gravitate towards that country.[122]

The absorption of Tuva into the USSR stimulated a large influx of Russians: by 1959 they constituted 40 percent of Tuva's population. Since then, with strong population growth among the indigenous population,[123] the Russian share has decreased. At the beginning of the 1990s, the relative Tuvan majority grew even faster, as Russians left the republic. The exodus was provoked by increasingly numerous and violent attacks by Tuvans. While malicious actions toward Russians by Tuvans have been dated to the 1970s by an article in *Literaturnaya Rossiya* (August 3, 1990), conditions worsened in the last years of Soviet power: the Soviet press attributed eighty-eight deaths in the first months of 1990 to interethnic hostility.[124] During the first half of 1990, about 3,000 Russians left Tuva.[125] Ethnic antagonism continues to simmer, and some Russian inhabitants have supported Zhirinovsky's call for the abolition of nationality-based administrative-territorial units.[126]

A Tuvan Popular Front formed in 1989, with members spanning much of the political spectrum. More radical Front members questioned the validity of Tuva's absorption into the USSR. The Popular Front and another nationalist party, the People's Party of Sovereign Tuva, lobbied for a referendum on seccession from the Rusian Federation in 1992. However, Tuva's Supreme Khural voted overwhelmingly (92 percent) against holding such a referendum. Deputies noted that over 90 percent of the republic budget comes from Moscow in the form of subsidies. Nevertheless, the newly adopted republican constitution allows for secession, and President Yeltsin has apparently taken heed, suggesting increased government subsidies to Tuva.[127]

## Conclusion

Walker Connor has suggested that "ethnonationalism appears to feed on adversity and denial" but "also appears to feed on concessions."[128] Confronted with the overwhelming physical and cultural degradation which the last several decades of Soviet power has wrought in their homelands, but recently freed from a fear-imposed silence to protest, indigenous people across Siberia now seek the power to reverse these processes of decline. In a bioregionalist analysis, they identify the foundations for the environmental and cultural destruction in the alienation from these lands from their guardianship. Without intimate ties to the land, *prishlie* have violated it, threatening long-term sustainability. With severed ties, indigenous peoples have suffered a disorientation strong enough to threaten cultural survival. National movements seek to restore indigenous control over land and resources, and in doing so, to regain command of their cultural, social and economic environments as well as their physical one.

The Siberian people do not necessarily refute the process of internationalization, but seek to realize its first stage, that of the full "flowering" of national identity. This, they feel, is requisite to true multiculturalism, as distinct from assimilation or acculturation. Currently, to partially withdraw from the external state is to draw on – and hopefully to develop – internal cultural strengths. Nationalists also look outward, past state boundaries, to forge cultural and political alliances with other nations, in their quest for self-determination.

Siberan peoples do not seek full sovereignty. Given the demographic makeup of Siberia, such a quest would prove futile. Rather, they accept the fact that they will remain part of Russian-dominated territorial units, whether these continue to answer to the Russian government or another political entity. They do pursue an increased voice in determining the future of the activities which most essentially define their cultures and the lands which support these activities. To date, advancement toward this goal has been limited, except in the case of the Sakha republic, where the titular nation commands key posts in the government, and the economic base of the republic is solid. Other peoples (Tuvans, Buryats) have fared less well, and those nations without republics, unable to pass any distinct legal code to improve rights, must depend on the Russian Federation to do so. Legal reform in Russia has begun to address Siberian concerns, but much progress is needed before the Siberian peoples are assured genuine self-determination of their futures.

## Notes

Research for this chapter was supported in part by grants from the International Research & Exchanges Board (IREX) and the National Council for Soviet and Eastern European Research, with funds provided by the National Endowment for the Humanities, the United States Information Agency, and the US Department of State ("Soviet-Eastern European Research and Training Act of 1983, Public Law 98–164, Title VIII, 97 Stat. 1047–50). None of these organizations is responsible for the contents or views expressed.

1 James Forsyth, *A History of the Peoples of Siberia. Russia's North Asian Colony 1581–1990* (Cambridge: Cambridge University Press, 1992), p. 100. *Prishlie* refer to those persons who have arrived fairly recently. Censuses however do not consider length of residency. The non-indigenous population doubled between 1939 and 1959 (Forsyth, *History of the Peoples of Siberia*, p. 405).

2 That is the North or regions "equated with the North" due to climatic and demographic-economic characteristics. For the definition of the Soviet "North," see S. V. Slavin, *The Soviet North. Present Development and Prospects.* (Moscow: Progress Publishers, 1972). A. I. Pika and B. B. Prokhorov (*Neotraditsionalizm na rossiyskom Severe*, Moscow, 1994, pp. 11–12), note changes in time over the regions included in both the "North" and the "regions inhabited by peoples of the North", two distinct, if overlapping geographical entities with policy implications.

The Soviet government recognized twenty-six "numerically small" Northern peoples, including the Sami (Lapps), who live on the Kola Peninsula, in the European North of the RSFSR. (This number dipped to twenty-two peoples for the 1959 census, and twenty-three for the 1970 and 1979 censuses.) Others (e.g. Kereks, Soyots), consider themselves distinct peoples but were not recognized as such by the Soviet government.

3 During the Tsarist period they had also been lumped together for policy purposes, but with other peoples as well.

4  Later simply Peoples of the North (*narody Severa*), as distinguished from the more numerous Peoples of Siberia (*narody Sibiri*), including the Altays, Buryats, Khakassy, Tuvans, and Sakha. Most recently the former have adopted the term "Small-Numbered Peoples of the North" (*malochislennie narody Severa*); some persons also have begun to use the terminology, widespread in Canada for indigenous peoples, of *perviye natsii*, First Nations.

5  Henry R. Huttenbach, "Muscovy's Penetration of Siberia. The Colonization Process 1555–1689," in Michael Rwykin (ed.), *Russian Colonial Expansion to 1917* (London: Mansell, 1988), p. 76. For excellent coverage of native Russian contacts, see Forsythe, *A History of the Peoples of Siberia*, and Yuri Slezkine, *Arctic Mirrors. Russia and the Small Peoples of the North* (Ithaca: Cornell University Press, 1994).

6  Huttenbach, "Muscovy's Penetration of Siberia," p. 78.

7  George V. Lantzeff, *Siberia in the Seventeenth Century. A Study of the Colonial Administration*, University of California Publications in History. Vol. 30 (Berkeley: University of California Press, 1943), pp. 90–91.

8  Huttenbach, "Muscovy's Penetration of Siberia," p. 86; Lantzeff, *Siberia in the Seventeenth Century*, pp. 107–110.

9  *Ibid.*

10  Though Russians hunted furs, most of Siberia's "soft gold" was taken by indigenous peoples and turned over to the state as tribute or traded for Russian commodities.

11  Vladilen A. Tugolukov, *Idushie Poperek Khrebtov* (Krasnoyarsk: Krasnoyarskoe knizhnoe izdatelstvo, 1980), p. 101; see also Slezkine, pp. *Arctic Mirrors*, 104ff.

12  Marjorie M. Balzer, "Strategies of Ethnic Survival: Interaction of Russians and Khanty (Ostiak) in Twentieth Century Siberia," Ph.D. dissertation, Ann Arbor, MI, University Microfilms, 1980, pp. 334–335.

13  Slezkine, *Arctic Mirrors*, pp. 26, 27.

14  Zoya Sokolova, *Na prostorakh Sibiri* (Moscow: Izdatelstvo "Russkiy yazyk," 1981), p. 17.

15  Though mostly at the expense of indigenous structures of governance. See Slezkine *Arctic Mirrors*, 1994, chapter 7. Slezkine documents the shifting outlook of the Committee of the North itself.

16  The issue of national consciousness among the Peoples of the North is not well studied. Available Soviet sources which hold that these peoples had no national consciousness, but identified only with the clan, are suspect due to their adherence to a strict Morganian social evolutionary bias (see e.g. H.G. Levin and L.P. Potapoy, *The Peoples of Siberia* (Chicago: University of Chicago Press, 1964). However, if a national consciousness did exist prior to the Revolution among some or all of these peoples, it was nonetheless much strengthened by the creation of a literary language (a single one, in more than one case, for groups speaking a large number of dialects), a national elite, and the designation of official homelands for a number of the peoples. Slezkine (1992: 345–6) discusses the terminology commonly used (*narodnosti* instead of *narod* or *natsii*) by ethnographers regarding the northern peoples.

17  See Yu. V. Popkov, *Protsess internatsionalizatsii u narodnostey Severa.* (Novosibirsk: Nauka, 1990), chapters 2, 3; V. I. Boyko, *Sotsialnoekonomicheskoe razvitie narodnostey Severa* (Novosibirsk: Nauka), chapter 4.

18  N. Amylskiy, "Kogda zatsvetayut zharkie tsvety (O rabote tuzemnykh sovetov i sudov v Turukhanskom rayone)," *Severnaya Aziya*, 1928, no. 3, p. 55.

19  Tsentralnyy Gosudarstvennyy Arkhiv Oktyabrskoy Revolutsii (TsGAOR). Fond 3977: Komitet Severa pri VTsIKe. Op.1. Delo 300. "Protokoly tuzemnykh sobraniy Dalne-Vostochnogo kraya, Irkutskoy gubernii, Arkhangelskoy gubernii i Buryato-Mongolskoy ASSR." ll.77, 104.

20 K. A. Zabelin, "Ocherki po ekonomike Severo-Baykalskogo rayona," *Zhizn Buryatii*, 1930, no. 4, pp. 35–37.

21 TsGAOR, f.3977, op.1, d.300, l.100.

22 Amylskiy, "Kogda zatsvetayut zharkie tsvety," p. 55; Zabelin, "Ocherki po ekonomike," p. 42.

23 One of the okrugs, the Nenets National Okrug, is located in the European North. The Russian government created over twenty national *rayony* for several peoples, including those living beyond the boundaries of their eponymous national okrugs (see Forsyth, *History of the Peoples of Siberia* pp. 283, 285 (map), 327; and Slezkine, *Arctic Mirrors*, pp. 269–272, especially about the lack of awareness about these at top levels of government). These *rayony* soon lost their designation as specifically "national" territories.

24 The Vitimo-Olekma (Evenk) and the Okhotsk-Even National Okrugs were abolished less than a decade after their formation, in 1937–8. The remaining national okrugs were renamed autonomous okrugs in 1977.

25 Affirmative action policy also "invites accusations of reverse discrimination by increasingly nationalistic Russians" (Marjorie M. Balzer, "Ethnicity without power: the Siberian Khanty in Soviet Society," *Slavic Review*, 42, no. 4 (1983), 648.)

26 E.g., Alitet Nemtushkin, "Bol moya, Evenkiya," *Sovetskaya Kultura*, July 28, 1988; Yuriy Rytkheu, "Lozungi i Amulety," *Komsomolskaya Pravda*, May 19, 1988; Vladimir Sangi, "Otchuzhdenie," *Sovetskaya Rossiya*, September 11, 1988; author's fieldnotes, 1992, 1993, 1994.

27 I. S. Gurvich (ed.), *Etnicheskoe razvitie narodnostey Severa v sovetskiy period* (Moscow: Nauka, 1987), p. 94.

28 N. V. Isakova and V. V. Markhinin, "Vsaimodeystvie natsionalnykh kultur: problemy i poiski resheniy," Typescript of paper presented at the II Soviet–Canadian colloquium "Russia-Quebec," July–August 1990, pp. 10–11.

29 *Osnovnye Pokazateli Razvitiya Ekonomiki i Kultury Malochislennykh Narodov Severa (1980–1989 gody)* (Moscow: Goskomstat RSFSR. 1990), p. 9; A. I. Pika and B. B. Prokhorov, "Bolshie problemy malykh narodov," *Kommunist*. 1988, no. 16, p. 77.

30 Unemployment in 1987 ran between 15–18 percent, and was on the increase among eleven of the twenty-six Peoples of the North. V. I. Boyko, ed. *Kontseptsiya sotsial'nogo i ekonomicheskogo razvitiya narodnostey Severa na period do 2010 g.* (Novosibirsk, 1990), p. 45. See also Yeremey Aypin, "Ne neft'yu edinoy," *Moskovskie Novosti*, January 8, 1989, pp. 8–9.

31 David G. Anderson, 1992, "Property rights and civil society in Siberia: an examination of the social movements of the Zabaikal'skie Evenki," *Praxis International* 12(1): 89ff.

32 Pika and Prokhorov 1988, p. 80.

33 Author's fieldnotes, May, June, 1994. See also Aypin, "Ne neft'yu edinoy," which tells of immigrant workers in the oil rich areas of Western Siberia stealing sleds and winter clothing, poaching domesticated reindeer, and desecrating Khant burial grounds.

34 *Materialy Sezda Malochislennykh Narodov Severa* (Moscow, 1990.), This document has been translated, with preface, in *Indigenous Peoples of the Soviet North*, IWGIA Document 67, Copenhagen, July 1990.

35 "International Labour Organisation: Convention Concerning Indigenous and Tribal Peoples in Independent Countries," *International Legal Matters*, no. 28 (1989), 1386–1387; M. I. Mongo, "The Legislative Foundations of the National Policy in the Period of Perestroika and the Destiny of Small-Numbered Peoples of the North," Report prepared for the II Soviet-Canadian colloquium "Russia-Quebec," July–August 1990, p. 14.

36 See especially Ukaz Prezidenta Rossiyskoy Federatsii No. 397, "O neotlozhnykh merakh

po zashchite mest prozhivaniya i khozyaystvennoy deyatelnosti malochislennykh narodov Severa," April 22, 1992; Articles 4 and 42 of the Russian law on subsurface resources (*nedr*) also provides limited advantages to the northern Siberian peoples (*Zakon Rossiyskoy Federatsii* No. 2395–1, "O nedrakh," 21 April, 1992)

37  Proekt Zakona Rossiyskoy Federatsii, "O garantiyakh svobodnogo razvitiya korennykh malochislennykh narodov RSFSR" (typescript, nd); Proekt Zakona Rossiyskoy Federatsii "Osnoy Zakonodatelstva Rossiyskoy Federatsii o pravovom statuse korennykh malochilennykh narodov" (typescript, June 18, 1993).

38  V. I. Boyko, "The Peoples of the North of the USSR on the Way to Self-Government," typescript of paper presented at the II Soviet-Canadian colloquium "Russia-Quebec," July–August 1990, p. 11.

39  *Ibid.*, p. 15.

40  Postanovlenie Kabitnet Ministrov SSR i Sovet Ministrov RSFSR No. 84, "O dopolnitelnykh merakh po uluchsheniyu sotsialno-economicheskikh usloviy zhizni malochislennykh narodov Severa na 1991–1995 gody," March 1991.

41  A. I. Pika and B. B. Prokhorov (eds.), *Neotraditsionalism na Rossiystom Severe* (Moscow, 1994), pp. 3–4.

42  Of the so-called *Trevozhnyy Sever* group of Moscow–St. Petersburg. See *Ibid.*

43  A number of autonomous okrugs elevated their status to ASSR in 1990. These moves were not necessarily backed by the indigenous population of the okrugs, nor did they ameliorate the rights or political powers of the native peoples. To assume that the upgrading of the status of autonomous territories (okrugs, oblasts, and ASSRs) is in all cases a move in favor of greater sovereignty for native peoples is to ignore the ethnic composition of the territories and their leadership. What Bremmer refers to as "matrioshka nationalism" is nowhere more evident than in the Yamalo-Nenets Autonomous Okrug. Inhabitants of this region claimed rights to the gas and oil over which the Tyumen Oblast and Ruran Federation (and formerly the USSR) each also assert ownership. Yet it is the *prishlie*, not the Nentsy and other indigenous peoples of the Okrug, who rallied to upgrade the autonomy of, and therefore their control over, the okrug and its hard-currency generating resources.

44  For example, indigenous Siberians participated in an international symposium on reindeer husbandry, held in Norway in 1993.

45  The Sami of the Koala Peninsula, one of the Peoples of the North (but not of Siberia), have contacts across the border with Sami of Fennoscandia, and have participated in several pan-Sami conferences in recent years.

46  A non-governmental organization of Inuit and Yupik (Eskimos) from Alaska, Canada and Greenland, with NGO status at the UN.

47  Ronald Wixman, *The Peoples of the USSR. An Ethnographic Handbook* (Armonk, NY: M. E. Sharpe, 1984), p. 9

48  L. P. Potapov, "The Altays," in Levin and Potapov (eds); *The Peoples of Siberia*, p. 320.

49  Wixman, *The Peoples of the USSR*, p. 101.

50  Walter Kolarz, *The Peoples of the Soviet Far Easy* (New York: Frederick A. Praeger, 1954), p. 172.

51  L. P. Potapov, "The Khakasy," in Levin and Potapov, (eds), *The Peoples of Siberia*, pp. 345, 351.

52  *Ibid.*, p. 370.

53  Kolarz, *Peoples of the Soviet Far East*, pp. 173, 175.

54  Though barely – see table 5.2 for 1926 figures.

55  Kolarz, *Peoples of the Soviet Far East*, pp. 169, 177.

56  See note 25, above.

57  Most other Turkic peoples of the RSFSR were growing at rates between 15 and 25 percent during this period.

58  A. Tchoudoïakov, "La tragédies des chors," *Questions Sibériennes Bulletin No. 1, Peuples autochtones*, 1990, p. 31.

59  *Ibid.*, p. 32.

60  Kolarz, *Peoples of the Soviet Far East*, p. 175.

61  Wixman, *The Peoples of the USSR*, p. 189, Dimitri Shimkin, pers. comm., July 1986.

62  Juha Janhunen, "Ethnic Activism among the South Siberian Turks," *Questions Sibériennes Bulletin No. 1, Peuples autochtones*, 1990, pp. 57–60.

63  *Ibid.*, p. 59

64  Vera Tolz, "Regionalism in Russia: The Case of Siberia," *RFE/RL Research Report* 2(9), February 26, 1993.

65  *Segodnya*, September 1, 1994

66  The Soviet of the Gorno-Altay ASSR also declared the establishment of an "ecological economic zone," and indicated its plans to attract foreign investment in this zone to develop such relatively low-impact commercial activities as medicinal plant collection and tourism. (FBIS-SOV-90-212).

67  Tolz, "Regionalism in Russia," p. 4

68  Caroline Humphrey, *Karl Marx Collective. Economy, Society and Religion in a Siberian Collective Farm* (Cambridge: Cambridge University Press, 1983), p. 28.

69  K. V. Vyatkina, "The Buryats," in Levi and Potapov (eds.), *The Peoples of Siberia*, p. 209.

70  Humphrey, *Karl Marx Collective* p. 27; Robert A. Rupen, "The Buriat Intelligentsia," *Far Eastern Quarterly*, 10, no. 3 (1986), 385, 386.

71  Rupen, "Burial Intelligentsia," p. 385.

72  *Ibid.*, p. 384. The Japanese sponsored a pan-Mongol congress in Chita in 1919, attended by Buryats, which promoted a Greater Mongol State and called for the expulsion of Russian colonists living east of Lake Baikal (Kolarz, *Peoples of the Soviet Far East*, p. 119).

73  Humphrey, *Karl Marx Collective*, p. 31.

74  Kolarz, *Peoples of the Soviet Far East*, p. 123.

75  See Boris Chichlo, "Histoire de la formation des territoires autonomes chez les peuples Turco-Mongols de Sibérie," *Cahiers du Monde Russe et Soviétique*, 27, nos. 3–4 (1987), especially p. 369, for "before" and "after" maps.

76  Kolarz, *Peoples of the Soviet Far East*, p. 123.

77  The Buryat SSR Council of Ministers adopted a resolution to this effect in September 1991, which evoked demonstrations from opposed parties. FBIS-SOV-91-77, September 12, 1991, p. 81; FBIS-SOV-91-194, October 7, 1991, p. 61.

78  Postanovlenie Verhovnogo Soveta Buryatskoy Sovetskoy Sotsialisticheskoy Respublike, "O postanovlenie TsIK USSR ot 26 sentyabrya 1937 g. 'O razdelenie Vostochno-Sibirskoy oblasti na Irkutskuyu i Chitinskuyu oblasti' v chasti razdeleniya Buryat-Mongol'skoy ASSR," April 26, 1991, published in *Vedomosti Verkhovnogo Soveta Respubliki Buryatiya*, (*VVSRB*), 3 (1992), 29; Postanovlenie Verkhovnogo Soveta Respubliki Buryatiya, "O reabilitatsii narodov Buryati," June 3, 1993, in *VVSRB*, 8 (1993), 134.

79  *Vedomosti Verkhovnogo Soveta i Soveta Ministrov Buryatskoy SSR*, 1 (1991), 29–32.

80  Zakon Respubliki Buryatii, "O yazykakh narodov Respubliki Buryatii," June 10, 1992, in *VVSRB* 5 (1993), 20. Tolz, "Regionalism in Russia," p. 6, noted that in 1991 seventeen of the republic's sixty-three officially registered newspapers (27 percent) were published in Buryat.

81  Postanovlenie Verkhovnogo Soveta Respubliki Buryatiya, "O reabilitatsii narodov Buryatia," June 3, 1993, in *WSRB*, 8 (1993), 134. This decree also condemned the treatment of other nationalities in the Buryat Republic.

82 Information on the presidential elections and the recent political situation in Buryatia, especially regarding cultural revitalization and Evenk/Buryat relations (see main text below), is based on casual conversations and "participant observation" conducted in the republic, April-August 1994, and on newspaper, radio and television reporting during this period. See also Marjorie Mandelstam Balzer, "From Ethnicity to Nationalism: Turmoil in the Russian Empire," in James R. Millar and Sharon L. Wolchik (eds.), *The Social Legacy of Communism* (Cambridge: Cambridge University Press, 1994), pp. 74–79, who notes the assessment of Buryat leaders themselves: Buryat "ethnicity" is more "patriotic than "nationalist" (p. 74).

83 Zakon Buryatskoy SSSR, "O pravovom statuse evenkiyskikh selskikh (poselkovykh) Sovetov narodnykh deputatov na territorii Buryatskoy SSR," January 17, 1991, in *VVSRB*, 3 (1992) 65–70 (and revisions to this, published in *VVSRB*, 8 (1993), 154–155; Polozhenie, "O statuse Bauntovskogo evenkiyskogo rayona Respubliki Buryatii," No. 354–XI, June 4, 1993, in *VVSRB*, 8 (1993), 150–154. About 2,000 Evenki live in Buryatia. A small number of Soyots live in the southwest of the republic: they also are fighting for increased recognition and power.

84 See G. Fondahl, "The Reindeer Riders," *Earthwatch*, 12, no. 2 (Jan. Feb. 1993), 17, for more information on the Evenki in Buryatia.

85 Kolarz, *Peoples of the Soviet Far East*, p. 116. The Soviet government also early on encouraged contact between the Buryats, Khalka Mongols, and the other Mongol people of the USSR, the Kalmyks. For instance, in 1931 Moscow hosted a conference for these three nations, the topic of which was language reforms, including the adoption of a Latin alphabet for all three groups (Kolarz, *Peoples of the Soviet Far East*, p. 115, n).

86 Rupen, "Buriat Intelligentsia," p. 388.

87 *Ibid.*, p. 392, esp. n 24, p. 394.

88 S.B. Pomishin of the Baykal Institute of Rational Resource Management, Ulan-Ude has spearheaded this effort.

89 This section is based in part on information from an interview with political scientist Greg Poelzer. Poelzer worked in Sakha in 1992 and 1993 and visited again in November 1994. I thank him for also loaning me a number of documents. I also thank Marjorie Mandelstam Balzer, the United States' foremost expert on Sakha, for sharing with me several recently published and forthcoming manuscripts of hers. See especially, Majorie Mandelstam Balzer, "A State Within a State: The Sakha Republic (Yakutia)," in Stephen Kotkin and David Wolff (eds.), *Rediscovering Russia in Asia: Siberia and the Russian Far East* (Armonk: M. E. Sharpe, 1995).

90 Goskomstat RSFSR, *Natsional'nyy Sostav Naseleniya RSFSR po dannym vsesoyuznoy perepisi naselenie 1989 g.* (Moscow: Respublikanskiy informatsionno-izdatelskiy tsentr, 1990), p. 152. The Sakha population has been increasing in proportion, due to higher relative birth rates more than outmigration of non-Sakha, and by 1994 approached 40 percent (Balzer, "A State Within a State," 1995).

91 Terence Armstrong, *Russian Settlement in the North* (Cambridge: Cambridge University Press, 1965), p. 113.

92 *Ibid.*

93 Kolarz, *Peoples of the Soviet Far East*, p. 103.

94 The Sakha population dropped between 1926 and 1959 (table 5.1). This is attributed primarily to severe losses during the collectivization drive (Wixman, *Peoples of the USSR*, p. 220).

95 Ann Sheehy, "Racial Disturbances in Yakutsk," *Radio Liberty Research Report* 251/86, July 1, 1986. Minor disturbances date to the 1960s: see Balzer, "A State Within a State," and Marjorie M. Balzer, "Yakut," *Encyclopedia of World Cultures, Volume*

*VI. Russia and Eurasia/China*, ed. Paul Friedrich and Norma Diamond (Boston: G. K. Hall & Co., 1994), p. 84.

96 Balzer, "Yakut," pp. 404–407. Less dramatic but telling events also evidenced the interethnic tensions. *Izvestiya* published an article in 1987 about a number of Sakha teachers who had been allegedly fired for incompetency, but claimed that their dismissal was due to their nationality. Complaints against one centered around her grading Russian students more harshly than Sakha students; her response was that Russian teachers did the same to Sakha. Sakha teachers were also accused of "preaching nationalism." *Izvestiya*, July 22, 1987.

97 Balzer mentions the discussed, if unlikely, division of Sakha along North-South lines, proposed by Slavs who resent what they perceive as excessive Sakha sovereignty movements (Balzer, "A State Within a State," and "Yakut," p. 83). She also notes the difficult position of persons of mixed ethnic background, who "feel they are asked to choose, both officially and unofficially, one dominant ethnic loyalty . . ." (Balzer, "A State Within a State").

98 *Konstitutsiya (Osnovnoy Zakon) Respubliki Sakha (Yakutiya)*, Yakutsk: Natsionalnoe izdatelstvo Respubliki Sakha (Yakutiya), 1993; FBIS-SOV-90–231, November 30, 1990, p. 87; *Report on the USSR*, August 23, 1991, p. 36.

99 Balzer, "A State Within a State"; Poelzer, personal communication, 1994.

100 People who have left have tended to keep their houses, as a contingency, which has only exacerbated the extreme housing shortage in urban areas and fueled further discontent regarding *prishlie* on the part of both the Sakha and the Russian old-timers.

101 Piers Vitebsky, "Reindeer Herders of Northern Yakutia: A Report from the Field," *Polar Record*, 25, no. 54 (1989), 217.

102 Kolarz, *Peoples of the Soviet Far East*, p. 102. For the location of these regions see map 10 in James Forsyth, *A History of the Peoples of Sibiera* p. 285.

103 Kolarz, *Peoples of the Soviet Far East* p. 102.

104 Almost half of the Evenk population of Russia lives in Sakha (only 14 percent live in the Evenk Autonomous Okrug). In 1979, 85 percent of the Evenks living in the Yakut ASSR spoke Sakha as their first language. See V.I. Boyko, "Chislennost, rasselenie i yazykovaya situatsiya u narodnostey Severa na sovremennom etape," in *Problemy Soveremennogo Sotsialnogo Razvitiya Narodnostey Severa* (Novosibirsk: Nauka, 1987), pp. 40, 47.

105 *Konstitutsiya . . . Sakha*, Article 42.

106 *Ibid.*, Article 43.

107 *Sovetskaya Rossiya*, August 19, 1989. National rayons were abolished in the 1930s; this is the first instance of this level of national territorial recognition being granted since then.

108 Evens also proposed the establishment of two national okrugs, but with no success to date. Pika and Prokhorov (eds.), *Neotraditsionalism na Rossiyskom Severe*, p. 78. Pika and Prokhorov note that the share of Evens in the two proposed okrugs would be 3 percent and 4 percent.

109 Balzer, "A State Within a State," 1995.

110 Robert A. Rupen, "The Absorption of Tuva," in Thomas T. Hammond (ed.) *The Anatomy of Communist Takeovers* (New Haven: Yale University Press, 1975), p. 149.

111 *Ibid.*, p. 150.

112 Chichlo, "Histoire de la formation des territoires autonomes," pp. 380–381.

113 Statement made by "representative of the Russian and Tuvan peoples," June 18, 1918, during the concomitant meetings of the Fift Congress of Russian Population of Uryankhai and the Congress of Uryankhai Khoshuns (indigenous leaders). Quoted in Yu. L. Aranchyn, *Istoricheskiy put tuvinskogo naroda k sotsializmu* (Novosibirsk: Nauka, 1982), p. 74.

114  Chichlo, "Histoire de la formation des territoires autonomes," p. 381.

115  *Ibid.*

116  Kolarz, *Peoples of the Soviet Far East*, p. 156.

117  Aranchyn, *Istoricheskiy put tuvinskogo* . . . p. 107.

118  *Ibid.*, p. 167. The alphabet was changed to Cyrillic in 1941.

119  Rupen, "The Absorption of Tuva," p. 151.

120  Kolarz, *"People of the Soviet Far East*, pp. 167–168.

121  See also L. P. Potapov, "The Tuvans," in Levin and Potapov (eds), *The Peoples of Siberia*, p. 388.

122  Kolarz, *People of the Soviet Far East*, p. 168.

123  The rate of growth among the Tuvan population between 1959 and 1970 appeared low, though during this period, Tuvan population grew from 57 percent to 59 percent of the republic's population. Anderson and Silver suggest that one explanation for the apparent low rate of growth is a permeable border with Mongolia which has allowed emigration. This might have been one way which Tuvans dealt with threats to their cultural integrity in the past. See Barbara Anderson and Brian D. Silver, "Some Factors in the Linguistic and Ethnic Russification of Soviet Nationalities: Is Everyone becoming Russian?" in L. Hajda and M. Beissinger (eds), *The Nationalities Factor in Soviet Politics and Society.* (Boulder, CO: Westview Press, 1990), p. 118.

124  *Report on the USSR*, August 10, 1990, p. 27, from *Izvestiya*, July 3, 1990.

125  Ann Sheehy, "Russians the Target of Interethnic Violence in Tuva," *Report on the USSR*, September 14, 1990, p. 16. Sheehy also notes that Tuvans have condemned the accounts of events in their republic in Russian newspapers as highly biased, portraying the Tuvans very unfavorably.

126  *CDSP*, 46, no. 26 (1994), 13.

127  Sheehy, "Russians the Target of Interethnic Violence in Tuva;" Tolz, "Regionalism in Russia," p. 8; *CDSP*, 46, no. 24 (1994), from *Segodnya*, June 17, 1994. See also Balzer, "Yakut," pp. 69–74.

128  Walker Connor, "The Politics of Ethnonationalism," *Journal of International Affairs*, 27, no. 1 (1973), 21.

# Siberia: chronology of events

*June 1986*

Clashes occur between Russians and Yakuts in the city of Yakutsk.

*1989*

Khakass, Altai, and Shor representatives unite to form the Siberian Cultural Center (SCC) which lobbies for increased Siberian autonomy, language development, and protection from environmental degradation.

The "Free Tuva" Popular Front is established, and many members come out in support of independence.

The Sakha Omuk organization is established to preserve and revive Sakha (Yakut) culture.

*July 1989*

24–28   Russian Eskimos participate in a meeting of the Inuit Circumpolar Conference. ICC delegates had come to Russia on an official invitation in November 1988, two years after Moscow had forbidden Russian Eskimos to attend an earlier ICC meeting.

*March 1990*

30–31   The Association of Small Peoples of the North holds its founding congress.

*August 1990*

5       It is announced that 3,000 people, largely Russians, have fled Tuva in 1990 because of violent interethnic conflict which has taken the lives of nearly 100 people.

15      The autonomous region of Khakassia declares itself a republic. The Russian government confirms the existence of the Republic of Khakassia on July 3, 1991.

*September 1990*

27      Yakutia issues a declaration of sovereignty, upgrading the ASSR to republican status and changing its name to the Yakut-Sakha SSR.

29      The Chukchi Autonomous Okrug announces its desire to break away from Magadan Oblast and upgrade to republican status.

*October 1990*

3    The "Siberian Agreement" association is formed to promote the economic interests of several Siberian republics, autonomous okrugs, and regions. The association disavows separatism.

8    The Buryat Supreme Soviet upgrades the ASSR to republican status and designates both Buryat and Russian as official languages.

16    The Koryak Autonomous Okrug proclaims itself a republic (it later agrees to retain autonomous okrug status).

18    The Yamal-Nenets Autonomous Okrug declares itself sovereign from Tyumen Oblast. The neighboring Khanty-Mansi Autonomous Okrug soon follows suit.

25    The Gorno-Altai Autonomous Oblast is upgraded to full republican status. (It remains under the jurisdiction of the Altai Krai until 1992.)

*November 1990*

14    The Nenets Autonomous Okrug proclaims itself a republic. (It later agrees to retain autonomous okrug status, albeit as an equal member of the federation.)

*March 1991*

17    In Tuva, 91 percent of voters (81 percent turnout) support the preservation of the union in the all-union referendum. In Buryatia, 84 percent of voters (82 percent turnout) support the union. In Yakutia, 77 percent of voters (79 percent turnout) support the union.

*June 1991*

12    In Russian presidential elections, Yeltsin loses to Ryzhkov in the Aga-Buryat Autonomous Okrug, the Republic of Gorno-Altai, and Tuva.

*July 1991*

3    A German Autonomous Raion is created in the Altai Krai.

*August 1991*

27    A mass protest organized by the Democratic Burtyatia movement is held in Ulan-Ude to demand the resignation of the Buryat leadership for supporting the Moscow coup attempt.

*September 1991*

22    The Buryat-Mongol People's Party denounces the Russian Federation's draft constitution for failing to define a new relationship between the center and the republics.

30    The Trans-Baikal Russian Union is formed in Ulan-Ude to protect Russian interests in Southern Siberia.

*December 1991*
21    In the first Sakha presidential elections, Mikhail Nikolayev, former parliamentary chairman, is victorious with over 70 percent of the vote.

*January 1992*
22    Khakassia holds elections to a 100-seat Supreme Soviet, the first parliamentary body in the republic's history.

*February 1992*
13    The Buryat Supreme Soviet explicitly endorses participation in the Russian Federation, making Buryatia the first republic to do so.
31    Yakutia's Supreme Soviet approves a draft treaty with Russia allowing the republic to maintain its own gold, diamond, and hard-currency funds.

*March 1992*
11    A meeting of the Association of Autonomous Formations opens in Khanty-Mansiisk to discuss the draft federal treaty.
23    The Negedel National Unity Movement is officially registered in Buryatia.
27–28    A Congress of People's Deputies of Siberia is held in Krasnoyarsk. One of the organizers is the Independent Siberia Party. Delegates call for greater independence and the right to levy their own taxes.

*April 1992*
3    The Koryak Autonomous Okrug officially breaks away from Kamchatka Oblast.
27    Sakha's new constitution comes into force.
The Union of Arctic and Far Northern Cities is founded.

*May 1992*
7    The Gorno-Altai Republic changes its name to the Altai Republic.

*June 1992*
17    The Chukot Autonomous Okrug is officially removed from under the jurisdiction of Magadan Oblast.
20    The Popular Front of Tuva and the People's Party of Sovereign Tuva begin to collect signatures in favor of holding a referendum on Tuva's independence but end the campaign when they face local opposition.

*November 1992*

18–19    Negedel sponsors the convocation of an unofficial Buryat National Assembly which makes several proclamations regarding Buryat state- and nation-building, including renaming Buryatia the Buryat-Mongol Republic and annexing the Aga-Buryat and Ust-Orda Buryat Autonomous Okrugs.

*January 1993*

13    The Buryat Supreme Soviet declares that the National Assembly was illegal and its decisions invalid.

*February 1993*

11    Sakha announces the publication of *Lachil* (Fire), a newspaper printed in the Even, Evenki, Yukagir, and Chukchi languages.

*June 1993*

3    The Buryat government denounces the 1937 decree breaking Buryatia into three territories and officially recognizes the Aga-Buryat and Ust-Orda Buryat Autonomous Okrugs as equal members of the Russian Federation.

*September 1993*

29    Supreme Soviet leaders from thirteen Siberian regions threaten to withhold taxes, seize national property, and interfere with elections if Yeltsin does not rescind his decree disbanding parliament.

*October 1993*

12    The Sakha Parliament dissolves itself, making it the first republican parliament to do so.

21    The Tuvan Parliament adopts a republican constitution pending its acceptance in a December referendum.

*December 1993*

12    54 percent of voters in Tuva (62 percent turnout) support the adoption of a new republican constitution which contains clauses in conflict with the Russian constitution (for which only 31 percent of voters cast their vote). A new parliament (the 32-deputy Supreme Khural) is also elected.

18    In Altai, parliamentary elections are held to the new El Kuraltai. Sakha also holds its parliamentary elections.

21    The Khakass Supreme Soviet cancels parliamentary elections which were scheduled for March 1994.

*January 1994*

6    Kaadyr-ool Bicheldey is elected parliamentary chairman in Tuva.

13–14    The Altai Krai and Kemerovo oblast pull out of the "Siberian Agreement" association on the grounds that it had become overly politicized.

*February 1994*

3    Valery Chaptynov is appointed parliamentary head in Altai. Vladimir Petrov is reappointed chairman of the republican government.

15    The head of the Yamal-Nenets Autonomous Okrug, Lev Bayandin, is removed for exceeding his authority. He is replaced by Yuri Neyelov.

22    The Buryat Parliament accepts the republic's new constitution.

*March 1994*

20    Elections are held to the Aga-Buryat Autonomous Okrug's duma with 60 percent turnout, significantly higher than most other local elections.

*July 1994*

1    In Buryatia, presidential elections are held. Leonid Potapov, a Buryat-speaking ethnic Russian, beats the Buryat Aleksandr Ivanov with 72 percent of the vote. Elections are held simultaneously to the 65-seat Supreme Khural.

7    The Siberian Agreement coordinating committee for culture meets in Gorno-Altaisk.

19    Mikhail Semenov, a Buryat, is elected parliamentary chairman in Buryatia.

*December 1994*

3    The Congress of Khakassian People is held in Abakan. Delegates express their concern for the plight of native Khakass.

*February 1995*

3    Deputies from Far East legislative bodies issue a resolution demanding that Moscow pay its debts to the region or else they will withdraw their support of the Russian government.

*May 1995*

25    Khakassia adopts its first constitution. In it, the republic is described as a "member" of the Russian Federation and not a "state."

*June 1995*

29   Sakha becomes the fifth republic to sign a power-sharing treaty with Moscow.

*July 1995*

11   Buryatia signs power-sharing agreements with Moscow.

# Part III
# The "new" Eastern Europe

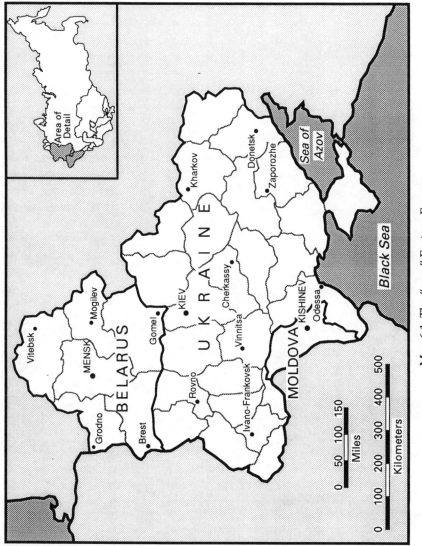

Map 6.1 The "new" Eastern Europe

**Ukraine**

- International boundary
- ★ National capital
- Railroad
- Road

0    100    200 Kilometers
0    100    200 Miles

Lambert Conformal Conic Projection, SP 47N/62N

Boundary representation is
not necessarily authoritative.

# 6 Ukraine: from empire to statehood

ALEXANDER MOTYL AND
BOHDAN KRAWCHENKO

Conventional wisdom holds that Ukraine is a hotbed of nationalism and that nationalism was responsible for Ukrainian independence. But while nationalists and nationalism have made a difference in Ukrainian history, Ukraine's relationship with other states and power centers has largely determined the directions its society, politics, and economy have taken. Developments within the system of states to which Ukraine belonged deprived it of its medieval freedoms, and similar external developments also prepared it for and then thrust it toward statehood. Nationalists pushed the process along, but without the decay of totalitarianism and the collapse of the Soviet empire their efforts could not have transformed Ukraine from a colonial territory into an independent polity.

In the twentieth century, Ukrainian nationalists tried three times to build their own state: first in 1917–1921, when they failed; then in 1941–1945, when they failed again; and in 1989–1991, when they finally succeeded. Success came the third time not because the nationalists tried harder or because they were stronger, but because the external conditions were right. Indeed, they were so right that sovereign Ukraine's leading nationalist proved to be the same person as Soviet Ukraine's leading anti-nationalist – Leonid Kravchuk. In a word, independence was not so much won by, as bequeathed to, Ukrainian nationalists.

## Ukraine's early history

*Okraina* means borderland, and indeed Ukraine has been a borderland for much of this millennium. Things were different from the early tenth century through to the mid thirteenth, when Ukraine comprised the heartland of one of medieval Europe's largest states, Rus'. Kiev, its capital, was a major center of trade, Orthodox Christianity, and old Slavic culture and, thus, a formidable political rival of Constantinople. Kievan Rus's preeminent ruler, Yaroslav the Wise (1036–1054), codified its laws, established a stable administration, and thereby created the conditions for a golden age of culture. At a time when Moscow was an insignificant settlement while St. Petersburg, obviously, did not even exist, Yaroslav cemented his state's international ties by marrying his daughters to the kings of France, Hungary, and Norway.[1]

Once Rus' collapsed under the impact of internecine warfare and the Mongol invasions in the mid-thirteenth century, however, Ukraine became a political *okraina*, a frontier zone that for several centuries remained at the intersection of the continually shifting borders of the Grand Duchy of Lithuania, the Ottoman Empire, the Polish – Lithuanian Commonwealth, the Crimean Tatar Khanate, and Muscovy. The continued existence of Ukraine as a politically undefined territory, however, was incompatible with two interrelated world historical trends: the growth of the international system of states and the emergence of the modern state. The packaging of the world into modern states, a process that began with the Peace of Westphalia in 1648, meant that borderlands such as Ukraine could not remain beyond the reach of some state or states. No less important, the transformation of the European state from a coercive, tax-gathering, and war-fighting apparatus to a bureaucratic structure concerned with permanently administering and supervising a subject population – a development that coincided with the division of the world among states and the development of new technologies and forms of political organization in the seventeenth and eighteenth centuries – made Ukraine's integration into some state inescapable as well. After 1648, in other words, not only was Ukraine's familiar frontier status, especially in Europe, impossible, but incorporation into a state necessarily entailed integration into the administrative, coercive, and financial systems supervised by some political elite.

Ironically, although borderland status transformed Ukraine into a political no-man's land, it also contributed enormously to a cultural, religious, and educational revival in the sixteenth and seventeenth centuries, one that produced many of the elites that eventually came to staff the Russian church and polity. To be sure, a precarious existence at the intersection of several states had the effect of assimilating local Ukrainian elites, who generally concluded that alignment with the culture and politics of Poland, Lithuania, or Muscovy would enhance their interest. By the same token, however, Ukraine's position at the point where so many cultures and religions met and clashed also produced cross-cultural fertilization and religious assertiveness – two processes that contributed greatly to a dynamic religio-cultural revival in the sixteenth and seventeenth centuries. The central event was the Counter-Reformation, which militant Jesuits utilized as a means for converting the Ukrainian Orthodox population to Catholicism. In 1596, their efforts bore fruit at the Union of Brest, whereby several formerly Orthodox bishops pledged allegiance to the Vatican on condition that their distinct eastern Orthodox liturgical rites be retained. In turn, the Catholic offensive provoked an Orthodox counter-offensive, led by Prince Konstantyn Ostrozsky and the Kiev Metropolitan Petro Mohyla.[2] Orthodox lay brotherhoods dedicated to a religious revival sprouted throughout the country; the clergy was mobilized in defense of the faith; and the intellectual foundations for the movement were laid with the establishment of the Ostrih Academy and the Kiev Mohyla Collegium, both institutions of higher learning dedicated to training Orthodox intellectuals.

By the mid seventeenth century, therefore, Ukraine had become a center of cultural and religious activity – a fact also reflected in the painting and architecture of the period and in the unusually high literacy of its population. One of the central fault lines in modern Ukrainian history also emerged at this time – the division between a European-oriented Catholic west and a Moscow-oriented Orthodox east. That division was mirrored in political realities. Despite unstable and shifting borders, Poland controlled most of the Right-Bank Ukraine (i.e. the lands west of the Dnieper), while Muscovy controlled most of the Left-Bank Ukraine. As long as such a condition persisted, Ukrainian culture remained open to a variety of external influences and continued to be vibrant. By the late eighteenth century, however, Ukraine's ambiguous political status had come to an end. In a portent of things to come, authoritarian Muscovy defeated chaotically democratic Poland, with the result that Ukraine's window to the West was closed. The three partitions of Poland bequeathed most of the Right Bank to Russia, with only eastern Galicia going to Austria and remaining open to the Western world.

Incorporation and integration into Russia was in most respects a disaster for Ukraine. Culturally, the region became a barren province within several generations, as most of its elites moved north or adopted Russian language and culture. In a trend that contravened European developments, the literacy rate actually declined. Religiously, Ukraine was reduced to an appendage of the Moscow Patriarchate, and the intellectual debates that characterized the seventeenth century withered away. Economically, Ukraine became a Russian hinterland, serving almost exclusively as a source of agricultural products and raw materials. Socially, Ukraine lost its educated elites and became a country of ignorant and impoverished peasants set against a Russian and Polish landlord class and Jewish merchants. And politically, Ukraine lost the capacity for self-rule that it had had in the seventeenth century and was transformed into a backwater of Russia.

## The Ukrainian Cossacks

The mid seventeenth century represented post-Rus' Ukraine's best chance of reestablishing an independent political existence. Due to Ukraine's borderland status, something in the nature of a primitive political elite had come into existence by the late sixteenth century – the Cossacks. Cossackdom emerged as a haven for escaping serfs, slaves, and peasants beyond the bounds of established political authority in the vast Ukrainian steppes. Their lair was the Sich, an island stronghold on the south Dneiper. From there the Cossacks launched attacks on Turks and Tatars and defended their autonomy from the encroachments of Poles and Russians. Their exploits became the stuff of Ukrainian legend and the basis of Ukrainian national identity.[3] In time, some of these "social bandits" were coopted by the Polish authorities, who "registered" them as frontier allies of the *Rzecz Pospolita* or Commonwealth. Even so, both registered and unregistered Cossacks continually engaged in rebellions against the expansion of Polish rule and obligations throughout most of the sixteenth and seventeenth centuries.

The Cossack rebellions culminated in the Great Insurrection led by their chieftain, Hetman Bohdan Khmelnytsky, in 1648. Cossack defense of their prerogatives merged with popular dissatisfaction with the harshness of Polish landlord rule and Orthodox opposition to the Counter-Reformation to produce a massive revolt that encompassed all strata of Ukrainian society. As Khmelnytsky's armies defeated the Poles in several battles, Orthodox battled Catholics and peasants massacred Jews. In the end, Khmelnytsky established an independent Cossack state. Independence was short-lived, however, as in 1654, facing military threats on all sides, Khmelnytsky signed a treaty with the Tsar of Muscovy at Pereyaslav.[4] Several decades of incessant warfare then followed, as Ukraine was transformed into a battleground among Turks, Tatars, Poles, Russians, and Ukrainians. By the late seventeenth century, when the dust had settled the Right Bank, utterly devastated and largely depopulated, remained Polish, while the Left Bank, which survived the period of the "Ruin" more or less intact, remained home to the Hetmanate – but in a new incarnation, as an autonomous political unit subordinated to the Russian Tsar. The Ukrainian Hetmans defended their rights, but to no avail. Hetman Ivan Mazepa actually attempted to secede from Russia with the assistance of Charles XII of Sweden, but both went down to defeat at Poltava in 1709.[5] Finally, by the late eighteenth century, Catherine the Great, in her enthusiasm to establish a modern bureaucratic state, abolished the Hetmanate and destroyed the Sich as well.[6]

Could the Cossacks have succeeded in maintaining an independent polity? An analysis of the international environment suggests that the answer is no. For reasons directly related to Ukraine's peculiar status as an unincorporated territory situated at the intersection of several realms, Ukrainian elites lacked the means to assert their political will over the long run. Although the Cossacks were formidable fighters, they were, in the final analysis, no match for the well-organized and better-supplied armies of the Turks, Russians, Tatars, and Poles. Seen from this point of view, Khmelnytsky's temporary success seems to have been due to the international "correlation of forces" in general and in Eastern Europe in particular. Poland had been weakened by the Thirty Years War, Muscovy had just emerged from the Time of Troubles, while the Ottomans were pursuing empire in the Balkans and southeastern Europe. With a power vacuum in Ukraine, the Cossacks were able to assert themselves temporarily; once this window of opportunity was closed, and Ukraine was transformed into a battleground among Poles, Russians, Ukrainians, Turks, and Tatars in the 1670s, state-building became well-nigh impossible.

Relative Ukrainian weakness was due to three other factors as well, all related to Ukraine's extended existence on the margins of several political realms. For some 400 to 500 years, Ukraine was the site of attempts at annexation, plunder, and buffer maintenance by Poles, Ottomans, Tatars, and Muscovites. The constant incursions of all four into the no-man's land separating them destabilized Ukrainian society and made indigenous Ukrainian attempts at concerted state-building exceedingly difficult. At the same time, such destabilizing conditions ensured that Ukraine would be the site of continual rebellions, uprisings, and revolts from the sixteenth century through to the eighteenth, precisely the time of the most concerted Polish, Muscovite, Tatar, and Ottoman attempts to control the territory.

Furthermore, Ukraine's geographic features – flat steppelands amidst virtually no natural boundaries – have made it a natural invasion and migration route from east to west, for Sarmatians, Goths, Alans, Huns, Mongols, and many others, and from west to east for the armies of Poland, France, and Germany. As there are few places that lend themselves to the sort of urban fortifications that were common in the Middle Ages in Western and Central Europe, the geography of Ukraine was conducive neither to easy defense nor to the development of settled stable societies in general and cities in particular. In turn, the relative lack of prosperous cities, a condition aggravated by the fall of Byzantium in 1453 and the concomitant elimination of the north–south trade routes that had contributed to Kiev's strength in the tenth and eleventh centuries, deprived the region of much-needed capital and other resources. Not surprisingly, Ukraine would remain a political vacuum until modern states emerged and began dividing up the world.

## The nineteenth century and after

Thanks to the modernization that radiated outward from the Moscow–Petersburg region, the nineteenth century witnessed the former Ukrainian borderland's progressive integration into the Russian polity and economy. Urbanization, industrialization, and transportation went hand in hand, as did education, communication, and social and ethnic differentiation. A Ukrainian working class began emerging in the late nineteenth century in the mining industries of the Donbass and in the oil industry of the Carpathian foothills of Galicia. A tiny Ukrainian bourgeoisie also came into existence. Tensions with Jews grew as competition for jobs and housing in rapidly growing cities intensified. In all these respects, however, nineteenth-century developments in Ukraine differed little from developments in Russia as a whole – which is simply to say that the country in its entirety was undergoing rapid change. To be sure, a distinctly Ukrainian national intelligentsia was making itself heard, especially toward the end of the century, and its self-perceptions did differ somewhat from those of the Russian intelligentsia – if only because the tsarist regime assiduously pursued cultural Russification to the point of even banning Ukrainian-language publications.[7] But, inasmuch as separatism was on virtually no one's agenda before 1917, Ukrainian and Russian intellectuals cannot be said to have had fundamentally different political aspirations at the start of World War I. Liberals, socialist revolutionaries, social democrats, conservatives, and reactionaries were evident in Ukraine, as throughout the entire empire. Democracy, socialism, and autonomy may have been desired goals, but independence remained the aspiration of only a handful of Ukrainians.

Nevertheless, despite the Ukrainian elite's utter lack of interest in separation from Russia initially, in a preview of perestroika, several years of massive instability transformed Ukraine into something approximating a country. World War I debilitated the tsarist polity, economy, and society. The Bolshevik revolution of 1917 destroyed tsarism, while the Civil War that lasted until 1921 forced the non-Russian elites to fend for themselves and choose sides. Ukrainians were compelled to build a state and to respond to the military and political challenge of the Bolsheviks and the Whites. As identical developments in state- and nation-building were also taking place in Finland, Poland, Belarus, the Baltics Georgia, Armenia, Azerbaijan, and Turkestan, it clearly was the collapse of the Russian polity and economy, and not non-Russian nationalism *per se*, that impelled Russia's constituent provinces and imperial peripheries to opt for nationalism and pursue independence. Simply put, independence not only began to make sense to Ukrainian elites, but by 1918 was the only option that offered them refuge from imperial collapse and Bolshevik takeover. So belated an appreciation of the benefits of independence meant that Ukrainian elites were completely unprepared for the demands of statehood. They lacked an army, a bureaucracy, and a citizenry willing to defend their state. As a result, Ukrainian leaders generally improvised. They reacted to events in Russia, they squabbled over utopian schemes, they shifted positions and changed alliances, they fought on several fronts – and in the end they lost.

## The Ukrainian revolution

The first to lose were the democrats who established the Ukrainian People's Republic in 1917. Unable to stop the Bolshevik invasion of early 1918, they were forced to conclude a separate peace with Germany and Austria-Hungary – a desperate move that earned them the contempt of the West. In

April, the Central Powers replaced the democratic nationalists with General Pavlo Skoropadsky, whose authoritarian policies proved so unpopular that the democrats were able easily to forge a broad-based coalition that swept him from power in November. Once again, however, the democrats failed at building a stable state. Chaos swept the country, as demobilized soldiers assisted land-hungry peasants in expropriating landlord property, warlords assumed control of most of the country, and a myriad of parties, movements, and armies vied for power. As Ukraine became a borderland once again, as Germans, Austrians, Poles, Bolsheviks, Whites, and Ukrainians of various political hues, from monarchist to anarchist, fought over the territory, a situation remarkably similar to the Ruin of the 1670s emerged. Unskilled, untrained, and unprepared Ukrainian nationalist elites, lacking armies, industries, bureaucracies, and popular bases, were no match for such confusion. Left-wing nationalists believed that social revolution alone could save the cause; in time, they allied with the Bolsheviks. Right-wing nationalists believed that a strong military and a strong state were the only answer; they looked to Symon Petliura, a social democrat-turned-general, for inspiration. Ironically, by 1918 both sides had become irrelevant, as events in Ukraine assumed a life of their own. The fact is that no one was in charge. What historian Arthur Adams called the "Great Peasant Jacquerie" devastated the country. Millions of Ukrainians and Russians died, falling victim to war or disease. Perhaps as many as 100,000 Jews were killed or wounded in pogroms initiated by Ukrainian peasants, warlords, and soldiers under Petliura's putative command, by Russian Whites, and by the Bolsheviks. By 1920, the nationalists, or what remained of them, had to flee.[8]

Under conditions such as these it was virtually certain that the Russian Bolsheviks would win control of Ukraine. Given Bolshevik organizational, military, and industrial superiority, Ukraine could not escape Bolshevik reassertion of central control on its own. The Bolsheviks possessed a genuinely well-disciplined cadre party; they inherited the bulk of the former tsarist army; and their control of Russia's largest urban centers provided them with the industrial base without which victory in a sustained war would have been impossible. Not surprisingly, only where German or Allied intervention was strong enough and lasted long enough, as in Finland, Poland, and the Baltic states, did independent states actually manage to sustain themselves.[9]

Although the imperial relationship between Soviet Russia and Soviet Ukraine closely resembled that between Petersburg and the Hetmanate in the eighteenth century, it represented a major step forward – from the point of view of Ukrainian elites – over that practiced by the tsars in the nineteenth century. Then, Ukraine had had virtually no distinct; by 1924, it could boast of having the elite it had lost in the late eighteenth century.[10] Elite or no, however, Soviet rule devastated Ukraine. Ukraine's population suffered enormous losses: millions died in the Great Famine of 1932–1933, and millions were shot, exiled, or incarcerated during the Stalinist Terror of the 1930s and 1940s.[11] As if Soviet rule were not enough, millions more perished during World War II as a result of Nazi Germany's genocidal policies toward Jews, who were slated for immediate destruction, and Ukrainians, who were to serve as *Untermenschen*.

But Soviet rule also decimated the very elites it created: first, during the 1930s, when the Ukrainian national Communists were purged and the budding Ukrainian intelligentsia was destroyed; then in 1939–1941, when the west Ukrainian elites were subjected to a terror that played a major role in inclining the population of Galicia to support Germany's attack on the USSR; in the late 1940s, when "Ukrainian bourgeois nationalism" again became the target of Stalin's ire; and, finally, for most of the 1960s and 1970s, when the Ukrainian dissident movement was crushed in several waves of secret police repression.[12]

In addition, Ukraine's culture and language were subjected both to the homogenizing influence of "Sovietization" and to the psychologically dislocating impact of "Russification." Ukraine not only became a cultural backwater with almost no ties to the rest of the world but also lost most of its historical memory. Ukraine's economy was subordinated to the dictates of planners in Moscow, who transformed it radically in the 1930s at an enormous cost in human lives and with the effect of destroying its agriculture, depleting its mineral deposits, poisoning its land, air, and water, creating inefficient monster industries, and producing a demoralized working-class population.[13] Finally, Ukraine's society was atomized, its diverse organizational forms destroyed, and its population regimented in officially sponsored institutions.

In a word, Ukraine – its population, its elites, its culture, its economy, and its civil society – fell victim to a totalitarian state, whose central Russian elite exerted imperial control over its satraps in the republics. Nevertheless, the creation of an administratively bounded, symbolically sovereign territory called the Ukrainian Soviet Socialist Republic, forced industrialization and rapid urbanization, the development of a relatively modern educational, social, and communications system, and the emergence of a Ukrainian political class endowed with a certain bureaucratic structure and some administrative skills effectively transformed what had been a backward province into a potentially viable Ukrainian state.[14] Ukraine had finally acquired all the prerequisites of statehood and could, as a result, become a state. Thanks to Soviet policies, Ukraine's administrative bureaucracies supervised its economic development, which in turn provided the territory with the urban resources and capital that state-building requires and that Ukraine had historically lacked.

In the early 1960s, a new Ukrainian political elite comprised of individuals with modern skills had come into being and found itself frustrated politically and economically by a hypercentralized system which refused to recognize it as a force, or share power with it. Led by Petro Shelest, who became the republic's first party secretary in 1963, Ukraine's leadership could not even sanction the construction of a pedestrian underpass in Kiev without first having obtained permission from Moscow.[15] Attempting to consolidate their position, the new elite made an effort to "re-Ukrainize" the political apparatus by opposing the influx of non-Ukrainian cadres into the republic.[16] The new elite also sought its own ideology to justify its claims and found sources of legitimacy in its own unique national heritage.

Correspondingly, Shelest sought to upgrade the status of Ukrainian culture and language in the republic. In 1965, Ukraine's Minister of Higher Education Yurii Dadenkov called for sweeping reforms in the educational establishment, including preferential admittance to higher educational institutes for Ukrainian speakers, mandatory Ukrainian proficiency for all instructors, and gradual conversion to a completely Ukrainian-language educational system.[17] While such a policy was not looked favorably upon by Moscow and did not make significant advances, Ukrainian-language textbooks at the post-secondary level did increase from 17 percent of the total (in 1968) to 40 percent in 1972.[18] The publication of other Ukrainian-language books and newspapers also increased under Shelest.

By the 1970s, Ukraine was actually in the position of being able, if external conditions permitted, of translating its symbolic sovereignty into genuine sovereignty. Brezhnev's ascension to power, however, led to a tightening of control in Ukraine, and in May 1972 Shelest was purged. He was accused of a number of anti-Soviet transgressions: misinterpreting the Soviet federal system, promoting "elements of economic autarkism," failing to acknowledge nationalist deviations in the CPU and Ukrainian cultural circles during the 1920s, idealizing Ukrainian Cossacks, and ignoring the positive influence of Russian culture on Ukrainian culture and education.[19] In a clear reference to Shelest, the new party leader, Volodomyr Shcherbytsky, admonished those standing "on the side of reactional nationalist philistinism" and criticized "the unprincipled tolerant attitude on the part of individual leading cadres toward manifestations of national limitedness and localism."[20]

Shelest's removal was engineered by the Brezhnev leadership and occurred at a time when Moscow was introducing new centralist initiatives. The purge that followed Shelest's fall was the most thorough since Stalin's time. Every major institution in Ukraine was affected by the purge, and at the regional, city, and district levels, a quarter of the secretaries responsible for ideology were replaced.[21] Shelest's position had been supported by virtually the entire Ukrainian apparatus, and his ouster was backed by only three of the twenty-five oblast first secretaries. But with his fall, autonomism as a movement suffered a major setback. Since the conditions that gave rise to it did not change, however, its reemergence within Ukraine in the late 1980s remained part of the historical agenda.

## Socio-economic factors and cultural assertion

The drive for independence was motivated by a number of factors, not all of which carried the same weight in different parts of the republic. Overall, however, there was a profound realization that the USSR was disintegrating as a socio-economic and political formation. The centralized bureaucratic system was seen as a brake on economic and social development and modernization. Moscow had nothing to offer – it was neither a source of technological know-how, nor an international financial center. It was merely an apparatus of repression and control

Neither was Ukraine tied to the center by virtue of its membership in a single, unified market, as the USSR was never that. Ukraine itself could not even be considered a single market. Rather, what existed were monopolistic structures and a mono-ministerial branch economy. All talk of economic integration was ludicrous when factory X, thousands of miles away, supplied factory Y with goods which Y could get from an enterprise across the street. In many cases transportation costs were higher than production costs. And before Ukraine's economy could be integrated into a larger market, not to speak of the world market, a Ukrainian market had to be first established with all of the institutions of a modern economy – a bank, currency, customs service, and economic statistics.[22] As for ties with other republics, these had to be developed through bilateral treaties. There was no pressing economic reason why Ukraine's exports of meat to oil-producing Tiumen had to be mediated by a Moscow ministry. It was far more efficient to do so directly (Indeed, starting in 1991 all of Ukraine's food exports to other republics were direct deals bypassing Moscow.)

Except in the western parts of Ukraine, the motor force for independence was socio-economic in nature. It could hardly be otherwise given that decades of Russification had weakened the traditional determinants of a Ukrainian national identity. Moreover, the largest Russian population outside the RSFSR lived in Ukraine (11.3 million in 1989). According to census data, every tenth Ukrainian was acculturated into Russian culture or Russified, and three-quarters of Ukrainians knew Russian. While only one-third of the total population of Ukraine gave Russian as their mother tongue, language data drawn from the general population census is an unreliable indicator of language use. A comprehensive 1988 survey of parents of first-grade students in Kiev found that only 16.5 percent of respondents used Ukrainian in the home, and only 4.7 percent used the language at work.[23] Moreover, in the 1988–1989 school year, only 47.5 percent of pupils studied in Ukrainian-language schools. Most large cities of the

Donbass or southern Ukraine did not have a single Ukrainian-language school until recently. In 1987, only 14 percent of lectures at Kiev University were delivered in Ukrainian. Only four Ukrainian-language records were produced between 1980 and 1985. Since the mid-1970s, with one exception, all scientific journals in Ukraine were published in Russian. Output of books per capita in Ukraine in 1991 was 0.9, as compared to 12.7 for Russia.[24]

As Soviet sociological investigations have pointed out, the system of attitudes on national relations depends not so much on cultural orientation, that is, the Russification of an individual's cultural pattern, as on a complex combination of social, economic, and cultural interests.[25] The fact of the matter is that Ukraine's economy, its society and environment had been ravaged at the hands of the Moscow center, and this in turn spurred the growth of a movement for independence. The dominance of socio-economic factors in the sovereigntist discourse helps explain why surveys show that 45–50 percent of Russians in the republic favored Ukraine's independence.[26]

The drive for statehood was thus largely motivated by a profound realization of just how mismanaged and ravaged Ukraine's economy had been at the hands of the Moscow center. Until 1990, 95 percent of Ukraine's economy was controlled by Moscow, which was responsible for the distribution of over 90 percent of what was produced in the republic. Less than a quarter of Ukraine's national income remained in the republic – the rest was repatriated to the center.[27] Also, Moscow's investment and pricing policy discriminated against Ukrainian industry.[28] Some 113 billion roubles were taken from Ukraine to the center annually, through taxation and profits, and all of Ukraine's hard currency earnings went to Moscow – 30–34 billion roubles annually. Every year 365 million roubles gathered by Ukrainian customs went to the center.[29]

This policy had serious consequences in all spheres of life. Expenditures on the development of basic science research per capita in Ukraine was 6.3 roubles, in Russia 25.5; per capita expenditure on culture in Ukraine was 3.8 roubles, in Russia 12.8; per capita investment in housing was 94 and 145 roubles respectively.[30] These and many other statistics received wide publicity, and most citizens of Ukraine agreed with Prime Minister Fokin in 1990, "Our only hope, our only chance of improving the situation is economic independence."[31]

The environmental devastation of Ukraine at the hands of Moscow was one of the most powerful leitmotifs of independence agitation. Ukrainians saw their nuclear experience as an example of Moscow's environmental imperialism, on a par with dumping toxic waste in Africa. The catastrophe at Chernobyl in May 1986 had not yet come to symbolize the Ukrainian experience in the Soviet Union, but its mishandling by the Party authorities in Moscow and Kiev greatly contributed to the erosion of Party legitimacy.

As Serhii Odarych, secretary-general of Rukh observed, "Chernobyl helped us understand that we are a colony."[32]

Chernobyl was but part of the story. Southern Ukraine had been so polluted by industry and mindless land improvement projects that this fertile steppe region had Ukraine's highest infant mortality and most appalling longevity rates. In Mykolaiv oblast, the average longevity of males dropped from 65.2 years in 1988 to 63.4 by 1989. Scientists warned of the erosion of Ukraine's gene pool: 46 percent of the republic's secondary school children experienced chronic illness of one kind or another. Only 5–8 percent of graduates of secondary schools could be considered healthy. 80 percent of pregnant women in Ukraine became ill (in the early 1980s, the figure was 30 percent), and 40 percent of pregnant women had miscarriages. Ukraine's birth rate was the lowest in the USSR – 13.3 per 1,000 of the population.[33]

But at the same time there was a realization that Ukraine had considerable economic and social potential if only it could get control of its resources. Ukraine had high grade ores and metallurgical coal; it was a large exporter of cement to the Middle East; its exported electric power for which it did not receive a kopeck, and its climatic and soil conditions could support a flourishing agriculture. In 1991, President Kravchuk quoted with pride a German study evaluating all republics of the USSR on the basis of their potential to integrate into the European market. In a scoring based on 100 points, Ukraine took first place with 83 points, Latvia, Estonia, and Lithuania obtained 77, the RSFSR 72, Georgia 61 and so forth down to Tajikistan with 18.[34]

The unbelievable economic incompetence of the central government also served to convince the Ukrainian political class that sovereignty was an indispensable component of crisis management. Ukrainian officials complained that the Moscow government was printing money with abandon, and thereby causing inflation, whereas the Ukrainian government was engaged in the impossible task of trying to take out of circulation surplus roubles (800 million roubles were burnt in Ukraine in 1990). Gorbachev's and Prime Minister Pavlov's decrees, said one factory director from Dnipropetrovsk, "are ruining our economy."[35]

## Stirrings of nationalism

Perestroika's destruction of the Soviet system was the background on which Ukraine's hesitant march toward independence took place. Few Ukrainians actually desired the creation of their own state, even as late as 1989.[36] That most of the population then proceeded to vote for such a measure in late 1991 was, to be sure, partly the result of a bitter political struggle waged by Ukrainian nationalists against the Communist regime. Far more so, however, this turnaround was the result of Gorbachev's demolition of Soviet totalitarianism.

As late as September 1989 the republic was still ruled by an ardent Brezhnevist, Volodymyr Shcherbytsky, the first secretary of the Communist Party of Ukraine (CPU). Nationalist activity was confined to the renewal of some of the dissident organizations that had been crushed in the 1970s, such as the Helsinki Group, to the formation of several others, most prominent of which was the Ukrainian Culturological Club, and to the agitation of Ukrainian writers – in particular Ivan Drach and Dmytro Pavlychko, both of whom discovered a talent for mobilizational politics. Organizations such as the Helsinki Group focused on the defense of human rights, while those such as the Culturological Club concentrated mostly on the "ecology" – i.e., the existential status – of Ukrainian culture and language.[37]

This nascent national and democratic movement viewed with envy Moscow's relatively liberal atmosphere – a certain provincial ferocity had always characterized communist rule in Ukraine. As the prominent poet Ivan Drach quipped in June 1989, "In Moscow they clip your nails, but in Kiev they cut your fingers off."[38] The Ukrainian intelligentsia urged Mikhail Gorbachev to end "Ukrainian exceptionalism" and allow the winds of glasnost and perestroika to blow in Ukraine.[39] Shcherbytsky's policy of resisting all measures aimed at political and economic modernization was becoming increasingly untenable since it clashed with Gorbachev's program. Indeed, Shcherbytsky's presence in Ukraine was a liability, given the growing radicalization of public opinion in the wake of the Chernobyl nuclear disaster. At the same time, spurred by the example of the Baltic republics, former dissident circles in Galicia pressed for the launching of Ukraine's own version of a people's front, envisaged initially as a movement in support of Gorbachev's reforms. On September 8, 1989 the People's Movement for Restructuring – "Rukh" (the word means "movement" in Ukrainian) held its constituent congress in Kiev.[40] Two weeks later Gorbachev flew to Kiev to oversee the ouster of Shcherbytsky.[41]

Volodymyr Ivashko, who replaced Shcherbytsky, was an unimaginative but conciliatory apparatchik. Nevertheless, Shcherbtsky's removal was significant step on the path to independence. In power since 1972, when he initiated a vicious crackdown on dissent, Shcherbytsky had embodied the ultraloyal non-Russian official, committed to Communist rule and to the preservation of Moscow's empire. His retirement, and eventual death in early 1990, removed one of the major obstacles to the development of a nationalist movement by permitting the hitherto monolithic Party elite to divide into pro- and anti-perestroika factions.

In contrast with the events that were rocking Central Europe in 1989, however, that year Ukraine still appeared – and largely was – quiet. Rukh's first major attempt at mobilizing mass public opinion took place on January 22, 1990, the anniversary of the declarations of independence and of unity (*sobornist'*) of the Ukrainian People's Republic in 1917 and 1918, when the movement attempted to replicate the Baltic "human chain" of several months before.[42] Incredibly, or so it seemed at the time, close to half a million Ukrainians turned out to join hands on the highways and roads between Kiev and Lviv. The action was a foretaste of things to come.

## 1990: the decisive year

In March of 1990, elections to the republican Supreme Soviets took place. Although the democratic opposition in Ukraine had only a month to campaign, and was not represented in all of the electoral districts, it still managed to win nearly a third of the new parliament's seats.[43] Since all parliamentary debates were broadcast live on radio and television, the opposition now had access to a national audience and skillfully exploited this opportunity. The Communist majority – the "Group of 239" – still controlled the legislature, but for the first time in Soviet Ukrainian history a vigorous opposition emerged and made itself heard. Most important perhaps, although the democrats lacked numbers, they quickly showed that they outclassed the Communists in political and oratorical skills – a fact of no small consequence in the next year and a half.

Events in other republics also pushed Ukraine in a nationalist direction. Estonia, Latvia, and Lithuania had declared sovereignty, by which they meant the primacy of their laws over Soviet laws, in 1988–1989. In March 1990, Lithuania went even further and proclaimed independence, an act that resulted in Gorbachev's imposing an economic blockade and Lithuania's suspending the declaration. That summer all the other republics followed in the Balts' footsteps and also declared their sovereignty.

So, in Ukraine, political initiative had clearly passed to the side of the opposition. Rukh's membership had grown to over 500,000, and other unofficial groups such as the Ukrainian Language Society, *Zelenyi svit* ("Green World") and Memorial also gained strength.[44] Throughout the summer, thousands thronged parliament as it debated Ukraine's own declaration of sovereignty. The document was passed almost unanimously on July 16, 1990.[45] The Ukrainian parliament had responded to the growing economic and political disarray in the Soviet Union and asserted its newly-found prerogatives in populist fashion, thus getting on the bandwagon led by the Balts.

On July 22, 1990, with Kiev still reeling from the drama of the passage of this act, Ivashko ignominiously resigned from all of his Ukrainian posts and moved to Moscow as second secretary of the CPSU Central Committee. Lacking charisma, he had not been able to interact with the public and quickly became an object of popular derision. Nor did he have the political skill to plot measures that would have held the unfolding national movement in check, a weakness which made him lose the support of key sectors of the communist hierarchy in Kiev.

Leonid Kravchuk, a former ideological secretary of the Central Committee of the CPU, replaced Ivashko as head of Ukraine's parliament. His elevation to this post surprised many. What undoubtedly played a role in his selection was the fact that Kravchuk had earned his spurs as the party's only capable public debater against Rukh, and thus could be expected to keep order in Parliament. The dour and tough industrial administrator Stanislav Hurenko became first secretary of the CPU.[46] A team was thus put in place which could, perhaps, challenge the gains of the national movement.

Throughout the autumn of 1990, in concert with the major provocations which Moscow unleashed in the Baltics, steps were taken in Ukraine to roll back the challenge to communist authority. Demonstrations near parliament were banned; troops were massed outside of Kiev; the communist majority in parliament changed procedures and restricted the opposition's use of the air waves; administrative obstacles were raised to thwart the work of democratically-controlled regional and local soviets; and a radical nationalist deputy, Stepan Khmara, was arrested in a crude provocation. Khmara languished in prison since the communist majority voted to strip him of his parliamentary immunity.[47] Democratic deputies began to wonder who would be arrested next. Ukraine was rife with rumors that direct presidential rule or martial law was about to be imposed. Indeed, instructions on whom to arrest, and what organizations to ban under the terms of a state of emergency, were circulated to reliable functionaries in oblast soviets.[48]

This conservative backlash poured cold water on the euphoria which had followed the adoption of Ukraine's declaration of sovereignty. The nation, it seemed, had been duped. It appeared that the declaration was destined to remain on paper only, and the opposition accused the communists of voting for Ukraine's sovereignty only to surrender it under the terms of a new union accord. (It would look better politically if a "sovereign" Ukraine signed a new treaty of union.)

Resistance to this strategy came from a totally unexpected quarter – Ukraine's students. Their actions captured the public's imagination, forced the resignation of Vitalii Masol, the chairman of the Council of Ministers, and committed parliament to strict conditions for the signing of a union accord, namely, the prior passage of a constitution enshrining Ukraine's sovereignty.

The student movement which unfolded in the early days of October 1990 carried out some of the most remarkable mass actions Ukraine had ever seen. It began with a small group of hunger strikers who camped on October Revolution square in downtown Kiev. They were quickly joined by hundreds of others and the square was turned into a miniature Woodstock. Post-secondary institutions throughout Ukraine went on strike and an all-Ukrainian student strike committee was formed. On October 16, some 150,000 people marched on parliament – naval cadets in the front rows with marshaling provided by over one thousand Afghan veterans. The crowd was an unusual conglomerate of social layers – vocational students and punkers, university students and the intelligentsia, workers and white-collar staff. Student leaders addressed parliament and their demands were broadcast live on radio and television. For the next two days the city was seized with tension. The government refused to negotiate with the student strike committee, and armored vehicles prowled about the city. Yet the students held firm.

On October 18, unexpectedly, a large column of workers from Kiev's largest factory marched on parliament in support of the students. They chanted only one word, their factory's name – "Arsenal." Workers tipped the balance. That evening the government reported that it would meet all student demands.[49] The prime minister, Vitalii Masol, was replaced with Vitold Fokin, who promised the immediate introduction of economic and political reforms.[50] Large segments of the population finally realized that change, substantive change, was inevitable and that Ukraine really could control its own destiny.

No less significant, however, while the government had remained inactive and the police were pursuing diversionary tactics against the nationalists, Kravchuk had not abandoned the sovereignty line. Indeed, against expectations, he became one of the most forthright defenders of Ukrainian sovereignty – the only position, as he no doubt realized, that permitted him to retain power, keep the conservatives and Gorbachev at bay, and continue to court the nationalists.

That October Rukh held its Second Congress, which together with the student strikes marked another turning point in the politics of Ukrainian nationalism. The movement condemned the Communist Party and expressly came out in favor of Ukrainian independence.[51] Ironically, their action put both the hardline Communists and the national Communists in a bind: inasmuch as both had supported sovereignty, they had to distance themselves from the maximalist demands of Rukh without appearing to contradict their pro-Ukrainian stance. Kravchuk especially had to maneuver between Rukh-style nationalism and what was probably his own preference, a looser Soviet Union with greater powers for Ukraine and the other republics. By late 1990, it was Rukh that set the political agenda and determined the political discourse.

Rukh's language was palatable to Communists such as Kravchuk because it was nationalist, but neither chauvinist, nor racist, nor anti-Semitic; it had at its core the attainment of statehood for the Ukrainian people, whom Rukh carefully defined in non-ethnic terms that permitted Russians, Jews,

Poles, and others to take part in and support its cause.[52] Such a nationalism was at least as potentially appealing to Communists, as it promised them the opportunity of continuing to serve as an elite, if not the only elite, within a future Ukrainian state.

## The union falls apart

Without painstaking preparatory work – the launching of some 350 unofficial newspapers, the establishment of Hyde Park corners in every major city, rock festivals and conferences, and the communication of a new national message by increasingly bold journalists working in radio, television, and the press – it would be impossible to imagine the surprising turn of events which unfolded during the miners' strike of February and March 1991. Echoing students, miners from russified Donbass raised as their first political demand the immediate constitutional sovereignty of Ukraine and the reduction of Moscow's powers to that of a coordinating center of a commonwealth of sovereign states. In the words of Serhii Besaha, the miners' spokesman who addressed Ukraine's parliament on March 22, 1991, "The political demands raised by the miners require decisive measures on the part of Ukraine's parliament . . . People of freedom-loving Ukraine understand our position: we are in a difficult situation and can get out of it only by Ukraine becoming fully sovereign."[53] The settlement that was reached between the miners and the government once again committed Parliament to acting in earnest on the question of sovereignty. And this time it was the sector of Ukraine's population – the majority Russian Donbass population – that was most likely to resist state-building measures which had been won over to a sovereigntist perspective.

The role of Ukraine's "Piedmont" – Galicia – loomed large in all national mobilizations. Donbass miners, for example, were first exposed to ideas of independence by their colleagues on the strike committee from the Lviv-Volyn' coal basin. Part of Austria before 1918, and then of interwar Poland, Galicia had escaped the devastation of Stalinist rule. When the Soviets occupied the area after the Second World War they confronted an active and militant national movement which had penetrated the masses down to the last village.[54] Under glasnost, the national movement there rapidly established hegemony, and spread to other areas of Western Ukraine (especially Volhynia). In the March 1990 elections, the Communist Party for all intents and purposes collapsed in Galicia, and an aggressive program of de-Sovietization of public life was undertaken: the removal of visible symbols of Soviet rule (such as Lenin monuments), changes to the school curricula, and the like. A more radical market reform, beginning with serious moves to de-collectivize agriculture, was initiated. Later, in the March 17, 1991 referendum on the fate of the "Union" (see below), the three Galician oblasts had their own third ballot which asked voters whether or not they wished Ukraine to be an independent state. Independence received the support of close to 90 percent of voters.[55]

An important part of the drive for sovereignty was the adoption of a program of Ukrainization. Although the Ukrainian language had been recognized as the official state language in November 1989, the Masol government "froze the project" and nothing was done until Fokin (a Russian) became prime minister.[56] 300 Ukrainian-language schools opened up, as well as several thousand Ukrainian-language classes in Russian schools.[57] Ukrainian was introduced in political and economic administration, and management staff in factories such as the giant Antonov aircraft works began taking intensive Ukrainian-language classes.

As one observer noted, "For the first time since the eighteenth century we see in Ukraine a profound crisis of loyalty to the imperial center."[58] A concomitant of this process was the legitimation of a Ukrainian national identity. The rediscovery of Ukrainian history and culture became a mass phenomenon. The three-million strong Ukrainian diaspora and its numerous centers of Ukrainian studies and publishing houses contributed substantially in this respect. For the first time since the 1920s, agencies such as the media and the educational system began to communicate a national message.

In 1991, politics in Ukraine entered into a new period, that of primary state-building. Increasingly, the power of initiative in the drive for sovereignty moved from the streets into the corridors of state and economic institutions. Of course the foundations for this development lay in the pressure which the new mass movements had exerted on the existing political elite. The partial democratization of the political order which had occurred, and the prospect of imminent elections, forced sectors of the political elite to think seriously about their future. Public opinion polls in Ukraine revealed that the popularity of the party apparatus had sunk to abysmally low levels.[59] In November 1990, Leonid Kravchuk's popularity among Kievans was so low that he did not even figure in the top twenty most popular politicians.[60] But by June 1991, after he had become closely identified with the sovereignty issue, Kiev polls showed him to be the preferred candidate for President of Ukraine. He was chosen by 54 percent of respondents. Hurenko, the first secretary of the CPU, could not even garner 1 percent support.[61] The Party, to quote I. Tarapov, rector of Kharkov State University, was "gripped by crisis."[62] The party's unpopularity hastened calls for the establishment of an independent Ukrainian Communist Party as a way of marking distance from the Moscow apparatus.[63] The CPU took a partial step in this direction by adopting its own statutes, a move criticized by some hardliners as the beginning of the federalization of the party.[64]

Throughout 1991 state structures gained greater significance and served as the hothouse for a new political class. The introduction of a rudimentary multi-party system, the removal of party cells from all factories, democratic control of local governments and the separation of powers between the Party and the state served to enhance the role of state structures.[65] Moreover, parliament began to resemble a real legislature. Unicameral, with a budget twice that of Russia's, Ukraine's Supreme Soviet nurtured a core of professional full-time politicians.[66] Parliamentary commissions, in which the opposition played an active role, took numerous legislative initiatives, while the relationship between party and state became strained. At a session of the Presidium of the Supreme Soviet, Ivan Pliushch, the deputy head, reportedly told Hurenko, "gone are the days when instructors from the Central Committee will tell the Council of Ministers what to do." In most oblasts and cities, the head of the state apparatus wielded more power than the party boss.[67] Emblematic of the balance of forces between the two institutions was the Presidium's decision to strip Hurenko of the use of his private airplane and give it to Kravchuk instead.

The center of political gravity, therefore, shifted away from the preeminent all-Union structure – the Party – towards the Ukrainian state, whose logic of existence was bound up with an expansion of its prerogatives. This served to factionalize the party elite and draw a sizable number of its members, namely, enterprise directors, government ministers and the like, into a group popularly called "the centrists" or "communists-sovereigntists." Thus, on many crucial votes in parliament, over a third of the so-called "Communist majority" could be counted on to vote with the opposition. The break in party ranks proved decisive in the debate on the March 1991 referendum on the new union. Despite the opposition of the party leadership, almost half the communist members of parliament voted in favor of adopting the second "Ukrainian" question which negated the one formulated by Gorbachev (see below).[68] Communist discipline in parliament slipped: many communist deputies did not even bother to turn up at CPU parliamentary faction meetings. The June 16, 1991 gathering, for instance, was attended by only 184 out of 324 deputies.

The communists' rapprochement with the opposition was also dictated by their fear of the latter's ability to unleash social unrest on a massive scale. In the face of initiatives such as the establishment of the All-Ukrainian Union of Solidarity Committees of Toilers, a new trade union patterned closely after Solidarity which held its founding congress on June 23, 1991, communists understood the advantages to be had from coopting the opposition. The new trade union supported radical social, political, and economic reform, and full Ukrainian independence. The opposition, in turn, felt unprepared to take power, and decided to use this rapprochement to push the new centrists into taking real measures to build Ukrainian statehood.

Politics in a country as diverse and large as Ukraine is a complex matter.

The strategy adopted by Ukraine's leadership was not to irritate Moscow with bold symbolic gestures. Rather, it preferred a low-key, incremental approach. The March 1991 referendum on the Union is a case in point. Rather than challenge Moscow's right to hold the referendum in Ukraine, parliament instead placed its own question on the ballot. Whereas the Kremlin's question asked people to decide whether or not they wished to remain in the USSR on the basis of renewed federalism, the Ukrainian question asked people whether they wished to be part of a Commonwealth of Sovereign States whose Ukrainian membership would be based on Ukraine's declaration of sovereignty. Kravchuk urged people to vote "yes" for both, saying that the first question merely asked "are you for a Union?" whereas the second asked "what kind of Union do you want?"[69] In its massive propaganda campaign the Communist apparatus totally ignored the second question, but to no avail: 70 percent of voters supported the Kremlin's question, and 80 percent Ukraine's question.[70] Kravchuk interpreted this as a mandate to accelerate the process of the "sovereigntization" of Ukraine and the transformation of the Union into a Commonwealth of Sovereign States with the center playing a loose coordinating role.[71]

Throughout 1991 the parliament had a full agenda, as some sixty laws fundamental to establishing Ukrainian statehood were considered. In the first instance the focus was on creating instruments for independent economic policy. Thus, Ukraine was to nationalize All-Union property by the end of 1991; all external trade was to be placed under the republic's jurisdiction. Ukraine established its own customs service and independent national bank, and the first plans were made to introduce a separate Ukrainian currency. Measures were adopted making all USSR Presidential decrees null and void unless they were passed by Ukraine's parliament. A commission on external and internal security was created as the first step in the formation of a ministry of national defense and a national army.[72] In the area of foreign relations, parliament passed a resolution instructing the Cabinet to take measures to establish "diplomatic, consular, and trade relations with foreign states" in order to implement "the Declaration of State Sovereignty of Ukraine in the Field of External Relations." The first major diplomatic breakthrough came in June 1991 when, on the basis of a direct bilateral agreement, Ukraine and Hungary opened consulates. Ukraine was the first Soviet republic to take such a measure.[73]

Ukraine's attitude towards the Union accord is an example of its quiet, determined approach. Unlike the first six republics which opted for full independence, Ukraine participated in the talks, but it drove a hard bargain. For example, Ukraine wanted to retain the right to form an internal army, and argued for relatively weak structures at the Union level. (Kravchuk, for example, was opposed to a Union constitution.) The Union government was not to be allowed to raise taxes in Ukraine. Rather, the republic was to fully control taxation, and transfer funds to the All-Union budget to pay for central programs which Ukraine had agreed to. Before any accord could be signed, All-Union property had to be in the hands of the republic. These demands, taken in concert with the imminent introduction of Ukrainian currency, were designed to deprive Moscow of the mechanisms of policy implementation. Resisting Gorbachev's haste in concluding a new Union treaty, Ukraine dragged out the process. The logic was that the more sovereign Ukraine became, the stronger its bargaining position would be.

Thus Ukraine proposed an elaborate process for the signing of the Union accord which would have postponed the act for at least six months. Ukraine had first to pass its own constitution enshrining its sovereignty, then Parliament was to debate the draft treaty "word by word," then it was to send a delegation to negotiate with other republics and produce a second draft. Only at this point could the accord be signed. Ukraine was insisting that different republics join the Union at different times and under different conditions.[74] Interestingly, the vast majority of communists agreed on the wisdom of this approach while the opposition realized that some kind of treaty had to be signed: one which would begin the process of the *de-montage* (dismemberment) of the Empire, to quote Mykhailo Horyn, a radical oppositionist deputy.

In a statement to Ukraine's parliament, Leonid Kravchuk summarized Ukraine's new mission:

> We are proceeding in stages [and] affirming Ukraine's sovereignty in all spheres – economic, social, international, cultural – in all aspects of our life ... These are the first steps to independent statehood. Some people may not understand this, but this is for real. It is such a pleasure to watch those deputies who are conscious of the fact that they are the creators of an independent state, a state which does not look submissively to the center, and which is not a colony.[75]

Vitold Fokin declared, "The time has come for us to focus our energy, intellect, and knowledge for a real rebirth of Ukraine as an independent, economically independent, industrially developed state, which will occupy its rightful place in the international community. This is our historic chance."[76]

## Independence and its consequences

The August coup was decisive in moving independence forward in Ukraine. For the first two days of the coup Kravchuk appeared hesitant in condemning the Emergency Committee. But as soon as it became evident that the *putsch* was doomed, he went further than the leaders of the other republics: as well as intensifying his anti-Communist rhetoric, he supported a declaration of independence before the Ukrainian parliament that was quickly passed on August 24, making the country independent contingent upon ratification in a general referendum.[77] In this way Kravchuk showed himself sensitive to changes in public opinion, which had grown considerably more anti-Moscow as the extent of the farcical coup, pitting Gorbachev against his once-trusted lieutenants, became known.

Increasing stimuli in the drive for Ukraine's independence came, then, from events taking place in Moscow itself. Belligerent statements from Yeltsin's advisors, including vice-president Aleksandr Rutskoi and press secretary Pavel Voshchanov, on what should constitute the frontiers of an independent Ukraine increased local distrust towards Russian rule of any kind. Russian nationalist demagoguery from Vladimir Zhirinovsky raised concerns about political leadership in Russia. One article in a Russian newspaper which discussed the option of a nuclear strike on Ukraine should Kravchuk refuse to give up his strategic arsenal did nothing to increase trust in Russia at the critical juncture when Ukraine was contemplating its constitutional future.[78] The Ukrainian parliament's initial proclamation of state sovereignty on July 16, 1990, had not appeared to stir up such Russian backlash to the extent that the post-coup declaration of independence had. Political developments within Russia were to remain of ongoing concern to Ukraine even with independence within grasp. As Kravchuk put it to the Rukh Congress held in late February 1992, "Remember, when there is a frost in Russia on Thursday, there will be frost in Kiev by Friday."[79]

Not a small part in Kravchuk's proclamation of independence was played by the diplomatic spadework he carried out in 1991 which, admittedly, was still being overshadowed in the West by Gorbachev's own international skills. In October 1990 Ukraine concluded an important agreement with its one-time overlord, Poland, which recognized the existing border between the two countries. On subsequent official visits to Western states – Germany, France, Switzerland, Canada, and the US – Kravchuk prepared foreign leaders for Ukrainian independence while establishing contacts with Western businessmen and renewing relations with Ukrainian communities abroad. His ability to undertake such extended foreign visits was linked, in turn, to political stability prevailing at home, and, relatedly, the absence of serious unrest among Ukraine's own national minorities.

By the end of November, Ukraine's "historic chance" for independence was about to be seized. The State Council of the USSR failed to approve Gorbachev's new Union treaty at a meeting outside Moscow; one newspaper presciently titled its story "Gorbachev's Waterloo at Novo-Ogarevo."[80] Kravchuk made clear his now uncompromising opposition to a Union of Sovereign States as Gorbachev had envisioned it: "A confederation and a united state are two incompatible, mutually exclusive things. When will we stop deceiving our own peoples? Half-hearted measures, vagueness, matters left unsaid, endless attempts to evade the tough questions – how long can this go on? I won't participate in this deception."[81]

The final act in the drama of Ukraine's independence was the December 1, 1991 referendum. With a turnout of 84 percent, the proposal received support throughout the country. In Western Ukraine, whose intense political activism has already been remarked upon, over 90 percent of voters favored independence. In industrialized oblasts which were markedly russified such as Donetsk, Dnepropetrovsk, Zaporozhe, and Kharkov, support for independence did not dip below 83 percent. The Crimea, with its ethnic Russian majority and its fairly recent (1954) incorporation into Ukraine, 54 percent cast ballots for independence.[82] Even the nationalists had not expected such a resounding vote of support; indeed, many feared that the population might actually vote *against* independence. But their fears were unwarranted. Kravchuk and his former comrades, all of whom were also fearful, but of being accused of insufficient patriotism and, perhaps, even complicity in the coup, supported independence and decided to use the old Party machine to that end. Several months of old-style "agitation and propaganda," incessant parliamentary debates that excluded other options as unpatriotic, methodically staged rallies by Rukh and other nationalist organizations, the careful courting of key Russian and other ethnic constituencies, and a media barrage concerning the historical inevitability of independence made the difference.[83] That continued membership in the Soviet Union meant having to live with the widely despised Gorbachev, that the other republics were also jumping ship, and, finally, that the Bush administration signaled its support of independence several days before the referendum only added to the persuasive appeal of genuine statehood.[84]

The referendum confirmed two facts. One was that the nationalist agenda was completely victorious and set the terms of debate. The other was that the former Communists under Kravchuk had managed to retain influence by appropriating that agenda and, far more important, translating it into reality. The resultant political reality in Ukraine was thus especially complex. Independence was won by people who for the most part had fought independence all their lives. The first of independent Ukraine's many Communist benefactors was, of course, Gorbachev, whose destruction of totalitarianism forced all of the republics to be free. The second such benefactors were the coup leaders, who banged the last nail into the USSR's coffin. The third were Kravchuk and his circle, who recognized that independence was the necessary condition of their survival in post-coup conditions. To be sure, the *bona fide* nationalists did make a large difference. They mobilized the masses and developed the program that eventually became Kravchuk's. On their own, however, the nationalists could not have destroyed the system and rallied the entire population around the flag of independence. Only established elites, in Moscow and in Kiev, could do that and did, by initiating and continuing a process – perestroika – that ineluctably led to the destruction of totalitarianism and, then, to the collapse of empire.

That Ukrainian independence came so abruptly, so suddenly, and so unexpectedly had enormous consequences for the future of the country. Virtually no one in or out of the government was prepared for independence or its aftermath. Inexperienced and untrained, Ukraine's postimperial elites had to cope with the herculean task of transforming a colony into an independent state and creating everything that totalitarianism had destroyed or stifled.

The collapse of totalitarianism left an institutional vacuum within the Ukrainian society and economy, while the collapse of empire left an institutional vacuum within the Ukrainian polity. In a word, Ukraine lacked a civil society, a market, and a state, and without these it could hardly have had a coherent sense of national identity, democracy, and rule of law. It did possess a highly educated citizenry and numerous informal organizations, extensive blackmarketeering and organized crime, and administrators, former dissidents, and would-be elites. None of these translated into *institutions* – established behavioral procedures and rules of the game.

The task before Ukraine was immense: the construction of all the characteristics of a "normal" country. Some reflection would have suggested that attaining all these goals quickly and simultaneously in a country devastated by seventy years of totalitarianism and several hundred years of imperialism was impossible. Moreover, the obstreperous nature of Ukraine's postimperial and post-totalitarian legacies meant that the rapid and full-scale introduction of the market – when defined as a set of economic institutions – was equally impossible. Markets presuppose effective, rule of law states; without rule of law, marketization becomes tantamount to the kind of gangster capitalism that has taken root in Russia. Premature "Big Bang" approaches are, thus, a guarantee of the nonattainment of the market and, perhaps, of the discreditation of reform in general.[85]

## Kravchuk's achievements

Although convention wisdom holds that the Kravchuk administration was an unmitigated disaster for Ukraine, the reality is rather more complex.[86] Kravchuk's Ukraine experienced both successes and failures with respect to building a state, an elite, a nation, a civil society, a democracy, and a market. Thanks to Kravchuk, the picture in Ukraine has not been one of unmitigated disaster.

President Kravchuk assumed formal power in a territorial space inhabited by people who were not yet a nation, administered by bureaucrats who did not yet comprise a state, and with the support or against the wishes of political activists who were only a half-elite. At a minimum,

Ukraine could be a meaningful term only if its inhabitants were Ukrainian citizens and its activists were genuine elites. In turn, independence could be a meaningful synonym for sovereignty only if there were a state capable of exercising effective decision-making authority. Kravchuk's overriding goal, therefore, had to be to create all three – a nation, a state, and an elite. His good fortune lay in the mutually supportive relationship between nation-building and state-building on the one hand and authority-building on the other. His bad luck lay in the incompatibility between the pursuit of these goals and elite incompleteness.[87]

What little there was of a Weberian state in Ukraine in late 1991 was supplemented with elements of stateness that bode relatively well for the future. In contrast to Russia, the Ukrainian presidency and parliament were on the way to becoming institutions, and not mere arenas of (armed) struggle. Some ministries, especially that concerned with foreign affairs, became more or less competent. Some elites, especially those with extended training in Western educational institutions or in several newly established Ukrainian institutes, acquired badly needed expertise in administration and policy making. The army became a more or less coherent fighting force apparently dedicated to defending Ukraine. Last but not least, the symbolic accoutrements of statehood – international recognition, hymns, flags – became natural and normal.

Similar gains could be claimed on the nation-building front.[88] Although Russian doubts about the wisdom of Ukrainian independence may have grown, secessionist movements were nascent at best, and ethnic Russian identification with Ukraine as a homeland appeared to be strong. By the same token, an exclusivist Ukrainian nationalism was still confined to some marginal political groups and to parts of Western Ukraine. Although it is much too premature to claim that a coherent Ukrainian nation has come into being, a *narod Ukrainy* may already exist, especially if the willingness to communicate in both Russian and Ukrainian, the absence of ethnic tensions, and the continued nonpoliticization of ethnicity indicate the existence of such an entity.[89]

Purveyors of scenarios of Ukraine's inevitable collapse have frequently suggested that, lured by the promise of economic prosperity in Russia, the ethnic Russians of the Donbass would press for secession from Ukraine.[90] Upon closer examination, the argument appears quite weak. Aside from the fact that secessionist movements the world over have been and still are notoriously unsuccessful, Donbass Russians have little incentive to embark on such a move. Their support of Ukrainian independence in late 1991 reflected the belief that life would be better in an independent Ukraine;[91] in other words, their commitment to "Russianness" and Mother Russia as an ethnic homeland appeared minimal. If so, then, for them, life in Ukraine will continue to be better than life in Russia. In energy-poor Ukraine, they have economic, political, and ethnic clout; in energy-rich Russia, they would be sacrificed to the interests of the more efficient Kuzbass, reduced to but one region in an enormous country, and have no ethnic card to play.

Crimea is somewhat different, less because it would make more political, economic, or ethnic sense for its inhabitants to join Russia – consider that even in Yeltsin's Russia Crimea would lose its putative sovereignty and enjoy far less genuine autonomy – and more because of the presence of the Black Sea Fleet. Crimea's transformation into a Trans-Dneister republic is not implausible, but, civil war aside, its successful secession would still depend far more on Russia's willingness to absorb it – and thereby set a precedent for its own dismemberment – than on Ukraine's incapacity to prevent it.[92] And in light of the mess that is Crimea's economy, there is virtually no incentive for Russia to annex an impoverished region.

Civil society may have done best in independent Ukraine. Although it, too, is still in a nascent stage, the large and burgeoning number of autonomous nonstate organizations, groupings, and proto-institutions is encouraging evidence of a civil society-in-becoming. The revival of churches, the multiplication of self-styled political parties, the emergence of numerous social, cultural, and ethnic organizations all portend the development of a public sphere that could act as a barrier between the citizenry and the state and as a breeding ground for further private political, social, and economic initiatives.

Democratization received passing grades as well, especially when compared to the retrograde processes that took place in Russia, where the struggle between parliament and president led to deinstitutionalization, the legitimation of violence as a means of political struggle, and the emergence of an all-powerful president with indisputably dictatorial inclinations. Although the Ukrainian government was deadlocked for most of 1992 and 1993 – and that did impede reform – deadlock was also a sign of growing institutionalization and of the recognition by political elites that balance of power is central to democratic politics. No less important was the ability of the Ukrainian parliament and president to agree peacefully on general elections in 1994.[93]

Economic reform was the Achilles' heel of Kravchuk's Ukraine. The karbovanets collapsed, hyperinflation ravaged the country, and privatization, even of the service sector, was minimal. None of this was good news, of course, but it is catastrophic only if one assumes that the economy determines everything and that nothing else matters. The economy *is* important, but states and nations and civil societies and democracies also matter, especially in post-totalitarian, post-imperial circumstances.

## Leonid Kuchma and the future of Ukraine

These largely encouraging developments, while not directly attributable to Kravchuk, were possible because of the policies he pursued. By building a state and a nation and by forging an elite, Kravchuk permitted a variety of important political, social, and cultural processes to take place within a relatively consensual elite framework. In a word, Kravchuk enabled institutions to take root and institutionalization to begin. As a result, Ukraine became more coherent after two and a half years of Kravchuk, but its movement toward greater coherence also highlighted the desperate straits of a country incapable of overcoming quickly the legacies of totalitarian rule. And yet, although Ukraine's condition in mid- to late 1994 was difficult, the country was actually better positioned to embark on economic reform and succeed than it had ever been.

President Leonid Kuchma came to power with several inestimable advantages. First and foremost, thanks to Kravchuk's slow, plodding, and unspectacular policies, some of the preconditions of the market and marketization were finally in place. Elected president of Ukraine on July 10, 1994 with 52.1 percent of the popular vote (but with considerable regional variations in popularity – see table 6.?),[94] Kuchma could successfully introduce a radical economic reform package in October of that year in large part due to Kravchuk's having made such a move possible with his patient construction of a nation, a state, and an elite. Secondly, because of the progressive economic decline experienced by Ukraine's population since late 1991, the impact of radical economic reform could not be as disruptive as it might otherwise have been. The population wanted change, any change; it was inured to economic pain; its expectations were virtually nonexistent; and things could hardly get worse with or without reform. Thirdly, Ukraine's elites and institutions had not only grown accustomed to one another, but they, too, in large measure came to adopt the view that continued economic decline was impermissible and that something, anything, had to be done. Despite the parliamentary majority enjoyed by Ukraine's Communists and Socialists, even many of them were inclined to accept reform for want of a better alternative.

Kravchuk also made Kuchma's successes on the international front possible. It was the Tripartite Agreement among presidents Yeltsin, Clinton, and Kravchuk in January 1994 that transformed Ukraine into a country worthy of Western support.[95] Once the nuclear issue was resolved, on paper at least, the door was open both to inclusion in the Partnership for Peace and to economic assistance, if, as indeed happened, radical economic reform were to become a priority on the president's agenda.

Last but not least, Kravchuk's policies toward Russia also paved the way for Kuchma. In essence, those policies – insistence on an equitable division of the Black Sea Fleet and of Soviet property, insistence on Russia's recognition of Ukraine's sovereignty and territorial integrity, promotion of ethnic Russian rights within Ukraine, and rejection of Russian-led reintegrationist schemes – were both reasonable, differing little from what most states would pursue, and understandable, reflecting a historically grounded

Ukrainian mistrust of Russian intentions in general and of objectively imperious Russian attitudes in particular. Not surprisingly, Kuchma's policies differed little from Kravchuk's in terms of substance. Indeed, Kuchma appeared to be no less committed to Ukrainian independence than his predecessor – hardly a surprising development in light of the inclination of all leaders to promote the interests of the states they run.[96] What did change was the atmospherics, the rhetoric. Kuchma's style was less assertive, less confrontational, than Kravchuk's. As a result, Kuchma's election was greeted with enthusiasm by Russian elites. But style only goes so far. It can smooth over differences and reduce tensions, but it cannot resolve genuine disagreements. And these, for better or for worse, are likely to typify the Russo-Ukrainian relationship for as long as Russia remains a great and imperialist power with tenuous democratic institutions.

All in all, things looked relatively well for Ukraine in 1996. Its relationship with Russia was more or less stable; its relations with the West were improving in leaps and bounds; and, most impressive perhaps, the country that many analysts predicted would collapse seemed poised to embark on an economic reform that would complement its state- and nation-building efforts and possibly result in a genuinely normal – that is to say, a severely traumatized though viable – post-Soviet state. Naturally, the political, economic, social, and cultural problems Ukraine inherited from the past would take years, perhaps even generations, to overcome. And Russia's brooding presence would never be reassuring. But as an independent state, Ukraine was here to stay.

## Notes

1 Orest Subtelny, *Ukraine: A History* (Toronto: University of Toronto Press, 1988), p. 35.

2 See S. N. Plokhii, *Paptsvo i Ukraina. Politika rimskoi kurii na ukrainskikh zemliakh v XVI-XVII vv.* (Kiev: Vyshcha shkola, 1989).

3 See, for instance, Frank Sysyn, "The Reemergence of the Ukrainian Nation and Cossack Mythology," *Social Research*, 58, no. 4 (Winter 1991), 845–863, as well as "The Cossack Chronicles and the Development of Modern Ukrainian Culture and National Identity," *Harvard Ukrainian Studies*, 14 no. 3/4 (December 1990), 593–607.

4 Whether the Treaty of Pereyaslav was actually intended to merge Ukraine with Russia or merely establish an alliance between two equal partners has been the focus of historical controversy. J. Basarab (ed.), *Periaslav 1654: A Historiographical Study* contains a good discussion of the controversy. See, particularly, Ivan Rudnytsky's introduction, "Periaslav: History and Myth," pp. xi-xxiii. The standard Soviet interpretation of the treaty can be found in Appendix 8, "Theses on the Three-Hundreth Anniversary of the Reunion of the Ukraine with Russia (1654–1954)," pp. 270–88.

5 Depending on one's point of view, Mazepa – whom Peter I considered a close ally – is seen as a traitor to the crown or, alternatively, a national hero. For a treatment of this issue, see Orest Subtelny, "Mazepa, Peter I, and the Question of Treason," XXI, 158–83.

6 For an analysis of the period, as well as a detailed description of the Hetmanate, see Zenon Kohut, *Russian Centralism and Ukrainian Autonomy* (Cambridge MA: Harvard Ukrainian Research Institute, 1988).

7 In the words of Petr Valuev, the czar's minister of internal affairs, the Ukrainian language "never existed, does not exist and shall never exist." Subtelny, *Ukraine*, p. 282. On the suppression of Ukrainian language and culture, also see Basil Dmytryshyn's introduction to Fedir Savchenko, *The Suppression of the Ukrainian Activities in 1876*, Harvard Series in Ukrainian Studies, vol. 14, 1970, pp. xv–xxvii. On the development of the Ukrainian national intelligentsia, see Zenon Kohut, "The Development of a Little Russian Identity and Ukrainian Nationbuilding," 559–576, and Andreas Kappeler, "The Ukrainians of the Russian Empire, 1860–1914" both in Andreas Kappeler (ed.), *Comparative Studies on Governments and Non-Dominant Ethnic Groups in Europe, 1850–1940: The Formation of National Elites* (Dartmouth: New York University Press,), pp. 105–131 and pp. 559–576 respectively. A study of Ukrainian cultural absorption can be found in George Luckyj, *Between Gogol' and Shevchenko*, Harvard Series in Ukrainian Studies, vol. 8, 1971.

8 For a detailed examination of revolutionary Ukraine, see Taras Hunczak (ed.) *The Ukraine 1917–1921: A Study in Revolution* (Cambridge MA: Harvard Ukrainian Research Institute, 1977).

9 In striking contrast, all of Austria-Hungary's successor states survived, because what remained of Vienna was far too weak to reassert control over the former Habsburg domains.

10 Indeed, the 1920s saw a period of Ukrainization never before experienced under Russian rule, with the opening of Ukrainian-language schools and institutes of higher education, the publication of Ukrainian books, journals, and newspapers. Many of the gains made due to Ukrainization, however, were eradicated in the next decade alongside the purges of the Ukrainian political and cultural elite. See James E. Mace, *Communism and the Dilemmas of National Liberation: National Communism in Soviet Ukraine, 1918–1933* (Cambridge, MA: Harvard Ukrainian Research Institute, 1983) and George O. Liber, *Soviet Nationality Policy, Urban Growth, and Identity Change in the Ukrainian SSR, 1923–1934* (Cambridge: Cambridge University Press, 1992).

11 The standard text on collectivization and the famine in Ukraine is Robert Conquest, *The Harvest of Sorrow* (New York: Oxford University Press, 1986). On the impact of the Stalinist purges on Ukraine, see Conquest, *The Great Terror: A Reassessment* (New York: Oxford University Press, 1990), pp. 227–34 and also Subtelny, *Ukraine*, pp. 417–421.

12 On repression in Ukraine, see Ivan Bilas, *Represyvno-karal'na systema v Ukraini, 1917–1953*, vols. 1–2 (Kiev: Lybid', 1994).

13 On the economy, see George Chuchman and Mykola Hersymchuk (eds.), *Ekonomika Ukrainy: mynule, suchasne i maibutnie* (Kiev: Nankova dumka, 1993).

14 More on Soviet Ukraine can be found in a number of works, including Bohdan Krawchenko, *Social Chance and National Consciousness in Twentieth-Century Ukraine* (Edmonton: Canadian Institute of Ukrainian Studies, 1985); Borys Lewytzkyj, *Soviet Ukraine, 1953–1980* (Edmonton: Canadian Institute of Ukrainian Studies, 1984); and Subtelny, *Ukraine*.

15 "Ukrainian Communist Document," *Meta*, no. 2 (1976), 40.

16 Helene Carrere d'Encausse, *Decline of an Empire: The Soviet Socialist Republics in Revolt* (New York: Newsweek Books, 1979), p. 214.

17 *The Ukrainian Herald Issue 6: Dissent in Ukraine* (Baltimore, 1977), p. 33. This is a translation of the Ukrainian *samvydav* (*samizdat*) journal *Ukrainsk'kyi visnyk*; and *Narodna osvita*, p. 149.

18 *Presa Ukrainsk'koi RSR, 1918–1975*, table 51.

19  The accusations were outlined in an unsigned review article of Shelest's book *Ukraino nasha radiansk' ka* (Kiev, 1970): "Pro seriozni nedoliky ta pomylky odniiei knyhy," *Komunist Ukrainy*, no. 4 (1973), 77–82.

20  *Pravda Ukrainy*, April, 20 1973.

21  Maksim Sahaydak (comp.), *The Ukrainian Herald Issue 7–8: Ethnocide of Ukrainians in the USSR* (Baltimore, 1976), pp. 125–151; and Iurii Badz'o, *Vidkrytyi lyst do Prezydii Verkhovnoi rady Soiuzu RSR ta Tsentral'noho komitetu KPRS* (New York, 1980), pp. 50–55.

22  Valerii Popovkin, "Suchasnyi stan ekonomiky Ukrainy i shliakhy vykhod Ukrainy z ekonmichnoi kryzy," Scientific-research Institute of State Planning Commission of the Ukrainian SSR, Kiev, March 2, 1991.

23  S. A. Voitovych, I. O. Martyniuk, "Perspektyvy'neperspektyvnoi' movy," *Filosofs'ka i sotsiolohichna dumka*, no. 5 (1989), 22.

24  *Narodnoe obrazovaniie i kul'tura v SSSR* (Moscow, 1989), p. 88; *Literaturna Ukraina*, June 11, 1987; *Holos Ukrainy*, February 2, 1991.

25  See Bohdan Krawchenko, *Social Change and National Consciousness in Twentieth-Century Ukraine* (London: Macmillan, 1985), pp. 216–217.

26  *Vechirnii Kyiv*, February 2, 1991.

27  Report of First Rukh Congress, *Suchasnist'*, no. 12, December 1989, p. 43.

28  *Radians'ka Ukraina*, February 28, 1991. See also *Vechirnii Kyiv*, March 14, 1991 and *Holos Ukrainy*, April 4, 1991.

29  *Komsomol'skoe znamiia*, June 7, 1991; *Ukraina Business*, no. 7, February 1991; *Literaturna Ukraina*, February 27, 1991.

30  *Vol'ne slovo*, December 13, 1990.

31  *Literaturna Ukraina*, April 5, 1990.

32  *The Economist*, April 17, 1991.

33  *Holos Ukrainy*, March 3, 1991 and Serhii Plachynda's remarkable articles on the environmental crisis in Ukraine published in *Literaturna Ukraina*, March 14 and 21, 1991.

34  *Holos Ukrainy*, April 3, 1991. See also *Literaturna Ukraina*, February 27, 1991.

35  *Robitnycha hazeta*, February 26, 1991.

36  O. V. Haran', *Ubyty drakona. Z istorii Rukhu ta novykh partii Ukrainy* (Kiev: Lybid', 1993), p. 31. See Taras Kuzio and Andrew Wilson, *Ukraine: Perestroika to Independence* (New York: St. Martin's Press, 1994), pp. 110–113.

37  On the Ukrainian Culturological Club and other organizations, see Kuzio and Wilson, *Ukraine*, pp. 63–79.

38  *Literaturna Ukraina*, July 9, 1987.

39  *Ibid.*, June 4, 1987.

40  A summary of Rukh's constituent congress, held in Kiev on September 8, 1989, can be found in *Izvestia*, September 11, 1989 (translation in *Current Digest of the Soviet Press*, XLI, 37, p. 1).

41  Kuzio and Wilson, *Ukraine*, pp. 100–101. For more on Shcherbytsky, also see Vitalii Brublevskii, *Vladimir Shcherbitskii: pravda i vymysly* (Kiev: Dovira, 1993).

42  *Izvestia*, January 22, 1990 (trans. in CDSP, XLII, 4, p. 30).

43  Kuzio and Wison, *Ukraine*, pp. 125–129.

44  *Vechernii Kyiv*, February 18, 1991.

45  The Supreme Soviet voted overwhelmingly for the Declaration, 355–4. TASS, July 16, 1990. The Declaration can be found in *Argumenty i fakti*, No. 29, 1990.

46  For more on Hurenko, see Roman Solchanyk, "The Communist Party and the Political Situation in Ukraine: An Interview with Stanislav Hurenko," *RFE/RL Report on the USSR*, December 14, 1990, p. 12.

47  Khmara was arrested on November 17, 1990, for his alleged participation in an assault on a policeman during protests held on Revolution Day the week before. He was

released on parole five months later, on April 5, amid protests and strike threats, but was re-arrested ten days later on the grounds that he had been participating in illegal meetings and inciting insurrectionary activity. His trial, which began in May, was postponed several times due to lack of order in the courtroom. Ultimately, the Ukrainian parliament restored Khmara's immunity in September 1991, following the banning of the Communists and the declaration of state independence. TASS, November 21, December 7, 1990, May 12 and September 4, 1991; Radio Kiev, December 13, 1990; *Komsomolskaya Pravda*, April 16, 1991.

48 March 29–30, 1991.

49 See Solomiia Pavlychko, *A Kiev Diary* (Edmonton: Canadian Institute of Ukrainian Studies, 1991).

50 Masol declared his intention to resign on October 16 and stepped down on October 23. Fokin assumed the premiership three weeks later. *Izvestia*, October 17, 1990; TASS, November 2 and November 14, 1990.

51 Haran', *Ubyty drakona*, pp. 124–143.

52 See Haran', *Ubyty drakona*, pp. 66–67, and *Suchasnist'*, January 1991, no. 1, pp. 56–60, 76–86.

53 Session of Ukraine's Supreme Soviet, March 22, 1991.

54 See Ivan L. Rudnytsky, *Essays in Modern Ukrainian History* (Edmonton: Canadian Institute of Ukrainian Studies, 1987), p. 470.

55 *Za vil'nu Ukrainu*, March 19, 1991.

56 *Kul'tura i zhyttia*, February 2, 1991.

57 *Osvita*, January 25, 1991.

58 Yurii Badzio speaking at conference on "Natsional'ne vidrozhenia – Ukrains'ka perpektyva," Republican Association of Ukrainian Studies, February 16, 1991.

59 V.S. Nebozhenko, "Vybory – shliakh do demokratii," *Filosofs'ka i sotsiolohichna dumka*, no. 8, 1990, p. 4.

60 *Ukraina Business*, no. 2, January 1991.

61 "Tsentr Vyvchennia hromads'koi dumky – 'Demos'," typescript, table 12.

62 *Krasnoe znamiia*, December 9, 1990.

63 *Prykarpats'ka pravda*, December 12, 1990.

64 *Ibid.*, December 18, 1990.

65 *Krasnoe znamiia*, December 29, 1990; *Robitnycha hazeta*, January 1, 1990; *Naddniprians'ka pravda*, December 8, 1990.

66 Central Ukrainian Television, February 3, 1991.

67 *Radians'ka Ukraina*, June 14, 1991.

68 *Holos Ukrainy*, no. 4, 1991.

69 Interview with L. Kravchuk on Central Ukrainian Television, March 12, 1991.

70 *Moloda hvardiia*, March 20, 1991.

71 *Holos Ukrainy*, March 29, 1991.

72 "Postanova Verkhovnoi Rady Ukrains'koi RSR. Pro poriadok dennytsu orhanizatsiiu roboty tret'oi sesii Verhovnoi Rady Ukrains'koi RSR," February 1991; *Ukraina Business*, no. 23, June 1991.

73 "Deklaratsiia pro derzhavnyi suverenitet Ukrainy. Zovnishn' opolitychna khronkia," typescript, n.d.

74 Chrystia Freeland, "Ukraine and the (Dis-) Union Treaty," typescript, June 1991. See also her report in *Financial Times*, May 30, 1991.

75 *Holos Ukrainy*, March 29, 1991.

76 *Vechirnii Kyiv*, March 12, 1991.

77 The declaration passed by a vote of 346–1. The text of the declaration can be found in *Pozacherhova sesiia verkhovnoi rady Ukrains'koi RSR: Dvanadtsiatoho sklykannia. Biuleten'*, no. 1–2 (Kiev: Verkhovna Rada URSR, 1991).

78 The article was published in *Nezavisimaya gazeta*. A Russo-Ukrainian nuclear war over

borders or over Ukraine's treatment of its large Russian minority were other scenarios that were considered in a *Reuters* dispatch of December 4, 1991.

79  *Holos Ukrainy*, March 1, 1992.

80  *Rossiiskaya gazeta*, November 28, 1991.

81  *Izvestia*, November 26, 1991.

82  In simulataneous presidential elections, Kravchuk was popularly elected president of Ukraine with 62 percent of the vote (Rukh activist V. Chornovil came in second, with 23 percent).

83  See Kuzio and Wilson, *Ukraine*, pp. 184–191.

84  *New York Times*, November 28, 1991.

85  See Alexander Motyl, "Reform, Transition, or Revolution? The Limits to Change in the Postcommunist States," *Contention*, 4, no. 1 (Fall 1994), 141–160.

86  For instance, Eugene B. Rumer, "Will Ukraine Return to Russia?" *Foreign Policy*, no. 96 (Fall 1994), 129–144.

87  For more on these dynamics, see "Ukraina postkomunistychna: superechnosti ta perspektyvy sotsial'no-politychnoho rozvytku," *Politychna dumka*, no. 1 (1993), 11–34; and "Ukraina: liderstvo, elita, vlada," *Politychna dumka*, no. 3 (1994), 16–43.

88  According to a poll conducted in February-March 1994, 34 percent of Ukraine's residents felt they "belonged" to the "Ukrainian population as a whole," 29 percent – to the "population of the region or city" they lived in, 8 percent – to the "population of the region (oblast or several oblasts)" they lived in, and only 17 percent to the "population of the former Soviet Union." "A Political Portrait of Ukraine," *Democratic Initiatives*, no. 4 (Kiev, 1994), p. 19.

89  See Ian Bremmer, "The Politics of Ethnicity: Russians in the New Ukraine," *Europe-Asia Studies*, vol. 46, no. 2, 1994. For a less optimistic reading, see Dominique Arel, "Ukraine under Kuchma: Back to 'Eurasia'?" *RFE/RL Research Report*, vol. 3, no. 32, 19 August 1994.

90  See Kuzio and Wilson, *Ukraine*, pp. 197–199.

91  *The Independent*, December 7, 1991. In the Donbass, where ethnic Russians make up over half the population, over 80 percent of voters opted for independence.

92  On Crimea, see Oleksii Haran' *et al.*, "Ukraina ta Krym u rosiis'kykh neopolitychnykh kontseptsiiakh," and Pavlo Khriienko and Iurii Kolesnykov, "Krym: Amplitudy hromads'koi dumky," *Politychna dumka*, no. 3 (1994), 93–102.

93  See Dominique Arel and Andrew Wilson, "The Ukrainian Parliamentary Elections," *RFE/RL Research Report*, vol. 3, no. 26, 1 July 1994, pp. 6–17.

94  Dominique Arel and Andrew Wilson, "Ukraine under Kuchma: Back to 'Eurasia'?" *RFE/RL Research Report*, vol. 3, no 32, 19 August 1994, p. 1.

95  TASS, January 14, 1994.

96  See, for instance, *The Ukrainian Weekly*, January 22, 1995, p. 1.

# Ukraine: Chronology of events

### 1986
Chernobyl

### September 1989
8    Rukh (The Ukrainian People's Movement for Restructuring) holds its constitutent congress.

28    The anti-reform Volodomyr Shcherbytsky is removed from his post as First Secretary of the Communist Party and is replaced by Volodymyr Ivashko.

### October 1989
27    A language law is adopted which makes Ukrainian the official language and offers "governmental status" to other languages spoken in areas which are dominated by non-Ukrainians.

### January 1990
22    Almost one million people form a human chain from Lviv to Kiev in a Rukh-organized commemoration of the 1918 declaration of independence and union of the western and eastern parts of Ukraine.

### March 1990
4    The Rukh-led opposition wins nearly a third of the seats in elections to the Supreme Soviet.

10    An anti-Communist rally in Kiev draws 50,000 people.

31    Defying a ban by Kiev authorities, tens of thousands of Ukrainians participate in mass meetings in support of Lithuanian independence.

### April 1990
30    The Helsinki Union human rights movement transforms itself into the Republican Party of Ukraine, led by Levko Lukyanenko.

### May 1990
15    The State Commission on Crimean Tatars reveals its program to return Tatars to their historical homeland in the Crimea between 1991 and 1996.

### June 1990
4    Ivashko is elected chairman of the Supreme Soviet.

22  Stanislav Hurenko replaces Ivashko as First Secretary of the Communist Party.

28  Vitalii Masol is re-elected Chairman of the Council of Ministers (Prime Minister), a post he had held since 1987.

*July 1990*

11  Parliamentary chairman Ivashko tenders his resignation.

16  The Supreme Soviet adopts a declaration of sovereignty in a vote of 355–4.

23  Leonid Kravchuk, a former ideological secretary of the Communist Party, is elected chairman of the Supreme Soviet.

*September 1990*

30  60,000 people rally in Kiev for greater independence from Moscow.

*October 1990*

2  A pro-independence demonstration in Kiev draws 200,000 people. Students erect a tent city in Kiev's Revolution Square during the protest.

10  The student protestors declare a hunger strike and demand rejection of the new union treaty, full sovereignty and independence for Ukraine, an end to Communist Party domination, and radical social and economic reforms. Several parliamentary deputies join in their hunger strike.

16  Tens of thousands gather in front of the Supreme Soviet in support of the students' demands.

18  The hunger strike ends after the government agrees to meet all of the students' demands, including Prime Minister Masol's resignation.

22  Masol resigns and is replaced by Vitold Fokin.

28  At its second congress, attended by 2,300 delegates, Rukh condemns the Communist Party and announces its support for Ukrainian independence.

*November 1990*

17  Stepan Khmara, a nationalist deputy, is stripped of his parliamentary immunity and arrested on charges of assaulting a police officer.

*March 1991*

17  In the referendum on the preservation of the Soviet Union, 70 percent of voters (84 percent turnout) support the USSR's continued existence. 80 percent support a second

question posed by the Ukrainian government on remaining part of a union in which membership is based on Ukraine's declaration of soverignty.

*June 1991*

27 In Kiev, 2,000 demonstrators demand that the Supreme Soviet reject the proposed Union Treaty. Deputies agree to postpone discussion of the treaty until September.

28 At a Congress of Crimean Tatars in Simferopol', delegates vote to declare Tatar sovereignty over the Crimean peninsula.

*July 1991*

?? The Crimean Supreme Soviet adopts a constitution for the autonomous republic.

*August 1991*

19–23 Anti-coup protests take place in Kiev and other cities.

24 Parliament issues a declaration of independence.

30 The Communist Party is banned.

*September 1991*

15 50,000 people gather in Kiev to demand independence.

*October 1991*

18 The Ukrainian government refuses to sign a treaty on economic union which is signed by 8 other republics.

24 The Supreme Soviet announces that Ukraine will be a nuclear-free state.

*November 1991*

6 A trade and cooperation agreement is signed with Russia.

*December 1991*

1 In a republican-wide vote, 90 percent choose independence. More than 80 percent support independence in eastern oblasts, and in Crimea, 54 percent. On the same day, Supreme Soviet chairman Leonid Kravchuk is elected president with 62 percent of the vote. His closest challenger, Rukh leader Vyacheslav Chornovil, receives 23 percent (up to 75 percent in Galicia).

5 Kravchuk declares he will not sign a Union Treaty, economic or otherwise.

10 Parliament ratifies the Minsk agreement on creating the CIS.

13 Kravchuk decrees the nationalizing of army and air force units, as well as the Black Sea fleet.

*Janurary 1992*

31   400 million rubles are allocated for efforts to resettle Crimean Tatars.

*February 1992*

13   The parliamentary group New Ukraine is formed.
26   The Crimean parliament upgrades its status from the Crimean ASSR to the Republic of Crimea.

*March 1992*

2   At its third congress, Rukh calls for Ukraine to leave the CIS.
18–20   Crimean Tatars stage a protest in Kiev calling for the restoration of an autonomous Crimean Tatar state and increased government assistance for resettlement. Police forcibly disperse protestors.
25   Rafat Chubarov, deputy chairman of the Crimean Tatar *Mejlis*, addresses parliament and requests the restoration of Tatar autonomy in Crimea.
28–29   The Organization of Ukrainian Nationalists (OUN), which led the Ukrainian Soviet resistance after World War II sponsors a conference in Kiev.

*April 1992*

29   Parliament passes law on Crimea's status, in which it is confirmed that the republic is a constituent part of Ukraine and cannot secede without the approval of its people.

*May 1992*

1–2   At the third congress of the Ukrainian Republican Party, Stepan Khmara and his supporters break away from the party to form their own political group.
5   The Crimean parliament votes 118–28 in favor of the republic's independence and schedules a referendum for August to confirm their resolution. The next day, deputies appear to back down, approving an amendment to the Crimean constitution which acknowledges that the republic is a part of Ukraine.
13   Parliament annuls Crimea's declaration of independence and demands that the Crimean parliament rescind the declaration.
15   Kravchuk refuses to sign the CIS collective security pact.
21   The Crimean parliament repeals their declaration of independence and cancels the scheduled referendum. Meanwhile, the Russian parliament declares the 1954 transfer of Crimea to Ukraine to be retroactively illegal.

*August 1992*

2   Several political parties and organizations, including the Republican Party, the Democratic Party, *Prosvita*, and the Union of Ukrainian Students, form a coalition at the Congress of National Democratic Forces and call for a resignation of the cabinet, new parliamentary elections, and Ukraine's withdrawal from the CIS.

17   In honor of Ukraine's first Independence Day, Kravchuk declares an amnesty for prisoners serving sentences for various minor offenses.

24   Thousands gather in Kiev's Independence Square and in other cities to celebrate Ukrainian Independence Day.

*September 1992*

30   Prime Minister Fokin and his cabinet resign after being assigned blame for the poor state of the Ukrainian economy.
Militia tear down a Crimean Tatar shantytown near Alushta in Crimea. Clashes ensue and several Tatars are arrested.

*October 1992*

2   Valentyn Symonenko is appointed acting prime minister.

6   Demanding the release of Tatars arrested on 1 October, protestors besiege the Crimean Supreme Soviet building in Simferopol'. The arrested Tatars are quickly released and presented to the protestors.

7   Students erect a tent city in Kiev's Independence Square on the anniversary of the 1990 hunger strike and demand the holding of new parliamentary elections and Ukraine's withdrawal from the CIS. The protest continues for more than two weeks.

9   The Crimean Supreme Soviet bans the Tatar organization Mejlis.

13   Leonid Kuchma is appointed Prime Minister.

*November 1992*

12   The ruble is suspended as legal tender, making the karbovanets coupon the sole legal currency in Ukraine.

*December 1992*

4–6   At its fourth congress, the Rukh movement resolves to become a political party.

*January 1993*

4–5   Kravchuk and several other political leaders denounce the draft CIS charter to be signed on 22 January.

18   Several thousand gather in Kiev to demand that Ukraine leave the CIS and retain its nuclear weapons.

20   1,000 gather in Simferopol in support of Crimean independence.

22   The Ukrainian government refuses to sign the CIS charter.

*July 1993*

9   The Russian parliament declares Sevastopol part of Russia and the headquarters of a unified Russian Black Sea Fleet.

*September 1993*

9   Two weeks after his reformist deputy Viktor Pynzanyk resigns, Prime Minister Kuchma tenders his resignation.

21   Parliament accepts Kuchma's resignation. Kravchuk appoints Deputy Prime Minister Efim Zvyhailsky as acting prime minister.

*October 1993*

5   The Communist Party of Ukraine is reregistered.

14   The Constitution of the Crimean Republic is ratified.

*November 1993*

7   Yurii Osmanov, leader of the National Movement of Crimean Tatars, is murdered.

10   Parliament passes a law making all paramilitary organizations illegal.

*Janurary 1994*

16   Pro-Russian candidate Yurii Meshkov wins first-round elections in Crimean presidential race. Runoffs are scheduled for 30 January.

18   The prominent Crimean Tatar Iskender Memetov is fatally shot.

30   Meshkov is elected President of Crimea with 73 percent of the vote, defeating parliamentary chairman Mikhail Bagrov who receives 23 percent.

*February 1994*

12   Militia raid the headquarters of the Ukrainian National Self-Defense Organization, the paramilitary wing of the ultranationalist Ukrainian National Assembly.

13   Russian economist Evgenii Saburov is appointed First Deputy Prime Minister of Crimea (the post of Prime Minister does not exist).

24   Parliament gives Crimea a month to bring the republic's Constitution and legislation in line with Ukraine's.

*March 1994*

27　First-round elections to a new parliament (the 450-seat Rada) are held with 75 percent turnout. Subsequent rounds are scheduled for later in April. In the Donetsk and Lugansk oblasts, a referendum is held in which voters overwhelmingly express approval for a federal state structure, the adoption of Russian as a second state language, and the signing of the CIS charter.

In Crimean parliamentary elections (including second-round elections in April), the *Rossiya* bloc wins 67 percent of the vote and takes 58 of 97 seats. *Kurultai* takes all 14 of the seats reserved for the Crimean Tatars. In a simultaneous referendum, 78 percent vote in favor of restoring the 1992 constitution and 83 percent in favor of dual citizenship.

*April 1994*

10　After follow-up elections, Communist and socialist parties succeed in capturing over 40 percent of parliamentary seats. 112 seats remain to be filled.

*May 1994*

18　Oleksander Moroz, the head of the Socialist Party, is elected speaker of the parliament.

19　The Crimean leaders accuse the Ukrainian interior ministry of deploying troops to the peninsula to effect an overthrow of the Crimean government.

20　Crimean parliament votes 69–2 to restore the republic's May 1992 constitution. The Ukrainian parliament gives Crimea 10 days to repeal its decision. Ukrainian troops reportedly continue to gather in the peninsula.

30　The Crimean deadline passes, and the Crimean parliament refuses to rescind its vote. Kiev decides not to take any drastic measures.

*June 1994*

7　The Crimean parliament rejects a power-sharing agreement proposed on 3 June which would reaffirm the precedence of the Ukrainian constitution and the republic's place in Ukraine.

16　Former prime minister Vitalii Masol is reappointed as prime minister, replacing acting prime minister Efim Zvyahilsky.

26　In first-round presidential elections, 69 percent of the electorate vote, and Kravchuk receives 38 percent of the vote. Former Prime Minister Kuchma follows, with 31 percent. In the Galician oblasts of Lviv, Ternopil, and Ivano-Frankivsk, Kravchuk receives over 87 percent of the vote, while Kuchma receives less than 4 percent. Runoff elections are scheduled for July.

*July 1994*

- 10   Kuchma is elected president, with 52 percent of the vote (72 percent voter participation).
- 24   Run-off parliamentary elections result in the election of 32 new deputies.

*August 1994*

- 7   27 more deputies are elected in yet another round of parliamentary elections, for a total of 393 members, of which 219 are independent and 106 belong to the Communist, Socialist, or Agrarian parties.
- 17   The Christian Liberal Party of Crimea, founded in the spring, suspends operations after the successive murders of its first three leaders.

*September 1994*

- 7   The Crimean parliament adopts a law mandating that the law on the presidency come into line with the Crimean constitution, specifically doing away with the President's status as head of state as well as his right to appoint city and district chief administrators.
- 11   Meshkov issues a decree dissolving parliament and all district soviets. The parliament refuses to comply. The next day, Meshkov agrees to rescind his decree if parliament repeals their amendments to the law on the presidency.
- 15   The Crimean parliament votes no-confidence in the government and demands its dismissal. Deputy Prime Minister Saburov submits his resignation which Meshkov refuses to act upon.
- 22   Meshkov rescinds his decree unilaterally.
- 23   Ukrainian parliament gives Crimean parliament until 1 November to bring their laws in line with the state constitution.
- 25   Former President Kravchuk is elected a parliamentary deputy in Western Ukraine with 87 percent of the vote.
- 29   The Crimean parliament votes for a law introducing the post of Prime Minister and designating the Prime Minister, rather than the president, the head of the executive branch.

*October 1994*

- 5   In a vote of 67–5, the Crimean parliament amends the republic's constitution to allow the introduction of the prime minister's post.
- 6   The Crimean parliament appoints Anatoly Franchuk, Kuchma's son-in-law, prime minister while Saburov remains head of the still-in-place Meshkov-appointed government.
- 18   The Communist Party is legalized after 201 of 393 deputies

present vote to rescind the August 1991 resolution banning the party.

*November 1994*

16   Parliament adopts the Nuclear Non-Proliferation Treaty by a vote of 301–8.

18   Having permitted their deadline to elapse, parliament annuls Crimea's declarations of sovereignty and independence as well as other documents adopted by the Crimean parliament, but takes no further action.

20   Nine more parliamentary seats are filled in another round of run-off elections. Four more are scheduled for December and elections to the remaining 43 seats are put off indefinitely.

*March 1995*

1   Prime Minister Masol resigns. His deputy Yevgenii Marchuk is appointed acting Prime Minister.

17   Parliament votes 247–60 to rescind Crimea's constitution and several of its laws.

22   In retaliation, the Crimean parliament removes Franchuk from his post and replaces him with Anatolii Drobotov.

31   Kuchma issues a decree placing the Crimean government under direct jurisdiction of the Ukrainian Cabinet of Ministers and reinstating Franchuk.

*May 1995*

10   Thousands of Crimean Tatars participate in a demonstration in Simferopol to demand that Crimean officials conduct investigations of the attacks and murders plaguing Tatars over the last several months.

# 7    Belarus: from statehood to empire?

JAN ZAPRUDNIK AND MICHAEL URBAN

The history of the lands that comprise Belarus[1] is a history of political contention. In one epoch or another, Poles, Lithuanians, Russians and – for briefer intervals in wartime – Germans have laid claim to, invaded and exercised dominion over these territories. Relatedly, Belarus's history itself has been an object of contention. As might be imagined, the reconstructions of the past performed by those with aspirations for Belarusan nationhood have contrasted sharply with the interpretations of historical events associated with those written from the perspective of, say, Polish or Russian domination. Whereas the latter would emphasize the inseparable affinity between the Belarusan people and the nation then exercising sovereignty over them, thus justifying the political status quo, the former would highlight the integrity and uniqueness of Belarus, thereby making the case for future independence.

This struggle over Belarus's past has never been sharper than it is today,[2] a fact that reflects the emergence of a powerful nationalist movement in Belarus locked in political combat with the remnants of the Communist regime. In the same way that the historiographic controversy over the past is simultaneously a political contest over Belarus's future, so the outcomes of this political contest have already altered the terms of debate and narrowed some of the differences between the contending parties. For example, historic symbols of Belarusan nationhood, such as the flag and coat of arms, that long had been outlawed by the communist authorities who, until mid-year 1990, had publicly associated them with fascism, have since been officially recognized.[3]

As this illustration with respect to national symbols as well as others concerning language and national sovereignty that we discuss below – would suggest, Belarus has only recently completed the long journey to nationhood. However, the political form which its nationhood might take – whether independence or some type of association with neighboring peoples – remains for the moment unclear. Certainly, it will be influenced by a number of diverse factors, not all of which lie within the scope of this study. Our focus falls on what can be regarded as the principal moment the development of a national consciousness. Reference to Belarus's troubled and often tragic past provides an understanding of how this con-

276

# Belarus

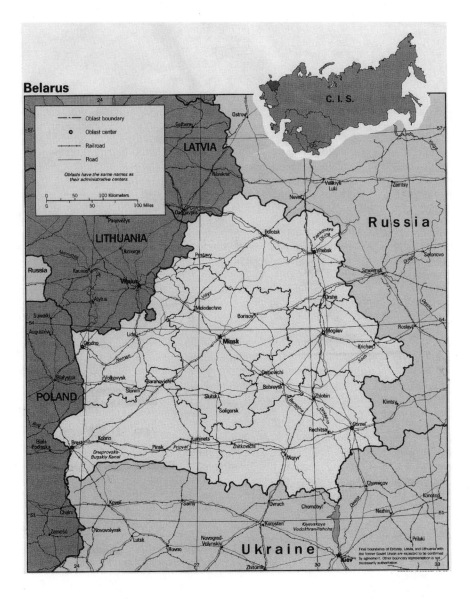

**LATVIA**

**LITHUANIA**

**POLAND**

**Russia**

**R u s s i a**

**U k r a i n e**

**C. I. S.**

Oblast boundary
Oblast center
Railroad
Road

*Oblasts have the same names as their administrative centers.*

0    50    100 Kilometers
0    50         100 Miles

Dstrov
Grabeny
Rēzekne
Daugavpils
Nevel'
Velikiyb Luki
Zemtsy
Polotsk
Zapadnaya Dvina
Vitebsk
Smolensk
Safonovo
Orsha
Roslavl'
Mogilev
Krichev
Minsk
Borisov
Molodechno
Volya
Postavy
Vilnius
Ukmerge
Kaunas
Alytus
Lida
Grodno
Nemen
Volkovysk
Baranovichi
Slonim
Osipovichi
Bobruysk
Slutsk
Soligorsk
Zhlobin
Klintsy
Gomel'
Rechitsa
Berezina
Dnepro
Sozh
Desna
Kobrin
Brest
Pinsk
Pripyat'
Zhitkovichi
Luninets
Mozyr'
Chernigov
Konotop
Dneprovsko-Bugskiy Kanal
Bug
Biała Podlaska
Chełm
Kovel'
Sarny
Ovruch
Chernobyl'
Nezhin
Priluki
Zamość
Novovolynsk
Lutsk
Rovno
Novograd-Volynskiy
Korosten'
Kiyevskoye Vodokhranilishche
Zhitomir
Kiev
Suwałki
Augustów
Białystok
Paņevēžys

Final boundaries of Estonia, Latvia, and Lithuania with the former Soviet Union are expected to be confirmed by agreement. Other boundary representation is not necessarily authoritative.

sciousness has emerged and how it has been retarded. It accounts for the unusual situation in which an identifiable national group that has for centuries occupied a particular territory has only in the past few years begun to exhibit in full the signs of nationhood.

## Belarus and the Belarusans

The origin of the name, Belarus ("White Russia"), is obscure. In some accounts it is said to derive from the white complexion of the population or from their white dress.[4] In others it has been traced to an administrative designation for those areas lying beyond the Russian lands that had been required to pay a regular tax to the Tatars during the years of their hegemony in Russia.[5] Whatever the initial derivation of its name may have been, however, Belarus first displayed a number of features of national identity during the period in which it was incorporated in the multiethnic state comprised of the Grand Duchy of Lithuania, Rus' and Samogitia (beginning in 1386), for the Belarusan language then served as the official language of the region's chancellery, courts, diplomacy and literature.[6]

The relative autonomy that Belarus had enjoyed within the Grand Duchy of Lithuania was diminished when the latter entered into political union with the Kingdom of Poland in 1569. Polish influence in the area succeeded in bringing much of the Belarusan Orthodox hierarchy under the authority of the Vatican. The Uniate Church thereby created in 1596 retained the Eastern rite while simultaneously embracing a number of Roman Catholic dogmas.

The subsequent expansion of Muscovy into the area brought Poles and Russians into direct and violent competition for control of Belarus.[7] Both sides regarded Belarus as a constituent unit of their respective states, and accordingly, each side promoted its religious and cultural policies in those areas of Belarus under its jurisdiction.

The partitions of the Polish-Lithuanian Commonwealth effected by Russia, Prussia and Austria in 1772, 1793 and 1795 fully incorporated the Belarusan lands within the Russian empire. By that time, however, the Belarusan nobility had already identified itself with Poland, as evinced by their acceptance of Roman Catholicism and the Polish language. Moreover, strong memories of the historical attachment to Lithuania persisted among the upper strata of the population, which, since the interests and policies of the Lithuanians and Poles had in the past been by no means identical, meant that neither had these strata fully acculturated along Polish lines.

The policy of the tsars in the lands "returned" to the Russian fold aimed at Russifying the population and converting them from the Uniate to the Russian Orthodox faith. The inscription on a coin minted under the order of Catherine II summed up the attitude of the empire toward the Belarusan lands: "What was torn away has been returned." Her successors, however showed themselves more obliging toward Polish interests in Belarus. This was particularly true during the reign of Alexander I (1801 1825), who allowed his friend, the Polish prince Adam Czartoryski, to handle educational policy in the annexed territories. As a consequence of Czartoryski's school reform and the growing prominence of the university at Wilno (Vilnius), the influence of Polish culture in Belarus during this period of Russian rule became even stronger than it had been in the previous epoch.

It was also at the University of Wilno, as recent research has shown, that "a foundation for Belorussian [Belarusan] national thought" was laid.[8] There, a circle of Uniate professors from the Bielastok region had assembled a collection of ancient documents written in Belarusan that inspired the idea of regaining autonomy for the Grand Duchy of Lithuania and restoring thereby the Belarus language and the Uniate religion to official status within it. The pronounced Polish nationalism amongst most students and professors at Wilno at this time, however, all but guaranteed an unhappy future for the project. Indeed, by 1830 when rebellion broke out in the western regions of the empire, the insurrection in Belarus evinced a clearly Polish orientation.

The tsarist government's response to the rebellion was severe. In addition to the physical repression that it visited on the active participants, it introduced a number of measures designed to eradicate "foreign" influences from cultural life. Wilno University was closed. Russian replaced Polish as the language of government and in educational institutions. In 1839 the Uniate Church, to which most Belarusans belonged, was abolished. In the following year, Nicholas I even banned the terms "Belorussian" ["Belarusan"] and "Lithuanian" in reference to the provinces of Vitebsk, Mogilev, Vilna and Grodno, because of the allegedly separatist overtones. At the same time, the laws of the Statute of the Grand Duchy of Lithuania (first published in Belarusan in 1588) were replaced by the Russian code. It was at this juncture that the term *Zapadnaya Rossiya* ("Western Russia"), first made its appearance. According to this appellation and the "theory" of *zapadno-russizm* ("Western Russianism") that accompanied it, those ethnographic distinctions that had set Belarusans apart from Great Russians were purely the product of artificially imposed Polish influences. *Zapadno-russizm* quickly became the secular creed of Orthodox priests, bureaucrats and school officials. Its obvious intention was "to destroy all that could remind anyone of Belorussia [Belarus] and Lithuania as separate national regions with their own historical, cultural, and linguistic traits."[9]

Administrative prohibitions constituted one side of the russification policy. The other concerned appeals to the distant past when, during the era of Kievan Rus', all "Russians" belonged to the same church and used the same written language. But the Romantic thrust of the new historiography also contained implications that cut in the opposite direction. For by reopening or rewriting (as the case may have been) the pages of the past, the new doctrines rekindled interest in Belarusan history that had only recently been retrieved by the scholars at Wilno University. A famous graduate of this university, the Belarusan-born Polish poet Adam Mickiewicz, articulated this revived historical consciousness while teaching in Paris in his later years:

> The Belorussian [Belarusan] language which is also called Russinian or Lithuanian . . . is spoken by approximately ten million people. This is the richest and purest tongue, ancient in origin and wonderfully developed. During the period of Lithuania's independence grand dukes spoke it and used it in their diplomatic correspondence.[10]

In the middle of nineteenth century, the idea of a Belarusan national identity began to crystalize among some students at the re-opened university at Wilno.[11] For the time being, however, it was largely connected to the Polish language the language of the instruction at the university – and to the memory of a common polity. Accordingly, the nobility and some segments of the peasantry in Belarus joined the Polish uprising of January 1863. Although the uprising failed, it marked a new stage in the development of a national consciousness. Kastus Kalinowski (1838–1864), the young and dynamic leader of the rebellion in Belarus, succeeded in publishing the first clandestine newspaper in the Belarusan language, *Mužychaja Praŭda* ("Peasants' Truth"). Kalinowski subsequently became one of Belarus's most celebrated national heroes. His words written on the eve of his execution in Wilno "For I say to you from beneath the gallows, my People, that only then will you live happily, when no Muscovite remains over you"[12] would inspire succeeding generations of Belarusan nationalists. In the period immediately following the 1863 uprising, however, the national idea languished.

The key to an understanding of why the national movement remained weak throughout the nineteenth century and why its exponents were usually advocates of union with Poland and Lithuania, rather than outright independence, lay in Belarus's social structure. As Thomas Hammond has argued, national consciousness and its attendant political movements arose among the various peoples of East Europe in the context of economic and demographic shifts which concentrated a critical mass of the population in towns whose social and occupational differentiation was sufficient to support an intelligentsia.[13] This intelligentsia would then press for their own group interests – a dominant representation in the civil service and the professions – by championing the vernacular and the national idea against the extant dominion of the respective empires, Russian, German or Austrian, under whose dominion they had fallen.[14] Importantly, the spread of literacy made possible the attraction of a mass following, as emerging national literatures communicated a sense of nationhood to expanding circles of people.

Table 7.1. *Nationalities of the five Belarusan provinces of the northwestern region, 1897*

| Nationality | Number | Percent of the area's total population | Number in towns | Percent of given group in towns |
|---|---|---|---|---|
| Belarus | 5,408,420 | 63.5 | 137,608 | 2.6 |
| Jews | 1,202,129 | 14.2 | 553,997 | 46.0 |
| Russians | 492,921 | 5.9 | 185,027 | 37.8 |
| Ukrainians | 377,487 | 4.5 | 9,461 | 2.6 |
| Poles | 424,236 | 4.9 | 122,785 | 28.5 |
| Lithuanians | 288,921 | 3.3 | 5,201 | 1.7 |
| Latvians | 272,775 | 3.1 | 3,843 | 1.4 |
| Germans | 27,311 | 0.3 | 13,365 | 48.0 |
| Tatars | 8,448 | 0.1 | 5,094 | 61.0 |
| Others | 19,658 | 0.2 | 7,293 | 37.0 |
| Total | 8,522,306 | 100.0 | 1,043,854 | 12.3 |

*Source:* Calculated from V. N. Pertsev *et al.* (eds.), *Dokumenty i materialy po isterii Belorussii, 1900–1917*, vol. 3 (Minsk: Academy of Sciences of the BSSR, 1953), p. 30.

In Belarus, however, the great mass of the native population in the last century remained on the land, leading lives that had been essentially unaltered for centuries. Literacy rates among these Belarusan speakers were, of course, exceedingly low and the language of instruction in the primary schools was itself not Belarusan but Russian.[15] In the towns, where a national consciousness may have caught on, Belarusans were vastly outnumbered by Jews, Russians, Poles and other nationalities (as the figures in table 7.1 from the 1897 census would indicate). Moreover, this census revealed that only some 7.3 percent of urban dwellers in these provinces spoke the Belarusan language.[16] Whereas non-Belarusans in the countryside retained their national identities as, say, Poles or Lithuanians, Belarusans commonly referred to themselves simply as "the locals."[17] The identification of the category "Belarusan" with the rural population poor, backward and overwhelmingly illiterate was in fact so strong that in the 1906 records of the Russian State Duma where the respective nationalities of the deputies were listed, some from the North-Western Region (Belarus) were described as "peasant-Belarusan" or "Belarusan-peasant."

Nationalist leaders were, of course, acutely aware of these facts. In 1884, for instance, the underground populist journal, *Homom*, noted that:

> The Belarusan people, a plebeian nation, are still awaiting the
> emergence of their intelligentsia. Until now, their talents have served

either Polish or Great Russian culture. Mutely but persistently they have protested against the treacherous attempts to polonize or to russify them, and both cultures, forcibly foisted on them, have failed to take root. Piously they have preserved the foundation of their life while awaiting the emergence of their own intelligentsia who would not uproot those foundations but develop and improve them.[18]

In the face of a considerable number of archaeological, ethnographic and philological publications in the latter years of the nineteenth century that attempted to show that Belarus was merely a province of either Poland or Russia, nationally-oriented Belarusan intellectuals began to draw their own conclusions. For example, many such studies portrayed the Belarusan language as a "dialect" of Russian and consequently categorized its speakers as Russian by nationality. However, even while the name "Belarus" remained taboo and the Belarusan lands were known officially as the "North-Western Region," the census of 1897, as we have seen, did enumerate Belarusan speakers in the Region. Consequently, Belarusan intellectuals, such as the academician, Yefim Karski, could call attention to the close link between language and nationality for all the peoples of East Europe and argue that language for the Belarusans had been "an inseparable indicator of the Belarusan nationality during its centuries-old history."[19]

The revolutionary ferment characteristic of the Russian empire at the turn of the century propelled the Belarusan national movement onto a new stage of political activism. In 1902, the Circle of Belarusan National Education was founded by a student group in St. Petersburg. The Circle transformed itself in the following year into the Belarusan Socialist *Hramada* (BSH), a self-professed political party, complete with a program for Belarusan autonomy. With the lifting of the prohibition against publishing in the Belarusan language that followed the 1905 Revolution, the BSH launched a weekly, *Nasa Niva* (*Our Soil*), that grew into a center for a revival of Belarusan national consciousness until its closure in 1915. The *Nasa Niva* movement was led by the brothers, Ivan and Anton Lutskievich – an archaeologist and publicist, respectively – and by two towering figures from the world of letters, Janka Kupala and Jakub Kolas. This movement culminated in the All-Belarusan Congress of 1917 and the proclamation of the Belarusan Democratic Republic on March 25, 1918.

Although Belarus enjoyed a brief period of formal independence (terminated by the Polish invasion in the following year), questions have remained with respect to the maturation of nationhood at this time. On one hand, the existence of a Belarusan government owed much to the political convulsions besetting surrounding states and to the presence of German forces in the region when independence was proclaimed.[20] On the other, the movement for independence lacked a mass base in the population. Both the indigenous nobility and bourgeoisie were overwhelmingly non-Belarusan. Belarusans made up a sizeable proportion of those in the lower

Table 7.2. *Belarusan-speaking population of the five Belarusan provinces of the northwestern region according to their religion, 1917*

| Religion | Number | Percentage |
|----------|--------|------------|
| Orthodox | 4,384,217 | 81.0 |
| Roman-Catholic | 994,210 | 18.5 |
| Old-Believers* | 25,495 | 0.47 |
| Lutherans | 643 | 0.03 |
| Total | 5,404,565 | 100.00 |

* Karski explains this category: "These are mostly Great Russians who use Belorussian elements in their language, but otherwise they generally have not mingled with Belorussians."

Source: Ye. F. Karski, *Etnografischeskaya karta belorusskago plemeni* (Petrograd: Belorussian National Committee of the All-Russian Soviet of Peasant Deputies, 1917), p. 27.

civil service and in the teaching profession, but most of these individuals were new arrivals from the countryside. The great majority of Belarusans on the land had little or no notion of national identity, much less national independence, taught as they had been by their clergies in the Orthodox and Catholic Churches that their religion bound them to either the Russian or Polish nations (see table 7.2 for respective figures). Indeed, only one nationalist delegate from Belarus was elected in 1917 to the All-Russian Constituent Assembly, and he has been described as a disguised Russian socialist.[21] Belarus's path to nationhood, then, has been a longer and in many ways more difficult one than those of surrounding peoples. It would remain for future generations, again beset by contradictory and largely inhospitable circumstances, to advance further along it.

## A Soviet Belarus

During the interwar period, the Belarusan lands were divided between Poland and Soviet Russia. The Treaty of Riga (1921), which ended the Russo-Polish War, placed some 38,600 square miles of Belarus – and nearly 3.5 million Belarusans – under Polish sovereignty. In these "western territories," the newly reconstituted Polish state directed an increasingly brutal policy of polonization at the local population, aimed at extirpating all media by which a Belarusan identity might be expressed and sustained. Until broken by mass arrests and political trials that followed Joseph Pilsudski's coup in 1926, the Belarusan Peasant-Workers' Hramada, which numbered at its peak about 150,000 members, had been able to organize the Belarusan population for its self-protection, including armed resistance.

When the Hramada was destroyed, the political orientation of the resistance became increasingly radical, with the Communist Party of West Belarus, an organization linked closely to countrymen and communists across the border, assuming a leading role. The Polish authorities enacted even harsher measures in reply and by the end of the 1930s many thousands of Belarusans had suffered imprisonment, fines, confiscation of property, cultural and religious persecution, and internment in concentration camps.[22]

The approximately 5 million Belarusans under Soviet rule were incorporated into the Belarusan Soviet Socialist Republic (BSSR) that was proclaimed January 1, 1919. By 1926, the BSSR included the Mogilev and Vitebsk provinces, the capital of Minsk and its surrounding districts, and the districts of Gomel and Rechitsa.[23] Initially, conditions here contrasted sharply with the anti-Belarusan measures employed by Poland in the western territories. Throughout most of the 1920s, the new communist state devoted considerable effort to reviving, establishing and developing national cultures. For Belarusans in the BSSR, this meant an unprecedented flowering of nationhood that for the first time reached the masses of people on the land through literary campaigns and official support for the native literature and culture.[24] The Belarusan State University, the first university to be built on Belarusan soil, along with a Belarusan Academy of Sciences were founded in Minsk. Moreover, Belarusans occupied leading positions in government and administration at all levels.

By the end of the decade, however, these policies were reversed. Nationally oriented elites became targets for repression throughout the USSR and the Belarusan experience was typical of this pattern. Belarusans were expelled from important posts in every sector and replaced by non-Belarusans, imported from other parts of the USSR to fill politically sensitive positions. In similar fashion, a considerable number of Belarusan officials were exported to other regions of the USSR. During the thirties, with the jailing of those accused of "nationalism" and succeeding waves of repression visited on the cultural expression of nationhood, national consciousness perforce moved underground.[25]

Yet, like the proverbial "mole of revolution," the development of this consciousness remained busy, albeit in ways that did not upset the surface of life of Stalinism. The industrialization of Belarus in the thirties drew hundreds of thousands from the countryside to the cities. Whereas Belarusans comprised only about two-fifths of the BSSR's urban population in the mid-twenties,[26] by the end of the forties they had come to represent an overall majority in the urban centres.[27]

The Second World War represented a pivotal experience in the making of the Belarusan nation. Its prelude, the Molotov-Ribbentrop Pact and its secret protocols, incorporated the western territories into the BSSR. When the German armies rolled eastward in 1941, however, they rapidly overran the entire Belarusan Republic and established an especially harsh regime of occupation. Suffice it to say that by the time of liberation, all of the BSSR's cities lay in ruins – in Minsk, only one building remained standing – and that Belarus had lost a quarter of its population to Soviet deportations and executions (1939–1941), the widespread terror practised by the German occupiers, banditry and guerrilla war, and, of course, conventional warfare.[28]

In the face of the prospect of the physical liquidation of the Belarusan nation, a Soviet-sponsored partisan movement became increasingly active in the German zone of occupation. Not only did partisan ranks swell in response to the widespread terror practised by the German invaders, but the leadership of the Belarusan partisans – frequently lacking communication links with their formal superiors in the Soviet armed forces – enjoyed considerable autonomy in staging their operations and in administering those areas that they had liberated.[29]

This wartime experience would prove seminal in shaping postwar politics in the BSSR. On the one hand, the bulk of the former partisan leadership embarked on political careers in the postwar period. Without doubt, their shared wartime experiences contributed a cohesiveness to this group that characterized it as an identifiable faction in Belarusan politics. By the mid-fifties, this faction dominated the BSSR's top party and governmental positions.[30] When their leader, K.T. Mazurau, was rewarded with the office of First Deputy Chairperson of the USSR's Council of Ministers and a seat on the Politburo in 1965 for his participation in the coalition that deposed N.S. Khrushchev, he brought a number of partisans with him to Moscow, thus establishing an influential presence for this faction at the all-union level. On the other hand, the partisans were able to promote at least a limited version of Belarusan national identity within the BSSR. Drawing on their experiences in the resistance, they portrayed the liberation, indeed, the salvation, of Belarus as the result of the heroic *national* resistance of the Belarusan people within the larger framework of the tremendous sacrifice and achievements of the *Soviet* people. This adroitness in the use of symbology – the framing of a national identity in terms not antagonistic to Moscow – was no small achievement during a postwar epoch in which the various peoples of the USSR were officially regarded as "growing together" to form one "Soviet people." Accordingly, the state-sponsored rites and ceremonies commemorating the liberation of the BSSR would feature prominently the contribution of the Belarusan partisans. Along these same lines, Mazurau's successor in the Republic, P.M. Masherau, who would often attend these ceremonies wearing native costume, became the first leader of the BSSR to address his countrymen on solemn occasions in their native tongue.[31]

The period of partisan leadership in the BSSR, which ended definitively with Masherau's death (or, perhaps assassination[32]) in 1980, is also noteworthy on two other counts pertinent to the formation of the Belarusan nation. First, patterns of elite mobility in the USSR demonstrate that the influence of Moscow over recruitment and promotion to important positions in the structures of the party-state had been negligible. Despite the impressive formal powers over key personnel decisions in the BSSR that lay in Moscow's hands, the actual career patterns of officials in the BSSR primarily had been determined by factors indigenous to the Republic, principally, the patronage of former partisans and rival groups. Within the framework of the Soviet order, then, the BSSR had been since the mid-sixties, if not earlier, a self-governing republic.[33]

Second, the postwar economic development of the BSSR has been, by Soviet standards at least, impressive. Minsk, whose industrial base had to be rebuilt from scratch after World War II, numbered among the leading industrial cities of the USSR.[34] Around the Republic, postwar construction of metal-working and machine-building industries had come to form the basis of an agro-industrial complex noted for the production of heavy trucks and agricultural machinery which, along with an integrated potassium mining and chemical fertilizer sector,[35] had enabled the BSSR to become one of the top agricultural producers in the Soviet Union.[36] Again, by Soviet standards, the light industrial sector performed remarkably well, making the BSSR one of the best supplied republics in terms of consumer goods.[37] Demographic changes, of course, accompanied the Republic's economic growth. Whereas as recently as 1970 only about one-third of the population had resided in cities, the urban-dwelling proportion of Belarus's 10 million inhabitants had nearly doubled by 1985.[38]

These factors – the relative autonomy of the BSSR's political elites in the post-Stalin period and the industrialization and attendant urbanization of Belarus – might be regarded as determining, rather than as casual, forces shaping the development of a national consciousness. That is, in neither case do they exhibit some unidirectional influence pushing either toward or away from nationhood. In general terms, of course, a relatively high degree of self-government might be counted as a positive factor in this respect. Similarly, the emergence of an urban industrial society in recent decades would appear to provide that ingredient so long absent in Belarus's history, namely, an educated majority of Belarusans concentrated in urban areas who would represent for the first time a mass audience potentially receptive to the ideas of nationhood long associated with the cultural intelligentsia.

However, in specific context, these same factors, can have – and, in the case at hand, have had – the reverse effect. Economic development in the BSSR, for instance, seems to have sustained a large measure of conservatism among the Republic's political elites. As one observer, a Belarusan deputy to the USSR's Congress of People's Deputies, has noted, a relatively prosperous, orderly and unreformed BSSR had been a living example that "developed socialism" (the shibboleth of the Brezhnev era) had continued to function reasonably well and, therefore, that perestroika was uncalled for.[39] In equal measure, the political faction that replaced the partisans during the early 1980s as the dominant force in Belarusan politics distinguished itself by its conservatism, earning for the BSSR the sobriquet "Soviet Vendeé," after the 1793 seat of French counterrevolution.[40] This orientation appears to have been shaped by the particular career histories of the group in question, nearly all of whom had been upwardly-mobile industrial workers who launched their political careers in Minsk's leading enterprises.[41] The rapid advancement of their individual careers against the backdrop of the group's success in coming to power in a republic where a palpable degree of material success within the status quo had been maintained would suggest ideal conditions for the development of a conservative orientation in politics.

## The politics of nationhood

In the same way that a modern Belarusan identity was forged during the period of partisan resistance when the continued existence of the Belarusan people was at stake, so the broad manifestation of national consciousness in recent years has been fired by three concerns, the measure of whose combined effect has been of equal impact on the fate of the nation. The first of these involved the steady decline of the native tongue as the primary language for ethnic Belarusans in the BSSR, dropping from 80.5 percent in 1970 (already the lowest figure for any of the Soviet republics[42]) to 74.2 percent in 1979.[43] The equally steady rise in Russian language usage among ethnic Belarusans – again far and away the highest rates among any of the non-Russian republics[44] – and the ongoing decline of schooling and print media in Belarusan, had convinced a sizeable number of the BSSR's cultural elite that the nation faced the very real prospect of linguistic extinction.[45]

On December 15, 1986, twenty-eight Belarusan intellectuals took the first public action on this issue by going over the heads of their superiors in the cultural establishment and addressing a letter of petition to then General Secretary of the Soviet Communist Party, Mikhail Gorbachev. This letter – also signed by a number of rank-and-file workers and subsequently endorsed by the BSSR's Writers' Union – observed that since "language is the soul of the nation," the General Secretary's intervention was now required "to save the Belorussian [Belarusan] people from spiritual extinction."[46] They went on to advise him that "we can now observe a noticeable growth of national awareness" that, in turn, "is provoking a hostile reaction from the bureaucracy," and to argue that the Belarusan language "must be protected by [new] legislation."

The appendix which accompanied this letter – "A Proposal for Radical Improvement of the Status of the Belarusan Language, Culture, and

Patriotic Education in the BSSR" – soon took on the character of a general political program for a number of "informal" groups and youth associations that had begun to form in the Republic. On December 26, 1987, more than thirty of these independent groups convened near Minsk and issued "An Appeal of the Initiative Group of the Confederation of Belarusan Youth Associations to Belarusan Youth" which lent a sharp edge to the general desiderata contained in the "Proposal" of the twenty-eight by reconfiguring the standard Soviet concept of "internationalist duty." "The cause of self-determination for the Belarusan youth movement," stated the "Appeal,"

> has ripened not only because of internal reasons. We are watched with hope and concern by the peoples of Estonia, Latvia and Lithuania. They are waiting for us to join the formidable wave of national upsurge that is rolling over the Baltic region. In Belorussia's [Belarus's] joining this surge, there is the assurance of the irreversibility of the revolutionary changes in the Baltic republics as well as throughout the entire Soviet Union, which means that it is our internationalist duty to do so.[47]

At its second convention (January, 1989) – held in Vilnius because authorities in the BSSR, already alarmed by the growth and independent direction taken by the youth movement, refused to sanction such meetings – the sixty-six groups now represented in the Confederation of Belarusan Youth Societies issued another "Appeal" which addressed the issues of national renewal, democratization, a multi-party system, economic reform, the formation of all-Belarusan units in the armed services, and language and cultural policy. Moreover, turning the tables on the authorities again (this time with reference to Belarus's hitherto nominal membership in the United Nations), the "Appeal" argued for Belarusan independence and the opening of foreign relations with other countries.

The second issue igniting the nationalist movement was the discovery by the archaeologist, Zianon Pazniak, that genocidal executions had been carried out by the Soviet regime from 1937 to 1941 in the Kurapaty wood near Minsk. The publication of Pazniak's findings in the Writers' Union weekly, *Litaratura i Mastactva* (June 3, 1988), which documented the existence of over 500 mass graves where lay the remains of an estimated 300,000 innocent victims, mobilized a broad public protest. On June 19, 1988, some 10,000 people marched to the site of the killings to commemorate the dead and demand a full investigation of the tragedy by an independent civil commision. The reply from officialdom was an attenuated inquiry which those outraged by the butchery at Kurapaty regarded as a cover-up.[48] Activists therefore created Committee-58 (after the notorious article in the criminal code under which the exterminations had been conducted) to pursue the investigation. At its meeting in October 1988, this group founded the Martyrology of Belarus, a group whose purpose, in the words of the renowned writer and highly-regarded man-of-conscience Vasil Bykau, was "to compile a great martyrology of our losses and our martyrs. This would be laid as a cornerstone in the foundation of our national consciousness, would become an important element of our historical memory."[49] Martyrology's five-member Civic Council included representatives of its four constituent organizations – the BSSR's Union of Cinematographers, Writers' Union, Union of Artists and the editorial board of *Litaratura i Mastactva* – along with Pazniak who was elected president. At its founding meeting, Martyrology established a political organization, the Belarusan Popular Front (BPF), also with Pazniak as president. The BPF's first act, a demonstration drawing 10,000 people on October 30, 1988 which both revived the national custom of *Dziady* (remembrance of the dead) and coincided with USSR's "Day of Remembrance" for the victims of Stalin's terror, was forcibly dispersed by police beatings, dogs, water cannon and noxious gas. Subsequent protests against this violence were dismissed by the BSSR's Procuracy and Supreme Soviet, thus dampening any hopes that the authorities might be open to accommodation and dialogue.[50]

Kurapaty symbolized for the growing national movement a past tragedy for Belarus to which the present regime would respond with only cover-ups and repression. The third major concern sparking the movement, the nuclear disaster at Chernobyl, represented a new and immediate danger to the survival of the nation. Although 70 percent of the fallout from Chernobyl had landed on two-fifths of the BSSR's territory and directly threatened the lives of some 2.2 million people, the Republic's authorities took little action to address the crisis except to suppress information and falsely reassure the population that they had no cause for alarm. Everyday life was permitted to continue in the contaminated zone, the inhabitants thus compounding their exposure to high-level radiation by ingesting locally raised vegetables, meat and milk containing concentrations of radionuclides that exceeded permissible limits many times over.[51]

Focusing on these three threats to the Belarusan people – the gradual loss of the native language, the massacres at Kurapaty and the ruin brought by the Chernobyl disaster – and accusing the communist regime of either agency or complicity in each, the BPF staged a rally in Minsk's Dynamo stadium on February 19, 1989 that drew over 40,000 supporters. This event, which occurred as part of the election campaign to the USSR's Congress of People's Deputies, marked a turning point in the struggle between the nationalist movement and the communist authorities. Inasmuch as the elections allowed for a limited amount of competition,[52] the BPF was able to go beyond the politics of protest and mount a challenge to the authorities that would be decided at the ballot box, rather than by police truncheons or rigged courts. Despite the huge advantages enjoyed by the communists, and the repression employed against their opponents, the BPF contributed to the defeat of at least seven of the BSSR's top officials at the polls and managed to elect eight of its own candidates to the new Soviet legislature.[53]

The battle between the BPF and the regime intensified enormously in the advent of the March 1990 elections to the Supreme Soviet and local soviets in the BSSR.[54] The BPF, which had by now grown to over 100,000 members,[55] formally constituted itself in Vilnius in June 1989 – a venue that at once bespoke the regime's continued hostility to the movement by again refusing it a meeting place in the BSSR and symbolizing the historic bonds between the Belarusan and Lithuanian peoples. In fending off the electoral challenge presented by the BPF, the authorities resorted to a number of devices, many of highly questionable legality, to insure an outcome favorable to themselves. Their control of the nomination process and the commissions formally encharged with monitoring it meant that hundreds of would-be opposition candidates were arbitrarily refused places on the ballot, while representatives of the regime were easily registered, often in safe rural districts without genuine competition. Candidates' access to the voters – either through the mass media or via face-to-face encounter in meeting halls – was, again, lopsided in favor of those preferred by the regime.

The authorities' coarse manipulations of the electoral process reflected their worries over the situation confronting them. For instance, one survey of public opinion conducted at the outset of the elections found that 90 percent of respondents took a dim view of any candidate associated with the apparatuses of the Communist Party, the Komsomol, the soviets or the trade unions.[56] Moreover, the regime's blatant disregard for procedural regularity and any measure of evenhandedness proved more than their junior partner, the Komsomol, could abide. As election day approached, the Komsomol passed a resolution claiming that the behavior of the authorities had caused the public to lose confidence in the BSSR's leadership and that "the leaders . . . must honestly and in a politically responsible way evaluate their own actions."[57] Additionally, the Komsomol inaugurated a new organization, Democratic Consent, that sought to foster dialogue and cooperation between the opposition and those elements in the party-state who might be committed to perestroika. Although this remained impossible for the moment, the results of the elections fundamentally altered the constellation of political forces in the Republic and increased the chances that at least some elements in the regime might seek some form of accommodation with other elements appearing in the political process.

Although representatives of the nomenklatura fared well as candidates in the essentially non-competitive rural districts where the political culture tended toward passivity, in the larger cities they were decimated at the polls. Given that a number of prominent communists were rejected by the voters, that only about one-quarter of the deputies elected were officials from the party or government apparatuses, and that the largest bloc of successful candidates was composed of intellectuals and technical specialists (many of whom were associated with the BPF), it was already clear when the new Supreme Soviet convened on May 15, 1990 that the old leadership would be unable to command a majority in the legislature, despite the fact that most of the deputies were members of the Communist Party and that regionally-based deputies' groups had been organized by the communist apparatus in an attempt to enforce party discipline in the legislature.[58]

The initial voting in the Supreme Soviet indicated the change that the elections had induced in the BSSR's political life. For the office of Chairperson of the Supreme Soviet, N. I. Dzemiantsei (Dementei), the incumbent, failed on the first ballot. Although he succeeded in the second round, his nominee for First Deputy Chairman, I. G. Moshko (Second Secretary of the Grodno Obkom) encountered such stiff opposition from the legislators that his name was withdrawn before a vote was taken. In his stead, the BPF's candidate, S. S. Shushkevich (then Vice-Rector of Belarusan State University) was elected as First Deputy Chairperson. In like fashion, V. F. Kebich retained his post as Chairperson of the BSSR's Council of Ministers, but the opposition was able to defeat his nominees to the positions of First Deputy Chairperson, Deputy Chairperson, and those to four of the ministries and three of the heads of state committees.

These votes highlighted the fact that although the old authorities had managed to hold on to power, their grip on it seemed far more tenuous than ever before. In a context now ripe for compromise, Dzemiantsei and Shushkevich forged a tactical alliance on the seminal question of Belarus's political future. Abandoning the less flexible members of their respective blocs in the legislature, they reached agreement on what was described in Dzemiantsei's proposal of June 12 to the BSSR's Supreme Soviet as "real political and economic sovereignty [and] the re-establishment of independence for the Belorussian Soviet Socialist Republic."[59] It was left to the legislature to fill out Dzemiantsei's general proposal, and the Declaration on State Sovereignty that was eventually passed on July 27 (henceforth an official holiday in the BSSR known as Independence Day) went considerably beyond the basic conceptions of the supremacy of Belarusan law on Belarusan soil and Belarusan ownership of all economic and natural resources contained in Dzemiantsei's plan. In its final version, the Declaration announced that the BSSR had become a nuclear-free zone, that it was officially neutral in international affairs, and that it reserved the right to raise its own army and security forces, as well as establish its own national bank and issue its own currency.[60] Nationhood, so long the dream of Belarusan nationalists, had been proclaimed by the government of Soviet Belarus.

Table 7.3. *National composition of Belarus, 1926–1989*

| Nationalities | 1926 in 1000s | 1926 in % | 1959 in 1000s | 1959 in % | 1970 in 1000s | 1970 in % | 1979 in 1000s | 1979 in % | 1989 in 1000s | 1989 in % |
|---|---|---|---|---|---|---|---|---|---|---|
| Belarusans | 4,017 | 80.6 | 6,532 | 81.1 | 7,240 | 81.0 | 7,568 | 79.4 | 7,897 | 77.8 |
| Russians | 384 | 7.7 | 658 | 8.2 | 938 | 10.4 | 1,134 | 11.9 | 1,341 | 13.2 |
| Poles | 98 | 2.0 | 539 | 6.7 | 383 | 4.5 | 403 | 4.2 | 417 | 4.1 |
| Ukrainians | 35 | 0.6 | 133 | 1.7 | 191 | 2.1 | 231 | 2.4 | 290 | 2.9 |
| Jews | 407 | 8.2 | 150 | 1.9 | 148 | 1.6 | 135 | 1.4 | 112 | 1.1 |
| Others | 42 | 0.9 | 42 | 0.4 | 52 | 0.6 | 61 | 0.7 | 71 | 0.9 |

*Source:* H. I. Kaspiarovic, "Etnademahraficnyja pracesy i miznacyjanalnyja adnosiny u BSSR," *Viesci AN BSSR. Seiryja hramadskich navuk* (Minsk), no. 5 (1990), 83.

## Interethnic relations

To date, Belarus has not evinced any of the varieties of interethnic conflict that surfaced in the Soviet Union during the years of perestroika. In part, this may be due to the fact that the indigenous nationality, as indicated in table 7.3, has not been overwhelmed as it has in, say, Estonia and Latvia with a large Russian immigration threatening to displace it as the majority group. But it also has seemed to reflect the traditional pattern of tolerance and goodwill toward other national groups historically associated with the Belarusan people. On the one hand, this has been evident in the nationalist movement. In its official charter, for instance, the BPF defines itself as:

> a mass socio-political movement [with the goal of] creating a society, and renewing the identity, of the Belarusan nation based on the principles of democracy and humanism, securing the conditions for a free and full-fledged development of the cultures of both the majority of the inhabitants and Belarus's national minorities."[61]

Similarly, Vasil Bykau has stressed this same point in his message to the founding congress of the BPF by noting that:

> Our movement for *pierabudova* [perestroika] is national in form and democratic in content. All the nationalities that comprise the Belarusan state will find a place within it. We are not excluding from it our brothers, the Russian people, with whom we share our land and fate, who for a long time have innocently suffered together with us. Nor do we exclude the tragic Jewish nation with whom we have shared the modest fruits of our land during the entire course of our history. The Poles and Lithuanians are our brothers, and we have countless examples of shared and truly fraternal coexistence.[62]

On the other hand, the government has been equally sensitive to the matter of interethnic relations in the Republic. In the preamble to the Declaration of State Soveriegnty, it has reaffirmed "respect for the dignity and the rights of the people of all nationalities who reside in the Belarusan SSR." Moreover, the Declaration itself specifically avoids the privileging of any national group in the Republic. "Citizens of the Belarusan SSR of all nationalities," it reads, "constitute the Belarusan people." And while the January 1990 Law on Languages in the Belarusan SSR does establish Belarusan as the official language of state, it allows for a period of from three to ten years' transition to its use. The Ministry of National Education has also drafted comprehensive plans for schools in which the respective languages of instruction include Russian, Ukrainian, Polish, Lithuanian, Yiddish, and Tatar.[63]

Perhaps as a consequence of sovereignty and Belarus's particular path to nationhood, the concept of the political state – rather than language, as in the past – has become the primary focus of the nation today. To be sure, concerns for reviving and developing the Belarusan language and culture remain much in evidence. Yet instances of Russian language publication and Russian speakers in Belarus endorsing Belarusan independence have also become commonplace. This overall allegiance to the Belarusan state, as well as governmental provisions for protecting minority languages and cultures, suggests that Belarus will continue to avoid the interethnic conflicts that have beset most of the former Soviet republics.

## The perspectives on Belarusan sovereignty and independence

The idea of the Belarusan people living in a Belarusan state has developed in the modern period from a project embraced by relatively narrow circles of intellectuals into an established political reality. At the same time, however, defining a concept of sovereignty pertinent to this state has been another bone of contention for organized political forces in the country. Prior to the coup d'etat staged in Moscow on August 19, 1991, it appeared that the government would opt for a limited form of sovereignty and the retention of Belarusan membership in a "renewed" federal union.[64] In this respect, they appeared to have a solid base of support in the population. For example, one poll of 33,000 respondents from all districts of the BSSR had found that "over 80 percent of those questioned condemn separatist attempts but actively support the idea of full sovereignty for the Republic."[65] Others, conducted on the eve of the USSR's March 17, 1991 referendum on a "renewed union," indicated that about four out of five citizens of the BSSR were opposed to secession.[66]

For its part, the BPF had consistently opposed all plans that would establish close political bonds between Belarus and Moscow. Until mid-summer of 1991, they had advocated the creation of an East European Commonwealth in which Belarus would join Ukraine, Lithuania, Latvia and Estonia. Pazniak, the BPF's Chairman and leader of the opposition in the BSSR's Supreme Soviet, has argued that such a commonwealth would be postulated on both geopolitics and history. Half a millennium of our common history, he has remarked, "tells us much more than 200 years of imperial bondage."[67]

Although this proposal for a commonwealth was discussed at several meetings of Belarusan, Ukrainian and Baltic leaders, little progress toward its realization was recorded. As these negotiations proved fruitless, the BPF modified its approach. In its August "Appeal" to the Belarusan people, it registered its opposition to the draft of a new Union treaty then under discussion and called for independence. Moreover, the BPF argued that the immediate future would be regarded as "a transitional period" and that the BSSR should join with other Soviet republics in "a commonwealth of sovereign states based on principles of confederation in which each state would be sovereign, where there would be no general laws and common organs of power, where common actions would be coordinated, and problems solved collegially on the basis of inter-state treaties."[68]

Although when promulgated, this Appeal may have appeared to have been no more than a far-fetched proposal reflecting neither the orientations of the majority of the legislature nor the opinions of most citizens, the coup that was launched in Moscow just five days later changed everything. Not only did the coup attempt succeed in destroying the very union that the plotters had risked all to save, but its result thoroughly discredited the unionist bloc in the BSSR and swung the political balance dramatically toward the position advocated by the BPF. At the extraordinary session of the BSSR's Supreme Soviet on August 24, N. I. Dzemiantsei was forced to resign as Chairman due to his support for the coup.[69] Shortly thereafter, Prime Minister Vechaslau Kebich and his cabinet resigned from the Communist Party citing the complicity of the Party's hierarchy in the coup attempt.[70]

The BSSR's Supreme Soviet returned to session in mid-September. In addition to changing the name of the country to the Republic of Belarus, it passed a battery of laws that initiated the transfer of all armed forces and units of state security on Belarusan soil – excepting strategic nuclear forces – to the jurisdiction of the Belarusan Council of Ministers.[71] The creation of an Armed Forces of the Republic of Belarus was thus emblematic of the radical change affected by the failed coup in the entire political structure of the Soviet Union. There no longer seemed to be any "center" that could hold. Stanislau Shushkevich, who officially replaced Dzemiantsei as Chairman of the Supreme Soviet at this session, reflected this change as well. Although he spoke at the September session in favor of Belarusan membership in a larger union,[72] by December he was meeting with Russian President Boris Yeltsin and Ukraine head Leonid Kravchuk to bury the old union and inaugurate a Commonwealth of Independent States[73] – a political structure apparently identical to that advocated since August by the BPF. Indeed, the Belarusan delegation to subsequent conferences of the member states of the Commonwealth has not only included representatives of the BPF, but the delegation itself has adopted the BPF's view of the Commonwealth "as a civilized form of transition to independence."[74] While the eventuality of such independence would remain contingent on a myriad of factors and considerations too complex to invite prediction, the remarkable journey to nationhood only recently completed by the Belarusan people would already count as an accomplished fact.

## A precarious independence

Independence is a process with many variables of which, in the case of Belarus, the geopolitical element is of primary significance. Geopolitically, an independent Belarus is a vulnerable state.

A look at the history of East-West military conflicts confirms the strategic importance of the Belarusan plain, situated squarely on a swath between Berlin and Moscow. It was a result of this central location that Minsk, the Belarusan capital, lay totally ruined at the conclusion of World War II, which brought death to every fourth inhabitant of the country.

Since the collapse of the Soviet Union, Belarus has gained geostrategic importance for Moscow because of Russia's weakened position vis-a-vis the Baltic states and Ukraine. The significance of the country for Russia's defense is graphically reflected in the facts that at the time of the dissolution of the Soviet Union there were 23 rocket bases and 42 military airfields on Belarusan territory;[75] and ten percent of the country's territory was under the jurisdiction of the "military structures."[76]

At the beginning of its independence, Belarus had to sustain one military person for every 43 inhabitants, while in Ukraine, for example, there was one soldier for every 98 inhabitants, in Kazakhstan – one for 118, in Tajikistan – one for 528, and in Russia – one for 634.[77]

Former Prime Minister Veachaslau Kebich had no illusions as to Russia's potential military dominion over his country. In an interview given to a Moscow newspaper Kebich admitted: "If a conflict arose today between Russia and some state to the west of it, would they ask us to allow the passage of Russian planes over our territory? Nobody would ask us."[78]

Russian intelligence seems to be at home in Belarus. Early in 1994, in the course of debate over a monetary union between Belarus and Russia entailing a partial abdication of Belarusan sovereignty, Member of Parliament Uladzimir Novik asked a pertinent question: "Who formulates such a policy? The government of a sovereign Belarus or foreign intelligence services?" His answer: "Rather the latter."[79] At the end of the year, this charge was repeated in a formal "Statement" by twenty-one members of Parliament representing the BPF, who objected to the government's inactivity in a situation where "Russian special agencies set out our policy."[80]

The trend of drawing closer to Russia started immediately after the declaration of independence. One of the co-signatories of the Belavezha agreement dismantling the Soviet Union, Belarusan Prime Minister Kebich, came to the conclusion that the economic woes of his state were a direct result of the severance of ties among the CIS states. To remedy the situation, Kebich saw no other way than to reestablish close relations with Russia as the keystone of the CIS.

The Kebich period in the history of sovereign Belarus (July 1990–July 1994) was marked by continuous economic decline, heated controversy over Belarus's military alliance with Russia, and an impasse over a merger of the two countries' monetary systems.

The issue of a collective defense with Russia pitted Prime Minister Kebich, who favored it, hoping for economic advantages, and Chairman (Speaker) of the Supreme Council (Soviet) Stanislau Shushkevich, who spoke ardently against it, defending his state's declared neutrality. Meanwhile both leaders were under constant fire from the democrats and nationalists in the parliament who demanded the resignation of both of them. The opposition, led by the 27-member Belarusan Popular Front faction and some of its allies, kept pressing for a referendum on the dissolution of the Supreme Soviet and the holding of new elections. The mood of the electorate, disturbed by the falling standard of living, was conducive to such a step. By mid-April 1992, within two months, over 442,000 signatures in support of the referendum were collected. However, members of the conservative parliament, bent on serving their full five-year term, overwhelmingly rejected the demand.

Eventually, Shushkevich was the first to fall in this political battle. Not only was he forced to sign the collective security treaty, in January 1994 he was posted in a vote of at confidence, 209–36.

One of Shushkevich's victories was the ratification of the START-I treaty. In May 1992, along with Ukraine and Kazakhstan, Belarus agreed to destroy or turn over all strategic nuclear warheads on its territory to Russia. To achieve this, the START-I Treaty had to be ratified. For some time, however, parliament dragged its feet on the ratification while seeking international guarantees of security. One of the most outspoken advocates of the ratification was Chairman Shushkevich who urged Belarus to get rid of nuclear missiles as soon as possible. Only by divesting itself of nuclear weapons, reasoned Shushkevich, would Belarus stand a chance to get rid of Russian troops located on its territory. How soon could it happen? "We planned to do it in seven years," says Shushkevich, "then changed it to five, now we are thinking of doing it in two and a half years."[81] On February 4, 1993, START-I was ratified by the Supreme Soviet in a vote of 218–1.

It is one of the paradoxes of the situation that the most serious threat to the independence of Belarus dwells in the nation's defenders, the army whose commanders are skeptical if not outright hostile to the idea of sovereignty. While the republic's armed forces have been downsized from an estimated peak of between 180,000 and 240,000 at the outset of independence to the stated goal of between 60,000 and 90,000, there were still an estimated 40,000 Russian strategic troops in Belarus at the end of 1994. Their total withdrawal, according to Belarusan Defense Minister General Anatol Kastenka, was to be expected "before 1996."[82] However, Belarusans had strong doubts that this will happen.

Russia has been building two important military stations in Belarus: one serving space defense, the other feeding radio signals to Russian surface ships and submarines in the Atlantic and the Mediterranean. Using its economic leverage Moscow managed to conclude a series of agreements with Minsk which will allow Russia to maintain those stations for the next twenty-five years.[83] Also, in November 1994, Belarus and Russia signed a package of military agreements on the "status of Russian military units, part of the strategic forces, temporarily stationed in Belarus." Russian General Staff Chief General Mikhail Kolesnikov told the Russian Duma that the agreement "legalizes the presence of Russian forces in Belarus."[84]

The precariousness of Belarus's sovereignty is underlined not only by the presence of Russian "strategic forces," but also by the composition and pro-Russian orientation of the national army's commanders. At the outset of independence, the ethnic composition of the officer corps in Belarus's military was "about twenty percent Belarusans, over fifty percent Russian, and Ukrainians slightly more than Belarusans."[85] In February 1993 the proportion of native Belarusans in the officer corps, according to the Defense Minister General-Colonel Pavel Kazlouski, grew to "about forty percent,"[86] still far from corresponding to the numerical place of Belarusans in their state (77.8 percent in 1989; see Table 5.3). It may take years before the republic will have its own politically reliable army grounded in Belarusan nationhood.

Over 40,000 Belarusan natives served in 1993 in the armed forces of other ex-Soviet republics. Many of them wished to return home for either patriotic or economic reasons. However, possibilities for repatriation are limited, largely because of the financial shortages from which the Belarusan state is suffering. Meanwhile efforts are being made to instill new spirit into the armed forces of the newly independent Belarus. On December 31, 1992, all servicemen (those with Belarusan citizenship) swore allegiance to the Republic of Belarus. Patriotically-minded Belarusan officers see a chance of fortifying their state's security by raising and spreading national consciousness through implementation of the law "About Languages" (in effect as of September 1, 1990) that makes Belarusan the only official language. The newspaper of the Belarusan Language Society, Naša Slova (*Our Word*), reported in September 1992: "Members of the Belarusan

Association of Servicemen have indicated to everybody that without a Belarusan Army in which the Belarusan language would be heard and Belarusan history and culture would be respected, there can be no independent Republic of Belarus."[87] The Association's task is an uphill struggle because of the small number of its adepts. However, some progress is being made. Teaching of the Belarusan language was provided for a small group of students of the Minsk Higher Military Engineering School, and the Defense Ministry "has been considering the issue of Belarusization of the military."[88]

The victory of Alaksandr Lukashenka in the presidential elections in July 1994 assured further continuation of the rapprochement with Russia. At the outset of his presidency, Lukashenka made it clear that he would not "initiate" any pullout of the Russian strategic forces from Belarus and would make an effort to revitalize the industrial military complex by gaining Russian orders.[89] "With Belarus in a vulnerable economic position," observed the *Christian Science Monitor*, "the new president, Alexander Lukashenka, may be easily influenced to maintain close ties to Russia."[90]

Furthermore, slow as it has been, the process of building up a patriotically conscious army has been hampered even more by the election of this pro-Russian President. Lukashenka appointed army commanders who favor even less "Belarusization of the military." But the situation grew more precarious in the wake of Russia's military onslaught on Chechnya. In regard to the latter development, *Narodnaja hazieta* (People's Newspaper), the parliamentary daily, observed that "Russia is entering a new phase of complex relationships between Moscow and the so-called national borderlands" and noted that "Moscow has traditionally placed little confidence in diplomacy but counts more on tanks." Commenting on Moscow's "iron grip in the Caucasus" and recalling similar Russian "deeds" in Budapest, Prague, and Kabul, the newspaper concluded that "the most resistant fortresses are the heads of those in the Kremlin who design such 'grand' policies."[91]

## Economic hurdles: dependency on Russia for energy and markets

The economy is at the very base of Belarus's independence. Prime Minister Viachaslau Kebich, in one his major speeches in December 1992, outlining "the pillars" of statehood of his nation – economy, morality, and culture – said about "pillar" number one: "Authentic statehood and independence begin with an independent and strong economy."[92]

The problem is that Belarus has inherited from the Soviet Union a distorted economy. After World War II, the country became an appendix to the Russian military industrial complex in disregard of its natural resources and considerable agricultural potential. Belarus is a graphic example of the economic bondage created under the former Communist regime by what could be called Moscow's industrial colonialism. During the pre-independence decades, the Belarusan SSR was turned into an "Assembly Shop" for the Soviet Union. Industry made up 70 percent of the republic's Gross National Product and was heavily engaged in feeding the USSR's war potential with machinery and electronics. Over eighty percent of Belarus's industrial output was exported to other Soviet republics, mainly to Russia. From Russia, to a similar extent, Belarus received energy and raw materials.[93]

Belarus's labor force is about five million. Of this number, until the early 1990s up to 400,000 were employed in the defense industry. After the proclamation of independence in August 1991, with an oversized army, the heavy burden of Chernobyl-related expenses, and growing unemployment, Belarus found itself in a situation where solutions are seen by the conservative government to lie in a close association with Russia.

The numerically small opposition, on the other hand, has been calling for a "return to Europe," an invitation that is supported by cultural considerations and historical tradition, now being refurbished by part of the intelligentsia. The government rejects such calls, maintaining that the country has little to offer to Western markets whereas there are buyers in the East. In addition to this realistic economic argument, there is a strong cultural and ideological bias within the official establishment and part of the population propelling them toward Russia. On the other hand, the government has insisted, in the spirit of the Declaration of State Sovereignty and the Constitution, that the Republic's independence will be preserved. What is vitally important now, say officials, is to avert the threatening social catastrophe by means of continuous employment.

By and large, freedom and independence are measured by the standard of living which, in the case of Belarus, has gone down dramatically during the early 1990s. Reacting to this shift, the nationalist opposition, which had been concerned largely with cultural issues, has lately shifted its attention to the economy and a quest for regional cooperation to counterbalance Russia's economic potential. In May of 1993, the Belarusan Popular Front's leader, Zianon Pazniak, together with Ukraine's Vyacheslav Chornovil and Lithuania's Vytautas Landsbergis, concluded that one of the gravest problems their republics are facing is the energy crisis. The three leaders further expressed their hopes that the solution for this problem not be connected with the economy of Russia which, in their opinion, has been hopelessly sinking. However, precisely where a solution to their energy problem lies, the three leaders did not specify. With the energy crisis deepening, it becomes clear that Russian economic pressure against the independence of Belarus (as well as other states in the region) has not yet run its full course. The war in Chechnya, of course, will only further disrupt the economic recovery of both countries.

Oil, gas, and raw materials for industrial production remain the basic commodities that Belarus lacks and for which it pays Russia with manufactured goods. However, Belarus has to accept the prices and trade conditions Moscow imposes, thus drastically reducing the competitiveness of Belarusan exports. For example, in 1994 Belarusan enterprises had to pay for Russian oil and gas from 2.5 to 3.5 times more than Russians did. There were, in addition, import and export fees imposed on Belarusan goods. To overcome these hurdles, Prime Minister Kebich was ready to barter away part of his state's sovereignty, i.e., to merge his country's currency (called *zaichile* (bunny) because of the picture on its one-ruble note) with Russia's and to subsume his republic's budget to that of Russia. This move evoked a world-wide reaction because of its political significance implying restoration of the Russian empire. "Belarus bunny falls victim to the prowling Russian bear," reported a British newspaper.[94] The proposed merger was also contoversial in Minsk and in Moscow for both political and economic reasons. "For Russia, the deal is terrible," wrote London's *Economist*. "It would bring into the rouble zone a country of 10 million people with inflation of 50 percent a month."[95]

While the controversy over the merger of the Belarusan and Russian monetary systems was dragging on, accompanied by a deepening economic crisis in Belarus, Prime Minister Kebich was voted out of office in July 1994. He lost dismally in the presidential contest to his populist rival, Aleksandr Lukashenka.

## The presidential republic

On March 15, 1994, the Belarusan Parliament adopted a Constitution which replaced that of 1978. The new Fundamental Law makes Belarus "a unitary, democratic, social State governed by the rule of law" where "the individual shall be the highest value of society and the State." "Democracy in Belarus," states the Constitution, "shall be realized on the basis of a diversity of political institutions, ideologies, and opinions." The Constitution gives the president enormous powers: elected for a five-year term (maximum of two terms), he is both head of the state and head of the government. The president appoints and dismisses ministers (key posts are filled with the approval of parliament); appoints justices; conducts international negotiations; signs treaties and laws; has the right to cancel acts and suspend decisions of lower executive authorities and local councils; heads the National Security council; is Commander-in-Chief of the Armed Forces; and can introduce martial law.

The new Constitution, which was drafted with Prime Minister Kebich in mind as president, reflects the authoritarian instinct of the conservative majority in the legislature who believed that a strong presidential hand would halt the republic's economic deterioration and prevent Belarus from

drifting too far away from Russia. On the other hand, the democratic deputies who went along with the majority in voting for the Constitution had
to give in on many points in order to create a badly needed legal barrier
that would somehow confirm the gains of recent years for national statehood and hinder the nomenklatura's drive to reincorporate the republic
into the Russian empire. One of the major achievements benefiting the
cause of the national revival was reconfirmation in the Constitution of the
official status of the Belarusan language (Article 17).

## The Lukashenka presidency

The first popularly elected president of independent Belarus, Alaksandr
Lukashenka (Lukashenko), came to power riding a wave of electoral disen-
chantment. The 39-year old presidential candidate made his name known
briefly before the contest as the chairman of the parliamentary Anti-
Corruption Committee. With his sweeping accusations of Prime Minister
Kebich's government, avowed friendship toward Russia, fulminations at
corrupt officials, and populist promises to take care of the the voters' needs,
Lukashenka was handed the reins of power by the electorate in relatively
clean elections.[96]

Having obtained a clear mandate from the voters (82 percent of those
who voted cast their ballots in his favor) and empowered extensively by
the freshly adopted constitution, the new president embarked immediately
on the path of rescuing the economy and restructuring the government. In
his inaugural address to the Supreme Soviet, President Lukashenka
announced first of all "reinforcement of state regulations and the establishment of a regime of harsh discipline," promised "no return to command
administrative methods in the economy," and pledged that "stimulation of
the national economy's development will be conducted by economic means
with absolute guarantees of defense of the right to private property." Lukashenka also expressed his readiness to collaborate with the International
Monetary Fund, without whose blessings, he knew, there would be no
badly-needed foreign investments.[97]

He brought into his presidential team a host of "Young Turks" marked
not so much by their expertise as by their allegiance to the Chief. The first
steps of Lukashenka's new administration were wobbly, slowed down by
the President's inability to complete the formation of his Cabinet of Ministers, as well as early desertions from his inner circle. The economic Anti-
Crisis Program announced within the first Hundred Days failed to take off.
By 1995, consumers faced skyrocketing prices and an increased monthly
inflation rate of about forty percent.

The situation was compounded by a constitutional crisis. The division
of power among the three branches of government, postulated by the Constitution, is fuzzy in many areas. The prerogatives of the national and

regional legislatures and the executive organs as well as the competence of the Constitutional Court clashed when the President moved to appoint his candidates as heads of regional councils (soviets), the so-called, "Presidential Vertical." Without a law regulating the rights of the press, the President's office tried to prevent publication of a stinging report in the parliament on corrupt officials and the continuing misuse of public funds within the new administration, in whose ranks there were many carryovers from the previous government. In the ensuing controversy over publicity of the report, having fired the editor of one daily, *Sovetskaya Belorussiya*, President Lukashenka threatened to dismiss other recalcitrant editors if they failed to follow the government line.[98] While some Minsk newspapers appeared in the latter days of December 1994 with blank spaces where the report exposing corruption would have been printed, or did not appear at all, the independent *Svaboda* published the document clandestinely (No.49, December 1994) in the "Lukashenka Publishing House."

As the year 1994 drew to an end, the Supreme Council's crowded agenda included such basic draft bills as the Law about the Supreme Soviet, the Law about Electing Deputies to the Supreme Soviet, the Law about the Presidency, the Law about the Cabinet of Ministers, and the Law about the Press.

March 1995 marked the expiration of the five-year term of the current parliament. Extending its life span for two more months, the parliament scheduled elections for May 14, 1995. As far as the parliament is concerned, this would be the first free expression of the voters' preferences. The principle of representation was majoritarian, favored by both the conservatives in the Supreme Soviet and by the Lukashenka administration.

In order to stem the proliferation of political parties, whose number grew to about thirty by the end of 1994, the parliament established a 500-member minimum membership "threshold" and ordered their registration by April 1, 1995. This measure will undoubtedly dampen further political development. Facing public inertia and financial shortages, the democratic opposition parties have been planning to form an electoral bloc in expectation of increasing their clout in the new legislature. Their success, however, has been limited, taking into consideration the wide phenomenon of nostalgia for the old times of relative security in evidence in Belarus.

## Political climate, culture, and national reawakening

As a result of historical circumstances, Belarusan society is politically apathetic to a greater degree than elsewhere in Eastern and Central Europe. By and large, the Belarusan people are not convinced that the pluralistic system they have seen up till now has been designed to improve their daily lot. What the population has experienced so far is chaos and corruption. Not being able to rely on their own organizational resources to fight it,

Belarusans look to the state to take care of them. For its part, the state is still present in almost every sphere of life. Besides the economic grip that the state has on people's lives, there is a major psychological impediment – a lack of differentation of such concepts as "state," "government," and "self-government" (civil society). Generally, citizens do not distinguish between the powers of officialdom, on the one hand, and their own civil and human rights and organizational prerogatives, on the other. The all-inclusive concept of "State" (*dziarzava*) is a hindrance to grassroots initiatives and movements and an intimidating factor in the growth of non-governmental organizations. The deepening economic crisis and almost total dependence of the citizenry in their daily activity on the public sector prevents the disassembly of this all-powerful concept of "State" into its components as a civil society.

The prevailing wait-and-see attitude, which seems to be a central feature of the Belarusan national character, and an absence of sharp political divisions have, along with a retarding effect on democratic reforms, also their advantages. One of these is a relatively stable political climate and the other – the absence of ethnic or religious strife. A U.S. Congressional report on implementation of the Helsinki Accords said: "A CSCE Rapporteur Mission visited Belarus in March 1992 and reported favorably, in terms of human rights and respect for national minorities, on the Belarus Declaration of Independence."[99]

Since the beginning of Gorbachevian perestroika, slow progress has been made toward reconfirmation of Belarusan nationhood in terms of public agencies, cultural programs, and national consciousness. While members of the older generation, especially war veterans and many among the governmental cadres, clamor for the stability of bygone days, patriots and nationalists root for an independent state where freedom and national pride would supply the building energy and civic morale. Much hope in this regard is pinned on the program of Belarusization (de-Russification) of educational and cultural institutions. The task, of course, is enormous because of decades of living according to the gospel from Moscow. Nevertheless, changes are tangible. Thus, whereas in the mid-1980s there was not a single Belarusan-language secondary or even primary school in any of the republic's cities or towns, in 1994 619,000 youths were instructed in Belarusan as compared with 896,000 taught in Russian.[100]

The switch to Belarusan as the language of instruction is not proceeding without protests and incrimination in nationalism. Minister of Education Vasil Strazhau, a Lukashenka appointee, speaking of the unhappiness of some Russian-speaking parents over their children being educated in Belarusan-language schools, explained that "the pace of growth of national consciousness lags considerably behind the pace of the transition of education to the Belarusan language." Strazhau sees a day when Belarusan will be used everywhere in the state.[101] For the time being, however, higher education in the country is still largely in Russian due to a lack of instructors, textbooks, and, to no small degree, resistance to change among teachers, administrators, and the public at large.

Russian is also spoken predominantly in official places. The election to the presidency of Lukashenka, who speaks Russian almost exclusively, has activated Moscow-oriented parties and movements in Belarus. Moreover, the results of a May 1995 referendum, in which voters overwhelmingly approved of making Russian a state language, integrating the Belarusan economy with Russia's and returning to Soviet-era state symbols, makes to the country's independence considerably less stable.

## Foreign relations

Since the proclamation of independence (August 25, 1991), Belarus has been recognized by over one hundred countries. Minsk has established diplomatic relations with nearly seventy of them. There were 21 foreign missions (embassies or consulates) in the Belarusan capital at the end of 1994. The number of the country's own foreign embassies, because of financial constraints and a lack of personnel, has been limited to major Western nations (Germany, France, England, The United States, Canada), Poland, the Baltic neighbors, and the CIS states.

In February 1992, Belarus became a member of the Conference on Security and Cooperation in Europe (CSCE). In the same year it joined the International Monetary Fund (IMF), the World Bank, and the European Bank for Reconstruction and Development. Minsk also gained observer status at the General Agreement on Tariffs and Trade (GATT).

Little known in the West, Belarus has been in the news mainly in connection with the issue of nuclear arms (tactical weapons and 81 intercontinental ballistic missiles) inherited from the Soviet Union. In May 1992, along with Ukraine and Kazakhstan, Belarus agreed to destroy or turn over all strategic nuclear warheads on its territory to Russia. To achieve this, the START-I Treaty had to be ratified. After protracted discussions, on February 4, 1993, START-I was confirmed along with the approval of the Non-Proliferation Treaty. These measures brought immediate results in the sphere of Belarusan-American relations. President Clinton in a telephone call to Chairman Shushkevich "assured the Belarus leader that the U.S. will provide Belarus with security guarantees."[102] Minsk was rewarded with the grant from Washington of most favored nation status in trade relations with the United States[103] followed by notification from the U.S. State Department of an increase in American aid (from $8.3 million to $65 million) to Belarus for its "bold and positive" steps in approving the START-I and Non-Proliferation Treaties.[104]

The latest chapter in the process of international recognition of the Republic of Belarus in return for its renunciation of nuclear arms was the signing in Budapest, at a CSCE summit, of a Protocol by which the Presidents of the United States and Russia and the Prime Minister of the United Kingdom agreed to guarantee the independence, sovereignty, and existing borders of Belarus. At the same gathering, similar guarantees were also accorded by the three powers to Kazakhstan and Ukraine.[105]

After a lengthy delay, caused most probably by negotiations with Moscow concerning economic/military agreements, Belarus finally joined NATO's Partnership for Peace program, leaving Tajikistan as the only country on the territory of the former Soviet Union not to have joined.[106]

Belarus's future international behavior will hinge largely on the country's economic condition, particularly its ability to secure alternative sources of energy and choice of markets to reduce its dependence on Russia. Before that happens, however, the change will require a considerable public airing of the problem. Thus far, the issue of foreign policy orientation is little debated in the mass media for various reasons, the principal of which are a lack of exposure to world problems, traditional timidity in tackling foreign-policy issues, and strict control of the press, radio, and television by the government.[107]

Some democratic politicians propound the idea of a loose economic association of the states between the Baltic and the Black Seas, others urge Belarus to join the Vise grad Group (Poland, Hungary, the Czech Republic, and Slovakia). Neither move is imminent, however, until there is a shift from the present conservative to a more liberal makeup of the country's parliament.

### Notes

1 We have employed throughout the terminology adopted as official as of 19 September 1991: "Belarus" rather than "Belorussia"; "Belarusan" rather than "Belorussian."

2 For examples, see: S. Kurganskii, "Polupravda – ne pravda," *Sovetskaya Belorussiya,* June 7, 1989; V. Korzun, "Po sledam odnoi besedy," *Politicheskii sobesednik,* no. 12, 1989.

3 Mikhail Tkachev, interviewed by Aleksandr Shagun, "Vsadnik s mestom nad gorodom," *Soyuz,* no. 43, October, 1990, p. 9.

4 *Etnahrafija Bielarusi. Encyklapiedyja* (Minsk: Bielaruskaja Savieckaja Encyklapiedyja, 1989), p. 77.

5 Nicholas P. Vakar, *Belorussia: The Making of a Nation* (Cambridge, MA: Harvard University Press, 1956), pp. 1–4.

6 *Encyklapiedyja litaratury i mastactva Bielarusi* (Minsk: Bielaruskaja Savieckaja Encyklapiedyjia, 1984), vol. I, pp. 364–367.

7 P.N. Milyukov, *Natsional'nyi vopros. Proiskhozhdeniye natsional'nosti i natsional'nye voprosy v Rossii* (Prague: Free Russia Publishers, 1925), p. 154.

8 Aleh Latysonak, "Bielastoccyna i narodziny bielaruskaje dumki," a lecture at the Byelorussian Institute of Arts and Sciences in New York, February 23, 1991.

9 Academy of Sciences of the BSSR, Institute of History, *Historyja Bielaruskaj SSR* (Minsk: Nauka i technika, 1972), vol. I, p. 586.

10 A.A. Lojka, V.P. Rahojsa, compilers, *Bielaruskaja litaratura XIX stahoddzia. Chrestamatyja* (Minsk: Vyšejšaja škola, 1988), p. 32.

11 Academy of Sciences of the BSSR, Institute of History, *Historyja Bielaruskaj SSR*, p. 515.

12 Jan Zaprudnik and Thomas E. Bird, *The 1863 Uprising in Byelorussia: "Peasants' Truth" and "Letters from beneath the Gallows" (Texts and commentaries)* (New York: Kreceuski Foundation, 1980), p. 68.

13 Thomas T. Hammond, "Nationalism and National Minorities in Eastern Europe," *Journal of International Affairs*, vol. 20, no. 1, 1966, pp. 9–31.

14 Zygmunt Bauman, "Intellectuals in East-Central Europe: Continuity and Change," *East European Politics and Societies*, vol. 1, Spring, 1987, pp. 171–172.

15 Vakar, *Belorussia*, pp. 34–36.

16 Stephen L. Guthier, "The Belorussians: National Identification and Assimilation, 1897–1970," (part 1), *Soviet Studies*, vol. 29, January, 1977, p. 43.

17 Vakar, *Belorussia*, p. 78.

18 S. Ch. Aleksandrovič *et. al.* (comps.), *Bielaruskaja litaratura XIX stahoddzia. Chrestamatyja* (Minsk: Vyšejšaja škola, 1971), pp. 193–194.

19 Ye. F. Karski, *Etnograficheskaya karta Belorusskago plemeni* (Petrograd: Belorussian Regional Committee of the All-Russian Soviet of Peasant Deputies, 1917), p. 1.

20 Vakar, *Belorussia*, p. 105.

21 *Ibid.*, p. 97.

22 *Ibid.*, pp. 121–133. On the Belarus Peasant-Workers' Hramada inside Poland, see Aleksandra Bergman, *Sprawy bialoruskie w II Rzeczypospolitej* (Warsaw: Panstwowe wydawnictowo naukowe, 1984), pp. 33–37.

23 Ivan S. Lubachko, *Belorussia Under Soviet Rule, 1917–1957* (Lexington, KY: University of Kentucky Press, 1972), p. 129.

24 Helene Carrere d'Encausse, *Decline of an Empire* (New York: Newsweek Books, 1979), pp. 24–28.

25 Lubachko, *Belorussia Under Soviet Rule*, pp. 111–118; Vekar, *Belorussia*, pp. 146–149.

26 Vakar, *Belorussia*, pp. 141–142.

27 *Narodnoe khozyaistvo Belorusskoi SSR v 1981 g.* (Minsk: Belarus, 1982, pp. 3, 5.

28 Jan Zaprudnik, "Belorussia and the Belorussians"; Zev Katz *et al.* (eds), *Handbook of Major Soviet Nationalities* (New York: The Free Press, 1975), p. 52.

29 K.T. Mazurov, *Nezabyvaemoe* (Minsk: Belarus', 1984), *passim.*

30 I.M. Ignatenko *et al.*, *Istoriya Belorusskoi SSR* (Minsk: Nauka i tekhnika, 1977), p. 145.

31 Although Masherov spoke Belarusan rather poorly, many people were moved by a feeling of national pride by the fact that he had chosen to speak in that language.

32 See Amy Knight, "Pyotr Masherov and the Soviet Leadership: A Study in Kremlinology," *Survey*, 26 (Winter, 1982), 151–168.

33 Michael E. Urban, *An Algebra of Soviet Power: Elite Circulation in the Belorussian Republic 1966–1986* (Cambridge: Cambridge University Press, 1989).

34 P.U. Brovka *et al.*, *Belorusskaya Sovetskaya Sotsialisticheskaya Respublika* (Minsk: Glavnaya redaktsiya Belorusskoi Sovetskoi entsiklopedii, 1978), pp. 587–588.

35 *Ibid.*, pp. 134–135; V. P. Borodina *et al.*, *Soviet Byelorussia* (Moscow: Progress, 1972), pp. 82–85, 134–135.

36 N. Matukovskii, "40 tsentnerov i bol'she," *Izvestiya*, September 9, 1987.

37 Brovka *et al.*, *Belorusskaya*, pp. 271–280; Borodina *et al.*, *Soviet Byelorussia*, pp. 93–95; V.P. Vorob'eva *et al.*, *Vitebsk* (Minsk: Nauka i tekhnika, 1974), pp. 197–198; V. Ya. Naumenko, *Brest* (Minsk: Nauka i tekhnika, 1977), pp. 123–135.

38 *Izvestiya*, December 16, 1985. The 1989 census recorded a population of 10.2 million in the BSSR and noted continued migration to urban centers. M. Shimanskii, "Kto zhivet v Belorussii," *Izvestiya*, March 13, 1990,

39  Alexander Zhuravlyov, "Not to miss a chance," *Moscow News*, no. 48, December 3–10, 1989, p. 11.

40  This term was initially coined by the Belarusan writer, Ales' Adamovich, in his "Oglyanis' okrest," *Ogonek*, no. 39, September 24–October 1, 1988, pp. 28–30. It has subsequently gained considerable currency throughout the Soviet Union. See, for instance, "Ekho tragedii," *Daugava*, no. 1, 1989; Kathleen Mihalisko, "Georgii Tarasevich – Prime Culprit in 'The Vendee' of *Perestroika*," *Radio Liberty Report on the USSR*, RL 299/89, June 14, 1989, p. 18–20.

41  Urban, *Algebra*, pp. 70–73, 98–135.

42  Stephen L. Guthier, "The Belorussians: National Identification and Assimilation 1897–1970" (part 2), *Soviet Studies*, 29 (April, 1977), 272–274; Brian Connolly, "Fifty Years of Soviet Federalism in Belorussia," in R.S. Clem, ed., *The Soviet West* (New York: Praeger, 1975), pp. 114–115.

43  Michael Kirwood, "Glasnost', 'The National Question' and Soviet Language Policy," *Soviet Studies*, 43, no. 1 (1991), 68–69.

44  *Ibid.*

45  Roman Szporluk, "West Ukraine and West Belorussia," *Soviet Studies*, 31 (January, 1979), 76–77.

46  *Letters to Gorbachev: New Documents from Soviet Byelorussia*, 2nd edn (London: The Association of Byelorussians in Great Britain, 1987).

47  Jan Zaprudnik, "Belorussian Reawakening," *Problems of Communism*, 38 (July–August, 1989), 27.

48  Adamovich, p. 29; "Ekho tragedii", *Daugava*, 1989.

49  *Press-hrupa "Navina paviedamlaje"* (Minsk), Samizdat (n.d.), p. 2.

50  Evgenii Budinas, "Ternii pravdy," *Vek XX i mir*, no. 3, 1989, pp. 26–31.

51  See, for instance, Vasil' Bykov, "Gumanizm 'nevozmozhno uchredit' . . .," *Znamya yunosti*, February, 1989, p. 3; Ales Adamovich, "Belorussia's Calamity," *Moscow News*, no. 41, October 15–22, 1989, p. 12; Yevgeniya Albats, "The Big Lie", *ibid.*, no. 42, October, 1989), pp. 8–9; Evgenii Konoplya, "Ostorozhno, zona otchuzhdeniya," *Soyuz*, no. 7, February 12–18, 1990, p. 12.

52  On the organizational advantages enjoyed by the Communist Party in the all-union elections of 1989, see Michael E. Urban, *More Power to the Soviets: The Democratic Revolution in the USSR* (Aldershot, UK and Brookfield, VT: Edward Elgar, 1990), chapter 5.

53  Zaprudnik, "Belroussian Reawakening," p. 49.

54  For a full account of these elections, see Michael E. Urban, "Regime, Opposition and Elections in the Belorussian Republic," in Darrell Slider (ed.), *Elections in the USSR* (Durham, NC: Duke University Press, forthcoming).

55  Kathleen Mihailsko, "Year in Review: Belorussia," *Radio Liberty Report on the USSR*, RL 583/89, December 15, 1989, p. 21. Mihailsko also points out that the Communist Party of Belorussia had been alone among republic-level communist parties in the USSR in forbidding its members to join a popular front and that the BPF lost a large number of its most active members as a result of this decision.

56  G. Akulova, ". . . Zainteresovany v silnykh Sovetov," *Sovetskaya Belarussiya*, January 7, 1990.

57  Mikhail Shimanskii, "Zayavlenie byuro Tsk LKSM Belorussii, *Izvestiya*, March 1, 1990.

58  V.V. Baranovskii *et al.*, "Ob etike glasnosti i demokratii," *Sovetskaya Belorussiya*, May 19, 1990.

59  N. Dementei, "Zapistak Verkhovnomu Sovetu Belorusskoi SSR o gosudarstvennom suverenitete respubliki," *Sovetskaya Belorussiya*, June 20, 1990.

60  "Deklaratsiya o gosudarstvennom suverenitete respubliki," *Sovetskaya Belorussiya*, June 20, 1990.

61 Radio Liberty, Belorussian Service, June 29, 1989. See also Zaprudnik, "Belorussian Reawakening," p. 51.
62 *Litaratura i Mastactva*, July 7, 1989.
63 *Nastaunickaja hazieta* (Minsk), October 10, 1990.
64 See, for instance, the interview given by Dzemiantsei to N. Matukovskii, "Sud'bu ne nazyvayut, a vybirayut," *Izvestiya*, February 14, 1991.
65 Evgenii Babosov, "Effekt bumeranga," *Kommunist Belorussii*, no. 12, December, 1990, p. 46.
66 Three such polls are discussed in M. Shimanskii, "Belorussiya: soyuzy byt'!," *Izvestiya*, March 14, 1991.
67 Z. Pazniak (an interview), "Slach u budučyniu," *Bielarus* (NY: Byelorussian-American Assoc., no. 375, November 1990).
68 *Zviazda*, August 14, 1991.
69 Aleksandr Shagun, "Srazhayas' nasmert', nomenklatura ukhodit so stseny," *Soyuz*, no. 35, August 28–September 4, 1991, p. 9.
70 Radio Moscow, August 28, 1991.
71 *Viedamasci Viarchounaha Savieta Respubliki Bielarus*, no. 30, 1991, pp. 22–27. This transfer was completed in early 1992, "Belarus' primeryaet dospekhi," *Rossiiskaya gazeta*, January 13, 1992, p. 2.
72 The proclamation and Agreement in the Creation of the Commonwealth of Independent States can be found in *Rossiiskaya gazeta*, December 10, 1991, p. 1.
73 *Niecarhovaja Sostaja Siesija Viarchounaha Savieta Bielaruskaj SSR Dvanaccataha Sklikannia (Biuleten)*, no. 2, September 17, 1991, p. 5.
74 See the interview given to Igor Sinyakevich by a member of the Belarusan delegation, Leonid Borshchevskii, "Belorusskaya delegatsiya ser'eznee drugikh otneslas' k peregovoram," *Nezavisimaya gazeta*, December 28, 1991, p. 3.
75 Statement by Piotra Sadouski, Chairman of the parliamentary Committee for International Affairs, *Navainy BNF*, No. 6, September 1991.
76 General Piotr Chaus, Minister for Defense of the Republic of Belarus, in an interview with correspondent Viacheslav Zenkovich, *TASS*, Minsk, January 11, 1992.
77 *Zviazda*, February 13, 1992.
78 *Nezavisimaya gazeta*, October 5, 1993.
79 *Svaboda*, No. 1, January 1994.
80 *Narodnaja hazieta*, December 13, 1994.
81 *FBIS-SOV*, January 29, 1993, p. 52.
82 *Foreign Broadcast Information Service Daily Report: Soviet Union* (henceforth *FBIS-SOV*), October 19, 1994, p. 32.
83 *Reuter*, Minsk, January 6, 1995.
84 Radio Free Europe/Radio Liberty. *Daily Report*, No. 225, November 30, 1994.
85 *Zviazda*, January 10, 1992.
86 *Zviazda*, February 23, 1993.
87 *Naša slova*, No. 35, September 2, 1992.
88 *Naša slova*, No. 31, August 5, 1992.
89 *Narodnaja hazieta*, July 14, 1994.
90 *Christian Science Monitor*, July 25, 1994.
91 *Narodnaja hazieta*, December 6, 1994.
92 *Sovetskaya Belorussiya*, December 23, 1992.
93 *Delo*, 1993, No. 1–2, pp. 9–13.
94 *The Independent*, January 26, 1994.
95 *Economist*, January 15, 1994, p. 76.
96 For the background of the presidential elections and the victor's biography, see *Belarusian Review*, Vol. 6, No. 2 (Torrance, CA, Summer 1994), pp. 1–9.
97 *Narodnaja hazieta*, July 19, 1994.

98  *Zviazda*, December 28, 1996.

99  *Implementation of the Helsinki Accords*, "Human Rights and Democratization in the Newly Independent States of the former Soviet Union," Compiled by the Staff of the Commission on Security and Cooperation in Europe, Washington, DC, January 1993, p. 77.

100  *Zviazda*, November 11, 1994.

101  *Narodnaja hazieta*, December 17–19, 1994.

102  *FBIS-SOV*, February 11, 1993, p. 39.

103  *FBIS-SOV*, February 19, 1993, p. 50.

104  *Newsday*, March 27, 1993.

105  *New York Times*, December 6, 1994; *Zviazda*, December 6, 1994.

106  Embassy of the Republic of Belarus. *Press-Release*, Washington, January 12, 1995.

107  For a discussion of foreign-policy mechanism and problems, see Jan Zaprudnik, "Development of Belarusian National Identity and Its Influence on Belarus's Foreign Policy Orientation" in: Roman Szporluk, ed., *National Identity and Ethnicity in Russia and the New States of Eurasia* (Armonk, NY: ME Sharpe, 1994), pp. 129–149.

# Belarus: chronology of events

*December 1986*

15  Twenty-eight leading intellectuals address a letter to
Gorbachev proposing the establishment of a plan to develop
Belarusan language and culture.

*December 1987*

26  The Confederation of Belarusan Youth Associations,
composed of more than thirty informal groups, issues an
appeal to the populace to support the cause of
self-determination.

*June 1988*

19  Thousands march to Kurapaty, the site of the mass graves
of victims executed by the Soviet regime from 1937–41,
to commemorate the dead and demand a full
investigation.

*October 1988*

The Belarusan Popular Front is established at a meeting of
another organization – the Belarus Martyrology, Zianon
Pazniak, archaelogist and discoverer of the Kuropaty graves,
is elected president.

30  10,000 people attend a memorial demonstration organized
by the Belarus Martyrology in honor of the victims of
Stalin. The demonstration is forcibly broken up.

*January 1989*

The Confederation of Youth Association issues an appeal
supporting independence and the establishment of foreign
relations.

*February 1989*

21  40,000 people attend a rally in support of BPF candidates
running in the March 1989 elections to the USSR Congress
of People's Deputies.

*July 1989*

28  N. I. Dementei replaces G.S. Tarazevich as chairman of the
Supreme Soviet.

*September 1989*

30  A rally protesting the government's negligence in attending

to the effects of the 1986 Chernobyl disaster attracts 30,000 participants.

*January 1990*

27    A Law on Language is adopted which establishes Belarusan as the official state language but allows for a transitional period of three to ten years.

*March 1990*

4    Elections to the Supreme Soviet are held. 8 BPF candidates gain seats.

*April 1990*

11    Vechaslav Kebich replaces M. Kovalyov as Chairman of the Supreme Soviet's Council of Ministers (Prime Minister).

*May 1990*

19    Dementei, the incumbent chairman of the Supreme Soviet, is reappointed to his position, but the BPF candidate Stanislau Shushkevich is elected First Deputy Chairman.

*July 1990*

27    The Supreme Soviet adopts a declaration of state sovereignty, which says that Belarus is a nuclear-free zone and neutral in international affairs, and reserves the right to raise its own army and security forces and establish its own national bank and currency.

*November 1990*

7    During a Revolution Day celebration, 13 nationalists break through a police cordon to wreath a statue of Lenin with Belarusan national symbols.

*March 1991*

17    In the all-union referendum on preserving the union, 83 percent of Belarusan voters (83 percent turnout) support the union.

*April 1991*

8–12    Tens of thousands participate in republican-wide strikes and demonstrations to protest poor economic conditions.

*August 1991*

24–25    With 50,000 protestors outside the Supreme Soviet, parliamentary chairman Dementei is forced to resign due to his support of the attempted coup in Moscow. As well, the Supreme Soviet temporarily suspends the Communist Party and gives the July 1990 declaration of sovereignty the force of law.

*September 1991*

18 Shushkevich is elected chairman of the Supreme Soviet.

*December 1991*

10 The Supreme Soviet ratifies the Minsk agreement creating the CIS. A new Communist Party of Belarus is formed to replace the Communist Party of the BSSR.

*January 1992*

6 The Popular Front initiates a signature-gathering campaign for a referendum on dissolving the Communist-dominated Supreme Soviet and holding new elections.

*February 1992*

23 Several thousand gather in Minsk in support of the Popular Front's referendum campaign.

*April 1992*

13 The Party of Popular Accord, organized by reformist former Communists, holds its founding congress.

*May 1992*

12 The Central Election Commission announces that 383,000 signatures have been gathered in the referendum campaign, 33,000 more than are required.

15 Shushkevich refuses to sign the CIS collective security pact, despite strong parliamentary support for the agreement.

*August 1992*

12 The United Agrarian Democratic Party is officially registered.

*October 1992*

9 The Popular Movement of Belarus is formed, uniting a number of pro-communist, pro-Russian political groups. The Belarus Research-and-Production Congress, an industrial movement, holds its founding conference.

29 Despite the fact that the referendum campaign collected more than the necessary 350,000 signatures, the Supreme Soviet votes 202–35 to reject it.

*February 1993*

3 The Communist Party, suspended in August 1991, is officially permitted to resume activity.

4    The START-1 treaty is ratified by the Supreme Soviet in a vote of 218–1.

*April 1993*

9    Parliament votes 188–34 to sign the CIS collective security pact, but Shushkevich again refuses to sign it and insists that a referendum be held to decide the issue.

*June 1993*

9–11    The First World Congress of Belarusans is held in Minsk.

*July 1993*

1    The Supreme Soviet passes a vote of no-confidence in Shushkevich 168–27, but it is not binding as a quorum of deputies had not been met.

15    A citizenship law is passed which grants automatic citizenship to all residents of Belarus.

22    Shushkevich signs the Nuclear Non-Proliferation Treaty.

*September 1993*

8    Kebich and Russian Prime Minister Viktor Chernomyrdin sign a preliminary agreement on Russian-Belarusan monetary union.

11    The conservative Popular Movement of Belarus sponsors a Congress of the Belarusan People which is attended by 1,300 delegates.

*November 1993*

8    The Belarusan Trade Unions Federation announces that it has collected 738,000 signatures, more than twice the amount required, in favor of a referendum in support of early parliamentary elections.

9    500 demonstrators gather in front of the Supreme Soviet building to call for the government's resignation.

18    The Supreme Soviet ratifies the monetary union treaty.

24    The Supreme Soviet makes the Belarusan *rubel* the sole legal currency in the country in preparation for monetary union with Russia.

*Janurary 1994*

3    Shushkevich signs the CIS collective security pact.

18    The Belarusan parliament ratifies the CIS charter.

26    Amid accusations of governmental corruption and facing widespread opposition by a pro-Russian parliament, Shushkevich is ousted as parliamentary chairman (and head of state) in a vote of no-confidence: 209 to 36. Kebich survives a similar vote: 101–175.

28 Myachyslau Hryb is elected Chairman of the Supreme Soviet.

*February 1994*

2 A National Strike Committee, headed by a number of trade unions, calls for nationwide strikes to demand the resignation of Kebich's government and early parliamentary elections. As many as 20,000 workers participate in the strike on 15 February.

7 The BPF issues a statement denouncing the impending monetary union.

*March 1994*

15 The Supreme Soviet ratifies a new Constitution.

*April 1994*

12 Kebich and Chernomyrdin sign a new agreement on monetary union to establish free-trade and ruble zones. The Chairman of the Belarusan national bank, Stanislau Bahdankevich, denounces the agreement as unconstitutional and refuses to sign it.

*June 1994*

1 The rubel becomes Belarus' sole legal tender.

23 In presidential elections, Aleksander Lukashenko receives 45 percent of the votes, placing him ahead of Prime Minister Kebich (17 percent), former Supreme Soviet chairman Shushkevich, and BPF leader Pazniak. Lukashenko and Kebich are scheduled to compete in runoff elections.

*July 1994*

10 In second-round elections, Lukashenko is victorious with 80 percent of the vote (70 percent voter participation).

11 Kebich and his cabinet resign.

*September 1994*

15 In an interview, Russian Prime Minister Chernomyrdin acknowledges that it is currently impossible to establish a monetary union with Belarus.

*October 1994*

6 Parliament amends law on local government to eliminate all rural soviets, as well as those of towns and cities, and replace them with nonelected administrations. In raions and oblasts, executive power is granted to soviet executive committee chairmen appointed by the president.
Lukashenko justifies the amendments as necessary measures to enact rapid economic reform.

*December 1994*

22–23    Several newspapers come out with blank spots where the printers, under presidential orders, removed a transcript of a speech made by deputy Sergei Antonchik accusing top officials of corruption. Parliament subsequently condemns Lukashenko for this act of censorship.

*January 1995*

4    A rally is held on Minsk's Independence Square to protest the censorship and demand that the language of instruction at Belarus State University be switched to Belarusan. As the police disperse protestors, one organizer, Professor Mikola Savitsky, is beaten and detained.

6    Lukashenko and Yeltsin sign a set of agreements on Russian-operated military installations and preparing for the mutual convertibility of the Russian and Belarusan rubles.

*February 1995*

9    It is announced that nearly 800 residents of Gantsevichi signed a petition to protest the construction of a nearby missile-attack early warning system owned and operated by Russia.

21–22    Lukashenko and Yeltsin sign a treaty of friendship, as well as eight other agreements on matters including joint operation of customs service and border patrol.

*March 1995*

21    Lukashenko suggests that the Supreme Soviet dissolve itself voluntarily.

30    Lukashenko schedules a four-question referendum for May on dissolving the Supreme Soviet, restoring ties to Russia, restoring Soviet-era state symbols, and making Russian Belarus' second state language.

*April 1995*

11–12    Nineteen Popular Movement deputies declare a sit-in hunger strike to protest the May referendum. They are removed at gunpoint from the parliamentary building by special forces troops.

*May 1995*

14    In parliamentary elections, only 18 of 260 seats are filled. In a simultaneous referendum (65 percent turnout), 83 percent of voters support the introduction of Russian as a second state language, 82 percent support economic integration with Russia, 75 percent support the return to the Soviet-era flag and emblem, and 78 percent support the introduction of a strong presidency.

28 In second-round parliamentary elections, 102 seats are filled. Additional rounds of elections are postponed indefinitely, as is the convening of the new parliament.

# 8 Moldova: caught between nation and empire

WILLIAM CROWTHER

## Introduction

The republic of Moldova declared its independence on August 27, 1991 amid the turbulence that characterized the collapse of the Soviet Union. Since that time it has been plagued by economic crisis, domestic political instability, and a nearly continuous separatist crisis. Its foreign policy situation has been complicated by the presence of Russian military units on its territory, as well as by its ambiguous relationship with Romania.

Despite these challenges a great deal of progress has been achieved in the three years that have passed since independence. Harmonious minority relations predominate in the bulk of the republic, and substantial progress has been made toward resolution of the separatist crisis. An initially extremely antagonistic political situation in the republic has been moderated over time. A second round of democratic elections has been held successfully, allowing for a peaceful transfer of power to a new legislative majority, and a new constitution has been put into effect. Finally, Moldova has begun the process of developing an independent position for itself in the international community, based on its own interests and identity.

What are the principle dynamics that have characterized Moldova's evolution since independence? What factors have been primarily responsible for shaping its progress so far? Those are the main questions that will be addressed in this chapter.

## Historic background

The roots of the current republic of Moldova stretch back to the historic principality of Moldova. Bessarabia, the territory located between the Dniester and Prut rivers which comprises the bulk of modern Moldova, was the eastern region of the traditional principality, most of which is now part of Romania. Along with Walachia to its west, historic Moldova was one of the two main regions in southeastern Europe populated by Romanian-speaking people.[1] The origin of this population dates back to the period

**Moldova**

International boundary

★ National capital

Railroad

Road

0    25    50 Kilometers

0    25    50 Miles

*Lambert Conformal Conic Projection, SP 40N/56N*

from 105 AD to approximately 270 AD, when Roman colonists inter-mingled with the local population before retreating beyond the Danube.

Located as it is at the boundary between powerful competitors, the Russians, the Ottoman Turks, and the Austrians, Moldova has been the site of conflict throughout its existence. An independent principality established in the mid fourteenth century which included the territory of the present Moldovan republic was short lived. During the second half of the fifteenth century it came under increasing pressure from the Ottoman empire, and was finally reduced to the status of a tributary state. The current differentiation between eastern and western Moldova began to develop in the beginning of the eighteenth century. Territory on the left bank of the Dniester river now included in Moldova was ceded by the Ottoman Empire to Russia in 1792.[2] The remainder of current Moldova, Bessarabia, was annexed by Russia following the Russo-Turkish war of 1806–1812. Western Moldova was united with Walachia in 1859 through the joint election of Alexandru Ion Cuza as Prince of both principalities in January 1859, forming the basis of modern Romania.[3]

Russia's Imperial rulers encouraged a substantial influx of migrants into Moldova, including Russians and Ukrainians, as well as Bulgarians and Gagauz colonists from the Balkan peninsula. Most of the population was engaged in agricultural production, which was the primary economic activity of the region. Russia, however, did not retain its grip on Moldova. The territory changed hands again as a consequence of the Russian revolution, when leaders in Bessarabia formed a National Council (the *Sfatul rii*) and voted to unite with Romania in 1918. Meanwhile, in October 1924, Russia's new communist authorities formed a competing political unit, the Autonomous Soviet Socialist Republic (ASSR) of Moldavia. The Moldovan ASSR, whose capital was Tiraspol, encompassed fourteen districts (raions) on the left bank of the Dniester and was administered as part of the Ukrainian Soviet Socialist Republic.

## Soviet Moldova and the independence movement

Along with Latvia, Lithuania, and Estonia, Moldova was among those territories whose fates were determined by the Molotov-Ribbentrop agreement, which allied Stalin's USSR with Nazi Germany. In June 1940 Bessarabia was occupied by Soviet troops, and the Soviet Socialist Republic of Moldova was formed on August 2, 1940. Eight of the fourteen raions that made up the Moldovan ASSR were then joined with Bessarabia to form a new Soviet Socialist Republic of Moldova. Districts to the north of the current republic, and the area between the Dniester and the Prut to the South were incorporated into Ukraine, leaving the present republic of Moldova landlocked.

The post-war years were a period of intense political and social upheaval for Moldova. Many ethnic Romanians, especially members of the middle and upper classes, fled the country for Romania. At the same time, substantial migration from other Soviet republics occurred to meet the labor demands generated by an ambitious industrialization effort. As a consequence the ethnic structure of Moldova's population was changed significantly. From 1941 to 1959 the proportion of Russians in the population grew from approximately 6 percent to 10 percent, and that of Ukrainians from 11 percent to 14 percent. The Moldovan share of the population declined from 69 percent to 65 percent during the same years. By 1970, Moldovans made up only 35 percent of the republic's urban population, while approximately 28 percent was Russian, and another 19 percent was Ukrainian.[4]

The impact of Soviet development policy acted to intensify hostility toward Russia that had already been engendered by annexation. Industrialization in Moldova transformed the distribution of occupations among ethnic groups. Non-Moldovan presence in the urban economy was reinforced, leaving Moldovans in less skilled and less highly paid urban occupations, and in the agricultural sector. The effect was most marked in the early post-war period, but continued to play a role up to the end of the Soviet regime. At the end of the Soviet period, in 1987, non-Moldovans accounted for 52 percent of positions in industry, 49 percent in party and state leadership positions, and 63 percent in scientific work. The disproportionate role of non-Moldovans in the urban economy was manifested particularly in regard to the most influential positions.[5]

Animosity was also generated by Moscow's cultural policy in Moldova, which presented special problems because of the artificial nature of its boundaries with Romania. Moscow undertook a determined effort to cut Moldovans off from Romania, and differentiate them from their co-nationals outside the borders of the USSR. While legitimate questions clearly existed during the inter-war period, as they do now, concerning the national identity of the Moldovan population and its relationship with the Romanians, Soviet authorities dogmatically asserted that Moldova's national identity was distinct and separate from that of Romania. In the realm of linguistic policy, the decision was taken in the mid-1920s to employ the Cyrillic script for writing the Moldovan language on the grounds that it could be better expressed graphically in this form. While Moldovans themselves disagreed on this issue prior to the formation of the ASSR, the commitment to Cyrillic clearly sharpened the line between Romanian and Moldovan, and located Moldova culturally in closer proximity to its Slavic neighbors.[6] Intellectuals who rejected the view that Moldovan was a separate language were subject to political repression.[7]

The treatment of the rural population following the reoccupation of Bessarabia was also ruthless, and produced deep seated hostility to Communist leaders. During 1946 and 1947, Moldova experienced a serious drought. Republican officials failed to reduce compulsory grain collections in response, inducing a famine that claimed the lives of several thousand people. On the heels of this disaster the peasants were subjected to forced collectivization, in the course of which more than 30,000 people were deported.

Moldova did experience substantial economic development under Soviet rule. During the ASSR period Tiraspol and the neighboring areas were the site of substantial industrial activity. Following World War II the new republican capitol, Chisinau, joined Transdniestria as a manufacturing center. In addition to further developing its traditional strengths in food processing, textile, machine tool, and electronics industries were introduced. By the end of the Soviet period, industry accounted for more than one third of Moldovan Gross National Product.

But while Moldova made relative progress, it failed to keep pace with changes occurring elsewhere. In 1987 Moldova was the fourth least urbanized of the Soviet republics, followed only by Uzbekistan, Kyrgystan, and Tajikistan.[8] Capital investment and industrial employment rates were below national averages, and as late as the early 1980s Moldova produced lower national income per capita than any other non-central Asian republic. With respect to its attainments in education, Moldova occupied the last place within the USSR.[9]

It was under such difficult conditions that Moldova entered into the political transformation that swept the Soviet Union in the second half of the 1980s. Reforms introduced in Moscow by Mikhail Gorbachev were critical in creating conditions in which Moldovans' aspirations for change could be given open expression. As in the Baltic republics, reform in Moldova was initiated by the republican intelligentsia. Prominent members of the Moldovan cultural elite organized the Democratic Movement in Support of Restructuring to press both for democratization (in support of Gorbachev's reform agenda), and also for the end of cultural repression in the republic. Their efforts focused on revision of Moldova's language laws, in particular provisions mandating Russian as the language of public communication, and Cyrillic versus Latin script for use in written Moldovan.

Despite limited concessions on the part of republican authorities, political unrest escalated through 1988 and 1989. On August 27, 1989, pro-reform activists staged a massive demonstration, the "great national assembly" in central Chisinau, which attracted more than 100,000 people. This proved to be a critical turning point in the movement for greater autonomy. On August 31, 1989 the republic's Supreme Soviet passed a version of the state language law favorable to the reformers. Political initiative then shifted to the Moldovan Popular Front which had been formed early in the preceding month, largely by leaders of the Democratic Movement in Support of Restructuring.

This initial phase of Moldova's transition to democracy was accompanied by intense interethnic conflict. The prospect of the Romanian speaking majority gaining political influence touched off a sharp response by the Russian-speaking inhabitants of the republic. Many Russians gravitated toward *Edinstvo*, a pro-Russian group whose strongest base of support was in the heavily industrialized cities on the left bank of the Dniester river. *Gagauz-Halki*, the main organization representing Moldova's Gagauz minority during the early transition period, aligned itself with the Russian activists, and demanded that the southern districts where their population was concentrated should be granted political autonomy.

In this context of escalating ethnic tension, campaigning for legislative elections, held in February and March 1990, fed the process of nationalist mobilization. The activists from both the Moldovan and minority communities depicted their opponents in threatening terms in order to gain electoral support. For both sides, the campaign was employed as a vehicle for building organizational infrastructure within their respective communities. In the end, however, it was the ethnic Moldovan opposition that benefited most. Approximately one third of deputies elected to the republican Supreme Soviet deputies were supporters of the Moldovan Popular Front. With the additional support of centrist deputies, the Popular Front was able to command a majority of the votes in the new legislature and backed the appointment of Mircea Snegur as chairman of the Supreme Soviet with Popular Front support, despite his prominent position on the Moldovan Communist Party. Ion Hadarca, President of the Popular Front Executive Council, and other Front members also took up leadership positions in the legislature. Mircea Druc, another member of the Popular Front hierarchy, was appointed Prime Minister

The shift in political control to the Moldovan opposition was accompanied by increasingly serious confrontation. A series of provocative actions by the new majority fueled minority concerns with regard to their future in a republic controlled by the titular nationality.[10] Their initial experience gave minority representatives little reason to develop confidence in emerging democratic institutions. Following a series of street confrontations in the capital, 100 Russophone deputies opposed to the Popular Front withdrew from the republican Supreme Soviet in May 1990. Local governments in the majority Russian-speaking cities of Tiraspol, Bender and Ribnitsa each passed measures suspending application of central government edicts in their territories.[11]

By the late summer of 1990, separatist forces were beginning to consolidate themselves, with evident encouragement and support from patrons in Moscow. In the southern region representatives of the Muslim Gagauz minority announced the formation on August 21, 1990 of their own republic in the five raions where their population was concentrated.[12] Local authorities in the Transdniestrian region followed suit days later, declaring the formation of the Transdniestrian Moldovan Soviet Socialist Republic.[13] While little inter-ethnic conflict occurred within the main territory of Moldova (Bessarabia), tension and sporadic fighting occurred between separatists and the Moldovan government, reaching a peak with the open battles of mid-1992.

The climax of the independence movement initiated during the mid-1980s was touched off by the August 1991 attempted coup in Moscow. The Moldovan government's response was immediate and unequivocal; it denounced the coup plotters and declared independence, founding the new Republic of Moldova on August 27, 1991.[14] Leaders of the separatist regions, in contrast, declared their support for the coup plotters. When their hopes were dashed by events in Moscow, they asserted their independence from Moldova and their commitment to uphold the values of the former Soviet Union. Thus did Moldova begin its existence with its sovereignty challenged, its political elite internally divided, and its government controlled by nationalist ideologues.

## Independent Moldova

### The search for political consensus
Throughout the first months of its independence Moldova was racked by factional infighting as elites struggled to define a new political course. The republic's economy suffered not only under the impact of the collapse of the Soviet Union, but also from a lack of clear policy direction and administrative organization. Meanwhile Transdniestria's leaders, encouraged from Moscow and emboldened by the support that they had begun to receive from Russia's 14th Army, which was headquartered on their territory, became increasingly bellicose.

The impact of the separatist crisis was evident not just in the minority regions, but also in the way political attitudes began to take shape within the Moldovan community. Militarization of the crisis and a growing sense of external threat played into the hands of nationalist elements within the Moldovan political elite. Extremists successfully focused legislative and governmental activity on a narrow "national" agenda, drawing on backing from mass supporters, whose often violent street demonstrations they openly encouraged. Within this environment moderates found themselves marginalized, and unable to effectively articulate a reform agenda tailored to attract support from all of Moldova's ethnic communities. Partial resolution of the situation was achieved in May 1991 through the dismissal of Prime Minister Mircea Druc and his replacement by the less radical Valeriu Muravschi. President Mircea Snegur found himself increasingly at odds with his Popular Front patrons, and began to distance himself from the organization. He moved to consolidate his position as a powerful and independent political actor by holding direct popular elections (over Popular

Front objections) to confirm him in the office of president. The results of the election, held on December 8, 1991, were overwhelming. Snegur, who ran unopposed, received 98.2 percent of the votes cast. While these actions limited the nationalist faction's ability to determine governmental policy, Popular Front deputies remained a powerful force within the legislature.

Across the Prut, the Transdniestrian leadership evolved in an increasingly reactionary direction. Their efforts to gain control of the right bank city of Bendery (Tighina) in mid-1992 had the unintended consequence of triggering a second phase in the post-independence realignment. President Snegur, under pressure from nationalists in the parliament, responded to the Bender crisis with force, touching off a conflict that quickly escalated into full scale battles between Moldova's nascent army and both Transdniestrian forces and 14th Army units. Given the Russian military's support for Transdniestria, little or no possibility existed for Moldova to achieve its ends through the use of force. The conflict quickly deteriorated into a bloody stalemate which enjoyed almost no support from a highly skeptical Moldovan population. In the following months political conditions in Moldova took a sharp turn, at least in part as a consequence of popular attitudes concerning the war.

In a clear signal that the balance of political forces had shifted, Moldova's last (and decidedly reformist) Communist Party First Secretary, Petru Luchinschi, was named Ambassador to Russia. Luchinschi, once the highest ranking ethnic Moldovan Communist Party official outside his home republic was able to use his access to the Moscow political elite to promote accommodation. A second prominent reform communist, Andrei Sangheli, quickly followed Luchinschi back to the center of the political stage, replacing Prime Minister Muravschi.[15] Sangheli's new government represented a marked departure from the preceding regime. It included within its ranks significantly improved minority representation.[16] It promised a more efficient economic reform program, and promoted a more moderate approach to the nationality question.

By taking a more flexible approach, Moldova's government was soon able to reduce the level of ethnic hostility inside the area under its control. While no resolution was achieved, the level of violence involved in the separatist dispute with Transdniestria was brought down to more manageable levels as well. But the ascendence of leaders labeled "pro-Moscow" and the shift in policy direction precipitated a strong backlash from the more extremist elements of the Popular Front, who saw themselves slipping from power. The stalemate produced by Popular Front deputies' obstructionism in parliament, taken in combination with popular dissatisfaction with the failing economy, forced a final step in the republic's political reorientation.

In December 1992, President Snegur, who supported the more conciliatory course undertaken by Sangheli, touched off a crisis by delivering a speech to the republican parliament in which he laid out a foreign policy course based on the pursuit of national independence. Snegur warned against the extremes of either unification with Romania or reintegration into a reinforced form of the Confederation of Independent States.[17] His public opposition to efforts to promote unification with Romania further soured relations between himself and the Popular Front, and at the same time sharpened divisions between moderates and more extreme nationalists within the Front itself. Fallout from the speech was almost immediate. In early January 1993 Alexandru Moghanu, the pro-Popular Front chairman of the Parliament, offered his resignation, pointing to the differences between himself and President Snegur and complaining about the growing influence of elements within the government that favored the previous political system (e.g. reform communists). Moghanu was immediately replaced by Petru Luchinschi, who returned from his post as ambassador to Moscow to take up the leadership of the parliament.[18]

Luchinschi's election brought to a close the Moldovan leadership realignment. With his ascendence, the three top positions in the political hierarchy of the republic, the presidency, the prime ministership, and the parliamentary chair, were all held by reform communists, each a former member of the Moldovan Communist Party politburo.

On the other hand the Popular Front of Moldova (which had renamed itself the Christian-Democratic Popular Front of Moldova at its Third Congress in early 1992), had declined into almost complete disarray by early 1993. Moderate intellectuals who had added tremendously to the Popular Front's prestige during its rise to power founded a competing organization, the "Congress of the Intellectuals." Through the Congress, they sought to repair the damage done to their cause by the radicals, and to promote a less extreme nationalist agenda. The moderate dissenters, including such key Popular Front leaders as Ion Hadirca, first president of the Popular Front, and Alexandru Moshanu, were dismissed from the organization.

As a consequence of nearly continuous factional infighting and defection, the ability of the once unassailable Popular Front to dominate legislative activity was broken. Popular Front voting strength in the legislature was reduced from half to only approximately twenty-five deputies by late 1993.

With the Front thus in decline, the bloc of Agrarian deputies (the *Viata Satului* parliamentary club) emerged as the single most influential force in Moldova's legislature. The success of this group resulted primarily from its ability to maintain cohesion throughout the continuous disruption and fragmentation that occurred within the parliament. Agrarian success was attributable to a variety of factors. The Viata Satului deputies were, for the most part associated with the republican agro-industrial complex, either as village mayors or collective farm managers. As reform communists, many held a common ideological orientation. They also shared substantial material interests, both with respect to reform issues, and with respect to questions of resource allocation. Furthermore, they maintained a powerful presence in the Ministry of Agriculture, which had become the new institutional home for many of their former colleagues, the rural district communist party committee first secretaries, who had needed new positions after the Communist Party was banned in Moldova, immediately following the failed August 1991 Moscow coup attempt. This link with the ministry provided both a channel of influence within the government, and a sizeable pool of organizational and physical resources that could be employed to mobilize supporters in the rural constituencies. With support from Socialist Party (former Communist) and independent deputies, the Agrarians were able to consolidate their political influence. Taken together the combination of a common policy orientation and constituency, political experience, and an institutional power base made the Agrarians a potent political force.

This shift in favor of the Agrarians and their Socialist Party allies brought the legislature into much closer alignment with the government. But given the degree of fragmentation that existed among deputies, it remained impossible to develop and implement a constructive legislative agenda. While unable to implement their own program, nationalists remained able to block legislation that ran counter to their interests. A series of key reforms, generally agreed to be necessary, were stalled due to legislators' inability to agree on issues relating to the national question. Local government reform, efforts to resolve the separatist crisis, clarification of Moldova's relationship with the CIS, and a projected new constitution all languished. Moldova's triumvirate of top leaders took little time to conclude that the legislature was no longer viable. Despite efforts of the Romanian nationalist faction to resist, the Agrarian coalition orchestrated a vote to dissolve the legislature. Early elections were called for a new parliament, with a date set for February 27, 1994.

Legislation establishing the electoral rules to be employed was enacted on October 14, 1993. It was decided that the new legislature should be considerably smaller than its predecessor, with 104 as opposed to 380 deputies. This smaller size, it was hoped, would be less conflict prone and more manageable than the Soviet-era Supreme Soviet. Elections were to be based on a closed party list proportional representation system, with a 4 percent threshold requirement for legislative representation.

Negotiations leading to the promulgation of the electoral law were substantially complicated by the long-standing separatist conflict. The establishment of territorial constituencies was dependent on passage of a new law on local administration that would have established new sub-national administrative boundaries. But the nature of these sub-national units was the subject of intense debate between nationalists and moderates in Chisinau, and the Transdniestrian separatists. Furthermore, if existing boundaries were employed and elections were not successfully held in Transdniestria, then the Tiraspol leadership could claim that the new legislature did not include its representatives, and hence was not legitimate. In order to avoid this impasse Moldovan leaders decided to employ a single national electoral district. While not ensuring participation in the separatist region, this mechanism allowed elections to go forward, selecting a body of delegates whose constituency was the entire republic, regardless of their individual places of residence.

Campaigning in Moldova's first entirely post-Soviet elections focused on competing reform strategies, polarization over the country's international position, and disagreement over the best course in dealing with interethnic relations and resolving the separatist conflict. Thirteen separate parties and electoral blocs took part in the elections. The primary policy confrontation ran along the foreign policy cleavage, with "pro-Romanian" forces arrayed against parties which maintained a "pro-CIS" orientation. The main forces on the pro-CIS side of the divide consisted of the Agrarian Democrats, which argued for economic but not military or political participation in the CIS, and the Socialist Party, which campaigned in an electoral bloc with the more extreme pro-Russian Edinstvo movement and supported full CIS participation. Confronting these forces was an array of pro-Romanian parties consisting primarily of the Christian-Democratic Popular Front, which supported full unification with Russia, and the Congress of the Intellectuals, which campaigned as part of the Bloc of Peasants and Intellectuals and supported a more gradual unification.[19]

Significant differences also existed over the country's economic future. Several small parties represented focused economic interests. The Reform Party, for example, was mostly supported by urban professionals and was committed to rapid marketization and privatization. Alternatively Democratic Labor Party, while favoring privatization as well, represented the interests of the managers of large scale industrial enterprises. Among the major competitors, both the Socialist Party and the Agrarian Democrats called for a slower transition to capitalism and the maintenance of a socialist orientation. On the rural property issue the Agrarian Democrats argued strongly in support of maintaining some form of collective landholding in agriculture, preferably through the transformation of state farms into peasant cooperatives.

Campaigning for the elections was itself controversial. Members of the pro-Romanian parties, in particular, complained of irregularities, and suggested that they were often excluded from fair access to the rural constituencies where the Agrarian influence was strongest and in some cases even subjected to physical coercion. Polling places were open in the Gagauz separatist region by agreement with the Gagauz leadership, and voting went on there without disruption. Transdniestria's authorities refused to allow voting to take place on the territory that they controlled, but several thousand crossed the Dniester and voted in west bank polling places. International observers concluded that the elections were open and fair, and there appears to be no reason to conclude that fraud or coercion played an important role in the final vote.

As indicated in table 8.1, the results of the first post-communist elections marked a sharp reversal from the politics of the previous period. Nationalist and pro-Romanian forces were overwhelmingly rejected in favor of parties supporting Moldovan independence and closer alignment with the CIS. The main beneficiaries of the dramatic shift in voter sentiment were the Agrarian Democrats, who won 43 percent of the vote and 56 out of 104 seats in the legislature. Another 22 percent of the vote was taken by the Socialist Party/Edinstvo Bloc, which captured 28 parliamentary seats. None of the pro-Romanian parties did well at the polls. Strongest among them was the Bloc of Peasants and Intellectuals, which gained 9 percent of the vote and 11 seats. The once dominant Christian-Democratic Popular Front's electoral Alliance won only 7.5 percent of the vote and took the remaining 9 seats in the new parliament. None of the other five parties and blocs that fielded candidates topped the 4 percent threshold required for participation in the national parliament.[20]

In addition to clarifying the "Romania" versus "CIS" question, the 1994 voting results also clearly reflected the emerging (post Popular Front) division of political forces in the republic. While the Agrarian Democrats' strong showing at the polls derived from their party's popularity among voters in the rural districts, the Socialist Party/Edinstvo alliance dominated voting in nearly all urban centers, including the capital. This urban-rural cleavage would play a strong role in the life of the new legislature.

The 1994 legislative election results had an immediate impact on the course of Moldovan politics. Top leadership positions, having been realigned prior to the elections, changed little. Andrei Sangheli remained in charge of the government as Prime Minister, and Luchinschi returned as chairman of the new parliament. But with a legislative majority and a high degree of policy consensus with President Snegur, the Agrarian government was able to act quickly on foreign and domestic policy commitments. Agreement was reached on the establishment of Gagauz autonomy agreement, clearing the way for resolution of that separatist issue.[21] Resolution of the Transdniestrian crisis proved more difficult to achieve. The tenor of discussions with Moscow improved significantly. But despite the efforts of the Agrarian government in Chisinau, Transdniestria's leadership remained intractable in their demand for independent status. After long delay, a new constitution was ratified by the parliament on July 29, 1994. It set the groundwork for Moldova to become a democratic republic, established a semi-presidential system with provision for separation of powers, and guaranteed basic human rights.[22] It called for permanent neutrality and banned the basing of foreign troops on its territory. The 1994 constitution also reflected the "Moldovan" orientation of the new political majority. References to Romanian language and Romanian people that had appeared

Table 8.1. *1994 Moldovan election results*

| Party | Percent of votes | Number of seats |
|---|---|---|
| Christian-Democrat Popular Front bloc | 7.53 | 9 |
| Victims of the Communist totalitarian regime of Moldova | 0.94 | 0 |
| National Christian Party | 0.33 | 0 |
| Social Democratic bloc | 3.66 | 0 |
| Bloc of peasants and intellectuals | 9.21 | 11 |
| Democratic Party | 1.32 | 0 |
| Socialist Party/Edinstvo Movement bloc | 22.00 | 28 |
| Women's Association of Moldova | 2.83 | 0 |
| Ecologist Party "Green Alliance" | 0.40 | 0 |
| Democratic Agrarian Party | 43.18 | 56 |
| Republican Party | 0.93 | 0 |
| Democratic Labor Party | 2.77 | 0 |
| Reform Party | 2.36 | 0 |
| Total | | 104 |

in the draft document were removed in favor of Moldovan language and the Moldovan people. Less action was immediately apparent in pressing economic initiatives, unsurprising given the cautious stance of both the Agrarian Democrats and the Socialist Party with respect to the transition to a capitalist economy.

## Economic reform

Moldova is located in a region that has historically been principally agricultural, subject to rural poverty, and weakly developed. Traditional Moldova's urban economy was based almost entirely on trade in agricultural products, food processing, and some limited consumer goods production. Prior to the mid eighteenth century, the entire region suffered as a consequence of periodic warfare and political instability. Bessarabia, when it was included in "Great Romania" in the interwar period, was considered backward in comparison to the other regions of the country. Administration from Bucharest brought with it little in the way of economic advantage, and Bessarabia remained an economic backwater up until the outbreak of the Second World War.

More than any other factor, the impact of Soviet rule was responsible for shaping the contours of the current Moldovan economy. As a Soviet republic, Moldova experienced substantial industrial development. Urban areas, especially Chisinau, Tiraspol and the neighboring areas along the Dniester, experienced substantial industrial growth. This fundamentally altered both the production and employment profiles of the country. While manufacturing activity increased, agriculture continued to play a central role in Moldova's economy, accounting for 42.4 percent of national income produced at the end of the Soviet period.[23] Industry accounted for approximately 38 percent of Moldovan Net Material Product.[24]

Until its independence, Moldova's economy was organized along standard Soviet lines. Industry was state owned, as was commerce and finance. Approximately one third of industrial enterprises were subordinated to USSR economic ministries (nationalized on independence), and two thirds were subordinated to republican authorities. The organizational backbone of Moldova's agricultural sector prior to independence was the system of approximately 390 state farms and 600 collective farms, covering over 600,500 hectares of terrain, and at the end of the Soviet period employing approximately 168,000 persons.

On achieving its independence in 1991, Moldova, like other former Soviet republics, faced staggering economic problems. The disruption of the broader economic structures of the former USSR, in which Moldova's economy remained firmly embedded, had an immediate negative effect. The Moldovan economy was trade dependent, with an imports plus exports to GDP ratio of more than 50 percent. The vast majority of this trade was directed to other Soviet republics, and was negatively affected by the demise of the Union. Among the most pressing near term difficulties created by the collapse of inter-republican trade was Moldova's almost complete lack of energy resources. Moldova is dependent on external sources for coal, oil, and natural gas to fuel its electric power generation plants. As energy resources became increasingly scarce, industrial enterprises were forced to reduce production.

Chisinau's political conflict with Transdniestria further complicated the economic situation. Substantial industrial assets, approximately one third of Moldova's total capacity, are located in the separatist region. Disruption of traditional economic ties with enterprises located there has negatively affected the rest of the national economy. The concentration of nearly all of Moldova's electric power generation capacity in the Transdniestrian region has been a source of disruption as well. Furthermore, Russian authorities have periodically withheld energy supplies to Moldova in order to gain leverage in ongoing negotiations over the fate of Transdniestria and the 14th Army.

Worsening an already difficult situation, Moldova's initial post independence leadership proved inept in economic management. Initial reform efforts lacked coherence, and were badly implemented. Basic disagreement within the political elite concerning the pace and direction of reform led to stalemate and economic drift.

As a consequence of the factors outlined above (complicated further by negative climatic conditions) Moldova has suffered from a dramatic economic decline in the first half of the 1990s. Production plummeted in both industry and agriculture, collectively declining by 35 percent between 1990 and the end of 1992.[25] As industrial production fell off and former Soviet markets collapsed, Moldova's foreign trade dropped by 34 percent in a single year, 1991.[26] The effects of the economic crisis on the population were severe and immediate. Wages declined by 33 percent in 1991 and a further 42 percent in 1992. The real extent of the impact on employment is difficult to assess but can be assumed to be substantial. Unemployment rates have been artificially low due to the policy of retaining unneeded workers on enterprise payrolls. Such workers are often not paid for long periods, partially paid, or sent on unwanted vacations.

The Moldovan policy response to the economic crisis was slow to take shape, despite several legislative initiatives. General legislative programs were promulgated in both 1990 and 1991. Bankruptcy and new ownership laws recognizing the right to private and various forms of collective property were passed in 1992. Efforts at privatization began with the formation of a Privatization Commission, and initiation of an inventory of national assets during 1992.[27] But the actual implementation of reform and privatization efforts was hindered by basic disagreements between political factions in the legislature, and between the legislative and executive branches. Administrators in the Privatization Commission complained of sabotage, both by enterprise managers and governmental authorities. Furthermore, as the separatist conflict progressed, the Popular Front leadership became increasingly focused on this crisis and broad foreign policy matters, leaving economic issues unresolved.

Thus, through 1993, reform and privatization proceeded at a sluggish pace. An initial privatization voucher auction was held in Chisinau in October 1993, but met with little success, managing to sell a total of seven shops and two cafes. The situation was further complicated by ill-conceived tax legislation which negatively affected private enterprises, reducing the interest of the population in gaining ownership. Plans as of 1993 called for selling 1,550 enterprises around the country by the end of 1994. No plans have been made for the privatization of strategic sectors, including defense, telecommunications, transport, and chemicals.

With the decline of the Popular Front and consolidation of the new Agrarian leadership in 1993 and early 1994, Moldova's economic reform efforts took on increased consistency. Despite some initial hesitation concerning the policy orientation of the Agrarian Democratic party leadership and their Socialist Party allies, Western economic authorities, including the World Bank and the International Monetary Fund, have reacted positively to the new government. Industrial privatization is expected to continue at a moderate pace. In November 1993 Moldova introduced its own national currency, the Moldovan leu, which will allow authorities to gain control over monetary policy.

Agricultural privatization, a focus of political debate in Moldova since independence, is a key part of the Agrarian legislative agenda. The Agrarian faction has argued that unrestrained rural privatization would be a disaster in Moldova, which has the highest rural population density of any former Soviet republic. Rather than individual plots, the Agrarian program calls for transformation of the system of Soviet collective farms and state farms to be transformed into joint stock companies, owned by their peasant employees.[28]

Despite substantial movement in the realm of economic reform, however, the Moldovan government has as yet been unable to stem the tide of economic decline. 1994 saw continued loss of production, with agricultural output dropping by 26 percent in comparison to 1993 levels, and industrial production reduced by 30 percent in the same period.

## Foreign policy

Almost inevitably, given its history and geography, international relations have been at the center of Moldova's political concerns since independence. Moldova is a small land-locked nation, surrounded by larger and more powerful neighbors. Control over the region has been contested for centuries. Its heterogeneous population gives rise to controversy as well. Once included within the boundaries of Romania, Moldova is populated primarily by a Romanian-speaking people. This raises the possibility of irredentist claims from Bucharest. But Moldova is also the home of a substantial minority population, including large numbers of Russians and Ukrainians. Relations between the Moldovan majority and these minorities raises concerns among their conationals outside Moldova.

As Soviet political institutions that underpinned the structure of regional relations since the end of World War II deteriorated at the end of the 1980s, conflict immediately arose concerning Moldova's status. Even before it declared independence the new republic faced challenges to its sovereignty from Transdniestrian and Gagauz separatist movements. Conflict between the central government and the minority populations quickly threatened to spill over internationally. Hence Moldova's main diplomatic efforts in the first years of its pre-Soviet existence focused on ending the separatist conflicts and stabilizing relations with regional powers, including in the first instance, Romania and Russia.

The conflict between Moldovan authorities and the two separatist regions traversed the boundary between domestic and international politics. In rejecting Moldovan authority, Transdniestria's leaders entered into a civil conflict with the Chisinau government. But from its inception, their efforts relied on support that they were able to procure from various points of contact within Russia itself. When the Transdniestrians organized a congress in order to assert their independence in late 1990, Soviet Ministry of Interior troops were on the scene to guarantee their security.[29] When economic separation from the republic followed, Moscow provided access to an alternative financial infrastructure that minimized the impact of secession. Similarly links between Russian industry and Transdniestria assured enterprises in the breakaway region of markets and access to raw materials.[30]

As the conflict became increasingly militarized, Russian support of Transdniestria again played a crucial role. The presence of the 14th Army on Transdniestrian territory effectively excluded the possibility of Moldovan military victory as a path to resolution of the conflict. Furthermore, the transfer of weapons from the 14th Army's arsenal to Tiraspol's militia forces provided the separatists with a significant advantage in their conflict with Chisinau. The Transdniester republic's connection with the Russian military was also critical at the high point of the armed conflict in mid-1993. When Moldovan forces managed to briefly gain the upper hand in fighting for the city of Tighina (Bender), 14 Russian Army tanks intervened on the side of the separatists, and turned the tide of battle.

Why did Russia extend such support to the Transdniestrian separatists? This question is not easily answered in a definitive sense, given the political morass that exists in Moscow. But clearly considerable interests are at stake in the conflict for various actors. Traditional foreign policy concerns provide a partial explanation. As Soviet era security relations broke down, Russia required new arrangements to maintain its regional influence. Retaining a significant military force in Moldova would advance this purpose, but Russia's proposal for a long term basing agreement was rejected by the new government in Chisinau. Furthermore, Moldova's initial Popular Front leadership was actively hostile to Moscow, and reluctant to enter into the network of Russo-centric post-Soviet international agreements. Fueling the separatist crisis provided Russia with leverage that could be used to prod Moldova into committing itself to CIS political and security arrangements, a tactic that was successfully employed in its relations with Georgia.

A second set of concerns derives from the presence of large numbers of ethnic Russians in the separatist region.[31] Beginning with the clashes over Moldova's language law, the fate of the Russian minority developed into a matter of intense public interest in Russia, where it received broad mass media coverage that was generally hostile to the Moldovan government. The issue took on particular significance for nationalist groups, which became increasingly influential during the early 1990s. The leadership of the Tiraspol government, headed by Igor Smirnov, was quick to build bridges to extremists in Moscow. Through them, Tiraspol recruited volunteers for the militia and sought to influence Russian political and military leaders. The Transdniestrians also reciprocated, providing support to their compatriots when possible. Forces from Tiraspol were reported to be actively engaged in a series of reactionary causes inside Russia, including the dispatch of volunteers to the Russian White House to participate in the attempted overthrow of Yeltsin in September–October 1993.[32]

The appointment of General Aleksandr Lebed to command of the 14th army in mid-1992 further complicated the situation. Once in Transdniestria, Lebed promptly indicated his strong support for the Russian minority, if not for the Tiraspol government, with which he often found himself at odds. Despite repeated warnings from his superiors to restrain himself, Lebed became a constant presence in the public media, remarking upon the political situation. He stated flatly that he would not "abandon" Transdniestria's Russians. By taking this outspoken and uncompromising stand, attacking Moldovan nationalists as "fascists," the Tiraspol leaders for their corruption, and Moscow for its timidity, Lebed became a force to be reckoned with among Russian conservatives. Rising from the status of an obscure regional commander to that of a national political figure, Lebed exercised near veto power over decisions that affected the status of the 14th Army.

Given the links between the Russian nationalists and Transdniestria, efforts to end the separatist conflict through accommodation with Chisinau and a troop withdrawal agreement would make moderates in Moscow vulnerable to attack from right wing forces. Boris Yeltsin, occupied in fending off challenges from competitors ranging from his one time vice-president, Alexander Rutskoi, to Vladimir Zhirinovsky, has had to handle the issue with care on domestic political grounds, regardless of its foreign policy implications.

Furthermore, there has been good reason to question the extent of President Yeltsin and the Ministry of Defense leadership's ability to dictate conditions to Russian military forces in Transdniestria. The 14th Army has strong local ties in Transdniestria through the draft, and the presence of many retired officers and soldiers in the local population. One of its previous commanders, General Yakovlev, heads Tiraspol's defense forces. Directions from Moscow to the 14th Army have been vacillating at best, and at times have been openly contradictory to actions taken on the ground. In August 1994, Moscow announced that the status of the 14th Army was to be reduced to that of an "operating group," and that its staffing was to be cut back dramatically. General Lebed (who was at the time in Moscow) was offered the position of commander of Russian forces in Tajikistan. In the final instance, however, the Ministry was unable to make this decision hold. President Yeltsin publicly announced his support for Lebed, who turned down the post in Tajikstan and returned to his command in Transdniestria. General Lebed publicly criticized the downsizing of the 14th Army, and the decision was subsequently suspended.[33]

Russian diplomats have become deeply engaged in the Transdniestrian dispute. In July 1992 the worst of the fighting in the conflict was brought to an end through an agreement mediated by Moscow. The cease fire accord placed peacekeepers in Transdniestria (including Russian 14th Army forces in this role along with Moldovans and Transdniestrians). Round after round of negotiations were then held but with little progress. Moldova demanded complete withdrawal of the 14th Army, sovereignty over Transdniestria, and no linkage between the two issues. Russia expected withdrawal to be linked to the fate of Transdniestria, hedged on the question of transferring 14th army assets to the Transdniestrians, and pressed for an agreement on long term basing rights for the 14th Army on Moldovan territory. Finally the Transdniestrian authorities, bolstered by support from Russia, held out for federation with Moldova, which would, in essence, recognize their independent status.

The deadlock on Transdniestria was broken in the 10th round of negotiations only as a consequence of political realignment in Moldova. Once the Popular Front was marginalized and the Agrarian Democrats began to consolidate their hold on parliament, the Moldovan government's negotiating position became increasingly conciliatory. In 1993 Chisinau undertook to entice the separatists back into the republic by offering substantial regional autonomy, along with assurances that there would be no union with Romania. Broad concessions were extended to both the Gagauz and the Transdniestrians. The Gagauz responded positively to these overtures, came to terms with Chisinau, allowed elections to be held in their territory in February 1994, and agreed to rejoin the republic.[34] Tiraspol, in contrast, merely escalated its demands in order to block reconciliation efforts.

This recalcitrant stance, however, is likely to become increasingly difficult to sustain. In January 1994 Moldova accepted the Conference on Security and Cooperation in Europe (CSCE) peace plan for Transdniestria, winning high marks from Western authorities for its willingness to extend autonomy and human rights guarantees to the minority regions. Following the Agrarian success in the February 1994 parliamentary elections, Moldova signalled its intention to move closer to the CIS (while remaining firmly independent), and distanced itself from Romania. Moscow, in response, began to moderate its support for Tiraspol. On August 10, 1994 Russia and Moldova initialed an agreement, over the objections of Tiraspol, calling for the withdrawal of the 14th Army, with its equipment, within three years. In a major concession, Moldova accepted that the troop withdrawal should be synchronized with a political solution to the separatist conflict. While the agreement was thus subject to interpretation, and by both sides did not represent a final settlement to the conflict, it clearly was a major step forward and must be seen by the Transdniestrian separatists as a signal that their support in Moscow is beginning to slip.

The Transdniestrian dispute has continually impinged upon other aspects of Moldova's foreign policy, driving its relationship with Russia in particular. During the period of escalation in the conflict Moldovan nationalist sentiment intensified, complicating negotiations intended to define Moldova's role in the CIS. President Snegur signed the Almaty declaration creating the Commonwealth of Independent States on December 31, 1991. But Moldova's parliament, strongly influenced by the Popular Front, refused to ratify the agreement. Even as the power of the Front waned, coolness toward participation in post-Soviet international structures characterized Moldova's foreign policy.

Rather than developing ties with Russia immediately following its independence, Moldova moved toward Romania, seeking an alternative source of diplomatic and economic support, much to the delight of nationalist advocates of unification. Chisinau also sought to develop a closer relationship with Ukraine, which was at the time engaged in its own dispute with Moscow concerning the status of the Crimea and the Black Sea Fleet, and which could potentially be of substantial aid in restricting access to the separatist region. But once the euphoria of independence began to fade, the inadequacy of these efforts quickly became clear. Romania and Ukraine could be of no substantial assistance should the separatist conflict escalate into a military contest with Russia, and would clearly work to avoid being drawn into any such situation. Neither could they provide an alternative to Moldova's long standing economic ties with Russia and other former Soviet republics.

Playing on Moldova's vulnerabilities, Russian leaders employed various methods, including its control over vital raw materials and its influence on events in Transdniestria, to induce Moldova to participate more fully in CIS institutions. In mid-1993, Moscow imposed non-CIS customs duties and taxes on Moldovan products, pressuring the republic to decide definitively on membership in the organization. But pro-Romanian forces retained sufficient influence in the Moldovan legislature to counter these efforts and resist a foreign policy realignment by less hostile members of the Moldovan political hierarch, such as President Snegur and Petru Luchinschi. In August 1993, well after Sangheli's national unity government was in place, the Moldovan parliament declined membership in the CIS. After consultation with party leaders, however, President Snegur signed the agreement despite the legislative deadlock, gambling that a new parliament would support his position. With the 1994 change in government, the Agrarian Democrats and their Socialist Party allies undertook to redefine Moldova's position more comprehensively. While holding to the position that it would not participate in CIS military and diplomatic agreements, Moldova became more actively involved on the economic plane.

In an obvious contradictory trend, as Chisinau warmed toward the CIS relations between Romania and Moldova have become increasingly hostile. This has marked a sharp reversal of earlier trends. Romania was the first state to recognize Moldovan independence. Romanian nationalists welcomed the early victories of the Popular Front, and saw Moldova's "Romanianism" as a natural phenomenon. But Romanians badly misinterpreted their eastern neighbors, focusing almost entirely on common aspects of their history, and the cultural homogeneity of Romanian speakers. Romania was very slow to recognize and react to the republic of Moldova's very real cultural divergence from the region to the west of the Prut. Moldova's assertion of its own identity immediately drew criticism from Bucharest, where those identifying as "Moldovan" are held to have been "denationalized," or "Russified" by the Soviet experience. This denationalization critique, which is also expressed by now marginalized Popular Front leaders, became a source of growing resentment on the part of the very large majority of Moldovans, and a cause of alarm among members of Moldova's minority communities.

Moldova's twin separatist crises have also exacerbated Moldovan/ Romanian relations. The prospect of unification with Romania was the primary cause for concern among members of Moldova's Russian speaking population in the late 1980s and early 1990s. For the Gagauz, in particular, inter-war rule from Bucharest is recalled as a bitter period of ethnic oppression. Efforts by minority activists to obstruct movement in the direction of reunification were central to the outbreak of ethnic conflict. In this environment of heightened concern over the unification issue, virtually all aspects of the relationship between Bucharest and Chisinau became politically charged, read by all parties as indications of movement toward or away from unification. High profile members of the Moldovan Popular Front appealed to a pan-Romanianist constituency on both sides of the border, contending that moderate elements in the Moldovan government were betraying them to Moscow. Given this dynamic it is unsurprising that the policy of Moldovan moderates often seemed vacillating. Constantly under attack, they shifted back and forth from efforts to mollify the minority communities and calm Moscow, to nationalist rhetoric necessitated by a nationalist "bidding war" with their more extreme competitors. Only after the final forced break with the Popular Front in 1993 was the situation clarified, through the moderates' definition of an independent "Moldovan" position.

Nationalist politics complicated the foreign policy environment in Romania as well. On purely diplomatic grounds, Romania has little or nothing to gain from instability on its eastern border. Annexation of Moldova, even if possible, would not be of any substantial material advantage. Moldova is neither a source of economic wealth of strategic influence. While achieving the withdrawal of Russian military forces from the region would no doubt be of interest to Bucharest, that end is hardly likely to be achieved by encouraging Moldovan extremists. Romanian President Ion Iliescu has sought to maintain a positive relationship with the Russian republic, a task that is clearly more easily achieved without the complication of conflict in Moldova.

But while Romania's foreign policy interests seem limited, it has proved

difficult for any national political leader in Romania to take a public position against unification. Nationalists forces (in particular the Greater Romania Party and the Party of Romanian National Unity), are becoming
increasingly influential in Romania, and have made unification with Moldova an article of political faith. They have been sharply critical of Iliescu's
failure to achieve unification immediately on Moldova's independence.
They have continued to bring pressure to bear on Romania's government
from the right, and struggle to maintain public interest in the reunification
issue.

Romanian nationalists have interpreted concessions extended to the
Gagauz and Transdniestrian separatists during 1994 as a failure to
defend "Romanian" national sovereignty, and as tantamount to treason
against the Romanian nation. The introduction to Article 13 of the
1994 Moldovan constitution – a provision establishing Moldovan, not
Romanian, as the state language of the republic – generated a barrage
of intensely vitriolic attacks from Romania, whose nationalist leaders
took it as a repudiation of their national heritage. This has in its turn
provoked Moldovan suspicion of and hostility toward Romanian interference. Much has also been made of Romanian funding of the
nationalist political effort in Moldova, and the granting of Romanian
citizenship to prominent Moldovan nationalists. Hence in a matter of
four years since independence relations between the two Romanian
speaking countries have degenerated from warm cooperation to cool
hostility.

## Conclusion

The republic of Moldova has confronted a series of critical challenges
during its brief history as an independent state. Created out of the
disintegration of the Soviet Union, it suffered under the political and
economic afflictions common to all of the former Soviet republics. Soviet
era political structures required radical reform or dismantling. New institutions had to be created to carry out tasks previously addressed by
Soviet authorities. Newly mobilized forces had to be incorporated into
the political system. Dissociation from the economic structures of the old
system, currency fluctuations generated by policy decisions undertaken in
Moscow, and the collapse of markets have produced severe economic
and social dislocation.

Moldova's transition to democratic politics was further complicated
by factors particular to the republic. Challenges to its sovereignty
mounted by Transdniestrian and Gagauz separatists both polarized the
population and distracted political elites from other policy areas that
demanded their attention. Moldova's historic relationship with Romania
called into question the basic identity of the new state. Was Moldova

intended to be sovereign and independent, or was it merely a transitional stage on the path to incorporation into Romania? This question both generated ongoing foreign policy difficulties, and divided the Romanian speaking population against itself.

The republic's initial leaders appeared to be overwhelmed by the combination of the multiple demands facing them and, in many cases, their own lack of political experience. During the brief period of Popular Front dominance, a series of ill-conceived policy decisions alienated the Russian speaking minorities, polarized Moldovans, and provoked a foreign policy crisis. Politics in the wake of the nationalists' ascendence was necessarily dominated by the effort to redress the negative effects of their rule. By late 1994, this task had been largely achieved. A fundamental political realignment marginalized radical nationalists within the Romanian speaking community, first on the leadership level, and with the February 1994 elections, within the legislature as well. Once in control of the main organs of government, moderate forces reshaped political discourse in the republic. They focused their efforts on issues that cut across nationality lines and pursuing an ethnically inclusive strategy. Central to this effort was their intentional self-definition as "Moldovan." This, along with forceful assertion of national independence from Romania, broke both the foreign and domestic policy deadlocks, winning back the acceptance of minority communities and opening the way for serious negotiations with Moscow.

Having successfully carried out its second set of democratic legislative elections and enacted a new post-Communist constitution, Moldova is well on its way toward successful democratic consolidation. Clearly, daunting tasks remain to be addressed. The economic transition is only at its beginning, and basic questions concerning the nature of Moldova's future economic model remain unanswered. While the Gagauz have been successfully reincorporated into Moldova, Transdniestrian leaders as yet remain obdurate. Finally, the strong showing of the Socialist Party/Edinstvo coalition in parliamentary elections indicates that collectivist sentiment remains strong in the republic, giving rise to the possibility of serious dispute between conservatives and more reformist forces. All this having been said, however, Moldova has made considerable progress, and is now better situated to contend with the challenges facing it than at any time since independence.

## Notes

1 Two useful histories of both Moldova and Walachia are Vlad Gheorghescu's *The Romanians* (Columbus, Ohio: The Ohio State University Press, 1991), and Robert Seton-Watson's *A History of the Roumanians* (London: Archon Books, 1963).

2  Barbara Jelavich, *History of the Balkans: Eighteenth and Nineteenth Centuries* (New York: Cambridge University Press, 1983), p. 112.

3  Vlad Gheorghescu, *The Romanians* (Columbus, OH: The Ohio State University Press, 1991), pp. 146–148.

4  Viktor Kozlov, *The Peoples of the Soviet Union* (Bloomington IN: Indiana University Press, 1988), p. 64. On the other side of the coin, in 1970 Moldavians made up 78.2 percent of the rural population. Yu. V. Arutyunyan, *Opyt Etnosotsiologicheskovo Issledovaniya Obraza Zhizni: Po Materialam Moldavskoy SSR* (Moscow: Nauka, 1980), p. 36.

5  Mihai Patrash, "Migration: The State of the Problem and the Path to its resolution under conditions of Self-Financing," *Literatura i Arta*, no. 6, February 8, 1990, p. 6.

6  The most extensive work on this issue has been done by Charles King. King's work suggests that the question of Moldovan identity during the interwar period is much more complex than has been depicted by Western specialists who generally argue that the USSR supressed a "Romanian" identification by the population in question. See Charles King, "Who are the Moldovans?" paper presented at Romanian Studies Day, School of Slavonic and East European Studies, London (13 January, 1995); "The Politics of Language in Moldova, 1924–1994" D. Phil. dissertation, Oxford University, 1995.

7  Among those singled out for persecution were those who publicly expressed support for the Latin alphabet prior to the Ninth Moldovan Regional Communist Party Congress, held in May 1938, at which favoring Latin script for written Moldovan was denounced as an expression of "bourgeois-nationalism." A. Morar, N. Movilyanu, and I Shishkanu, "How the Latin Alphabet Was Arrested," *Moldova Socialist*, June 17, 1989, p. 3; *Sovietskaya Moldavia*, June 17, 1989, p. 2.

8  James H. Bater, *The Soviet Scene: A Geographical Perspective* (New York: Edward Arnold, 1989), p. 84.

9  In 1959 only 264 Moldovans per 1000 population had higher education, in contrast to the USSR average of 361 per 1000. By 1984 the situation had improved dramatically, to 620 per 1000 population, much closer to the USSR average of 686 per 1000. But relative to other republics Moldova lost ground, moving to last place within the USSR. Michael Ryan and Richard Prentice, *Social Trends in the Soviet Union From 1950* (New York: St. Martin's Press, 1987), p. 74.

10  Popular Front representatives, for example, entered a motion restoring the pre-revolutionary Moldavian flag as the symbol of the republic. The measure passed in the legislature but was widely and conspicuously disregarded by its opponents. Selection of a new parliamentary leadership also became a source of political confrontation. Those appointed to high level posts were overwhelmingly ethnic Moldovans, leaving minority activists little hope that their interests would be represented in deliberations on key issues. Moldovans accounted for 69.62 percent of entire legislature, but for 83.3 percent of the leadership. All five of the leading positions in the Supreme Soviet were held by ethnic Moldovans, as were eighteen of twenty positions in the new government. *Moldova Socialist*, June 26, 1990, pp. 2–3; *Moldova Socialist* May 13, 1990, p. 1.

11  For the central government's response to these actions see *Moldova Socialist*, May 13, 1990, p. 1. On conditions in Bender, see S. Agnail, "Meetings during Work Time," *Moldova Socialist* May 4, 1990, p. 3.

12  Foreign Broadcast Information Service, FBIS-SOV-90-162, August 21, 1990, p. 92.

13  E. Kondratov, "Moldova's Unity Threatened," *Isvestia*, Sept. 3, 1990, p. 2, in *Current Digest of the Soviet Press*, 42, no. 2, 35 (1990), 27.

14  Vladimir Socor, "Moldavia Proclaims Independence, Commences Secession from USSR," *RFE/RL Report on the USSR*, October 18, 1991, pp. 19–20.

15  Sangheli was a former Communist Party raion committee first secretary and later a member of the republican Council of Ministers. He played a prominent role in the

removal of the reactionary Simion Grossu from the position of party first secretary at the end of the Soviet period.

16 *Moldova Suverana*, August 20, 1992, p. 1.

17 "Poporul Trebuie Intrebat i Ascultat," *Moldova Suverana*, December 26, 1992, p. 1.

18 *Moldova Suverana*, February 6, 1993, p. 1.

19 For a profile of all of the main parties that participated in the 1994 elections, see Vladimir Socor, "Moldova's Political Landscape: Profiles of the Parties," *RFE/RL Research Report*, 3, no. 10 (March 11, 1994), 6–14.

20 This included the politically influential and intellectually powerful Social Democratic party, which had high hopes for the election, but was shut out by competitors with better grass roots organization.

21 For a complete account of the Gagauz agreement, see Vladimir Socor, "Gagauz Autonomy in Moldova: A Precedent for Eastern Europe?" *RFE/RL Research Report*, 3, no. 33 (August 26, 1994), 20–28.

22 *Constitu ia Republicii Moldova* (Chiinau: Direcia de Stat pentru Asigurarea Informational, MOLDPRES, 1994).

23 *Economia Na ionala a Republicii Moldova* (Chiinau, Moldova: Departmentul de Stat Pentru Statistica, 1992), p. 8.

24 Not surprisingly, food processing was a central component of manufacturing activity, accounting for 40.4 percent of total industrial production. *Economia Na ionala a Republicii Moldova* (Chiinau, Moldova: Departmentul de Stat Pentru Statistica, 1992), p. 318.

25 *Moldova: Moving Toward a Market Economy* (Washington, D.C.: The World Bank, 1994), p. 5.

26 The ration of Moldovan imports plus exports to GDP was 50 percent in 1990, and 33 percent in 1991. *Moldova: Moving Toward a Market Economy* (Washington, D.C.: The World Bank, 1994), p. 7.

27 The aggregate results of this inventory became the basis of a calculation of the total industrial wealth of Moldova. Each citizen is to be provided with coupons endowing them with a share in this total amount based on the number of years that they have been employed in the economy. Twenty-five years of work in the republic equals 25 coupon points, ten years provides ten points. Employees of cooperative and state farms were also provided with coupons on the basis of their term of employment in the agricultural sector. Enterprise employees will be allowed to purchase up to 30 percent of the value of their enterprises at nominal value.

28 Each family with members working on a state or collective farm was entitled to 0.75 acres of the farm's property, but could not resell this land until 2001.

29 E. Kondratav, "Moldova's Unity Threatened," *Isvestia*, Sept 3, 1990, p. 2, reported in *Current Digest of the Soviet Press*, 42, no. 35 (1990), 27–28.

30 For a more detailed discussion of the political situation in Transdniestrian region during this period, see Vladimir Socor, "Moldova's 'Dniester' Ulcer," *RFE/RL Research Report*, 2, no. 1 (January 1, 1993), 12–16.

31 While Russian speakers comprise a majority of Transdniestrians (about 25 percent Russians and 28 percent Ukrainians), the largest single ethnic group in Transdniestria is Moldovan, with a little more than 40 percent of the population.

32 For a full account of links between the Transdniestrian forces and conservatives in Russia, see Vladimir Socor, "Dniester Involvement in the Moscow Rebellion," *RFE/RL Research Report*, 2, no. 46 (November 19, 1993), 25–32,

33 For accounts of the key decisions in this rather bewildering chain of events, see *The Current Digest of the Former Soviet Press*, 46, no 32 (September 7, 1994), 15–16; *The Current Digest of the Former Soviet Press*, 46, no. 33. (September 14, 1994), 23–24; *The Current Digest of the Former Soviet Press*, 46, no. 36 (October 5, 1994), 21–22.

34 See Vladimir Socor "Gagauz Autonomy in Moldova: A Precedent for Eastern Europe?" *RFE/RL Research Report*, 3, no. 33 (August 26, 1994), 20–28.

# Moldova: chronology of events

*December 1988*
> 28   Parliament releases a report recommending the adoption of Moldovan as the state language and a transition to Latin script.

*June 1989*
> 25   70,000–80,000 demonstrators participate in a rally organized by the Popular Front of Moldova to protest the USSR's annexation of Moldova in 1940.

*August 1989*
> 27   More than 100,000 participate in a demonstration in Chisinau in support of the adoption of Moldovan as the state language. Several thousand Russians (and Gagauz) hold alternative rallies denouncing the law.
> 29   A series of strikes in Russian enterprises to protest the language law culminates with 80,000 workers on strike in a hundred factories.
> 31   The language law is adopted making Moldovan the official language of the republic (the first republic to adopt such a law) and ordering the transition to Latin script. Russian is declared the language of interethnic communication. Gagauz is declared the official language in Gagauz-dominated areas.

*November 1989*
> 7   Anti-government demonstrations turn violent on Revolution Day.
> 12   The Gagauz Movement (*Gagauzi Khalk*) holds its first congress and declares the establishment of a Gagauz ASSR. The Moldovan Supreme Soviet insists the declaration is illegal.
> 16   Petr Luchinski replaces Semen Grossu as first secretary of the Communist Party.

*January 1990*
> 10   Petr Poskar is appointed chairman of the Council of Ministers (prime minister).
> 27   The city of Tiraspol votes to become a self-governing, independent territory.

*February 1990*
> 25   Elections to the Supreme Soviet are held. Approximately

one-third of the deputies are supporters of the Popular Front.

*April 1990*

27    Mircea Snegur, a moderate Communist, is elected chairman of the Supreme Soviet. A state flag is adopted on the same day.

*May 1990*

6    The border to Romania is opened. An estimated 150,000 Moldovans venture across (as do 200,000 Romanians).

23    100 Russian-speaking deputies withdraw from the Supreme Soviet after several of them are physically attacked by protestors.

25    Prime Minister Poskar resigns citing opposition to his government from the Supreme Soviet. He is replaced by Mircea Druc.

*June 1990*

23    The Supreme Soviet issues a declaration of sovereignty.

24    Thousands of Romanians cross the border to Moldova and call for reunion on the 50th anniversary of Moscow's annexation.

*July 1990*

27    Parliament annuls all decisions of the November Gagauz congresss and rejects the notion of autonomous territories within the republic.

*August 1990*

19    At a congress of Gagauz deputies in Komrat, attendees announce the formation of a Gagauz republic outside the boundaries of the Moldovan SSR, and schedule parliamentary elections for October 28.

21–22    The Moldovan parliament declares the Gagauz decision unconstitutional and outlaws *Gagauzi Khalk*.

*September 1990*

2    The government of the Dnestr region proclaims the establishment of a "Dnestr republic" (Transdniestria) and declares that only USSR laws will be valid on its territory.

3    Parliament decides to institute presidential rule and elevates parliamentary chairman Snegur to the post of president. Alexandru Mosanu takes his place as Supreme Soviet chairman.

*October 1990*

26    A state of emergency is declared in the Gagauz region and

public meetings are banned for a two-month period.
29   In a compromise, a moratorium is declared for both the
      Gagauz parliamentary elections and parliament's rejection
      of Gagauz autonomy.

*November 1990*

2    Six people die when Moldovan MVD troops clash with
      Transdniestr forces when attempting to clear a roadblock in
      Dubosari.
15   A funeral service for Dumitru Moldovanu, who was
      stabbed and killed in an argument with a Russian who had
      insulted the republic's flag, turns into a mass
      demonstration. Attacks on Russian-speakers in Chisinau by
      gangs of Moldovan youth followed.
25   Transdniestria holds its own parliamentary elections: of 60
      deputies, 25 are Russian, 18 Ukrainian, and 12 Moldovan.
29   Igor Smirnov is elected chairman of the Dniestr parliament.

*December 1990*

16   200,000 people gather at a demonstration in Chisinau to
      demand the rejection of the proposed union treaty.
23   A rally calling for civic concord degenerates into a brawl.

*February 1991*

4    Grigori Yeremei replaces Luchinski as party first secretary.
19   Parliament votes against holding the March referendum on
      the union's preservation.
21   A coupon system is introduced
28   Snegur issues a decree providing for Ukrainian-language
      schools in areas dominated by ethnic Ukrainians.

*March 1991*

17   Despite a Moldova boycott, the Dniestr and Gagauz regions
      hold the all-union referendum on the preservation of the
      union, with almost universal approval for the union in each
      region.

*April 1991*

8    The Independent Moldovan Communists Party is
      established with a predominantly-ethnic Moldavian
      membership.

*May 1991*

21   Two Gagauz leaders submit a plan to parliament requesting
      that the Gagauz region receive autonomy and become a free
      economic zone in return for respecting Moldova's territorial
      integrity. Stepan Topol, chairman of the Gagauz Supreme
      Soviet, is against the plan.

28    Following a no-confidence vote, Prime Minister Druc is replaced by Valeriu Muravschi. Popular Front supporters of Druc riot.

*June 1991*

5    Parliament passes a law on citizenship which grants automatic citizenship to all who resided in the republic before June 23, 1990, those who lived on the territory before June 28, 1940 and their descendents, and all who are born on Moldovan soil.

*August 1991*

23    The Communist Party is declared illegal and all of its property is nationalized.

23    Topol and Mihail Kenderelian, another Gagauz leader, are arrested on charges of supporting the Moscow coup.

27    Parliament issues a Declaration of Independence.

*September 1991*

2    At a congress in Komrat, Gagauz delegates issue a declaration of independence, demand the release of Topol and Kenderelian, and propose the creation of a confederation of Moldova, the Gagauz republic, and the Dniestr republic.

*October 1991*

14    The Popular Front announces a boycott of the presidential elections scheduled for 8 December.

22    Transdniestria's parliament requests full membership in a new Union.
The Agrarian Democratic Party holds its founding congress.

24    The Dniestr leadership declares that the region will also boycott the December 8 presidential elections.

30    A decree is issued which nationalizes all Soviet enterprises on Moldovan territory.

*November 1991*

3    Thousands gather in a rally organized by the Popular Front to denounce the upcoming presidential elections.

*December 1991*

1    Refusing to participate in presidential elections, the Dniestr and Gagauz regions hold their own elections. Topol is elected president in the Gagauz region with over 90 percent of the vote while Smirnov is elected president of Transdniestria with 65 percent of the vote. A majority of voters in both regions also vote for independence in simultaneous referenda.

8  With election regulations tailored to eliminate potential opponents, the Popular Front boycott, and the withdrawal of two other candidates, Snegur receives 98 percent of the vote (83 percent voter participation).

13  In clashes with police, more than ten die in Transdniestria.

*January 1992*

3–12  Forces loyal to the Dniestr leadership launch multiple attacks on government buildings in Bendery and Dubosari. Police, under orders to avoid bloodshed at all cost, do not return fire.

31–3  Numerous attacks on Moldovan policemen and others by Dneister militia.

*February 1992*

16  At a congress, the Popular Front declares that its highest goal is reunification with Romania. Also, the Front changes its name to the Popular Christian-Democratic Front.

24  A decree is issued which declares that all residents of Moldova will be offered citizenship.

*March 1992*

2–3  In Dubosari, Dnestr forces seize police headquarters after police surrender their arms. They proceed to block off the region.

29  Following a month of escalating violence, a state of emergency is declared, and government troops are ordered into Transdniestria. A war ensues and lasts until June.

*April 1992*

1  Yeltsin places the Soviet 14th Army based in Transdniestria under Russian jurisdiction.

5  Rutskoi expresses support for Transdniestria's independence in a visit to Tiraspol.

*May 1992*

15  Moldova does not sign the CIS collective security pact.

20  Several units of the 14th Army join the Dnestr forces.

27  Parliament denounces 14th Army actions as outside interference and passes a resolution demanding its withdrawal.

*June 1992*

30  Prime Minister Muravschi and his cabinet resign amid mass discontent over declining living standards.

*July 1992*

1  Andrei Sangheli is confirmed by parliament as new prime minister.

7–8    Following more than a thousand deaths and tens of thousands of refugees, troops are disengaged in Transdniestria. Russian parliament agrees to permit the use of the 14th Army for peacekeeping operations.

21    The Moldovan government signs an agreement with Moscow which includes the maintenance of trilateral peacekeeping units and the establishment of a security zone. The Popular Front issues an appeal demanding Moldova's withdrawal from the CIS and attacks the government's decision to permit Russian peacekeepers in Transdniestria.

24–26    In Chisinau, the Popular Front stages a protest, in which armed soldiers participate, to demand Snegur's resignation. Protestors disperse after Snegur meets with Front representatives.

*August 1992*

13    Armistice declared in the Dniestr region.

19    The state of emergency which had been in effect since March is ended.

28    Parliamentary chairman Alexandru Mosanu asserts that the government seeks reunification with Romania.

*September 1992*

Schoolteachers and students in Transdniestria launch a strike to protest the reintroduction of the Russian alphabet in Moldovan-language schools.

*November 1992*

29    Several thousand supporters of the Popular Front demonstrate in favor of reunification with Romania.

*December 1992*

24    Snegur proposes a referendum to decide whether Moldova should remain completely independent, reunite with Romania, or join the CIS.

25    Smirnov admits that Dniestr residents are being conscripted into the Russian 14th Army.

*January 1993*

22, 25    Dniestr and Gagauz regions sign pacts of friendship and cooperation with Abkhazia, agreeing to come to each other's aid in case of attack.

29    The pro-Romanian Mosanu resigns after a majority of deputies threaten to walk out if he does not support the holding of the referendum.

*February 1993*

4     Petru Luchinschi, former first secretary of the Moldovan Communist Party, is elected parliamentary chairman.

*March 1993*

9     Leaders of the Dniestr and Gagauz regions call for the establishment of a "Moldovan Confederation."

*April 1993*

6     At an emergency congress of Gagauz parliamentary deputies, delegates reject a proposed draft constitution as it fails to spell out the rights of national minorities.

*May 1993*     Moderate members of the Popular Front, which had formed a "Congress of Intellectuals," are expelled from the Front.

30     The Social Democratic Party of Moldova holds its founding congress.

*July 1993*

19     The Popular Front accuses the government of engaging in a policy of repression.

*August 1993*

4     Parliament votes 162–101 to ratify Moldova's membership in the CIS, but fails to gain the simple majority required.

10     After their attempt to dissolve parliament fails, a majority of deputies resigns, effectively dismantling the legislature. New elections are scheduled for February 1994.

*September 1993*

9     The Gagauz parliament requests admission to the CIS.

*October 1993*

22     More than 700 demonstrators occupy the last Moldova school in the city of Bendery to protest a ban on the Latin script.

*November 1993*

29     Moldova leaves the ruble zone, making the *lei* the sole official currency.

*December 1993*

9     The Dniestr supreme court hands down a death sentence to Moldovan nationalist Ilie Ilascu and extends jail sentences to five others who were accused of murder during the 1992 conflict. Moldova and Romania, as well as Russia and the CSCE, condemn the ruling and ask for lenience.

*January 1994*

19    The Dniestr government forbids the holding of Moldova's parliamentary elections in the region and declares a 6-week state of emergency.

*February 1994*

3    The Romanian foreign ministry asserts that a proposed referendum to confirm Moldova's independence must have the participation of Romanian citizens if it is to be valid. Sangheli responds on February 16: "they in Bucharest must understand once and for all that Moldova is an independent state."

27    In elections to the new 104-seat parliament, the Agrarian Democratic Party wins 43 percent of the vote (56 seats) followed by the Socialist Party/Edinstvo bloc (22 percent and 28 seats). The Bloc of Peasants and Intellectuals gains 9 percent and 11 seats, while the Christian-Democratic Popular Front wins only 7.5 percent (9 seats).

*March 1994*

6    In referendum, 90 percent of voters (66 percent participation) affirm their support of Moldova's independence.

29    Luchinschi is reappointed parliamentary chairmen. Two days later, parliament reelects Prime Minister Sangheli.

*April 1994*

8    Parliament ratifies CIS membership for Moldova.

*May 1994*

23    Officers of the 14th Army reveal that nearly all the leaders of Trandnestria have received Russian citizenship.

*June 1994*

7    Parliament votes overwhelmingly to remove "Awake ye Romanian," the Romanian national anthem, as the Moldovan state anthem.

*July 1994*

6    The CSCE calls for the "unconditional and full withdrawal" of the 14th Army.

13    Transdnieistria ministry of education asserts that use of the Latin script is punishable by law.

28    Parliament ratifies the new Constitution in a vote of 81–18. The Constitution defines Moldova as a "single" state, makes Moldovan (not Romanian) the official language, safeguards the freedom of use of non-state languages, declares the country's permanent neutrality, bans the

stationing of foreign troops on its soil, and provides for the autonomy of the Transdniester and Gagauz regions. Parliament adopts law on making the Gagauz region a national-territorial autonomous unit, granting the region its own elected governing bodies, three official languages, and the right of secession in the case of reunification with Romania.

*August 1994*

11 Tenth-round of talks between Moscow and Chisinau on the 14th Army's withdrawal end with the two agreeing that the troops will leave in three years' time.

13 Alexei Mocreac, leader of the pro-Moldovan "Integrity" movement, is arrested in the Transdniester region. Two ethnic Russians who are political opponents of the Dniestr regime were also arrested a few weeks before.

*October 1994*

21 Prime Minister Sangheli signs a treaty with Chernomyrdin on withdrawing the 14th Army within three years. General Lebed', head of the 14th Army, and Smirnov insist that the treaty won't stand.

*March 1995*

5 In a referendum in Gagauzia, 29 of 36 villages vote to establish autonomy in accord with state law.

26 In a referendum in Transdniestria, 91 percent of voters oppose the withdrawal of the 14th Army. Local elections are held simultaneously.

*April 1995*

27 Students halt a month-long protest campaign which gathered up to 10,000 people at rallies after Snegur agrees to amend the article of the Constitution which declares that the official state language is Moldovan, and not Romanian.

Part IV

# The Baltics

Area of Detail

Gulf of Finland

BALTIC SEA

Narva

Rakvere • • Ahtme
TALINN •

ESTONIA

Parnu • • Tartu
• Viljandi

• Valga

Gulf of Riga

LATVIA

Ventspils •

RIGA •
Jurmala • Daugava R. • Daugavapils
Liepaja • • Jelgava

LITHUANIA

• Taurage
Kaunas •
VILNIUS •

Alytus •

0   25   50   75   100
Kilometers

0   25   50   75
Miles

Final boundaries of Estonia, Latvia, and Lithuania with the
USSR are expected to be confirmed by agreement. Other
boundary representation is not necessarily authoritative.

Gulf of Riga

**LATVIA**

Baltic
Sea

SOVIET UNION

POLAND

SOVIET UNION

## Lithuania

—— International boundary
★ National capital
—•— Railroad
—— Road

*Lithuania has no internal administrative divisions.*

0        50 Kilometers
0              50 Miles
*Lambert Conformal Conic Projection, SP 47N/62N*

# 9 Lithuania: rights and responsibilities of independence

ALFRED ERICH SENN

Although, in the 1980s, Lithuanians constituted only about one percent of the population of the Soviet Union, the nation played a leading role in the collapse of the Soviet system. The Lithuanians began to speak of independence in the winter of 1988–1989; they led the way in demanding the breakup of the CPSU (December 1989); they were the first to vote the Communist Party out of power (February 1990); they were the first to challenge Moscow directly by declaring the independence of their republic (March 1990). Later, the Lithuanians were the first successor state of the FSU to elect the heirs of the Communist Party *back* into power (October-November 1992).

In origin, the confrontation between the Lithuanians and the central authorities in Moscow combined questions of nationality rights with demands to decentralize the Soviet state, and it involved a clash of fundamentally opposed ideas of "statehood." Soviet ideologists had claimed that a nationality could best realize its potential as part of a multinational workers' state directed from Moscow, and they had denounced "bourgeois nationalism" as a false doctrine built on class oppression. As Lithuanians asserted a stronger national consciousness in 1988 and 1989, they insisted that a nationality could best realize its potential when it ruled itself as a sovereign national state. The resulting conflict shook the Soviet state to its foundations.

## Lithuanian national consciousness

Lithuanian national consciousness has both religious and secular roots. Latin Christianity, which came to Lithuania in the fourteenth century as a result of the political union of the Grand Duchy of Lithuania and the Kingdom of Poland, brought the Lithuanians into the western cultural tradition, but it also resulted in the Polonization of the upper classes. When a Lithuanian national movement developed at the end of the nineteenth century, lower clergy struggled to assert their own identity against the Polish church hierarchy while some Lithuanian nationalists considered the Catholic Church a negative influence in the national development of their people.[1] In the last years of tsarist rule in Russia, the priesthood constituted one of the few occupations in Lithuania open to Lithuanian intellectuals, and in the first years of Lithuanian independence after World War I, the Catholic Christian Democratic bloc dominated Lithuanian politics.

In the Soviet years, Lithuanians constituted the bulk of Roman Catholics in the USSR, and in the 1980s there were over 600 churches still functioning in the republic while there were only a handful in the rest of the Soviet state. (The Uniate church in Ukraine was banned, and therefore it did not enter into such counts.) The Catholic church, moreover, constituted a legal haven for people wanting to display some sort of resistance to the regime, and many dissidents in fact could not distinguish between their own religious and national feelings.[2]

The secular roots of Lithuanian national consciousness include the Lithuanian language and a historical memory that spans seven centuries, beginning with the pre-Christian Lithuanian Grand Duchy of the thirteenth and fourteenth centuries and emphasized by the establishment of an independent state, proclaimed by Lithuanian spokespersons on February 16, 1918. Hampered by the historic domination of Polish language and culture, Lithuanian language and culture had suffered still another blow in the nineteenth century when the Russian government banned the publication of the Lithuanian language in Latin characters. Only in the period of independence between the two World Wars could Lithuanian culture develop freely according to its own dynamic.[3]

On July 12, 1920, the Soviet Russian government formally recognized Lithuanian independence. The period of independence also brought new problems: In October 1920, Polish forces seized Vilnius, which the Lithuanians claimed as their capital, and for almost the entire interwar period, Kaunas served as the country's "provisional" capital, thereby intensifying a rivalry between the two cities that continues to the present day. In addition, in 1926 a coup, led by the military, overthrew the democratic, constitutional government, installing an authoritarian regime under Antanas Smetona, that ruled until the Soviet invasion of 1940.[4] But as a member of the League of Nations and even a two-time champion of European basketball, Lithuania had held a recognized place among the states of Europe and the world.

The Soviet invasion in June 1940 put an abrupt end to Lithuanian independence, and the USSR incorporated the land as a constituent republic. The Soviet authorities also encouraged the minority nationalities of the republic in their complaints against the Lithuanians, thereby stimulating national conflicts – especially with the Jews – that had not seriously threatened the society before. In 1941 Soviet authorities deported thousands of Lithuanians. From 1941 to 1944 Lithuania lay under German occupation, and when Soviet forces returned, many Lithuanians took up arms to resist the reimposition of the Soviet order. In all the Soviets killed, imprisoned, or deported some five to seven percent of the republic's population. A partisan movement, the "forest brethren," continued to fight until 1953, and after its suppression, the Lithuanians only sullenly accepted the realities of Soviet rule.[5]

After 1953 organized resistance was virtually impossible, but in the Khrushchev years of the late 1950s and early 1960s, the deportees who returned from exile and prison camps would forget neither their own experiences nor their nation's independent existence. Actions by individuals repeatedly embarrassed the authorities: In 1969 a Lithuanian seaman, Simas Kudirka, evoked an international incident by jumping from a Soviet ship onto an American one, and in 1972, Romas Kalanta, a young man who had thought of becoming a priest, immolated himself in a park in the heart of Kaunas. In a singular organized action, underground activists published the samizdat *Chronicle of the Catholic Church*, defying efforts of the Soviet authorities to find their center of operation.[6] After the signing of the Helsinki Accords in 1975, dissidents dared to form a Helsinki Watch group in Lithuania. Soviet authorities soon deported most of the group's original activists, but despite numerous arrests, dissidents continued to challenge the regime.

In the early 1980s, Lithuanians, including intellectuals and party members, focused on a number of cultural and environmental issues. Writers and philologists feared for the future of the language in the face of the regime's Russification policies that started schoolchildren with Russian before Lithuanian and required that all doctoral dissertations be written in Russian. Environmental problems, on the other hand, threatened the physical existence of the nation. The newly growing chemical industry polluted both land and water, and the Chernobyl meltdown of 1986 raised the specter of something similar occurring in Eastern Lithuania at the Ignalina Atomic Energy plant, which had been built on the Chernobyl model and which, when complete, would be the largest atomic plant in the world. Taking advantage of the Soviet regime's encouragement of "informal organizations," Lithuanians brought out their private concerns in public discussion.[7]

In 1987 and 1988, the Soviet order began to crumble. On August 23, 1987, dissidents organized a public meeting in Vilnius to mark the forty-eighth anniversary of the Molotov-Ribbentrop pact of 1939 whereby the Soviet Union and Nazi Germany had divided Eastern Europe between themselves. During the winter of 1987–1988, the authorities tried to reassert their control of the public dialogue, but while they harassed demonstrators and spectators, they faced growing challenges.

In June 1988 a group of Vilnius intellectuals, responding to Gorbachev's calls for "democratization" and the establishment of a government "ruled by law," organized themselves as the Lithuanian Movement for Perestroika (Lietuvos Persitvarkymo Sajudis), or, as it became better known, *Sajudis*. Sajudis spokespersons, all of whom held responsible positions in Soviet society, at first eschewed political goals, limiting themselves to stressing concerns about the cultural rights and the environmental protection of the Lithuanian nation.[8]

As an expression of Lithuanian national feeling, Sajudis quickly won broad support and became the spearhead of a powerful national movement. It organized mass rallies that brought together as many as 150,000 people, maybe four percent of all the Lithuanian-speaking people in the world. When it held its constitutional convention in October 1988, Sajudis became a republican-wide organization with public ambitions. At the same time, since it did not restrict its membership, more radical elements in the population, particularly people from Kaunas and the other cities of Lithuania, joined and eventually dictated its politics. Whereas the Vilnius intellectuals had advocated reform, many of the activists from other parts of the republic did not consider anything in the Soviet system to be worth saving, and they began to speak of the possibilities of political independence.[9]

The Soviet authorities were of two minds in assessing the developments in Lithuania. Although Aleksandr Yakovlev, Gorbachev's closest advisor, endorsed the efforts of the Sajudis intellectuals, republican party leaders sought support among the conservatives in Moscow. The Soviet military objected to the Lithuanians' complaints about the treatment of their young men in the armed forces, and both the party and the KGB encouraged the minority nationalities of Lithuania, in the name of "internationalism," to oppose the growing national consciousness of the Lithuanians.[10] Nevertheless, even the Lithuanian Communist Party (LCP) experienced reform: In October 1988 Algirdas Brazauskas, with the support of Sajudis sympathizers, became First Secretary of the Party. As a party reformer, he became a popular figure in Lithuania and throughout the Soviet Union, but he faced criticism both at home and in Moscow.[11]

The major minorities in Lithuania were Russians (in 1989, 9.4 percent, mostly in cities throughout the republic) and Poles (about 7.0 percent, concentrated in the city of Vilnius and in the rural districts in the south east) (see table 9.1). For the most part, these people considered themselves citizens of the Soviet Union rather than of Lithuania, and many rallied to the so-called "interfront" – in Lithuania it took the form of an organization called "Unity" (*Edinstvo* or *Jedność*) – criticizing the efforts of the Lithuanians to free themselves of Moscow's controls.[12] Lithuanians in turn considered these people hostile to the idea of a Lithuanian national state.

During the winter of 1988–1989, Brazauskas leaned toward placating Moscow while Lithuanian activists surged ahead. When Lithuanians protested Gorbachev's move to strengthen the power of the central government in November and December 1988, Brazauskas urged moderation on his compatriots, fearing that Moscow might establish a tighter direct control

Table 9.1. *National composition of Lithuania, 1989*

| Nationalities | Population | in % |
|---|---|---|
| Total population | 3,675,000 | 100.0 |
| Lithuanians | 2,925,300 | 79.6 |
| Russians | 345,450 | 9.4 |
| Poles | 257,250 | 7.0 |
| Belarusans | 62,475 | 1.7 |
| Ukrainians | 44,100 | 1.2 |
| Other | 40,425 | 1.1 |

*Source: Natisional'nyi sostav naseleniya SSSR* (Moscow: Finansy i statistika, 1991).

Table 9.2. *National makeup of urban population, 1989*

| | Lithuanians | Russians | Poles | Belarusans | Other |
|---|---|---|---|---|---|
| Vilnius | 50.5 | 20.2 | 18.6 | 5.3 | 5.2 |
| Kaunas | 88.0 | 8.3 | 0.6 | 0.7 | 2.4 |
| Klaipeda | 63.0 | 28.2 | 0.5 | 2.7 | 5.6 |
| Siauliai | 85.0 | 10.5 | 0.3 | 0.9 | 3.3 |
| Druskininkai | 79.3 | 8.7 | 5.5 | 3.8 | 2.7 |
| Palanga | 87.2 | 8.9 | 0.4 | 1.2 | 2.2 |
| Neringa | 88.5 | 8.1 | 0.4 | 1.0 | 1.9 |
| Snieckus* | 7.7 | 64.2 | 6.4 | 11.0 | 10.7 |

* The Russian population has reportedly declined by at least 10 percent since 1989 as the result of emigration from the republic.
* Sniekus is now named Visaginas.

*Source:* National Minorities in Lithuania (Vilnius: Centre of National Researches of Lithuania, 1992).

over the republic, and he criticized the growing nationalist feeling in the republic. As of February and March 1989, he seemed to be turning away from the high hopes of the previous fall.[13]

In the spring the situation changed after Sajudis achieved an overwhelming victory in the election of deputies for the USSR Congress of People's Deputies (CPD) in Moscow. Sajudis leaders were now openly speaking of their desire to reestablish Lithuania's independence, and their candidates won thirty-six of the forty-two seats contested in Lithuania. Brazauskas even owed his own electoral victory to the decision of Sajudis leaders that in view of the danger of Moscow's taking action, they should let him run unopposed. Brazauskas in turn recognized that he had to cooperate with

Sajudis leaders, and he now worked more closely with Vytautas Landsbergis, the President of Sajudis, in presenting a common front toward Moscow.[14]

The Lithuanian delegation took advantage of the political stage offered them at the First Session of the CPD, demanding political sovereignty for their republic, republican economic self-sufficiency, and an official investigation of the secret protocols to the Nazi-Soviet agreements of 1939 whereby the Germans had recognized the Baltic as part of the Soviet sphere of influence. At one point, most of the Lithuanian delegation walked out of a CPD session to emphasize their argument that they considered the Soviet regime an unconstitutional occupation regime in their republic.[15]

The CPSU looked askance at Brazauskas's inclination to work with Sajudis and to seek a popular constituency in Lithuania. As a member of the presidium of the CPD, Brazauskas did not participate in the parliamentary walk-out, but he subsequently endorsed the idea of making the LCP independent of the Moscow party. CPSU spokespersons vigorously denounced this policy, and in August, after the Lithuanian Supreme Soviet had challenged the legality of Lithuania's incorporation into the USSR in 1940, CPSU leaders, in the name of the party Central Committee, warned that the failure of the LCP to control events in Lithuania could have dire consequences for the Lithuanian people. Brazauskas held his course, opening the way for a multi-party system in Lithuania and then supervising the LCP's split with the CPSU in December 1989.[16]

In January 1990, Gorbachev visited Lithuania, officially to try to heal the split in the Communist Party but ultimately to keep Lithuania in the Soviet fold by appealing directly to the Lithuanian people.[17] The visit accomplished little, other than putting the Lithuanians in the center of world attention. In February 1990, back in Moscow, Gorbachev accepted a CPSU Central Committee resolution condemning the LCP's action and declaring support for a splinter group of the LCP that professed loyalty to Moscow while at the same time criticizing Gorbachev's reform program. Forced to choose between reform and keeping Lithuania, Gorbachev tried to hold the empire together.[18]

Thoughts of independence now predominated among the Lithuanians. Brazauskas favored a gradual process, "step by step," trying to keep conflict with Moscow to a minimum; radical nationalists insisted to the contrary that sharp conflict with Moscow was inevitable and that therefore the Lithuanians should move as quickly as possible. Gorbachev's decision to work with rump party loyalists, organized as the LCP/CPSU, crippled Brazauskas's position as a mediator between Vilnius and Moscow: Gorbachev himself was moving toward confrontation, and at the end of February when voters overwhelmingly elected Sajudis supporters to the Lithuanian Supreme Soviet, it was only a matter of time before the Lithuanians would declare their independence of Moscow.

The action came quickly. Having won a two-thirds majority in the new parliament, Sajudis deputies, led by the nationalists, on March 11 elected Vytautas Landsbergis as chairman of the Supreme Soviet, in essence the president of the republic. (After this Lithuanians insisted that the parliament should be called "Supreme Council" in English.) Then, in a carefully orchestrated series of votes, the deputies declared the restoration of the Lithuanian republic that had existed until the state's incorporation by the Soviet Union in 1940. Insisting that they had no obligations toward the Soviet constitution, they spoke of dismantling the occupation regime.[19]

Although the LCP accepted its fall from power peacefully – thereby endorsing the transfer of power from party to government – Gorbachev feared that the dominoes would begin to fall elsewhere. He demanded that the Lithuanian parliament rescind its declaration, and the Soviet army demonstratively flexed its muscles, sending tanks on nightly drives through the city of Vilnius. Soviet authorities encouraged strikes by Russian workers against the Lithuanian government, and Gorbachev threatened to take territory, including the cities of Vilnius and Klaipeda, from the Lithuanians. Western leaders held back and urged the Lithuanians to negotiate with Moscow.[20]

In the middle of April 1990 Gorbachev imposed a blockade on Lithuania, stopping the shipment of oil and gasoline while permitting only about 20 percent of the normal deliveries of natural gas to the republic. He also banned the shipment of other goods, such as coffee and sugar, that supposedly could be sold for hard currency. At the same time he made sure Moscow loyalists in the Polish regions of the southeast received supplies as usual, and the CPSU encouraged demands for Polish autonomous regions within Lithuania. (Some Poles in Lithuania openly dreamed of establishing a Polish Soviet Socialist Republic as part of the USSR.) To Moscow's suprise, the Lithuanians resisted the pressure; although the blockade ravaged the Lithuanian economy, Gorbachev found himself embarrassed by the lingering impasse.

Once started, the blockade did not lend itself to easy solution. Even after Gorbachev had shown a desire to end it, the Lithuanians still argued among themselves as to what to do. The Lithuanian prime minister, Kazimiera Prunskiene, an economist, and Brazauskas, also an economist by training and now her deputy for economic affairs, favored negotiating with Gorbachev as soon as possible. Landsbergis and his advisors preferred to wait to deal with Boris Yeltsin and the newly assertive government of the RSFSR. Only at the end of June did Landsbergis finally agree to promise a "moratorium" on legislation supporting the declaration of March 11, and Gorbachev immediately lifted the blockade.[21]

The Lithuanian Supreme Council's debate on the proposed moratorium marked the beginnings of party politics. Nationalist deputies objected to Prunskiene's acceptance of a moratorium, but a "Center faction" of Sajudis deputies announced their support for Prunskiene's policies. On the other hand, deputies from other cities of Lithuania tended to gather for tea in the hotel in which they were all housed, and from this "tea party," as it was called, there arose several right-wing parties, such as the March 11 Party and the Christian Democratic Party. (It now became the practice in Lithuania to consider the nationalists or "patriots," as they called themselves, the political Right, and this essay observes that practice.[22])

By the end of summer the parliamentary majority – which could not be accurately measured because the parliament did not keep comprehensive voting records – and the cabinet of ministers were at loggerheads. Although Landsbergis, who looked to the nationalists for his support, had accepted the idea of a moratorium, he aligned himself with the parliament and delayed the start of negotiations with Moscow. This confrontation, with both domestic and international ramifications, drifted on into the fall and winter.

Frustrated by the failure of the blockade, resurgent conservative forces in the Soviet government and the CPSU drew up new plans. The new CPSU CC secretary for organizational questions, Oleg Shenin, undertook advising the rump LCP/CPSU on how to unseat the Lithuanian government, while leaders of the military and the KGB began making their own plans. In Lithuania itself, the LCP/CPSU set about mobilizing Russian and Polish workers for an assault on the government as it issued appeals for Gorbachev to establish "presidential rule," i.e. martial law.[23]

The culmination of this process came in January 1991, exactly on the anniversary of Gorbachev's visit a year earlier and in the shadow of the beginning of the Gulf War in which the western powers engaged Iraq. Soviet paratroopers moved into Lithuania, and on January 8 Russian workers, encouraged and protected by the military, attacked the parliament building. The Lithuanians pushed them back with a demonstration of mass support by unarmed citizens who gathered to defend the building with their bodies.[24]

At this same time, the Lithuanian government endured an internal crisis. Facing an imminent and sure vote of no confidence over the issue of price hikes, Prunskiene resigned. Landsbergis replaced her with a member of the Center faction, Albertas Šimenas.

On January 11, as the Simenas government took office, Soviet troops began occupying strategic buildings in Vilnius, and during the night of January 12–13, the troops took the television station and the television tower. Military spokespersons insisted that this was necessary to silence "tendentious" reporting, and they blamed Landsbergis for the deaths of fifteen persons who had stood in the way of the Soviet tanks.[25] Although Lithuanians expected an attack on the parliament building, the Soviet troops stopped, presumably because of the cries of protest across the Soviet Union and around the world.

The political tangle in Lithuania took a new twist on Sunday, January 13, when nationalists in parliament installed a new prime minister, Gediminas Vagnorius, who would remain in office for about eighteen months. It would be his cabinet that saw the Lithuanian state win general world recognition of its independence.

In the aftermath of the "January events," as the Lithuanians call them, Moscow and Vilnius remained at an impasse for seven months. Soviet troops, now clearly playing the role of an occupying army, controlled the streets and supported the LCP/CPSU; the Landsbergis administration nevertheless continued to function. The situation proved embarrasing for Gorbachev, who continually denied any responsibility for the violence in Vilnius, and in July, when Soviet special forces murdered a team of Lithuanian border guards during US President George Bush's visit to Moscow, the scandal reached an international level. Gorbachev assured Bush that the KGB would investigate the situation.[26]

The "August Putsch" of 1991 in Moscow finally resolved the impasse in Lithuania. Even as Gorbachev returned to Moscow from the Crimea, the leaders of the KGB in Lithuania fled the republic, and the military spirited off the leaders of the LCP/CPSU to hiding in Russia. The Landsbergis-Vagnorius government now ruled the land, and recognitions of Lithuanian independence tumbled in from around the world.

## Independent Lithuania

The Lithuanians soon discovered that independence again brought problems. Soviet troops remained as a quasi-occupying force and posed a constant threat; the economy, severely damaged by Gorbachev's blockade, was still tied to the collapsing Soviet economy; debate raged as to which former Soviet institutions should be scrapped and which should be saved; and, of course, the Lithuanians had to assume new responsibilities toward the minority nationalities in their new state.

The Lithuanian republic was a "national state," that is to say, its leaders considered "Lithuania" to be an ethnoregional concept blending language and territory into a single whole with its own distinctive political imperatives. Although nationalists insisted, "A large part of ethnic Lithuania's territory is outside the borders of the Lithuanian SSR,"[27] governmental leaders nevertheless tended to accept the boundaries of the Lithuanian SSR as their frontier. In practice, this of course meant that while the Lithuanians constituted 80 percent of the population, other nationalities, of uncertain loyalty, comprised one-fifth of the population.

The Lithuanian government had prepared for its new authority by accepting the "zero-option" concept of citizenship, making all persons residing and working in Lithuania as of 1989 eligible for citizenship.[28] Whether the individuals accepted the opportunity to get a Lithuanian passport or not was another question, but the Lithuanians were in this way able to avoid the controversial publicity that the Latvians and the Estonians received on the citizenship question. The Lithuanian government also accepted the organization of minority groups as communities and supported the development of schools for the major groups.

Leaders of the minority nationalities now had the opportunity – which they had never had in Soviet times – to mobilize their own communities and build their own power bases. The Jewish population of the republic had heretofore basically supported Sajudis, and Jewish leaders seemed to agree that the government itself supported no anti-Jewish policies. The Lithuanians nevertheless faced a barrage of criticism from Jewish groups abroad over their efforts to rehabilitate people sent by the Soviet authorities to camps and into exile.[29]

The Russians, of course, presented a unique problem as a formerly dominant nationality now demoted in status. Whereas Russians formerly could force their language onto any meeting in Lithuania as a matter of course, now they considered it a victory when they could convince the Lithuanians to use Russian in speaking with them directly. The provisions for citizenship, however, softened the problems in that they allowed Russians who took Lithuanian passports to share in the distribution of "checks" for the distribution of state property. Many Russians used these to buy their apartments or otherwise to acquire real property, and those who chose to emigrate could then sell the property and leave with a nestegg that would help them start elsewhere. By the mid 1990s, the Russian population of the republic had declined to less than 9 percent with a minimum of rancor. For the Russians remaining, the problems have focussed mainly on trials of daily life – school texts, teachers, border crossings, and so forth.[30]

The Poles of Lithuania had begun reasserting their national heritage in 1988, in the shadow of Sajudis's activity. Some supported the Lithuanians, but many supported Moscow. (The LCP/CPSU had its strongest following in the Polish regions.) The Polish community, to be sure, had experienced great difficulty under Soviet rule. In the aftermath of World War II, much of its intelligentsia took advantage of the offers by Soviet authorities to let them emigrate to Poland. In the latter 1980s, although some Poles had moved to Lithuania to take advantage of the Polish schools there, many Polish families were sending their children to Russian schools, believing that such training would best prepare them for life. After 1989, however, attendance at Polish schools began to grow, and Polish leaders demanded recognition by both church and state in Lithuania. In the fall of 1991, the Lithuanian government suppressed local self-government in the Polish regions in the southeast, charging that the local powers had consistently supported the reactionary forces in Moscow.

The demands of the Poles covered all aspects of life, ranging from the establishment of a Polish university to the celebration of Polish-language masses in the Vilnius cathedral and a prohibition on Lithuanians' moving into the Polish regions around the city of Vilnius. When Lithuanians suggested that the Poles send their children to universities in Poland, Polish spokespersons replied that they might not come back and that therefore this was contrary to the interests of the community. After 1991 Polish leaders received considerable support from the Polish ambassador in Vilnius, who acted much more forcefully on behalf of his compatriots than the Russian ambassador did for his, but even so they criticized Warsaw for not doing enough for them.[31]

For the Lithuanians, on the other hand, the problems with the minority nationalities in the state constituted only a sideshow to their own concerns about dealing with their Soviet heritage. Nationalists devoted considerable effort to breaking up institutions like the trade unions, once called the "building blocks of communism," and also the collective farms. Carrying through the idea of "restoring" Lithuania as the independent state it had been in the 1930s, they "revived" political parties, newspapers, and even social organizations that had existed before Soviet rule.

One aspect of Soviet rule that the Lithuanians could not quickly eradicate, however, was the social poison left by the activity of the KGB, the eyes and ears of the Soviet authorities. In fleeing Lithuania after the August putsch, the KGB left behind an enormous archive, one of the largest police archives in Eastern Europe, which, while admittedly incomplete, provided rich fishing grounds for political vendettas. The parliament named a committee, headed by a former political prisoner, to supervise the archive, and favored individuals were able to root through the documents for their own purposes. Continuing the distrust that the Soviet authorities had sown among the people in their time, Lithuanians exchanged charges of having cooperated with or worked for the KGB, and several individuals who had been members of the Sajudis Initiative Group in 1988 had to retire from political life.[32]

Landsbergis called for continued national unity and wanted Sajudis to mobilize the people behind his government. Sajudis, however, was drifting to the political right, and it no longer enjoyed the broad popular base that it had in 1988 and 1989. In an effort to keep alive the national spirit of confrontation with Moscow, the government maintained the defensive fortifications built around the parliament building in January 1991, but that spirit waned quickly. The Sajudis majority in parliament disintegrated, and Landsbergis at times insisted that he represented only a minority of the deputies. He therefore called for creating a strong presidency independent of the parliament. The Sajudis organization supported him and forced a referendum on the question.

The campaign for the referendum ran through the winter and spring of 1992. Seeing that there was relatively little enthusiasm for the issue, Landsbergis proposed adding a second referendum, this one demanding that Soviet troops leave Lithuania by the end of 1992. With the center faction's figuring prominently in the maneuvering, the parliament foiled him by scheduling the two referenda for separate days. In May 1992, although a majority of the votes cast favored the institution of the presidency, the referendum failed because it did not win the support of an absolute majority of eligible voters. On June 14, the 51st anniversary of the deportations of 1941, the voters overwhelmingly endorsed the demand that the Soviet troops leave by the end of the year.[33]

After his idea of a presidency had failed, Landsbergis accused his opponents of carrying out a "creeping revolution," and he called for new parliamentary elections in October 1992. Preparatory to the vote, Landsbergis signed an agreement with the Russian government providing for the evacuation of all Soviet troops by August 31, 1993.[34] In addition, the parliament approved putting a new constitution to a popular vote at the same time.

The elections proved to be a complete surprise. Many Lithuanians had expected "a Polish result," with a number of small parties winning seats in the parliament, but instead they produced what they called a "Nicaraguan result," whereby pollsters proved to be completely wrong. Respondents had probably misled the pollsters because they feared saying that they would vote for Brazauskas's LDLP (Lithuanian Democratic Labor Party, the heirs of the Lithuanian Communist Party). The LDLP won an absolute majority of the 141 seats in the parliament; the voters also approved the new constitution for Lithuania, establishing a strong presidency and renaming the legislature the "Seimas," the name used for the Lithuanian parliament of the 1920s.[35]

To complete the restructuring of government, the Lithuanians now had to elect a president by direct ballot, and the voting was set for February 14, 1993. Brazauskas, who replaced Landsbergis as chairman of the parliament, announced his candidacy, and after some hesitation, Landsbergis announced that he would not run. Stasys Lozoraitis, the Lithuanian ambassador in Washington, leaped into the political ring as Brazauskas's opponent.

Landsbergis's accomplishments during his two and one-half year tenure are difficult to evaluate. On the one hand, he led Lithuania in confrontation with Moscow and emerged triumphant over Gorbachev; for that many Lithuanians revere his name. On the other hand, he accomplished little in creating institutions to lead the country out of the Soviet experience. In 1990 he insisted that the parliament was the vessel of Lithuania's sovereignty; in 1992 he referred to the same deputies as a pack of curs. He now retired to his self-designated post as "leader of the opposition," and in the spring of 1993, together with Gediminas Vagnorius he supervised the formation of a party that claimed to represent the best values of Sajudis, "Union of the Fatherland (Conservative Party)."[36]

The presidential election campaign brought into sharp focus another underlying problem of Lithuanian statehood, namely the relationship of the new state to the old Lithuanian emigration. Emigration had been a major phenomenon of Lithuanian life since the nineteenth century, but the most recent mass emigre movement were the "Displaced Persons" of World War II, Lithuanians who were in western Europe at the end of the war and refused to return to their homeland. These Lithuanians had created emigre institutions that had actively opposed Soviet rule in Lithuania. They welcomed the collapse of the Soviet system, but in 1988–1992 they found that their ideal of Lithuania did not necessarily coincide with the realities of life in the republic.

Lozoraitis represented a special dimension of this question in that the United States had refused to recognize the Soviet Union's incorporation of the three Baltic states in 1940 and had instead continued to deal with the diplomatic corps of the republics. When the individuals holding these positions died, they were succeeded by people who had provisional status. Lozoraitis's father had been the doyen of the Lithuanian diplomatic service in 1940, and by the late 1980s, Lozoraitis, who had himself left Lithuania as a young boy, had succeeded to this position. In September 1991, after the collapse of the Soviet Union, Landsbergis had accredited Lozoraitis as the ambassador of the reestablished republic.

In his election campaign against Brazauskas, Lozoraitis enjoyed broad support among political figures on the right and in the center of the political spectrum, but he had to confront the thought that an emigre could not understand the experiences and priorities of a society emerging from a half-century of Soviet rule. Émigrés, who supported him with enthusiasm, resented such challenges to their own understanding of the situation in Lithuania, and when Lithuanian voters chose Brazauskas, many emigres despaired of the behavior of the people. When Brazauskas visited Chicago in the fall of 1994, the editor of the major Lithuanian-American daily called for a boycott, insisting that "he is not our president."[37]

Brazauskas owed his victory to his own personal popularity and also to his party, which had seemed broken and battered in 1990–1991 but which rallied and reformed for the campaigns of 1992. As of 1994 it was the largest and best organized of Lithuania's political parties; its program had changed drastically since the years of Soviet rule. Many LCP figures had in fact left the party to engage in business, and when the LDLP began to organize for the elections, they returned, at the same time bolstering the party coffers.

## Lithuania's present and future

In its first two years in power, the LDLP showed signs of a split between more liberal and more traditional deputies in the parliament, but the party's majority stayed intact. The LDLP's prime minister, Adolfas Šleževičius, at first tried to form a coalition government, but after more than half the ministries had changed hands in his first fifteen months in office, some party leaders demanded the removal of non-party members from the cabinet. Right wing parties have sought to challenge the government on almost all fronts: demands for early elections failed in 1994, but in August 1994 they forced the holding of a referendum aimed at indexing savings accounts, the value of which had fallen precipitously as a result of inflation, especially in 1992–1993. Had the referendum passed, the Brazauskas government would have faced a serious crisis, but low voter turnout defeated it.[38]

In foreign policy, Brazauskas found relations with Russia to be the key issue. In their struggle against Gorbachev in 1990 and 1991, Lithuanian leaders were delighted to receive support and encouragement from Boris Yeltsin in Moscow; his public criticisms of Moscow's policy during the "January events" had been particularly welcome. Dealing with Yeltsin after the August putsch, however, proved to be more problematic.

The issues involved general problems of economic relations with Russia and the very specific question of Kaliningrad. As a highly militarized Russian exclave between Poland and Lithuania, Kaliningrad presented a battery of problems, the most urgent of which involved Russian military transport across Lithuania. Although the Lithuanian political right called any arrangement with Moscow tantamount to a military union, western diplomats and consultants urged the Lithuanians to find an acceptable compromise.

The Lithuanian government balanced its negotiations with Moscow by asserting that it belonged to "Europe." (Lithuanian journalists made considerable use of the thought that the geographic "center" of Europe lies close to Vilnius.) In January 1994, Brazauskas put Lithuania first in line among the successor republics of the USSR to apply for the NATO Partnership for Peace, and the Lithuanian government worked intensively to win entrance to other western European organizations.

The Lithuanians watched with great concern as Russia maneuvered to be recognized as the official international peacekeeper for Eastern Europe. Like other East Europeans, the Lithuanians identified this specter as "Yalta-2," conjuring up an image of Russia's reestablishing a sphere of influence that could reincarnate the Soviet empire. The problem of Lithuania's economic and political relations with Russia nevertheless remained a key to the republic's future, conditioning as it does future economic and political prospects.

An undiscussed question that the Lithuanians, like many other East Europeans, have not resolved is the function of government in post-Soviet society. The Lithuanian government inherited a centralized system from the Soviets, and although it officially favors "privatization," the government still controls much of the economic life, setting many prices. The discussions of relations between the nationalities in the republic have focused on the role and obligations of the government: The government must not persecute the nationalities, but what must it do for them? Leaders of both the Landsbergis and the Brazauskas administrations have talked of government laws defining freedom of the press, apparently dissatisfied with leaving the definition of the principle to the courts as guided by the constitution. The Lithuanians struggled for the decentralization of authority in the Soviet system; that decentralization has reached the point of political independence, and now they must define the scope of their own government's authority.

## Notes

1 As an example of the tensions among Catholics in Lithuania, the father of the Lithuanian composer M. K. Čiurlionis lost his life-long job as a church organist when he subscribed to Lithuanian newspapers to the disapproval of the church's Polish priest. See Jadvyga Čiurlionyte, *Vospominaniia o M. K. Chiurlenise* (Vilnius: Vaga, 1975), pp. 27–28; Jonas Basanavičius, "Autobiografija," *Lietuviu tauta* (Vilnius), 5: 95–96.

2 See V. Stanley Vardys, *The Catholic Church, Dissent and Nationality in Soviet Lithuania* (New York: Columbia University Press, 1978).

3 For a useful and interesting account of Lithuanian traditions, see Algirdas Julien Greimas and Saulius Žukas, *La Lithuanie. Un des Pays Baltes* (Vilnius: Baltos Lankos, 1993). For a useful aid in assessing the development of Lithuanian print culture in the 1920s and 1930s, see *Lietuvisku knygu sistematinis katalogas. Rinkoje esančios knygos*, ed. Isidorius Kisinas (Kaunas: Lietuvos Knygu Leidejai, 1938).

4 For a chronology of the events of 1939–1941, see Liudas Truska and Vytautas Kancevičius, *Lietuva Stalino ir Hitlerio sanderio verpetuose* (Vilnius: Mintis, 1990).

5 On the life in exile see the diary kept by Onute Garbštiene, published in English as *Hell in Ice* (Vilnius: Ethnos' 91, 1992).

6 The chronicle was published in English translation by Lithuanians in the United States. For documentation of opposition to Soviet rule, see *Nenugaletoji Lietuva*, ed. Algimantas Liekis (Vilnius: Valstybines Leidybos Centras, 1993); Tomas Remeikis, *Opposition to Soviet Rule in Lithuania 1945–1980* (Chicago: Institute of Lithuanian Studies, 1980).

7 On the events of 1987–1988, see Alfred Erich Senn, *Lithuania Awakening* (Berkeley: University of California Press, 1970), translated into Lithuania as *Lietuva bundantie* (Vilnius: Mokslas, 1992).

8 On the formation and activities of the Sajudis Initiative Group, see the group's irregular newsletter, *Sajudžio žinios*.

9 For an introduction to Sajudis politics, see the stenograms of Sajudis's Constituent Congress in October 1988, *Steigiamojo Seimo stenogramos* (Vilnius: Lietuvos Persitvarkumo Sajudis, 1988).

10 See Vadim Bakatin, *Izbavlenie ot KGB* (Moscow: Novosti, 1992), p. 49.

11 On Brazauskas's installation, see Senn, *Lithuania Awakening*, pp. 198–216.

12 See interviews with Jan Ciechanowicz in *Lithuania* (Warsaw, in Polish), (1990) 56–58, and in *LAD*, October 15, 1989; and interview with Anicet Brodowski in *Vil'nius* (Vilnius, in Russian), 2 (1991), 84–93.

13 See Brazauskas's memoirs, *Lietuviškos skyrybos* (Vilnius: Politika, 1992); Alfred Erich Senn, *Gorbachev's Failure in Lithuania* (New York: St. Martin's, 1995), pp. 49–59.

14  Brazauskas, *Lietuviškos skyrybos*, pp. 47–60.

15  On the work of the Lithuanians in the CPD and their relationship with Gorbachev, see Kazimiera Prunskiene, *Leben für Litauen* (Frankfurt: Ullstein, 1992), pp. 63–194.

16  See Brazauskas, *Lietuviškos skyrybos*, pp. 71–94.

17  For an account of the impact of Gorbachev's visit, see Alfred Erich Senn, "Gorbaciovas reklamuoja Lietuvą" and "Su Akiračių veliava," *Akiračiai*, nos. 2, 3 (1990).

18  See *Materialy plenuma tsentral'nogo komiteta KPSS. 5–7 fevralia 1990 g.* (Moscow: Politizdat, 1990).

19  See the parliamentary debates, *Lietuvos Respublikos Aukščiausiosios Tarybos (pirmojo šaukimo) Pirmoji Sesija*, vol. 1 (Vilnius: Valstybinis leidybos centros, 1990)

20  On the relations between Gorbachev and U.S. President George Bush, see Michael R Beschloss and Strobe Talbott, *At the Highest Levels* (Boston: Little, Brown and Company, 1993).

21  On the blockade see *The Road to Negotiations with the U.S.S.R.*, 2nd edn (Vilnius: State Publishing Centre, 1991), pp. 1–128; also, Senn, *Gorbachev's Failure in Lithuania*, pp. 103–114.

22  See the interview with Virgilijus Čepaitis, "Ar reikalinga Kovo 11-tos Partija?" *Akiračiai*, 10 (1990), 5.

23  On Moscow's preparations to act in Lithuania, see A. S. Cherniaev, *Shest'let s Gorbachevym* (Moscow: Progress-Kul'tura, 1993), pp. 337–339; *Nezavisimaia gazeta*, January 29, 1991.

24  For an eyewitness account of the "January events," see my *Crisis in Lithuania January 1991* (Chicago: Akiračiai, 1991).

25  See the official Soviet report, published in *Tarybu Lietuva*, June 12, 1991.

26  See Senn, *Gorbachev's Failure in Lithuania*, p. 150.

27  Declaration of the Sajudis Seimas, January 20, 1990, in Lithuanian Reform Movement Sajudis, *Lithuanian Way* (Vilnius: LPS, 1990), pp. 79–80

28  The citizenship law of November 3, 1989, was published in *Lietuva – Litva – Lithuania* (Vilnius: Atgimimas, 1989), pp. 35–46 (in the Russian edition).

29  Cf. *The New York Times*, September 5, 1991. In March 1995, Algirdas Brazauskas, now the president of Lithuania, visited Israel and made a formal public apology for the role of Lithuanians in the Holocaust of World War II. See also G. Arganovskii and I. Guzenberg, *Litovskii Ierusalim* (Vilnius: Lituanus, 1992)

30  See *Russkie v Litve – problemy i perspektivy* (Vilnius, Alena, 1992).

31  See Saulius Girnius and Anna Sabbat-Swidlicka, "Current Issues in Polish-Lithuanian Relations," in Radio Free Europe, *Report on Eastern Europe*, January 1, 1990, pp. 39–50; Steve Burant, "Polish Lithuanian Relations: Past, Present, and Future," *Problems of Communism*, May-June 1991, pp. 67–84. Cf. the interview with the Polish ambassador in Lithuania, "Istorijaistorikams, gyvenkime del ateities," *Respublika*, April 6, 1993.

32  On the character of the archive, see Romuald J. Misiunas, *The Archives of the Lithuanian KGB* (Köln: Berichte des Bundesinstituts für ostwissenschaftliche und internationale Studien, 1994); also the series "Voratinklis," published in *Lietuvos aidas* in 1992.

33  Landsbergis's speeches can be found in his *Atgavę viltį* (n.p., n.d.) and his *Laisves byla* (Vilnius: Lietuvos aidas, 1992). His proposal to establish a presidency received 69.4 percent of the vote, but it did not win the required absolute majority of registered voters since less than 60 percent of the voters had turned out.

34  See *Negotiations with the Russian Federation Concerning the Withdrawal of Russian Military Forces from the Territory of the Republic of Lithuania* (Vilnius: Supreme Council, 1992).

35  *Constitution of the Republic of Lithuania* (Vilnius: Supreme Council of Lithuania, 1992). For an ongoing review of Lithuanian politics, see *Lithuania Today: Politics &*

*Economics*, a monthly publication of the Lithuanian European Institute in Vilnius; the first issue appeared in the summer of 1992.

36 On Landsbergis's views, see also Alfred Erich Senn, "Metmenys V. Landsbergio politinei biografijai," *Akiračiai*, 1991/8; and Senn, "The Political Culture of Independent Lithuania: A Review Essay," *Journal of Baltic Studies*, 23, no. 3 (1992), 307–316.

37 *Draugas* (Chicago), September 27, 1994. Brazauskas received 60 percent of the vote. See *Lietuvos rytas*, February 17, 1993.

38 Even though the referendum failed, the political right claimed victory. See the analysis of the results in *Lietuvos aidas*, August 30, 1994. The right in fact dominated elections to organs of local self-government in the spring of 1995.

# Lithuania: chronology of events

*August 1987*
27    In Vilnius, a demonstration organized by the dissident
        Freedom League (established in 1978) protests the
        Molotov-Ribbentrop pact.

*February 1988*
16    A demonstration is held to commemorate the 70th
        anniversary of independence.
        Police harass protestors and arrest several leaders.

*June 1988*
        Sajudis is founded.
14    Sajudis and the Freedom League hold separate
        demonstrations in remembrance of the mass deportations of
        1941.
24    20,000 gather at a rally organized by Sajudis and attended
        by several delegates to the 19th Party Conference, including
        Algirdas Brazauskas, a Central Committee Secretary.

*July 1988*
        100,000 Lithuanians attend a rally in Vilnius to hear
        a report from Lithuanian participants in the party
        conference.

*October 1988*
22–24    Sajudis holds its founding congress.
           Brazauskas is elected First Secretary of the Communist
           Party.

*January 1989*
        A rally in Lithuania calls for the removal of all Soviet
        troops from the Baltics.

*February 1989*
        Sajudis calls for full sovereignty.

*March 1989*
        Sajudis wins 36 of Lithuania's 42 seats in elections to the
        USSR Congress of People's Deputies.

*May 1989*
18    The Supreme Soviet adopts a law on sovereignty.

*August 1989*

22 Lithuania declares that the 1940 annexation to the USSR is invalid.

23 Almost two million demonstrators in the Baltics participate in a human chain of protest on the 50th anniversary of the Molotov-Ribbentrop pact.

*November 1989*

3 Citizenship law is passed which makes all residents in 1989 eligible for citizenship.

*December 1989*

21 The Lithuanian Communist Party secedes from the USSR Communist Party.
The Lithuanian legislature votes 243–1 to abolish the clause in its constitution which grants the Communist Party a monopoly on power.

*February 1990*

24 In elections to the Supreme Soviet, Sajudis-backed candidates win approximately 80 percent of the seats. The Lithuanian Supreme Soviet is the first republican government to be freely elected in the USSR.
Vytautas Landsbergis is chosen chairman of the Supreme Council. Kazimiera Prunskiene is appointed prime minister. Brazauskas and Ozolas become deputy prime ministers.

*March 1990*

11 The Lithuanian Supreme Soviet declares Lithuania to be an independent state by a vote of 124–0 (with six abstentions). A non-communist, Vytautas Landsbergis, is elected president. Gorbachev announces that the declaration is illegal and insists that the republic can only secede after a referendum with a two-thirds "yes" vote, a five-year waiting period, and approval of the Soviet parliament.

*April 1990*

An embargo on oil and gas supplies to the republic is initiated by Gorbachev.

*June 1990*

Landsbergis announces a moratorium on the independence declaration, and the embargo is lifted.

*December 1990*

Changes are made to the language law to provide for a

more gradual transition to Lithuanian in non-Lithuanian areas.
The Lithuanian Communist Party changes its name to the Democratic Labor Party.

*January 1991*

Soviet paratroopers move into Lithuania.

8   Russian workers storm the parliament building but are pushed back by a mass of unarmed citizens.

11  Prunskiene resigns in the face of an upcoming no-confidence vote over recent price hikes. She is replaced by Albertas Simenas.

12–13  Soviet troops take control of the Vilnius TV tower and station. When confronted by a mass of protestors, they fire on the crowd, killing fifteen people. Gorbachev claims he did not order the violence.
Simenas disappears and is replaced by the more nationalist Gediminas Vagnorius. 200,000 rally in Moscow to protest Lithuanian crack-down and call for Gorbachev to resign.

*February 1991*

9   In a referendum on independence, more than 90 percent vote in favor.

*May 1991*

200,000 rally for Lithuanian independence in Vilnius.

*June 1991*

Soviet troops set up checkpoints in Vilnius. Lithuanians hold a vigil around the parliament building in Vilnius to help prevent an army attack.

*July 1991*

30  Six Lithuanian border guards are murdered by Soviet OMON troops.

*August 1991*

21  Parliament reaffirms is 1990 declaration of independence and bans the Communist Party.
The National Independence Front is formed in Lithuania. Lithuania demands the removal of Soviet forces from its territory.

*September 1991*

6   The Soviet government recognizes Lithuania's independence.

*October 1991*

5   The Baltic Council, comprised of the leaders of Lithuania,

Latvia, and Estonia, issues a joint statement demanding the immediate withdrawal of Soviet troops from their territories.

*December 1991*

11    A citizenship law which was passed on 6 December takes effect. All those who resided in Lithuania prior to 15 June 1940, as well as their descendants who are residing in Lithuania; all those who received citizenship by 3 November 1991 according to previous legislation; and all those who fulfill the law's requirements are automatically granted citizenship. To be naturalized, residents must demonstrate a working knowledge of Lithuanian and have lived in Lithuania for the past ten years.

*Janurary 1992*

30    The 25-member Sajudis faction, the largest in parliament, splits with the formation of the Sajudis Santaros faction which takes ten deputies.

*February 1992*

1–2    Russia agrees to withdraw the 100,000 troops estimated to be stationed in the Baltic states.

*March 1992*

6    The Council of Baltic Sea States (including the Baltic states plus seven others) is established.

*May 1992*

16    Prime Minister Vagnorius declares his intent to resign, citing his inability to govern in the face of left-wing parliamentary opposition.

17    Thousands of Sajudis supporters gather in Vilnius in support of the 23 May referendum on establishing a strong presidency.

23    While 69 percent of those voting (58 percent turnout) support the adoption of a strong presidency, the referendum fails as it does not gather a majority of all eligible voters.

26    Landsbergis accuses left-wing opposition of planning a "creeping coup" and calls for new parliamentary elections and a three-month freeze on replacing high officials.

*June 1992*

14    In a referendum, an overwhelming majority of voters support the removal of Soviet troops by the end of the year.

*July 1992*

14    Prime Minister Vagnorious resigns.

21    Aleksandras Abisala is elected Prime Minister.

*August 1992*
6    Russia asks for $7.7 billion from the Baltic states in exchange for withdrawing its troops from the region by 1994.

*September 1992*
8    Landsbergis and Yeltsin sign an agreement arranging for the removal of all Soviet troops by September 1993.

*October 1992*
1    Temporary coupons are issued to take the place of the ruble until the national currency, the *litas*, is introduced.
25    Elections to parliament (the 141-seat Seimas) and a referendum on the constitution are held. Following second-round elections in November, the Lithuanian Democratic Labor Party (the former Communists) wins 73 seats. Second-place Sajudis wins 30. On the referendum, 75 percent of those voting support the constitution and the establishment of a strong presidency.

*November 1992*
25    Algirdas Brazauskas, the LDLP head, is elected chairman of the Seimas and acting president by a vote of 81–4.
26    Prime Minister Aleksandras Abisala and his cabinet resign.

*December 1992*
2    Bronislovas Lubys is chosen as Prime Minister.

*February 1993*
14    In presidential elections, Brazauskas is elected president, defeating Landsbergis's endorsed candidate Stasys Lozoraitis, the ambassador to the United States.
25    Jursenas is confirmed chairman of parliament.
26    Lubys resigns and is replaced by Adolfas Slezevicius.

*April 1993*
The Homeland Union (Conservative Party), led by Landsbergis and Vagnorious, is founded.

*June 1993*
Lithuania becomes a member of the Council of Europe.

*July 1993*
20    The litas replaces the temporary coupon as the sole legal tender.

*August 1993*
    31    Russia meets the deadline to withdraw all of its troops from Lithuanian soil.

*May 1994*
    23    Gediminas Vagnorious, chairman of the Homeland Union, reports that the necessary 300,000 signatures have been gathered to hold a referendum on illegal privatization and compensation of savings.

*June 1994*
    2    Prime Minister Adolfas Slezevicius announces that his government will resign as more than half of his cabinet is to be changed.
    13    The Baltic states establish a joint Baltic Council of Ministers.
    16    The government survives a no-confidence vote 51–65 (71 needed to pass).

*August 1994*
    27    The Fatherland-sponsored referendum fails due to low voter turnout (37 percent).

*November 1994*
    13    The Baltic Assembly issues a statement regarding the need to demilitarize the Russian Kaliningrad oblast and restore its cities' historical German names.

*March 1995*
    25    In local elections to 1,488 seats, the Homeland Union wins the most seats at 426, followed by the LDLP at 297 and the Christian Democratic Party (247).

*April 1995*
    12    Lithuania becomes an associate member of the European Union.

# 10 Latvia: restoring a state, rebuilding a nation

NILS MUIZNIEKS

Moscow recognized the independence of Estonia, Latvia, and Lithuania on September 6, 1991, thereby formally bringing to an end Soviet rule in the Baltic states. This was the second time the Soviet central government recognized Baltic independence this century; the first recognition came under Lenin, when the Soviet Union signed peace treaties in 1920 renouncing "forever" all claims to Baltic territory. "Forever" lasted but twenty years, as Stalin annexed the Baltic States in 1940. Independence signifies a reversal of the consequences of World War II for the Balts and a restoration of the status quo ante. Here, we consider the events that led to the second incarnation of the Latvian state and post-independence efforts to undo the legacy of Soviet rule.

A broad-based Latvian nationalist movement emerged soon after Mikhail Gorbachev assumed power in 1985 and initiated liberalizing reforms in the Soviet Union. Diverse groupings coalesced into a Popular Front in 1988 that sought to promote perestroika and the decentralization of authority from Moscow. In short order, however, the movement came to espouse the more far-reaching goals of democracy and the restoration of independence. The goal of independence came to have virtually unanimous support among ethnic Latvians and substantial backing among the other nationalities in the republic. The neutrality or support of non-Latvians was critical for the movement's success: Latvians constituted only 52.0 percent of the 2,666,567 inhabitants of the republic in 1989. Russians comprised the bulk of the remainder with 34.0 percent, followed by Belarusans with 4.5 percent, Ukrainians with 3.5 percent, and Poles with 2.3 percent.[1]

The impetus for independence was varied. For Latvians fearful of demographic minoritization and linguistic Russification due to Slavic immigration, independence signified control over Latvia's borders and expanded opportunities to nurture Latvian culture. Representatives of all nationalities could agree on the desirability of separation from the Soviet social order, based on the Communist Party and central planning, and the creation of a new order, based on democracy and the market. For many, faith in the viability of an independent Latvia rested on the memory of the twenty-year period of statehood between the two world wars. The independence move-

## Latvia

—— International boundary
★ National capital
—— Railroad
—— Road

*Latvia has no internal administrative divisions.*

0        50 Kilometers
0        50 Miles

*Lambert Conformal Conic Projection, SP 47N/62N*

**Baltic
Sea**

**Gulf
of
Riga**

*Irbe Strait*

**ESTONIA**

*Lake
Peipus*

*Lake
Pskov*

**SOVIET
UNION**

**LITHUANIA**

**SOVIET
UNION**

Hiiumaa
Haapsalu
Leie
Paide
Mustvee
Gdov
Sareyere
Jõgeva
Muhu
Virtsu
Võhma
Pärnu
Viljandi
Vorts-
Järv
Tartu
Kihnu
Elva
Põlva
Rūjiena
Valga
Võru
Pechory
Pskov
Aloja
Burtnieku
Ezers
Ostrov
Kolka
Ruhnu/
Saar
Valmiera
Strenci
Limbaži
Alūksne
Ventspils
Mērsrags
Cēsis
Ugale
Stende
Sigulda
Gulbene
Pyatalovo
Jūrkalne
Kuldīga
Tukums
Jūrmala
**Riga★**
Ogre
Ērgļi
Lubāna
Kārsava
Skrunda
Saldus
Skrīveri
Pļaviņas
Lubānas
Ezers
Liepāja
Dobele
Jelgava
Jēkabpils
Rēzekne
Ludza
Zilupe
Eleja
Bauska
Rāznas
Ezers
Mažeikiai
Biržai
Krāslava
Kuršenai
Joniškėlis
Pandelys
Palanga
Telšiai
Pakruoj
Šiauliai
Panemunelis
Daugavpils
Kretinga
Druya
Klaipėda
Radviliškis
Turmantas
Voropayevo
Kelmė
Panevėžys
Dūkštas
Šilutė
Utena
Tauragė
Kēdainiai
Ukmergė
Soвetsk
Jonava
Postavy

Final boundaries of Estonia, Latvia, and
Lithuania with the USSR are expected
to be confirmed by agreement.

ment was imbued with the historical memory of that era and the violence that attended its closing.

## Latvia before Soviet power

A modern Latvian national consciousness emerged only in the latter half of the nineteenth century when the territory of Latvia was a province of the Russian empire. Baltic German barons held the leading political and economic posts, and the vast majority of Latvians were peasants. The small but active Latvian intelligentsia considered the Baltic German nobility to be its primary adversary. Many Latvian activists welcomed the erosion of Baltic German control over provincial life that was a consequence of the crown's policy of Russification after the 1880's. By 1905, national development had brought Latvians to the point of demanding autonomy within the Russian empire. Widespread peasant and worker unrest that year evoked harsh punitive expeditions by the imperial army, leading a part of the intelligentsia to begin formulating more far-reaching political goals.[2]

World War I and the collapse of the Russian Empire provided the opportunity for the proclamation of an independent Latvian state in 1918. The 1920 peace treaty with the Soviet Union guaranteed the new state's integrity. The Republic of Latvia soon gained international recognition, pursued a neutral foreign policy, and became a member of the League of Nations.[3] In domestic policy, Latvia was notable for its radical land reform, rapid economic growth based on agricultural exports, and progressive welfare system. From 1920 to 1934, Latvia had a parliamentary democracy in which the Social Democrats were the largest single political party. As in much of Eastern Europe during that era, however, the Great Depression engendered social tensions and political polarization that set the stage for authoritarianism. Karlis Ulmanis, one of the founders of Latvia, engineered a bloodless coup in 1934 and ruled through the bureaucracy and the army until World War II. The mild authoritarianism of Ulmanis's regime contrasted starkly with developments to the East, where Stalin was pursuing policies of collectivization, forced draft industrialization, and political terror that took millions of lives.

## From independent state to Soviet republic

The signing of the Molotov-Ribbentrop Pact by Nazi Germany and the Soviet Union on August 23, 1939, marked the beginning of the Soviet encroachment on Latvia's sovereignty. A secret protocol of the pact placed Latvia, along with Estonia and Lithuania, in the Soviet sphere of influence. Soon thereafter, the three Baltic governments submitted to growing Soviet intimidation and signed mutual assistance treaties allowing Soviet bases and troops on their territories. As in postwar Eastern Europe, the presence of Soviet troops was followed by terror and rigged elections. The hand-picked Baltic governments soon tendered requests to join the Soviet Union, which were quickly granted in August of 1940. The following months wit-nessed coordinated campaigns of Sovietization in all three Baltic republics, capped by massive deportations. On one night alone – June 13–14, 1941 – around 15,000 individuals were deported from Latvia to the GULag. Total population losses stemming from deportations, executions, and evacuations during the first year of Soviet occupation have been estimated at over 30,000.[4]

When German forces attacked the USSR and invaded the Baltic republics at the end of June in 1941, many Latvians welcomed them. Some Latvians did so because they were right-wing extremists; most, however, felt a sense of relief that further Soviet terror and deportations would be halted, and many of them hoped that the new invaders might permit the restoration of independence. Nazi Germany had no interest in restoring Latvia's inde-pendence; rather, the new occupiers sought to use Latvia's human and economic resources for their own purposes. While some Latvians suffered under Nazi rule, others participated in one of the darkest chapters of Lat-via's history: collaboration with the Nazis in exterminating most of the local Jewish population.[5]

The return of the Soviet army in 1944 led over 100,000 people to flee for the West. Thousands more resisted, either fighting alongside the retreating Germans or engaging in guerilla warfare. As the Red Army destroyed all resistance, the Soviet authorities reintroduced their own distinctive brand of terror. In 1945–1946, an estimated 60,000 people were deported from Latvia, to be followed by 43,000 more during collectivization in 1949.[6] The armed guerilla resistance was wiped out by the early 1950s, though passive resistance continued for years. The extreme violence employed to cow the population into submission continues to shape both ethnic and inter-state Russian-Latvian relations to this day.

Some Russians in Latvia came to brand any anti-Soviet or anti-Russian sentiment among Latvians as a manifestation of fascism. Many Latvians, on the other hand, came to associate the brutality of Stalinism with Russians. The alien ethos of the new regime in Latvia was intensified by Soviet cadres policy. Those members of the Latvian elite that had not fled to the West or perished in the GULag were little trusted by the authorities. The Communist Party of Latvia (CPL) was minuscule when the Soviets arrived, numbering less than 1,000 in 1940 and perhaps 5,000 in 1945.[7] These factors pushed the authorities to import Russian and Soviet-born and Soviet-educated Russian Latvians to fill leading posts in in the immediate post-war era. Members of the latter group often spoke no Latvian, and but for their names, were indistinguishable from Russians. Thus, embedded in the Stalinist political system was an element of ethnic domination: as Russian cadres dominated politics in Moscow, Russians and Russian Latvians assumed most of the key posts in the local Latvian power structure.[8]

## Latvia under Khrushchev and Brezhnev

From 1957 to 1959, during the Khrushchev thaw, "national communists" briefly gained the upper hand within the leadership of the Communist Party of Latvia. Led by Deputy Chairman of the Council of Ministers Eduards Berklavs, this group attempted to slow the influx of Slavic settlers into Latvia, promote native cadres, expand the use of the Latvian language in the educational system and in party affairs, and increase republican autonomy in management of the economy. This attempt to put a Latvian face on communist rule was quelled in the summer of 1959, when Berklavs and nearly 2,000 other officials were purged.[9] The Communist Party of Latvia never truly recovered a national face after the purge. The figures on the nationality composition of the CPL bear this out: as late as early 1989, well before the CPL crumbled, Latvians accounted for only 39.7 percent of the 184,182 party members and candidates, less than the Russian share of 43.1 percent.[10]

The 1959 purge was a turning point in postwar Latvian history. It doomed party nativization and economic experimentation and marked the onset of stepped up immigration and a renewed campaign of cultural Russification that would last for the next thirty years. Many Latvians came to associate the subsequent era and its pathologies with the leadership of two Russian Latvians: Arvids Pelse and Augusts Voss.

From 1960 to the late 1980s, Pelse and Voss presided over the rapid growth of heavy industry for which the republic's supply of labor, raw materials, and consumption patterns were unsuited. For example, the percentage of all industrial workers in Latvia employed in the labor intensive sectors of machine construction and metal work rose from 26.4 percent in 1960 to 39.4 percent in 1980.[11] This development strategy required the importation of workers from other republics.

Unfortunately, data on migration flows in the late 1940s are unavailable. However, Latvia did witness substantial migration to and from other Soviet republics throughout the rest of the post-war era (see table 10.1). Immigration exceeded emigration almost every year until 1989, when the pattern was reversed. As suggested by the figures in table 10.2, the overwhelming majority of immigrants were eastern Slavs (Russians, Belarusans, Ukrainians), whose combined share of Latvia's population rose from 10.3 percent in 1935 to 42.0 percent in 1989. As a result of non-native immigration, Latvian wartime losses, post-war deportations and low birth rates, the Latvian share of the population fell from 77.0 percent in 1935 to 52.0 percent by 1989.

Table 10.1. *Migration flows into and out of Latvia, 1951–1988 (thousands)*

|           | Arrived | Departed | Net immig. | Avg./yr |
|-----------|---------|----------|------------|---------|
| 1951–1960 | 377.2   | 307.6    | 69.6       | 7.0     |
| 1961–1970 | 327.4   | 220.8    | 106.6      | 10.7    |
| 1971–1980 | 389.2   | 290.6    | 98.6       | 9.9     |
| 1981–1988 | 283.2   | 202.9    | 80.3       | 8.0     |

*Source:* LR Valsts Statistikas Komiteja, *Latvija Skaitlos/Latvia in Figures 1992* (Riga, 1993), p. 32.

Table 10.2. *The ethnic composition of Latvia, 1935–1989 (percentage of the total population)*

|            | 1935 | 1959 | 1979 | 1989 |
|------------|------|------|------|------|
| Latvians   | 77.0 | 62.0 | 53.7 | 52.0 |
| Russians   | 8.8  | 26.6 | 32.8 | 34.0 |
| Belarusans | 1.4  | 2.9  | 4.5  | 4.5  |
| Ukrainians | 0.1  | 1.4  | 2.7  | 3.5  |
| Poles      | 2.5  | 2.9  | 2.5  | 2.3  |
| Others     | 10.2 | 4.2  | 3.8  | 3.7  |

*Source: Etnosituācija Latvijā, Fakti un Komentāri* (Riga: LR Valsts Statistikas Komiteja and Zinatnu Akademijas Filozofijas and Sociologijas Instituts, 1994), p. 4.

The influx of Slavic immigrants, the declining share of Latvians, and Soviet policies of Russification transformed the linguistic environment. Most Latvians and other non-Russians were compelled to learn Russian, while most non-Latvians had neither the incentive nor the opportunity to learn Latvian. The Soviet authorities had destroyed the interwar cultural infrastructure of Latvia's non-Russian minorities, thereby facilitating their linguistic Russification. As a consequence, many non-Latvians became monolingual speakers of Russian, while most Latvians became bilingual speakers of their native language and Russian.

By the last Soviet census in 1989, 68.7 percent of all Latvians claimed a command of Russian, while only 22.3 percent of all Russians claimed a knowledge of Latvian. Latvian-language knowledge among members of the three next largest ethnic groups ranged from 9.8 percent among Ukrainians, 18.0 percent among Belarusans, to 37.6 percent among Poles. Many members of these groups had adopted Russian as their native language. This was the case among 64.7 percent of all Belarusans, 49.3 percent of all

Ukrainians, and 54.2 percent of all Poles. Only 62.3 percent of the total population claimed knowledge of Latvian, while 81.6 percent claimed to know Russian in 1989.[12]

Discontent with hyper-industrialization, Slavic immigration, Russification, and other pathologies of communist rule in Latvia could not be openly voiced before the era of glasnost in the late 1980s. Indeed, the few dissidents that raised the banner of nationalism or democracy during the 1970's were harshly repressed.[13] Unlike their Lithuanian counterparts, Latvian dissidents lacked an organizational base such as the Catholic Church. Open resistance was rare. Despite the pressures outlined above, there was little assimilation: 97.4 percent of Latvians considered Latvian their native language in 1989. The large proportion of non-native immigrants in the republic, however, led to a relatively high proportion of mixed marriages, indicating a slow erosion of Latvian group boundaries. In the 1980s, about 20 percent of all marriages involving a Latvian were mixed – one of the highest shares for the titular nationality of any union republic.[14] The overwhelming majority of Latvians, however, neither assimilated nor actively joined the ranks of the dissidents.

A more common response appeared to be either a turn to consumerism or cultural activism. Latvia and its Baltic neighbors consistently had the highest relative levels of consumption per capita of all the union republics,[15] a feature that might have blunted some political dissatisfaction during the Khrushchev and Brezhnev years. While some Latvians might have turned to consumerism, others sought refuge from the pressures for political conformity in culture. By the mid-1970s, the vibrant Latvian cultural scene led some Western observers to detect in Latvian efforts to protect and extend their cultural values a "conscious commitment to nationalism."[16] While some of Latvia's cultural output had political undertones, there is little evidence that most cultural activity exemplified more than an affirmation of humanistic values against the dead hand of Soviet ideology. Ultimately, any judgements about the political significance of consumerism or cultural activism during the Brezhnev years fall into the realm of speculation. Other than the economic and demographic data, the only "hard" evidence about the state of the Latvian nation before perestroika comes from interviews with emigres.

One study conducted in the early 1980s asked respondents about their perception of trends in the "power of the local nationality" in the non-Russian republics. Of the respondents mentioning the Baltic republics, 59 percent perceived the power of the Baltic nationalities to be decreasing, as Russians immigrated more, held the decisive positions in society, and imposed their culture on natives. The perception of decreasing power in the Baltics contrasted sharply with the perceived gains or stable positions of other republican nationalities.[17] It was only under Gorbachev that circumstances would permit Latvians to act to recoup their power position and voice their grievances about Soviet policy in Latvia since World War II.

## Latvia at the dawn of the Gorbachev era: 1985–1987

One of Gorbachev's first moves as general secretary was to accelerate the personnel changes begun under Andropov as a means of breaking up entrenched republican machines and reasserting central control in the periphery after the "benign neglect" of the Brezhnev years.[18] In Latvia, the post of first secretary had already changed hands in 1984 with the accession of Boris Pugo, the Russian Latvian former KGB chief in the republic. Far-reaching personnel turnover in Latvia was implemented in the first two years of Gorbachev's reign with the passing away and retirement of many beneficiaries of the 1959 purges. Key changes in 1985 included the rise of moderate Latvians Anatolijs Gorbunovs and Janis Vagris to the posts of Central Committee secretary for ideology and chairman of the Presidium of the Supreme Soviet, respectively.[19] While Gorbachev was reasserting central control on personnel matters, he was loosening control in other realms by reducing official coercion and advocating glasnost.

The impact of glasnost in Latvia, as in the other Baltic republics, was profound. When Gorbachev legitimized a reevaluation of history, especially that of the Stalin era, he unwittingly gave Baltic activists the sanction to question the circumstances of the Soviet annexation of the Baltic states, and thus, the legitimacy of Soviet rule. Glasnost in Latvia was given a boost from outside actors when a conference on US-Soviet relations organized by the Chautauqua Institution, the Eisenhower World Affairs Institute, and the USSR–USA Society, took place September 15–19, 1986, in Jurmala, Latvia. The town-hall type conference featured speeches in which American representatives reaffirmed their government's non-recognition of the Soviet annexation of the Baltic states.[20] The event also spurred unofficial activism: several Latvian dissidents attempted to create a nationalist organization called Helsinki '86 and submit complaints to the conference, for which they received several-month prison terms.

Soon after the conference ended, unofficial activists of a less controversial nature – environmentalists – took advantage of the opportunities provided by glasnost. In Latvia, as in many areas of the Soviet Union, one of the first issues to elicit mass protest was environmental destruction. Why the environment became an early focus of discontent throughout the Soviet Union is not difficult to understand. The Chernobyl disaster and the slow official reporting on its effects evoked outrage and suspicion that the authorities were covering up other health hazards as well. From a political point of view, environmentalism was a relatively safe topic. It could be portrayed as a matter of efficiency and the rational employment of resources – technical, not political problems. Moreover, the environment could bring together activists of widely divergent ideological inclinations: nationalists decrying the rape of their native soil and technocrats concerned with economic rationality.

In Latvia, the specific issue that elicited a popular outcry was the construction of a hydroelectric dam on Latvia's most cherished river, the Daugava. Popular mobilization against the project was sparked when journalist Dainis Ivans and writer Arturs Snips published an article criticizing the project in a mid-October 1986 issue of a popular Latvian-language cultural weekly. In the following months, a debate about the project raged in the weekly, and grass-roots activists organized meetings and a letter-writing campaign against the project. Over 30,000 people of all nationalities signed letters protesting the dam – an astounding achievement for that period. The public outcry led the Latvian Council of Ministers to set up a commission to review the project, which was finally canceled in the summer of 1987.[21] The campaign was a critical experience of empowerment for many activists. It was, for example, the political baptism of Dainis Ivans, who was later elected president of the Popular Front.

Public activism against the dam coincided with the emergence of several independent association, some of which had distinctly political and nationalist agendas. A small group of mostly young, Latvian counterculture activists that had been organizing expeditions to repair old churches and monuments since 1984 coalesced into the Environmental Protection Club (VAK) in 1987. In many ways, VAK resembled Western green movements, with their holistic approach to the environment, inclusiveness, aversion to structure, and disdain for authority. VAK lent a political coloring to ecological activism by linking it to democratization. The group's manifesto stated that "democratization is not a dessert that will be brought to us on a platter from Moscow. Democratization will have to be won by struggle in every factory, farm, or office . . ."[22] At the outset, however, VAK was tame in comparison to Helsinki '86, which regrouped in early 1987 after its founders were released from incarceration as part of a broader amnesty of political prisoners throughout the USSR.

Helsinki '86 was the first openly nationalist unofficial organization to appear in Gorbachev-era Latvia.[23] Small in membership and harshly repressed by the regime, Helsinki '86 wrote letters to Moscow, appeals to the West, and assorted memoranda. It called for the restoration of Latvia's independence, an end to the Sovietization and Russification of Latvia, and observance of international human rights norms. Denied access to the media, the group reached only a limited audience through the circulation of *samizdat*. In the summer and fall of 1987, however, Helsinki '86 created shock waves throughout Latvia by organizing demonstrations in the heart of Riga at the Freedom Monument, a symbol of Latvia's independence. The "calendar demonstrations" were organized to publicly commemorate the anniversaries of key events in Latvian history: the deportations of June

14, 1941, the signing of the Molotov-Ribbentrop Pact on August 23, 1939, and the declaration of Latvia's independence on November 18, 1918. Despite the detention of several organizers and official harassment, thousands participated, attesting to the latent support for nationalism among the Latvian population.[24]

Though several Helsinki '86 activists were exiled to the West and those remaining in Latvia were to play only marginal roles in subsequent events, the group was extraordinarily influential during the gestation period of the Latvian nationalist movement in 1987. Helsinki '86 provided a heroic example by facing down fear, repression, and official threats to openly advocate nationalist goals. It articulated numerous demands that would later gain wide currency: the elevation of Latvian to the status of state language, the halt to unregulated immigration from other republics, and, ultimately, the restoration of Latvia's independence. Both Helsinki '86 and VAK pioneered the use of non-violent demonstrations, petition campaigns, appeals to international law, and the delegitimation of Soviet rule by filling in historical "blank spots" – tactics that came to be employed by the broader Latvian nationalist movement in following years.

Groups such as Helsinki '86 and VAK, however, could not attract a mass following in the absence of media coverage. Composed primarily of counterculture youth, they were short on skilled professionals and political savvy. Though some links between these "informal groups" and the official cultural, academic and media elite had been forged during the campaign against the hydroelectric dam in 1986–1987, it was only in 1988 that the intelligentsia jumped on the nationalist bandwagon.

## The emergence of a mass nationalist movement: 1988

At the beginning of 1988, the intelligentsia took the lead in reexamining and commemorating the historical events that occasioned the demonstrations of the previous summer. In early March, the Writers' Union established two commissions to rehabilitate victims of Stalinism. More significantly, the cultural unions organized an official demonstration at the end of the month commemorating the 1949 demonstrations. Official sanction for the ceremony opened the floodgates of popular participation, and some 25,000 people attended the ceremony.[25] Soon thereafter, the Latvian cultural elite followed the example of its Estonian counterpart, which had already begun to engage in political activity outside the confines of the Communist Party.[26]

The Latvian cultural elite entered the political arena at an expanded plenum of the Writers' Union on June 1–2 devoted to "Pressing Problems of Soviet Latvian Culture on the Eve of the 19th CPSU Conference."[27] The most prominent theme was the perceived threat of Latvian ethnic annihilation. The sense of looming disaster was highlighted in numerous speeches decrying immigration and its demographic consequences, linguistic Russ-ification, economic centralization, and environmental degradation. Numer-ous taboos were broken: one speaker called the events of 1940 an "occu-pation"; several condemned Russian chauvinism; others openly criticized the Party leadership. Though the plenum served as a forum for the pent-up grievances of almost fifty years, it also produced a detailed resolution chart-ing a course of action and witnessed the first effort to create an autonomous political organization.[28]

The resolution was a comprehensive political program calling for Lat-via's "sovereignty" within the Soviet Union. At that stage, "sovereignty" was understood to entail local control over the natural resources, budget, borders, and foreign policy of the republic. While decentralization was por-trayed as being in the interests of all of Latvia's inhabitants, the resolution unequivocally demanded priority status for Latvians. The CPL and the government were urged to consider one of their main tasks to be "the preservation and renewal of the Latvian nation." Moreover, pointing to the precedents of Georgia, Armenia, and Azerbaijan, the resolution rec-ommended that Latvian be granted the status of state language. National demands were accompanied by liberal democratic ones, such as the demand to halt censorship, guarantee the inviolability of postal and other forms of communication, separate the legislative and executive branches of govern-ment, and support the nomination to leading posts of non-Party members.

The plenum witnessed the first moves towards the creation of a new political organization to implement the resolution. An initiative group led by journalist Viktors Avotins circulated a document arguing the need for a "democratic popular front of Latvia."[29] The committee charged with pre-paring the plenum's resolution deleted any mention of a front from the text, marking the start of a complicated game of cat-and-mouse by the Communist Party leadership, the cultural elite, and the informal groups. The Party was on the defensive thereafter.

Decisive action on the part of the Party leadership in Latvia was compli-cated by a number of factors. After the Nina Andreyeva controversy pitted Stalinists against reformers within the all-Union political elite, Moscow began sending mixed signals. At the local level, the leadership of the CPL reacted in confusion to popular mobilization. The leaked minutes of a crisis Central Committee plenum of the CPL on June 18 revealed a leadership deeply divided and fearful of reform "from below."[30] Despite signs of growing disarray, the Party apparatus successfully stymied numerous efforts to create a popular front initiative group over the next month.

In late July and early August, however, a front organizing committee eluded Party tutelage by finding refuge in the Writers' and Artists' Unions, from which the expertise of lawyers, economists, and other skilled pro-fessionals could be tapped.[31] The climate for activism improved after an early August visit by liberal politburo member Aleksandr Yakovlev, who seems to have told the Party leadership in Latvia to stop resisting the inevitable and take a more active role in influencing events.[32] The first chairman of the Popular Front, Dainis Ivans, later recalled that "in August, in many factories, the Party committees urged workers to join the TF [Popular Front]; many of these tried to disrupt work at the first Congress."[33]

The leaders of the informal groups, especially of Helsinki '86 and VAK, remained suspicious of the establishment intellectuals and reform communists organizing the popular front during the summer. Considering the idea of independence rather than democracy to be of the utmost priority, some of the more militant members of the informal groups had already founded "Latvia's National Independence Movement" (LNNK) in late June.[34] Despite the suspicions of the militants and the Party's efforts to maintain some influence, the front initiative group rapidly gathered force. By September 20, 2,300 Popular Front local chapters had formed with over 80,000 members.[35] At the same time, hundreds of thousands of people participated in letter-writing campaigns to legalize the national flag and make Latvian the state language.[36]

Faced with this groundswell of organizational activity and popular mobilization, Moscow and the republican leadership moved to defuse popular discontent. On September 29, the Supreme Soviet declared Latvian the state language and legalized the long-banned independence-era national flag.[37] On the eve of the front's founding congress, Moscow intervened to shuffle the republic's leadership in preparation for more trying political times. Boris Pugo was promoted to head the Party Control Commission in Moscow, Janis Vagris became first secretary of the CPL, and Anatolijs Gorbunovs became the chairman of the Supreme Soviet. These personnel shifts weakened the conservatives, signalled the vulnerability of the regime to mobilization, and rendered the founding congress an occasion for celebration.

On October 8–9, 1988, over 1,000 delegates representing 115,000 dues paying members of over 2,300 local chapters convened in Riga for the founding congress of the Popular Front of Latvia (LTF). Eighty-eight percent of the delegates were ethnic Latvians; one third were members of the Communist Party.[38] Though new CPL leader Vagris addressed the gathering, so did representatives of Helsinki '86, VAK, LNNK, and religious groups. The assembled delegates gave speeches; adopted statutes, a program, and resolutions; and elected a leadership body.[39]

The program went beyond the resolution adopted by the Writers' plenum and placed the Front more clearly in competition with the Communist Party, stating that the LTF "does not recognize as democratic the monopoly rights of any political organization to rule society and public life." Political sovereignty, according to the program, entailed the republic's right to veto legislation affecting its interests. Economic sovereignty would permit Latvia to issue its own currency after a shift to republican self-financing on

January 1, 1990. The program was also more assertive in demanding a Latvian ethnic veto by guaranteeing Latvians a majority vote in representative bodies at all levels. Moreover, the program called on the Latvian government to promote the voluntary return of immigrants (in the euphemistic parlance of that time, "victims of Stalinist nationality policy") to their places of origin – a demand bound to raise the shackles of immigrant Slavs. Though the program asserted Latvian prerogatives, it also supported the right of all nationalities to cultural autonomy (including minority-language schooling).

Janis Peters, the influential head of the Writers' Union, turned down the chairmanship of the Front and nominated Dainis Ivans, the journalist who rose to prominence in the campaign against the hydro-electric dam. The congress endorsed Ivans and elected a ninety-nine member Governing Council, which, in turn, elected an eighteen member board to run the day-to-day affairs of the Popular Front. The board came from diverse backgrounds: most members were Latvian, two were Russian, and one was Jewish. It contained prominent radicals such as Eduards Berklavs, the "national communist" purged in 1959 who had recently joined LNNK, and Ints Calitis, a dissident active in VAK. It also featured several party members, including the editor of the Latvian-language Komsomol daily. In theory, all major decisions required approval of the Governing Council. In practice, the board and its staff were to become the key actors in formulating policy, maintaining contacts with local chapters, and dealing with the republic's leadership.

## The Popular Front ascendant

Although Communist Party first secretary Janis Vagris had pledged to cooperate with the Front at its congress, the Central Committee issued a statement several days later criticizing the anti-Soviet and secessionist calls made at the congress and expressing concern about the underrepresentation of members of the Russian-speaking community in the Front and its leadership.[40] Indeed, attracting the support of the republic's non-Latvian populaton was one of the most serious challenges leadership of the Front faced.

The overwhelming majority of the Front's eventual membership of 200,000 to 300,000 members (perhaps as many as 90 percent) were Latvians.[41] Though the leadership and program of the Front were moderate, anti-immigrant sentiment was strong among the membership at large. Even progressive members of the Russian-speaking community could be expected to have strong qualms about the Front, whose program was based on the priority of the Latvian nation. The Russian-speaking masses could not be expected to yield their privileged status on language issues and the like without a fight.

To stave off this brewing conflict, the Popular Front's leaders moved quickly to assure minority groups (and Russians in particular) that they supported minority cultural autonomy and sought to foster interethnic dialogue. In November and early December 1988, the Popular Front supported the foundation of eighteen National Cultural Societies for Russians, Poles, Jews, and other minority groups.[42] Then, in cooperation with the Communist Party leadership, the Popular Front helped to organize a Nationalities Forum in early December to air ethnic grievances.[43] Despite these efforts to reach out to minority populations, large segments of the Russian-speaking community remained passive or outright hostile towards the Popular Front. Ethnic polarization had already begun with the Writers' plenum, where the Russian-speaking community heard the pent-up grievances of Latvians for the first time. Polarization accelerated, however, soon after the founding of the Popular Front, when a Russian-dominated "Internationalist Front of the Workers of the Latvian SSR" (Interfront) emerged.[44] The Interfront,[45] which held its founding congress in January 1989, cast itself as the defender of the Russian-speaking community, though it never attracted more than a vociferous minority of conservative Communist Party members, workers and managers in the military-industrial complex, and retired military officers. The Interfront's aim was to uphold the leading role of the Party and oppose the adoption of Latvian as the state language and other changes that threatened the privileged status of Russian-speaking immigrants. To this end, the Interfront stoked fears that republican sovereignty and the erosion of Communist Party rule would leave Slavic immigrants in the position of second-class citizens under the resurgent Latvians. Yet with its Brezhnev-era rhetoric, the Interfront, for most Latvians, was more an object of ridicule than concern in late 1988 and early 1989.

A greater challenge to the Popular Front was posed by Moscow's proposals in late October 1988 to constitutionally limit democratization and republican rights. In the first instance of what was to become extensive cooperation, the Popular Front moved rapidly to coordinate with its Estonian and Lithuanian counterparts a letter-writing campaign against the proposed amendments. By the end of November, Latvian Supreme Soviet chairman Gorbunovs reported that a million signatures against the changes had been gathered, thereby demonstrating the depth of the Front's support.[46] Assisted by the Front's legal experts, Gorbunovs then successfully lobbied Moscow to change several points in the draft document.[47]

The spring 1989 elections to the Congress of People's Deputies provided the Popular Front with another opportunity to test its base of support and to gain access to the halls of power in Moscow. Engaging in a lively electoral campaign, the Front successfully promoted the election of reformist communists, as well as several of its own more moderate leaders. Electoral success was the product of both an effective campaign and ethnic gerrymandering: some rural Latvian-dominated electoral districts contained

28,000 voters while multiethnic urban districts contained 150,000 voters each.[48] Once in Moscow, the Front's deputies, in cooperation with their counterparts from Estonia and Lithuania, succeeded in pushing through the creation of a special commission on the Molotov-Ribbentrop Pact. Baltic deputies soon became disillusioned with the Congress and the new USSR Supreme Soviet as majorities of both institutions were hostile towards Baltic aspirations.[49] But while the Front's moderate leaders were in Moscow promoting the republic's sovereignty within a reformed union framework, those who remained in Latvia were busy advocating a more radical agenda.

## Towards independence

While the Front's initial program called for "sovereignty" within the Soviet Union, many Front activists and informal groups supported full independence. Through the spring of 1989, the leaders of the Front were subject to multiple pressures: criticism from Helsinki '86, VAK, LNNK and emigre groups on the Front's ambiguous position on independence; the growing radicalization of the Front's rank-and-file; and the example of more assertive Fronts in Estonia and Lithuania. When LNNK convened for a congress on May 28 and loudly raised the banner of independence, the Front was forced to act in order to regain the political initiative: three days after the LNNK Congress, those Front leaders who were not in Moscow issued an appeal to the rank-and-file calling for a discussion of complete independence for Latvia.[50] This appeal presented the moderates in Moscow with a *fait accompli*. Even the Front's chairman, Dainis Ivans, had not been informed of the decision beforehand.[51] Once issued, the appeal could not be easily retracted, and the goal of independence was soon ratified by local chapters of the Front and the Governing Council.

With its decision to support independence, the Front aligned itself with the more radical informal groups, and set itself on a collision course with Moscow. This conflict first came to a head with the "Baltic Way" demonstration of August 23, 1989 – the fiftieth anniversary of the signing of the Molotov-Ribbentrop Pact. The three Baltic popular fronts mobilized nearly 2 million people to form a human chain stretching from Tallinn through Riga to Vilnius.[52] The mass action was meant to demonstrate to the world the lack of legitimacy of Soviet rule in the Baltics. Three days later the CPS Central Committee issued a statement harshly criticizing the Baltic movements.[53]

Popular Front leaders, however, were generally more moderate than the membership at large or the more militant groups on the political flanks who were quick to cry "Betrayal" at the first sign of compromise. Having coalesced into a "Citizens' Movement" over the summer, the more radical nationalists pushed for a rapid break with the Soviet Union and the election of an alternative parliament. This movement claimed that only those who were citizens of interwar Latvia and their direct descendants, not the hundreds of thousands of post-war immigrants, had the right to determine Latvia's fate. By the beginning of 1990, the Citizen's Movement had gathered 900,000 signatures in favor of independence, thus carrying out, in effect, an unofficial referendum.[54]

Another factor that facilitated the radicalization of the Latvian and other Baltic movements was the example of the East European revolutions of late 1989 and early 1990. That the East European states could go their own way without Moscow intervening must have raised doubts in the minds of some Baltic activists that Gorbachev was willing to use force to preserve the internal empire. When the newly elected Lithuanian Supreme Soviet declared independence on March 11, 1990, Moscow's reaction was mild, and throughout the Baltic region many held strong hopes that a path to independence could be negotiated. The imposition of an economic blockade on Lithuania soon thereafter was a sobering reminder that Moscow had other means of pressuring the Baltic republics. However, candidates supported by the Popular Front ran on a platform of independence during the elections in March and April. The Front's opposition was in disarray and the Communist Party of Latvia split largely along ethnic lines into pro-Soviet and pro-independence factions in early April.[55] When the final results of the elections were counted, candidates supported by the Front had trounced conservative communists and representatives of the Interfront.

On May 4, 1990, over two-thirds of the Latvian Supreme Soviet voted for the restoration of independence. In the hope of avoiding Lithuania's fate, Latvian legislators made their declaration conditional, calling for a "transitional period" of indeterminate length leading to complete independence from the Soviet Union.[56] The electoral success of pro-independence forces was striking in view of the demographic situation in Latvia: pro-independence candidates won the votes of not only an overwhelming number of Latvians, but also those of many non-Latvians.

In late 1990 and early 1991, the new Latvian government made little headway on economic and political reforms as Moscow used its economic and military power to obstruct most changes. For over a year, the government unsuccessfully sought diplomatic support from the West and negotiations with Moscow. Yet the West responded timidly for fear of undermining Gorbachev, who had in turn, thrown in his lot with the conservatives and thereby avoided negotiations with the Balts.

Within Latvia, the pro-Soviet movement caused some instability. Though this movement represented only a minority of the non-Latvian population, it had some support from Soviet military and security personnel stationed in Latvia. On repeated occasions, Moscow resorted to shows of force by the army and special MVD "black beret" troops. The intimidation tactics backfired, steeling the resolve of independence advocates and pushing non-Latvians into the pro-independence camp. When the Latvian government held a plebiscite on independence on March 3, 1991, 74 percent of the voters opted for independence.[57] Analyses of the voting results and sociological surveys from that period indicate that 90 to 95 percent of all Latvians supported independence, while the corresponding figure for non-Latvians was between 38 and 45 percent.[58]

The conservative trend in Moscow reached its peak in August 1991, when leaders of the Communist Party and security organs carried out a short-lived coup. At the height of the coup attempt, the Latvian and Estonian governments declared full independence, thereby ending their "transitional periods" and aligning themselves with Lithuania.[59] The failed coup emasculated the Soviet central government and boosted the influence of Boris Yeltsin, whom the Balts had supported since his ouster from the Politburo in 1987. The resurgent RSFSR recognized Baltic independence on August 24, and numerous Western countries followed suit. When recognition by the central Soviet government came on September 6 it was practically an anti-climax.

## Post-Soviet Latvia

Though Latvia and Yeltsin's RSFSR had been allies in the struggle against Gorbachev, the honeymoon was short-lived. Soon after independence, relations became strained over the lingering Russian military presence in Latvia. At the time of the coup, between 50,000 and 80,000 Soviet military personnel were stationed in Latvia.[60] When first Gorbachev, then Yeltsin delayed the troop withdrawal and attempted to link it to other issues, such as the status of Latvia's Russian-speaking community, historical Latvian suspicions of Russian intentions were immediately rekindled. These suspicions were exacerbated by the not altogether voluntary accession of almost all the former Soviet republics to the Commonwealth of Independent States, the emergence of the doctrine of the "near abroad," and the rise of Zhirinovsky. After several years of arduous negotiations and mutual recriminations, Latvia and Russia finally signed a packet of agreements on April 30, 1994. According to the agreements, Russia was obliged to finish the troop withdrawal by the end of August 1994 and grant preferential trade status to Latvia. In return, Russia was granted permission to continue using an early warning radar station on Latvian territory for several more years, and 22,000 Russian military pensioners were allowed to remain in Latvia.

While tensions centered on the troop issue, Moscow also protested Latvia's treatment of the post-war immigrant population. In preparation for new elections, Latvia's parliament adopted a resolution on October 15, 1991 "restoring" citizenship to those who were citizens of interwar Latvia

Table 10.3. *Registered citizens and non-citizens by ethnicity, January 1994*

| Ethnicity | Citizens | Non-citizens | Total |
|-----------|----------|--------------|-------|
| Latvian | 1,355,259 | 22,031 | 1,377,290 |
| Russian | 278,087 | 444,399 | 722,486 |
| Belarusan | 20,455 | 82,849 | 103,304 |
| Ukrainian | 3,929 | 59,853 | 63,782 |
| Polish | 38,333 | 24,060 | 62,393 |
| Lithuanian | 7,062 | 26,206 | 33,268 |
| Jewish | 6,638 | 8,074 | 14,712 |
| Gypsy | 6,146 | 673 | 6,819 |
| Other | 4,393 | 22,316 | 26,709 |

*Source:* Department of Citizenship and Immigration data, Diena, January 26, 1994.

and their descendants.[61] The next step was to be a decision on expanding the body of citizens to include at least some of the post-war immigrants and their descendants. After considerable controversy, however, the parliament ruled that it lacked the authority to decide such an important issue, because it had been elected in 1990 by all inhabitants of the republic and Soviet military personnel stationed in Latvia, and not just citizens. Thus, a decision on expanding the franchise was left to a new parliament, the Saeima, which was elected by citizens alone in the summer of 1993.[62]

With the October 15 resolution, two-thirds of the population of Latvia qualified for immediate citizenship, while one third (approximately 700,000) had to await the election of a new parliament and the adoption of a law setting out naturalization procedures. The citizen/non-citizen divide did not fall entirely along ethnic lines, as many non-Latvians with roots in interwar Latvia also had their citizenship "restored" (see table 10.3). But the ethnic issue was salient enough – except for 22,000 Russian Latvians, almost all non-citizens were non-Latvians.

In June 1993, Latvia's citizenry elected a new parliament, the Saiema, which finally adopted a Law on Citizenship on July 22, 1994.[63] The general requirements for naturalization under the complex law are five years of residency after May 4, 1990 and command of the Latvian language. Some categories of non-citizens (e.g. retired Soviet military officers, KGB) are forever barred from naturalization. Other categories are eligible for priority naturalization: spouses of citizens, ethnic Latvians, people who finished a Latvian-language school, etc. Most may submit naturalization applications according to a complex timetable from 1996 to 2003. Naturalization will undoubtedly be a lengthy process and the language requirement will be an insuperable barrier for many non-citizens.

Table 10.4. *Migration flows into and out of Latvia, 1989–1993 (thousands)*

|      | Arrived | Departed | Net immig. |
|------|---------|----------|------------|
| 1989 | 20.9    | 26.3     | −5.4       |
| 1990 | 17.0    | 25.4     | −8.4       |
| 1991 | 12.6    | 23.8     | −11.2      |
| 1992 | 4.6     | 51.8     | −47.2      |
| 1993 | 3.1     | 31.3     | −28.2      |

*Source:* LR Valsts Statistikas Komiteja, *Latvija Skaitlos/Latvia in Figures 1992* (Riga, 1993), p. 32; LR Valsts Statistikas Komiteja, *Latvija Skaitlos/Latvia in Figures 1993* (Riga, 1994), p. 21.

Making command of Latvian a requirement for citizenship was a continuation of earlier measures aimed at defending and promoting the Latvian language. In March 1992, the Latvian parliament adopted strict amendments to the 1989 Law on Languages making knowledge of Latvian a prerequisite for many posts in government and in the state and private sectors of the economy.[64] After passage of the law, tens of thousands of people were required to undergo language examinations and, often, remedial language instruction. A parliamentary decision of August 1992 permits employers to annul the contracts of employees whose knowledge of Latvian is insufficient for the performance of their duties.[65] Though there have been no reports of mass layoffs, the adjustment has been painful for many non-Latvians.

While many non-Latvians have been adversely affected by citizenship and language legislation, all of Latvia's population has struggled through the difficult transition to a market economy. Over 1992 and 1993, inflation was high and incomes stagnated. Accordingly, purchasing power fell 24 percent and real personal incomes dropped by 40 percent.[66] The economic problems were moderated somewhat by the introduction of Latvia's own currency, the *hat*, in the spring of 1993. The hat steadily gained in valve in relation to all Western currencies. By mid-1994 the economy appeared to have stabilized, and slow growth was even anticipated for the remainder of the year.

As a result of the citizenship controversy and changes in language policy, as well as the economic crisis of 1992–93, a sizeable number of non-Latvians have emigrated to Russia, Belarus, and Ukraine. Since 1989, emigration has exceeded immigration every year through at least 1993 (a larger than normal outflow took place in 1992, however, when tens of thousands of families accompanied withdrawing Russian military personnel) (see table 10.4). Non-Latvian leaders have warned that the departure of many young, educated people is weakening and "lumpenizing" the Russophone community. Most Latvians, however, have welcomed the process, as it has eased long-standing fears of being demographically "swamped" by Russophones. As a result of emigration, the Latvian share of the total population has increased since 1989, and stood at 54.2 percent in 1994.[67]

While many Russophones have had difficulty adapting to conditions in post-Soviet Latvia, some representatives of non-Russian minorities have taken advantage of the new opportunities offered to rebuild the minority cultural infrastructure destroyed by Soviet rule. In cooperation with the Latvian authorities and, often, their respective foreign embassies, non-Latvian activists have established a network of full-time minority schools. In addition to funding schools with Latvian and/or Russian as the language of instruction, for 1993–94, the state financed Polish, Ukrainian, and Jewish high schools (grades 1–12), Estonian and Polish middle schools (grades 1–9), several Polish primary schools (grades 1–4), and individual classes for Lithuanians and Gypsies.[68] The primary complaints uttered with respect to these schools have concerned the lack of both resources and legislation defining the status of minority schools.[69]

Ethnic politics in post-Soviet Latvia, then, has been characterized by the interplay of three processes: Latvians have asserted what they consider to be their political and cultural "birthright," Russian-speakers have struggled to adapt to their new status as minorities, and non-Russian minorities have sought to revive the cultural pluralism of the 1920s. Increasingly, Latvian politicians describe their goal as the creation of a "national multicultural state." Whether this is an attempt to square a circle or move towards a new synthesis is, as yet, unclear. For now, it has meant the entrenchment of Latvian as the sole state language, an openness to educational and cultural pluralism, and a decisive political role for Latvians until non-citizens become fully integrated into Latvian society.

## Notes

1 State Committee for Statistics of the Republic of Latvia, *Latvija Skaitlos/Latvia in Figures 1993* (Riga, 1994), p. 18.

2 For a cogent examination of developments in Latvia during this period, see Andrejs Plakans, "The Latvians," in Edwards C. Thaden (ed.), *Russification in the Baltic Provinces and Finland, 1855–1914* (Princeton: Princeton University Press, 1981), pp. 207–84.

3 For a history of interwar Latvia, see Georg von Rauch, *The Baltic states: The Years of Independence, Estonia, Latvia, Lithuania, 1917–1940,* (Berkeley and Los Angeles: University of California Press, 1974).

4 Peteris Zvidrins and Inta Vanovska, *Latviesi: Statistiski Demografisks Portretejums* (Riga: Ainatne, 1992), pp. 44–45.

5 For an overview of the period of Nazi occupation, see Romuald J. Misiunas and Rein Taagepera, *The Baltic States: Years of Dependence, 1940–1990* (London: Hurst & Company, 1993), pp. 49–69.

6  The estimate of 60,000 is that of Misiunas and Taagepera, *ibid.*, p. 73. The 1949 tally of 43,000, based on new archival research, was first published in *Cina*, March 4, 1988.

7  Cited in Misiunas and Taagepera, *The Baltic States*, table 6, p. 359.

8  On the role of Russians and Russian Latvians in the CPL at the dawn of Soviet rule in Latvia, see Ilga Apine, "Nomenklatura Latvija 1940–1941. gada," *Latvijas Zinatnu Akademijas Vestis*, Part A, no. 11, 1993, pp. 20–26.

9  See Juris Dreifelds, "Latvian National Consciousness and Group Demands Since 1959," in George W. Simmonds (ed.), *Nationalism in the USSR and Eastern Europe in the Era of Brezhnev and Kosygin* (Detroit: University of Detroit Press, 1977), pp. 136–516.

10  Padomju Latvijas Komunists, no. 6, June 1989, p. 29.

11  Latvijas PSR valsts Statistikas Komiteja, *Latvija Sodien: Socialekonmisku Aprakstu Krajums* (Riga, 1990), p. 74.

12  All language data calculated from the census results as published in Latvijas Valsts Statistikas Komiteja, *1989, Gada tautas Skaitisanas Rezultati Latvija, Statistisks Biletens*, part 2, (Riga, 1991), pp. 41–42.

13  For a survey of dissent in Latvia, see Ludmilla Alexeyeva, *Soviet Dissent: Contemporary Movements for National, Religious and Human Rights* (Middletown, CT: Wesleyan University Press, 1985), pp. 97–105.14 Data on mixed marriages in Latvia and elsewhere in the Soviet Union for 1978 and 1988 may be found in *Journal of Soviet Nationalities*, 1, no. 2 (Summer 1990), 163–168.

15  See, e.g., the data in Gertrude E. Schroeder, "Nationalities and the Soviet Economy," in Lubomyr Hajda and Mark Beissinger (eds.), *The Nationalities Factor in Soviet Politics and Society* (Boulder CO: Westview Press, 1990), table 4, p. 51.

16  Janis John Penikis, "Latvian Nationalism: Preface to a Dissenting View," in Simmonds (ed.), *Nationalism in the USSR and Eastern Europe in the Era of Brezhnev and Kosygin*, p. 159.

17  Rasma Karklins, *Ethnic Relations in the USSR: The Perspective from Below* (Boston: Allen and Unwin, 1986), p. 81.

18  For an overview of personnel changes at the dawn of the Gorbachev era, see Thane Gustafson and Dawn Mann, "Gorbachev's Next Gamble," *Problems of Communism*, 36 (July–August 1987), 1–20.

19  For a summary of personnel changes in 1985–1986, see Romuald J. Misiunas and Rein Taagepera, "The Baltic States: Years of Dependence, 1980–6," *Journal of Baltic Studies*, 20, no. 1 (Spring 1989), 66–67.

20  For the proceedings of the conference, see Edvins Berkos *et al.* (eds.) *Jurmalas Dialogi* (Riga: Avots, 1987). See also Dzintra Bungs, "After the Jurmala Conference: Imperfect Glasnost'," *Radio Free Europe Research*, Baltic Area Situation Report (hereafter, cited as RFER BA SR), no. 8, December 9, 1986.

21  For a review of the entire incident, see Nils R. Muiznieks, "The Daugavpils Hydro Station and Glasnost in Latvia," *Journal of Baltic Studies*, 18, no. 1 (Spring 1987), 63–70.

22  *Staburags*, no. 1, January-February, 1988, p. 5. For an overview of VAK's activities, see Juris Dreifelds, "Latvian National Rebirth," *Problems of Communism*, 38, no. 4 (July–August, 1989).

23  For an overview of the membership and goals of the group, see Dzintra Bungs, "One-and-a-half Years of Helsinki '86," RFER BA SR, no. 2, February 16, 1988.

24  For a *samizdat* account of the June 14 demonstration, see *Auseklis* (Riga), no. 1 (September, 1987), 7–10. For an overview of the latter demonstrations, see Dzintra Bungs, "The Latvian Demonstration of 23 August 1987," RFER BA SR, no. 7, October 28, 1987, and "A Survey of the Demonstrations on November 18," RFER BA SR, no. 9, December 18, 1987.

25  On the emergence of public activism on the part of the intelligentsia, see Dreifelds, "Latvian National Rebirth," p. 83.

26 See Toomas Ilves, "The People's Front: the Creation of a Quasi Political Party," RFER BA SR, no. 5, May 20, 1988.

27 The speeches of the participants were published in *Literatura un Maksla*, no. 24, June 10, no. 25, June 17, no. 28, July 1 and no. 29, July 8, 1988.

28 The resolution is printed in *Literatura un Maksla*, no. 24, June 10, 1988.

29 For an account of the initiative group by Valdis Steins, one of its members, see *Atmoda*, no. 24, June 12, 1989. The original document has not been published.

30 The minutes were never published in Latvia. Excerpts were published in the Swedish newspaper *Dagens Nyheter*, October 16, 1988, translated in *Foreign Broadcast Information Service*, October 21, 1988, pp. 59–64.

31 For detailed documentation of the emergence of Latvia's front, see Nils Raymond Muiznieks, "The Baltic Popular Movements and the Disintegration of the Soviet Union," Ph.D. dissertation, University of California at Berkeley, 1993, pp. 221, 225–226, 228.

32 See Dzintra Bungs, "Yakovlev in Latvia: An Exercise in Socialist Pluralism," RFER BA SR, no. 9, August 26, 1988.

33 *Atmoda*, October 2, 1990.

34 For a *samizdat* account of the meeting at which LNNK was formed, see the group's newsletter, *Neatkariba*, no. 1, September 1988. For a Western report, see Dzintra Bungs, "New Group for Latvian Independence Formed," RFER BA SR, no. 7, July 13, 1988.

35 *Padomju Jaunatne*, September 22, 1988.

36 For the flag campaign, see *Padomju Jaunatne*, September 28, 1988; for the language campaign, see *Padomju Jaunatne*, October 5, 1988.

37 *Cina*, September 30, 1988.

38 Membership figures provided by Janis Peters at the congress. See *Latviias Tautas Fronte, Gads Pirmais* (Riga: Latvijas Tautas Frontes Izdevnieciba, 1989), p. 11. For the breakdown of delegates according to ethnicity and Communist Party membership, see *New York Times*, October 10, 1988, p. A3, and *Washington Post*, October 10, 1988, pp. A1, A36–37.

39 All the speeches and documents adopted at the congress may be found in *Latvijas Tautas Fronte. Gads Pirmais.*

40 *Padomiu Jaunatne*, October 15, 1988.

41 These figures are cited in J. Brolish, "Perestroika i natsionaloye protsessy v sovetskoy Latvii," *Chto delat'* (Moscow: 1989), p. 183.

42 See *Latviias PSR Tautu Forums, Foruma Orgkomitejas Specializlaidums* (Latvian SSR Nationalities Forum, Special Publication of the Forum Organizing Committee), December 10–11, 1988, pp. 2–3.

43 For speeches and resolutions of the Forum, see *Latviias PSR Tautu Foruma Materiali* (Riga: Avots, 1989).

44 See the interviews with Interfront spokesmen in *Cina*, October 30, 1988, and in *Pravda*, November 26, 1988.

45 For an overview of the Interfront, see Nils R. Muiznieks, "The Pro-Soviet Movement in Latvia," *Report on the USSR*, 1, no. 34, August 24, 1990.

46 *Padomiu Jaunatne*, November 24, 1988.

47 See Dreifelds, "Latvian National Rebirth," p. 87.

48 Valerii A. Tishkov, "An Assembly of Nations or an All-Union Parliament?" *Journal of Soviet Nationalities*, 1, no. 1 (Spring 1990), 113.

49 See Nils R. Muiznieks, "The Evolution of Baltic Cooperation," *Report on the USSR*, 2, no. 6, July 6, 1990.

50 For the text of the appeal, see *Atmoda*, June 5, 1989.

51 Author's interviews with Dainis Ivans and other Front leaders in Riga, June 1989. This version of events is similar to that in Dreifelds, "Latvian National Rebirth," p. 88.

52 See Dzintra Bungs, "Balts Mark 50th Anniversary of Molotov Ribbentrop Pact," RFER BA SR, no. 8, September 11, 1989.
53 For a text of the statement, see *Pravda*, August 27, 1989.
54 See Nils R. Muiznieks, "The Committee of Latvia: An Alternative Parliament?" *Report on the USSR*, 2, no. 29, July 20, 1990.
55 See Dzintra Bungs, "Latvian Communist Party Splits," *Report on the USSR*, 2, no. 17, April 27, 1990.
56 *Cina*, May 5, 1990.
57 Voter turnout was 87.57 percent. *Diena*, March 5, 1991.
58 For a voting analysis, see Ilmars Mezs, *Latviesi Latviia: Etnodemografisks Apskats* (Kalamazoo, MI: LSC Apgads, 1992), pp. 49–50. For sociological survey data, see B. Zepa, "Sabiedriska Doma Parejas Perioda Latvija: Latviesu un Cittautiesu Uzskatu Dinamika (1989–1992)," *Latviias Zinatnu Akademijas Vestis*, Part A, no. 10 1992, p. 23.
59 For English-language texts of the declarations, see *The Baltic Independent* (Tallinn), August 30-September 5, 1991, p. 3.
60 Precise figures were never disclosed. This estimate was provided by Sergei Zotov, the head of Russia's negotiating team with Latvia to *Diena*, March 10, 1992.
61 For an English-language text of the October 15 resolution, see Standing Commission on Human Rights and National Questions, *About the Republic of Latvia* (Riga: Supreme Council of the Republic of Latvia, 1992), pp. 51–53.
62 For an exposition of the view that the Supreme Council had no authority to enact a new law on citizenship, see Standing Commission on Human Rights, *Human Rights Issues* (Riga: 5th Saeima – Republic of Latvia, 1993), pp. 74–75.
63 For a text of the law, see *Latvijas Vestnesis*, August 11, 1994.
64 For a text of the amended law in English, see *About the Republic of Latvia*, pp. 76–80.
65 Diena AP MP, August 28, 1993.
66 State Committee for Statistics of the Republic of Latvia, *Latvija Skaitlos/Latvia in Figures 1993* (Riga, 1994), p. 27.
67 *Latvijas Vestnesis*, July 28, 1994.
68 For detailed data on minority schools, see *Latvijas Vestnesis*, July 5, 1994.
69 See the letter by Raffi Kharajanyan, the chairman of the Association of National Cultural Societies, in *Baltiiskaia Gazeta*, April 15, 1994.

# Latvia: chronology of events

**1985**

Moderate Janis Vagris is appointed chairman of the Presidium of the Supreme Soviet. Anatolijs Gorbunovs is appointed Central Committee secretary of ideology.

*July 1986*

The organization Helsinki '86 is established and calls for an end to Russification and the restoration of Latvian independence.

*September 1986*
15–19    A conference on US–Soviet relations is held in Jurmala, in which American representatives reaffirm the United States nonrecognition of the Soviet annexation of the Baltic states. Over 30,000 people sign letters protesting a proposal to build a hydroelectric dam on the Daugava river (the project is cancelled the following year).

*June 1987*
14    Demonstration organized by Helsinki '86 is held to commemorate the mass deportations of 1941.

*August 1987*
23    A demonstration is held to commemorate the signing of the Molotov-Ribbentrop Pact.

*November 1987*
18    A demonstration is held in honor of the 1918 declaration of independence.

*January 1988*

The Russian-speakers' association, Interfront, holds its founding congress.

*March 1988*

200,000 demonstrate in Riga against the Latvian Party Central Committee's condemnation of "anti-Soviet and separatist" currents in the republic. 25,000 gather in a ceremony in remembrance of the 1949 deportations.

*June 1988*
1–2    The Writers' Union holds a meeting on "Pressing Problems

of Soviet Latvian Culture on the Eve of the 19th CPSU Conference." Participants issue a resolution calling for decentralization and sovereignty.

18    Party first secretary Boris Pugo convenes an emergency meeting of the Central Committee and denounces participants in the Writers' Union meeting.

21    The National Independence Movement of Latvia is established.

*September 1988*

Supreme Soviet declares Latvian the state language and legalizes the independence-era flag.

*October 1988*

Vagris replaces Pugo as party first secretary. Gorbunovs becomes chairman of the Supreme Soviet.

8–9    The founding congress of the Popular Front of Latvia is held, drawing over 1,000 delegates representing over 100,000 members. 88 percent of delegates are ethnic Latvians. The journalist Dainis Ivans is elected chairman. The Popular Front coordinates a letter-writing campaign with its Estonian and Lithuanian counterparts to campaign against Moscow proposals to limit the pace of reform.

*November 1988*

30    Gorbunovs reports that he has received around one million signatures against Moscow's proposals.

*March 1989*

Elections to the Supreme Soviet are held.

*1989*

A Law on Languages is adopted which makes Latvian the official language.

*April 1989*

14    Soviet tanks roll into Riga.

*May 1989*

28    At a congress, the National Independence Movement declares its goal of independence.

31    Popular Front leaders issue an appeal for the discussion of independence.

*August 1989*

Representatives of several pro-independence groups gather at a conference in Riga to coordinate their demands.

The Latvian Popular Front declares a goal of "complete independence" at their 2nd Congress.

23  Almost two million demonstrators in the Baltics participate in a human chain of protest on the 50th anniversary of the Molotov-Ribbentrop pact.

*December 1989*
10  Local elections are held, with nationalist candidates taking about 70 percent of the seats.

*May 1990*
4  Over two-thirds of the Supreme Soviet vote for a declaration on the illegality of the 1940 occupation and restoration of independence. The Equal Rights parliamentary faction does not participate in the vote.

*October 1990*
23  Parliament amends the constitution to allow the passage of laws with a majority vote (and only 1/3 of deputies present) and constitutional amendments with a 2/3 majority vote (and half of the deputies present).

*December 1990*
12  An explosion rocks the Latvian Communist Party Central Committee's Public Policy Center.
15  Interfront holds its third congress and declares its support for economic independence and sovereignty within the framework of a new union structure.

*January 1991*
20  Five are killed when Soviet OMON troops storm the headquarters of the Latvian Interior Ministry in Riga.

*March 1991*
3  In a referendum, 74 percent of voters support independence. Parliament passes a law to protect minorities in the republic.

*May 1991*
22–23  Riga special police carry out armed attacks on customs stations.

*June 1991*
20  Parliament adopts a law declaring the onset of a transitional period to independence. The 1922 Constitution is declared in force, and it is forbidden to change or repeal any articles relating to Latvia's independence or territorial integrity.

*August 1991*
21  Parliament issues a declaration of independence.
23  The government asserts that the coup leaders have no authority in Latvia.

Parliament bans the Communist Party.
24 Yeltsin recognizes Latvia's independence.

*September 1991*
6 The Soviet government recognizes Latvia's independence.

*October 1991*
15 Citizenship is "restored" to all citizens of interwar Latvia and their descendants. Two-thirds of residents qualify.
5 The Baltic Council, comprised of the leaders of Lithuania, Latvia, and Estonia, issues a joint statement demanding the immediate withdrawal of Soviet troops from their territories.

*February 1992*
1–2 Russia agrees to withdraw the 100,000 troops estimated to be stationed in the Baltic states.

*March 1992*
Parliament adopts amendments to the 1989 Law on Languages making knowledge of Latvian a prerequisite for many government posts.
6 The Council of Baltic Sea States (including the Baltic states plus seven others) is established.

*May 1992*
7 The Latvian ruble is introduced as a parallel currency.

*July 1992*
20 The Latvian ruble becomes the sole legal tender.
25 A citizenship law is passed which mandates a 16-year period of residency and knowledge of Latvian.

*August 1992*
6 Russia asks for $7.7 billion from the Baltic states in exchange for withdrawing its troops from the region by 1994.

*September 1992*
16 Several political leaders call upon the government of Prime Minister Godmanis to resign.

*October 1992*
21 The cabinet, except for the minister for economic reforms, survives a vote of no-confidence.
30 Yeltsin suspends troop pullout due to concern of infringement of ethnic Russians' rights.

*December 1992*

1    Protestors from several Russian organizations call for former Party first secretary Alfred Rubiks' release from prison and equal rights for citizens and noncitizens.

*June 1993*

5–6    Elections to the 100-seat Saiema, Latvia's parliament, are held. Latvia's Way, led by chairman of the parliament Gorbunovs and Foreign Minister Andrejevs, wins the most seats at 36.

*July 1993*

6–7    Parliament convenes and confirms the reestablishment of Latvia's 1922 Constitution. Guntis Ulmanis of the Farmer's Union is chosen president by parliament, after the leading candidate Zigfrids Meierovics (a Latvian from the U.S.) withdraws from the race.

8    Valdis Birkavs is confirmed as prime minister

*October 1993*

6    Three pro-communist organizations are banned.

18    The Latvian ruble is withdrawn from circulation, and the *lat* is made the sole official currency.

*March 1994*

15    An agreement with Russia is signed which grants Russia possession of the Skrunda radar station until 31 August 1998, after which the station is to be dismantled.

*April 1994*

30    Five agreements are signed with Russia which require that all Russian forces be withdrawn by the year 2000, although most of the 7,000 troops are to be pulled out by 31 August 1994.

*May 1994*

29    The first post-independence local elections are held in Latvia with about 60 percent participation. Primarily anti-communist, pro-Latvian candidates are successful.

*June 1994*

13    The Baltic states establish a joint Baltic Council of Ministers.

21    Parliament adopts a new Law on Citizenship which retains naturalization quotas and is condemned by the OSCE. Preferential naturalization is to be given to residents with one ethnic Latvian parent; those who came to Latvia before 17 June 1940; Lithuanian and Estonian minorities; spouses of Latvian citizens who have been married for ten years; and

those who have completed the highest course in Latvian language. Soviet military retirees are not to be granted citizenship. Others may apply for naturalization from 1 January 1996 with preference given to Latvian-born applicants. From the year 2000, all others may be naturalized at the rate of 0.1 percent of Latvia's total citizenship per year.

28  In response to criticism, Ulmanis returns the Law on Citizenship to parliament for further consideration.

*July 1994*

11  The Farmers' Union withdraws from its ruling coalition with the government party, Latvia's Way. Three Farmers' Union ministers resign.

14  Birkavs resigns his post as Prime Minister.

22  A modified Law on Citizenship is adopted and goes into effect following Ulmanis' endorsement in August.

*August 1994*

18  Prime Minister-designate Andrejs Krastins, of the National Independence Movement, does not get enough votes in parliament (35–27, with 28 abstentions) to approve his new government.

*September 1994*

13  Parliament approves a new cabinet organized by Latvia's Way (out of 25 cabinet members, 12 are from Latvia's Way and 2 previously belonged to the Farmers' Union). Maris Gailis is selected prime minister.

*October 1994*

20  Parliament ratifies the April 30 agreements with Russia on social guarantees for military pensioners and the status of the Skrunda radar station. 100 opponents protest outside parliament.

*November 1994*

13  The Baltic Assembly issues a statement regarding the need to demilitarize the Russian Kaliningrad oblast and restore its cities historical German names.

*January 1995*

31  Latvia becomes a member of the Council of Europe.

*April 1995*

12  Latvia becomes an associate member of the European Union.

# 11 Estonia: independence redefined

TOIVO U. RAUN

Emerging in the late 1850s, the Estonian national movement followed a pattern similar to that of most other smaller peoples of eastern and northern Europe in the second half of the nineteenth century.[1] The "national awakening" of the 1860s and 1870s as well as the ensuing decades before the beginning of the twentieth century emphasized cultural development, e.g., folklore collection, literature, music, education, and journalism, to name only the most prominent concerns. It was only with the Russian Revolution of 1905 that the opportunity arose for mass political participation and the pursuit of a concrete political program – autonomy within a democratic and federalized Russian state.[2] Before 1917, the maximum Estonian political objective remained limited to the goal of autonomy, since anything more far-reaching appeared utopian given the existing constellation of forces.[3]

Before the crisis that spelled the end of the Soviet Union, the key period in Estonia's political development was undoubtedly the two decades of independence during the interwar era. This experience, which distinguished Estonia, Latvia, and Lithuania from the other former union republics in the USSR, left a powerful legacy that could not be erased by the nearly five decades of Soviet rule. Indeed it informed all unofficial political activity in Estonia after 1940. Thus, it is crucial to bear in mind that what took place in August-September 1991 was regarded by all Estonian political forces as the *restoration* of independence and not merely the emergence of a successor state to the Soviet Union. Nevertheless, Europe and the world had changed a great deal in the intervening fifty years, and Estonia and the other two Baltic states faced new challenges in redefining their status in the international state system of the 1990s.

## Demographic trends

In order to understand Estonia's distinctive demographic circumstances at the present time, it is necessary to briefly review population trends in historical perspective (see tables 11.1 and 11.2). The first modern census in the region that became Estonia in the twentieth century took place in 1881 under tsarist rule and indicated that ethnic Estonians constituted 90 percent

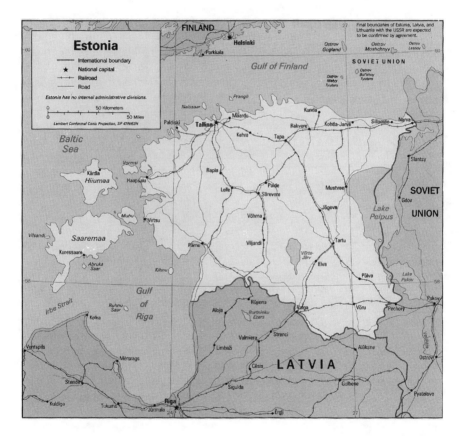

**FINLAND**

● Porkkala

■ **Helsinki**

*Gulf of Finland*

*Ostrov Gogland*

*Ostrov Moshchnyy*

*Ostrov Lesnoy*

27

Final boundaries of Estonia, Latvia, and Lithuania with the USSR are expected to be confirmed by agreement.

**S O V I E T   U N I O N**

*Ostrov Malyy Tyuters*

*Ostrov Bol'shoy Tyuters*

## Estonia

— International boundary
★ National capital
+—+ Railroad
— Road

*Estonia has no internal administrative divisions.*

0 ──── 50 Kilometers
0 ──── 50 Miles
*Lambert Conformal Conic Projection, SP 47N162N*

*Baltic Sea*

Naissaar

△ Prangli

● Kunda

Maardu

Paldiski

● **Tallinn** ★

Kehra

Rakvere ● Kohtla-Järve ● Sillamäe ● Narva

● Tapa

● Slantsy

Vormsi

Kärdla ●
*Hiiumaa*

Haapsalu ●

● Rapla

● Lelle

● Paide
● Särevere

● Mustvee

○ Gdov

**SOVIET**

*Muhu*

● Virtsu

● Võhma

● Jõgeva

*Lake Peipus*

**UNION**

Vilsandi

*Saaremaa*

Kuressaare ●

△ Abruka Saar

● Pärnu

● Viljandi

*Võrts-Järv*

● Tartu

● Elva

● Põlva

*Lake Pskov*

58

58

Kihnu ○

*Gulf of Riga*

Ruhnu ○ Saar

Irbe Strait

Kolka ●

● Rūjiena

Aloja ●

*Burtnieku Ezers*

● Valga

● Võru

Pechory ●

● Pskov

Ventspils ●

● Valmiera

Strenči ●

Alūksne ●

Ostrov ●

Mērsrags ●

Limbaži ●

Stende ●

Cēsis ●

**LATVIA**

Pyatalovo ●

Kuldiga ●

Tukums ●

**Riga** ★

Jūrmala ●

Sigulda ●

Gulbene ●

Ērgļi ●

27

60

60

Table 11.1. *Major ethnic groups in Estonia (thousands)*

|  | 1934[a] | 1959 | 1970 | 1979 | 1989 |
|---|---|---|---|---|---|
| Estonians | 993.5 | 892.7 | 925.1 | 947.8 | 963.3 |
| Russians | 92.7 | 240.2 | 334.6 | 408.8 | 474.8 |
| Ukrainians | — | 15.8 | 28.1 | 36.0 | 48.3 |
| Belarusans | — | 10.9 | 18.7 | 23.5 | 27.7 |
| Finns | 1.1 | 16.7 | 18.5 | 17.6 | 16.6 |
| Jews | 4.4 | 5.4 | 5.3 | 5.0 | 4.6 |
| Germans | 16.3 | 0.7 | 7.9 | 3.9 | 3.5 |
| Latvians | 5.4 | 2.9 | 3.3 | 4.0 | 3.1 |
| Swedes | 7.6 | — | — | — | — |
| Others | 5.4 | 11.5 | 14.6 | 17.9 | 23.8 |
| Total | 1,126.4 | 1,196.8 | 1,356.1 | 1,464.5 | 1,565.7 |

[a] Prewar borders.

*Sources:* Egil Levits, "Die demographische Situation in der UdSSR und in den baltischen Staaten unter besonderer Berücksichtigung von nationalen und sprachsoziologischen Aspekten," *Acta Baltica*, 21 (1981), pp. 63–64; *Eesti arvudes 1920–1935* (Tallinn: Riigi Statistika Keskbüroo, 1937), p. 12; Riina Kionka, "Migration to and from Estonia," *Report on the USSR*, 2, no. 37 (1990), p. 20; Kalev Katus, "Rahvus: sakslane; elukoht: Eesti," *Aja Pulss*, no. 22 (1990), p. 10; Ene Tiit, "Eesti rahvastik ja selle probleemid," *Akadeemia*, 5 (1993), p. 2118.

Table 11.2. *Major ethnic groups in Estonia (%)*

|  | 1934[a] | 1959 | 1970 | 1979 | 1989 |
|---|---|---|---|---|---|
| Estonians | 88.2 | 74.6 | 68.2 | 64.7 | 61.5 |
| Russians | 8.2 | 20.1 | 24.6 | 27.9 | 30.3 |
| Ukrainians | — | 1.3 | 2.1 | 2.5 | 3.1 |
| Belarusans | — | 0.9 | 1.4 | 1.6 | 1.8 |
| Finns | 0.1 | 1.4 | 1.4 | 1.2 | 1.1 |
| Jews | 0.4 | 0.5 | 0.4 | 0.3 | 0.3 |
| Germans | 1.5 | 0.1 | 0.6 | 0.3 | 0.2 |
| Latvians | 0.5 | 0.2 | 0.2 | 0.3 | 0.2 |
| Swedes | 0.7 | — | — | — | — |
| Others | 0.5 | 1.0 | 1.1 | 1.2 | 1.5 |
| Total[b] | 100.1 | 100.1 | 100.0 | 100.0 | 100.0 |

[a] Prewar borders.
[b] Due to rounding off totals are not always 100.0%.
*Sources:* See Table 11.1.

of the total population.[4] As suggested in table 11.2, this proportion remained stable until the onset of Soviet rule. Ironically, the impact of wartime upheaval and Soviet border manipulation led to a temporary increase in the Estonian share of the population, probably rising to 97 percent in 1945 (within Soviet-era borders).[5] Thereafter, however, a precipitous decline occurred in the ethnic Estonian proportion, mainly as a result of massive in-migration by Russians and other East Slavs along with the Stalin-era deportation of tens of thousands of Estonians to remote regions of the Soviet Union. Although the rate of decline of the Estonian share of the population slowed in the 1970s and 1980s, only the Latvians among other union republic nationalities in the USSR had suffered such a drastic weakening of their demographic position by 1989. By the time of the Gorbachev era, a sense of demographic vulnerability lent an evident urgency to the Estonian movement for renewed self-determination. It is particularly noteworthy that the number of ethnic Estonians has not yet reached the pre-World War II level, and given the age structure of the population, it is not likely to do so in the foreseeable future.

No censuses have been conducted in the post-Soviet era, but it is clear that a considerable population decline has taken place, largely as a result of out-migration by Russians and other non-Estonians. At the beginning of 1995, the Estonian Statistical Office estimated a total population of 1,491,000 (nearly 75,000 less than in 1989), consisting of about 956,000 Estonians and 535,000 non-Estonians. Thus, the ethnic Estonian share had risen to just over 64 percent.[6]

## Historical background to 1918

Before the twentieth century the major political theme of Estonian history was external domination. Given its favorable geopolitical location on the Baltic littoral the region of traditional ethnic Estonian settlement attracted the intervention of larger peoples. Following the German-Danish conquest of the early thirteenth century, Estonia was also ruled by Poles, Swedes, and – beginning with Peter the Great in the early eighteenth century – Russians. Despite periodic change in formal suzerainty the key elites in Estonia from the thirteenth to the twentieth centuries remained the Baltic German nobility and merchants. Socially, the most striking aspect of Estonian development was the absence of a native nobility and clergy. After 1200, ethnic Estonians were relegated to the lower echelons of both rural and urban society, and anyone who rose to a higher social station was assimilated by the German-speaking elites. Serfdom dominated as the institution organizing daily life from the fourteenth to the early nineteenth centuries. The model for the Baltic nobility was the German states, with which it had close cultural and social ties, and when emancipation of the peasantry came in 1816–1819, it was characteristically based on the Prussian example of a decade earlier.[7]

The Estonians were Christianized "by fire and sword" as part of the medieval crusades, but it is doubtful that Catholicism penetrated very deeply into the consciousness of the common people. In the early sixteenth century the Protestant Reformation, in the form of Lutheranism, swept Scandinavia and the eastern Baltic region, including Estonia, but it was probably only with pietism in the eighteenth century that a living religious faith reached the Estonian peasantry. Perhaps the most important legacy of Protestantism in Estonia was a non-religious one: the early rise of mass literacy, beginning in earnest under Swedish rule in the seventeenth century. By the time of the emancipation of the Estonian peasantry around 1820, roughly four-fifths of younger-generation Estonians (excluding young children) could probably read, and this proportion increased in the course of the nineteenth century. According to the 1881 census, 95 percent of ethnic Estonians, fourteen years of age and older, were able to read.[8] This phenomenon no doubt contributed to the relatively rapid spread of national consciousness.

From a twentieth-century perspective, one of the most significant aspects of the Estonian experience in the decades preceding the Russian Revolution of 1917 was the phenomenon of increasing social mobilization, especially through the establishment of grass-roots organizations and societies. These associations focused on cultural and socioeconomic concerns such as music (both choral and orchestral), theatre, education, temperance, and the promotion of scientific agriculture.[9] By fostering citizen participation and local initiative these organizations contributed notably to the beginnings of a modern civil society. Beginning in the mid-1880s, the tsarist regime's ill-founded attempts at cultural Russification in education (requiring the use of Russian as the language of instruction at all levels of education), religion (promoting the spread of Russian Orthodoxy among Lutheran Estonians), and the introduction of Russian as the language of administration proved counterproductive. The St. Petersburg government lacked the means and the will to implement such policies in a systematic way, and applying these measures in a half-hearted manner only served to further strengthen the developing sense of national identity among the Estonian population.[10]

As suggested above, all political movements in the late Russian Empire were severely circumscribed except during the unique opportunity afforded by the Revolution of 1905. As was the case with other nationalities, the Estonians acquired a useful political education during the upheaval, affording them preparation for the more sweeping revolutionary change in 1917. In the waning years of the tsarist regime, Estonian elites also gained political experience through participation in municipal government – especially in Tallinn where they controlled the city administration from 1904 on – and as representatives to the four State Dumas (1906–1917).[11]

## The first independence era, 1918–1940

The emergence of Estonian independence in the wake of the Russian Revolution must be seen in the context of both external and internal factors. The unprecedented international situation created by the temporary collapse of *both* the Russian Empire and Imperial Germany, the two traditional great powers in the Baltic region, offered a unique opportunity, and at key points in the years 1918–1919 the fledgling Estonian state received considerable aid from both Great Britain and Finland. Nevertheless, it would be a mistake to ignore the role of internal readiness for independence by Estonian society.

Although limited to only two decades, interwar independence left an important cultural, political, and socioeconomic legacy. During these years the process of building a modern Estonian culture reached fruition, including the standardization of the written language and the unfettered evolution of various forms of high culture. Most importantly, particularly in view of what lay ahead during the decades of Soviet rule, a native-language educational system from the elementary to the postgraduate level became firmly established. These developments in the 1920s and 1930s were instrumental in helping the Estonians withstand the later challenges of cultural Sovietization and Russification.[12]

Politically, the interwar era offered a mixed picture, as was the case nearly everywhere in the successor states. In Estonia a decade and a half of liberal democracy (1920–1934) was followed by six years of moderate authoritarianism (1934–1940). The Constitution of 1920, reflecting the idealism and euphoria of liberation from tsarist rule, virtually eliminated the executive branch and placed political power in a democratically elected legislature and ultimately in the voters themselves through provisions for initiative and referendum. From the five parliamentary (*Riigikogu*) elections that were held in the years 1920–1932, a workable, if fragmented, multi-party system developed.

Fueled by growing dissatisfaction resulting from economic uncertainty in the early 1930s, a right radical movement based among the veterans of the war of independence against Soviet Russia made a bid for power. The bid was unsuccessful, however, Konstantin Päts, arguably the leading founder of Estonian independence in 1918–1920, carried out a preventive coup in March 1934. Päts in turn instituted a traditionalist authoritarian regime, based on the established agrarian, business, and military elites.[13] In the East European context of the 1930s, the Päts regime was a mild one, eschewing political executions and even amnestying its opponents on both right and left in 1938. Nevertheless, the authoritarian system also halted Estonia's political evolution and contributed to internal divisions, leaving a fragmented society to face the international crisis of 1939–1940.[14]

With 88.2 percent of the population in 1934 belonging to the titular nationality, interwar Estonia was ethnically one of the most homogeneous of the successor states in East Central Europe. In that year the leading minorities were Russians (8.2 percent), Germans (1.5 percent), Swedes (0.7 percent), Latvians (0.5 percent), and Jews (0.4 percent). About 80 percent of the Russian population lived in the areas bordering on the Soviet Union.[15] Ethnic tensions remained at a low level, despite some lingering Estonian resentment against the Baltic Germans. Estonian-Russian relations did not present any particular problems. In 1925, parliament passed a law on cultural autonomy that permitted minority groups of at least 3,000 individuals the right to establish governing bodies to organize their cultural affairs, particularly state-supported education in the mother tongue. Since the law was extraterritorial in nature, it proved especially attractive to those minorities who were dispersed throughout the country, i.e., the Germans and Jews.[16]

In 1919, a sweeping land reform expropriated and redistributed the large estates (mainly held by Baltic German nobles), eliminating most of the landless population in the countryside over the next two decades and creating a stable agrarian sector. Building on the pre-independence base, Estonian industrial output expanded moderately in 1920s, predictably declined during the Depression, and took a major leap forward in the late 1930s – especially with the much increased mining of oil-shale deposits in the northeastern part of the country. Estonia remained an overwhelmingly rural country in these years with the urban proportion increasing only gradually from 25.0 percent in 1922 to 32.8 percent in 1939.[17]

Admitted to the League of Nations in 1922, Estonia became a member of the expanded international community in the 1920s and 1930s. However, its search for security in the interwar period was never resolved. Attempts at a regional alliance that would have included states bordering on the Baltic Sea foundered on the disparity of the perceived interests of the potential participants, and even the much less ambitious Baltic Entente, established in 1934 by Estonia, Latvia, and Lithuania, had no teeth in its military clauses. Any hopes based on the League of Nations crumbled in the 1930s as this institution repeatedly showed its inability to deal with international aggression.[18] The eclipse of Estonian independence was sealed in the secret protocol to the Molotov-Ribbentrop Pact on August 23, 1939, a cynical deal between two totalitarian states that contravened existing conventions of international law and assigned Estonia to the Soviet sphere of influence.[19] Under threat of invasion by overwhelming force in September 1939, Estonia agreed to permit Soviet military bases manned by 25,000 troops on its territory, and in June 1940, as the West was preoccupied with the fall of France, Stalin used the same means to force a "people's government" on Estonia and the other two Baltic states. Estonia now came under full military occupation as the USSR increased its troop strength in the country to some 115,000 men.[20] Following Soviet-style sham elections in July, Estonia was formally "admitted" to the USSR in August 1940.

## From World War II to Gorbachev

The demographic impact of the Second World War and the ensuing Stalinist decade on the population of Estonia was devastating. During the war the main components of population losses included Soviet and German deportations and forced military mobilization, wartime casualties (military and civilian), executions (especially of Jews and political opponents), and flight to the West. As a result, the Baltic German, Swedish, and Jewish communities in Estonia – the first two of which traced their origins back to the thirteenth century – virtually ceased to exist, and the ethnic Estonian population declined by about 20 percent during the war alone. Under Stalin, arrests and deportations continued, although not quite at the level estimated by Western observers before the glasnost' era. In addition, the clashes of the pro-independence guerrilla movement with Soviet forces led to considerable loss of life in the late 1940s.[21]

In view of the forced nature of Estonia's annexation by the Soviet Union, the pervasive acts of regime-sponsored violence against the population, and the continuing military occupation, it is not surprising that the Soviet regime never gained any appreciable legitimacy among the ethnic Estonian population. True to his deep-seated distrust even of communists who had lived outside the USSR, Stalin based Soviet rule in Estonia – especially following the purge of 1950 – on so-called Russian-Estonians, i.e., Sovietized ethnic Estonians who had spent most of their lives in the USSR. Although native Estonian communists did rise in the ranks of the party in the post-Stalin era, they never attained decisive leadership positions until the Gorbachev era. It is characteristic that over a period of nearly four decades the post of first secretary of the Communist Party of Estonia (CPE) was held by two Russian-Estonians: Johannes (Ivan) Käbin (1950-1978) and Karl Vaino (1978-1988). Moreover, the perceived foreignness of the CPE was heightened by the strong non-Estonian (mainly Russian) presence in its ranks, ranging in the post-Stalin era from 56 percent in 1953 to a low of 48 percent in the 1970s.[22] In contrast to some parts of the Soviet Union, e.g., Lithuania or the Caucasian republics, the phenomenon of national communism was weakly developed in Estonia. After the purge of "bourgeois nationalists" under Stalin, the CPE elite was naturally wary of asserting republican rights. To some extent Johannes Käbin, who re-Estonianized his first name in the 1960s, moved in the direction of national communism in that decade, e.g., in his tolerance of more open cultural expression, but he stopped short of any decisive moves.[23]

Under Stalin, peaceful dissent was impossible, and the Estonian resistance in the first postwar decade took the form of a guerrilla movement of "forest brethren" (Est. *metsavennad*) who were based in the thickly wooded rural areas of the country. The guerrillas clearly did not expect to defeat the Soviet regime by their own efforts, but hoped to hold out until pressure from the Western powers would force the Soviet Union to withdraw from Estonia. Leaving aside patriotic motivations, the forest brethren were mainly comprised of veterans who had been conscripted into the German military and feared arrest, and those seeking to avoid deportation or other forms of repression. Estimates of the total number involved in guerrilla activity at one time or another in the years 1944–1953 vary widely, ranging from about 15,000 to 40,000.[24] The forest brethren likely had substantial support among the civilian population since a protracted resistance would have been near impossible without it.

In the post-Stalin era, dissent in Estonia emerged in the late 1960s on the Moscow model, expressing similar frustration at the unfulfilled expectations of reform engendered by de-Stalinization. The small band of dissidents in Estonia demanded both civil and national rights, including among the latter the restoration of Estonian independence. By the late 1970s, as the CPE adopted an increasingly harder line following Karl Vaino's advent to power and despite various forms of repression and arrests, the scope and social base of dissent broadened and led to some cooperation with other Balts, most notably in a memorandum on self-determination on the fortieth anniversary of the Molotov-Ribbentrop Pact in 1979. Estonian dissidents produced a number of samizdat publications in the late 1970s and early 1980s and greeted the rise of Solidarity in Poland with particular enthusiasm. In a broader sense, Tartu University, the leading institution of higher learning in Estonia, served as a center of intellectual opposition. The most striking example of dissent in the late Brezhnev era came in the "Letter of the Forty" in October 1980, a signed, open letter to various newspapers from forty leading intellectuals decrying the growth of ethnic tensions in Estonia and speaking out for the Estonian language whose role in public life, education, and the media was in visible decline.[25]

As elsewhere in the Soviet Union, the scope of outright dissent among the Estonian population remained limited since the penalties for overt opposition, although usually not murderous in the post-Stalin era, still constituted a strong deterrent. On the other side of the spectrum a considerable element, but still a minority, of the ethnic Estonian population collaborated directly with the Soviet regime for various reasons, most typically for personal gain. In the three decades between Stalin and Gorbachev, however, the great majority of Estonians might be termed "conservationists" in the sense that they quietly and in their own way sought to preserve Estonian national identity, integrity, and inherited cultural tradition.[26]

As the sphere of activity least subject to manipulation by the Soviet authorities, culture played a key role in the struggle for national survival under Soviet rule. In the Stalin era a rigid intepretation of the doctrine of socialist realism and a persistent campaign against "bourgeois nationalists" among Estonian writers, composers, artists, and others had a chilling impact on cultural output. However, parallel to the post-Stalin thaw elsewhere in the Soviet Union, a remarkable cultural rebirth took place in Estonia during the 1960s, never directly questioning official guidelines, but gradually expanding their parameters beyond recognition. This decade witnessed the coming of age of the first Soviet-era generation, who had not lived through the horrors of the Stalin era as adults, and it was also joined by representatives of older generations, a number of whom had only recently returned from deportation or the camps. Jaan Kross (1920-), Estonia's leading writer in the post-Stalin period, spent eight years as a deportee (1946–1954), but returned to his homeland to publish a series of powerful historical novels exploring the Estonian condition.[27] In the late Brezhnev era the heavy-handed promotion of Russian as the "language of friendship and cooperation" among the nations of the USSR provoked a strong reaction, as seen in the "Letter of the Forty" noted above. Although the letter was not published in Estonia before the glasnost era, it became widely known in the early 1980s through samizdat as well as Western radio broadcasts and had a far-reaching impact on the Estonian population, providing a significant lift to national morale at a bleak time.[28]

Under Stalin, in place of the balanced economic development of the interwar era, Estonia underwent the same wrenching experience of forced industrialization and collectivization of agriculture as the Soviet Union had in the 1930s. The rapacious mining of oil shale in northeastern Estonia during the decades of Soviet rule depleted most of the republic's reserves of this valuable resource and created massive air and water pollution in the region.[29] The exceedingly rapid pace of industrialization under Stalin led to an astonishing growth of urbanization from 31.3 percent in 1945 to 52.5 percent in 1953, a trend which was enhanced by the Estonian fear of continued rural deportations in these years. The rate of increase slowed in the 1950s and 1960s, and the level of urbanization reached 65.0 percent in 1970 before stabilizing in the 1980s at 70–72 percent.[30] The collectivization of agriculture destroyed the well-functioning family farmsteads (139, 991 in 1939 with an average size of 23 ha) and replaced them with increasingly larger collective and state farms. By 1975, their average land area had reached 7,174 ha.[31] Although agricultural productivity made a notable recovery in the post-Stalin era, the uprooting of the agricultural population from its individualist traditions left a bitter legacy.

## The Gorbachev era and the restoration of independence

When Mikhail Gorbachev opened the floodgates to change in the USSR, the Baltic peoples were best poised among Soviet nationalities to take advantage of the opportunity. The historical memory of two decades of independence had remained alive through a modern oral tradition, and the Balts were well aware of the fact that the United States and other leading Western powers had never recognized their forced incorporation into the USSR. Moreover, the Estonians had a unique window on the West through Finnish television, accessible in Tallinn and the northern third of the country.

By 1987, clear signs of a rebirth of civil society, drawing in part on the experience of pre-Soviet times, appeared in Estonia. Environmental protests, especially by students at Tartu University in spring 1987, against plans for expanded phosphate mining in north-central Estonia began the process of social mobilization. On August 23, the anniversary of the Molotov-Ribbentrop Pact, Estonian dissidents – several of whom had only recently been released from custody – organized a demonstration of 2,000–5,000 participants in Tallinn that for the first time publicly questioned the legitimacy of Soviet rule.[32] Although one of the leaders of the demonstration was forced to emigrate, this event emboldened Estonian society as it tested the limits of glasnost. By 1988, the intelligentsia became increasingly involved in the movement for change, especially at a landmark plenum of the leadership organs of the cultural unions in April. Writers, artists, composers, journalists, and others broke significant taboos at this meeting, including offering criticism of the party elite by name and calling for genuine federalism in the Soviet system.[33]

During 1988, the inchoate movement for renewal in Estonia became increasingly politicized, and Estonia took the lead in the USSR with two major firsts: the establishment of a popular front in April and passage of a declaration on sovereignty in November. Led by reformist communists such as Edgar Savisaar and Marju Lauristin, the Estonian Popular Front sought to consolidate and channel the reawakened civic energies of the population and to prod the CPE toward fundamental reform. At the front's founding congress in October, Savisaar stressed its centrist and stabilizing role in the unfolding pluralism of Estonian political life.[34] At this relatively early stage in the Gorbachev era the CPE still played a significant role, especially after Vaino Väljas replaced Karl Vaino as first secretary in June 1988 and became the first native Estonian to hold that office since 1950. Väljas took a strong autonomist position, advocating the decentralization of the USSR, and his leadership was decisive in the nearly unanimous passage of a declaration on sovereignty – meaning primacy of republican laws over all-Union ones – by the Estonian SSR Supreme Soviet in November. Moscow protested strongly, but the ESSR legislature reaffirmed its position in December by a more divided vote (150 to 91).[35]

During the latter half of 1988, the political scene in Estonia became increasingly checkered. As a reaction to the formation of the Estonian Popular Front, there appeared in summer 1988 a self-styled Internationalist Movement (Intermovement, for short), claiming to speak for the Russian and other non-Estonian population of Estonia, and – on the other side of the political spectrum – the Estonian National Independence Party (ENIP), led by former dissidents who unequivocally advocated the restoration of independence.[36] Thereafter, a wide range of political parties and organizations emerged as the possibility of significant transformation became increasingly palpable.

In the course of 1989 public opinion among the ethnic Estonian population shifted increasingly toward full independence from the USSR. Gorbachev and the central authorities in Moscow failed to address the nationalities issue in any meaningful way nor in the case of Estonia and rejected a project for self-management and economic autonomy, first proposed in September 1987 by four Estonian intellectuals.[37] Beginning in February 1989, a new factor was a grass-roots organizing campaign by the Estonian Citizens' Committees, a movement based on the principle of legal continuity from the interwar republic and seeking the voluntary registration of individuals born in independent Estonia and their descendants. By early 1990, over half of the ethnic Estonian population had registered as citizens, and this massive organizing effort and its appeal to historical continuity helped push public opinion toward the goal of independence. In February 1990, the movement held elections for a non-Soviet Congress of Estonia, an alternative parliament backed by the ENIP and other "national radical" groups.[38]

Events elsewhere in the Soviet bloc, especially in Eastern Europe and the other two Baltic states, had a marked impact on developments in Estonia. The fall of communist rule in Poland in summer 1989 without Soviet intervention, i.e., the withering away of the Brezhnev doctrine, suggested that the restoration of Estonian and Baltic independence might not be the impossible dream that it had appeared to be a few years earlier. During the era of glasnost there was much interaction and crossfertilization among the Baltic movements for change, most strikingly through the Estonian and Latvian Popular Fronts and Lithuania's Sajudis, e.g., the Baltic Assembly held in Tallinn in May 1989. The most dramatic instance of Baltic cooperation and solidarity came on the fiftieth anniversary of the Molotov-Ribbentrop Pact in August 1989, as the three popular fronts organized a massive human chain of over one million people linking the three Baltic capitals over a distance of some 400 miles. Moscow's threats following the demonstration merely served to further fuel Estonian and Baltic sentiment for independence.[39] When the Estonian Popular Front explicitly endorsed full independence in October 1989, it proved to be the final step in the consolidation of Estonian public opinion on this issue. Polls indicate that Estonian support for independence grew rapidly from 64 percent in September 1989 to 96 percent in May 1990. Among non-Estonians the increase was from 9 to 26 percent.[40]

The key question in Estonia in early months of 1990 became the following: what institution could most effectively serve as the vehicle for bringing about renewed independence? By March 1990, two newly elected rivals had emerged – the non-Soviet Congress of Estonia and the ESSR Supreme Soviet. Although they agreed to cooperate at first and many individuals were deputies to both bodies, the Supreme Soviet had a distinct advantage since it possessed legislative and administrative authority within the existing political system. On March 30, the Supreme Soviet (or in the now more appropriate translation of the Estonian *Ülemnõukogu*, "Supreme Council") declared Soviet power illegal in Estonia, since the country had been unlawfully occupied and annexed in 1940, and proclaimed the beginning of a period of transition that would culminate in the restoration of an independent Estonia.[41] This was a more cautious formulation than that passed by the Lithuanian legislature three weeks earlier, reflecting Estonia's more delicate demographic balance. The major political casualty at this stage of the developing independence movement was the CPE. It lost its "leading role" in public life by action of the ESSR Supreme Soviet in February 1990, and during the next year it also lost most of its membership as most ethnic Estonians no longer saw any need to be associated with a Soviet-era institution. In January 1991, the much shrunken CPE split into pro-independence and pro-CPSU wings.[42]

The period March 1990–August 1991 witnessed a continuing stalemate between the new Estonian government led by Edgar Savisaar, based on the Estonian Popular Front as the single largest entity in the Supreme Council, and Moscow. Estonia and the other two Baltic states argued that they constituted a special case since they were forcibly joined to the USSR after being recognized members of the international community for two decades, but Gorbachev refused to negotiate seriously, presumably fearing the ripple effect of any territorial changes in the Soviet Union. In January 1991, Estonia escaped the bloody crackdown that occurred in Lithuania and Latvia, largely because of the strong resistance in those two states and also support from Boris Yeltsin who traveled to Tallinn during the crisis and spoke out for the Baltic right to self-determination.[43] Estonia boycotted Gorbachev's all-Union referendum on the future of the USSR and instead held its own poll on the restoration of independence in March. With all permanent residents eligible to vote, the result was a strong 78 percent "yes," including about 30 percent of the non-Estonian voters.[44] The abortive August 1991 coup in Moscow provided the final, unexpected turn on the road to Estonian independence. On August 20, the Supreme Council, noting that the Soviet coup had "made it impossible to restore the national independence of the Republic of Estonia through bilateral negotiations with the USSR," unilaterally affirmed Estonian independence and established a Constitutional Assembly delegated from both the Supreme Council and the Congress of Estonia. This body was to draft a new constitution and present it to the electorate for a referendum. The resolution also called for parliamentary elections on the basis of the new constitution to be held in 1992.[45]

It is noteworthy that much of the symbolism of the movement for Estonian self-determination and independence in the Gorbachev era was tied to the image of "awakening" and specifically to the national awakening of the nineteenth century. The term was used not so much in the sense of "regaining" national consciousness, which obviously had not been lost under Soviet rule, as in the notion of reconnecting with the Estonian past and its cultural traditions, which had become increasingly inaccessible through deliberate Soviet policy. Historical continuity was exemplified by the use of the national song festival tradition, begun in 1869, as a vehicle for expressing Estonian solidarity in the present.[46] As noted above, the other major source of inspiration was the interwar independence era which provided the symbols of political continuity, e.g., the state flag, the preeminent role of the Estonian language in public life, and the idea of a constitutional, multiparty democracy. Among the several parallels between the process of establishing Estonian independence in the wake of the Russian Revolution and achieving its restoration during the Gorbachev years, perhaps the most striking are the following: (1) the collapse of empire combined with an internal Estonian readiness to take advantage of the opportunity, and (2) the rapid shift of Estonian public opinion from the goal of autonomy to complete independence in the context of systemic crisis.

## Domestic politics and economic transition, 1991–1994

Once the Soviet Union and the United States recognized Estonian independence in September 1991, the country's return to the ranks of the international community seemed remarkably simple. However, the challenges facing the fledgling state were enormous. Above all, Estonia had to redefine its existence as an independent entity, both in internal affairs and in its relations with the external world.

Among the former republics of the Soviet Union, Estonia became a pacesetter in both political and economic development in the early postcommunist era. In June 1992, by overwhelming approval in a referendum, it adopted the first post-Soviet constitution.[47] Reacting against the legacy of the authoritarian era of the late 1930s, the makers of the new constitution returned to the liberal democratic tradition of the 1920s and assigned political supremacy to the *Riigikogu* (State Assembly), a unicameral parliament with 101 members elected for a four-year term. The *Riigikogu* has ultimate authority over legislation, treaties with foreign countries, the appointment of the prime minister and other leading officials, and the longevity of governments. Parliament also elects the president by a two-thirds majority vote for a term of five years. The Constitutional Assembly's intention was that the powers of the president be more ceremonial than real. Nevertheless, he represents the state in international relations, has the first two choices in nominating a prime minister, and can force parliament to reconsider legislation.[48]

Estonia also held the first post-Soviet parliamentary elections in September 1992 which resulted in a right-of-center majority and led to the formation of a coalition government consisting of three electoral blocs or parties: Fatherland (30 seats), the Moderates (12), and the ENIP (11). Overall, nine parties or blocs achieved representation in the *Riigikogu*, and in contrast to the Soviet era, the legislature was monoethnic in composition, largely because of the nature of the 1938 citizenship law that Estonia reinstated in November 1991.[49] All citizens of Estonia in June 1940 and their descendants were automatically considered citizens. Naturalization required two years of residence (counting from March 30, 1990 – the beginning of the transition period to restored independence) and an additional one-year waiting period, a modest level of competence in Estonian, and an oath of loyalty to the constitution. Thus, the first naturalized citizens could appear only in spring 1993, i.e., after the September 1992 elections and as a result of Stalin's border changes in 1945 and the upheavals of World War II, very few Russians and other non-Estonians within Estonia's current borders were descendants of persons living there before June 1940.[50]

In a compromise among opposing views in the Constitutional Assembly, it was decided that as a one-time exception a direct presidential election for a four-year term would be held at the same time as the parliamentary one in September 1992. If no candidate received a majority, the decision would be left to the new *Riigikogu*. In the election the popular former chair of the Estonian SSR Supreme Soviet Arnold Rüütel finished first (41.8 percent of the vote), but lost to the writer and ex-foreign minister Lennart Meri (29.5 percent) in the subsequent runoff in parliament by a tally of 59–31.[51]

The 1992 elections marked the major turning point in Estonia's political evolution after August 1991. During the first post-Soviet year the governments were dominated by reformist ex-communists often associated with the Estonian Popular Front, e.g., Prime Ministers Edgar Savisaar (b 1950) and Tiit Vähi (b. 1947).[52] In contrast, the new cabinet formed by Mart Laar (b. 1960) in October 1992 represented a new political generation and also one that with few exceptions was free of previous communist ties. Despite commanding only a slim parliamentary majority at the beginning and facing various defections in the course of its tenure, the Laar government managed to survive for nearly two years until September 1994, outlasting any of the cabinets of the previous democratic era (1920–1934). The vote of no-confidence was 60–27, with the opposition citing the "incorrect conduct of state affairs" as the main reason, e.g., a questionable arms deal with Israel and the secret sale of surplus Russian rubles to Chechnya.[53] In view of the Laar government's longevity, it is not surprising that its approval rating dwindled; in September 1994, less than 10 percent of the eligible voters supported the parties still in the ruling coalition. There is also no question that the approaching regular parliamentary elections in March 1995 raised the stakes in political infighting during much of 1994.[54]

Overall, the *Riigikogu* became increasingly fragmented as numerous splits among the parties and blocs took place, making it difficult for parliament to play the intended leading role in national politics. The major beneficiary of parliamentary weakness was the presidency. For example, President Meri played an activist role in the legislative process, e.g., his intervention on the issue of the law on aliens in June-July 1993 and in the making of foreign policy.[55] It is also clear that after only two years of experience under the new constitution the working relationship between the branches of government was still in the process of evolution.

In the economic sphere Estonia took rapid and bold steps in comparison to other former Soviet republics, especially in the early introduction of its own currency, the *kroon* (crown), in June 1992. This action allowed the country to escape the runaway inflation of the "ruble zone" and to begin the process of diversifying its trade relations. The newly re-established Bank of Estonia resisted the temptation to print new money and to extend subsidies to the industrial sector. As a result inflation quickly came under control, falling from a monthly rate of 90 percent in January 1992 to 1.7 percent in May 1993. For 1993, Estonia was in a virtual tie with Latvia for the lowest annual inflation rate among ex-Soviet republics (36 percent).[56] The country also escaped dependence on trade with Russia and other successor states, and by the latter months of 1992, Finland had replaced Russia as Estonia's leading trading partner. For all its success, however, Estonia could not avoid the pain of economic transition. Inequality of wealth and income increased sharply with the agricultural sector lagging especially far behind, and pensioners and other low-income groups were hard hit by free market prices.[57]

## Ethnic relations

During the decades of Soviet rule in Estonia, ethnic tensions were forced beneath the surface by the stringent political system and the official myth of the "friendship of peoples." In the glasnost era, as social problems began to be faced with increasing frankness, the nationality issue immediately came to the forefront, especially in view of the drastic changes in Estonia's ethnic composition since World War II. The reality of relations among nationalities was much more complex than a superficial glance at them would suggest. For example, although the Intermovement made a noisy entrance on the political scene in 1988, it received only limited support among the Russian and other non-Estonian population.[58] It would be equally misleading to assume that most Estonians were overtly hostile to all

Russians. Despite obvious tensions, the fact is that ethnic relations have remained non-violent and manageable in Estonia, and opinion polls indicate that the situation is gradually improving. Indeed, a comparison of two surveys in December 1988 and February 1993 showed that relations among nationalities had changed substantially for the better. Among Estonians, those classifying ethnic relations as "very poor and poor" declined from 55 to 12 percent, while among non-Estonians (mainly Russians) the proportion fell from 39 to 9 percent.[59] Furthermore, a study by the Estonian Academy of Sciences at the end of 1993 found that the share of non-Estonians ("Russian-speakers") who had a positive view of Estonian independence had doubled since 1990 from about 30 to 60 percent.[60]

Despite the protracted ethnic violence in a number of postcommunist countries, the prospects for a continued non-violent solution to the ethnic tensions in Estonia remain favorable. There is a strong tradition of non-violence inherited from Estonia's interwar political culture which could be seen in Estonian dissent in the post-Stalin period and during the independence movement in the glasnost era. Both the Estonian Popular Front and the Estonian Citizens' Committees stressed grass-roots mobilization and non-violent resistance, drawing in part on earlier East European examples such as Solidarity and the Prague Spring. Moreover, the problem of ethnic relations in Estonia is less intractable than in other post-communist regions such as Mountainous Karabagh or Bosnia and Herzegovina because no deep-seated historical antagonisms are involved. Although 475,000 ethnic Russians resided in Estonia in 1989, their number was only about 20,000 in 1945, if postwar borders are used.[61]

On the other hand, if the Estonian authorities choose to pursue a serious policy of integration of non-Estonians, the enormous scope of the task is suggested by the fact that fully 26.3 percent of Estonia's population was foreign-born in 1989, one of the highest proportions in Europe.[62] Although there has been some out-migration by Russians and other non-Estonians since August 1991, this has involved only a small minority of the total non-Estonian population, and there is no indication that a massive wave of emigration will occur in the foreseeable future, especially if Estonia's economy continues to perform substantially more effectively than that of Russia.[63] In short, the great majority of non-Estonians in Estonia are there to stay.

Russians and other non-Estonians became more actively involved in politics with the first post-Soviet local elections in October 1993. Only citizens could be candidates, but all permanent residents eighteen years of age and older who had lived in a given locality for five years were eligible to vote. It is noteworthy that non-Estonian voters participated in the election much more actively than Estonian ones. In Tallinn, where one third of the country's population is located, two mainly ethnic Russian groups won 42 percent (27 of 64) of the seats. There, and in other areas where non-

Estonians were elected, moderate Russian candidates, i.e., those who supported an independent Estonia, were more successful than opponents of Estonian statehood.[64]

It is striking that the great majority of Russians and non-Estonians have taken a wait-and-see position on the issue of citizenship. By August 1994, only about 40,000 persons had become naturalized as citizens of Estonia while another 50,000 or so opted for Russian citizenship. It appears that many non-Estonians, including those for whom the language test presents no obstacle, fear the consequences of making a choice, especially if political sovereignty in Estonia should change.[65] In terms of integration, the most challenging region is the urban areas of northeastern Estonia, e.g., Narva — where ethnic Estonians comprised only 4.0 percent of the population in 1989. Although there is growing interest in learning Estonian among the Russians of Narva (85.9 percent of the population) and in placing their children in Estonian schools, the city lacks the resources, human and material, to provide these services.[66]

Among non-Estonians, Russians face the most difficult task of adaptation to life in post-communist Estonia, given their previously privileged position during the decades of Soviet rule. An opinion poll among Russians living in northern Estonia in late 1994 indicated that attitudes toward Estonian independence were directly related to economic and educational status: the higher the income and educational level, the more positive were Russian views of the Estonian state. Among the respondents, 77 to 89 percent noted the following problem areas in life in Estonia: unemployment, demands for knowledge of Estonian for citizenship and employment, the process of acquiring citizenship, and making ends meet economically. In this poll Russian attitudes toward the monoethnic Estonian parliament were mainly negative, a view that may begin to change following the electoral success of "Our Home is Estonia" in the March 1995 elections.[67]

## Foreign policy

Given geopolitical realities, relations with Russia are and will remain Estonia's most significant foreign policy challenge. During the first three years after the restoration of independence, the issue of ex-Soviet troops in Estonia dominated all others. From an estimated figure of over 100,000 in the late Brezhnev era, their numbers fell to about 25,000 in summer 1992 and to some 2,400 at the end of 1993.[68] Nevertheless, Russia showed great reluctance to come to any formal agreement on a withdrawal, especially after the success of extremist parties in the December 1993 Duma elections, and Moscow often tied the troop issue to the question of treatment of ethnic Russians in Estonia. However, at the end of July 1994, Presidents Meri and Yeltsin reached a dramatic and unexpected compromise in Moscow. Russia agreed to withdraw the rest of its troops by August

31, 1994 while Estonia accepted the principle of "social guarantees" for the slightly more than 10,000 retired ex-Soviet and Russian military officers living in Estonia.[69] There is little doubt that Western diplomatic intervention played a major role in promoting the agreement, and the already existing timetable for military withdrawal from Germany and Latvia – set for August 31 – put additional pressure on Moscow. A number of other questions remain on the agenda, including Stalin's annexation of about 5 percent of Estonian territory to the RSFSR in 1945. However, with a few exceptions in the southeast, these regions are entirely non-Estonian today, and it is unlikely that the West will support any Estonian claims on this issue.

The larger question in Estonian-Russian relations concerns to what extent and for how long will an imperial mentality inform Russian thinking. As the main successor to the Soviet Union, Russia has been living through an identity crisis, compounded by economic and political instability. By claiming special rights in the "near abroad," which includes Estonia and the other two Baltic states, Moscow is capable of contributing to potentially explosive situations. As Carl Bildt suggests, Russia's relations with the Baltic states are a possible "litmus test" with regard to the future direction of Moscow's foreign policy in general. It may well be, however, that Russia will focus mainly on the current members of the Commonwealth of Independent States, especially Belarus and Ukraine, while asserting a "peacekeeping" role in the Caucasus and Central Asia.[70] For Estonia the challenge will be to remain level-headed and to deal with its large Russian community according to internationally acceptable norms.

Although Estonia, Latvia, and Lithuania have shown a predictable post-communist tendency to assert their individual independence, it is noteworthy that cooperation among the Baltic states has grown considerably, in marked contrast to the situation in the interwar era when they failed to work together in any meaningful way. On the one hand, periodic verbal attacks from Moscow have encouraged Baltic solidarity in foreign policy. On the other hand, Western representatives have noted that cooperation begins at home; i.e., if the Balts want to integrate with various European organizations, they need to show their ability to work together in a narrower context as well. In the economic realm the most important indication of Baltic cooperation was a free trade agreement, signed in September 1993, and political relations have developed through ties at both the governmental and parliamentary levels, e.g., the Baltic Council of Ministers, established in June 1994.[71] Beyond its Baltic neighbors, Estonia has also developed strong ties with the Scandinavian states, especially Finland and Sweden, and the level of political, economic, and cultural cooperation between these states can be expected to develop further.

In a broader context, Estonian foreign policy since the restoration of independence has sought to develop a wide range of international connections in order to avoid dependence on a bilateral relationship with Russia. In particular, Estonia has focused on acquiring membership in key European organizations. Although Estonia was able to join the Conference on Security and Cooperation in Europe almost immediately (October 1991), the process of admission to the Council of Europe was much more rigorous and included the obligation to hold democratic elections and meet the organization's strict standards on human rights. In a major success for its foreign policy Estonia was admitted to the Council of Europe in May 1993, despite Russia's vocal opposition.[72] Established in March 1992, the Council of Baltic Sea States includes ten states bordering on the Baltic Sea (Germany, Denmark, Norway, Sweden, Finland, Poland, Russia, and the three Baltic states) and holds significant potential for small countries like Estonia as a means to avoid isolation.[73] Like the East Central European states and its Baltic neighbors, Estonia has expressed strong interest in eventual membership in the European Union and NATO. Full membership in both of these organizations is a long-term prospect, but Estonia's relative economic success and political stability have made it a stronger candidate than many post-communist states.[74]

## Conclusion

In the movement for the restoration of independence during the Gorbachev era, Estonia could draw on two main models from its previous history: the nineteenth-century national movement and the interwar independence era. As the Soviet system began to crumble, Estonia and its two Baltic neighbors were perceived as a special case by much of the international community, in large part because of the twenty years of previous experience with statehood. It is not coincidental that the Baltic states achieved their renewed independence in August-September 1991, i.e., several months *before* the collapse of the Soviet Union, in contrast to the other union republics.

Nevertheless, Estonia in 1991 was far different from the state and society that had existed in 1940, and it did not rejoin the same international community from which it had been forcibly removed fifty years earlier. This changed situation posed significant challenges, especially on the domestic scene where Soviet rule had effected a distorted form of modernization and far-reaching demographic changes, forcing Estonia to redefine what its restored independence would mean. In contrast, Estonia's external prospects seemed considerably more propitious than half a century earlier. Europe and the world had become much more interconnected, and small states such as Estonia had many more opportunities for international integration, and possibly a more secure existence, than in the past.

NOTES

1 On this point, see especially Miroslav Hroch, *Social Preconditions of National Revival in Europe* (Cambridge: Cambridge University Press, 1985).

2 Toivo U. Raun, "Estonian Social and Political Thought," Andrew Ezergailis and Gert von Pistohlkors, eds., *Die baltischen Provinzen Russland zwischen den Revolutionen von 1905 und 1917* (Cologne: Böhlau, 1987), pp. 60–65.

3 Toivo U. Raun, "The Estonians and the Russian Empire," *Journal of Baltic Studies*, 15 (1984), pp. 130–140.

4 Toivo U. Raun, *Estonia and the Estonians*, 2nd ed. (Stanford: Hoover Institution Press, 1991), p. 247.

5 Luule Sakkeus, *Post-War Migration Trends in the Baltic States*, RU Series B, no. 20 (Tallinn: Estonian Interuniversity Population Research Centre, 1993), p. 5.

6 *Estonian Human Development Report 1995*, p. 30.

7 For a survey of these topics, see Raun, *Estonia*, chapters 2–4.

8 Toivo U. Raun, "The Development of Estonian Literacy in the 18th and 19th Centuries," *Journal of Baltic Studies*, 10 (1979), pp. 119, 122.

9 See Ellen Karu, "On the Development of the Association Movement and Its Socio-Economic Background in the Estonian Countryside," Aleksander Loit, ed., *National Movements in the Baltic Countries During the 19th Century* (Stockholm: Almqvist & Wiksell International, 1985), pp. 271–282 and Ea Jansen, "Voluntary Associations in Estonia: The Model of the 19th Century," *Proceedings of the Estonian Academy of Sciences: Humanities and Social Sciences*. 42 (1993), pp. 115–125.

10 See Toivo U. Raun, "The Estonians," Edward C. Thaden, et al., *Russification in the Baltic Provinces and Finland, 1855–1914* (Princeton: Princeton University Press, 1981), pp. 287–354.

11 Toomas Karjahärm, "Eesti linnakodanluse formeerumisest 1870-ndate aastate lõpust kuni 1914. aastani (linna-ja duuma valimiste materjalide põhjal)," *Eesti NSV Teaduste Akadeemia Toimetised: Ühiskonnateadused*, 23 (1973), pp. 251–265.

12 On Estonia in the interwar period, see Raun, *Estonia*, chapters 7 and 8.

13 For a recent study of the Estonian radical right, see Rein Marandi, *Must-valge lipu all – Vabadussõjalaste liikumine Eestis 1929–1937*, vol. 1: *Legaalne periood (1929–1934)* (Stockholm: Almqvist & Wiksell International, 1991).

14 Rein Ruutsoo, "Eesti omariiklus ja rahvuslik areng 1918–1940," Kaarel Haav and Rein Ruutsoo, eds., *Eesti rahvas ja stalinlus* (Tallinn: Olion, 1990), pp. 56, 59.

15 *II rahvaloendus Eestis*, 4 vols. (Tallinn: Riigi Statistika Keskburoo, 1934–1937), vol. 2, pp. 47–48.

16 Karl Aun, "The Cultural Autonomy of National Minorities in Estonia," *Yearbook of the Estonian Learned Society in America*, 1 (1951–1953), pp. 30–35; Georg von Rauch, *The Baltic States: The Years of Independence – Estonia, Latvia, Lithuania, 1917–1940* (Berkeley: University of California Press, 1974), pp. 140–142.

17 Raun, *Estonia*, pp. 125–129, 131.

18 For contrasting views on Estonian and Baltic foreign policy, see Edgar Anderson, "The Baltic Entente: Phantom or Reality?," V. Stanley Vardys and Romuald Misiunas, eds., *The Baltic States in Peace and War, 1917–1945* (University Park: The Pennsylvania State University Press, 1978), pp. 126–135 and Alexander Dallin, "The Baltic States Between Nazi Germany and Soviet Russia," *ibid.*, pp. 97–109.

19 On the Molotov-Ribbentrop Pact, see the special issue of the *Proceedings of the Estonian Academy of Sciences: Social Sciences*, 39, no. 2 (1990).

20 Raun, *Estonia*, pp. 141, 144.

21 Romuald J. Misiunas and Rein Taagepera, *The Baltic States: Years of Dependence, 1940–1980* (Berkeley: University of California Press, 1983), pp. 274–276, 279–280; Evald Laasi, "Mõnede lünkade täiteks," *Sirp ja Vasar*, November 27, 1987, pp. 3–4; Evald Laasi, "Sissisõjast Eestis 1945–1953," *Looming*, no. 11 (1989), pp. 1519–1527; Ene Tiit, "Eesti rahvastik ja selle probleemid," *Akadeemia*, 5 (1993), p. 1654.

22 *Kommunisticheskaia partiia Estonii v tsifrakh 1920–1980* (Tallinn: Eesti Raamat, 1983), pp. 108–109, 181–182.

23 Jaan Pennar, "Soviet Nationality Policy and the Estonian Communist Elite," Tönu

Parming and Elmar Järvesoo, eds., *A Case Study of a Soviet Republic: The Estonian SSR* (Boulder: Westview, 1978), pp. 122–123; *Eesti Aeg*, May 18, 1994, p. 13.

24  Misiunas and Taagepera, *Baltic States*, pp. 81–84; Evald Laasi, ed., *Vastupanuliikumine Eestis 1944–1949* (Tallinn: Nõmm & Co., 1992), p. 111; Mart Laar, *War in the Woods: Estonia's Struggle for Survival, 1944–1956* (Washington, DC: Compass Press, 1992), p. 155.

25  V. Stanley Vardys, "Human Rights Issues in Estonia, Latvia, and Lithuania," *Journal of Baltic Studies*, 12 (1981), pp. 275–278, 280–284, 289–296; Toivo U. Raun, "Language Development and Policy in Estonia," Isabelle T. Kreindler, ed., *Sociolinguistic Perspectives on Soviet National Languages: Their Past, Present and Future* (Berlin: Mouton de Gruyter, 1985), p. 30.

26  On "conservationism," see Alexander Shtromas, "The Baltic States," Robert Conquest, ed., *The Last Empire: Nationality and the Soviet Future* (Stanford: Hoover Institution Press, 1986), pp. 202–203.

27  On Jaan Kross, see Mardi Valgemäe, "The Antic Disposition of a Finno-Ugric Novelist," *Journal of Baltic Studies*, 24 (1993), pp. 389–394. Two recent English translations of his novels are *The Czar's Madman* (New York: Pantheon, 1993) and *Professor Martens' Departure* (New York: New Press, 1994).

28  Sirje Kiin, Rein Ruutsoo, and Andres Tarand, *40 kirja lugu* (Tallinn: Olion, 1990), pp. 49, 67–70.

29  Mare Taagepera, "Pollution of the Environment and the Baltics," *Journal of Baltic Studies*, 12 (1981), pp.264–265.

30  Raun, *Estonia*, pp. 183, 205, 234; *Eesti Aeg*, May 18, 1994, p. 12.

31  *Eesti entsüklopeedia*, 8 vols. & supplement (Tallinn: Loodus, 1932–1937), suppl., pp. 241–242; Alfred Kasepalu, "Sotsialistlike põllumajandusettevõtete arvust Nõukogude Eestis aastail 1944–1976," Edgar Tõnurist, ed., *Sotsialistliku põllumajanduse areng Nõukogude Eestis* (Tallinn: Valgus, 1976), p. 130.

32  Rein Taagepera, "Estonia's Road to Independence," *Problems of Communism*, 38, no. 6 (1989), pp. 15–16; "Glasnost in the Baltic: Summer Demonstrations," *Baltic Forum*, 4, no. 2 (1987), p. 3.

33  *Baltic Forum*, 5, no. 1 (1988), pp. 95–97; *Eesti NSV loominguliste liitude juhatuste pleenum 1.-2. aprillil 1988* (Tallinn: Eesti Raamat, 1988), pp. 157–158, 223.

34  *Rahvakongress: Eestimaa Rahvarinde kongress 1.-2. oktoobril 1988* (Tallinn: Perioodika, 1988), pp. 19–21.

35  *Homeland*, November 23, 1988, pp. 1–2; *New York Times*, December 8, 1988, p. A11.

36  *Homeland*, July 27, 1988, p. 2; Endel Pillau, ed., *Eestimaa kuum suvi* (Tallinn: Olion, 1989), p. 136.

37  On the self-management or IME (*Isemajandav Eesti*) project, see Toivo Miljan, "The Proposal to Establish Economic Autonomy in Estonia," *Journal of Baltic Studies*, 20 (1989), pp. 149–164.

38  Riina Kionka, "The Estonian Citizens' Committee: An Opposition Movement of a Different Complexion," *Report on the USSR*, 2, no. 6 (1990), pp. 30–33.

39  *Baltic Forum*, 6, no. 2, pp. 77–79.

40  *Homeland*, October 18, 1989, pp. 1–2; October 25, 1989, pp. 1–2; *The Estonian Independent*, May 30, 1990, p. 3.

41  Charles F. Furtado, Jr. and Andrea Chandler, eds., *Perestroika in the Soviet Republics: Documents on the National Question* (Boulder: Westview, 1992), pp. 102–103. The vote was 73–0 with 27 non-Estonian deputies present but not voting (*Homeland*, April 4, 1990, p. 1).

42  *Päevaleht*, January 27, 1991, p. 1.

43  *The Estonian Independent*, January 17, 1991, pp. 1–3.

44  *Ibid.*, March 7, 1991, pp. 1, 3.

45 Furtado and Chandler, *Perestroika*, pp. 108–109.
46 Rein Ruutsoo, "Rahvuslik identiteet ja riikliku iseseisvuse taastamine," *Looming*, no. 9 (1994), pp. 1267, 1270–1271.
47 *The Baltic Independent*, July 3–9, 1992, p. 1. With 66.3 percent of the eligible voters participating, 91.2 percent approved of the new constitution.
48 *Eesti Vabariigi põhiseadus/Republic of Estonian Constitution* (Tallinn: Eesti Vabariigi Riigikantselei, 1993).
49 *The Baltic Independent*, September 25-October 1, 1992, p. 9.
50 Dzintra Bungs, Saulius Girnius, and Riina Kionka, "Citizenship Legislation in the Baltic States," *RFE/RL Research Report*, 1, no. 50 (1992), pp. 38–39.
51 *Eesti Vabariigi põhiseadus/Eesti Vabariigi põhiseaduse rakendamise seadus* (Tallinn: Riigi Teataja, 1994), p. 29; *The Baltic Independent*, October 9–15, 1992, p. 1.
52 *Kes on kes Eesti poliitikas 1988–1992* (Tallinn: Eesti Entsüklopeedia, 1992), p. 83, *passim*.
53 *Postimees*, September 27, 1994, p. 3; *Helsingin Sanomat*, September 4, 1994, p. C1.
54 *Helsingin Sanomat*, September 23, 1994, p. C3; *Postimees*, June 18, 1994, p. 2.
55 *Helsingin Sanomat*, September 28, 1894, p. A2; *The Baltic Independent*, July 9–15, 1993, p. 1; July 16–22, 1993, p. 1.
56 *The Baltic Independent*, June 25-July 1, 1993, p. B3; *Postimees*, June 27, 1994, p. 8.
57 *The Baltic Independent*, June 25-July 1, 1993, p. B3; *Rahva Hääl*, August 13, 1994, p. 5; *Eesti Ekspress*, March 4, 1994, p. A6.
58 At the end of 1988, an opinion poll among "Russian-speakers" in Estonia indicated that 15 percent supported the Intermovement (*Homeland*, March 15, 1989, p. 2).
59 *Rahva Hääl*, March 31, 1993, p. 2.
60 *Helsingin Sanomat*, May 4, 1994, p. A2.
61 Toivo U. Raun, "Ethnic Relations and Conflict in the Baltic States," W. Raymond Duncan and G. Paul Holman, Jr., eds., *Ethnic Nationalism and Regional Conflict: The Former Soviet Union and Yugoslavia* (Boulder: Westview, 1994), pp. 171–174.
62 Kalev Katus, "Eesti rahvastiku tulevikujooned," *Looming*, no. 2 (1994), pp. 249–250; *Eesti Aeg*, May 11, 1994, p. 7.
63 According to the Russian State Statistical Committee, there was a net in-migration of 30,363 ethnic Russians from Estonia during the period January 1, 1991-October 1, 1993 (*Eesti Aeg*, March 16, 1994, p. 7).
64 *The Baltic Independent*, October 22–28, 1993, pp. 1, 4; *Helsingin Sanomat*, May 4, 1994, p. A2. In 1989, the population of Tallinn was as follows: Estonians – 47.4 percent; Russians – 41.2 percent; and others – 11.4 percent (Raun, *Estonia*, p. 249).
65 *Päevaleht*, August 10, 1994, p. 2; *Helsingin Sanomat*, August 21, 1994, p. C2. About 960,000 citizens in Estonia traced their roots back to the pre-1940 republic; some 880,000 were ethnic Estonians while approximately 80,000 were non-Estonians.
66 *Päevaleht*, August 17, 1994, p. 12. The population of Narva was 64.8 percent Estonian in 1934 (Raun, *Estonia*, p. 207), but deliberate Soviet policy, especially under Stalin, transformed the ethnic composition of the city.
67 Marika Kirch and Aksel Kinch, "Ethnic Relations: Estonians and Non-Estonians," *Nationalities Papers*, 23 (1995), p. 46; *Easti Express*, March 34, 1995, p. A4; April 13, 1993, p. A14.
68 Raun, *Estonia*, p. 232; Dzintra Bungs, "Soviet Troops in Latvia," *RFE/RL Research Report*, 1, no. 34 (1992), p. 19; *RFE/RL Daily Report*, no. 249, December 30, 1993.
69 *New York Times*, July 27, 1994, p. A1; *Postimees*, July 28, 1994, p. 4.
70 Carl Bildt, "The Baltic Litmus Test," *Foreign Affairs* (September/October 1994), p. 82; *Postimees*, July 20, 1994, p. 2.
71 Bildt, "Baltic Litmus Test," p. 72; *New York Times*, October 21, 1994, p. A6.
72 *The Baltic Independent*, September 17–23, 1993, p. 1; December 17–23, 1993, pp. 1–2; December 24, 1993-January 6, 1994, p. 1; *Postimees*, June 14, 1994, p. 1.

73 *Helsingin Sanomat*, May 12, 1993, p. A8; May 14, 1993, p. C2.
74 Eve Kuusmann, "Estonia and Cooperation in the Baltic Sea Region," Pertti Joenniemi and Peeter Vares, eds., *New Actors on the International Arena: The Foreign Policy of the Baltic Countries* (Tampere: Tampere Peace Research Institute, 1993), pp. 83–84.

# Estonia: chronology of events

*August 1987*
23   Several thousand attend a demonstration to commemorate the anniversary of the Molotov-Ribbentrop pact.

*September 1987*
Four Estonian intellectuals submit a project on republican self-management to Moscow.

*April 1988*
At a plenum of the leadership organs of Estonian cultural unions, several criticisms of the party elite and calls for genuine federalism are heard. The Estonian Popular Front, the first of its kind in the Soviet Union, is established.

*June 1988*
16   Vaino Valjas replaces Karl Vaino as First Party Secretary, becoming the first native Estonian to hold that office since 1950.

*August 1988*
21   The pro-independence Estonian National Independence Party is formed.

*October 1988*
1   The Estonian Popular Front, which began to form in April, holds its founding congress (and is officially registered in January 1989).

*November 1988*
1   The Supreme Soviet issues a declaration of sovereignty by a vote of 258–1 (with several abstentions) and asserts its right to veto all-union laws passed in Moscow.

*December 1988*
7   In a more divided vote (150 to 91), the Supreme Soviet reasserts its decision on sovereignty.

*January 1989*
15   The Russian speakers' movement, Intermovement, holds its founding conference.
18   A language law is adopted which makes Estonian the official republican language.

*February 1989*

The Estonian Citizens' Committee begins a campaign for the voluntary registration of Estonian citizens, defined to be residents born in interwar independent Estonia or their descendants.

*March 1989*

14  Anti-Estonian rallies are held in several cities.

*April 1989*

14  Soviet tanks roll into Tallin and Tartu.

*May 1989*

18  The Supreme Soviet votes for an economic autonomy program.

*August 1989*

9–17  Thousands of Russian factory and shipyard workers in Tallinn walk off their jobs in protest against language discrimination and the curbing of their voting rights.

23  Almost two million demonstrators in the Baltic states participate in a human chain of protest on the 50th anniversary of the Molotov-Ribbentrop pact.

*December 1989*

10  Nationalists gain a majority of seats in local elections.

*February 1990*

23  The Supreme Soviet eliminates the Communist Party's "leading role" in public life.

24  The Estonian Citizens' Committee holds elections to an alternative Congress of Estonia.

*March 1990*

18  Nationalists gain a majority of seats in elections to the 105-seat parliament.

25  The Communist Party of Estonia breaks from the CPSU.

29  Arnold Ruutel is reelected parliamentary chairman.

30  In a vote of 73–0 (with 27 abstentions), parliament declares Soviet power illegal in Estonia and proclaims the beginning of a transition period to independence.

*April 1990*

3  Edgar Savisaar is chosen as Prime Minister.

*January 1991*

The Communist Party splits into pro-independence and pro-CPSU wings.

*March 1991*

3    Boycotting the 17 March referendum on preserving the union, Estonia holds an alternative referendum in which 78 percent of voters (83 percent turnout) declare their support for independence.

*August 1991*

20    Parliament issues a declaration of independence.
24    Yeltsin recognizes Estonia's independence.

*September 1991*

6    The Soviet government recognizes the independence of Estonia.

*October 1991*

5    The Baltic Council, comprised of the leaders of Lithuania, Latvia, and Estonia, issues a joint statement demanding the immediate withdrawal of Soviet troops from their territories.

*November 1991*

6    Estonia reinstates the 1938 citizenship law granting automatic citizenship to all citizens of Estonia in June 1940 and their descendants. All other residents must have resided in Estonia for two years starting from 30 March 1990 before they can apply for naturalization. Applicants must demonstrate a minimum proficiency of Estonian language.

*January 1992*

16    Parliament agrees to grant Prime Minister Edgar Savisaar emergency powers to resolve the country's economic crisis.
23    After widespread protest against parliament's decision, Savisaar resigns.
27    Tiit Vahi confirmed as new prime minister.

*February 1992*

1–2    Russia agrees to withdraw the 100,000 Soviet troops estimated to be stationed in the Baltic states.
26    The citizenship law goes into effect.

*March 1992*

6    The Council of Baltic Sea States (including the Baltic states plus seven others) is established.
21    Several thousand Russians protest in Tallinn against price hikes and the proposed citizenship law which would prevent most Russians from gaining automatic citizenship.

*May 1992*

12    A signature campaign begins for a referendum on disbanding parliament and holding new elections.

*June 1992*

28    In a referedum, 91 percent of voters (with 66 percent participation) vote for the passage of the new constitution.

*July 1992*

25    A citizenship law is passed which bars most ethnic Russians from becoming citizens automatically.

27    Estonian and Russian troops exchange shots in Riga.

*August 1992*

6    Russia asks for $7.7 billion from the Baltic states in exchange for withdrawing its troops from the region by 1994.

*September 1992*

20    Only citizens are allowed to participate in both presidential and parliamentary elections to the 101-seat Riigikogu. Parliamentary chairman Arnold Ruutel leads with 42 percent, followed by former foreign minister Lennart Meri (30 percent). Meri's Fatherland (Isamaa) party wins the most seats, 28, followed by the leftist Secure Home (18) and the Popular Front (16). As no presidential candidate received a majority vote, the president is to be selected by parliament. Isamaa forms a governing coalition with the Moderates (with 12 seats) and ENIP (with 11).

*October 1992*

6    Meri is selected President by the State Assembly by a vote of 59–31.

7    Parliament declares the end of the transitional period to full independence.

8    Mart Laar is appointed Prime Minister.

30    Yeltsin suspends troop pullout due to concern of infringement of ethnic Russians' rights.

*November 1992*

28    At its 22nd congress, the Communist Party changes its name to the Estonian Democratic Labor Party.

*December 1992*

1    Six Slavic organizations write up a charter for a Community of Russian-speaking Residents of Estonia.

*January 1993*

30    Founding congress of the Russian-speakers' Representative Assembly opens. The Assembly supports legislative activity to defend the rights of the Russian-speaking population.

*March 1993*

12    Militia take control of the town of Padilski, the site of a Russian naval base which had barred the entrance of government officials.

*May 1993*

12    Estonia is admitted to the Council of Europe.

*June 1993*

21    Parliament passes Law on Aliens, which requires all noncitizens to apply for residence permits and decide which citizenship to adopt.

*July 1993*

16–17    Narva and Sillamae hold referendums on gaining autonomous national-territorial status, and over 90 percent of those voting (54 percent and 61 percent turnout) express support. The Supreme Court later rules that the referendums are invalid.

*September 1993*

15    Parliament adopts a law on education which includes a clause mandating the phaseout of all non-Estonian language high schools by the year 2000.

*October 1993*

17    In the first post-Soviet local elections, only citizens are eligible to run, but all permanent residents 18 and older who had lived in a given locality for five years are eligible to vote. In Tallinn, Russians win 42 percent of the seats.

27    A law granting minorities wide cultural autonomy is approved by parliament.

*November 1993*

13    The Estonian Popular Front dissolves itself after members decide that all of its goals have been accomplished.

*June 1994*

11    Isamaa reelects Prime Minister Laar as its chairman, following a warning by Laar that he would resign his premiership if not reelected.
The Baltic states establish a joint Baltic Council of Ministers.

30    Isamaa fragments, retaining only half of its 22
parliamentary seats.

*July 1994*

26    After last-minute talks on troop withdrawal, Russia agrees
to withdraw the remaining 2,000 troops by 31 August. In
return, Estonia promises to grant the 10,000 military
pensioners in Estonia certain "social guarantees."

*August 1994*

31    Russia meets its deadline for troop withdrawal.

*September 1994*

7    Former prime minister Vahi accuses Laar of permitting the
illegal sale of 2 billion Russian rubles to Chechnya.

26    In a vote of 60–27 (with one abstention), parliament
supports a no-confidence motion again Prime Minister Laar
who is subsequently dismissed from office.

*October 1994*

1    The Russian Party of Estonia, the first Russian-speakers'
party, is founded.

8    The more moderate United People's Party of Estonia,
made up of several Russian-speakers' organizations, is
established.

13    Parliament votes against the President's candidate for Prime
Minister, Siim Kallas, the President of the Bank of Estonia,
Kallas had intended to continue the radical reforms Laar
had initiated.

27    Andres Tarand, formerly Minister of the Environment, is
elected Prime Minister.

*November 1994*

13    The Baltic Assembly issues a statement regarding the need
to demilitarize the Russian Kaliningrad oblast and restore
its cities historical German names.

*December 1994*

11    Russian citizens in Estonia unite under the umbrella Union
of Citizens of Russia.

*January 1995*

19    Parliament adopts a new law on citizenship mandating that
prospective citizens must have lived in Estonia five years
before applying for citizenship and imposing a one-year
waiting period following application. The law only applies
to residents who moved to Estonia beginning in July 1990.

*March 1995*

5   In parliamentary elections, the left-of-center Coalition Party/ Rural People's Union bloc wins 42 seats. They are joined by the Centrist Party to form a government coalition with 57 of 101 seats.

*April 1995*

5   Tiit Vahi, leader of the Coalition Party/Rural People's Union bloc, is elected Prime Minister, a position he held in 1992.

12   Estonia becomes an associate member of the European Union.

Part V
# The Transcaucasus

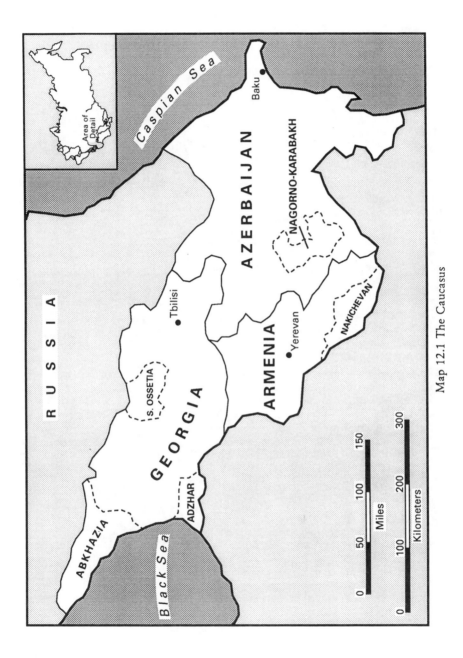

Map 12.1 The Caucasus

# Azerbaijan

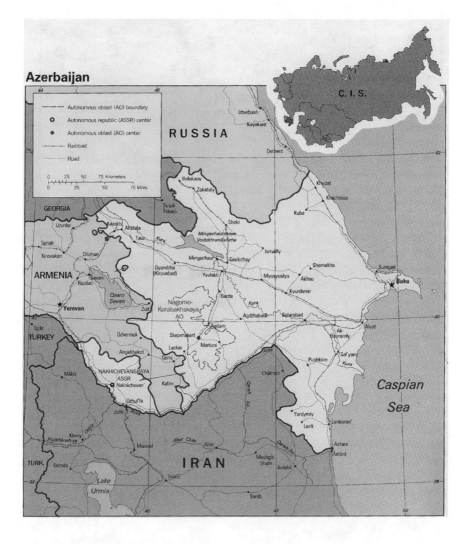

C. I. S.

RUSSIA

Izberbash

Kayakent

Derbent

Belokany

Zakataly

Tsiloti-Tskaro

Sheki

Khudat

Khachmas

Kuba

GEORGIA

Uzunlar

Kazakh

Akstala

Taúz

Kura

Mingechaurskoye
Vodokhranilishche

Ismailly

Spitak

Kirovakan

Dilizhan

Mingechaur

Geokchay

Shemakha

Sumqait

Gyandzha
(Kirovabad)

Yevlakh

Myusyuslyu

Akhsu

Baku

ARMENIA

Sevan

Razdan

Kyurdamir

Ozero
Sevan

Zod

Barda

Kura

Yerevan

Nagorno-
Karabakhskaya
AO

Agdzhabedi

Sabirabad

Alyat

Iğdır

TURKEY

Dzhermuk

Stepanakert

Agdam

Ali-
Bayramly

Angekhakot

Lachin

Goris

Martuni

Arax

Pushkino

Sal'yany

Kura

NAKHICHEVANSKAYA
ASSR

Mákú

Kafan

Chálmeh

Nakhichevan'

Dzhuffa

Jolfa

Arax

Yardymly

Lenkoran'

Lerik

Caspian

Sea

Rúdkháneh-ye

Khvoy

Maraad

Ahar Chay

Ahar

Qareh Su

Astara

Astárá

TURK.

Salmás

IRAN

Meshgin
Shahr

Ardebil

Lake
Urmia

Tabriz

Sarāb

# 12   Azerbaijan: searching for new neighbors

SHIREEN T. HUNTER

## Azerbaijan: An Historical and Ethno-cultural background

The country which constituted the Soviet republic of Azerbaijan and which, since the end of the USSR, has become the Republic of Azerbaijan, has a long and checkered history, a mixed ethno-cultural legacy, and an ethnically and religiously heterogeneous population. Even the very name of the republic is a matter of controversy. Indeed, the appellation "Azerbaijan" was first affixed to the present republic only in 1918, when – following the chaotic situation which the Bolshevik revolution of 1917 created in the tsars' empire – an independent republic was created under the auspices of the Ottoman forces, which were occupying part of the country. Prior to this date, this region was known as "Arran" to Iranian and Islamic historians and geographers, and as Albania-Caspia to the Romans.[1] However, by the early seventeenth century, the name Arran had lost its usage and various regions of what is now the Republic of Azerbaijan were known by their local names, such as Shirvan, Gandja, and Dagistan.[2] Indeed, the only region known historically by the name "Azerbaijan" was what is today the Iranian province of Azerbaijan.

When the republic of Azerbaijan was first created in 1918, some Iranian Azeris thought of changing the name of their province to "Azadistan" (The Land of Freedom). This was largely because of their fear of the irridentist and expansionist ambitions of the new republic and their Ottoman allies.[3] This apprehension later proved to be justified, as the Bolsheviks, who reconquered the region between 1920–21, created an elaborate irridentist myth about a historic and united Azerbaijan which had been divided in 1813 and 1828 as a result of Russo-Iranian imperial rivalry. The communists also popularized the notion of "Northern" and "Southern" Azerbaijans, divided in the manner of the Koreas or Vietnam before the latter's reunification. Over the years, a whole literature of grief over the separation of the so-called Northern and Southern Azerbaijans came into being, and thus the myth was internalized by large numbers of Azeris, including the nationalist forces which came to the fore following the introduction of *glasnost* in the Soviet Union.[4]

The historic facts, however, are somewhat different from the myth. Iran did not divide Azerbaijan in the context of a conspiracy with Tsarist Russia. Instead, Iran lost its Transcaucasian possessions to Russia – including parts of the present republic of Armenia – following two series of wars in 1804–

437

1812 and 1824–1828. Indeed, the Treaty of Turkmenchai, signed in 1828, not only deprived Iran of its Transcaucasian possessions, but also established the regime of "capitulation" in Iran, and thus opened it to extensive Russian and other foreign influence. For this reason, the treaty is known as "shameful" (Nangin) by the Iranians.

Azerbaijan also has an ethnically and culturally composite character and an essentially bifurcated sense of identity. This derives from the fact that the Transcaucasus – including Azerbaijan – has been at the crossroads of major ethnic migrations and a meeting place of civilizations which have included the Greco-Roman, the Christian, the Iranian and the Turko-Islamic. In the case of Azerbaijan, Iranian civilization, in both its pre- and post-Islamic versions, has exerted the greatest influence, even after the introduction of Turkic elements into the region and Azerbaijan's linguistic Turkification.[5]

In addition to those peoples which have been characterized as indigenous to the region and whose origins and ethnic affiliations are not clear, the Transcaucasus has witnessed two major waves of ethnic migration. The first wave consisted of the Indo-Europeans, who entered the region in the first (perhaps even the second) millennium BC, and extended south and east. The second wave consisted of Turkic peoples, who entered the region in significant numbers in the late tenth and eleventh centuries although Turkic elements had been present in close proximity to the region by the sixth century.

The introduction of Turkic elements into the region weakened, but did not eliminate, the indigenous population. On the contrary, accounts of Islamic geographers as late as the fourteenth century point to the existence of two distinct Turk and Tajik communities. What did happen over five centuries was the linguistic Turkification – or, as the Azeri historian Ahmad Kasravi has put it, the self-Turkification – of the indigenous population of the region.[6] But with the Iranian literary renaissance which followed the Arab invasion, Persian became the literary, and in many instances, the court language of the northern and eastern reaches of the Muslim lands.

This interaction of Turkic and Iranian elements created a certain cultural duality in Azerbaijan, and led to divisions between those Azeris who want a totally Turkic culture and those who prefer a blending of these elements and the development of a uniquely Azeri synthesis. Moreover, not all of the Iranian people of the region became linguistically Turkified. In Azerbaijan today, for example, it has been estimated that there are up to one million Talysh, who are ethnically and linguistically close to the inhabitants of Iran's northern provinces of Gilan and the region known as Tawalesh. There is also a significant Kurdish population which, together with the Persians, formed the largest group of Iranian peoples entering the region in the first millennium BC. There are also a small number of Tats, who speak various Iranian dialects, and the Lezgdin – one of the so-called

Table 12.1. *National composition of Azerbaijan,*
*1989*

| Nationalities | Population | in % |
|---|---|---|
| Total population | 7,021,000 | 100.0 |
| Azeris | 5,806,400 | 82.7 |
| Russians | 393,200 | 5.6 |
| Armenians | 393,200 | 5.6 |
| Lezgins | 140,400 | 2.0 |
| Kabardinians | 42,100 | 0.6 |
| Other | 245,700 | 3.5 |

*Source: Natisional'nyi sostav naseleniya SSSR*
(Moscow: Finansy i statistika, 1991).

indigenous people of the Caucasus – who have lived in the region since before the settlement of the Indo-Europeans (see table 10.1)[7]

The existence of these groups gives the Republic of Azerbaijan an ethnically heterogeneous character, a factor which has had significant, and mostly negative, implications for its evolution during the last several years. Coupled with Azerbaijan's cultural duality, this heterogeneity has eroded Azerbaijan's sense of national cohesion and has made it vulnerable to the manipulation of external forces seeking to influence its evolution and to gain, or regain – as has been the case with Russia – a controlling influence over its destiny.

Sectarian differences further contribute to the fragmentation of Azeri society. After the reunification of Iran in the late fifteenth century under the Safavids which resulted in its gradual Shi'aization, the vast majority of the inhabitants of the diverse regions that today constitute the Republic of Azerbaijan also adopted Shi'ism. Historically, this factor has played an important role in shaping the collective self-identity of the Azerbaijanis and the focus of their loyalties, deciding the fate of the rivalry which developed between reunited Iran and the Ottoman empire over the allegiance of these peoples. Thus these regions, plus parts of what is now the republic of Armenia – including its capital Yerevan – remained under Iranian sovereignty until their capture by Russia in 1828.

Currently, 75 percent to 80 percent of the population of Azerbaijan is nominally Shi'a, and 20 percent to 25 percent is Sunni. There is a small number of Christians – mostly concentrated in the Armenian-inhabited region of Nagorno-Karabakh – and a very small number of Jews, approximately thirty thousand. The Shi'a population is mostly concentrated in Baku and the southern part of the country close to the Iranian border, while the North is more Sunni. During the seventy years of communist rule, the practice of Islam declined, and its influence as a component of peoples' individual and collective self-identity greatly diminished, especially among the urbanized elites. Nevertheless, Islam still forms an important part of Azeri popular culture and self-identity. As a result, it also plays some role in determining what perceptions different segments of society hold regarding their immediate neighborhood and the broader world, as well as the way they view Azerbaijan's relations with other countries. Accordingly, the more Islamically-oriented Shi'a population feels closer to Iran, whereas the Sunnis and the more secular nationalists are drawn to Turkey and/or Russia.[8]

## The Soviet legacy

The legacy of the Soviet era engendered a whole range of problems – most notably, its seemingly intractable interethnic and territorial disputes. The most consequential of these is the Armenian-Azeri dispute over Nagorno-Karabakh, an Armenian-inhabited enclave in Azeri territory which resulted from Soviet-era gerrymandering. Another example is the autonomous republic of Nakhichevan, which is separated from the rest of Azerbaijan by Iranian and Armenian territories. Moreover, Soviet historical revisionism – and at times outright falsification – has given the Azeris an incorrect vision of their history and origins, with considerable implications for their internal evolution and the character of their external relations. Azeris inherited from the Soviet Union a faction-ridden bureaucracy and polity, as well as a clientist mentality. The Soviet experience significantly eroded Azerbaijan's strong entrepreneurial and mercantile traditions.

This combination of factors has made the transition to a post-communist economy and society extremely difficult. The problem of economic transition has been made worse by the highly centralized and planned nature of the Soviet economy. Particularly damaging was the practice of allocating specific production tasks and quotas to various republics. This resulted in peripheral economies, which were often based on a single commodity and highly dependent on the center, and hence excessively vulnerable to fluctuations in the central economy. Because of this over-dependence on Moscow, Azerbaijan, like many post-Soviet states, has found it difficult to integrate itself into the international economic system. Declining investment in the maintenance and upgrading of Russia's oil and gas field installations, for instance, has meant a reduction in demand for Azerbaijan's oil industry-related products.

Finally, the military, bureaucratic, and political networks which developed in the Soviet era have shown a great deal of resilience. Even after the USSR's official demise, they have exerted considerable influence on the evolution of ex-Soviet republics by shaping, for instance, bureaucratic infighting and power struggles within these countries, as well as their external orientation. In Azerbaijan, they have facilitated Moscow's bid to regain influence over its former republic. Given the existence of other competitors with Russia, this factor has contributed greatly to Azerbaijan's chronic instability since the start of the Gorbachev reforms in 1987.[9]

## Azerbaijan's external setting

Azerbaijan's development during the last few years has been affected not only by internal factors, but also by its external geopolitical setting. The Transcaucasian region (of which Azerbaijan is a part) is of great strategic importance to both its neighbors and to the great powers by virtue of its proximity to Russia, Turkey and the Black Sea, and Iran (and hence the Persian Gulf and the Middle East). Azerbaijan is also of interest to outside actors, most notably Turkey and the West, because of its vast oil and gas reserves. Consequently, since the late 1980s, a large number of countries have had a keen interest in the character of Azerbaijan's political system and its external orientation.

During the last several years, therefore, these actors have tried to influence Azerbaijan's internal developments and its external policies in directions more compatible with their own interests. In the process, they have manipulated Azerbaijan's specific characteristics and vulnerabilities, most notably the fragmented nature of its society and polity and its interethnic problems. In this respect, Moscow's policies, both during the period of reform between 1987–1991 and since the collapse of the Soviet Union, have been especially important. Prior to Soviet collapse, the reckless manipulation of Azerbaijan's internal divisions by competing power centers in Moscow exacerbated the republic's domestic conflict, worsening the Armenian–Azeri dispute and contributing to the chronic instability of Azeri politics. Following independence, Russia's efforts to bring Azerbaijan under its influence led to the fall of Abufazl Elcibey and continued to add tension to Russian-Azeri relations in the Aliev era.[10]

Iran, another significant player, has been more worried about the disruptive and adverse effects of instability in Azerbaijan (and the Transcaucasus in general) on its own security. Iran has been particularly concerned about the growth of nationalist, pan-Turkist, and irredentist tendencies in Azerbaijan and their potential impact on its own territorial integrity. Consequently, Iran's policy towards Azerbaijan has been very cautious and has concentrated on establishing economic ties and correct political relations.

The Western policy (especially of the United States) of containing the spread of Islamic extremism in the Muslim regions of the former Soviet Union has also had a significant impact on Azerbaijan's fate during the last several years. Western states have encouraged Turkey to play a prominent role in the region and have sought to prevent an increase of Iranian influence. Also, the West's determination to gain control over Azerbaijan's oil and gas reserves has enabled Azerbaijan to resist, more than it could otherwise, Russian pressures for it to submit to Russian hegemony. However, Western support has not gone so far as to favor Azerbaijan in its conflict with Armenia.

The interplay of these external factors and Azerbaijan's specific features have, in the final analysis, determined the direction of both its domestic evolution and its external policies in the last several years.

## Perestroika and the emergence of the Azerbaijan Popular Front

When in 1987 Mikhail Gorbachev embarked on his policy of reform, Azerbaijan was still undergoing a process of transition to the post-Brezhnev era. After Brezhnev's death, Azerbaijan's KGB head and Party boss Haidar Aliev gained membership to the USSR Politburo, and Kamiran Bagirov, another staunch Brezhnevite, became the First Secretary of the Azeri Communist Party. However, both these men rapidly fell victim to Gorbachev's policy of purging personalities associated with Brezhnev-era stagnation: Bagirov was replaced by Abdurrahman Vesirov in 1985, and Aliev was forced out of the Politburo in 1987.

Compared to the situation in some other Soviet republics, nationally oriented political groupings were slow to emerge in Azerbaijan. Moreover, early groups were not concerned with politics per se, but focused mostly on cultural issues, such as restoring historic names to towns and places, changing the Cyrillic alphabet to either Latin or Arabic, and reasserting Azerbaijan's indigenous culture. Because of the widespread influence of the idea of a Russo-Iranian conspiracy to divide Azerbaijan, and hence the belief in the inevitability of eventual reunification, certain groups also promoted the theme of the reunification of the two Azerbaijans. In addition to these new groups, some of the old pre-Soviet parties, such as *Mussavat*, resurfaced, and a variety of Islamic groups also emerged. The latter groups mostly operated underground, however, thus making an accurate assessment of their strength problematic.[11]

One group which did come to exert considerable influence in Azerbaijan was the Azerbaijani Popular Front (APF). Neither a political party itself nor, as its name would suggest, a coalition of political parties, the APF originated in a gathering of mostly academic figures. Later, however, the APF would acquire the characteristics of a political party. The first information about the APF's formation emerged in an article by Babak Adalati in an Azeri literary magazine in November 1988. Later, Etibar Mammadov, a historian at Baku University, announced the formation of the APF and the list of its founding members, some of whom would occupy high positions in the APF-dominated government which came to power in June 1992. Most of the founders of the APF were Azeris, but the original list also included two Russians.[12]

In early 1989, the APF circulated its draft program, which consisted of six chapters outlining its views on political, economic, and social issues. Initially, the APF's goals were limited to helping achieve perestroika's goals. Because of this, Azerbaijan's communist leadership did not object to the formation of the APF, and there was even some effort at cooperation.[13] However, as the power struggle between reformists and conservatives throughout the Soviet Union intensified and the latter became concerned about the activities of reformist groups, the relationship between the APF and the Azeri communist establishment – notably, the party's first secretary, Abdurrahman Vezirov – became strained. Vezirov even accused the APF of wanting to become an alternative to the Communist Party.

It has been suggested that the APF's formation was initially sanctioned by Moscow as a way of putting pressure on Vezirov, whom Gorbachev wanted to remove because of his conservatism and support for Yegor Ligachev. Later developments – including the fact that the APF was allowed to play a limited role in Azerbaijan's political life after Vezirov's fall and the coming to power of Ayaz Mutalibov – lend some credence to this theory.

In 1989, the APF went through a process of both fragmentation and expansion. Some of its original founders either were imprisoned or left the party. At the same time, it also acquired many new adherents. Meanwhile, the APF's goals expanded from merely helping promote perestroika to seeking greater independence for Azerbaijan. Its ideology also became more nationalist, pro-Turkish, and to some degree, pan-Turkist. The election of Abulfazl Aliev (who later called himself Elcibey – meaning "envoy of the people") as chairman of the APF executive board during its founding conference on July 16, 1989, was a clear indication of this trend, as Elcibey was a self-avowed Kemalist and a proponent of Azerbaijan's eventual federation with Turkey.[14]

## The importance of Karabakh

The Karabakh conflict has been central to the evolution of events in Azerbaijan since 1987. Both the Azeris and the Armenians believe that, for at least 3,000 years, the region has been part of their respective countries, and their scholars have done excellent work in support of each's views.[15] The fact is, however, that the region, like other parts of the republic, has had a checkered history and has witnessed many changes in the makeup of its population and the identity of its political masters.

Like the rest of what is now the republic of Azerbaijan and parts of the present day republic of Armenia, the Karabakh region was part of Iran until 1828, when, by the terms of the Treaty of Turkmenchai, Iran ceded

all of its Transcaucasian possessions to Russia. Following the Russian revolution of 1917, a scramble for power and influence in the region ensued
between the Ottomans and the British.[16] Meanwhile, both the Armenians
and the Turkic-speaking population of what came to be known as the
republic of Azerbaijan set up independent republics. By 1920, the Karabakh region was made part of the new republic of Azerbaijan. The Armenians, however did not recognize this decision, and war broke out between
the two new republics.[17]

When the Bolsheviks entered the region in November 1920 and tried to
redraw the map of the area, they decided that the three regions of Nakhichevan, Karabakh, and Zangezur should become part of Armenia. This
decision was reversed in 1921, and Nakhichevan and Karabakh were given
to Azerbaijan. This change of heart was prompted by regional politics, and
most notably the new Russian Soviet's desire to reach an understanding
with the nationalist forces in Turkey under the leadership of Mustafa
Kemal, who were battling for the control of Turkey with the forces of the
weakened and discredited Ottoman Sultan in Istanbul. In view of the difficult Turkish-Armenian relationship, the Turkish nationalist forces did not
want Turkey to have common borders only with Armenia, nor had they
completely given up Ottoman ambitions for influence in Azerbaijan. Thus
Nakhichevan was made part of Azerbaijan in order to give Turkey a border
with that republic.[18]

After becoming part of Azerbaijan, Nakhichevan underwent a gradual
process of de-Armenianization. Although in 1920 its population was
almost evenly divided between Armenians and Azerbaijanis, presently there
are almost no Armenians there. Indeed, one of the fears of the Karabakh
Armenians is what they call the potential "Nakhichevanization" of Karabakh. Partly in response to this fear, the region was turned into an autonomous oblast within Azerbaijan in 1923. But this compromise was not
accepted by either the Armenians of Karabakh nor those of Armenia
proper, who pressed Soviet authorities for a change in the *oblast's* status.
Throughout the communist period, tensions between the Azeri and Armenian communities continued to simmer beneath the general oppression and,
at times, led to clashes.[19]

Several explanations have been offered for the existence and intensity of
hostility between the two peoples. Some observers have emphasized the
religious factor, namely Azerbaijan's Islamic and Armenia's Christian traditions. Others have emphasized ethnic differences. No doubt, both factors
have played a role in generating sustained mutual hostility. Especially
important has been the Armenians' bitter historic memory of their encounter with the Turks, with whom the Azeris are identified. Yet, religious and
ethnic differences alone do not explain the extent and longevity of the conflict. Indeed, such differences have not prevented peaceful coexistence
between Armenians and non-Armenians in other places, as illustrated by

the history of Armenian–Iranian relations, including those between the Iranian Armenians and the largely Turkic-speaking population of the Iranian province of Azerbaijan.[20]

Two other factors best explain the longevity and intractability of the Karabakh dispute. The first factor is that the Karabakh region has special emotional and historic significance for both Armenians and Azeris. For Armenians, as Professor Richard Hovannissian has put it, Karabakh represents the only place that a flicker of Armenian independence survived until 1828, albeit under Persian suzerainty. Karabakh also represents the only part of historic Armenia, outside the borders of the republic of Armenia, where the majority of the population is still Armenian. On the other hand, for Azeris the region represents the place where their national consciousness was first awakened. In the late nineteenth century and the early twentieth, Nagorno-Karabakh was a center of Azeri cultural renaissance. Indeed, the Karabakh issue has been the principal impetus behind the emergence of Azeri nationalism in recent years.[21]

The second factor has been the manipulation of this issue by internal political forces as a means of gaining popular support. This has been especially true of Azerbaijan, where the nationalists of the APF have used the Karabakh issue to drum up support. External actors have also used the crisis to advance their own aims. Russia, the West, Turkey, and Iran have all had an impact on the evolution of the Karabakh problem. Of all the external actors, however, the role of Russia has been most pivotal.

## Russian military intervention and the fall of Vezirov

International attention was awakened to the Karabatch problem and Armenian-Azeri relations in early 1988, after anti-Armenian riots in the Azeri industrial city of Sumgait from 28 February to 1 March 1988. The tragic events of Sumgait marked a decisive turning point in the evolution both of the Nagorno-Karabakh conflict and of Azerbaijan's internal political scene. In retaliation for the Sumgait events, Armenia expelled close to 200,000 Azeris who then flooded the Azeri capital of Baku. Following this event, a series of strikes and demonstrations took place in both Azerbaijan and Armenia. As the situation deteriorated, Moscow placed Nagorno-Karabakh under its direct rule in January 1989, but, unwilling or unable to resolve the Karabakh problem, it restored Azeri control to the region in November.[22]

The year 1990 began with large-scale anti-Armenian clashes in Baku, triggered to a great extent by the difficulties caused by the influx of large numbers of Azeri refugees. Other observers, however, have alleged that these riots (as well as those in Sumgait) were instigated by Moscow in order to pave the way for the introduction of Russian troops. It is impossible to determine with any certainty the accuracy of these claims. But it should be noted that – as later developments illustrate – the manipulation of interethnic disputes had become an important tool in the power struggle among competing factions in Moscow and the republics. The conservatives used these disputes to show the dangers involved in glasnost, while supporters of both Gorbachev and Yeltsin used them to rid themselves of unwanted elements in the republics. Thus, irrespective of whether he had instigated the Baku riots, Gorbachev warned of an imminent Muslim extremist threat and, under the pretext of protecting the Armenians, sent Russian troops into Baku in January 1990 and established martial law. Following these events, First Secretary Vezirov fell and was replaced by Ayaz Mutalibov.

## The Mutalibov era

From the beginning of his rule, Ayaz Mutalibov was handicapped by the fact that he had come to power in the shadow of Russian tanks. The intervention of the Russian military had resulted in the death of a large number of civilians and had generated strong anti-Russian feelings among the Azeri population. Nevertheless, during the early days of his rule, it seemed that Mutalibov and the pro-Gorbachev elements of Azerbaijan's communist establishment had succeeded in consolidating power.[23] What followed was a period of cohabitation – or, as Professor Ronald Suny has put it, the "condominium" of communist and nationalist forces.[24] This meant that the communist establishment increasingly adopted a nationalist facade and, at the same time, allowed some elements within the nationalist movement to have limited participation in political life. In early 1990, Mutalibov seemed to share Gorbachev's view that the socialist system could be reformed and rendered more effective: "a new concept of socialism is, if you like, a necessity for our times. People are disenchanted not with the idea of the socialist ideal, but with the way it has been put into practice . . ."[25]

In September 1990, Mutalibov ran unopposed for the presidency of Azerbaijan and was duly elected. In October 1990, parliamentary elections were held. Reflecting the limited *modus vivendi* reached between the communist establishment and the nationalists, the APF was allowed to take part in the elections, and it managed to send twenty-five of its members as delegates to the parliament. Beneath the surface of relative stability and compromise, however, rifts emerged within Azerbaijan's communist establishment, and between Mutalibov and Hassan Hassanov, the chairman of Azerbaijan's Council of Ministers, who had developed a close relationship with the APF.

### Mutalibov and the international system

As noted earlier, because of geo-strategic importance, the Transcaucasus, in general, and Azerbaijan, in particular, had become of interest to major regional and international actors. However, until the mid-1990s, most of these actors had viewed their relations with this region in the context of their overall relations with Moscow. Thus, their principal concern was to prevent regional developments from adversely affecting their relations with Moscow. The West was also concerned about the potentially adverse consequences of events in the periphery on the process of reform in Moscow and on Gorbachev's position. Therefore, when Russian troops moved into Baku, the West did not protest. Despite Gorbachev's opportunistic manipulation of the "Islamic menace," and his warnings to Tehran not to take advantage of instability in Azerbaijan, Iran responded that events in Azerbaijan were an internal Soviet affair.[26] Meanwhile, the Turkish president, Turgut Ozal, who was visiting Washington, DC when Moscow dispatched its troops to Baku, said that in his view, events in Azerbaijan were of more concern to Iran than to Turkey, because the Azeris are Shi'a.[27]

At an unofficial level, both Western and neighboring countries began to develop their ties with various emerging political forces. Turkey, in particular, cemented its ties with the APF. The ultra-nationalists of the party of Alpaslan Turkes were especially active in Azerbaijan. Iran, meanwhile, tried to cultivate the more Islamically-oriented segments of the Azeri population. But because Iran was still undergoing a difficult transition to the post-Khoemeini era, and had yet to normalize its relations with the West, it did not want to run the risk of antagonizing Moscow. Consequently, it adopted a cautious approach toward the region.[28]

There was no broad consensus on the principal outlines of Azerbaijan's foreign policy. This reflected Azerbaijan's ethnic and sectarian heterogeneity, its mixed Irano-Turkic culture, and its legacy of long Russian domination. Because of the military intervention by Moscow, anti-Russian feelings were very strong among the population. However, pro-Russian elements were still influential within the country's political and bureaucratic establishment; and a minority of linguistically-Russified Azeris also shared pro-Russian sentiments.

As the APF was taking shape during 1990–91, its members were strongly pro-Turkish, and to varying degrees, Pan-Turkist. Other groups were oriented towards Islam, and, to some degree, Iran. The Iranian-speaking Talysh were also mostly pro-Iran. Thus, despite the fact that Mutalibov was pro-Russian, Azerbaijan's relations with Russia during his tenure were not easy. Because of strong anti-Russian feelings, Mutalibov adopted an ambiguous, wait-and-see attitude toward Gorbachev's new Union Treaty in 1991. During this period, Azerbaijan also expanded its relations with both Turkey and Iran.[29]

## The fall of Mutalibov

The interaction of a number of factors, some of which had also played key roles in Vezirov's ouster, led to Mutalibov's downfall. These factors were: (1) continued power struggles in Moscow – this time between Mikhail Gorbachev and Boris Yeltsin – which culminated in the Soviet Union's dismantlement; (2) power struggles in Azerbaijan, notably between Mutalibov and an increasingly combative APF; (3) the Nagorno-Karabakh conflict and the reverses suffered by Azeri forces; and (4) intensified regional and international rivalry for influence in Azerbaijan, as the process of the Soviet Union's disintegration accelerated in 1991. This last factor especially benefited the APF, which, because of its pro-Turkish and anti-Iranian tendencies, had become attractive to the West.

Among the more immediate causes of Mutalibov's ouster, his alleged support for the attempted coup of August 1991 and Azerbaijan's reverses in the Nagorno-Karabakh conflict particularly stand out. It has been alleged that, when the August 1991 coup attempt took place, Mutalibov, who was visiting Iran, was pleased at the prospect of a conservative comeback. Although Mutalibov has strenuously denied this allegation, Yeltsin and his entourage remained suspicious of him. But the event which precipitated Mutalibov's removal was the fall of the Azeri region of Khodjali to the Armenian forces of Nagorno-Karabakh in February 1992 and the death of large numbers of Azeri civilians. These events led to massive protests in Baku against Mutalibov. The APF, in particular, attributed these defeats to Mutalibov's "deliberate delay" in creating a national army. However, there were also rumors that APF supporters in the army had intentionally performed poorly, so that they could use these defeats as a pretext to unseat Mutalibov. Yet others have attributed Azeri defeats to Russian help provided to the Armenian side.

It is difficult to assess the accuracy of these claims, but in view of later events, APF sabotage and Russian assistance to Armenia cannot be dismissed out of hand. In the wake of popular outrage over events in Khodjali, in March 1992 the Azeri parliament forced Mutalibov to resign. Yaqub Mammadov, the dean of the Baku Medical Institute, was appointed interim prime minister, and it was agreed that presidential elections would be held on June 7, 1992.

The APF, which had played an important role in the ouster of Mutalibov, was not happy with the appointment of Mammadov and preferred to have its ally, Hassan Hassanov, as his temporary successor. It is tempting to speculate that, had this occurred, later troubles might have been averted and the APF might have come to power through bureaucratic processes rather than through what amounted to a *coup d'etat*. What followed was an excessively tense period, extending from March to mid-May 1992, and was dominated by continuous power struggles and the war over Nagorno Karabakh, which became increasingly intertwined. Meanwhile, a series of international mediation efforts were undertaken with the aim of reaching a cease-fire.

Azerbaijan suffered further reverses in the war. In May, the Azeri town of Shusha fell to Armenia forces. Both the supporters of Mutalibov and those of the APF tried to use the fall of Shusha to propel themselves to power. At first, it seemed that Mutalibov would regain power. Indeed, on May 14 the Azeri parliament voted to reinstate Mutalibov, a move which prompted the interim prime minister to declare his satisfaction that the "political vacuum in the republic was filled." However, this apparent victory for Mutalibov was extremely short-lived. The very same day, the APF called Mutalibov's reinstatement a *coup d'etat* and staged demonstrations in which its armed militia took part. After minor skirmishes between the APF militia and certain elements of the military, by May 16 Mutalibov was out of power for good.

## The APF government

Immediately after the final removal of Mutalibov, the APF speedily proceeded to place its supporters in key government positions. To begin with, the APF replaced the head of Azeri television with one of its own supporters, an act which gave it an important – some would say unfair – advantage during the electoral campaign. Also, declaring the Azeri parliament a relic of the communist era and thus unrepresentative, the APF gave more weight to the National Council until new parliamentary elections were held. The Council had been created during the presidency of Mutalibov, at the insistence of the APF. Its membership consisted of the twenty-five APF members of parliament, plus twenty-five chosen from among other members.

The period between the effective coming to power of the APF and presidential elections was very short. There was thus little time for political organization and adequate campaigning. For a time, because of the continued war in Nagorno-Karabakh and the fear that election campaigning could degenerate into armed clashes, it was not even clear whether presidential elections would actually take place. However, they were held as scheduled on June 7, 1992, and the APF candidate, Abulfazl Elcibey, was elected president. Although the elections themselves were not marred by massive fraud, the political playing field was far from level. Indeed, because of its control over the governmental apparatus and substantial assistance from abroad – notably Turkey – the APF was in a highly advantageous position compared to other parties.

The political philosophy of the APF, at least at the rhetorical level, was secular and democratic, and its government's stated goal was to create a secular system where the rights of all Azeris would be protected, irrespective of their ethnic or sectarian background. To implement this philosophy, the government set up committees in the parliament and in the president's office to draft election laws under which parliamentary elections were to be held. In addition, committees were formed to examine which system of government – presidential or parliamentary – was better suited to Azerbaijan's conditions.

During the APF government, some efforts at political liberalization were undertaken, and a large number of political parties emerged. However, with few exceptions, most of these parties did not have either the popular base or the organizational strength needed to play an effective role. Indeed, most of the parties were either vehicles for the personal ambitions of their leaders or fronts for external powers. Moreover, because the government controlled access to media and allocated buildings to house party headquarters as well as paper on which to print party publications, opposition parties were disadvantaged. Accordingly, during the APF government, those parties with a nationalist and, to varying degrees, Pan-Turkist ideology fared better than others.[30]

In the economic field, the APF favored a free-market system, but because of its short tenure, the government could not leave a significant imprint. The burden of the war, along with the continued internal and regional power struggles, hampered the government from initiating reforms and realizing the country's vast potential, especially in the energy sector.[31] Thus Azerbaijan's economic conditions declined, and the living standards of most people eroded. In the meantime, a new upper class emerged and engaged in primarily non-productive activities, such as acting as middlemen for various regional and international businesses. This situation angered those whose conditions had worsened and ultimately contributed to the APF government's downfall.

Culturally, the APF pursued a policy of remolding Azerbaijan in the image of Turkey, and it introduced linguistic changes to bring the Azeri Turkic dialect closer to post-Ottoman, modern Turkish. This policy, however, was not well received by non-Turkic speakers and exacerbated Azerbaijan's ethnic and linguistic divisions. These ethnic divisions were later manipulated by outside forces against the government.

The APF government's foreign policy was pro-Turkish, pro-West, anti-Russia, and anti-Iran. Having good relations with Turkey and the West made eminent sense from the point of view of Azerbaijan's interests. However, because this policy was accompanied by Pan-Turkist inclinations, included a hostile attitude toward Iran, and was unresponsive to Russian interests, it proved damaging both to Azerbaijan and to Elcibey's government. It created serious fears in Iran and Russia, and prompted them to adopt a pro-Armenian posture in the Nagorno-Karabakh conflict. Moreover, Elcibey's pro-Turkish policy contributed to Russia's determination to replace him, exacerbating, as it did, Russia's concern about the potential impact of events in the Transcaucasus on its own security and territorial integrity – most notably with respect to its Turkic-speaking minorities.

# The fall of Elcibey

By the winter of 1992–93, after being in power for only a few months, the position of the APF government had already weakened, and Baku was buzzing with rumors that Haidar Aliev would soon return to national politics. Aliev, who had already returned to prominence in Azerbaijan by his election as chairman of the Nakhichevan parliament in September 1991, was expected to win a seat in the upcoming parliamentary elections, which were scheduled to take place in April 1993. However, the government, rapidly losing its popularity, was reluctant to hold elections and argued that they would be inappropriate while the war in Nagorno-Karabakh was continuing. Indeed, the Nagorno-Karabakh conflict was to soon be the catalyst for the fall of yet another Azeri government.

Immediately after the APF government came to power, Azeri forces made some modest advances in the war. However, because of factors discussed earlier – most notably the worsening of relations with Russia which was partially caused by the APF government's refusal to join the CIS – the tide of the war turned against Azerbaijan. This was largely prompted by Russian assistance to the Armenian side, as part of a broader policy of reintegrating the Transcaucasus into the Russian sphere of influence.[32] As with events in Khodjali in 1992, the fall of the Azeri region of Kelbedjar to Armenian forces in April 1993 set in motion a process which led to Elcibey's ouster. The significance of the fall of Kelbedjar lay in the fact that it was in the territory of Azerbaijan proper and not in Nagorno-Karabakh.

Following the fall of Kelbedjar, the government postponed elections indefinitely and declared a state of emergency. It also ordered a parliamentary probe into malpractice in the defense establishment, imprisoned some key defense figures, and removed a key military commander, Surat Husseinov, from his post. Shortly after his removal, Husseinov gathered his supporters and launched an open rebellion against the government from his stronghold of Gandja.[33]

The Elcibey government's reactions to Husseinov's challenge was a mixture of compromise and defiance. Early on, President Elcibey sent an envoy to Husseinov to convince him to ease the siege of Gandja. When these efforts failed, the government tried to relieve the city by the use of military force. That strategy failed as well, however. On June 9, Husseinov called for the resignation of both President Elcibey and the speaker of the parliament, Issa Gambarov. On June 13, as Husseinov's troops were advancing toward Baku, Gambarov resigned. Two days later, Haidar Aliev was appointed to replace him. Gambarov's resignation was followed by Elcibey's flight from Baku on June 18, and five days later, Husseinov and his troops entered Baku.

At this time, it was widely speculated in Baku that Husseinov's actions were part of a larger scheme orchestrated by Moscow to bring Aliev back to power. Moscow was clearly unhappy with Elcibey and his policies. However, it is not clear whether Aliev or Mutalibov was Moscow's first choice to replace Elcibey.

Some observers believed that Mutalibov was Moscow's first choice, but Aliev managed to parlay himself into power.[34] Others have noted that the Moscow leadership was ambiguous about Mutalibov. On the one hand, Mutalibov would have been very responsive to Russian desires. But on the other hand, Moscow was concerned about his lack of decisiveness. Moreover, some of President Yeltsin's entourage still remembered Mutalibov's alleged support for the 1991 coup. Regardless of Russia's real preferences, it welcomed Elcibey's departure. In any case, Aliev's relations with Moscow would prove just as difficult.

## The Aliev era

The first days of Aliev's coming to power were confused. On the domestic front, Elcibey's departure had created a constitutional vacuum and various forces were still jockeying for power. Internationally, Elcibey's ouster had generated strong negative reactions from the West. Turkey, in particular, reacted angrily, accusing Russia of fomenting unrest. Then Turkish foreign minister Hikmat Cetin stated in a letter to the United Nations that his government intended to support Azerbaijan's "lawful authorities." He further described the Husseinov rebellion as an army mutiny aimed at overthrowing the democratically elected government.[35] There were also reports that Elcibey, in hiding in his native village of Ordubad, was receiving discreet council from high-ranking Turkish officials late into the night.[36]

The European countries and the United States also expressed support for Elcibey.[37] However, as it became evident that there was no chance of Elcibey's return, the Western powers tried to make the best of an unfavorable situation. Turkey, which in the past had had close dealings with Aliev – both during the Soviet era and during the time of Aliev's tenure as president of the autonomous republic of Nakhichevan – moved quickly to consolidate its relations with Aliev. Reversing its earlier position, Turkey declared that "... Aliev came to power in Azerbaijan within the democratic process."[38]

During the period immediately after Elcibey's ouster, Aliev faced a significant challenge in legitimizing his rule and consolidating his power. The first step in this process was the holding of a referendum on the fate of Elcibey. Elcibey had earlier indicated that he would accept the verdict if the referendum were held in a fair manner. The referendum was held on August 28, 1993, and, as expected, Elcibey was stripped of his position. This was followed by presidential elections on October 3, 1993. These elections were even less fair than those of June 1992. In addition to Aliev, only two obscure figures – Zakir Tagiev from the "Himmat" party and Kirar Abilov – ran as candidates.[39]

After being elected president, Aliev set out to form his cabinet. Surat Husseinov, who had been instrumental in propelling Aliev to power, occupied the posts of prime minister and minister of defense. Initially, in order to co-opt the nationalists and elements of the APF, as well as to placate Turkey, Aliev offered the post of foreign minister to Etibar Mammadov, leader of the Nationalist Independent Party and a well-known pro-Turkish political figure. When Mammadov refused this offer, Aliev turned to Hassan Hassanov, Azerbaijan's ambassador to the United Nations. Since Hassanov had had good relations with the APF and was also known for his pro-Turkish sentiments, his appointment was intended to send a signal to Turkey that Azerbaijan was not turning away from it.

## Recasting Azerbaijan's foreign policy and the Nagorno-Karabakh conflict

One of the principal criticisms directed at Elcibey was that he had damaged Azerbaijan's interests by overly antagonizing Russia and Iran. The general expectation was thus that Aliev would move to remedy the damage done by Elcibey, and, in this way, improve Azerbaijan's position in the Nagorno-Karabakh conflict.

Relations with Iran improved considerably during 1993–1994. However, the kind of rapprochement which was expected in Russian-Azeri relations has not taken place. Indeed, since the beginning of 1994, Azerbaijan's policy has evolved in a pro-Western and pro-Turkish direction without, however, the excesses of the Elcibey period. In May 1994, Azerbaijan joined NATO's Partnership for Peace (PFP) program in defiance of Russian objections. Moreover, after initially suspending negotiations, Azerbaijan finally signed an agreement with a consortium of Western oil companies in September 1994, also in defiance of Russian wishes.[40]

The westward trend in Azerbaijan's policy, despite earlier expectations about a dramatic shift in favor of Russia, have resulted from the following two factors. First was the change in the West's attitude toward Russia and the new republics. Until late 1993, the approach taken by the West – notably, the United States – toward the CIS was generally Russo-centric.[41] Moreover, most Western policy makers had come to accept a special role for Russia in the republics of the former Soviet Union, with few exceptions – primarily the Baltic states, and, to some extent, Ukraine. However, two developments – namely, the growing involvement of the Russian military in interethnic disputes, notably in Georgia, and the growing strength of hard-liners in Moscow – led to a shift in the West's position. An important turning point were the Russian parliamentary elections of December 1993, when ex-communists and hard-line nationalists made a strong showing. This change in Western focus provided countries such as Azerbaijan with a Western option and made it somewhat easier for them to resist Russian pressures.

A second factor was Russian unwillingness to help Azerbaijan in the Nagorno-Karabakh conflict as a quid pro quo for the latter's adoption of a pro-Russian posture. Quite the contrary, Armenian forces continued their advances into Azeri territory. By October 1993, nearly one-fifth of Azeri territory was occupied by Armenian forces, and Armenian–Azeri clashes had reached the Iranian border in the Khoda Afarin region. These Armenian advances had also led to an outpouring of Azeri refugees from the Armenian-occupied regions, bringing the total Azeri homeless population to close to one million. These developments gave rise to two kinds of speculation – namely, that Aliev was not Moscow's man, and therefore, the Russians wanted to be rid of him; and that the Russians wanted to force Aliev to join the CIS.[42]

Indeed, despite considerable popular opposition, Azerbaijan joined the CIS. It became clear, however, that this step would not satisfy Russia, which soon revealed that it had other demands. Foremost among them was the stipulation that Azerbaijan agree to the stationing of Russian troops on the Azeri–Iranian border, as part of Russia's broader strategy of bringing the Transcaucasus under its control. But even if Aliev had wanted to comply with the Russian demands, he could not do so because of considerable domestic opposition. Moreover, such a move would have antagonized Turkey and the Western powers, which, in turn, could have used their supporters in Azerbaijan to weaken Aliev. At this point, it is important to note that, while Azerbaijan's relations with Turkey had warmed considerably at the official level, animosity toward Aliev remained in some Turkish circles, especially among the nationalist and Pan-Turkist elements close to Elcibey.[43]

The continued strains in Russian–Azeri relations also had a negative effect on attempts to resolve the Nagorno-Karabakh conflict. During the presidency of Abulfazl Elcibey, the focus of the mediation efforts in the Nagorno-Karabakh conflict had shifted to the Conference on Security and Cooperation in Europe (CSCE). By 1993, however, the Russian attitude toward the role of the CSCE had become, at best, ambivalent. Indeed, Russia had come to see the CSCE's involvement as a potential impediment to its own plans to become the sole peacemaker, peacekeeper, and arbiter of interethnic disputes in the CIS. After Elcibey's departure, Russia thus stepped up its mediation efforts and appointed Vladimir Kazimirov as a special envoy.[44]

As part of an overall strategy of repairing relations with Russia, Aliev initially welcomed the Russian initiative. He also said that the CSCE had not been effective in its mediation efforts. However, it soon became clear that there were considerable differences between the Russian and Azeri positions on how to resolve the conflict. For instance, the Azeris demanded that all Armenian forces be withdrawn from occupied Azeri territories before a cease-fire could be established, and negotiations proceed on the final status of Nagorno-Karabakh. By contrast, the Russian plan provided, first, for a cease-fire followed by withdrawal of Armenian forces from most Azeri territories, and only then the start of negotiations. The Russians believed that the final status of the town of Shusha and the Lachin corridor, linking Nagorno-Karabakh to Armenia, should be left to the last stage.[45]

The Russians and the Azeris also differed on the composition of peace-keeping forces. The Russians wanted the bulk of such a force to consist of their own troops, while the Azeris preferred a more balanced distribution and the participation of other forces, including Turkish troops. Russia managed to organize a cease-fire agreement between the two belligerents, but there was not much progress on the other fronts. In the meantime, because of growing Western concern over the evolution of events in Russia – the CSCE once again became more active in mediation efforts.[46] The Azeris, too, in line with their overall shift toward a more pro-Western foreign policy, advocated the CSCE as the principal instrument for resolving the Karabakh conflict.

## The record of the Aliev presidency

During the first eighteen months of his presidency, Haidar Aliev did not prove to be the savior that Azerbaijan was waiting for. Azerbaijan's internal and external problems had, at least to that point, proved to be too many and too intractable even for his political and bureaucratic skills. On the domestic political front, Aliev has faced numerous challenges to his authority. Opponents have included supporters of ousted president, Elcibey, who were especially active in the Nakhichevan area, and an army commander of Talysh origin, Akram Himmatov, who during the early days of Aliev's coming to power, rebelled and announced the creation of an independent Talysh-Mughan republic.[47] To a considerable degree, Aliev succeeded in suppressing these challenges. However, this success came at the price of reversing even the very modest steps taken toward democratization and political institution-building. Activities of opposition groups were severely curtailed, and their newspapers were closed. Similarly, because of these measures, many of the political parties which had emerged in 1992–93 lost all effectiveness, and many of them completely disappeared from the scene.

Regarding the vitally important issue of Nagorno-Karabakh, Aliev was, in his first eighteen months in power, no more successful than his predecessors in finding an acceptable solution or in improving Azerbaijan's performance on the battlefield. On the contrary, Azerbaijan continued to lose territory to Armenia. As a result of these difficulties, Azerbaijan's economic situation also continued to deteriorate, and in 1994, it was estimated that 50 percent of the Azeri population lived below the poverty line.

Aliev did have one important success, which, if not reversed by political turmoil, could dramatically improve Azerbaijan's economic conditions. This was the signing of an agreement between Azerbaijan and the international oil consortium for the exploitation and export of Azerbaijan's oil and gas. If implemented, the agreement will lead to massive foreign investment in Azerbaijan's energy sector – an estimated $8 billion – and will provide a general boost to its economy. However, as of the completion of this chapter, the implementation of the agreement was not certain. First, the issue of the route of the pipeline to carry Azeri oil and gas has not been determined. Russia insists that the oil should be exported through its ports, while Turkey is trying to become the principal transit route. Second, Russia has insisted that Azerbaijan does not have the right to unilaterally sign contracts regarding the oil in the Caspian Sea, which Russia regards as the property of all countries surrounding the Caspian. Finally, the future stability of Aliev's government is far from secure. Indeed, after the oil agreement was signed in late September 1994, Aliev's authority was challenged by Surat Husseinov, the same military commander who had forced out Abulfazl Elcibey. When Husseinov mounted a military rebellion in early October, many observers concluded that his actions might have been prompted by Moscow, which clearly was not happy with the Azeri oil deal, and, indeed, Aliev accused Russia of complicity.[48] Aliev won in this power struggle, and Husseinov was dismissed from the government. However, it was not at all clear that this would be the last challenge to Aliev's authority.

## Aliev's foreign policy

Compared to Elcibey, Aliev's performance in the foreign policy area during his first two years has been impressive. Despite early misgivings on the part of the West and Turkey about Aliev's coming to power, he has managed to establish excellent relations with both.

Iranian–Azeri relations have also improved considerably during Aliev's presidency. In October 1993, Iran's president, Hashemi Rafsanjani, visited Baku and, in July 1994, Aliev travelled to Tehran. However, as relations rapidly improved between Azerbaijan and the West, relations with Iran did not expand as much as initially expected. In addition to the Western factor, there have been some fundamental sources of tension between Iran and Azerbaijan, most notably the latter's irredentist claims on Iranian territory. It should be remembered that in 1981, Aliev had expressed the hope that the two Azerbaijans would be united during his lifetime.

At the same time, Azerbaijan's relations with Russia have proved to be more of a challenge than initially expected. Indeed, one of Aliev's attractions was that he would be able to mend the rift with Russia, and thereby induce Moscow to help Azerbaijan in the Nagorno-Karabakh conflict. However, there are also some fundamental conflicts of interest between Russia and Azerbaijan regarding Russia's regional and economic aspirations. Unless the West decides to provide extensive military and economic support to Aliev's government, disagreements with Russia could prove extremely costly for Azerbaijan.

In short, the Aliev government has had a reasonably good record in the foreign policy area. Nevertheless, the country still faces a tremendous challenge in trying to balance its own diverse interests and those of its neighbors, most notably Russia, which are keenly interested in the evolution of Azerbaijan's internal and external policies.

## Conclusion and future outlook

Neither the period of glasnost and perestroika, nor the post-independence period, has resulted in greater economic prosperity and political freedom for Azerbaijan. On the contrary, both of these periods have been marked by an upsurge in political tensions and chronic instability, bloody interethnic disputes resulting in territorial losses and large numbers of refugees, and a steady deterioration in the country's economic conditions.

Four factors have helped to produce these sad results. The first factor has been the unleashing of forces which had been kept dormant for many decades, coupled with the cumulative effect of years of Soviet political and economic mismanagement. The second factor has been the haphazard way in which the devolution of the Soviet Union occurred. Particularly damaging have been the extensive and drawn-out power struggles in Moscow. Also damaging has been the manipulation of rival forces in the former Soviet republics in these competitions for power. The third factor has been the heterogeneous character of Azerbaijan's society and polity, deep divisions within its political elite, and the poor quality of its leadership. The final factor has been Azerbaijan's sensitive geo-strategic position and resources which elicit strong attention from external actors. Wide ideological differences and diverging economic and political interests among these actors have placed Azerbaijan in an extremely sensitive position. They have created a situation in which any shift by Azerbaijan in one direction would prompt a negative reaction from other interested parties.

None of these factors is likely to change anytime soon. On the contrary, there is a reasonable chance that they will be aggravated, an outlook which does not augur well for Azerbaijan's immediate future. In particular, the evolution of regional and international events – most notably, developments in Russia, the evolution of Russian policy toward the Transcaucasus, and the evolution of Russian-Western relations. These developments would turn Azerbaijan into a battleground of great power rivalries, with potentially highly-adverse consequences for its stability and well-being.

## Notes

1 For a detailed analysis of the origins of the name Azerbaijan and its geographical borders, see Enayatollah Reza, *Azerbaijan Va arran ya Albania-e-Ghafghaz* (Azerbaijan and Arran or Albania of Caucasus) (Tehran: Entesharat-e-Iran Zamin, 1360 [1980–81]).

2 A good account of this process is provided in a nineteenth-century Persian book written by a native of Baku, Abbasghuliagha Bakikhanov, called "Gulistan-e-Eram" (Garden of Eden). The book was republished in 1917 by the History Institute of Azerbaijan SSR.

3 See Ahmad Kasravi, *Tarikh-e-Hidjdahsaleh-e-Azerbaijan* (The 18 year history of Azerbaijan) (Tehran: Amir Kabir publishing, 1353 [1974]), p. 874.

4 For a detailed analysis of these issues, see Shireen T. Hunter, *The Transcaucasus in Transition: Nation-building and Conflict* (Washington, D.C. and Boulder Colorado: Center for Strategic and International Studies/Westview Press, 1994).

5 The Azerbaijani poet, Balgohlan Shafizadeh, in a poem called "Vatan" (Homeland), calls Azerbaijan the flame of the great Zardusht's (Zoroaster) faith. Quoted in Audrey L. Allstadt, *The Azerbaijani Turks* (Stanford, CA: Hoover Institution Press, 1992), p. 180.

6 See Ahmad Kasravi, *Azeri Ya Zaban-e-Bastan-e-Azerbaijan*, (Azeri or the ancient language of Azerbaijan) (Tehran: Sharq publishing, 1308 [1932]). As proof of this process, Kasravi produces examples of Azeri Persian, which is still spoken in some remote villages of Iranian Azerbaijan.

7 On major ethnic migrations to the region, see Charles Allen Burney and David Marshall Lang, *The People of the Hill: Ancient Arrat and Caucasus* (New York: Praeger Publishers, 1971).

8 For example, according to Linda Feldman, "Some Azeris talk of Iran as their own". See "Islamic Revivalism Stirs in Azerbaijan," *Christian Science Monitor*, October 30, 1990.

9 For details, see Hunter, *The Transcaucasus in Transition*, pp. 58–96

10 The following are some of the early informal groups which emerged in Azerbaijan: (1) *Kizilbash,* named after the elite troops of the founder of the Safavid dynasty, Shah Ismail. This was a nationalist group and advocated the unification of the two Azerbaijans; (2) *Birlik*, which is also a nationalist group. Some observers have also attributed Islamist tendencies to this group; (3) *Dirchelich* (Renaissance), also with nationalist tendencies, especially in regard to reassertion of Azeri culture; (4) the "Greens" which, like their counterparts in other parts of the Soviet Union, were mostly concerned with environmental issues. On Birlik's origins and ideology, see Mirza Michaeli and William Reese, "The Birlik Society in the Azerbaijani Democratic Movement," *Report on the USSR, RFE/RL*, vol. no. 25, September 25, 1989.

11 See text.

12 Some of the early members of the APF included Abufazl Aliev, Etibar Mammadov, Towfik Qassimov, Issa Gambarov, Najab Najafov, and Sabit Bagirov. Most of these people assumed high positions when the APF came to power. Others, however, split from the APF. Initial membership of the Front also included two Russians, Anatoli Grachov and Georgi Tkachenko. See *Ibid.*

13 For example, in April 1989, Vezirov met with the APF members. As power struggles between the reformists and the conservatives intensified, however, the relationship between Vezirov's entourage and the APF became strained. According to some reports, in private Vezirov criticized the APF. *Ibid.*

14 Note the following statement by Elcibey during an interview with the Turkish daily, *Miliyat*: "We do not support the idea of uniting with Turkey. However, the idea of a confederal state may be discussed in 20 or 30 years. Once we achieve our independence

we shall help the Central Asian republics to become independent. Perhaps then we can establish a confederal state with them." Reprinted in *Foreign Broadcasting Information Service (FBIS) Sov*, July 20, 1990, p. 103.

15 On the roots of the conflicts from an Armenian view, see "The Karabakh File," (Cambridge, MA: Zoryan Institute); also Audrey L. Alstadt, "Nagorno-Karabakh: The Apple of Discord in the Azerbaijan SSR", *Central Asian Survey*, 7, no. 4 (1988).

16 For an analysis of great power rivalry in this region, see Firuz Kazemzadeh, *Struggle for Transcaucasia: 1917–1921*: (Birmingham: Temple Press, 1951).

17 For an analysis of relations between Armenia and Azerbaijan in this period, see Richard C. Hovannissian, *The Republic of Armenia from Versailles to London 1919–1920* (Berkeley: University of California Press, 1982).

18 On the Russo-Turkish agreement, see Richard C. Hovannissian, "Armenia and the Caucasus in the Genesis of Soviet-Turkish Entente", *International Journal of Middle East Studies*, 4, no. 2 (1973). However, even with this compromise, Turkey could not have much of a border with Azerbaijan. It was only after a deal with Iran in the context of demarcating the frontier that Turkey acquired the short border with Azerbaijan.

19 For example, in 1968 clashes broke out between the Armenians and the Azeris in Stepanakert, the capital of KKAO. These riots were triggered by the alleged killing of an Armenian pupil by an ethnic Azeri teacher and the failure of the Azeri authorities to charge him with murder. Tensions continued during the 1970s and, in 1977, led to increased Armenian–Azeri clashes. See "Special Issue: Crisis in the Caucasus", *United States Department of State*, no. 15 (August 1988), 1.

20 Since the eighteenth century, the Armenians have found a reasonably safe refuge in Iran. The wholly Armenian city of Julfa, Isfahan, which was built in the seventeenth century during the rule of Shah Abbas Safavi, is a good example of this coexistence.

21 On the relationship between the Nagorno-Karabakh conflict and the rise of Azeri nationalism, see Mark Saroyan, "The Karabakh Syndrome and Azeri Politics," *Problems of Communism*, 39 (Sept. Oct. 1990).

22 Several reasons have been cited for Moscow's inability to resolve the Karabakh problem early on. One was the lack of experience and knowledge on the part of Gorbachev about ethnic problems and the manipulation of interethnic disputes by rival forces in Moscow. See Ludmilla Alexeyeva, "Unrest in the Soviet Union," *Washington Quarterly*, 13, no. 1 (Winter 1990); also, Mark Saroyan, "Trouble in the Transcaucasus," *Bulletin of Atomic Scientists*, 45, no. 2 (March 1989); also, Quientin Peel, "Dagger at the Heart of Perestroika," *Financial Times*, January 18, 1990.

23 The following comment by an observer of the Azeri scene illustrates this perception: "The Azerbaijani communist party was reborn, like a phoenix from the ashes of the burnt party membership cards." Quoted in Elizabeth Fuller, "The Azerbaijani Presidential Elections: A One Horse Race," *RFE/RL Report on the USSR*, 3, no. 37, September 13, 1991.

24 See Ronald Grigor Suny, *Looking Toward Ararat* (Bloomington, IN: Indiana University Press, 1992), p. 235.

25 See Elizabeth Fuller, "Azerbaijani Presidential Elections.

26 For example, in a letter to then Soviet Foreign Minister Edward Shevardnadze, Iran's Foreign Minister emphasized Iran's "adherence to the principle of non-interference in other nation's affairs." see "Velayati on Helping Resolve Azerbaijan's Crisis," *FBIS/MES*, April, 22 1991.

27 See "Turkish Azeris Protest Massacres", *Turkish Daily News*, January 20–21 1990.

28 Ozal's statement created an uproar in Turkey, and opposition leaders accused him of pushing Azerbaijan into Iran's arms. Not everyone in Iran agreed with this low-keyed approach. Indeed a number of influential clerical figures warned that with Iran's passive posture Azerbaijan was falling under the influence of Turkey and the Wahabi of Saudi

Arabia. One of these clerics was the Ayatollah Musravi Ardabili, who warned against Saudi supported Wahabi activists and urged more vigorous Iranian diplomacy in the region. See *FBIS/MES*, April 22, 1991.

29 During the Mutalibov era, a number of agreements on economic and cultural cooperation were signed between Azerbaijan and Iran and Turkey. See "Iran and Soviet Azerbaijan Sign Memorandum of Understanding on Economic, Cultural and Political Cooperation," *Keyhan*, December 4, 1991.

30 The most important of these parties included the National Independence Party of Etibar Mammadov, the New Azerbaijan party of Haidar Aliev, the New Mussavat party of Issa Gambarov, and the Social Democratic party of Zardusht Alizadeh. For details see Hunter, *The Transcaucasus in Transition*.

31 The issue of the route of the pipeline for carrying Azerbaijan oil and gas became particularly entangled with regional and international rivalries, especially the competition between Russia and Turkey. For details see *Ibid.*

32 On the evolution of Russia's post-Soviet foreign policy, especially in regard to the former Soviet republics or the so-called "Near Abroad," see *Ibid.*; also Mohaiddin Mesbahi, "Russian Foreign Policy and Security in Central Asia and the Caucasus," *Central Asian Survey*, 112, no. 2 (1993), and Susan Crowe, "Russia Asserts its Strategic Agenda," *RFE/RL Research Report*, 2, No. 50, December 17, 1993.

33 Among those military leaders who were affected by these moves were the deputy defense minister, Baba Nazarli, and the head of the general staff, Major General Shahin Musayev.

34 For details, see Hunter, *The Transcaucasus in Transition*.

35 See Daniel Sneider, "Turkey and Russia Back Rivals in Azerbaijan Power Struggle," *Christian Science Monitor*, June 30m 1993.

36 *Ibid.*

37 *Ibid.*

38 See "Cetin on Azerbaijan Policy," *Turkish Times*, June 15, 1993.

39 On Azerbaijan's presidential elections, see "Azerbaijan: La Paticipation a l'election presidentielle a été élevée," *Le Monde*, October 5, 1993; also "Azerbaijan Presidential Elections Undemocratic," *RFE/RL Daily Report*, no. 193, October 7, 1993.

40 On the signing of the oil agreement, see Steve Levine, "Oil Companies to Sign Azerbaijan Extraction Deal," *Financial Times*, 19 September 1994; also "Oil Concerns Set $8 Billion Accord with Azerbaijan," *International Herald Tribune*, September 21, 1993.

41 On the West's Russo-centrism, see, among others, Paul Goble, "Ten Issues in Search of a Policy: America's Failed Approach to Post-Soviet States," *Current History*, 92, no. 576 (October 1993).

42 During the parliamentary debate on Azerbaijan's joining the CIS, Aliev said: "There was no pressure from Russia at all. I never felt such a pressure." See "National Assembly Meets to Discuss Joining of CIS," *FBIS/SOV*, September 21, 1993.

43 For example, there was an assassination attempt against Aliev in which a Turkish national was implicated.

44 On the Russian mediation efforts, see Elizabeth Fuller, "The Karabakh Mediation Process", *RFE/RL Research Report*, 3, no. 23, June 10, 1994.

45 In fact, the Russian mediator, Kazimiron, likened these two regions to the problem of Jerusalem, implying that they would have to be tackled in the last phase of a peace process. *BBC Summary of World Broadcasts*, May 12, 1994.

46 For details of the reactivation of the CSCE process, see Hunter, *The Transcaucasus in Transition*.

47 This development is an example of the political consequences of Azerbaijan's heterogeneous society. Separatist tendencies have also existed among the Lezgins. Himmatov's fate is not clear. According to some reports, he was apprehended by government forces. Other reports allege that he fled to Iran.

48 Reacting negatively to the signing of the oil deal, the spokesman of the Russian Foreign Ministry said "Azerbaijan was trying to tamper with the Soviet-Iranian border. Russia considers this inadmissable and comes out against unilateral attempts by Baku to spread its jurisdiction over certain sections of the Caspian Sea." "Azeri President Accuses Russia," *Financial Times*, October 6, 1994.

# Azerbaijan: chronology of events

*February 1988*
20    The soviet of the Nagorno-Karabakh oblast votes to request that the oblast join Armenia.
28–29    Anti-Armenian riots occur in Sumgait, resulting in more than thirty deaths.

*May 1988*
21    Abdul Rakhman Vezirov is appointed first party secretary

*November 1988*
22–28    Mass demonstrations and strikes are held in Baku, and incidents of anti-Armenian violence are widespread. Several thousand Armenians flee Azerbaijan, while many Azeris depart from Armenia as well.

*January 1989*
20    Local government organs in Nagorno-Karabakh are replaced by a Moscow-appointed Special Administration Committee, led by industrialist Arkadii Volsky.

*July 1989*
16    The nationalist Azerbaijani Popular Front holds its founding congress.

*August 1989*
16    Nagorno-Karabakh soviet deputies declare the oblast to be independent from Azerbaijan.

*September 1989*
13    After initiating a blockade of Nagorno-Karabakh, the Popular Front agrees to end the blockade if Vezirov legalizes the organization and agrees to declare sovereignty for the republic.
16    The Supreme Soviet asks Moscow to withdraw the Special Administration Committee.
23    The Supreme Soviet issues a declaration of sovereignty which includes the provision that Azeri is the official language of the republic.

*November 1989*
28    Moscow withdraws the Special Administration Committee and returns Nagorno-Karabakh to Azeri rule.

*December 1989*
31–2, 6 Thousands of Azeris tear down border posts at the
Azeri-Iranian border.

*January 1990*
13 Wide-scale attacks on Armenians in Baku take place.
Sixty-six are killed and 220 injured. 10,000 Armenians and
many Russians are evacuated from Azerbaijan.
15 A state of emergency is declared in Azerbaijan, and Soviet
troops are sent to the republic to restore order.
17 Tens of thousands gather in an anti-government protest in
front of the Communist Party Central Committee building
in Baku.
20 Soviet troops enter Baku, using artillery, tank, and naval
gunfire to break a blockade of the city's port and raid the
offices of the Popular Front. 150 are killed. The same day
Vezirov is removed. He is replaced four days later by Ayaz
Mutalibov, chairman of the Council of Ministers (Prime
Minister), as First Party Secretary. Hasan Hasanov replaces
Mutalibov as Prime Minister.

*September 1990*
30 In Supreme Soviet elections, the Democratic Azerbaijan bloc
gain 40 of the 350 seats (including 25 Popular Front seats).

*January 1991*
9 Several Azeris and Armenians are killed in two different
incidents of violence in Nagorno-Karabakh.

*February 1991*
500,000 rally in Nagorno-Karabakh for a transfer of
Nagorno-Karabakh to Armenian control.

*March 1991*
1 More deaths occur in interethnic shootouts.
17 In the all-union referendum on preserving the union, 93
percent of Azerbaijani voters (75 percent turnout) support
the union. In Nakhichevan, 87 percent of voters support the
union, but there is only a 21 percent turnout.

*April 1991*
30 Soviet troops and Azerbaijani militia crack down to
Armenian insurgents in Western Azerbaijan. Thirty-five
Armenians are killed in an assault on the villages of
Getashen and Martunashen.

*May 1991*
16 1,500 Armenians are forcibly deported from

Nagorno-Karabakh by Azerbaijanis; 1,200 more are forced to leave their homes and live in tents.

*July 1991*
13–14    Several Armenians are killed in attacks on villages in the Geranboi (Shaumyan) region. Troops order the inhabitants of the village to leave their homes.

*August 1991*
30    The Supreme Soviet issues a declaration of independence and lifts the state of emergency in the republic which had been imposed in January 1990.

*September 1991*
6    Tens of thousands protest against upcoming presidential elections in Popular Front-sponsored demonstrations.
8    Mutalibov is victorious in unopposed presidential elections, following the last-minute withdrawal of opposition candidate Zardusht Ali Zadeh and a Popular Front boycott. 91 percent of voters support Mutalibov. While an 84 percent turnout was officially reported, opposition estimates place turnout as low as 25 percent.
14    In a demonstration in Baku, 5,000 supporters of the Popular Front call for new parliamentary and presidential elections.

*October 1991*
18    Following a Supreme Soviet vote of 174–35 against signing the interrepublican economic treaty, Mutalibov refuses to sign.

*November 1991*
26    Parliament votes to abolish the autonomous status of Nagorno-Karabakh.

*December 1991*
10    In a referendum on independence in Nagorno-Karabakh, 91 percent of the Armenian population turns out to vote amid an Azeri bombardment of the capital city of Stepanakert and several assassinations. 99.8 percent vote for independence.
26    Parliament adopts law to reintroduce the Latin alphabet.
29    In a referendum on independence, 99 percent of voters (95 percent turnout) vote in favor.

*January 1992*
30    Renewed fighting in Nagorno-Karabakh breaks out following the downing of an Azeri helicopter over the republic.

*February 1992*

17    The People's Front attacks Mutalibov for his moderate
      stance in the war against Armenia and demands his
      resignation.

26–27  The region of Khojali, between Nagorno-Karabakh and
      Armenia, falls to Armenian forces of Nagono-Karabakh.
      Hundreds of Azeris are killed.

28    Three soldiers from ex-Soviet troops are killed in
      Nagorno-Karabakh by Armenian artillery attack.

29    CIS high command orders troops to be withdrawn from
      Nagorno-Karabakh.

*March 1992*

3     Armenian protestors prevent CIS troops from withdrawing
      from Nagorno-Karabakh. One soldier is killed after refusing
      to surrender his weapon.

5     Parliamentary chairwoman Elmira Kafarova resigns and is
      replaced by Yagub Mamedov. The next day Mutalibov
      resigns after being blamed for serious defeats in
      Nagorno-Karabakh. He agrees to transfer power to a
      50-member National Council made up equally of opposition
      and communist deputies. Mamedov is appointed Acting
      President.

10    Armenian fighters in Nagorno-Karabakh release 10 CIS
      army officers captured the day before.

*April 1992*

4     Prime Minister Hasan Hassanov resigns and is replaced by
      Feyruz Mustafaev.

14    Artur Mkrtchyan, chairman of the Nagorno-Karabakh
      parliament, is assassinated in Stepanakert.

27    100,000 gather in Baku to show support for Abulfaz
      Elcibey's candidacy in June presidential elections.

*May 1992*

9     Armenian forces seize the Azerbaijani town of Shusha,
      reportedly with little resistance.

12    Armed supporters of Mutalibov encircle the parliament
      building and demand that the parliament convene.

14    At an extraordinary session, parliament restores Mutalibov
      to power, cancels presidential elections, disbands the
      National Council, and declares a state of emergency. Ragim
      Huseinov is appointed prime minister.

15    Heidar Aliev, Chairman of the Nakhichevan parliament and
      former first party secretary, declares Mutalibov's
      reinstatement illegal and calls upon the People's Front to
      cooperate in establishing legal rule. People's Front
      supporters prevent Mutalibov from leaving the country to

attend a CIS summit and seize the parliamentary building, the presidential palace, and television headquarters.

17–23   Nakhichevan is attacked by Armenian forces.

18   Armenian forces capture the town of Lachin, thus securing a corridor between Armenia and Nagorno-Karabakh.
Mamedov resigns and is replaced by Isa Gambarov in both posts. Parliament hands over power to the National Council.

*June 1992*

7   Abulfaz Elcibey, leader of the Popular Front, is elected president in popular elections, with 59 percent of the vote (76 percent turnout). Nizami Suleimanov of the Democratic Union of Azerbaijani Intellectuals wins a little less than third of the vote.

*August 1992*

13   The Nagorno-Karabakh parliament declares a state of emergency in the republic.

15   The national currency, the *manat*, is introduced, to be used alongside the ruble. The Nagorno-Karabakh prime minister Oleg Esayan and his cabinet resign. Karen Baguryan is appointed acting parliamentary chairman to replace Georgii Petrosyan.

*October 1992*

3   A shadow cabinet is formed under Mamedov's leadership.

7   The National Council votes 43–1 against joining the CIS.

*December 1992*

24   In a demonstration staged by the Turan trade union calling for the resignation of the government, some 200 protestors are detained.

25   Demonstrators protesting against a parliamentary decision to rename the state language "Turkish" are beaten and arrested.

*Janurary 1993*

2   The Movement for Democratic Reform calls upon the government to free those jailed in the December 24 protest, dissolve the parliament, and hold new elections.

26   Prime Minister Ragim Huseinov resigns after giving a speech condemning the breaking off of relations with Russia. He is replaced by his first deputy Ali Masimov.

*February 1993*

21   Defense minister Rakim Gaziyev is removed from his post, as well as Murshud Mamedov, the head of the Ganja city administration.

22  Surat Huseinov, the commander of Azerbaijani troops in northern Nagorno-Karabakh, is relieved of his command after he surrenders a number of Azeri towns to Karabakh forces. Huseinov goes to Gandjha where he establishes an opposition headquarters.

*April 1993*

2–3  Armenian troops take the region of Kelbajar. It is estimated that Armenian forces now control nearly 10 percent of Azerbaijani territory.

2  A state of emergency is declared in Azerbaijan.

28  Panakh Huseinov, a founding member of the Popular Front, is appointed prime minister.

*June 1993*

4–6  Government troops launch an attack on Surat Huseinov's headquarters in Gandjha. Huseinov withstands the attack, seizes control of key locations in the city, takes government officials hostage, and demands the resignation of Prime Minister P. Huseinov and Parliamentary chaiman Isa Gambarov.

7  P. Huseinov resigns.

9  S. Huseinov demand's Elcibey's resignation and threatens to overthrow the government if he refuses.

13  Gambarov resigns.

15  In a vote of 37–3, Geidar Aliev is appointed chairman of the Supreme Soviet, which had not operated since the Popular Front's seizure of power in May 1992, as well as acting president.

17  Elcibey flees Baku but insists that he remains president.

23  Huseinov's troops enter Baku.

24  Parliament impeaches Elcibey.

30  Parliament appoints Surat Huseinov Prime Minister in a vote of 38–1, after an attempt by Aliev to install Etibar Mamedov, leader of the National Independence Party of Azerbaijan, fails.

*July 1993*

1  Huseinov calls for general mobilization as Armenian forces continue their incursion into Azeri territory.

3  Thousands of Elcibey supporters are attacked by security forces but allowed to proceed with a demonstration.

16  Gambarov is arrested for his involvement in ordering the June assault on Huseinov's headquarters.

17  Government militia seal the headquarters of the Azerbaijan Popular Front and violently break up a Popular Front demonstration.

26  The *manat* becomes the sole legal tender in Azerbaijan.

*August 1993*
29    Elcibey receives a vote of no-confidence (97 percent) in a popular referendum (93 percent turnout).

*September 1993*
1    Parliament schedules new presidential elections for 3 October.
20    Parliament elects to rejoin the CIS.
24    Thousands gather at a Popular Front demonstration in Nakhichevan to protest Azerbaijan's membership in the CIS.

*October 1993*
3    Presidential elections are held, and Heidar Aliev receives 98.8 percent of the vote (97.6 percent turnout). Two other candidates ran.
30    New Armenian offensive is launched in Azerbaijan, and several hundred are killed. Karabakh forces take the Beilagandski region, the last stronghold in southwestern Azerbaijan.
Azerbaijan joins the CIS.

*December 1993*
8    Separatist Alikram Gumbatov, who had declared an autonomous Talysh-Mugan Republic centered on the town of Lenkoran, is arrested.

*February 1994*
2    A bomb explodes in the main Baku train station, killing 5 people.

*March 1994*
19    A bomb explodes in the Baku metro, killing twelve people

*May 1994*
5    Leaders of Armenia, Nagorno-Karabakh, and Russia sign an agreement on a cease-fire in Nagorno-Karabakh. Azerbaijan follows suit on 8 May.
7    The Democratic Party of Azerbaijan holds its founding congress.
13    Police forcefully prevent 150 members of the Society for the Defense of Women from protesting the Nagorno-Karabakh cease-fire agreement.
The Baku headquarters of the Popular Front are invaded by 300 armed persons.
14    Police blockade the Baku office of the Popular Front's newspaper *Azadlyg* and force employees to vacate the premises.
16–20    A second cease-fire agreement is concluded which outlines

the details of CIS peacekeeping troop deployment.

31    Ex-foreign minister Tofik Gasymov and first deputy
chairman of the Popular Front Ibrahim Ibrahimly are voted
out of parliament upon Aliev's urging.

*July 1994*

3    A bomb explodes in the Baku metro, killing seven people.
Aliev accuses anti-independence forces of terrorism.

*August 1994*

18    Police raid the office of *Azadlyg* and detain ten Front
members.

*September 1994*

10    Police forcibly break up a Popular Front rally held to protest
the draft treaty on ending the war for Nagorno-Karabakh.
Several are wounded and about a hundred people are
arrested.

20    Aliev signs an agreement on the "contract of the century"
giving a consortium of Western oil companies the right to
extract oil from Azerbaijan's Caspian Sea shelf. The Russian
government refuses to acknowledge the agreement as legal
and demands participation in further negotiations, even
though the Russian firm Lukoil had already been given a 10
percent share in the deal.

21    Ex-Defense Minister Ragim Gaziyev and three others escape
from a pretrial detention center where they were being held
on charges of treason. Gaziyev reportedly takes refuge at the
Russian-controlled Shabalinskaya Radar Station.

29    Deputy speaker Afiyaddin Dzhalilov (rumored to be Aliev's
illegitimate son) and head of the presidential guard Shamsi
Ragimov are assassinated.

*October 1994*

2    Prosecutor General Ali Omarov announces the detention of
three suspects in connection with the recent murders.
Members of the OPON special police (under the direction of
Deputy Minister of Internal Affairs Rovshan Javadov) storm
the Prosecutor's office and take Omarov, his deputies, and
other employees hostage. They demand the release of the
suspects and the removal of Minister of Internal Affairs
Usudov, who had been considering disbanding the OPON.

3    The OPON troops release the hostages and return to their
base which is subsequently surrounded by government
troops.
Aliev declares a 60-day state of emergency.
Javadov is dismissed from his post but later reinstated.

4    In Gandjha, OPON members seize the mayor's building and

take the mayor hostage. They are joined by troops loyal to Prime Minister Surat Huseinov.

In Baku, thousands gather in front of the presidential palace to express support for Aliev.

5     Huseinov assures Aliev that the president has his full support. Javadov denies staging a coup.

100,000 gather in Baku's Freedom Square in support of Aliev.

6     Parliament dismisses Huseinov from his posts as prime minister and parliamentary deputy. His deputy Fuad Guliyev is appointed acting prime minister.

8     After being accused of provoking the seizure of his offices, Prosecutor-General Omarov resigns.

20     After Huseinov joins ex-Defense Minister Gaziyev at the Gabalinskaya radar station on October 12, they are reportedly flown to Russia.

*December 1994*

22     The Nagorno-Karabakh parliament elects Robert Kocharyan, head of the republic's State Defense Committee, as president.

*March 1995*

12     OPON troops attempt to seize power in the districts of Akstafa and Kazakh.

14     Usudov dissolves the OPON.

Government forces lay seige to OPON headquarters in Baku.

15     Aliev removes Javadov from his post as Deputy Minister of Internal Affairs.

17     Government troops succeed in taking OPON headquarters, and the rebellion is put down. In the fighting, about 30 people die, including Javadov.

# 13 Armenia: paradise regained or lost?

NORA DUDWICK

## Introduction

Four years after Armenian independence and eight years after the first massive, sustained nationalist demonstrations in the USSR, the bloom is off the rose. Conditions in independent Armenia are reminiscent of the first independent Armenian republic which arose out of the ashes of World War I, when Armenia declared independence after the collapse of the Russian Empire and the short-lived Transcaucasian Federation. Between 1918 and 1920, led by the revolutionary party which had struggled for the liberation of the Turkish Armenians, the Armenian government "had to start from scratch and create everything from ruins and chaos."[1] Simon Vratsian, the republic's prime minister, later wrote that Armenia had been completely unprepared for independence, and compared its declaration of independence "to the birth of a sick child."[2] Armenia was surrounded by hostile countries, with thousands of destitute refugees pouring over the border. Famine and malnutrition were widespread, and 20 percent of the population died during the first year of independence. Cut off from Russian supplies, the economy destabilized and inflation soared. By 1920, the defeated government signed over its power to the Bolsheviks, and Armenia entered the Russian orbit as a Soviet republic.

Seventy years later, Armenia again embraced independence with mixed fear and elation. As in 1918, the party which spearheaded the nationalist movement committed itself to the task of replacing the political and economic structures of the socialist state with a free-market, democratic government. Despite hopeful Western pronouncements about Armenia's progress, it is not yet clear in what direction this transition is actually leading Armenia.

Independent Armenia has grappled with war on its borders, a ruined infrastructure (this time, not so much from war as from the 1988 earthquake), and over 200,000 refugees. Cut off from Soviet economic support, the economy is in shambles. Despite Armenia's pioneering agricultural privatization, much of the population suffers from poverty, and the difficulties of earning of living have driven as much as 25 percent of the population from the republic since independence. Armenians now wonder if their joy at achieving independent statehood after centuries of

471

subordination to the great empires of Europe and the Middle East was premature.

How Armenians confront the future and weigh the past suggests that the direction in which Armenia will move is conditioned not only by free market requirements, but also by history. Not only is history central to Armenians' self-conceptions, but the way in which Armenians respond to contemporary problems grows out of their understanding and interpretation of their own past. In order to outline for the reader the contours of post-Soviet Armenia, this chapter will therefore begin by placing Armenia and the Armenian people in a broad social and historical context.

## The origins of the Armenian people

Despite the Armenians' difficult geopolitical position at the crossroads of warring peoples and empires, they have nevertheless maintained a continuous existence on a portion of their ancient territories for over two millennia. It has yet to be ascertained whether Armenians originated in western Asia Minor, or whether they were indigenous to the highlands of eastern Anatolia. Nor is it known where the name "Armenia," or the indigenous name, "Hayastan," originates,[3] although Greek and Persian sources refer to "Armina" and "Armenians" as early as 500 BC.[4] According to these sources, Armenian tribes first appeared around 600 BC.

Early Armenia was made up of feuding dynastic principalities with shifting alliances. This pattern continued throughout the medieval period, making Armenia prey to large neighboring empires. At the same time, it probably ensured the survival of a distinct ethnic identity, since part of Armenia was always able to maintain some autonomy and thereby resist assimilationist pressures.[5]

The adoption of Christianity as the state religion at the beginning of the fourth century and the creation of a phonetic, thirty-six character alphabet a century later under Church sponsorship played a major role in establishing a distinctive Armenian identity, for "in a real sense, Armenians did not even fully become 'Armenians' until they acquired their own distinctively Armenian religion . . ."[6] In 451 AD, at the Battle of Avarair, St. Vardan Mamikonian and his men died resisting the Persian Empire's attempt to impose Zoroastrianism on the Armenians. Armenians still commemorate this date, less for its religious significance than as a symbol of their willingness to martyr themselves in defense of their nation.[7]

After the sixth-century schism between the Armenian church and the World Council of Churches, Armenia formed a distinct cultural unit between the Classical west and the Persian east.[8] Split between the Persian and Roman (and later, Byzantine) empires by the end of the fifth century, Armenians continued to enjoy relative autonomy despite rendering nominal fealty to their imperial rulers.[9]

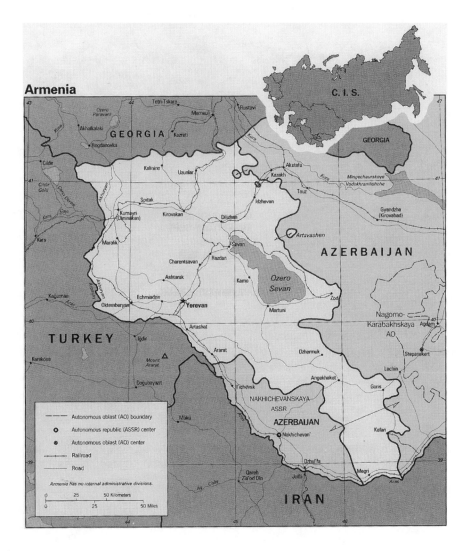

# Armenia

Waves of invasions by Turkic tribes from Central Asia in the eleventh century, followed by the Mongol invasions of the thirteenth and fourteenth centuries, stimulated Armenian migration to cities throughout Europe, Russia, and the Middle East, where they formed a far-flung network of diaspora communities. By the end of the fifteenth century, the Ottoman Turks had established themselves in Constantinople and begun consolidating their power into Anatolia. The Ottoman Empire ruled religious minorities through their religious leaders; thus, the Patriarch of the Armenian Apostolic Church became the functional head of the Armenian *millet*, or ethno-religiously defined "nation." The Church became the single most important institution of Armenian life within the Ottoman Empire,[10] and "from the fifteen to the late nineteenth century, whoever led the Church spoke for what there was of the nation."[11]

A sixteenth-century treaty between the Ottoman and Persian Empires divided Armenia into a western portion under Ottoman hegemony, and an eastern portion under Persian hegemony. This boundary transformed Armenia into a frequent theater of war, as military campaigns, pillage, deportations and famine during the following centuries reduced the Armenian population, ultimately turning Armenians into a minority in their home territories.[12] In contrast to the impoverishment of the Armenian heartland, however, a prosperous commercial bourgeoisie developed in the urban diaspora. It was among these communities that a nationalist consciousness first developed as Armenians, as permanent "outsiders," turned their attention to the plight of the distant but longed-for homeland. In the cities, they were also exposed to the revolutionary and nationalist currents which swept Europe in the eighteenth and nineteenth centuries. As in Europe, nationalism among Armenians developed unevenly among social groups and regions, beginning with a cultural and literary phase which gradually developed into a militant campaign for the "national idea."[13]

## The birth of Armenian nationalism

The "prehistory" of Armenian nationalism can be traced to the communities of the diaspora, where a cultural renaissance began in the sixteenth century. Use of the printing press by Armenian commercial entrepreneurs led to a stream of publications in Armenian, including the first printed Armenian Bible (Amsterdam, 1666), and the first journal of Armenian affairs (Madras, 1794). Such publications disseminated European Renaissance ideas among Armenians.[14] A very significant factor in the Armenian cultural awakening was the rediscovery and republication of Armenian classical religious, literary and historical texts by the Mekhitarist monks, an Armenian Benedictine order founded in Venice in the eighteenth century.[15] The Mekhitarists aimed their efforts at the culturally backward Armenian communities of the Ottoman Empire, "but they were careful not to transform cultural views into political trends."[16] Historical and mytho-logical Armenian heroes who had resisted foreign domination were offered to Armenians primarily as sources of pride and spiritual values. The concept of the "nation," however, remained cultural rather than political. Within the Ottoman Empire, where the bulk of the Armenian population still formed an impoverished, semi-literate, often Turkish or Kurdish-speaking mass, the "nation" as a self-conscious entity consisted primarily of the *millet's* clerical and wealthy classes.[17]

Following the Mekhitarists' modification of the ancient literary language, *grabar*, Khatchatur Abovian popularized a radically modified vernacular with the publication of his novel, *Verk Hayastani* ("wounds of Armenia"). This vernacular subsequently became the medium of a nationalistic literary revival. Appeals were made to Armenians in the Ottoman empire to "wake up . . . from your death-inviting slumber of ignorance, remember your past glory, mourn your present state of wretchedness and heed the example of other enlightened nations . . ."[18]

In the mid nineteenth century, cultural practices, as summed up by the concept of "nation," gradually displaced religion as the guarantor of ethnic identity for a new Armenian middle class of doctors, lawyers, writers, tea-chers, and small manufacturers who challenged elite control over social and political life in the *millet*.[19] This new liberal class achieved a limited democratization of the *millet* administration, which then directed its atten-tion to spreading literacy and enlightenment among the Armenian popu-lation. But most liberals focused their efforts within Constantinople, for as one liberal editor wrote, "the Patriarch is there, the progressive and edu-cated elements of the nation are there. In one word, the great strength of nation is there."[20]

The growth of cultural nationalism in the urban centers contrasted with the lack of national consciousness in the rural hinterland, "where the very concept of Armenia as an idea or living concept was lost at times for the mass of Armenians,"[21] until it was rediscovered and reinvented by intellec-tuals in the nineteenth century. The cultural awakening in the cities, how-ever, stimulated a new generation of educated provincial Armenians. These included the self-taught clergyman from Van who eventually became Cath-olicos, Mkrtich Khrimian, who in his concern for the welfare of the masses, "began a shift in Armenian political thought from an abstract nationalism to a concrete populism . . ."[22] As patriotism became redefined as love of the fatherland, the nation became more strongly linked to a particular terri-tory, a further step in the development of a political program.

Despite the *millet* reforms and the guarantees for Armenian security which the victorious European powers forced the Ottoman Empire to make, the economic and political situation in the provinces steadily deterio-rated after the Russo-Turkish War of 1877–78. The war had devastated the Armenian countryside, and the Sultan Hamid's repression against the Armenians for their perceived pro-Russian orientation and increased politicization resulted in the "Hamidean massacres" of 1895–96, which took approximately 300,000 Armenian lives.[23]

Russia's annexation of the Crimea and Eastern (Persian) Armenia introduced new security and prosperity to Armenians living in the Russian Empire.[24] As in the Ottoman Empire, a new generation of secular, nationalist intellectuals emerged by mid-century. Their socialist and revolutionary ideology had a profound impact on the programs of the Armenian political parties. Although two of these parties, the Hunchak party (Geneva, 1887), and the Dashnak party (Tbilisi, 1890) were founded outside Armenia proper, they directed their efforts primarily at the six eastern *vilayets* (provinces) of the Ottoman Empire, where most Turkish Armenians lived. The increased oppression and large-scale massacres in the Ottoman Empire and the example of the successful Balkan resistance movements radicalized their programs. The parties' dearth of manpower and economic strength, the lack of active support from the Armenian religious and economic establishment, internecine conflicts, and a futile reliance on assistance from the European powers, however, resulted in the ultimate failure of the nineteenth-century revolutionary movement to secure its aims.[25]

## The 1915 Genocide

Armenian nationalist aspirations in the Ottoman Empire came to an abrupt halt during World War I, when the Young Turk government and ruling Committee of Union and Progress seized on the war as an opportunity to eliminate the Ottoman Empire's troublesome Armenian population. In the organized slaughter which peaked between 1915 and 1917, about one million[26] Armenians were executed or died during forced marches across Turkey to the deserts of present-day Syria.[27] Refugees poured into Russian Armenia, where they constituted at least one fourth of the population by the beginning of the 1920s.[28]

It is impossible to exaggerate the significance of the *mets eghern* (great slaughter) for contemporary Armenian thinking, both in Armenia and in the diaspora. The genocide virtually eliminated Armenians from nine-tenths of their historical territories in Turkey, leaving them only the small fragment in the Russian Transcaucasus to call their own. Throughout the Middle East, Europe, and North America, it created new or vastly enlarged diaspora communities, where the memory of the genocide served as a virtual "charter of identity," even for those who had not directly experienced it.[29]

## The first independent Armenian republic

With the collapse of central power which followed the October Revolution in 1917 and the withdrawal of Russian troops from the Transcaucasus, Armenia, Azerbaijan, and Georgia declared independence. In 1918, the

Table 13.1. *Distribution of the Armenian population in 1988*

| | | | |
|---|---|---|---|
| Soviet Union | 4,600,000 | Latin America | 100,000 |
| Armenia | 3,100,000 | Canada | 50,000 |
| United States | 750,000 | Balkans (Bulgaria, | 50,000 |
| Middle East, | | Greece, Romania | |
| Libya, Egypt, | | Australia | 25,000 |
| and Ethiopia | 475,000 | Far East | 12,500 |
| Western Europe | 400,000 | Africa | 5,000 |
| Iran | 140,000 | | |

Source: Adapted from Claire Mouradian, *De Stalin à Gorbatchev. Histoire d'une république soviétique: l'Arménie* (Paris: Editions Ramsay, 1990), p. 169.[30]

"Armenian republic began its existence under the leadership of the Dashnak Party, on about 4,500 square miles (12,000 square kilometers) of bleak rugged terrain, crammed with refugees, devoid of the bare essentials of life, and surrounded by hostile forces ... it became the "Land of Stalking Death," as famine, contagion, and exposure swept away nearly 200,000 people during the ensuing year.[31]

During the war with Turkey, harvests had decreased by 40 percent, the land under cultivation by a third, and industrial production had almost ceased. The Turkish invasion and occupation of 1918 left two hundred villages and half the vineyards in the Ararat valley in ruins.[32] By 1919, the republic was overwhelmed by almost 300,000 refugees, and new refugees poured in daily from the North Caucasus and Azerbaijan."[33]

## The sovietization of Armenia

Sovietization of the republic occurred "as a measure of last resort by the defeated, discouraged, and disintegrating Dashnak government of independent Armenia," which signed away its powers on December 2, 1920.[34] According to a British eyewitness, "people were amazed, incredulous, but for the most part apathetic. Anyhow, they thought it would be better to have the Russians back and to lose their independence than to be massacred by the Turks."[35]

The Armenian peasantry was collectivized in the 1930s, despite a vigorous resistance from 1930 to 1934, led by traditional village leaders and occasionally supported by rural Communists.[36] By 1975, only 20 percent of the labor force worked in agriculture and forestry, with 38 percent of the labor force in industry and 42 percent in services. With two-thirds of the population living in cities and towns, Armenia had completed the transition from an agrarian to an urban, industrialized society.[37]

# Exploring the limits of nationalism

The character of the relationship between the Armenian population and the Soviet regime between 1920 and 1990 frequently shifted, depending on the period and social group considered. Attitudes ranged from sincere conviction, especially among first-generation Communists, that they were building a new society, to the opportunism of new local elites whose status depended on their support for the regime, and disaffection or even hostility among many Turkish Armenian refugees,[38] repatriates, and the tens of thousands of families affected by Stalin's purges.[39]

The Armenian Church never became the focus of dissident nationalism, but played a consistently cautious, accommodating role in relation to the Soviet state. It had already lost many of its social and educational functions as well as its influence among the intelligentsia before sovietization, although the peasantry remained devout.[40] But right up to the present, it has retained a national significance for Armenians for its historical role in providing leadership and preserving Armenia's scholarly and literary heritage through centuries of statelessness. For people living in an environment where medieval churches and carved stone crosses seem part of the natural landscape, and where "Armenianness" was defined for centuries in terms of Christianity, history, Church and "the nation" are not easily compartmentalized.[41]

Throughout the Soviet period, Armenians tried to expand the domain of a permissible nationalism which would still conform to Soviet requirements of "national in form, socialist in content." Paradoxically, nationalism in the Soviet Union was unintentionally encouraged by the status of "the nation" as the only domain in which a limited contestation of political issues was allowed (as long as it was couched in the idiom of culture). For Armenians living in their titular republic, the defense of their "nation" – whether of the Armenian language, Church, cultural heritage, or history – functioned simultaneously as an attempt to heal the physical and psychological trauma of the genocide and to protect local interests and traditions.[42]

# The institutional framework of nationalism

Initially, Soviet authorities encouraged the staffing of local government with Armenians and the development of the Armenian Communist Party. By the end of 1933, 89.2 percent of local Party members were Armenian. Up until 1936, "ambitious youths did not have to cease being Armenian, they had to become Soviet Armenians."[43]

During these years, Armenia acquired the structures of national statehood and a network of cultural institutions. Yerevan State University opened in 1921,[44] and an Armenian affiliate of the Academy of Sciences

Table 13.2. *Ethnic composition in Armenia*

|  | 1979 | | 1989 | |
| --- | --- | --- | --- | --- |
|  | thousands | % | thousands | % |
| Armenians | 2,725 | 89.7 | 3,076 | 93.7 |
| Azerbaijanis | 161 | 5.3 | 41 | 1.4 |
| Russians | 70 | 2.3 | 51 | 1.6 |
| Kurds | 51 | 1.7 | 65 | 1.8 |
| Others | 30 | 1.0 | 50 | 1.5 |
| Total | 3,031 | 100.0 | 3,283 | 100.0 |

*Source*: figures taken from Mouradian, *De Staline à Gorbachev*, p. 165.

was founded in 1935, followed by several national museums, libraries, and archives.[45]

The centralization of authority under Stalin in the 1930s, however, drastically reduced the autonomy of Armenia's government and Communist Party. The Great Purge began with the mysterious death in 1936 of the Armenian first secretary, Aghasi Khanjian (generally assumed to be the work of Laurentii Beria). None of the sixteen members of the Bureau of the Armenian Party's Central Committee of 1936 still held their posts in 1937. The purges destroyed two generations of intellectuals, and replaced the remaining "old Communists" and the second generation of Communist Party leaders with "apparatchiks" rather than revolutionaries, controlled by and dependent on the center.[46] By 1947, "Armenians were required to be more than Soviet Armenians; they had to be Armenian Soviets."[47]

The zigzag policy toward nationalism in Armenia since the 1920s reflects the paradox that achievement of centrally-determined policies depended on the abilities of local leaders to mobilize local populations, which they could best do when perceived as responsive to local interests. The high degree of nativization in the post-Stalin period (in 1964, Armenians made up 91.8 percent of Party membership, but only 88 percent of the population),[48] combined with the republic's ethnic homogeneity, created a "palpable native cast" to the way local bureaucracy perceived its own welfare and that of the republic.[49] During the 1960s, a movement toward greater economic decentralization allowed the Armenian government to somewhat increase its independence from Moscow and solidify local support by making more concessions to local nationalism. Installed in 1974 as first secretary after an essentially local career, Karen Demirchian, like his predecessor, Anton Kochinian, was able to manipulate national feelings and strong traditional networks of mutual assistance to solidify his personal position.

## Language and nationalism

Discussion about Armenian and Russian bilingualism in Armenia has been a way of describing and arguing political issues, including Russian cultural hegemony and Moscow's political control. Armenian nineteenth-century enlightenment figures recognized the symbolic significance of language; in the first Armenian vernacular grammar, published in 1866, the authors used the impoverished, Turkified state of Armenian vernacular speech as a metaphor to describe the "incursions and devastations" occurring under the Ottomans.[50] Language remains an emotive issue for Armenians, who consider their language, an archaic branch of Indo-European, and its ancient alphabet a factor contributing to their long survival as a distinct ethnic entity. Even in Turkish-speaking Armenian communities of the Ottoman Empire, it was not uncommon for Armenians to write Turkish in the Armenian alphabet.[51]

The new Soviet government encouraged the employment of the Armenian language in administration and education, where it served as the "transmission belt" for disseminating Marxist-Leninist ideology and Soviet policies.[52] Nevertheless, mastery of Russian was seen as important to advancement. In the 1930s, the number of Armenian children in Russian schools increased due to parents' desire to assure their children's upward mobility. In 1927, 98.5 percent of all pupils in Armenia attended Armenian schools;[53] by 1987, this figure had decreased to 75 percent.[54]

This trend disturbed many Armenian cultural figures, who accused the local party elite of alienation from their own culture and national interests.[55] The poet, Gevork Emin, asserted that the republic's schools were graduating pupils who spoke neither Armenian nor Russian fluently,[56] and the ethnographer, Hambartsum Galstian, claimed that the fact that most Armenian children entered the Russian-language classroom with no prior knowledge of Russian impeded learning and even emotional development.[57] Delegates to the 1981 Congress of the Armenian Writers' Union warned that the increased voluntary use of Russian posed a serious threat to the vitality of Armenian language and culture, and that an ever-growing number of pupils were enrolling at Russian schools since the adoption of the requirement that dissertations must be submitted in Russian.[58] In 1987, the popular poet, Silva Kaputikian, warned that the position of Armenian in the republic was still diminishing every year, even in strictly local institutions.[59] Galstian and Kaputikian, both of whom played a visible role in the early days of the Karabakh movement, were among those who introduced the issue into the political agenda of the late 1980s.

## Reinterpreting the past

Even sharper battles over nationalism were fought in the arenas of literature and historiography, as Armenian writers and scholars worked to con-

struct a past which ratified and legitimized national claims and aspirations. After the creation of Soviet Armenia, the intellectual and cultural
establishment undertook the task of firmly establishing the Armenian historical claim to its territory. A toponymic reform replaced Turkish and
Russian place-names with new Armenian names. This change effectively erased from popular memory the fact that Muslims had formed a
majority of the region's population during the first half of the nineteenth
century.[60]

Grief over the genocide, nostalgia for the lost territories in Turkey,
and pride in Armenia's rich cultural heritage were allowed a limited
expression as long as Armenians publicly acknowledged the "progressive
historical role" of Tsarist Russia and the Soviet Union in Armenian
history. During the Twenties, Soviet Armenian authorities invited well-
known Armenian writers, composers, and artists living outside the republic to work in Armenia. The first decade of Soviet power saw a cultural
renaissance, a period that "would later be looked back upon fondly as
a period of relative freedom and great creativity."[61] In the 1930s, many
writers were arrested on charges of nationalism, and a whole generation
of Armenia's most talented literary figures, including Aksel Bakunts and
the poet Eghishe Charents, perished in Stalin's purges.[62] During World
War II, however, authorities authorized limited concessions to harness
Armenian nationalist feelings to the war effort, and the Church "began
to enjoy a respite from Soviet persecution, if not from Soviet
control."[63]

After the war, the campaign against nationalism began anew as contemporary Armenian writers were condemned for "idealizing the historical
past," and popular nineteenth century authors such as *Raffi* (the pseudonym for Hakob Melik-Hakobian) were banned for their "bourgeois
nationalism."[64] Following Stalin's death, banned works were republished
and writers rehabilitated, some, such as Charents and Bakunts, posthumously. Historical themes appeared with greater frequency in literature, and
monographs were published on the ancient, medieval and early Soviet periods of Armenian history.

The exploration of diaspora themes, especially the Western Armenian
experience, signalled a shift from "national consciousness based on the
identification of the nation with a specific territory" to one based on "a
more inclusive conception of ethnic experience unfettered by political
borders."[65] This new construction of nationality on the basis of ethnic
and cultural practices sought to incorporate Armenian diaspora communities into a single Armenian nation. This trend is exemplified by literature
on the genocide. The first major work, Jon Kirakosyan's *The First World
War and the Western Armenians*, was published in 1965, followed in the
late 1970s and 1980s by a spate of studies under Kirakosyan's
sponsorship.[66]

# Dissident nationalism in Armenia

The post-Stalin era in Armenia saw a "complex interplay" between official nationalism, the highly regulated expression of "national pride, patriotic sentiments, even a certain glorification of the past," and the dissident nationalism of public protest and unsanctioned political organizations.[67] To the extent that Armenian demands were directed at Turkey, they were not perceived as threats to Soviet hegemony. On the contrary, Armenia remained "a 'loyal millet' within the Soviet Socialist world."[68]

Nevertheless, in contrast to the intellectuals' protests, which were confined to the realm of culture, radical dissent arose among a small group of people born toward the end of the Stalin era into working-class or lower-middle-class families.[69] Many of these families had repatriated from or had roots in Turkish Armenia, and the national question was inextricably bound up with their personal fate. These young Armenians often instrumentalized human rights issues to serve the "Armenian Cause" (Armenian irredenta), in a system where the only authorized political space was the national, and where the heavy burden of the Armenian past and the ongoing reality of the national question made it difficult for them to think politically in universalistic terms.[70]

The first known Armenian group with a nationalist agenda, the Union of Patriots, appeared as early as 1956 at Yerevan State University.[71] It was followed in 1963 by the Union of Armenian Youth, which continued for three years.[72] The National Unification Party (NUP), formed in Yerevan in 1966, called for an independent Armenia which would include Western Armenia, Nakhichevan[73] and Karabakh. The leaders were arrested in 1968, and the nineteen-year-old Paruir Hairekyan, who was to renew his call for independence during the Armenian nationalist movement of the late Eighties, took over the leadership until his arrest in 1969.[74]

Despite the small numbers involved in radical protest, during the 1960s the first massive outbreak of national feeling occurred in Yerevan. On April 24, 1965, as public officials, representatives of the Armenian Apostolic Church, and delegates from the diaspora gathered in the Spendiarian Opera Theater to commemorate the 50th anniversary of the Armenian genocide, an estimated 100,000 people gathered outside, demanding the return of Armenian lands seized by the Turks and asking for Soviet assistance.[75] Police broke up the demonstration and many of the student-age participants, including future leaders of the Armenian national movement such as Vazgen Manukian and Levon Ter-Petrossian, spent several days in jail,

It is evident that the national issue had already become the focus of considerable student activity. Manukian later claimed that it was at this time the idea of independence was born among Armenian youth. In March 1967, for example, thirty-two students were expelled from the university for nationalist, anti-Soviet activity.[76] At Yerevan State University in the

1970s, a group of reform-minded Komsomol (Communist Youth League) members attempted to democratize university policies by engineering the election of popular candidates.[77]

As a result of the 1965 demonstrations, the first secretary, Yakov Zohrabian, one of Nikita Khrushchev's team popular among Armenians for his perceived honesty and sympathy for national issues, was replaced. Although his successor, Anton Kochinian, publicly criticized Armenian nationalism, it was during his regime that the first monument to the 1915 genocide was erected. This imposing structure thereafter allowed April 24 commemorations to be channeled toward a precise and institutionalized space.[78] In the following years, additional monuments were erected to heroes of the Armenian liberation struggle in the Ottoman Empire and the battles against Turkish troops during and after the First World War, in a similar effort to assuage and defuse national feelings.[79]

In 1977, a small group of Armenian dissidents, including several NUP founders, established the Armenian Helsinki Watch Group to monitor compliance with the Helsinki Accords and to work for Armenian membership in the United Nations. An NUP announcement in June 1977 described civil rights violations in Armenia and enumerated the "anti-nationality policies of the central and republic governments." According to the Helsinki Watch Group, these included the destruction of national customs and language, the privileging of Russian over Armenian schools, linguistic Russification, and the ongoing violation of Karabakh Armenians' civil rights. By February 1978, with its members in prison and awaiting sentencing, the group had been crushed.[80] Ensuing investigations tried to discredit the NUP and the Armenian Helsinki Watch Group by linking them to an explosion which occurred January 8, 1977, in the Moscow metro. Three young workers, including a former NUP member (posthumously rehabilitated in 1986), were tried secretly in Moscow and executed in 1979.[81]

The early Eighties saw continuing arrests and trials for the dissemination of *samizdat* urging independence for Armenia.[82] A visitor to Soviet Armenia in 1984, just before the era of glasnost, recorded the spectrum of attitudes, from the unabashed pro-independence nationalism of an Armenian "repatriate" from the Middle East, to the more accommodationist expressions of Party members, and the belief that Soviet protection provided a guarantee for at least a remnant of Armenia.[83]

## The birth of the Karabakh movement

In February 1988, a concerted movement developed among the Armenian population in Nagorno-Karabagh, with the single goal of attaching the region to Armenia. That month, mass demonstrations began in Karabagh. In response, the largest demonstrations since 1965 took place in Armenia.

Within months, these spontaneous collective actions evolved into a movement with a broad agenda of democratic and social reforms.

The history of Nagorno-Karabakh is now bitterly disputed by Armenian and Azerbaijani scholars, who have put forth elaborate historical arguments to demonstrate the ethnic continuity of their own people on this territory. Armenians consider Nagornyi ("mountainous") Karabakh[84] to be a historically Armenian region with special significance for Armenian national consciousness,[85] where Armenian *meliks* (princes) had retained a degree of autonomy under Muslim rule up until the nineteenth-century Russian conquest. By the nineteenth century, however, it had also become "an important site of Muslim intellectual and political development," which even more than Baku, "served as the focal point of emerging Azerbaijani identity . . ."[86]

After annexation by Russia, Nagornyi Karabakh, Zangezur (now in southeast Armenia) and most of present-day Azerbaijan were incorporated into a single province. Despite Nagornyi Karabakh's largely Armenian population, the construction of roads and rail lines bound it ever more tightly to Baku, and Armenian workers streamed from Zangezur and Nagornyi Karabakh to work in the thriving Baku oil industry.[87]

When Armenia and Azerbaijan became independent republics in 1918, Zangezur, Nakhichevan, and Nagornyi Karabakh became the objects of bitter contention between the Armenian, Azerbaijani, and Ottoman armies. After Sovietization, the new Soviet authorities awarded Nakhichevan and Nagornyi Karabakh to Azerbaijan and in 1923, the Nagorno-Karabakh Autonomous Oblast was created. Comprising an area of 1,700 square miles and separated from Armenia by a narrow corridor, the new oblast excluded several contiguous Armenian-populated districts.[88]

Karabakh Armenians periodically protested to Moscow that Azerbaijan severely neglected the oblast's infrastructure, and despite cultural rights guaranteed by the Soviet constitution, prevented contacts with Armenia. They pointed to the relative decline in the oblast's Armenian population as evidence of ethnically discriminatory policies used by Azerbaijan to drive Armenians from their homeland. This decline coincided with the gradual political, economic, and cultural Azerbaijanization of the republic, consistent with Soviet state policies encouraging development of republic-based "national" identities to replace regional or kin-based identities. Throughout the Soviet Union, minorities such as the Armenians in Azerbaijan, as well as Azerbaijanis in Armenia, found themselves treated as factually non-indigenous, and excluded from republic-based cultural development.[89]

Resistance to Azerbaijani rule never completely died in Nagorno-Karabakh. After Stalin's death, the Karabakh Armenians protested more openly, sending hundreds of letters, petitions, and delegations to Moscow. A petition addressed to Khrushchev in 1964 detailed the transfer of local

Table 13.3. *The population of Nakhichevan and Nagorno–Karabakh*

|  | 1914 | 1926 | 1959 | 1970 | 1979 |
|---|---|---|---|---|---|
| *Nakhichevan* | | | | | |
| Armenians | 53,700 | 11,300 | 9,500 | 5,800 | 3,400 |
| Azeris | 81,300 | 93,609 | 127,000 | 189,700 | 229,700 |
| *Nagorno–Karabahk* | | | | | |
| Armenians | 170,000 | 117,000 | 110,000 | 121,100 | 123,100 |
| Azeris | 9,000 | 13,600 | 18,100 | 27,200 | 37,200 |

*Source*: figures are taken from Mouradiau, *De Staline à Gorbatchev*, p. 414

enterprises to regions lying outside the oblast, and the neglect of agriculture, industry, roads, water and energy supplies.[90] Three years later, an appeal to the Soviet authorities and to the Armenian people referred to the "hundreds of requests to the Central Government in Moscow and to the government of Azerbaijan" regarding the harassment, murder, and imprisonment of Armenians in Nagorno-Karabakh.[91] Additional complaints concerned the unavailability of Armenian instructional and cultural materials, lack of facilities for receiving television broadcasts from Armenia, and symbolic Azerbaijani appropriation of Armenian historic and cultural achievements.[92] During the 1960s and 1970s, expulsion from the Party and loss of employment forced many Armenian protesters to emigrate from Nagorno-Karabakh.[93]

Pressures for change built up throughout 1987. Prominent Armenians such as Zori Balayan, a Moscow-based writer for *Literaturnaia gazeta*, with roots in Karabakh, the historian Sergo Mikoyan (son of Anastas Mikoyan, late president of the Soviet Union), and Abel Aganbegyan, Gorbachev's economic advisor, publicly expressed optimism regarding an imminent resolution of the Karabakh problem. On October 19, 1987, the day after a demonstration against the planned construction of a chemical enterprise,[94] hundreds of Armenians gathered at the Opera Theater in Yerevan in response to reports that Azerbaijanis had attacked Armenians living in the village of Chardakhlu in Azerbaijan. Meanwhile, activists in Armenia and Karabakh circulated petitions calling for a referendum on attaching Karabakh to Armenia.[95] The petitions were sent to Moscow in January 1988, with tens of thousands of signatures. These activities culminated in February 1988, when Karabakh Armenians, led by the *Krunk* ("crane") Committee, composed of their political and economic elite, began strikes and demonstrations in Stepanakert, the capital of Nagorno-Karabakh. On February 20, Nagorno-Karabakh's Soviet (Council) of Peoples' Deputies passed a resolution requesting the Armenian and Azerbaijani Supreme Soviets to approve Nagorno-Karabakh's transfer to Armenia.[96]

## The rise of political activism in Armenia

In Yerevan, activists disseminated news of the events unfolding in Nagorno-Karabakh at a February 18 protest against the planned construction of a new chemical plant in Abovian, a town outside Yerevan. For those in Armenia, Karabakh had more than territorial significance. The Karabakh Armenians' allegations that Azerbaijanis were trying to force them to abandon their homeland evoked bitter memories of the 1915 genocide of Armenians in the Ottoman Empire and the loss of traditional territories to the Turks, as well as bloody Armenian-Azerbaijani conflicts[97] in 1905 and 1918 in Azerbaijan. On February 19, several hundred people gathered at the Opera Theater to show their support for the Karabakh Armenians. During the course of the week, the number of demonstrators increased exponentially after the Politburo refused to consider border changes, and the official news agency, TASS, branded the demonstrators as "nationalists" and "extremists." The students, teachers, and intellectuals who made up the demonstrations on the first days were soon joined by blue collar workers as well as agricultural workers from the countryside. The crowds dispersed at the end of the week at the urging of Zori Balayan and Silva Kaputikian, two prominent Armenian cultural figures, who returned from discussions with First Secretary Mikhail Gorbachev and Politburo member Alexander Yakovlev in Moscow with guarded assurances of a favorable outcome.

The massive demonstrations provided tangible evidence for the impotence of the Armenian Communist Party authorities, who were unable to provide responsive leadership, but unwilling to suppress the movement by force. Before the crowds dispersed, the organizers asked people to select trusted representatives from their work collectives to serve as communication links between the organizing committee and the rest of the population. The formation of this loose network marked the birth of the grassroots nationalist movement in Armenia.

In Armenia, movement leadership consisted of an *ad hoc* organizing committee, soon dubbed the "Karabakh Committee," composed of young intellectuals, mainly non-Party, without direct connections to government. They decided on strategy and tactics, and took primary responsibility for articulating a program and disseminating correct information at "public meetings." An informal, fluctuating group of intellectuals and writers (many with family roots in Karabakh) played an advisory role, generating documents to legitimate Armenian claims to the broader Soviet and Western audience. The composition of the Karabakh Committee gradually changed, as advocates of extreme positions were expelled so as to avoid provocations and maintain a moderate face to the rest of the country.

The network of committees which formed at enterprises, institutes, university departments, and schools disseminated information about developments in Karabakh, organized collective actions, and forced through some of the political reforms first proposed by Gorbachev. The Karabakh Committee soon achieved credibility with the population during their frequent "informational" meetings and careful analyses of events. They also received *de facto* recognition from local Party authorities, with whom they held periodic negotiations to defuse tense situations.

This focus on democratization was diverted early on, however, by ethnic violence, which both Armenians and Azerbaijanis suspected to be a deliberate provocation on the part of Communist Party authorities to discredit the nationalist movements which had taken hold in both republics. On February 28, the deputy prosecutor of the Soviet Union announced on Baku Radio that two Azerbaijani men had been killed during interethnic clashes in Agdam just outside Nagorno-Karabakh. Apparently in response to the news, Azerbaijani mobs attacked, the same day, the Armenian population of Sumgait, a depressed and heavily polluted industrial city near Baku and home to 16,000 Armenians (out of a total population of 250,000). The attacks, which lasted until March 1, resulted in at least thirty-two deaths (twenty-six of which were Armenian), hundreds of injuries, and destroyed or vandalized apartments and shops.[98] The violence occurred with the apparent complicity of local authorities – tellingly, neither the local police nor Soviet troops intervened for three days. Armenians were angered by the failure of Soviet and Azerbaijani authorities to condemn the violence as a premeditated attack on an ethnic community rather than as acts of individual "hooliganism." The impact of the Sumgait events considerably increased the animosity between the ethnic communities, and culminated in the mass deportation of Armenians from Azerbaijan and Azerbaijanis from Armenia.

Although the Karabakh issue had become part of an agenda which activists in Armenia used to further their struggle for perestroika and glasnost, Armenians in Nagorno-Karabakh used Gorbachev's slogans of perestroika and glasnost to legitimate their single-minded struggle to join Armenia.[99] In the context of increasing violence in the oblast, they even voiced their willingness to accept Russian rule as an alternative to remaining under Azerbaijani jurisdiction.

On March 24, 1988, acknowledging "serious deficiencies" in Nagorno-Karabakh, the Politburo in Moscow proposed a 1.4 billion ruble development package for the oblast to be administered by the Azerbaijani government. Armenians in Karabakh rejected this offer because it failed to address the political problems, and because they doubted the Azerbaijani authorities would use the funds to their benefit. Instead, they reiterated their demand for transfer on the basis of the Soviet Constitution, which asserted the rights of national self-determination.

On July 18, 1988, however, the Presidium of the Supreme Soviet of the

USSR resolved in Azerbaijan's favor the constitutional impasse between the concept of national self-determination to which the Armenians appealed, and the requirement that a republic had to agree to border changes, cited by Azerbaijan. In retrospect, it is clear that Armenians underestimated the extent to which Azerbaijanis perceived Armenian demands as a threat to territorial integrity, and by extension, to Azerbaijani national identity. They also overestimated the ability or desire of central authorities to effectively resolve a dispute whose historic and contemporary ramifications were more complex than Armenians acknowledged.

In August 1988, the Karabakh Committee articulated an agenda which addressed environmental problems, corruption, freedoms of press and speech, and Communist Party reforms. By fall 1988, the Armenian Communist Party, under the leadership of Suren Harutiunian, frequently consulted the Karabakh Committee to defuse potential confrontations between the population and Soviet troops, present in Yerevan since February 25, 1988. In October 1988, as the result of write-in campaigns, two movement activists, Ashot Manucharian and Khachik Stamboltsian, were elected to the Armenian parliament on anti-corruption and environmentalist platforms.

On December 7, 1988, the two-way deportation which followed Sumgait was interrupted by a disastrous earthquake in north west Armenia. The earthquake levelled cities, towns and villages, destroying over a third of Armenia's manufacturing capacity and leaving 25,000–30,000 dead and 530,000 homeless. The earthquake increased Armenian bitterness toward the Communist authorities, whom they blamed for the shoddy highrise construction in an area of known seismological activity, and for their ineptness in organizing assistance to the stricken area.

Local and central authorities used this period of distraction and grief to arrest eleven members of the Karabakh Committee in December 1988 and January 1989.[100] For the next six months, the most salient fact of political life in Armenia was their detention, which itself triggered further protests and political organization. In response to local and international campaigns, the Committee members were released in May 1989 without trial. In November 1989, during a founding congress, they became part of a 36-member board of the *Hayots Hamazgayin Sharzhum* (Armenian All-National Movement, or HHSh), an umbrella group for the dozens of groups, parties, and political activists who had entered the political scene since February 1988.

The HHSh brought together three groups with distinct but overlapping agendas. One wing advocated democratic reforms in an all-Union context, the other wing concentrated exclusively on the Karabakh issue, while the center concerned itself with all political and cultural issues affecting the Armenian people. The movement as a whole mobilized a vast reservoir of discontent among a population fed up with official cant and hypocrisy, pervasive corruption, severe environmental pollution, and a declining living standard, and aroused by Gorbachev's promises of radical reform.

By May 1990, however, the Armenian public was demoralized by Moscow's continued refusal to accede to Karabakh's demands for unification and its inability to halt the debilitating rail blockade of Armenia and Nagorno-Karabakh which Azerbaijan had begun in 1989. They were also burdened by the continued impact of the earthquake and ongoing interethnic violence. In January 1990, in response to a new outburst of violence, Baku's large, prosperous, and well-integrated Armenian community fled Azerbaijan and Soviet troops brutally occupied the city.[101] By the end of the year, ethnic conflict had resulted in a complete population exchange between the republics. 160,000 Azerbaijanis had fled from Armenia, and 400,000 Armenians from Azerbaijan (excluding Nagorno-Karabakh).

## The Karabakh conflict in Azerbaijan

In Nagorno-Karabakh, Armenians continued work stoppages and protests. In January, 1989, Moscow replaced the local organs of government with a "Special Administration Committee," and sent Arkadii Volskii as the representative of the Central Committee and the presidium to act as chair. Although initially welcomed by the Armenian population, Volskii's Committee failed to halt tensions in the oblast. Moscow restored Azerbaijani administrative control over the region less than a year later, in November 1989. The Armenians were quick to accuse the new administration of further weakening the Armenian position in Nagorno-Karabakh.[102]

For Azerbaijanis, Karabakh became the symbol of challenge to Azerbaijan's territorial integrity and sovereignty. Armenian activism triggered the formation of an Azerbaijani Popular Front, which put forth a platform calling for democratic reforms and the reassertion of control in Nagorno-Karabakh. Faced by lack of grass-roots support and the rigid refusal of the Azerbaijani Communist leaders to engage in discussion, the Front adopted an increasingly nationalistic, anti-Armenian program.[103] In an effort to halt Armenian separatism, it organized a rail blockade of Nagorno-Karabakh and Armenia which disrupted reconstruction in the earthquake ravaged regions of Armenia and put Nagorno-Karabagh and adjacent Armenian-populated districts in a virtual state of siege. Armenians responded by instituting periodic "counterblockades" of Nakhichevan.[104]

## The transition to independence

Demoralized by the earthquake, the escalating bloodshed in Karabakh and on the republic's border, and Moscow's seeming hostility to their demands, less than half the electorate participated in the May 20, 1990, elections to the Armenian Supreme Soviet. After several rounds of voting, the HHSh emerged as the largest single faction in the new parliament. On August 4, 1990, Karabakh Committee member Levon Ter-Petrossian, a respected scholar of ancient Middle Eastern languages, became chairman of the parliament. This signalled the end of the Communist Party's monopoly on political life in Armenia.

Compared to the other Soviet republics, Armenia was slow to raise the issue of independence. Under tsarist rule, Armenians had prospered in Russia and the Transcaucasus as a bilingual and bicultural bourgeoisie. Despite the impact of Stalinism (the purges of 1936–37 and deportations in 1949), Armenia's elite remained more favorably disposed towards Russia than its counterparts in Georgia or the Baltic republics. Reluctance to demand independence also resulted from the belief that the absence of Soviet protection would make Armenians vulnerable to Turkish expansionism.

After the new Armenian parliament convened, however, it adopted a Declaration *on* Independence (as opposed to a declaration of independence) in August 1990, which affirmed the supremacy of the Armenian constitution and laws on Armenian territory, endorsed Armenia's right to pursue an independent foreign policy, and affirmed freedoms of speech, press and conscience, and a multi-party system. The document also announced Armenia's intention to work toward the establishment of a national army, organs of state and public security, and a national bank and currency.

Armenia boycotted the All-Union referendum on the continued existence of the Soviet Union, set for March 17, 1991. Instead, with confidence based on the republic's 93 percent ethnic homogeneity, Armenia invoked the new Soviet "Law on Mechanics of Secession" and organized a republic-wide referendum on secession for September 1991. The vote, held shortly after the unsuccessful August 1991 putsch against Mikhail Gorbachev, was overwhelmingly in favor of secession. On October 16, 1991, Levon Ter-Petrossian became independent Armenia's first popularly elected president. Armenians greeted independence with great enthusiasm, pouring into the streets to celebrate when the result of the referendum was reported.

## Independence and its woes

Despite the enthusiasm with which Armenians greeted it, independence caused an abrupt change in status for Armenia. It was transformed from a province of the powerful Soviet state, to a tiny – the size of Belgium – landlocked, resource-poor, and vulnerable republic bordering hostile or unstable neighbors.[105] Armenia was no longer part of an integrated all-Union market, with guaranteed supplies of raw materials, energy and markets. As in the other former Soviet republics, the standard of living declined precipitously for the majority of the population.

Espousing support for free market principles, in February 1991, the parliament passed a pioneering Land Reform Act, which gave households the right to own, buy, sell, lease, and pass on land to their heirs. People on state and collective farms, even if they had worked outside the agricultural sector in industry or services, received a plot of farmland, a garden, and in many cases, livestock. The government's assumption that private ownership would stimulate increased harvests failed to materialize, however, because few would-be farmers could afford increasingly expensive seed, fertilizer, pesticide, and animal feed, and lacked storage and distribution capacity. Land privatization did succeed, however, in creating an effective social safety net for the rural population, which was at least able to feed itself.[106]

While many ordinary citizens were plunged into poverty, Soviet-era political elites were able to use connections and access to resources to maintain and improve their positions, while entrenched government-mafia networks profited from privatization and opportunities for war-profiteering. By 1995, small-scale production had almost ceased, as small entrepreneurs, discouraged by the large bribes required to obtain bank loans, premises, materials and dependable eletricity supplies, abandoned their efforts or moved their businesses to Russia or other republics. At the same time, growing numbers of people from every profession attempted to supplement their incomes through trade with neighboring countries and retail sales in Armenia.

Although Soviet structures no longer functioned, relations of mutual trust, obligation, and accountability had not yet developed between the citizenry and their elected or appointed officials. This distrust also resulted from the pervasive anti-state mood and fear of parties and ideologies which were a Soviet-era legacy. The government, headed by the activists who had ousted the Communist regime, lost public confidence for failing to arrest the downward economic spiral, end the war, or control flagrant corruption and crime. A skilled diplomat abroad, Ter-Petrossian proved an aloof leader at home who avoided nationalist demagogery, but was criticized for his perceived detachment from the suffering of the population.

Four years after independence, the effect of the ongoing war, blockade, energy shortages, and economic mismanagement was depressingly apparent. High food prices and massive unemployment and underemployment had forced Armenians to search for new coping strategies, the most successful of which were subsistence gardening, labor emigration and trade. The government's inability to subsidize health services, public education, and transportation, or even guarantee steady supplies of electricity and gas, increased daily hardship and extinguished the enthusiasm and political involvement Armenians had demonstrated in 1991. As citizens of one of the first republics to be supplied with electric power after Sovietization, Armenians bitterly joked that they had achieved the distinction of becoming the first republic to go from the space age to the stone age. Conditions had become so harsh that an estimated one in three or four Armenians had left the republic by 1995.[107]

Conditions also took their toll on cultural and intellectual life. Schoolteachers, citing their inadequate salaries and the loss of public respect for their work, left their positions in droves, to be replaced only in part by university students and pensioners. The bilingual and bicultural intellectual elite were depressed by the surge of cultural nationalism and the isolating and provincializing implications of independence. Once part of a network of world-class science and scholarship, Armenian researchers and scholars had access to the best Soviet universities in Moscow, Leningrad (St. Petersburg), Novosibirsk, Tartu and Kiev. They became known, within the Soviet state and internationally, through their publications in Russian-language Soviet journals and state-wide conferences. The Soviet budget financed a network of research institutes and academies and subsidized the cultural life that small embattled Armenia can no longer afford. Many Armenian cultural and intellectual figures came to feel themselves expendable. Some tried to develop commercial ventures or sought funds from abroad to finance their research, while others abandoned their professions for business, or emigrated abroad.

## From ethnic conflict to war

A grave consequence of independence was the transformation of an intra-state conflict between two Soviet republics over the status of Nagorno-Karabakh into a full-fledged civil war involving at least two sovereign states (Azerbaijan and Armenia) and threatening to draw in Russia, Turkey, and Iran. In 1991, during "Operation Ring," Soviet troops assisted Azerbaijani forces in deporting Armenian villagers from Karabakh, ostensibly for harboring provocateurs from Armenia. Later that year, Karabakh Armenians unilaterally declared Nagorno-Karabakh and adjacent Armenian-populated districts to be an independent republic. They began to construct a government and organize an army. Feuled by armed provocations and spiraling human rights abuses on both sides, and a continued air bombardment of Stepanakert, the conflict escalated towards all-out war.

By the end of 1993, Karabakh Armenian forces were organized into an effective, well-trained army, supplied by weapons seized or purchased from Soviet troops in Karabakh (and later from Russia) and seized from Azerbaijan, as well as by an undisclosed amount of assistance from Armenia and the diaspora. As well, perhaps in exchange for permission to site two military bases in Armenia, Russian military assistance to the Karabakh Armenians intensified. Aside from the large number of former Soviet Army officers in the ranks of the Karabakh "defense forces," Russian troops allegedly assisted Armenian forces in taking the Azerbaijani region of Kelbadjar, between Armenia and Nagorno-Karabakh, in April 1993. With such assistance, Karabakh forces were able to establish a broad land corridor joining the former oblast to Armenia and occupy a wide swath of land around Karabakh. In the process, they destroyed Azerbaijani towns and villages in and around Nagorno-Karabakh and turned an estimated one million Azerbaijanis (less than a third of which were from Nagorno-Karabakh) into refugees in their own republic. While the Republic of Armenia maintained that the conflict was strictly between Azerbaijan and Karabakh, it devoted a sizable part of its budget to supporting Karabakh.[108]

For Azerbaijan, the war has not only been an economic and human catastrophe, it seriously destablized a succession of regimes. In Armenia, by contrast, the war initially helped maintain internal harmony, since opposition parties were reluctant to challenge the Armenian leadership given the existence of an external threat. As well, the spoils of war eased some of the pressure on the economy. Nevertheless, assistance to Nagorno-Karabakh and the influx of Armenian refugees from Azerbaijan, and later from Abkhazia as a result of the Georgian conflict, placed huge economic and social burdens on Armenia. And while the war and blockade served as useful scapegoats for the republic's dismal economic state; waste, corruption, and mismanagement of Armenia's limited resources were also significant contributors.

## Foreign and domestic relations

With independence, Armenian leaders have developed a pragmatic view of relations with their neighbors. The inability of Europe and the United States to help resolve the war through individual mediators or the eleven-member Minsk group established by the Conference on Security and Cooperation in Europe (CSCE), and Turkey's refusal to establish diplomatic and trade links until ethnic Armenian forces withdraw from Azerbaijani territory, have convinced many Armenians that they must retain close links with their large, powerful Russian neighbor. Furthermore, they are aware that a significant portion of the remittances from abroad which helped much of the population survive the last few years has come from Armenians working in Russia.

The government of Armenia has also called upon its prosperous, worldwide diaspora to help rebuild the country and expand international links. Large-scale diaspora involvement began after the 1988 earthquake, as Armenian organizations and individuals donated time and money to help rebuild Armenia's shattered infrastructure and arrange medical treatment for survivors. After independence, diaspora Armenians were invited to participate in the economic and political restructuring; several were appointed to high government posts. Diaspora political parties such as the centrist and largely pro-government Ramgavar and Hunchak parties, and the nationalist Dashnaktsutiun (Armenia Revolutionary Federation), established themselves in Armenia. But as much as diaspora and homeland Armenians have begun to unify, clashing visions of Armenia continue to divide many. Irredentist claims on Turkey, demands that Turkey acknowledge and make reparations for the 1915 genocide, and the militant stance on Karabakh of many diaspora Armenians have often conflicted with government policy.

At the end of 1994, this ideological and power struggle between diaspora nationalists and government leaders erupted and was resolved in a manner which demonstrates the fragility of democratic practice in Armenia. On December 17, the assassination of former Karabakh Committee member and Yerevan mayor, Hambartsum Galstian, shocked the country. Having left politics for business, Galstian had become a fierce critic of the government. Accusing the nationalist Dashantstiun of Galstian's murder, President Ter-Petrossian suspended the activities of the organization, by now the single largest opposition party, and almost a dozen affiliated publications. He charged them with harboring a clandestine terrorist organization whose members were engaged in sabotage, drug trafficking, and political assassinations, all aimed at destabilizing Armenia. Despite the Dashnaktsutiun's history of terrorism in the Ottoman Empire and Europe, many Armenians felt the government had violated its own laws by the manner in which it closed down the party and arrested its members. Many suspected government complicity in several brutal assaults made on the defendants' lawyers and the death of one of the accused while in custody.[109]

## Past, present and future

How far does contemporary Armenia resemble the first independent republic? Despite many similarities between the Armenia of 1918–20 and the Armenia of 1991–95, both of which had been thrust into independence in catastrophic economic conditions, there are also fundamental differences. The first Armenian republic had virtually no industry. A provincial backwater, its agriculture had been ruined during the First World War and in subsequent battles with Turkish troops. In the course of its two year existence, it lost significant territories – Karz and Ardahan districts – but gained a population of destitute refugees, most of whom, like the native population, were uneducated peasants.

By 1991, Armenia had a highly developed industry and a strong intellectual and cultural infrastructure. But if World War I had wrecked the first republic's agriculture, the Soviet collapse and Armenian independence proved disastrous for the second republic's industry and culture. Lack of energy and supplies brought Armenia's enterprises to a virtual standstill, although they began to make a recovery by 1995.

Despite the influx of urban, educated Armenians from Azerbaijan, Armenia experienced a net outmigration which included its most capable and educated citizens. In contrast to the first republic, which surrendered vast chunks of Armenian land but gained in population, the current republic has thus sacrificed infrastructure and population in a struggle over what Armenians consider historically Armenian territory.

Speaking to a diaspora audience in New York on the third anniversary of independence in September 1994, President Levon Ter-Petrossian asserted that the two republics were no longer comparable. Despite its severe economic problems, Armenia had already become a stable, functioning multi-party democracy actively engaged in the task of restructuring its government and economy. He reminded his compatriots that the republic had already been in existence one year longer than the first Armenian republic had survived. This, he said, had special meaning for a people who live so much in their past, for it signified that Armenia had "passed the test of time" and become "an irreversible and indisputable reality."[110]

Yet, like Janus,[111] Armenia presents one face to the international community, another to its own citizens. Since independence, Armenia has become an integrated member of the world community: it has joined many international organizations, opened almost two dozen embassies, and signed international covenants and treaties. Armenia's prosperous global diaspora can take some credit for the rapidity and success of this integration.

The face the Armenian state presents to its own citizens is less benign. Ordinary citizens still deal with a chaotic combination of Soviet-era and post-independence laws, bureaucratic inertia, and most important, a political culture conditioned by seventy years of Soviet rule. A multitude of political parties and independent newspapers notwithstanding, Armenian citizens have hardly more control over their own lives than they did before independence. Devoting its energy to survival, the populace has become apathetic and uninvolved.

Referring to the coups and wars that have wracked their neighbors, Armenian leaders boast that Armenia is the most stable state in the region. But stability is not a synonym for democracy, another of the Armenian leadership's stated goals. How the government balances the desire for political stability, economic growth, and national pride with respect for political and human rights will determine the shape of Armenia's future.

## Notes

1 Ronald Grigor Suny, *Looking Toward Ararat: Armenia in Modern History* (Bloomington: Indiana University Press, 1993), p. 127,

2 Christopher, J. Walker, *Armenia: The Survival of a Nation*, revised 2nd edn (New York: St. Martin's Press, 1990), p. 257.

3 Walker, *Armenia*, p. 20 This is a good, overall introduction to Armenian history,

1800–1900. The revised edition also includes a brief discussion of the Karabakh movement.

4 Heroduts, Strabo, and Xenophon describe Armenia's wealth of flocks, natural products, metals, precious stones, and the fame of her soldiers. For a discussion of classical references to Armenia, see Robert W. Thompson, "The Armenian Image in Classical Texts," in Richard G. Hovannisian (ed.), *The Armenian Image in History and Literature* (Malibu, CA: Undena Publications, 1981), pp. 9–25. See also David Marshall Lang, *The Armenians: A People in Exile*, new edn (London: Unwin Paperbacks, 1988, pp. 39–48.

5 Ronald Suny, *Armenia in the Twentieth Century* (Chico, CA: Scholars Press, 1983), p. 4.

6 Ronald Suny, "Some Notes on the National Character, Religion, and Way of Life of the Armenians," unpublished paper presented at the Lelio Basso Foundation Conference, Venice, October 18–20, 1985, p. 6.

7 Significantly, even for the monk Eghishe, the first chronicler of this event, Vardan's death had more than just a religious meaning. According to Eghishe, Vardan and his men fought the Persians to defend their traditional Armenian customs and way of life, an interpretation which suggests that a sense of distinctiveness existed among Armenians, at least among the princely strata, at least 1,500 years ago. The dating of Elishe's history of Vardan is controversial, however, Soviet Armenia scholars consider him a contemporary of Vardan, while Robert W. Thompson places his account toward the end of the sixth century. See his commentary in Thompson (translator), *Elishe. History of Vardan and the Armenian War* (Cambridge: Harvard University Press, 1982), pp. 1–8 Cyril Toumanoff, *Studies in Christian Caucasian History* (Washington, DC: Georgetown University Press, 1963).

9 Walker, *Armenia*, p. 21.

10 Khajig Tololyan, "The Role of the Armenian Apostolic Church in the Diaspora," *Armenian Review*, 41, no. 1–161 (Spring 1988), 56.

11 *Ibid.*, p. 57.

12 According to Armenian Patriarchate figures of 1882, there were 2,660,000 Armenians in the Ottoman Empire, of whom 1,630,000 lived in the six eastern vilayets. According to Walker, these estimates are probably too high. Nevertheless, most sources agree that Armenians formed about a third of the population of Eastern Anatolia by the end of the nineteenth century, although in many regions, they were the largest single minority. Walker, *Armenia*, pp. 95–96.

13 Eric Hobsbawm, *Nations and Nationalism Since 1780* (Cambridge: Cambridge University Press, 1990), p. 12.

14 Henry Jewel Sarkiss, "The Armenian Renaissance, 1500–1863," *The Journal of Modern History* 9, no. 4 (December 1937), 437–438.

15 *Ibid.*, p. 441.

16 Gerard J. Libaridian, "Nation and Fatherland in Nineteenth century Armenian Political Thought," *Armenian Review*, 36, no. 3 (Autumn 1983), 71–90.

17 *Ibid.*, p. 71.

18 Quoted from the liberal Armenian newspaper, *Hayastan*, published in Constantinople, *ibid.*, p. 76.

19 Until the emergence of a liberal middle class, the *millet* was dominated by an oligarchy of bankers, rich merchants, and government officials known as the *amira* class.

20 Libaridian, "Nation and Fatherland," p. 78.

21 Ronald Suny, *Looking Toward Ararat: Armenia in Modern History* (Bloomington: Indiana University Press 1993), p. 6.

22 Libaridian, "Nation and Fatherland," p. 79.

23 Walker, *Armenia*.

24 Ronald Suny, "The Formation of the Armenian Patriotic Intelligentsia in Russia: The First Generations," *Armenian Review*, 36, no. 3 (Autumn 1983), 25.

25 This section draws on Louise Nalbandian's *The Armenian Revolutionary Movement: The Development of Armenian Political Parties through the Nineteenth Century* (Berkeley: University of California Press, 1967), one of the definitive works on the Armenian revolutionary movement. See also Anaide Ter Minassian, *Nationalism and Socialism in the Armenian Revolutionary Movement* (Cambridge: The Zoryan Institute, 1984); this short monograph covers the period 1885–1914.

26 Exact mortality figures are difficult to determine, because of uncertainties in the pre-1915 census figures for Armenians in the Ottoman Empire. For a thoughtful discussion of this issue, refer to Daniel Panzac, "L' enjeu du Nombre: La Population de la Turquie de 1914 a 1927," *Révue du monde Musulman et de la Mediteranées*, 50, no. 4 (1988). Panzac estimates the number of casualties at about 900,000.

27 See Richard G. Hovannisian (ed.), *The Armenian Genocide in Perspective* (New Brunswick: Transaction, 1987), for a useful collection of historical and comparative essays on the genocide.

28 Mark Saroyan, "Beyond the Nation-State: Culture and Ethnic Politics in Soviet Transcaucasia," *Soviet Union/Union Sovietique*, 15, nos. 2–3 (1988), 222.

29 See Jenny Phillips, *Symbol, Myth and Rhetoric: The Politics of Culture in an Armenian-American Population*, (New York: AMS Press, 1989), for an extended discussion of this theme, based on her field research.

30 Where she has provided a range of figures, I have averaged them to produce a single estimate for a given region.

31 *The Republic of Armenia: From Versailles to London, 1919–1920, Vol. 2* (Berkeley: University of California Press, 1982. A third volume is forthcoming.

32 Hovannisian, "Caucasian Armenia," p. 13.

33 Richard Hovannisian, "Caucasian Armenia Between Imperial and Soviet rule: The Interlude of National Independence," in Occasional Paper No. 99, Kennan Institute for Advanced Russian Studies (1980), *The Republic of Armenia: The First Year, 1918–1919. Vol. 1*, (Berkeley: University of California Press, 1971).

34 Suny, *Armenia in the Twentieth Century*, p. 41.

35 *Ibid.*, p. 41.

36 *Ibid.*, pp. 107–108.

37 Suny, *Armenia in the Twentieth Century*, p. 75.

38 Matossian, *Impact*, p. 61.

39 Approximately 200,000 Armenians entered Soviet Armenia as refugees after 1921, as "repatriates" after World War II, mainly from the Middle East and Europe, and as migrants from other Soviet republics. See Hovik Meliksetian, *Hayrenik-Spiurki Arnchutiutnere ev Hayrenatartsutiune: 1920–1980 tt.* (Yerevan: Yerevan State University, 1985) for figures on the repatriation. The postwar climate of hardship and distrust led to hostility toward the immigrants, many of whom left Armenia when emigration subsequently became possible. Armenians in Armenia, Georgia, and Azerbaijan with suspected Dashnak connections were arrested in June 1949, and deported to the Altai region; many returned to Armenia after Stalin's death. According to popular accounts, there were many repatriates among the deportees.

40 Matossian, *Impact*, pp. 90–91.

41 See Mouradian, *De Staline à Gorbatchev*. She devotes a full chapter to the role of the Armenian Church in Soviet Armenia, pp. 361–403.

42 For Soviet Armenians living outside their titular republic, on the other hand, a strong sense of national identity often proved a hindrance to economic or social success; therefore, these communities experienced high rates of intermarriage and loss of ethnic traditions. Suny, *Armenia in the Twentieth Century*, p. 77.

43 *Ibid.* p. 133.

44  A university had actually been founded at Leninakan in 1920, during the period of the republic.

45  Mouradian, *De Staline à Gorbatchev*, p. 239

46  Mouradian, *De Staline à Gorbatchev*, p. 90; Suny, *Armenia in the Twentieth Century*, p. 91.

47  Matossian, *Impact*, p. 163.

48  Mouradian, *de Staline à Gorbatchev*, p. 87.

49  Gregory Gleason, *Federalism and Nationalism: The Struggle for Republican Rights in the USSR* (Boulder: Westview Press, 1990), p. 87.

50  Rouben Adalian, "Theory and Rationality in Armenian Thought: Arsen Aytenian's Analysis of the History of the Armenian Language," *Sonderdruck aus Handes Amsorya* (1987), p. 650.

51  Claire Mouradian, "Nation, realités et fantasmes: Le cas Arménien," *Raison Présente*, no. 86 (1988), 122.

52  Matossian, *Impact*, p. 38.

53  Mouradian, 1962, op. cit., p. 38.

54  These figures were provided to me in March, 1991, by Ruben V. Sarkissian, an educational specialist working in the Armenian Ministry of Education.

55  O.L. Zakarian, "Neskol'ko zamechanii o natsional' nom iazike i dvuiazichii," In L. A. Abramyan, G. R. Simonian *et al.* (eds.), *National'nie voprosy novoe myshlenie* (Yerevan: Yerevan State University, 1989), p. 188.

56  Elizabeth Fuller, "Armenian Writers' Congress Focuses on Language Teaching," *Radio Liberty Research*, RL 242/81, June 18, 1981, p. 2.

57  Hambartsum Galstian, "Nekotorie aspekty Armiano-russkogo dvuiazichiia (po materialiam etnosotsiologicheskogo obsledovaniia naseleniia Yerevana)," *Sovetskaia Etnografiia*, no. 6, 1987. According to his figures, Armenian–Russian bilingualism in Armenia as of 1979 was 34.6 percent overall, and 57.1 percent in Yerevan. More than 20 percent of Yerevan Armenians speak Russian with greater fluency, and Russian is the native language for 11 percent of Armenian families in Yerevan.

58  Fuller, "Armenian Writers' Congress," p. 2.

59  Silva Kaputiklan, "Our Motherland – Large and Small," *Armenia Today*, no. 5 (103) (1987), 13. This article is translated and condensed from the original, which appeared in *Pravda* (May 7, 1987), 2nd edn, pp. 3, 6.

60  According to George A. Bournoutian, Armenians formed a majority in Eastern Armenia until the mid fourteenth century, when Turkic tribes settled in the region. Until the Russian annexation of the Erevan khanate (which is somewhat larger than present-day Armenia) in 1828, Armenians constituted less than 20 percent of the population, with Muslims (Persians, Kurds, and Turkic tribes) comprising over 80 percent. The subsequent departure of Muslims and influx of Armenians after the annexation brought Armenians up to 50 percent of the population by 1832. See his *Eastern Armenia in the Last Decades of Persian Rule, 1807–1828: A Political and Socioeconomic Study of the Khanate of Erevan on the Eve of the Russian Conquest* (Malibu, CA: Udena Publications, 1982), pp. 73–74

61  Suny, *Armenia in the Twentieth Century*, p. 50.

62  See Matossian, *Impact* chapter 8. See Marzbed Margossian and Jack Antreassian (eds.), *Across Two Worlds: Selected Prose of Eghishe Charents* (New York: Ashod Press, 1985) for an overview and assessment of nationalist and revolutionary themes in Charents' work.

63  Matossian, *Impact*, p. 162.

64  *Ibid.*, pp. 167–168.

65  Saroyan, "Beyond the Nation-State," p. 227.

66  *Ibid.*, p. 228.

67  Suny, *Armenia in the Twentieth Century*, p. 78.

68 *Ibid.*, p. 78

69 Mouradian, *De Staline à Gorbatchev*, p. 274.

70 *Ibid.*, p. 268.

71 p. 253.

72 Ludmilla Alexeyeve, *Soviet Dissent: Contemporary Movements for National, Religious, and Human Rights* (Middletown, CT: Wesleyan University Press, 1985), p. 123.

73 Nakhichevan was once home to a mixed population of Armenians and Muslims, but after its incorporation into Azerbaijan, as an Autonomous Republic, its Armenian population sharply declined, a fate Armenians fear for Karabakh.

74 Hairekyan spent seventeen years on and off in detention before his exile from the Soviet Union. He returned in 1989 to take up a seat in the Armenian parliament and to head an opposition party. See "Secret Political Trials in Soviet Armenia," *The Armenian Review* 31, no. 323 (1979), 365–409, for a *samizdat* transcript of Hairekyan's trials.

75 Suny, *Armenia in the Twentieth Century*, p. 78. Alexeyeva, *Soviet Dissent*, p. 123.

76 Mouradian, *De Staline à Gorbatchev*, p. 258.

77 One of these, Ashot Manucharian, later a leader of the ANM, was voted first scretary of the university Komsomol, but removed after several weeks on a technicality.

78 Mouradian, *De Staline à Gorbatchev*, p. 288.

79 *Ibid.*, p. 321.

80 In "Documents: 'The Armenian Public Group' and the 'Helsinki Accord," *The Armenian Review*, 31, no. 4–124 (April 1979), 427–429.

81 Mouradian, *De Staline à Gorbatchev*, pp. 266–268.

82 *Ibid.*, pp. 266–268; Alexeyeva, *Soviet Dissent*, p. 132.

83 Gary Thatcher, "Armenia, The Soviet Republic That Welcomes Foreigners," *The Armenian Mirror-Spectator*, 52, no. 11 (Sept 29, 1984) (reprinted from the *Christian Science Monitor*, Sept. 24, 1984).

84 "Nagornyi Karabakh" refers to the region, which includes several Armenian-populated districts outside oblast boundaries. "Nagorno-Karabakh" refers to the official administrative unit, the Nagorno-Karabakh Autonomous Oblast. The conflict has drawn in the districts lying outside oblast boundaries, however.

85 See, for example, the article which translates the words of the Russian poet, S. Goredetsky, on the significance of Karabakh for Armenian national memory "*Gharabaghi masin S. Gorodetsku sakav haitni hodvatse*," by Anushavan Zakarian and Alpert Karatyan, in *Erekoyan Erevan*, October 27, 1988, p. 3.

86 Richard Hovannisian, "Nationalist Ferment in Armenia," *Freedom at Issue* (November-December 1988), p. 30.

87 *Ibid.*, p. 30.

88 *Ibid.*, p. 33.

89 Mark Saroyan, "The Karabagh Syndrome in Azerbaijani Politics," *Problems of Communism* (September-October, 1990), pp. 3–4. This article provides an insightful analysis of the Karabagh conflict from the Azerbaijani perspective.

90 Gerard J. Libaridian (ed.), *The Karabagh File: Documents and Facts on the Question of Mountainous Karabagh 1918–1988* (Cambridge, MA: The Zoryan Institute, 1988), pp. 44–46.

91 *Ibid.*, pp. 47–48.

92 Complaints range form physical neglect of Armenian historical monuments, to the Azeri attribution of Armenian churches and carved stone crosses to the Causcasian Albanians, whom the Azeris claim to be forebears of the modern Azeri people. These complaints are detailed in B. Galoyan and K.C. Khudaverdian (eds.), *Nagornyi Karabakh, Istoricheskaia spravka* (Yerevan: Armenian Academy of Sciences, 1988).

See also B. S. Mirzoian, "Nagornyi Karabakh," *Soviet Anthropology and Archeology*, 29, no. 2 (Fall 1990), 12–33.

93 Elsewhere in Azerbaijan, where they lacked even nominal institutional structures of oblast-based cultural autonomy, Armenians either lived in monoethnic villages, or found a *modus vivendi* in the city with their Azeri neighbors. Especially in Baku, they became part of an ethnically mixed, Russian-speaking elite whose members, in the words of Armenian refugees from Baku, exemplified the "new Soviet person" and regarded themselves as loyal "Bakintsis," whose primary affiliation was to the "internationalist" city of Baku.

94 In the 1980s, provoked by growing public alarm over the effect of pollution from Armenia's many chemical plants, radioactive leaks from the nuclear power station, and a sharp drop in the level of Armenia's largest lake, Sevan, an ecology movement coalesced, and attracted many intellectuals who later became active in the Karabakh movement.

95 According to Elizabeth Fuller, "Moscow Rejects Armenian Demands for Return of Nagorno-Karabagh," from *Radio Liberty Research*, RL 91/88 (Feb 29, 1988), p. 2, some 75,000 signatures were gathered. According to Fuller, the petition was organized by Robert Nazaryan, one of the organizers of the Armenian Helsinki Watch group; see "Armenians Demonstrate for Return of Territories form Azerbaijan," *Radio Liberty Research*, RL 441/87 (October, 20, 1987), p. 2.

96 Christopher J. Walker (ed.), *Armenia and Karabagh: The Struggle for Unity* (London: Minority Rights Publications, 1991), pp. 121–122. Walker's account provides a detailed description of the first period of the movement. Also, Walker, *Armenia: The Survival of a Nation*, and Suny, *Looking Toward Ararat*, chapters 12 and 14. Gerard Libaridian's report, "The Question of Karabagh: An Overview," (Cambridge, MA, June 1988), prepared for the Zoryan Institute, is a very perceptive interpretive account of the movement's political, social and cultural significance. My account here is also based on my own observations and interviews in Armenia, 1987–91.

97 Some historians refer to these conflicts as the Armenian-Tatar wars, "Caucasian Tatar" being the preferred Russian designation at the time for the Azeri-Turkish speaking inhabitants of Transcaucasia.

98 See Samrel Shahmunation (ed.), *The Sumgait Tragedy: Pogroms Against Armenians in Soviet Azerbaijan. Vol. 7, Eyewitness Accounts*, (Cambridge: Zoryan Institute 1990), collection compiled by the journalist Shahmunation from hundreds of taped interviews with survivors of the pogrom.

99 See Levon Abrahamian, "The Karabagh Movement as Viewed by an Anthropologist," *Armenian Review* 43, no. 2–3 (1990), 68–69.

100 Those arrested were: Babken Araktsian, Hambartsum Galstyan, Samvel Gevorkian, Rafayel Ghazarian, Samson Ghazarian, Alexan Hakopian, Ashot Manucharian, Vazgen Manukian, Vano Siradeghian, Levon Ter-Petrossian, and David Varanian, along with Igor Muradian and Khachik Stamboltsian (activists but not Committee members). It was never clear whether authorities in Moscow or Armenia called for the Committee's arrest. Current consensus, however, places responsibility for the initiative with Moscow.

101 The issue of the troops' entry into Baku remains contentious. Although troops were stationed just outside Baku, they did not receive orders to shoot until most of the violence had run its course, at which time they entered, killing over 100 Azeris in the process. It had been acknowledged by some Soviet authorities that troops entered to prevent an anti-Soviet takeover of authority in Azerbaijan. See, for example, Igor Beliaev, "Baku: Before and After," *The Literary Gazette International*, 1, issue 3, No. 1 (March 1990), 6–7.

102 See, for example the open letter to the Supreme Soviet of the USSR and the Special Administration Committee protesting that Azeri authorities were sending Meshketian

Turks and Azeri refugees in Nagorno-Karabakh to destabilize it demographically, "Bats Namak KhSHM Geraguin khohrtin, LGhIM Hatook karavarman komitein," *Khorhrtayin Gharagah*, Nov. 15, 1989. The article by S. Ishkhanian, "Hoghe mern el Durs korek," in the same issue of this paper, accused Azeris of disrupting communications and transport between Armenia and Azerbaijan.

103 See Saroyan, "Beyond the Nation-State." Also see the report by Robert Cullen, "A Reporter At Large (Armenia and Azerbaijan): "Roots," in *The New Yorker*, April 15, 1991.

104 Azerbaijan's blockade of Karabagh and Armenia was considerably more effective than Armenia's counterblockade, since Nakhichevan borders the friendly neighboring states of Turkey and Iran.

105 Interestingly, the Islamic Republic of Iran has proved to be the most restrained and neutral of Armenia's neighbors. Despite Armenia's perceived anti-Muslim sentiments, most Armenians acknowledge their cultural debt to Iran, under whose hegemony part of Armenia existed for centuries. Iran, unwilling to encourage separatism among its own Azeri population, has demonstrated neutrality and restraint in its dealings with Armenia.

106 See *Armenia: Agriculture and Food Sector Review*, World Bank, June 10, 1994, and Sharon Holt, "Women, Poverty and Land Privatization," forthcoming.

107 According to the Armenian State Committee on Statistics, the officially registered population in January 1994 was 3.7 million, while unofficial estimates put migration as high as one million.

108 Officially, Armenia maintains that it devotes only 5 percent of its GDP for humanitarian and other support for Nagorno-Karabakh. Outside observers have suggested that a considerably greater part of the Armenian budget has been devoted to military assistance.

109 For an overview of these events, refer to *Covcas Bulletin: Nationalities-Conflicts and Human Rights in the Caucasus*, vol. 5, 1995 which provides useful bi-monthly summaries of the Armenian and diaspora media.

110 Translated in the *Daily News Report from Armenia*, September 27, 1994, produced on-line each day by the Armenian Assembly of America.

111 This metaphor was suggested to me by Dr. Igor Barsegian, Armenian Academy of Sciences Institute of Philosophy and Law.

# Armenia: Chronology of events

*October 1987*
18   Hundreds gather in Yerevan to protest clashes in the
Armenian village of Chardakhlu, in Azerbaijan, and to call
for the annexation of Nagorno-Karabakh.

*January 1988*
A petition is signed by 75,000 Armenians demanding the
annexation of Nagorno-Karabakh.

*February 1988*
18–24   In Yerevan, demonstrations and strikes in support of
annexing Nagorno-Karabakh are held throughout the week
and attract nearly one million participants. Protestors
disperse after leaders reassure them that the matter is under
discussion.

*September 1988*
100,000 participate in an anti-Soviet demonstration in
Yerevan.

*December 1988*
7   Earthquake hits in southern Armenia, killing thousands.
11 members of the Karabakh Committee organizing relief
efforts are arrested by Communist authorities and only
released 6 months later.
The Armenian National Movement is founded.

*December 1989*
The Armenian Supreme Soviet votes to unite with
Nagorno-Karabakh region.

*January 1990*
10   The Supreme Soviet votes to include Nagorno-Karabakh in
the republican budget and allow its residents to vote in
Armenian parliamentary elections.

*April 1990*
V. Movsisyan is elected first party secretary, replacing S.
Arutyunyan.

*May 1990*
20   Parliament is elected.

24  Armenian gunmen open fire on Soviet troops. The troops return fire, killing six.

27–28  Clashes with police occur when tens of thousands gather to demand formal political ties with Nagorno-Karabakh and to protest against the earlier violence.

*August 1990*

4  Levon Ter-Petrossian is elected parliamentary chairman. Parliament issues a declaration of independence.

*November 1990*

30  S. Pogosyan replaces Movsisyan.

*February 1991*

20  Thousands gather in Yerevan to declare their solidarity with Nagorno-Karabakh.

*March 1991*

17  Armenia boycotts the all-union referendum on preserving the union.

18  A poll conducted in Armenia indicates that 80 percent of Armenians support secession from the USSR.

*September 1991*

4  Armenia nationalizes all Communist Party property.

21  In a referendum on independence, 99 percent of voters (95 percent participation) support secession.

23  Parliament issues a declaration of independence.

*October 1991*

17  Levon Ter-Petrossian is elected president with 83 percent of the vote.

*March 1992*

25  State of economic emergency declared in response to an economic blockade imposed by Azerbaijan.

*May 1992*

9  Armenian forces seize the Azerbaijani town of Shusha, reportedly with little resistance.

17–23  Nakhichevan is attacked by Armenian forces.

18  Armenian forces capture the town of Lachin, thus securing a corridor between Armenia and Nagorno-Karabakh.

*June 1992*

16  Leaders of the Dashnak party and the Association for National Self-Determination call upon the government to resign for its conciliatory stance in Nagorno-Karabakh.

29 Ter-Petrossian attacks the nationalist Dashnaktsutyun Party
for its unwillingness to enter negotiations in
Nagorno-Karabakh.

*July 1992*
29 Khosrov Arutyunyan is appointed Prime Minister,
replacing the acting prime minister, Vice-President Gagik
Arutyunyan.

*August 1992*
9 Ter-Petrossian, invoking the CIS collective security pact,
asks for intervention in the Nagorno-Karabakh region citing
Azerbaijiani aggression.
14 3,000 rally to call for the resignation of Ter-Petrossian.
17 Attempted assassination of Ter-Petrossian. President
later survives no-confidence vote called in
connection with setbacks in war with
Azerbaijan.

*January 1993*
22 A pipeline explosion in Georgia cuts Armenia's gas supply
in half.

*February 1993*
2 Prime Minister Khosrov Arutyunyan is dimissed
after openly criticizing the government's 1993 draft
budget and economic plan. First deputy prime minister
Hrant
Bagratyan is appointed acting prime
minister.
5 100,000 demonstrate to demand the resignation of
Ter-Petrossian, the dissolution of parliament, and the
creation of a new constitution.
10 The opposition Dashnaks (Armenian Revolutionary
Federation) turn down an offer by Ter-Petrossian to form a
coalition government.
11 Another Georgian pipeline explosion retricts gas supplies to
Armenia.
12 Bagratyan appointed prime minister.
18 About 8,000 gather in a protest organized by the Union of
National Self-determination to call for the dissolution of
parliament.
20 Tens of thousands demonstrate in protest against dire
economic condition and call for the resignation of
Ter-Petrossian.

*April 1993*
2–3 Armenian troops take the region of Kelbajar. It is estimated

that Armenian forces now control nearly 10 percent of
Azerbaijani territory.

*July 1993*

7   15,000 people gather in a demonstration organized by the
Association for National-Self Determination to demand the
resignation of Ter-Petrossian.

*August 1993*

24   The UN Security Council demands Armenia's withdrawal
from Azerbaijan.

*November 1993*

22   The national currency, the *dram*, replaces the ruble as the
sole legal currency in the republic.

*July 1994*

1   20,000 demonstrators organized by the
National-Democratic Union gather to denounce the
government for political persecution.

15   Anti-government rally with 20,000–50,000 demonstrators is
held in Yerevan

*August 1994*

19   Vasgan I, the 130th Catholicos of All-Armenians for the
last 39 years, dies.

*December 1994*

17   The former mayor of Yerevan, Humbartsum Galstyan, is
murdered. Ter-Petrossian accuses the Dashnaks of
complicity.

29   Ter-Petrossian suspends the Dashnaks for six months.

*Janurary 1995*

26   Three Dashnak leaders are arrested.

*March 1995*

16   A treaty is signed with Russia establishing a Russian
military base in Armenia, thereby granting the Russian
troops already stationed in Armenia official legal status.

*June 1995*

Several opposition parties are banned from running in the
July parliamentary elections.

15   Opposition parties call for postponing the elections.

21   Clashes occur between opposition and government
supporters.

# 14    Georgia: the trauma of statehood

STEPHEN F. JONES

The transition from communism to democracy in Central Europe and the USSR highlights the continuing legacy of Soviet political culture. The collapse of communism led, in many cases, to quasi-democratic hybrids led by pseudo-democratic chauvinists. New leaders, many of them ex-apparatchiks, have established the legislative and institutional framework for pluralist democracy, but have failed to break old habits of Soviet paternalism. They have replaced the "cognitive monopoly" of communism with a morally fervent nationalism, and the majority of the population, inexperienced in civic politics and undergoing tremendous political and economic anxiety, loudly supports these new ethnic hegemonies.[1] In the context of today's crisis, the often violent history of these multiethnic societies has made the recovery of national identity and the rehabilitation of memory a dangerous challenge to democratic development. The problems of state-building and what Guiseppe di Palma calls the "crafting of democracy" are magnified in an ethnically segmented society like Georgia.[2] Questions concerning the distribution of power among the different ethnic groups has been transformed into a challenge to the new state's legitimacy and a test of its commitment to democratic change.

Georgia is the latest, but not the last demonstration of the tension between liberalism and nationalism, between majority and minority rights. The impact of perestroika and the breakdown of central control transformed Georgian nationalism from a force for liberation and democratization to one of ethnic hegemonism and anti-pluralism. After the accession to power of Zviad Gamsakhurdia's authoritarian nationalist government in October 1990, Georgia resembled Andrei Sakharov's description of the republic as a "little empire."[3] The atmosphere of national chauvinism undermined the qualities of tolerance, consensus and compromise necessary for multiethnic cooperation and pluralism. Both the Georgian opposition and the ethnic minorities found themselves threatened by a new political paternalism acting in the name of national freedom. The Georgians' dream of liberation following the fall of Soviet power, and the prediction of many Sovietologists that the structural and social changes in the USSR over the last twenty years would inevitably lead to pluralism, turned out to be overly optimistic.

*Derived from 1989 Soviet Census*

Breakdown by Regions
Region  1 : Kareli ................15.4 % Ossetian
        2 : K'aspi ................10.1% Ossetian
        3 : Axmet'a ................11.1% Ossetian, 10.1% Ingush
        4 : Lagodexi ................17.9% Azerbaijani
        5 : Sagarejo ................26.3% Azerbaijani
        6 : Gardabani ................42.5% Azerbaijani
        7 : Tetric'qaro ................23.1% Greek, 12.4% Armenian
        8 : C'alk'a ................61% Greek, 28.5% Armenian
        9 : Axalkalaki ................91.3% Armenian
        10 : Aspinza ................19.1% Armenian
        11 : Axalcixe ................42.8% Armenian
        12 : Bogdanovk'a ................89.6% Armenian
        13 : Dmanisi ................63.9% Azerbaijani
        14 : Bolnisi ................66% Azerbaijani
        15 : Marneuli ................76.3% Azerbaijani, 10.4% Armenian

Map 14.1 Regions with more than 10% non-Georgian Population

# Georgia

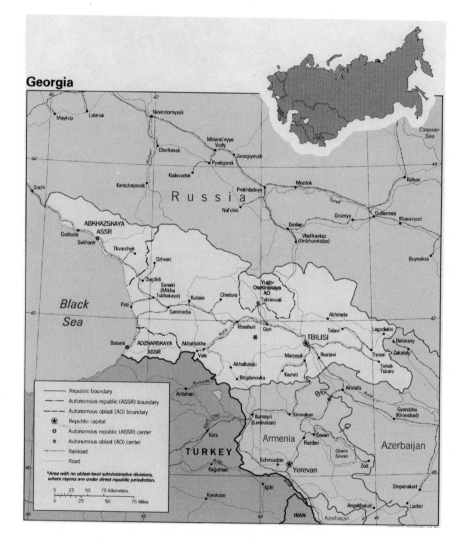

Maykop
Labinsk
Nevinnomyssk
Mineral'nyye Vody
Cherkessk
Georgiyevsk
Pyatigorsk
Kislovodsk
Karachayevsk
Mozdok
Kizlyar
Sochi
**R u s s i a**
Prokhladnyy
Nal'chik
Beslan
Groznyy
Gudermes
Khasavyurt
**ABKHAZSKAYA ASSR**
Gudauta
Vladikavkaz (Ordzhonikidze)
Sukhumi
Tkvarcheli
Buynaksk
Dzhvari
Zugdidi
Senaki (Mikha Tskhakaya)
**Yugo-Osetinskaya AO**
Poti
Kutaisi
Chiatura
Tskhinvali
**Black Sea**
Samtredia
Akhmeta
Khashuri
Gori
Telavi
Lagodekhi
Batumi
**ADZHARSKAYA ASSR**
Akhaltsikhe
**TBILISI**
Belokany
Vale
Marneuli
Rustavi
Tsnori
Zakataly
Akhalkalaki
Kazreti
Tsiteli-Tskaro
Bogdanovka
Ardahan
Akstafa
Kumayri (Leninakan)
Kirovakan
Gyandzha (Kirovabad)
Kars
**Armenia**
Sevan
Razdan
**Azerbaijan**
**TURKEY**
 Echmiadzin
Ozero Sevan
Zod
Kağızman
**Yerevan**
Stepanakert
Karaköse
Iğdır
**IRAN**
Angekhakot
Lachin
Azerbaijan

Caspian Sea

- Republic boundary
- Autonomous republic (ASSR) boundary
- Autonomous oblast (AO) boundary
⊛ Republic capital
○ Autonomous republic (ASSR) center
⊛ Autonomous oblast (AO) center
Railroad
Road

*Area with no oblast-level administrative divisions, where rayons are under direct republic jurisdiction.

0  25  50  75 Kilometers
0  25  50  75 Miles

Table 14.1. *National composition of Georgia, 1926–1989*

| | 1926 | | 1939 | | 1959 | | 1979 | | 1989 | |
|---|---|---|---|---|---|---|---|---|---|---|
| | Pop. in 1000s | % of total pop. | Pop. in 1000s | % of total pop. | Pop. in 1000s | % of total pop. | Pop. in 1000s | % of total pop. | Pop. in 1000s | % of total pop. |
| Total | 2,677 | 100.0 | 3,540 | 100.0 | 4,044 | 100.0 | 4,993 | 100.0 | 5,443 | 100.0 |
| Of whom: | | | | | | | | | | |
| Georgians | 1,788 | 66.8 | 2,174 | 61.4 | 2,601 | 64.3 | 3,433 | 68.8 | 3,787 | 70.1 |
| Armenians | 307 | 11.5 | 414 | 11.7 | 443 | 11.0 | 448 | 9.0 | 437 | 8.1 |
| Russians | 96 | 3.6 | 308 | 8.7 | 408 | 10.1 | 372 | 7.4 | 341 | 6.3 |
| Azeris | 144 | 5.4 | 188 | 5.3 | 154 | 3.8 | 256 | 5.1 | 307 | 5.7 |
| Ossetians | 133 | 4.2 | 149 | 4.2 | 141 | 3.5 | 160 | 3.2 | 164 | 3.0 |
| Abkhaz | 57 | 2.1 | 57 | 1.6 | 63 | 1.5 | 85 | 1.7 | 95 | 1.8 |
| Greeks | 54 | 2.0 | 85 | 2.4 | 73 | 1.8 | 95 | 1.9 | 100 | 1.9 |
| Others | 118 | 4.4 | 165 | 4.7 | 162 | 3.9 | 144 | 2.9 | 212 | 3.1 |

*Source:* This data is taken from Ann Sheehy, "Data from the Soviet Census of 1979 on the Georgians and the Georgian SSR," *Radio Liberty Research 162/80*, p. 10. V. Jaoshvili, *Sakartvelos Mosaxleoba XVIII–XX Sauk'uneebshi*, Tbilisi, 1984. *K'omunist'i*, January 13, 1990. p. 2.

The Georgian route to nationalist authoritarianism, attenuated since the election of Eduard Shevardnadze as Georgian head of state in October 1992, should be seen in the context of Soviet Georgian political culture and the political and economic chaos brought on by the Union's collapse. Chaos and uncertainty has led to authoritarian sentiment in all post-Soviet societies, but in Georgia's case these authoritarian tendencies took on virulent form. Among the numerous factors which can explain this situation, this chapter shall concentrate on three: Georgians' relations with their minorities, the Soviet civic and political legacy, and the personality of Zviad Gamsakhurdia. The final part of the chapter will look at how Shevardnadze has coped with this authoritarian legacy since he assumed the leadership of the republic in March 1992. What is the nature of post-Gamsakhurdian society and has Shevardnadze put democracy on a firmer base in Georgia?

## Georgian-minority relations

### The pre-Soviet period

Georgia is a complex multiethnic state (see table 14.1). Historically, Georgian–minority relations, although characterized by mutual prejudice and national sterotypes, have on the whole been peaceful. Notable exceptions to this occured in 1918–21, when Georgia was independent; in the 1970s, when Moscow's economic and political control declined in the republic;

and again today, when Georgia is fighting for political and economic survival. Moscow's weakening influence has almost always coincided with an economic or social crisis. While there is not necessarily a direct causal relationship between the decline of Moscow's power and the rise of ethnic conflict in Georgia, the economic and social disruption which accompanied Moscow's decline has always had a measurable impact on power relationships between ethnic groups in the republic.

In 1918, Georgia regained its independence from the Russian empire.[4] For three years until 1921, when Georgia was reincorporated into the Soviet state, Georgia's moderate socialist leaders established a polity based on universal suffrage, popular participation and public contestation for power. The conditions were hardly propitious for democratic development. Georgians were at war with the Turks, the Russian Volunteer Army, and the Armenians. They were subject to an economic blockade by the Allied powers, faced problems of internal Bolshevik subversion, and after rapidly emptying the government treasury, experienced economic chaos and hyperinflation. Nonetheless, the Georgian socialists established a democratic legislature, a quasi-independent judiciary, and tolerated competing nonsocialist interest groups and organizations.

Initially, Georgia's minorities, who numbered 30 percent of the total population, were given special status and one quarter of the Georgian parliament's seats. Abkhazia was granted a degree of autonomy, although South Ossetia was not.[5] By 1919, after a number of revolts in non-Georgian areas, inspired in the Georgians' view by the Bolsheviks, relations with the minorities soured. When a Constituent Assembly replaced the parliament in 1919, minority quotas were removed. The Georgian socialists, fighting for their state's physical survival, turned to Georgian nationalism as a source of legitimacy and political mobilization. A Georgianization program was launched in the schools and government administration, and the Georgian Social Democratic party, which was overwhelmingly Georgian, became the sole source of political patronage and power. In this situation, the Armenians, Ossetians, Abkhazians and other minorities, who had organized their own national soviets in 1917–18, began to fear they would be locked into a position of permanent inferiority.

Social and economic resentments among non-Georgians, combined with a newly discovered national consciousness that local Bolsheviks exploited, led to a series of armed conflicts with the Georgian National Guard.[6] The revolts in non-Georgian areas, which entered Soviet mythology as resistance to Menshevik oppression, have become part of today's competing ethnic histories. The Georgian suppression of the June 1920 revolt in Ossetia is interpreted by Ossetians as part of a Georgian strategy aimed at national genocide. They compare this period to the struggle of Armenians in Nagorno-Karabakh against the Azeris.[7] In contrast, the Georgians view it as the first attempt by Ossetians to seize Georgian territory and break up the Georgian state. Ossetian and Georgian newspapers have further enflamed the current conflict by reprinting reports from 1920 of the fighting between Ossetians and Georgians which highlight the atrocities and reinforce brutal national sterotypes.[8] Similar conflicts between Abkhazians and Georgians in 1918–21 have also become historical lessons of ethnic incompatibility for both sides.

The ethnic conflicts of 1918–21, which extended to Muslim districts in Ajaria and Armenian districts in the south, underlined the weakness of Georgian democracy. Although the Georgian government could legit-imately claim it was fighting for the integrity of the new state, its methods – occupation, military governors and military tribunals – reflected an inability to incorporate ethnic minorities into the political system. Argu-ably, if economic conditions and the threat of invasion from Russia and Turkey had not been so pressing, and if the government had had a less corrupt and more effective civil administration, these ethnic disputes might have been resolved in a more democratic manner. As it was, the experience of Georgian rule reinforced the minorities' alienation from the new Georg-ian state and led Georgians to view the minorities as a potential "fifth column." This situation has been repeated today, although the Russians are no longer Bolsheviks and the Turks publically support Georgian territorial integrity. But the consequences of ethnic conflict are as threatening now as they were in 1918–1921 to Georgia's embryonic democracy.

## The Soviet period

After 1921, the conflict between national rights and political pluralism in Georgia was transformed into a struggle over power sharing between terri-torially defined ethnic groups. In 1922 and 1931, the Ossetians and Abkh-azians gained Autonomous Region and Autonomous Republic status respectively.[9] Policies of affirmative action (*korenizatsiia*) gave them limited protection from Georgian dominance. Under the stewardship of Lavrentii Beria, from the 1930s onwards Georgian minorities were pressured to assimilate into the majority Georgian population.[10] In the 1930s, when other non-Russians had their alphabets "Cyrillicized," the Abkhazians had theirs "Georgianized" and all native language schools in Abkhazia and South Ossetia were closed.

After Stalin's death, most minority rights were restored, but the loosening of central control combined with increasing Georgian hegemony in the republic's political and cultural life, reawakened minority anxieties over their demographic and cultural decline. Georgians occupied positions of power in Tbilisi, dominated the informal structures of the second economy, and controlled republican networks that ensured professional advancement and wealth. Despite the positive results of affirmative action in Abkhazia,

South Ossetia and other minority districts, non-Georgians accused Tbilisi of deliberately neglecting them and of forcing them, as socially and linguistically disadvantaged minorities, to accept inferior jobs.[11]

In the 1970s, party boss Eduard Shevardnadze's anti-corruption campaign and his attacks on "half-baked" nationalism increased minority anxieties as their own ethnic networks of mutual support and self protection came under scrutiny. Shevardnadze admits in his autobiography that in the 1970s and 1980s "interethnic friction had broken out in virtually all the regions in Georgia," and between 1972–79, more than fifty resolutions of the Georgian Central Committee and the Georgian Council of Ministers addressed the economic and cultural concerns of minorities in Abkhazia and South Ossetia and local Georgians in Ajaria.[12]

The most public case of ethnic conflict under Shevardnadze occured in Abkhazia.[13] Since the 1950s, a conflict had smoldered between Georgian and Abkhazian historians concerning the ethnic identity of Abkhazia's first settlers. In the 1950s and 1960s, some Georgian historians publically challenged the view that Abkhazians were indigenous to Abkhazia, suggesting that they had settled in later centuries, displacing the original Georgians.[14]

The drafting process of the 1978 "Brezhnev" constitution brought the Abkhazian-Georgian conflict to a head. In December 1977, 130 Abkhazian intellectuals sent to the CPSU Central Committee and the Supreme Soviet of the USSR a litany of complaints about political and cultural discrimination by Georgians. They demanded the secession of Abkhazia from Georgia and its union with the RSFSR.[15] This letter was followed in 1978 by demonstrations, petitions, and the defacement of Georgian signs and monuments. Moscow installed a new Abkhazian party leadership in April and coordinated with Tbilisi a package of concessions ranging from economic investment in the region to increased publishing and broadcasting in the Abkhazian language. In 1979, the Sukhumi Pedagogical Institute was transformed into an Abkhazian State University and quotas were established to increase the number of Abkhazian students in higher education.[16]

These conciliatory measures did not go far enough to relieve Abkhazian anxieties. Abkhazian demands for the constitutional right to secede and the removal of Georgian as a state language in Abkhazia, were rejected. The Georgians were anxious to protect their own minority status within the USSR. They had secured their own concessions as a result of dramatic protests in the spring of 1978 against Moscow's attempt to remove Georgian's status as a state language. A series of resolutions, following a barrage of articles in the Georgian press, called for more comprehensive instruction in the Georgian language and the systematic publication of materials promoting Georgian.[17] In this context, pro-Abkhazian measures only intensified Georgian resentments. As the plurality in Abkhazia (see map 14.1), Georgians claimed they were suffering reverse discrimination. And the Abkhazians, regardless of their political gains in leading party and government posts, remained demographically insecure, making up only 15.1 percent of their own republic's population in 1979. Moscow continued to use Georgian cadres as their primary conduit of economic and political control in the Georgian republic, and Georgians retained their monopoly over the republic's cultural, historical and political symbols. In turn, the Abkhazians felt affirmative action programs were not enough to prevent their eventual cultural extinction.

## Perestroika

Perestroika and glasnost intensified ethnic anxieties in the republic. The economic crisis and the absence of central power, the emergence of ethnically based political parties and the rehabilitation of bitter national memories raised the stakes of ethnic competition. The minorities' demands for cultural and educational equality, and for greater political and economic representation challenged the Georgians' belief that they, as the titular and autochtonous group in the republic, were entitled to privileged status and control. Stimulated by a history of foreign invasion, Russification, and traditionally weak demographic representation in the republic's periphery, Georgians' deep national insecurity encouraged them to support nationalist policies designed to protect majority, rather than minority, rights.

Central to the programs of the myriad of Georgian parties and associations that have emerged since 1988 are demographic concerns and Georgianization of the republic's administrative and cultural institutions.[18] The Communist Party of Georgia, before it was ousted from power in multiparty elections in October 1990, was no exception. In an attempt to prevent its political marginalization, it published a draft *State Program for the Georgian Language* in November 1988, which advocated an increased role for Georgian instruction in all republican schools, including a Georgian language test for entry into higher education.[19] This was a challenge to most of the minorities, who spoke Georgian badly, if at all. Other measures included programs for the promotion of Georgian history and the defense of historical monuments, a law restricting immigration, and the institutionalization of previously unofficial Georgian national holidays.[20] The creation of republican military units, comprising only Georgians, and the resettlement of Georgians in areas dominated by the minorities, must have seemed particularly threatening. Although these attempts at Georgian state-building were understandable, in an atmosphere of growing chauvinism, fanned by the slogan "Georgia for the Georgians," the minorities felt increasingly insecure.

Their apprehensions were not eased by discussion of the citizenship law in the summer of 1990, when Gamsakhurdia proposed that eligibility be limited to those residents whose forebears lived in Georgia before the annexation of 1801. The citizenship law which eventually took effect in June 1990 was less discriminatory, granting citizenship to all those who were "permanent residents" with a legal source of support. But the electoral law which had passed nine months earlier prevented all regionally based parties in the republic from registering for the elections, effectively disenfranchising non-Georgians who wished to vote for ethnically based parties. As a result, non-Georgians either boycotted the elections in October or voted for the Georgian communist party which was seen as the best protection for minority groups.[21] The few Georgian electoral blocs and parties, such as "Democratic Georgia" and "Accord, Peace and Renaissance," which took a more moderate line toward the minorities and proposed constitutional provisions for the protection of their rights and incorporation into the political system, received almost no electoral support.

The winners of the election were the members of Zviad Gamsakhurdia's Round Table-Free Georgia Bloc, which gained 54 percent of the vote. After the election, minority access to economic and political power was virtually eliminated. Although Abkhazians retained ex-officio posts in the Georgian Council of Ministers, the Supreme Soviet Presidium and the Committee for the Supervision of the Constitution, the new parliament contained almost no minority representation, except in the opposition communist party. Nationalist arguments for special treatment on the basis of prior settlement, history, or by dint of numbers became the new language of Georgian politics, and censuses, borders and toponyms took on new meaning. Attempts by ethnic minorities to carve out spheres of cultural or economic sovereignty were perceived by the Georgian government as a challenge to its people's spatial and social homogeneity. The government elaborated a theory of minority rights based on the assumption that members of minorities with a relatively recent history of settlement in Georgia, such as the Ossetians or Azeris, qualified neither for an inalienable right to residence in the republic nor for equal status with the dominant ethnic group.[22]

The new Georgian government based much of its ethnic policy on the distinction between "indigenes" and "settlers." The abolition of the South Ossetian autonomous region by the Georgian government in December 1990, which led to a bitter war, was justified by the latters' "settler" status. The Georgian government asserted that Ossetians only began to arrive in Georgia in the nineteenth century and that they were illegally granted an autonomous region by the Bolsheviks in 1922 as a reward for their anti-Georgian activity during the civil war of 1918–21. President Gamsakhurdia called on South Ossetians to return to their "real" homeland in neighboring North Ossetia. The flight of Ossetian refugees from the region since the war began there in December 1990 has partially fulfilled this agenda, although 12,000 local Georgians also fled.[23] By autumn 1991, the Azeris also began to leave in significant numbers, and the Russian Dukhobors in Bogdanovka (since renamed Ninoc'minda) have already returned to Russia. In an agreement between Daghestan and Georgia reminiscent of the forced population exhanges following World War II in Poland, Czechoslovakia and elsewhere, the Avars from northeastern Georgia agreed to an exchange for Georgians living across the border in southern Daghestan, although it is unlikely that it will now take place.[24] Despite Shevardnadze's more inclusive policies, the accelerated migration of minorities has continued.[25]

The drive for ethnic homogenization and the promotion of Georgian hegemony came at great cost. In July 1989, before the war in Ossetia began, bloody clashes over Abkhazian education rights in the Autonomous Republic's capital of Sukhumi left 14 dead and over 500 wounded.[26] Armenians and Azeris clashed with Georgians over rights to land and cultural monuments. The Georgian Muslims, known as Ajarians, protested the Gamsakhurdia government's Christianization program, including its encouragement of mass baptisms in Muslim areas and the appointment of Georgian Orthodox priests as government officials. They strongly resisted the attempted removal of Ajaria's autonomous status.

The Ossetians and Abkhazians also began to organize themselves as formal opposition forces. With overwhelming support, the Ossetian popular front *Adamon Nykhas* (Popular Shrine) and its Abkhazian equivalent, *Aidgilara* (Unity), used the existing soviet structures to promote regional control and express dissatisfaction with their exclusion from power. In August 1990, the Abkhazian Supreme Soviet, with a bare quorum, declared its state sovereignty. A few weeks later in September, the South Ossetian Regional Soviet declared a South Ossetian Democratic Soviet Republic.[27] While the South Ossetian Soviet was shortly thereafter abolished by the Georgian government, it continued its illegal existence and in December 1991, proclaimed the region's independence. The Abkhazian Supreme Soviet continued its "war of laws" with the Georgian parliament, but intense hostility between the two power centers led in August 1992 to full-scale war. After Georgia's defeat in September 1993, largely a result of Russian military aid to the Abkhazian secessionists, Abkhazia secured *de facto* independence.

The Gamsakhurdia government's single-minded pursuit of Georgianization alienated the vast majority of the republic's non-Georgian population. With the exception of a system of ethnic power sharing devised in Abkhazia in August 1991, reminiscent of the Lebanese system before the civil war, no attempt was made to incorporate non-Georgians into the representative bodies of the republic.[28] The Gamsakhurdia constitution devoted only ten short articles to the autonomous republics and restricted their rights in innumerable ways, leaving them with almost no recourse against a powerful center and president. Decisions of the autonomous republics' higher bodies could be challenged or rejected by a host of institutions and bodies in Tbilisi.[29] The persistent exclusion of the minorities from real power stymied the development of democracy in Georgia. The philosophy of majority rights encouraged a siege mentality where any opposition to Georgian hegemony was seen as a threat to national unity and to the state's interests.

## The Soviet legacy

### The problems of transition

In the elections of October 1990, and again in October 1992, every Georgian party trumpeted the virtues of political pluralism and the free market. Zviad Gamsakhurdia's coalition, the Round Table-Free Georgia bloc, presented a program which hardly differed from that of its opponents. It called for independence, a multiparty system, the sanctity of law, a market economy, and guarantees of civil rights such as freedom of religion and the independence of the media. On the other hand, also in common with the opposition, the program advocated laws to strengthen Georgian majority rights: more restrictions on immigration, laws defending the sovereignty of the Georgian language, and a new citizenship law with a narrower definition of prerequisites. But overall, the program, with its call for human rights' guarantees based on UN declarations, could not be called authoritarian.[30]

The election campaign in October 1990 was peaceful. Based on a mixed system of proportional and majority representation, Gamsakhurdia's bloc received 155 of the 250 Supreme Soviet seats. The Communist Party of Georgia, which received 64 seats or 29.6 percent of the vote, formed the only significant opposition. The Popular Front, which presented a program almost indistinguishable from Gamsakhurdia's, but was represented by more mainstream intelligentsia figures, came a poor third with twelve seats.[31] Although the new Supreme Soviet was predominantly nationalist, the new government under Prime Minister Tengiz Sigua, formerly Director of the Metallurgy Institue in Tbilisi and Chairman of the moderate Rustaveli society, comprised a number of former government officials and academics and was technocratic rather than ideological in character.[32] A law of transition was passed which envisaged a gradual and negotiated path to independence. In the euphoria of victory and with the full support of the newly elected Supreme Soviet, Gamsakhurdia's government began the relatively uncomplicated process of symbolic deconstruction. All references to "socialism" were removed from the constitution, the supremacy of all-Union law was ended, the republic's name was changed, the hymn and flag were replaced, civil and criminal codes were amended, the draft into the Soviet army was annulled and the provincial party bodies removed. Throughout, any actions taken against Moscow were greeted with unanimous acclaim.[33]

But the construction of a democratic state is a difficult process. Robert Dahl, writing twenty years ago, concluded that a country which has "little or no experience with the institution of public contestation and political competiton and lacks a tradition of toleration toward political oppositions" is unlikely to develop a democratic system quickly. Neither is it likely to endure.[34] Guiseppe Di Palma suggests that an analysis of structural preconditions is a poor historical guide to successful transitions to democracy, but agrees that economic instablility, a hegemonic nationalist political culture and the absence of a strong and nondependent middle class – all characteristics of Georgia – would impede a transition to democracy.[35] The Soviet past had left Georgians without constituencies, institutions and practices conducive to a pluralistic power structure. Unlike their counterparts in post-authoritarian regimes such as Spain and Greece, where autonomous societies and institutions had been allowed to develop, the Georgian leaders were forced to use exclusively, as Benedict Anderson calls it, "the wiring of the old state." The danger, as Alexander Yakovlev points out, is that a country then begins to regenerate "in itself the vices of the past in new wrappings."[36]

In Georgia, the Soviet legacy of official nationalism, distrust of one's opponents, paternalism, hegemonism, censorship, the personalization of politics, and a corrupt and unaccountable bureaucracy had a particularly strong influence on the young state. They were all passed on, virtually unaltered, to the new regime. A politically unsophisticated population distrustful of institutions and inexperienced in the mechanisms of "checks and balances" or managed conflict, and rebounding from seventy years of Russian oppression, supported Gamsakhurdia's single-minded drive for unity and independence. This occurred despite a program that putatively rejected the Soviet political inheritance.[37]

## The new legislative program

Gamsakhurdia's new government, in its legislative program and constitution, parroted the model of Western style pluralism. It passed liberal laws on citizenship, set up a system of local self government and strengthened the independence of the judiciary by extending judges' terms to few years and banning any party membership among them.[38] In December 1990, a law on the status of deputies guaranteed them parliamentary immunity and substantial rights to question and supervise the executive, and in August 1991, laws on political associations and the freedom of the press were passed restricting government controls.[39] From spring 1991 onwards, a whole series of new laws expanded the sphere of personal ownership and laid the basis for private commercial activity. In particular, legislation authorized the sale of government businesses and government owned housing.[40] By autumn 1991, a "Rechtstaat" existed on paper, with a division of powers, rights of public contestation, a multiparty system, and a free press. A Committee for the Supervision of the Constitution was established, with members elected for few years, to overrule any laws which transgressed the constitution.

Despite this impressive legislative activity, laws were flawed by omission or vagueness, and betrayed a continuing concern for tight regulation by government. The law on political associations, for example, made it relatively easy for the Ministry of Justice to refuse registration to any party organization. Apart from requiring a long list of information on finances, expenditure, and the nature of the party's internal organization, the Ministry could refuse registration if the organization interfered "with the normal working of state organs." The Procurator General could ban a party for three months if, among other things, it "crudely broke its own rules." The law on the press was also hazy. Newspapers could be taken to court "for malevolently using freedom of the press, [and] spreading facts not corresponding to reality . . ." or for printing "false and unchecked information, and conscious disinformation . . ." Ostensibly laudable, such vague formulations encouraged arbitary and inequitable enforcement.[41]

The constitution, amendable by a two-thirds majority of the Supreme Soviet, remained heavily "interventionist," despite enormous improvements in defense of civil rights. A whole section was devoted to the spiritual and aesthetic welfare of its citizens, in which the state stipulated equal relations between spouses, and emphasized motherhood and the filial duties of children.[42] But more significantly, the new constitution continued the legacy of strong state regulation in the economy and a powerful executive branch. The laws on the prefecture and the presidency, passed in February and April 1991 respectively, and subsequently incorporated into the constitution, severely restricted the representative bodies in the regions (the *sakrebuloebi*) and the center. The prefects, described as the supreme regional powerholders, were directly responsible to and appointed by the President and the Supreme Soviet. They had enormous powers over the *sakrebulo* and could dismiss it, with the Supreme Soviet's consent, at any time. They controlled most of the regional budget and all local appointments, which allowed them to build up personal networks. They rapidly acquired a reputation for corruption and played a crucial role in getting busloads of Gamsakhurdia's supporters to Tbilisi in September, 1991, when the government was besieged by anti-government demonstrations.[43]

The presidential system dominated the legislatures of the center and autonomous republics in similar fashion. Many of the president's powers, such as appointment and dismissal of the cabinet and its prime minister, were to be taken "with the agreement" of the Supreme Soviet, although it is unclear whether the legislature had veto rights. The president could cancel any resolutions or orders of the cabinet. His rejection of a bill could be overturned by a two-thirds vote in the legislature, but he could then call a referendum or dismiss the Supreme Soviet after "consulting" his prime minister and the chairman of the House. There was no limitation on the number of terms the president could serve and he could be removed only on charges of treason by three-quarters of the assembly vote. As commander in chief, he had personal control over the National Guard and other military appointments, and could declare various degrees of presidential or emergency rule, during which time the legislature did not need to be consulted at all. The president was advised by a presidential council, but had the power to issue both decrees and instructions without consulting anybody. He could also suspend the force of laws, decrees and instructions of the legislative and executive organs of the autonomous republics.[44]

## Relations with the opposition

Democracy above all else requires mutual trust and shared principles of political behaviour, but both the Georgian government and its opponents proved incapable of establishing a normative framework of political competition. Opposition to Gamsakhurdia fragmented. The most vociferous opposition groups developed in the National Congress, a body elected in the fall of 1990 as an alternative national forum to the Supreme Soviet. Dominated by the National Democratic Party of Gia Čanturia and the National Independence Party of Irakli Cereteli, two young nationalist dissidents imprisoned in the 1980s, the National Congress mobilized supporters onto the streets and organized hunger strikes to protest government policies. Initially, Congress leaders, who dubbed themselves "the irreconcilables," took a more radical stand than Gamsakhurdia on relations with the USSR. They called for a more rapid move to secession and demanded the expulsion of Soviet "occupation" troops (how it was not clear). Gamsakhurdia, who, after much pressure, agreed to the presence of Soviet troops in South Ossetia, was accused of collaboration with Moscow.

After the October 1990 elections to the Supreme Soviet, the National Congress groups were increasingly marginalized. However, taking advantage of the government's increasing authoritarianism, the "irreconcilables" successfully redefined themselves as defenders of democracy. When the paramilitary organization *Mkhedrioni* ("Horsemen"), which was allied to the National Congress, was disbanded by force in February 1991 with the help of Soviet troops and its leader, Jaba Ioseliani, imprisoned without trial, it only served to bolster the new found image of these groups as persecuted democrats.[45]

Parliamentary opposition was ineffective. The Georgian Communist party, undergoing an internal crisis since its defeat at the polls in October 1990, was extremely defensive. The deputies were expelled from the Supreme Soviet after the August coup and its remaining property nationalized. The other parties were too small to have any influence. The Round Table-Free Georgia Bloc representatives were docile until the September 1991 events (see below), and needed no party whip to vote *en bloc* for government legislation.

The upper levels of the professional intelligentsia, while critical, were intimidated by the cultural monopolism of Gamsakhurdia's ministries. They were regularly insulted by the president as "a false intelligentsia" with links to the communist "mafia." Deprived of their traditional role as *vox populi*, they were isolated by the new political hegemony.[46] They continued to snipe at the government in the press and give interviews to Western correspondents, but were heavily outnumbered by journalists and writers prepared to defend Gamsakhurdia, his policies, and his image.

That situation changed dramatically in August 1991 after a perceived ambivalence to the Moscow putsch by Gamsakhurdia and his demotion of the Georgian National Guard.[47] A parliamentary opposition led by a number of Gamsakhurdia's former allies from the Round Table-Free Georgia Bloc created Charter '91, a group of at least forty-nine deputies. It linked up with the extraparliamentary opposition, disgruntled ministers, military commanders, and resentful intellectuals, to form a coalition which finally overturned Gamsakhurdia's government by force in January 1992. They accused Gamsakhurdia of economic mismanagement, hostility to the Western powers, crude manipulation of personnel, disrepect for the law and suppression of the opposition.

Throughout Gamsakhurdia's period in office, relations between opposition and government were characterized by intense animosity and an absence of consensus. Unable to shed the policies of direct action, civil disobedience, ultimatums and violence which had been so successful in the final years of communism, the bloody battle for power in December 1991 was a culmination of the boycotts, strikes, occupations, rallies, and physical threats that had been the resort of all parties during the previous year. Gamsakhurdia, with overwhelming support in the Supreme Soviet and among the electorate, had seen no need to compromise or respond to opposition constituencies. At the time, as Robert Dahl might have put it, the costs of not incorporating the interests or anxieties of opposition groups had seemed insignificant.[48] Gamsakhurdia dismissed the extraparliamentary opposition as "criminals" and "bandits," and characterized his five presidential opponents in May 1991 as unworthy.

But in some sense Gamsakhurdia was right. The opposition had no social base. It had been unable to mobilize any real challenge to Gamsakhurdia's one-party hegemony. Gamsakhurdia had received 87 percent of the popular vote for the presidency (the first such election in the USSR) in May 1991. His nearest rival, V. Advadze, had received 240,243 votes compared to Gamsakurdia's two and a half million.[49] (Results were likely skewed somewhat due to an intimidation campaign against the opposition as well as the heavy bids of the government-controlled mass media, but the election itself was generally considered to be free.) This dramatic unevenness of power forced the opposition into extreme and demonstrative exhibitions of resistance. The Congress parties refused to disarm their paramilitary organizations or vacate occupied government buildings, and they constantly disrupted civil life with street barricades and long rallies. These parties, like Gamsakhurdia, failed to make the transition to accomodation and gradualism. They were wedded to fixed principles inherited from their moral crusade against communist oppression. Impatient at being consigned to an insignificant and permanent minority status for at least five years (the term of the Supreme Soviet), they were unable to accept the notion of democratic choice and uncertain outcome, a quality essential to a competitive political market.[50]

By the winter of 1990, both government and opposition had become trapped in an escalating cycle of verbal and physical assault. The language used by most parties, repeated in the predominantly pro-government press, resembled the hysterical phraseology of the 1930s. "Enemy of the people," "traitor to the nation," or "bandits" were common appellations. Gamsakhurdia's call to his supporters in September 1991, after some anti-government demonstrators had been killed by loyal National Guard troops, was typical: "The Kremlin's infernal machine has been activated with the help of Georgian traitors based in Moscow. I urge the Georgian people to rise up and destroy those traitors . . . I am ready to go to the people and, through rallies and demonstrations, to arouse the Georgian people and smash all our enemies . . ."[51]

The government daily *Sakartvelos Respublika* (The Republic of Georgia) ran a column entitled "Agents of the Kremlin in Georgia" which indiscriminately attacked all forces in the opposition, from the "irreconcilables" to liberal intellectuals. At a meeting in March 1991 between representatives of the liberal intelligentsia and the government, a university professor commented that the atmosphere of enmity and the language of extremism now helped her understand how the terror of the 1930s began.[52]

## The rule of law?

Georgian democracy was undermined less by legislative flaws than by the selective way in which these laws were interpreted. Thus despite a relatively liberal press law, the government maintained its monopoly over the media by controlling paper supplies, personnel appointments, and by intimidating and closing opposition papers. By the winter of 1991, there were only two or three independent newspapers. Oppositionist papers like *Molodezh Gruzii* (Young Georgia) and *Akhalgazrda Iverieli* (Young Iverian) were closed down, allegedly due to paper shortages. Those with the largest circulation, such as *Sakartvelos Respublika*, *Eri* (Nation), and *Svobodnaia Gruziia* (Free Georgia) were declared official government newspapers, and like almost all others, including the formerly liberal *Literaturuli Sakartvelo* (Literary Georgia), became supine followers of government policy.

Television, under the management of a Gamsakhurdia appointee, cancelled outspoken critical programs. *Sagamos Shvidobisa* (Good Evening), a popular current affairs program, for example, was axed in the spring of 1991 after it implied Georgia was moving toward totalitarianism. During the presidential elections in May 1991, despite a law stipulating equal air-time for all candidates, Gamsakhurdia enjoyed much more exposure. After the August coup, when Gamsakhurdia was attacked on all sides for alleged collaboration with the State Committee for the State of Emergency, some Georgian journalists were arrested, Russian newspapers were temporarily banned, and several foreign correspondents were physically attacked.[53] In September 1991, when the coverage of opposition demonstrations was cen-sored and broadcasts from Moscow were not aired, 189 TV journalists took part in a protest strike. In a letter to the government, they accused the TV management of "Bolshevik-like methods," called for an end to the "dictat" of the Department of Georgian Radio and TV, including the removal of its General Director, and the establishment of an alternative channel for the opposition.[54] The *casus belli* of the split in Gamsakhurdia's Round Table ranks in September, when forty-nine deputies abandoned the government benches in protest, was the president's refusal to allow TV coverage of parliamentary debates on the shooting of anti-government demonstrators on September 2. Significantly, when Tengiz Sigua and Tengiz Kitovani, Gamsakhurdia's former prime minister and commander of the National Guard respectively, organized direct action against the government in late September, the TV studios were the first buildings they occupied.

Restrictions on the press were accompanied by an increasingly tight hold on executive power. The KGB was transformed into a National Security Department in August and September, as part of an attempt to concentrate executive power within a streamlined cabinet of ministers, it became a min-istry. Along with the Ministry of Justice and the Ministry of Defense, it was made directly subordinate to the president. The units of the National Guard which had not defected to Kitovani, were put under presidential control on September 9.[55] In the following weeks, Gamsakhurdia estab-lished a National Security Council with wide ranging emergency powers, suspended the law on political associations, and declared a state of emerg-ency in Tbilisi.[56] None of these measures was ratified, as required by law, by the Supreme Soviet. Thus ended any pretension that body might have had about its capacity to resist presidential will. Gamsakhurdia had forced all channels of power under his control.

The Supreme Court, which had already proved its loyalty to Gamsakhur-dia by approving the legally dubious decision to expel the sixty-four com-munist party members from the Supreme Soviet in August, and the Com-mittee for the Supervision of the Constitution, provided no resistance to cynical abuse of the law. They failed to prevent the arrest of opposition leaders, and in November, they did not protest when the term of imprison-ment without charge was extended to nine months if necessitated by the case's "complexity" or "special circumstances."[57]

## The Gamsakhurdia factor

Elsewhere I have argued that the Soviet legacy, in the context of post-Soviet economic and political economic chaos, produces systems prone to populist authoritarianism.[58] In the case of Georgia, a major factor was the figure of Zviad Gamsakhurdia. Born in 1939 into the family of Konstantine Gamsakhurdia, one of the most popular Georgian novelists and a staunch patriot, Zviad was brought up, in his own words, to recognize Georgia as an "enslaved state."[59] A specialist in American literature, he rapidly became one of Georgia's most well-known dissidents. In 1974 he was a co-founder, with Merab Kostava and Viktor Rckhiladze, of the Georgian Initiative Group for Human Rights, and in 1976 of the Georgian Helsinki Watch Group. After publishing a series of *samizdat* journals and campaigning on issues of corruption in the Georgian church, Russification and the plight of national monuments, he was arrested in April 1977 for anti-Soviet propaganda, but released in June 1979 after a televised retraction. On his return, he continued his dissident activities and became a leading figure in the Georgian nationalist movement. The death of Kostava in a car accident in October 1989 left Gamsakhurdia the most popular leader of the Georgian nationalist movement.[60]

Gamsakhurdia was a complex figure. His actions must be seen in the context of a fanatical commitment to Georgian independence. His deeply expressed religious feelings, for example, are less metaphysical than part of a nationalist ideology that views the Georgian church as the embodiment of Georgian nationhood. Despite a constitutional provision separating church and state, Gamsakhurdia openly promoted the Christianization of the republic. He deliberately undermined Islam among Georgians in Ajaria, and appointed a priest to the prefecture of Akhalcikhe, a heavily Muslim-populated area.[61] His writings and speeches were infused with a Messianic vision of Georgia's future. His most popular work, *Sakartvelos sulieri missia* (Georgia's Spiritual Mission), depicts Georgian christianity as a militant ideology in defense of the nation, but at the same time as a source of Georgia's "special spiritual purpose" to mediate between East and West.

This work, which was eulogized in the government press as "a new stage in Georgian culture and science," reminds one of the fantastic pseudo-racial concoctions of nineteenth-century pamphleteers. It is a jumble of mythological theories taken as fact, depicting Georgia as the embodiment of "ancient spiritual wisdom" and the source of a powerful "proto-Iberian culture" which spread throughout the Ancient world. At one stage, he points out that Japhet, son of Noah and the mythological ancestor of Georgians, is identical to Jupiter, "the planet of the white race."[62] This pamphlet, typical of the nationalist's mind with its search for past glory and distinctiveness, reveals a dangerously naive and irrational personality. There is not a trace of skepticism in the work. Georgia is a superior culture.

The consequence of this deeply held ethnocentrism was a policy aimed at the limitation of the smaller and inferior cultures which shared Georgian historical territory.

Gamsakhurdia's other characteristics were a sense of paranoia, a conspiratorial frame of mind, virulent anti-communism, and a tendency to self-glorification. The first three might be traced to his own experiences in the Soviet Union when he was constantly persecuted by the KGB. His speeches ubiquitously referred to foreign agents, traitors, and conspiracies hatched by his "enemies" in Moscow. Colleagues who broke with Gamsakhurdia became traitors, and critical intellectuals became Moscow's tools. "Tbilisians" who supported the opposition were "cruelly deceived." A key conspirator against both Gamsakhurdia and Georgia (the two presumed identical by Gamsakhurdia) was Shevardnadze, who, Gamsakhurdia alleged, masterminded the "civil junta" which finally overthrew his government in January 1992.[63]

Gamsakhurdia viewed himself as the last in a long line of Georgian national heroes, all of whom, in his words, have embodied "sacrifices on the altar of the fatherland." The struggle for Gamsakhurdia was between "good and evil." If he were removed, Georgia would become "the victim of total anarchy, and Georgia's existence, its future in general, will be in question." Comparing himself to de Gaulle, Gamsakhurdia argued that a strong presidency corresponded to the "historical laws and characteristics" of the Georgian people, and that it was the only means for Georgia's salvation.[64]

The above is not intended to suggest that Gamsakhurdia was directly responsible for the authoritarianism and violence in Georgia. He was, after all, elected by 87 percent of those who voted in the presidential elections. His "dictatorial tendencies" were not perceived as a threat by most Georgians, who did not take part in the fighting which finally ousted him. The Georgian political culture contributed just as much to the paternalism and violence which characterized Gamsakhurdia's reign as the Soviet legacy, a point pursued below.[65] But Gamsakhurdia's paranoia, his refusal to enter serious dialogue with the opposition, and his manipulation of the law undoubtedly contributed to an atmosphere in which mutual accommodation and trust were rejected.

## Shevardnadze to the rescue?

Shevardnadze came to power in March 1992 at the invitation of the Georgian Military Council, a praetorian body which had assumed power after the removal of Gamsakhurdia the previous January. Since then, Shevardnadze has discovered that Boris Yeltsin's paradoxical dictum about post-Soviet Russia – that it is harder to destroy things than create them – applies to his own country.[66] By 1995 Shevardnadze had still not settled fundamental questions of legitimacy, institutional authority, and political stability. There are numerous reasons for this. I will deal with four: the influence of Georgian and Soviet political cultures, the continuing absence of central power, the war with Abkhazia, and Shevardnadze's own predilection for caution and balance.

## Legacies of the past

The structural and psychological burdens of the Soviet period discussed above, were transformed by Gamsakhurdia into pillars of a populist-authoritarian system. Exploiting wide social divisions in Georgian society which existed between a socially undifferentiated mass and a cozy politico-cultural elite on the one hand, and between Tbilisi and the provinces and Georgians and non-Georgians on the other, Gamsakhurdia fragmented the country into regions, nationalities, and haves and have-nots. His populism placed the people (or street) above representative politics, principle above accomodation, and loyalty to the state and its leader above democratic control.

Shevardnadze's attempts to democratize this Gamsakhurdian political culture have had limited impact. An illustration of this is the post-Soviet Georgian legislature. Elected in October 1992, it is characterized by intense factionalism among its over twenty-six parties and poor discipline, including frequent absent quorums and violent rhetoric directed against "internal enemies" and the head of state. It has also largely failed to fulfill its legislative or executive control functions. This is partly due to the laws determining its powers. The August 1992 electoral law and the Law on State Power and the Temporary Regulation of the Georgian Parliament, both passed in November 1992, created a parliament of weak mini-parties subject to almost no disciplinary control by parliamentary authorities.[67] The war in Abkhazia also created a highly emotional atmosphere which undermined productive debate.

But Georgian and Soviet political culture remain critical factors in the parliament's failure. A reaction against Soviet discipline combined with Georgians' own reliance on "egocentric networks," expressed as a rejection of formal collective power in favor of a system of clients and patrons, has led to ineffective and undisciplined parties without grass roots support among the population. The parties' use of patron–client networks, a Georgian tradition reinforced by the Soviet system, has contributed to a neglect of constituents' concrete interests by party members. The collapse of Soviet power has increased the patronage powers of pseudo-clans and regional bosses, undermining the organizational effectiveness of Georgian parties and embryonic civic institutions.

Parliamentary consensus and the formation of alliances and majorities, essential to a smoothly working legislature, has been partially obstructed by Georgians' own values of "honor and shame." Parliamentary insults, characterized by extreme epithets such as "traitor," "thief," and "coward" have left little room for compromise and have driven parliamentarians into fierce and public enmity. In addition to such cultural (or ethical) obstacles, the Soviet system left Georgians unprepared for policy formulation, process, or accountability. Confusion about rules and responsibility affect all Georgian institutions from the parliament and ministries to the police and judiciary. The result is a discredited political system, with particular venom directed at Georgian parliamentarians whose disputes and *ad hominem* attacks in the parliamentary chamber are televised daily. Shevardnadze has exploited parliamentary incompetence to increase his own powers, but in the long term the poor reputation of parliament and other civic institutions will undermine both democracy and Shevardnadze's popularity.

### The collapse of central power

Georgia has been one of the least successful of the newly independent states in creating new forms of governance to replace the "wiring of the old state." It shares with other former Soviet republics absent legacies such as the rule of law, an effective tax system, accountable bureaucracies, legislative control of the executive, and a government partnership with the public. These have all contributed to Shevardnadze's inability to "institutionalize" Georgian democracy. The economic catastrophe has compounded institutional atrophy, leaving ministries unable to implement elementary bureaucratic tasks such as paying local government officials, including the police. The institutional anarchy was reflected by serious disputes between the Ministries of Defense and Security at the end of 1992 which led to mutual terrorist attacks, and by Shevardnadze's need to temporarily assume the posts of prime minister and interior minister in 1993. In July and September of that same year, Shevardnadze was granted extraordinary powers to deal with crises in the government and in Abkhazia.[68]

As head of state, Shevardnadze has a large apparatus which parallels the government, but despite full use of his prerogatives to issue decrees and states of emergency, he has only limited authority in the country, particularly in the regions. Leaving aside Abkhazia and South Ossetia which have *de facto* separated from Georgia under Russian protection, the rest of the country is divided among local ethnocracies and regional potentates. Ajaria is controlled by Aslan Abashidze, chairman of its Supreme Council, who bases his legitimacy on descent from a famous ruling clan as much as on Tbilisi's authority and his own election. The southern regions of Akhalcikhe, Akhalkalaki, Dmanisi, Ninocminda, Marneuli and Bolnisi are largely under local Armenian or Azeri control. Samegrelo (Mingrelia) in western Georgia is still deeply resentful of metropolitan Georgia, which sent its troops to defeat Mingrelian rebels who supported Gamsakhurdia's attempt to regain his presidency in September–November 1993. This collapse of central power and the country's division among regional barons echoes Georgia's past which, prior to the Russian annexation, was characterized by internecine conflict and regional challenges to the center.

One of the symptoms of the power vacuum in Georgia was the rise of armed militias. The two most powerful were the National Guard and *Mkhedrioni*. Led respectively by Tengiz Kitovani and Jaba Ioseliani, both nonprofessional soldiers, they played a leading role in the overthrow of Gamsakhurdia and the return of Shevardnadze. The National Guard, although it was recognized as the official defense force in Georgia under Gamsakhurdia and Shevardnadze until the fall of 1992, never resembled a professional army. It lacked discipline, an *esprit de corps* and professional expertise. Its loyalty was to its commander Tengiz Kitovani, who used it like a personal militia, often ignoring the orders of the Supreme Commander of the Armed Forces, whether it was Gamsakhurdia or Shevardnadze. One of Shevardnadze's primary tasks was to "civilianize" these armed militias, but by the autumn of 1994, he had only partially succeeded. In the absence of a professional army, its creation stymied by economic collapse, the war in Abkhazia, and the lack of professional personnel, the armed militias under Kitovani and Ioseliani became the powerbrokers in Georgian politics. Both Kitovani and Ioseliani demonstrated their independence from Shevardnadze when they raided Russian military bases in Georgia, opposed Shevardnadze's peace making, and publically threatened his government.[69] The worst case of such disobedience was Kitovani's decision to lead his troops into Abkhazia, which resulted in the thirteen month-long war.

With the removal of Kitovani as defense minister in May 1993 and the appointment of a professional soldier, Vardiko Nadabaidze, to this position in April 1994 following the brief tenure of Giorgi Qaqarashvili, a professional army subject to civilian authority began to emerge. But Shevardnadze's attempts to integrate *Mkhedrioni* into the armed forces, including an award of state committee status which guarantees it a cabinet seat, has not worked. *Mkhedrioni* has gone through serious internal strife, but remains a body personally loyal to Ioseliani. As former chairman of the State of Emergency Provisional Committee, and since July 1994 a deputy chairman of its replacement, the Emergency Coordinating Commission, Ioseliani has great influence within government. But his real power lies outside the institutional framework. Georgian politics has become "feudalized," fractured politically and geographically into unofficial power centers dominated by holders of important political office but who run their spheres of influence on the basis of informal networks, mutual favors and obligations. Such a situation which undermines embryonic institutional relationships, a legal framework for economic reform, the security of citizens, accountability and process, has made formal governance precisely that – formal.

## The war

Shevardnadze brought the South Ossetian secessionist war to an end three months after his arrival, although it remains a truce rather than a resolution. He was unable to prevent the outbreak of a second secessionist war in Abkhazia however. This was partly due to the indiscipline of Georgia's armed forces as well as the Georgian political establishment's inability to find a constitutional solution, but it was just as much a result of the support of the local Russian military and the Russian government for the Abkhazian leaders' uncompromising demands.[70] The war left around 20,000 dead and a quarter of a million refugees in Georgia alone. The country was transformed into a military camp and the state forced to divert its limited economic resources from domestic to military needs. Money was printed uncontrollably and by the war's end, inflation had reached 9,000 percent. Georgia's economic devastation, with GDP, industrial output, and labor productivity down to the level of the 1960s, can be explained by many factors, from the rupture in trade relations and the absence of energy resources to the government's own mistakes, including the issue of a worthless national currency and massive credits to bankrupt industries.[71] But the war in Abkhazia gave the economy no respite. It destroyed much of the infrastructure in the west, drove up prices of oil and food, prevented the harvesting of crops and the collection of revenues, discouraged foreign investment, and ended supplies by rail and road from the north as Russia declared an economic blockade until the war was resolved. It also gave an excuse to the former Georgian *apparatchiki* still in power to stall reform.

But the war's impact went further than economic dislocation and decline. Gamsakhurdia, taking advantage of the political, mobilized his own supporters in Samegrelo in an attempt to retake power in Tbilisi. The short civil war which ensued from September to November 1993 intensified political divisions. It led Shevardnadze, in order to preserve his power and the integrity of the state, to invite Russian troops to put down the rebellion. Thankful for Russian aid, Shevardnadze brought Georgia back into the CIS in October and signed bilateral military agreements which placed significant limitations on Georgia's sovereignty.[72] The war also had a dramatic effect on crime. Armed soldiers with no employment prospects returned to cities, and in particular Tbilisi, where there were no effective or honest police forces. Kote Gabashvili, the mayor of Tbilisi, called this Georgia's own "Vietnam syndrome."[73] Parliament was affected dramatically, its attention drawn to emotional themes of territorial sovereignty and the Abkhazian enemy, with little time left for the detail of economic and social legislation.

The war did not create a sense of solidarity among Georgians, only enmity and accusations of betrayal. Shevardnadze's perceived appeasement of the Russian government, which had supplied the Abkhazians with military hardware and personnel, was particularly divisive, leading to bitter opposition. Inevitably, war also denuded civil liberties, increased secrecy, and reduced accountability. Shevardnadze was forced to introduce curfews and states of emergency in numerous parts of the country.

But the war produced one positive result. It created a sense of realism, an understanding that patriotism was not enough, that the country's problems could not be solved by Western powers and that Georgia's political and economic stability could not be achieved without a *modus vivendi* with Russia. But should the government fail to achieve moderate success in the peace negotiations with Abkhazia (which in 1995 still looked unlikely) or in the economy, then this pragmatism will turn to deeper despair, making the construction of a popularly supported democracy even more difficult.

## The Shevardnadze factor

Shevardnadze's priority on his return to Georgia was to promote conciliation among a polarized Georgian population and between Georgians and their minorities. Despite the war in Abkhazia and the brief civil war, he has stemmed Georgia's mutinies with policies of political balance and inclusion, caution, and, when necessary, no policies at all.[74] While this has preserved the state, no doubt a priority for Shevardnadze and all Georgians, it has had negative side effects, from economic stagnation and corruption at all levels to widespread popular cynicism and ineffective state building.

It is impossible to explain here the multiple pressures and forces Shevardnadze must deal with to maintain his authority, but his most surprising failure – given his reputation as a reformer and "new thinker" – has been his passivity in the field of economic and political reform. He faced considerable constraints, such as the need to deal with powerful paramilitary leaders, secessionist and civil wars, institutional atrophy, and an unimaginable economic crisis. Yet there were policy choices which he refused to consider or simply postponed. This applies in particular to personnel and economic decisions. In the two and a half years since coming to power, Shevardnadze's adherence to the principle of balance between opposing political forces and loyalty to discredited colleagues has stalled reform, perpetuated the disintegration of institutional power, and undermined his credibility. Shevardnadze skillfully manipulated political rivals Kitovani and Ioseliani and has secured regional and political bases through the appointment of officials such as Prime Minister Otar Pacacia and Vice Premier Avtandil Margiani, representatives of powerful Mingrelian and Svan lobbies repectively.[75] But the cost has been the alienation of reformers in parliament and a disunited cabinet of rivals chosen for their political bases rather than competence. This encouragement of personal power over institutional process is reinforced by Shevardnadze's reliance on a prefecture system in the regions.

Shevardnadze's response to criticism of his personnel decisions has led him to defend politicians long after their policies or personal behaviour, including suspected embezzlement, have discredited them. Thus Shevardnadze defended Tengiz Sigua and his cabinet when its economic incompetence and moral improbity was apparent to all (Sigua's cabinet finally resigned in August 1993). Shevardnadze's current defense of Jaba Ioseliani, including the latter's appointment to a commission to fight corruption in the autumn of 1994, has led to incredulity among the population, aware of his close links to the economic mafias that currently dominate Georgia's economy. Shevardnadze's appointments to the cabinet left economic reformers in a permanent minority. Vice Premier Roman Gociridze who was responsible for economic reform in Tengiz Sigua's cabinet was isolated, and Vice Premier Temur Basilia, his counterpart in the current cabinet led by Otar Pacacia, is similarly powerless against a conservative cabinet and unreformed ministries.

The absence of economic reformers in the government and Shevardnadze's own passivity toward economic reform has contributed to popular skepticism about the efficacy of market reform. Despite a legislative reform base, including laws on entrepreneurship, investment, privatization, tax collection, and land ownership which have been passed under Shevardnadze, there has been practically no implementation. Privatization has been primarily "spontaneous" at the lower levels of the retail and trade industries, or disorganized and damaging to economic improvements, as in the countryside.[76] Until the summer of 1994, Shevardnadze supported the soft credit policies of former president of the National Bank Demur Dvalishvili, who was replaced in August 1993 after accusations of bribery. Such policies led to calamitous inflation and all its corollaries, from worthless salaries and pauperization to absent revenues and massive budget deficits. The lack of economic reform from Shevardnadze led the mayor of Kutaisi, Tamar Shashiashvili, to introduce his own reform program for western Georgia, although it is difficult to see how it could succeed without macroeconomic change coordinated by the center.

In the summer of 1994, a series of decrees, economic summits and a change in Shevardnadze's tone suggest that in conjunction with a crackdown on economic crime, he is beginning to respond to the financial crisis.[77] This is in part due to the depth of the economic disaster, Shevardnadze's own growing unpopularity, and powerful pressures from international financial organizations such as the European Union, World Bank and IMF. Georgia's dependence on foreign aid to feed its population and the danger of being swallowed up by the Russian ruble economy has left Shevardnadze little choice. But despite Shevardnadze's support for a series of radical decrees in August 1994 for the liberalization of prices, the legalization of "hidden" privatization, an end to subsidies of non-profitable enterprises, administrative cuts, and banking and welfare reform, questions about its implementation have been raised by reformers within Georgia, including Vice Premier Basilia, the minister responsible for reform.

# Conclusion

Georgia's experience since independence in 1991 illustrates many of the problems evident in other post-totalitarian societies. It shows that free elections do not always produce democracy, that there are subtler factors – historical, structural and psychological – that determine its success or failure. Georgia's authoritarian experience was not inevitable. The legacy of statism, the popular distrust of institutions, and the lack of a legal culture, were not insurmountable obstacles. There were alternative strategies that might have ensured a less bloody transition. As Guiseppe Di Palma has so elegantly phrased it, "crafting" a democracy is possible even in the most difficult of situations. It is now up to Shevardnadze and his government to devise the alternative strategies Gamsakhurdia so emphatically rejected. The experience so far is mixed, and even Shevardnadze's own realization that accommodation and incorporation are the premises on which all democracies are built may not be enough to secure it.

## Notes

The author would like to thank Professor Edwina Cruise and Dr. Tatuna Grdzelidze for their comments and suggestions on a previous draft of this article.

1 For discussion of the problems faced by ex-communist regimes in the transition to democratic change, see Guiseppe Di Palma, *To Craft Democracies: An Essay on Democratic Transitions* and the series of articles in *World Politics*, 44, no. 1 (October 1991), devoted to "Liberalization and Democratization in the Soviet Union and Eastern Europe." The theoretical context of this article draws much from both these sources.

2 Di Palma, *To Craft Democracies*.

3 See the interview with Andrei Sakharov in *Ogonek*, no. 31, 1989, p. 27.

4 Georgia declared its independence on May 26, 1918 after brief participation in a Democratic Federal Republic of Transcaucasia from April 1918. For a short outline of this period, see Stephen F. Jones, "Transcaucasia: Revolution and Civil War," in H. Shukman (ed.), *The Blackwell Encyclopedia of the Russian Revolution* (Oxford: Basil Blackwell, 1988), pp. 232–239. See also Firuz Kazamzadeh, *The Struggle for Transcaucasia (1917–1921)* (Oxford: George Ronald, 1951).

5 For the national breakdown in Georgia during this period, (1897 census figures) see V. Jaoshvili, *Sakartvelos mosakhleoba XVIII–XX saukuneebshi* (Mecniereba, Tbilisi, 1984), p. 112. Abkhazia was formally granted autonomy in February 1921, on the eve of the collapse of the Georgian republic. The Abkhazian National Soviet had only limited opportunities of self-rule before then.

6 The most significant in Ossetian districts were in March 1918, December 1919, and June 1920. In Abkhazian districts, the National Guard was constantly involved in suppressing nascent revolts, particularly in the spring and summer of 1918.

7 For the Ossetian point of view, see *Osetino-Russkaia tema etnoperestroechnykh urokov*, (No publisher) Pichidzhen, 1991. See especially pp. 38–41. The Georgian view of Georgian-Ossetian relations is expressed in A. Menteshashvili *Iz istorii vzaimootnoshenii Gruzinskogo, Abkhazskogo i Osetinskogo narodov*: (Tbilisi: Znanie, 1990), pp. 65–80.

8 See for example *Sakartvelos Respublik'a* No 40, 2.28.91., p. 4; No 41, 3.1.91., p. 4.

9 In fact, the Abkhazian republic was intitially granted "treaty status" in 1921 as an

independent republic associated with Georgia. Its change of status in 1931 represented a demotion.

10 See Darrell Slider "Crisis and Response in Soviet Nationality Policy: the Case of Abxazia," *Central Asian Survey*, Vol. 4, No. 4, 1985, pp. 51–68.

11 *Ibid.* and Elizabeth Fuller "The Azeris in Georgia and the Ingilos: Ethnic Minorities in the Limelight," *Central Asian Survey*, Vol. 3, No. 2, 1984, pp. 75–86. See also her "Marneuli: Georgia's Potential Nagorno-Karabagh?," Radio Liberty, *Report on the USSR*, 477/88, pp. 1–5.

12 Elizabeth Fuller "Large-Scale Measures to Improve the Teaching of the Georgian Language," *Radio Liberty Research*, 157/80, p. 2. See also *Kommunisticheskaia partiia Gruzii v rezoliutsiiakh i resheniiakh s"ezdov, konferentsii i plenumov Ts.K.*, Vol. 4 (1972–80), Sabchota Sakartvelo, Tbilisi, 1980, pp. 898–901.

13 Slider, *ibid.* See also Elizabeth Fuller "Kapitonov on Nationality Relations in Georgia," *Radio Liberty Research*, 125/78, pp. 1–5 and *Kommunisticheskaia partiia Gruzii*, ibid. pp. 795–804, 881–886, 888–891.

14 Extracts from these disputes in the 1950s and 1960s are included in *Mat'iane*, Tbilisi, 1989, pp. 3–49. *Mat'iane* was the journal of the Georgian Helsinki Group led by Zviad Gamsaxurdia, and is biased. It contains a section from Georgian historian Pavle Ingoroqva's book *Georgi Merchule* published in 1954, which suggests Abkhazians have been in the region for only 300 years. Abkhazians claim they have been there two millenia.

15 Slider, *ibid.* See also Ronald G. Suny "Georgia and Soviet Nationality Policy" in Stephen Cohen, Alexander Rabinowitch and Robert Sharlet (eds.), *The Soviet Union Since Stalin*, (London: Macmillan, 1980), pp. 200–226.

16 Slider, *ibid.*

17 Ann Sheehy "The National Languages and the New Constitutions of the Transcaucasian Republics," *Radio Liberty Research*, 97/78, pp. 1–12; Elizabeth Fuller "Manifestations of Nationalism in Current Georgian-Language Literature," *Radio Liberty Research*, 106/80, pp. 1–6; *idem.* "Eduard Shevardnadze Speaks on Recent Achievements in Georgian Literature and on the State of the Georgian Language," *Radio Liberty Research*, 146/80, pp. 1–2.

18 See, for example the programs of the National Democratic Party ([Paris], *Gouchagi*, No 18. 1989, pp. 33–37) and the program of the Georgian Union for National Justice (Tbilisi: *Uc'xebani*, No. 1, October 1988).

19 *Komunisti*, November 3, 1988, pp. 2–3. A later version was published in August 1989 which added the language requirement. I have not been able to obtain a copy of the second version, but was informed of the new stipulation by a reliable informant.

20 For the Georgian History state program, see *Komunisti*, 2.7.89, pp. 2–3; the law on immigration is in *Komunisti*, 26 November, 1989, p. 1.

21 Those parties which attained seats in the new Georgian Supreme Soviet elected in October 1990, were as follows:

| | |
|---|---|
| Round Table-Free Georgia Bloc | 155 deputies (53.95 percent) |
| Georgian communist party | 64 deputies (29.57 percent) |
| Georgian Popular Front | 12 deputies (1.93 percent) |
| Democratic Georgia | 4 deputies (1.65 percent) |
| All-Georgian Rust'aveli Society | 1 deputy (2.32 percent) |
| Liberation and Economic Rebirth | 1 deputy (1.46 percent) |
| Independents | 9 deputies |

The remaining parties, which shared the rest of the vote between them, failed to receive any seats. In Abkhazian and Ossetian districts, there was a boycott or very low turnout. The Georgian Communist Party did particularly well in the southern periphery in Armenian and Azeri districts, and in the rural districts of Ajaria. For full details on the election results, see *Axali Sakartvelo*, 11.16.90, p. 3, and *Zaria Vostoka*, November 9 and November 14, 1990.

22 Numerous examples of this view can be found in the speeches of President Gamsakhurdia. See, for example, his speech justifying the abolition of South Ossetia's regional autonomy in *Sakartvelos Republika*, December 12, 1990, p. 1,4.

23 In 1989, there were 164,000 Ossetians in Georgia. Sixty five thousand of them lived in South Ossetia. Reports have suggested 50,000 to 100,000 refugees. These numbers may include Georgians and Ossetians outside South Ossetia, but it is likely that the largest proportion are Ossetians from South Ossetia. On refugee estimates, see *Foreign Broadcast Information Service Daily Report: Soviet Union* (henceforth FBIS-SOV), 91–214, p. 71 and 91–217, p. 73.

24 "Avars Leave Georgia," *Moscow News*, No. 21, (May 26-June 2), 1991, p. 4.

25 See Guram Svanidze, *Spravka o rezul'tax sotsiologicheskogo issledovaniia obshchestvennogo mneniia naseleniia g. Tbilisi ob emigratsii i prichinax ee obuslavlivaioshchix*, (Tbilisi: Caucasian Institute for Peace, Democracy, and Development, 1994), Svanidze cites figures suggesting that voluntary emigration from Georgia was 59,000 in 1990, 75,000 in 1992 and 50,000 in the first half of 1993. In 1992, 50 percent of those emigrating were Russian.

26 For reports on Abkhazian events, see *Current Digest of the Soviet Press* (henceforth CDSP), XLI, No. 29, 1989, pp. 14–16. See also *Komunisti*, July 18, 1989, pp. 1–3 and July 19, 1989, p. 3.

27 For a review of the events in South Ossetia, see Elizabeth Fuller "The South Ossetian Campaign for Unification," *Report on the USSR*, No. 49, 1989, pp. 17–20, and *idem.* "South Ossetia: Analysis of a Permanent Crisis," *Report on the USSR*, No. 7, 1991, pp. 20–22.

28 The "Law on Introducing Changes into the Abkhazian ASSR Law on Electing Deputies to the Abkhazian ASSR Supreme Soviet," which was introduced in August 1991, guaranteed ethnic quotas in parliament, with each ethnic group voting for its own "ethnic" deputies. The elected posts in the Supreme Soviet were also ethnically reserved, *Svobodnaya Gruziya*, 31 August 1991 (trans. in *FBIS-SOV*, 91–176, p. 80) and 12 September 1991 (trans. in *FBIS-SOV*, 91–186, pp. 59–60). For a discussion of the similarities with the Lebanese system, see Donald Horowitz "Ethnic Conflict Management for Policymakers" in Joseph Montville (ed.) *Conflict and Peacemaking in Multiethnic Societies*, (Lexington Books, 1989), p. 126.

29 See chapters 7 and 8 in *Sakartvelos respublik'is k'onst'it'ucia* as amended until October 1991. (no publisher, pp. 63). The author has a copy.

30 For an English translation of the program, see "The Election Block (sic) 'Round-Table Free Georgia,' Political Platform." The author has a copy.

31 For a report on the conduct and result of the elections, see *Report on the Supreme Soviet Election in Georgia*, November, 1990. Prepared by the Staff of the U.S. Commission on Security and Cooperation in Europe.

32 For the cabinet appointees and their backgrounds, see *Zaria Vostoka*, 11.23.90, p. 2.

33 For these early laws and amendments, see Akhali Sakartvelo, Nos. 2 (15 November), 4 (16 November), 7 (22 November), 1990.

34 Robert A. Dahl *Polyarchy and Oppostion: Participation and Opposition*, (New Haven: Yale University Press 1971), p. 208.

35 Di Palma, *To Craft Democracies* ... p. 3.

36 Benedict Anderson *Imagined Communities: Reflections of the Origin and Spread of Nationalism*, (rev. ed.), London and New York, Verso, 1991, p. 160. The Yakovlev quotation is cited in Julie Wishnevsky "Russia: Liberal Media Criticize Democrats in Power" in *RFE/RL Research Report*, Vol. 1, No. 2, p. 6, 1992.

37 Benedict Anderson notes that "even the most determinedly radical revolutionaries always, to some degree, inherit the state from the fallen regime." *ibid.* p. 159.

38 *Sakartvelos respublik'is k'onst'it'ucia*, Chs. 21 and 22. See also *Sakartvelos Respublik'a*, No. 19, 29 December, 1990, p. 3.

39 For the draft law on the status of deputies, see *Sakartvelos Respublik'a*, No. 16, 25 December, 1990, p. 1. For the law on political associations, see *Sakartvelos Respublik'a*, No. 160, 14 August, 1991, p. 4. For the draft law on the press, which was passed on 30 August 1990 almost unchanged, see *Sakartvelos Respublik'a*, No. 20, December 30, 1990, p. 1.

40 See, for example, *Sakartvelos Respublik'a*, Nos 155–156 (8 August), 181 (18 September), 211 (30 October), and 214–215 (2 November) 1991, for laws on privatization and demonopolization.

41 *Sakartvelos Respublik'a*, No. 160, 14 August, 1990, p. 4. and *ibid.*, No. 20, December 30, 1990, p. 1.

42 *Sakartvelos respublik'is k'onst'it'ucia*, Chs. 5 and 6, pp. 10–19.

43 For the powers of the prefects, see *ibid.*, Chs. 17 and 188, pp. 51–53. See also *Sakartvelos Respublik'a*, No. 24 (5 February) 1991, p. 3.

44 *Sakartvelos respublik'is k'onst'it'ucia*, Ch. 13 pp. 40–45. See also *Sakartvelos Respublik'a*, No. 90, 16 April, 1991, p. 1.

45 For more detailed discussion of these groups and the National Congress, see Stephen F. Jones "Glasnost, Perestroika, and the Georgian Soviet Socialist Republic," in *Armenian Review*, Summer/Autumn 1990, Vol. 43, Nos. 2–3, pp. 127–152.

46 For Gamsakhurdia's derisory assessment of Georgian intellectuals, see his press conference, reported in *Sakartvelos Respublik'a*, No. 38, 26 February, 1991, p. 1.

47 For Gamsakhurdia's response to the August coup before its outcome was clear, see *Sakartvelos Respublik'a*, No. 163, 21 August, 1991, p. 1. Although not forceful and aggressive in his condemnation of the coup leaders, Gamsakhurdia appealed to the West to support the forces of democracy in the USSR, and in particular, to help the republics threatened by "military aggression." The National Guard was demoted from its independent status and placed under the control of the Georgian Ministry of Interior.

48 Dahl's first axiom on successful democratization was that "the liklihood that a government will tolerate an opposition increases as the expected costs of toleration decrease." Gamsakhurdia viewed the oppostion as fragmented and powerless. The costs of its suppression initially looked like a good risk. Dahl, *ibid.*, p. 15.

49 For the Presidential election results, see *Komsomolskaya Pravda*, 14 August 1991 (trans. in *FBIS-SOV*, 91–159, p. 48).

50 For discussion of this point, see Di Palma, *ibid.*, pp. 40–43.

51 *Izvestiya*, 10 September 1991 (trans. in *FBIS-SOV*, 91–176, p. 77).

52 For a report of this highly revealing meeting, in which members of the university community in particular, condemned the new "atmosphere of fear" created by the government, see *Tavisupali Sakartvelo*, 22 March, 1991, p. 2.

53 See *Gruziya spektr*, No. 19, 9–15 September 1991; *Izvestiya*, 12 September 1991 (trans. in *FBIS-SOV*, 91–177, p. 88–90, 93); FBIS-SOV 91–178, p. 93; 91–204, p. 70; 91–181, pp. 75–77. Tengiz Sigua, in an interview in mid-November, suggested two government emissaries were sent to Moscow on the eve of the coup to make a deal with the leaders (*Gouchagi*, Paris, No. 26, December 1991, pp. 15–16). I am grateful to Tatiuna Grdzelidze for the information about TV programming.

54 *Sakartvelos Respublik'a*, No 194, 5 October, 1991, p. 4.

55 *FBIS-SOV*, 91–174, p. 89; 91–175, p. 93; 91–190, pp. 66–67.

56 *FBIS-SOV*, 91–214, p. 72; 91–186, p. 59. *Sakartvelos Respublik'a*, No. 185, 24 September, 1991, p. 1.

57 *Sakartvelos Respublik'a*, No.213, 1 November, 1991, p. 1.

58 Stephen F. Jones "Populism in Georgia: the Gamsaxurdia Phenomenon," Donald Schwartz and Razmik Panossian (eds.), *Nationalism and History: the Politics of Nation*

Building in Post-Soviet Armenia, Azerbaijan and Georgia, (Toronto: University of Toronto Center for Russian and East European Studies, 1994).

59 *FBIS-SOV*, 91–007, p. 82.

60 For a biography of Gamsakhurdia, see *Sakartvelos Respublik'a*, No. 89, 8 May, 1991, p. 1.

61 *Sakartvelos Respublik'a*, No. 51, 15 March, 1991, p. 2.

62 *Samshoblo*, No. 22, November 1990, pp. 4–5.

63 *Svobodnaya Gruziya*, 19 September 1991 (trans. in *FBIS-SOV*, 91–191, p. 78; 91–196, pp. 66–67). For the ultimate expression of this paranoia, see the government declaration of September 25, "Message to the Georgian People and to the States and Peoples of the World," which names film directors, journalists and political leaders in Tbilisi and Moscow as members of an anti-government plot. This declaration, which was rejected by the majority of Gamsakhurdia's own parliamentary followers, was probably the first step in Gamsakhurdia's plan to launch mass arrests among the opposition. See *Sakartvelos Respublik'a*, No. 186, 25 September, 1991, p. 1.

64 See *Svobodnaya Gruziya*, 11 October 1991 (trans. in *FBIS-SOV*, 91–205, pp. 66–69).

65 This is an argument also put forward by Professor Ghia Nodia of the University of Tbilisi. See his "The Political Crisis in the Republic of Georgia" presented at the Kennan Institute, Washington, October 25, 1991.

66 Boris Yeltsin *Boris Yeltsin. The Struggle For Russia*, (Trans. Catherine A. Fitzpatrick), (New York: Random House, 1992), p. 158.

67 For these laws see *Svobodnaia Gruziia, 15 August 1992 and Sakartvelos parlament'is ucqebani* (Tbilisi), No. 1, 1992, pp. 24–36 and 7–23 respectively.

68 For an account of Shevardnadze's relationship to the legislature, see Stephen Jones "Georgia's Power Structures," *Radio Free Europe-Radio Liberty Research Report* (henceforth *RFE-RL*), Vol. 2, No. 39, 1 October 1993, pp. 5–9.

69 For example, in September 1993, Ioseliani publically accused Shevardnadze of accumulating dictatorial powers, which led briefly to Shevardnadze's resignation.

70 For an assessment of Russian involvement in the Abkhazian drive for secession, see Thomas Goltz "Letter from Eurasia: the Hidden Russian Hand," *Foreign Policy*, No. 92, Fall 1993, pp. 92–116; S.M. Chervonnaia *Abkhaziia-1992: Postkommunisticheskaia Vandeiia* Mosgopechat'. Moscow, 1993; and Catherine Dale "Turmoil in Abxazia: Russian Responses," *RFE-RL*, Vol. 2, No. 34, 27 August 1993, pp. 48–57.

71 For an account of the Georgian economy in 1992 in English, see *Georgia: a Blueprint for Reforms*, (Washington D.C.: The World Bank, 1993). There are also monthly reports in English on the state of the Georgian economy in *The Georgian Chronicle*, a publication of the Caucasian Institute for Peace, Democracy and Development (CIPDD), based in Tbilisi. Reports are available by electronic mail (cipdd@cipdd.ge).

72 For example, instead of the 20,000 remaining Russian troops leaving unconditionally by 1995 as was originally agreed in May 1993, the October agreement permitted Russia to keep three military bases, have joint use of all Georgia's ports and airfields, and help patrol Georgia's borders.

73 Kote Gabashvili used this expression in an interview with me in July 1993. Gabashvili was appointed Ambassador to Germany in October 1993.

74 For discussion of Shevardnadze's policies toward Georgia's national minorities, see Stephen F. Jones, "The Unbearable Freedom: Georgia on the Precipice," *Armenian International Magazine*, October 1993, pp. 16–21.

75 The Svans, like the Mingrelians, have their own language and a strong regional identity. The Svans live in the mountainous regions of north Georgia and in the last few years have acquired a reputation for banditry.

76 See, for example, "Legal, Financial and Institutional Organization of Agriculture: Synthesis of Observations on the Georgian Agricultural Crisis," (Draft report

November 1992–July 1993), Commission of the European Communities (TACIS). In 1993, of 762 state facilities privatized, only 18 were manufacturing units. Five hundred and sixty six were trade facilities. Cited in *The Georgian Chronicle*, February-March, 1994, p. 15.

77 See *The Georgian Chronicle*, Vol 3, Nos. 5 (May), 7 (July) and 8 (August), 1994 for details of these new laws and decrees.

# Georgia: chronology of events

*December 1988*

A draft State Program for the Georgian Language is published. The program calls for a Georgian-language test for entry into higher education.

*March 1989*

19  30,000 signatures are gathered for a petition demanding that Abkhazia be granted the status of a full Union republic (the status it enjoyed from 1921–1930).

*April 1989*

9  At least 20 people are killed and 200 wounded in Tbilisi when a peaceful pro-independence demonstration is forcibly broken up by Army and MVD troops. Attempts are made to distance Gorbachev from the massacre, leading to the replacement of Georgia's party secretary and premier.

23  2,000 members of the Democratic Union rally in Moscow to protest the killings in Tbilisi; forty-seven are arrested.

*July 1989*

15–17  Interethnic clashes resulting in more than 15 deaths ensue following an attempt by Georgians to establish a branch of Tbilisi State University in Sukhumi (in the Abkhaz ASSR).

24  20,000 Georgians march for independence in Tbilisi.

*October 1989*

14  Prominent dissident Merab Kostava dies in a car accident, leaving Zviad Gamsakhurdia the most popular leader of the nationalist movement.

*March 1990*

20  Elections to the Supreme Soviet are postponed until September to allow time for opposition parties to take part.

*April 1990*

9  200,000 rally in Tbilisi to press for independence and to protest the April 1989 massacre.

*August 1990*

25  The Abkhaz Supreme Soviet (with ethnic Georgian delegates boycotting the session) declares the ASSR to be a sovereign

republic, independent from Georgia. The Georgian Supreme Soviet annuls the declaration.

The opposition (but anti-Gamskhurdia) National Congress is founded and is dominated by the National Democratic Party (of Gia Chanturia) and the National Independence Party (led by Irakli Tsereteli).

### September 1990

20    The South Ossetian soviet declares the region to be a sovereign republic. The Supreme Soviet insists that the declaration is invalid.

30    Unofficial elections are held to the alternative National Congress, with the greatest number of votes won by the National Independence Party. Turnout is estimated at over 50 percent.

### October 1990

28    In parliamentary elections, Zviad Gamsakhurdia's Round Table-Free Georgia bloc receive 54 percent of the vote and 155 of 250 seats, followed by the Communist Party with 30 percent (64 seats). Third-place Popular Front takes only 2 percent (12 seats). Several Abkhazian and South Ossetian districts boycott the election.

### November 1990

15    Tengiz Sigua, former director of the Metallurgy Institute in Tbilisi and Chairman of the moderate Rustaveli society, is elected prime minister.

### December 1990

Vladislav Ardzinba is elected chairman of the Abkhaz Supreme Soviet.

9    South Ossetia holds elections to form a regional parliament.

10    The South Ossetian parliament votes to withdraw from Georgia and declare sovereignty for the region.

11    Parliament abolishes the autonomous status of the South Ossetian region and its parliament. The parliament continues to operate illegally.

### January 1991

20    Two Georgian policemen are killed, in a shootout in South Ossetia.

### February 1991

19    The paramilitary organization *Mkhedrioni*, associated with the National Congress, is forcibly disbanded and its leader Jaba Ioseliani is imprisoned without trial a day after

denouncing Gamsakhurdia and vowing to establish another party.

23–24  Six more Georgians are killed in South Ossetia.

*March 1991*

17  Georgia boycotts the referendum on preserving the Soviet Union. Abkhazia allows it to proceed: 52 percent of voters participate, 99 percent vote in favor of the USSR.

30  In a referendum on independence, 98 percent vote for secession.

South Ossetian extremists burn four Georgians to death.

*April 1991*

9  In line with the 30 March referendum, parliament issues a declaration of independence.

*May 1991*

Georgians kill seven in South Ossetia.

26  Zviad Gamsakhurdia is elected president with 87 percent of the vote. No voting is held in South Ossetia or Abkhazia.

*July 1991*

5  A law on citizenship is adopted which provides automatic citizenship to residents who have lived in Georgia for 10 years and who have a command of the Georgian language.

*August 1991*

64 Communist deputies are expelled from the Supreme Soviet.

18  Sigua is forced to resign when he is blamed for Georgia's poor economic conditions.

*September 1991*

2  Militia fire upon anti-government demonstrators. Television coverage is not allowed.

6  A number of former Gamsakhurdia allies form Charter '91, which counts at least 49 deputies as members.

23  Gamsakhurdia establishes a national security council, bans most independent political associations, and declares a state of emergency.

16  10,000 rally in Tbilisi to demand Gamsakhurdia's resignation.

25  Gamsakhurdia issues a declaration in which he names a number of prominent media and political figures as members of an anti-government plot.

29  Elections are held to the Abkhaz Supreme Soviet. Second-round elections are held on 13 October and 1 December.

*October 1991*

6    In clashes between pro- and anti-government protestors, 2 die and 74 are injured.

30    Parliament rejects Georgian participation in the new treaty on economic union.

*December 1991*

20–21    10,000 demonstrate to demand Gamsakhurdia's resignation.

21    The South Ossetian Supreme Soviet declares the republic independent from Georgia.

22–23    Fighting breaks out between loyal government troops and the rebel National Guard.

*January 1992*

2    The opposition forms a Military Council and declares that they have assumed power. Tengiz Sigua, forced to resign as Prime Minister in August, is reappointed to the position.

3    Several deaths occur when Gamsakhurdia supporters are fired upon by Military Council militia.

6    Gamsakhurdia flees Georgia.

15–16    Gamsakhurdia returns to Georgia and heads towards Tbilisi with armed followers.

17–27    Gamsakhurdia followers battle Military Council forces in numerous towns.

19    99 percent of South Ossetian voters choose in a referendum to secede from Georgia and reunite with North Ossetia.

24    A state of emergency is declared in Abkhazia.

30    Abkhazian parliament debates the possibility of secession. Several thousand rally in Tbilisi in support of Gamsakhurdia.

*February 1992*

2    Gamsakhurdia loyalists clash with Military Council supporters in Tbilisi.

6    Sukhumi, the last Gamsakhurdia outpost, is taken by Military Council forces.

*March 1992*

10    Military Council transfers power to a State Council, to be led by Eduard Shevardnadze, who returned to Georgia on 7 March.

12    Parliament convenes in Grozny and is addressed by Gamsakhurdia, who denounces the State Council as illegal.

*April 1992*

1–2    Clashes between government forces and Gamsakhurdia supporters in Poti result in the deaths of 13.

9    A rally to commemorate the third anniversary of the killing

of demonstrators by Soviet troops turns into a protest calling for the State Council's resignation and CIS troop withdrawal.

16  The South Ossetian parliament asks to be placed under Russian sovereignty.

*June 1992*

24  An attempted coup by Gamsakhurdia loyalists is put down by security forces.

*July 1992*

14  Russian and Georgian peacekeeping troops are deployed along the border with South Ossetia.

23  With 35 (of 65) deputies voting in favor, the Abkhazian parliament reinstates the 1925 Constitution declaring the republic to be a sovereign state.

25  The State Council declares the Abkhaz declaration invalid.

*August 1992*

4  The state of emergency is lifted and an amnesty for supporters of Gamsakhurdia is called.

11  Interior Minister Gventsadze and 11 other officials are kidnapped by Gamsakhurdian loyalists and held in Abkhazia. 3,000 National Guard troops, led by Tengiz Kitovani, pour into Abkhazia to prevent the kidnappers' escape.

14–15  Abkhaz Interior Ministry troops open fire on National Guard units, killing up to 50. The Abkhaz government declares the Georgian troop movement to be an illegal "occupation." The Georgian troops withdraw.

18  The National Guard reenters Sukhumi and launches an attack on the Abkhaz parliament building. 5 people are killed.

22  The Confederation of Mountain Peoples of the Caucasus calls upon its members to send volunteers to defend Abkhazia's sovereignty.

25–26  Another 50 die in skirmishes between Abkhaz and Georgian militia. Fighting continues through September.

*September 1992*

10  Six members of the National Democratic Party are kidnapped by Gamsakhurdia supporters in Western Georgia.

*October 1992*

1–6  Abkhaz guerillas retake almost half of Abkhazian territory. The Russian military is accused of arming and assisting

Abkhazian forces. Fighting in Abkhazia continues throughout the month.

11    In popular elections, Shevardnadze is elected chairman of parliament (there is no presidential post) with 90 percent of the votes. He subsequently forms the State Defense Council to rule the country. 10 percent of the population does not participate as no voting takes place in nine regions in Abkhazia, South Ossetia, and western Georgia. Elections to parliament are held simultaneously. The *Mshvidoba* (Peace) bloc comprised of former communists receives the most seats with 29, followed by the 11 October bloc (18).

*November 1992*

21    The political movement "Citizens' Union" holds its founding congress with Shevardnadze as its chairman. The movement calls for a reassertion of control over Abkhazia and rapid economic reform.

*January 1993*

29    The government asks the United Nations to send peacekeeping forces to Abkhazia.

*March 1993*

11    Parliament passes a Law on Citizenship, which grants universal citizenship to residents of Georgia. Knowledge of Georgian is not a prerequisite. As well, Abkhaz is made a second state language in Abkhazia.

17    Georgian troops repel an Abkhaz attack on Sukhumi. The government reiterates accusations of Russian involvement.

26    Faced with ruble shortages, parliament elects to introduce parallel coupons.

*April 1993*

9    Several thousand Gamsakhurdia supporters hold a demonstration in Tbilisi on the anniversary of the 1989 suppression of a pro-independence rally.

*May 1993*

6    Tengiz Kitovani is removed from his post as Defense Minister.

11    10 die in an attack on a Russian army base by Mkhedrioni members seeking arms after Shevardnadze suspends the Defense Council, of which Mkhedrioni head Ioseliani had been a prominent member.

17    Agreement is reached with Russia on the withdrawal of 20,000 Russian troops by 1996.

*July 1993*

1   An Abkhaz offensive on Sukhumi results in at least 30 deaths. The Defense Ministry asserts that 2,000 Russian soldiers entered Abkhazia overnight.

6   Shevardnadze declares martial law in Abkhazia.

21   United Nations endorses the use of Russian peacekeeping forces in Abkhazia.

*August 1993*

2   Georgia withdraws from the ruble zone, making the coupon sole legal tender (to eventually be replaced by the *lari*).

6   Prime Minister Tengiz Sigua and his cabinet resign following a no-confidence vote in Parliament. Shevardnadze is appointed interim prime minister and given two weeks to form a cabinet.

20   Otar Patsatsia is elected Prime Minister by a vote of 126–17 (with 6 abstentions).

28   Gamsakhurdia supporters occupy three towns in western Georgia.

*September 1993*

2   62 deputies from the Gamsakhurdia parliament convene a shadow parliament.

14   Shevardnadze tenders his resignation but then stays in office after thousands rally in his support and the parliament grants him emergency powers and promises to suspend its activities for three months.

27   Sukhumi finally falls to Abkhazian troops. Zhiuli Shartava, the pro-Georgian Prime Minister of Abkhazia, is executed.

28   Having returned to Georgia, Gamsakhurdia calls upon Shevardnadze to resign.

30   Abkhazian troops occupy the last town in Abkhazia held by Georgian troops.

*October 1993*

2–29   Gamsakhurdia loyalists capture key towns in western Georgia.

8   Shevardnadze announces that Georgia will join the CIS, and signs a decree approving membership on the 22nd.

9   An agreement is signed which allows Russia to keep three military bases in Georgia, have joint use of all ports and airfields, and help patrol the country's border.

22–6   Georgian troops retake territory held by Gamsakhurdia forces.

*November 1993*

4   Russian troops land in western Georgia to defend against Gamsakhurdia forces.

30      Peace talks begin between Abkhazia and Georgia.

*January 1994*
5       It is announced that Gamsakhurdia is dead, presumably by
        suicide.

*February 1994*
10      The Abkhazian parliament declares the republic
        independent from Georgia.

*March 1994*
30      Parliamentary elections are held in South Ossetia, with 80
        percent voter turnout, but are not considered legal by the
        Georgian leadership. Second-round voting is scheduled for
        10 April.

*April 1994*
9       Thousands gather in Tbilisi on the five-year anniversary of
        the Soviet military intervention. Gamsakhurdia supporters
        hold a counter-demonstration.

*May 1994*
19      A prominent Gamsakhurdia supporter is arrested in Tbilisi
        and charged with treason, inciting interethnic conflict, and
        organizing armed resistance.
23      Seven parties which belonged to the pro-Gamsakhurdia
        Round Table/Free Georgia coalition announce the reentry of
        the coalition into politics.
25      34 political parties sign a declaration on National Accord
        and Unity.
26      On the anniversary of the 1918 declaration of
        independence, approximately 3,000 gather in Tbilisi to call
        for Georgia's withdrawal from the CIS, annulment of all
        agreements with Abkhazia, and the resignation of
        Shevardnadze. 1,000 Gamsakhurdia supporters gather in a
        separate rally.

*June 1994*
9       Yeltsin signs a decree on the deployment of peacekeeping
        forces in Abkhazia.

*July 1994*
10      An anti-government demonstration with 200,000
        participants is forcibly broken up.

*August 1994*
1       Irakli Tsereteli, head of the National Independence Party,
        ends a three-week hunger strike to demand Shevardnadze's

resignation after he receives a promise that an emergency parliamentary session would be held.

12   The emergency session is not held, as only 80 of 224 deputies are present (118 are needed).

*September 1994*

12   Two Russian peacekeepers are killed in Abkhazia by unknown assailants several days before the anticipated return of Georgian refugees to an Abkhazian-held district.

*November 1994*

26   The Abkhazian parliament elects parliamentary chairman Vladislav Ardzinba as the first president of the republic. Sokrat Dzhindzholia, former chairman of the Council of Ministers, is selected as the new chairman of parliament. Parliament also adopts a new constitution declaring Abkhazia to be a sovereign state and a subject of international law. The new constitution is condemned by Shevardnadze.

*December 1994*

3   Georgy Chanturia, the chairman of the National Democratic Party, is assassinated.

*Janurary 1995*

13   Deputies Tengis Kitovani (ex-Defense Minister and head of the National Liberation Front) and Tengiz Sigua (ex-Prime Minister) set off with about 1,000 supporters to "liberate" Abkhazia. They are halted by state militia and arrested.

# Part VI
## Central Asia

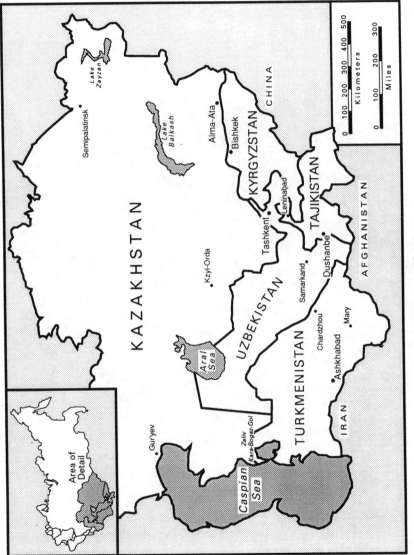

Map 15.1 Central Asia

# 15 Kazakhstan: pushing for Eurasia

MARTHA BRILL OLCOTT

## Introduction

For its first two years of independence, Kazakhstan celebrated December 16 as the Day of the Republic, to mark the date in 1991 when the collapse of the USSR left the republic with little choice but to take formal independence. That date was also important, for it commemorated the day in 1986 when riots had erupted in Almaty (then Alma-Ata), in some ways beginning the cycle of unrest which led to the failure of Gorbachev's government, and the collapse of the Soviet Union. By this calendar, then, Kazakhstan was approaching its fourth anniversary by the end of 1994.

However, in July 1994 the republic's legislature adopted a resolution moving the Day of the Republic to October 25, to mark the date in 1990 when Kazakhstan, still part of the USSR, first declared itself to be a sovereign republic.[1] As a consequence, Kazakhstan may now claim to be entering not its fifth year of existence as a state, but rather its sixth.

Small as it is, this shift of the national holiday is indicative of a number of changes which the republic is undergoing as the process of state-building continues, and the state begins to formulate *de facto* legitimacy, substantiating the *de jure* independence which Kazakhstan had forced upon it by the dissolution of the USSR. It also is a sign of greater official recognition of Russian sensitivities, as the 1986 disturbances that the December date commemorated had far more emotive meaning to Kazakhs than to Russians. At the same time, it also reflects a certain official nostalgia for the time when Kazakhstan had both the freedom of sovereignty and the security of being part of a larger whole, a condition to which President Nazarbaev, at least, would like very much to have his country return.

At the root of the republic's problems is the fact that Kazakhstan was the only Soviet republic in which the titular nationality was a minority population; according to the last Soviet census, taken in 1989, Kazakhs constituted 39.5 percent of the population, while Russians were 37.7 percent. Combined with the Ukrainians (5.4 percent) and the Belarusans (1.1 percent), the Slavs were 44.2 percent of Kazakhstan's population. When combined with the largely Russified Germans (5.8 percent), "Russian-speakers" formed a bare but absolute majority of the republic,[2] many of whom moreover are settled in nearly homogenous communities in the

Table 15.1. *Population of Kazakhstan, 1939–1994*

|  | 1939 | 1951 | 1961 | 1971 | 1981 | 1989 | 1994 |
|---|---|---|---|---|---|---|---|
| Population, in thousands | 6,094 | 6,813 | 10,236 | 13,211 | 15,053 | 16,536 | 16,870 |

*Sources: Natisional'nyi sostav naseleniya SSSR.* Finansy i statistika, Moscow, 1991; *Panorama*, 16 July 1994.

republic's north, hard against Russia's southern and Siberian cities. (See tables 12.1–12.3)

Although there has been a steady decline in the number of Russians and other non-Kazakhs, coupled both with a high Kazakh birthrate and government-sponsored settlement of "foreign" Kazakhs, most of them from Mongolia and China, demography still leaves the Kazakhs at a slight numeric disadvantage. Kazakhstan's official demographic projections indicate that by the end of 1994, Kazakhs will be 44.3 percent of the country, while Russians, Ukrainians, Belarusans and Germans will be 45.6 percent.[3]

For most of the Soviet period, Kazakhstan's leaders boasted of the republic's demographic variety, as an example of true Soviet multinationalism. The break-up of the USSR, and the failure of the Commonwealth of Independent States (CIS) to emerge as a transnational functional equivalent has increasingly made Kazakhstan's divided nature a liability, requiring that every aspect of statecraft become a delicate balancing act, avoiding offense to the ever-more skittish Russians while satisfying Kazakhs who are pressing for ever greater control of the republic's political, public, and – especially – economic affairs.

Kazakhstan's need for a larger multinational environment to guarantee stability has made Kazakhstan's President, Nursultan Nazarbaev, a consistent supporter of any political program which would continue some form of the old Soviet Union. Nazarbaev now says that the increasing disintegration of the USSR prompted him (and some other republic leaders) to propose reorganization of the USSR into a federation of sovereign states,

Table 15.2. *National Composition in Kazakhstan, 1926–1979*

|  | 1926 | 1939 | 1959 | 1970 |
|---|---|---|---|---|
| Kazakhs (%) | 57% | 38% | 30% | 36% |
| Russians (%) | 20% | 40% | 43% | 41% |
| Other (%) | 23% | 22% | 27% | 23% |

*Sources:* Derived from *Natisional'nyi sostav naseleniya SSSR.* Finansy i statistika, Moscow, 1991.

Table 15.3. *National composition of Kazakhstan, 1989–1994*

| Nationalities | 1989 | | 1994 | |
|---|---|---|---|---|
| | Population | in % | Population | in % |
| Total population in thousands | 16,536 | 100.0 | 16,870 | 100.0 |
| Kazakhs | 6,535 | 39.5 | 7,474 | 44.3 |
| Russians | 6,228 | 37.7 | 6,042 | 35.8 |
| Germans | 958 | 5.8 | 614 | 3.6 |
| Ukrainians | 896 | 5.4 | 857 | 5.1 |
| Uzbeks | 332 | 2.0 | 372 | 2.2 |
| Tatars | 328 | 2.0 | 331 | 2.0 |
| Belarusans | 183 | 1.1 | 178 | 1.1 |
| Azeris | 90 | .5 | 102 | .6 |
| Other | 986 | 6.0 | 900 | 5.3 |

*Sources:* Derived from *Kazakhstan b tsifrakh (kratkii statisticheskii sprovachnik).* Kazinformtsentr, goskomstata respubliki Kazakhstan, 1993 and *Panorama,* 16 July 1994, as cited in Ian Bremmer and Cory Welt, "The Trouble with Democracy in Kazakhstan," *Central Asian Survey,* forthcoming.

in December 1990, only to be rebuffed by Gorbachev.[4] When the August 1991 coup failed, it was Nazarbaev who introduced plans for a new "union" government to the Supreme Soviet of the USSR.[5] When it was clear that the USSR was dead, and the new Commonwealth of Independent States was announced as a sort of replacement, Nazarbaev embraced the new entity, thus sealing Gorbachev's fate. More recently, Nazarbaev was moved to propose the creation of a Eurasian Union, which would create a supranational government of member nations, headed by a Council of Presidents.[6] The response of other governments, however, was far from enthusiastic.

Although 1994 saw a steady rise in political demonstrations, as well as increasing reports of clashes between Kazakhs and members of other nationalities (mostly Cossacks), Kazakhstan has nevertheless managed to survive enormous political and economic upheavals in relative peace. This continued stability is largely due to the popularity of Nursultan Nazarbaev, head of Kazakhstan since June 1989, who satisfies Kazakh national pride because he is a Kazakh, but who also reassures Russians, because he was a prominent Soviet. The Russians also know that Nazarbaev is far more likely to be sympathetic to them than would be any possible successor, who would inevitably be Kazakh.

As "stretching" Kazakhstan's independent existence further into the past suggests, however, the search to find a basis of political legitimacy which is acceptable to both Kazakhs and Russians is growing more urgent, even as it becomes more difficult.

## Whose homeland?

As might be inferred from recent statistics, that 37.8 percent of the republic's Russians see Kazakhstan as their sole "motherland," while another 43.0 percent see it as one of their two "motherlands,"[7] Kazakhs and Russians share many goals for the republic's future. There was strong common support for Nazarbaev's economic program, introducing private property and a free market, just as both Russians and Kazakhs appear hesitant to sanction turning agriculture over exclusively to private cultivation. However, the question of whether Kazakhstan is to be a multinational society, an ethnic hybrid of Kazakhs and Russians, or a Kazakh homeland continues to bedevil domestic politics.

Much of the problem stems from the history of Kazakhstan's unification with Russia, which Kazakhs and Russians interpret differently. Although there were as many as 1.6 million Russian settlers in the region before the revolution,[8] 38 percent of the Russians now living in Kazakhstan were born elsewhere,[9] and the overwhelming majority of the rest are first- or second-generation descendants of Soviet-period settlers. The Russians still consider Kazakhstan, or at least its northern oblasts, to be a part of Russia, voluntarily ceded to the Russian Tsars by Kazakh Khans in return for Russia's protection.

Although they do not dispute the basic facts, that Abdul' Khayr, Khan of the Small Horde, swore an oath of loyalty to Empress Anna Ivanovna in 1731, and that Khan Ablai of the Middle Horde did the same in 1740,[10] Kazakh historians argue that the Khans intended these alliances to be for shortlived, strategic purposes.[11] Certainly, subsequent Russian relations with the Middle Horde (whose territory was found in northeastern Kazakhstan around the Irtysh river) bear out this interpretation. For forty years Khan Ablai was able to play the Russians and the Chinese off against one another, protecting his territory from invasion without fully sacrificing his sovereignty.

After Ablai's death, however, the Russians stretched a series of forts and Cossack outposts across Middle Horde territory. This first Russian expansion was achieved peacefully, but in the 1840s, when they moved further southward, into the remaining territory of the Middle Horde and that of the Great Horde, the Russians encountered considerable armed resistance, led by Ablai's grandson, Kenisary Qasimov. There was also fighting in the 1860s, when Russia used troops to annex territory in western Kazakhstan which belonged to the Small Horde. Kazakh historians now insist that this armed resistance is proof that their territory was conquered, and not voluntarily annexed.[12]

To local Russians, however, these same facts mean that Kazakhstan is understood as an extension of the Siberian frontier. The term "Kazakhstan," or land of the Kazakhs, was not used during the colonial period, when Kazakh territory was divided between two administrative districts, the Steppe region, and Turkestan, encompassing Semirech'e and Syr Darya. Colonial officials hoped that the land of these districts, and especially the Steppe, would help alleviate Russia's growing land problem. To that end they pursued an aggressive policy meant to achieve the settlement of the Kazakhs and other nomads, and so free up land for European homesteaders.

After the revolution, when the boundaries of the Kazakh republic were being drawn up, the northernmost part of the Steppe territory was attached to two Siberian oblasts, and the rest, plus most of the former *guberniias* of Syr Darya and Semirech'e, became an autonomous part of the Russian Federation (briefly as an autonomous oblast, then from 1924–1936 as an autonomous republic). Finally, in 1936, Kazakhstan was awarded full union republic status.

Most of Kazakhstan's non-Kazakh residents came to the republic during the Soviet period. Russians and Ukrainians came in two waves, as deported kulaks in the 1920s and 1930s, and as virgin lands "enthusiasts" in the 1950s. The kulaks were dispersed throughout the republic. The virgin lands settlers were dispatched to the six northern oblasts, where even today, non-Kazakhs still constitute up to 80 percent of the population.[13]

Kazakhstan also has a considerable population of other deported nationalities. Volga Germans, Crimean Tatars, and Koreans were all forcibly settled in the region just prior to and during World War II. In addition to these groups there are also indigenous minority communities, of which the Uzbeks, Dungans and Uighurs are the most numerous.[14]

The Kazakhs believe that this ethnic mix is continued proof that their colonial overlords, Russian and Soviet alike, followed deliberately discriminatory, even genocidal, policies, in order to render the Kazakhs a minority in their own republic. One of the first public statements of these complaints, made by Kazakh poet Olzhas Suleimenov at the First Congress of Peoples' Deputies in June 1989, remains among the most complete and forceful. Kazakhs were subjected to: forced settlement at the end of the nineteenth century; political repression on the eve of the revolution; famine during the civil war; near annihilation by Stalin in the 1930s; the final disruption of their traditional culture with the invention of the virgin lands in the 1950s; and finally, systematic poisoning of their environment by the Soviet military industrial complex over the forty year post-war period. These wrongs, Suleimenov stated, had cost four million Kazakhs their lives.[15]

## The Almaty uprising and the beginning of Moscow's end

The popularity and political skills of long-time republic leader Dinmukhammed Kunaev, a Kazakh, as well as ingrained caution bred of the Soviet experience, kept the Kazakhs silent about this deep sense of grievance until December 1986, when Kunaev was forced into retirement, replaced by Gennadi Kolbin, a Russian who had no previous connection to Kazakhstan.

The scale and nature of the disturbances which followed the announcement of this change have still not been completely revealed. Official press accounts at the time tried to dismiss the three days of protest as the work of disturbed and rowdy nationalist youth,[16] while Kazakh nationalists maintained, as they continue to do today, that a spontaneous but peaceful public demonstration turned violent because of official provocation.[17] Official sources claim two deaths, while unofficial estimates range from 58 to over 250.[18]

The impact of the disturbances on republic political life, however, are less disputed. Kolbin used the unrest as grounds to try to force out the rest of Kunaev's political organization. Although there was not a full-scale purge, many republic figures, especially in the educational system, were subjected to public criticism. The threat of dismissal and public disgrace inhibited any temptation most prominent Kazakhs might have had to demonstrate "Kunaev-like" leadership, meaning in practice that they avoided anything which might be construed as nationalist.

Olzhas Suleimenov, Kunaev's official nationalist gadfly,[19] who during the December riots had gone out onto Brezhnev Square (now Republic Square) to assure demonstrators that Kazakhstan's new leadership would protect their national rights,[20] was by January attacking the policies of his former protector. Even Nursultan Nazarbaev, then Chairman of the Council of Ministers, and so the republic's senior Kazakh politician, was sharply critical of Kunaev, his former mentor, implying that the Almaty riots were a violent outburst of destructive nationalism that grew naturally out of the corrupt leadership style of the Kunaev era.[21]

Although both men now depict their attitudes toward the December 1986 disturbances, and their actions during them, quite differently, it is clear that the anti-Kunaev crackdown, led by Kolbin but orchestrated in Moscow, made it impossible while Kolbin was in charge for Kazakhstan's leaders to develop political programs which favoured *any* national community in the republic.

Nonetheless, the Almaty uprising, and the crackdown it provoked, stimulated the development of Kazakh nationalism, deepening the Kazakhs' sense of having been victimized by Moscow. By contrast, the republic's Russians saw the disturbances as proof of the need for Kolbin's campaign against "unhealthy nationalism." This was especially true in the heavily Russian north, which is far removed from Almaty, and thus from the many eye-witnesses who knew that government accounts of the event were false. However, one of Kolbin's attempts to address Kazakh grievances, by increasing the public role of the Kazakh language as a preliminary step toward an eventual transition to Kazakh as an administrative language,[22] served to anger both ethnic groups. Failure to commit resources to training teachers convinced the Kazakhs that Kolbin's efforts were empty gestures, while the Russians were further assured that they had no need to learn what they considered an alien tongue.

Despite the Communist Party's tight control over public discussion under Kolbin, which kept the issue of nationality entirely out of the 1989 election campaign for the new USSR Congress of People's Deputies, Kolbin's last days in Kazakhstan were spent coping with more riots, this time between North Caucasian oil workers and Kazakhs in the western Kazakhstan town of Novy Uzen.

Kolbin was already scheduled for replacement, but the riots undoubtedly hastened the appointment of Nazarbaev, who became head of Kazakhstan's Communist Party on June 22, 1989. An ethnic Kazakh, who not only speaks Kazakh (something of a rarity among the Russified elite) but who also has an obvious love and respect for his people's customs, Nazarbaev was immediately popular among the Kazakhs. He quickly found support among the Russians as well, because of his background as a metallurgist and economic manager, a person who was well used to working with Russians.

Although he had almost no experience outside the republic, Nazarbaev soon proved himself to be an adroit politician, able to function effectively on an all-union level, and even an international one. More importantly, Nazarbaev was also able to span the gaps between the republic's two major nationalities during a period of rising nationalism, while also remaining loyal to Soviet President Mikhail Gorbachev and his program of reform.

Nazarbaev understood that Kazakhstan had to become more overtly the homeland of the Kazakhs, but he recognized too that the increased visibility of Kazakh culture, language, and history should not alienate the republic's large Russian and European population. Among the measures he undertook was to sponsor legislation which would make Kazakh the state language of the republic, almost immediately in regions where Kazakhs were 70 percent or more of the population, but with a delay of five years in regions where non-Kazakhs were in the majority.[23] When Russians, especially those in the north, objected that even that delay was far too short, Nazarbaev brokered a compromise which delayed implementation until January 1, 2000.

Nazarbaev also oversaw the rehabilitation of Kazakhstan's national communists who had been purged during the Stalin era,[24] although his administration tread gingerly around the historical significance of such Kazakhs as Ali Khan Bukeikhanov (1869–1932) and Mir Yakup Dulatov (1885–1935), who had been central actors in the anti-Bolshevik Alash Orda government at the time of the revolution.

No such hesitation was evident in the official rewriting of the history of collectivization in Kazakhstan. Kazakh historian Manash Kozybaev, with full approval of the Kazakhstan Communist Party leadership, published a series of articles which revealed publicly for the first time that millions of Kazakhs died at the hands of the regime during the early 1930s.[25]

However, just as the Kazakhs were learning more about their history, so too were the Russians. Viktor Kozlov, a historian at the Institute of Ethnography in Moscow, first raised the question of Kazakhstan's northern boundaries and Russia's historic right to Eastern Kazakhstan.[26]

Although Kozlov subsequently disavowed the implications of his work, Cossacks and descendants of other pre-revolutionary Russian homesteaders began to band together, to demand greater local autonomy, or even separation.

Nazarbaev distrusted Russian and Kazakh nationalist groups alike, making it equally difficult for Russian groups like *Edinstvo* ("Unity") and Kazakh informal organizations like *Zheltoksan* ("December") and *Azat* ("Freedom") to gain access to the media or legal registration.

In general, Nazarbaev was a very cautious politician during the last Soviet years. He defended Gorbachev's plans to create "a strong center and strong republics," and claimed that the introduction of "self-administration and self-financing" was a sufficient achievement for the republics.[27] It was not until July 1989, when coal miners' strikes spread from Russia to Kazakhstan, that Nazarbaev began to speak of a need to gain partial control of the republic's mineral wealth.[28]

## Nazarbaev, president of Soviet but sovereign Kazakhstan

Nazarbaev's virtually complete control of political life in Kazakhstan meant that in the March 1990 elections for a new republic Supreme Soviet, the Communist Party took 95 percent of the 360 seats.[29] One of the first acts of this new legislature, on April 24, 1990, was to elect Nazarbaev the first president of Kazakhstan. In his maiden presidential address, Nazarbaev was still speaking only of "Kazakh self-finance and self-administration."[30] That quickly changed however, when Russia's Supreme Soviet voted for sovereignty in June 1990.

The sovereignty question split the Kazakh and Russian populations unlike any previous issue. Russians, used to thinking of Kazakhstan as merely a part of a whole which was ruled from Moscow, now faced a republic sovereignty bill which, in draft, demanded that they formally recognize Kazakhstan as the Kazakh's homeland, in which the Kazakh language, culture, and history would have a special place.[31] For their part, the Kazakhs felt the bill gave them too little, by also granting that the republic was multinational, with almost equal status given to Russian and Kazakh. The atmosphere was not helped by Moscow's decision to publish Aleksandr Solzhenitsyn's essay, "How Are We To Build Up Russia?," in the Soviet press, which among other things proposed that northeast Kazakhstan was a part of historic Russia which should be "returned."[32]

Nazarbaev's control of the legislature, as well as the compromises written into the legislation which made the Kazakhs only first among equals in the republic and stressed the equal rights of all citizens, regardless of nationality,[33] meant passage of the sovereignty bill, adopted 25 October 1990, was never in doubt. However, the process had made everyone in the republic acutely aware of how tense Russian-Kazakh relations could easily become. It was largely for that reason that in the months remaining to the Soviet Union, Nazarbaev emerged as Gorbachev's staunchest ally in the fight to keep the union together. At the same time, though, Nazarbaev also modified the wording of republic ballots during the March 17, 1990 referendum on the continuation of a Soviet Union so that a "yes" vote also strengthened the republic's claim to sovereignty.[34]

Similarly, throughout spring and summer 1991 Nazarbaev vigorously defended the premise that the transition to a market economy must be based on preserving the USSR as "a single economic space;"[35] however, Nazarbaev also demanded ever-expanding economic control of Kazakhstan's mines and other resources.[36]

With Gorbachev's political credibility in visible decline, Nazarbaev also took great pains to work out his earlier political differences with Russian president Boris Yeltsin. Yeltsin paid a well-publicized trip to Kazakhstan in mid-August, signing an agreement of cooperation on August 16, 1991, that recognized the existing borders between the two republics.[37]

The attempted coup of 19–21 August occurred immediately afterward. The coup had no immediate resonance in Kazakhstan; Nazarbaev's first appeal called only for unity and warned the population not to respond to possible acts of provocation.[38] It was not until the second day that Kazakhstan's president condemned this attempted seizure of power.

Nazarbaev worked strenuously in what turned out to be the last three months of the USSR's existence to protect Kazakhstan's interests, but the rapidly shifting political environment meant that this defense sometimes appeared inconsistent, or even contradictory. His conviction that independence would be economic suicide for the republics in general and Kazakhstan in particular caused Nazarbaev to support Gorbachev, in such gestures as presenting a hastily reworked version of a new union covenant to the hurriedly assembled deputies, just after the coup.

The gathering momentum for republican independence, however, made any sort of continuation of the union seem increasingly unlikely, so Nazarbaev also began to shift his administrative apparatus around, in anticipation of the increased financial responsibility. In October 1991 Nazarbaev appointed a number of economists and managers to high posts, including Yerik Asanbaev (an economist) as Vice-President, Uzakbai Karamanov (head of old SovMin) as chairman of a new Council of Ministers, and

Daulet Sembaev (former head of Nazarbaev's economic advisory council) as Vice-Premier. These are Kazakhs, but his choice for Prime Minister fell on Sergei Tereshchenko, a Ukrainian agronomist who not only had gotten his degree in Chimkent, but, a great rarity, had also mastered the Kazakh language.[39]

Nazarbaev won an enormous vote of public confidence in the republic's presidental elections that were held on December 1, 1991. Though he ran unopposed (the leader of *Zheltoksan* had failed to get the 100,000 petition signatures necessary for him to appear on the ballot), Nazarbaev got over 98 percent of the vote, with more than 80 percent of all eligible voters participating. These people had cast their votes for the president of a Soviet republic, but just a week later Nazarbaev became the president of a *de facto* independent nation, when the presidents of the three Slavic republics agreed to dissolve the Soviet Union.

## Independent Kazakhstan

Sources close to him report that Nazarbaev was stunned by the dissolution of the USSR,[40] although Kazakhstan's president has subsequently tried to downplay this apparent Slavic rejection of the non-Slavs by saying that he had seen the 8 December 1991 agreement but refused to sign it, because he had not been given the time to read it.[41] Stunned or not, Nazarbaev recovered quickly, convening the heads of the Central Asian republics in Ashgebat, thus raising the spectre of a "Turkestani union." This persuaded Yeltsin and the others to agree to expand the original document of dissolution, which was signed in Almaty. At the same meeting the CIS was created, in the form which it held until late 1993.

His awareness of Kazakhstan's dependence upon Russia made Nazarbaev one of the strongest advocates of the CIS, which he spent much of 1991–1993 struggling to nurture. It was Nazarbaev who, as he put it, "strong-armed" the other CIS presidents into accepting a unified inter-republic banking alliance in November 1992,[42] just as he lobbied forcefully for a jointly-directed CIS defense establishment.[43] Because these were just two among many CIS policies which either were never adopted or remained adopted but unobserved, Nazarbaev became increasingly frustrated, leading him by the end of 1992 to wonder "Does the CIS even exist, or is this a trick?"[44]

Nazarbaev worked as hard, and with more result, to create a functional replacement for the Communist Party, which was outlawed after the August 1991 coup.[45] The first attempt was the Socialist Party, founded right after the failed coup. When that party failed to develop a popular following, Nazarbaev began to distance himself from it.

Nazarbaev's next effort at building a party constituency was the People's Congress, formed in autumn 1991. This party is led by two Kazakh poets,

Olzhas Suleimenov and Mukhtar Shakhanov, and was designed to be a loose "rally-style" organization which was formed on the base of Suleimenov's large national anti-nuclear movement, Nevada-Semipalatinsk. The organization was more popular than the Socialists had been, but it did not prove malleable enough for Nazarbaev, because Suleimenov has strong personal political ambitions of his own, which have continued to grow since independence.

Nazarbaev's most recent effort at party organizing is the Union of People's Unity for Kazakhstan, or SNEK, formed in early 1992, which by 1994 was formally identified as the government party.

Although Nazarbaev is not the legal head of any of these parties, his close political control of the republic has permitted Kazakhstan to proceed further than have any of the other CIS states in creating the institutions of a new state. Nazarbaev faced the same sort of resistance in his communist-era Supreme Soviet as Yeltsin had in his, Nazarbaev did not have to storm parliament in order to establish what the constitution calls a "strong presidential democracy." Although the 1993 Constitution created a national parliament, or Majlis, and a system of lower level bodies, the President has the right to make virtually all appointments in the republic. And although the state's 19 oblasts have elective representative councils, executive power is wielded by presidentially-appointed *hakims*, which makes the entire republic administration an extension of the President.[46] Kazakhstan's new constitution, voted on in a public referendum in August 1995, placed even greater power in Nazarbaev's hands, especially since a referendum of April 1995 has extended his presidency until 2001.

In carving out a foreign policy for his new state, Nazarbaev has stressed repeatedly that Kazakhstan will be neither eastern nor western, neither Islamic nor Christian; rather the state should be a bridge between both. Kazakhstan was quick to join "neutral" international bodies like the UN, OSCE, NATO Coordinating Council, Partners For Peace, and OPEC (in which it has observer status) but, unlike the other Central Asian states, Kazakhstan did not immediately accept full membership in the Economic Coordinating Council, because of that body's domination by Iran and Turkey. Nazarbaev has hosted visits by the Iranian Foreign Minister and President, but was the last of Central Asia's leaders to make *haj* to Mecca, which he put off doing until September 1994.

## Kazakhstan and Russia

The reality which has continued to dominate Kazakhstan since independence, however, is that of its Soviet heritage. Although it has enormous potential wealth, Kazakhstan began independence with a badly under developed and deteriorating physical infrastructure, which moreover had been deliberately designed so as to bind the republic to other parts of the

Soviet Union, and above all to Russia, with whom Kazakhstan continues to do 70 percent of its business. Soviet policies had turned the state into a supplier of raw materials to Russian industries and a consumer of Russian-made goods. The most glaring example of this is oil; despite Kazakhstan's enormous petroleum resources, which are presumed to rival or even surpass those of Kuwait, the republic remains a net importer of petroleum products. The republic has no pipeline which could carry oil from the pump in western Kazakhstan to the central and eastern industrial centers, nor does it have a refinery capable of processing Kazakhstan's sulphur-rich oil. As a consequence, Kazakhstan has not only piled up an enormous debt to Russia – said to have been 547.6 billion rubles in 1993 – but the republic also remains vulnerable to Russian political pressure, which has been applied at least once; in the summer of 1992, when Kazakhstan attempted to establish customs checkpoints on its borders, Russia responded by halting all fuel shipments, bringing Kazakhstan's grain harvest to a standstill. The checkpoints were removed, and gas shipments resumed.

Nazarbaev's determination to remain within the "ruble zone" had enormous economic impact on Kazakhstan. The freeing of Russian prices, on 1 January 1992, set off inflation in Kazakhstan which the state had no means of controlling, because Russia was the sole emission source of currency, as well as the major supplier of goods. Throughout 1992 Kazakhstan was having to buy goods at new, inflated ruble prices while still supplying raw materials on previous contracts, at old, pre-inflation prices.

The disadvantages of this were further exacerbated by the central bank's slowness in clearing payments, which could take up to six months. At the beginning of 1993 a clearing-house system of "book-keeping" rubles was established, which was intended to speed settlement of inter republic accounts. Instead this led to creation of a huge trade imbalance, which Russia began to interpret as debt. In August 1993, when Moscow withdrew pre-1992 rubles from circulation, the Yeltsin government refused to ship Kazakhstan new rubles until the debt was cleared, with payment now demanded in hard currency. Without any of the new rubles, Kazakhstan was forced to keep the old rubles in circulation, prompting a flood of billions of old rubles from the other republics, where they were otherwise worthless. As a result, Kazakhstan's inflation in 1993 was about 2,500 percent.

Despite being chained to a hyper-inflation which he had no means of controlling, Nazarbaev remained committed to remaining tied economically to Russia. In October 1993 he managed to convince a reluctant parliament to accept the package of conditions which Russia had demanded of republics wishing to receive new rubles, even though this in effect passed control of such central economic questions as budgeting, customs, taxes, and investment policy to Moscow.

In November 1993 Russia tightened its conditions for inclusion in the "ruble zone" still further, demanding that ruble nations deposit their gold reserves in Russia. It was only then that Nazarbaev balked, putting the *tenge* into circulation instead, with the backing of the international financial community. Introduced at approximately 5 to the US dollar, the tenge had fallen to about 50 to the dollar by September 1994.

## Kazakhstan and the future

In December 1993, immediately after the departure from Almaty of US Vice President Gore, Nazarbaev dissolved the Supreme Soviet which had been elected in 1990, and called elections for the new Majlis, to be held in March 1994. Although this dissolution was of questionable constitutionality, Nazarbaev needed to create a more tractable partner for the executive tasks of economic and political transformation, as well as to capitalize on his own popularity before the effects of Kazakhstan's changing economy began to bite harder at the population. As it was, Kazakhstan's national income for 1993 was only 60 percent of what it had been in 1991, while per capita income was only 84.5 percent of the average for the CIS.

The new Majlis had only 177 seats, of which 42 were filled from a Presidential list. Nevertheless, great care was taken to insure that most of the new deputies would be people loyal to Nazarbaev. Registration and voting procedures made it very difficult for nationalist groups of any sort to be placed on the ballot, and districts were drawn so as to create Kazakh pluralities whereever possible. As a result, 105 of the 177 new deputies were Kazakhs, while 49 were Russian (another 17 were "European"). The largest single party representation was for SNEK (33 seats), followed by the Congress Party (9 seats) and the Socialists (8 seats). To the Russian population, the results of that voting only exacerbated the effects of Nazarbaev's political appointments, about 80 percent of which have gone to ethnic Kazakhs.

In March 1995 Kazakhstan's Constitutional Court unexpectedly ruled that the 1994 parliamentary elections had been illegal. After an almost token appeal, Nazarbaev dissolved the parliament. Using powers granted him by the 1990–1993 parliament, Nazarbaev reappointed his Prime Minister, Akesham Kazhegeldin, (who had replaced Sergei Tereshchenko in 1994) and began to introduce a number of economic and political charges by presidential decree. His presidency extended until at least 2001, Nazarbaev also undertook a fundamental rewriting of the constitution which, among other things, will create a weaker, bi-cameral legislature.

The demography of Kazakhstan is slowly but perceptibly moving in the Kazakhs' favor. Government policy has sponsored the relocation of about a half million "foreign" Kazakhs, mostly from China and Mongolia; about one-third of the Kazakhs in the latter are said to have repatriated.[47] Most have been settled in the northeastern and central oblasts, where there are

Russian majorities. Because the "foreign" Kazakhs are primarily still pastoral nomads who know no Russian, the psychological impact of this "Kazakhification" is greater than simple numbers might suggest.

Political considerations make statistics on Russian out-migration unreliable, but there is little question that many "Europeans" are departing. 200,000 Germans a year are said to be leaving, and the number of Russians and Russian-speakers moving to Russia are put at more than 300,000 per year since 1990.[48] In addition, birthrates among Russians and Ukrainians have fallen so low that more of these peoples are dying than are being born, while Kazakhs have a birthrate of 19.7 per thousand.[49]

As a consequence, the Russian community of Kazakhstan has increasingly felt itself to be facing a long-term threat, which has made demands for greater local autonomy more frequent. Russia too has attempted to apply pressure, demanding since mid-1993 that Kazakhstan permit its ethnic Russians to have dual citizenship, a courtesy which Russia does not extend to Kazakhs living within its boundaries. Kazakhstan has steadfastly refused, but it did quietly extend the deadline by which people must choose their citizenship, until 15 March 1995.[50] After the closure of parliament it was extended again, and may be postponed until the year 2000. Nazarbaev also agreed to re-examine some of the conditions of the republic's language laws, to soften the impact of the imposition of Kazakh in areas where the population remains overwhelmingly Russian. In addition, Russia and Kazakhstan have reached agreement on a treaty of reciprocity which obviates much of the need for dual citizenship.

There is a constituency within Russia for "reclaiming" the northern territories, as is articulated most powerfully by Aleksandr Solzhenitsyn,[51] just as there is some sentiment for self-rule among Russians in Kazakhstan.[52] However, the only group which seems inclined to become violent about the issue of Russian separatism are the Cossacks, descendants of Russia's imperial front-line troops, who first came to the region three hundred years ago. Not only are they demanding the right to bear arms which their fellows across the Russian border enjoy, but they are beginning to speak ominously of being the "Serbs" of Kazakhstan, who will "withstand."[53]

For the most part Kazakhstan's Russians seem inclined to stay where they are, whether because they do not see better places for themselves in Russia, because they are unable to sell their holdings in Kazakhstan, or because of simple inertia. One consequence of this is that Kazakhstan is losing the most desirable Russians, who have skills or talents which can be easily employed elsewhere. Because Russians stay, however, it does not mean that they are willing to see themselves as subject to Kazakhs, or to see their children as having blighted futures, because of favoritism shown to Kazakhs.[54]

Nazarbaev's awareness of his continuing vulnerability to demographic issues not only made him put more Russians back into government, but also has kept him an advocate of supranational governing bodies, for which he is willing to exchange considerable national autonomy. His most recent attempt to create such a body was the proposal, in June 1994, to establish a Eurasian Union of States. Although the member states of such a union would retain their nominal sovereignty, in practice executive decisions would pass to a Council of Presidents, whose decisions would be binding upon the members. This Union would have a common defense policy, common economic policies, and a single currency.

The weaker states of the old union, such as Kyrgyzstan, which could only gain from such an arrangement, have enthusiastically endorsed Nazarbaev's proposal, but most of the other states remain cool. Most important is Russia, which not only remains indifferent, but has begun in autumn of 1994 to insist on proprietary rights to mineral and oil extraction contracts being let by other states, including Kazakhstan.

In the absence of a workable supranational entity, Kazakhstan is increasingly going to seem two nations, contained within a single border. As that occurs, the preservation of stability is to become an increasingly important criterion for decisionmaking. The lesson which Nazarbaev and all of Central Asia's leaders seem to have drawn from the civil war in Tajikistan is the high cost of instability, whatever its cause. For Nazarbaev, preservation of public order will take precedence over all other considerations, including defense of individual liberties, continuation of economic or political reforms, and creation of a civil society based upon laws. This is clearly demonstrated by the dissolution of parliament on a thin pretext, the extension of Nazarbaev's term in office, and the hasty rewrite of the Constitution.

Just what stability is, and how it is to be preserved, though, is going to become an increasingly delicate calculation in the face of demands for separatism, or even for local autonomy. For example, the Constitutional Court's decision about the illegality of voting procedures did not encompass the elections for local councils, but it could be extended to them, if necessary. However, the greater power which Nazarbaev has given to Russians and Russian interests since March 1995 suggests that he is unlikely to try to restrain the growing assertativeness of the northern local councils. If he does not, however, he will be likely to face demands for similar freedoms from the southern, Kazakh-dominated, local councils. This will present Nazarbaev with the choice either of permitting significant further dilution of central authority, or of refusing to the Kazakh councils rights and freedoms which he has already given to the Russian councils.

A similar difficulty obtains for crime, which has proliferated since the collapse of Moscow's authority. A large percentage of this crime is petty, of the sort which prompts warnings that western visitors should not now wander freely about Almaty. What influences the climate of public opinion more, though, is the evidence of official corruption, which grows more visible every month. In autumn 1994 there were a series of scandals about high government officials, or members of their families, who had abused their positions in pursuit of substantial private fortunes, with some bribes reported to reach into the millions. These scandals gave the final push to the Tereshchenko government, in October 1994. Although there is considerable corruption among the Russian population too, Kazakh control of government functions such as export licensing has meant that illegal privatization has disproportionately favored the Kazakhs, further feeding Russian dissatisfaction. Nazarbaev could attempt to impose much tighter public security, but only at the risk of alienating the increasingly powerful families of the Kazakh elite.

The greatest problem, however, remains that of Russia. Despite formal protestations to the contrary, Russia shows every sign of regarding Kazakhstan as still "theirs." Russia has imposed itself as a partner in an Omani-Kazakhstan deal to build the pipeline for the Tengiz oil field, and Russian companies are said to be buying significant positions in other Kazakhstan companies, as well as setting up joint-ventures.[55] As noted above, the Russian government is also flexing considerable financial muscle, which has both forced Kazakhstan to adopt a currency it has tried to avoid, and made it very difficult for that currency to succeed. The tenge has stabilized in 1995, but remains vulnerable should Russia wish to intervene.

President Nazarbaev has instituted an ambitious 3-stage program of social and economic transformation, which has as its goal turning Kazakhstan into a new "Asian tiger" by the beginning of the next century. Certainly the republic has the physical resources to make such a dream a possibility, while the government and legislature have shown the ability to put at least the first stages of the necessary legal and political framework for such a transformation into place.

If Kazakhstan can continue this precarious balancing act for as little as five more years, then the chances of an economic rescue seem bright. By extending his presidency until 2001, President Nursultan Nazarbaev has taken upon himself the role of hard-pressed keystone in this "bridge between East and West," kept in place as much for what each constituency feels he prevents the other constituencies from doing as it is for what the constituencies feel he does for them.

However, the continued and increasing dislocations of that transformation, amplified as they are by Kazakhstan's ever-present demographic realities, make it ever more possible that one side or the other of Kazakhstan's precarious balancing act might be tempted to – or might feel pushed to – try to tip the republic's political balance in their direction. Since the chances of another such "balancer" as Nazarbaev emerging are remote, particularly as the demands of Nazarbaev's balancing act make the fostering of potential successors dangerous and impossible, the results of any such attempt would probably be bloody.[56]

## NOTES

1 Kazakh radio, 14 July 1994, as reported in *Central Eurasia. Daily Report,* FBIS-SOV-94-136, 15 July 1994, p. 52.
2 *Soiuz,* no. 32, August 1990.
3 *Panorama* n. 28, 16 July 1994, p. 1.
4 *Izvestiia,* 11 March 1994, p. 4.
5 *Kazakhstanskaia pravda,* August 27, 1991.
6 The complete proposal is printed in *Nezavisimaia gazeta,* 8 June 1994.
7 *Karavan,* 22 July 1994, p. 4.
8 *Karavan,* 24 June 1994, p. 1.
9 *Karavan,* 22 July 1994, p. 4.
10 For details see Martha Brill Olcott, *The Kazakhs* (Stanford: Hoover Institution Press, 1987), esp. chapter 2.
11 *Kazakhstanskaia pravda,* May 16, 1991.
12 The well known Kazakh historian E. Bekmakhanov was sent to a labor camp for merely *implying* that Kenisary Kasimov was a hero, in his *Kazakhstan v 20–40 gody XIX veka* (Alma Ata, 1947).
13 Kazakhs comprise 27.2 percent of the population of East Kazakhstan, 28.9 percent of Kokchetau, 22.9 percent of Kustanai, 18.6 percent of North Kazakhstan, 28.5 percent of Pavlodar and 22.4 percent of Tselinograd oblast. *Ekonomika i zhizn,* no. 5, 1990, p. 70.
14 However, collectively they account for less than three percent of the population. *Soiuz,* no. 32, August 1990.
15 *Kazakhstanskaia pravda,* June 8, 1989.
16 *Kazakhstanskaia pravda,* December 19, 1991.
17 *Turkestan,* no. 1, February, 1990.
18 See *Pravda,* December 18–21, 1986; the fifty-eight deaths by the MVD are in addition to these two. They are mentioned in *Literaturnaia gazeta,* no. 48, November 28, 1990, p.11. Kazakh informants who have read the complete text of the Shakhanov Commission report on the Almaty riots claim that they admit to 268 deaths. The full version of the report has yet to be published. The summary of the report is found in *Kazakhstanskaia pravda,* September 28, 1990.
19 Suleimenov had been a major cultural figure in the republic since the early 1960s. He achieved "notoriety" in 1976 with the publication of *Az i ia,* an attempt to present "Igor's Tale" from a Turkic viewpoint. Attacked by the full force of the USSR's academic establishment, he survived with a brief public recantation and a great deal of support from Kunaev.
20 Interviews with bystanders of the December 1986 demonstrations, May 1990.
21 *Kazakhstanskaia pravda,* March 16, 1987; *Kazakhstanskaia pravda,* March 17, 1987; "Istselenie," *Druzhba narodov,* no. 9, 1987, pp. 195–209.
22 *Kazakhstanskaia pravda,* February 18, 1987.
23 *Kazakhstanskaia pravda,* August 25, 1989.
24 *Kazakhstanskaia pravda,* July 26, 1989, and December 9, 1989.
25 *Partinaia zhizn' kazakhstana,* no. 6, 1990, pp. 85–90.
26 V. I. Kozlov, "Natsional'nyi vopros: paradigmy, teoriia i politika," *Istoriia SSSR,* no. 1, 19990, pp. 3–21, see especially pp. 11–12.
27 *Daily Report. Soviet Union.* FBIS-SOV-89-107, October 27, 1989, as translated from *Sovetskaia Rossiia,* October 19, 1989.
28 *Izvestiia,* July 21, 1989.
29 *Kazakhstanskaia pravda,* April 25, 1990.
30 *Kazakhstanskaia pravda,* April 25, 1991.
31 *Kazakhstanskaia pravda,* October 11, 1991.

32  *Komsomol'skaia pravda*, September 19, 1990.

33  *Kazakhstanskaia pravda*, October 28, 1991.

34  *Izvestiia*, February 13, 1991.

35  *Daily Report. Soviet Union*, FBIS-SOV-91–116, June 17, 1991, pp. 101–103, a transcription of Central Television broadcast from June 14, 1991.

36  *Radio Liberty on the USSR*, August 9, 1991, pp 13–15.

37  The Yeltsin commitment is reported in FBIS-SOV-91–169, 30 August 1991, p. 125.

38  *Kazakhstanskaia pravda*, August 19, 1991.

39  Interviews by author, March and May 1992,

40  *Argumenty i fakty*, #2, 1993, p. 2.

41  FBIS-SOV-92, 226, 23 November 1992, p. 46.

42  FBIS-SOV-92–185, 23 September 1992, p. 42.

43  *Argumenty i fakty*, #2, 1993, p. 2.

44  It has subsequently been legalized again, but its membership is small.

45  Constitution of the Republic of Kazakhstan.

46  *Ardyn Erh*, 24 February 1994, p. 3, as reported in *Daily Report. Central Eurasia*, FBIS-USR-94–078, 21 July 1994, p. 92.

47  *Moscow News*, n. 20, May 1994, p. 3, as reported in *Daily Report. Central Eurasia*, FBIS-USR-94–065, 20 June 1994, p. 96.

48  *Krasnaia zvezda*, 1 June 1994, p. 3.

49  *Panorama*, n. 28, 16 July 1994.

50  *Moscow News*, n. 20, May 1994, p. 3, as reported in *Daily Report. Central Eurasia*, FBIS-USR-94–065, 20 June 1994, p. 96.

51  Radio Free Europe/Radio Liberty Daily Report, 25 July 1994.

52  The group *Lad* (Harmony) demanded self-rule for East Kazakhstan oblast just after the March elections. *Nezavisimaia gazeta*, 31 March 1994, p. 3.

53  *Moscow News*, n. 20, May 1994, p. 3, as reported in *Daily Report. Central Eurasia*, FBIS-USR-94–065, 20 June 1994, p. 96.

54  One indication of "reverse discrimination" is the admissions patterns to Al Farabi State University, where 79.5 percent of the new students are Kazakhs, as opposed to 14.6 percent Russian. *Kazakhstanskaia pravda*, 28 June 1994, p. 2.

55  Interviews by author, April, May, and October, 1993.

56  In Nazarbaev's words: "God grant that no one should stir up Kazakhstan on ethnic grounds. It would be far worse than Yugoslavia." *Kazakhstanskaia pravda*, 23 November 1991, p. 1.

# Kazakhstan: chronology of events

*December 1986*
16 Dinmukhammad Kunaev is replaced as Communist Party First Secretary by Gennadi Kolbin, an ethnic Russian.
17 A protest demonstration in Almaty against Kunaev's removal turns violent, resulting in clashes with police and numerous deaths.

*June 1989*
16 Fighting breaks out between Kazakhs and Lezgin oil workers in Novy Uzen. A month-long curfew is imposed.
22 Nursultan Nazarbaev replaces Kolbin as Party first secretary.
At the Soviet Congress of People's Deputies, poet Olzhas Suleimenov makes the first public statements accusing Russians of carrying out a deliberate policy to render Kazakhs a minority in their own republic.

*July 1989*
20–21 Miners in Karaganda go on a 2-day strike.

*August 1989*
22 A language law is adopted which makes Kazakh the state language and provides for the development of Kazakh-language instruction in schools and a gradual transition to Kazakh in government and business spheres.

*March 1990*
25 In elections to the Supreme Soviet (including later runoffs), 94 percent of the 360 deputies elected are Communists. One-quarter of the seats were reserved for public organizations, and no informal organizations ran their own slate of candidates.

*April 1990*
24 Supreme Soviet elects Nazarbaev to the post of republican president.

*September 1990*
28 The Supreme Soviet issues a report on the 1986 riots in which several senior members of the Communist Party are accused of complicity and criminal activities.
29 It is decreed that in Russian-dominated areas,

Kazakh-language services will only have to be provided beginning in 1995 but must be fully bilingual by the year 2000.

*October 1990*

25    The Supreme Soviet adopts a declaration of sovereignty, in which Kazakhs are described as the first among the republic's nationalities.

*March 1991*

17    In the all-union referendum on preserving the union, 94 percent of voters (88 percent turnout) support the union. The question is phrased to use the word "states" as opposed to "republics."

*August 1991*

16    Nazarbaev and Yeltsin sign an agreement of cooperation which recognizes the existing borders between Kazakhstan and Russia.

*September 1991*

7    The Communist Party is dissolved and replaced by the Socialist Party, composed primarily of ethnic Russians and assimilated Kazakhs.

14–15    In Uralsk, Cossacks take part in a four-hundredth anniversary celebration. Large protests are staged by Kazakh national movements.

*October 1991*

5    The People's Congress of Kazakhstan is formed to oppose the reigning Socialist Party (the former Communists).

*November 1991*

16    The Union of Cossacks has its registration revoked after it is determined that its bylaws are unconstitutional.

*December 1991*

1    Nazarbaev is elected President by popular vote, receiving 98 percent of the vote (80 percent participation) in an uncontested race. His only potential opponent, Hasan Kozhakhmetov (the leader of the Kazakh nationalist movement Zheltoqsan) could not enter the race as he did not procure the requisite 100,000 signatures.

13    The Chief Mufti of Kazakhstan is assaulted by several supporters of Alash.
Kazakhstan joins the CIS.

16 The Supreme Soviet issues a declaration of independence.
19 A citizenship law is adopted which grants automatic citizenship to all residents of Kazakhstan.

*May 1992*

15 Kazakhstan signs the CIS collective security treaty.
23 Nazarbaev agrees to transfer Kazakhstan's nuclear weapons to Russia.
25 A treaty of friendship and cooperation with Russia is signed.

*June 1992*

17–23 Demonstrations led by opposition movements Azat, Zheltoqsan, and the Republican Party are held to demand the formation of a coalition government. Attracting some 5,000 participants, the demonstrations are broken up on 23 June.
26 The Communist Party is denied the right to re-register.

*August 1992*

19 History professor Karishal Asanov is arrested for writing an article accusing Nazarbaev of disrespect for Kazakh nationalism.
27 The editors of the newspaper *Birlesu* are tried on charges of insulting the Prime Minister and mayor of Almaty, and calling for the overthrow of the constitutional order.

*September 1992*

27 At a secret congress, the Russian organization Lad is founded.
29 The First World Congress of Kazakhs is held in Almaty.

*October 1992*

29 The First Congress of Germans in Kazakhstan is held in Almaty.

*December 1992*

7 Some 15,000 residents of Ust-Kamenogorsk rally to demand the adoption of Russian as an official language, dual citizenship, and greater autonomy for East Kazakhstan.

*January 1993*

28 The Constitution is ratified by the Supreme Soviet.

*February 1993*

6 The pro-Nazarbaev Union of Popular Unity of Kazakhstan (SNEK) holds its founding congress.

*May 1993*
22–23   After broadcasting a news feature regarding the difficulties
        ethnic Russians face in Kazakhstan, Russian journalists
        Aleksandr Svyazin and Andrei Kondrashov lose their right
        to practice journalism in the country.

*August 1993*
22      Dinmukhammed Kunaev dies.

*October 1993*
6       Former head of the Azat movement, Kamal Ormantaev,
        establishes the National-Democratic Party.
        The Supreme Court overturns the ruling on Asanov.

*November 1993*
15      Kazakhstan leaves the ruble zone, making the *tenge* the sole
        official currency.

*December 1993*
6       Following mass resignations of local and regional deputies,
        43 Supreme Soviet deputies resign and call upon parliament
        to dissolve itself.
8       After almost 200 of parliament's 350 deputies resign, the
        remaining parliamentarians vote to dissolve the Supreme
        Soviet and call for new elections to be held on 7 March.

*March 1994*
7       Parliamentary elections are held, with supporters of the
        pro-Nazarbaev SNEK receiving about 30 seats. 42 seats
        (nearly one-quarter of the 177-member Supreme Kenges)
        are filled from a "state list" of handpicked pro-Nazarbaev
        candidates.
9       CSCE observers denounce the elections for multiple
        violations and undemocratic procedures.
16      The Communist Party is finally permitted to reregister.
23      Nazarbaev in London publically suggests that CIS
        states should come together to form a new "Eurasian
        Union."
29      An agreement on the Baikonur space center is signed, which
        gives Russia a twenty-year lease on the complex and allows
        Baikonur employees to be subject to Russian law.

*April 1994*
13      Russian journalist Boris Suprunyuk is arrested on charges of
        inciting interethnic discord through his articles detailing the
        difficulties of Russians in Kazakhstan.
20      Abish Kekilbaev is elected parliamentary chairman.

*May 1994*

14   Several political movements, including Azat, Zheltoqsan, Lad, and the Communists gather to discuss coordinating government opposition.

16   Twelve opposition members are arrested when attempting to conduct a hunger strike in front of the Supreme Soviet building.

27   A majority of deputies (111) vote for a nonbinding resolution of no-confidence in the government.

*June 1994*

9   Nazarbaev proposes to move the capital from Almaty to Akmola.

14   A week after insisting that the government is to remain in place for the next 15 months, Nazarbaev replaces several top ministers.

*July 1994*

1   The Society for the Assistance of the Semireche Cossacks are registered, making them the first official Cossack organization in independent Kazakhstan.

6   Parliament votes to transfer the capital to Akmola, although the move is not expected to occur until after the year 2000.

*September 1994*

7   Boris Suprunyuk is pronounced guilty and receives a suspended two-year prison sentence.

16   Minister of Economics Mars Urkumbaev and Minister of Internal Affairs Vladimir Shumov are removed from office for ostensibly "violating moral and ethical standards."

*October 1994*

11   Prime Minister Tereshchenko and his cabinet are forced to resign after Nazarbaev accuses them of failing to carry out a program of economic reform.

12   Akezhan Kazhegeldin (Tereshchenko's deputy) is elected prime minister.

*November 1994*

18   The Supreme Court overturns the ruling on Suprunyuk.

25   Cossack ataman Fyodor Cherepanov is kidnapped in Ust-Kamenogorsk. He escapes from captivity on 2 December after the Kazakh government reportedly paid a $900,000 ransom.

30   Following several illegal protests, the Society for Assistance to Semireche Cossacks is banned for several months on the grounds that it possesses illegal armed units.

*January 1995*

13   100,000 coal miners begin a strike in Karaganda and Ekibastuz.

20   Nazarbaev and Yeltsin sign an agreement on establishing Joint Armed Forces.

*February 1995*

3   Northern chapters of the People's Congress and Lad agree to work together to oppose Nazarbaev's policies.

*March 1995*

7   The Constitutional Court rules, after deliberating for a year, that constitutional violations had occured in the March 1994 parliamentary elections.

8   Both Nazarbaev and Kekilbaev send objections to the Constitutional Court, but the Court overrules them two days later.

11   Parliament votes (illegally) to amend the constitution to allow it to suspend the Constitutional Court and its decisions. Nazarbaev declares that the parliament is an unconstitutional body and its decisions are devoid of any legal force. He dissolves the parliament and transfers all legislative authority to himself. The entire government resigns, in acknowledgement that it had been confirmed by an illegitimate parliament, but is immediately reconfirmed by Nazarbaev. 72 deputies stage a hunger strike to protest parliament's dissolution, but only 22 remain the following day.

15   Several ex-deputies announce the creation of an alternative People's Parliament of Kazakhstan, but it gains little support.

*April 1995*

29   In a referendum seeking to extend Nazarbaev's term of office until 2001, 95 percent of voters (91 percent participation) support the move. Widespread accounts of electoral violations lead to unofficial estimates of only 20–30 percent participation.

# 16 Uzbekistan: the politics of national independence

GREGORY GLEASON

Uzbekistan's path to independence presents many puzzles for the outsider.[1] In comparison with the other former Soviet republics, Uzbekistan's leadership is one of the most authoritarian, yet at the same time it is among the most popular. In economic terms, Uzbekistan's leadership is one of the most successful, yet it is among the least popular abroad. Many Uzbeks pride themselves on the degree to which Uzbekistan's politics is distinguished from the political free-for-all of post-Soviet Russia. They claim that Uzbekistan's political culture is marked by dignity and sense of civilization. At the same time, the outside world criticizes Uzbekistan as the worst offender of human rights among the post-Soviet republics. Uzbekistan has difficult diplomatic relations with the "realist" Great Powers, yet pursues a hardline realist foreign policy within Central Asia.

How are we to understand Uzbekistan? One approach to appreciating the seemingly contradictory aspects of Uzbekistan's national politics is to see it as a country that has just undergone the wrenching process of decolonization. It has been catapulted to independence, found itself racked with internal competition for power, forced into full participation in the international trading community, called upon to recreate virtually all new institutions of government, and taken upon itself the responsibility for maintaining regional security in Central Asia.

## Uzbekistan: nation and state

The substance of modern nationhood in Uzbekistan owes much to the historical influence of Marxist ideology on Central Asian political development during the past seven decades. The Marxist interpretation of history stresses that "nations" – the ethnic collectivities of like-minded who see themselves as belonging to the same fraternal community – are little more than a temporary by-product of capitalist economic relations. Among Marxists, Lenin in particular emphasized that nations were transitional social formations. Lenin the theoretician was convinced that nations would eventually lose their importance at the same time that class consciousness among the workers increased. But Lenin the tactician also realized that nationalism had a great appeal in the popular psychology. To harness this

*571*

appeal, Lenin agreed to the idea of granting national groups "autonomy," "self-government" and "national statehood" within the new socialist order that he established after the Russian revolution. Lenin's plan was to recognize nations by granting them federal rights within the Soviet system of government.[2] Hence the emergence of the principle of "national-statehood" (*natsional'naia gosudarstvennost'*). This principle lies at the foundation of the Soviet state Lenin designed, despite the fact that for theoretical reasons Lenin had always been antagonistic to federal solutions.

Lenin's tactical compromise was successful in many parts of what later became the Soviet Union, for it enabled him to attract the support of nationalist groups to the aims of the Revolution. In Central Asia, however, nations, and thus nationalism, did not exist. No working class existed. The political institutions that existed were subordinated to the Khanates rather than to institutions of a popularly-based republic. The intellectuals drew most of their inspiration from Koranic teachings. The peasants tended to identify with a particular tribe, valley or oasis rather than with some large national group.

In an effort to make reality conform to the principles of the ideology, Soviet policy in Central Asia embarked upon the creation of nations. National categories would be created, it was reasoned, and national groups would emerge to fill these categories. The borders of the Central Asian republics, on the basis of Marxist ideological presuppositions, were artificially imposed during the early years of Soviet power. At the turn of the century, the political map of Central Asia had been divided into three major Khanates, each one of which was associated with oasis and river agriculture: Kokand, Khiva, and Bukhara. The golden days of prosperity associated with the ancient Central Asian "Silk Road" had long since faded. Gone too was the mythic age of enlightened rule by benign despots. The Emirs governed as unenlightened but all-powerful petty tyrants. The political landscape was dominated by struggles between the Emirs of Bukhara and Khorezm, among the feuding local "revolutionary" factions, and among the internally divided Russian settler population.[3] The territorial borders of these oasis societies were challenged by the influence of the Tsarist government as it expanded into Central Asia in the competition with the British empire over regional influence in the heart of Asia. What the British and Russian troops encountered was groups of sedentary peoples, who called themselves "sarts," along the oases valleys and nomads in the hills and deserts. The sarts later became known as the Uzbeks and the nomads as the Turkmen, Karakalpak or Karakyrgyz.

Now, with the coming of the new ideology, a major goal was to create the appropriate "states" for Central Asia. At first, Moscow, absorbed by the Civil War, could do little, but by the spring of 1920, Moscow's attention returned to Central Asia. A plan for redistricting was worked out by the "Turkcommission." Lenin reviewed the Turkcommission's report and

## Uzbekistan

- International boundary
- *Wiloyat* or *respublika* boundary
- ★ National capital
- ⊛ *Wiloyat* or *respublika* capital
- Railroad
- Road

*The city of Tashkent (Toshkent Shahri) has status equal to that of a wiloyat.*

| 0 | 100 | 200 Kilometers |
| 0 | 100 | 200 Miles |

*Lambert Conformal Conic Projection, SP 47N62N*

**KAZAKHSTAN**

Embi

Shalqar

Zhezqazghen

Aral

Beyneü

*Aral Sea*

Qyzylorda

Sariqamish Kuli

Müynoq

QORAQALPOGHISTON

Qünghirot

RESPUBLIKASI

Nukus

Türkistan

Zhambyl

Bishkek

Kara-Balta

Shymkent

TOSHKENT

NAMANGAN

**KYRGYZSTAN**

Syrdariya

Uchquduq

Dashhowuz

Urganch

**N A W O I Y**

KHORAZM

Shardara Boʻgazi

Tashkent

Chirchiq

Angren

Namangan

ANDIJON

Jalal-Abad

Andijon

Osh

Aydar Kuli

JIZZAKH

Düzün (Koʻkhoʻ)

FARGʻONA

**BUKHORO**

Newoiy

Guliston

Khujand

**KYRGYZSTAN**

Bukhoro

SAMARQAND

Samarqand

Jizzakh

SIRDARYO

FARGHONA

Qizil-Suu

**TURKMENISTAN**

Charjew

Qarshi

QASHQADARYO

Zarefshon

**TAJIKISTAN**

Dushanbe

Ashgabat

Bojnürd

Mary

Denow

Küsob

Khorügh

Qürghonteppa

Bartang

Murghab

Darya-ye Pani

Rude Atrak

Qaraqum Kanaly

SURKHONDARYO

Termiz

Konduz

Chitral

**PAKISTAN**

Sabzevár

Neyshábür

Mashhad

Mazár-e Sharif

Kondüz

Meymaneh

**AFGHANISTAN**

**I R A N**

Qushqy

Daryá-ye Morgháb

Kabul

concluded that the "political map" of Turkestan needed to be redrawn to contain three primary units, "Uzbekia, Kirgizia and Turkmenia."[4] Lenin thought it necessary, as well, to "specify in a detailed fashion how these three would be combined into one group."[5]

The First Congress of Soviets, meeting in Moscow in December 1922, adopted the Union Treaty. The Treaty recognized the Turkestan Autonomous Soviet Republic as a part of the RSFSR, one of the four original republics of the Soviet Union.[6] The Bukharan Peoples' Republic and the Khorezm Peoples' Republic were both still outside of the union, ostensibly because they were not "socialist."[7] They were soon to be brought inside the socialist structure. As two Central Asian writers assert, Lenin and the other communists "never considered the Bukharan and Khorezm Peoples' Republics to be permanent government structures for the peoples of Central Asia."[8]

In 1924, Moscow's attention returned to the subject of redistricting in Central Asia. A major land reform was enacted.[9] A number of party meetings raised the issue of the optimal design. An idea surfaced that there should be a "Central Asian Federation" consisting of Kyrgyz, Uzbek, and Turkmen republics as well as Karakirgiz (Kyrgyz)[10] and Tajik autonomous oblasts.[11] On June 12, 1924, the RCP(b) CC Politburo issued a resolution "On the National Redistricting of the Republics of Central Asia." According to two notable Uzbekistan scholars, the criteria for redistricting included: consideration of the local ethnic make up; irrigation district management authority; economic specialization of the regions; the suitability of urban areas for the management of agricultural areas; and the distribution of the ethnic groups.[12] A resolution passed at the October 27, 1924 meeting of the Central Executive Committee of the USSR provided for the redivision of the Turkestan ASSR according to the "principle of self-determination of nationalities" into: the Uzbek Soviet Socialist Republic (within which was included the Tajik Autonomous Soviet Socialist Republic); the Turkmen Soviet Socialist Republic; the Karakyrgyz Autonomous Oblast (incorporated into the RSFSR); and the Kyrgyz Autonomous Soviet Socialist Republic (also incorporated into the RSFSR).[13] The new Uzbek government formalized the arrangement on December 5, 1924, with the passage of a "Declaration of the Revolutionary Committee of the Uzbek Republic."[14] A number of major border changes affecting the Uzbek republic followed, but the principle of the ethnic Uzbek control of Uzbekistan was firmly established at this point.[15]

The First Congress of Soviets of the Uzbek SSR, in February 1925, passed a "Declaration on the formation of the Uzbek Soviet Socialist Republic," chose a Central Executive Committee, and approved the Council of Peoples Commissars for the Uzbek Republic. On May 13, 1925, the Third Congress of Soviets of the USSR officially incorporated the Uzbek and Turkmen republics into the USSR, bringing the number of republics in the union to six. At this point, the redistricting was technically completed. By 1926, the Uzbek SSR (not including the area that later became Tajikistan) had a population of 5,272,800, about 66 percent of whom were ethnic Uzbeks.[16]

Over the years of Soviet power, because of party control, the artificiality of the borders, and the fact that most decisions, ultimately, rested on the shoulders of Moscow rather than the provinces, the inter-republican and inter-ethnic group borders in Central Asia had little significance. As the president of Uzbekistan, Islam Karimov, recently lamented "During all the years of Soviet power, Uzbekistan, in reality, was not a state."[17]

## Control over political institutions

Although the republican borders and intra-republican delineations (such as the Karakalpak Autonomous Republic) were artificial creations and enjoyed none of the "national-statehood" supposedly guaranteed them in successive Soviet constitutions, the administrative jurisdictions that these borders introduced did eventually gather a great deal of importance. Political boundaries do not only represent territorial divisions on a map, they also represent structures of political authority and systems of reciprocal exchange. Uzbekistan's political boundaries became the basis for formal political institutions. These institutions were originally in the hands of Moscow's power brokers, but, over the years of Soviet power, such institutions as the local party organizations, the economic ministries and the related production agencies, the Uzbek cultural and scientific establishments, the agricultural organizations, the construction organizations and the educational institutions increasingly were captured by local interests. With the advent of perestroika and political reform at the center, the formal Central Asian political borders acquired a real significance.

The core of Uzbekistan's politics today is the contestation for the control of these institutions by different groups. How have these groups competed in the past to control resources? Given the agricultural orientation of the Uzbekistan economy, the key resource was control over land. Ethnic Uzbeks fared very well in the division of land in the original districting of Central Asia. They captured the most agriculturally productive region in Central Asia, the Fergana valley. In addition, they gained the watersheds and the associated irrigated agricultural areas of the Chirchik river (which runs through Tashkent), the Zerafshan river (which runs through both Samarkand and Bukhara), and the Surkhan-Darya (a major feeder of the Amu-Darya).

The Uzbeks did not succeed in claiming the main water course of the Amu-Darya downstream from the southern Soviet border and upstream from Urgench. This area went to the Turkmen. The Uzbeks later claimed the fertile Khivan oasis areas around Urgench, even though this area was landlocked within the area acknowledged to belong to the Karakalpak. The

Table 16.1. *National composition of Uzbekistan, 1989*
*(principal nationality groups)*

|  |  | percent of total |
|---|---|---|
| Total | 19,810,077 |  |
| Uzbek | 14,142,475 | 71.00 |
| Russian | 1,653,478 | 8.30 |
| Tajik | 933,560 | 4.70 |
| Kazakh | 808,227 | 4.00 |
| Tatar | 467,829 | 2.30 |
| Karakalpak | 411,878 | 2.00 |
| Kyrgyz | 174,907 | 0.80 |
| Ukrainian | 153,197 | 0.70 |
| Turkmen | 121,578 | 0.60 |
| Jew | 65,493 | 0.03 |
| Armenian | 50,537 | 0.02 |
| Azeri | 44,410 | 0.02 |

*Source: Pravda Vostoka*, June 15, 1990, p. 3.

Kazakhs received the valuable agricultural lands along the Syr-Darya below Chardara. The Russians had relatively close relations with the Kazakhs. The Russians, therefore, may have insisted that the lower Syr-Darya valley not be considered within the core of Central Asia. The big losers in the division were the Tajiks and Kyrgyz. The Tajiks received national statehood in the form of an autonomous republic in the far south. But the large numbers within Uzbekistan received little. The Kyrgyz were given the grazing lands but gained little of the prime agricultural land of the Fergana valley.

Early Moscow policy emphasized "korenizatsiia" (nativization) of cadres. The motivation of this policy was the assumption by Moscow officials that local administrations needed local support which could most easily come from local leaders who were recognized as representing local interests. In Uzbekistan this policy came by 1928 to be identified as "Uzbekizatsiia" although this was more a slogan than a policy.[18] The fact remains, however, that the Turkic-speaking Uzbek majority managed to use nativization to gain a privileged position within the republic. The power establishment of the Khiva oasis in the Fergana valley was relegated to a provincial status as was the Persian-speaking power establishment of the Samarkand and Bukhara oases. Over the years, the Uzbek majority increased their share of the minority group by gradually accumulating the Turkic-speaking tribal groups and assimilating them in the Uzbek "nation." By the early 1990s, the Uzbeks comprised more than 70 percent of the Uzbekistan population.

At the commanding heights of Uzbekistan's leadership, "nativization" meant that natives would rule, but they would do so in accordance with Moscow's designs. This implied a certain contract between the local officials and their Moscow patrons. The first class of Central Asian surrogate leaders who adopted this contract were men like Akmal Ikramov who became the Uzbek party first secretary and Faizulla Khodzhaev who became the Uzbek republic's first prime minister.[19] Both men cooperated with Moscow in part from ideological commitment and in part from self-interest. The careers of both men ended tragically in the purges of 1937. Both have since been rehabilitated. This generation of initial leaders was succeeded mainly by appointees from the center. During the Second World War, a substantial Slavic immigration took place as war industries were transported to Central Asia. Slavs assumed many of the key administrative and political posts during this period. The postwar generation saw a re-establishment of local leadership. A rapid series of leaders in Uzbekistan followed the accession to power of Nikita Khrushchev. Then first secretary of the Communist Party of Uzbekistan, Amin Irmatovich Niyazov, was demoted in December 1955, just months after Khrushchev became first secretary of the CPSU. Niyazov was transferred to a minor republican ministry in Uzbekistan.[20] His replacement, Nuriddin Akramovich Mukhiddinov, who was Chairman of the Uzbekistan Council of Ministers under Niyazov, served for two years as Secretary before being brought to Moscow as a Secretary and member of the Presidium of the CPSU Central Committee, where he remained until the XXII CPSU Congress in 1961. His successor, Sabir Kamalovich Kamalov, had served as Chairman of the Uzbekistan Council of Ministers before being appointed first secretary of the CPUz late in December 1957. Kamalov's tenure as CPUz First Secretary lasted just over a year. He was ousted from his party post in March 1959, for "mistakes" in party work.[21] The CPUz first secretary's mantle was then handed to Sharaf Rashidov who retained it until his death in 1983.

Rashidov's death coincided with the accession to power of Yuri Andropov in Moscow. Andropov initiated an anti-corruption campaign throughout the USSR. But the efforts to root out corrupt officials in Central Asia were especially enthusiastic. The personnel changes in Uzbekistan started with investigations into the "cotton affair."[22] As Moscow investigators conducted a routine investigation into embezzlement in Uzbekistan cotton procurement agencies, they discovered what to them seemed a labyrinthine network of political corruption.[23] The campaign that had begun as an effort to catch a few local criminals mushroomed into Central Asia's most extensive political purge. Between 1984 and 1987, some forty of sixty-five party secretaries in UzSSR were replaced.[24] Over 260 new secretaries of city and district party committees were elected. One-third of all the chairmen and vice-chairmen of regional party committees were changed. The result of the purge was that an entirely new generation of Central Asian officials

Table 16.2. *Oblasts, UzSSR*

|  | Territory (sq. km) | Date of formation | Population (1/89) |
|---|---|---|---|
| UzSSR | 447.4 | 1924 | 19,906,000 |
| Karakalpak ASSR | 165.5 | 1936 | 1,214,000 |
| Andizhan Ob. | 4.2 | 1941 | 1,728,000 |
| Bukhara Ob. | 143.2 | 1938 | 1,141,000 |
| Dzhizak Ob. | 20.5 | 1973 | (discontinued) |
| Kashkadarin Ob. | 28.4 | 1964 | 1,594,000 |
| Namangan Ob. | 7.9 | 1967 | 1,475,000 |
| Navoi Ob. |  | 1982 | (discontinued) |
| Samarkand Ob. | 24.5 | 1938 | 2,778,000 |
| Surkhandarin Ob. | 20.8 | 1941 | 1,255,000 |
| Syrdaryn Ob. | 5.1 | 1963 | 1,316,000 |
| Tashkent Ob. | 15.6 | 1938 | 2,157,000 |
| Fergana Ob. | 7.1 | 1938 | 2,153,000 |
| Khorezm Ob. | 4.5 | 1938 | 1,016,000 |

Source: *Narodnoe khoziastvo Uzbekskoi SSR, 1979* (Tashkent: Statistika, 1980), p. 6; *Ezhegodnik, Bol'shaia Sovetskaia Entsiklopedia* (Moscow: BSE, 1988); *Pravda Vostoka*, March 29, 1989.

was installed. By the late 1980s, Uzbekistan's managerial elite was the youngest in the union; some 45 percent of party committee secretaries were under forty. Eventually the most powerful official in Uzbekistan, the Uzbek Communist Party first secretary, Inomzhon Usmankhodzhaev, was removed by the scandal and sentenced to twelve years in jail.

The cotton affair not only resulted in death sentences for local Central Asian kingpins, but implicated numerous local and regional officials in a web of political corruption leading from the Central Asian cotton plantations to the heights of political power in Moscow. Among those toppled by the affair were Nikolai Shchelokov, a former Minister of Internal Affairs and his first deputy, Yuri Churbanov, a son-in-law of the late Leonid Brezhnev. The notoriety surrounding the trial made the two special investigators who broke the case popular heroes in Russia.[25] It also made them among the most hated figures among Central Asian circles where the anti-crime campaign was seen as an ethnic Russian backlash against local Central Asian gains.

As perestroika got underway in Uzbekistan then, the internal political situation was "tense." The native party and administrative apparatus had just suffered the worst personnel purge in Uzbekistan's history. There was gathering public anxiety over declining standards of living in the republic. There were bitter conflicts between Moscow administrative officials – both party and government – and the local officials in Uzbekistan.[26] Moscow officials saw Uzbekistan as the most economically inefficient, difficult to manage, and politically corrupt of the Soviet republics. Uzbekistan officials saw the Moscow administrative elite as having reneged on promises to aid the republic through changes in water policy, assistance for the unemployed, measures to alleviate ecological disasters, and increases in prices for agricultural goods and primary commodities.

A turning point was the first USSR Congress of Peoples' Deputies in the spring of 1989. Uzbek officials spoke out publicly, voicing criticism of policies toward the republic, focusing on the regionalization of the Central Asian economy. Rafik Nishanov decried the "monstrous" cotton monoculture of the region as having brought "Uzbekistan not only to an economic stand-still, but having produced mass ecological decay and mass illness."[27] Tulepbergen Kaipbergenov bemoaned the state of the Aral Sea, saying that his presentation was "not to cry over the Aral; the Aral needs water, not tears."[28]

Political reform in Moscow meant a political reform in Uzbekistan as well. The last hurried session of the old Uzbek republic Supreme Soviet, meeting for only two days, passed a series of amendments and decrees that paralleled the USSR electoral changes that were passed in December 1988. New draft elections laws, one for republican elections and one for local elections, were introduced and then, following a brief discussion period, were spirited through the Uzbek Supreme Soviet on October 20, 1989. The next day a new language law naming Uzbek as the government language of the republic was passed.[29] The last decrees issued by the departing parliament were the resolutions establishing the timing of the republican and local elections.[30] Both were set for the same day, February 18, 1990.

The most important aspect of the election in the Uzbek republic was the nomination process. It is also the aspect of the election on which we have the least reliable information. Individuals only had the right to nominate candidates from within recognized organizations or institutions. Some groups, for instance the "informals" (*neformaly*), were thereby effectively excluded from participation. The voter turnout in the general election was high, especially in the rural areas.[31] 9,385,740 people, or 93.5 percent of the eligible voters, cast ballots.[32] The initial round of voting on February 18, 1990, selected 368 deputies. In the first election, 386 of the districts filled their seats.[33]

By the time the new Supreme Soviet convened its first session on March 24, 1990, only the first and second round of elections had been completed.[34] According to the public announcements, 463 of the deputies were sworn in at the new session.[35]

The republican and local elections in the Uzbek republic changed the landscape of local politics. Groups that had previously lobbied through informal networks now found that taking their message to the public was

Table 16.3. *Uzbek Soviet Socialist Republic Peoples' Deputies, February 18, 1990, first ballot*

| | |
|---|---|
| 500 | electoral districts |
| 174 | districts had only a single candidate |
| 177 | district had two candidates |
| 149 | districts had three or more candidates |
| 1,094 | candidates altogether |
| 93.5 | percent of voters participating |
| 386 | deputies chosen |

another method of advancement. However, it is not clear that the substance of local politics changed appreciably or quickly with this political reform.

One good example of the continuity in Uzbekistan politics is the outcome of the all-union referendum on whether to retain the USSR in the form of a "renewed union of sovereign states." During the campaign period, the idea of staying with the union received broad support from such groups as the Uzbekistan republican Soviet of Women and many Moslem clerics. Both before and after the referendum, the overwhelming majority of local economists and technical specialists spoke in favor of retaining the Union.[36] In the referendum itself, Uzbek voters virtually unanimously voted in favor of retention of the union.[37]

Table 16.4. *Results of the USSR federal referendum within the Uzbek Soviet Socialist Republic*

| | Registered voters | % "for" | % "against" |
|---|---|---|---|
| Uzbek SSR | 10,287,938 | 93.7 | |
| Karakalpak ASSR | 584,208 | 97.6 | 1.8 |
| Andizhan | 903,734 | 94.0 | 4.6 |
| Bukhara | 845,237 | 96.1 | 3.1 |
| Dzhizak | 360,035 | 94.8 | 4.3 |
| Kashkadarin | 760,051 | 94.6 | 4.2 |
| Namangan | 756,947 | 91.7 | 6.9 |
| Samarkand | 1,114,339 | 93.5 | 5.4 |
| Surkhandar | 602,816 | 97.6 | 1.8 |
| Syrdar | 282,928 | 95.4 | 3.9 |
| Tashkent | 1,144,617 | 92.8 | 6.0 |
| Fergana | 1,130,981 | 94.3 | 3.5 |
| Khorezm | 500,199 | 97.1 | 2.1 |
| Tashkent City | 1,273,846 | 88.1 | 10.5 |

*Source: Savet Uzbekistani, March 21, 1991.*

Like the other republics of the former Soviet Union, Uzbekistan declared "national sovereignty" in 1990. But, at least for Uzbekistan, in 1990 the definition of "socialist national sovereignty" was a peculiar one; it meant sovereignty *within* the confines of the USSR. Uzbekistan did not have a developed anti-colonial nationalist movement nor did Uzbekistan's political leadership expect that the Soviet Union would disintegrate. After the abortive coup d'etat in Moscow in August 1991, Uzbekistan's leadership reevaluated the situation. Only then did real consideration of national independence begin.[38] The adoption of the "Alma-Ata Declaration" in December 1991 brought an end to the USSR and brought "sudden independence" to Uzbekistan.[39]

## State building and civil rights

When political intrigue in Moscow culminated in the paralysis of the central Soviet government in August 1991, Uzbekistan moved quickly to reconfigure its internal political structures. After a period of hesitation on whether to support the political coup against Gorbachev, the Karimov government began taking steps to consolidate its powers. Karimov resigned from the CPSU on August 23. On August 26, the Ministry of Internal Affairs and the KGB were both nationalized and legally subordinated to the Uzbekistan President. The property of the Uzbek Communist Party was nationalized on August 30. The Uzbek party itself changed its form, becoming officially the Peoples Democratic Party (PDP) the following month. The Uzbek republic was finally declared an independent and sovereign state on September 1.

The Uzbekistan declarations of sovereignty and independence were less far-reaching than those in other Soviet republics. They were designed to be instruments used in negotiations with Moscow rather than in redesigning the Uzbek system of governance. By the first months of 1992, however, the new Uzbek government was forced to assume the responsibilities of the old regime. The new government took on a highly personalistic shape, with the office of the president at the epicenter. While the legislature continued to function it did so mainly in an advisory capacity, subordinated to the office of the presidency. A parliamentary decree in July 1992 provided for the withdrawal of the authority of a People's Deputy if the deputy was charged with "anti-constitutional actions aimed at undermining the state structure."[40] The president presided over a presidential council, the economic ministries, a new system of regional administration, and the legislature.

In the summer of 1992 a Consultative Council was established. The Council included the Prime Minister, his first deputy, district administrators (the *hakims*), specialists from the ministries, and the chairmen of the Uzbek and Karakalpak Supreme Soviets. The Karakalpak Autonomous Republic was brought under the direct supervision of the Uzbekistan government, and the chairman of the Karakalpakstan Supreme Soviet and Chairman of the Karakalpakstan Council of Ministers were forced to resign.

Uzbekistan established several new institutions of government. The legislative branch is headed by the Oliy Majlis (Supreme Council). The executive branch is headed by the President, who is the highest official of government and state power. The judiciary is a three-tiered system consisting of the Constitutional Court, Supreme Court, and Arbitration Court.

The Uzbekistan Constitution was adopted by the parliament in December 1992. The Constitution describes a secular, democratic state in which "the people are the sole source of state power." The preamble to it notes that one of the principal goals of the people of Uzbekistan is to "create a humane and democratic rule of law." It guarantees rights of freedom of speech, assembly, and religion, as well as the rights to express one's national heritage. According to the Constitution, the highest organ or power is the legislature. But it also describes a unitary "presidential form of government," identifying the president as the "head of state and executive authority in the republic." The powers of the executive include: the right to represent the state abroad; appoint and recall diplomats; form the government and head it; establish and dissolve ministries and other government organizations; appoint and dismiss the prime minister and his deputies, members of the Cabinet, and the procurator-general and his deputies; nominate appointees to the Constitutional Court, Supreme Court, and Board of the Central Bank; appoint and dismiss judges of regional, district, city and arbitration courts; appoint and dismiss Hakims for violations of the law; suspend or repeal acts of Hakims; sign all laws of the Oliy Majlis or return them for reconsideration; declare state of emergency; serve as Commander-in-Chief of the Armed Forces; declare war; award orders and medals; rule on matters of citizenship; issue amnesty and pardons; and form and dismiss heads of the national security service.

The president is elected by direct, secret – but not competitive – election for a term of five years. According to the Constitution, a president can hold the office no more than two terms. After state service, the president becomes a lifetime member of the Constitutional Court.

What the Constitution does not say is also important. There are no meaningful lower tiers of independent authority (i.e., no federal divisions), the vice president is not mentioned and no relationship is specified between the President and a political party.

The Oliy Majlis functions as an advisory and legitimating instrument, not as a deliberative body. Article 10 of the Uzbekistan Constitution states that the "Oliy Majlis and President of the Republic, elected by the people, shall have the exclusive right to act on behalf of the people." The powers of the legislature include drafting of laws; passing of laws; promulgation of laws; appropriation of funds; and enforcement of laws. The legislature does not possess subpoena power or the power to hold hearings. Oversight of the executive branch is limited to confirmation of certain Executive appointments[41] and access to information.

The judicial system consists of three branches: a) a Constitutional Court, charged with deciding questions of the constitutionality of legislative or executive decisions; b) a Supreme Court, the highest judicial body of civil, criminal, and administrative law; c) an Arbitration Court, charged with deciding questions of economic management. The Constitutional Court has the right to decide cases of disputes between the legislature and executive and to rule on the constitutionality of legislative and executive decisions. Ostensibly to deter politicization of the judiciary, all members of the Constitutional Court and judges are forbidden from joining political parties. In theory, the judiciary is independent; in practice, however, the judiciary is subordinate to the executive in virtually all matters.

There are four major territorial divisions: the Autonomous Republic (Karakalpakstan), the district, region, and city. The Constitution specifies in a general way the "competence" of the lower administrative units. But the Constitution makes clear that the authorities of these lower administrative units are delegated, not independent. This new prefectural system of administration shifted the twelve former oblasts to districts headed by a *hakim*. All of the *hakim* appointments announced in March were ethnic Uzbeks, all had been previous oblast party committee secretaries, and all were members of the Peoples Democratic Party of Uzbekistan, the party headed by Islam Karimov.

The political process is also carefully monitored and controlled. The Central Electoral Commission (CEC), a fourteen member board established by the parliament on the advice of the president, is responsible for oversight of the nomination process, the campaigning, and the organization of the election. Campaign financing and publicity is managed by the CEC. According to the election law passed in December 1993, the right to nominate candidates is reserved to registered political parties, veliats (districts) legislative councils, and the Karakalpak parliament. Moreover, political parties must satisfy the additional condition that they have been registered with the Ministry of Justice no less than six months prior to the election and have collected the signatures of 50,000 voters supporting their participation in the election. These and other restrictions on the nomination process make it possible for the government to exercise a determinative influence on the preselection of candidates. The most recent legislative elections held on December 25, 1994, found Karimov supporters taking a clear majority of the parliament's seats.

Uzbekistan's new government institutions strike a sharp contrast with those of civil societies designed to protect the interests of the citizen with respect to the state. The assumption underlying the structure of government is that civil rights proceed from the rights of the collectivity, and not that the government derives its authority from the consent of the governed.

## The "national question"

In the few years since independence, the "national question" has assumed an entirely new character in Uzbekistan. The decree on Uzbekistan citizenship adopted on July 28, 1992, granted citizenship to all persons living on the territory, without regard to national origin, social status, race, sex, education, language, or political views. (Dual citizenship, was excluded, however.)[42] But Karimov's policy since independence has been to encourage the groundswell of popular support for the celebration of Uzbek national identity.

According to Soviet nationality theory, nationality was calibrated principally by three measures: ethnicity, language, and a common history. Where Soviet policy attempted to eradicate national identity and national consciousness, Karimov has made it the defining feature of the republic. Where Soviet policy attempted to relegate indigenous languages to a second class status relative to the Russian language, Karimov has reversed this process. Where history was lost (or destroyed) in the Soviet period, Uzbek history is now being recovered (or recreated). In short, the new institutions of government in Uzbekistan are designed to maximize the prerogatives of the state to achieve social goals.

The Uzbek language is not one language, but a family of related languages. The Uzbek literary language – the Fergana dialect of Uzbek – is the language of the media, but it is not always comprehensible to all Uzbeks. In general, there are three other linguistic groups: one includes speakers of the other Turkic languages; a second includes speakers of Persian (Tajik); and a third includes virtually everyone else, that is, speakers of Russian. The new government emphasis on Uzbek, however, is sure to impose a single, comprehensible linguistic convention on the country in a short time. In September 1992, the General Director of the Uzbek National Information Agency announced that the agency, beginning January 1, 1993, would produce information only in the Uzbek language.[43] The Russian language street signs of the Soviet period have virtually disappeared in Uzbekistan, remaining only in Tashkent and a few other areas with a higher concentration of Russian-speakers.

The difficult situation of the Russian-speaking population in Uzbekistan was underscored late in 1989 with the passage of the new law on the official language in Uzbekistan. Article 5, which calls for a transition from Russian to Turkic, was not to come into effect for eight years, that is, until 1997, but the passage of the law prompted a speedier than anticipated transition.[44] Many people were thus caught in the transition of the Uzbek language from the status of a minority language to that of the majority language.

Often the Russian speakers are regarded as former "occupiers" or "colonizers." Some Uzbeks have expressed the feeling that the despoilers of their native lands should leave or even make restitution for what they have done in Uzbekistan.[45] In light of this, fear for the future, and particularly for the future of their children, has convinced many to leave Uzbekistan.[46] 1990 was a year of debate among many Russians whether the time had come for a return to the "Russian homeland."[47] Many of those who could leave for Russia did so, often at great expense to Uzbekistan. As one analyst warned in 1990, if the trend toward migration was not reversed, in two to three years the technologically advanced production sectors in Central Asia would experience a "catastrophic shortage of technological specialists" leading to, ultimately, to the "Angolicization" of the Central Asian economy.[48] Yet catastrophic consequences have not occurred, perhaps because there are many ethnic Russians and members of other non-Uzbek ethnic groups who have resigned themselves to staying in "stable" Uzbekistan rather than risking relocation to their ethnic homelands.

## Uzbekistan's role in Central Asia: leader or partner?

One lesson of the transition to independence is that, in a world of growing global interdependence, national self-determination does not mean what it did a century or even fifty years ago. When Kemal Ataturk, the "Father" of the modern Turkish state, championed the independence of Turkey some seventy-four years ago, he could prevail in a "go it alone" strategy of national development. In contrast, the leaders of the newly-independent former Soviet states have no such luxury.

### Reign of personalism

Central Asian leaders were not prepared for the trade and security implications of independence, nor for the political infighting which started as soon as independence began. But what Central Asia was perhaps the least prepared for was the deluge of influences from the outside world. Soon after independence came voluntary assistance programs by churches and cultural groups. Some humanitarian assistance came to Uzbekistan in the form of the U.S. sponsored "Operation Provide Hope," a program which began its activities in early 1992. Soon afterward, the European Union established the Program of Technical Assistance for Commonwealth of Independent States (TACIS). The U.S. Peace Corps arrived in late 1992. The European Bank for Reconstruction and Development opened a mission in Tashkent; the International Monetary Fund (IMF) and the World Bank opened permanent offices. By 1994, Uzbekistan was no longer terra incognito to the outside world. For better and for worse, Uzbekistan became accustomed to diplomats, business people, tourists, do-gooders, and some do-not-so-gooders. Uzbek officials came to feel that the outside world was more difficult to adjust to than they had expected.[49] Many in Uzbekistan began to talk about doing things in an "Uzbek way."

The most common explanation for the Uzbek propensity to political unorthodoxy is that the Uzbek culture of authority is distinctively different than it is elsewhere.[50] According to defenders of the Uzbek approach to authority, the relationship between the citizen and the state in Uzbekistan is determined not by the influence of political institutions, but by centuries of highly developed tradition regarding the proper way to make public decisions.

The peoples of present-day Uzbekistan are the heirs of the ancient settled regions of Central Asia. Their styles of behavior are very different from, for instance, their Tajik and Kyrgyz neighbors. Traditions of tribal democracy and inter-tribal confederation that were strong among the nomadic peoples of the mountains and the plains are contrasted in Uzbekistan with traditions of hierarchy and authoritarianism among the settled peoples of the river valleys and oases. An outsider who sits down at the negotiating table to observe Kyrgyz interacting with Uzbeks is likely to conclude that the cultural differences are much greater between them than between, for instance, European neighbors.

The authoritarianism of the settled peoples of Central Asia has long been apparent to outsiders. Some scholars have sought explanation for these cultural differences by noting that the functions of regimentation and centralization required by the nature of the irrigated oasis society produced an effect on the structure of power. In his highly criticized interpretation of the origins of "Oriental despotism," Karl Wittfogel argued that the demands that emerged from the necessity to centrally manage an irrigation system produced a socio-political organization which he characterized as the "hydraulic society."[51] Wittfogel's thesis is that unlike the individualistic political culture that developed in many water-rich agrarian societies, semi-arid agricultural societies often required a high level of centralized decision making. The demands of the hydraulic society resulted in the emergence of the "managerial state," the economic, administrative and political functions of which were concentrated in a ruling class consisting of landowners, land managers, and the military.

Outsiders, even when they are sensitive to the great differences among the groups of Central Asia, often assess Central Asian values in terms of their distinctive acceptance of hierarchy. Perhaps the most visible aspect of the public culture of these countries is the great importance associated with *hurmat*, the ideas of "deference" or "respect."

In present day Central Asian life, the origins of *hurmat* are not hard to find. *Hurmat* begins in the family. Personal life is family life in Central

Asian societies. Property is communal, *palov* (the preferred Central Asia dish) is shared, elders are deferred to without question, and the subordinate position of women in society is reinforced through the family structure. Authority is personalized and personal loyalties are deeply rooted. Obligation tends to be focused on an individual, not an idea.

The power of personalism in Uzbekistan is illustrated by the country's president, Islam Karimov. Born in the same year as the great Stalinist purge, 1938, Karimov was a party worker who rose through the financial bureaucracies of the republic. Karimov was not an Uzbek nationalist, but neither was he a "socialist cosmopolitan" in the mold of Kazakhstan's Nazarbaev or Kyrgyzstan's Akaev.

Although Karimov initially supported the August 1991 coup attempt in Moscow and opposed the breakup of the USSR, he moved quickly to champion national values once the Soviet Union disintegrated in December. In the ethnically Uzbek northern province of Tajikistan, many people refer to Karimov – whom they regarded as their protector in the Tajik civil war – as *Islam-Aka* (Father Islam). Their deference to Karimov is not "political," it is familial.[52]

The most visible political opposition movements in Uzbekistan in the period of Soviet disintegration were Birlik (Unity) and Erk (Will). Birlik's case, in particular, is illustrative of political consolidation in Uzbekistan. Less a democratic movement than a reflection of the elation of independence, Birlik started early in 1990 as only a small group of intellectuals. It quickly discovered broad popular support, however, through drawing attention to pressing problems, spearheading protest efforts and generally awakening Central Asian citizens from a state of political passivity. Birlik's leaders defined its main goals as achieving economic and political sovereignty while restoring the cultural values of the people of Uzbekistan.[53]

The ability of Birlik to mount such a broad appeal was viewed as threatening by the communist party elite ruling the country. To counter this threat, Uzbekistan's political leadership adopted a two-pronged policy – the government absorbed many of Birlik's younger recruits and adopted many of the slogans, at the same time it brutally suppressed Birlik's leaders.[54] Birlik was allowed by the government officially to register as a public organisation in November 1991, but did not succeed in getting on the ballot in the parliamentary elections. In connection with the harassment, arrests, beatings, and attempted assassinations of Birlik's leaders, as well as other opposition figures, the Karimov regime quickly gained a reputation as a systematic violator of human rights.[55]

Karimov's concentration of power under the general idea of presidential leadership provoked charges of dictatorship by some of his closest collaborators. Shukurulla Mirsaidov, a former first secretary of the Fergana communist party organization as well as vice-president of Uzbekistan, resigned as a deputy of the Uzbekistan parliament in August 1992, claiming, in a letter to his constituents, that an authoritarian regime was being established with the connivance of the Uzbek parliament.[56] On September 8, 1992, Mirsaidov also resigned as vice-president of Uzbekistan.

Ethnic Russians may insist that patterns of "Khanstvo" based upon unquestioning respect for elders, deference to authority, and the perceived "impoliteness" of public criticism make democracy impossible in Uzbekistan.[57] Be that as it may, the style of "authoritarian democracy" that has surfaced in Uzbekistan is definitely different from the party-led totalitarianism of the past – it is more closely related to forms of politics that came long before the existence of the communist party.

## Uzbekistan's "Asian path"

Uzbekistan's authoritarian political culture puts its leaders in a position to play a more direct role in determining the macroeconomic policy of the country than would be the case in a more pluralistic culture. In the immediate period following the breakup of the USSR, President Karimov elaborated a strategy for economic development in Uzbekistan that fits a textbook model of a populist leader.[58] Karimov's goal is to preserve political stability by improving living standards and creating an atmosphere of stable public expectations.

At the time of independence Uzbekistan was confronted with a choice between principal models of development. The chief contenders included the continuation of state socialism with a combination of bureaucratism and neo-Marxist ideology, the liberal democratic western model with a combination of political pluralism and the hurly-burly of an open market, the "Little Tigers" model with a combination of strong state paternalism and neo-mercantilism, and the Chinese model with a combination of authoritarian political rule and a mercantilist economic development strategy.

In the early months of independence, Karimov and his advisors criticized what they considered the gathering chaos in Russia and the economic travail of the liberal democracies of Latin America. They argued that the European path and the North American path were inappropriate for a country like Uzbekistan. The "Uzbek Path" that emerged by the end of 1993 was clearly closer to the "Asian Path" than to the European.

Uzbekistan's macroeconomic policy stressed the state control of a managed market during the transitional period. Karimov's often repeated dictum of conservatism – "You do not tear down your old house before you are finished building the new one" – was invoked again and again at various levels of the bureaucracy to justify the continuation of policies (and the perpetuation of offices) that existed prior to the Soviet breakup. The state adopted a pro-business approach, but one which relied heavily upon a collusive marriage between private firms and bureaucratic agencies. The state adopted an export-oriented economic policy, but it relied upon family connections of government officials and stressed the foreign marketing of primary commodities such as cotton and gold which could be easily controlled by the government. And the state adopted a private-property orientation, but it was one that emphasized the good of the state rather than individual rights as the basis for property relations.

In theory, Uzbekistan adopted a pro-business posture to use the market as an engine of economic growth. But satisfying the conditions necessary to create markets did not always square well with the entrenched interests of the bureaucratic apparatus of economic decision-making. The case of foreign trade policy is illustrative. In June 1990, the Uzbek republic passed a law "On the formation of a Government Committee of the Uzbek SSR on foreign trade and external contacts,"[59] which assert the republic's right to conduct an independent foreign economic policy. But the law also emphasized the role of the Uzbek government in coordinating all economic, commercial and scientific-technical relations with foreign countries. The legislation was essentially designed to create an export-led "para-statist" organization to promote trade.

Presidential decrees passed in the following two years sought to promote trade and boost foreign investment. The first series of decrees, adopted in the summer of 1992, relieved agricultural enterprises of a Value Added Tax and offered incentives for foreign investment. In early 1994, a package of trade reform measures included provisions for cancellation of import duties, a moratorium on taxes for joint ventures, exclusion of foreigners from double taxation, and a convention on solution of interstate investment disputes backed by $1.5 billion of Uzbekistan gold reserves in foreign banks. Yet the pro-trade decrees were implemented by the state bureaucracy which frequently responded to cues other than those of the market.

An illustration of the difficulties of trading under this politically controlled economic environment is the series of hotels built by an Indian firm in downtown Tashkent, Samarkand, and Bukhara. A dispute over how profits from the enterprise would be distributed led the Uzbekistan government to suspend the project. The hotels, 90 percent complete and clearly the most modern hotel facilities in the country, have sat vacant for more than two years while the personalities involved have worked to sort out their differences. Other deals have been more successful; for instance, Mercedes-Benz has opened a truck factory in Khorezm, a South Korean/Uzbek joint venture is producing television sets, and Uzbekistan has announced plans to open an airplane factory with Ukraine, but the economic risks inherent in the centrally controlled Uzbek system surely has driven many firms away.

Uzbekistan's efforts to privatize have met with similar mixed results. In the spring of 1993, thousands of apartment buildings and private homes were privatized. Particularly in the large cities such as Tashkent and Samarkand, tenants became owners for nominal sums, and then were free to sell their privately owned apartments on the open market for relatively large amounts of money. In Tashkent, apartments that were purchased from the state for only dollars became worth thousands of dollars.

Privatization of public assets was more complicated. In late 1993, plans were adopted by GKI, the government committee on property, to auction off some public assets such as restaurants, small factories, hotels, and unfinished buildings. An initial auction in Namangan in February 1994 was very successful. Perhaps because of the initial success, the privatization process came under a great deal of criticism for alleged insider trading, culminating in the removal of the Director of GKI in late 1993. The privatization of land was even more problematic. In late 1994, probably in an effort to defuse criticism of the privatization process, the Karimov government announced the real privatization of agricultural land. Although this decree has not yet been implemented, if it is carried out Uzbekistan would become the first of the ex-Soviet governments to truly privatize land.

The privatization experience illustrates one of the most difficult challenges for Uzbekistan's economy, the problem of economic corruption. Corruption in much of the developing world is systemic and enduring. Uzbekistan's experience is best illustrated by the cotton affair, which, after independence, became a symbol of foreign manipulation. The cotton convicts became a celebrated cause among the working Uzbek populace.[60] In the atmosphere of political independence, Karimov pardoned those charged with economic crimes, in many cases restoring individuals to positions of influence and prestige. The problem of economic corruption endures. The fusion of economic and political power in Uzbekistan makes obtaining a trade license, gaining a trade concession, or acquiring property a transaction that requires both government connections and a willingness to increase the incentives of responsible officials.

Uzbekistan is tied to its neighbors by a common geography and culture and is linked to them by common trade, security, and environmental interests. The outlines of Uzbekistan's new role within the community of Central Asian states is not yet clear, but competing visions of Uzbekistan's future role in Central Asia have begun to emerge. The leading question in Uzbekistan's future is whether Uzbekistan will assume the posture of a partner or a leader among the new states of Central Asia.

The role of Uzbekistan starts with the question of the identity of Central Asia itself: Is Central Asia one region or many states? If it is one region with "artificial borders," to what extent can they be changed and by whom? As the Soviet Union was moving toward disintegration, the leaders of the Communist Party met in the summer of 1990 to adopt a critically important political principle. They agreed that Central Asia was one cultural unit but many political entities,[61] pledged that they would abstain from any effort to change borders and recognized the right of each of the "republics" to independent and separate existence.[62]

This formula on the one hand gave lip service to the idea of a unified "cultural space" in Central Asia, and on the other hand managed to salvage the political institutions with which each of the leaders was associated. It was a compromise which allowed them to reject the colonial yoke imposed by Moscow and at the same time reject sentiment in favor of the creation of a greater "Turkestan." This idea of a unifed Turkestan had been around for a long time, but it was not possible to openly propose or even discuss it during the Soviet period. But as the Soviet Union was unravelling, unification became a real alternative. As one journalist expressed it, "the question of the creation of a union of the five Central Asian republics was swirling around the halls of the capitals of the republics" during the July 1991 meeting of the presidents.[63] After the August 1991 putsch in Moscow was repulsed, the sentiment in favor of uniting the Central Asian republics intensified. A historian at Tashkent State University observed in October 1991, "The country we call the Soviet Union is gone. I dream to live in a time that we will form a United States of Asia.[64]

The resurgence of Islamic tradition initially also played an important, albeit limited, role in supporting a united Central Asia. Prior to the Soviet breakup, "official Islam" – that is the ecclesiastical institutions that were in reality controlled by the KGB – remained conservative. For example, Kazi Zakhidzhan, a Soviet-period Islamic cleric, argued in favor of "Soviet patriotism." A former Mufti of Tashkent, Muhammad Sadiq Yusupov, who was elected in 1989 to the USSR Congress of Peoples Deputies, helped to restore calm in Fergana after the interethnic riots. He also led the Islamic faithful in a campaign to retain the Soviet Union when this issue was put to popular vote in March 1991.

But after the breakup, Islam quickly reestablished its position as the leader of Uzbek culture. The role of Islam is everywhere visible in Uzbekistan where public prayer and respect for the five pillars of Islam is manifest. At the same time, however, the Karimov regime has steadfastly opposed the political aspect of Islam. The regime has identified the republic as a secular government and has systematically sought to exclude anti-regime Islamic movements, branding them as products of foreign adventurism. Those Muslim organizations which attempted to sponsor more rapid change were isolated by the Uzbek authorities. For instance, the "All-Union Islamic Party of Renewal" was allowed to register as a party in Moscow, but the branch in Uzbekistan was declared illegal and its meetings were broken up.

In matters of national security, Karimov has adopted a realist hardline. His arguments resonate among the citizenry primarily because of the events in Tajikistan, where political independence produced new opportunities for opposition forces to openly challenge the claim of the former members of the communist apparat to lead the post-communist government.[65] Rather than producing democracy, however, the situation brought civil war. By mid-1992, the Tajik civil war became the defining element in security relationships in Central Asia.[66]

Events in Tajikistan propelled Uzbekistan in the direction of developing an independent military capacity. As the Soviet Union broke up, the Central Asian states became heir to various components of the Soviet military-industrial complex, including both conventional and high-tech weaponry.[66] After independence, Uzbekistan did not have nuclear weapons, but it did have a large cadre of nuclear science specialists.[67] Kyrgyzstan, Tajikistan and Uzbekistan had uranium mines, many located in the Fergana Valley, all of which are under Uzbekistan's protection.[68] A major storage and testing facility for Soviet biological and chemical weapons was previously located on Resurrection Island in the Aral Sea.

The changing military profile in Uzbekistan is apparent. In June 1993 Karimov announced a major program to reconfigure the scientific and engineering establishment of Uzbekistan to provide the low-tech answers to their regional security problems. For instance, a major diesel engine factory in Tashkent which previously supplied engines for Soviet tanks had been shuttered and closed for almost two years. In the spring of 1993 the factory was reopened to produce engines for troop transport vehicles for local needs. By the end of 1994, the most prestigious institute for study of young Uzbeks was not the Law Faculty of the Ministry of Justice, or Tashkent State University of the Ministry of Education, but the Military Academy of the Ministry of Defense.

## After independence

We usually think of a transition to national independence as ushering in a period of "new policies" driven forward by an anti-colonial nationalist program designed to restore autonomy and self-determination. But very little of this description applies to the politics of national independence in Uzbekistan. The politics of the "new Uzbekistan" can hardly be described as a break with tradition. Nationalism was not an important element in the establishment of the present leadership. This was clearly a case of revolution "from above"; virtually the entire political and economic leadership is a carry over from the Soviet period. Uzbekistan's national independence did not "restore" autonomy and national self-determination, for Uzbekistan never existed as an independent political unit prior to its capture in the late nineteenth century by Russia. Uzbekistan did not achieve "splendid isolation" and complete autonomy, for its infrastructure was tightly meshed with that of the former USSR in such a way that immediate disentanglement would have been suicidal.

If the politics of independence in a country as proud, self-confident, and richly rooted in tradition as Uzbekistan teaches us any lesson, it is that autonomy in the modern period is necessarily limited and constrained. Globalization, economic interdependence, and the communications revolution have limited the scope of independence. Traditional nation-state conflicts such as economic nationalism and security competition have constrained new state leaders even further. Uzbekistan is linked to the other countries of the CIS in ways that will continue to dominate Uzbekistan's political agenda for many years to come.

## NOTES

Research for this article was made possible with the help of the United States Institute of Peace, the Hoover Institution at Stanford University, and the University of New Mexico. The author gratefully acknowledges this assistance.

1 In the last two years, the political institutions of the former USSR have changed substantially. Conventions of popular usage of political terminology will no doubt change as well though perhaps more slowly. "Ozbekistan" is the Latin transliteration of the Uzbek language name for Uzbekistan. The more familiar variant, "Uzbekistan," is the Russianized version. With the passage of the Uzbekistan's "Law on Languages" in December 1989 declaring Uzbek to be the official language of the republic and with Uzbekistan's Declaration of Independence of August 31, 1991, the practice of transliterating from Uzbek to Russian to English is no longer justified. In deference to established patterns of usage, however, many of the terms used in this article derive from the Russianized versions of Uzbek words. Transliterations are from either the Russian according to the Library of Congress system or from the Uzbek according to the system presented in Edward Allworth, *Nationalities of the Soviet East: Publications and Writing Systems* (New York: Columbia University Press, 1971).

2 See Gregory Gleason, *Federalism and Nationalism: The Struggle for Republican Rights in the USSR* (Boulder, CO: Westview Press, 1990), chapter 2.

3 For an account of the main contests between the local groups and the Russians, see Michael Rywkin, *Moscow's Muslim Challenge*, revised edn (Armonk, NY: M.E. Sharpe, 1990), chapter 2.

4 V.I. Lenin, *Polnoe Sochinenia*, vol. 41, p. 436. A suggestion that Lenin attached a great deal of importance, if only unconsciously, to the unifying aspect of the common Turkic language, was the notable omission of the Persian speaking group, the Tajiks. Lenin, it should be noted, had never been in Central Asia and thus had to rely upon his lieutenants' accounts for descriptions of the political situation there.

5 V.I. Lenin, *Polnoe*, vol. 41, p. 436.

6 The republic had four oblasts: the Zakaspiiskaia oblast (roughly today's Turkmenistan); the Ferganskii oblast (roughly today's southern Kazakhstan and Kyrgyz SSR); and the Syrdarinskaia oblast (covering most of today's Uzbek SSR and parts of the Kazakh SSR along the Syr-Daria river).

7 Mysteriously, Soviet historical sources are remarkably inconsistent in the identification of the political units of the early period. For instance, sources will refer frequently to the "Khorezm Peoples, Republic" but use the appreviation "KhPSR." Some sources, indeed, in the same article refer to it variously as the "Khorezm Soviet People Republic" and the "Khorezm Peoples Soviet Republic." See Sh. Z. Urazaev, "Uzbekskoi sovetskoi natsional'noi gosudarstvennosti – 60 let," *Obshchestvennye nauki v Uzbekistane*, no. 5, 1984, pp. 3–8, esp. p. 4.

8  A. Agzamkhodzhaev and Sh. Urazaev, "Natsional'no-gosudarstvennomu razmezhevaniiu respublik Sovetskoi Srednei Azii – 60 let," *Sovetskoe gosudarstvo i pravo*, no. 10, 1984, pp. 25–33, at p. 26.

9  On the land and water reform in Central Asia, see Frank A. Ecker, "Transition in Asia," Ph.D. dissertation, University of Michigan, 1952.

10  Russians for some time previously had referred to the Kazakhs as Kyrgyz and to the Kyrgyz as Karakyrgyz.

11  Agzamkhodzhaev, p. 30.

12  A. Agzamkhodzhaev and Sh. Urazaev, "Natsional'no-gosudarstvennomu . . .," p. 29. James Critchlow examines the argument that Faizulla Khodzhev's support for the land reform was lukewarm in light of his nationalist as opposed to internationalist leanings. See James Critchlow, "Did Faizulla Khojaev Really Oppose Uzbekistan's Land Reform?" *Central Asian Survey*, vol. 9, no. 3, 1990, pp. 29–41.

13  Agazamkhodzhaev, p. 31.

14  Khodzhaev, vol. II, p. 415.

15  Two border changes which are critical and should be mentioned are the 1924 subordination of the Karakalpaks to the RSFSR and the 1929 transformation of the Tajik Autonomous Republic into a union republic. The Karakalpaks were switched to Uzbekistan subordination with the adoption of the Stalin Constitution of 1936. The Karakalpak Autonomous Republic declared sovereignty on December 14, 1990. For a discussion, see S. Nietullaev, "Trudnyi put'k soglasiiu," *Pravda Vostoka* April 4, 1991, p. 3.

16  See Lee Schwartz, "Regional Population Redistribution and National Homelands in the USSR," in Henry R. Huttenbach, *Soviet Nationality Policies: Ruling Ethnic Groups in the USSR* (London: Mansell Publishing Company, 1990), p. 133.

17  See A. Alimmov and A. Mursaliev, "Nas uchili prygat' cherez kapitalizm," *Komsomol'skaia pravda*, March 3, 1991, p. 1.

18  See Bernard V. Oliver, "Korenizatsiia," *Central Asian Survey* vol. 9, no. 3, 1990, pp. 77–98.

19  For a description of the various ideological gradations within this group see the chapter "Muslim National Communism," in Alexandre Bennigsen and Chantal Lemercier-Quelquejay, *Islam in the Soviet Union* (London: Pall Mall Press, 1967), pp. 101–119.

20  Niyazov had been First Secretary of the CPUz since 1950. After his demotion he was appointed Minister of Communal Economy, a ministry which was abolished just over a year afterward. He later served for a short period as an agricultural secretary of the CPTu. The data on Niyazov and the other personalities discussed here are taken from a number of sources, the most useful of which is Grey Hodnett and Val Ogareff, *Leaders of the Soviet Republics, 1955–1972* (Canberra: Australian National University, 1973). Additional data is from various editions of *Who's Who in the U.S.S.R*, compiled by the former Institute for the Study of the USSR (Austria: Intercontinental Book and Publishing Company, Ltd.), Herwig Kraus, compiler: Herwig Kraus, "The Composition of Leading Organs of the CPSU, (1952–1982)," Supplement to the Radio Liberty Research Bulletin (Munich: 1982); Directory of Soviet Officials, Volume II, Union Republics (US State Department, June, 1966); various editions of *Directory of Soviet Officials, Volume III: Union Republics* (National Foreign Assessment Center, US Government, Washington, DC); and the author's own files.

21  See Sh. Ziiamov, *Kadrovaia politika KPSS v deistvii*, (Tashkent: Uzbekistan, 1980), pp. 24–25.

22  See Gregory Gleason, "Nationalism or Political Corruption? The Case of the Cotton Scandal in the USSR," *Corruption and Reform*, vol. 5, no. 2, 1990, pp. 87–108.

23  See Ann Sheehy, "Major Anti-Corruption Drive in Uzbekistan," *Radio Liberty Research Bulletin*, RL 324/84, August 30, 1984, pp. 1–17; James Critchlow, "Further

Repercussions of the 'Uzbek Affair'," *Report on the USSR*, vol. 2, no. 18, 1990, pp. 20–22.

24 This figure is cited by I. Usmankhodzhaev, *Partiinaia zhizn'*, no. 1, January, 1986, pp. 28–33.

25 The investigators, Telman Gdlyan and Nikolai Ivanov became so popular for their anti-corruption campaigns that they were elected to the Congress of People's Deputies in the Soviet Union's first free elections in March 1989. The two continued to assert that there was evidence to implicate other high-ranking officials, including Egor Ligachev, who, as a Politboro member, was a chief executive official in the USSR. Amid the growing political ferment in 1989, the charges of corruption in high places garnered Gdlyan and Ivanov widespread public support among the Soviet citizenry and, as well, many powerful enemies. The two were eventually accused of having used illegal methods for gathering testimonies and evidence. In April 1990, the USSR Supreme Soviet opened a debate over whether to revoke Gdlyan and Ivanov's immunity to prosecution. The multiple ironies of the situation were summed up by one commentator who said of Gdlyan that we do not know whether to call him "Knight of Law and Order" or the "Evil Genius of Perestroika" (Savchenko).

26 The citizens of Uzbekistan, as the citizens of many other areas in the USSR, ponder the significance of their republic's name. It is a multinational republic. But many of its names, in Uzbek, in Russian, in Tajik as in English tend to give precedence to the dominant ethnic group. Is it "Uzbekistan?" Is it the "republic of Uzbekistan?" The "Uzbek republic?" Or the "Uzbek SSR?" In the eyes of Uzbekistan's citizens, it is inaccurate and often very misleading to refer to the republic's citizens as "Uzbeks" unless one refers specifically to the ethnic group. *"Ozbekistanlar"* ("Uzbekistanis") sounds contrived. A good solution has not yet been reached.

27 'Vystyplenie deputata Nishanova, R.N.," *Pravda Vostoka*, June 2, 1989, p. 2.

28 *Pravda Vostoka*, June 1, 1989, p. 1.

29 Both laws were passed on October 20, 1989. The text of the laws was published in *Pravda Vostoka* on October 24 and 25, 1989. See "O vyborakh narodnykh deputatov Uzbekskoi SSR," *Pravda Vostoka*, October 24, 1989, and "O vyborakh deputatov mestnykh sovetov narodnykh deputatov Uzbekskoi SSR," *Pravda Vostoka*, October 25, 1989.

30 These decrees were passed on October 19 and 20, 1989, respectively. See *Pravda Vostoka*, October 21, 1989, p. 1.

31 Some questions were raised with respect to high voter turnout. One newspaper reporter observed that the reported turnouts of over 98 percent in some areas were surely fictitious. As he put it in terms that Uzbekistan's citizens could easily appreciate, "even if they sold meat and oranges at the voting booths you couldn't get that kind of turnout." I. Khisamov, "My vybiraem, nas vybiraiut," *Pravda Vostoka*, March 3, 1990, p. 2.

32 This is a high voter turnout by cross-national comparative standards. In comparison with previous Soviet elections, however, it is low. The turnout for the 1987 local elections in Uzbekistan, for instance, was 99.84 percent. See *Pravda Vostoka*, June 27, 1987, p. 1.

33 In one of the districts, the candidate was apparently disqualified and the election was not held.

34 This was the first session of the twelfth convocation.

35 The reader will note that this figure does not correspond with the election return data presented in the official election outcomes. These would set the total number of elected deputies at 460.

36 See Anvar Agzamkhodzhaev, "Na chem stoit soiuz," *Pravda Vostoka*, April 16, 1991, p. 3.

37 The referendum on the Soviet federal principle was held on March 17 in most of the

USSR. In Uzbekistan, 9,830,782 ballots were counted. 9,196,848 voted in favor. Thus only about 6 percent of the votes were in favor of withdrawal from the Union.

38 Islam Karimov, Put', *obnovlenie* (Tashkent: Fan, 1992).

39 For background on Central Asia in general, see Martha Brill Olcott, "Democracy and Statebuilding in Central Asia: Challenges for U.S. Policy Makers," *Demokratizatsiya*, vol. 2, no. 1, 1993/94, pp. 1139–50; Nancy Lubin, "Pollution, Politics, and Public Opinion in Central Asia," *Demokratizatsiya*, vol. 2, no. 1, 1993–94, pp. 102–107; Paul B. Henze, "Turkestan Rising," *Wilson Quarterly* Summer 1992, pp. 48–58; Roger D. Kangas, "Uzbekistan: Evolving Authoritarianism," *Current History*, April 1994, pp. 178–182.

40 INTERFAX (30 July 1992).

41 Prime Minister, First Deputy PM; Deputy PMs, Procurator-General and his Deputies, and Chairman of Board of State Bank.

42 *FBIS-SOV-92-146* (29 July 1992): 42.

43 *Moscow Radio Mayak* (26 September 1992).

44 Not everyone thinks that the transition to a native language standard will be damaging to the position of the Russians. As one commentator noted, when the local groups have returned to their native languages they will tend to be separated from one another. "The Russian-speaking population will strengthen their position because the means of communication between different speaking republics naturally will be Russian." Alisher Il'khamov, "Vozmozhno li 'Uzbekskoe chudo' ili Rynochnaia ekonomika s vostochnym litsom," *Zhizn i ekonomika* (Tashkent), no. 11, 1990, p. 7.

45 Shakhimarden Kusainov, "Eta zemlia nam Bogom dana," *Munosabat*, no. 1, January, 1990, pp. 7–8.

46 Sergei Tatur, "Vmeste podnimat' Uzbekistan," *Zvezda vostoka*, no. 1, 1991, pp. 3–17.

47 'Bezhentsy v Rossii: Chto dal'she?" *Pravda Vostoka*, November 28, p. 3.

48 Timur Pulatov, "Dogonim i peregonim Angolu!" *Moskovskie novosti*, 14, October 1990, p. 7.

49 Uzbekistan has repeatedly been involved in symbolic diplomatic standoffs with the United States. Karimov rebuffed the US Ambassador to the CIS, Strobe Talbott, in September 1993, by offering a lecture on what the US could gain from relations with Uzbekistan. In January 1994, Uzbekistan detained and then deported one of America's leading Central Asian specialists, William Fierman, in what was visibly a symbolic gesture. Such incidents notwithstanding, the Uzbekistan government's fundamental willingness to cooperate with the US and its desire for American technical assistance was manifest in such positive steps as the signing of the bilateral agreement on technical assistance of March 1, 1994.

50 For a general defense of the culture of personalism in Uzbekistan, see C (pseudonym), "One Man Rule in Uzbekistan: A Perspective from Within the Regime," *Demokratizatsiya*, vol. 1, no. 4, 1993, pp. 44–55.

51 Karl A. Wittfogel, *Oriental Despotism* (New Haven: Yale University Press, 1957).

52 While this is unusual for North Americans, it is not atypical for most of the world. Nor is it foreign to the western intellectual tradition. Aristotle, one will recall, begins his discussion of politics with the structure of the family.

53 Mikhailova, "Nachalo," *Zvezda Vostoka*, no. 4, 1990, pp. 73–81.

54 During his trip to the Central Asian states in February, 1992, US Secretary of State James Baker III met with Birlik's leader, Abdurakhim Pulatov, as an indication of the commitment of the United States government to the principle of political pluralism.

55 See for instance, Human Rights in Uzbekistan *Helsinki Watch*, May 1993; "Straightening Out the Brains of One Hundred: Discriminatory Political Dismissals in Uzbekistan," *Helsinki Watch*, April 1993, vol. 5, issue 7; and Wendy Sloane, "Uzbekistan Cracks Down on Human Rights Activists," *The Christian Science Monitor*, 24 May 1994, 7.

56  Radio Rossli broadcast of August 21, 1992. FBIS-SOV-92 (24 August 1992): 50. 57
    On traditions of deference to authority, see Gregory Gleason, "Fealty and Loyalty:
    Informal Authority Structures in Soviet Asia," *Soviet Studies*, vol. 43, No. 4, 1991, pp.
    613–628.
58  Sheila Marnie and Erik Whitlock, "Central Asia and Economic Integration," *RFE/RL
    Research Report*, vol. 2, no. 14, April 1993, pp. 34–44.
59  The law was passed on June 12, 1990. See Anvar Khamidovich Rasulev, "Proryv na
    vneshnii rynok," *Zhizn' ekonomika*, no. 10, 1990, pp. 54–57.
60  See Gregory Gleason, "Nationalism or Political Corruption? The Case of the Cotton
    Scandal in the USSR," *Corruption and Reform*, vol. 5, no. 2, 1990, pp. 87–108.
61  'Zaiavlenie rukovoditelei of the Uzbek SSR, Kazakh SSR, Kirgiz Tadzhik SSR and
    Turkmen SSR, *"Kommunist Uzbekistana* no. 8, 1990, pp. 56–58.
62  The agreement to retain present borders is important because there are numerous
    territorial disputes among the Uzbeks and other groups of Central Asia. There are
    demands for: secession of Karakalpakia from Uzbekistan; separation of a part of the
    Mangyshlak oblast of Kazakhstan and its addition to Turkmenistan; separation of the
    part of the Tashauz and Chardzhua veliats on the Amu-Darya river from Turkmenistan
    and their addition to Uzbekistan; separation of the northern part of the Bukhara oblast
    from Uzbekistan and its addition to Karakalpakia; separation of the south-eastern part
    of Karakalpakia and its addition to the Khorezm oblast of Uzbekistan; separation of
    the southern part of the Chimkent oblast of Kazakhstan and its addition to Uzbekistan;
    separation of the Zeravshan valley of Uzbekistan and its addition to Tajikistan; and
    separation of the Surkhandarin valley of Uzbekistan and its addition to Tajikistan.
63  Vitalii Portnikov, "Turkestan poiavitsia osen'iu?" *Nezavisimaia gazeta*, 27 July 1991.
64  Edward A. Gargan, "In Central Asia, Many Dream of Union Under Islam's Flag," *The
    New York Times* October 11, 1991, p. 1.
65  One of the best documentary sources on the war is A. Rudenko, *Tadzhikistan v Ogne*
    (Dushanbe: Irfon, 1993).
66  See Christopher J. Panico, "Uzbekistan's Southern Diplomacy," *RFE/RL Research
    Report*, vol. 2, no. 13, 26 March 1993, 39–45; Bess Brown, "Tajik Civil War Prompts
    Crackdown in Uzbekistan," *RFE/RL Research Report*, vol 2, no. 11, 12 March 1993,
    pp. 1–6.
67  Before the Soviet breakup, tactical nuclear weapons were deployed in all of the Central
    Asian republics. In 1990, Turkmenistan was thought to have 125 tactical nuclear
    weapons, Uzbekistan was thought to have 105, and Kyrgyzstan and Tajikistan were
    each both believed to have 75. Kazakhstan, the only Central Asian country to have
    both strategic and tactical nuclear weapons, was believed to have a total of 1,800
    nuclear weapons, counting both categories. In an informal protocol to the Strategic
    Arms Reduction Treaty (SALT), signed by presidents Bush and Gorbachev in July
    1991, Gorbachev was asked expeditiously to direct the withdrawal of ground-based
    tactical nuclear weapons from their places of deployment to safe storage areas within
    Russia. Withdrawal of the Central Asian tactical nuclear weapons to secure facilities
    within Russia was reportedly carried out prior to the August 1991 coup attempt.
68  In Uzbekistan, a law went into effect in August 1992 that binds the republic to three
    non-nuclear principles: not to locate, not to produce, and not to acquire nuclear
    weapons. *FBIS-SOV-92–153* 7 August 1992, p. 76.

# Uzbekistan: chronology of events

*April 1989*
    10    Soviet troops enter Tashkent following a nationalist demonstration.

*June 1989*
    3–4    Rioting breaks out in the Fergana region of Uzbekistan between Uzbeks and Meskhetian Turks, resulting in a few hundred deaths and almost a thousand injured.

*October 1989*
    21    The Supreme Soviet adopts a language law which makes Uzbek the official government language.

*February 1990*
    18    94% of eligible voters participate in elections to the 460-member Supreme Soviet.
    27    The Erk (Will) Democratic Party holds its founding congress in Tashkent.

*March 1990*
    24–31    Parliament creates a presidential post and appoints First Party Secretary Islam Karimov to the position. Shukurulla Mirsaidov is appointed chairman of the Council of Ministers (Prime Minister), and Mirzaolim Ibragimov is appointed parliamentary chairman.

*June 1990*
    20    Parliament issues a declaration of sovereignty.

*March 1991*
    17    In the all-union referendum on preserving the union, 94% of voters (95% turnout) support the union.

*July 1991*
    Uzbeks set up an international association, *Fl*, to develop cultural and economic cooperation between Soviet Uzbeks and Uzbek diasporans.

*August 1991*
    23    Karimov resigns from the Communist Party
    30    Property of the Communist Party is nationalized.

*September 1991*

    1    Parliament adopts a declaration of independence.

   14    The Communist Party renames itself the People's Democratic Party of Uzbekistan and is registered four days later.

*October 1991*

        Uzbeks try to retrieve the throne of the Khans in the Hermitage in St. Petersburg, claiming it belongs to the Uzbek people.

*November 1991*

   19    The Birlik (Unity) popular front is officially registered. The Council of Ministers is abolished. Mirsaidov is transferred to the position of vice-president.

*December 1991*

   13    Uzbekistan joins the CIS.

   29    Islam Karimov is elected president with 86% of the vote. His only competitor, poet Muhammed Saleh, chairman of Erk, receives 12%. A simultaneous referendum on independence gains almost unanimous approval.

*January 1992*

    8    The position of Vice-President is abolished and Mirsaidov is appointed state secretary.

   13    Abdulkhashim Mutalov is appointed Prime Minister.

17–18    Six die in a clash with police when a student demonstration begun as a protest against price increases turns into a demand for Karimov's resignation. Karimov accuses the opposition of staging the disturbance, but promises the students lower prices.

   23    Journalist Abdurashid Sharif is assaulted after he is blamed for exaggerating casualty figures in the clash.

*May 1992*

   15    Uzbekistan signs the CIS collective security treaty.

   28    Birlik's headquarters are ransacked and activists beaten.

   30    A treaty of political, economic, and cultural cooperation with Russia is signed.

*June 1992*

   29    Birlik co-chairman Abdurakhim Pulatov is assaulted.

*July 1992*

    2    Birlik and Erk supporters hold a demonstration to demand new elections, and several protestors are arrested.

28   A law on citizenship is adopted which grants universal citizenship.
29   Pulat Akhunov of Birlik is arrested.

*August 1992*

4    The Fatherland Progress Party is officially registered, presumably to demonstrate the existence of a multiparty system.
14   Babur Shakirov, a dissident who spent 10 years in labor camps, is arrested on charges of attempting to convene a shadow parliament.
15   Shukhrat Ismatullaev, a co-chairman of Birlik, is arrested and released.

*September 1992*

1    Karimov declares a general amnesty of political prisoners to celebrate the first anniversary of independence.
7    Mirsaidov resigns as a parliamentary deputy in protest against Karimov's imposition of an authoritarian regime.

*October 1992*

19   Pulatov of Birlik is attacked in the Tashkent metro (for the third time in six months).

*December 1992*

8    The Supreme Soviet adopts a new constitution.
9    Abdulmanov Pulatov, chairman of the Human Rights Committee of Uzbekistan and brother of Abdurakhim Pulatov, is arrested in Bishkek when attending a human-rights conference.
10   Parliament elects to suspend Birlik.
15   Akhunov begins a one-year prison sentence.

*January 1993*

28   Abdulmanov Pulatov is sentenced to three years in jail but immediately freed under the conditions of the February 1992 amnesty.

*February 1993*

26   Despite several efforts of Muslim clergy to depose him on grounds of collaborating with the KGB, Mufti Muhammad-Sadyk Muhammad Yusuf is reelected to the post of chairman of the Muslim Religious Board of Central Asia. Poet Vasilya Inoyatova is sentenced to two years in prison for an article she wrote which allegedly insulted the president, but she is immediately amnestied.
27   Erk leader Muhammed Saleh is arrested.

*April 1993*
13    Erk is evicted from its headquarters in Tashkent.

*May 1993*
5    Ismatullaev is severely beaten in Tashkent.

*June 1993*
18    Mirsaidov, now a leader of the Democratic Movement Forum, is found guilty on corruption charges, sentenced to three years in prison, and immediately amnestied.

*August 1993*
6    Six opposition leaders found guilty of seeking to overthrow the government, including Shakir Babirov, are sentenced to three to five years in prison and immediately amnestied.
18    Akhunov's sentence is extended for three years on charges of narcotics possession.
24    A car bomb explodes near Mirsaidov's home.
28–29    Inoyatova and a member of Birlik are placed under house arrest to prevent them from attending a conference in Almaty.

*September 1993*
2    Karimov signs a law restoring the use of the Latin alphabet. The transition to Latin characters is to be complete by the year 2000.
24    Five alleged members of the Islamic opposition group Adolat are sentenced to 10–15 years of forced labor for attempting to overthrow the government.

*November 1993*
12    Karimov announces the introduction of the national currency, the *som*.
15    After being recalled to Uzbekistan on charges of misusing state funds, Muhammad Malikov, ambassador to the United States, defects and asks the U.S. government for political asylum. Malikov asserts his innocence and says he opposes Karimov's human rights violations and suppression of opposition movements.
23    Three leaders of Erk receive two-year suspended sentences.

*December 1993*
8    The Supreme Soviet adopts a new Constitution.

*March 1994*
3    Three leaders of Erk are arrested.

*May 1994*

12    Inoyatova is arrested in Kazakhstan on her way to a human rights conference in Almaty (her colleague Talib Yakubov was arrested two days earlier).

*June 1994*

12    A new political party, Istiqlal Yoli (Independence Path), is founded under the guidance of Shadi Karimov, who was previously a member of both Birlik and Erk.

*November 1994*

1    Under pressure from various human rights groups, Karimov issues a decree pardoning five political prisoners

4    Five members of Erk (and two others) are brought to trial on charges of attempting to forcibly seize power and training fighters in Turkey to that end.

*December 1994*

25    In parliamentary elections (including later runoffs), 69 seats are won by Karimov's People's Democratic Party, 14 by Vatan Tarakkiyeti (Progress of the Fatherland), and 167 from local councils, over 40 of which are PDP members. Another 47 belong to the Adolat (Justice) Social Democratic Party of Uzbekistan, which is led by Mirsaidov.

*February 1995*

18    Adolat holds its founding congress.

23    Erkin Khalilov is elected chairman of parliament.

*March 1995*

25    Muhamed Saleh of Erk and Abdurakhim Pulatov of Birlik (both living outside Uzbekistan) issue a joint statement declaring that the movements will consolidate their efforts to oppose President Karimov.

26    In a referendum on extending Karimov's term of office through the year 2000, 95% of voters (91% participating) support the president.

31    The Erk members on trial are found guilty on all counts and sentenced to five to twelve years of hard labor.

# 17 Tajikistan: reform, reaction, and civil war

MURIEL ATKIN

As the Soviet regime underwent reform and then collapse in the late 1980s and early 1990s, the inhabitants of Tajikistan, like those of the other successor states, grappled with the problem of how much of the old order to dismantle in fact as well as in name. In Tajikistan, this power struggle escalated into a civil war, which began in May 1992 and was decided by December of that year, when supporters of a Soviet-style monopoly of power by elements of the old ruling elite seized the capital city, Dushanbe. After that, all opposition political organizations were banned and the news media was tightly censored. Some prominent members of the opposition went into exile but others, as well as some members of the ruling elite who had been willing to accept reforms, were jailed or killed. A general breakdown of order made life perilous for ordinary citizens in parts of the country. Limited fighting has continued since 1993, pitting the regime's forces, aided by troops from Russia, Uzbekistan, Kazakhstan, and Kyrgyzstan, against elements of the opposition based both within Tajikistan and in exile in Afghanistan. Peace talks between representatives of the two sides began in 1994, but, as of this writing, had produced few results. The conflict killed tens of thousands of people and displaced hundreds of thousands of others (precise, impartial tallies were unavailable) in a country where the total population numbered about 5.2 million on the eve of the civil war.

There were many reasons people took sides in the Tajikistan conflict. Neither side was homogeneous or motivated by a sole concern. A discussion of all the facets of this complex tragedy lies beyond the scope of a single essay. The link between nationalism and the quest for a post-Soviet political system will be the focus of attention here.

## Links to reforms elsewhere in the former Soviet Union

After decades during which the Soviet regime defined and regulated national identity in ways which were often restrictive and sometimes demeaning, Tajiks, like members of other nationalities, sought to take control of the interpretation of their own nationhood. At the same time, many of the issues that concerned Tajiks, including economic problems and

### Tajikistan

|  | International boundary |
| --- | --- |
|  | Oblast boundary |
|  | Autonomous oblast (AO) boundary |
| ★ | National capital |
| ⊙ | Oblast center |
| ○ | Autonomous oblast (AO) center |
|  | Railroad |
|  | Road |

An oblast is named only when its name
differs from that of its administrative center.

0     75 Kilometers
0     75 Miles

Lambert Conformal Conic Projection SP 12N/38N

KAZAKHSTAN

KYRGYZSTAN

Talas

Arys

Chimkent

Toktogul'skoye
Vodokhranilishche

Chardara

Chirchik

Tashkent

Angren

Uchkurgan

Kara-
Kul'

Akhangaran

Namangan

Gagarin

Syrdar'ya

Andizhan

Gulistan

Kokand

Fergana

Osh

Khudzhand
(Leninabad)

Kanibadam

Dzhizak

Chkalovsk

UZBEKISTAN

Ura-
Tyube

Sulyukta

Kyzyl-Kiya

KYRGYZSTAN

Zeravshan

Ayni

Pendzhikent

Kashi

Kyzyl-Suu

LENINABADSKAYA OBLAST'

Surkhob

CHINA

Ozero
Karakul'

Area with no oblast-level administrative divisions.

Dushanbe

Ordzhonikidzeabad

Denau

Tursunzade

Nurek

Gorno-

Murgab

Shurchi

Kofarnikhon

Kulyab

Bartang

Badakhshanskaya

Taxkorgan

Dzhargurgan

Kalininabad

Kurgan-
Tyube

A.O.

Termez

Vakhsh

Kunduz

Kirovabad

Feyzabad

Khorog

Kholm

Lasht

AFGHANISTAN

PAKISTAN

Baghlan

Gilgit

Boundary representation is
not necessarily authoritative.

exasperation with Communist hard-liners, were not unique to any nationality but reflected problems that were perceived widely in the Soviet Union
and its successor states, although some were given a national coloration in
the Tajik context.

There was a tendency in some quarters to treat the Asian republics of
the former Soviet Union as so exotic as to be incomparable to the rest of
the successor states. Therefore, before taking a closer look at developments
in Tajikistan, it is worth noting that Tajiks who placed nationality issues
in the political foreground were attentive to developments in other republics and the center. The first Congress of People's Deputies in Moscow in
1989 demonstrated to such Tajiks how effective representatives from the
Baltic and Caucasian republics as well as Moscow and Leningrad were as
advocates of their own national or regional interests and how Tajikistan's
representatives suffered by comparison.[1] The efforts of nationalists in other
republics, including Russia, Armenia, and Lithuania, to enhance the position of their respective national cultures as the reform era provided new
opportunities for doing so also served as an example to Tajiks.[2] A prominent component of discussions of Tajikistan's economic problems in the
final years of the Soviet era included comparisons with other Soviet republics (see below).

The rally which reformers organized in downtown Dushanbe in reaction
to the August 1991 attempted coup by Communist hard-liners in Moscow,
included not only an expression of Tajik interests but also praise for both
Yeltsin and Gorbachev. The demonstrators also held a minute of silence
for the "national heroes" in Moscow who died opposing the coup.[3]

Reform-minded political groups in Tajikistan, which all advocated Tajik
national interests in some sense, cooperated with and were helped by
reformers in other formerly Soviet republics. One example of this was the
platform of the Democratic Party of Tajikistan (DPT), which was derived
from those of the Democratic Party of Russia and the Social Democratic
Association.[4] When Tajikistan's regime refused to allow the DPT to publish
the first issue of its newspaper in the republic, the party arranged to have
it published in Lithuania with the help of Sajudis. The DPT was also in
contact with similar parties in other then-Soviet republics.[5] Similarly, a
Tajik cultural organization, Mehr, that faced harassment from the Tajikistani regime was allowed to organize and publish a newspaper by Moscow's
reformist city government. The severe repression of dissenting views after
the civil war prompted the publishers of the leading opposition newspaper,
*Charoghi ruz*, to shift their operations to Moscow. Some of the political
refugees from the civil war also sought a haven in Moscow. During Tajikistan's presidential election campaign in the fall of 1991, Davlat Khudonazarov was the joint candidate of the opposition coalition, both secular and
religious. He had been one of Andrei Sakharov's supporters in the Congress
of People's Deputies and won a public endorsement for his candidacy from

Boris Yeltsin.[6] Those in Tajikistan who sought the dismantling of the old Soviet system of rule in their country hoped for the support of a reformist Russia in their power struggle against the defenders of the old order but that was not to be. Ironically, from the latter stages of Tajikistan's civil war, the Russian government sided with those who fought against Tajikistan's opposition coalition.

None of this meant that people engaged in Tajik-oriented politics were incapable of formulating objectives or identifying grievances without outside guidance. It did mean that such political leaders, while emphasizing the particular, were well aware of the broader context in which they operated.

## Suppression and assertion of national interests

The long-standing Soviet condemnation of national feeling, except in the pallid form dictated by the regime itself, continued into the Gorbachev era but produced a backlash. The Gorbachev regime continued the practice of its predecessors in presenting "internationalism," which really meant an emphasis on the interests of the center of power, as occupying a lofty moral plane. In contrast, the regime treated nationalism as linked to, and no better than, "chauvinism." In practice, the epithets "nationalism" (or "national narrowness") and "chauvinism" were readily applied to any display of interest in one's national heritage or current concerns that fell outside the confines of the officially authorized version. The Dushanbe regime, in keeping with the policy set in Moscow, extolled internationalism and criticize Tajiks' attention to national interests as late as 1989.[7]

Yet this hard line proved unsustainable. In a climate of waning repression and growing nationalism in a number of republics, Tajiks reacted against the long-standing Soviet practice of manipulative nationality politics as well as Moscow's centralizing and Russianizing practices, to press what they considered their national interests with increasing vigor. Even Tajikistan's Communist leadership found it politically useful to espouse Tajik national interests, as a departure from the extreme emphasis on command from the center made it desirable for republic-level officials to seek the support of republic-level constituencies.

## Origins of a Tajik state

There was some irony in this, in the sense that the contemporary republic of Tajikistan and the emphasis on a Tajik political-national identity were creations of the Soviet era. Yet these took on meaning in their own right during the course of this century.

The boundaries of Tajikistan reflect neither a traditional Tajik polity nor the geographic distribution of the Tajik population within what was Soviet Central Asia. The territory which comprises Tajikistan was often part of larger states or divided among a number of regional or supra-regional powers. Even the Samanid kingdom (875–999), which, according to Soviet Tajik historiography, was a Tajik state and presided over the emergence of the Tajiks as a distinct, consolidated people with a flourishing culture,[8] ruled very little of what became twentieth-century Tajikistan directly from its capital in Bukhara. Most of the modern state's territory was ruled through local vassals; the mountainous southeast was outside the Samanid realm entirely.

During the 1920s, the Soviet regime subdivided its Central Asian holdings into nationally-defined republics. As part of that process, Moscow's fiat established Tajikistan as an autonomous republic within the new Uzbekistan Soviet Socialist Republic in 1924. The core of this Tajikistan ASSR was formed from the eastern regions of the old emirate of Bukhara (comprising much of what subsequently became central and southern Tajikistan) and, further north (the Panjakent area), a small part of the tsarist-era governorship-general (and, briefly, the autonomous republic) of Turkestan. The following year, the remote Pamir highlands, along the border with Afghanistan and China, were reassigned from the Turkestan republic to Tajikistan under the name of Gornyi (Mountainous) Badakhshan.[9] In 1929, Moscow separated Tajikistan from Uzbekistan and made it a Union Republic in its own right. At that time part of the populous, economically important Fergana Valley was transferred from Uzbekistan to become the northern-most part of Tajikistan (Leninobod province).

## Tajiks as a people

Although the idea of a Tajik nation-state was a twentieth-century invention, the ethnic designation "Tajik" was used for many centuries to refer to Persian-speakers, in contrast to various Turkic peoples, wherever these groups lived in contact with each other. (However, the designation of their language as Tajik rather than Persian was imposed by Soviet policy, in keeping with the more general practice of differentiating nationalities from kindred peoples living outside the Soviet Union.) By the twentieth century, the area of its use had contracted to Central Asia, part of Afghanistan, northeastern Iran, and China's Xinjiang. According to the 1989 Soviet census, some 4.2 million Tajiks lived within Soviet borders, of whom nearly 3.2 million lived in Tajikistan; the vast majority of the rest, more than 900,000, lived in Uzbekistan.[10] The exact number of Tajik inhabitants of either Tajikistan or Uzbekistan was subject to question for reasons which had to do with ethnic politics (see below). There were also more than 4 million Persian-speakers in Afghanistan, a majority of whom were called "Tajiks." Several tens of thousands of Tajiks lived in the oases of China's Xinjiang.

The designation of Tajiks or other Central Asian peoples by ethnic names did not mean that a majority of them perceived such categories as the proper basis for constituting states when the Soviets first reshaped the region into nationally-defined republics. However, decades of Soviet rule in Tajikistan, entailing both the institutionalization of national identity and transgressions against national feeling, made nationality politics important there. Contemporary Tajik nationalists saw their people not as the "formerly backward people" they were called for decades in Soviet rhetoric but as heirs to a synthesis of the western and eastern forms of Iranian civilization (representing the Iranian plateau and Central Asia) that had its roots in antiquity. At the same time, many of these nationalists, especially those belonging to the cultural intelligentsia, decried what they perceived as the low level of knowledge of this rich heritage and even of the national language among most Tajiks. They blamed Soviet policies for depriving them of their birthright and wanted to use the power of the state to remedy the situation.[11]

## Tajik nationalism in the ascent

That Tajikistan's Communist leadership perceived such sentiments to have a widespread following in the republic was reflected by its shift in 1989 to policies which addressed nationalist grievances. This took various forms, including the appearance of increasingly explicit articles in the official press (many authored by people who later became active in the opposition) reflecting nationalist concerns, the establishment of a Tajikistan cultural foundation to preserve the Tajik heritage, the identification of political figures by nationality in the press, and the restoration of the historic name, Khujand, of Tajikistan's second largest city, known for most of the Soviet era as Leninobod. The republican regime's most important concession to nationalist feeling was the enactment of the language law of 1989, which, among other things, gave Tajik primacy over Russian as the state language, although it did not exclude the use of Russian. The law also advocated a return to the Arabic alphabet and called for the use of Tajik, not Russianized or Russian personal and place names.[12] However, that law had little practical effect on language policy in the turbulent years which followed. Its most significant impact may ultimately prove to have been the antipathy it inspired in Russians.

The old ruling elite did not have a monopoly on expressions of Tajik nationalism. For example, there was a ground swell of public support among Tajiks, especially in Dushanbe, for improving the status of the Tajik language months before the legislature passed the language law. Alternative political organizations, which began to operate openly in the final years of the Soviet era, articulated nationalist concerns. Among their common themes were calls for sovereignty, in an economic as well as a political sense, and the full, unhindered cultural development of the Tajiks.[13] The terms in which sovereignty and independence were discussed gave the impression that these were seen in no small part as ways of improving the republic's bargaining position as relations among the Union republics were renegotiated at the end of the Soviet era, rather than the pursuit of complete independence and the daunting problems that would bring. Only after the Soviet Union dissolved in December 1991 did Tajikistan become an independent state.

The strength of nationalism among ordinary Tajiks, especially the rural majority, was harder to gauge because of the dearth of reliable information. Communist Party officials and non-Tajiks living in Dushanbe tended to portray rural Tajiks as a primitive, anarchic menace lacking a full-fledged ideology but capable of xenophobia and Islamic fanaticism. Even many educated, urban Tajik nationalists viewed ordinary Tajiks, especially those in the countryside, as ignorant of their national heritage and given to a local rather than a national form of identity.[14] Ironically, in the political power struggle in newly independent Tajikistan, some members of the urban ruling elite played an active role in fomenting local antagonisms in their pursuit of victory (see below).

There were examples of behavior by ordinary Tajiks that suggested that by the 1990s, their political awareness in general and their sense of national identity had become stronger than others assumed. Rural as well as urban Tajiks (and non-Tajiks) rallied in the mass, anti-government demonstrations in Dushanbe following the collapse of the attempted coup of August 1991. They were motivated primarily by the kind of opposition to the Communist elite that was widespread in the Soviet Union by then, but also invoked national reawakening.[15]

Tajik nationalism also affected the discussion of other issues of which it was not the primary component, especially the low standard of living, unemployment, and environmental concerns. Both the ruling elite and the opposition blamed much of Tajikistan's economic woes on Moscow's policies, which they depicted as, in essence, exploitative and colonial.[16] The high level of unemployment in Tajikistan was the target of criticism on the grounds that Moscow's policies did not provide adequate training for Tajiks to fill new industrial jobs but relied instead on importing workers from elsewhere in the USSR. This made Dushanbe's acute housing shortage even more of a political problem because the imported workers and Russians often received priority in housing assignments.[17]

## Ethnic minorities

Any discussion of nationality politics in Tajikistan must take account of the fact that neither the Tajiks nor other nationalities were tidily defined by state borders. Millions of Tajiks and other Persian-speakers lived outside Tajikistan, while roughly 40 percent of the people who lived within its

Table 17.1. *National composition of Tajikistan, 1989*

| Nationalities | Population | % |
|---|---|---|
| Total population | 5,093,000 | 100.0 |
| Tajiks | 3,172,900 | 62.3 |
| Uzbeks | 1,196,900 | 23.5 |
| Russians | 387,100 | 7.6 |
| Tatars | 71,300 | 1.4 |
| Kyrgyz | 66,200 | 1.3 |
| Other | 198,600 | 3.9 |

*Source: Natisional'nyi sostav naseleniya SSSR. Finansy i statistika*, (Moscow, 1991).

borders (as of the 1989 census) belonged to other nationalities. Even some of the people who were classified as Tajiks according to Soviet policy had an additional identity as members of other ethno-linguistic groups. The most important of these in the political turmoil of the 1990s were the seven groups known collectively as the Pamiris, whose homelands lay in the mountains of southeastern Tajikistan and adjoining parts of Afghanistan. Their languages belong to the eastern branch of the Iranian linguistic family (in contrast to Tajik/Persian, which belongs to the western branch), although traditionally they used Persian as their written language; in the Soviet era it was common for educated Pamiris to know Russian as well. They adhered historically to the Isma'ili sect of Shi'a Islam, which distinguished them both from the Sunni majority in Central Asia and the Imami Shi'i majority in Iran. Soviet policy toward the Pamiri peoples was assimilationist, with education and publications generally being available in Tajik or Russian but not in the Pamiri languages. This began to change in the final years of the Soviet era,[18] but the stereotyping of Pamiris as supporters of the opposition during the civil war prompted a retreat from such concessions.

The largest minority within Tajikistan was composed of Uzbeks, who numbered some 1.1 million inhabitants and thus constituted roughly 23 percent of the population as of the 1989 census (see Table 17.1).[19] By the late Soviet era, the Uzbek language was used to some extent in Tajikistan's schools and mass media. However, there were no Uzbeks in the republic's highest political offices. (A rumor among members of the opposition alleged that Rahmon Nabiev, the president of Tajikistan from November 1991 to September 1992, was really an Uzbek.) The fact that more than 16 million Uzbeks lived in Central Asia as a whole and that the government of the neighboring state of Uzbekistan was hostile to the reform movement in Tajikistan made the Uzbeks a force to be reckoned with in post-Soviet politics. The government of Uzbekistan encouraged anti-Tajik sentiment among the Uzbek inhabitants of southern Tajikistan. After the speaker of Tajikistan's Supreme Soviet, Safarali Kenjaev, was forced out of office by opposition demonstrations in Dushanbe (May 1992), he began to organize his own fighting force, for which he drew heavily on the Uzbek minority. He used this force in his unsuccessful attempt to seize Dushanbe in October 1992. The fighters who took Dushanbe in December of that year were trained in Uzbekistan and received tanks and armored vehicles from that country.[20] Clashes between Uzbek and Tajik inhabitants of western and southwestern Tajikistan continued into 1994.[21]

Russians constituted the next most numerous minority in Tajikistan, and in terms of positions of influence occupied by its members, a more powerful one than the Uzbeks until the end of the Soviet era. The more than 388,000 Russians comprised just over seven percent of the population according to the 1989 census.[22] Even before the outbreak of civil war, the Russian minority's relations with the Tajiks began to deteriorate. In the last few years of the Soviet era, Tajiks became increasingly open about their resentment of Russians over various matters, including the preferential treatment in employment and housing mentioned above and the inability of most Russian inhabitants to speak Tajik.[23] Russians' worries increased because of the 1989 law making Tajik the primary state language. This did more than raise the prospect of their being required to learn a language few had shown any interest in learning. It also raised fears of Russian children being denied a good education in their own language which would stress the Russian cultural heritage and train them well for desirable careers. Tajikistan's low standard of living and the misperception of the February 1990 riots in Dushanbe as anti-Russian added to the Russians' worries.[24] In the 1990s, the sharp drop in the standard of living and the dangers raised by the civil war accelerated the emigration of Russians as well as members of other nationalities. In the absence of a census, estimates put the Russian population remaining in Tajikistan by 1994 at 70,000 to 120,000; they continued to leave at the rate of perhaps several thousand a week.[25]

During the power struggle in 1992, both sides courted national minorities. The opposition did so by trying to present itself as inclusive, as seeking the well-being of all of Tajikistan's peoples.[26] This was undermined not only by the general escalation of interethnic tensions but also by the occasional public outbursts of Shodmon Yusuf, the head of the DPT, whose threats against Russians, although not opposition policy, understandably increased Russians' fears. Members of the ex-Soviet elite sought to present themselves to the minority nationalities as the only alternative to oppression at the hands of Tajik chauvinists and Islamic militants.[27]

## Dushanbe riots of February 1990

The perception noted above that Tajiks were discriminated against in housing in Dushanbe created an atmosphere in which rumors that falsely alleged that large numbers of Armenian refugees from Azerbaijan had fled to Dushanbe and received priority in housing assignments there found a receptive audience among some Tajik inhabitants of the city. This led to a large demonstration in February 1990. The demonstrators' underlying grievances were not about the Armenians but about general dissatisfaction with the standard of living and the unresponsive political leadership, but those rumors had struck a raw nerve.

When republican Ministry of Internal Affairs forces fired on demonstrators, rioting swept the city.[28] Order was restored in a few days but this outburst of violence in the capital of the republic heightened political anxieties. Various elements of Tajikistani society, including Tajik reformers, supporters of the old Soviet order, and members of the Russian minority, saw the February events as a warning that their worst fears would come to pass. However, different elements had different fears, ranging from the stifling of reform and perpetuation of repression to Islamic revolution and the persecution of non-Muslims.

## Challenge to the Soviet political system

The political reforms of the Gorbachev era penetrated only weakly into Tajikistan. Proponents of change gained some leeway to organize and express their views by 1989, but no opposition parties obtained legal recognition until 1991. The 1990 legislative elections were uncontested. When supporters of the old Soviet order attempted a coup in Moscow in August 1991, Tajikistan's leadership appeared to support them. The large demonstrations in Dushanbe in the wake of the coup set the stage for the Supreme Soviet to oust the president, Qahhor Mahkamov, also the Communist Party first secretary. This was accompanied by the short-lived suspension of the Communist Party of Tajikistan, and the dismantling of a large statue of Lenin in central Dushanbe. The old guard soon recovered its composure and staged a successful coup of its own on September 23, 1991. This brought to power Rahmon Nabiev, who had been party first secretary in the republic from 1982 until forced out by Gorbachev in 1985. In November, Nabiev became Tajikistan's first directly elected president. The election was genuinely contested but was also rigged to ensure Nabiev's victory.[29]

In the following months, the Nabiev government took a number of steps which indicated that it intended to lead newly independent Tajikistan back to the kind of authoritarian rule which had existed before the late-Soviet reforms. Nabiev made repeated attempts in late 1991 and the first half of

1992 to establish a presidential guard, in essence his private army, outside the normal chain of command and answerable directly to him. Individual opposition figures as well as political parties were targeted by the regime. For example, Mirbobo Mirrahim, a vocal nationalist, was tried and convicted for his role in the peaceful demonstrations in Dushanbe in the wake of the August 1991 coup attempt; the key witness against him was the speaker of the Supreme Soviet, Safarali Kenjaev. Both the DPT and the Islamic Movement Party were harassed. Two veteran government officials were punished for not having sided with the old guard during the demonstrations of August and September 1991; Dushanbe's mayor, Maqsud Ikromov was arrested and Minister of the Interior Mahmadayoz Navjuvonov was fired because he had refused to use his troops against the demonstrators.[30]

Opposition to continued politics as usual did not end, despite the chill in the political climate. By the spring of 1992, the opposition had coalesced around the leadership of four political groups and a prominent individual. The DPT advocated the establishment of a parliamentary democracy. Leaders of the Islamic Movement Party (called the Islamic Revival Party in Russian) spoke of the creation of an Islamic state as an eventual objective but for the near-term endorsed the political and economic reformist goals of their secular allies. Rastokhez ("revival") was most noted for its emphasis on Tajik nationalism. La'li Badakhshon ("ruby of Badakhshan") combined calls for democratization at the republic level with advocacy of autonomy for Badakhshan; its membership was comprised predominantly of Pamiris. The country's most influential religious figure, *Qadi* Akbar Turajonzoda, was not a member of any political party but supported political and economic reforms as well as recognition of Muslims' rights to practice their faith openly and without hindrance.

In March 1992 a new wave of opposition demonstrations began in Dushanbe, on Shohidon Square. The demonstrators demanded Ikromov's release from jail, an end to the government's authoritarianism, economic reforms, and the ouster of Speaker Kenjaev, one of the most determined supporters of the old order.[31] Tensions increased in late April and early May, as Nabiev and the legislature appeared to make some concessions but then reneged, while Kenjaev summoned people from the southern province of Kulob to begin counter-demonstrations on Dushanbe's Ozodi Square. Some of the opposition demonstrators responded by becoming increasingly confrontational. Matters came to a head in May, when a march by some opposition demonstrators towards KGB headquarters led to shooting and several demonstrators' deaths. At that point, Nabiev appeared to yield and agreed to the formation of a coalition government. The opposition did not try to remove Nabiev himself, for fear that that would destabilize the country. A majority of positions in the new government went to veteran members of the ruling elite, some of whom were willing to reach an accommodation with reformers, others of whom were not; a few positions went to opposition figures, including Davlat Usmon, one of the founders of the Islamic Movement Party, who became deputy prime minister, and Mirbobo Mirrahim, of Rastokhez, who became chairman of the state television and radio committee.

This apparent compromise did not lead to the establishment of a stable transitional regime. Instead, the supporters of the old politics worked to undermine reform. The Supreme Soviet refused to enact reforms or to disband, as the May 11 compromise had stipulated, so that a new assembly could be created, with half of the membership to be drawn from the Supreme Soviet, half to be drawn from the opposition. Nabiev had sent automatic weapons to demonstrators on Ozodi Square. They returned to Kulob Province and launched a campaign of terror against supporters of the opposition there.[32] The fighting subsequently extended to the neighboring province to the west, Qurghonteppa, where most of the civil war was fought. Elements of the opposition also resorted to violence. Amid the bitterness of civil conflict and the general breakdown of order, the fighting became increasingly ugly. More and more supporters of the opposition held President Nabiev personally accountable. On September 7, 1992, he was seized by a group of armed men at Dushanbe airport and forced to resign. (He was then released. He lived in retirement in his native province of Leninobod until his death, apparently from natural causes, in 1993.)

A Nabiev protégé, Akbarsho Iskandarov, became acting president. He was not adamantly opposed to reforms but neither was he able to wield power effectively. The coalition government as a whole was unable to handle the country's crisis. At the same time, ex-communists fought on in the south and gained territory, and legislators from Leninobod Province refused to come to the capital for meetings of the Supreme Soviet, thus denying it a quorum. In a desperate attempt to end the conflict, Iskandarov and the coalition government resigned in November. At that point the Supreme Soviet, dominated by ex-communists and their supporters, convened in Khujand, the capital of Leninobod Province, and chose a new government which excluded the opposition. The office of president was abolished. The head of state became the speaker of the Supreme Soviet, Imomali Rahmonov, a protégé of Sangak Safarov, the leader of the neo-Soviet fighters in the south. The ex-communists fought on, aided by forces from Russia and Uzbekistan, until they captured Dushanbe in December 1992 and installed the new government in the capital.[33]

The installation of the new government was followed by a crackdown on supporters of the opposition. Many opposition members were seized and killed; others were given multi-year prison sentences or held prisoner for more than a year. Some prisoners were believed to have been tortured; two died in captivity in 1994 under questionable circumstances. Almost none faced any semblance of due legal process. Prominent opposition figures who went into exile were charged in absentia with political crimes. Opposition parties were banned; the mass media came under the regime's tight control; and journalists who did not follow the regime's line were harassed, arrested, or killed.[34]

Although the outcome of the civil war was decided by December 1992, fighting on a smaller scale continued after that date, especially in the mountainous region northeast of Dushanbe and in the southeast of the country, as well as along the border with Afghanistan. The proliferation of weapons in the central and southern regions of the country combined with the lack of effective law enforcement provided favorable conditions for a sharp increase in violent crimes, both political and otherwise, in Dushanbe and points south. The victims of these assaults included a deputy prime minister and several Russian officers. Responsibility for the killings was not ascertained.

## Russian involvement in Tajikistan after 1992

Russia became more deeply embroiled in Tajikistan's affairs after the outcome of the civil war had been decided. With an extension of credit, budget subsidies, and an infusion of currency (Russian rubles), Moscow actively supported the Dushanbe regime.[35] Material which Moscow had refused to provide the short-lived coalition government went to its successor, to help it establish its own army.[36]

Russian military units in the form of the 20th Motorized Rifle Division and border guards accounted for by far the largest number of troops in Tajikistan. By 1995 they probably numbered about 23,500.[37] (Small numbers of troops from Uzbekistan, Kyrgyzstan, and Kazakhstan were also part of the CIS joint peacekeeping force led by a succession of officers from the Russian military.) Russian troops participated in operations against opposition fighters within Tajikistan and provided logistical aid to Tajik forces in such operations. The Russian units engaged in combat numerous times with exiled opposition fighters who launched cross-border raids from their bases in Afghanistan.[38] This has cost the lives of Russian soldiers and added to the intensity of the debate between supporters of Russian involvement and advocates of withdrawal.[39] On several occasions, Russian forces staged land-based and aerial bombardment of sites in northern Afghanistan, resulting in the deaths of Afghanistani civilians who inhabited villages near the border.[40]

## 1994 elections

In an effort to affirm its legitimacy, the government of Tajikistan held presidential elections in November 1994. (The office of president, which had been abolished in November 1992, was revived in a new constitution which was endorsed in a referendum held simultaneously with the vote for president.) Russian civilian as well as military officials (including the commanders of the CIS joint peacekeeping force and the borderguards) endorsed the candidacy of Imomali Rahmonov, the *de facto* head of government since the civil war. Russia delivered billions of rubles to Tajikistan on the eve of the election, with the result that the Rahmonov regime was able to enhance its public image by paying employees' wages which had been months in arrears.

Ultimately, Imomali Rahmonov won with more than 60 percent of the votes cast. The election offered one alternate candidate in the person of the former prime minister, Abdumalik Abdullojonov, who was at the time of the election Tajikistan's Ambassador to Moscow. No figures associated with opposition parties were able to run or have access to the mass media within Tajikistan; opposition parties remained banned. Rumors in Tajikistan predicted that the results would be fixed in Rahmonov's favor. The Conference on Security and Cooperation in Europe rejected the bona fides of this electoral process and refused to send monitors. After the balloting Abdullojonov charged electoral fraud. Human Rights Watch/Helsinki called the vote tainted by intimidation and slanted news coverage. However, a spokesman for the Russian Foreign Ministry hailed the vote as internationally verified proof of both democracy at work in Tajikistan and the lack of popular backing for the opposition there.[41]

## Peace negotiations

Attempts to end the intra-Tajik conflict through negotiations mediated by the United Nations came to naught in 1993. After delays, talks finally began in April 1994. They were to proceed by stages and meet in different capitals. (The first four sessions were held in Moscow, Tehran, Islamabad, and Almaty). Observers from Russia, Iran, Pakistan, and Afghanistan, as well as the UN mediator also attended. Given the difficulties in overcoming the two sides' objections, it was significant that several stages of talks were held at all. The negotiation process led to the declaration of a cease fire in September 1994 that was extended to run until January 1995. One critical test of the peace process, the exchange of prisoners between the two sides, was agreed upon at the third stage of the talks, in October 1994. However, fighting continued despite the cease-fire, and the negotiations had produced no political compromises by the spring of 1995. The future of the talks was uncertain as of this writing.

## Regional and "clan" factionalism

The civil war in Tajikistan was often characterized as based on rivalries between clans or tribes to which regional labels were applied, with the

Leninobodis and Kulobis pitted against the Gharmis and people from Gornyi Badakhshan. The implication was that the source of conflict was an age-old blood feud rather than contemporary power politics and ideology. In fact, the conflict was rooted in Soviet and post-Soviet politics; and the inhabitants of these four regions did not form homogeneous blocks. The central issue was whether the ruling elite of the Soviet era would maintain its monopoly of power and the benefits that went along with that while preserving much of the Soviet political and economic order in the post-Soviet era.

People who did especially well under the old order, or who benefited from the patronage of those who did, were most likely to want to preserve it. That included people from Leninobod, among them Qahhor Mahkamov and Rahmon Nabiev, and people from Kulob, like Safarali Kenjaev, Sangak Safarov (the career criminal who headed the ex-communist militia based in Kulob), and Haidar Sharifov (the *imam* of Kulob's main mosque and a neo-Soviet activist.) However, there were veteran politicians from the regions usually described as pro-opposition who also had successful careers under the old order and supported its preservation, such as Narzullo Dustov (Nabiev's vice-president from November 1991 to May 1992) and Akbarsho Iskandarov (who succeeded Kenjaev as speaker of the Supreme Soviet in May 1992), who were from Gornyi Badakhshan. (Iskandarov later changed his stance somewhat during his short term as acting president.) Some prominent opposition figures were from Leninobod, including many of the members of Rastokhez.

At the grass-roots level, people voiced support for the opposition and attempted demonstrations in the provinces of Leninobod and Kulob. They did not play a conspicuous role in politics in those provinces in 1992 or since because the ruling regime used intimidation and repression to silence dissenters there.[42] (In December 1992, the victorious ex-communists merged Qurghonteppa and Kulob into a single province, named Khatlon.) Supporters of the ex-communists within Qurghonteppa Province fought its pro-opposition leadership during the civil war.

During the course of the civil war, regionalism gained in importance as the basis for society's polarization. The fact that different provinces were controlled by rival political groups and that an armed force composed of Kulobis and Uzbeks spearheaded the neo-Soviets' drive for victory in the civil war reinforced the significance of regional identity. The winter of 1992–1993 saw neo-Soviets take vengeance not only on opposition activists who fell into their hands but also on Pamiris and Gharmis in general.[43]

After the civil war, the alliance between ex-communists from Leninobod and Kulob showed signs of strain. Kulobis acquired many of the key positions in the new government. This marked a change from the Soviet era, when Leninobodis had been the most favored. The highest state office went to the Kulobi Imomali Rahmonov. The highest-ranking Leninobodi was

Abdumalik Abdullojonov, the prime minister; but he was forced out of office in December 1993 in a power struggle with Rahmonov.

## Islam and opposition politics

Those who defended the privileges of the old ruling elite claimed repeatedly that the power struggle in Tajikistan pitted proponents of modern, secular democracy against radical Islamicizers, whose secular coalition partners were mere window dressing.[44] This argument owes more to political self-justification than an accurate description of the Tajikistan opposition.

President Nabiev and his domestic allies themselves had invoked Islam to garner public support. The widely respected and influential Islamic figure, *Qadi* Turajonzoda, and the leaders of the Islamic Movement Party stated repeatedly, in various settings, that they considered an Islamic state an ultimate ideal but that its realization in Tajikistan, if that were ever to occur at all, lay decades in the future and in any event could not be forced on an unwilling public. In the power struggle of the 1990s, they supported the presidential candidacy of the secular reformer Davlat Khudonazarov (as a Pamiri of Isma'ili ancestry, a member of a religious minority) and the general opposition demands for political democratization and economic reforms along market-oriented lines. Moreover, Muslim inhabitants of Tajikistan had varying notions of the place of Islam in their lives. For some, it was at least as important in a cultural and social sense as in a strictly religious one. For some, Islam meant the traditional practices of their particular family, village, or urban quarter and not of people outside those groups. Others sought a break with customary practices in the pursuit of a more thoroughly Islamic society; however, they did not all agree on what that alternative ought to be. Still others focused on learning more about the teachings of their faith, a process which began so recently that its outcome cannot yet be predicted.[45]

## Relations with other Central Asian states

The fact that the Central Asian states were not ethnically homogeneous was one of several factors which complicated relations between Tajikistan and its neighbors in the late-Soviet and early-independence eras. The Stalinist approach to inter-republican relations, which survived until the Gorbachev era, focused all republics' dealings on Moscow. The changing climate of reform-era politics made possible increased direct contacts and cooperation among republics. However, the weakening of the old controls also allowed more inter-republican antagonisms to surface.

In some ways, Central Asians found advantages to cooperating on governmental and nongovernmental levels. Representatives of the Central Asian republics, Tajikistan included, voiced support in principle for cooperation in addressing economic and environmental problems, as well as in scholarly matters, although little was actually accomplished in the first half of the 1990s.[46] New political groups which advocated change also expressed a desire for cooperation across republican borders. The reasons lay not only in the regional economic and environmental problems and the cultural similarities among peoples but also in the hostility advocates of change faced from the still-powerful forces which favored the *de facto* continuation of Soviet-style politics.[47]

Yet the Central Asian states also reacted to their economic and environmental problems by treating their neighbors as competitors. Tajikistan and its neighbors tried to keep consumer goods and other high-demand items, including fuel, from leaving their territory or charged much higher prices for them.[48] Access to water was a particularly contentious issue in a region plagued not only by natural aridity but also by the policies of central economic planners which misused and polluted much of the water that was most readily available. Both Tajikistan and Kyrgyzstan, where many of Central Asia's rivers originate, mistrusted the designs of the down-river republics, Uzbekistan and Turkmenistan, on their water. In addition, a border dispute over land and water led to local violence and acrimonious relations between Tajikistan and Kyrgyzstan at the end of the Soviet era.[49]

## Relations with Uzbekistan

There was also an ethnic dimension to the tensions between Tajikistan and the other Central Asian states, above all, Uzbekistan. Alone among the major indigenous nationalities of the region, the Tajiks were Persian-speakers rather than speakers of Turkic languages. Even though there was a tradition of close contact and mutual cultural influences between the Tajiks and the Uzbeks, the friction between them became significant by the close of the Soviet era. Tajik nationalists argued that Uzbeks had denied since the 1920s that the Tajiks constituted a distinct nationality, characterizing them instead as Uzbeks who had stopped speaking their original tongue.[50] The main expression of this dispute, before the civil war in Tajikistan eclipsed all other issues, was over the status of the Tajik inhabitants of Uzbekistan. According to the 1989 census, Tajiks numbered more than 900,000 of that country's more than 20 million inhabitants. Tajik nationalists' estimates were much higher, ranging between three and four-and-a-half million.[51] The discrepancy in population figures was part of the larger argument made both by the Tajik opposition and the ruling regime: that the cities of Bukhara and Samarkand and their environs were inhabited predominantly by Tajiks in the 1920s, when they were assigned to Uzbekistan, and had remained predominantly Tajik ever since. According to this argument, the Uzbeks deliberately undercounted Tajiks and used various methods to force their assimilation.[52] However, no major political figure in Tajikistan went so far as to advocate the redrawing of state borders to transfer Bukhara and Samarkand to Tajikistan. Given that the Uzbeks outnumbered the Tajiks several times over, any attempt to press irridentist claims would have been reckless indeed.

At the close of the Soviet era, Uzbek officials made some short-lived gestures to conciliate the Tajik minority.[53] However, the civil war in Tajikistan gave the Karimov government the basis to cite the dangers of interethnic conflict and militant, political Islam to justify domestic repression aimed not only at the Tajik minority but also at Uzbek critics of the regime.[54]

In addition to providing aid to the forces within Tajikistan during the civil war there, Uzbekistan also sent in its own troops to aid the ex-communists' final drive toward Dushanbe, and subsequently participated in attacks on the remnants of opposition forces within Tajikistan.[55]

## The role of Islam in international relations

In a region where Sunni Islam was an important part of the cultural as well as spiritual traditions of the great majority of the indigenous inhabitants, one may wonder whether this supranational bond might serve, in the post-Soviet era, as a unifying force that is stronger than ethnic differences. Yet a shared religion did not prevent conflicts among Central Asians before or during the Soviet era. One reason is that Islam means different things to different Central Asians in general, just as it do to different Tajiks.

Another reason Islam was not as powerful a unifying force in practice as it was in theory was that it became strongly linked to national identity among Central Asians in the past half century.[56] One reflection of this national coloration of Islam was that, as the power of the Soviet system eroded, the authority of the Muslim Spiritual Administration of Central Asia and Kazakhstan, a Stalinist creation, weakened considerably while religious figures in individual republics gained in authority. The Islamic establishment in several republics, including Tajikistan, broke away from the regional body and set up independent administrations.

Once again, the fact that Tajik nationalists worried about their prospects as an Iranian people in a predominantly Turkic region played a role. A number of Tajik intellectuals voiced the concern that any supranational Islamic movement would be dominated by the Turkic peoples of the former Soviet Union.[57] The Tajikistan branch of the Soviet-wide Islamic Revival Party subsequently became a separate party. One of its founders, Davlat Usmon, voiced no interest in the creation of a supranational Islamic state. Apart from the fact that he considered such a state impracticable, he also saw it as undesirable because, to him, national differences mattered.[58]

## Relations with Iran

Ethnicity, language, and culture also link Tajiks to the much larger number of Persian-speakers living outside the former Soviet Union, especially in Iran and Afghanistan. The Tajiks' interest in the Persian cultural world was not simply a desire to emulate Islamic political activists in Iran or Afghanistan. The interest predated by decades the rise of militant Islamic political movements there in the late 1970s. Soviet policy toward this kinship was oddly ambivalent. On the one hand, the official line designated the Tajiks a distinctive Soviet nationality, separate from people living in non-Soviet lands. On the other hand, Moscow's foreign policy found uses for the Tajiks' links to Persian cultural heritage, using them as a showpiece, for instance, to demonstrate to delegations from Iran (and other states) in cultural festivals the Soviet commitment to preserving its peoples, cultural identities.

The Iranian government, rumors to the contrary notwithstanding, did not foment Islamic revolution in Tajikistan. Political tranquility across Iran's northeastern border looked more important to the country's rulers than the radical Islamicization of the Central Asian successor states.[59] Tehran counseled moderation in the opposition's dealing with the ex-Communists during the 1992 confrontations.[60] Some defeated opposition figures ended up in exile in Iran, among them *Qadi* Turajonzoda. Although Iran criticized the suppression of the opposition it also began rebuilding relations with the new Tajik government. In addition, it continued its working relationship with the government of Uzbekistan, despite the latter's intervention in Tajikistan on the side of the hard-liners and the repression of the opposition within Uzbekistan, whether secular or religious, Tajik or Uzbek. Symbolic of this was President Ali Akbar Hashemi-Rafsanjani's visit to Uzbekistan in October 1993, which led to expanded diplomatic and economic contacts between the two states.[61] A similar pattern applied to Iran's relations with Russia.[62] When peace talks began in 1994 between the new Dushanbe regime and members of the opposition, Iran endorsed a negotiated settlement and along with Russia and other states sent observers to the talks. Tehran was the site of the second round of those talks, in June 1994.

## The Afghanistan factor

The attitudes of Tajiks in Tajikistan towards Afghanistan were in many ways similar to their attitudes toward Iran but were complicated by the prolonged war over who should rule in Kabul. While the Soviet army was engaged in that war, the proximity of and cultural similarities between Tajikistan and Afghanistan made Tajiks useful to Moscow as it strove to solidify Communist rule in Afghanistan. Moscow used Soviet Tajiks (and other Central Asian peoples) to work in Afghanistan's government, educational, and scholarly systems. It presented Tajikistan as an example to show organized delegations from Afghanistan and as a place to educate young Afghanistanis. Tajiks from Tajikistan saw tours of duty in the Soviet military in Afghanistan from the invasion in 1979 until 1988.[63]

In the late Soviet and early independence periods, there were allegations that Afghanistan's *mujahidin* were important backers of Tajikistan's opposition. Much of this information came from partisan sources, including supporters of the old order and those who wished to justify a Russian military presence in Tajikistan. The basic pattern of the rhetoric on the subject after the collapse of the Soviet Union drew on propaganda formulas which had become well established in the Soviet era: that Afghanistan's *mujahidin* were tools of foreign countries hostile to the Soviet Union and that criticism of the Soviet status quo was unwarranted, disloyal, and the product of externally-inspired subversion. The widespread alarmism over an alleged Islamic "fundamentalist" menace lent credibility to the allegations of Afghanistani machinations.[64]

The conflict in Afghanistan and its cross-border implications is too complex an issue to be treated here in depth but a few key points may be summarized. Afghanistan was not the primary source of the weapons used in Tajikistan's civil war of 1992. Most of the weapons came from the north side of the border, from armed forces within Tajikistan (voluntarily or by force) and from other formerly Soviet republics (especially Uzbekistan). Only a small fraction of the arms were smuggled from Afghanistan, by men traveling in small groups and carrying a limited number of weapons.[65]

The change of Tajik government in 1992 was accompanied by an exodus of people from Tajikistan to Afghanistan; most estimates put the number at 60,000. Most of the refugees were noncombatants fleeing the violence against people and property which was part of the victors' advance. A majority of those who had fled to Afghanistan probably returned to Tajikistan by late 1994, some to face renewed violence and discrimination in addition to the hardship of rebuilding their lives in a region devastated by war.[66]

A small minority of the refugees who went to Afghanistan staged periodic raids into Tajikistan. There was no impartial, verifiable tally of the number of people involved; the prevailing guess among Western sources was at most 5,000. They received some assistance from two different, mutually hostile groups of Afghanistani *mujahidin*, the predominantly Pushtun, radical Islamist Hizb-i Islami and the predominantly Tajik Jami'at-i Islami.[67] However, most of the information about the raids came from the Russian border guards stationed in Tajikistan or from other Russian sources. These were partisan sources, which had a vested interest in exaggerating the exiles' military threat for a variety of reasons.[68]

There was no independent corroboration of the claim that crossborder raids sometimes involved as many as a few hundred men.[69] Nor was there corroboration of Russian claims that Afghan *mujahidin* or militants from several Arab countries participated in the attacks to any significant degree. Moreover, information from Russian military sources themselves undercut the credibility of the alarmist stories. In 1993 and 1994, Russian military sources warned frequently of imminent, major attacks by exile fighters that never happened. Many of the border violations in those years were neither major nor combat related; the smuggling of consumer goods was a common reason for border crossings.[70]

One possibility for cross-border realignments which was much bruited for a time but did not materialize was the creation of a new state uniting Tajiks in northern Afghanistan and southern Tajikistan. This prediction was predicated on the faulty assumption that ethnicity must always be decisive in politics. Tajiks in southern Tajikistan were themselves bitterly divided between supporters of the opposition and the ex-communists; the victory of the latter ruled out any redrawing of what had previously been the Soviet-Afghanistan border. The Afghan Tajik *mujahidin* commander Ahmad Shah Mas'ud, of the Jami'at-i Islami, was engaged in a fierce power struggle within post-Communist Afghanistan against the forces of perennial rival Gulbeddin Hekmatyar, of the Hizb-i Islami, and Mas'ud's erstwhile ally, Rashid Dostum, the Uzbek commander of Afghanistan's airforce. Thus, Mas'ud's attention had to be focused on domestic affairs.

## Conclusion

The conflict in post-Soviet Tajikistan was a particularly destructive form of the troubles which all the successor states faced in replacing a political and economic order which had become so deeply entrenched and which had ended, at least in a formal sense, so suddenly. Tajikistan's political leaders, whether reformers or conservatives, neither anticipated nor sought the complete dissolution of the Soviet Union that occurred at the end of 1991. Conservatives hoped to maintain their positions; reformers hoped for a modified Union which could aid them in addressing their country's problems. The collapse of the old order solved nothing for Tajikistan but instead threw the country's problems into high relief.

The transition in Tajikistan bore a resemblance to the decolonization of Western states' empires a generation earlier. The borders of the newly independent states of Central Asia had been drawn by colonial masters with scant consideration for the preferences of those encompassed or divided by those lines. That set the stage for troubled relations between states and also between states' dominant and minority nationalities. Furthermore, the very concept of a national identity with political connotations was largely a recent development; it owed a great deal to a quasi-colonial Soviet nationality policy, which encouraged it in some ways while thwarting it in others. The process of defining Tajik national identity and of asserting its claims over those of older, regional identities or of patron-client networks was still evolving by the time independence made these competing loyalties crucial. The analogy with decolonization also applied to the reaction of the Russian inhabitants of Tajikistan, many of whom became alienated from a place which was becoming less like the homogeneous, Russianized, Soviet center.

Ultimately, the turmoil in Tajikistan hinged on two essential issues. One was the attempt to end the monopoly of political power by the cliques which had been favored by the Soviet system. How accepted or participatory any challengers to that system might have become was never tested, nor was the challengers' competence in wielding political power. Their only chance was a limited one, as part of a coalition government that ruled for a few months in 1992 amidst the widening chaos of a civil war. The other essential issue was the role Islam would play in this predominantly Muslim country. The call simply for freedom to practice the religion after decades of Soviet repression was widespread but beyond that there was much disagreement. However, the stereotype which equated interest in Islam with extremism, intolerance, and violence was a powerful weapon in the politics of independent Tajikistan. This provided the rationale for the suppression of the opposition as a whole.

## NOTES

1 S. Davlatov, "Vaqti amal ast," *Tojikistoni soveti*, July 16, 1989, p. 3; R. Ataev and D. Kabiliov, "Kto idet nevernoi dorogoi?" *Komsomolets Tadzhikistana*, September 6, 1989, p. 1; A. Vahhobov, "Khomushi ba ki lozim?", *Tojikistoni soveti*, June 13, 1989, p. 2; T. Barki, "Vstrechaias"s deputatom," *Komsomolets Tadzhiistana*, December 20, 1989, p. 6.

2 S. Ayub, "Nomo niz ta"rikhand," *Adabiyot va san"at*, October 13, 1988, p. 11; B. Karimov, "Dar poyai vazifahoi nav," *ibid.*, November 9, 1989, p. 12; A. Mukhtorov, "Ta"rikhdoni khudshinosist," *Gazetai muallimon*, March 4, 1989, p. 3; "Mas"uliayati buzurg meboyad," *Tojikistoni sovet*, July 25, 1989, p. 2.

3 TadzhikTA, "Shikasti suiqasdchiyon–piruzi demokratiya," *Tojikistoni soveti*, August 27, 1991, p. 2.

4 M. Khudoiev, "Gotovnost' k dialogu, no na printsipal"noi osnove," *Kommunist Tadzhikistana*, July 3, 1990, p. 1.

5 Foreign Broadcast Information Service [FBIS], *Daily Report. Soviet Union*, October 5, 1990, p. 105; F. Karimov, "Muloqoti namoyandagoni quvvajoi demokratii," *Tojikistoni soveti*, May 15, 1991, p. 2.

6 R. Evans and R. Novak, "Moscow: Periphery of Power," *Washington Post*, September 25, 1991, p. A25.

7 Typical of this are S. Tabarov, "Sarvati bebahoi ma"navi," *Tojikistoni soveti*, December 12, 1986, p. 3; "Kalomi navisand–vositai muhimi tarbiyai internatsionali," *Adabiyot vas san"at*, June 11, 1987, p. 3; Tadzhikta, "Vopityvat" ubezhdennykh bortsov za delo partii," *Kommunist Tadzhikistana*, September 3, 1986, p. 2; "Politicheskii kharakter partiinogo rukovodstva: opyt i problemy," *Komsomolets*

*Tadzhikistana*, April 14, 1989, p. 2; "O prakticheskikh merakh realizatsii v respublike reshenii sentiabřskogo (1989 g.) Plenuma TsK KPSS," *Kommunist Tadzhikistana*, 1990, no. 2 (February), p. 19.

8 From the perspective of Persian-speaking Iranians, the Samanids played an important role in the revival of Persian culture after the Arab conquest.

9 The historic name "Badakhshan" is also used now for a province in northeastern Afghanistan.

10 T.W. Karasik, ed., *USSR. Facts and Figures Annual*, vol. 17 (Gulf Breeze, FL.: Academic International Press, 1992), pp. 444, 449.

11 M. Atkin, "Tajiks and the Persian World," in *Soviet Central Asia in Historical Perspective*, ed. B.F. Manz (Boulder, CO: Westview Press, 1994), pp. 129–133.

12 'Qanuni zaboni Respublikai Sovietii Sotsialistii Tojikiston," *Tojikistoni soveti*, July 30, 1989, p. 1.

13 For example, "Az rui aqli solim," *Adabiyot va san'at*, August 16, 1990, p. 1; "Ustav i programma organizatsii 'Rastokhez' (Vozrozhdenie) Tadzhikskoi SSR," *Rastokhez*, 1990, no. 5, pp. 2, 3.

14 B. Berdieva, "Hama rosti juyu mardonagi," *Omuzgor*, July 25, 1989, p. 7; Atkin, "Tajiks," p. 130.

15 F. Muhammad, "Maromi mo: khudshinosi, beddorii millat," *Tojikistoni shuravi*, September 10, 1991, p. 2; M. Egamzod, "Dushanbe, Maidoni Ozodi, 2–3 oktiabr. In chi hukumat, in chi mardum?" *Jumhuriyat*, October 4, 1991, p. 3.

16 A few examples of this oft-repeated argument are: "Durnamoi rushdi mo," *Adabiyot va san'at*, July 13, 1989, p. 2; H. Muhammadiev, "Barodari man boshi, barobari man bosh!", *ibid.*, September 7, 1989, p. 3; N. Yodgori, "Narkhi pakhta va sathi zindagi," *Tojikistoni soveti*, January 6, 1990, p. 2; S. Mirzoev, "Tadzhikistan! Kakov tvoi zavtrashnii den'?", *Sogdiana*, 1990, no. 3 (October) p. 1; R.K. Alimov, Sh. Shoismatulloev, and M. Saidov, "Migratsionnye protsessy i natsional'nyi vopros," *Kommunist Tadzhikistana*, 1990, no. 5 (May), p. 12; the comments by prominent opposition figure Mirbobo Mirrahim in "Natsional'nyi vopros i mezhnatsional"nye otnosheniia v SSSR: Istoriia i sovremennost'," *Voprosy istorii*, 1989, no. 5 (May), p. 84; comments made by Tajiks in the author's presence.

17 A. Sattorov, "Dardhoi miyonshikan," *Omozgor*, October 3, 1989, p. 4; "Soobshchenie komissii prezidiuma Verkhovnogo Soveta Tadzhikskoi SSR po proverke sobytii 12–14 Fevralia 1991 g. v Dushanbe," *Sogdiana*, 1990, no. 3 (October), p. 3; Alimov, Shoismatulloev, and Saidov, "Migratsionnye protsessy," p. 11; Q. Kholiqov, "Oilai baradaroni mo: tajriba, problema, peshomadho," *Adabiyot va san'at*, April 13, 1989, p. 3; Helsinki Watch, *Conflict in the Soviet Union. Tadzhikistan* (New York and Washington, DC: Human Rights Watch, 1991), p. 13.

18 'Mas"uliyati buzurg," p. 2.

19 Karasik, ed., *USSR. Facts and Figures Annual*, p. 450.

20 A. Dubnov, "Katastrofa v Tadzhikistane," *Novoe vremia*, no. 4, 1993 (January), p. 13); N. Vladimirov, "Sataniiskaia okhota," *Vek*, no. 3, 1993, p. 10, as photocopied in *ibid.*, January 25, 1993, p. 36; *Kommersant-Daily*, December 15, 1992, as translated in FBIS, *Daily Report. Central Eurasia*, December 16, 1992, p. 48; S. Tadjbakhsh, "The Bloody Path of Change: The Case of Post-Soviet Tajikistan," *The Harriman Institute Forum*, vol. 6, no. 11 (July 1993), p. 8.

21 I. Rotar', "Predstaviteli vlastei i oppozitsii vstretiatsia v Moskve," *Nezavisimaia gazeta*, March 10, 1994, p. 3.

22 *Ibid.*, p. 449

23 See, for example, Muhammadiev, "Barodari man boshi."

24 Helsinki Watch, *Conflict*, pp. 5, 19, 20, 21, 22, 36, 52; Alimov, Shoismatulloev, and Saidov, "Migratsionnye protsessy," p. 13.

25 Russian Press Digest, July 13, 1994; G. Khasanova, "V Tadzhikistane, kotoryi

polnostiu zavisti ot pomoshchi Moskvy, skoro ne ostanetsia ni odnogo russkogo," *Izvestiia*, May 6, 1994, p. 3.

26  Dushanbe Radio, in Russian, May 11, 1992, as translated in FBIS, *Daily Report. Central Eurasia*, May 12, 1992, pp. 59-60; Interfax, June 12, 1992, as republished in ibid., June 15, 1992, p. 49; S. Shermatova, "We Are Ready For a Dialogue With Russia, And Only With Her," *Moscow News*, August 11, 1993; S. Gretsky, "Qadi Akbar Turajonzoda," *Central Asia Monitor*, no. 1, 1994, p. 23.

27  ITAR–TASS, July 18, 1992; Interfax, October 22, 1992, as republished in FBIS, *Daily Report. Central Eurasia*, October 23, 1992, p. 62; Dushanbe radio, in Russian, October 24, 1992, as translated in FBIS, *Daily Report. Central Eurasia*, October 26, 1992, pp. 71–72.

28  'Soobshchenie komissii," pp. 2–4; Helsinki Watch, *Conflict*, pp. 22–23, 25, 40, 41.

29  Russian Press Digest, December 4, 1991; Reuters, November 25, 1991; R. H. Krieble and S. M. Loui, "'Democracies' Still Precarious," *The Christian Science Monitor*, January 8, 1992, p. 19

30  E. Pain, "Internationalization of the Tajik Conflict," *Moscow News*, November 4, 1992; *Human Rights and Democratization in the Newly Independent States of the Former Soviet Union* (Washington, DC: Commission on Security and Cooperation in Europe, 1993), p, 225; *Izvestiia*, May 14, 1992, as translated in FBIS, *Daily Report. Central Eurasia*, May 18, 1992, p. 49.

31  S. Mirzov, "Millatu oini tojik dar khatar," *Jomi jam*, 1992, no. 6 (April), p. 3; Reuter Library Report, March 24, 1992.

32  A. Azamova, "Kuliab ne sdaetsia," *Moskovskie novosti*, no. 25, 1992, p. 9.

33  J. Krauze, "L'Armée russe abandonne Douchanbe aux communistes," *Le Monde*, December 13–14, 1992, p. 20; Agence France Presse, December 17, 1992; The Reuter Library Report, December 14, 19, and 21, 1992; A. Dubnow, "Katastrofav Tadzhikistane," *Novoe Vremia*, no. 4, 1993 (January), *Current Digest of the Post-Soviet Press*, vol. 45, no. 3 (February 17, 1993), p. 12.

34  *Current Digest of the Post-Soviet Press*, vol. 45, no. 2 (February 10, 1993, p. 25; Russian Press Digest, August 13, 1994; Congressional Testimony, "Memorandum," to Chairman Tom Lantos, Member of the House Subcommittee on International Security, International Operations and Human Rights, and Interested Parties, From Pamela B. Cohen and Micah H. Naftalin, April 26, 1994; press releases, Human Rights Watch/ Helsinki, October 19 and 20, 1994; U.S. Department of State Dispatch, "Tajikistan Human Rights Practices, 1993," January 31, 1994; Inter Press Service, October 26, 1994; S. Erlanger, "Tajik Ex-Communists Prosecute Opposition," *New York Times*, January 10, 1993, p. 15.

35  S. Erlanger, "In Ex-Soviet Lands, Russian Army Can Be a Protector or an Occupier," *The New York Times*, November 30, 1993. S. LeVine, "Tajikistan Swaps Soviet Roubles for Russian Ones," *Financial Times*, January 7, 1994, p. 4.

36  A. Karpov, "Rossiiskaia diviziia uidet iz Tadzhikistana," *Izvestiia*, October 7, 1993; Interfax, April 10, 1993, as reprinted in FBIS, *Daily Report, Central Eurasia*, April 13, 1993, p. 15.

37  R. "Boudreaux, "Struggling with the 'Tajik Problem'," *Los Angeles Times*, October 25, 1994; Agence France Presse, April 29, 1995.

38  Interfax, April 10, 1993, as reprinted in FBIS, *Daily Report, Central Eurasia*, April 13, 1993, p. 15; *Moskovskie novosti*, May 23, 1993), as translated in *ibid.*, May 21, 1993 (sic.), p. 5; The Reuter Library Report, February 23, 1993; Boudreaux, "Russian Copters Attack Tajik Rebels," *Los Angeles Times*, April 12, 1995; Reuters, April 12, 1995.

39  The two costliest incidents occurred on July 13, 1993, when 25 Russians were killed and April 7–16, 1995, when 41 died.

40  The Reuter Library Report, August 4, 1993 and September 14, 1993; Reuters, August

1, 1993; Deutsche Presse-Agentur, January 24, 1995: Agence France Presse, July 26 and 17, 1993, February 24, 1995, and May 18, 1995; Boudreaux, "Russian Copters"; Agence France Presse, April 22, 1995; Reuters, April 12, 1995.

41 Agence France Presse, November 9, 1994; I. MacWilliam, "Ex-Communist Declared Victor in Disputed Tajik Race," *Los Angeles Times*, November 8, 1994, p. A9; Deutsche Presse-Agentur, November 4, 1994; Official Kremlin International News Broadcast, November 10, 1994 (English transcript by Federal Information Systems Corporation.)

42 Azamova, "Kuliab ne sdaetsia"; M. Nuriyon, "Tojikistonro digar qismat makun," *Jumhuriyat*, April 4, 1992, p. 4; Kh. Nazrulloev, "Strasti po Tadzhikistanu," *Nezavisimaia gazeta*, April 4, 1993, p. 4; O. Panfilov, "Tadzhikistan blizok k grazhdanskoi voine," *Nezavisimaia gazeta*, June 20, 1992, p. 3; Interfax, September 28, 1991, as reprinted in FBIS, *Soviet Union. Daily Report*, September 30, 1991, p. 97; Congressional Testimony, *Memorandum*, to Chairman Tom Lantos, April 26, 1994.

43 Dubnov, "Katastrofa," pp. 39–40; G. Tett, "The night that friends turned into murderers," *Financial Times*, February 19, 1994, p.XIII

44 Representative of the numerous examples of that argument is an interview with Imomali Rahmonov; U. Babakhanov, "Kazhetsia, v Tadzhikistane oboidutsia bez ιgolubykh kasok'," *Komsomol'skaia pravda*, January 12, 1993, p. 1.

45 This subject is too complex and contentious to be treated in depth in this essay. The argument is developed at some length in the author's, "Islamic Assertiveness and the Waning of the Old Soviet Order," *Nationalities Papers*, vol. 20, no. 1, Spring 1992, p. 62, and "Islam as Faith, Politics, and Bogeyman," in ed. Michael Bourdeaux, *The Politics of Religion in Russia and the New States of Eurasia* (Armonk, NY: ME Sharpe, 1995.)

46 See, for example, "regional'noe ekonomicheskoe sotrudnichestvo: opyt, problemy, perspektivy," *Agitator Tadzhikistana*, 1989, no. 18 (September), p. 3; FBIS, *Daily Report. Soviet Union*, July 17, 1990, pp. 86–88; "Az rui maslihati dustoni hammusobiqa amal mekunem," *Tojikistoni soveti*, August 16, 1989, p. 3; "Hamkori duston," *Tojikistoni soviet*, September 10, 1991, p. 2.

47 Helsinki Watch, *Conflict*, p. 58; P. Goble, "Central Asians Form Political Bloc," *Report on the USSR*, July 13, 1990, pp. 19–20; F. Karimov, "Muloqoti namoyandegoni quvvahoi demokratii," *Tojikistoni soveti*, May 15, 1991, p. 2.

48 See for example, FBIS, *Daily Report. Soviet Union*, June 4, 1990, p. 116; *ibid.*, p. 119.

49 H. Atokhonov, "Azamati navbati dar Vakhsh," *Tajikistoni soveti*, October 19, 1989, p. 2; "Voda kak prichina pozhara," *Literaturnaia gazeta*, January 16, 1991, p. 8; G. Gleason, "The Struggle for Control over Water in Central Asia: Republican Sovereignty and Collective Action," RFE/RL *Report on the USSR*, vol. 3, no. 25, June 21, 1991, p. 17; "Konflikt na granitse Kirgizii i Tadzhiksitana," *Turkestan*, 1990, no. 1, January–February, p. 5; TadzhikTA, "Dar sharoiti vaqti komendanti," *Tojikistoni soveti*, July 19, 1989, p. 1.

50 Atkin, "Religious, National, and Other Identities in Central Asia," in *Muslims in Central Asia*, ed. J. A. Gross (Durham, NC: Duke University Press, 1992), pp. 50–52.

51 Karasik, ed., *USSR. Facts and Figures Annual*, p. 444; "Natsional'nyi vopros," p. 13; B. Firuz, "Didu bodide muborak!", *Adabiyot va san'at*, April 20, 1989, p. 4; Muhammadiev, "Barodari man boshi"; and comments made in the author's presence.

52 See, for example, R. Masov, "Far'yodi qurboniyon: nido as safhai ta'rikh," *Omuzgor*, July 18, 1989; Q. Davlatov, "Seb ne, olma," *ibid.*, November 7, 1989, p. 3; A. Istad, "Qonuni madaniyat zarur," *Adabiyot va san'at*, August 10, 1989, p. 10; D. Ruziev, "Ki durugh meguyad? Vazir yo vakili anjuman?", *Tojikistoni soveti*, October 20, 1989,

p. 3; N.B. Khotamov, "Iz sovetskoi pressy," *Sogdiana*, 1990, no. 1 (February), p. 3; "Na ruinakh ambitsii," *Sogdiana*, 1990, no. 1 (February), p. 3.

53 See for example, FBIS, *Daily Report. Soviet Union*, September 24, 1990, p. 104; *ibid.*, September 28, 1990, p. 104.

54 Agence France Presse, September 18, 1992; A. Azamova, "Nuzhna li musul″manam demokratiia?" *Moskovskie novosti*, no. 39, 1992, p. 9.

55 Kh. Nazrulloev, "Strasti po Tadzhikistanu," *Nezavisimaia gazeta*, April 4, 1993, p. 4; Agence France Presse, August 7, 1993; *Current Digest of the Post-Soviet Press*, vol. 45, no. 3 (February 17, 1993), p. 12; *Kommersant-Daily*, December 15, 1992, as translated in FBIS, *Daily Report. Central Eurasia*, December 16, 1992, p. 48; S. LeVine, "Afghans fuel war on ex-Soviet territory," *Financial Times*, May 12, 1993, p. 5.

56 A. Bennigsen and C. Lemercier-Quelquejay, *L'Islam en Union soviétique* (Paris: Payot, 1968), pp. 188, 216.

57 Helsinki Watch, *Conflict*, p. 13; statements made in the author's presence.

58 'Partiia, kotoroi ofitsial′no u nas net," *Komsomolets Tadzhikistana*, November 21, 1990, p. 2.

59 This was the argument made by *Tehran Times*, a newspaper believed to echo the views of the Iranian foreign ministry; The Reuter Library Report, September 9, 1992. A Russian Foreign Ministry official also rejected the notion of Iranian trouble-making in Tajikistan (as quoted in East European Markets, February 19, 1993.)

60 S. Erlanger, "Tajik Ex-Communists Prosecute Opposition," *New York Times*, January 10, 1993, p. 15.

61 The Reuter Library Report, October 20, 1993.

62 See for example, The Reuter Library Report, January 27, 1993.

63 Atkin, "Religious, National, and other Identities," p. 58; TadzhikTA, "Dar safi pesh," *Tojikistoni soveti*, December 9, 1989, p. 3.

64 Atkin, "Islamic Assertiveness," pp. 56–57.

65 A. Azamova, "Tajikistan asks Russia for arms for its interior troops," *Moscow News*, September 23, 1992; *Holos Ukrainy*, October 16, 1992, as translated in FBIS, *Daily Report. Central Eurasia*, October 21, 1992, p. 45.

66 D. Sneider, "Refugees Rebuild in Tajik Village," *The Christian Science Monitor*, May 19, 1994, p. 6; R. Bonner, "Tajik Civil War Fades, but the Brutality Goes On," *New York Times*, November 26, 1993, p. A3; The Reuter Library Report, September 8, 1993.

67 J. Rettie, "Struggle for the legacy of empire," *The Guardian*, August 21, 1993, p. 11.

68 Those included the power struggle between Russia's Ministry of Security, which controlled the border guards, and its Ministry of Defense, which controlled regular army troops in Tajikistan, as well as the need to demonize the enemy to divert attention from blunders made in defending the border and the Russian armed forces' efforts in general to prevent cuts in their budget.

69 See for example *Krasnaia zvezda*, May 25, 1993, as translated in FBIS, *Daily Report. Central Eurasia*, May 28, 1993, p. 52; ITAR-TASS, as reprinted in *ibid.*, April 25, 1994, p. 46; ITAR-TASS, September 2, 1993; Agence France Presse, December 11, 1993.

70 Between January and October 1993, according to the border guards' first deputy commander-in-chief, Aleksandr Tymko, there were 150 border violations; in only fifty of these incidents did the border guards on the scene consider a response necessary. Similarly, a spokesman for the border guards stated that in the first eight months of 1994, there were 229 border violations but only 48 of them led to armed clashes (ITAR-TASS, October 11, 1993; *Agence France Presse*, September 6, 1994). Russia's Minister of Defence, Pavel Grachev, stated that only Tajiks (from Tajikistan), but no

citizens of Afghanistan, were involved in the border incursions (*Russian Press Digest,* September 7, 1993). At the time he made that statement (September 1993) Russia was trying to improve its relations with Afghanistan. Even if Grachev only denied Afghanistani involvement in the fighting because it served Russian diplomacy to do so, that meant that claims about Afghanistani involvement could be made or dropped depending on the political expediency of the moment.

# Tajikistan: chronology of events

*June 1989*
13–14   Tajiks and Kyrgyz clash in a dispute over water and land ownership on the republics' border, resulting in one dead and several wounded.

*July 1989*
22   A language law is adopted which makes Tajik the official state language.

*February 1990*
11–14   A mass protest demonstration is staged in Dushanbe in response to rumors that Armenian refugees were to be given housing preference. MVD forces fire on demonstrators and riots ensue. Thirty-seven are killed and eighty wounded.
25   Elections to the Supreme Soviet are held. Kakhar Makhkamov is appointed parliamentary chairman.

*May 1990*
25   Makhkamov is elected Communist Party first secretary.

*August 1990*
24   The Supreme Soviet issues a declaration of sovereignty.

*November 1990*
22   200 members of the Democratic Party of Tajikistan go on a hunger strike after the government refuses their demands to hold popular presidential elections, permit them to hold a congress, and end the persecution of opposition.
30   The Supreme Soviet elects Makhkamov president. Kadriddin Aslonov replaces him as parliamentary chairman.

*December 1990*
1–2   The government permits the Democratic Party to hold a congress.

*March 1991*
17   In the all-union referendum on preserving the union, 96% of voters (94% turnout) support the union.

*August 1991*
31   President Makhkamov resigns following mass antigovernment demonstrations organized by the

Democratic Party, the Rastokhez (Rebirth) Popular Front, and the illegal Islamic Renaissance Party. Aslonov becomes acting president.

*September 1991*

22    Aslonov bans the Communist Party, and the Islamic Renaissance Party is legalized. The mayor of Dushanbe Maksud Ikramov orders the removal of a prominent statue of Lenin in the city.

23    Parliament removes the ban on the Communists, declares a state of emergency, and removes Aslonov, replacing him with Rakhmon Nabiev, former head of the Tajik Communist Party, who is also appointed acting president.

23–30    Thousands defy a ban in Dushanbe to protest the power shift.

*October 1991*

6    Nabiev withdraws his post to campaign in presidential elections.

*November 1991*

24    Nabiev is elected president, with 58% of the vote. The opposition candidate, filmmaker Davlatnazar Khudonazarov, receives 30%. An 85% turnout is reported.

*December 1991*

2    Safarali Kenjaev is elected parliamentary chairman.

13    Tajikistan joins the CIS.

*January 1992*

6    The ban on the Communist Party is removed.

9    Prime Minister Izatullo Khayeev resigns for health reasons and is replaced by Akbar Mirzoev.

*March 1992*

6    Mayor of Dushanbe Maksud Ikramov is arrested.

26–28    Tens of thousands rally in numerous demonstrations to support Ikramov and demand his release as well as the holding of new parliamentary elections. These protests are matched by pro-government demonstrations.

*April 1992*

11    The parliament of the Gorno-Badakhshan Autonomous Region upgrades the territory to the Pamir-Badakhshan Autonomous Republic.

20    Protestors begin forming armed groups and several parliamentary deputies are taken hostage by members of the rebel national guard.

22    Acceding to the opposition, parliamentary chairman Kenjaev resigns.

*May 1992*

3    Kenjaev is restored to his post by parliament.

5    Four people are killed when fighting breaks out between pro- and anti-government forces. Nabiev declares a state of emergency.

6–7    After heavy fighting, opposition forces take control in Dushanbe and form a governing Revolutionary Council.

10    Nabiev signs a pact with the opposition agreeing to include opposition figures in a coalition government.

20    Authorities in Leninobod and Kulyab oblasts refuse to recognize the legitimacy of the new government and threaten to secede.

*August 1992*

24    State prosecutor Nurullo Khuvaidullaev is murdered in Dushanbe.

27    Eight members of the Democratic Party of Tajikistan and Lali Badakhshan are killed.

30    Prime Minister Mirzoev resigns.

31    Opposition forces storm the presidential palace and demand Nabiev's resignation.

*September 1992*

2    Parliamentary leaders and cabinet members pass a no-confidence resolution and demand Nabiev's resignation.

4    Russia, Kazakhstan, Kyrgyzstan, and Uzbekistan send troops to Tajikistan to prevent arms and drug smuggling from Afghanistan.

7    Nabiev is seized in the airport while attempting to flee Dushanbe and is forced to resign.

Parliamentary chairman Iskandarov assumes presidential duties and asserts that the opposition does not intend to establish an Islamic state.

17    Iskandarov approves the entry of Russian peacekeepers.

21    Abdumalik Abdullojanov is appointed acting prime minister.

*October 1992*

13    The Islamic National Salvation Front dissolves itself and calls upon its supporters to back Iskandarov.

24–25    Heavy fighting occurs in Dushanbe, and Communist rebels demand restoration of the pre-May political order.

26 A state of emergency is declared in Dushanbe.

**November 1992**

6 Iskandarov authorizes Russian soldiers to disarm militants.

10 Communist rebels surrounding Dushanbe call upon the government to resign or risk a blockade.

12 Iskandarov resigns, as well as the whole Presidium of the Supreme Soviet and the Council of Ministers.

16 Parliament opens meeting in Kojand.

19 Imomali Rakhmonov, a supporter of Nabiev, is elected parliamentary chairman.

20 Abdullojanov is elected prime minister.

27 The Supreme Soviet abolishes presidential rule and declares the country a parliamentary republic, with Rakhmonov as head of state.

**December 1992**

4–13 Communist forces reassert complete control over Dushanbe.

**March 1993**

29 Sangak Safarov, head of the pro-Communist People's Front, is killed, along with one of his military commanders.

**April 1993**

11 Former president Nabiev dies of a heart attack.

13 Khudonazarov, living abroad, is charged with inciting civil war.

**May 1993**

25 A treaty on political, economic, security, and military cooperation with Russia is concluded.

**June 1993**

13 Parliamentary elections are held for 19 districts to replace deputies who were killed or had fled the country in the last year. No opposition groups are permitted to participate.

20 Gorno-Badakhshon officials announce that they are abandoning their quest for independence.

21 The Supreme Court bans four main opposition parties.

23 Parliament opens its first session since the start of the civil war.

**July 1993** Frequent battles on Tajik–Afghan border throughout the month, with Russian participation.

28 Government declares amnesty for all opposition fighters who put down their arms by 9 September.

*December 1993*

18    Prime Minister Abdullojanov is forced to resign after being blamed for the Tajik economy's failure to improve. He is appointed ambassador to Russia.

27    Abduzhalil Samadov is appointed prime minister.

*Janurary 1994*

4    Rakhmanov declares that the Russian ruble is to be the country's sole legal currency.

*May 1994*

29–31    Five Russian officers are murdered in four separate incidents.

*June 1994*

15    Deputy defense minister Ramazan Radzhabov is assassinated outside of Dushanbe.

18–27    Peace talks held in Tehran fail, and no cease-fire is reached.

*July 1994*

20    Supreme Soviet adopts a draft constitution which restores the office of president.

22    Rebels attack government forces near Dushanbe, reportedly capturing 36 soldiers.

26–28    Fighting ensues between government and rebel forces. 30 of the captured soldiers are found to have defected to the opposition.

*August 1994*

9–11    Journalists Maksud Huseinov and Muhammadrahim Saidar are arrested for distributing the outlawed opposition newspaper *Charogi ruz.*

18    Television head Davlatati Rakhmonaliev is assassinated.

21–25    10 Russian border troops die in battles with rebels on the Tajik–Afghan border.

*November 1994*

6    Parliamentary chairman Emomali Rakhmonov is elected president with 60% of the vote (reported 95% voter participation). His only opponent Abdumalik Abdullodzhanov wins 35%. The Constitution is simultaneously accepted when 90% of voters support its passage in a referendum.

10    A 54-man prisoner exchange occurs, fulfilling one of the major demands of the opposition.

*February 1995*

26    Elections to the new 181-seat parliament, the Majlisi Oli, are held with 85% turnout. 40% of the 161 seats filled go

to deputies of the old parliament, and most others are also associated with the communists.

*April 1995*

8–15    Intense fighting on the Tajik–Afghan border renews, and more than 25 border guards from a Russian-Kazakh battalion are killed.

20–26    Third-round negotiations with the opposition end in Moscow with little progress reported.

*May 1995*

10    The Tajik ruble is introduced, replacing the Russian ruble as the sole legal tender in Tajikistan.

20–30    Fourth-round negotiations are held in Almaty.

# 18   Turkmenistan: just like old times

DAVID NISSMAN

When the Soviet Union was still intact, Turkmenistan was the fourth largest union republic in terms of territory and one of the smallest in terms of population. Prior to the Russian conquest of Turkmenistan in the late nineteenth century, the dominant political forces in the region were the khanates of Khiva and Kokand to which the Turkmens were nominally subordinate. In theory, the Turkmen tribes were compelled to pay an annual tribute to whichever khanate claimed control over them and provide military troops for the khanates' defense whenever necessary. This tribute was paid in years when the Turkmen tribes, individually or collectively, felt that their military strength was inadequate to repel the khan's tax collectors. The dominant forces in Turkmen life were the tribe, the clan, the family, and Islam, and outside interference with the Turkmen way of life was minimal. For centuries there had been no uniquely Turkmen state structure superior to that of the collective will of the tribe and its elders, and no enforceable laws governing the society save for Islam and its body of common law as interpreted by the local Turkmen clergy.

The Turkmens did not live in cultural, commercial or political isolation. Their literature was written in Chagatay, the lingua franca of the Turks of Central Asia, and a number of Turkmen poets made major contributions to Central Asian literature in the centuries preceding the Russian conquest. The Turkmen clergy were educated in the dominant Muslim educational institutions of the period, in Bukhara, Iran, Iraq and Egypt, and were thus exposed to the ideas and influences which pervaded these major centers of Muslim training. At the same time, as Moscow's power and influence grew in the eighteenth and nineteenth centuries, the larger tribal–clan confederacies sent regular diplomatic and trading missions to Russia and Iran. Defeat by Tsarist forces in the late nineteenth centuries changed all this; under Russian rule, Turkmenistan became a backwater.

Under the Tsar, few changes took place in Turkmenistan: the climate, which varies from intense cold in the winter to suffocating heat in the summer, was unattractive to settlers from other parts of the Russian Empire, and the land was inhospitable to farmers due to the lack of a developed irrigation system. It remained an oasis culture, the steppes being exploited for the animal herds, sheep, goats, and horses for which

**Turkmenistan**

- International boundary
- *Welayat* boundary
- ★ National capital
- ◉ *Welayat* capital
- Railroad
- Road

0       200 Kilometers
0       200 Miles

*Lambert Conformal Conic Projection, SP 12N/38N*

KAZAKHSTAN

Aqtaū

KAZAKHSTAN

Aral Sea

Müynoq

Qünghirot

Nukus

Uchquduq

Bekdash

Garabogazköl Aylagy

Sariqamish Köli

Sarygamysh Köli

Dashhowuz

Urganch

Caspian

Gyzylgaya

DASHHOWUZ WELAYATY

UZBEKISTAN

Nawoiy

Zarafshon

Turkmenbashi (Krasnowodsk)

BALKAN WELAYATY

LEBAP

Bukhoro

Samarqand

Sea

Nebitdag

Gumdag

Yerbent

WELAYATY

Chärjew

Qarshi

Gyzylarbat

AHAL WELAYATY

Sumbar

Ashgabat

MARY

Gowurdak

Esenguly

Etrek Daryasy

Nidir Airaū

Bojnürd

Mary

Garagum Kanaly

Kerki

Bandar-e Torkeman

Tejen

Bayramaly

Sari

Gorgān

WELAYATY

Sheberghän

Shährüd

Kushaf Rüd

Saragt

Sebzevar

Neyshabūr

Mashhad

Murgap Daryasy

Meymaneh

IRAN

Darya-ye Murghäb

Tayyebat

AFGHANISTAN

Gönabäd

Herat

Hariröd

Gushgy

Deyhuk

Shindand

Delärām

Turkmenistan had been famous for centuries. The new Russian conquerors selected the small Turkmen town of Ashgabat as the seat of occupation, and to this end built a fortress there in 1881. Subsequently, Ashgabat became a major railroad and industrial center as the Russians deepened their control over the region. Major changes only took place after the Bolshevik revolution in 1917.

Turkmenistan's present borders were established under the Anglo-Russia Treaty of 1895. A major consequence of this border agreement is that a substantial number of Turkmens living in Iran and Afghanistan were ultimately isolated from the Turkmens of Turkmenistan, especially during the Soviet period. There are now approximately 2.5 million Turkmens in Turkmenistan, between 1–2 million Turkmens in Iran and another million in Afghanistan. Only since the onset of glasnost in Turkmenistan (somewhat later than in the rest of the USSR) have contacts between Turkmenistan, Iran and Afghanistan been revived. Of equal or, in the short term, greater importance is that renewed contact with the exile Turkmen community – those who had fled from Bolshevism to the West or the Middle East – provides the previously isolated Turkmens of the former Soviet Union with a greater diversity of political and economic views than ever before.

Turkmenistan was proclaimed a republic in October 1924 when Central Asia was divided administratively by the Bolshevik government in Moscow. This process was officially termed national-state demarcation (*razmezhevanie*). Prior to the creation of the Turkmenistan Soviet Socialist Republic, Moscow's policy was directed at eliminating wealthy landholders, reducing the influence of the tribes who controlled pasturage and could raise their own armies, and dismantling the Islamic clergy, who were considered to be a strong anti-Bolshevik force.

Anti-Soviet sentiment remained strong through the early 1930s. The Basmachi movement, which was active throughout Central Asia and surfaced beginning in 1928 even within the highest circles of Turkmenistan's government, resulted in punitive countermeasures by Moscow. Turkmen resistance to Moscow's policies reached a crescendo in 1931 with an uprising in Kara Kum. In the end, however, the Red Army was victorious, and Moscow prevailed in all instances of Turkmen resistance to its policies. Many Turkmen fled to Iran and Afghanistan; the final death toll of those who remained is still unknown.

During the early Soviet period, a policy of *korenizatsiya*, or nativization of Turkmen cadres in leadership positions of the state and economy was introduced. But in the early 1930s resistance to central authority increased among the Turkmen leaders of Turkmenistan. As a consequence, party and government leaders were charged with fomenting sedition, and an extensive purge of the apparatus ensued. Simultaneously, korenizatsiya was replaced by Sovietization.

While pan-Turkism was never a factor that dominated domestic politics in the Central Asian Turkic republics, Russia's fear of it as an emerging movement compelled them to place limits on the extent of interrepublican contact. In the early 1920s, the Turks of the Soviet Union had decided collectively to shift from the Arabic alphabet to a Latin script, called the Common Turkic Latin alphabet. This consisted of a common pool of graphemes representing consonants and vowels from which each republic could draw in order to construct the writing of their own literary languages. In this way, differences between each of the Turkic languages would be more clearly delineated than in the older Arabopersian script (which lacked graphemes that could represent the Turkic vocalic systems). The purpose of this reform was to promote literacy. This alphabet remained in use until the beginning of 1940 when Stalin decreed that all Turkic languages be changed immediately to various variations of the Russian alphabet. In the case of Turkmen, the phonetic system of which differs from the languages of other Turkic languages in Central Asia, this meant that Turkmen's long vowels could no longer be differentiated from the short. It is worthy of note that one of Turkmenistan's first post-Soviet moves in the area of cultural reform was the readoption of a variation of the Latin alphabet it had been forced to abandon in 1940.

The onset of the Second World War continued the development of industrialism begun in the 1930s. This brought with it some of the benefits of modernization: the emergence of a modest working-class and national intelligentsia, increased social-economic mobility, new employment patterns, and some urbanization. The irrigation network was expanded and the development of the cotton industry was accelerated at the cost of the more varied oasis agriculture that had dominated earlier. This, combined with the building of the Karakum Canal in 1954 (the largest irrigation project in the USSR), caused major ecological problems and severe damage to the Aral Sea.

The postwar period was marked by frequent accusations of nationalism directed at the Turkmen leadership and frequent purges of the Turkmen political hierarchy. Following Khrushchev's destalinization speech in 1956, however, resistance to the highly centralized Soviet state became more successful. By the 1970s Turkmen officials were able to demand more powers from the all-union government in budgetary and planning matters. The Soviet policy of treating cotton, gas, and oil as raw materials to be exported from Turkmenistan and processed elsewhere was increasingly criticized by the Turkmen leadership. The fact that Turkmenistan lagged behind all other republics on most economic indicators exacerbated the sense of deprivation.

Turkmens demonstrated extraordinarily high retention of the native language into the 1980s (over 98 percent). At that time, approximately one-third of the republic's population belonged to other nationalities (see table

Table 18.1. *National composition of Turkmenistan, 1989*

| Nationalities | Population | % |
|---|---|---|
| Total population | 3,523,000 | 100.0 |
| Turkmen | 2,536,600 | 72.0 |
| Russians | 334,700 | 9.5 |
| Uzbeks | 317,100 | 9.0 |
| Kazakhs | 88,100 | 2.5 |
| Tatars | 38,700 | 1.1 |
| Other | 207,800 | 5.9 |

*Source: Natisional'nyi sostav naseleniya SSSR. Finansy i statistika,* (Moscow, 1991).

18.1.). Although Russians had begun to emigrate from Turkmenistan in the late 1970s, they still made up 10 percent of the population in 1989. Other minorities included Kazakhs and Uzbeks who were indigenous to the region and lived close to the borders of Kazakhstan and Uzbekistan respectively, and peoples such as Kurds, Baluch and Koreans, many of whom had been resettled in Turkmenistan as the result of Stalin's deportation of whole nationalities in the early 1940s.

The August 1991 coup in the USSR changed nothing in Turkmenistan. The Turkmenistan Communist Party was dismantled in name only and S. A. Niyazov, formerly first Secretary of the Central Committee of the Turkmenistan Communist Party, retained his position as the duly elected president (in an election in which he was the only candidate). Dissident movements, including non-communist democratic reform movements, continued to be either suppressed by authorities or, in general, passed over in silence by the Turkmen media.

Despite numerous campaigns directed against it over several decades, tribalism is still strongly felt in Turkmenistan. A "Round Table" discussion among prominent social activists touched on this recently in the context of nationalism: one participant maintained that nationalism per se is not a problem in Turkmenistan but that "among Turkmens themselves incorrect tribal–clan relations and tribal prejudices . . . are not only disturbing, but also do considerable harm." He noted that at the opening of the academic year at the Turkmen State University students are allocated rooms without regard to their rayon or oblast "but only a short time later only people from the same villages occupy the same rooms."[1]

Turkmen political unity can be said only to have become a reality in the twentieth century. The two factors which transcend tribal and the putative Soviet national concept imposed on the Turkmens in the Stalin period are language and religion, Islam. To be added to this, perhaps, is a third, somewhat more elusive factor – "Turkmenism" – which has only recently been raised for public discussion. Basically, it is an attempt to define what makes an individual exclusively a Turkmen, as opposed to a Turk, a Muslim, a communist, or a democrat.[2] Since nations have risen and fallen throughout history without defining, or even contemplating what made them unique, it can be assumed that this question is peripheral to the main issue, which is Turkmenistan's future as a nation.

## Turkmen nationhood

Turkmenistan declared itself a sovereign nation on August 22, 1990 and independent slightly more than a year later; at the same time, the Niyazov government stressed its willingness to remain within the Soviet Union. No voices of direct dissent were raised in the media but, in fact, an organized movement searching for political alternatives had already begun to take shape. Unlike most of the other Central Asian republics, the Turkmen democratic and anti-communist movements had received no coverage in the Turkmen mass media, save the occasional denunciation directed at either the movements themselves or their more active members. In January 1990, the director of the Ideology Department of the Central Committee of the Turkmen Communist party assailed a group of "non-formals" within the Turkmen Academy of Sciences by claiming that they were misusing glasnost and pluralism in their attacks on the Communist Party.[3] A month later, Turkmenistan's First Deputy Procurator announced that "measures" were to be taken against "juridically unregistered movements." Specifically, he mentioned a movement called *Agzybirlik* ("Solidarity") as a target of these measures.[4] The attitude of the party elite towards political pluralism was expressed clearly by a party official in the Academy of Sciences: opposition to any party which is "unable to make a contribution to perfecting socialism."[5]

Despite the frequent criticism directed at informal organizations, political and social dissent continued to spread. An official Turkmen Writers Union spokesman noted that "tendencies to deny the political primacy of the CPSU and its organizational and political leadership are not going without a significant influence on Turkmen literature and writers."[6] The failure of the August 1991 coup clearly caught the Turkmen ruling hierarchy unprepared, although in the coup's immediate aftermath no important Turkmen official lost his position.

Along with democratic movements such as Agzybirlik, more extreme nationalist trends have also found fertile soil in Turkmenistan. In May of 1989, city-wide riots took place in Ashkhabad and Nebitdag. While these were initially attributed to hooliganism, later interpretations of these events cast a different light on the occurrences. A roundtable discussion at the Turkmenistan Council of Trade Unions stressed efforts by "scandal-mongers and extremists" to stir up feelings of nationalism among Turkmen youth.[7] A few months later, a commentator on social issues complained that "windbags" were aiding and abetting nationalism and "exploiting the quarrelsome nature of petty chauvinist groups."[8] On the other hand, the TuSSR Procuracy has admitted that the May riots are attributable to a number of "unresolved," but unspecified social problems;[9] shortly thereafter, a "letter to the editor" asserted that the emergence of nationalism was not only built on "unresolved social problems, but also the distance between the party leadership and the people."[10] If that is indeed the case, this distance has not closed in post-coup Turkmenistan.

Events in other parts of the Soviet Union have not lacked an impact in Turkmenistan. The press carried reports of a meeting between a people's judge and students in Gokdepe allegedly in response to students' expressions of support for "extremist forces in Uzbekistan" and other parts of the country.[11] In an effort to counter this type of influence, the press started printing "letters to the editor" decrying the Baltic independence movements.[12] This campaign, however, was unable to counter the effect of news of independence movements and alternative political approaches in other republics a year later, when a discussion between historians, political scientists and journalists debating the advantages of remaining in the Soviet Union concluded that it was "regrettable" that there were some people in the republic under the influence of media coming from dissident republics.[13]

## Turkmenistan's government and constitution

At the 25th Congress of the Communist Party of Turkmenistan in the Autumn of 1991, the party decided to dissolve itself. In its place, the Turkmenistan Democratic Party (TDP) was organized, and on December 16th, 1991 S. A. Niyazov, who was elected president of Turkmenistan the previous year, signed a decree officially conferring TDP membership on former TCP members. As a by-product of this change, Turkmenistan, the territory of which had been divided into four oblasts, which in turn, were composed of a number of rayons, began to redivide territorial–administrative boundaries into five veliats – Akhal (formerly Ashkhbad Oblast), Balkan, Tashauz, Mary and Leban (formerly Charjou).[14] These are governed by velis appointed by and responsible to the president, and each veliat is composed of *ils* administered by *hakims* appointed by the veli and responsible to him.

## The TDP and the opposition

According to its program, the TDP pledged to initiate and carry out reforms in economics, politics, and culture; democratize all aspects of Turkmenistan's society; cultivate and develop Turkmen history and national traditions; act without regard for nationality or personal beliefs and promote the equality of all citizens; and eliminate state control over certain branches (primarily manufacturing and industrial) of the economy. It is unclear to what extent the TDP Program will be carried out in fact; one thing is clear: since Niyazov was elected president (October 27, 1990) there have been regular human rights violations in Turkmenistan. As has been documented by Helsinki Watch, "criticism of the government is suppressed, censors approve only what is in harmony with government policy, and residents who dissent or who have contact with dissidents . . . are put under de facto house arrest."[15]

Early in 1992 the Peasants' Party of Turkmenistan was organized. Its draft program describes it as a "parliamentary-type" of party. The Peasants' Party defines its goals as defending the interests of farmers and peasants, workers in the agroindustrial industry, and the rural intelligentsia (physicians, teachers, and agricultural technicians). It advocates a free economy, the peasant's right to own the land under cultivation and the right to bequeath this land to heirs. Its current membership is unknown. While officially registered, it is considered to be inactive.[16]

There is also an unregistered Democratic Party of Turkmenistan which was established on December 22, 1990. It claims to work toward uniting the efforts of all democratic parties in Central Asia.[17] But the Democratic Party has been refused registration by the Turkmenistan Ministry of Justice. According to its president, Dudymurat Khojamukhammed (now in exile): "if the president wishes to register a party, it is registered; if he does not, he can stall under the pretext that the party does not exist."[18] It claimed a membership of 1,500 in 1992.

On September 1, 1989, Agzybirlik, the Society for the Protection of the Turkmen Language, was registered with the presidium of the Academy of Sciences TSSR. Its original platform was independence from the USSR and a greater emphasis on Turkmen language and history. Agzybirlik was officially closed on January 15, 1990 because they wished to mark the anniversary of the battle of Gok-Depe, when Turkmenistan was forcibly annexed by the Russian Empire.[19] Akmuhammed Velsapar, secretary of Agzybirlik's press service, commented on the government's refusal to register the organization, "It's interesting that before the fall of the USSR they declared us a 'CIA organization,' but now we are a 'KGB organization.'"[20] At the time, Agzybirlik's membership numbered 1,000.

Connected to the reform movement in Moscow is the Movement for Democratic Reform. It includes some former Communist Party members and two deputies in Turkmenistan's Supreme Soviet, and is generally considered to be more willing to accommodate itself to Turkmenistan's current regime.[21]

Finally there is Genesh ("Council"), founded in August 1991. It is a coalition formed by Agzybirlik, the Democratic Party of Turkmenistan and the Movement for Democratic Reform, and is supposed to coordinate the work of all the opposition groups.[22]

Article 1 of Turkmenistan's Constitution, adopted on May 18, 1992, defines Turkmenistan as a "presidential republic."[23] It has a President, a Prime Minister, and a parliament called a Supreme Soviet. In addition, government also includes a *khalk maslakhaty* ['people's council'] which has responsibility for the passage of constitutional amendments. Helsinki Watch has pointed out that "with few exceptions ... all members of this ostensibly highly powerful body are appointed, not elected, greatly diminishing its ability to function as a representative body, and compromising the principle and practice of separation of powers."[24] On the rayon and oblast level, Turkmenistan has representative government in the form of Soviets of Peoples Deputies who are elected directly by the people. Advising the president is the Presidential Council, whose members are appointed by the president. There are also a number of committees at the cabinet level, most important of which is the National Security Committee. During the Soviet period, many industrial and other institutions were under the control of All-Union ministries; as of January 1, 1992, these devolved to the government of Turkmenistan. Some Turkmen ministries had existed on paper alone or had purely ceremonial functions, such as the Ministry of Foreign Affairs. Following independence, this ministry actually began to play a foreign policy, diplomatic, and consular role; others, such as the Ministry of Defense, had never existed at all in Turkmenistan and are now in their initial stages.

The Constitution contains many guarantees that do not exist in practice.[25] The report by the Organization on Security and Cooperation in Europe (OSCE), in a discussion of the current government's record vis-à-vis the Constitution, has noted a number of vague areas:

> For example, Article 27 states that "Freedom of meetings, rallies and demonstrations *in the procedure established by legislation* is guaranteed," leaving the legislature open to pass laws that curtail that right, rather than guaranteeing the right absolutely. Similarly, Article 28 states that "Citizens have the right to create political parties and other public associations operating within the framework of the Constitution and the laws." Article 28 also lays out that basis on which political parties can be prohibited by the government, including those parties which "encroach on the health and morals of the people." The vague wording here causes concern that any opposition to the government could be seen as an encroachment on the "health and morals of the people," especially in view of the fact that an October 1991 resolution declared that demonstrations and hunger strikes in public places were illegal because, among other things, they were a threat to "public health."[26]

The seemingly repressive controls imposed by the government of Turkmenistan are consistently justified by Turkmenistan's officials who assert the need for "stability."[27] This "stability" led the OSCE to conclude that:

It may be that Turkmenistan will remain the most "stable," or stagnant, of the Central Asia countries, especially if the level of government repression remains unchanged. For in addition to the repressive policies, the government has a large reserve of natural resources on which to mollify the population economically, unlike many of the other former Soviet republics. Turkmenistan's natural gas reserves are third only to those of Russia and the United States; that alone, given Turkmenistan's relatively small population of 3.5 million, may "buy" Niyazov the compliance he demands.[28]

# Islam in Turkmenistan

Islam manifests itself in almost every aspect of Turkmen life, and anti-Muslim propaganda conducted in Central Asia has been ineffective. At the present time, Islam is especially powerful among women and the youth. In 1988, an article in the Turkmen CP daily pointed out that mollas, ishans and faith healers are still active, "especially in the vicinity of 'holy' places" and added that "primarily, unemployed women and certain other groups of the population have fallen under their influence." Above all, "it has been demonstrated by sociological studies conducted in rural regions that more than 46% of nonbelievers follow religious traditions when they get married and during the course of religious holidays." The same survey established that 61.2% of female believers are housewives. Another survey conducted at three Turkmen schools found that 80% of the students "wear beads against the evil eye, multicolored strings, amulets, talismans and other religious ornaments."[29]

Until the late 1980s, it would have been safe to say that in Turkmenistan, Islam, especially the unofficial kind which had predominated and only now is merging with the officially recognized state structure, was closely linked with native tribal and clan institutions. In the last few years, however, Turkmen Islam has been increasingly subject to external influences. In the late 1980s, Iranian radio and television stations such as Radio Gurban and Bender Turkmen began broadcasts in Turkmen aimed at disseminating Islam among the population. Iran's Islamic centers also began to send letters to the inhabitants of Krasnovodsk Olast certifying that they had been awarded the title "hajji" externally.[30] There have also been reports that Hekmatyar's Islamic Party of Afghanistan has been successful in bringing its ideology across the border into Turkmenistan[31] and that an attempt was made by two alleged Tajik "apple sellers" in a kolkhoz market in Ashkhabad to recruit soldiers among the Turkmens to conduct a *jihad* (holy war).[32] In light of statements made by Abdureshid Saidov, head of the Islam Democratic Party, to the effect that Islam was incompatible with Marxism-Leninism,[33] one can readily understand why Turkmenistan's government, which is staffed almost completely by members of the former Marxist-

Leninist regime, is treading very carefully when it comes to Turkmenistan's Muslims, especially in view of the "illegal religious pamphlets" now in circulation in the country.[34]

In 1989 the Kazi-Imam of the believers of Turkmenistan proposed that the illegal Muslim clergy be integrated into the official ranks of the accepted mollas and be allowed to minister to the Muslim population. According to him, "progressive thinking" religious functionaries could also include members of the non-official clergy, referred to generally as "pseudomollas." He pointed out that "official religious representatives are still unable to serve all religious believers, especially those in distant places."[35]

In a subsequent statement made at a meeting in Kalinin Rayon, he claimed that the only bad mollas, or "pseudomollas," are those "who do not refrain from cheating people in their own self-interest, who make no distinction between virtue and vice, who do not understand genuine religious views and cannot tell the difference between good deeds and sin."[36]

Another consequence of the official change in attitude towards religion in Turkmenistan is an increase in mosque construction. While there were only four mosques in Turkmenistan in 1985, this number increased to 70 by June of 1990, and by 1994, to a few hundred. There are also a number of noted religious shrines in Turkmenistan, often centered in Muslim grave-yards or near tombs of prominent Muslims of the medieval period: the most notable of these are Ag-ishan, near Bakherden in Krasnovodsk Oblast; Babagammar, or Gammarbaba, to whom there are two shrines, one in Yoloten Rayon, the other in Kushgy Rayon; and Saragtbaba, built near the mausoleum of the eleventh-century Muslim mystic Abu'l-Fazl near Saragt.[37]

Nevertheless, with independence, the Turkmen government has declared itself to be a secular society, and church and state are separated. According to Article 6 of Turkmenistan's Constitution, religious practices are free, but private religious instruction is forbidden.[38] There are also other conditions placed on the practice of religion. Under Article 3, which guarantees freedom of conscience, it is stated that "exercising the freedom to profess a religion or other convictions is subject only to those restrictions which are necessary to safeguard public safety and order, life and health of the people, and morale . . ."[39] The vagueness of the wording permits the government enormous latitude in interpreting the concepts of public safety, order and morale. On June 1, 1992, the Kazi Hajji Nasrullah ibn Ibadulla officially registered the Kaziate of Turkmenistan, responsible for the administration of religious affairs, with the Turkmen Ministry of Justice. This was, however, under the condition that the Ministry of Justice officials maintain a "working relationship with the religious representatives."[40]

## Turkmen as a state language of the TSSR

Statements in the "letters to the editor" columns of the Turkmen daily and weekly newspapers generally make the claim that the key to a strong national identity is a strong national language, and that the national language is only strong when it acquires the status of the "state language." To this end, after a debate lasting over a period of several months, at the end of May 1990 Turkmenistan passed a Language Law which in effect placed Turkmen on equal par with Russian. The debate on the language question was and is intense and covers a number of issues aside from its acquisition of official status: the re-Turkmenification of place and personal names, language purification and its opposite, Russification, and the role of the Russian language in independent Turkmenistan.

Immediately after the creation of a Soviet government in Turkmenistan, Russian was declared a state language, and various measures were taken to assure that cadres coming into the republic had the opportunity to learn it. Pygam Azymov, a leading Turkmen linguist and academician, pointed out in a recent article that "enthusiasm for and interest in studying Turkmen began to weaken" in the late 1930s and 1940s. As a consequence Turkmen fluency among urban intelligentsia and their children is extremely low at the present time. One side effect of this decline is that the language is rarely used as a mode of communication in ministries and leading organizations and, as claimed by Azymov, has been "misused" by the media. He places the blame for the present situation on "we linguists, the Turkmen intelligentsia, party and Soviet workers."[41] Azymov's article, which appeared in the republican party daily, attracted many letters supporting his position. Two weeks later, the same newspaper carried letters from a writer who, expressing his support for Azymov, complained that "most meetings and gatherings and even Turkmen feasts in this city [Ashkhabad], are not held in Turkmen"; on the same page, the chairman of the Young Scholars council at the Magtymguly Institute of Language and Literature maintained that "local youth in the city view the study of Turkmen with indifference" and proposed that Turkmen language requirements be imposed at all institutions of higher learning because "if entrance and graduation examinations in Turkmen were to be introduced, nobody would look on the study of Turkmen with disdain.[42] Five days later it was urged in another letter that the requirement that dissertations be submitted in Russian be eliminated.[43] With independence, language legislation encompassing many of the suggestions enumerated above did, in fact, become a priority.

On the other hand, Russification had made few inroads into the majority rural population. The 1979 All-Union census revealed that only 25.4 percent of the local population could speak Russian freely, and these were mostly in the cities; in the last fifteen years, the number of fluent Russian-speakers decreased further. As one observer has commented, "the basic component of our [younger] population does not know Russian."[44]

Language and language reform issues raised in debates occurring in the pages of the Turkmen press have become reliable markers indicating the form Turkmen nationalism and national pride will take in the future. Turkmen-language successes have included the imposition of Turkmen language requirements at institutions of higher learning, expansion of the urban Turkmen kindergarten networks, an increase in Turkmen academic publishing, the establishment of language purification (or "translation") commissions, and an increase in introducing Turkmen courses for non-local bureaucrats working in predominantly national areas. All of these are required in order to comply with the language law, but the extent to which they can be implemented in a short time is open to question. For these moves to be effective, full cooperation between all institutions within the republic is a basic requirement. A number of recent articles in the press point out that there are many shortcomings in the execution of the massive language program.

## Turkmen diaspora relations

Following official, and hence public, recognition that it had become politically feasible to establish contact with Turkmens abroad, the Central Committee of the Turkmen Communist Party passed the decree "On The Establishment Of A Turkmenistan Society For Relations With Conationals Abroad" in July 1990.[45] A few months later, the Vatan ("Fatherland") Society was established with the stated goal of focusing on the "close to three million Turkmens" of Iran and Afghanistan.[46] A three-day First International Conference of World Turkmens was convened in Ashkhabad in May 1991, which was attended by Turkmens from Afghanistan, Turkey, Syria, Great Britain, Germany and Iran.[47] At the conference, a mixture of local and diaspora Turkmens created the World Humanitarian Association of World Turkmens.[48] The role and importance of these contacts increased considerably after Turkmenistan gained independence.

Turkmenistan's relations with Turkmens abroad have not, until recently, been a matter of discussion outside very narrow circles. Until the Afghanistan war and the upsurge of Turkmen language religious propaganda beamed at the TSSR from Iran, the issue was rarely mentioned in the media, mass or scientific, at all. As late as 1958, a Turkmen historian noted that "not one ethnographic study of Turkmen ethnography exists in the Turkmen language if one does not count articles published in journals of the 1930s."[49] The significance of this omission in Turkmen research into their own ethnogenesis became apparent when articles began to appear in the Turkmen literary newspaper in the mid 1960s, announcing at first the presence of Turkmens in Turkey and Sinkiang, and then the presence of large numbers in Iraq who were even publishing works in their own language in the multilingual Iraqi literary journal *Yengi Yraq (New Iraq)*.[50] Since the Iraqi Turkmen may be Azeris instead of ethnolinguistic Turkmens, reference to them was subsequently reduced to almost nothing for the next twenty years, as were all efforts to establish contact. In 1966, a work on the Turkmens abroad was to have been published by the Institute of History of the TSSR Academy of Sciences because "the production of scientific work dealing with the Turkmens living in foreign countries has great scientific, theoretical and political importance."[51] The work never appeared, and the Turkmens abroad were forgotten until the Soviet march into Afghanistan.

One can only speculate why Turkmenistan lagged behind other union republics in relations with their own countrymen abroad. The Turkmen of Iran and Afghanistan (by far the largest diaspora communities) are related by blood with the Soviet Turkmens and many of the Afghan and Iranian Turkmens are descendants of former Basmachis. These relationships did not surface in the public media until recently, and did so on the basis of a decision by Moscow which established direct trade and other relations between oblasts of the TSSR with the Afghan provinces of Badkhyz, Farab and Herat. The latter two contain substantial numbers of Turkmens.

In the late 1980s Turkmen media began a campaign, stimulated primarily by Moscow, for the establishment of closer relations with Afghan Turkmens. The first objective was to open a dialogue. On February 11, 1989, G. A. Borovik, chairman of the Soviet Committee for the Defence of Peace and vice president of the World Peace Council met with activists from the TSSR republic Committee for Defence of Peace in Ashkhabad to discuss the role of Turkmenistan, which shares a common border of over one thousand kilometers with Afghanistan, in helping to regulate the Afghan situation following the withdrawal of Soviet troops. He urged that "republic writers, artists, war and labor veterans must join widely in peaceful, creative action . . . maintain relations with organizations in Afghanistan, Iran and Pakistan and certain people, including Turkmens living in these countries, and be especially active." He added that "local activists in Tajikistan have talked with Afghan Mujahidin; it is possible that such meetings can be very useful"; and exhorted his fellows to "broadly exploit the participation of religious workers" in this movement.[52]

The purpose of these new contacts was to develop cultural, especially linguistic ties with their Afghan compatriots. For several years *Goresh* (struggle), a Turkmen newspaper in the Arabic script, has been published in Kabul for distribution to Turkmens throughout Afghanistan. In a recent visit to Chardzhou its editor, Mukhammet Emin Khemra, discussed the language problems involved in putting out the newspaper (which has a circulation of 5,000 and is distributed in eleven provinces), especially after the Soviet withdrawal. He said: "At the present time the language problem has turned into one of the most pressing questions before press and state workers. The Afghan Turkmens consist of representatives from various tribes, each of them speaking its own dialect. In short, Afghan Turkmens are still far from developing a common Turkmen literary language. Thus ... Turkmen linguistic scholars must provide help in this urgent problem."[53] Similar developments have occurred in relations with the Turkmens of Iran. Efforts to alleviate the language problems have increased in intensity since Turkmenistan was able to establish its own diplomatic and cultural relations with Afghanistan and Iran.

## Turkmen foreign affairs

Turkmenistan basically conducts foreign affairs on two levels. As a member state of the Commonwealth of Independent States, it maintains relations with Russia and the other CIS members which remain its strongest trading partners. As a new member of the world community, it has been recognized by more than forty other nations, including the United States, and is a member of the United Nations as well as the Islamic Cooperation Organization. Turkmenistan is also a signatory of the Final Act of the Helsinki Convention, a hypocritical position considering that many of the freedoms considered to be inalienable rights by the other signatories have been disregarded by the Turkmen government. President Niyazov has defined Turkmenistan's foreign policy as one of "positive neutralism," the meaning of which is largely unclear.

Following independence, the first two countries to recognize Turkmenistan were Iran and Turkey, and Turkmenistan has developed strong relations with both. Turkey is training Turkmen specialists and participating, on an equal basis with Russia, in training Turkmenistan's armed defense forces. For its part, Iran was quick to begin active commercial relations, not only in providing such goods as clothing and shoes to Turkmen consumer networks, but also in offering the services of Iranian petroleum and natural gas experts. One of Niyazov's greatest international achievements, in fact, took place at a meeting of a planned Central Asian confederation shortly after the formation of the CIS: Niyazov made a backroom deal with an Iranian observer to construct a railway link between Turkmenistan's cities and Iran, track for which is being laid at the present time. Iran and Turkmenistan share a long, common border and it is only natural that it become one of Turkmenistan's closest, non-former-Soviet allies.

The United States was also quick to establish diplomatic representation in Ashkhabad. At present, Turkmenistan enjoys Most Favored Nation (MFN) status with the US, although American officials have often expressed concern about Turkmenistan's implementation of the Helsinki Accords.

NOTES

1 *Sovet Turkmenistany*, 19 November 1988, p. 3
2 The discussion was launched in a two-part essay by the Turkmen commentator on sociopolitical affairs Tirkesh Jumageldiyev, *Sovet Turkmenistany*, September, 22–23 1990.
3 B. Soyunov *Sovet Turkmenistany*, January, 28 1990.
4 Sh. Khojamberdiyev, *Sovet Turkmenistany*, February, 17 1990.
5 B. Mammetyazov, deputy secretary of the party bureau of the Magtymguly Institute of Language and Literature, *Mugallymlar Gazeti*, March, 25 1990.
6 A. Atabayev, acting chairman of the TuSSR Writers Union, *Sovet Turkmenistany*, February 27, 1991. A short story which depicts the atmosphere of this time by the Turkmen writer Atageldi Atabayev has been translated into English: see "Guests," *Icarus*, vol. 16, Winter 1995, pp. 81–94.
7 *Sovet Turkmenistany*, July, 22 1989.
8 Y. Durdyyev, *Mugallymlar Gazeti*, September, 2 1989.
9 *Sovet Turkmenistany*, July, 26 1989.
10 *Sovet Turkmenistany*, July, 26 1989.
11 S. Atamukhammedov, *Mugallymlar Gazeti*. December, 3 1989.
12 See, for example, *Mugallymlar Gazeti*. January, 5 1990 and *Sovet Turkmenistany*, March, 27 1990.
13 *Sovet Turkmenistany*, April, 10 1991.
14 Law on Constitution's Implementation (Ashkhabad: *Turkmenskaya Iskra*, May 19, 1992, pp. 1,3) as reported in Foreign Broadcast Information Service (FBIS), *Daily Report: Central Eurasia*, June 24, 1992, pp. 101, 102.
15 Helsinki Watch, *Human Rights in Turkmenistan* (New York: Helsinki Watch, July 1993), p. 1.
16 Helsinki Watch, *Human Rights in Turkmenistan*, p. 6.
17 Commission on Security and Cooperation in Europe, "Turkmenistan," *Implementation of the Helsinki Accords: Human Rights and Democratization in the Newly Independent States of the Former Soviet Union* (Washington, DC: US Government Printing Office, January 1993), p. 179.
18 Helsinki Watch, *Human Rights in Turkmenistan*, p. 7.
19 Commission on Security and Cooperation in Europe, "Turkmenistan," p. 179.
20 Helsinki Watch, *Human Rights in Turkmenistan*, p. 8.
21 Commission on Security and Cooperation in Europe, "Turkmenistan," p. 179.
22 *Ibid*, p. 179.
23 Turkmenskaya Iskra, May 19, 1992.
24 Helsinki Watch, *Human Rights in Turkmenistan*, pp. 2–3.
25 See David Nissman, "Turkmenistan [Un]transformed," *Current History*, April 1994, pp. 183–186 for a discussion of Turkmen constitutional issues and their bearing on human rights.
26 Commission on Security and Cooperation in Europe, "Turkmenistan," p. 181.
27 Helsinki Watch, *Human Rights in Turkmenistan*, p. 2.
28 Commission on Security and Cooperation in Europe, "Turkmenistan," p. 188.
29 B. Saryyev, *Sovet Turkmenistany*, August 10, 1988.
30 N. Kulyyev, head of the Turkmenistan House of Scientific Atheism, *Sovet Turkmenistany*, January 8, 1989.
31 Interview with P. M. Arkhipov, Chairman TuSSR KGB, *Sovet Turkmenistany*, February 25, 1990.
32 S. Khanov and A. Yusubov, *Sovet Turkmenistany*, April 7, 1989.
33 *Mugallymlar Gazeti*, March 11, 1991.

34 Report from the Ideology Commission of the Turkmenistan Communist Party, *Sovet Turkmenistany*, June 7, 1991.
35 *Sovet Turkmenistany*, January 8, 1989.
36 *Sovet Turkmenistany*, January 22, 1989.
37 David Nissman, "Iran and Soviet Islam," *Central Asian Survey* (Oxford: Society for Central Asian Studies, December 1983), pp. 45–60.
38 Helsinki Watch, *Human Rights in Turkmenistan*, p. 2.
39 Commission on Security and Cooperation in Europe, "Turkmenistan," *Implementation of the Helsinki Accords: Human Rights and Democratization in the Newly Independent States of the Former Soviet Union* (Washington, DC: US Government Printing Office, January 1993), pp. 182–183.
40 Turkmeninform, "Kaziate Registered," *Turkmenistan* (Ashkhabad, June 3, 1992), p. 3.
41 P. Azymov, *Sovet Turkmenistany*, February 9, 1989.
42 *Sovet Turkmenistany*, February 23, 1989.
43 *Sovet Turkmenistany*, February 28, 1989.
44 A. Atayev, *Sovet Turkmenistany*, November 11, 1988.
45 *Sovet Turkmenistany*, July 1, 1990.
46 *Sovet Turkmenistany*, July 13, 1990.
47 *Mugallymlar Gazeti*, May 22, 1991.
48 Interview with M. Aydogdyev, *Sovet Turkmenistany*, May 22, 1991. Aydogdyyev is both a member of the directorate of the Humanitarian Association of World Turkmens and advisor to Turkmenistan's president on nationality affairs.
49 Sh. Annaklychev, *Turkmenskaya Iskra*, August 16, 1958.
50 Ata Jykyev, *Adebiyat ve Sungat*, January 8, 1966 and Ashyr Meredov, *Adebiyat ve Sungat*, January 8, 1966.
51 B. Myradov, *Mugallymlar Gazeti*, March 24, 1967.
52 *Sovet Turkmenistany*, February 15, 1989.
53 *Mugallymlar Gazeti*, February 19, 1989.

# Turkmenistan: chronology of events

*December 1988*

16    Imam-Kazi Ibadullayev, a distinguished Muslim leader, meets openly with party workers. The meeting is prominently reported in the party media.

*March 1989*

7    The republican party newspaper, *Soviet Turkmenistany*, fills a page with thirty-four letters to the editor encouraging wider public use of Turkmen and recommending its adoption as a state language.

*May 1989*

1    May Day riots occur in Ashkhabad and Nebitdag.

*September 1989*

1    Agzybirlik, the Society for the Protection of the Turkmen Language, is registered.

*January 1990*

The director of the Central Committee Ideology Department accuses informal groups of misusing glasnost and pluralism.

15    Agzybirlik is shut down for its anti-Russian activities.

*February 1990*

The First Deputy Procurator announces that measures are to be taken against unregistered social movements and particularly singled out Agzybirlik.

*May 1990*

A language law is adopted which gives Turkmen equal status with Russian.

*August 1990*

22    The Supreme Soviet issues a declaration of sovereignty.

*October 1990*

27    Sapurmad Niyazov is elected president in unconstested elections with 98% of the vote.

*December 1990*

22    The Democratic Party of Turkmenistan is established but is later refused registration.

*March 1991*

17    In the all-union referendum on preserving the union, 98% of voters (98% turnout) support the union.

*May 1991*

The first International Conference of World Turkmens is held.

*August 1991*

Niyazov declares his support for the coup leaders.

*October 1991*

26    In a referendum, 94% of voters choose independence for Turkemenistan. The next day, the Supreme Soviet issues a declaration of independence.

*December 1991*

13    Turkmenistan joins the CIS.
16    The Communist Party of Turkmenistan changes its name to the Democratic Party of Turkmenistan.

*January 1992*

9    Akbar Mirzoev is appointed prime minister, replacing Izatullo Khaeev who resigned for health reasons.

*May 1992*

15    Tajikistan signs the CIS collective security treaty.
18    The Supreme Soviet adopts a new Constitution. Turkmenistan is the first Central Asian state to do so.

*June 1992*

8    A three-year military cooperation agreement with Russia is signed.
17    Turkmenistan joins the Islamic Conference Organization.
21    Niyazov is re-elected president of Turkmenistan, with 99.5% of the vote.

*July 1992*

The government-sponsored "opposition" Peasant Justice Party is founded.

*February 1993*

18    Niyazov requests a halt to the practice of naming buildings, streets, and public transport after him.

*April 1993*
>15   Niyazov issues a decree mandating that Latin replace the Cyrillic script for writing Turkmen by 1996.

*May 1993*
>3   Niyazov proposes an educational policy mandating that all citizens of Turkmenistan be competent in Turkmen, Russian, and English.

*November 1993*
>1   Turkmenistan leaves the ruble zone, making the *manat* the sole official currency.

*December 1993*
>3   The Democratic Party of Turkmenistan (the former Communists, led by Niyazov) proposes that the 1997 presidential elections be cancelled.
>23   An agreement on dual citizenship is signed with Russia, the only agreement of its kind in the CIS
>27   Niyazov announces that the Peasants' Party would be permitted to officially register, even though it has less than the 1,000 members formally required. The Peasants' Party becomes Turkmenistan's second legal political party.

*January 1994*
>15   99.9% of voters choose in a referendum to permit Niyazov to forgo presidential elections until the year 2002. Only 212 (out of almost 2 million) vote against the president.

*April 1994*
>19   A Council on Religious Affairs that reports to the president is established.

*September 1994*
>23   Niyazov orders his security ministries to do everything in their power to subdue government opponents.

*October 1994*
>4   Murat Esenov, editor of the opposition paper *Turkmen ili*, is physically attacked in Moscow and suffers serious wounds.
>20   Arrests begin of people listed in a notebook seized from Esenov.
>28   Russian citizens Khashali Karayev and Mukhammetkuli Aimuradov of the dissident Turkmenistan Foundation are arrested in Tashkent and deported to Ashkhabad.

*November 1994*

6    Dissident Yusup Kuliev is released from prison but beaten and re-arrested later in the month.

24    Esenov is arrested in Moscow by Russian Federal Counterintelligence Service agents and held at the Lefortovo pretrial detention center, apparently under agreement with the Turkmen Prosecutor General's office.

25    Kholmurat Soyunov, another Turkmen journalist, is also arrested and held at Lefortovo.

*December 1994*

11    Elections are held to the 50-seat Khalk Maslakhaty. Only one seat had more than one candidate, and turnout was 99.8%. Two Russians and three Uzbeks are elected.

21    Esenov and Soyunov are released when no evidence is found to support the accusations against them, which included attempted assassination of Niyazov.

26    Sakat Muradov is reappointed parliamentary chairman.

27    Niyazov suspends the national celebration of his birthday (19 February) and restores the Karakum canal's proper name (it had been changed to the Turkmenbashi canal in December 1992).

# 19  Kyrgyzstan: the politics of demographic and economic frustration

EUGENE HUSKEY

## Introduction

In May 1991, the first competitively-elected parliament in Kyrgyz history adopted a new land law, an unremarkable document save article two, which described the land and natural resources of Kyrgyzstan as the wealth (*dostoianie*) of the ethnic Kyrgyz. The declaration by itself had no legal force, and detailed provisions of the law made clear that all ethnic groups in the republic, from Russians to Uzbeks to Dungans, enjoyed equal rights in the use, possession, and alienation of land. Yet the political and psychological fallout from article two was immediate. The non-titular nationalities of the republic vigorously protested this special claim of the ethnic Kyrgyz. To prevent a worsening of the already tense ethnic relations in the republic, the new president of Kyrgyzstan, the reform-minded scholar, Askar Akaev, vetoed article two as contrary to the constitution.[1] Ethnically-neutral language was later substituted for the offending article.

In Kyrgyzstan and the other former Soviet republics, episodes such as this pose the most fundamental questions about the use of state power to establish, or reassert, the identity and pre-eminence of the titular nationality. If an ethnic group gives its name to a territory, is it entitled to craft policy on language, land, citizenship, and political representation that assures it a leading role among the ethnic groups of the republic? This question assumes special urgency in republics such as Kazakhstan, Latvia, and Kyrgyzstan, where the titular nationality represents a minority or bare majority of the territory's population. Whereas in the Russian Federation or Georgia, the assertiveness of the titular group in the transition from Communist rule smacks of "superiority-complex" nationalism,[2] in Kyrgyzstan it may be viewed as an effort to sustain a fledgling, and threatened, nation. To understand the relationship between the contemporary Kyrgyz state and nation, let us begin with a brief review of the political, cultural, and demographic heritage of the Kyrgyz.

## The prehistory of Kyrgyz nationalism

The modern Kyrgyz formed as a people in the mountain ranges and foot-hills of inner Asia. Their ancestors were the Turkic tribes of the Altai and

Names and boundary representation are not necessarily authoritative.
Lake Balkhash
KAZAKHSTAN
Burylbaytal
Sarkand
Taldy-Kurgan
Saryozek
Khorgos
Panfilov
Ili
Chu
Kapchagay
Kapchagayskoye Vodokhranilishche
Zhanatas
Turkestan
Karatau
Alma-Ata
Kaskelen
Kegen
Dzhambul
Kara-Balty
Bishkek (Frunze)
Tokmak
Cholpon-Ata
Narynkol
CHUSKAYA OBLAST'
Talas
Arys'
Chimkent
Issyk-Kul' (Rybach'ye)
Ozero Issyk-Kul'
Przheval'sk
ISSYK-KUL'SKAYA OBLAST'
Chatkal
Toktogul'skoye Vodokhranilishche
Ozero Song-Kel'
Chirchik
Tashkent
Kara-Kul'
Naryn
Kara-Say
UZBEKISTAN
Tash-Kumyr
Aksu
Angren
Namangan
Kok-Yangak
Syrdar'ya
Dzhalal-Abad
Aksay
Toxkan He
Gulistan
Khudzhand (Leninabad)
Kokand
Andizhan
Fergana
Kara-Kul'dzha
Osh
CHINA
Kyzyl-Kiya
Sulyukta
Ura-Tyube
Ayni
Zeravshan
Kyzyl-Suu
Surkhob
TAJIKISTAN
Dushanbe
Ordzhonikidzeabad
Vakhsh
Murgab
Kulyab
Kurgan-Tyube
Pyandzh
Taxkorgan
AFGHANISTAN
Khorog
Feyzābād
Kondūz
Lasht
PAKISTAN
Kyrgyzstan
International boundary
Oblast boundary (approximate)
National capital
Oblast center
Railroad
Road
Information on the 1990 reorganization of administrative divisions is incomplete. It is not clear whether the administrative center of Issyk-Kul'skaya Oblast' is Issyk-Kul' or Przheval'sk. An oblast is named only when its name differs from that of its administrative center.
0 50 100 150 Kilometers
0 50 100 150 Miles
Lambert Conformal Conic Projection, SP 47N/62N

Irtysh, the Mongols, and the ancient peoples of the Tian-Shan, the mountain range that has been home to the Kyrgyz for at least five centuries.[3] By the end of the 18th century – late in comparison to the peoples of Europe and the Caucasus – the Kyrgyz had developed an ethnic consciousness which was linked to a common territory around the Tian-Shan, to a nomadic, or semi-nomadic economy, and to a legend, Manas, that told of the group's glorious past.[4] One must not confuse, however, the rise of an ethnic consciousness with the rise of nationalism, if by nationalism one means the desire "of a community to assert its unity and independence vis-a-vis other communities and groups."[5] The loyalties of the Kyrgyz, like those of other Central Asians, most notably the Kazakhs, lay first with family, clan, and tribe. It was only their subordination to Russian rule, beginning in the mid-19th century, that planted the seeds of nationalism among the Kyrgyz. As Donald Carlisle argues, "the history of Soviet Central Asia should be read as an attempt to create modern nations . . . where previously there were only ethnic groups."[6]

Lacking a national ideal as well as modern arms and political organization, the Kyrgyz offered little resistance to the expansion of the Russian Empire into Kyrgyz lands in the 1860s and 1870s. In effect, the encroachment of the Russians presented the Kyrgyz with a Hobson's choice: remain loyal to the rulers of the Kokand kingdom, the Central Asian khanate that had been governing the Kyrgyz and neighboring groups with increasing brutality, or submit to the domination of the technologically and culturally advanced Russians.[7] While Soviet historiography clearly overstated the welcome extended to tsarist rule in Kyrgyzstan (with such titles as *The Voluntary Entry of Kyrgyzstan into Russia and its Progressive Consequences*[8]), post-Soviet historiography must be careful not to exaggerate the scale of opposition to Russian suzerainty over the region.

Relations between the Kyrgyz and Russians deteriorated rapidly, however, after the turn of the century, in part due to the encroachment of Russian settlers into traditional Kyrgyz grazing lands. In northern Kyrgyzstan, then a part of the Semirech'e district of the Russian Empire, the indigenous population declined by almost nine percent from 1902 to 1913 while that of Russian settlers increased by ten percent.[9] Predominantly Russian cities sprung up where Kokand forts had once stood. Among these was Pishpek (later Frunze, most recently Bishkek), the future capital, which had 14,000 residents by 1916, 8,000 of them Russian.[10]

Mounting resentment against Russian expansionism exploded in the summer and fall of 1916, following the tsar's infamous decree of 25 June. To fill labor divisions for the war in Europe, the decree ordered the mobilization of all Central Asian men aged 19 to 43. The Central Asians responded to this "requisition of aliens" (*rekvizitsiia inorodtsev*) for a distant war by attacking the symbols and representatives of Russian authority. Fierce, if lopsided, battles occurred throughout Kyrgyzstan between the local Kyrgyz and the tsar's punitive brigades. None was more alarming for the authorities than the seige of Tokmak in northern Kyrgyzstan, where 5,000 crudely-armed Kyrgyz repeatedly attacked a small garrison of Russian troops. The seige of Tokmak, beaten back with the loss of 300 Kyrgyz and two Russians, was followed by massacres of the civilian Kyrgyz population, carried out by armed Russian settlers as well as by tsarist reinforcements.[11] The result was what one contemporary Kyrgyz writer called "the unknown genocide." Out of an estimated population of 780,000 in 1916, 100–120,000 Kyrgyz are believed to have been killed in the uprisings.[12] An equal number sought refuge in China through the treacherous, icy passes of the Tian-Shan.[13] Many refugees perished en route; others died in the first winter, having lost their herds. The survivors would return to their former grazing lands in Soviet Kyrgyzstan by the mid-1920s to rejoin a people who now had a rallying point for national unity.[14]

The uprisings of 1916 were followed only a year later by the Bolshevik Revolution, whose legacy for the Kyrgyz nation will remain a subject of dispute well beyond the collapse of the Soviet Union.[15] At least through the prism of Western historiography, with its emphases on nation building and state formation, the creation of the Soviet state was in some respects a godsend for the Kyrgyz. Once the resistance to the Bolsheviks had been defeated in the region, the Kyrgyz acquired for the first time their own political community. Formed originally on October 14, 1924 as the Kara-Kirgiz autonomous region within the Turkestan republic of the USSR, Kyrgyzstan underwent several name changes and administration redesignations before emerging in 1936 as the Kirgiz Soviet Socialist Republic. Formal constitutional provisions notwithstanding, the Kirgiz Republic was not an autonomous political community. Yet the very linkage of the Kyrgyz to a proto-state, and the development of at least the symbols of Kyrgyz cultural and political identity, created important pre-conditions for the rise of a Kyrgyz national consciousness.

In the formative years of Soviet Kyrgyzstan, the central authorities in Moscow seemed intent on creating the foundations for indigenous rule in the region, within the parameters of Soviet power.[16] A law of 1924 mandated the translation of all government documents in the region into Kyrgyz and other major Central Asian languages. Furthermore, 10 of the 13 members of the Communist Party's first Orgburo in the Kara-Kirgiz region were ethnic Kyrgyz, as were 13 of the 17 members of the highest state body in the region, the oblast revolutionary committee (*oblrevkom*).[17] But the demographic features of the region insured that the ethnic Kyrgyz would at first play only a limited role in the formation of a modern state bureaucracy. In the early 1920s, there was not a single ethnic Kyrgyz with a higher education; at best 20,000 (less than five percent) were literate, and many of these were from so-called hostile classes.[18] Thus, the administration of the territory fell largely to the Slavs and Tatars. In May 1925, ethnic Kyrgyz accounted for only 319, or 10.8 percent, of the 2,950 regional and local administrative personnel in the region.[19]

A gradual indigenization of political life in Kyrgyzstan continued, however, until the mid-1930s. To prepare the rising generation of Kyrgyz for leadership positions, the new regime offered short courses and, in a few cases, more extensive training in educational institutions of European Russia. These freshly-trained "Soviet" Kyrgyz cadres were then enlisted in large numbers during the *vydvizhenstvo* campaign of the late 1920s to manage the local economy and society. An edict of December 1932 envisioned a full indigenization of the republican apparatus by June 1934. But in 1933, the first wave of Stalinist repression intervened to halt the indigenization drive, and by 1938 the first generation of the Soviet Kyrgyz elite had been swept away in the purges.[20] Many of the purged had combined a commitment to Bolshevism with a desire to nourish their Kyrgyz and Turkic heritage.

While maintaining the symbols of Kyrgyz national autonomy, Stalinism launched policies that deepened Slavic domination of the region. Perhaps the most important of these was a cadres policy that placed in leading party and government posts Kyrgyz who were obsequious toward Russian culture and central political authority. It also placed in oversight positions in Kyrgyzstan Slavic personnel, usually seconded from posts in Russia, to serve as the republic's second party secretary, its KGB head, and its procurator. Few republics could match Kyrgyzstan for the malleability and sycophancy of its leaders. Especially notable in this regard were the illiterate miner, Turabai Kulatov, who was a prime minister and supreme soviet chairman of the republic in the late Stalinist period, and Turdakun Usubaliev, the Communist Party first secretary from 1961 to 1988. On the eve of the Gorbachev era – and his own removal from office – Usubaliev noted that:

> Sixty years is just a brief moment in the history of Kirgizstan ... but it was indeed during this period that its age-old dream of happiness became a reality.[21]

The rhetoric of subservience masked inexorable conflicts between center and republic over investment and resource allocation. In a planned economy, Usubaliev and other Kyrgyz leaders believed that political fealty and reliable deliveries of output to the center strengthened their claims to new projects and scarce supplies. To remind the center of its obligation to its faithful vassal, Usubaliev deluged Moscow ministries with claims for resources.[22] Obseqiousness had its limits, which were quickly crossed when economic development of the region was at stake.

In general, the terms of exchange between center and periphery were highly unfavorable for the Kyrgyz, at least in terms of linguistic and demographic developments in the republic. Russification of the Kyrgyz language began in earnest immediately after Stalin's first wave of terror against the Kyrgyz elite. A party directive of June 1934 ordered the further enrichment of the Kyrgyz language "by the maximum use of sovietisms and international, multinational terminology through the Russian language . . ."[23] This policy was facilitated by the adoption in 1940 of the Cyrillic alphabet for written Kyrgyz (its script had been Arabic until 1926, Latin thereafter). Increasingly in the postwar era, Russian began to displace Kyrgyz as the language of politics and commerce in the republic. A new generation of Kyrgyz urban residents was brought up on Russian and was often unable to converse with rural Kyrgyz. Many older Kyrgyz in the cities reserved their native language for private discourse. In short, Kyrgyz was rapidly marginalized in its homeland. Not a single new Kyrgyz-language school was opened in the capital of Frunze (Bishkek) after the 1930s.[24] By the 1980s, only three of Frunze's 69 schools used Kyrgyz as the primary language of instruction.[25] At the end of Soviet rule in Kyrgyzstan, only four percent of the 5.6 million books in Frunze's Lenin Library were in Kyrgyz, and of books requested by readers, only two percent were in Kyrgyz.[26]

The Russification of the Kyrgyz language had its parallels in economic development in the republic. In the postwar era, Soviet power brought modern industry and transportation to a traditional society that lacked the most rudimentary physical infrastructure. Yet economic modernization of the region largely bypassed the ethnic Kyrgyz. The most advanced enterprises were built in the cities, staffed largely by Slavs, and managed by all-union ministries in Moscow. At the end of the 1980s, enterprises of all-union subordination accounted for 38 percent of the republic's economy and offered employees access to the best housing and social services.[27] Relatively few employees of such enterprises were ethnic Kyrgyz. The Kyrgyz made up only 6.3 percent of employees in the electric energy sector and 11 percent of personnel in machine construction and metalworking.[28] In all, only 13 percent of the republic's engineers and technicians were Kyrgyz.[29] Of particular concern to many Kyrgyz was the reluctance of the central ministries to train an indigenous working class, preferring instead to import Slavic workers en masse.[30]

The influx of Slavic workers into Kyrgyzstan in mid-century created one of the conditions for the rise of Kyrgyz nationalism at the end of the century.[31] The demographic challenge to the Kyrgyz had several dimensions. First, it rendered the titular nationality, the Kyrgyz, a minority within its own republic. If the Kyrgyz accounted for two-thirds of the territory's population in 1926, their share of the population had dropped to 40.5 percent by the end of the 1950s (see table 19.1). At this time the Kyrgyz outnumbered the Russians by a margin of only four to three. Although the immigration of Slavs continued after the end of the 1950s, by 1989 the higher birth rate among the Kyrgyz and other indigenous Central Asian

Table 19.1. *National composition of Kyrgyzstan*

|  | 1926 | 1939 | 1959 | 1970 | 1980 | 1989 | 1993 |
|---|---|---|---|---|---|---|---|
| Total Population | 1,001,700 | 1,458,200 | 2,066,100 | 2,933,200 | 3,588,500 | 4,257,755 | 4,469,324 |
| Kyrgyz | 668,700 | 754,300 | 836,800 | 1,248,800 | 1,687,400 | 2,229,663 | 2,526,361 |
|  | 66.8% | 51.7% | 40.5% | 42.6% | 47.0% | 52.4% | 56.5% |
| Russians | 116,800 | 302,900 | 623,600 | 855,900 | 911,700 | 916,558 | 840,506 |
|  | 11.7% | 20.8% | 30.2% | 29.2% | 25.4% | 21.5% | 18.8% |
| Uzbeks | 106,300 | 151,600 | 218,900 | 333,000 | 426,200 | 550,096 | 604,241 |
|  | 10.6% | 10.4% | 10.6% | 11.4% | 11.9% | 12.9% | 13.5% |
| Ukrainians | 64,200 | 137,300 | 137,000 | 120,000 | 109,300 | 108,027 | 93,261 |
|  | 6.4% | 9.4% | 6.6% | 4.1% | 3.0% | 2.5% | 2.1% |
| Germans | 4,300 | 11,800 | 39,900 | 89,800 | 101,100 | 101,309 | 44,421 |
|  | 0.4% | 0.8% | 1.9% | 3.1% | 2.8% | 2.4% | 1.0% |
| Tatars | 4,900 | 20,000 | 56,300 | 69,400 | 72,000 | 70,068 | 68,230 |
|  | 0.5% | 1.4% | 2.7% | 2.4% | 2.0% | 1.6% | 1.5% |
| Kazakhs | 1,700 | 23,900 | 20,100 | 22,000 | 27,400 | 37,318 | 41,364 |
|  | 0.2% | 1.6% | 1.0% | 0.8% | 0.8% | 0.9% | 0.9% |
| Dungans | 6,000 | 5,900 | 11,100 | 19,800 | 26,700 | 36,928 | NA |
|  | 0.6% | 0.4% | 0.5% | 0.7% | 0.7% | 0.9% |  |
| Uighurs | 8,200 | 9,400 | 13,800 | 24,900 | 29,800 | 36,779 | NA |
|  | 0.8% | 0.6% | 0.7% | 0.8% | 0.8% | 0.9% |  |
| Tajiks | 7,000 | 10,700 | 15,200 | 21,900 | 23,200 | 33,518 | 35,534 |
|  | 0.7% | 0.7% | 0.7% | 0.7% | 0.6% | 0.8% | 0.8% |
| Others | 13,600 | 30,400 | 93,400 | 91,600 | 108,000 | 137,491 | 215,406 |
|  | 1.4% | 2.1% | 4.5% | 3.1% | 3.0% | 3.2% | 4.8% |

Source: *Narodnoe khoziaistvo Kirgizskoi SSR* (Frunze, 1982), p. 16; *Vestnik statistiki*, no. 4, 1991, pp. 76–78; *Chislennost' postoiannogo naseleniia Kyrgyzskoi Respubliki po natsional'nostiam na 1 ianvaria 1993* (typescript in possession of author).

peoples in the republic allowed the Kyrgyz to claim a bare majority of the republic's population (52.4 percent).

The uneven distribution of ethnic groups across the republic exacerbated the effects of Slavic migration. Certain areas were largely unaffected by the influx, notably the Naryn oblast, a mountainous region where the Kyrgyz still make up over 97 percent of the population.[32] By contrast, Frunze developed in effect as a Russian city. In 1959, less than 10 percent of Frunze's population was ethnic Kyrgyz, and even as late as 1989 the Kyrgyz represented less than 23 percent of the capital's population.[33] With Russians and Ukrainians comprising 45 percent of the urban population outside of Bishkek, and the Uzbeks accounting for a majority of the population in Osh, the Kyrgyz cannot even claim a plurality of the republic's urban population. While it is an exaggeration to assert, as one Kyrgyz did recently, that the Slavs created in the cities of Kyrgyzstan an "impenetrable national boundary,"[34] they have certainly dominated urban life in the republic. For the majority of the Kyrgyz, who live in the countryside, the cities have been alien and inhospitable.

## The emergence of Kyrgyz nationalism

Because the first stirrings of Kyrgyz nationalism appeared in the second half of the 1980s, it is tempting to view them as outgrowths of Gorbachev's policies of glasnost and democratization. That conclusion would be a mistake. The policies of the center did on occasion arouse national indignation, as in the appointment of the Russian Gennadii Kolbin in December 1986 to head the Communist Party in neighboring Kazakhstan, whence discontent spread briefly to Kyrgyzstan. The policies associated with Gorbachev also facilitated the expression of national interests and the organization of groups to press national claims, both within and outside the state apparatus. But the origins of the national explosion in Kyrgyzstan at the end of the 1980s lie in a volatile mixture of economic and demographic frustration.

Even before Gorbachev assumed power in 1985, rural areas in Kyrgyzstan were in crisis. Coupled with a stagnant economy, the high birth rate of preceding decades had produced a generation of rural youth without jobs in the village or the skills and desire to find work in the cities. Whereas the rural population of the USSR from 1959 to 1989 declined by 18 percent, it doubled in the same period in Kyrgyzstan.[35] By the end of the 1980s, at least 110,000 persons were unemployed in the republic, with the highest concentration among village youth.[36] Many more rural folk were underemployed. In the Osh oblast, the largest and most agriculturally-oriented region in Kyrgyzstan, 45 percent of the employed earned 125 rubles a month or less at a time when the average monthly salary was 180 rubles.[37] The collapse of the economy in the early 1990s only deepened the crisis in the countryside. According to President Akaev, by 1991, 140,000 persons were unemployed – three-quarters of them under 30 years of age – and 500,000 had a monthly income of less than 75 rubles.[38]

In a pattern long familiar in the developing world, the excess population of the Kyrgyz countryside reluctantly sought work and shelter in the cities.[39] But the cities had neither space nor services for them. Most of the new Kyrgyz settlers in the cities lived not in carefully-rationed apartments but in overcrowded dormitories or the "corners" of private homes. Some set up shanties in open land on the outskirts of the cities only to have them torn down by the authorities. Conscious of the relatively well-housed Russians in the cities, one Kyrgyz complained that he felt "a guest in his own home."[40]

In the summer of 1989, frustrated Kyrgyz settlers in Frunze formed Ashar, the first major independent association in the republic. Ashar soon counted among its members 5,000 of the 20,000 families waiting for suitable housing in the city.[41] Exploiting rumors of the resettling in Frunze of Armenian refugees from the crisis in the Caucasus, Ashar seized land on the outskirts of the city for the construction of a shantytown (*samostroi*), an action that threw the party and government leadership in Kyrgyzstan into a panic. After succeeding Usubaliev in 1986, the first secretary of the Communist Party of Kyrgyzstan, Absamat Masaliev, prided himself on the maintenance of traditional politics and a quiescent society in the republic. As late as the spring of 1989, Masaliev had suppressed attempts to form a Kyrgyz national front akin to those already in place in other Soviet republics. But proscribing Ashar threatened to alienate a desperate and growing segment of Kyrgyz society and set it against the ruling Kyrgyz and Russian elites. After lengthy discussions with the authorities in Moscow, Masaliev acquiesced in the recognition of Ashar, though he was soon frustrated by the inability of the local authorities to limit its activities to housing matters.[42]

The recognition of Ashar in the summer of 1989 represented the takeoff point for social movements in Kyrgyzstan. By the beginning of 1990 there were 13 independent associations in the republic; a year later the number exceeded 36. Many of these groups were explicitly nationalist in orientation. In terms of membership, they were generally segregated along ethnic lines, although a few Russians joined predominantly Kyrgyz groups.[43] A defining moment in the development of the Kyrgyz national movement came in late May 1990, when 24 informal groups favoring democratic reform and Kyrgyz national revival formed the Democratic Movement "Kyrgyzstan" (DDK). Over 300 delegates from throughout the republic met in Frunze to advance a program that called for, *inter alia*, a sovereign republic, a civil society and market economy, and a reassessment of Kyrgyz history, especially the uprisings of 1916.[44] Within three months, membership of the movement was estimated at 100,000, with half of that number drawn from Frunze.[45]

In the summer of 1990, competing claims advanced by new ethnically-based associations in the Osh region led to interethnic violence that fundamentally transformed the political landscape in Kyrgyzstan. In contrast to Frunze, land claims by the ethnic Kyrgyz were handled with less success in Osh, where unemployment and land hunger were more acute and local politicians were more willing to support openly Kyrgyz nationalism. The ethnic Kyrgyz in Osh resented the relative wealth and prominence of the local Uzbeks, who controlled, according to one estimate, 80 percent of the city's trade. The Uzbeks, for their part, claimed that their economic and demographic presence in the region was not translated into political power.[46] Only one of the 25 party first secretaries of local districts and cities was an Uzbek and only 4.7 percent of leading department posts in soviets in the region were held by Uzbeks (85 percent were occupied by Kyrgyz).[47] This perception of political disenfranchisement fed Uzbek irredentism, which had deep historical roots in the region.

In May 1990, Ashar's counterpart in Osh, Osh Aimagy, demanded land on which to settle ethnic Kyrgyz families who were unable to find housing. The regional party first secretary, Usen Sydykov, agreed to allot Osh Aimagy 32 hectares of a predominantly Uzbek collective farm on the outskirts of Osh. The reaction of local Uzbeks was swift and dramatic. They seized the occasion to advance a range of political claims, including home rule for an Uzbek region in southern Kyrgyzstan and the recognition of Uzbek as the official language of the territory. There were even calls for the incorporation of parts of Kyrgyzstan into Uzbekistan.[48]

The refusal of the Kyrgyz political leadership to satisfy the Uzbek demands or to reverse its land grant ignited widespread violence between the Kyrgyz and Uzbek communities in the Osh region, the latter supported by compatriots from Uzbekistan who crossed the republican border in the early stages of the fighting. Facing what one observer called "10 Sumgaits,"[49] the republic called in the Soviet Army and MVD to restore order. During a week of rioting in early June, thousands of homes and buildings were destroyed and 230 people were killed, 161 in the Uzgen district alone. The Osh events exposed and deepened divisions in the republic's political leadership and hastened the downfall of first secretary Masaliev, who had been one of the most vocal opponents of perestroika in the USSR.

Disputes over land and water resources were the most violent interethnic encounters in the first years of national strife in Kyrgyzstan,[50] but no question excited more debate than the revival of the Kyrgyz language. Following the lead of other republics, Kyrgyzstan began to draft a new law on language in the summer of 1989.[51] The debate surrounding the language law, adopted by the republic's supreme soviet in September 1989, brought into the open long-suppressed ethnic tensions. Whereas the Kyrgyz welcomed the elevation of their language to a preeminent position in the republic, Slavic residents viewed with alarm the recognition of Kyrgyz as the state language, despite the simultaneous recognition of Russian as the language of interethnic communication.[52] One of the most controversial elements of the law was Article 8, which required management and professional personnel – a stratum that the Slavs dominated – to have the ability to speak Kyrgyz to their workers or clients. Unlike most provisions of the law, which were originally to be phased in by 1997, Article 8 was to take effect immediately.[53] Responding to the draft law, Russian managers of all-union enterprises in the republic organized letter-writing campaigns that criticized the law as divisive.[54]

The language debate destroyed the official discourse on ethnic relations in Kyrgyzstan, a discourse that had for decades denied tensions or conflicts of interests among ethnic groups in the republic. For the first time, recriminations against Russians became commonplace in the press. In an intemperate article in *Literaturnyi Kirgizstan* at the beginning of 1990, a Kyrgyz writer complained that the Russians despoiled the rural landscape with their trash-strewn picnic sites and the urban landscape with their queues. It was the Russians' hoarding genes (*geny zapasaniia*), she insisted, that kept them in lines.[55] The local Russian response to such criticism ranged from chauvinist to internationalist.[56]

Even if the language law increased the use and visibility of Kyrgyz only modestly in the first years after its adoption – due both to the reluctance of non-Kyrgyz to study the language and the absence of instructional materials and qualified teachers[57] – it spawned symbolic changes that served a rising Kyrgyz nationalism. Shops, squares, and cities gave up their Russian and Soviet labels to assume Kyrgyz names. The republic itself acquired a spelling in Russian that more closely approximated its pronunciation in Kyrgyz.[58] At the end of 1991, a new tote board, in Kyrgyz only, was installed in the parliament. And the number and edition size of Kyrgyz-language periodicals rose in comparison with those in Russian. Such reforms inspired among the ethnic Kyrgyz a new sense of ownership of the republic.[59]

While the deepening bond between nation and state in Kyrgyzstan represented a renascence for the Kyrgyz, it alienated many other ethnic groups in the republic, in the first instance the Slavs. The Russians and Ukrainians began to form their own national organizations, such as the Fund for Slavic Literacy and Culture (*Fond slavianskoi pis'mennosti i kul'tury*) and later Soglasie. Both organizations received assistance directly from the government of the Russian Federation.[60]

Reacting to the indigenization of cultural policy, the violence in Osh, and the weakening industrial sector, Slavs began to leave Kyrgyzstan in significant numbers in the early 1990s. For the first time in the contemporary history of Kyrgyzstan, the exodus of Slavs from the republic exceeded the in-migration. From 1989 to 1993, over 100,000 Slavs abandoned Kyrgystan. In the same period, more than half of the country's 100,000 Germans departed.[61] Alarmed by the loss of its Europeans settlers, who were a valuable economic and political resource for the Russified Kyrgyz elite, Akaev introduced numerous measures to stem the tide of emigration. Among the most important of these were the establishment of the Slavonic University in Bishkek in 1993 and a May 1994 decree postponing the implementation of the language law.[62]

## Democratization, nationalism, and marketization in Kyrgyzstan

The discussion to this point has emphasized the cleavages between the Kyrgyz and other ethnic groups, cleavages deepened by the rise of electoral politics, the liberal policies on political expression and association, and the breakup of the Soviet Union. But as national agendas are formed and acted on, other forces are at work that restrain the development of a pure politics of cultural pluralism. The sources of these restraints lie in social attitudes as well as state policy. Kyrgyz attitudes toward the Russians, for example, are by no means unswervingly hostile. To the contrary, the Kyrgyz have generally exhibited respect toward Russians and Russian culture, sometimes to the point of deference. In a letter to ethnic Kyrgyz living in Moscow, a Kyrgyz woman invoked the folk wisdom: "where there are Russians there is truth" (*tam, gde russkie, est' i pravda*).[63] In his own way, a reformist member of the republic's parliament, also an ethnic Kyrgyz, expressed a similar sentiment in regard to Russian language.

> I would not have the right to call myself a son of my people without knowing the Kyrgyz language. But without a deep knowledge of Russian, I would not consider myself a complete man [*polnotsennym chelovekom*].[64]

For a century, Russia has been the touchstone for the development of Kyrgyz language, culture, and politics. While that psychological dependency is in part a source of Kyrgyz nationalism, it also binds Russians and Kyrgyz to an extent that is virtually unparalleled in relations between Russians and titular nationals in other successor states.

Kyrgyz attitudes toward the Uzbeks, the other major national minority in the republic, are more ambivalent. While sharing a Turkic and Islamic heritage[65] with the Uzbeks, the Kyrgyz have been suspicious of calls for pan-Turkic or pan-Islamic unity, fearing that such movements could lead to the hegemony in Central Asia of the larger and historically more prominent Uzbek nation.[66] The Kyrgyz fear of Uzbekization was evident in a 1991 article that pointed to the decline of persons claiming Kyrgyz ethnicity in the Andizhan district of Uzbekistan, from 107,000 in 1906 to only 72,900 in 1989.[67] For the Kyrgyz, Uzbekization appears more insidious than Russification. The latter affects language and culture, the former ethnic identity itself.

Relations within as well as between ethnic groups have shaped the course of Kyrgyz nationalism. If Kyrgyz national claims have been more modest than those of most titular nationalities of the former USSR, it is in part because of the lack of unity among the Kyrgyz, and especially their elite. Clan and tribal loyalties continue to temper Kyrgyz nationalism.[68] Equally important barriers to Kyrgyz solidarity may be found in regional and urban/rural distinctions.[69] Party and government elites in Kyrgyzstan have long been divided into northern and southern "families," a division that colored the purges of the 1930s and facilitated central control of the republic thereafter.[70] Long-simmering tensions between the northern and southern Kyrgyz elites boiled to the surface at the end of 1990 following the ouster of the southerner Masaliev as republican leader. Distressed by the erosion of their traditional dominance of key republican posts, some southern Kyrgyz began to agitate for structural changes that would insure greater autonomy for their region. These proposals ranged from dividing the republic into two regions, with equal representation from each in republican bodies, to the formation of a Kyrgyz federation, with northern and southern republics.[71] Pushing the case for political devolution even further, one Kyrgyz writer favored the creation of five autonomous regions in the republic, one for each oblast. Such a confederation would have been coordinated by a rotating collective presidency.[72] The advocates of devolution and power-sharing are motivated less by a desire to promote regional social and economic development than to protect local political networks.

Potentially the most serious division among the Kyrgyz runs along urban-rural lines. The urbanized quarter of the ethnic Kyrgyz population has appropriated the language and at least some of the cultural values of the Russians, who dominate the cities of Kyrgyzstan, especially its northern tier. As suggested earlier, Kyrgyz urban youth raised in the postwar era resemble in many respects second generation immigrants. They know smatterings of the language and traditions of their elders but feel more at home in their Russified surroundings. In short, they have assimilated. The rise of a Kyrgyz national consciousness stranded many of these urbanized Kyrgyz between two cultures. The predicament has been especially acute for the rising generation of Kyrgyz politicians, typified by an incident in 1991 involving Ulukbek Chinaliev, the first secretary of the Frunze city Communist Party committee. Not knowing Kyrgyz, Chinaliev could only address his Kyrgyz audience in Russian, while immediately after his speech, an ethnic German, raised in the countryside, spoke to the audience in Kyrgyz.[73]

Whether the tensions between urbanized and rural (or recently urban) Kyrgyz can be contained is as yet unclear. At the beginning of 1992, the urbanized Kyrgyz elite appeared to be in firm control of the state apparatus and leading nationalist organizations. As one might expect, they showed considerable sensitivity to the economic and cultural claims of non-urbanized Kyrgyz. But a Russified – some would prefer the term Sovietized – elite must remain vulnerable to a new and more atavistic wave of Kyrgyz nationalism that could be unleashed by populist politicians or movements.

Maintaining a multiethnic ruling coalition has grown ever more difficult amid the proliferation of political parties,[74] the indigenization of language policy, and a market reform that is increasing economic hardships and social stratification. The ethnic Kyrgyz are especially vulnerable in the transition to a market-oriented economy. As a group, they have neither the education and skills of the Slavs nor the commercial traditions of the Uzbeks or Koreans living in Kyrgyzstan. Ethnic Kyrgyz account for 75 percent of agricultural labor in Kyrgyzstan and only a quarter of the industrial workforce, where the jobs and conditions have traditionally been more desirable.[75] Perhaps more disturbing, Kyrgyz youth have been reluctant to pursue careers in industry and construction.[76] In a more competitive and open economy, then, ethnic Kyrgyz as a group may fall further behind the Uzbeks, the Koreans, and the Russians in terms of economic well-being. This has created strong pressures on a Kyrgyz-dominated state to adopt measures to "defend" the titular nationality. Among the many concessions to Kyrgyz nationalist sentiment was the formation in 1992 of a national land trust, which reserved half of newly-privatized land for ethnic Kyrgyz.[77]

If the Kyrgyz have thus far held their own in an economy in transition, it is due in large measure to their domination of bureaucratic posts that grant access to foreign funds and that facilitate insider trading in the denationalization of state property and resources. At a meeting of the Security Council in the summer of 1994, Akaev lamented the high level of corruption in ruling circles. He estimated that only half of the people in government were actually working; the rest occupied themselves with private business or building dachas.[78]

## Askar Akaev and the political economy of Kyrgyzstan

Rising economic deprivation in Kyrgyzstan has complicated efforts to sustain ethnic harmony and open, competitive politics.[79] The industrial economy of Kyrgyzstan all but collapsed after the breakup of the Soviet Union. By 1994, more than 50 factories were idle. Industrial production had fallen by a third in one year.[80] To be sure, the rupture of inter-republican purchase and supply links and the loss of labor discipline undermined the economies of all the newly independent states. But Kyrgyzstan faces special problems with its small market, its relative paucity of mineral wealth, its distance from developed economies, and its poor transportation links, both domestically and internationally.[81] Moreover, the peculiar geography of the Soviet economy left Kyrgyzstan with a host of unsustainable enterprises, among which were a torpedo plant – in a country without a navy – and a sugar refinery designed to process tropical cane from Cuba rather than native beetroot. Further impeding efforts to stabilize the Kyrgyz economy were several natural disasters in the early 1990s, including earthquakes and landslides, which required state funding for humanitarian assistance and reconstruction efforts.

As the Russian Federation curtailed its deliveries of subsidized fuel to Kyrgyzstan in 1992, mounting social pressures and budget deficits encouraged President Akaev to seek assistance abroad. In an extraordinary display of the politics of international grantsmanship, the leadership of Kyrgyzstan attracted well over half a billion dollars in foreign aid within three years.[82] The largest share of the funding came from international and regional organizations, such as the IMF and the Islamic Bank, though individual countries also contributed generously to Kyrgyzstan. The United States, for example, had committed over $100 million in grants and loans to Kyrgyzstan by the end of 1994.[83]

What explains the success of Akaev's fund-raising campaign? Put simply, Kyrgyzstan captured the imagination of the West. The idea of Kyrgyzstan as "an island of democracy" and "the Switzerland of Asia" appealed to international donors, who were anxious to assist a progressive regime in Central Asia.[84] The inflated rhetoric aside, there was much to recommend Kyrgyzstan to the West. At its inception, independent Kyrgyzstan had a free and vigorous press, an openness to fundamental economic reform, and a popular president with liberal political instincts. Politics in Kyrgyzstan stood in sharp contrast to the authoritarianism, whether veiled or open, of its neighbors.

Akaev and the Kyrgyzstan leadership became hostages, however, to their own success. The immediate issue was not debt service – the repayment terms were generous – but satisfying the political and economic expectations of their donors. In some cases, the cost of foreign largesse was clear and politically affordable. An initial infusion of 64 million dollars from the IMF was tied explicitly to the introduction of a national currency, the som, in May 1993.[85] But the leadership of Kyrgyzstan found it increasingly difficult, and unpalatable, to meet escalating foreign demands on the country's monetary, fiscal, and privatization policies.[86] Set against the marketizing demands of the West was rising popular pressure for paternalistic policies by the state.

By the mid-1990s, contradictions abounded in Kyrgyz economic policy, as Akaev sought to satisfy both foreign and domestic constituencies. On the one hand, he introduced by decree a liberal foreign investment policy and an innovative program to develop small business. But to shore up declining support at home, Akaev also increased social welfare payments and recruited traditional elites to key positions in regional and national government, measures that retarded the liberalization of the economy and alarmed Western financial institutions. The new deputy premier for agrarian policy was the former Communist Party General Secretary, Zhumgalbek Amanbaev, whose ideas on land reform differed markedly from those espoused earlier by Akaev. "Private property in land," Amanbaev argued, "is not a dogma ... Today it is premature. But within a decade – we'll see."[87]

Akaev's concessions to domestic economic critics formed part of a broader turn to the right in the politics of Kyrgyzstan. Through the summer and fall of 1994 the president employed methods of rule normally associated with authoritarian leaders. He closed two leading opposition newspapers, including *Svobodnye gory*, the official parliamentary organ.[88] He cooperated in a successful plot – launched ostensibly by a group of deputies – to prorogue parliament.[89] And in anticipation of new parliamentary elections, he put before the nation a plebiscite designed to replace the constitutionally-mandated unicameral assembly with a bicameral parliament. As expected, the nation followed the script of plebiscitarian democracy and approved creation of the new assembly, thereby violating the May 1993 Constitution, which had provided for amendments through parliamentary action alone.[90] In a further violation of the Constitution, Akaev insisted on the eligibility of regional executive officials for seats in one of the chambers of the new parliament.[91] Much like the Federation Council in Russia, this chamber in Kyrgyzstan was designed to be an infrequently-convened assembly of regional leaders, who were tied to the presidency through patronage.[92] According to the widely respected speaker of the parliament, Medetkan Sherimkulov, such a chamber in Kyrgyzstan will lead to "the institutionalization of the policy of regionalism in the worst sense of the term."[93]

Kyrgyzstan's shift to the right has endangered its political and economic ties to the West. In a harsh speech in September 1994, Strobe Talbott, the American official charged with relations with the former USSR, made clear the linkage of economic assistance to Western standards of democratic development.

> The stakes are very high. The reputation of Kyrgyzstan as a democratic country is one of its most valuable resources for the international community. The absence of this resource will place in doubt the entire political basis for large-scale aid from the United States.[94]

This speech, and a similar message conveyed to Akaev in person by James Collins, a State Department emissary, reminded Kyrgyzstan of the limits of national sovereignty in the new world order. In language full of ambiguity and contradiction, Talbott warned that the West would be viewing parliamentary elections in February 1995 as "a decisive test of democracy in Kyrgyzstan."[95]

The defining moment for democratic development in Kyrgyzstan may in fact have come earlier, at the end of 1993, when an increasingly isolated president forged an informal ruling alliance with conservative regional executives, the *akimy*.[96] Surrounded by a corrupt national bureaucracy and a moribund parliament, Akaev turned to the governors of Kyrgyzstan's six regions to provide efficient administration of the country. He gambled that the popularity and patronage powers of the presidency would enable him to control a group of shrewd and experienced local politicians.[97] But it is as yet unclear whether the president or the *akimy* have the upper hand in this relationship. As the results of the October 1994 local elections make clear, politics in the regions is far from open and contested. In the Issyk-Kul' region, for example, of the 888 seats in the local assemblies (*zhogorku kenesh*), only 169 were contested.[98] The *akimy* are able to govern much as Communist Party first secretaries did under the old regime.[99]

An equilibrium between presidential and akimiat power seems in place at the moment, based on mutual dependency. Whereas Akaev relies on the *akimy* to implement policies on the ground, the *akimy* need the cover of Akaev's national and international legitimacy. The relationship is, however, inherently unstable, as the liberalizing and centralizing instincts of the president compete with the traditionalist and devolutionary aims of local elites. For the duration of this unlikely alliance, politics in Kyrgyzstan will bear the marks of a struggle between two distinct visions of the future.

## NOTES

1 "Zemel'nyi kodeks respubliki Kyrgyzstan," *Slovo Kyrgyzstana*, June, 11 1991, p. 3; "Veto Prezidenta otvechaiet chaianiiam vsekh liudei dobroi voli," *Slovo Kyrgyzstana*, June, 28 1991, p. 3. President Akaev was one of the few leaders of Soviet republics to publicly condemn the August 1991 coup in its initial stages. For portraits of Akaev, see "Portrety bez ramok (Prezident Kirgizstana Askar Akaev)," *Literaturnyi Kyrgyzstan*, (January 1991) pp. 116–120; N. Andreev, "Askar Akaev: svobodnyi Kyrgyzstan dolzhen byt' sil'nym," *Izvestiia*, October 10, 1991, p. 2; and E. Huskey, "Askar Akaev," in Joseph Wieczynski, *The Gorbachev Encyclopedia* (Salt Lake City: Charles Schlacks Publisher, 1993), pp. 30–34.

2 No one better exemplifies the ugly face of Russian nationalism than Vladimir Zhirinovsky. In an interview with an American correspondent in January 1992, Zhirinovsky claimed that, once in power, he would "immediately change the foreign policy radically. In two days, I would do away with such countries as Kazakhstan and Kirghizia, because . . . there is not a single scholar in the USA or elsewhere in the world who would be able to locate such political entities as Kazakhstan and Kirghizia on the map of the world." *MacNeil/Lehrer Newshour*, January, 13 1992.

3 'The question of the origins of the Kyrgyz nation is among the most complex and controversial aspects of the ethnic history of Central Asia." With these words S. M. Abramzon opens his seminal work on the Kyrgyz. *Kirgizy i ikh etnogeneticheskie i istoriko-kul'turnyi sviazi* (Leningrad: Nauka, 1971), p. 10. As this and other works illustrate, the question of the ethnogenesis of the Kyrgyz is by no means closed. See *Istoriia Kirgizskoi SSR*, vol. 1, ed. V.M. Ploskikh et al. (Frunze: "Kyrgyzstan", 1984), and Esen Uluu Kylych, "K dinastii karakhanidov – Kirgizov?," *Slovo Kyrgyzstana*, 7 September 1991, p. 10. Among non-specialists the identity of the modern Kyrgyz is confused by the use of the name to describe an older tribe along the Enisei River in southern Siberia and by the Russians' use of the term well into this century to describe the Kazakhs. The Kyrgyz were often referred to as the Kara-Kirgiz to distinguish them from the Kazakhs.

4 S.M. Abramzon, *Kirgizy i ikh etnogeneticheskie i istoriko-kul'turnye sviazi*, pp. 22–23.

5 D. Thomson, *Europe since Napoleon* (Harmondsworth: Penguin, 1966), p. 119.

6 Donald S. Carlisle, "Uzbekistan and the Uzbeks," *Problems of Communism*, September-October 1991, p. 24.

7 A. Arzymatov, "V sostav Rossii: Vkhozhdenie? Prisoedinenie? Zavoevanie?," *Slovo Kyrgyzstana*, June, 1 1991, p. 10; Hélène Carrère d'Encausse, "Systematic Conquest, 1965 to 1834," in *Central Asia: 120 Years of Russian Rule*, ed. E. Allworth (Durham: Duke University Press, 1989), p. 134. It should be noted that the southern Kyrgyz were more hostile to the encroachment of the Russians than the northern Kyrgyz.

8 This is the subtitle of the second volume of the authoritative Soviet history of the republic. *Istoriia Kirgizskoi SSR*, vol. 2, ed. S.I. Il'iasov et al. (Frunze: "Kyrgyzstan", 1986). For an argument that Russians were the lesser evil in Kyrgyz national

development, see I. Boldzhurova, "Ne zabludit'sia v istorii," *Slovo Kyrgyzstana*, September 17, 1994, p. 7. The greater evil in her view: the Chinese.

9  Osmon Ibraimov, "Neizvestnyi genotsid," *Slovo Kyrgyzstana*, April, 20 1991, p. 10.

10  Ian Murray Matley, "Population and Land," in *Central Asia: 120 Years of Russian Rule*, p. 105.

11  Osmon Ibraimov, "Neizvestnyi genotsid," *Slovo Kyrgyzstana*, April, 20 1991, p. 10.

12  "Znaia pravdu istorii, ne pred'iavliat' drug drugu schet za svoikv," *Slovo Kyrgyzstana*, April, 6 1991, p. 3; G. Krongard, "Spravedlivost' trebuet pravdu," *Slovo Kyrgyzstana*, July, 13 1991, p. 3.

13  Osmon Ibraimov, "Neizvestnyi genotsid," *Slovo Kyrgyzstana*, April, 20 1991, p. 10.

14  An authoritative Soviet account of the 1916 uprisings in Kyrgyzstan may be found in *Istoriia Kirgizskoi SSR*, vol. 2, ed. S.I. Il'iasov *et al.* (Frunze: "Kyrgyzstan", 1986), pp. 337–345.

15  For a Soviet account of the revolution itself in Kyrgyzstan, see A. G. Zima, *Velikii Oktiabr' v Kirgizii* (Frunze: "Ilim," 1987).

16  *Istoriia Kirgizskoi SSR*, vol. 3, ed. K.K. Karakeev *et al.* (Frunze: "Kyrgyzstan", 1986), pp. 319–337.

17  Dzh. Dzhunushaliev, "Politika korenizatsii: opyt i problemy," *Kommunist Kirgizstana*, no. 1, 1990, pp. 69–70.

18  *Ibid.*

19  *Ibid.* On the background of members of "elected" bodies in early Soviet Kyrgyzstan, see Z. Kurmanov, "Tochka zreniia," *Slovo Kyrgyzstana*, July, 13 1991, p. 6.

20  One member of this elite was Torekul Aitmatov, the father of the internationally-known novelist, Chingiz Aitmatov. For a discussion of Torekul Aitmatov's life and its influence on his son's work, see Joseph P. Mozur, *Doffing "Mankurt's Cap," Chingiz Aitmatov's "The Day Lasts More than a Hundred Years" and the Turkic National Heritage* (Pittsburgh: The Carl Beck Papers in Russian and East European Studies [no. 605], 1987).

21  "Vorotnikov Speaks at Frunze," *Foreign Broadcast Information Service (Soviet Union)*, 15 October 1984, R9, citing Moscow Domestic Service in Russian, 1600 GMT, October, 13 1984.

22  See "Kirgiz Party Chief Usubaliev Retires," *Radio Liberty Research Bulletin*, November, 1985, p. 3.

23  Dzh. Dzhunushaliev, "Istoki 'belykh piaten' istorii," *Kommunist Kirgizstana*, no. 5, 1990, p. 65.

24  Ch. Aitmatov, "Voronii grai nad opolznem. Oshskie razdum'ia, god spustia," *Slovo Kyrgyzstana*, August, 2 1991, p. 2.

25  Even in the approximately 1,000 schools in the republic where Kyrgyz was the language of instruction, the teachers trained in Russian in their substantive fields. ". . . chtoby v kazhdoi dushe byl pokoi," *Sovetskaia Kirgiziia*, September, 13 1989, p. 3.

26  "Na osnove svobodnogo razvitiia i ravnopraviia iazykov," *Sovetskaia Kirgiziia*, September, 28 1989, p. 3. In general, Kyrgyz-language works were poorly represented in every cultural field. Of the fifty works in the repertory of the Kyrgyz Theater of Opera and Ballet in 1989, only four were in Kyrgyz; and of the 5577 films in the inventory of Kirgizkiioprokat, only 9 percent were dubbed into Kyrgyz. *Ibid.*

27  R. Osmonalieva, "Ob'ektiven li voliuntarizm?," *Kommunist Kirgizstana*, no. 10, 1990, p. 81. Only in light industry, where the Kyrgyz comprise 35 percent of the workforce, does the titular nationality make up at least a third of an industrial sector. *Ibid.*

28  *Ibid.*

29  Dzh. Dzhunushaliev, "Politika korenizatsii: opyt i problemy," *Kommunist Kirgizstana*, no. 1, 1990, p. 75.

30  On the correlation between ethnicity and employment in Central Asia, see Nancy

Lubin, *Labor and Nationality in Soviet Asia: An Uneasy Compromise* (Princeton: Princeton University Press, 1984).

31 For an excellent overview of demographic trends in Central Asia, see M. Rywkin, *Moscow's Muslim Challenge: Soviet Central Asia*, revised edition (Armonk, NY: ME Sharpe, 1990), ch. 5.

32 A. Zhakypov, "Komuz ne dlia frantsuvoz," *Sovetskaia Kirgizia*, 10 September, 10 1989, p. 2.

33 M. Guboglo, "Demography and Language in the Capitals of the Union Republics," *Journal of Soviet Nationalities*, no. 4, 1990, p. 7.

34 "O prioritetakh," *Murok*, no. 1, November 1990, p. 2. *Murok* was an irregularly issued newsletter published in Moscow by ethnic Kyrgyz who sought more rapid reform of the republic's political and economic system. For insightful articles on the Kyrgyz communities in Moscow and St. Petersburg, numbering about 3,000 in each city, see A. Gorodzeiskii, "Moskovskie kirgizy," *Literaturnyi Kirgizstan*, no. 11, 1990, p. 82, and N. Ablova, "'Belyi parokhod v ust'e Nevy, ili kirgizy goroda Pitera," *Literaturynyi Kirgizstan*, nos. 7–8, 1990, pp. 112–117.

35 E. Abildaev, "Rabochii klass Kirgizii: Osobennosti razvitiia," *Kommunist Kirgizstana*, nos. 8–9, 1990, p. 135.

36 V. Rumiantsev, "Sluzhba zaniatosti i rynochnaia ekonomika," *Kommunist Kirgizstana*, no. 11, 1990, pp. 42–48.

37 "Ozdorovit' i stabilizirovat' obstanovku (s plenuma oshkogo obkoma Kompartii Kirgizii)," *Sovetskaia Kirgiziia*, August, 15 1990, p. 2.

38 "Deistvovat' vzveshenno, obstoiatel'no, soobscha," *Slovo Kyrgyzstana*, January 15, 1991, p. 2.

39 On the problem of overpopulation of the Central Asian countryside, see Boris Z. Rumer, *Soviet Central Asia: "A Tragic Experiment"* (Boston: Unwin Hyman, 1989), ch. 6.

40 S. Usenov, "Vozvrat k srednevekov'iu?!," *Murok*, no. 1, 1990, pp. 2–3.

41 V. Ponomarev, *Samodeiatel'nye obschestvennyi organizatsii Kazakhstana i Kirgizii, 1987–1991 (opyt spravochnika)* (Moscow: Informatsionnoe agentstvo "Aziia", 1991), p. 84.

42 "Na osnove svobodnogo razvitiia i ravnopraviia iazykov," *Sovetskaia Kirgiziia*, 28 September 1989, p. 5; S. Usenov, "Vozvrat k srednevekov'iu?!," *Murok*, no. 1, 1990, pp. 2–3. By the beginning of 1991, a corporatist-style relationship existed between Ashar and the local authorities in Frunze (Bishkek). E. Denisenko, "Ashar deistvyet, i on prav," *Slovo Kyrgyzstana* May 8, 1991, p. 7.

43 Russian reformers began to leave these groups, however, after the Osh events and after the rise of Yeltsin in the Russian Federation, which attracted many of them to Russia. A. Kniazev, "Russkii vopros," *Literaturnyi Kirgizstan*, no. 1, 1991, pp. 109–115. An exception was G. Kaliuzhnaia, a Russian elected chairman of the Sokuluk branch of the DDK. "Lider DDK v raione – russkaia," *Slovo Kyrgyzstana*, September 6, 1991, p. 1.

44 "Programma Demokraticheskogo dvizheniia 'Kyrgyzstan'" [document in possession of the author]. The rules of the organization may be found in *Frunze shamy*, August 28, 1990.

45 V. Ponomarev, *Samodeiatel'nye obshchestvennye organizatsii Kazakhstana i Kirgizii, 1987–1991*, pp. 96–97. For biographies of the co-chairmen of the Democratic Movement "Kyrgyzstan", Topchubek Turganaliev and Zhypar Zheksheev, see "Portrety bez ramok," *Literaturnyi Kirgizstan*, no. 12, 1990, pp. 89–94. Turganaliev was among a number of members of the DDK who went on a hunger strike outside the parliament building in Frunze to demand reform of what until that time had been an unreconstructed political system. The defeat of Masaliev and the election of Akaev coincided with this hunger strike. For an assessment of the rise of contested politics in

Kyrgyzstan, see E. Huskey, "Electoral Politics in Kyrgyzstan, 1989–1990," *Europe-Asia Studies* (forthcoming).

46 For the result of opinion polls among local residents on the origins of the Osh disturbances, see A. Elebaeva, "Mezhnatsional'nye otnosheniia: mif i real'nost'," *Slovo Kyrgyztana*, August, 3 1991, p. 4.

47 "Ozdorovit' i stabilizirovat' obstanovku (s plenuma oshkogo obkoma Kompartii Kirgizii)," *Sovetskaia Kirgiziia*, August, 15 1990, p. 2.

48 Since the 1920s, when Turkestan was divided, the boundaries between Kyrgyzstan and Uzbekistan have been disputed. See T. Ozhukeeva, ". . . i rezali derzhevu, kak tort (istoki territorial'nykh konfliktov v SSSR)," *Slovo Kyrgyzstana*, November, 2 1991, p. 10.

49 Dzhamin Akimaliev, "Igra bez pravil," *Literaturnyi Kirgizstan*, no. 11, 1990, p. 88.

50 Disturbances on a smaller scale broke out on the Kyrgyz-Tajik border concerning water rights. This dispute, whose roots go back to the drawing of territorial boundaries in the 1920s, soured relations between the Kyrgyz and Tajik leaders in the late 1980s and early 1990s. For a brief review of the dispute, see A. Kniazev, "Zalozhniki zakholustiia," *Literaturnyi Kirgizstan*, no. 5, 1990, pp. 98–104. At stake is 24,000 hectares of Kyrgyz territory claimed by Tajikistan. "Zachem vvodit' liudei v zabluzhdenie?," *Slovo Kyrgyzstana*, May 24, 1991, p. 1.

51 See A.S. Pigolkin and M.S. Studenkina, "Republic Language Laws in the USSR: A Comparative Analysis," *Journal of Soviet Nationalities* (forthcoming). Reform of language policy had begun in Kyrgyzstan in October 1988 with the adoption of a party directive "O national'no-russkom dvuiazychii, uluchshenii prepodavaniia i izucheniia kirgizskogo, russkogo i drugikh iazykov narodov SSSR v respublike." "O proekte Zakona o gosudarstvennom iazyke Kirgizskoi SSR (Doklad sekretaria TsK Kompartii Kirgizii, predsedatelia Komissii zakonodatel'nykh predpolozhenii Verkhovnogo Soveta Kirgizskoi SSR deputata M.Sh. Sherimkulova)," *Sovetskaia Kirgiziia*, September 28, 1989, pp. 2–3.

52 See, for example, the comments of the ethnic Russian procurator of Kyrgyzstan, G.I. Ivantsov. "Na osnove svobodnogo razvitiia i ravnopraviia iazykov," *Sovetskaia Kirgiziia*, 28 September 1989, p. 4.

53 "O gosudarstvennom iazyke Kirgizskoi SSR," *Sovetskaia Kirgiziia*, 29 September 1989, pp. 1–2.

54 One collective letter, signed at 10 am on 16 September 1989, bore 1623 signatures. "Obsuzhdaetsia proekt Zakona o iazyke," *Sovetskaia Kirgiziia*, September 12, 1991, p. 1.

55 U. Midinova and E. Turaliev, "O ıpiknikakh', dlinnykh ocherediakh . . . i drugikh malopriiatnykh veshchakh," *Literaturnyi Kirgizstan*, no. 1, 1990, pp. 123–126.

56 A Russian from the Alamedinsk district wrote that he did not feel guilty before the Kyrgyz people because his ancestors brought with them to Turkestan agriculture, infrastructure, and civilization. V. Ermakov, "Ostat'sia, chtoby vozrodit'sia," *Literaturnyi Kyrgyzstana*, no. 5, 1991, pp. 104–105. See also E. Chernova, "Trudoresursnyi faktor i mezhnatsional'nye otnosheniia," *Kommunist Kirgizstana*, no. 6, 1990, p. 61. The reaction of the Central Asian minorities to the law was less immediate and less alarmist. The law did provoke resentment, however, among the Uzbeks in southern Kyrgyzstan. Uzbeks objected that they already knew a second language, Russian, and Kyrgyz would be a third. In their compact ethnic community in the Fergana valley, many argued, Uzbek and not Kyrgyz should be the official language.

57 "Nuzhen dialog, a ne protivosostoianie," *Sovetskaia Kirgiziia*, December 16, 1989, p. 3.

58 "Respublika ishchet imia," *Slovo Kyrgyzstana*, December 13, 1990, p. 1. Changing the spelling of the republic in Russian from Kirgizstan to Kyrgyzstan caused considerable

resentment among the Russians, who claimed their language was being interfered with by forcing it to deny Russian rules of pronunciation. "I dukh, i bukva," *Sovetskaia Kirgiziia*, December 9, 1990, p. 3. By the end of 1993, Russian-language publications in Kyrgyzstan began to return to the original spelling of the republic – Kirgizstan.

59 On the implementation of the language law, see E. Huskey, "The Politics of Language in Kyrgyzstan," *Nationalities Papers* (forthcoming).

60 V. Alekseev, "'Slavianskie vesti'," *Sovetskaia Kirgiziia*, December 19, 1990, p. 1. *Soglasie*, formed in July 1994, has considerable support in the Russian business community. It has ties to the Congress of Russian Communities, an organization uniting Russians throughout the near abroad. Aleksandr Brasov, "Soglasie: drugogo puti prosto net," *Slovo Kyrgyzstana*, October 8, 1994, p. 6.

61 "Iurgen Sheller: Moi deviz – Sapere aude!" *Slovo Kyrgyzstana*, February 26, 1994, p. 3.

62 In September 1994, the Government published a *postanovlenie* setting out specific steps designed to implement the May decree of the president. In all organizations with a majority of non-Kyrgyz, internal communications may be conducted in Russian as well as Kyrgyz until the final expiration date for introducing the state language. The new date is to be January 1, 2005, according to a bill to be drafted for parliament by the Ministry of Justice. "Kak umen'shit' migratsiiu," *Slovo Kyrgyzstana*, September 14, 1994, p. 3. As the *akim* of Bishkek, Zhumabek Ibraimov, points out, however, the exodus of Russians will only stop if industry in Kyrgyzstan can be revived. In 1993, 30,000 Russians left Bishkek alone. "Khochu, chtoby Bishkek stal stolitsei edinomyshlennikov," *Slovo Kyrgyzstana*, June 28, 1994, p. 2.

63 A. Gorodzeiskii, "Moskovskie kirgizy," *Literaturnyi Kirgizstan*, no. 11, 1990, p. 82.

64 Dzhamin Akimaliev, "Igra bez pravil," *Literaturnyi Kirgizstan*, no. 11, 1990, p. 92.

65 The roots of Islam are less deep in Kyrgyzstan than among the more sedentary peoples of Central Asia. As Abramzon points out, although Islam came to Kyrgyzstan in the sixteenth and seventeenth centuries, it had hardly taken hold even by the nineteenth century. S.M. Abramzon, *Kirgizy i ikh etnogeneticheskie i istoriko-kul'turnye sviazi*, pp. 255–275. For a sophisticated analysis of the role of Islam in the rise of a Kyrgyz ethnic consciousness, see Guy Imart, "The Islamic Impact on Traditional Kirghiz Ethnicity," *Nationalities Papers*, nos. 1–2, 1986, pp. 65–88. It is still unclear to what extent Islam will serve as a catalyst in the formation of contemporary Kyrgyz nationalism.

66 Recent meetings of independent democratic associations and parties in Central Asia have called for retaining the territorial status quo. The leaders of these organizations specifically rejected the idea of a pan-Turkic state, Turan. E. Denisenko, "Slozhenie sil na ostrove demokratii," *Slovo Kyrgyzstana*, May 31, 1991, p. 2. The permanent headquarters of this federation of Central Asian democratic organizations is to be in Bishkek, remarkable testimony to the pace of reform in Kyrgyzstan, which as late as the fall of 1989 was seen by many to be the most backward republic politically in Central Asia.

67 K. Bobulov, "Pravda i lozh'," *Slovo Kyrgyzstana*, March 1, 1991, p. 3.

68 For a discussion of Kyrgyz tribes and clans, see S. M. Abramzon, *Kirgizy i ikh etnogeneticheskie i istoriko-kul'turnye sviazi*, pp. 24–34, 189, and *passim*.

69 The head of the presidential department for interethnic relations, A. Dzhusupbekov, argued in early 1993 that "intraethnic disagreements and interregional tensions are particularly worrying for me and my associates. It is problem number one, and must not be underestimated. Tajikistan will serve as an example." "Igra na grani fola, no bez udaleniia s polia," *Slovo Kyrgyzstana*, January 23, 1993, p. 6.

70 Azamat Altay, "Kirgiziya During the Great Purge," *Central Asian Review*, no. 2, 1964, p. 102. I am grateful to Joseph Mozur for bringing this source to my attention. A. Dzhusupbekov, "Net proroka v svoem otechestve," *Slovo Kyrgyzstana*, August 17, 1994, p. 2. One southern commentator noted in 1992 that the theory of "checks and

balances" required a firm division of government portfolios between northerners and southerners. Only in this way, he argued, could southerners insure adequate representation in governing institutions in Bishkek. Mamat Karataev, "Produkt 30-minutnoi deiatel'nosti nekrupnogo mozga, ili Razgovor s samim soboi po povodu stat'i K. Mambetalieva," *Slovo Kyrgyzstana*, October 22, 1992, p. 7.

71  "Deistvovat' vzveshenno, obstoiatel'no, soobshcha," *Slovo Kyrgyzstana*, January 15, 1991, p. 2.

72  A. Biialinov, "Kirgizskaia Federativnaia Respublika: byt' ili ne byt'?," *Sovetskaia Kirgiziia*, November 24, 1990, p. 2.

73  K. Mambetaliev, "Uvazhitel'noe gostepriimstvo – ili bratskoe sokhoziaistvovanie?," *Literaturnyi Kirgizstan*, no. 8 (1990), p. 87.

74  As of the fall of 1994, the most influential parties in Kyrgyzstan were the Communist Party and Ata-Meken, the latter a recently-formed party generally supportive of the president. Among the other major parties were Erkin Kyrgyzstan, DDK, Asaba, the Social-Democratic Party, the Agrarian Party, and the Republican Popular Party. For the level of popular support enjoyed by these parties, see Kusein Isaev, Emil' Niiazov, and Karybek Zhigitekov, "Komu otdat' svoi golos i nadezhdu," *Slovo Kyrgyzstana*, September 24, 1994, p. 5.

75  E. Abildaev, "Rabochii klass Kirgizii: osobennosti razvitiia," *Kommunist Kirgizstana*, nos. 8–9, 1990, p. 134. On the educational "lag" of indigenous Central Asian nationalities, see Martha Brill Olcott, "Central Asia: The Reformists Challenge a Traditional Society," in *The Nationalities Factor in Soviet Politics and Society*, ed. L. Hajda and M. Beissinger, (Boulder, CO: Westview Press), pp. 266–267.

76  Even in the urban vocational training schools, only 15 percent of ethnic Kyrgyz opt for industrial courses, with most preferring trade-related subjects. *Ibid.*, pp. 135–138.

77  By the middle of 1994, one-third of the state farms – those considered unprofitable – had closed and more than 20,000 private farmers were tilling the land. Nur Dolay, "Le Kirghizstan cherche sa voie," *Le monde diplomatique*, December 1994, p. 5. According to the prime minister, Adas Dzhumagulov, the remaining state and collective farms were to close by the end of 1994 unless they raised grain or were tribal (*plemennye*) in membership. "Proshchal'noe slovo kolkhozam i sovkhozam," *Slovo Kyrgyzstana*, November 25, 1994, p. 2.

78  A. Barshai, "Dve opasnosti groziat gosudarstvu – odna izvne, drugaia iznvnutri," *Slovo Kyrgyzstana*, August 26, 1994, p. 1. For a detailed account of how officials acquired state property for a song, see the procurator-general's report in A. Sharshenaliev, "Da, znakomye vse familii!" *Slovo Kyrgyzstana*, August 17, 1994, p. 2. See also V. Niksdorf, "Deputaty reshili borot'sia za chistotu svoikh riadov," SK, May 31, 1994, p. 1.

79  For popular reactions to the economic crisis, see Richard B. Dobson, *Kyrgyzstan in a Time of Change: A Report on Ten Focus Groups in 1994* (Office of Research, USIA, October 1994).

80  "Apas Dzhumagulov: U nas slishkom malo vremeni chtoby tratit' ego na politicheskie batalii . . .," *Slovo Kyrgyzstana*, May 20, 1994, pp. 2–3.

81  Due to a lack of reliable supplies of jet fuel, Kyrgyzstan has been unable to open a direct air route to any foreign capital save Moscow, and even service to Moscow has been interrupted for long stretches. In 1992, the Kyrgyz writer and diplomat, Chingiz Aitmatov, failed in his effort to open an air route, Luxembourg–Bishkek–Hong Kong.

82  Along with Akaev, the foreign minister, Roza Otunbaeva, has been instrumental in enhancing Kyrgyzstan's image in the world community. Until early 1994, she was the Kyrgyz ambassador in Washington. See "Roza Otunbaeva: Vlast' dolzhna byt' sil'na, no nado li ee protivopostavliat' demokratii?" *Slovo Kyrgyzstana*, September 3, 1994, p. 6, where Otunbaeva emphasizes the importance of Kyrgyzstan's image for its geopolitical position.

83 For a list of aid commitments as of the middle of 1993, see L. Lozovskaia, "Den'gi perechisliat MVF, vsemirnyi Bank, Iaponia . . .," *Biznesmen K* [Bishkek], no. 15 (June 1993), p. 3, and N. Aiyp, "Obzor nedeli," Res Publica [Bishkek], June 5, 1993, p. 1.

84 According to a former colleague, Akaev had the following to say about aid negotiations with the West: "When I became a politician, I understood that it is an art to call various things by the same name. And I, and Nazarbaev [the president of Kazazhstan], and Karimov [the president of Uzbekistan], are of course building different things, but we call it democracy, because that pleases you in the West . . ."

"Kogda politik Askar Akaev okazyvaetsia v patovoi situatsii, uchenyi Askar Akaev govorit: 'ia chto-nibud' pridumaiu . . .," *Slovo Kyrgyzstana*, October 1, 1994, p. 6.

85 E. Huskey, "Kyrgyzstan Leaves the Ruble Zone," *RFL/RL Research Report*, September 3, 1994, pp. 38–43.

86 It is instructive that the government commission drafting the new tax code of Kyrgyzstan is headed by the 31 year-old representative of the IMF in Bishkek, David Robinson. "Devid Robinson: Kyrgyzstan? O'kei! MVF i vpred' budet podderzhivat' vas," *Slovo Kyrgyzstana*, October 22, 1994, p. 3.

87 "Vozrashchenie," *Slovo Kyrgyzstana*, April 8, 1994, p. 2.

88 Accused publicly of inciting anti-semitic and anti-Chinese feelings, these papers had most likely run afoul of the authorities by investigating charges of corruption in the president's entourage. Earlier in the year, a scandal surrounding the letting of a gold mining contract had forced out Prime Minister Tursunbek Chyngyshev. ". . . na menia zh parusami makhnuli," *Slovo Kyrgyzstana*, November 12, 1994, p. 5.

89 In July 1994, 105 deputies signed an open letter calling for the "self-closure" (*samorospusk*) of parliament. "Narod dolzhen znat' pravdu!" *Slovo Kyrgyzstana*, July 22, 1994, p. 1. At the next session of the parliament in September, a majority of the deputies boycotted the assembly, which led to the resignation of the government and the formal closing of the parliament by the president. The president's decision was later upheld by a local court.

90 85 percent of those voting supported the proposed changes to the constitution on an 86 percent turnout. The only areas that supported the amendments less enthusiastically were the Bazar-Korgon district of Jalal-Abad oblast and the Bakai-Atin district of Talas oblast, by 51.69 percent and 72.13 percent, respectively. "Rezul'taty itogov golosovaniia na referendume Kyrgyzskoi Respubliki 22 oktiabria 1994 goda – po pervomu voprosu," *Slovo Kyrgyzstana*, October 28, 1994, p. 6.

91 "Pis'mo Prezidenta," *Slovo Kyrgyzstana*, October 28, 1994, p. 2; "Sprosit' i vyslushat' narod – ne v etom li segodnia real'naia demokratiia v Kyrgyzstane?" *Slovo Kyrgyzstana*, September 27, 1994, p. 1.

92 Again as in Russia, the president laid down the new electoral rules himself. Zakon Kyrgyzskoi Respubliki o vyborakh deputatov Zhogorku Kenesha Kyrgyzskoi Respubliki, *Slovo Kyrgyzstana*, October 28, 1994, pp. 3–5.

93 A bicameral assembly would also reduce Sherimkulov's power in any future parliament. "U zakona net privilegii," *Slovo Kyrgyzstana*, October 5, 1994, p. 2. Earlier a reform-oriented secretary of the Central Committee of Kyrgyzstan, Sherimkulov had used the office of speaker to further the politics of consensus advanced by Akaev. Sherimkulov was in many respects the guarantor of stability during the first years of independent Kyrgyzstan. Personal interview with Medetkan Sherimkulov, Bishkek, June 9, 1993.

94 "Stavki ochen' vysoki'," *Slovo Kyrgyzstana*, September 24, 1994, p. 4.

95 Kusein Isaev, Emil' Niiazov, and Karybek Dzhigitekov, "Esli ne k khramu doroga, to zachem ona?" *Slovo Kyrgyzstana*, November 19, 1994, p. 8.

96 It was at this point that Akaev's popularity rating was at its lowest. See Kusein Isaev, Emil' Niiazov, and Karybek Dzhigitekov, "Esli ne k khramu doroga, to zachem ona?" *Slovo Kyrgyzstana*, November 19, 1994, p. 8. In a perceptive critique of Akaev's

alliance with the *akimy*, Zhapar Zheksheev, one of the founders of the DDK, notes that the local executives will hardly be in his pocket (*karmannye*), as he believes. The liberal, national press is poorly distributed in the provinces and the *akimy* have their own allies in the White House in Bishkek. "Dlia demokratii u nas slishkom tverdaia zemlia," *Slovo Kyrgyzstana*, October 22, 1994, p. 5. The *akimy* also appear to have veto power over the appointment of local representatives of the central ministries. Personal interview with Tologon Rakhmanovich Rakhmanov, Head of Administration, Kalinin district. Kara-Balta, Kyrgyzstan, June 11, 1993.

97 Several regional *akimy* have been personally close to Akaev, perhaps most notably Abdygany Erkebaev, the head of the Osh oblast. For a revealing portrait of this politician, see "Abdygany Erkebaev: Nastupit vremia, kogda intellektualy ustupiat mesto professionaliam," *Slovo Kyrgyzstana*, September 24, 1994, p. 3.

98 "'Vybory i referendum sostoialis'!" *Slovo Kyrgyzstana*, October 25, 1994, p. 1. In the Naryn oblast, 105 of the 692 electoral districts were contested. In Talas oblast, half of the 464 seats were contested. *Ibid*. Precise figures were not available for the remaining regions.

99 Indeed, many of the *akimy* had served as party secretaries before 1991. One of the more progressive of these is Gennadii Valerivich Davidenko, the former *akim* of the Panfilov district. Davidenko noted that in comparison with the party secretaries, the *akimy* enjoy more independence and are less bound by directives from above. Personal interview, Kaindy, Kyrgyzstan, June 11, 1993.

The *akimy* recently sponsored the formation of a new party, the Social Democrats, which appears set to compete against the still powerful Communist Party for the rural and traditional vote in Kyrgyzstan. One plank of the party's platform is direct election of *akimy*. "Rezoliutsiia II s'ezda SKPK," *Slovo Kyrgyzstana*, October 4, 1994, p. 3.

# Kyrgyzstan: chronology of events

*1989*

The first major independent association Ashar, originally established to lobby for suitable housing, is permitted to register.

*September 1989*

Language law is adopted which makes Kyrgyz the state language and Russian the language of interethnic communication. One article requires that all management and professional personnel speak Kyrgyz. Russian-speakers are outspoken in their opposition to the law.

*February 1990*

2  Elections to the Supreme Soviet are held.

*April 1990*

9  Absamat Masaliev is elected chairman of the Supreme Soviet.

*May 1990*

26  24 informal groups come together to form the Democratic Movement "Kyrgyzstan."
A housing lobby organization in Osh is granted several hectares of land belonging to an Uzbek-dominated collective farm. Local Uzbeks respond by calling for autonomy for the region and adoption of Uzbek as the official language.

*June 1990*

4  Following the Kyrgyz leadership's refusal to acknowledge the Uzbek demands, rioting breaks out, resulting in mass destruction of homes and building and more than 200 deaths. Troops from the Soviet Army and MVD are called in to restore order.

*July 1990*

8  Several thousand Uzbeks participate in a demonstration to demand an investigation of the killing of B. Sarymsakov the day before as well as policies to promote Uzbeks and Uzbek language.

10  Ethnic violence continues in Osh.

*September 1990*
18    114 deputies join the parliamentary bloc "For Democratic Renewal and Civil Harmony."

*October 1990*
28    The Supreme Soviet elects Askar Akaev, president of the Kyrgyz Academy of Sciences, as president of the republic.

*December 1990*
10    The Supreme Soviet issues a declaration of sovereignty. Masaliev resigns as parliamentary chairman and is replaced by M. Sherimkulov.

*January 1991*
22    Vice-President Nasirdin Asanov is appointed prime minister, replacing Apas Dzhumagulov (who had served in the post since 1986). He is replaced as vice-president by German Kuznetsov.

*February 1991*
5    The Supreme Soviet changes the name of the republic's capital from Frunze to Bishkek.

*March 1991*
17    In the all-union referendum on preserving the union, 95% of voters (93% turnout) support the union.

*April 1991*
6    Dzh. Amanbaev replaces Masaliev as first party secretary.

*May 1991*
The Supreme Soviet adopts a law on land which describes the republic's land and natural resources as the wealth of the Kyrgyz nation. Amidst public outcry by non-Krygyz, President Askar Akaev vetoes the statement, and it is replaced with ethnically-neutral language.

*Summer 1991*
The presidential party National Unity is formed.

*August 1991*
The Supreme Soviet issues a declaration of independence and bans the Communist Party.

*October 1991*
13    Akaev receives over 95% of the vote in uncontested presidential elections.

*November 1991*
 29  Prime Minister Isanov dies in a car accident.

*December 1991*
 13  Kyrgyzstan joins the CIS.

*February 1992*

Tursunbek Chyngyshev is appointed prime minister.

*May 1992*
 15  Kyrgyzstan signs the CIS collective security treaty.

*December 1992*
 15  At a meeting, human rights activists demand the
     release from jail of Uzbek participants of the human
     rights conference held in Bishkek the week
     before.

*May 1993*
 4   Parliament adopts Kyrgyzstan's first post-Soviet
     constitution.
 10  Kyrgyzstan leaves the ruble zone, making the *som* the sole
     official currency.

*June 1993*
 3   The Society for Furthering the Protection of Human Rights
     in Central Asia appeals to Akaev to release from prison 3
     ethnically-Tajik television journalists.

*July 1993*

Former Vice-President and First Vice-Premier German
Kuznetsov, a prominent member of Kyrgyzstan's Russian
community, emigrates.

*November 1993*
 9   The Slavonic University, a project aimed at convincing
     Russian-speakers to stay in Kyrgyzstan, is opened in
     Bishkek.

*December 1993*
 8   A pan-Central Asian Congress of Non-Governmental
     Humans Rights Organizations is held in Bishkek.
 13  Prime Minister Tursunbek Chyngyshev and his government
     are dismissed by Akaev after Chyngyshev fails to survive a
     no-confidence vote regarding accusations that he had sold
     gold reserves abroad.
 14  Apas Dzhumagulov, former chairman of the Council of
     Ministers, is appointed prime minister.

*January 1994*

21    A Kurultai (Assembly) of the People of Kyrgyzstan is convened in Bishkek to discuss ways of uniting Kyrgyzstan's is multiethnic population.

30    In a referendum asking if Akaev should finish out his term of office, 96% (98?) voting (95% participation) supported the president.

*July 1994*

20    Akaev's call for press restrictions on 14 July is heavily criticized by Kyrgyz press and media organs.

*September 1994*

5    165 of 320 deputies announce their intention to not participate in a parliamentary meeting scheduled for later in the month, effectively dissolving the legislative body. Prime Minister Dzhumagulov and his cabinet resign but agree to stay in their posts until a new cabinet is formed.

12    The Congress of Democratic Forces of Kyrgyzstan call for simultaneous parliamentary and presidential elections.

*October 1994*

22    In a referendum, 85% of voters (86% participation) support a proposal to change the constitution to allow the election of a bicameral parliament. Local elections are held with most of the seats unconstested.

*January 1995*

5    First-round elections to the new bicameral parliament, the Zhogorku Kenesh, are held. Following second-round elections on 19 February, 78 deputies are elected: 28 to the 30-seat Legislative Assembly, and 50 to the 75-seat Assembly of People's Representatives. Only five seats are won by Russians.

*March 1995*

28    Mukar Cholponbaev, the former minister of justice, is elected chairman of the Assembly of People's Representatives. Almambek Matubraimov is elected chairman of the Legislative Assembly.

*April 1995*

5    Dzhumagulov is reappointed prime minister.

# Part VII
# Conclusion

# Conclusion: from matrioshka nationalism to national interests

RAYMOND TARAS

Nationalist assertion among the many peoples that formed part of the USSR was a complex phenomenon. Like nested Russian wooden dolls, there seemed invariably to be an inner component to a national entity. The Russian Federation consists of scores of non-Russian nationalities, and the other fourteen states that became independent after the dismantling of the USSR in 1991 also have varying numbers and proportions of national minorities. The Soviet collapse removed only the outermost shell of the matrioshka structure. Since 1991 we have continued to witness largescale human tragedies resulting from competing nationalist claims: the brutal war in the Russian republic of Chechnya, the festering conflict over Nagorno-Karabagh between Armenia and Azerbaijan, and the successful Abkhazian uprising against Georgian rule, to identify only the bloodiest armed struggles. The actions taken to suppress "subnationalism," as it is manifested by minorities in the new states, are carried out to promote newly-defined national interests, such as territorial integrity, social unity, and national security.

## New states, new politics, new approaches

Whether we study the causes of nationalist assertion in the fifteen independent states, the processes that characterize such assertion, or the political outcomes that have resulted and are by no means final, we are struck by the sheer number of unique cultures, the politicized nature of their nationalism and, perhaps most problematically, the often equal moral weight of contending nationalist claims. An exponential learning curve has subsumed not only area and regional studies specialists but large sections of the interested citizenry in many parts of the world. Arguably, laypeople are more sensitized to the legitimacy of Chechen or Siberian peoples' grievances today – as they are to those of Russian minorities "stranded" in the new states of Eurasia – than they were to that of the Baltic nations' struggle for independence from the Soviet Union in the late 1980s. Indeed, a number of previously-obscure nationalities now expect an informed understanding of their grievances from external actors. Clearly, specialists and non-specialists alike have learned immensely from the nationalities revolution that is ongoing on the Eurasian continent.

To match the rise of nationalism in the contemporary world, the number and variety of explanatory theories concerned with modern nationalism has increased significantly. To be sure, in the expansive 1990s literature addressing the subject, discursive analyses have far outnumbered formal social science theories. Thus, in his wide-ranging examination of the major modern thinkers on nationalism, Ernest Gellner, the doyen of nationalism research, was content to report about the new wave of nationalist assertion in this way. Following the first eruption of nationalism that occurred in the aftermath of the collapse of empires in 1918, "This second great post-imperial eruption of nationalism takes place in a different and new ideo-logical climate, one in which the old link between territory and wealth has been broken, and the new political supremacy of growth-states established, and one in which Left and Right extremism has lost much of its conviction and repute."[1] Growth-states have been conspicuously absent in post-Soviet space, and Gellner may be right in implying that the desire to create them may overwhelm states organized primarily in terms of a nationalist agenda. Still, to suggest that the appeal of right-wing extremism has thereby been eroded does not square with the evidence presented in many of our case studies.

British scholar Anthony Smith has also influenced recent debates on nationalism. In particular, he has described the vise that national identity has established on contemporary politics. He is not optimistic that global forces carving out alternatives to such identity – pan-nationalisms, trans-national corporations, functional international regimes, telecommuni-cations – will succeed. For "Through the rediscovery of an ethnic past and the promise of collective restoration of the former golden age, national identity and nationalism have succeeded in arousing and inspiring ethnic communities and populations of all classes, regions, genders and religions, to claim their rights as 'nations,' territorial communities of culturally and historically cognate citizens, in a world of free and equal nations."[2] Affirming national identity is perceived to be the means to attaining the modern utopia of sovereignty.

Irish essayist Conor Cruise O'Brien is no less troubled by the contemporary phenomenon of nationalism. "Any nationalism inherently finds it hard to understand any other nationalism or even to want to understand it." Especially when nationalism takes on a religious, spiritual dimension transcending mere politics, that is, when it develops into "holy nationalism," it becomes intractable. As a former United Nations diplomat, then, O'Brien underscored how "The management of holy nationalism is the greatest problem in peacekeeping."[3]

The discursive, frequently polemical, approach that has recently been dominant in the analysis of nationalism, is discernable in American writings as well. In depicting the international havoc flowing from a renewal of nationalist sentiments, Senator Daniel Patrick Moynihan chose the term "pandaemonium," that is, the name in *Paradise Lost* that John Milton gave to the capital of Hell.[4] Journalist William Pfaff decried how "Too much academic and analytical discussion of nationalism ignores the importance of the communal attachments and conviction of identity (and 'authenticity') provided by nationality." He seems to be suggesting that rigorously-organized, rationalist, value-free inquiry is ill-suited to understand the quasi-atavistic and primordial nature found in nationalist identity and assertion. Pfaff ascribes demonic qualities to nationalism, which he views as having trampled most other political forces underfoot. "The twentieth century has belonged to nationalism. Nationalism destroyed western imperialism and the colonial system, and also destroyed the ideological internationalisms which have been the distinctive political phenomena of the twentieth century, Leninism and Nazism. Nationalism has installed nations nearly everywhere."[5]

Although in the 1990s nationalism was more evident as a feature of politics in many parts of the world and, justifiably, received greater scholarly attention than at any time since World War II, less new theoretical ground has been broken than might be expected. Probably the most notable conceptual breakthrough was in distinguishing between civic and ethnic forms of nationalism. According to Liah Greenfeld, the civic basis of membership in a national collectivity involves open and voluntaristic criteria; the ethnic basis of such membership is inherent and it is either acquired or not and, if acquired, not subject to change.[6] The civic versus ethnic distinction has shaped the work of scholars such as Rogers Brubaker and even journalists such as Michael Ignatieff.[7]

Yet such a dichotmous approach to community membership is apparent in earlier treatments of nation- and state-building. The historical period in which eminent Jewish theologian Martin Buber was writing had much in common with the post-Soviet era because it involved incipient statehood, in his context for Israel. His observations appear, therefore, to be especially salient to the study of nations emerging from the Soviet yolk.

In an essay written in 1949, just after the creation of the State of Israel, Buber rhetorically asked: "We have full independence, a state, and all that appertains to it, but where is the nation in the state? And where is that nation's spirit?"[8] While hardly a popular view to take after the birth of Israel, Buber expressed concern about "group egoism" and the nationalist program it engendered; while accepting its mobilizing efforts, he was alarmed about how egoism could produce extremism, for in hothouse conditions nationalism would know no bounds. For Buber, "formal nationalism" – in most respects similar to what has recently been termed ethnic nationalism – disclaimed that the nation was based on anything other than a national task and as a result "formal nationalism sanctions a group egoism which disclaims responsibility." Buber's critique of official Zionism went further and was cast in terms of moral postulates: "A foundation on which the nation is regarded as an end in itself has no room for supernational ethical demands."[9] Put in theological terms, "To be limited to one's self is to be condemned to die; to live for what is limitless is to be freed from death."[10]

Only encounters with other nations with programs of their own would, in Buber's view, lead to full recognition that other groups have rights, that is, would correspond to a civic basis for nationalism. Extrapolating this principle from Talmudic teaching led Buber to a conclusion whose relevance remains clear for the post-Soviet landscape: "There is no scale of values for the function of peoples. One cannot be ranked above another."[11]

Buber's approach to the national question was grounded in subtle distinctions: peoplehood involved a unity of fate; nationality, a collective awareness of this unity; and nationalism, an overconscious sentiment. Or as Michael Walzer summarized Buber, "Peoplehood is an impulse, nationality an idea, nationalism a program. The program is conceived in difficulty; it aims to mobilize the nation so as to overcome some deficiency in its common life."[12] Buber was not satisfied with such restrictive teleology and his quest was for the realization of universalist values – justice and truth.

> Coincidentally, his moral case for a civic-based Israeli state seemed to come to full fruition only in the wake of the collapse of the Soviet Union. For in 1993 the Israeli government concluded a peace accord with the Palestine Liberation Organization Palestinian self-rule in Gaza and the West Bank.

If some of the more recent theorizing about nationalism turns out, then, to have earlier counterparts, it does not detract from the impressive scholarship conducted in the 1990s empirically investigating the phenomenon. A rekindled interest in established paradigms addressing nationalism has also characterized the new empiricism.[13] The extensive fieldwork into nationalism that explicitly connects this phenomenon to political organization and objectives permits us to speak of a transition in the scholarly literature from ethnography to "nationology." This neologism refers specifically to the study of the political boundaries that national groups seek to delineate rather than simply identifying their cultural markers.

Our study has described the ongoing process of nationalist assertion in the fifteen new states of Eurasia. The pathways taken by these different peoples to power are, as we have read, similar in some respects – for example, opposition to centralized rule of the kind exhibited by the past Soviet system – and dissimilar in others. In the case of European peoples more than in the case of Soviet Muslims, the overriding political objective has been to regain national identities rather than create them. In addition to national identity, however, the case studies have examined the more tangible problems of political organization (setting up parties and movements) and institution-building (defining rights, responsibilities, and separation of powers). Many of these are inseparable from implementing nationalist agendas.

It is almost a cliche to assert that in studying different nation-states (like Russia, the Baltics, or Armenia and Georgia) as well as state-nations (the Central Asian countries and, some would add, Belarus or Moldova), we should avoid superimposing on complex historical phenomena and processes one schema, one etiology. No single theory can account for the historical path travelled in the early 1990s in the former Soviet Union by Balt and Turkic peoples, Uniates and Buddhists, industrialized sectors and communities of reindeer herders. Social scientists must perenially be on their guard against accepting any form of determinism, whether of the discredited Marxist historical kind or the more appealing *fin-de-siècle* varieties–nationalist, capitalist, liberal-democratic. Not all the most important events chronicled in this volume can be explained by the phenomenon of nationalism, nor by the power of the free market or liberalism.

The remaining three sections of this chapter attempt to move beyond these problems. The next section examines the issue of ethnic political mobilization. Beginning with the early years of perestroika and glasnost, this analysis seeks to capture the processes of nation-building or -rebuilding. What are the principal theories that offer alternative understandings of this phenomenon? Which framework appears to provide greatest explanatory power for the rise of nationalism in the last years of the USSR? What methodology can most parsimoniously present and order the empirical findings on ethnic political mobilization reported in the individual chapters? Then the chapter considers what type of association, if any, may exist between the early ethnically-mobilizing states and their current political priorities. This examination is conducted in the hope of shedding light on the important but not easily testable hypothesis whether ethnic mobilization can be sustained for a longer period and, if so, under what general background conditions.

The following section returns to the framework advanced in the introductory chapter. It examines the degree to which titular nationalities, non-titulars, and the Soviet center interacted with each other as hypothesized during the process of state formation. Patterns of ethnic interaction that have become evident since the establishment of fifteen independent states are also assayed. This section seeks, then, to describe political strategies followed by national groups. Evidence concerning these strategies provided by our case studies is ordered in terms of different combinations of interaction among titular and non-titular groups. This syncretic analysis reveals emerging patterns in an otherwise murky system of interaction.

The final section concerns new forms of international interaction and regional cooperation among the independent states. It considers the impact that national and ethnic conflicts may have on the international politics that are emerging and, conversely, the ways that actors in the international system can mediate such conflicts. The potential for new axes of ethnic conflict, as well as for conciliating cleavages through third-party mediation, is assessed.

## Ethnic political mobilization: its influence and endurance

A central problem bedevilling comparative research is that of finding a sufficient number of cases that can be meaningfully compared. A sizeable body of social science literature has been concerned with macro–political issues and has sought to interpret significant historical outcomes-social revolutions, regime changes, collapse of empires. As a result, as Charles Ragin indicated, "when a comparativist interprets significant historical outcomes, he or she selects extreme values on a more general dependent variable." If it is to be manageable, comparative research has to adopt a limited perspective: "the problem of having too few societies on which to test theory is compounded by the fact that the interests and goals of comparative social science (and scientists) often dictate the design of studies with a small number of cases."[14] Fortunately, the felicitious appearance of fifteen cases of statehood in place of the USSR made the methodological problem of a small *n* irrelevant.

Ragin developed a methodology for conducting qualitative comparative research based on Boolean analysis. Potential causal variables are identified in various combinations with each other, thereby revealing key causal conjunctures. Once such conjunctures are specified, more traditional, case-oriented elaboration can be conducted. Through use of the two approaches, causal explanation and historical interpretation can be combined.

Ragin tested the explanatory power of three major theories of ethnic political mobilization. The first is the developmental perspective. It views ethnicity as a primordial category that manifests itself when regional economic inequality has adverse effects on a subnation. As Ragin summarized this perspective, "the underlying basis for mobilization according to developmental logic is the failure to integrate the subnation, not its relative poverty per se."[15] Examples from this book are the Islamic republics of the former USSR as well as autonomous republics of the Russian Federation like Chechnya and, to a lesser degree, Tatarstan. The peoples of these areas appear not to have been fully drawn into national economic life, producing their alienation and subsequent revindications.

A second theory of ethnic mobilization is the reactive ethnicity perspective. In contrast to the developmental approach, it points to the infiltration of a subnational area by members of the dominant cultural group – not its isolation – for engendering a "cultural division of labor" and the ethnic backlash to it. To invoke Ragin again: "The dominant strata come to be seen as alien by the lower strata, and the culture of the lower strata becomes stereotyped as inferior by members of the dominant strata."[16] A clear illustration of reactive ethnicity was the Baltic peoples' sense of having been infiltrated by large-scale Russian in-migration (especially true in Estonia and Latvia).[17]

The third approach to ethnic mobilization can be termed the ethnic competition perspective. For a non-dominant nation to be competitive, it needs to be large enough to challenge the core. Further, abundant natural resources and wealth enhance the prospect of political mobilization, thereby requiring resource mobilization. Under conditions of competition, "Ethnic political mobilization is sparked when ethnic groups (dominant and subordinate) are forced to compete with each other for the same rewards and resources."[18] Of former constituent republics of the USSR, only Ukraine was in a position to challenge Russian dominance. In many of the new Eurasian states, notably Kazakhstan and Ukraine, sizeable Russian minorities represent ethnic competition to the titular nations.

What were the most important causal variables producing ethnic political mobilization distinct to each of the three perspectives? According to Ragin, these were: 1) the size of national groups (from the competition perspective); 2) the linguistic proficiency of "isolated" groups (from the developmental perspective); 3) the relative wealth of "infiltrated" groups (from the reactive ethnicity perspective); and 4) economic growth or decline (from all three perspectives). Adapting Ragin's coding to the Soviet context, nations we have considered to be those titular nationalities represent at least 10 percent of the overall population of the former USSR. Coding the size variable presented no problem since no nation came close to this figure other than Russia and Ukraine. As a result, in table 20.1, these two are coded as large (1) and the remaining titular nations as small (0) on the size variable (S).

Soviet statistical data over the years concurred that titular nationalities of union republics in overwhelming numbers declared their nationality language to be their native tongue; all, therefore, would have been coded 1 on the linguistic base variable, making the variable insignificant.[19] In the specific context of the USSR, ethnic homogeneity of a republic was a significant factor producing variations in political mobilization since it tells us something about the degree of unity and cohesiveness of a population. Republics where titulars accounted for at least 75 percent of the population were coded 1 on the ethnic homogeneity variable (H); those with minorities of 25 percent or more were coded 0.

With regard to relative wealth (W), Ragin's measurement was regional variations in production per capita; relative wealth was coded 1 when such production was equal to or greater than the average. The index employed here was national income per capita during 1981–1985, before economic rot really set in. Those republics with national income levels at or above the Soviet average were coded 1, those below it were coded 0.[20]

Finally, Ragin defined the growth variable (G) in terms of net population in-migration, which he took to signify advancing economic status. Given the relative immobility of the population of Central Asia, which would skew results if this index was applied to the Soviet case, combined with the ready availability of more direct indices of advance or decline, I do not follow Ragin here. One possible measure that could be used was the average annual rate of growth of consumption per capita between 1960 and 1985 – an especially revealing factor in a centrally-planned economy stressing growth of heavy industry.[21] But in keeping with the interpretation of the growth variable offered by Ragin, a region or republic's economic advance or decline would be more accurately measured by levels of gross fixed investment per capita over time. As Gertrude Schroeder put it, "If the central government had been determined to equalize levels of development among nationality groups, this policy presumably would have been most apparent in the allocation of investment."[22] More than migration patterns, growth or decline in the Soviet context seemed more a function of fixed investment. Those republics whose level of investment in 1981–85 was equal to or higher than 1961–65 levels were coded 1; those whose share of investment fell over this time were coded 0.

Table 20.1 presents coded data providing the basis for a Boolean analysis of the fifteen then Soviet republics. The outcome variable is defined as ethnic mobilization (N). More specifically, since our case studies provided abundant evidence of ethnic mobilization encompassing titular and non-titular nationalities across the Soviet Union as the center began to disintegrate, the outcome variable is narrowed to ethnic mobilization in support of national sovereignty. Where in our case study chapters, authors have documented extensive evidence of a high degree of such mobilization – seen in the formation of mass organizations such as national fronts, recurrent large-scale pro-independence demonstrations, and extra-constitutional means (like various forms of civil disobedience) – all intended to accelerate and enhance a republic's independent control of its own affairs, such outcomes are coded as positive (1). Lesser degrees of mobilization, evidenced only in the Central Asian cases (and summarized in the following section), are coded negatively (0).

Returning to the three general theories of ethnic mobilization, we recall that the developmental perspective emphasizes ethnic homogeneity but also growth or decline: the image is of a culturally distinct but economically isolated nation. It would be coded in Boolean terms as Hg (uppercase letters indicate presence of a condition, lowercase indicate absence, and multiplication indicates logical AND). Reactive ethnicity focuses on the predatory behavior of the dominant nation involving erosion of ethnic and economic

Table 21.1 *Data on first-order titular Soviet nationalities*

|  | S | H | W | G | E |
|---|---|---|---|---|---|
| Russia | 1 | 1 | 1 | 1 | 1 |
| Ukraine | 1 | 0 | 1 | 0 | 1 |
| Belarus | 0 | 1 | 1 | 1 | 1 |
| Moldova | 0 | 0 | 1 | 1 | 1 |
| Lithuania | 0 | 1 | 1 | 1 | 1 |
| Latvia | 0 | 0 | 1 | 1 | 1 |
| Estonia | 0 | 0 | 1 | 0 | 1 |
| Georgia | 0 | 0 | 1 | 1 | 1 |
| Armenia | 0 | 1 | 1 | 0 | 1 |
| Azerbaijan | 0 | 1 | 0 | 0 | 1 |
| Kazakhstan | 0 | 0 | 0 | 0 | 0 |
| Uzbekistan | 0 | 0 | 0 | 0 | 0 |
| Tajikistan | 0 | 0 | 0 | 0 | 0 |
| Turkmenistan | 0 | 0 | 0 | 0 | 0 |
| Kyrgyzstan | 0 | 0 | 0 | 0 | 0 |

S = Size of nation
H = Ethnic homogeneity
W = Relative wealth
G = Growth or decline
E = Ethnic mobilization for sovereignty

bases (hw). Ethnic competition highlights the size and wealth of the subordinate nation (SW).

In Boolean analysis the absence of a cause has the same logical status as its presence. The Table depicts the absence of ethnic mobilization for sovereignty in Central Asia at the time the Soviet Union was unravelling. The combination of causal conditions for lack of mobilization was small population, lack of ethnic homogeneity, limited wealth, and economic decline (shwg). Conversely, of the ten cases of mobilization, two combinations of causal conditions explain half of the cases. The first was when relative wealth and economic advance were combined with small size and ethnic heterogeneity (Georgia, Latvia, and Moldova), expressed in unreduced Boolean terms as shWG. The second was when relative wealth, economic advance, and homogeneity were combined with small size (Belarus and Lithuania), that is, produce sHWG.

Boolean minimalization is based on the rule that when two Boolean expressions differ in only one causal condition, then that causal condition can be regarded as irrelevant since the outcome remains the same. Thus, whether a nation was characterized by homogeneity or not, it could still pursue mobilization (expressed as sHWG combining with shWG to produce sWG). Further minimization[23] produces the final reduced Boolean equation:

$$E = HWG + sWG + hWg + sHg$$

where + signifies logical OR. That is, our studies revealed mobilization took place under causal conjunctures where nations were relatively wealthy and economically growing but were either small (Belarus, Georgia, Latvia, Lithuania, Moldova) or at least were ethnically homogeneous (Russia); or they were not advancing but were wealthy and ethnically heterogenous (Estonia, Ukraine) or were small and homogeneous (Armenia, Azerbaijan). No single cause appeared necessary or sufficient to produce mobilization since each appeared only in a subset of a combination of conditions. Relative wealth came closest to being a necessary condition, appearing in nine of the ten instances of ethnic mobilization. Azerbaijan was the exception, but it was the "richest" of the republics coded as poor and also represented the only one of the six Soviet Muslim republics that was ethnically homogeneous. When we factor the Boolean expression above, the centrality of wealth becomes apparent:

$$E = W(HG + sG + hg) + sHg$$

The equation reveals two contradictory contexts (HG and hg) which require W to be present for E to occur.[24] It therefore draws our attention to the third causal combination, sG in the presence of W and indeed, as noted above, a relatively wealthy but small Soviet republic that was economically advancing represented the most common profile of a politically mobilizing nation in our study (five of ten cases).

Two of the three theories explaining ethnic mobilization receive support from this Boolean analysis. The developmental perspective stressed the probability of mobilization under conditions of ethnic homogeneity but economic decline (Hg). This equation is a prime implicant of sHg identified in Armenia and Azerbaijan. Except for populous Ukraine, it was never probable that the ethnic competition perspective (SW) would be substantiated in the Soviet case, given the near-hegemonic position of Russians in the old Soviet Union. And indeed Ukraine with its size and wealth fit the competition perspective (though its ethnic heterogeneity and economic decline were also important factors here). A surprising finding was that the reactive ethnicity perspective (hw), which in the Soviet case would confirm that subject nations rose up against Russian infiltration into their republics and that they expressed their frustration with their own limited wealth, was not borne out by the analysis. To the contrary, a weak ethnic and economic base was more closely linked with failure to mobilize.

This short exercise in Boolean analysis is not intended to reduce the collapse of the Soviet empire to a simple algebraic statement. Referring back to Ragin, Boolean analysis is a holistic approach and views cases in terms of combinations of values as well as comparing cases with different combinations. It is also primarily an inductive method, simplifying complexity: "It starts with a bias toward complexity – every logically possible combination of values is examined – and simplifies this complexity through experiment-like contrasts – procedures which approximate the logic of the ideal social scientific comparison."[25] While also variable-oriented, it is easily compatible with qualitative interpretative analysis. Indeed, "the results of Boolean-based analysis provide important signposts for more detailed historical examination of specific cases, using a traditional case-oriented approach," as has characterized this book.[26] Finally, in the specific area of interest to nationalism studies, "Boolean analysis does more than simply confirm complexity. It shows the key combinations of causal conditions linked to ethnic political mobilization."[27]

In this spirit of follow-up inquiry, can we draw an association between the ethnically-mobilized former Soviet republics and the more nationalist-oriented independent states of the second half of the 1990s? From the case studies it is clear that Russia and the Baltic republics seem best to have sustained ethnic political mobilization but for very different reasons. In the case of Russia it is the desire to regain power and prestige that has shaped political discourse and given hope to many ambitious political leaders. For Estonia, Latvia, and Lithuania, it is the consciousness of their smallness and vulnerability that in large measure keeps these nations mobilized. The causal conjunctions – primarily the resource and growth potential that characterize them – that first drove these four nations to strive for independence may continue to contribute to their nationalist assertion. But these conjunctions appear to represent secondary rather than primary causes of persistent nationalism. On the other hand, the more nationalist discourse of Central Asian presidents owes much to their now more optimistic assessment of their states' resource and growth potential.

The two cases of electorally-determined reversals of nationalist agendas are Belarus and Ukraine. Since at the time of independence in 1991 they were characterized by contrasting conjunctural causes, it is logical to assume that it is some characteristic they share that has led each to vote more pro-Russian leaders into power. That characteristic is obviously Slavism. The factors that promoted ethnic mobilization in the late 1980s have failed to sustain nationalism through the 1990s and, apparently, cultural determinants have now overriden them.

There seems to be little or no association, therefore, between variables triggering ethnic mobilization and those needed to maintain it. As a result, it is important to distinguish heuristically between the two sets of conditions that initially give rise to national assertion and those that keep it alive. The chapters in this book have made clear the changing political context of nationalism.

## Patterns of ethnic interaction in post-Soviet space

What have been the dominant patterns of interethnic relations in the area that used to comprise the Soviet Union and that contained over 100 nationalities? The introductory chapter depicted four principal actor-types in the Soviet context (Figure 1.1): the center (Soviet power), first-order titular nationalities (of the union republics), second-order titular nationalities (of the autonomous republics), and non-titular nationalities (peoples without their own administrative status). There were fifteen conceivable dyads connecting the four actor-types (center-center interaction is empirically-vacuous). These could be reduced to six substantive types of interaction: integration, assimilation, liberation, competition, domination, and collusion. Let me synthesize the findings reported in the case studies in terms of this framework of ethnic interaction.

Only central authority – the old USSR – sought integration. It aimed at creating a sovietskii narod which would normatively integrate first- and second-order titular peoples, and it failed in this effort. Since the Soviet breakup, theoretically fifteen new centers of state power have emerged. But political reality suggests otherwise: central power established in the capitals of Georgia, Moldova, Tajikistan – to name the most clearcut cases only – has been unable even to perform the elementary task of territorial integration, let alone national integration. The old political center, in Moscow, has been emasculated and has given up on the project of forging a sovietskii narod, a niesovietskii narod, or even realizing the idea of "e pluribus unum." But this is not to say that it is no longer a center at all. The transformed center in Moscow now strives for political, economic and military integration across much of post-Soviet space. It wields far more power over this space than Brussels does over Europe, if less than it wielded prior to 1991.

Soviet failure at integrating first-order titulars (Lithuanians, Georgians, Uzbeks) was matched by its general failure at integrating second-order titulars: Tatars, Chuvash, Bashkirs and Mari in the Middle Volga; Chechens, Balkars and Karachai (all deported peoples) in the north Caucasus, and Yakuts, Buryats and Tuvans in Siberia. Case studies of these regions suggest that the Russian Federation has also not enjoyed complete success in integrating these autonomous republics.

When the old Soviet center sought assimilation of non-titulars, such as Crimean Tatars, Lithuanian Poles, Volga Germans, or Russian or Moldovan Jews, evidence of some linguistic success was apparent. Crimean Tatars proved exceptional in having a high rate of maternal language retention but, simultaneously, they demonstrated a high rate of knowledge of Russian as a second language. We can suggest, therefore, that central Soviet authority succeeded – and then only partially – when it bullied the weak. With Soviet collapse, bullying by Moscow initially became more difficult and Crimean Tatars and Volga Germans swiftly advanced their own political agendas. One unusual finding in research into second-order titulars was how Soviet authorities sought assimilation of certain groups, but not necessarily into Russian culture. Thus Gail Fondahl described the efforts at "Yakutizing" many peoples of the north, which met with resentment and then resistance.

The interethnic relationship depicted as liberation was characteristic of interaction initiated by first-order titulars towards the center, second-order titulars towards their first-order cohorts, and non-titulars towards all titulars. Chapters in this volume have documented the origins, methods, and strategies of national liberation from Soviet control by the former union republics. Particularly instrumental in undermining the ancient regime was the emancipatory struggle undertaken by the Russian federation under the leadership of President Yeltsin. John Dunlop identified other, more determined Russian nationalists who circumscribed Yeltsin's ability to manoeuvre on nationality issues. Processes of nation-building (following in-migration beginning in 1976 and accelerating in the late 1980s) and state-building (setting up the same republic institutions in Russia that other republics had had for many years) provided the basis for attaining Russian statehood. Simultaneously, among Russia's own minority peoples, Chechens and Tatars led the way in seeking their own liberation from Moscow's rule. And while the Russian military was ordered to quash the Chechen secession in 1994, Dunlop's chapter documents how Russian public opinion was split on the issue of using troops to manage hot spots in the near abroad.

In the case of Ukraine, Bohdan Krawchenko and Alexander Motyl described how an acute sense of economic exploitation propelled the liberation struggle. As in the Baltic republics, nationalist and democratic movements coalesced and expanded the agenda of liberation into national as well as political freedom. As Krawchenko and Motyl make clear, Ukraine's first president, Leonid Kravchuk, was particularly imaginative in the realm of institution-building – a critical aspect in consolidating statehood.

In Belarus, national liberation was given momentum by the republic's economic development producing industrialization and urbanization. Jan Zaprudnik and Michael Urban highlighted the importance of the native language in nation-building, but they also referred to the impact of revelations made in 1988 about mass executions carried out under Stalin which created a Belarus martyrology. In assessing political developments since independence, the authors stressed the reserve and skepticism that average Belarusans began to harbor about their young democractic system and new state. Moldova's national struggle was wracked by the problem of Gagauz and Transdniestrian separatism, which was aided and abetted by patrons in Moscow, as William Crowther showed. The government of Moldova responded by adopting a flexible approach designed to reduce the level of ethnic hostility within the country. Seeking to allay fears on the part of its minorities that it might become a nationalist Romanian state, Moldova enacted a constitution in 1994 that established Moldovan rather than Romanian as the national language.

The Baltic republics had led the struggle of nations for independence from the USSR, and Lithuania had led the Baltic peoples. Lithuania's deep-felt desire for liberation from the Soviet center was grounded in several key factors: its historic identity and attendant emotional attachments (thereby making explanations centering on economic exploitation or repressive Soviet policies second-order causes); its earlier experience of statehood (not just in the interwar period but as part of a commonwealth with Poland in the sixteenth century); and widespread perceptions of Russification. Given such powerful motivations for statehood, Alfred Senn argued that the country's first president, Vytautas Landsbergis, seemed unconcerned with creating state institutions. In neighboring Latvia, the fact that the republic's ruling Communist Party did not even have a Latvian majority made the sense of being ruled from without more acute. Nils Muznieks pointed out, in addition, that violence used by Soviet troops to produce submission of Latvian nationalists itself affected the pathway of Latvian nationalism. While an agreement on Russian troop withdrawal was signed in 1994, the Latvian authorities faced other problems with Russia, in particular, their alleged disenfranchisement of the Russian minority and the adoption of a tough citizenship law requiring non-Latvians to demonstrate command of the Latvian language. Toivo Raun also underscored Estonia's historical experience, especially memories of the independent interwar republic, as a catalyst for the independence struggle. The demonstration effect produced by other anti-Soviet movements in the region was crucial, too, as was the national symbolism of solidarity and awakening. Raun thus stressed the interconnectedness of the liberation struggles and, in the post-Soviet period, of small state efforts to achieve national security and international integration.

The thrust for liberation from the center characterized the Transcaucasus as well. Shireen Hunter described the rich history of Azerbaijan, the efforts made to rediscover the past, often requiring mythification of history and identity, and the competing influences of Iran and Turkey. But she also brought attention to the efforts made by the Yeltsin administration to rein in Azerbaijan and take the oil weapon out of its hands. Nora Dudwick chronicled the methods used by Armenians to expand the domain of per-missible nationalism throughout the Soviet period, but she also pointed to the country's long-standing relationship with Russia, serving as insurance against Turkish revanchism. Despite some success in the war in Nagorno-Karabagh, Armenia remained relatively weak militarily as well as economi-cally, casting a shadow on its regained independence. The third new state in the Caucasus faced the greatest difficulties in asserting its political independence. Thinly-disguised Russian intervention in Georgia's internal politics and in its civil war with the Abkhazians left the Shevardnadze leadership unable to exert control over its own territory. Stephen Jones traced the "Georgianization" program pursued by onetime leader Gamsakhurdia and showed how its insensitivity to minority rights backfired against the authorities in Tbilisi.

While the Central Asian republics of the former USSR did not engage in large-scale ethnic mobilization for sovereignty before 1991, they have since been busy establishing political structures and cultivating a sense of nationhood. Kazakhs are a minority in their own territory and as with other states possessing regions with disaffected ethnic groups (Transdniestria, Abkhazia, Crimea) they are susceptible to Russian meddling in the country. Even if demography is on its side, as Martha Olcott noted, Kazakhstan is marked more by its Soviet pedigree than most of the other new states. At the same time, President Nazabarev has been very active in seeking new forms of regional cooperation as well as trying to maintain links with Russia (as through the ruble zone).

Internal ethnic fragmentation also characterized Uzbekistan when it found itself an independent state. Gregory Gleason considered that greater contestation occurred among groups within the country than had taken place between Tashkent and Moscow. He provided an extended list of territorial disputes existing between various groups in Central Asia and cautioned about the potential for conflict, especially between Uzbeks and Russian minorities, the Kyrgyz, and the Tajiks.

In the case of Tajikistan, statehood brought in its wake a a bloody civil war in 1992 that opposed ex-communist elites and a democratic opposition. Both sides exploited Islamic fundamentalism, regional divisions, and non-Tajik minorities for their own purposes. Muriel Atkin made clear that it was inaccurate to cast the civil war as a clash between traditional clans or between communists and fundamentalists. She also drew attention to the irony of a civil war being fought in a Tajik territorial state that, like Tajik political-national identity itself, was a Soviet creation. Independence left Tajikstan with neighbors it did not trust, an economy that was not self-sufficient, and social and environmental problems not resolvable by a small country on its own.

The inhabitants of Turkmenistan, too, were largely unclear about their nationhood when statehood unexpectedly arrived. David Nissman stressed how language was turned into an instrument intended to catalyse a national identity. Embryonic post-independence "nationalist" orientation was also exemplified by increased contacts with co-nationals in Afghanistan and Iran. While making some inroads into national integration, politically Turkmenistan remained a highly-authoritarian state.

A variety of factors accounted for the emergence of nationalist sentiment in Kyrgyzstan, according to Eugene Huskey. These included demographic and economic frustrations of the Kyrgyz, the related phenomena of large-scale Slav immigration, urban centers with non-Kyrgyz majorities, the declining status of the Kyrgyz language, and an increasing sense of economic inefficacy. While remaining close politically to Yeltsin, President Akaev became aware of the need to engage in the nation- and state-building that was a functional requirement of independence.

In summary, the majority of the titular nations of the former Soviet republics engaged in struggles for liberation from the center, then with independence, often faced struggles for greater political independence by the minorities found on their territories. Within the Russian Federation, before the Chechnya secession flared up, disturbances had already occurred in Sakha. Tatars number close to seven million but were persuaded to sign a treaty with Moscow that considerably expanded their political autonomy but kept them within the Federation structure. It remains unclear whether such asymmetrical solutions to subnationalist assertion within Russia defuse or incite minority claims for expanded rights. We still do not know whether peoples whose identities are very distinct (Chuvash, Mari), who are sizeable (Bashkirs, Mordovians), or who are sitting on enormous natural resources (Yakuts and other peoples of Siberia) are likely to press for political liberation from the new Moscow center. The Chechen precedent may be misleading since this nationality group in the north Caucasus was traditionally regarded by Russians and others in the region as exceptionally determined.

The ethnic competition that characterized relations between titular nations of the Soviet republics now involves, of course, competition for allies, trading partners, and markets in the international arena. The war between Armenia and Azerbaijan over Karabagh is a rare post-Soviet case of military struggle between newly-independent states. In general, the case studies of the Baltics and Central Asia revealed a remarkable degree of cooperation among the republics preceding the Soviet collapse. Other examples from this period included Belarus cooperation with Lithuania and, most significantly, common interests pressed in Ukraine and Russia by democratic forces. But if the thrust of Soviet power made interrepublican cooperation a possibility in the Gorbachev era, more recent events show less reason for optimism. Despite the creation of the Commonwealth of Independent States precisely for the purpose of encouraging greater cooperation among the member-states, differing national interests have impeded realization of this objective.

The chapters on Russia's minorities also furnish considerable evidence of competition among them: Tatars and Chuvash, Chuvash and Mari, Chechens and Ingush, Ingush and Ossetians, Yakuts and other peoples of Siberia. Alan Frank and Ronald Wixman remarked on how Soviet policy sought to diminish Tatar influence in the Middle Volga region through support of the Chuvash. Jane Ormrod showed how Soviet dissolution of the North Caucasus Mountain Republic in 1924 constituted an effort to split up rebellious groups. In time the peoples of the North Caucasus were drawn into conflicts on the basis of national identities that had begun as ethno-linguistic designations and which still had little resonance in popular consciousness. Just as the Soviet central authorities regularly scripted competition between neighboring groups where cooperation might otherwise have developed, so the Chechen case suggests how the Russian Federation has prevented regional solidarity from taking shape.

Domination may often be the objective of titular nations in relations with their minorities. In the Soviet period the hierarchy of nations was embodied in constitutional provisions according different status to groups within a republic. Grievances expressed since 1991 by Tatars, Buryats, Germans, and Jews suggest that they have felt oppressed not only under Soviet power but also within the framework of the Russian Federation. Abkhazians in Georgia, Gagauz in Moldova, Poles in Lithuania, and Russians in many of the new states also claim oppression by their new overlords. Predictably, collusion also commonly appeared between an aspiring central power and the ethnically dispossessed. This book has indicated how, in the mid-1990s, a resurgent Russia colluded with minorities to destabilize politics in many of the successor states.

## Ethnic conflict and international relations

Is it true to say that what were only a short time ago the internal affairs of the USSR have since become transformed into foreign policy issues for the new states of the kind found in interstate relations in other parts of the world? Related to this, since nationalism was central in the Soviet collapse, what does international relations tell us about the metamorphosis of ethnic-based conflicts into international problems?

Ethnic conflict is the dominant form of contemporary political violence and occurs in most parts of the world.[28] Stephen Ryan described how such conflict was commonplace in the first world, manifested as ethnic revival; in the second world, triggered by erosion of central authority; and in the third world, saddled with the legacy of decolonization (artificial borders, dominant cultural groups as neo-colonizers).[29] He then outlined how regional powers became involved in ethnic disturbances. From our case studies we observed how such states as Turkey, Iran, and Afghanistan were drawn in varying degrees into the politics of the Caucasus and Central Asia. Both the United Nations and the Organization for Security and Cooperation in Europe sought to mediate ethnic conflicts in places like Chechnya, Nagorno-Karabagh, and Tajikistan. In the new states of Europe, NATO's Partnership for Peace program is often viewed as the first step in extending a Western security umbrella over the Baltic region, Ukraine, Belarus, and Moldova. Many of the smaller, more vulnerable ethnic groups appeal for support for their cause to the West when an appeal to Russia is impractical or undesirable.

In linking nationalist assertion to international conflict, James Mayall captured the paradoxical and contradictory nature of this relationship: "Ostensibly, the world has been made safe for nationalism," yet "the ideal of 'true' popular national sovereignty has never been wholly domesticated." If it had been, Mayall pursued, then a world consisting of about 8,000 identifiably separate cultures would not have been compressed into under 200 independent states.[30]

The implications of ethnic-based conflicts for international politics are very serious. Such conflicts within Russia and the neighboring new states have more potential to become internationalized, thereby generating international conflicts, "not because aggression by states has become less likely, but because conflicts within many states have become more likely."[31]

The internationalization of ethnic conflict may occur under any of the following sets of conditions. First, protracted ethnic conflicts within states may spill over into the international arena by tempting "outside powers to intervene in these conflicts to pursue their own self-interest. . . ."[32] Such outside intervention might trigger the intensification of the conflict into a wider regional war. Second, in cases where an ethnic group is spread over more than one state but is a majority in none, ethnic conflict in one state may have a spill over effect in another state with a similar ethnic minority, which may either support its co-nationals in their struggle and put pressure on its own state to take measures to help them or try to make common cause with its co-nationals. Third, conflict can arise in situations "where a dominant group in one state is separated from co-nationals, who make up a minority group in one or more other states," causing it to pursue an aggressive irredentist policy with the aim of redrawing the territorial and political boundaries of the state and redeeming its lost co-nationals. Ill-treatment of fellow nationals in another state and their "right" of self-determination are the common justifications offered for irredentism. Fourth, ethnic conflicts can spill over into the international arena through international terrorism. Increasingly, disaffected ethnic groups have resorted to terrorism in their efforts to seek concessions from whoever they are struggling against and to publicize their cause internationally. Fifth, ethnic conflicts frequently become internationalized because groups with irredentist or secessionist demands actively seek outside support. "Since ethnic groups are rarely able successfully to confront intransigent state authorities, they need external allies."[33] External allies often provide diplomatic, financial, and military support to such groups; in rare cases, as in Afghan support for anti-communist Tajik rebels, even armed intervention may be provided. Finally, internal ethnic conflicts often get internationalized through refugee flows. Massive influx of refugees who flee their own state for fear of persecution creates two different kinds of problems for the receiving state. Myron Weiner writes:

> To grant a refugee political asylum on the grounds of persecution is, of course, to condemn the state which has been persecuting its citizens. But far more conflictual is the massive refugee influx which imposes a large economic and political burden upon the receiving country.[34]

This has been one justification for external intervention in the affairs of the country producing the refugees.

The most immediate impact of ethnic nationalist movements has been on state- and nation-building in multinational societies like Russia, Ukraine or Georgia, mainly in the form of separatism and demand for independence. Such demands have often been justified by those making it in the name of ethnic separateness and the right of national self-determination.

Since ethnic conflicts are potentially dangerous for international security and are deeply connected with issues of war and peace, human rights, and growing democratization after the end of the Cold War, in recent years the literature on ethnic nationalism and conflict has increasingly focused on the hitherto neglected international dimension. An area where research has just begun involves the use of the concept of the security dilemma and realist international theory as well as imperatives of national security to "explain and predict the probability and intensity of military conflict among groups emerging from the wreckage of empires."[35] In this context, Barry Posen's work on the emergence of ethno-nationalist and religious conflicts among recently independent states in the Eurasian region is an important contribution.

The author analyses the linkage between the security dilemma of states and inter-state ethnic conflict within the context of an "emerging anarchy" as a result of the breakdown or dissolution of imperial order. Posen's argument is that in a situation of emerging anarchy (which the breakup of the imperial communist regimes created in the Eurasian region) the primary concern of the successor "entities" (states as well as host of groups that aspire for statehood) is security. Since the key to security is power, these entities are in natural competition for power. This intense competition for power in turn creates the security dilemma and leads to ethnic conflict between these successor entities.

Posen argues that the security dilemma becomes intense as a result of two factors. First, it becomes difficult for states to signal their defensive intention (i.e., limited objectives) when their offensive and defensive military forces are more or less identical. Since the military technology and organization (often taken as the main factor distinguishing offense and defense) of the successor groups is likely to be rudimentary, their military strength becomes largely a function of their "groupness" or "cohesion."

Because the cohesiveness or groupness of the collectivities are likely to be more than the empires they emerge from, this is likely to provide them an inherent offensive military capability. But because all sides are likely to stress their groupness and cohesion, each might seem threatening to the other. In this atmosphere, the only way to assess the intentions of other groups is to use the knowledge of history; assessments which, given prevailing conditions, would rarely meet objective scholarly standards. The result, as Posen argues, is a "worst-case analysis" where every group thinks the others are its enemies.

The second factor which intensifies the security dilemma is the belief in the superiority of offensive over defensive action. This is affected by technology and geography. Technology is a crucial variable in the offense-defense balance. Political geography is a situational variable which often provides an offensive advantage and an incentive for preventive war. In the context of the dissolution of empires, recovering ethnic enclaves inhabited by one's ethnic kin might provide the incentive for rapid offensive military action. At the same time, the tactical offensive advantage which an ever-expanding area of homogeneous population provides may induce a group to "ethnically cleanse" (i.e., induce the other group's population to leave) areas it controls.

This intense security dilemma is further linked to the groups' sense of opportunity or vulnerability. In either case the outcome is offensive military action in order to press home a temporary military advantage or to acquire a military advantage before the other side has time to shore up its forces. The preoccupation of great powers and international organizations with other pressing matters might provide further incentive for offensive military action. The outcome of this security dilemma, then, Posen suggests, is intense ethnic conflict among the successor states and groups in the aftermath of the collapse of imperial order.

Posen's work provides a dynamic model linking causal inputs from the external environment (in his case inputs affecting state or group security) with the outbreak of intense nationalism among and offensive or aggressive behavior by states/groups. However, his focus on inter-state conflict in the context of the collapse of imperial order may be excessively delimited by the contextual features of the collapse. Our case studies highlight the many variants of nationalist assertion and their transformation over time. We can advance the important, if prosaic, conclusion that some nations' security dilemmas are more acute and more enduring than those of other nations.

It is how Russia has defined its security dilemma in different terms throughout the 1990s that has most markedly affected ethnic war and peace in Eurasia. From the initial starting point under Yeltsin of recognizing the international equality of all the successor states, Russia has subsequently regarded international relations in the Soviet successor states as not of the same variety as international relations occurring in other parts of the world. For increasingly-revanchist Russian leaders, the states of the "near abroad" are more than just Russia's natural sphere of influence, if not any more merely Soviet gubernates. Indeed, for these leaders, it is the refusal to recognize the international aspect of ethnic conflict that is key to their political mindset. And that, in turn, hardens the resolve of many of these nations not to be drawn completely into Russia's orbit. The struggle over interpretative paradigms is, therefore, part of the wider struggle for power and independence among the successor states.

## NOTES

1 Ernest Gellner, *Encounters with Nationalism* (Oxford: Blackwell, 1994), pp. xi–xii.
2 Anthony D. Smith, *National Identity* (Reno, NV: University of Nevada Press, 1991), p. 170.
3 Conor Cruise O'Brien, *God's Land: Religion and Nationalism.* (Cambridge, MA: Harvard University Press, 1988), p. 80.
4 Daniel Patrick Moynihan, *Pandaemonium: Ethnicity in International Politics* (New York: Oxford University Press, 1994), p. 24.
5 William Pfaff, *The Wrath of Nations: Civilization and the Furies of Nationalism* (New York: Touchstone Books, 1993), pp. 40, 30.
6 Liah Greenfeld, *Nationalism: Five Roads to Modernity* (Cambridge, MA: Harvard University Press, 1992), p. 11.
7 Rogers Brubaker, *Citizenship and Nationhood in France and Germany* (Cambridge, MA: Harvard University Press, 1992), Michael Ignatieff, *Blood and Belonging: Journeys into the New Nationalism* (New York: Farrar, Straus, and Giroux, 1993).
8 Martin Buber, "Should the Ichud Accept the Decree of History?" in Paul R. Mendes-Flohr (ed.), *A Land of Two Peoples: Martin Buber on Jews and Arabs* (Oxford: Oxford University Press, 1983), p. 250.
9 Martin Buber, "Nationalism," in Buber. *Israel and the World: Essays in a Time of Crisis* (New York: Schocken, 1978), p. 25.
10 Martin Buber, "The Gods of the Nations and God," in Buber, *Israel and the World* p. 198.
11 Buber, "Nationalism," in *Israel and the World* p. 221.
12 Michael Walzer, *The Company of Critics: Social Criticism and Political Commitment in the Twentieth Century* (New York: Basic Books, 1988), p. 66.
13 The rediscovered (and reprinted) earlier texts include: John Breuilly, *Nationalism and the State* (Chicago: University of Chicago Press, 1993). Eric Hobsbawm, *Nations and Nationalism Since 1780* (New York: Cambridge University Press, 1990). Hugh Seton–Watson, *Nations and States: An Enquiry into the Origins of Nations and the Politics of Nationalism* (Boulder, CO: Westview Press, 1977). A return to earlier scholarship has been facilitated by the publication of compendiums, notably, Omar Dahbour and Micheline R. Ishay, eds., *The Nationalism Reader* (Atlantic Highlands, NJ: Humanities Press, 1995).
14 Ragin, *The Comparative Method* p. 11.
15 Ragin, *The Comparative Method,* p. 134. Three expositions of the developmental perspective are Clifford Geertz, *Old Societies and New States: The Quest for Modernity in Asia and Africa* (New York: Free Press, 1963); Talcott Parsons, "Some Theoretical Considerations on the Nature and Trends of Change of Ethnicity," in Nathan Glazer and Daniel Moynihan, eds., *Ethnicity: Theory and Experience* (Cambridge: Harvard University Press, 1975), pp. 56–71; Stein Rokkan, *Citizens, Elections, Parties* (New York: McKay, 1970).

16  Ragin, *The Comparative Method*, p. 135. Elucidation of the reactive ethnicity perspective can be found in Ernst Gellner, *Thought and Change* (Chicago: University of Chicago Press, 1969); and Michael Hechter, *International Colonialism: The Celtic Fringe in British National Development* (London: Routledge and Kegan Paul, 1975).

17  The strength of reactive ethnicity is associated in large measure with the strength of central oppression. But was anti-Sovietism stongest in those republics where Stalinism was most brutal? For a start in making this connection, see Jim Nichol, *Stalin's Crimes Against the Non-Russian Nations: The 1987–1990 Revelations and Debate* (Pittsburgh: University of Pittsburgh, Carl Beck Papers in Russian and East European Studies, 1991), no. 906. For national grievances articulated in speeches at the May–June 1989 Congress of Peoples' Deputies session that could be compared in terms of reactive ethnicity, see Oleg Glebov and John Crowfoot, eds., *The Soviet Empire: Its Nations Speak Out* (London: Harwood Academic Publishers, 1989).

18  Ragin, *The Comparative Method*, p. 136. Examples of the ethnic competition approach include Michael Hannan, "The Dynamics of Ethnic Boundaries in Modern States," in Hannan and John Meyer, eds., *National Development and the World System* (Chicago: University of Chicago Press, 1979), pp. 253–277; Francois Nielsen, "Toward a Theory of Ethnic Solidarity in Modern Societies," *American Sociological Review* 50, 1985, 133–149. The resource mobilization view is described in Charles Tilly's magisterial *From Mobilization to Revolution* (Reading, MA: Addison-Wesley, 1978).

19.  See 1959 through 1989 data on nationality language use in table 4 of Graham Smith (ed.) *The Nationalities Question in the Soviet Union* (New York: Longman, 1990), pp. 366–367. Only Belarus, as reported in this table as well as in Urban and Zaprudnik's chapter, had cause for linguistic insecurity.

20  The source for these data is table 2 on average annual growth of national income and industrial production by republic reported by Gertrude E. Shroeder, "Nationalities and the Soviet Economy," in Lubomyr Hajda and Mark Beissinger, eds., *The Nationalities Factor in Soviet Politics and Society* (Boulder, CO: Westview Press, 1990), p. 47. If personal income distribution was used, the coding would not vary; see Table 8 of Smith, *The Nationalities Question*, p. 371. Note that Ukraine's national income (as well as personal income) was just marginally below the Soviet average. If we also take into account that the significant interval is between Ukraine and the republic ranked below it (Azerbaijan), Ukraine should be coded 1 on relative wealth.

21  A source on per capita consumption is Table 4 of Schroeder, "Nationalities and the Soviet Economy," p. 51. If instead of rate of change, relative levels of per capita consumption were employed, differences would be seen to have widened in the 25-year period, in particular between the Baltics at one end of the spectrum and Central Asia on the other. But republic rankings remained very stable over this time.

22  Schroeder, "Nationalities and the Soviet Economy," pp. 52–53. My source for republic levels of gross fixed investment per capita, 1961–65 to 1981–85 compared, is Table 5 of Schroeder, p. 53.

23  SHWG is combined with sHWG to produce HWG; ShWg is combined with shWg to produce hWg; and SHwg is combined with sHWg to produce sHg.

24  Ragin suggested that when faced with such contradictions, we should search for an additional variable to include in the causal combination. One possible factor might be industrial or agrarian society. Thus wealth, combined with homogeneity, growth and an agricultural economy could produce mobilization (Belarus, Lithuania) as when it was combined with no homogeneity, no growth, but sizeable industrial enclaves. (Estonia, Ukraine). For more on resolving contradictions in Boolean analysis, see Ragin, *The Comparative Method*, pp. 113–118.

25  *Ibid.*, p. 101.

26  *Ibid.*, p. 170.

27  *Ibid.*, p. 149.

28 For an overview, see Rodolfo Stavenhagen, "Les conflits ethniques et leur impact sur la societe internationale," in *Revue Internationale des Sciences Sociales*, no. 127. (Fevrier 1991), pp. 123–138.

29 Stephen Ryan, *Ethnic Conflict and International Relations* (Aldershot: Dartmouth Publishing, 1990) pp. x-xi.

30 James Mayall, *Nationalism and International Society* (Cambridge: Cambridge University Press, 1991), pp. 50, 64.

31 Myron Weiner, "Peoples and States In a New Ethnic Order?," *Third World Quarterly*, vol. 13, no. 2 1992, p. 320.

32 Ryan, *Ethnic Conflict and International Relations*, p. 22.

33 *Ibid.*, p. 222.

34 Weiner, "Peoples and States In a New Ethnic Order?," p. 221.

35 Barry R. Posen, "The Security Dilemma and Ethnic Conflict," *Survival* vol. 35, no. 1 Spring 1993, p. 43.

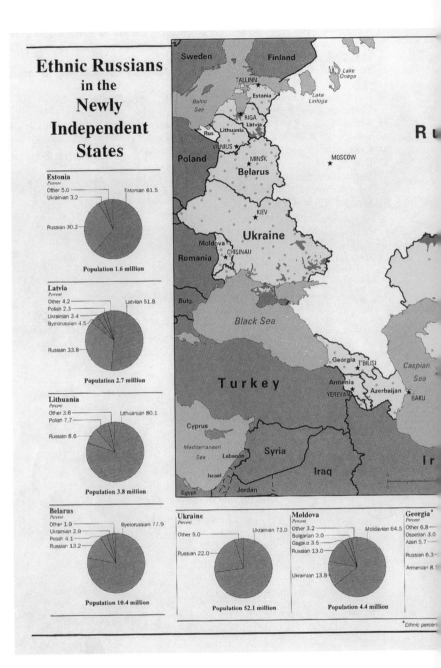

# Ethnic Russians in the Newly Independent States

### Estonia
*Percent*

Other 5.0
Ukrainian 3.2
Estonian 61.5
Russian 30.3

**Population 1.6 million**

### Latvia
*Percent*

Other 4.2
Polish 2.3
Ukrainian 3.4
Byelorussian 4.5
Latvian 51.8
Russian 33.8

**Population 2.7 million**

### Lithuania
*Percent*

Other 3.6
Polish 7.7
Lithuanian 80.1
Russian 8.6

**Population 3.8 million**

### Belarus
*Percent*

Other 1.9
Ukrainian 2.9
Polish 4.1
Russian 13.2
Byelorussian 77.9

**Population 10.4 million**

### Ukraine
*Percent*

Other 5.0
Ukrainian 73.0
Russian 22.0

**Population 52.1 million**

### Moldova
*Percent*

Other 3.2
Bulgarian 2.0
Gagauz 3.5
Russian 13.0
Ukrainian 13.8
Moldavian 64.5

**Population 4.4 million**

### Georgia*
*Percent*

Other 6.8
Ossetian 3.0
Azeri 5.7
Russian 6.3
Armenian 8.5

*Ethnic percen

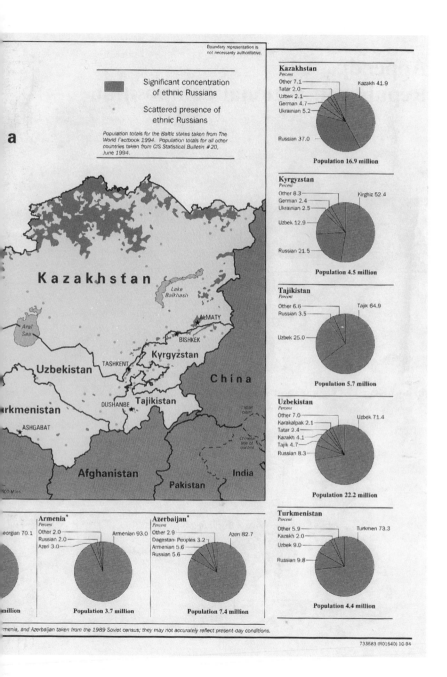

Boundary representation is not necessarily authoritative.

Significant concentration of ethnic Russians

Scattered presence of ethnic Russians

Population totals for the Baltic states taken from The World Factbook 1994. Population totals for all other countries taken from CIS Statistical Bulletin #20, June 1994.

a

**Kazakhstan**
Percent
Other 7.1 — Kazakh 41.9
Tatar 2.0
Uzbek 2.1
German 4.7
Ukrainian 5.2
Russian 37.0
Population 16.9 million

**Kyrgyzstan**
Percent
Other 8.3 — Kirghiz 52.4
German 2.4
Ukrainian 2.5
Uzbek 12.9
Russian 21.5
Population 4.5 million

**Tajikistan**
Percent
Other 6.6 — Tajik 64.9
Russian 3.5
Uzbek 25.0
Population 5.7 million

**Uzbekistan**
Percent
Other 7.0 — Uzbek 71.4
Karakalpak 2.1
Tatar 2.4
Kazakh 4.1
Tajik 4.7
Russian 8.3
Population 22.2 million

**Turkmenistan**
Percent
Other 5.9 — Turkmen 73.3
Kazakh 2.0
Uzbek 9.0
Russian 9.8
Population 4.4 million

Kazakhstan
Lake Balkhash
ALMATY
BISHKEK
Kyrgyzstan
TASHKENT
Uzbekistan
China
Aral Sea
rkmenistan
DUSHANBE Tajikistan
ASHGABAT
Indian claim
Chinese line of control
Afghanistan India
Pakistan

**Armenia***
Percent
eorgian 70.1
Other 2.0 — Armenian 93.0
Russian 2.0
Azeri 3.0
million
Population 3.7 million

**Azerbaijan***
Percent
Other 2.9 — Azeri 82.7
Dagestani Peoples 3.2
Armenian 5.6
Russian 5.6
Population 7.4 million

menia, and Azerbaijan taken from the 1989 Soviet census; they may not accurately reflect present-day conditions.

733583 (R01640) 10-94

# Appendix A
# Republican national composition

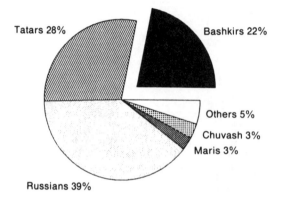

1. Bashkhortostan 1989 population 3,043,133

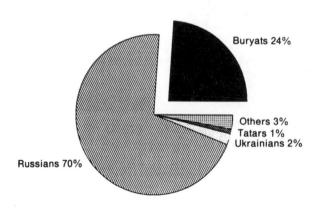

2. Buryatia 1989 population 1,038,252

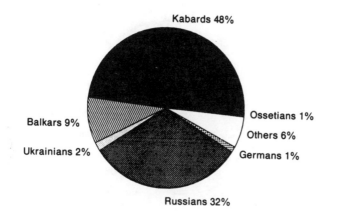

**3. Kabardino-Balkaria 1989 population 753,531**

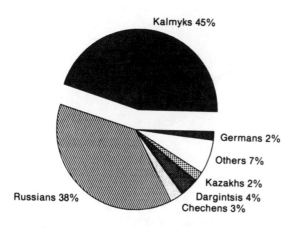

**4. Kalmykia 1989 population 322,579**

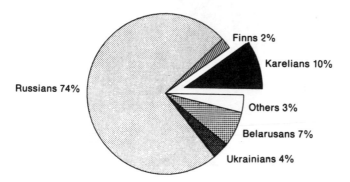

**5. Karelia 1989 population 790,150**

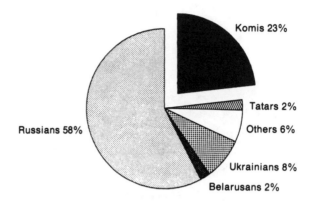

6. Komi ASSR 1989 population 1,250,847

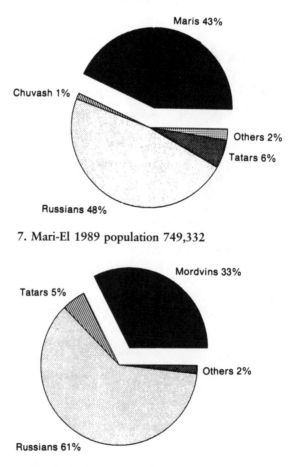

7. Mari-El 1989 population 749,332

8. Mordovia 1989-population 963,504

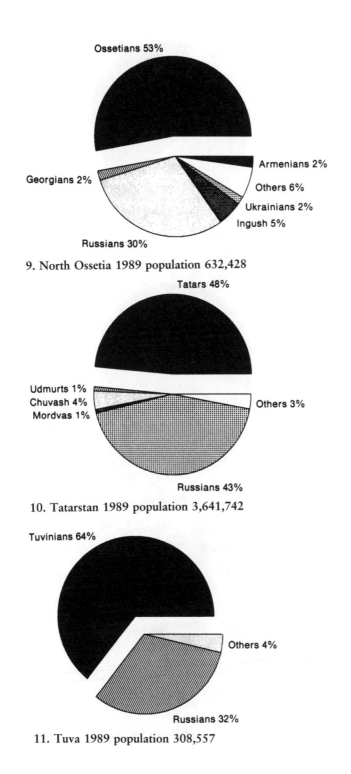

Ossetians 53%

Armenians 2%

Georgians 2%

Others 6%

Ukrainians 2%

Ingush 5%

Russians 30%

9. North Ossetia 1989 population 632,428

Tatars 48%

Udmurts 1%
Chuvash 4%
Mordvas 1%

Others 3%

Russians 43%

10. Tatarstan 1989 population 3,641,742

Tuvinians 64%

Others 4%

Russians 32%

11. Tuva 1989 population 308,557

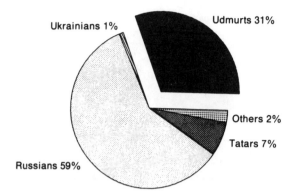

12. Udmurtia 1989 population 1,605,663

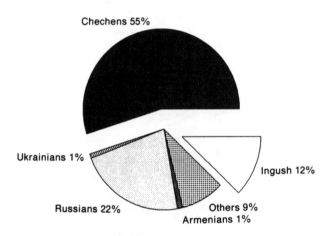

13. Chechen-Ingushetia 1989 population 1,338,023

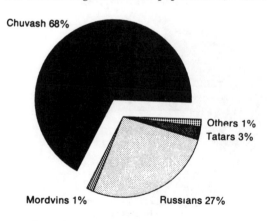

14. Chuvashia 1989 population 1,338,023

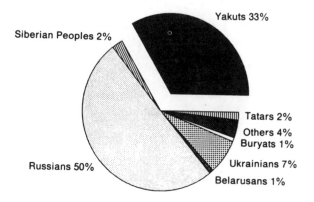

**15. Sakha 1989 population 1,094,065**

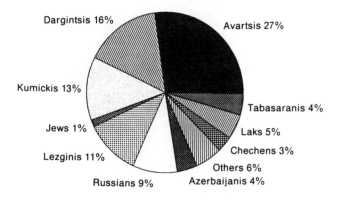

**16. Dagestan 1989 population 1,802,188**

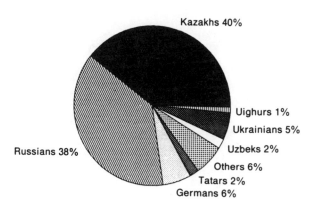

**17. Kazakhstan 1989 population 16,463,115**

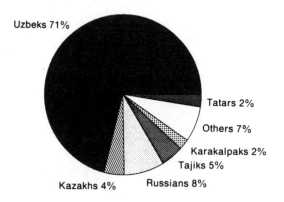

Uzbeks 71%

Tatars 2%

Others 7%

Karakalpaks 2%

Tajiks 5%

Kazakhs 4%

Russians 8%

18. Uzbekistan 1989 population 19,808,077

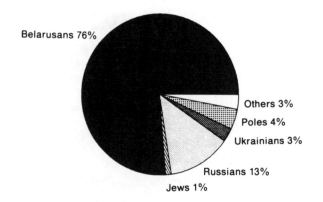

Belarusans 76%

Others 3%

Poles 4%

Ukrainians 3%

Russians 13%

Jews 1%

19. Belarus 1989 population 10,149,248

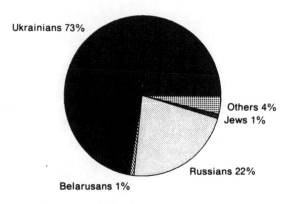

Ukrainians 73%

Others 4%

Jews 1%

Russians 22%

Belarusans 1%

20. Ukraine 1989 population 51,449,479

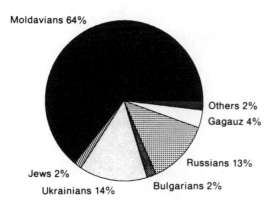

Moldavians 64%

Others 2%

Gagauz 4%

Russians 13%

Jews 2%

Ukrainians 14%   Bulgarians 2%

**21. Moldova 1989 population 4,322,363**

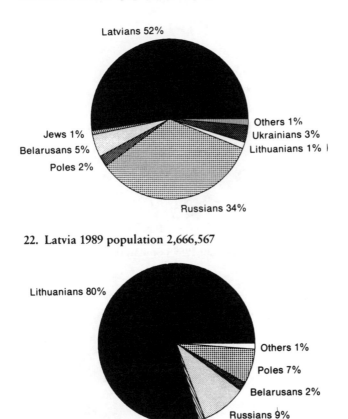

Latvians 52%

Others 1%

Jews 1%

Ukrainians 3%

Belarusans 5%

Lithuanians 1% |

Poles 2%

Russians 34%

**22. Latvia 1989 population 2,666,567**

Lithuanians 80%

Others 1%

Poles 7%

Belarusans 2%

Russians 9%

Ukrainians 1%

**23. Lithuania 1989 population 3,673,362**

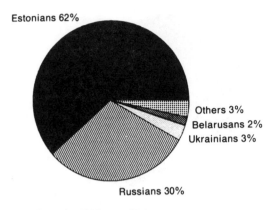

Estonians 62%

Others 3%
Belarusans 2%
Ukrainians 3%

Russians 30%

24. Estonia 1989 population 1,565,662

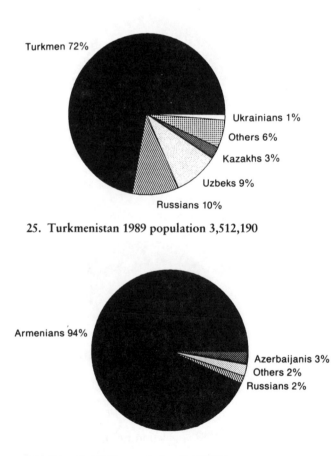

Turkmen 72%

Ukrainians 1%
Others 6%
Kazakhs 3%
Uzbeks 9%

Russians 10%

25. Turkmenistan 1989 population 3,512,190

Armenians 94%

Azerbaijanis 3%
Others 2%
Russians 2%

26. Armenia 1989 population 3,304,353

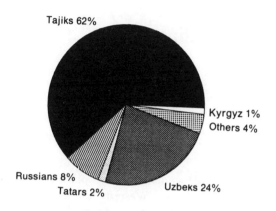

27. Tajikistan 1989 population 5,089,593

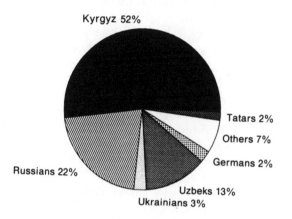

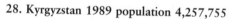

28. Kyrgyzstan 1989 population 4,257,755

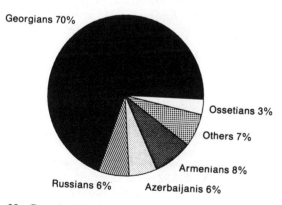

29. Georgia 1989 population 5,395,841

# Further reading

The creation of fifteen independent states in place of the Soviet Union has changed the research agenda for Western scholars. Where studies of the center made most sense in the past and research on "peripheral" nations was treated as indeed peripheral to the field of Soviet studies, examination of the new countries is the future of the new wave of scholars who specialize in the post-Soviet nations.

The list below is selective, encompassing book-length studies published over the past two decades that focus primarily on the political aspects of nationality questions. Corresponding in large measure to the organization of this volume, the bibliography is divided into parts treating the Soviet center, Russia and its nations, the Baltics, the new Eastern Europe, the Caucasus and Central Asia. Some of the books included under the center are comparative studies of two or more republics that are usually informed by "top-down" or "outside-in" perspectives. Several guides to nations of the USSR and to Marxist theories of nationalism are also included in this section.

Since the collapse of the Soviet Union, scholars have begun to redress the balance that for many years had weighed in favor of the perspective from Moscow. Many new monographs have been written on the politics of the post-Soviet states. Russia's politics has, of course, received special attention but political science research on the other countries has also expanded. Looking to the future, cross-national comparative research (shorn of the Moscow perspective) will likely prove one of the most interesting fields of inquiry for post-Soviet scholars.

## The Center

Amalrik, Andrei. *Will the Soviet Union Survive Until 1984?* New York: Harper and Row, 1970.

Azrael, Jeremy R. (ed.). *Soviet Nationality Policies and Practices.* New York: Praeger, 1978.

Bahry, Donna. *Outside Moscow: Power, Politics, and Budgetary Policy in the Soviet Republics.* New York: Columbia University Press, 1987.

Bialer, Seweryn (ed.). *Politics, Society, and Nationality inside Gorbachev's Russia.* Boulder, CO: Westview Press, 1989.

Bremmer, Ian and Norman Naimark (eds.). *Soviet Nationalities Problems.* Stanford, CA: Center for Russian and East European Studies, 1990.

Bremmer, Ian and Ray Taras (eds.). *Nations and Politics in the Soviet Successor States.* Cambridge: Cambridge University Press, 1993.

Buttino, Marco, *In a Collapsing Empire: Underdevelopment, Ethnic Conlfcts, and Nationalisms in the Soviet Union.* Milano: Fondazione Giangiacomo Feltrinelli, 1993.

Carrere d'Encausse, Helene. *Decline of Empire: The Soviet Socialist Republics in Revolt.* New York: Newsweek Books, 1979.

Carrere d'Encausse, Helene. *The End of the Soviet Empire: The Triumph of the Nations.* New York: Basic Books, 1993.

Colton, Timothy J. and Robert Legvold, *After the Soviet Union: From Empire to Nations.* New York: WW Norton, 1992.

Conner, Walter. *The National Question in Marxist-Leninist Theory and Strategy.* Princeton, NJ: Princeton University Press, 1984.

Conquest, Robert (ed.). *The Last Empire: Nationality and the Soviet Future.* Stanford, CA: Hoover Institution Press, 1986.

Denber, Rachel (ed.). *The Soviet Nationality Reader.* Boulder, CO: Westview Press, 1992.

Diuk, Nadia and Adrian Karatnycky. *The Hidden Nations: The People Challenge the Soviet Union.* New York: William Morrow, 1990.

Diuk, Nadia and Adrian Karatnycky, *New Nations Rising.* New York: John Wiley & Sons, 1993.

Gleason, Gregory. *Federalism and Nationalism: The Struggle for Republican Rights in the USSR.* Boulder, CO: Westview Press, 1990.

Glebov, Oleg and John Crowfoot (eds.). *The Soviet Empire: Its Nations Speak Out.* London: Harwood Academic Publishers, 1989.

Hajda, Lubomyr and Mark Beissinger (eds.). *The Nationalities Factor in Soviet Politics and Society.* Boulder, CO: Westview Press, 1990.

Huttenbach, Henry R. (ed.). *Soviet Nationality Policies: Ruling Ethnic Groups in the USSR.* London: Mansell Publishing Company, 1990.

Kaser, Robert J. *The Geography of of Nationalism in Russia and the USSR.* Princeton: Princeton University Press, 1994.

Karklins, Rasma. *Ethnic Relations in the USSR: The Perspective from Below.* Boston: Allen and Unwin, 1986.

Katz, Zev, Rosemarie Rogers, and Frederic Harned (eds.). *Handbook of Major Soviet Nationalities.* New York: Free Press, 1975.

Kozlov, Victor. *The Peoples of the Soviet Union.* Bloomington, IN: Indiana University Press, 1988.

Mandel, William M. *Soviet but not Russian: The "Other" Peoples of the Soviet Union.* Palo Alto, CA: Ramparts Press, 1985.

Mandelbaum, Michael, ed. *The Rise of Nations in the Soviet Union: American Foreign Policy and the Disintegration of the USSR.* New York: Council on Foreign Relations, 1991.

Motyl, Alexander. *Will the Non-Russians Rebel? State, Ethnicity and Stability in the USSR.* Ithaca, NY: Cornell University Press, 1987.

—— *Sovietology, Rationality, Nationality: Coming to Grips with Nationalism in the USSR.* New York: Columbia University Press, 1990.

Motyl, Alexander J. (ed.). *Thinking Theoretically about Soviet Nationalities.* New York: Columbia University Press, 1992.

Nahaylo, Bohdan and Victor Swoboda. *Soviet Disunion: A History of the Nationalities Problem in the USSR.* New York: Free Press, 1990.

Odom, William E. and Robert Dujarroic, *Commonwealth or Empire? Russia, Cultural Area, and the Transcaucacus.* Indianapolis: Hudson Institute 1995.

Olcott, Martha Brill (ed.). *The Soviet Multinational State: Readings and Documents.* Armonk, NY: ME Sharpe, 1990.

Parrott, Bruce and Karen Dawisha, *Russia and the New States of Eurasia.* (Cambridge: Cambridge University Press, 1994).

Rywkin, Michael, *Moscow's Lost Empire.* (Armonk, NY: ME Sharpe, 1994).

Shlapentokh, Vladimir, Munir Sendich, and Emil Payin, eds. *The New Russian Diaspora: Russian Minorities in the former Soviet Republics.* Armonk, NY: ME Sharpe, 1994.

Simon, Gerhard. *Nationalism and Policy Toward the Nationalities in the Soviet Union.* Boulder, CO: Westview Press, 1991.

Smith, Graham (ed.). *The Nationalities Question in the Soviet Union.* New York: Longman, 1990.

Suny, Ronald Grigor, *The Revenge of the Past.* Stanford: Stanford University Press, 1993.

Szporluk, Roman. *Communism and Nationalism: Karl Marx Versus Friedrich List.* New York: Oxford University Press, 1991.

——*National Identity and Ethnicity in Russia and the New States of Eurasia.* Armonk, NY: ME Sharpe, 1994.

Tillett, Lowell. *The Great Friendship: Soviet Historians on the Non-Russian Nationalities.* Chapel Hill, NC: University of North Carolina Press, 1969.

Wixman, Ronald. *The Peoples of the USSR: An Ethnographic Handbook.* Armonk, NY: ME Sharpe, 1988.

Zaslavsky, Victor. *The Neo-Stalinist State: Class, Ethnicity, and Consensus in Soviet Society.* Armonk, NY: ME Sharpe, 1982.

Zwick, Peter. *National Communism.* Boulder, CO: Westview Press, 1983.

### Russia and its Nations

Allworth, Edward (ed.). *Ethnic Russia in the USSR: The Dilemma of Dominance.* New York: Pergamon Press, 1980.

Allworth, Edward (ed.). *Tatars of the Crimea: Their Struggle for Survival.* Durham, NC: Duke University Press, 1988.

Bobrick, Benson, *East of the Sun; The Epic Conquest and Tragic History of Siberia.* New York: Poseidon Press, 1992.

Carter, Stephen K. *Russian Nationalism: Yesterday, Today and Tomorrow.* London: Pinter, 1990.

Conquest, Robert. *The Nation Killers: The Soviet Deportation of Nationalities.* London: Macmillan, 1970.

Dienes, Leslie. *Soviet Asia: Economic Development and National Policy Choices.* Boulder, CO: Westview Press, 1987.

Dunlop, John. *The Faces of Contemporary Russian Nationalism.* Princeton, NJ: Princeton University Press, 1983.

Dunlop, John B., *The Rise of Russia and the Fall of the Soviet Empire*. Updated ed., Princeton, NJ: Princeton University Press, 1995.

Fisher, Alan W. *The Crimean Tatars*. Stanford, CA: Hoover Institution Press, 1978.

Forsyth, James. *A History of the Peoples of Siberia: Russia's North Asian Colony*. Cambridge: Cambridge University Press, 1992.

Gitelman, Zvi. *A Century of Ambivalence: The Jews of Russia and the Soviet Union. 1881 to the Present*. New York: Schocken Books, 1988.

Humphrey, Caroline. *Karl Marx Collective: Economy, Society and Religion in a Siberian Collective Farm*. Cambridge: Cambridge University Press, 1983.

Isham, Heyward, ed., *Remaking Russia: Voices from Within*. (Armonk, NY: ME Sharpe, 1995).

Kempe, Frederick. *Siberian Odyssey: A Voyage into the Russian Soul*. New York: Putnam's Sons, 1992.

Krasnov, Vladislav. *Russia Beyond Communism: A Chronicle of National Rebirth*. Boulder, CO: Westview Press, 1991.

Kremenyuk, Victor A., *Conflicts in and around Russia: Nation-Building in Difficult Times*. (Westport, CT: Greenwood, 1994).

Laqueur, Walter. *Black Hundred*. New York: Harper Collins Publishers, 1993.

Lincoln, W. Bruce. *The Conquest of a Continent: Siberia and the Russians*. New York: Random House, 1994.

Nekrich, Aleksandr M. *The Punished Peoples: The Deportation and Fate of Soviet Minorities at the End of the Second World War*. New York: Norton, 1978.

Pinkus, Benjamin. *The Jews of the Soviet Union: A History of a National Minority*. Cambridge: Cambridge University Press, 1988.

Ro'i, Yaacov. *The Struggle for Soviet Jewish Emigration, 1948–1967*. Cambridge: Cambridge University Press, 1990.

Rorlich, Azade-Ayse. *The Volga Tatars: The Profile of a People in National Resilience*. Stanford, CA: Hoover Institution Press, 1986.

Slezkine, Yuri. *Arctic Mirrors: Russia and the Small Peoples of the North*. Ithaca: Cornell University Press, 1994.

Smith, Hedrick. *The New Russians*. New York: Random House, 1991.

Swearingen, Rodger (ed.). *Siberia and the Soviet Far East: Strategic Dimensions and Multinational Perspective*. Stanford: Hoover Institution Press, 1987.

Yanov, Alexander. *The Russian New Right: Right-Wing Ideologies in the Contemporary USSR*. Berkeley, CA: Institute of International Studies, 1978.

——*The Russian Challenge and the Year 2000*. Oxford: Basil Blackwell, 1987.

Wood, Alan (ed.). *The History of Siberia: From Russian Conquest to Revolution*. London: Routledge, 1991.

## Baltic States

Allworth, Edward (ed.). *Nationality Group Survival in Multi-Ethnic States: Shifting Support Patterns in the Soviet Baltic Region*. New York: Praeger, 1977.

Clemens, Walter Jr. *Baltic Independence and Russian Empire*. New York: St. Martin's Press, 1991.

Gerner, Kristian. *The Baltic States and the End of the Soviet Empire*. London: Routledge, 1993.

Hiden, John and Patrick Salmon. *The Baltic Nations and Europe: Estonia, Latvia, and Lithuania in the Twentieth Century*. London: Longman, 1991.

Karklins, Rasma, *Ethnopolitics and Transition to Democracy: The Collapse of the USSR and Latvia*. Baltimore: Johns Hopkins University Press, 1994.

Lieven, Anatol. *The Baltic Revolution*. 2nd ed. New Haven: Yale University Press, 1994.

Misiunas, Romuald and Rein Taagepera. *The Baltic States: Years of Dependence, 1940–1990*. Updated ed. Berkeley: University of California Press, 1993.

Parming, Tonu and Elmar Jarvesoo. *A Case Study of a Soviet Republic: The Estonian SSR*. Boulder, CO: Westview Press, 1978.

Raun, Toivo U. *Estonia and the Estonians*. 2nd ed. Stanford: Hoover Institution Press, Stanford University, 1991.

Senn, Alfred Erich. *Lithuania Awakening*. Berkeley: University of California Press, 1990.

Shen, Raphael. *Restructuring the Baltic Economies: Disengaging Fifty years of Integration with the USSR*. Westport: Praeger, 1994.

Sprudzs, Adolf. *The Baltic Path to Independence: An International Reader of Selected Articles*. Buffalo: WS Hein, 1994.

Taagepera, Rein. *Estonia*. Boulder, Co: Westview Press, 1992.

Trapans, Jan Arveds (ed.). *Toward Independence: The Baltic Popular Movements*. Boulder, CO: Westview Press, 1991.

Vardys, V. Stanley. *The Catholic Church. Dissent and Nationality in Soviet Lithuania*. Boulder, CO: Westview Press, 1978.

Vardys, V. Stanley and Romuald J. Misiunas. *The Baltic States in Peace and War*. University Park, PA: Penn State University Press, 1978.

von Rauch, Georg. *The Baltic States: Years of Independence, 1917–1940*. Berkeley, CA: University of California Press, 1974.

## The New Eastern Europe

Armstrong, John Alexander. *Ukrainian Nationalism*. 3rd ed. Englewood, CO: Ukrainian Academic Press, 1990

Bahry, Romana M., ed. *Echoes of Glasnost in Soviet Ukraine*. North York, Ontario: Captus Press Publications, 1989.

Bruchis, Michael. *Nations – Nationalities – People: A Study of the Nationalities Policy of the Communist Party in Soviet Moldavia*. Boulder, CO: East European Monographs, 1984.

Brym, Robert J. *The Jews of Moscow, Kiev, and Minsk: Identity, Antisemitism, Emigration*. New York: New York University Press, 1994.

Dzyuba, Ivan. *Internationalism or Russification? A Study in the Soviet Nationalities Problem*. New York: Monad, 1974.

Hosking, Geoffrey (ed.). *Church, Nation and State in Russia and Ukraine*. Basingstoke: Macmillan, 1991.

Krawchenko, Bohdan. (ed.), *Social Change and National Consciousness in Twentieth-Century Ukraine*. London: Macmillan, 1985.

Krawchenko, Bohdan (ed.). *Ukraine after Shelest*. Edmonton, Alberta: University of Alberta, Canadian Institute of Ukrainian Studies, 1983.

Kuzio, Taras and Andrew Wilson. *Ukraine: Perestroika to Independence.* Houndmills, Basingstoke, Hampshire: Macmillan, 1994

Lewytzkyj, Borys. *Politics and Society in Soviet Ukraine, 1953–1980.* Edmonton, Alberta: University of Alberta, Canadian Institute of Ukrainian Studies, 1984.

Liber, George. *Soviet Nationality Policy, Urban Growth, and Identity Change in the Ukrainian SSR, 1923–1934.* Cambridge: Cambridge University Press, 1992.

Little, David. *Ukraine: The Legacy of Intolerance.* Washington, DC: United States Institute of Peace, 1991.

Lubachko, Ivan S. *Belorussia Under Soviet Rule, 1917–1957.* Lexington: University Press of Kentucky, 1972.

Manoliu-Manea, Maria (ed.). *The Tragic Plight of a Border Area: Bessarabia and Bucovina.* Arcata, CA: Humboldt State University Press, 1983.

Marples, David R. *Ukraine under Perestroika: Ecology, Economics, and the Workers' Revolt.* London: Macmillan, 1991.

Motyl, Alexander J., *Dilemmas of Independence: Ukraine after Totalitarianism.* (New York: Council on Foreign Relations Press, 1993).

Potichnyj, Peter (ed.) *Ukraine and Russia in Their Historical Encounter.* Edmonton: Canadian Institute of Ukrainian Studies Press, University of Alberta, 1992.

Solchanyk, Roman (ed.). *Ukraine, from Chernobyl' to Sovereignty: A Collection of Interviews.* New York: St. Martin's Press, 1992.

Subtelny, Orest. *Ukraine: A History.* 2nd ed. Toronto: University of Toronto Press, 1994.

Urban, Michael. *An Algebra of Soviet Power: Elite Circulation in the Belorussian Republic 1966–1986.* Cambridge: Cambridge University Press, 1989.

Vakar, Nicholas P. *Belorussia: The Making of a Nation.* Cambridge, MA: Harvard University Press, 1956.

Zaprudnik, Jan. *Belarus.* Boulder: Westview Press, 1993.

## Transcaucasia

Allen, W. *A History of the Georgian People.* New York: Barnes and Noble, 1971.

Altstadt, Audrey L. *The Azerbaijani Turks.* Stanford: Hoover Institution Press, 1992.

Bournoutian, George A., *A History of the Armenian People.* Costa Mesa, CA: Mazda Publishers, 1993.

Chorbajian, Levon, Patrick Donabedian, and Claude Mutafian. *The Caucasian Knot: The History and Politics of Nagorno-Karabagh.* London: Zed Books, 1994.

Goldenberg, Suzanne. *Pride of Small Nations: The Caucasus and Post-Soviet Disorder.* London: Zed, 1994.

Hovannisian, Richard G. *The Armenian Genocide in Perspective.* New Brunswick, NJ: Transaction Books, 1986.

Hunter, Shireen. *The Transcaucasus in Transition: Nation-Building and Conflict.* Washington, DC: Center for Strategic and International Studies, 1994.

Lang, David M. *The Armenians: A People in Exile.* London: Unwin Hyman, 1988.

Libaridian, Gerard J. (ed.). *Armenia at the Crossroads: Democracy and Nation-hood in the Post-Soviet Era*. Watertown, MA: Blue Crane Books, 1991.

Libaridian, Gerald J., ed. *The Karabagh File: Documents and Facts on the Region of Mountainous Karabagh, 1918–1988*. Cambridge: Zoryan Institute, 1988.

Matossian, Mary K. *The Impact of Soviet Policies in Armenia*. Leiden, Holland: E.J. Brill, 1962.

Rost, Yuri. *Armenian Tragedy*. London: Weidenfeld and Nicolson, 1990.

Shahmuratian, Samuel, (ed). *The Sumgait Tragedy: Pogroms against Armenians in Soviet Azerbaijan*. Cambridge: Zoryan Institute, 1990.

Suny, Ronald Grigor, *Looking toward Ararat: Armenia in Modern History*. Bloomington: Indiana University Press, 1993.

——*The Making of the Georgian Nation*. 2nd ed. Bloomington: Indiana University Press, 1994.

Suny, Ronald Grigor (ed.). *Transcaucasia: Nationalism and Social Change*. Ann Arbor, MI: University of Michigan Press, 1983.

Swietochowski, Tadeusz. *Russian Azerbaijan 1905–1920: The Shaping of National Identity in a Muslim Community*. Cambridge: Cambridge University Press, 1985.

Walker, Christopher J., *Armenia: The Survival of a Nation*. 2nd ed. New York: St. Martin's Press, 1990.

## Central Asia

Adshead, Samuel Adrian M. *Central Asia in World History*. New York: St. Martin's Press, 1993.

Akiner, Shirin. *The Early History of Central Asia*. London, Kegan Paul, 1989.

——*Islamic Peoples of the Soviet Union*. London: Kegan Paul International, 1983.

Akiner, Shirin (ed.). *Cultural Change and Continuity in Central Asia*. London: Kegan Paul, 1991.

——*Political and Economic trends in Central Asia*. London: Kegan Paul, 1991.

Allworth, Edward. *The Modern Uzbeks: From the Fourteenth Century to the Present*. Stanford, CA: Hoover Institution Press, 1990.

——*Central Asia, 130 Years of Russian Dominance: A Historical Overview*. 3rd ed. Durham: Duke University Press, 1994.

——*The Nationality Question in Soviet Central Asia*. New York: Praeger, 1973.

Banuazizi, Ali and Myron Weiner. *The New Geopolitics of Central Asia and its Borderlands*. Bloomington: Indiana University Press, 1994.

Bennigsen, Alexandre and Marie Broxup. *The Islamic Threat to the Soviet State*. New York: St. Martin's, 1983.

Bennigsen, Alexandre and S. Enders Wimbush. *Muslim National Communism in the Soviet Union*. Chicago: University of Chicago Press, 1979.

—— *Muslims of the Soviet Empire*. London: Hurst, 1986.

Black, Cyril. *The Modernization of Inner Asia*. Armonk, NY: ME Sharpe, 1991.

Carrere d'Encausse, Helene. *Islam and the Russian Empire: Reform and Revolution in Central Asia* Berkeley: University of California Press, 1988.

Critchlow, James. *Nationalism in Uzbekistan: A Soviet Republic's Road to Sovereignty*. Boulder, CO: Westview Press, 1992.

Ehteshami, Anoushiravan, ed. *From the Gulf to Central Asia: Players in the New Great Game*. Exeter: University of Exeter Press, 1994.

Eickelman, Dale F. (ed.). *Russia's Muslim Frontiers: New Directions in Cross-Cultural Analysis.* Bloomington: Indiana University Press, 1993.

Ferdinand, Peter, *The New States of Central Asia and Their Neighbors.* New York: Council on Foreign Relations Press, 1994.

Fierman, William (ed.). *Soviet Central Asia: The Failed Transformation.* Boulder, CO: Westview Press, 1991.

Gross, Jo-Ann (ed.). *Muslims in Central Asia: Expressions of Identity and Change.* Durham: Duke University Press, 1992.

Haghayehgi, Mehadad. *Islam and Politics in Central Asia,* New York: St. Martins Press, 1995.

Hauner, Milan, *What is Asia to Us?: Russia's Asian Heartland Yesterday and Today.* London: Routledge, 1992.

Hayit, Baymirza. Islam and Turkestan under Russian Rule. Istanbul: Can Matbaa, 1987.

Hiro, Dilip. *Between Marx and Muhammad.* London: HarperCollins, 1994.

Hopkirk, Peter. *The Great Game: Struggle for Empire in Central Asia.* New York: Farrar, Straus & Giroux, 1994.

Hostler, Charles Warren. *The Turks of Central Asia.* Westport, CT: Praeger, 1993.

Lewis, Robert A. (ed.). *Geographic Perspectives on Soviet Central Asia.* New York: Routledge, 1992.

Lubin, Nancy. *Labor and Nationality in Soviet Central Asia.* Princeton, NJ: Princeton University Press, 1984.

Malik, Hafeez, (ed.). *Central Asia: Its Strategic Importance and Future Prospects.* New York: St. Martin's Press, 1994.

Manz, Beatrice (ed.). *Soviet Central Asia in Historical Perspective.* Boulder, CO: Westview Press, 1992.

Mandelbaum, Michael, ed. *Central Asia and the World: Kazakhstan, Uzbekistan, Tajikistan, Kyrgyzstan, and Turkmenistan.* New York: Council on Foreign Relations Press, 1994.

Manz, Beatrice F. (ed.). *Central Asia in Historical Perspective.* Boulder, co: Westview Press, 1994.

Medlin, William K., William M. Cave, and Finley Carpenter, *Education and Development in Central Asia; A Case Study of Social Change in Uzbekistan.* Leiden, Brill, 1971.

Mesbahi, Mohiaddin (ed.). *Central Asia and the Caucasus after the Soviet Union: Domestic and International Dynamics.* Gainesville, FL: University Press of Florida, 1994.

Nazmlein, Vitaly (ed.). *Central Asia and Transcaucasia: Ethnicity and Conflict.* Westport, CT: Greenwood Press, 1994.

Olcott, Martha Brill. *The Kazakhs.* Stanford, CA: Hoover Institution Press, 1987.

Paksoy, H. B., (ed.). *Central Asia Reader: The Rediscovery of History.* Armonk, NY: ME Sharpe, 1994.

Rakowska-Harmstone, Teresa. *Russia and Nationalism in Central Asia: The Case of Tadzhikistan.* Baltimore, MD: Johns Hopkins University Press, 1970.

Rashid, Ahmed. *The Resurgence of Central Asia.* Karachi [Pakistan]: Oxford University Press, 1994.

Rywkin, Michael. *Moscow's Muslim Challenge: Soviet Central Asia.* rev. ed. Armonk, NY: ME Sharpe, 1990.

Rumer, Boris Z. *Soviet Central Asia: "A Tragic Experiment."* Boston: Unwin Hyman, 1989.

# Index